GOOD BEER GUIDE 1996

EDITED BY JEFF EVANS

BOOKS

Campaign for Real Ale Ltd.
230 Hatfield Road, St Albans,
Herts. AL1 4LW

CONTENTS

Editor: Jeff Evans. **Deputy Editor:** Jill Adam. **The HQ Team:** Stephen Cox, Iain Loe,
Richard Smith, Malcolm Harding, Jo Bates, Mike Benner, Cressida Feiler, Su Tilley,
Jean Jones, Clare Stevens, Mandi Gilling, Mick Green, Gary Fowler, Fiona Whyte.
Design: Rob Howells. **Cover Photograph:** Tom Dobbie. **Cover Map:** David Atkinson.
Maps: Perrott Cartographics, Machynlleth. **Illustrations:** Nick Asher *(pages 5-8)*.

Published by Campaign for Real Ale Ltd., 230 Hatfield Road, St Albans, Herts. AL1 4LW.
Tel. (01727) 867201. **Typeset by** Create Publishing Services, Bath. **Printed by** WSOY, Finland

ISBN 1 85249 008 X   © Campaign for Real Ale Ltd. 1995/96

This guide could not have been produced without the tireless efforts of nearly 50,000
CAMRA members. Special thanks once again to CAMRA Regional Directors, to those
members who helped with pub surveys and those who provided information on beers
and breweries.

INTRODUCTION

One night, 25 years ago, four drinking companions on a pub crawl in Chester were collectively grumbling about the beer in their glasses. It was expensive, it was fizzy and it had little flavour, apart from a nasty sickliness. All was not well in the world of beer.

The big breweries were largely at fault. They had bought up and closed down small breweries right across the country and in place of traditionally brewed beers for local palates, they had introduced fizzy, pasteurised 'keg' beers, brewed at giant beer factories and advertised on national television to give them some appeal. The surviving smaller brewers had followed suit with their own keg beers and, in some cases, had even gone so far as to spoil their good, traditionally-brewed cask beer by forcing it to the bar with carbon dioxide (a process known as 'top pressure' dispense).

The four friends moved on the next day to a boozy holiday in Ireland. On their travels, through bars stocked with beer even worse than Chester could offer (the stout apart), they formed, as a bit of a lark, the Campaign for the Revitalisation of Ale. A couple of years later, this half-hearted attempt at beer consumerism was inaugurated as an official movement, complete with a paid secretary. The name became the snappier Campaign for Real Ale and, much to everyone's surprise, it attracted thousands of instant supporters, many of whom had been waiting for just such an organisation to come along. CAMRA was born.

In the quarter-century which has followed, CAMRA has had much to cheer – the revival of cask-conditioned 'real' ale, the limitation of brewery take-overs, the introduction of the guest beer law and the application of more flexible licensing hours are just four of its more obvious achievements. The last few years have been particularly good – nearly 150 new breweries opening up and CAMRA membership rocketing up towards 50,000. Yet, as CAMRA looks to build on its first 25 years, a shadow has been thrown over the silver jubilee celebrations.

BACK FROM THE DEAD

Just when you thought it was safe to go back into the pub, the spectre of the early 1970s is set to haunt your favourite watering hole. Keg beer is making a comeback bid. This sad parody of genuine ale seemed to be disappearing down the brewery plug hole, but now the marketing men and the brewery scientists have discovered a way to resuscitate this lifeless corpse. As Roger Protz reveals on page 9, new 'nitrokeg' looks set to muscle in on the cask ale market, encouraged by

3

blandness amongst nationally-available real ales and the success of 'draught' beers in a can. Using a less fizzy, mixed nitrogen/carbon dioxide gas dispense system, the national 'blands' are becoming available in nitrokeg form, served from fonts which resemble cans of beer with a handpump stuck on the top, just to confuse the unwary drinker.

The success of the new Caffrey's Irish Ale proves that not everyone thinks nitrokeg beer is a bad thing. This brand has gained a big following with little promotional effort from Bass. CAMRA's concern, however, is that publicans will be encouraged to install such beers at the expense of cask-conditioned brews – beers which by any standard taste so much better. It is like having 'proper' bread replaced by flabby white sliced.

We know just how badly the big brewers want these keg products to succeed, after all they are wildly profitable and far less complicated to handle than 'real' beer. Their motives are transparent. Advertising money which had briefly been placed behind cask beer has already been diverted to the nitrokeg equivalents. The fear is that the cask version will gradually be phased out in favour of mass-marketed nitrokeg, echoing events 25 years ago and having ramifications throughout the whole British brewing industry.

The freshness, the levels of flavour and the natural effervescence of cask-conditioned beer trounce the homogenised, dead tang of tasteless, cold keg any day. Some people no doubt are happy to drink keg beer, but we do not want it foisted upon all drinkers as happened once before. That is why CAMRA will not allow keg – however trendily it may be packaged – to kill off the real ale revival and will not stand by as drinkers' preferences are yet again sacrificed to the brewery accountant's balance sheet. If, like us, you appreciate real ale, please help us to defend it and nip the new keg boom in the bud. Details of how to join the Campaign can be found on page 546.

BREWING REALITIES

It is opportune at this point to look more closely at keg beer and real ale, to explain further why CAMRA has so fiercely defended traditional brewing. For much of the brewing process the two beers, keg and real, share the same ritual, although towards the end they go their own separate ways and this makes all the difference to the finished product.

All beer begins with malted barley. This is barley grain which has been partially germinated to help release vital sugars needed for the brewing process and then kilned to prevent further germination. The degree of kilning also dictates the character of the malt; the more 'baked' the malt the darker the colour and the roastier the taste. Some are toasted black for bitter, coffeeish flavours; others are merely lightly crisped for a sweeter or nuttier taste. The malt is crushed at the brewery and then combined in a vessel called a mash tun with hot water (known as 'liquor' in the trade). This liquor

has usually been treated to remove unsuitable chemicals or to emulate the natural brewing waters of towns like Burton upon Trent.

After an hour and a half's mashing and stirring, a thick, sweet porridgey liquid called wort is formed. This is then run off from the mash tun and diverted into a boiler known as a copper, leaving behind the spent grain, which is sprayed – or 'sparged' – to extract any last sugars and then sold for animal fodder. In the copper, the wort is boiled up with hops which add bitterness and sometimes herby, spicy or floral characters. Like malts, hops come in various forms. Some are very bitter; others milder. Some evidence themselves in the aroma; others are expressed in the taste. Hops also act as a preservative. They can be added as whole hop flowers or as compressed pellets. Some brewers use hop oils (concentrated hop extract), but it is widely considered that such oils provide inferior flavour. The hops are added at various stages of the boil and sometimes other 'adjuncts' are also introduced. These include sugars which add to the fermentability of the wort and maize which helps produce a good head on the finished beer, but such additives (and other less wholesome ingredients) are always hotly opposed by purists.

After an hour or two in the copper, the hops are strained out and the hopped wort is run off and cooled. When the temperature has dipped sufficiently, the wort is pumped into a fermenting vessel, yeast is added ('pitched' is the technical term) and fermentation begins. Yeast is a single-celled fungus whose value to the brewer lies in its ability to turn the sugars in the wort into alcohol and carbon dioxide. Each yeast, however, also has its own character which is skilfully harnessed and preserved by brewery chemists. Many breweries use the same yeasts for decades, ensuring that the brewery maintains its own style and individuality. The yeast is reprocessed and reused after each brew, with any excess generated sold to companies like Marmite.

During the first few days of fermentation, the yeast works furiously with the wort, growing quickly and covering the wort with a thick, undulating duvet of foam. Most is skimmed off, but some sinks into the brew and continues to work, eating up the sugars and generating more carbon dioxide and alcohol. A few days later, this 'primary fermentation' is deemed over and cask and keg beers go their separate ways.

Keg beer is filtered, pasteurised and chilled, effectively

killing off or removing any living yeast still in the brew. It is then packed into pressurised containers known as kegs and shipped off to the pub. Keg beer requires no further care. It contains no sediment which needs to settle and the only life it has is provided by canisters of gas which are applied in the pub to pump it to the bar. In the bad old days, this gas was carbon dioxide, applied at such a pressure as to render the beer excessively gassy. In the bad new days, the gas is part carbon dioxide and part nitrogen, a combination which takes away the fizz but fails to redeem the beer in any other way. These 'nitrokeg' beers are still dead products, served at a sufficiently low temperature to negate whatever flavour they might have.

Cask beer is not filtered, pasteurised or chilled. After primary fermentation, the 'green beer' is transferred to a conditioning tank where further, more gentle fermentation occurs as the yeast becomes more tired and the sugars are further reduced. This conditioning rounds the harsh edges off the beer and extinguishes unpleasant tastes. A few days later, the beer is simply drawn off ('racked') into casks for delivery to the pub. Sometimes brewing sugars or hop leaves are added to the cask to stimulate further fermentation or to induce a hoppy nose. The only additive otherwise is finings, a glutinous substance derived from fish which sticks to the yeast particles in the beer and drags them to the bottom of the cask, thus helping the beer to 'drop bright'. Because yeast is still present in the brew, the beer is fermenting all the time. This helps to round out the flavours even further and gives a good, fresh taste when sampled. The cask has to be vented to prevent build up of naturally occurring carbon dioxide, but no gas needs to be applied. The beer is drawn to the bar by simple pumps – the handpump is the most common, though electric pumps are also widely used in some parts of the country. A number of pubs in Scotland still use compressed air to push the beer to the bar and many pubs make a virtue out of the simple, gravity dispense system whereby a tap is opened in the cask and the beer flows by gravity straight into the glass or jug. Some publicans apply carbon dioxide or nitrogen gas to casks in their cellar, in an effort to prolong their shelf life by stopping oxygen reaching the beer. This so-called blanket pressure is opposed by CAMRA as it stops the beer from maturing properly and can make it gassy, like the old keg beers. A system known as the cask-breather only allows gas into the cask at atmospheric pressure and is therefore less likely to fizz up the beer, but it still inhibits proper conditioning and is again not accepted by CAMRA.

Consequently, cask beers subjected to any form of gas blankets are not counted as real ales for the purpose of this book.

Those are the bare bones of beer brewing. Each brewery, of course, has its own subtly different methods and uses recipes which combine various types of malts with various types of hops, in greater or lesser quantities. Lager, incidentally, follows a similar procedure but is fermented at a much lower temperature than ale, using a yeast strain which sinks to the bottom of the wort. Hence lager is a bottom-fermented beer and ale a top-fermented one. Lager also undergoes longer conditioning at the brewery, at near freezing temperatures. On the Continent, this 'lagering' can last months; most British lagers barely stay longer than a week or two in the brewery, with inevitable consequences for their taste. (British lagers are also, on the whole, much weaker than their European counterparts, are usually pasteurised and are subject to over-carbonation in the keg and at the point of sale.)

THE GOOD BEER GUIDE

So how does the *Good Beer Guide* work? Entries are chosen by CAMRA branches at special selection meetings. At these meetings, they evaluate all the likely contenders and vote on which pubs to include in the book. Some clubs and off-licences may also be included, if the branch considers that they make significant contributions to the local real ale scene. These and the pubs are formally surveyed each year and the information is passed to CAMRA head office for processing. Branches see proofs of their entries and can recommend changes right up to the last possible moment before the *Guide* goes to press. We believe this provides the most up to date research system employed by any guidebook. Our members are pub enthusiasts who know the pubs in their area extremely well and use them all year-round. They don't base their judgements on one or two formal visits. Readers' recommendations are extremely useful and sometimes offer another viewpoint which our branches are always keen to bear in mind when considering their selections, but reader recommendation alone does not guarantee entry to the *Guide*, as it does with some other publications.

There is only one criterion used in selecting pubs, namely the quality of the real ale on sale. This is, after all, the *Good Beer Guide*. Readers are sometimes bemused because some of Britain's prettiest pubs are not featured. We don't doubt that the pubs are attractive and may provide other excellent facilities. But if the beer is not always up to scratch then

these pubs are not selected for the *Guide*. That doesn't mean to say that the book does not include wonderful, picture postcard pubs. It certainly does. However, next to the thatched rustic gems you will find noisy town boozers, all sharing the common theme of serving excellent cask-conditioned ale.

READING THE ENTRIES

English pubs are listed first, followed by pubs in Wales, Scotland, Northern Ireland and the offshore islands. Pubs are arranged alphabetically by county, with all the Yorkshires listed under Y, the two Sussexes under S, the three Glamorgans under G and Greater London and Greater Manchester under L and M respectively. Within each county, pubs are included in alphabetical order of place name, then alphabetically within each location.

An at-a-glance guide to reading pub entries is supplied on the inside front cover but, basically, each entry provides the following information: name of pub, address, directions and Ordnance Survey reference number (if tricky to find), telephone number (if available), opening hours, a brief description of the pub and its major features and, finally, a row of symbols highlighting its key facilities. For meals and accommodation, no assessment of quality is made, unless mentioned in the pub description. Just before this book went to press, the Government changed the law to permit all day (12 – 10.30) opening on Sundays. Readers are therefore advised to check a pub's new Sunday hours before visiting.

Central to each entry is the list of real ales sold. These are arranged alphabetically by brewery and where more than one beer from a brewery is sold its beers are listed in ascending order of strength. Seasonal beers, such as winter ales, are included but are clearly only available at certain times of the year. For further information on all beers, check the breweries section and the Beers Index at the back of the book.

Each county is headed by a location map, pinpointing where all the pubs are situated and also marking the independently-owned breweries and brew pubs in the county. These breweries are then named in the box beneath the map. For further information about the breweries, see the breweries section. Breweries and brew pubs owned by the national brewers are not included in the maps. To pull all the counties together, and to help readers identify neighbouring counties, a national map is provided on the inside back cover.

Here's to another 25 years of enjoyable drinking!

NEW KEG, NEW THREAT

Twenty-five years after CAMRA first rode to the defence of cask-conditioned ale, the big breweries are fighting back with a new type of keg beer. Roger Protz leads the counterattack.

T he final piece of the jigsaw clicked into place. 'We are doing everything we can to keep swan necks out – they lead to mixed gas which will lead to the disappearance of cask ale', the director of Greene King told a party of CAMRA members visiting the Bury St Edmunds brewery in 1995.

Cask-conditioned ale is under threat. If that seems a curious statement to make as the Campaign celebrates its quarter-century, when new micros blossom like mushrooms at dawn and pubs are awash with new beers, then it serves to emphasise that the giant national brewers have not changed their ways. They may have offered a gloved hand of friendship to CAMRA. But the knuckle-duster glints through the thin fabric. The beerage doesn't fight by Queensberry Rules. Its enthusiasm for real ale was always tempered by the inescapable forces that drive big brewing corporations to develop mass-marketed, high-volume brands that make up for their lack of character and quality with awesome profitability.

THE SICK SIXTIES

The first attack on the real ale citadel came in the 1960s with the creation of the 'Big Six' national brewers. With a national market to satisfy, they created first keg beers – pasteurised and pressurised ales – and then lager, Britain's feeble attempt to recreate genuine European, cold-fermented beers. Both beer styles were supported by million-pound promotions while cask beer was ignored or obliterated. Within a decade, the number of beer brands in the country was halved from 3,000 to 1,500 as the giants concentrated on such tongue-tingling delights as Tavern keg and Skol lager.

CAMRA, by both reasoned argument and ridicule, stopped keg almost dead in its tracks. It survived for a while in areas where cask ale found less support and in fast-turnover clubs with a 'stick it down yer neck' philosophy. But by the late 1980s even the most ardent supporters of keg among the big brewers were admitting that the beer style was dead in the mash tun. I recall a top marketing man from

Allied Breweries telling me that within a few years the keg version of the group's biggest-selling standard beer, Tetley Bitter, would be phased out. The future was all cask, he assured me, even in clubland. And then the penny dropped – literally.

The big brewers saw their profits declining inexorably if keg disappeared. Keg, including lager, is between two and four times more profitable than cask ale. Real beer is perishable. Allowed to ferment and mature naturally, it will stay in drinkable condition for only a few days once the cask is tapped and is open to the atmosphere. Keg, on the other hand, is dead beer, filtered and filleted in the brewery. It has a long shelf life. It will certainly not improve in its keg, but neither will it deteriorate. It requires no skill from publicans and no arcane rituals of soft and hard pegging that bring a well-matured cask beer to fruition. Above all, keg is wonderfully, orgasmically profitable. It had to be saved, but in a different form. And from Yorkshire, the Tetley Bitter men came riding to keg's salvation, brandishing aloft the symbol of a new age, the swan neck.

THE SWAN'S SONG

Yorkshire beer, brewed traditionally in two-storey fermenters known as squares and using yeast strains that are more reluctant to turn sugars into alcohol than greedier cultures, have always had a high level of natural carbonation and a full-bodied maltiness. To balance the maltiness, these beers are served through a tight sparkler attached to the spout of the beer engine. The beer is forced through tiny holes in the sparkler, which agitates the beer, forming a thick collar of foam and driving hop bitterness out of solution and into the head. The result is a beer with a good hoppy 'nose' and a smooth, creamy palate. In the 1980s the popularity of Yorkshire bitters saw the 'tight head' invade the south of England. In order to make delivery less irksome for southern bar staff, a new type of sparkler, inside a long curved pipe called a swan neck that reaches to the bottom of the beer glass, was developed (see Forever Blowing Bubbles).

There was nothing wrong with this method of delivery as long as it was confined to Yorkshire beers. But other brewers thought they would win greater custom for their ales if they followed suit. Suddenly southern beers, brewed to best express their aromas and flavours through a thin collar of foam, were being agitated, aerated and rendered bland by the all-pervading swan neck.

Big brewers with the money and the technology rushed to cash in on the craze for beers with several inches of Cadbury's Smash on top. In a separate move, Guinness had put a keg stout – Draught (sic) Guinness – in a can in which nitrogen gas was trapped under a small plastic widget. When the can was opened, the nitrogen was released, blended with carbon dioxide and presented in the drinker's

glass a beer that resembled Draught Guinness in a pub. A curious amalgam of the swan neck and the widget showed brewers how keg beer could be revived.

Suddenly a phalanx of famous cask ales, such as Boddingtons, Draught Bass and John Smith's, were widgetised. Britain's absurdly lax consumer protection laws could not prevent beers that had been filtered, pasteurised and pressurised from being presented as 'draught beers in a can'. Expensively advertised, they were enormously successful, appealing to a gullible and largely young audience that did not know or could not be bothered to work out the difference between the real and the unreal. History repeated itself, tragedy and farce dialectically intertwined. In the 1950s and 1960s the success of bottled beers encouraged brewers to put such artificially pressurised products into

bigger containers – kegs. Forty years on, the success of fake draught canned beers drove brewers to make them available in pub form. Nitrokeg was born.

As a result of the mixture of nitrogen and carbon dioxide, the new keg beers lack the unpleasant burp and bite of old-fashioned keg. They are smooth, bland and served at lager temperature. The biggest success of the new genre has been Caffrey's Irish Ale, brewed by Bass in Belfast. At least it cannot be said that Caffrey's is attempting to pass itself off as anything other than a keg beer, but its popularity has prompted rival brewers to produce nitrokeg versions of their existing cask-conditioned ales. When the likes of John Smith's Bitter comes both in real form and in nitrokeg, served from a giant can topped by a dummy handpump, is it any wonder that drinkers are confused? Tetley also offers the 'choice' of cask and nitrokeg. At the time of writing I believe that such dubious choice will manifest itself in nitrokeg versions of Courage Best Bitter and Directors Bitter.

BLURRING THE DISTINCTION

To paraphrase Reynold Scot, the Elizabethan exponent of the hop plant, no one 'with sense in his mouth' could mistake cask ale for keg. Unless, that is, the brewers had not been busily blurring the distinction. At the same time as the draught canned nonsense was being converted into bulk nitrokeg for pubs, brewing 'scientists' were beavering away to make cask ales more user friendly. The end result was bland beer, hyped as 'real ale' but largely devoid of the rich and ripe aromas and flavours of malt and hops that makes this unique style one of the wonders of the world of beer. New yeast strains which pack down quickly in the cask and allow beers to 'drop bright' within an hour or two of reaching the pub, and minimal amounts of yeast in the cask which mean that secondary fermentation is by no means guaranteed but may take place when the moon is in its last quarter and Mars is in the ascendancy, have resulted in 'real' ales which desperately lack character. Such bland cask ale, served increasingly cold to mask any residual flavour it may contain and with a deep collar of foam, not only blurs the distinction with nitrokeg but does not encourage drinkers to distinguish one from the other.

Real ale is being emasculated once again. The technology today is better and the marketing departments cleverer than in the 1960s. But the aim is the same: to switch drinkers from comparatively low-volume, low-profit cask ales to high-volume, high-profit keg. Just when CAMRA was saying that it was safe to go back into the pub, along come the brewing piranhas once more. The *Good Beer Guide* has never been more essential in order to help you avoid the quick and the dead.

Roger Protz edits CAMRA's national newspaper, What's Brewing. His latest book, The Ale Trail, traces the history of ale brewing from the Old World to the modern day.

THE PRICE IS RIGHT?

Stephen Cox examines the drinker's most common gripe – the price of a pint. Are we now paying over the odds and, if so, who's to blame?

T wenty-five years after CAMRA came into being, many things have changed. One of them hasn't – people are still complaining about beer prices, brewers' profits, and the Chancellor of the Exchequer. Let's try to dispel a few myths and really explore the price of your pint. To start, here's a little quiz.

TRUE OR FALSE?

❶ If beer prices had risen in line with inflation since 1971, pub prices would now average less than a pound a pint.

❷ The Chancellor profits more from your pint than either brewer or licensee.

❸ Tax is a lower proportion of the cost of a pint than it was in 1971.

For the answers, read on.

The price of a pint is a furious debating point. Customers and journalists constantly complain about rising prices driving people out of pubs. Wild comparisons are made with the Continent and with the dim and distant past. Brewers and other pub owners respond that the choice and price of beer in British pubs beats anything on the Continent. Despite battling against some of the highest taxes in Europe, they claim that their pubs offer some of the lowest prices. In so far as they admit at all that prices have risen in real terms, they claim it is to pay for better facilities for customers. Or it is the Chancellor's fault. In the middle are licensees, who agree that prices are driving people away from the pub, but who are adamant that absolutely everyone except themselves is to blame. Who's telling the truth?

The bald figures on beer prices since CAMRA was founded seem startling. A pint of beer cost 12p in 1971 and £1.43 in 1994 – nearly 12 times as much. If the price of a pint had risen with the retail price index (RPI), it would have been only 87p. Brewers argue that a fairer comparison than the general RPI is with the RPI 'catering' index, which looks at restaurants

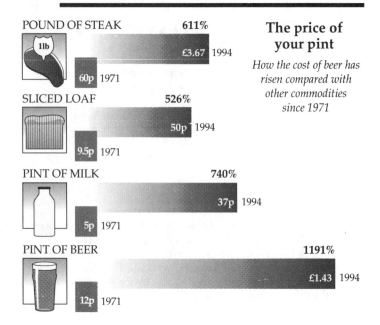

The price of your pint

How the cost of beer has risen compared with other commodities since 1971

POUND OF STEAK — 611%
1lb — £3.67 1994 — 60p 1971

SLICED LOAF — 526%
50p 1994 — 9.5p 1971

PINT OF MILK — 740%
37p 1994 — 5p 1971

PINT OF BEER — 1191%
£1.43 1994 — 12p 1971

and other 'outside the home' eating and drinking. But, had beer prices risen in line with this catering index, a pint would have cost less than £1.20 – still 16% less than the actual figure.

Above all, brewers like to avoid the retail price index completely and refer instead to wages, evaluating how long an employee has to work in order to earn the price of a pint. Indeed, it now takes fewer minutes of work to buy a pint than it did in 1971, yet it is also true that if wages are to be the measure of prices then most everyday items of food and drink are substantially cheaper than they were in 1971, as real wages have risen considerably in the last 25 years. On the 'wages' index, eggs and bread are just over half their 1971 price, milk and petrol around 40% cheaper, steak around 30% cheaper and beer only 21% cheaper.

So is the Chancellor to blame? There is no doubt that the tax on British beer is far too high and is damaging pubs and breweries throughout the country. Not only does the pub pint carry VAT, but also beer duty, an additional tax based on strength. A pint costing £1.43 incurs about 25 pence duty and 21 pence VAT, which means the Exchequer takes 46 pence out of the money you hand over the bar. On top of this, the Chancellor claims business taxes from the pub, taxes on the income of the pub staff, and taxes on profits made by both the licensee and the brewer.

This is all particularly mad given that a pint of the same strength in France incurs only four pence in duty. No wonder thousands of Brits flock to Calais each month to buy at knock-down prices. Is it surprising that well over a million pints of beer a day are brought into Britain from France by travellers and smugglers? All the same, the brewers can't place all the blame for rising prices at the Chancellor's door.

From 1971 to 1994, beer duty did rise steadily. VAT was

introduced, and increased twice. Yet the proportion of the price of a pub pint that goes to the Chancellor has actually declined since 1971. In that year, the Chancellor grabbed 36.6% of the price of the typical pub pint. This rose to 37.9% when VAT went up to 15%. Since then, however, the Chancellor's take has declined, and it is now well under a third, at 31.6%. So, the tax burden on the brewing industry is actually less today than it was in 1971. Yes, beer duty is still too high and should be cut. But that is not the whole picture.

BETTER FACILITIES?

Another argument put forward by brewers and other pub owners is that higher prices reflect higher standards. It is clear pubs have improved in many ways – better facilities for children, a greater choice of drinks (including soft), better food, more investment in the quality of the beer sold, etc. For those who like quiet, unspoiled pubs, with original features, a friendly governor, locally brewed beer, and conversation rather than electronic games and piped music, not all change is 'improvement'. But, however much people talk about the good old days, pubs have not wholly changed for the worse. It is also true, of course, that just about every sort of shop, restaurant or service industry has had to improve standards in the last 25 years. Remember supermarkets in 1971, or motorway service stations? Have pubs improved so dramatically compared with restaurants?

Pub refurbishments often result in vast sums of money being pumped into a pub, with little return except the loss of its individuality and the need for price hikes to pay for the changes. Millions of pounds go towards converting pubs into wine bars, back into pubs, then into 'alehouses'... whatever the fashion is. Each refurbishment is not expected to last more than a couple of years. Then further price rises are needed to cover the cost of the next refurbishment. CAMRA prices surveys reveal that smaller brewers' pubs are consistently cheaper than many free houses or the tied pubs of larger brewers. A major reason for this is that when the independent brewers spend on refurbishment, they spend more carefully and with a longer lifespan in mind.

There are other factors which must be taken into account when evaluating just why our beer is so expensive. For a start, cask beer has become a premium product. It used to be that keg beer was more expensive than cask. Now cask is edging ahead of keg, though the new breed of 'nitrokeg' beers will no doubt be heavily priced. The fact that the bigger brewers have taken to promoting cask ale and pushing it as a premium product has also brought the inevitable edging up of prices as advertising costs have had to be recovered. However, within the pub, cask still offers the best value in flavour and quality. Ordinary lager, for instance, remains as cheap to brew as cask but is up to 20 pence a pint more expensive to drink. Consider this a sort of tax on those stupid enough to believe lager advertising.

The brewers also like to compare the value of British beer with that of its continental neighbours, and here I think the industry does have more of a point. Much is heard about how much cheaper some European countries are for beer. But this really refers to the off-trade, where mega-brewers dump millions of litres of beer into hypermarkets at relatively cheap prices. Continental bars are not, in general, such good value. This is particularly true when you consider how much less tax those bars pay on their beer. If your local pub was suddenly allowed to pay French beer duty, it could cut 26 pence off a pint of Stella or Old Speckled Hen overnight, which leads to the conclusion that French bars charge extortionate prices. When you consider that most French bars have all the romance of a vertical quickie in Marseilles train station and offer poorer facilities and a worse choice of drinks than the British pub, the value seems even lower. The lustre of drinking in France comes solely from better weather, different scenery and longer opening hours – none of which are the café's responsibility.

PROFIT? WHAT PROFIT?

So, in conclusion, how much profit is really made on the sale of a pint? This depends on whether the pub is run by a brewery manager (an employee of the brewery), a tied tenant or lessee (who leases the pub from the brewery but is an independent business), or a free house owner. On your £1.43 pint, 46 pence goes to the Government. Around 27 pence is the cost of brewing the beer, getting it to the pub, advertising the product and furnishing the cellar so it has some chance of being drinkable. Thirty-two pence covers pub costs – wages, repairs, heating, lighting, insurance, rates, etc. The remaining 38 pence is 'profit'.

Beer
Where your money goes

Profit 38p

Pub costs 32p

Brewing 27p

Tax 46p

But before you assume that the brewery owners take home 38 pence for every pint sold, bear in mind that this has to cover running the company, supporting bad debts, paying the PR department, redesigning the corporate logo, sponsoring round the world yacht racing and, of course, investing millions in awful pub refurbishments. Bass claims the actual money that goes to shareholders is around 6p a pint, on which they then have to pay tax. Donations to this impoverished institution, the national brewery, will no doubt be welcome.

Finally, if you have read this article thoroughly, you will now know that the answer to all three quiz questions is 'true'.

Stephen Cox is CAMRA's Campaigns Manager.

FOREVER BLOWING BUBBLES

Mark Dorber looks at the rise of the swan neck and its effect on the beer in our glasses.

I n recent years, bars throughout Britain have been indulging in under-the-counter activities of a perfectly legitimate kind. The replacement of the traditional bar attachment, the short, simple down spout, with the more elegant looking piece of chrome-work, the swan neck, has, however, resulted in agitation beyond measure.

The use of the term swan neck to describe a 'structural part or contrivance having a curved cylindrical form like a swan's neck' can be traced back to the 17th century. However, modern day sightings of swan necks first in Yorkshire, then further afield, may be traced to the demise of the economiser (colloquially known in the trade as the auto-vac) in the early 1980s. This system, which involved recirculating beer spilled in the course of dispense into the beer engine, was deemed unhygienic by environmental health officers. To brewers and publicans, the virtue of the autovac was that lively beer could be pulled through a tight sparkler with all overspill being instantly reused. It was a cost-efficient method of achieving thoroughly aerated beer topped with a tight creamy head.

A HEALTHIER ALTERNATIVE

Tetley of Leeds needed to find a successor to the autovac. After extensive development work, Angram Design of Boroughbridge produced a non-adjustable sparkler with 16 small holes, fitted to a long or extended nozzle curved like a swan's neck and capable of reaching the bottom of a pint glass. For the publican, the key change was to replace top filling with bottom filling. Formerly, beer dispensed from a short spout was run down the side of the glass onto the emerging head. The bottom filling approach, made possible with the nozzle thrust deep into the glass, developed a head from the bottom which then floated up to the brim. The glass was lowered as it filled, to reduce the displacement effect of the pipe on the volume of beer in the glass. The nozzle always remained below the head, enabling the server to control the quality and size of the head being produced. It was a simple, intelligent solution to the problem of how to dispense

beer without substantial spillage and financial loss.

Brand managers for national brewers took note and Courage (John Smith's), S&N (Theakston) and Bass (Stones) followed suit. They realised that the swan neck/tight sparkler combination, attached to a quarter-pint beer engine, could create a long-lasting, visually distinctive head that could be consistently replicated not just in the tap rooms of Leeds, but nationwide. Moreover, they claimed their market research showed that customers preferred a creamy head and lacework. Whitbread patented their own 'North Star' sparkler to achieve the same effect and in their 'Cream of Manchester' campaign skilfully exploited the colour contrast of golden Boddingtons with a pure, white head. Appearance is extended to tactile images of texture, smoothness and softness – a step up from mother's milk – appealing to teenage scribblers in the City of London.

BUT WHAT ABOUT THE TASTE?

If the effect of the swan neck and tight sparkler on appearance is understood, then the general effects on the aroma, flavour and mouthfeel are less so. Experimental work by Dr Keith Thomas at the University of Sunderland confirms that dispensing beer through tight sparklers leads to substantial reductions in the amount of dissolved carbon dioxide in the body of the beer. The effect is to soften the mouthfeel both by reducing the acidity due to the removal of carbon dioxide from the body of the beer and by purging some of the prickly effervescence. Whereas the angels were dancing on the tongue, they are now walking on tiptoe perhaps.

Scientists at the University of Leuven in Belgium, meanwhile, have demonstrated that beer foam acts as a barrier to the perception of certain aromas, such as some malts and caramel, whilst enhancing other odours such as hoppiness. They point out that some light, fruity aromas like bananas and pear drops are barely perceptible through beer foam whilst off-flavours such as sulphur dioxide and acetic acid also become less apparent. Their broad conclusion is that if beer has a thick head then only if an aroma component is present in the beer foam itself will the taster be able to detect it.

SOUTHERN DISCOMFORT

In Britain, many southern brewers have long held the view that dispensing a beer through a tight sparkler 'brutalises' the palate of their flowery, hoppy beers. The subtle interplay of malt richness, balanced by the clean, dry bitter seasoning of whole leaf hops, wrapped around by soft, fruity, yeast, is lost, it is felt, by vigorous agitation. Bitterness levels fall by a small but significant amount. Flavour intensity is reduced. Some of the delicious volatile aromas are driven off by tight sparkler agitation, as is some of the palate tickling carbon dioxide, rendering the body of the beer flatter, duller and less quenching. From undulating downs to plain, so to speak.

Although the flavour profile of some beers is suited to the use of the swan neck and a tight sparkler (especially northern pale ales and milds), that of many beers is not. In the past, regional preferences and traditions dictated how beers were served. Increasingly, the sales momentum of successful national brands is used to dictate the choice of dispense equipment in pubs. Consistency of appearance is the new god. That a consistent appearance can be achieved by a gizmo suits the 'quick fix at low cost' mindset of some beer manufacturers. Delivering a head of the maximum size permissible under the industry's code of practice makes the retailers happy.

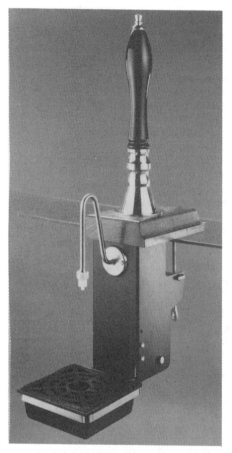

However, if publicans and other beer sellers believe in the primacy of prettiness over palate and sight over smell, then beer perforce will be 'flattened'. Highly carbonated cask ales cannot be served through tight sparklers either quickly or, crucially, without substantial fobbing and wastage. If cellar practices are therefore dictated by the dispense equipment requirement of lower carbonation levels then quality in the cask and glass will suffer. Swan necks per se do not affect beer flavour, but sparklers do. The sparkler should always be removed or adjusted (where possible) for the dispense of unsuitable beers or at the customer's request.

Respect for the visual appeal of tight creamy heads should be secondary to customers' desires for true tasting, full-flavoured beers with aromatic complexity and appeal. Methods of dispense, therefore, must always be the *servant* of best cellar practices and never their *master*.

Mark Dorber is joint licensee of The White Horse on Parsons Green, Fulham, SW6 and has been its cellarman since 1981. He is on the editorial advisory board of Brewing Techniques in the USA, and is a committee member of the British Guild of Beer Writers.

REAL ALE IN A BOTTLE

Barrie Pepper welcomes the revival of bottle-conditioned beers.

About 40 years ago I worked on the bar at Yates Wine Lodge in Blackpool during my summer holidays. Most of the time it was wine we sold; Cape Red, Australian White, Cyprus Commandaria and champagne at half a crown a glass. But there was a small and discerning custom for Draught Bass, Worthington White Shield and Bass Red Triangle.

The manager was called Peter Yates and, whilst he was one of the family, he still had to work for his living. He overlooked us from a glass-fronted cabinet high in the roof void. I was told it was to check that the firm got the cash and we didn't slip it into our pockets. But in my second week I found out differently. I was called to Mr Peter's office in the sky.

In fear and trepidation I climbed the narrow stairs, though I had no idea what sin I may have committed. In Mr Peter's eyes it was a cardinal one. I had poured the whole of a bottle of Red Label Bass into a glass – sediment and all. He

lectured me and suggested that any further infringement of this rule could involve sacking.

'White Shield and Red Label,' said Mr Peter, 'and Guinness stout for that matter, are classic, delicate beers and deserve careful treatment. Hold bottle and glass at eye level and pour it so that you can see when the sediment reaches the neck. Then stop. But always offer the bottle to the customer for he has paid for what is left inside and may want to drink it.'

Later on I learned that there are people who retain the sediment (it is not dregs) and just before finishing the glass pour it in, swirl it around and drink. It is said to 'keep you regular'. You must test its efficacy for yourself.

Peter Yates concluded by lecturing me on the glories of bottle-conditioned beers, dismissing with a wave of his hand other bottled beers that did not reach his benchmark. These even included Bass Blue Triangle and Worthington Green

Shield which he described as abominations. 'They are false prophets,' he declared. 'If you are asked for a pale ale make sure you hand over a real beer.'

REAL REVIVAL

Memory tells me that this is what he said. I may be wrong but when 'real ale' became the vogue 20 years on I recognised the phrase even if I did not understand it. But I did know what White Shield and Red Triangle were all about and I knew I liked them. And a long summer in Ireland during the 1960s gave me a similar taste for bottled Guinness.

Then along came the 1970s and the renaissance of real ale. By my count there were five bottle-conditioned beers on general sale when CAMRA was formed in 1971. They were Worthington White Shield (Red Triangle had gone the way of all flesh and Bass did not deny that there was a remarkable similarity between that and White Shield), Guinness Extra Stout (and here the connoisseurs voted for that brewed in Dublin against the one from Park Royal), Gale's Prize Old Ale (the corked half pints were preferred to the crown-topped nips), Eldridge Pope's Thomas Hardy's Ale (which we were advised to keep for ten years before drinking), and Courage Imperial Russian Stout (dated with its year of brewing and difficult to find).

The upsurge in the brewing of draught real ale spawned a smaller but quite significant revival of bottle-conditioned beers. Traquair House Ale was being produced at Scotland's oldest house at Innerleithen near Edinburgh by the twentieth Laird, Peter Maxwell Stuart. At first the naturally-conditioned product was sold only at the house, with a bright version in a few selected outlets in southern Scotland. Later its popularity and strength forced a widening of sales even into England.

Another bottle-conditioned beer on restricted sale was made at the Miners Arms at Priddy in Somerset. Despite its name this was not a pub and the home-brew could only be sold to accompany meals.

The most unusual brewery to pop out of the real ale explosion was John Boothroyd's York Brewery. It was actually based in Boroughbridge but its products were sold from a home brewing shop in York and these products were bottle-conditioned beers – nothing else. Sadly John closed down the brewing operation around 1980.

NEW FOR THE NINETIES

There was a halt to the initial progress in bottle-conditioned beers through the 1980s. Occasional ones popped up and often withered. Some made the grade and continued. Burton Bridge Burton Porter is a case in point, a wonderful, full-flavoured beer which deserves its success. And from the tiny Linfit brewery behind the Sair Inn at Linthwaite, near Huddersfield, Ron Crabtree cocked a snook at his large Irish competitor and produced English Guineas Stout (no relation).

The hiatus broke in the early 1990s and CAMRA recognised this perhaps prematurely. *Bottle-Conditioned Beers* was introduced as a category in the 1992 *Champion Beer of Britain* awards.

The following year I had the job of chairing the panel that judged this category. It is not an easy job like, for example, choosing the best out of six bitters. They were all of different styles: a stout, a strong ale, a porter, a pale ale, a no show and our old friend Worthington White Shield. Thomas Hardy's Ale won by a whisker and my panel whisked off for a pint of bitter.

One beer missing that year was Guinness Extra Stout which, up to April 1993, had been the best selling bottle-conditioned beer in the world, making its mark in around one hundred countries. The company decided to sterilise, pasteurise, homogenise and do whatever else was needed to kill off a brand of beer that had more advocates and adherents than any other. And at a time when not only were black beers coming back into fashion, so were bottle-conditioned ones. In the words of Roger Protz: 'Guinness must be out to lunch'.

The move forward was given strong support by some of the regional independent brewers. Eldridge Pope brought out their Hardy Country Bitter and the first time I tasted it I thought I was drinking draught. 'Real ale in a bottle' it certainly was. King & Barnes produced Festive and also Old Porter, Harveys brewed 1859 Porter and Shepherd Neame started bottling Spitfire which had had great success as a draught ale.

And the micros followed; in some cases led. Breweries like Borve at Huntly in the Grampian region have a portfolio of four. Commercial, Old Luxters and Masons Arms are others in the market. Some beers have become regulars after being brewed for a special occasion. Others are given a trial and then carried on.

Now a recent count takes the total to close to 50. And their success has given them another place at the Great British Beer Festival where they now have their own bar. CAMRA National Executive member David Hughes is most protective of bottle-conditioned beers; he loves and cherishes them; they are his baby. 'You can drink one on top of Snowdon,' he told me, 'which is somewhere you won't find a pint of Brains SA'. Well, maybe he can do that. I prefer mine in the comfort of my armchair.

A freelance journalist and author of many books on beer, Barrie Pepper is Chairman of the British Guild of Beer Writers.

TIME AND TIED

Ted Bruning untangles the chains which bind pubs and breweries and discovers who decides which beer you drink in your local.

F lak and hassle from disgruntled customers are part of life in the licensed trade. Sometimes it's the licensees' fault: it's up to them to keep the ale fresh and the toilets clean; if they don't, they can hardly be surprised when people complain. But more often, the cause of customer disgruntlement is outside the licensees' control, and they find themselves carrying the can for the cupidity, crassness or plain incompetence of some distant, nameless, and omnipotent functionary, thanks to a system which allows big breweries to control nearly all our pubs.

To add to the luckless licensees' dyspepsia, there's a common illusion that the Beer Orders that followed the Monopolies Commission enquiry into the brewing industry a few years ago have weakened the link between publican and brewer. You wish! Many and strong are the chains that bind; they're just longer and more twisted these days.

YESTERDAY AND TODAY

In the old days, as anyone familiar with the trade knew, there were **managers** directly employed by the brewers to run the bigger tied pubs. They were paid a wage and simply did as they were told. Then there were self-employed **tenant**s who ran the smaller pubs and paid rent for the privilege. Their contracts usually lasted one year or three years, and rents, which were traditionally modest to compensate for the higher beer prices charged by the brewery, were reviewed on a similar timescale. Like managers, tenants were tied to the brewer for everything down to the last salt and vinegar crisp. Next came independent **free traders**, on the face of it genuinely free to sell whatever they chose, but many tied to a brewery by means of a cheap loan with a supply agreement attached. Finally, just before the Monopolies Commission enquiry was announced, a new subspecies of tenant began to emerge in the estates of the national and larger regional brewers: long **lessees**, who were tied in the same way as tenants, but whose contracts stretched to 20 years in some cases and whose rents were higher as a pay off for longer 'security' of tenure.

In few cases, then, did the people behind the bar have much control over what they stocked, whether it was cask or keg beer, or indeed over any of the larger areas of policy. So it was no good having a go at them for the lack of variety available, the prices, or the standards of decoration and comfort: control lay elsewhere.

So how far did the Beer Orders actually go towards loosing the brewers' hold over the nation's pubs? As is so often the way, the legislation merely reinforced trends that were emerging anyway. Non-brewing pub chains and 'guest' ales are common features of the pub scene today; but both were in place before the Beer Orders, which simply hastened their progress. CAMRA believes that the pubgoer has won significant benefits from these changes, however fiercely brewery directors condemn them. Comparative surveys by CAMRA branches show a big increase in the number of pubs serving real ale in the last few years, with an even greater growth in the choice of real ales available, since each pub serves a larger number of ales. But to pubgoers wondering who really controls their locals, the split between ownership and tenure in the modern licensed trade, and the resultant degree of freedom allowed to publicans, remains a mystery. Here is a guide.

❑ **Traditional regional breweries** such as Eldridge Pope, Banks's, Vaux, and many others are not obliged to allow other breweries' products into their pubs, so it's no good insisting that your local brewery tenant should stock a greater choice. Some regionals allow guest ales; some have reciprocal deals, so that some Greene King tenants sell Marston's ales and vice versa. However, the discretion belongs to the brewer, not the tenant.

❑ **National brewery managed houses** – many of which appear under names like Brewer's Fayre, Toby Inns, Beefeater and so on – do not have to stock guest ales, although many of their parent companies (Bass, Whitbread, Carlsberg-Tetley, Scottish & Newcastle and Courage) carry wide ranges because the market demands it.

❑ **National brewery tenants and lessees** may stock a guest real ale of their own choice, in addition to any 'foreigners' offered by the brewery itself.

❑ **Free traders** divide along the same lines as before. The Beer Orders gave free traders tied by loan to the national brewers the same guest ale right as big brewery lessees. But interest rates on brewery loans are normally linked to sales volumes and therefore influence which beers are sold. Even genuine free traders can be swayed by offers of big discounts from the larger breweries – effectively an insidious form of tie.

❑ There have always been **non-brewing pub chains** such as Yates Wine Lodges, but now there are far more. Most of the chains which have appeared recently (see Pub Groups) were formed when the Beer Orders forced the big brewers to dispose of 11,000 pubs in an effort to improve choice and competition. But don't look for an interesting selection of ales from regionals and microbrewers: this generation of pub chains was in the main founded by former big brewery exec-

utives taking over pubs no longer required by the big brewers with financial assistance from big brewers, through loans like those offered to free houses but on a much greater scale. These companies run traditional managed houses and tenancies, so don't blame the licensee if you have to drink rubbish beers: it's all tied trade, just like the old days. The bitter irony is that many of these pubs fleetingly enjoyed the right to stock a guest ale when they belonged to the big breweries. Then they were sold, and the right was extinguished.

❑ Finally, there are the **alehouse chains.** Some of these – the likes of Wetherspoon's and the smaller Unicorn Inns and Tynemill Inns – are genuinely free and stock real ales from brewers large and small, although since they are all managed houses, the people behind the bar aren't the ones making the choices: somebody at head office does that, and discount is a big factor. The others – Hogshead, Firkin, T&J Bernard's, Festival Ale Houses – belong to the managed house divisions of the big brewers, so their managers don't break wind without permission. Tap & Spile is worth seeking out, though: it's part of Pubmaster, and is a notable patron of microbrewers, although, again, its pubs are managed and stocking is largely centrally dictated.

That outlines the tied house system as it officially exists today. There are, however, many sub rosa methods by which big brewers exert control over dissident tenants, and which CAMRA reports to the Office of Fair Trading whenever it discovers them. Big brewery area managers have sales targets to meet, and no one at head office turns a hair if they unlawfully threaten lessees with lines like: 'Sell a guest ale and you lose the discount on all your other beers', or: 'Sell a guest ale and your rent goes through the roof'.

Big brewers manipulate their estates to their own advantage, which is natural but not always to the public good. For instance, the one feature common to almost all the long leases around today is a fully-repairing clause transferring 'put and keep' responsibility from brewer to lessee. This has landed the lessee with the financial responsibility for internal and external repairs to the property, matters traditionally handled by the brewery under the old tenancy system. This, combined with the higher rents mentioned earlier, has liberated huge sums for the brewers to spend on developing their managed estates.

In effect, the lessees have been subsidising the creation of abominations such as Jumblie Villages and Scruffy Murphy's, and when their pubs are milked dry, they are sold for private housing, or, if they're not pretty enough for that, for redevelopment. Village pubs close in droves; great managed barns open on the proceeds. That's the free market: all for the best in the best of all possible worlds?

Ted Bruning is a freelance journalist and assistant editor of What's Brewing, CAMRA's monthly newspaper.

MINOR LAW, MAJOR HASSLE

Jill Adam reviews the implementation of the new children's certificate for pubs.

L egislation came into force on 3 January 1995 to allow licensees in England and Wales to apply for children's certificates. This brought them into line with publicans in Scotland, where new conditions for admitting children into pubs have been in force for over 12 months. It was fervently hoped by CAMRA and many in the brewing industry that the legislation would be worded in such a way that the inconsistencies in granting the new licences experienced in Scotland would not be repeated. Alas, it was not to be. Like the Beer Orders, overtly designed to help the smaller fish in the business, it has turned out to benefit the big players yet again.

To be fair to the Government, the legislation was drawn up with the intention of keeping demands on licensees to a minimum, but it made the mistake of leaving it up to local licensing authorities to determine exactly what conditions to impose on landlords who wish to open their pubs to families. The Home Office circular addressed to all licensing authorities simply stated:

'Before granting a children's certificate, licensing justices must be satisfied that the bar area to which the application relates constitutes an environment in which it is suitable for children under 14 to be present, and that meals and beverages other than intoxicating liquor will be available for consumption in that area ... (it) requires the licensee to display a notice in a conspicuous place within the certificated bar area, stating the effect of the certificate and of any conditions attached to it.'

NOT IN MY BACK YARD

The circular goes on to point out that during the Parliamentary debates on children's certificates, 'the Government's intention was that there will be the least possible alteration to the normal operation of the bars concerned ... (and it has) tried to put in place a regime ... that does not impose unnecessarily expensive and time-consuming burdens on the police and courts who will have to administer it, or the licensees'.

CAMRA's interpretation of this, and indeed that of the Brewers and Licensed Retailers Association, is that the decision as to whether a pub is suitable should be left to the licensee and the parents. All that the licensing authorities really need to do

The Family welcome.

Full menu served all day everyday
Family dining · Internal Play area

Garden & Play equipment

THE FAMILY PUB – THE ONLY WAY FORWARD, OR WILL GENUINE PUBS BE ALLOWED TO COMPETE? is inspect the premises to ensure the legal requirements are covered.

However, many licensing authorities appear to be taking on the role of nanny and adopting a NIMBY stance, i.e. 'whatever the Government may say, we're not letting kids willy-nilly into pubs around here'. In many parts of the country, when licensees have applied for children's certificates, they have been sent lists of conditions that would be more appropriate for a playgroup than a pub. For example, North East Suffolk Licensing Committee's list of 17 conditions included:

❑ Meals to be available at all times the certificate is operating.

❑ No smoking in the area.

❑ No gaming machines in the area; if a dartboard is in the area it is not to be used during the operation of the certificate.

❑ Nappy changing facilities to be provided in both male and female toilets, or a separate room provided for such a purpose. Low-level WCs, urinals and wash basins to be made available; the hot water supply to the latter to be thermostatically controlled to 39° C.

❑ Furniture and fittings to be of a safe design, i.e. no sharp-edged or glass tables, etc.

These are typical of instructions sent out by licensing boards around the country and fly in the face of the

Government's stated desire of not imposing unnecessary expense. From a health and safety point of view, of course, a lot of these requirements are desirable, but hardly essential – how many children use low-level urinals at home? It would also be more reasonable if similar conditions applied to other places that welcome children, such as cinemas, clubs and restaurants, but they do not. The irony is that even if a pub does adhere to such draconian measures, if that same pub has a good old family room (a room without a bar), none of these conditions apply.

WHY BOTHER?

It is the case that, faced with such high demands, pubs in many areas have either not bothered to apply for children's certificates, or have quickly withdrawn their applications. This is a pity, since, because of the parochial nature of licensing authorities, a perfectly suitable pub in one town may lose all its family trade to another house a few miles away where licensing authorities are less stringent. Or the national brewery chains which are determinedly opening pubs just to cater for families, may clean up the market by providing exactly what is wanted by the authorities, although not necessarily by the customers. Chains like Whitbread's Brewer's Fayre, along with certain magistrates, seem to think that the new law is a blueprint for a completely new kind of establishment, a 'children's pub', which is patently not the kind of place that most self-respecting CAMRA families would wish to visit.

TIME TO SEE SENSE

The children's certificate does not mean that all pubs have to allow in children. Indeed, in principle, it is a sensible way of opening up certain, suitable pubs to families whilst preserving others for adult use only. If only all licensing authorities would adopt the simple approach of Nithsdale District Council in Dumfries, which, after ensuring that premises are suitable for the under-14s, impose only two other conditions: that cooked meals be available while the licence is in operation and that the part of the premises set aside be clearly marked.

CAMRA is determined that children's certificates should succeed and will continue to campaign for children to be allowed into existing pubs where they can learn how to behave in a special kind of social environment and can witness alcohol being consumed in a sensible, grown up way – thus discouraging reckless, boozy experiments in their teenage years. It does not want to see a massive growth in licensed creches, courtesy of the big breweries.

Jill Adam has edited two editions of CAMRA's Pubs For Families and has been assistant editor of the Good Beer Guide for ten years.

Avon

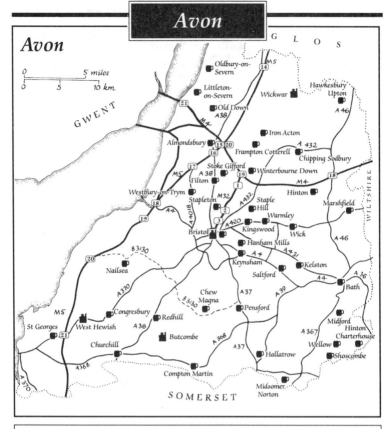

Avon

GLOS

GWENT

WILTSHIRE

SOMERSET

0 5 miles
0 5 10 km

Oldbury-on-Severn
Littleton-on-Severn
Hawkesbury Upton
Wickwar
Old Down
Iron Acton
Almondsbury
Frampton Cotterell
Chipping Sodbury
Stoke Gifford
Winterbourne Down
Filton
Hinton
Westbury-on-Trym
Stapleton
Staple Hill
Marshfield
Bristol
Warmley
Kingswood
Wick
Hanham Mills
Nailsea
Keynsham
Kelston
Saltford
Bath
Chew Magna
Pensford
Congresbury
Redhill
Midford
Hinton Charterhouse
St Georges
West Hewish
Butcombe
Wellow
Churchill
Hallatrow
Shoscombe
Compton Martin
Midsomer Norton

Butcombe, Butcombe; **Hardington**, Bristol; **RCH**, West Hewish; **Ross**, **Smiles**, Bristol; **Wickwar**, Wickwar

---

Almondsbury

Bowl Inn
16 Church Road, Lower Almondsbury
☎ (01454) 612757
11–3, 5 (6 Sat)–11
Courage Best Bitter, Directors; John Smith's Bitter; Wadworth 6X; guest beers Ⓗ
Pleasant, 17th-century pub with a good reputation for food in the bar and restaurant.
🛏 Q 🕭 🌣 🛏 ◑ ● P

Bath

Bell Inn
103 Walcot Street
☎ (01225) 460426
11.30–11
Courage Best Bitter, Directors; Fuller's London Pride; Smiles Best Bitter, Exhibition Ⓗ
Open-plan bar, renowned for its jazz and soul music.
🌣 ♣

Belvedere
25 Belvedere, Lansdown Road
☎ (01225) 330264
12–2.45, 5.30–11
Draught Bass; Hancock's HB Ⓗ
Welcoming, unpretentious local with a quiet lounge.
Q 🕭 ♣

Bladud Arms
Gloucester Road, Lower Swainswick (A46)
☎ (01225) 420152
11–3, 5.30–11
Butcombe Bitter; Oakhill Best Bitter; Wadworth 6X; Wickwar Brand Oak; guest beer (occasional) Ⓗ
Long, lounge-bar local with a public bar section. Skittle alley. No meals Sun eve.
🌣 ◑ ● ♣ P

Cross Keys Inn
Midford Road, Combe Down (B3110)
☎ (01225) 832002
11–2.30, 6–11
Courage Best Bitter; Ushers Best Bitter, Founders Ⓗ
Attractive Bath stone building with two traditional bars, and a large aviary in the garden. Interesting food. Ushers seasonal beers sold.
🛏 🌣 ◑ ● P ⚹

Fairfield Arms
1 Fairfield Park Road, Fairfield
☎ (01225) 310594
11–2.30 (3 Sat), 6–11
Courage Best Bitter; Ushers Best Bitter Ⓗ
Welcoming local, with an award-winning garden, on the north-eastern outskirts.
🌣 🕭 ♣

Forester's Arms
Bradford Road, Combe Down
☎ (01225) 837671
11–2.30, 5–11
Courage Best Bitter; Otter Bitter, Head; guest beer Ⓗ
Pub where the comfortable lounge has a skittle alley behind curtains. The spartan public bar has a pool table. No food Sat.
◑ 🕭 ♣ P

Avon

Golden Fleece
1–3 Avon Buildings, Lower
Bristol Road ☎ (01225) 429572
11–2.30 (3 Sat), 5.30 (4.30 Fri, 6
Sat)–11
**Courage Georges BA, Best
Bitter; guest beer** Ⓗ
Popular, street-corner local.
The guest beer changes daily.
Lunches Mon–Fri. Ⓖ ⊞ ♣ P

Hatchetts
6–7 Queen Street (off Queen
Sq) ☎ (01225) 425045
11–11
Beer range varies Ⓗ
Popular side-street free house
serving five, usually higher
gravity beers which change
daily. Beer prices are below
average for the area. No food
Sun. Ⓖ ⇌ (Spa)

King's Arms
1 Monmouth Place
☎ (01225) 425418
11–11
**Courage Best Bitter,
Directors; guest beer** Ⓗ
Former coaching inn, a
popular weekend music venue
for its mainly local clientele.
Sun lunch served.
⚘ ⇆ ⊞ ♣

Larkhall Inn
St Saviours Road, Larkhall
(400 yds off A4/A46 jct)
☎ (01225) 425710
11–2 (2.30 Fri), 6–10.30 (11 Fri & Sat);
12–2, 7–10.30 Sun
**Courage Best Bitter,
Directors** Ⓗ
Distinctive, suburban local. No
entry after 10.30 Fri or Sat.
⚏ Q ⚘ ⊞ ♣

Old Crown
1 Crown Hill, Weston
☎ (01225) 423371
11–2.30 (3 Sat), 6 (6.30 Sat)–11
**Draught Bass; Courage Best
Bitter; Smiles Best Bitter;
Wadworth 6X; Whitbread
Boddingtons Bitter** Ⓗ
A staging post during the Civil
War, this pleasant village local
has a spacious single bar and a
walled garden, popular with
families. Eve meals Wed–Sat;
no food winter Mon.
⚘ Ⓖ ▶ ♣

Old Farmhouse
1 Lansdown Road
☎ (01225) 316162
12–11
**Draught Bass; Butcombe
Bitter; Hall & Woodhouse
Tanglefoot; Wadworth 6X** Ⓗ
Lively local of character. Its
unusual sign is a caricature of
the landlord. Live jazz Wed–
Fri. No food Sun.
⚏ ⚘ Ⓖ ▶ ⊞ ♣ P

Porter Butt
York Place, London Road
☎ (01225) 425084

12–3, 5.30–11; 12–11 Sat
**Courage Georges BA, Best
Bitter, Directors; Marston's
Pedigree** Ⓗ
Two-bar local staging live
music in the 'Walcot Palais'
downstairs. Next to the bus
depot. No food Sun.
⚘ Ⓖ ⊞ ♣ P

Pulteney Arms
37 Daniel Street, Bathwick
☎ (01225) 463923
11.30–2.30, 5.30–11; 11–3, 5–11 Sat;
11–11 Sat
Smiles Best Bitter Ⓖ; **Ushers
Best Bitter; Wadworth 6X;
guest beer** Ⓗ
Comfortable pub near
Henrietta Park. The main bar
is a shrine to rugby; an
overspill room is popular with
students. Eve meals finish at
8.45. Ⓖ ▶ ⊞ ♣ ⚲

Rose & Crown
6 Brougham Place, Larkhall
(400 yds NW of A4/A46 jct)
☎ (01225) 425700
11–11
**Smiles Bitter, Best Bitter,
Bristol Stout, Exhibition;
guest beer** Ⓗ
Friendly, refurbished
suburban local. ⚘ Ⓖ ♣ ⚲

Star Inn
23 The Vineyards (A4 NE of
centre) ☎ (01225) 425072
12 (11 Sat)–2.30, 5.30–11
Draught Bass Ⓖ; **Wadworth
6X; guest beer** Ⓗ
Atmospheric classic town pub
where Bass is served from the
jug. Q ⊞ ♣

Bristol

Beaufort Arms
23 High Street, Clifton
☎ (0117) 9735906
11.30–2.30, 5–11; 11–11 Sat
Banks's Hanson's Mild Ⓔ,
Bitter; Marston's Pedigree Ⓗ
Comfortable, single-bar pub
with a small darts room. Pool
table. ♿ ♣ ⚲ ⊟

Brewery Tap
6–8 Colston Street
☎ (0117) 9213668
11–11; 7–10.30 Sun, closed Sun lunch
**Smiles Bitter, Best Bitter,
Exhibition; guest beer** Ⓗ
Small, friendly, wood-panelled
pub with a horseshoe bar. A
no-smoking extension offers
more space, but it can still get
crowded. Breakfast 8–11;
meals noon–8pm. Q Ⓖ ▶ ⚹

Cadbury House
68 Richmond Road,
Montpelier ☎ (0117) 9247874
12–11
**Courage Best Bitter; Wickwar
Brand Oak** Ⓗ
Busy, cosmopolitan pub. The

covered terrace opens in
summer to a pleasant garden.
Great jukebox; interesting
games. Alternative beers from
Wickwar may be stocked. Eve
meals finish at 6.30.
⚏ ⚘ Ⓖ ▶ ⇌ (Montpelier)
♣ ⚲

Hope & Anchor
38 Jacobs Wells Road, Clifton
☎ (0117) 9292987
12–11
Beer range varies Ⓗ
Popular, one-bar free house,
close to Clifton centre, selling
four changing beers, most
unusual for the area. Food is
served all day, interesting and
sensibly priced. Brewing may
resume this year. ⚘ Ⓖ ▶

Howlin' Wolf
155 St Michael's Hill
☎ (0117) 9735960
11–11
**Courage Best Bitter;
Wychwood Best; guest beer** Ⓗ
Basic one-roomer famous for
blues music. Blues
memorabilia adorns the walls.
⚲

Kellaway Arms
Kellaway Avenue, Horfield
☎ (0117) 9497548
11–3, 6.30–11; 11–11 Sat
**Courage Georges BA, Best
Bitter; Marston's Pedigree;
Smiles Best Bitter** Ⓗ
Comfortable, two-bar
suburban local, close to
Horfield Common: a large
public bar and a smaller
lounge. Slides in the garden.
No food Sun. Q ⚘ Ⓖ ⊞ ♣

King's Head
60 Victoria Street
☎ (0117) 9277860
11–3 (not Sat), 5.30 (7.30 Sat)–11;
12–3, 7.45–10.30 Sun
**Draught Bass; Courage
Georges BA, Best Bitter** Ⓗ
Small, unspoilt Victorian gem,
boasting a superb bar back
and a tramcar bar. Excellent
lunch snacks. Q ⇌ (T Meads)

Lion Tavern
19 Church Lane, Cliftonwood
☎ (0117) 9268492
12–2.30 (3 Sat), 6–11
**Butcombe Bitter; Courage
Georges BA, Best Bitter,
Directors; Marston's
Pedigree** Ⓗ
Traditional local in a quiet
area, popular eves with
students and much frequented
by Clifton folk. No meals Sun
eve. Ⓖ ▶ ⊞ ♣

Orchard
Hanover Place
☎ (0117) 9262678
11–3, 5–11
Draught Bass; Courage Best

Bitter; Smiles Bitter;
Wadworth 6X Ⓗ
Friendly, single-bar pub near
Brunel's *SS Great Britain*.
🏠 ◖ & ⌂

Phoenix

15 Wellington Street, St Judes
☎ (0117) 9558327
11.30–11
Draught Bass Ⓖ/Ⓗ; Oakhill
Best Bitter, Black Magic Ⓗ,
Yeoman; Wadworth 6X Ⓖ;
Wickwar Coopers WPA,
Brand Oak Ⓗ; guest
beers Ⓖ/Ⓗ
Archetypal, street-corner local
with a split-level single bar.
🏠

Prince of Wales

5 Gloucester Road, Bishopston
☎ (0117) 9245552
11–2.30, 5.30–11; 11–11 Sat
Butcombe Bitter; Courage
Georges BA, Directors Ⓗ
Busy, two-bar town pub, with
a courtyard. Popular with
locals and students.
Q 🏠 ◖ ♣

Princess of Wales

1 Westbourne Grove,
Bedminster ☎ (0117) 9493008
11–3, 5.30–11; 11–11 Fri & Sat
Draught Bass; Courage Best
Bitter; Whitbread Flowers
Original; guest beer Ⓗ
Clean, friendly, one-bar
back-street local. Live organ
music alternate weekends.
Good value lunches Mon–Fri.
🏠 ◖ ♣ 🍴

Robin Hood

56 St Michael's Hill,
Kingsdown (opp. Children's
Hospital) ☎ (0117) 9291334
11–3, 6 (5 Fri)–11
Adnams Extra; Hall &
Woodhouse Tanglefoot;
Smiles Best Bitter; Wadworth
IPA, 6X; guest beer Ⓗ
Refurbished, wood-panelled,
basic, one-room pub. Friendly
atmosphere. No food Sat. 🏠 ◖

Seahorse

15 Upper Maudlin Street (near
Royal Infirmary)
☎ (0117) 9299761
11–11
Smiles Bitter, Best Bitter,
Exhibition; guest beer Ⓗ
Attractively refurbished
Smiles pub, opposite the
brewery; reminiscent of an old
railway station 🏠 ◖ ▶ ♣

Swan With Two Necks

12 Little Ann Street, St Judes
(near end of M32)
☎ (0117) 9551893
11.30–3, 5–11; 11.30–11 Fri; 12–11 Sat
Hardington Bitter, Best Bitter,
Jubilee, Moonshine, Old Ale;
guest beer Ⓗ
Popular one-bar local,
refurbished in a basic style.

Other one-off beers from
Hardington occasionally
appear, along with interesting
guests. Q ◖ ♣

Chew Magna

Bear & Swan

South Parade
☎ (01275) 332577
11–3, 6–11; 11–11 Sat
Courage Best Bitter; Mole's
Tap Ⓗ
Stone pub with two bars: the
lounge extends through an
alcove. 🏠 🏠 ◖ ▶ P

Chipping Sodbury

Beaufort Hunt

72 Broad Street
☎ (01454) 312871
10.30–3, 5 (6.30 Sat)–11
Draught Bass; Tetley Bitter;
guest beer Ⓗ
Homely, two-bar, high street
local, ornately decorated. Very
good food. The guest beer
changes weekly. A house beer
is also sold. ◖ ♣

Churchill

Crown Inn

The Batch, Skinners Lane, (off
A38, S of A368/A38 jct)
☎ (01934) 852995
11.30–3, 5.30–11
Draught Bass; Butcombe
Bitter; Palmers IPA; RCH PG
Steam; guest beers Ⓖ
Unspoilt country pub on the
edge of the Mendips: two bars
with log fires and a wide
selection of ales, mainly from
SW independents.
🏠 Q 🍴 🏠 ◖ ▲ ♣ P

Compton Martin

Ring o' Bells

Bath Road ☎ (01761) 221284
11.30–3, 6.30–11
Draught Bass Ⓖ; Butcombe
Bitter; John Smith's Bitter;
Wadworth 6X; guest beer Ⓗ
Over 200 years old; a very
pleasant, two-bar pub offering
wonderful food, a well-
equipped family room, and a
safe garden.
🏠 🍴 🏠 ◖ ▶ ▲ ♣ P

Congresbury

Old Inn

Pauls Causeway (from A370,
right at village cross, then left)
☎ (01934) 832270
11.30–11
Draught Bass; Marston's
Pedigree Ⓖ; Smiles Bitter,
Best Bitter, Exhibition; guest
beer Ⓗ
Friendly, old village local with
two log fires. Eve meals
Wed–Sat. 🏠 Q 🏠 ▶ ♣ P

Filton

Filton Recreation Centre

Elm Park ☎ (0117) 9791988
12–2 (11.30–2.30 Thu & Fri), 6.30–11;
11.30–2, 4 (6 summer)–11 Sat; 12–2 (3
winter), 7–10.30 Sun
Butcombe Bitter; Ind Coope
Burton Ale; Smiles Best
Bitter; Tetley Bitter; guest
beer Ⓗ
Leisure centre bar open to the
public; the landlord is a
Burton *Master Cellarman*.
Weekly guest beer. Snacks
served. & ♣ P

Frampton Cotterell

Rising Sun

43 Ryecroft Road
☎ (01454) 772330
11.30–3, 7–11
Draught Bass; Butcombe
Bitter; Smiles Best Bitter;
Wadworth 6X; Wickwar
Coopers WPA; guest beer Ⓗ
Real, friendly local, a genuine
free house with a single bar
and a skittle alley. Avon
CAMRA *Pub of the Year* 1995.
Q 🏠 ◖ ♣ P

Hallatrow

Old Station Inn

Wells Road (A39)
☎ (01761) 452228
11–3, 5 (6 Sat)–11
Draught Bass; Oakhill Best
Bitter; Otter Ale; Wadworth
6X Ⓗ
Friendly village free house,
full of bric-a-brac.
🏠 Q 🍴 🏠 🍴 ◖ ▶ ♣ P

Hanham Mills

Old Lock & Weir

From Hanham go to bottom of
Abbotts Rd, turn right
☎ (0117) 9673793
11–11
Draught Bass; Marston's
Pedigree; Wadworth 6X; guest
beer Ⓗ
Welcoming pub over 300 years
old, on the Avon. A genuine
free house which welcomes
families and drinkers alike.
The beer range may expand.
🏠 Q 🏠 ◖ ▶ ♣ P

Hawkesbury Upton

Beaufort Arms

High Street ☎ (01454) 238217
12–3, 5.30–11; 12–11 Sat
Wadworth 6X; Wickwar
Brand Oak; guest beers Ⓗ
18th-century free house with
Victorian modifications and a
stable converted to a dining

Avon

area: a friendly two-bar local, close to the Cotswold Way. Well behaved families, walkers and cyclists welcomed. Eve meals Wed–Sun. Cider in summer.
🏚 Q ❀ ◑ ▶ ⊞ ▲ ♣ ⟲ P

Hinton

Bull
1½ miles SW of M4 jct 18
OS735768 ☎ (0117) 9372332
11–2.30, 7 (6 summer)–11
Draught Bass; Wadworth IPA, 6X Ⓗ**, Old Timer** Ⓖ
Mature, unspoilt country local with a large garden for children, an attractive bar and a lounge. Full meals are served in the restaurant.
🏚 Q ⛄ ❀ ◑ ▶ ⊞ ▲ ♣ P

Hinton Charterhouse

Rose & Crown
High Street ☎ (01225) 722153
11–11
Draught Bass; Butcombe Bitter; guest beer Ⓖ
Comfortable, panelled lounge and restaurant.
🏚 ❀ ◑ ▶ ⊞ ♣ P

Iron Acton

Rose & Crown
High Street ☎ (01454) 228423
5–11; 12–2.30, 6–11 Sat
Draught Bass; Hook Norton Old Hooky; Marston's Pedigree; Smiies Exhibition; Whitbread WCPA Ⓗ
Friendly, 17th-century village pub with two bars.
🏚 Q ❀ 🍽 ♣

Kelston

Old Crown Inn
Bath Road ☎ (01225) 423032
11.30–2.30 (3 Sat), 5–11
Draught Bass; Butcombe Bitter; Smiles Best Bitter; Wadworth 6X Ⓗ
Attractive, 18th-century coaching inn with a large garden, flagstone floor and original beer engines. Eve meals Thu–Sun; no lunches Sun. 🏚 Q ❀ ◑ ▶ P

Keynsham

Ship Inn
Temple Street
☎ (0117) 9869841
11–2.30, 6–11
Draught Bass; Courage Georges BA, Best Bitter; guest beers Ⓗ
Popular, two-bar community pub hosting barbecues in summer. Good value food.
❀ ◑ ♣ P

Kingswood

Prince Albert
130 Two Mile Hill
☎ (0117) 9610239
12–2, 5–11; 11–11 Fri & Sat
Hardington Bitter, Best Bitter, Jubilee, Moonshine; guest beers Ⓗ
Traditionally refurbished, quiet local; Hardington's second outlet. Q ♣

Littleton-on-Severn

White Hart
☎ (01454) 412275
11.30–2.30, 6–11; 11.30–11 Sat
Smiles Bitter, Best Bitter, Exhibition; Wadworth 6X; guest beers Ⓗ
Popular, 17th-century country pub, sympathetically enlarged. Avon CAMRA *Pub of the Year* 1994. Wide range of home-cooked food.
🏚 Q ⛄ ❀ 🍽 ◑ ▶ ♣ P ⤧

Marshfield

Catherine Wheel
High Street ☎ (01225) 892220
11–2.30 (not Mon), 6–11
Courage Georges BA Ⓗ**, Best Bitter** Ⓖ**; Ruddles Best Bitter; Wadworth 6X** Ⓗ**, Old Timer** Ⓖ
Thriving, welcoming, 17-century local. The new rear lounge was once the coal cellar. No food Mon.
🏚 Q 🍽 ◑ ▶ ⊞ ♣ P

Midford

Hope & Anchor
On B3110 ☎ (01225) 832296
12–2.30, 6.30–11
Draught Bass; Butcombe Bitter; Mole's Best Bitter Ⓗ
Large pub, split into eating and drinking areas, with a patio at the rear. Next to the remains of Midford station.
🏚 ❀ ◑ ▶ P

Midsomer Norton

White Hart
The Island ☎ (01761) 418270
11–3, 5.30–11
Draught Bass Ⓖ
Victorian establishment with many rooms, a minor classic. No food Sun.
🏚 ⛄ ◑ ⊞ ♣ ⟲

Nailsea

Blue Flame
West End OS449690
☎ (01275) 856910
12–3 (4 Sat), 6–11
Draught Bass; Oakhill Best Bitter Ⓗ**; Smiles Best Bitter, Exhibition; guest beer** Ⓖ

Wonderful, small cottage-style pub, popular with a mixed clientele.
🏚 Q ⛄ ❀ ⊞ ⅋ ▲ ♣ ⟲ P

Oldbury-on-Severn

Anchor Inn
Church Road
☎ (01454) 413331
11.30–2.30 (3 Sat), 6.30 (6 Sat)–11
Bass Worthington BB Ⓗ**, Draught Bass** Ⓖ**; Butcombe Bitter; Marston's Pedigree; S&N Theakston Best Bitter** Ⓗ**, Old Peculier** Ⓖ
Very popular, friendly village local: a converted 16th-century mill, with a well used garden in summer. Excellent good value, home-cooked food in both the bar and restaurant.
🏚 Q ❀ ◑ ▶ ⊞ ⅋ ♣ P

Old Down

Fox Inn
Inner Down ☎ (01454) 412507
12–3, 6–11
Draught Bass; Brains Bitter; Whitbread Flowers IPA Ⓗ
150-year-old, beamed, picturesque village pub, built from local stone; cosy, yet spacious. Flowers, hanging baskets, and a children's play area in the garden.
🏚 Q ❀ ♣ ⟲ P

Pensford

Rising Sun
Church Street
☎ (01761) 490402
11.30–2.30, 7–11
Ind Coope Burton Ale; Tetley Bitter; Wadworth 6X Ⓗ
Cosy, 15th-century, stone pub with a garden leading down to the River Chew (unfenced). Good value food (no eve meals Sun or Mon); book Sun lunch. Carlsberg-Tetley house beer. 🏚 ❀ ◑ ▶ ♣ ⟲ P

Redhill

Bungalow Inn
Winford Lane (from Bristol, 1st left after Lulsgate Airport)
☎ (01275) 472386
10.30–4.30, 6–11
Draught Bass Ⓔ**; Wadworth IPA, 6X** Ⓗ
50-year-old, cosy, brick bungalow. Large function room. Good value food (not served Sun).
🏚 Q ❀ ◑ ⅋ ♣ P

St Georges

Woolpack Inn
Shepherd's Way (off M5 jct 21)
☎ (01934) 521670
12–2.30, 6–11

Courage Best Bitter; guest
beers Ⓗ
17th-century coaching house
and woolpacking station: a
friendly, two-bar pub and
restaurant. Varying guest
beers (three in winter, up to
five in summer). Booking
advised for eve meals (good
value).
🚪 ⚘ ◖ ❙ ⚠ 𝍅 (Worle)
♣ P

Saltford

Bird in Hand

High Street ☎ (01225) 873335
11–2.30 (3 Sat), 6.30 (6 Fri & Sat)–11
Draught Bass; Courage Best
Bitter; Wadworth 6X; guest
beer Ⓗ
Large, food-oriented pub with
access from the Bath–Bristol
cycle track. Large garden.
🚪 ⛱ ⚘ ◖ ❙ ⌕ P

Shoscombe

Apple Tree

☎ (01761) 432263
12–3 (not Mon–Fri), 7–11
Draught Bass; Oakhill Best
Bitter; Otter Bitter; guest
beers Ⓖ
Friendly village local nestling
in a hidden valley.
🚪 ⚘ ⛁ ⌕ P

Staple Hill

Humpers Off-licence

26 Soundwell Road
☎ (0117) 9565525
12–2, 4.30–10.30; 11–11 Sat
Smiles Best Bitter, Exhibition;
Wickwar Brand Oak Ⓗ; guest
beers Ⓖ
Street-corner off-licence with
the widest beer range and
lowest prices for miles. Up to
three guest beers, often strong;
polypins available. ⌕

Stapleton

Mason's Arms

124 Park Road
☎ (0117) 9654383
11–3, 7–11

Butcombe Bitter; Courage
Best Bitter; guest beers Ⓗ
Cosy, friendly, two-bar pub.
The lounge is small,
comfortable and ornate; the
bar is larger and spacious.
Two or three guest beers.
⚘ ♣ ⌕

Stoke Gifford

Parkway Tavern

Hatchet Road
☎ (0117) 9690329
11.30–2.30, 5–11; 11–11 Fri & Sat
Banks's Mild, Bitter Ⓔ;
Camerons Strongarm;
Marston's Pedigree Ⓗ
Large, two-bar modern pub on
the northern edge of Bristol,
handy for Parkway Station.
No food Sun.
⚘ ◖ 𝍅 (Parkway) ♣ P ⊟

Warmley

Midland Spinner

4 London Road (A420)
☎ (0117) 9674204
11–11
Courage Best Bitter,
Directors; Marston's Pedigree;
John Smith's Bitter;
Wadworth 6X Ⓗ
Pleasant pub with a railway
theme, near the old London
Midland line, now used by
walkers and cyclists. Skittle
alley. 🚪 ⚘ ◖ ♣ P

Wellow

Fox & Badger

Railway Lane
☎ (01225) 832293
11–3, 6–11; 11–11 Fri & Sat
Butcombe Bitter; Exmoor Ale;
guest beer Ⓗ
Pretty Wellow's only pub: a
two-bar local where,
unusually, the public bar is
carpeted and the lounge bar
flagstoned. Parking difficult.
🚪 ◖ ❙ ⛁ ♣ ⌕

Westbury-on-Trym

Post Office Tavern

17 Westbury Hill
☎ (0117) 9401233
11–11

Draught Bass Ⓖ; Fuller's
London Pride; Otter Bitter;
Marston's Pedigree; Smiles
Bitter Ⓗ; guest beers Ⓖ/Ⓗ
Interesting pub featuring lots
of old GPO memorabilia. The
good menu includes
substantial home-made pizzas.
Q ◖ ❙ ⅃

Prince of Wales

84 Stoke Lane
☎ (0117) 9623715
11–3, 5.30–11; 11–11 Sat
Courage Georges BA, Best
Bitter; Marston's Pedigree;
Mole's Tap; Ushers Best
Bitter Ⓗ
Friendly pub in a residential
area displaying royal
memorabilia and sporting
items. Popular in summer for
its large garden (barbecues).
No-smoking area lunchtime.
⚘ ◖ ⛸ ♣ ⅃

Wick

Rose & Crown

High Street
☎ (0117) 9372198
11.30–2.30, 5.30 (6 Sat)–11 (11–11
Tue–Sat in summer)
Courage Best Bitter,
Directors; John Smith's Bitter;
Wadworth 6X Ⓗ
Comfortable, spacious inn
dating from 1640, with original
beams and three log fires.
Popular for its varied,
reasonably priced food (book
Sun lunch). Families welcome
in one bar.
🚪 Q ⚘ ◖ ❙ ♣ P ⅃

Winterbourne
Down

Cross Hands

Down Road
☎ (01454) 772777
12 (11 Sat)–11
Courage Georges BA, Best
Bitter; Smiles Best Bitter;
Wadworth 6X; Wickwar
Brand Oak; guest beers Ⓗ
Sewing machines feature in
this carefully extended and
refurbished old village local.
🚪 ⛱ ⚘ ⌕

BREW IT YOURSELF

Beer enthusiasts who enjoy making, as well as drinking, their
favourite tipple should look out for two comprehensive brewing
manuals which reveal how home-brew needn't taste of sterilising
fluid and plastic. *The CAMRA Guide to Home Brewing* (priced £6.99),
by Graham Wheeler, provides all the information you need to make a
start, plus tips for more experienced home-producers. *Brew Your Own
Real Ale at Home* (also priced £6.99), by Graham Wheeler and Roger
Protz, takes readers a step further and reveals how they can recreate
over 100 famous commercial brands. See page 544 for how to order.

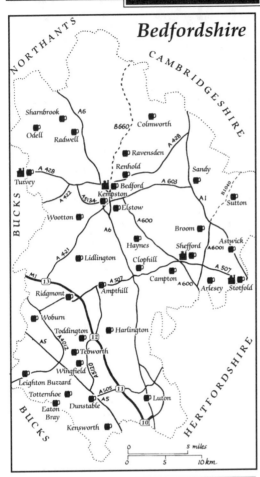

Bedfordshire

NORTHANTS

CAMBRIDGESHIRE

Sharnbrook · A6

Odell · Colmworth

Radwell · B660

Ravensden

Renhold · Sandy

Turvey · A428 · Bedford · A603

Kempston · A1

Elstow · Sutton

Wootton · A600

Broom

Haynes · Shefford · Astwick

Lidlington · Clophill · A6001

Campton · A600 · Arlesey · Stotfold

Ridgmont · Ampthill · A507

Woburn

Toddington · Harlington

Tebworth

Wingfield

Leighton Buzzard

Totternhoe · Dunstable · Luton

Eaton Bray · Kensworth

BUCKS

HERTFORDSHIRE

0 — 5 miles
0 — 5 — 10 km

 B&T, Shefford; **Stag**, Stotfold; **Nix Wincott**, Turvey; **Wells**, Bedford

Ampthill

Queen's Head
20 Woburn Street
☎ (01525) 405016
11–3, 5.30–11; 11–11 Fri & Sat
Wells Eagle, Bombardier; guest beer Ⓗ
Two small bars and a restaurant in a 17th-century listed building with a resident ghost. Live music on Sat nights, when the landlord performs. No meals Sun eve or Mon. Q ⛵ ◑ ▶ ♣

Arlesey

Three Tuns
86 High Street
☎ (01462) 731339
11.30–3, 5.30–11

Draught Bass; Morrells Bitter; guest beer (occasional) Ⓗ
Picturesque, 15th-century thatched pub in the village centre with a friendly atmosphere and an unusual collection of brasses.
⛵ ❀ ◑ ▶ ⌾ Ⓐ ♣ P

True Briton
27 Hospital Road
(off Station Rd)
☎ (01462) 731264
5.30–11; 11.30–3.30, 6–11 Sat
Fuller's London Pride; Tetley Bitter; guest beer Ⓗ
Very busy, friendly local, tucked away just behind the High Street – well worth seeking out. Open-plan, but with two separate bars, it fields an active pool team.
⌾ ♿ ♣ P

Astwick

Tudor Oaks
Taylors Road (A1, Baldock–Biggleswade road)
☎ (01462) 834133
11–11; 11–3, 6–11 Fri & Sat
Beer range varies Ⓗ
Pub featuring six handpumps which turn over six or seven different beers each week. Excellent value fresh food comes in huge portions. This part-16th-century, beamed building also boasts a Jacobean staircase and five fireplaces. Nightclub in a separate building Fri and Sat.
⛵ ❀ ⛵ ◑ ▶ ♣ P ⊟

Bedford

Fleur de Lis
12 Mill Street (E of A6)
☎ (01234) 211004
10.30–11; 12–2.30, 7–10.30 Sun
Wells Eagle; guest beers Ⓗ
Very well-run, one-bar, town-centre pub with a mixed clientele. Parking is difficult lunchtimes. Live music Tue eve. No food Sun. Upstairs meeting room. ◑

Queen's Tavern
120 Queen's Drive (off Goldington Rd via Polhill Ave and Haylands Way)
☎ (01234) 358514
11–2.30 (3.30 Sat), 5.30 (6 Sat)–11; 11–11 Fri
Greene King XX Mild, IPA, Abbot Ⓗ
Estate community pub with a lively public bar. Eve meals and Sun lunches served only if booked. ⛵ Q ❀ ◑ ⌾ P

Three Cups
45 Newnham Street (down Mill St from High St)
☎ (01234) 352153
11–11; 10.30–4, 7–11 Sat
Greene King IPA, Rayments Special, Abbot Ⓗ
Fine, traditional pub near the town centre with oak-panelled bars. A wide range of lunchtime food includes daily specials and full breakfasts. Greene King seasonal brews stocked. ❀ ◑ ▶ ⌾ ♣ P

Try also: Castle, Newnham St (Wells)

Broom

Cock
23 High Street
☎ (01767) 314411
12–2.30, 6–11
Greene King IPA, Abbot Ⓖ
Pub offering several rooms off a central corridor: no bar, the beer is served from the cellar

steps, straight out of the cask (Greene King's seasonal beers on handpump). Table skittles played. Good value meals (game a speciality). No food Sun or Mon eves. Well worth a visit.
🏚 Q 🌭 ⊛ ◖ ▮ ♣ P

Campton

White Hart
Mill Lane (off A507)
☎ (01462) 812657
6 (11 Sat) –11
Hook Norton Best Bitter; S&N Theakston Best Bitter; Wadworth 6X; guest beer Ⓗ
Popular, two-bar, open-plan village free house with a comfortable lounge and a dining area. Games dominate the public bar, which has a flagstone floor and an inglenook. Petanque played.
🏚 ⊛ ▮ ᶿ ♣ P

Clophill

Stone Jug
Back Street (off A6/A507 roundabout)
☎ (01525) 860526
1–3, 6–11
B&T Shefford Bitter; Courage Directors; S&N Theakston Best Bitter; John Smith's Magnet Ⓗ
Deservedly popular free house with guest beers to complement the regular range (NB a cask breather is sometimes used on these). Convenient for the Greensand Ridge Walk. No food Sun. Check before arriving with children. ⊛ ◖ P

Colmworth

Wheatsheaf
Wilden Road (¾ mile E of B660)
OS101574
☎ (01234) 862370
11–2.30, 6–11
Draught Bass; guest beers Ⓗ
17th-century country pub to the south of the village. Mind the low beams. Good, varied bar meals. Children's play area in the garden.
🏚 Q ⊛ ◖ 🔁 ♣ P ⅙

Dunstable

Highwayman
London Road (A5)
☎ (01582) 601122
11–2.30, 6–11
Wells Eagle, Bombardier, Fargo Ⓗ
Refurbished lounge bar of a medium-sized, two-star hotel, one mile south of the centre. Food is always available; the comfortable, new restaurant has an extensive menu and carvery. 🛏 ◖ ▮ ⅙ P

Star & Garter
147 High Street South
☎ (01582) 661044
11–11
Courage Best Bitter, Directors; guest beers Ⓗ
Traditional, two-bar pub with a comfortable lounge and a friendly welcome. Courtyard for families. ⊛ ♣

Victoria
69 West Street
☎ (01582) 662682
11–11
Tring Ridgeway; Whitbread Boddingtons Bitter; guest beers Ⓗ
Popular and friendly, town-centre pub with one, L-shaped bar. Good for games, including bar billiards and shove-ha'penny. No food Sun. ⊛ ◖ ♣

Eaton Bray

Hope & Anchor
63 Bower Lane
☎ (01525) 220386
11–3, 5–11; 11–11 Sat
Greene King IPA; Tetley Bitter; Wadworth 6X; Young's Bitter Ⓗ
Recently partly rebuilt, this low-beamed lounge bar and restaurant offers a homely, welcoming atmosphere, good food and a large garden.
⊛ ◖ ▮ P

Elstow

Swan
High Street (off A6)
☎ (01234) 352066
11–3, 7–11
Greene King IPA, Abbot Ⓗ
Old village pub near Elstow Abbey; one L-shaped room with a separate restaurant and a local clientele. Sun lunches should be booked (fresh produce is always used).
🏚 ⊛ ◖ ♣ P

Harlington

Carpenter's Arms
Sundon Road
☎ (01525) 872384
12–2.30, 5.30–11; 12–11 Sat
Banks's Bitter; Courage Best Bitter; Wadworth 6X Ⓗ
17th-century village pub featuring a low-ceilinged lounge, with copper-topped tables, and a small snug. The public bar has pool, darts, etc. The recommended upstairs restaurant does not open Sun or Mon eves.
🏚 ⊛ ◖ ▮ 🔁 🚲 ♣ P

Haynes

Greyhound
Northwood End Road
☎ (01234) 381239
11.30–3 (not Mon), 5.30–11
Greene King IPA Ⓗ
Old village pub extended to provide comfortable eating facilities. Cheap and good food attracts clients from local villages. Club-like atmosphere for drinkers; games teams are strongly supported. Greene King Abbot and seasonal beers are kept under cask breathers.
Q ⊛ ◖ ▮ 🔁 ᶿ ▮ ♣ P

Kempston

King William IV
56 High Street (A5134)
☎ (01234) 854533
11.30–2.30, 5.30 (6.30 Sat)–11
Wells Eagle, Bombardier, Fargo; guest beer Ⓗ
Attractive, genuine oak-beamed building which caters for a mixed clientele with one bar and a games room. Swings and slides in the nicely landscaped garden. No food Sun eve. ⊛ ◖ ▮ ♣ P

Try also: Griffin Bedford Rd (Greene King)

Kensworth

Farmer's Boy
216 Common Road
☎ (01582) 872207
11–11
Fuller's London Pride, ESB Ⓗ
Friendly well-kept village pub: a small public bar, a comfortable lounge and a dining area. Note the original Mann, Crossman & Paulin leaded windows. Excellent home-cooked food. Children's play area in the garden.
🏚 ⊛ ◖ ▮ 🔁 ▮ ♣ P

Leighton Buzzard

Black Lion
20 High Street
☎ (01525) 382510
11–3.30, 5.30–11; 12–2.30, 7–10.30 Sun
Ind Coope Benskins BB, Burton Ale; Tetley Bitter; guest beers Ⓗ
16th-century building, a pub since 1891. Crowded at lunchtimes and weekend eves; live music most Thus. No food Sun. Venue for the annual Leighton Buzzard beer festival (usually first weekend in July).
⊛ ◖

Hunt Hotel
19 Church Road, Linslade
☎ (01525) 374692
11–2.30, 5.30–11; 11–11 Sat

Bedfordshire

Draught Bass; Fuller's London Pride, ESB; Ringwood Fortyniner; Tetley Bitter Ⓗ
Modest hotel, tucked away in a quiet corner near the railway station, offering two bars and a restaurant. The beer range varies. ⍾ ◖ ▶ ⇌ P

Stag
1 Heath Road
☎ (01525) 372710
11–2.30, 6–11
Fuller's Chiswick, London Pride, Mr Harry, ESB Ⓗ
High quality renovation of a one-time basic Allied pub. The wedge-shaped, through-bar has an appetising food counter at the end. The landlord was runner-up in the brewery's annual cellarmanship competition. No food Sun. Tiny car park. ◖ ▶ P

Try also: Globe, Stoke Rd (Free)

Lidlington

Green Man
High Street
☎ (01525) 402869
12–3, 6–11
Greene King IPA, Abbot Ⓗ
17th-century thatched pub in a quiet village. A cosy lounge with an attached restaurant area offers a good varying menu (no food Sun–Tue eve). Handy for ramblers on the Greensand Ridge Path. Petanque played.
⍾ ⚘ ◖ ▶ ⊟ ⇌ ♣ ⌂ P

Luton

Bat & Barrel
104–106 Park Street
☎ (01582) 453125
11–11
Wells Eagle, Bombardier; guest beers Ⓗ
Attractive, half-tiled, two-bar town pub, near the university. Pool and Sky TV in the public; quieter lounge.
⚘ ⊟ ♣

Bird & Bush
Hancock Drive, Bushmead (off A6 on Bushmead Estate)
☎ (01582) 480723
11–3, 5–11; 11–11 Fri & Sat
Draught Bass; Hancock's HB; Young's Bitter or Special; guest beer Ⓗ
Opened in 1991, a community tavern with attractive Yorkshire flagstone and quarry tiled floors. Good bar food includes vegetarian options; Sun lunches only for booked groups of at least four people. No food Sun eve.
⚘ ◖ ▶ ⅙ ♣ P

Bricklayer's Arms
16–18 High Town Road
☎ (01582) 27482
11–2.30, 5–11; 11–11 Fri & Sat
Everards Beacon, Tiger, Old Original; guest beers Ⓗ
Friendly and unpretentious town pub, recently refurbished without changing its character. No carpets; old wooden casks are set here and there. Lunchtime snacks available.
⇌ ♣ P

Two Brewers
43 Dumfries Street
☎ (01582) 23777
12–11
B&T Shefford Bitter; guest beers Ⓗ
Friendly back-street local, popular with bricklayers, bankers and bikers. Yard for outside drinking. ⍾ ⚘ ♣

Odell

Bell
Horsefair Lane
☎ (01234) 720254
11–2.30, 6–11
Greene King IPA, Rayments Special, Abbot Ⓗ
Popular, thatched, multi-roomed village pub serving good food. The large garden near the river has a patio and an aviary of unusual birds. Path into Harrold Country Park. No food Sun eve. ⍾ Q ⚘ ◖ ▶ P

Radwell

Swan
Felmersham Road (1 mile off A6) OS004575
☎ (01234) 781351
12–2.30, 5–11
Wells Eagle, Bombardier Ⓗ
17th-century, thatched country inn with a restaurant and a quiet bar. Good quality food includes creative fish dishes (no meals Sun eve). Children welcome. ⍾ Q ⚘ ◖ ▶ P

Ravensden

Blacksmith's Arms
Bedford Road (B660, at crossroads 3 miles from Bedford) OS065545
☎ (01234) 771496
11–2.30, 6–11.30
Greene King IPA, Abbot; Whitbread Boddingtons Bitter; guest beers Ⓗ
Rural pub and restaurant with lounge and public bars. Family-run, it offers up to six guest ales from a range of over a hundred. The menu is based on fresh ingredients.
Q ⚘ ◖ ▶ ⊟ ⅙ ♣ P

Renhold

Three Horseshoes
42 Top End (1 mile N of A428)
☎ (01234) 870218
10.30–2.30, 6–11; 11–11 Sat
Greene King XX Mild, IPA, Abbot Ⓗ, Winter Ale Ⓖ
Friendly village pub with a children's play area in the garden. The public bar has traditional games and satellite TV. Good value home-cooked food includes fresh steaks and soups (no eve meals Sun or Tue). A long-standing outlet for mild.
⍾ Q ⚘ ◖ ▶ ⊟ ⅙ ♣ P

Ridgmont

Rose & Crown
89 High Street
☎ (01525) 280245
10.30–2.30, 6–11
Adnams Broadside; Mansfield Riding Bitter; Wells Eagle, Bombardier Ⓗ
Popular pub with extensive grounds, offering camping and caravanning facilities and barbecues in summer. The lounge bar has a 'Rupert' theme, and has a games area. In every edition of the Guide.
⍾ ⚘ ◖ ▶ ⊟ ▲ ♣ ⌂ P

Sandy

Bell
Station Road ☎ (01767) 680267
12–3 (4 Sat), 5 (7 Sat)–11
Greene King IPA, Abbot; guest beers Ⓗ
Friendly, one-bar local, opposite the station and handy for the RSPB HQ. Newly added restaurant and function rooms; four petanque pitches in the garden. Children welcome in the restaurant.
⍾ ⍾ ⚘ ◖ ▶ ⇌ ♣ P

Sharnbrook

Swan with Two Nicks
High Street ☎ (01234) 781585
11–3, 5–11; 11–11 Sat
Wells Eagle, Fargo; guest beers Ⓗ
Friendly village pub with a rear patio. Home-cooked food includes daily specials. Hood skittles played.
⍾ ⚘ ◖ ▶ ⊟ ♣ P

Shefford

Black Swan
1 High Street
☎ (01462) 811072
11–3, 6–11
B&T Shefford Bitter; Tetley Bitter; Vaux Samson Ⓗ

Friendly atmosphere in a pub serving home-made food from a vast menu seven days a week, including specials and Sun roasts. 🏠 Q ◑ ▶ ⅍ ♣ P

Stotfold

Stag
35 Brook Street
☎ (01462) 730261
12–2.30, 5–11, 12–11 Fri & Sat
Abel Brown's Lord Douglas Mild, Jack of Hearts; guest beers Ⓗ
Pub with a beer festival every week (over 250 different ales last year), including many unusual beers for the area. Two real ciders. The new brewery at the rear began production in spring 1995.
🏠 ❀ ⍾ ◑ ▶ ♣ ◔ P 🍴

Sutton

John o'Gaunt Inn
30 High Street
☎ (01767) 260377
12–3, 7–11
Greene King IPA, Abbot Ⓗ
Attractive pub in a picturesque village near a golf course. Good range of bar food; Sun lunches served. Table skittles are played and there is a floodlit boules court in the garden. 🏠 Q ❀ ◑ ▶ ⍾ ♣ P

Tebworth

Queen's Head
The Lane ☎ (01525) 87101
11–3 (3.30 Sat), 6.30 (7 Sat)–11
Adnams Broadside; Mansfield Riding Mild Ⓖ; **Wells Eagle** Ⓗ
Very welcoming, good-humoured pub with two small, popular bars. Good value food (no meals Sun). Quizzes, darts and conversation provide the entertainment.
🏠 ❀ ◑ ♣ P

Toddington

Angel
1 Luton Road
☎ (01525) 872380

11–2.30, 5–11 (11–11 Easter–Oct)
Courage Best Bitter; Ruddles Best Bitter; John Smith's Bitter; guest beers Ⓗ
Dating in part from the 16th century, this is an enterprising, entertaining and expanding pub, offering two (usually exotic) guest beers. Live jazz Thu eve and Sun lunch. An Italian restaurant is open Tue–Sat eves. Cream teas. Children's certificate.
🏠 ☙ ❀ ◑ ▶ ♣ P ⅍

Sow & Pigs
19 Church Square
☎ (01525) 873089
11–11
Greene King IPA, Abbot Ⓗ
Unpretentious and unpredictable pub with somewhat haphazard furnishing: the decor is strong on pigs. Visitors may find a sense of humour useful! In every edition of the *Guide*.
🏠 Q ❀ ◑ ♣ P

Totternhoe

Old Farm Inn
16 Church Road
☎ (01582) 661294
11–3, 6–11
Fuller's Chiswick, London Pride Ⓗ
Old village pub: a popular, traditional public bar with a low, boarded ceiling, and a quiet, comfortable lounge with a large inglenook. No meals Sun. 🏠 Q ❀ ◑ ▶ ♣ P

Turvey

Three Cranes
High Street (off A428)
☎ (01234) 881305
11–2.30, 6–11
Draught Bass; Fuller's London Pride, ESB; Smiles Bitter; Taylor Landlord; guest beers (summer) Ⓗ
17th-century coaching inn with an excellent range of food, including vegetarian

dishes, in both the bar and restaurant.
🏠 Q ❀ ⌷ ◑ ▶ P

Try also: Three Fyshes, Bridge St (Free)

Wingfield

Plough Inn
Tebworth Road
☎ (01525) 873077
12–3, 6–11
B&T Shefford Bitter Ⓗ, **Black Bat** Ⓖ; **Fuller's London Pride; guest beers** Ⓗ
Attractive, friendly and recently re-thatched village pub with a children's/pool room to the rear. Four ever-changing guest beers are normally available, plus Biddenden cider. Good food (no meals Sun eve). Local CAMRA *Pub of the Year* 1993 and 1994.
🏠 Q ☙ ❀ ◑ ▶ ⅍ ◔ P

Woburn

Royal Oak
40 George Street
☎ (01525) 290610
11–11
Greene King IPA, Rayments Special, Abbot Ⓗ
Multi-roomed, low-ceilinged, thatched pub of character. The pleasant garden features a covered patio area. Good food (no meals Sun eve); Greene King seasonal ales as available.
🏠 Q ☙ ❀ ◑ ▶ ♣

Wootton

Chequers
Hall End Road
☎ (01234) 768394
11–3, 5.30–11
Wells Eagle, Fargo; guest beers Ⓗ
16th-century coaching inn half a mile from the church, boasting three real fires, oak beams, brasses and a large garden. No eve bar meals winter Sun. Boules played in summer.
🏠 Q ❀ ◑ ▶ ⌷ ♣ P

A PINT OF SPECIAL

Not only are we witnessing a boom in new small breweries and, consequently, hundreds of new real ales, but established breweries, too, are looking to attract the attention of the discerning drinker by releasing seasonal and one-off brews. In addition to the standard range available in their tied houses, many independents now offer a special beer brewed in celebration of a local event or to catch the mood of the season.

Mansfield, Marston's, Greene King, Arkell's, McMullen, Fuller's and Ushers are amongst the regional brewers recreating old recipes and inventing new ales. Even the brewing giants have rushed into the fray. Ironically, it is something the micro-breweries have been doing for years.

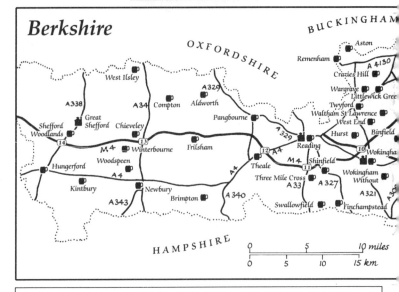

Berkshire

 Butts, *Great Shefford*; **Greenwood's**, *Wokingham*; **Hop Leaf**, *Reading*

Aldworth

Bell
Off B4009 ☎ (01635) 578272
11–3, 6–11; closed Mon except bank hols
Arkell's 3B, Kingsdown; Hook Norton Best Bitter; Morrells Bitter, Mild Ⓗ
Small, friendly, two-bar pub set admidst tranquil surroundings. Walk in and you go back in time to the old traditional pub. The hot rolls are well worth a try. National CAMRA *Pub of the Year* 1990 (and has not changed since). 🕍 Q 🕍 ⛲ ♣ P

Ascot

Stag
63 High Street (A329)
☎ (01344) 621622
11–3, 5.30–11; 11–11 Fri & Sat
Greene King IPA, Rayments Special, Abbot Ⓗ
Comfortable pub in the town centre, near the racecourse. The lounge is extensively ornamented with Victoriana. No lunches Sun. 🕍 ◖ ◗ ≠ ⛄

Aston

Flower Pot
Ferry Lane (down Aston Lane off A423) ☎ (01491) 574721
11–2.30, 6–11
Brakspear Mild, Bitter, Special, OBJ Ⓗ
Smart pub with its own landing stage, a short walk

from the River Thames: a basic public bar plus a smart lounge. Breakfast is served from 8am. No eve meals Sun.
🕍 Q 🕍 ⛵ ◖ ◗ ⛄ ▲ ♣ P

Binfield

Victoria Arms
Terrace Road North
☎ (01344) 483856
11–3, 5–11; 11–11 Sat
Fuller's Chiswick, London Pride, ESB Ⓗ
Stylish, multi-area pub with an interesting collection of bottles and bric-a-brac. Busy food trade. Built in 1856 and Fuller's *Country Pub of the Year* 1994. Large garden. Fuller's seasonal beers sold.
🕍 🕍 ◖ ◗ ♣ P ⛄

Bracknell

Old Manor
High Street
(opp. Met. Office roundabout)
☎ (01344) 304490
11–11
S&N Theakston Best Bitter, XB; Wadworth 6X; Younger Scotch; guest beer Ⓗ
Local CAMRA *Pub of the Year*: a town-centre Wetherspoon free house, originally the old manor house. Priest holes and escape tunnels were discovered during renovation. Period themes feature in each separate area. The guest beers change regularly.
Q ◖ ◗ ⛄ ⛄ P ⛄

Brimpton

Three Horseshoes
School Road ☎ (01734) 712183
11–3 (4 Sat), 6–11
Fuller's London Pride, ESB; Wadworth 6X *or* **Adnams Bitter** Ⓗ
Pleasant, Victorian, two-bar village pub, built by Mays of Basingstoke. The panelled lounge, with its fine old clock and old prints, is usually quiet. The larger bar offers darts, pool and a jukebox. No lunches Sun. Q 🕍 ◖ ⛄ ♣ P

Chieveley

Olde Red Lion
Green Lane (½ mile NW of M4, jct 13) ☎ (01635) 248379
11–3, 6 (5.30 Fri & Sat)–11
Arkells 2B, 3B, Kingsdown Ⓗ
Comfortable and friendly pub rescued by Arkell's which, while popular with passing trade, remains a village local. Oak beams, an open fire, and a wide range of pub games feature. 🕍 🕍 ◖ ◗ ⛄ ♣ P

Compton

Compton Swan Hotel
Cheap Street ☎ (01635) 578269
11–3, 5.30–11; 11–11 Fri & Sat; 12–3, 7.30–10.30 Sun
Adnams Broadside; Morland Original, Old Speckled Hen Ⓗ

Sympathetically refurbished pub drawing custom from near and far; a strikingly large pub which offers something for everyone yet remains cosy when required. Pets welcome. Good food. No meals Sun eve (except for residents).
🏠 🍴 ◖ ▶ ♿ ☘ ♣ P

Crazies Hill

Horns
Between A4 and A423, towards Warren Row OS799809
☎ (01734) 401416
11–3, 5.30–11
Brakspear Mild, Bitter, Old, Special, OBJ Ⓗ
Super country pub: no music, no machines, well worth a visit to all Brakspear's beers. A winner of many CAMRA awards. Eve meals Fri and Sat only (booking essential). No family area Fri/Sat eves.
🏠 Q ☞ ☘ ◖ ▶ 🍴 ☘ ♣ P

Eton

Waterman's Arms
Brocas Street
☎ (01753) 861001
11–2.30 (3 Fri & Sat), 6–11
Brakspear Bitter; Courage Best Bitter, Directors; Morland Old Speckled Hen; Ushers Best Bitter; Wadworth 6X Ⓗ
Building dating from 1542, and a pub since the mid-1800s. Its cosy single bar has an intimate atmosphere. The restaurant/conservatory covers the old courtyard and is suitable for families. No meals

Sun eve (except bank hol weekends). 🏠 ◖ ▶ ≷ (Central/ Riverside) ♣ ✄

Try also: Red Cow, Albert St, Slough (Courage)

Eton Wick

Pickwick
32 Eton Wick Road
☎ (01753) 861713
11.30 (12 Sat)–2.30, 5.30 (6 Sat)–11
Young's Bitter, Special, Winter Warmer Ⓗ
Built in 1840, this became a beer house in 1842. Originally the Grapes, the name was changed in 1984 to mean the 'pick of the Wick'. This single bar pub now specialises in Malaysian food prepared with herbs from its award-winning garden. No eve meals Sun/Mon. ☘ ◖ ▶ P

Finchampstead

Queen's Oak
Church Lane (opp. church)
OS794639 ☎ (01734) 734855
11.30–2.30, 6–11; 12–3, 6.30–11 Sat
(11.30–4, 6.30–11 summer Sat)
Brakspear Bitter, Special, OBJ Ⓗ
A winner: in this guide since 1981. It features a no-smoking bar and a large garden with a bar and a play area for kids. Barbecues in summer; Aunt Sally played. Pizzas are a speciality. Note the key fob collection.
🏠 Q ☘ ◖ ▶ ♿ ☘ ♣ P ✄

Frilsham

Pot Kiln
On Yattendon to Bucklebury road; not in village OS552731
☎ (01635) 201366
12–2.30, 6.30–11
Arkell's 3B; Morland Bitter, Old Speckled Hen; Morrells Mild Ⓗ
Remote, unspoilt pub overlooking beautiful wooded countryside. The building dates from the 16th century and its name was derived from a local brickworks. A good range of food includes vegetarian. The full menu is suspended Sun and Tue, when hot filled rolls are available. Phone to camp.
🏠 Q ☞ ☘ ◖ ▶ ☘ ♣ P ✄

Holyport

Belgian Arms
Holyport Street
(cul-de-sac off village green)
☎ (01628) 34468
11–3, 5.30 (7 winter)–11
Brakspear Bitter, Special Ⓗ
Old, wisteria-clad local by the village pond. The upstairs was

used as a Wesleyan chapel until 1835. The building became a Brakspear pub 99 years ago and changed its name from the Eagle in WWI because German POWs held locally saluted the inn sign. Separate eating area with a children's menu. No food Sun.
🏠 Q ☘ ◖ ▶ P

Horton

Five Bells
Stanwell Road
☎ (01753) 682193
11–3, 5–11
Webster's Green Label; Whitbread Boddingtons Bitter; guest beers Ⓗ
Quiet, 17th-century pub once owned by the church. It is now part of the Magic Pub Co. chain. The back garden overlooks lakes.
Q ☘ ◖ ▶ P

Hungerford

Downgate
Down View, 13 Park Street
☎ (01488) 682708
11–2.30 (3 summer), 6 (5.30 summer)–11
Arkell's 2B, 3B Ⓗ
Pleasant, small pub on the edge of the common with a good outlook. No eve meals Sun or Mon. Arkell's seasonal beers also sold.
🏠 ☘ ◖ ▶ ≷ ♣ P

Hurst

Castle
Church Hill
☎ (01734) 340034
11–3, 6–11
Morland Bitter, Old Masters, Old Speckled Hen; guest beer Ⓗ
Two-bar country pub opposite a 900-year-old church and beside a bowling green. Home-cooked food always available.
🏠 Q ☘ ◖ ▶ ☘ P

Try also: Wheelwrights Arms Davis Close (Wadworth)

Kintbury

Dundas Arms
Station Road
☎ (01488) 58263
11–2.30, 6–11; 12–2.30, 7–10.30 Sun
Morland Bitter; Wells Bombardier; guest beers Ⓗ
Attractive, 18th-century inn by the Kennet & Avon Canal (Lock 78), named after Lord Dundas who opened the canal in 1810. Very good, home-made bar and restaurant meals (no food Sun/Mon eves).
Q ☘ 🏠 ◖ ▶ ≷ P

Berkshire

Littlewick Green

Cricketers
Coronation Road
☎ (01628) 822888
11–2.30, 5.30–11
Brakspear Bitter; Fuller's London Pride; guest beers Ⓗ
Charming, unspoilt pub overlooking the village green and split into three drinking areas, one with a large log fire, one with a pool table. Open all day Sat, when there is cricket on the green.
🏚 Q ❀ ◖ ▶ ♣ P

Maidenhead

Hand & Flowers
15 Queen Street
☎ (01628) 23800
10.30–3, 5 (7 Sat)–11
Brakspear Mild *or* OBJ, Bitter, Old, Special; Whitbread Boddingtons Bitter Ⓗ
Small, homely Victorian pub in the town centre. An ex-plumber and a BT manager have made an outstanding start at this, their first pub, winning fans from as far afield as Hong Kong and the USA. Imaginative home cooking plus deluxe sandwiches. Occasional Sun breakfasts.
🏚 Q ◖ ▶ ⇌ ♣

Moneyrow Green

White Hart
SE from Holyport Green
☎ (01628) 21460
11–11
Morland IPA, Bitter Ⓗ
Picturesque pub over 400 years old, originally a hunting lodge in Windsor Royal Forest. The public resounds to the sound of bar billiards and dominoes. The saloon is dark and wood-panelled, with a sandstone fireplace and an air of class. No lunches Sun. Note: Tanner's Jack and Old Speckled Hen are kept under CO_2.
🏚 Q ❀ ◖ ⊞ ᵬ ♣ P

Newbury

Coopers Arms
39 Bartholomew Street
☎ (01635) 47469
11–3, 5–11; 11–11 Fri, Sat & Mon
Arkell's 3B, Kingsdown Ⓗ
Excellently refurbished traditional town pub, rescued by Arkell's after years of neglect by Courage: three drinking areas plus a new dining room with a no-smoking section at lunchtimes. Children are welcome in this room. Arkell's seasonal ales also sold.
◖ ⊞ ᵬ ⇌ ♣ P

Lion
West Street (off Northbrook St by McDonald's)
☎ (01635) 528468
11–3, 5 (7 Sat)–11; 11–11 Fri
Hall & Woodhouse Tanglefoot; Wadworth IPA, 6X, Farmer's Glory, Old Timer; guest beer Ⓗ
Popular pub with a good atmosphere. The wooden floor, interesting decor and alcove seating give character. New snug area; jazz memorabilia in places. Regular quiz and theme nights. Good, reasonably priced food. ◖ ▶ ᵬ

Lock, Stock & Barrel
104 Northbrook Street (just off main street, by canal bridge)
☎ (01635) 42730
11–11
Fuller's Chiswick, London Pride, ESB Ⓗ
Spacious, one-bar pub converted from a coffee shop on the bank of the Kennet & Avon Canal. Pleasant rooftop terrace. Fuller's seasonal beers also served. Open at 10am for coffee. Small no-smoking area lunchtimes. Wheelchair WC next to the bar.
❀ ◖ ᵬ ⇌ ⊬

Plough on the Green
1 The Folly, Greenham Road (on Stroud Green)
☎ (01635) 47269
12 (10.30 Sat)–11
Courage Best Bitter; Marston's Pedigree; Wadworth 6X; guest beers Ⓗ
Within sight of the racecourse, this was once the smallest pub in Newbury. It now features lots of nooks. A very large fountained patio, with overhanging greenery and an orchard garden, adds space. Heaving – of course! – on racedays.
🏚 ❀ 🛏 ◖ ᵬ ⇌ P

Old Windsor

Oxford Blue
Crimp Hill (off A308)
☎ (01753) 861954
11–11
Adnams Bitter; Tetley Bitter; Wadworth 6X Ⓗ
Dating from the 1600s, this verandah-fronted pub has an adventure playground at the rear. For adults that haven't grown up, a feast of airline models and memorabilia dominates the back bar. Altogether a welcoming, cosy pub. Q ❀ 🛏 ◖ ▶ ♣ P

Pangbourne

Cross Keys
Church Road
☎ (01734) 843268
11–3, 6–11

Lion (cont.)
Morland Bitter, Old Speckled Hen; guest beer (occasional) Ⓗ
Super, unspoilt, 17th-century village pub, where the patio garden backs on to the River Pang. Cosy, oak-beamed lounge and a more basic public bar. Just south of Whitchurch toll bridge on the Thames.
🏚 ♿ ❀ 🛏 ◖ ▶ ⊞ ⇌ ♣

Pinkneys Green

Stag & Hounds
1 Lee Lane ☎ (01628) 30268
11–2, 6–11
Gale's BBB, Best Bitter, HSB; Shepherd Neame Spitfire; Wells Bombardier; guest beer Ⓗ
Pub dating from 1820 and originally a Nicholson's beer house. A raised open porch leads to the bar; the dining area is non-smoking. Off-road parking opposite. Q ❀ ◖

Waggon & Horses
112 Pinkneys Green Road
☎ (01628) 24429
11–3, 5 (6 Sat)–11
Morland Bitter, Old Masters; guest beers Ⓗ
Traditional pub overlooking National Trust countryside. The lounge bar entrance is down an alley to the right. Steam fair second weekend in May. No food weekends.
🏚 ❀ ◖ ⊞ ♣ P

Reading

Butler
89–91 Chatham Street (just W of inner ring road)
☎ (01734) 391635
11.30–11
Fuller's, Chiswick, London Pride, ESB Ⓗ
Well-established pub close to the town centre, with a strong local following. Named after wine merchants who formerly occupied the premises. Guinness was once bottled on the site. Fuller's seasonal beers sold. 🏚 ❀ ◖ ▶ P

Dove
119 Orts Road (near canal, behind Reading College)
☎ (01734) 352556
11–2.30, 5.30–11; 11–11 Sat.
Brakspear Mild, Bitter, Old, Special, OBJ Ⓗ
Friendly town pub with a great community spirit. Irish folk music Wed; blues Thu.
◖ ♣ P

Fisherman's Cottage
224 Kennetside (on canal bank, off Orts Rd) ☎ (01734) 571553
11–3, 6–11; 11–11 Fri, Sat & occasionally Mon–Thu in summer
Fuller's Chiswick, London Pride, ESB Ⓗ
Tastefully extended,

traditional pub on the canalside, popular for food and outside summer drinking (rear garden and front terrace). A pleasant walk eastwards along the towpath from the town centre. Fuller's seasonal ales stocked. 🏚 ❀ ◑ ▶ P

Hobgoblin

2 Broad Street
☎ (01734) 508119
11–11; closed Sun lunch autumn–Easter
Beer range varies Ⓗ
Basic, friendly, town-centre local, offering beers from the Wychwood range, plus constantly changing guests. There are always seven real ales available, usually including a mild. Live music Thu eve. ⇌ ◔ ∠

Hop Leaf

163–165 Southampton Street (A33, one-way system, towards town centre)
☎ (01734) 314700
11–11
Hop Back Mild, Special, Wilt, Entire Stout, Summer Lightning; Hop Leaf Bitter Ⓗ
Former derelict Courage pub, totally revitalised by Hop Back Brewery, and now a thriving, community local with a brewhouse at the rear. Occasional special brews. Snacks Mon–Fri, till 7pm. Parking difficult. Highly recommended. ⛴ ♣

Horse & Jockey

120 Castle Hill (just W of inner ring road, near police station)
☎ (01734) 590172
11–11
Beer range varies Ⓗ
Recently refurbished pub with enlarged bar space and a horse racing theme. Three guest beers mainly from independent breweries, at very reasonable prices.
🏚 ❀ ◑ ▶ ♣ P

Sweeney & Todd

10 Castle Street (off St Mary's Butts) ☎ (01734) 586466
11–10.30; closed Sun eve
Adnams Bitter; Eldridge Pope Royal Oak; Wadworth 6X; guest beer Ⓗ
Now a Reading tradition, a pub in the back of, and below, a pie shop. Excellent, inexpensive food and moderately-pricey beer. Q ◑ ▶

Try also: **Corn Stores**, Forbury Rd (Fuller's); **Eldon Arms**, Eldon Tce (Wadworth)

Remenham

Two Brewers

Wargrave Road (A321 just before Henley)
☎ (01491) 574375

11–3, 6–11
Brakspear Bitter, Special Ⓗ
Friendly, near riverside pub, with a warm atmosphere. Handy for visiting Henley and just across the river from Brakspear's brewery. Beer prices vary during Henley Regatta week. Children welcome if eating.
🏚 ❀ 🚢 ◑ ▶ ♣ P

Shefford Woodlands

Pheasant Inn

Baydon Road (off A338 N of M4 jct 14) ☎ (01488) 648284
11–3, 5.30–11
Brakspear Bitter; Wadworth 6X; guest beers Ⓗ
Wooden boarded, country pub just off the motorway (hence popular with travellers, particularly sports fans). The basic public bar features painted 1930s fittings and Ring the Bull displays by local experts! The intimate lounge and small dining room offer a wide range of excellent food.
🏚 Q ❀ ◑ ▶ 🍴 ♣ P

Shinfield

Royal Oak

39 School Green
☎ (01734) 882931
11–11
Draught Bass; Morland IPA, Bitter, Old Masters, Old Speckled Hen; S&N Theakston XB Ⓗ
Popular village local where the extended lounge bar is famous for lunchtime and eve meals. Active teams in darts, cribbage, football, pool and cricket. There has been a pub in this location for over a century. ❀ ◑ ▶ 👤 ♣ P

Sunninghill

Duke's Head

Upper Village Road
☎ (01344) 626949
11–11
Beer range varies Ⓗ
Comfortable village local with a friendly landlord and an extensive food menu. No eve meals Sun.
🏚 Q ❀ ◑ ▶ 👤 ♣ P ∠

Swallowfield

Crown

The Street (just off B3349, old A33) ☎ (01734) 883260
11–3, 6–11
Morland Bitter, Tanner's Jack Ⓗ
Village pub which has been run by the same family for over 30 years: a large, friendly public bar and a smaller

---

lounge. Eve meals Thu–Sat only. Plenty of vegetarian choices on the menu.
🏚 ❀ ◑ ▶ 🍴 👤 ♣ P

Theale

Falcon

High Street (old A4)
☎ (01734) 302523
10.30–11
Archers Best Bitter; Courage Best Bitter; Wadworth 6X; guest beer Ⓗ
Old, two-bar coaching inn, near the site of the former Blatch's Brewery and close to the Theale swing bridge on the Kennet & Avon Canal. Parking is through the classic archway. No meals weekends.
Q ❀ ◑ ⇌ ♣ P

Three Mile Cross

Swan

Basingstoke Road (S of M4 jct 11) ☎ (01734) 883674
11–11
Courage Best Bitter, Directors; Marston's Pedigree; John Smith's Bitter; Wadworth 6X Ⓗ
17th-century coaching inn in a quiet village setting, with oak beams and an inglenook. Small, homely lunchtime restaurant (renowned for freshly home-cooked food).
🏚 ❀ ◑ ▶ P

Twyford

Duke of Wellington

High Street ☎ (01734) 340456
11–2.30, 6–11
Brakspear Mild, Bitter, Old, Special, OBJ Ⓗ
16th-century village pub with a busy public bar and a quieter, smart lounge. Good sheltered garden and play area. 🏚 Q ❀ ◑ 🍴 ⇌ ♣ P

Waltham St Lawrence

Star Inn

Broadmoor Road (B3024 from Twyford) ☎ (01734) 343486
11–3, 6–11
Wadworth IPA, 6X Ⓗ
Smart pub in a classy village deep in the Berkshire countryside. Nice garden for use in the summer; log fires in winter. The many public footpaths nearby lead to other places of interest. No meals Sun eve or Mon.
🏚 ❀ ◑ ▶ ♣ P

Wargrave

Bull

High Street (A321)
☎ (01734) 403120
11–2.30, 6–11

Berkshire

Brakspear Bitter, Special Ⓗ
17th-century pub with oak
beams and a huge open fire.
Good reputation for food. No
meals Sun eve. ♨ Q ✿ ⌂
◖ ▶ ⅋ ⇌ (not winter Sun)

West End

Plough

Plough Lane (off Twyford–
Wokingham road,
signed West End)
☎ (01734) 340015
11.30–3, 5.30 (6 Sat)–11
**Hall & Woodhouse Badger
BB, Tanglefoot; Wells Eagle;
guest beer** (occasional) Ⓗ
Small, rural local: a 14th-
century building newly
redecorated and originally
built as a keeper's cottage for
Windsor Great Park. Drag
hunts twice a year.
Q ✿ ◖ ▶ ⅋ ♣ P

West Ilsley

Harrow

☎ (01635) 281260
11–3, 6–11
**Morland Bitter, Tanner's Jack,
Old Speckled Hen; guest
beer** Ⓗ
Beautifully refurbished village
pub in the Berkshire Downs.
Cricket can be viewed on the
ground opposite without
leaving the front garden.
Handy for walkers on the
nearby Ridgeway. Very good
food: home-made pies are a
speciality – mail order
available.
♨ Q ✿ ◖ ▶ ⅋ ♣ P

White Waltham

Beehive

Waltham Road
☎ (01628) 822877
11–3, 5.30–11
**Brakspear Bitter; Whitbread
Boddingtons Bitter, Flowers
IPA, Original; guest beers** Ⓗ
Popular, friendly village local
opposite the cricket pitch,
fronted by a public bar with a
saloon to the right. The
landlord arranges trips to beer
festivals. Petanque in the fine
back garden. No food Sun eve.
Cider in summer.
♨ Q ✿ ◖ ▶ ⊞ ♣ ⌂ ⅋

Windsor

Prince Christian

11 Kings Road
☎ (01753) 860980
11–3, 5.30–11
**Brakspear Bitter; Fuller's
London Pride; S&N
Theakston Best Bitter** Ⓗ
Windsor's longest established
free house is but a short stroll

---

from the main tourist area. An
Irish air pervades the
atmosphere. No food Sat or
Sun. Q ◖ ▶ ♣

Two Brewers

34 Park Street
☎ (01753) 855426
10.30–11
**Courage Best Bitter;
Marston's Pedigree;
Wadworth 6X** Ⓗ
In a row of Georgian terraced
houses (part of the Queen's
Mews leading up to the Long
Walk at Windsor Castle), this
two-bar pub with three
drinking areas has an original
interior with half-panelled
walls and an off-sales servery.
The frontage has a wonderful
floral display even in winter.
Eve meals served Mar–Oct.
♨ Q ◖ ▶ ⊞
⇌ (Central) ♣

Vansittart Arms

Vansittart Road
☎ (01753) 865988
11–11
Fuller's London Pride, ESB Ⓗ
Comfortable Victorian-style
pub in a residential area,
offering several, cosy drinking
areas, one with a working
wood-fired range. All food is
home cooked. No meals Sun
eve. Fuller's seasonal ales sold.
♨ ✿ ◖ ▶ ♣

Winterbourne

Winterbourne Arms

¼ mile W of B4494
☎ (01635) 248200
11–3 (not Mon,
except bank hols), 6–11
Beer range varies Ⓗ
Tastefully refurbished, old
country village inn (formerly
the New Inn). Note the
rosewood-cabineted beer
engine on static display.
Excellent, freshly-prepared
food (no meals Sun eve).
Peacefully-set, despite
standing just ½ mile south of
the M4 (no immediate access).
♨ ✿ ◖ ▶ ♣ P

Wokingham

Duke's Head

56 Denmark Street
☎ (01734) 780316
11.30–3, 5.30 (5 Fri, 6 Sat)–11
**Brakspear Bitter, Special;
Whitbread Boddingtons
Bitter** Ⓗ
Comfortable town pub,
originally converted from
three cottages and popular
with business and passing
trades. Archives mention the
Duke's Head as 1791. No
food Sun. The skittle alley
is available for group hire.
✿ ◖ ⇌ ♣ P

Queen's Head

23 The Terrace
(A329 at top of Station Rd)
☎ (01734) 781221
11–3, 5.30–11
**Morland IPA, Bitter, Tanner's
Jack, Old Masters, Old
Speckled Hen** Ⓗ
Charming, single-bar pub
which retains its traditional
character. The local and
business regulars take an
active role in the many pub
sporting activities. The
rear garden is accessed
through the bar. Aunt Sally in
summer. No meals Sun.
Q ✿ ◖ ⇌ ♣

Ship

104–108 Peach Street
☎ (01734) 780389
11.30–3, 5–11; 11–11 Fri; 11–4,
6.30–11 Sat
**Fuller's Chiswick, London
Pride, ESB** Ⓗ
As its name suggests, a pub
with a nautical theme in two
separate bars and a games
room (16th-century in parts).
Lively and bustling at
weekends. Fuller's seasonal
beers sold.
✿ ◖ ⊞ ♣ P

Wokingham Without

Crooked Billet

Honey Hill (off B3430, 2 miles
SE of Wokingham) OS826667
☎ (01734) 780438
11–11
**Brakspear Bitter, Old, Special,
OBJ** Ⓗ
A gem of a traditional ale
house on the outskirts of
Wokingham; well worth
seeking out for both food and
drink. The ramp access and
real fire typify the welcome.
Several walks pass the pub.
Eve meals Tue–Sat.
♨ Q ✿ ◖ ▶ P

Woodspeen

Five Bells

Lambourn Road (2 miles
NW of Newbury on
Lambourn Valley road)
☎ (01635) 48763
11.30–3, 6–11
Draught Bass *or* **S&N
Theakston XB** *or* **Wells
Bombardier; Morland Bitter,
Old Speckled Hen** Ⓗ
Small, early Victorian pub in a
tiny hamlet at the bottom end
of the Lambourn Valley, near
the famous Watermill Theatre
at Bagnor, in an area
threatened with destruction
for Newbury's bypass.
Purchased from Courage and
extended to resemble a
restaurant.
☙ ✿ ⌂ ◖ ▶ ⅋ ♣ P ⅋

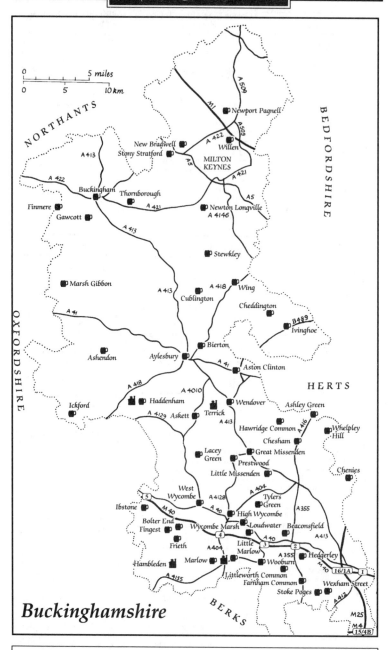

Buckinghamshire

 Chiltern, *Terrick*; **Old Luxters**, *Hambleden*; **Rebellion**, *Marlow*; **Vale**, *Haddenham*

Ashendon

Gatehangers
Lower End (lane by church)
☎ (01296) 651296

12–2.30, 7–11
Adnams Bitter; Hall & Woodhouse Badger BB; Wadworth IPA, 6X; guest beer Ⓗ
Formerly the Red Lion, this

400-year-old building, on a hilltop overlooking the northern Vale of Aylesbury, was once used as a courtroom. Imaginative food.
🚕 ❀ ◐ ▶ P

Buckinghamshire

Ashley Green

Golden Eagle
☎ (01442) 863549
11.30–3, 5.30–11; 12–4, 7–11 Sat
**Adnams Bitter; Draught Bass;
Greenalls Bitter, Shipstone's
Bitter, Original; Wadworth
6X** H
Traditional, 17th-century
village pub. Eve meals Mon–
Thu. ✿ ◖ ▮ & ♣ P

Askett

Three Crowns
Off A4030 ☎ (01844) 343041
12–2.30, 5.30–11
**Bass Worthington BB;
Hancock's HB; Whitbread
Flowers Original** H
Village pub with two simple
bars. Superior food cooked to
order (no meals Mon).
🏚 Q ✿ ◖
➤ (Monks Risborough) P

Aston Clinton

Rothschild Arms
82 Weston Road
☎ (01296) 630320
12–2.30, 5–11; 11–11 Fri & Sat
**Bass Worthington BB; M&B
Highgate Dark; Whitbread
Flowers Original** H
Friendly, one-bar, mid-terrace
local. Food only until 8.30pm
(8pm Sat) and none Sun.
Barbecues in summer.
🏚 ✿ 🏠 ◖ & ♣ P

Aylesbury

Aristocrat
1 Wendover Road
☎ (01296) 415366
11–3, 4.45–11; 11.30–11 Fri; 11–11 Sat
**Fuller's Chiswick, London
Pride, ESB** H
Welcoming, popular pub on
the outskirts of town. With its
good atmosphere it caters for
all ages, offering quizzes,
games, discos and live music.
Fuller's seasonal beers served.
No food Sun.
✿ 🏠 ◖ & ➤ ♣ P

Grapes
Market Square
☎ (01296) 83735
11–11
**Courage Best Bitter,
Directors; Vale Wychert** H
Narrow bar adjacent to the
civic centre. Wooden
floorboards and Victorian
decor provide a pleasant
atmosphere. The upstairs
restaurant only takes group
bookings for eve meals. ◖ ➤

Ship
59 Walton Street
☎ (01296) 21888
11–2.30 (3 Fri), 5–11

**Greene King Abbot; Tetley
Bitter; Wadworth 6X** H
Cosmopolitan, friendly pub by
the canal basin of the Grand
Union Canal; opposite the
controversial 'Blue Leanie'
office block. Discos Thu.
✿ ◖ 🏠 ▲ ➤ ♣ P

Beaconsfield

Greyhound
33 Windsor End
☎ (01494) 673823
11–3, 5.30–11
**Courage Best Bitter; Fuller's
London Pride; Wadworth 6X;
guest beers** H
Small, charming, unspoilt pub
with a cosy snug. Home-
cooked food in the bar and
restaurant area (no meals Sun
eve). Q ✿ ◖

Bierton

Bell
191 Aylesbury Road
☎ (01296) 436055
11–3, 6–11; 11–11 Sat
**Fuller's Chiswick, London
Pride, ESB** H
Small two-bar pub with a
thriving food trade (reasonable
prices). All food is home-
prepared. Fuller's seasonal
beers sold. ✿ ◖ ▮ ▲ ♣ P

Bolter End

Peacock
On B482 ☎ (01494) 881417
11.45–2.30, 6–11
**Ind Coope ABC Best Bitter;
Marston's Pedigree; Tetley
Bitter; guest beer** H
Pub dating from 1620, located
just west of Lane End: one
large room with several
distinct areas. The emphasis is
on freshly prepared, home-
cooked bar meals (no food Sun
eve). 🏚 Q ✿ ◖ ▮ ♣ P

Buckingham

Whale
14 Market Hill
☎ (01280) 815537
10–11
**Fuller's Chiswick, London
Pride, ESB** H
Welcoming, traditional market
town pub where gas lights are
a feature of the bar. The
lounge doubles as a restaurant.
Fuller's seasonal beers sold.
🏚 ✿ 🏠 ◖ ▮ ♣

Try also: New Inn, Bridge St
(Greene King)

Cheddington

Rosebery Arms
Station Road ☎ (01296) 668222
11.30–2.30, 5.30–11

**Wells Eagle, Bombardier;
guest beers** H
Old hotel, close to the scene of
the Great Train Robbery. The
bar was refurbished two years
ago. Good value food (no
meals Sun eve). ✿ ◖ ▮ ➤ ♣

Chenies

Red Lion
Off A404 ☎ (01923) 282722
11–2.30, 5.30–11
**Ind Coope Benskins BB;
Rebellion IPA; Tring
Ridgeway; Wadworth 6X** H
Friendly, busy village free
house, which attracts drinkers
and diners. No machines.
Amazing snug to the rear of
the dining room.
Q ✿ ◖ & P

Chesham

Black Horse
The Vale (Cholesbury Road,
2 miles N of centre)
☎ (01494) 784656
11–2.30, 6–11
**Adnams Bitter; Ind Coope
Benskins BB, Burton Ale;
guest beers** H
Comfortable old inn with an
enormous garden, popular
with eaters (sausages and
home-made pies). ✿ ◖ ▮ & P

Queen's Head
Church Street
☎ (01494) 783773
11–2.30, 5 (6 Sat)–11
**Brakspear Bitter, Special;
Fuller's London Pride; guest
beer** H
Old town pub with two bars.
Home-cooked pies a speciality.
🏚 ✿ ◖ ▮ ▲ ⊖ ♣ P ✂

Try also: Last Post, The
Broadway (Wetherspoon)

Cublington

Unicorn
High Street ☎ (01296) 681261
12–3, 5.30–11
Beer range varies H
Excellent, low-beamed village
local with open fires at each
end of a long bar. Separate
dining room (no meals Sun
eve). Five changing real ales.
Happy 'hour' 5.30–7pm.
🏚 Q ✿ ◖ ▲ ♣ P

Farnham Common

Yew Tree
Collingswood Road (A355, 1
mile N of village)
☎ (01753) 643723
11–11
**Morland IPA, Bitter, Old
Masters, Old Speckled Hen** H

Small country inn, 300 years old. Meals served in the lounge (all day breakfast from 8am). ⚒ ❀ ◖ ▶ ♣ P

Fingest

Chequers
☎ (01491) 638335
11–3, 6–11
Brakspear Bitter, Old, Special Ⓗ
Friendly, 15th-century pub opposite the church. The emphasis is on food (separate restaurant – no meals Sun eve). The large garden greatly extends the eating/drinking area in summer.
⚒ Q ☎ ❀ ◖ ▶ P ⅄

Finmere

Red Lion
Mere Lane (W of village)
☎ (01280) 847836
12–3, 5.30–11
Fuller's London Pride, ESB Ⓗ
Comfortable thatch and limestone, roadside pub with an inglenook. Frequently crowded. No eve meals Sun in winter. Aunt Sally played.
⚒ ❀ ◖ ▶ ♣ P ⅄

Frieth

Prince Albert
Moors End (100 yds from Lane End–Frieth road)
☎ (01494) 881683
11–3, 6–11
Brakspear Mild, Bitter, Old, Special Ⓗ, **OBJ** Ⓖ
Pub which has appeared in the *Guide* 21 times, offering superb atmosphere, location and hospitality. Josie's platefuls are a bonus at lunchtime (Mon–Sat). ⚒ Q ❀ ◖ ♣

Gawcott

Cuckoo's Nest
New Inn Lane
☎ (01280) 812092
11–3 (not Mon), 6–11
Hook Norton Best Bitter; Morland Old Speckled Hen; guest beer Ⓗ
Welcoming, two-bar village local. ⚒ Q ❀ ▤ ♿ ♣ P

Great Missenden

Cross Keys
High Street ☎ (01494) 865373
11–3, 5.30–11
Fuller's Chiswick, London Pride, ESB Ⓗ
400-year-old pub. High back settles feature in the bar area (where no dining is allowed in the eve, thus retaining a good atmosphere; eve meals in the dining area Mon–Sat).
⚒ Q ❀ ◖ ▶ ≢ P

Haddenham

Rising Sun
9 Thame Road
☎ (01844) 291744
11–3, 7–11; 11–11 Fri
Wells Eagle; guest beer Ⓗ
Small, friendly, one-bar village local, a free house since 1993 (purchased from Wells). Interesting guest beers; occasional mini-beer festivals. No lunches Sun. Cider in summer. ❀ ◖ ≢ ♣ ⌂

Hawridge Common

Full Moon
OS936069 ☎ (01494) 758262
12–3, 6–11
Courage Best Bitter; Morrells Bitter, Graduate; Ruddles Best Bitter; Ushers Best Bitter Ⓗ
Old English country pub, licensed for over 300 years. Radically extended but unspoilt. Q ❀ ◖ ▶ ♣ P

Hedgerley

Brickmould
Village Lane ☎ (01753) 642716
11–2.30, 5.30–11; 11–11 Sat & bank hols
S&N Theakston Old Peculier; Wadworth 6X; guest beers Ⓗ
Comfortable pub in a small village offering three drinking areas and home-cooked food. Note the aggregation of cats and dogs. ⚒ ◖ ▶ P

One Pin
One Pin Lane, Farnham Common ☎ (01753) 643035
11–3.30, 5.30–11
Courage Best Bitter, Directors Ⓗ
Traditional, two-bar pub. A brass plate in the lounge commemorates the landlord's 30 years' service. Wheelchair access is through the garden doors. No food Sun.
⚒ Q ❀ ◖ ▶ ▤ ♣ P

White Horse
Village Lane ☎ (01753) 643225
11–3, 5.30–11
Beer range varies Ⓖ
Family-owned, genuine free house, a picturesque local with a wonderful public bar. Seven beers. ⚒ Q ❀ ◖ ▤ ♣ ⌂ P

High Wycombe

Bell
Frogmoor ☎ (01494) 521317
11–3, 5.30 (7 Sat)–11
Fuller's Chiswick, London Pride, ESB Ⓗ
Cosy pub on the edge of the

town centre, a popular lunchtime venue which becomes a disco at weekends (it closes 2am Fri/Sat). Lunches Mon–Sat; eve meals Mon–Thu. Fish is a speciality. Fuller's seasonal ales.
🛏 ◖ ▶ ≢

Rose & Crown
Desborough Road
☎ (01494) 527982
11–3, 5–11; 11–11 Fri & Sat
Courage Best Bitter; Gale's HSB; Marston's Pedigree; Ushers Best Bitter; Wadworth 6X; guest beers Ⓗ
Wycombe's most interesting selection of beers is served in an L-shaped, corner pub with a busy office lunchtime trade (no lady weekends).
⚒ ◖ ≢ ♣ ⌂

Try also: Iron Duke, Duke St (Courage)

Ibstone

Fox
The Common
☎ (01491) 638289
11–3, 6–11
Brakspear Bitter; Fuller's London Pride; Greene King Abbot; guest beers Ⓗ
Popular pub offering high quality hotel accommodation and food in both the bar and restaurant. Large garden in superb countryside.
⚒ Q ❀ 🛏 ◖ ▶ P

Ickford

Rising Sun
Worminghall Road,
☎ (01844) 339238
12–3, 6–11
Bass Worthington BB, Draught Bass; Hancock's HB Ⓗ
Very attractive, 15th-century timber-framed, thatched coaching inn. The varied menu includes an 'Eat as much as you like' buffet lunchtimes. German food a speciality. Children's menu and play area. ⚒ ❀ ◖ ▶ ♣ P

Ivinghoe

Rose & Crown
Vicarage Lane (turn opp. church, then 1st right)
☎ (01296) 668472
12–2.30, 6–11
Adnams Bitter; Greene King IPA; Morrells Mild; guest beers Ⓗ
Hard to find, but worth the effort, this street-corner local has a comfortable lounge and a lively public bar on different levels. High quality food.
⚒ ◖ ▶ ▤ ♣

Buckinghamshire

Lacey Green

Pink & Lily
Pink Road, Parslows Hillock
OS828019 ☎ (01494) 488308
11.45–3, 6–11
**Brakspear Bitter; Chiltern
Beechwood; Courage
Directors; Wychwood
Hobgoblin; Whitbread
Boddingtons Bitter, Flowers
Original** Ⓗ
Lively, popular country pub
noted for food (no chips!). No
eve meals Sun. The snug is
original, unaltered and
dedicated to poet Rupert
Brooke. ♨ ✿ ◖ ▸ ₺ ♣ P

Little Marlow

King's Head
Church Road
☎ (01628) 484407
11–3, 5.30–11
**Brakspear Bitter; Marston's
Pedigree; Wadworth 6X;
Whitbread Boddingtons
Bitter; Young's Special; guest
beer** Ⓗ
One-bar village pub with
much character. Varied,
home-cooked meals are
always available. Function
room and new separate dining
room. Families very welcome.
♨ ✿ ◖ ▸ ₺ P

Little Missenden

Crown
Off A413 ☎ (01494) 862571
11–2.30, 6–11; 12–2.30, 7–10.30 Sun
**Draught Bass; Hook Norton
Best Bitter** Ⓗ**; Morrells Mild**
(summer) Ⓖ**, Varsity** Ⓗ
Authentic old village pub with
a genuine welcome. The small
single bar enjoys a two-bar
atmosphere and is decorated
with farm implements. No
food Sun. Cider in summer.
♨ Q ✿ ◖ ▲ ♣ ◔ P

Littleworth Common

Blackwood Arms
Common Lane (2 miles W of
A355) ☎ (01753) 642169
11–2.30, 5.30–11; 11–11 Fri, Sat &
bank hols
Beer range varies Ⓗ
Sited in idyllic woodland, the
one-time New Inn is a real ale
heaven. Over 900 beers are
sold each year, all from
independents. Foreign beers
are also stocked, one on
draught.
♨ Q ✿ ◖ ▸ ♣ ◔ P

Loudwater

Derehams Inn
5 Derehams Lane OS903907
☎ (01494) 530965

11–3, 5.30–11
Beer range varies Ⓗ
Cosy pub, hard to find and so
mainly catering for local trade.
Small car park. Lunches
weekdays.
♨ ✿ ◖ ♣ P

Marlow

Carpenter's Arms
15 Spittal Street
☎ (01628) 473649
11–11
Morrells Bitter, Varsity Ⓗ
Thriving workingman's local
of considerable character;
acquired by Morrells in 1992.
Fresh sandwiches always
available.
Q ✿ ⇌ ♣

Clayton Arms
Quoiting Square, Oxford Road
☎ (01628) 478620
11–2.30 (3 Sat), 5.30 (6 Sat)–11
**Brakspear Mild, Bitter, Old,
Special** Ⓗ
Town-centre gem with two
small bars – the original and
genuine local. A new kitchen
and outside patio are planned.
♨ Q ⇌ ♣

Prince of Wales
Mill Road
☎ (01628) 482970
11–11
Beer range varies Ⓗ
Friendly, back-street local with
two connecting bars – a
comfortable public and a
lounge with a dining area
(families welcome). No food
Sun eve. Four changing ales.
✿ ◖ ▸ ⇌ ♣ P

Marsh Gibbon

Greyhound
West Edge
☎ (01869) 277365
12–3.30, 6–11
**Fuller's London Pride; Greene
King IPA, Abbot; Hook
Norton Best Bitter** Ⓗ
Listed building, probably of
Tudor origin, rebuilt after a
fire in 1740. Thai cuisine,
steaks and quick business
lunches are popular.
♨ Q ✿ ◖ ▸ P

Milton Keynes: *New Bradwell*

New Inn
2 Bradwell Road
☎ (01908) 312094
11–11; 11–4, 6.30–11 Sat
**Adnams Broadside; Wells
Eagle; guest beers** Ⓗ
Lively, canalside inn serving
good value bar food; also a
separate restaurant.
♨ Q ✿ ◖ ▸ ⊟
⇌ (Wolverton) ♣ ◔ P

Stony Stratford

Bull Hotel (Vaults Bar)
64 High Street
☎ (01908) 567104
12–11
**Draught Bass; Fuller's
London Pride; Hook Norton
Best Bitter; Ind Coope ABC
Best Bitter; S&N Theakston
Old Peculier; Wadworth 6X** Ⓗ
Welcoming beer drinkers' pub:
a narrow bar with wood and
brick dating from the 18th
century. Breweriana and
Victoriana feature. Local
CAMRA *Pub of the Year*.
♨ 🛏 ◖ ▸ ₺ ♣ P

Fox & Hounds
87 High Street
☎ (01908) 563307
11–2.30, 6–11; 11–11 Sat
Courage Directors *or*
Marston's Pedigree *or*
**Wadworth 6X; Webster's
Yorkshire Bitter; guest
beers** Ⓗ
17th-century, two-bar pub
with a warm welcome.
Occasional special food nights.
No food Sun. ✿ ◖ ▸ ♣ P

Willen

Ship Ashore
Granville Square, Beaufort
Drive ☎ (01908) 609998
11–2.30 (3 Sat), 5 (6 Sat)–11
**Draught Bass; Fuller's
London Pride** Ⓗ
Modern estate pub with a bold
nautical theme, using timbers
and ship's fittings. A separate
dining area serves a wide
range of freshly prepared
meals (not Sun eve).
🐃 ✿ ₺ P ⌿

Newport Pagnell

Bull
33 Tickford Street (between
Iron Bridge and Aston-Martin
works) ☎ (01908) 610325
11.30–2.30 (3 Sat), 5.30 (6.30 Sat)–11
**Marston's Pedigree;
Whitbread Boddingtons
Bitter; guest beers** Ⓗ
Wonderfully modernised free
house with an adventurous
beer range. Food is varied and
excellent (no meals Sun eve).
Q ✿ 🛏 ◖ ▸ ⊟ ₺ ▲ ♣ P

Green Man
92 Silver Street (down Willen
Rd from High St)
☎ (01908) 611914
12–3, 6–11; 12–11 Sat
Banks's Hanson's Mild *or*
**Mild, Bitter; Camerons
Strongarm; Marston's
Pedigree; guest beers** Ⓗ
Family-run, wonderfully
unspoilt backstreet boozer,

46

with a cheerful public bar, a quiet lounge, lots of clocks and bric-a-brac. 🏚 🛏 ⊞ ▲ ♣

Newton Longville

Crooked Billet
2 Westbrooke End
☎ (01908) 373936
11–2.30, 5.30 (6 Sat)–11
Hook Norton Best Bitter; Wadworth 6X; guest beers H
Wood, brick and thatch pub, formerly a medieval barn. A wealth of genuine and add-on beams provides a tasteful interior, with a chimney breast segregating the dining area. No eve meals Sun.
🏚 ❀ ⑃ ▶ & ♣ P

Prestwood

King's Head
188 Wycombe Road
☎ (01494) 862392
11–11
Adnams Broadside; Brakspear Mild, Bitter, Old, Special; Tring Old Icknield Ale G
The ultimate antidote to the modern pub: traditional decor and atmosphere – no machines, no music, no draught lager, no meals (snacks only).
🏚 Q ❀ ⊞ ♣ ⏚ P

Stewkley

Swan
High Street North
☎ (01525) 240285
12–3, 6–11
Courage Best Bitter, Directors; Marston's Pedigree; Morland Old Speckled Hen H
Fine Georgian pub in the village centre. A good atmosphere prevails in the old, beamed interior which has a separate dining area. No eve meals Sun.
❀ ⑃ ▶ ♣ P

Stoke Poges

Rose & Crown
Hollybush Hill
☎ (01753) 662148
11–3, 5.30 (7 Sat)–11
Adnams Broadside; Morland Bitter, Old Masters, Old Speckled Hen (winter) H
Pre-war two-bar pub with a single entrance. Plush seating in both areas; cosy atmosphere.
Q ❀ ⑃ ♣ P

Thornborough

Lone Tree
Buckingham Road
☎ (01280) 812334
11–3, 5–11
Beer range varies H
Roadside, mainly food-oriented, one-bar pub with an inglenook and wood panelling. Ever-changing range of ales; original and extensive menu of freshly prepared food (booking advised). 🏚 Q ❀ ⑃ ▶ P

Tylers Green

Horse & Jockey
Church Road
☎ (01494) 815963
11–2.30, 5.30–11
Ansells Mild; Fuller's London Pride; Ind Coope Burton Ale; Tetley Bitter; guest beers H
Good all-round country village pub displaying a fine collection of horse brasses and livery. Food served at all times. Q ❀ ⑃ ▶ & ♣ P

Wendover

Shoulder of Mutton
20 Pound Street
☎ (01296) 623223
11–11 (11–3, 6–11 Mon–Wed, Jan–Feb)
Morland Old Speckled Hen; John Smith's Bitter; Whitbread Boddingtons Bitter, Flowers Original H
Early 17th-century former hotel, a rambling building with a large restaurant (open all day Sun) and an extensive garden. Good value bar meals.
❀ ⑃ ▶ ⇌ P

Try also: King & Queen, South St (Pubmaster)

West Wycombe

George & Dragon
☎ (01494) 464414
11–2.30, 5.30–11; 11–11 Sat
Courage Best Bitter, Directors; guest beer H
18th-century coaching inn with an original timbered bar. It is noted for its food and excellent garden.
🏚 Q ⏚ ❀ 🛏 ⑃ ▶ P

Wexham Street

Plough
☎ (01753) 662633
11–11
Ind Coope Benskins BB,

Burton Ale; Tetley Bitter; guest beer H
Originally three cottages, this pub's frontage is listed. The bar has a low, beamed ceiling, original internal doors and a flagstone floor. Reasonably priced, home-cooked food (also served 3–7 Sun).
🏚 Q ❀ ⑃ ♣ P

Whelpley Hill

White Hart
Off Bovingdon Market
☎ (01442) 833367
11–2.30 (4.30 Sat), 6 (6.30 Sat)–11
Draught Bass; Ind Coope Benskins BB; Whitbread Flowers IPA H
Homely country pub serving home-cooked food. The old Herts-Bucks county border used to separate the pub and is marked on the floor. Eve meals end at 8.30.
🏚 Q ❀ ⑃ ▶ & ▲ ♣ P

Wing

Cock Inn
High Street ☎ (01296) 688214
11–3, 6–11
Courage Directors; Webster's Yorkshire Bitter; guest beers H
Expensively restored free house with one bar, a 60-seater restaurant (extensive menu) and good facilities for disabled guests. Six ales (including four from far and wide). Seasonal beer festivals.
🏚 Q ❀ ⑃ ▶ & P

Wooburn

Queen & Albert
24 The Green
☎ (01628) 520610
11–3, 5.30–11; 11–11 Sat
Ind Coope Benskins BB, Burton Ale; guest beer H
Friendly local, popular with all ages. Good value bar food (no meals Sun, or winter Mon and Tue eves). Petanque piste available. ❀ ⑃ ▶ ♣

Wycombe Marsh

General Havelock
114 Kingsmead Road
☎ (01494) 520391
11–2.30 (3 Fri), 5.30 (5 Fri)–11
Fuller's Chiswick, London Pride, ESB H
Traditional family pub: smart, friendly and noted for its lunches. Eve meals Sat in summer. Fuller's seasonal ales.
🏚 ❀ ⑃ ♣ P

Remember to check neighbouring counties for even more choice. See the Key Map on the inside back cover to quickly find adjacent counties.

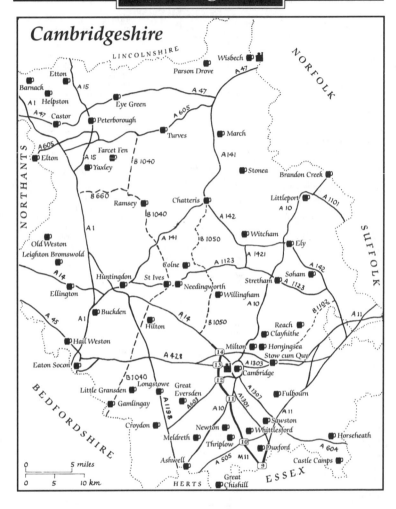

Cambridgeshire

 Ancient Druids, *Cambridge;* **Elgood's,** *Wisbech*

Ashwell

Jester
116 Station Road, Odsey
☎ (01462) 742011
11–11
Marston's Pedigree; Morland Old Speckled Hen; Whitbread Boddingtons Bitter, Flowers IPA, Original; guest beer H
Large, one-bar pub with various drinking areas. A local council award-winner for healthy menu and hygiene.
🏠 Q ♿ ❀ 🛏 ◑ ▸ ⇌
♣ P ⾕

Barnack

Millstone
Millstone Lane
☎ (01780) 740296
11–2.30, 5.30–11
Adnams Bitter; Everards Tiger, Old Original; guest beer H
Friendly, stone village local first recorded as a pub in 1672. The large main room has several alcoves; separate restaurant with a reputation for good, home-made food (no meals Sun/Mon eves). A winner of many local CAMRA awards. Q ❀ ◑ ▸ ♿ P ⾕

Brandon Creek

Ship
☎ (01353) 676228
11–3, 6.30–11 (11–11 summer Sat)
Adnams Bitter; Elgood's Cambridge Bitter; Hook Norton Old Hooky; guest beers H
A welcome find on a long dry stretch of the A10, offering a wide range of beers and an excellent bar menu. At the confluence of the Ouse rivers and ideal for motorists, walkers or sailors. Steeped in history.
🏠 Q ❀ ◑ ▸ ⌣ P

Buckden

Spread Eagle
High Street ☎ (01480) 810277
12–4, 6–11
**Adnams Broadside; Wells
Eagle** Ⓗ
16th-century coaching inn; a
friendly local. Note the
stained-glass panel showing
the Charles Wells eagle.
Separate area for pool. Cold
snacks. A cask breather is used
on guest beers. Q ❀ ♣ P

Cambridge

Cambridge Blue
85–87 Gwydir Street
☎ (01223) 61382
12–2.30, 6–11
**Nethergate IPA, Bitter, Old
Growler; guest beers** Ⓗ
Characterful terrace pub: a
no-smoking bar, a tiny snug
and a conservatory
complement the extended
main bar. Amazing collection
of hats; model railway in the
garden. Children welcome till
9pm. Guest beers usually
include a mild. No eve meals
Sun. ⏚ Q ☜ ❀ ◑ ♣ ♨ ✔

Cow & Calf
14 Pound Hill
☎ (01223) 576220
12–3 (2.30 Sat), 5.30 (7 Sat)–11
**Courage Best Bitter; Elgood's
Cambridge Bitter; Nethergate
Bitter; John Smith's Bitter;
Whitbread Boddingtons
Bitter; guest beers** Ⓗ
A traditional pub atmosphere
prevails in one of Cambridge's
few genuine free houses. The
beer range varies. Weekday
lunches. ⏚ ❀ ◑ ♿ ♣

Empress
72 Thoday Street (off Mill Rd)
☎ (01223) 247236
11–2.30, 6.30–11
**Marston's Pedigree;
Whitbread Castle Eden Ale;
guest beers** Ⓗ
Bustling, corner local where
something's always
happening. Four different
drinking areas within a
basically open-plan layout.
❀ ♿ ♣ ♨

Fountain
12 Regent Street
☎ (01223) 66540
11–11
**Marston's Pedigree; S&N
Theakston Best Bitter, XB,
Old Peculier; Young's
Special; guest beers** Ⓗ
Terrific reconstructed ale
house, retaining a traditional
atmosphere. High gravity
guest beers are expensive.
Note the display of European
bottled beers. Full menu 12–3,

restricted 3–8.30. All beers are
served via swan necks.
◑ ▶ ☷ ♨

Jug & Firkin (off-licence)
90 Mill Road ☎ (01223) 315034
10.30–1.30, 3–10; 10–10.30 Sat;
12–2.30, 7–9.30 Sun
**Adnams Bitter; Burton Bridge
XL; Fuller's London Pride;
guest beers** Ⓖ
Specialist independent off-
licence which stocks 300
bottled beers from Belgium,
Germany and the UK, plus
ciders and wine. The house
beer is brewed by Tolly
Cobbold. ♨

Mitre Tavern
17 Bridge Street
☎ (01223) 358403
11–11
**Ansells Mild; Eldridge Pope
Hardy Country, Royal Oak;
Ind Coope Burton Ale;
Marston's Pedigree; Tetley
Bitter; guest beers** Ⓗ
Attractively de-modernised
pub in ale house style. Usually
eight beers on tap. Open for
meals Sun afternoon until 7;
other eves meals finish at 8.30.
Limited eve menu in winter.
⏚ ◑ ▶ ✔

Red Bull
11 Barton Road, Newnham
☎ (01223) 352788
11–11
**Fuller's London Pride;
Marston's Pedigree; Morland
Old Speckled Hen; Wadworth
6X; Whitbread Boddingtons
Bitter** Ⓗ**; guest beers** Ⓖ
Whitbread Hogshead house,
vastly improved. Fewer guest
beers in summer (less
students). Meals served
12–10.30 Mon–Thu, 12–2
Sat–Sun. ⏚ ❀ ◑ ▶ P

St Radegund
129 King Street
☎ (01223) 311794
12–11
**Bateman XB; Fuller's London
Pride; Nethergate Bitter;
Taylor Landlord** Ⓗ
Small, characterful street-
corner local. 1994 CAMRA
Cambridge *Pub of the Year*.
Greek meze and real French
baguettes served. ◑

Tap & Spile (Mill)
14 Mill Lane (by river)
☎ (01223) 357026
11–11
Adnams Bitter; guest beers Ⓗ
First, and some would say
best, of the ale houses which
now abound in Cambridge.
Oak floors and exposed
brickwork feature. It overlooks
the mill pond where punts can
be hired; outside drinking on
the green. Eight beers.
Q ❀ ◑ ♨

Wrestlers
337 Newmarket Road
☎ (01223) 566554
12–11
**Adnams Broadside; Hall &
Woodhouse Tanglefoot;
Mansfield Bitter; Morland
Old Speckled Hen; Wells
Eagle, Bombardier** Ⓗ
Bustling, buoyant pub,
essentially one to experience
rather than scrutinise, its
character formed by the
clientele rather than fixtures
and fittings. Authentic Thai
bar meals and take-aways.
Live music twice a week.
⏚ ◑ ▶ ♣ ♨ 🍴

Castle Camps

Cock
High Street ☎ (01799) 584207
12–2, 7–11; 12–11 Sat
**Greene King IPA, Abbot;
Nethergate Bitter; guest
beer** Ⓗ
Pleasant, two-bar country local
with friendly staff and a good
range of food (not served Sun
eve/Mon lunch). Note the
cock mural in the alcove.
⏚ Q ❀ ⏚ ◑ ▶ 🍴 ♣ P

Castor

Royal Oak
24 Peterborough Road
☎ (01733) 380217
11–2.30, 6–11
**Ind Coope Burton Ale; Tetley
Bitter; guest beer**
(weekends) Ⓗ
Listed building with a
thatched roof and a low
beamed ceiling. The splendid
maze of passages and bars
provides considerable charm.
Popular with passing trade.
⏚ Q ❀ ♣ P

Chatteris

Honest John
24A–26 South Park Street
☎ (01354) 692698
11–2.30, 5.30–11
**Whitbread Boddingtons
Bitter, Wethered Bitter; guest
beer** Ⓗ
Former labour exchange,
dating from the 1950s, which
became a pub in 1977. See the
model car and ship collection.
Good value, home-made food.
Beware the keg cider on a fake
handpump.
Q ☜ ❀ ◑ ▶ ♿ ♣ P

Clayhithe

Bridge Hotel
☎ (01223) 860252
12–2.30, 6–11
**Adnams Bitter, Broadside;
guest beer** (summer) Ⓗ

Cambridgeshire

18th-century brick hotel with a lawn down to the River Cam (moorings). Large restaurant.
🏨 ⛵ ❀ 🛏 ◗ ▶ P

Colne

Green Man
East Street ☎ (01487) 840368
12–3, 7–11
Greene King IPA; Ind Coope Burton Ale Ⓗ
Comfortable, friendly two-bar village pub, dating from the 17th century. Mind the step down into the pub and the low, uneven door to the lounge. ❀ ◗ ▶ 🍴 ♣ P

Croydon

Queen Adelaide
High Street ☎ (01223) 208278
11.30–3, 6 (6.30 Jan–Feb)–11
Greene King IPA, Rayments Special; Whitbread Boddingtons Bitter Ⓗ
Large pub with several distinct drinking areas and a welcoming atmosphere. Good range of food.
🏨 ⛵ ❀ ◗ ▶ ♿ P

Duxford

Plough
51 St Peter's Street
☎ (01223) 833170
11–3, 5.30–11
Adnams Bitter; Everards Beacon, Tiger, Old Original; guest beers (occasional) Ⓗ
17th-century, refurbished thatched house offering a warm welcome. Excellent pub food at reasonable prices (eve meals Tue–Sat). Well situated for the Air Museum. Children welcome. 🏨 ❀ ◗ ▶ ♣ P

Eaton Socon

Crown
Great North Road
☎ (01480) 212232
11–2.30, 5.30–11; 11–11 Sat
Draught Bass; S&N Theakston Best Bitter; Tetley Bitter; guest beers Ⓗ
Always popular, ivy-clad free house, just off the A1. At least six ales. Book the restaurant.
❀ ◗ ▶ ♠ ♣ P 🍴

Miller's Arms
Ackerman Street (off Great North Road) ☎ (01480) 405965
12–2, 5.30–11; 12–11 Sat (& Fri in summer)
Greene King XX Mild, IPA, Abbot Ⓗ
Small village pub on the larger of Eaton Socon's greens. The garden boasts many children's facilities and offers live jazz and barbecues in summer. Popular with boaters from the

nearby river moorings. Lunches Tue–Sat.
🏨 ⛵ ❀ ◗ ♣ 🍴

Ellington

Mermaid
High Street ☎ (01480) 891450
12–2.30, 7–11
Draught Bass Ⓗ
Single-bar, friendly village pub which has changed little in recent years. 🏨 Q ❀ ◗ ♣

Elton

Black Horse
14 Overend
☎ (01832) 280240
11.30–3, 6.30–11
Adnams Bitter; Wadworth Farmer's Glory Ⓗ
Traditional village free house. The 400-year-old wall of what was the village gaol runs through the middle. Wide range of reasonably priced food in the bar and restaurant.
🏨 Q ⛵ ❀ ◗ ▶ ♠ ♣ P

Ely

Prince Albert
62 Silver Street
☎ (01353) 663494
11.30–2.30 (3 Thu & Fri), 7 (6.30 Thu & Fri)–11; 11–3.30, 7–11 Sat (11–3, 6.30–11 summer)
Greene King IPA, Abbot Ⓗ
Superb local where the emphasis is on beer. Delightful garden; public car park opposite. A cask breather is used on XX Mild occasionally.
Q ❀ ⧗ ♣

West End House
West End ☎ (01353) 662907
11–2.30 (3 Sat), 6–11
Courage Directors; Marston's Pedigree; Ruddles Best Bitter; Webster's Yorkshire Bitter; guest beer Ⓗ
Four drinking areas with a plethora of beams and low ceilings. Friendly staff, but unfriendly cat.
🏨 ❀ ♿ ♣

Etton

Golden Pheasant
1 Main Street
☎ (01733) 252387
11–11
Draught Bass; Bateman XXXB; Ruddles County; guest beers Ⓗ
Former 19th-century manor farmhouse with a large comfortable lounge, a family room and a restaurant. The garden (with aviary) seats over 200; permanent marquees for parties and beer festivals.
🏨 Q ⛵ ❀ ◗ ▶ ♿ ♠ ♣ P ✂

Eye Green

Greyhound
41 Crowland Road
☎ (01733) 222487
11–3.30, 6–11
Wells Eagle, Bombardier; guest beer Ⓗ
Popular, early 20th-century village local with a large garden, a comfortable lounge/diner and a public bar. No keg bitter sold.
🏨 Q ❀ ◗ ▶ 🍴 ♿ ♠ ♣ P

Farcet Fen

Plough
Milk and Water Drove, Ramsey Road (B1095)
☎ (01733) 844307
12–2.30, 7–11
Draught Bass; M&B Highgate Dark; John Smith's Bitter Ⓗ; **guest beer** Ⓖ
Welcoming, isolated fen pub, featuring a collection of brasses and kettles. Book the restaurant (only fresh produce used). No meals Wed.
🏨 Q ❀ ◗ ♣ P 🍴

Fulbourn

Six Bells
High Street ☎ (01223) 880244
11.30–2.30, 6.30–11; 11.30–11 Fri; 12–11 Sat
Ind Coope Burton Ale; Tolly Cobbold Mild; Whitbread Flowers IPA; guest beer Ⓗ
Village-centre pub maintaining traditional values. Home-cooked food in the bar or in the cottage-style restaurant; lunches Wed–Sun, eve meals Tue–Sat. Afternoon teas in the garden. 🏨 ❀ ◗ ▶ ♣ P

Gamlingay

Hardwicke Arms
The Cross ☎ (01767) 650727
11.30–3, 7 (6 Fri & Sat)–11
Draught Bass; Hancock's HB; Tetley Bitter; guest beer Ⓗ
Unchanged, popular one-bar local at the heart of the village. Busy on games nights. A pub with a wide appeal. No food Tue eve or Sun.
🏨 ⛵ ❀ ◗ ▶ ♣ P

Great Chishill

Pheasant
Heydon Road
☎ (01763) 838535
11.30–3 (may extend Sat), 6–11
Adnams Bitter; Ruddles Best Bitter; Wadworth 6X; guest beer Ⓗ
Old village pub and restaurant featuring beams, an inglenook, brasses, and a beautiful raised garden. 🏨 ❀ ◗ ▶ P

Great Eversden

Hoops
High Street ☎ (01223) 262185
12–3, 6.30–11
Marston's Pedigree; Wells Eagle; guest beer Ⓗ
Recently renovated village inn now opened out but retaining a separate Jacobean dining room. Food-oriented, but it retains local support. The huge garden has children's attractions. Eve meals Tue–Sat.
🏚 ❀ 🍴 🌘 🌓 ♣ P

Hail Weston

Royal Oak
High Street ☎ (01480) 472527
11–11
Wells Eagle, Bombardier; guest beers Ⓗ
Picturesque, thatched village pub which has a large garden (children's playground) and a pleasant family room with games (video). Eve meals Tue–Sat. 🏚 ♨ ❀ 🍴 🌓 ♣ P

Helpston

Bluebell
10 Woodgate (off B1443 towards Castor)
☎ (01733) 252394
11–2.30, 6–11; 12–2, 7–10.30 Sun
Draught Bass; Bateman XXXB; John Smith's Bitter; Webster's Yorkshire Bitter Ⓗ
Traditional, 17th-century village drinking house: stone-built, with a simple bar and a wood panelled lounge, featuring teapots and jugs. An excellent example of a dying breed of non-food pubs.
🏚 Q ❀ 🍴 🍺 ♣ ⌂ P

Hilton

Prince of Wales
Potton Road (B1040)
☎ (01480) 830257
11–2.30 (not Mon), 6–11
Adnams Bitter; Fuller's London Pride; guest beer (occasional) Ⓗ
Village pub offering a public bar, a warm welcome and good value food (no meals Mon). 🏚 ❀ 🍴 🌓 🍺 ♣ P

Horningsea

Crown & Punchbowl
High Street ☎ (01223) 860643
12–2.30, 7–11
Adnams Extra; Elgood's Cambridge Bitter; Greene King IPA Ⓗ
17th-century inn extended to include an hotel and restaurant. The quarry-tiled public bar is a delight.
🏚 🍲 ❀ 🍴 🌓 🍺 ♣ P

Horseheath

Old Red Lion
Linton Road ☎ (01223) 892909
11–11
Morland Old Speckled Hen; Ruddles Best Bitter; John Smith's Bitter; Wadworth 6X; guest beers Ⓗ
Large, modernised, old hotel; the well-reconstructed public bar has fires, stone flags and wood panelling. Children welcome in the restaurant.
🏚 🍲 ❀ 🍴 🌓 ♿ P

Huntingdon

Old Bridge Hotel
High Street (ring road)
☎ (01480) 52681
11–11
Adnams Bitter; B&T Shefford Bitter; guest beers Ⓗ
Imposing riverside hotel on the River Ouse. Many dining and function rooms offer a relaxed and friendly atmosphere. The guest beer changes weekly.
🏚 Q ❀ 🍴 🌓 ♿ P ⚥

Leighton Bromswold

Green Man
The Avenue ☎ (01480) 890238
12–2.30 (not Tue–Thu), 7–11; closed Mon
Hall & Woodhouse Tanglefoot; Mitchell's Original; Taylor Landlord; guest beer Ⓗ
CAMRA East Anglia *Pub of the Year 1992*: a comfortable, rural free house with a collection of breweriana and a wide and ever-changing range of guest beers. Hood skittles played. Good value food (no meals Sun). 🍲 ❀ 🌓 ♿ ♣ P

Little Gransden

Chequers
Main Road ☎ (01767) 677348
7 (11 Sat)–11
Greene King IPA; guest beer Ⓗ
Worth searching for, this three-roomed village pub has changed little in recent years. Friendly and welcoming, it serves a different guest ale each week. 🏚 Q ♣ P

Littleport

George & Dragon
Station Road ☎ (01353) 862639
11.30–11
Hall & Woodhouse Badger BB; Iceni Boadicea Chariot; Wells Eagle, Bombardier; guest beer Ⓗ

Despite the pre-war frontage this ex-Watney's pub was extant during the 1816 riots. Lots of games in a relaxed and comfy atmosphere. Crones cider. ⇌ ♣ ⌂ P

Longstowe

Golden Miller
High Street ☎ (01954) 719385
12–2.30, 6.30–11
Adnams Bitter; Eldridge Pope Royal Oak; Greene King IPA Ⓗ
Friendly village pub named after the 1934 Grand National winner, whose photographs adorn the walls. Separate dining room. No eve meals Tue. 🍲 ❀ 🌓 ♣ P 🍴

March

Rose & Crown
41 St Peter's Road
☎ (01354) 652879
11–2 (3 Sat), 7–11
John Smith's Bitter; Wilson's Mild; guest beer Ⓗ
150-year-old traditional pub, now the only real free house in March. The guest beer is often stout or porter. 🍴 ♣ ⌂ P

Meldreth

British Queen
High Street ☎ (01763) 260252
11–3, 5.30–11
Adnams Mild, Bitter; Greene King IPA; Morland Old Speckled Hen; Whitbread Boddingtons Bitter; guest beers Ⓗ
Pleasant, comfortable village local with a games room. Look for special offers on guest beers. No eve meals Sun.
🏚 Q ❀ 🌓 🍺 ♣ ⌂ P

Milton

Waggon & Horses
High Street ☎ (01223) 860313
12–2.30, 5–11; 12–11 Sat
Bateman XB; Nethergate Bitter; guest beers Ⓗ
Unassuming pub offering two changing guest ales. Curry night Fri; roast lunch Sun. No food Sat lunch or Sun eve.
🏚 ❀ 🌓 ⌂ P

Needingworth

Queen's Head
High Street ☎ (01480) 63946
11–11
Hop Back Summer Lightning; Smiles Best Bitter; Woodforde's Wherry; guest beer Ⓗ
Friendly, two-bar village local, with a strong domino following in the public bar.

Cambridgeshire

Always a good range of guest beers – many unusual for the area. Curries a speciality (take-away available). Handpumps are in the public bar. ❀ ◖ ▶ 🍴 ♣ ⟳ P

Newton

Queen's Head
☎ (01223) 870436
11.30 (11 Sat)–2.30, 6–11; 12–2, 7–10.30 Sun
Adnams Bitter, Old, Broadside, Tally Ho Ⓖ
A year-old firkin of Tally Ho is broached on Nov 5 every year at this pub which is now an institution. In every edition of the *Guide*. ⚔ Q ☞ ❀ ◖ ▶ 🍴 ▲ ♣ ⟳ P

Old Weston

Swan
Main Street ☎ (01832) 239400
12–3 (not Mon or Tue), 7–11
Adnams Bitter; Greene King Abbot; Hook Norton Old Hooky; Morland Old Speckled Hen; Nethergate Old Growler; Webster's Yorkshire Bitter Ⓗ
Characterful village pub with three rooms, plenty of beams and a good atmosphere. Lunches Wed–Sun; eve meals Wed, Fri and Sat.
⚔ ☞ ❀ ◖ ▶ ▲ ♣ P

Parson Drove

Swan
Main Road ☎ (01945) 700291
12–2 (3 Sat), 7–11
Elgood's Cambridge Bitter; guest beer (occasional) Ⓗ
Largely unspoilt fen village pub, built in 1541: a bar, lounge and restaurant. Live music Sat. No lunches on Tue.
⚔ Q ❀ 🍴 ◖ ▶ 🍴 ♣ P

Peterborough

Blue Bell
6 The Green, Werrington
☎ (01733) 571264
11–3, 6.30–11
Elgood's Cambridge Bitter, Greyhound; guest beer Ⓗ
White-painted, brick-built pub at the village centre. Dating from the 1890s, it has a modern interior and a very comfortable lounge. Extensive menu of home cooking; no eve meals Tue/Wed.
❀ ◖ ▶ 🍴 & ♣ P

Bogart's
17 North Street
☎ (01733) 349995
11–3, 5–11; 11–11 Fri, Sat & summer; closed Sun
Draught Bass; guest beers Ⓗ / Ⓖ

A traditional atmosphere prevails in this revitalised free house where walls are adorned with old film posters and breweriana. No pool or jukebox. The house beer is brewed by Eldridge Pope. Always a guest mild.
Q ❀ ◖ ⇌ ⟳

Charters Café Bar
Town Bridge ☎ (01733) 315700
12–3, 5–11
Adnams Broadside; Draught Bass; Fuller's London Pride; M&B Highgate Dark; guest beers Ⓗ
Dutch barge built in 1907, now moored upstream of the town bridge; a large bar below decks and a large restaurant above. Guest ales from small independents include milds, stouts and porters. Local CAMRA *Pub of the Year* 1994.
❀ ◖ ▶ ⇌ 🍴

Coach & Horses
39–41 High Street, Stanground
☎ (01733) 343400
11.30–2.30, 6–11; 11–11 Sat
Marston's Pedigree; John Smith's Bitter; guest beer Ⓗ
Popular, long-established local: two rooms, a large garden and a function room. Regularly changing guest beer. Traditional Sun lunch; no food Wed eve.
Q ❀ ◖ ▶ 🍴 & ♣ P

Durham Ox
76 Star Road ☎ (01733) 66565
11–3, 5–11; 11–11 Fri
Adnams Broadside; Wells Eagle, Bombardier; guest beer Ⓗ
Back-street local, built in 1854 and recently reopened after refurbishment.
⚔ Q ☞ ❀ ◖ ▶ 🍴 ♣ ✂

Fountain
2 Burghley Road
☎ (01733) 54533
12–3, 6–11; 11–11 Sat
Courage Directors; Everards Beacon, Tiger, Old Original; guest beers Ⓗ
1930s, two-roomed pub, close to the city centre, with a comfortable lounge and a friendly bar. Frequently changing guest beers. A local CAMRA *Pub of the Season*. No food Sun. ❀ ◖ 🍴 ♣

Hand & Heart
12 Highbury Street, Millfield
☎ (01733) 69463
10.30–3, 6–11
Courage Directors; Marston's Pedigree; Morland Old Speckled Hen; John Smith's Bitter, Magnet; Wilson's Mild; guest beer Ⓗ
The finest example in the area of an unspoilt, back-street local

where the beer range has increased and quality and price are as good as ever. Note the original Warwick's windows. Twice-yearly beer festivals. ⚔ Q ❀ 🍴 ♣ ⟳ 🍴

Old Ramblewood Inn
The Village, Orton Longueville
☎ (01733) 394444
12–3, 5.30–11; 12–11 Fri & Sat
Adnams Broadside; Draught Bass; Fuller's London Pride; Greene King IPA; M&B Highgate Dark; guest beer Ⓗ
Formerly the stables of Orton Hall, itself now an hotel, this pub has a cosy atmosphere, attractive gardens and a highly regarded, good value restaurant. ❀ ◖ ▶ & ▲ ⇌ (Orton Mere, Nene Valley Rlwy) P

Ramsey

Three Horseshoes
50 Little Whyte (left before church) OS289853
☎ (01487) 812452
12 (11 Sat)–3, 7–11
Younger Scotch, IPA; guest beer Ⓗ
Quiet, two-bar, back-street local with a friendly landlord. Choice of four reasonably priced, home-cooked meals lunchtimes (Sun lunch a speciality). Book eve meals.
Q 🍴 ◖ ♣ 🍴

Reach

Kings
Fair Green
☎ (01638) 741745
12–3 (not Mon), 7–11
Elgood's Cambridge Bitter; Greene King IPA; Nethergate Bitter; guest beer Ⓗ
Comfortable, split-level, beamed pub handy for the Devil's Dyke walk and the annual Reach Fair. All food is home-cooked, including the Round the World specials (available in the bar or the dining room). No food Sun eve or Mon. Impressive collection of games.
⚔ ❀ ◖ ▶ ♣ P

St Ives

Aviator
Ramsey Road
☎ (01480) 464417
11–2.30, 6–11
Courage Directors; Webster's Yorkshire Bitter; guest beers Ⓗ
L-shaped bar (eating area at one end) with an impressive range of handpumps, often offering something unusual. The decor is based on a flying theme. Note the 'Wall of Fame'. ❀ ◖ ▶ P

Oliver Cromwell

Wellington Street
☎ (01480) 465601
10.30–2.30, 6–11
Adnams Broadside; Elgood's Cambridge Bitter; Greene King IPA Ⓗ
Busy, one-bar pub largely unchanged in recent years, near the riverside quay and historic bridge. Note the ornate wrought iron sign bracket on the exterior, once part of the Ship, a former quayside pub. The pub clock keeps to GMT. Q ◖

Sawston

Greyhound

High Street ☎ (01223) 832260
11–2.30, 5–11
Brakspear Bitter; Nethergate IPA; Whitbread Castle Eden Ale, Flowers Original; guest beers Ⓗ
One of the oldest pubs in Sawston (the weatherboards are deceptive). The new restaurant extension features beams and glass whilst the garden is good for children.
🏠 ☀ ◖ ▮ P

Soham

Carpenter's Arms

76 Brook Street (off A142, opp. Cherry Tree pub)
☎ (01353) 720869
11–11
Adnams Broadside; Greene King IPA; guest beers Ⓗ
Pleasant, friendly, free house offering a good range of guest beers. Live music two or three times a month (phone for details). Good value lunches.
♿ ☀ ◖ ♣ 🚻

Stonea

Golden Lion

Sixteen Foot Bank (B1098 by level crossing)
☎ (01354) 680732
12–2 (not Mon), 7–11
Greene King IPA, Abbot; guest beer Ⓗ
Friendly, isolated country pub decorated with maps, traps and agricultural implements. Children's play area. Caravans for rent. 🏠 ☀ ◖ ▮ Å ♣ P

Stow cum Quy

Prince Albert

Newmarket Road (A1303, off A14) ☎ (01223) 811294

11.30–3, 5–11; 11.30–11 Sat
Greene King IPA; guest beers Ⓗ
Lively, friendly and welcoming roadhouse with loyal customers. Four guest pumps serve mild, ordinary, best and strong bitters. Beer festivals. Book eve meals. The first authenticated 1000-beer pub in the country.
🏠 ♿ ☀ ◖ ▮ 🚻 ♣ ◔ P 🚻

Stretham

Red Lion

High Street ☎ (01353) 648132
11–3, 6.30–11; 11–11 Sat
Ansells Mild; Greene King IPA; Ind Coope Friary Meux BB, Burton Ale; Nethergate Umbel Magna; Tetley Bitter Ⓗ
Superbly renovated and extended village inn, run with style and imagination. Games and sports nights usually feature a drinks promotion. Good value food in the bar or the candlelit conservatory; salads a speciality.
🏠 ☀ 🛏 ◖ ▮ 🚻 ♣ P 🔀

Thriplow

Green Man

2 Lower Street
☎ (01763) 208855
12–3, 6–11
Adnams Bitter; Hook Norton Best Bitter; Taylor Landlord; guest beers Ⓗ
Ex-Charles Wells village local saved from closure by a local campaign. It stands by the village green, opposite an old smithy. No food Sun eve.
🏠 ☀ ◖ ♣ P

Turves

Three Horseshoes

344 March Road
☎ (01733) 840414
11.30–2.15, 6.30–11; closed Tue
North Yorkshire Flying Herbert; Whitbread Boddingtons Bitter, Flowers Original; guest beers Ⓗ
Pub where the panelled bar features a collection of bric-a-brac, the large garden has a barbecue, patio and play area, and the restaurant offers an extensive menu.
Q ♿ ☀ ◖ ▮ 🚻 P 🔀 🚻

Whittlesford

Bees in the Wall

North Road ☎ (01223) 834289
12–2.30 (not always Mon–Thu), 6–11

Fuller's London Pride; Hook Norton Best Bitter; Morland Old Speckled Hen; Wadworth 6X Ⓗ
Bees do nest in the wall of this ex-Whitbread local with a well-appointed lounge bar and a traditional public.
🏠 Q ☀ 🚻 P

Willingham

Three Tuns

Church Street
☎ (01954) 260437
11–2.30, 6–11; 12–2.30, 7–10.30 Sun
Greene King XX Mild, IPA, Abbot Ⓗ
Classic, unchanging village local offering good company. Basic lunchtime snacks.
Q ☀ 🚻 ♣

Wisbech

Rose Tavern

53 North Brink
☎ (01945) 588335
12–3, 5.30–11
Butterknowle Conciliation Ale; Cains FA; guest beers Ⓗ
Cosy, one-roomed pub, a 200-year-old listed building, on the river close to Elgood's Brewery. Interesting guest beers. Q ☀ 🛏 🚻

Witcham

White Horse

7 Silver Street
☎ (01353) 778298
12 (not Mon)–3, 6.30–11
Greene King IPA; Nethergate Bitter; Whitbread Boddingtons Bitter; guest beer Ⓗ
Village local where the reputation for food has not dulled the enthusiasm for ale. Wide range of home-cooked meals in the restaurant, plus a new instant food counter for pizzas, pies, etc. in the no-smoking bar. No food Sun eve.
☀ ◖ ▮ Å ♣ P 🔀

Yaxley

Three Horseshoes

179 Main Street
☎ (01733) 242059
11–3, 6–11
Courage Directors; John Smith's Bitter; guest beer Ⓗ
Early 18th-century, thatched village local with an enormous garden. Sports theme in the bar; traps and old implements in the lounge. Large menu of home-cooked meals.
☀ ◖ ▮ 🚻 🛏 Å ♣ P

For further information about the beers listed in the above entries, check the breweries section at the rear of the book.

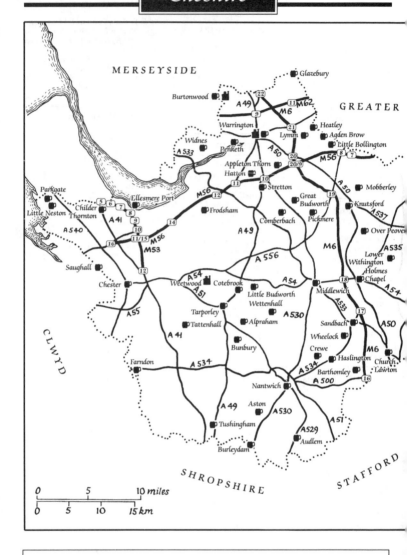

MERSEYSIDE

GREATER

CLWYD

SHROPSHIRE

STAFFORD

0   5   10 miles
0   5   10   15 km

 Beartown, Congleton; **Burtonwood**, Burtonwood; **Coach House**, Warrington; **Weetwood**, Weetwood

---

Agden Brow

Jolly Thresher
Higher Lane (A56/B5159 jct)
☎ (01925) 752265
11.30–3 (4 Fri & Sat), 5.30 (6 Sat)–11
Hydes' Anvil Mild, Bitter Ⓔ
Opened-out roadside pub with
a good reputation for food
(booking advised): a main
lounge plus a dining area and
darts room. Crown green
bowling green at the rear.
No food Mon.
⊛ ◖ ◗ ♣ P

Wheatsheaf
Higher Lane
(A56, 300 yds from B5159 jct)
☎ (01925) 752567
11.30–3, 5.30–11
**Hydes' Anvil Mild,
Bitter** Ⓔ
Large, single-bar pub
modernised in the 1980s,
with a darts/games area.
Popular with the locals.
There is a grassed
playground at the rear.
Good value meals (eves
Thu-Sun).
⊛ ◖ ◗ P ⊟

Alpraham

Traveller's Rest
Chester Road (A51)
☎ (01829) 260523
6–11; 12–3, 6–11 Sat
**McEwan 70/-; Tetley Walker
Mild, Bitter** Ⓗ
Deservedly in the *Guide*
for years and still a
largely unchanged, quiet
local on a main road
with its own bowling
green.
🏚 Q ⊛ ♣ P

Cheshire

MANCHESTER

DERBYSHIRE

Handforth
Kettleshulme
Wilmslow
Bollington
Prestbury A523
Higher Hurdsfield
A537
Henbury
Macclesfield
A34
A523
Eaton
A54
Wincle
Buglawton
Congleton
Timbersbrook
Newbold

SHIRE

Appleton Thorn

Appleton Thorn Village Hall
Stretton Road
☎ (01925) 261187
8.30–11; 8.30–10.30 Sun; closed Mon–Wed
Beer range varies H
This ex-village school now houses a true community social club. CAMRA *Club of the Year* for 1995. Six beers normally available. All visitors welcomed. Q ❀ P

Aston

Bhurtpore Inn
Wrenbury Road (off A530)
OS610469 ☎ (01270) 780917
12–2.30, 6.30–11

Hanby Drawwell; guest beers H
Former smallholding, attracting clientele from miles around. The name is a town in India with connections to Lord Combermere – a local dignitary. The regularly changing guest beers always include a mild. Local CAMRA *Pub of the Year* in 1993.
🍴 Q ❀ ◑ ▮ ⊟ ⅂ ▲ ⌂ P

Audlem

Bridge Inn
12 Shropshire Street (A525 by Bridge 78, Shropshire Union Canal) ☎ (01270) 811267
11–11
Bateman Mild; Marston's Bitter, Pedigree H
Originally a roadhouse prior to the canal being constructed, this was rebuilt in 1873 as a canal pub. Recent refurbishment has not affected its character: it is still a pub serving food rather than a food house serving beer. Friendly welcome.
🍴 ⏚ ❀ ◑ ⅂ ♣ P

Lord Combermere
The Square (A525/A529 jct)
☎ (01270) 811316
11–3.30, 6–11 (11–11 Easter–Oct)
Courage Directors; Marston's Pedigree; Ruddles Best Bitter; John Smith's Bitter H
Late 17th-century coaching inn with a bar area plus seven rooms off. No two doors have the same dimensions!
🍴 ❀ ◑ ▮ ♣ P

Barthomley

White Lion
Audley Road
☎ (01270) 882242
11.30 (5 Thu)–11
Burtonwood Mild, Bitter, Forshaw's, Top Hat H
Popular, black and white, thatched pub at the centre of a small, picturesque village. Dated 1614, it displays a list of 18 landlords. The church opposite was the scene of a massacre during the Civil War.
🍴 Q ⏚ ❀ 🛏 ♣ P

Bollington

Church House
Chapel Street
☎ (01625) 574014
12–2.30 (3 Sat), 5.30–11
Jennings Bitter; S&N Theakston Best Bitter; Taylor Landlord; Whitbread Boddingtons Bitter H
Popular, busy, corner terrace pub with a reputation for good food. Renovated church pews provide attractive seating in the lounge. 🍴 Q 🛏 ◑ ▮

Cotton Tree
3–5 Ingersley Road
☎ (01625) 576883
11–11
Vaux Bitter, Samson; Wards Mild H
Stone-built, corner local. The Bollington Building Society met here in the 1830s. Recently taken over by Vaux, it has been decorated throughout, and is now a good village pub.
🍴 Q ⊟ ⅂ ♣

Lord Clyde
36 Clarke Lane, Kerridge
OS924764 ☎ (01625) 573202
11–11
Greenalls Mild, Bitter, Original H
Small, one-room country pub, close to the Macclesfield Canal. It was named after Colin Campbell, a British general who was in charge at the outbreak of the Indian Mutiny. ❀ ♣ P

Try also: Vale, Adlington Rd (Free)

Buglawton

Church House
Buxton Road (A54)
☎ (01260) 272466
11.30–3, 6–11
Robinson's Hatters Mild, Best Bitter, Frederic's H
Classic, inter-war-style roomy pub, catering for local, passing and canal (⅓mile away) customers with excellent bar meals and a restaurant (closed Sat eve). The unusual pub sign is combined with a pigeon cote. Very good outside facilities for children.
🍴 Q ⏚ ❀ ◑ ▮ ♣ P

Try also: Robin Hood, Buxton Rd (Marston's)

Bunbury

Dysart Arms
College Lane ☎ (01829) 260183
12–3, 5.30–11; 11–11 Sat
Draught Bass; Tetley Walker Bitter H
A stone-floored public bar and a lounge with a large fireplace and an aquarium, in an 18th-century former farmhouse.
🍴 Q ❀ ◑ ▮ ⊟ ⅂ ♣ P

Burleydam

Combermere Arms
On A525 3 miles from Audlem
11–11
Bass Worthington BB; M&B Highgate Dark; guest beers H
Reputedly haunted, 16th-century free house, which welcomes families but has a

varied clientele. Several beer festivals each year. Cider in summer.
🏰 Q ⛐ ❀ ◐ ◑ ♿ ♣ ⌓ P

Burtonwood

Bridge Inn
Phipps Lane ☎ (01925) 225709
11–11
Burtonwood Mild, Bitter Ⓗ
Four-roomed pub, games- and sports-oriented; the licensee's mementoes from his rugby-playing days are displayed. It has a bowling green and a children's play area.
⛐ ❀ ◐ ⊞ ♣ P

Chester

Albion
4 Park Street ☎ (01244) 340345
11.30–3, 5.30–11; 11.30–11 Fri
Cains Bitter; Greenalls Mild, Bitter, Original; Stones Best Bitter Ⓗ
Victorian street-corner pub retaining three rooms, including a snug, and featuring a collection of old enamelled signs and sewing machine tables. Good, home-made food, featuring some unusual dishes, and definitely no chips! Eve meals Fri and Sat. 🏰 Q ◐ ◑ ⊞

Boot
Eastgate Street
11–11
Samuel Smith OBB, Museum Ⓗ
Very old building at the heart of the city, partly dating back to the 16th century (see the glass panel). ❀ ◐

Centurion
Oldfield Drive, Vicars Cross (Green Lane off A51, 1 mile from centre) ☎ (01244) 347623
11.30–3, 5.30–11; 11–11 Sat
Jennings Bitter; Marston's Pedigree; Robinson's Best Bitter; Tetley Walker Mild, Bitter; guest beer Ⓗ
Energetic modern pub holding regular beer festivals and charity fund-raising events. The beer range may vary. Children's play area in the garden. ❀ ⊞ ♿ ♣ P

Claverton's
Lower Bridge Street
11–11
Lees Bitter, Moonraker Ⓗ
Popular bar in the cellar of an historic building. Doormen at weekends prevent overcrowding. Food 12–8.
◐ ◑ ♿

Mill Hotel
Milton Street
11–11
John Smith's Bitter; Weetwood Best Bitter; Whitbread Boddingtons Bitter; guest beers Ⓗ
Enterprising and popular hotel bar and restaurant. A house beer, Mill Premium, is brewed by Coach House. Guest beers usually include a mild. Food until 10.30.
Q ⛐ ❀ 🛏 ◐ ◑ ♿ ⇌ P ⚡

Pop-In (Off-Licence)
43 Boughton ☎ (01244) 320013
12–10.15
Beer range varies Ⓖ
Specialist beer store stocking cask ales and imported beers (many bottle-conditioned), plus its own label bottled porter. Beers are below pub prices.

Talbot
33 Walter Street, Newtown
☎ (01244) 317901
11–11; 11–5, 7–11 Sat
Burtonwood Mild, Bitter Ⓗ
Warm, friendly, corner pub, popular with locals, close to the Northgate Sports Centre. Note the large collection of ornamental pigs in the bar. Parking is difficult.
⊞ ♿ ⇌ ♣ P

Childer Thornton

White Lion
New Road (200 yards off A41)
☎ (0151) 339 3402
11.30–3, 5–11; 11.30–11 Fri & Sat
Thwaites Best Mild, Bitter, Craftsman Ⓗ
Unspoilt, two-roomed country local with a warm reception for all. The snug is used by families at lunchtime but can get busy. No food Sun.
🏰 Q ❀ ◐ P

Church Lawton

Lawton Arms
Liverpool Road West
☎ (01270) 873743
11.30–3.30 (4.30 Fri), 5.30 (7 Sat)–11
Robinson's Hatters Mild, Best Bitter Ⓔ
Georgian local with a snug and a games room.
🏰 ❀ P ⊟

Comberbach

Drum & Monkey
The Avenue ☎ (01606) 891417
11.30–3, 5.30–11
Tetley Walker Bitter Ⓗ
Friendly, popular village local, convenient for Marbury Country Park. 🏰 ◐ P

Congleton

Moss Inn
140 Canal Road
☎ (01260) 273583
11–11
Bateman Mild; Marston's Bitter, Pedigree Ⓗ
Warm, cosy pub whose walls are laden with interesting artefacts. A thriving local trade is boosted by cyclists, walkers and canal users (100 yards away). Extensive smoke filter and extraction system. Eve meals 6–8, Tue–Fri.
❀ ◐ ◑ ♿ ⇌ ♣ P

Cotebrook

Alvanley Arms
Forest Road (A49)
☎ (01824) 760200
11.30–3, 6–11
Robinson's Hatters Mild, Best Bitter Ⓗ
Georgian country pub with decor and furnishings to match. A good range of quality bar meals predominates. Families welcome. Located on a fast bend so beware!
🏰 ❀ 🛏 ◐ ◑ P

Crewe

Albion
1 Pedley Street
☎ (01270) 256234
12 (7 Tue & Thu)–11
Tetley Walker Mild, Bitter; guest beer Ⓗ
Street-corner local with an emphasis on darts and dominoes, plus a pool room. The frequently changing guest beer comes from small breweries. ⊞ ⇌ ♣

George
645 West Street
☎ (01270) 213462
11–3, 7–11; 11–11 Sat
Tetley Walker Mild, Bitter; guest beer Ⓗ
Community pub near Crewe Park, with a convivial atmosphere. Families welcome. Constantly changing guests are sold at very reasonable prices. ❀ ◐ ♿ P

King's Arms
56 Earle Street
☎ (01270) 584134
11.30–3 (4 Fri & Sat), 7–11
Whitbread Chester's Mild, Chester's Best Bitter, Boddingtons Bitter, Trophy Ⓗ
Multi-roomed, town-centre pub to suit all tastes; friendly atmosphere. ⊞ ♣

Eaton

Waggon & Horses
Manchester Road (A34)
☎ (01260) 224229
11–3, 5.30 (6 Sat)–11
Robinson's Hatters Mild, Best Bitter Ⓗ

Pleasant, two-bar pub on a main road, with a large dining room. The popular bar menu includes children's portions.
🛏 Q ⅏ 🏵 ◑ ▮ ♣ P

Try also: Plough, Macclesfield Rd (Banks's)

Ellesmere Port

Grosvenor
2 Upper Mersey Street (near M53 jct 9) ☎ (0151) 355 1810
5 (12 Thu–Sat)–11
Burtonwood Bitter, Forshaw's Ⓗ
Large, two-roomed, basic boozer. 🚆 ♣ P

Straw Hat
Hope Farm Road, Great Sutton (off A41) ☎ (0151) 356 3335
12–11
Courage Directors; Marston's Pedigree; John Smith's Bitter Ⓗ
Modern estate pub hosting live music from predominantly local bands three nights a week. ♣ P

Try also: Sir Robert, Overpool Rd (Whitbread); **Sutton Way**, Thelwell Rd (Courage)

Farndon

Greyhound Hotel
High Street ☎ (01829) 270244
5.30–11; 12–3, 7–11 Sat
Greenalls Mild, Bitter, Original Ⓗ
Large, welcoming pub in a picturesque village close to the River Dee. Beware the keg cider on a false handpump. The accommodation is self-catering. 🛏 Q 🏵 🛌 ⅏ ♣ P

Frodsham

Rowland's Bar
31 Church Street
☎ (01928) 733361
11–11
Weetwood Best Bitter; Whitbread Boddingtons Bitter; guest beers Ⓗ
Very popular, single-room pub with a friendly atmosphere. Over 1000 different guest beers have been served from four pumps; 15 beers per week, plus guest cider. The food is recommended, with daily bar meals and a restaurant upstairs (booking advised). Q ◑ ▮ 🚆 ⏚ 🍴

Glazebury

Chat Moss
207 Warrington Road
☎ (01925) 762128
12–3, 5.30–11; 12–11 Fri & Sat (closed Mon–Tue eves in winter)

Burtonwood Mild, Bitter, Top Hat Ⓗ
Formerly George Stephenson's site office, now a large, comfortable lounge featuring plenty of locomotive photographs, plus a games area. No trains stop but the vibrations can be felt.
🛏 🏵 ◑ ▮ ⅏ ♣ P

Great Budworth

George & Dragon
High Street ☎ (01606) 891317
11.30–3.30, 6–11
Tetley Walker Bitter; guest beers Ⓗ
Picturesque village pub opposite the church, featuring a timbered lounge full of brasses, coppers and multi-coloured lanterns. Local CAMRA *Pub of the Year*.
⅏ 🏵 ◑ ▮ ⅙ ♣ P

Handforth

Railway
Station Road ☎ (01625) 523472
11–3, 5.30–11
Robinson's Hatters Mild, Best Bitter Ⓗ
Large, multi-roomed, pub facing the station; a thriving local, popular with all. No food Sun. Q ◑ ▮ 🚆 ♣ P

Haslington

Hawk
137 Crewe Road
☎ (01270) 582181
11–11
Robinson's Hatters Mild, Best Bitter, Frederic's Ⓔ
15th-century, multi-roomed inn, where an original wattle wall is on display. Dick Turpin is believed to have stayed here. Friendly atmosphere. Eve meals Fri and Sat.
⅏ 🏵 ◑ ▮ P 🍴

Hatton

Hatton Arms
Hatton Lane ☎ (01925) 730314
11–11
Greenalls Mild, Bitter, Original; Tetley Walker Bitter Ⓗ
Traditional village pub, based on old cottages. It retains multiple rooms and a real fire.
⅏ Q 🏵 ◑ ▮ P

Heatley

Railway
Mill Lane (B5159)
☎ (01925) 752742
12–11
Whitbread Boddingtons Bitter; guest beer Ⓗ
Large, multi-roomed, old-style pub catering for most tastes,

with a large, open garden and a play area. An ideal base for a stroll on the Bollin Valley section of the Trans-Pennine Trail. Sandwiches at all times; no lunches Sun. Q 🏵 ◑ ♣ P

Henbury

Cock Inn
Chelford Road (A537)
☎ (01625) 423186
11–3, 5–11
Robinson's Hatter's Mild, Best Bitter, Old Tom Ⓗ
Comfortable, main road pub just outside Macclesfield drawing both local and passing trade. Children welcome in the restaurant. No coaches. Q 🏵 ◑ ▮ ⅏ ♣ P

Higher Hurdsfield

George & Dragon
61 Rainow Road (B5470, Whaley Bridge road, ½ mile from canal) ☎ (01625) 424300
12–3 (not Sat), 7–11
Beer range varies Ⓗ
Small, friendly pub built of local stone, set back off the main road. Part of the structure is 400 years old. Bus stop outside. ◑ ⅙ ♣

Holmes Chapel

Swan
29 Station Road
☎ (01477) 532259
11–11
Samuel Smith OBB, Museum Ⓗ
Former coaching inn serving good food (large pizzas a speciality). Note the old black stove. The car park is reached by driving underneath the pub. ⅏ 🏵 🛌 ◑ ▮ ⅏ 🚆 P

Kettleshulme

Bull's Head
Macclesfield Road
☎ (01663) 733225
7–11; 7–10.30 Sun (12–3, 7–11 summer Sat; 12–3, 7–10.30 summer Sun)
Whitbread Boddingtons Bitter, Castle Eden Ale; guest beer Ⓗ
Friendly, stone-terraced pub situated in the centre of a village in the Peak National Park. Time has little changed the traditional character of its cosy lounge, public bar and darts area. ⅏ 🏵 ♣ P

Knutsford

Builder's Arms
Mobberley Road, (off A537)
☎ (01565) 634528
11.30–3, 5.30–11; 12–2, 7–10.30 Sun

Cheshire

Banks's Mild; Marston's Bitter, Pedigree Ⓗ
Delightful, busy pub in an attractive terrace on the outskirts of the town centre. A former Taylors Eagle Brewery pub, it has a keen games emphasis and is best approached from the road opposite the Legh Arms.
Q ❀ 🍴 ⬆

King Canute
21 Princess Street
☎ (01565) 633915
11.30–4.30, 7–11; 11–11 Sat
S&N Theakston Best Bitter; Webster's Yorkshire Bitter Ⓗ
Friendly, open-plan pub in the centre of town. Good range of reasonably priced food. It now enjoys a more mature clientele.
🍴 ▶ ⬆

White Lion
94 King Street
☎ (01565) 632018
11.30–11
Tetley Walker Bitter; guest beers Ⓗ
A black and white, timbered building from the mid-17th century, this pub was in existence long before a party of soldiers was billeted here during the 1745 Jacobite rebellion. Good food (no meals Sun).
🏨 Q ❀ 🍴 ⬆ ♣

Little Bollington

Swan with Two Nicks
Park Lane (off A57)
☎ (0161) 928 2914
11.30–3, 5.30–11
Whitbread Boddingtons Bitter, Flowers IPA, Castle Eden Ale Ⓗ
Rural pub licensed since 1880, now much extended into outbuildings at the rear to create a restaurant. Next to Bridgewater Canal and Dunham Deer Park (NT).
🏨 ❀ 🍴 ▶ P

Little Budworth

Shrewsbury Arms
Chester Road (A54)
☎ (01829) 760240
11.30–3, 6–11
Robinson's Old Stockport Bitter, Hartleys XB, Best Bitter, Frederic's Ⓗ
Just 20 minutes from Chester and five from Oulton Park motor racing circuit, this neat country pub features all the Robinson's bitters. It comprises a snug, a lounge and a small dining room where families are welcome. No meals Mon eve.
❀ 🍴 ▶ P

Little Neston

Harp Inn
19 Quayside (from Burton Rd down Marshlands Rd; left along Marsh Rd)
☎ (0151) 336 6980
11–11
Taylor Landlord; Whitbread Chester's Mild, Trophy; guest beers Ⓗ
Delightful, two-roomed pub served by one bar. The superb public bar has a real fire and low beams. This former miners' pub may be difficult to get to but it is a joy when you find it. Beware high tides!
🏨 Q ☕ ❀ 🍴 P

Lower Withington

Red Lion
Trap Street, Dicklow Cob, (B5392) ☎ (01477) 71248
11.45–2.30 (3 Sat), 5.30–11
Robinson's Dark Mild, Best Bitter Ⓗ
Large, rural pub with a restaurant, a lounge bar and a tap room for locals, close to Jodrell Bank radio telescope. The pump clip says Robinson's Best Mild but it is actually a very rare outlet for Dark Mild.
🏨 ❀ 🍴 ▶ 🍴 ♠ ♣ P

Lymm

Bull's Head
32 The Cross ☎ (01925) 752831
11.30–11 (11.30–3, 5.30–11 winter)
Hydes' Anvil Mild, Bitter Ⓔ
Thriving local with a friendly atmosphere: a comfortable lounge and a large basic bar. Close to the Bridgewater Canal. Q 🍴 🍴 ♣

Spread Eagle
Eagle Brow (A6144)
☎ (01925) 755939
11.30–11
Lees GB Mild, Bitter Ⓗ, Moonraker Ⓔ
Ornate village pub with a black and white facade, near Lymm Cross and canal moorings. Three varying rooms: a large, plush, split-level lounge, a cosy snug popular with locals, and a basic bar extended into the cottage next door. 🏨 Q 🍴 🍴

Macclesfield

Baths
40 Green Street (off A537)
6.30–11; 11–4, 6.30–11 Sat
Banks's Hanson's Mild, Bitter; Whitbread Boddingtons Bitter Ⓗ
Small, but thriving local. A nearby bowling green inspired

its original name, Bowling Green Tavern. The later name was derived from a public bath. The pub has outlived both. 🍴 ⬆ ♣

Chester Road Tavern
18 Chester Road
☎ (01625) 424683
11–3 (4 Fri & Sat), 6–11
Greenalls Mild, Bitter; Stones Best Bitter Ⓗ
Popular pub, on a now quiet street since the opening of the ring road. It hosts a keen dominoes school along with other pub games. 🍴 ♣

George & Dragon
Sunderland Street
☎ (01625) 421898
11–3 (4 Thu & Sat), 5.30 (7 Sat)–11; 11–11 Fri
Robinson's Hatters Mild, Best Bitter Ⓔ
Friendly pub serving good value food. Pool, darts and skittles are played. Close to both bus and railway stations. Eve meals Mon–Fri till 6.45.
Q ❀ 🍴 ▶ ⬆ ♣

Ox-Fford
73 Oxford Road
☎ (01625) 422092
12–3.30, 5–11; 11–11 Fri & Sat
S&N Theakston Best Bitter, XB; guest beers Ⓗ
Detached brick pub on a busy through road to Congleton. It was called the Oxford before being renamed.
❀ 🍴 🍴 ♣

Queens
5 Albert Place
☎ (01625) 422328
11–11
Holt Mild, Bitter Ⓗ
Large Victorian inn, opposite the station. The original brickwork has been restored by Holt's. It is now an honest drinking house serving very cheap beer. 🏨 🍴 ⬆ ♣

Middlewich

Big Lock
Webbs Lane (off A530, Northwich Rd, turn down Finneys Lane)
☎ (01606) 833489
11.30–11
Courage Directors; Ruddles Best Bitter; Webster's Yorkshire Bitter; guest beer Ⓗ
Former Allied keg pub, now offering an increasing number of real ales and good food. Handy for canal users. The house beer is brewed by Courage. ☕ ❀ 🍴 ▶ 🍴 ♣ P

Cheshire Cheese
Lewin Street (A533)
☎ (01606) 832097
11–4.30, 6.30–11

Burtonwood Mild; Cains
Bitter; John Smith's Bitter;
guest beer Ⓗ
Former Tetley keg pub sold to
Boddingtons in 1990 and
bought by Paramount in late
1994: a small, friendly pub
near the canal. Guest beers are
likely to be from Whitbread or
Courage. ✿ ◖ ♣

Mobberley

Bull's Head

Town Lane (off B5085)
☎ (01565) 873134
11–11
Tetley Walker Mild, Bitter;
Whitbread Boddingtons
Bitter; guest beer Ⓗ
Large, detached pub of late
17th-century origin, with a
bowling green to the rear. The
open-plan lounge has a central
fireplace. Limited parking. No
meals Sun. Occasional beer
festivals. ☎ Q ✿ ◖ P

Nantwich

Wilbraham Arms

58 Welsh Row
☎ (01270) 626419
11–11
Coach House Coachman's;
John Smith's Bitter;
Weetwood Best Bitter; guest
beers Ⓗ
Georgian fronted hotel just out
of the town centre and within
easy reach of the Shropshire
Union Canal. It stages a real
cider festival and live music
during the town's folk festival
in early Sept. ☎ Q ⌂ ◖ ◗
⊟ ▲ ✿ ♣ ⌁ P ⊟

Newbold

Horseshoe

Fence Lane (off A34 at Astbury
church, right after ½ mile)
OS863602 ☎ (01260) 272205
11–3, 6–11
Robinson's Hatters Mild, Best
Bitter, Frederic's Ⓔ
Isolated country pub, formerly
part of a farmhouse and
retaining a farming
atmosphere. Difficult to find
but worth the effort. A superb
children's play area has
swings, see-saw and climbing
frames. Good local trade but a
welcome is extended to
walkers and canal users. No
food Mon eve.
☎ Q ⛄ ✿ ◖ ◗ ♣ P

Over Peover

Parkgate Inn

Stocks Lane ☎ (01625) 861455
11–3, 5–11; 11–11 Sat
Samuel Smith OBB Ⓗ
Very smart, ivy-clad old pub
with several small, wood-

panelled rooms, including a
tap room. Annual gooseberry
competition Aug. Good food.
☎ Q ✿ ◖ ◗ ⊟ & ♣ P

Parkgate

Red Lion

The Parade ☎ (0151) 336 1548
12–11
Ind Coope Burton Ale;
Walker Mild, Best Bitter Ⓗ
Traditional lounge and bar
giving a superb view of the
Welsh hills across the Dee
estuary and marsh (famous for
birdlife). Locals numbers are
swelled by many summer
visitors. Kitchen utensils adorn
the lounge ceiling; Nelson, a
parrot, guards the bar. No
food Sun. Q ◖ ⊟ ♣

Penketh

Ferry Tavern

Station Road (off A562, follow
signs to yacht haven)
☎ (01925) 791117
11–3, 5.30–11; 11–11 Thu–Sat &
summer
Courage Directors; Ruddles
County; John Smith's
Magnet; Webster's Yorkshire
Bitter, Wilson's Mild; guest
beers Ⓗ
Welcoming, historic inn by the
Mersey. Two ever-changing,
independent guest beers are
chosen through a request
system. Lunchtime food is
often free for children; eve
meals (not served Sun) include
a full vegetarian menu. Over
100 whiskies. Garden play
area. ☎ ✿ ◖ ◗ P

Pickmere

Red Lion

Park Lane (off B5391)
☎ (01565) 733151
11.30–2.30 (3.30 summer), 5–11;
11.30–11 Sat
Tetley Walker Dark Mild,
Bitter; guest beer Ⓗ
Friendly, two-room country
pub with several comfortable
drinking areas and a large
garden. No meals Sun eve.
☎ ✿ ◖ ◗ ♣ P

Prestbury

Admiral Rodney

New Road (A538)
☎ (01625) 828078
11–3, 5.30–11
Robinson's Hatters Mild, Best
Bitter Ⓗ
Popular inn in an attractive
village terrace. A Grade
II-listed building, its original
front door became the back
door when the new road was
built through the village.
☎ Q ◖ ⇌ P

Sandbach

Lower Chequer

Crown Bank, The Square
☎ (01270) 762569
12–5.30, 7–11
Courage Directors; Marston's
Pedigree; Tetley Best Bitter,
County; guest beers Ⓗ
Former money-changing
house which dates from the
16th century, with a striking,
beamed frontage and interior.
Good atmosphere. Q ◖ ◗

Wheatsheaf

1 Hightown ☎ (01270) 762013
11.30–3, 5.30–11; 11.30–11 Thu & Sat
Bass Worthington BB,
Draught Bass; Tetley Walker
Bitter Ⓗ
Traditional town pub, in the
old part of the village. Popular
with a young crowd at
weekends, but a quiet pint can
be had most weekdays.
☎ Q ⌂ ◖ P

Saughall

Greyhound Inn

Seahill Road ☎ (01244) 880205
11.30–3, 5–11; 11.30–11 Sat
Whitbread Boddingtons
Bitter, Castle Eden Ale; guest
beer Ⓗ
Refurbished local, well worth
the bus ride from Chester;
only 200 yards from the Welsh
border. Eve meals finish at
8.30. Q ✿ ◖ ♣ P

Stretton

Ring O' Bells

Northwich Road, Lower
Stretton (A559, nr M56 jct 10)
☎ (01925) 730556
12–3 (3.30 Sat), 5.30 (7 Sat)–11
Greenalls Mild, Bitter,
Original Ⓗ
Friendly roadside local. The
comfortable bar retains a cosy
atmosphere and is warmed by
a welcoming log fire in winter.
There are also two small,
intimate snugs. Petanque is
popular in summer.
☎ Q ✿ ♣ P

Tarporley

Rising Sun

38 High Street
☎ (01829) 732423
11–3, 5.30–11
Robinson's Hatters Mild, Best
Bitter Ⓗ
This authentic old pub scores
heavily on almost all fronts: a
perennial *Guide* entry. The
excellent meals, in the bar and
restaurant, are renowned for
their quality and value.
Children welcome at
lunchtime or in the restaurant.
Q ◖ ◗ P

Swan Hotel

50 High Street
☎ (01829) 733838
11–11
Weetwood Best Bitter; guest beers Ⓗ
Elegant, family-run free house, an 18th-century coaching inn at the centre of picturesque Tarporley; two oak-beamed bars with open fires. Extensive range of English and French cuisine. Varied clientele; friendly atmosphere.
🏾 Q ⛄ ❀ ⇔ ◑ ◗ ♿ ♠ P

Tattenhall

Letters Inn

High Street
☎ (01829) 70221
11.30–3, 5.15–11
Cains Bitter; Whitbread Boddingtons Bitter; guest beers Ⓗ
Traditional country inn where bar meals are available at all times. No-smoking restaurant area.
🏾 Q ❀ ◑ ◗ ♣ ⅟

Timbersbrook

Coach & Horses

Dane in Shaw Bank
OS890618 ☎ (01260) 273019
11–3, 6–11
Robinson's Hatters Mild, Best Bitter Ⓔ
Situated high in the hills above Congleton, this small brick pub with surrounding farm buildings is half hidden from the main road as it winds upwards from the A537. The interior is mainly a large through-lounge, but there is also a tiny tap room.
🏾 ⛄ ❀ ◑ ◗ ⊟ ♿ ♠ P

Tushingham

Blue Bell Inn

Just off A41, 4 miles N of Whitchurch
☎ (01948) 662172
12–3, 6–11
Hanby Drawwell, Treacleminer; guest beers (occasional) Ⓗ
Delightful, award-winning country pub. Three timber-beamed rooms welcome locals, visitors and children. Good home-cooked food.
🏾 Q ⛄ ❀ ◑ ◗ P

Try also: Wheatsheaf Inn, No Man's Heath (Free)

Warrington

Lower Angel

27 Buttermarket Street
☎ (01925) 633299
11–4, 7–11
Ind Coope Burton Ale; Walker Mild, Bitter, Best Bitter, Winter Warmer; guest beer Ⓗ
Small, two-roomed, popular pub in the town centre with its own ghost: a multi-award winner from the local CAMRA branch. ⇌ (Central) ♣

Manx Arms

31 School Brow
☎ (01925) 230791
12–3.30 (4.30 Sat), 7–11
Vaux Mild, Bitter, Samson, Waggle Dance Ⓗ
Friendly rejuvenated, town-centre pub in a side street near the Cockedge shopping centre. Thriving local trade; visitors are always welcome. The beers may change within the Vaux range. ⊟ ⇌ (Central) ♣

Saracen's Head

381 Wilderspool Causeway
(A49, 1½ miles S of centre)
☎ (01925) 634466
11–11
Greenalls Mild, Bitter, Original; Tetley Walker Bitter; guest beer Ⓗ
A former brewery tap, this large, comfortable, multi-roomed pub retains its community focus. Regular family days. It has its own bowling green and children's zoo. The guest beer comes from the Greenalls list.
🏾 ⛄ ❀ ◑ ◗ ⊟ ♣ P

Wettenhall

Boot & Slipper

Long Lane OS625613
☎ (01270) 528238
11.30–3, 5.30–11
M&B Highgate Dark; Marston's Bitter, Pedigree Ⓔ/Ⓗ
16th-century coaching inn with a friendly atmosphere: a local eating house.
🏾 ❀ 🏾 ◑ ◗ ⊟ ♣ P

Wheelock

Commercial

Game Street ☎ (01270) 760122
8–11; 12–2, 8–11 Sun

Cains Bitter; Marston's Pedigree; Thwaites Bitter; guest beer (Thu) Ⓗ
Listed Georgian building, a former brew pub showing signs of former Birkenhead Brewery ownership. The superbly restored games room has a full-sized snooker table and table skittles. 🏾 Q ⛄ ⅟

Widnes

Millfield

Millfield Road
☎ (0151) 424 2955
11–11; 11–5, 7–11 Sat
Webster's Yorkshire Bitter, Wilson's Mild; guest beer Ⓗ
Busy, two-roomed back-street pub. ♣

Wilmslow

Farmer's Arms

71 Chapel Lane
☎ (01625) 532443
11–11
Whitbread Boddingtons Bitter; guest beers Ⓗ
Traditional Victorian town pub: several rooms with brasses and antiques. Very busy at times due to its good atmosphere. Note the etched lounge windows. Beautifully kept garden. Children's room upstairs. No food Sun.
🏾 ⛄ ❀ ◑ ◗

George & Dragon

Church Street
☎ (01625) 522802
11.30–3.30 (3 Thu), 6–11; 11–11 Wed & Fri
Bass Worthington Dark, BB, Draught Bass; Stones Best Bitter; guest beers Ⓗ
Excellent, large, multi-roomed community pub next to a church. Very large garden; keen emphasis on sport.
🏾 ❀ ◑ ⊟ ⇌ ♣ P

Wincle

Wild Boar

On A54 ☎ (01260) 227219
12–3, 7–11
Robinson's Hatters Mild, Best Bitter, Frederic's Ⓗ
Traditional, welcoming stone pub, high on the moors with warming open fires in cold weather. Fortnightly clay-pigeon shoots can make Sun lunchtimes very busy. A popular venue for sledging and skiing. 🏾 Q ❀ ◑ ◗ P

Some pubs may have extended their Sunday opening hours to take advantage of legislation introduced in late summer 1995. Readers are advised to check before visiting.

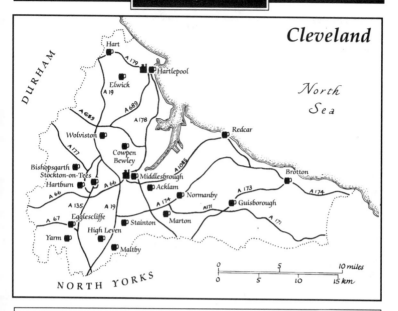

Cleveland

DURHAM

North Sea

NORTH YORKS

 Camerons, Hartlepool; **North Yorkshire**, Middlesbrough

Acklam

Coronation
Acklam Road (A1032/A1130 jct) ☎ (01642) 817599
11–11.30 (11 Sat)
Camerons Crown Special, Strongarm Ⓗ
Inter-war, brick-built pub, recently refurbished as a Wolverhampton & Dudley house, with a bar, lounge and a function room. Ⓓ 🏠 ♣ P 🍴

Try also: Master Cooper, Acklam Rd (Samuel Smith)

Bishopsgarth

Mitre
Harrowgate Lane
☎ (01642) 580238
11–11
Whitbread Boddingtons Bitter, Castle Eden Ale; guest beers Ⓗ
Former Nimmo's house built at the edge of a 1960s estate. Recently refurbished in 'Tithe Barn' style, it still has an emphasis on food (Beefeater), but also an ever-widening range of guest beers.
🏠 Ⓓ ♦ & P

Brotton

Malt & Hop
3 High Street
☎ (01287) 678300

12–4.30, 7–11; 11–11 Sat
Camerons Strongarm; Tetley Mild, Imperial; guest beers Ⓗ
Small, terraced pub in a former ironstone mining village. The lively bar serves a strong local trade; separate pool room and a quiet rear snug. Good value bar meals, and the best chips for miles! Children allowed in the snug.
Q Ⓓ ♦ ♣

Cowpen Bewley

Three Horse Shoes
☎ (01642) 561541
11–3, 6–11
Camerons Strongarm; S&N Theakston Best Bitter; guest beer Ⓗ
Homely village pub at one end of the green. A pub has been on this site for a very long time. The original was mentioned in the *Domesday Book*, but the present building is from the 1960s. Keen local following.
🏠 Q 🏠 Ⓓ ♦ ⅃ & ♣ P 🍴

Egglescliffe

Pot & Glass
Church Road (800 yds from A135 into village, turn right)
☎ (01642) 780145
11–3, 5.30–11
Bass Worthington BB, Draught Bass Ⓗ
Attractive village pub facing the church: two bars and a

function room. Its fascinating history includes a tale of ghostly nuns! The ornate bar fronts were carved by a former licensee from old furniture. Eve meals only by request.
Q 🏠 🏠 Ⓓ ⅃ & ♣ P

Elwick

McOrville
The Green (off A19 in village centre) ☎ (01429) 273344
11.30–3, 7–11; 11–11 Fri & Sat
Whitbread Boddingtons Bitter, Castle Eden Ale; guest beers Ⓗ
Country tavern on the village green serving an excellent, home-cooked lunchtime menu with eves set aside for drinkers. Live jazz once a month. The pub boasts an expanding collection of pigs.
🏠 🏠 Ⓓ & ♣ P

Guisborough

Tap & Spile
Westgate ☎ (01287) 632983
11–3, 5–11; 11–11 Thu–Sat
Beer range varies Ⓗ
Old, town-centre pub, refurbished in traditional style, with a no-smoking room at the rear (available for small functions). Up to eight real ales and a real cider on tap at any one time. Cleveland CAMRA *Pub of the Season* autumn 1994.
Q 🏠 Ⓓ ♣ ⌂ 🍴

Cleveland

Three Fiddles
34 Westgate ☎ (01287) 632417
11–11
Draught Bass; Whitbread Boddingtons Bitter; guest beer 🄷
Old coaching house in the town centre featuring framed photos and sketches of local views. Separate pool room.
Q ❀ 🛏 ◖ ◗ ♿ ♣

Voyager
The Avenue (Stokesley Rd jct)
☎ (01287) 634774
11–3, 6–11
Ind Coope Burton Ale; Tetley Bitter; Whitbread Castle Eden Ale 🄷
Modern estate pub of interesting architectural style, with split-level bars. Surrounded by lawns and mature trees, it holds barbecues and bonfire specials in the outside area. Wheelchair access to the restaurant only (closed Sun eve). Oversized glasses on request.
❀ ◖ ◗ P ⊟

Hart

Raby Arms
Front Street ☎ (01429) 274058
11–11
Whitbread Boddingtons Bitter, Castle Eden Ale; guest beers 🄷
Large family tavern at the village centre; five rooms of differing sizes and character. It caters very much for families with a large children's play area. ⛀ ❀ ◖ ◗ ♿ ♣ P ⚔

Hartburn

Masham Hotel
87 Hartburn Village
☎ (01642) 580414
11–11
Draught Bass; Black Sheep Special Strong; guest beers 🄷
Popular old local in a tree-lined conservation area. Its origins as a 'public house' can still be seen. The welcoming interior has several small drinking areas. Large garden.
Q ⛀ ❀ ♣ P ⊟

Hartlepool

Brewer & Firkin
2 Whitby Street
☎ (01429) 273564
11–11 (may vary)
Whitbread Boddingtons Bitter, Castle Eden Ale; guest beers 🄷
Large one-room pub with various levels to give areas of privacy. In a part of town receiving massive investment, it is handy for the town centre and the new museums complex. The Cask and Curry Club is popular on Fri. Up to six guest beers.
♨ 🛏 ◖ ⇌ ♣

Causeway
Elwick Road, Stranton (behind Camerons' Brewery)
☎ (01429) 273954
11–11
Banks's Bitter; Camerons Bitter; Strongarm; guest beers 🄷
Basic beer drinkers' pub: a large bar plus two cosy rooms, with beer served from a hatchway. Folk club Sun eve. No meals Sun lunchtime.
Q ⛀ ❀ ◖ ⊞ ♣ P

Gillen Arms
Clavering Road (off A179 in the estate) ☎ (01429) 860218
11–11
Whitbread Castle Eden Ale; guest beer 🄷
Large, modern, open-plan estate pub with two rooms and strong community links. The comfortable interior has quiet corners and a family conservatory.
♨ Q ⛀ ❀ ◖ ◗ ♿ ♣ P ⊟

Kirkham Hotel
South Crescent (end of Rowell St, opp. old breakwater)
☎ (01429) 266818
7 (12 Sat)–11
Federation Buchanan's Original; guest beer 🄷
Large, Victorian seafront pub overlooking a children's pool and play area: one large bar with a smaller, cosy lounge offering scenic views across the bay to Redcar. A recent base for the BBC's *Harry* series. Well worth the effort of finding. ♨ Q ❀ 🛏 ♣ P ⊟

Try also: New Inn, Durham St (Camerons)

High Leven

Fox Covert
Low Lane (A1044 Hilton jct)
☎ (01642) 760033
11–3, 5–11
Vaux Samson, Double Maxim 🄷
Distinctive cluster of white-washed brick buildings of farmhouse origin, with a comfortable, open-plan interior and a warm welcome for all. Function room upstairs. Strong emphasis on food.
♨ ❀ ◖ ◗ ♣ P

Maltby

Pathfinders
High Lane ☎ (01642) 590300
11–11
Whitbread Boddingtons Bitter, Castle Eden Ale, Flowers Original; guest beers 🄷
Large, one-roomed bar on two levels, with a separate dining area. It was renamed by a previous licensee, in honour of the wartime Pathfinder Squadrons. Several changing guest beers. Q ❀ ◖ ◗ ♿ ♣ P

Marton

Appletree
38 The Derby (Marton Manor Park Estate) ☎ (01642) 310564
11–11
Bass Worthington BB, Draught Bass 🄷
Modern estate pub serving a local patronage: a large but cosy lounge, plus a separate bar with pool and darts. Children welcome in the conservatory. Good bar lunches. ⛀ ❀ ◖ ⊞ ♿ ♣ P

Middlesbrough

Fly & Firkin
18 Southfield Road (opp. university amenities block)
☎ (01642) 244792
11–11
Firkin Bluebottle, Fly, Golden Aphid, Dogbolter; guest beer 🄷
Pub recently restyled into a spacious ale house with all beers brewed on the premises. Food is available all day every day. Live music Thu/Sun; wide range board/table games. ❀ 🛏 ◖ ◗ ♿ ⇌ ♣ P

Star & Garter
Southfield Road (opp. university student union building) ☎ (01642) 245307
11–11
Bass Worthington BB; Draught Bass; Butterknowle Conciliation Ale; S&N Theakston XB, Old Peculier; guest beers 🄷
This pub has won a CAMRA *Pub Preservation* award for its conversion from a workingmen's club, and boasts a fine Victorian-style bar. Winner of S&N's *Cellarman of the Year* award. Regular beer festivals. Popular with students. The large L-shaped lounge has a quiet eating area. Outside seating is in the car park. ❀ ◖ ◗ ⊞ ♣ P

Tap 'n' Barrel
86 Newport Road (near bus station) ☎ (01642) 219995
11–11; 11–4.30, 7–11 Sat
North Yorkshire Best Bitter, Fools Gold, Erimus Dark, Flying Herbert, Dizzy Dick; guest beers 🄷
Cosy pub near the town centre, converted from a shop

to a Victorian-style, gas-lit bar, with a children's/function room upstairs. The brewery tap of the North Yorkshire Brewing Company. Sun lunch served. ⚲ & ⇌ ♣ ◠

Tavern

228 Linthorpe Road
☎ (01642) 242589
11–11
S&N Theakston XB; Whitbread Boddingtons Bitter, Castle Eden Ale; guest beers Ⓗ
Large recently refurbished pub with 15, constantly changing guest beers. Regular events are held in the upstairs function room. Outdoor seating is in the car park.
❀ ㈤ ◑ & ♣ P

Try also: Malt Shovel, Corporation Rd (North Yorkshire)

Normanby

Poverina

45 High Street
☎ (01642) 440541
11–11
Camerons Strongarm; guest beer (occasional) Ⓗ
Old roadhouse, much extended in postwar years, which takes its name from a racehorse. Recently refurbished in typical Wolverhampton & Dudley style. Strong local patronage.
❀ ◑ & ♣ P ⊟

Try also: Norman Conquest Flatts Lane (S&N)

Redcar

Pig & Whistle

West Dyke Road (by Central station) ☎ (01642) 482697
11–11
Courage Directors; Marston's Pedigree; Morland Old Speckled Hen; John Smith's Magnet; guest beer Ⓗ
100-year-old, traditional pub in the town centre, featuring a collection of over 2500 pigs from all over the world. Games room. ⚲ 🍴 ⇌ ♣ ⊟

Turner's Mill

Greenstones Road (opp. Wm Turner's College)
☎ (01642) 475895
11–11
Bass Worthington BB, Draught Bass; guest beer Ⓗ
Attractive new Bass estate pub and restaurant, with pictures relating to the Turner family. Food is served throughout the pub. Wheelchair toilets and baby changing facilities; no-smoking area in the restaurant.
⚲ ❀ ◑ 🍴 & ♣ P

Yorkshire Coble

West Dyke Road (by racecourse) ☎ (01642) 482071
11–3, 6–11; 11–11 Fri & Sat
Samuel Smith OBB Ⓗ
Large Sam Smith's estate pub, drawing a strong regular clientele to its comfortable lounge, large functional bar and games room. Food is available throughout the pub. Outside seating is in the car park. ❀ ◑ ▶ 🍴 ⇌ ♣ P

Stainton

Stainton Inn

2 Meldyke Lane
☎ (01642) 599902
11–3, 6–11
Camerons Bitter, Strongarm Ⓗ
Imposing, Victorian red-brick pub in the village centre, with a strong emphasis on food.
❀ ◑ ▶ 🍴 & ♣ P ⊟

Stockton-on-Tees

Clarendon

72 Dovecot Street
☎ (01642) 607530
11–11
Camerons Strongarm Ⓗ
Classic, town-centre pub.
◑ 🍴 ⇌ ♣ ⊟

Cricketer's Arms

Portrack Lane (off Maritime Rd) ☎ (01642) 675468
11–11
Whitbread Boddingtons Bitter; guest beer Ⓗ
A warm, friendly atmosphere

prevails in this popular old, street-corner pub.
㈤ Q ◑ ▶ ♣ P

Fitzgerald's

9–10 High Street
☎ (01642) 678220
11–3, 6.30–11
Draught Bass; S&N Theakston Old Peculier; Taylor Landlord; Younger IPA; guest beers Ⓗ
Pub where an imposing red granite facade opens on to a split-level, open-plan interior. Mini-beer festivals throughout the year. Local CAMRA *Pub of the Year 1993*. ◑ ⇌ ♣

Sun

Knowles Street (off High St)
☎ (01642) 615676
11–4, 5.30–11
Draught Bass Ⓗ
Classic town-centre pub, reckoned to sell more Draught Bass than any other pub in Britain. ⊟ ⇌ ♣

Try also: Theatre, Yarm Lane (S&N)

Wolviston

Wellington

31–33 High Street
☎ (01740) 644439
11–11
Bass Worthington BB, Draught Bass; guest beers Ⓗ
Friendly, traditional village pub with a welcoming atmosphere: a tiny basic bar along with two separate, larger rooms. Folk club upstairs Thu night. Function room available. Wheelchair access from the rear car park.
Q ❀ ◑ & ♣ P

Yarm

Black Bull

High Street ☎ (01642) 780299
11–11
Draught Bass Ⓗ
Popular local with a long standing commitment to real ale. One of several old coaching inns in this conservation area.
❀ ◑ ▶ ⊟ &

BREWERY BOOM

Remember the 1970s cartoon in which the landlord of a keg beer pub dismissed a forlorn-looking customer with the words 'I've told a hundred people already this week, there's no demand for real ale'? Well, he was wrong then and even more wrong now. This edition of the *Good Beer Guide* lists over 50 brand new cask ale breweries. When added to the 85 new producers the book has introduced in the last three years, these ensure the real ale scene has not been brighter or more varied for many, many years. What better way to celebrate CAMRA's 25th birthday?

Cornwall

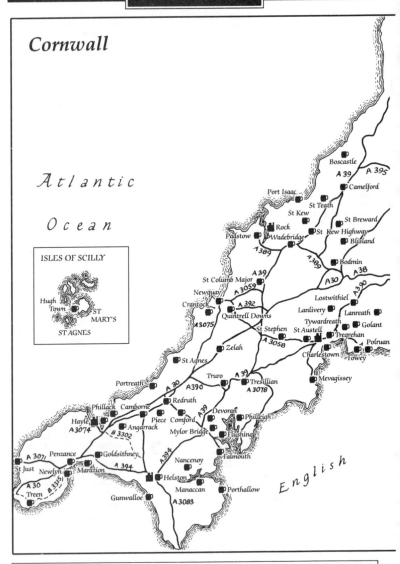

Atlantic

Ocean

ISLES OF SCILLY

Hugh Town
ST MARY'S
ST AGNES

Boscastle
A 39   A 395
Camelford
St Teath
Port Isaac
St Kew
St Breward
Rock   St Kew Highway
Padstow   Wadebridge   Blisland
A 389
A 39   A 389   Bodmin
St Columb Major   A 30   A 38
Newquay   A 3059   A 390
Crantock   A 392   Lostwithiel
Quintrell Downs   Lanlivery   Lanreath
A 3075   St Stephen   Tywardreath   Golant
St Austell   Tregrehan
Zelah   A 3058   Polruan
Charlestown   Fowey
St Agnes   Truro   A 39   Mevagissey
Portreath   A 30   A 390   Tresillian
A 3078
Phillack   Camborne   Redruth   A 39   Devoran
Hayle   Piece   Comford   Philleigh
A 3074   Angarrack   Mylor Bridge   Flushing
B 3302
Penzance   Goldsithney   Nancenoy   Falmouth
St Just   A 394
Newlyn   Marazion   A 394   Helston
A 30   Treen   B 3315   Manaccan   Porthallow
Gunwalloe   A 3083

English

 Bird in Hand, *Hayle*; **Blue Anchor**, *Helston*; **St Austell**, *St Austell*; **Sharp's**, *Rock*

Altarnun

Rising Sun
On Camelford road, 1 mile N of village
☎ (01566) 86332
11–3, 5.30–11
Exmoor Ale; Marston's Pedigree; Otter Ale; Whitbread Flowers Original; guest beer Ⓗ
Lively, 16th-century country inn on the edge of Bodmin Moor, offering ever-changing guest beers and good fare.
♨ 🐾 ⊛ 🛏 ◖▶ ▲ ♣ P

Angarrack

Angarrack Inn
32 Steamers Hill (off A30)
☎ (01736) 752380
11–3, 6–11
St Austell Bosun's, XXXX Mild, HSD Ⓗ
Attractive, welcoming and comfortable village pub offering an extensive and good value menu of home-cooking.
♨ ⊛ ◖▶ ▲ P

Blisland

Royal Oak
Village Green
☎ (01208) 850739
12–3, 6–11 (11–11 summer)
Draught Bass; Whitbread Flowers IPA; guest beers Ⓗ
Set on the only village green in Cornwall, this is a fine, granite pub. The boisterous public bar boasts a collection of

Cornwall

barometers. Lizards are housed in the family/games room. 🏚 🍺 🏵 🍴 🍷 🏰 ♣ P

Bodmin

Mason's Arms
5–9 Higher Bore Street (A389)
☎ (01208) 72607
11–3, 5–11; 11–11 Fri & Sat
Bass Worthington BB, Draught Bass; Fuller's London Pride; guest beers H
Historic town pub built before the Napoleonic Wars and reputedly holding the oldest continuous licence in Cornwall. Quiet lounge; good value food (eve meals in summer).
Q 🍺 🏵 🏰 🍷 🍴 🏰 ♣ P

Boscastle

Napoleon
High Street ☎ (01840) 250204
11–3, 6–11
Draught Bass; St Austell Tinners, HSD G
Attractive, 16th-century inn with several cosy rooms, set in the upper part of the village. Once a recruitment centre for the Napoleonic Wars. Prone to inpromptu folk singing.
🏚 Q 🍺 🏵 🏰 🍷 🍴 🏰 ♣ P

Botus Fleming

Rising Sun
Off A388 ☎ (01752) 842792
12–3, 6–11 (may vary in summer)
Draught Bass; Morland Old Speckled Hen; guest beer H
Unspoilt and unpretentious pub, tucked away in a quiet village on the outskirts of Saltash. Now in the third generation of family ownership. Good value Inch's cider. 🏚 🏵 🏰 🍴 ♣ 🍷 P

Callington

Coach Maker's Arms
Newport Square
☎ (01579) 382567
11–3, 6.30–11
Draught Bass; Fuller's London Pride; Greene King Abbot; guest beer H
300-year-old coaching inn with a warm, friendly atmosphere and a popular small bar. Good food; en suite accommodation.
Q 🏰 🍷 🍴 ♣ P

Camborne

Tyacks Hotel
Commercial Street
☎ (01209) 612424
11–11
St Austell Bosun's, XXXX Mild, Tinners, HSD H
18th-century former coaching inn, providing a very high standard of comfort and offering a good range of ales and wines and excellent cuisine.
Q 🏵 🏰 🍷 🍴 🏰 ♣ P

Camelford

Darlington Inn
Fore Street ☎ (01840) 213314
11–3, 6–11 (11–11 summer)
St Austell XXXX Mild (occasional), **Tinners, HSD** H
Renovated 13th-century coaching inn, with two comfortable rooms off the main bar, plus a family room. Cider in summer.
🏚 Q 🍺 🏵 🏰 🍷 🍴 ♣ 🍷

Charlestown

Rashleigh Arms
☎ (01726) 73635
11–11
Draught Bass; Ruddles County; St Austell Tinners; Tetley Bitter; Wadworth 6X; Whitbread Flowers Original; guest beers H
Large, friendly inn overlooking the famous port, comprising two large bars, a restaurant and a family room. Cornish Tourist Board commended accommodation.
Q 🍺 🏵 🏰 🍷 🍴 🏰 ♣ P

Comford

Fox & Hounds
On A393 ☎ (01209) 820251
11–3, 6–11
Draught Bass; St Austell XXXX Mild (occasional), **Tinners, HSD, Winter Warmer** G
Comfortable country pub with a restaurant specialising in home cooking. An old frieze in the snug has been restored to its former glory after being hidden by wallpaper for over ten years.
🏚 🏵 🍷 🍴 🏰 ♣ P

Crantock

Old Albion
Langurroc Road
☎ (01637) 830243
11–11
Courage Best Bitter; Morland Old Speckled Hen; Sharp's Cornish Coaster; John Smith's Bitter; Wadworth 6X; guest beers H
Picture postcard, thatched pub popular with holidaymakers visiting the superb sandy beach. A wide-ranging menu caters for most tastes. Live music often at weekends. No eve meals Sun–Wed in winter.
🏚 Q 🍺 🏵 🍷 🍴 ♣ P

Devoran

Old Quay Inn
St John's Terrace (off A39)
☎ (01872) 863142
11–3 (2.30 winter), 6 (7 winter)–11
Draught Bass; Whitbread Boddingtons Bitter, Flowers IPA H
Welcoming pub, home to thriving village teams. Fine views over Devoran Quay and creek. Limited parking.
🏚 🏵 🏰 🍷 ♣ P

Falmouth

Quayside Inn
Arwenack Street
☎ (01326) 312113
11–11

Draught Bass G; Courage
Directors; Ind Coope Burton
Ale; Ruddles County; Tetley
Bitter; Whitbread
Boddingtons Bitter H; guest
beers G

Large, two-bar pub,
overlooking the customs house
quay and harbour. The
upstairs bar boasts 218
whiskies; the downstairs bar
has a wide range of guest
beers. Live music Fri and Sat
eve. Twice yearly beer
festivals. No food Sun eve.
❀ ◖▮ ⇌ (The Dell) ♺

Seven Stars
The Moor ☎ (01326) 312111
11–3, 6–11
Draught Bass G; Ruddles
County H; St Austell HSD G;
John Smith's Bitter H; guest
beers G

Unspoilt by 'progress', a pub
in the same family for five
generations. The present
landlord is an ordained priest.
The lively tap room has casks
on display; quiet snug to the
rear. Q ❀ ⊟

Five Lanes

King's Head
Off A30 ☎ (01566) 86241
11–11
Butcombe Bitter H; St Austell
HSD; Sharp's Cornish
Coaster G; Tetley Bitter H;
guest beer G

16th-century coaching inn,
now bypassed. A flagstone
floor graces the public bar and
restaurant; good
accommodation. Five beers.
Worth looking for.
▦ ❀ ⋈ ⊟ ▮ ♣ ♺ P

Flushing

Royal Standard
St Peter's Hill (off A393)
☎ (01326) 374250
11–2.30 (3 Fri & Sat), 6.30–11; 12–2;
7–10.30 Sun (varies in winter)
Draught Bass; Whitbread
Boddingtons Bitter, Flowers
IPA H

Friendly local, run by the
present landlord for 30 years.
Home-made pasties and apple
pies are specialities (take-
aways available). Fine views of
the Penryn River from the
front patio, but beware of
swans in the road and high
spring tides. ▦ ❀ ◖▮ ♣

Fowey

Ship Inn
Trafalgar Square
☎ (01726) 832230
11–3, 6–11 (11–11 Easter & summer)
St Austell XXXX Mild,
Tinners, HSD H

This comfortable, one-bar pub
has historic connections with
Drake and Raleigh. A pleasant
local in a popular waterside
village.
▦ Q ☕ ⋈ ◖▮ ▮ A ♣

Golant

Fisherman's Arms
Fore Street ☎ (01726) 832453
11–3, 6–11
Courage Best Bitter; Ushers
Best Bitter, Founders
(summer) H

Charming village pub in a
delightful waterside setting
with views across the River
Fowey. Try the home-cooked
food. Extra riverside parking
at low tide. ▦ Q ❀ ◖▮ ♣ P

Goldsithney

Crown
Fore Street ☎ (01736) 710494
11–3, 6–11
St Austell Bosun's, XXXX
Mild, HSD H

Attractive, comfortable, village
pub with a very popular
restaurant (booking advisable).
Excellent, home-cooked bar
meals, too. ▦ ❀ ⋈ ◖▮ A

Gunwalloe

Halzephron
2½ miles SW of A3083 jct
☎ (01326) 240406
11–3, 6.30–11
Dartmoor Best Bitter H

Welcoming, comfortable inn
with woodwork partly from
old shipwrecks. It takes its
name from the nearby cliff and
was once the haunt of
smugglers. A well-appointed
award-winning pub.
▦ Q ☕ ❀ ⋈ ◖▮ A P

Hayle

Bird in Hand
Trelissick Road
☎ (01736) 753974
12–3, 6.30–11 (11–11 summer)
Courage Directors; John
Smith's Magnet; Wadworth
6X; Wheal Ale Paradise,
Miller's, Artists H

Friendly former coach house
with its own brewery, next to
Paradise Park bird gardens.
Live music most weekends.
Children welcome. Meals in
summer. ❀ ◖▮ A ⇌ ♣ P

Helston

Blue Anchor
Coinagehall Street
☎ (01326) 562821
10.30–11, 6 (may be all day if busy)
Blue Anchor Middle, Best,
Special, Extra Special H

The flagship of pub breweries:
a superb, unspoilt, rambling
granite building with a
thatched roof, dating from the
15th century. The famous
Spingo beers come from the
old brewhouse at the rear.
Good chat in its two friendly
bars. No jukebox or bandits.
▦ Q ☕ ◖▮ A

Isles of Scilly:
St Mary's

Bishop & Wolf
Main Street, Hugh Town
☎ (01720) 22790
11–11
St Austell XXXX Mild,
Tinners, HSD H

Named after two famous local
lighthouses, this lively pub has
a large bar, pool room and an
upstairs restaurant. The beer is
fined in the pub after
occasional rough crossings.
☕ ◖▮ A

Try also: Turk's Head, St
Agnes (Ind Coope)

Kilkhampton

New Inn
☎ (01288) 321488
11–2.30, 5.30–11
Draught Bass; guest beers H

Spacious, 15th-century village
pub that once boasted its own
brewery. The family room is
just off the main bar; quiet
front bar. Good, home-cooked
meals. ▦ Q ☕ ❀ ◖▮ ♣ P

Kingsand

Rising Sun
The Green ☎ (01752) 822840
11–3, 7–11
Draught Bass; Courage Best
Bitter; guest beer H

Former customs house, a
Grade II-listed building, in a
village of very narrow streets.
It is popular, yet quiet, and
stands on a coastal path.
Excellent food: sandwiches are
a speciality.
▦ Q ❀ ◖▮ A ♣

Lanlivery

Crown Inn
Off A390 ☎ (01208) 872707
11–3, 6–11
Bass Worthington BB,
Draught Bass; Sharp's Own
(summer) H

Comfortable, old-fashioned
pub, a listed building. The
restaurant has an inglenook
and a low-beamed ceiling.
Good accommodation in
pleasant country village
surroundings. ▦ Q ☕ ❀
⋈ ◖▮ ⊟ ▮ A ♣ P

Cornwall

Lanreath

Punch Bowl Inn
Off B3359 ☎ (01503) 220218
11–3, 6–11
Draught Bass; Whitbread Boddingtons Bitter; guest beer Ⓗ
Chaises-longues in the lounge and a large flagstoned bar are key features of this historic coaching house. Excellent food. ⏺ Q ☎ ⊛ ⋈ ◖ ❙ ⊟ ⅄ ♣ P

Launceston

Baker's Arms
Southgate Street
☎ (01566) 772510
11–3, 7–11; 11–11 Sat
Courage Directors; John Smith's Bitter; Wadworth 6X Ⓗ**; guest beer (occasional)** Ⓖ
Popular town pub next to the historic Southgate Arch: a cosy, wood-panelled lounge bar and a busy, games-oriented public. Good value home-cooking.
⏺ Q ⋈ ◖ ⊟ ♣

Lostwithiel

Royal Oak
Duke Street ☎ (01208) 872552
11–11
Draught Bass; Fuller's London Pride; Marston's Pedigree; Whitbread Flowers Original; guest beers Ⓗ
Busy, 13th-century inn renowned for good food. A stone floor in the bar contrasts with the comfortable lounge and restaurant. Guest beers come from small independent breweries; many unusual bottled beers available. Families welcome.
Q ⊛ ⋈ ◖ ❙ ⊟ ⅄ ≢ ♣ P

Manaccan

New Inn
☎ (01326) 231323
11–3, 6–11
Whitbread Flowers IPA, Castle Eden Ale; guest beer (summer) Ⓖ
Very traditional, thatched village pub serving good, home-cooked food. No jukebox or fruit machine.
⏺ Q ⊛ ◖ ❙ ⅄ P

Marazion

Station House
½ mile from A30
☎ (01736) 50459
11–11
Courage Best Bitter, Directors Ⓗ**; John Smith's Bitter; guest beer** Ⓗ

Large, one room pub/restaurant overlooking the beach and St Michael's Mount. Live music Thu; no jukebox. Good value, home-cooked food. Families welcome. ⊛ ◖ ❙ ⅋ P

Mevagissey

Fountain Inn
St George's Square
☎ (01726) 842320
11–11
St Austell XXXX Mild, Tinners Ⓗ**, Winter Warmer** Ⓖ
Traditional, olde-worlde, harbourside inn, licensed for 500 years. The two bars, with slate floors and beams, display historic photos. A separate restaurant is open March–Oct.
⏺ Q ⋈ ◖ ❙ ⅄ ♣

Mylor Bridge

Lemon Arms
Off A393 ☎ (01326) 373666
11–3, 6–11
St Austell Tinners, HSD Ⓗ**, Winter Warmer** Ⓖ
Friendly, one-bar village-centre pub, refurbished after a fire in 1994. Good food.
⏺ ⊛ ◖ ❙ ⅄ ♣ P

Nancenoy

Trengilly Wartha
Off B3291 OS731282
☎ (01326) 40332
11–3, 6–11 (may vary)
Dartmoor Best Bitter; St Austell XXXX Mild Ⓖ**; guest beers** Ⓖ/Ⓗ
Delightful, remote pub/hotel with owners who like to ring the changes with guest beers. Excellent, ever-changing menu. Wonderful country walks nearby.
⏺ Q ☎ ⊛ ⋈ ◖ ❙ ⅋ ♣ ⏏ P

Newlyn

Fisherman's Arms
Fore Street ☎ (01736) 63399
10.30–2.30, 5.30–11
St Austell XXXX Mild, Bosun's, Tinners, HSD Ⓗ
Popular old local with superb views over the busy fishing harbour and St Michael's Mount. Note the inglenook and intriguing ceiling display of memorabilia. Good, simple food. Very limited parking.
⏺ Q ⊛ ◖ ❙ ⅄ ♣ P

Newquay

Tavern
Mellanvrane Lane
☎ (01637) 873564
11–11
Bass Worthington BB,

Draught Bass; Sharp's Own; Stones Best Bitter; Whitbread Boddingtons Bitter; guest beers Ⓗ
Pub retaining some of its original, 14th-century manor house atmosphere, but now surrounded by modern housing. Games room extensions; live entertainment at weekends.
☎ ⊛ ◖ ♣ P ⊟

Padstow

Old Ship Hotel
Mill Square ☎ (01841) 532357
11–3, 6–11 (11 summer)
Draught Bass; Brains SA; Whitbread Boddingtons Bitter; guest beers Ⓗ
Agreeable retreat, just away from the harbour, with a sheltered outdoor drinking area and a restaurant. Live music.
Q ☎ ⊛ ⋈ ◖ ❙ ⊟ ♣ P

Penzance

Mount's Bay Inn
The Promenade, Werrytown
☎ (01736) 63027
11–2.30, 5.30–11
Draught Bass; guest beers Ⓗ
Small, friendly free house, on the seafront towards Newlyn. The open bar has an eating area to one side. Ever-changing guest ales.
⏺ Q ◖ ❙ ⅀

Phillack

Bucket of Blood
☎ (01736) 752378
11–2.30, 6–11
St Austell XXXX Mild, Tinners, HSD Ⓗ
Historic, friendly village inn close to Hayle beaches. The name originates from a local gory legend! Meals in summer.
⏺ Q ☎ ⊛ ◖ ❙ ⅄ ♣ P

Philleigh

Roseland Inn
On King Harry Ferry road
☎ (01872) 580254
11.30 (11 summer)–3, 6.30 (6 summer)–11
Draught Bass; Greenalls Bitter; Marston's Pedigree; guest beer (occasional) Ⓗ
Classic, 17th-century country pub in the heart of the Roseland Peninsula with slate floors and beams: a restaurant, a bar and a locals' snug. Good menu of home-cooked food. Cider in summer. ⏺ Q ⊛ ◖ ❙ ⏏ P

Piece

Countryman
On Four Lanes–Pool road
☎ (01209) 215960
11–11

Cornwall

Courage Best Bitter,
Directors; Morland Old
Speckled Hen; Sharp's Own;
John Smith's Bitter;
Wadworth 6X Ⓗ
Former count house for the
local tin mining community, a
welcoming, popular country
pub said to be haunted by
three maidens. Entertainment
and good food provided.
🏚 ✿ ◑ ▶ 🍴 🛏 ♿ ♣ ♠ P 🚬

Polperro

Blue Peter
The Quay ☎ (01503) 72743
11–11
St Austell Tinners, HSD;
guest beer Ⓗ
The smallest pub in Polperro,
reached by a flight of steps at
the harbour. Good food in a
convivial atmosphere.
🏚 ◑ ▶ ⟲

Crumplehorn Inn
The Old Mill ☎ (01503) 72348
11–11
Dartmoor Best Bitter; St
Austell XXXX Mild, HSD;
guest beer Ⓗ
Haunted inn converted from
an old mill mentioned in the
Domesday Book. Self-contained
chalets and B&B available.
🏚 Q ✿ 🚗 ◑ ▶ ♿ ♠ P

Polruan

Lugger Inn
The Quay ☎ (01726) 870007
11–3, 6–11 (11–11 summer)
St Austell XXXX Mild,
Bosun's, Tinners, HSD Ⓗ
Situated near the quay, served
by the Fowey passenger ferry,
this pub has a friendly,
nautical atmosphere.
🏚 ◑ ▶ 🍴 ♠ ♣

Porthallow

Five Pilchards
☎ (01326) 280256
11–2.30, 6–11 (closed Mon & Sun eve
in winter)
Greene King Abbot; guest
beers Ⓗ
Attractive, rural pub, only
yards from the beach, with
views across to Falmouth. Fine
collection of ships' lamps,
model ships and wreck
histories. 🏚 ✿ 🚗 ◑

Port Isaac

Shipwright's
The Terrace ☎ (01208) 880305
12–2.30 (3 summer), 7–11
Draught Bass; Whitbread
Flowers IPA; guest beer Ⓗ
Cheery, family-run pub with a
bistro. Excellent view over the
bay. Interesting display of old
shipwright's tools.
🏚 ✿ 🚗 ◑ ▶ ♣

Portreath

Basset Arms
From B3301 at bottom of hill
hairpin turn right
☎ (01209) 842077
11–2.30, 6–11 (11–11 summer)
Draught Bass; Dartmoor Best
Bitter; Tetley Bitter Ⓗ
Attractive, traditional pub
within easy reach of the sea. A
restaurant and new
conservatory provide
additional comforts.
✿ ◑ ▶ ♿ ♠ ♣ P

Quintrell Downs

Two Clomes
East Road (A392)
☎ (01637) 873485
12–2.30, 7–11
Beer range varies Ⓗ
18th-century free house which
takes its name from the old
clome ovens either side of the
open log fire. Self-catering
chalets.
🏚 Q ♋ ✿ ◑ ▶ ♿ ♠ ⛵ ♣ P

Redruth

Tricky Dickie's
Tolgus Mount (off old Redruth
bypass) ☎ (01209) 219292
11–3, 6–11 (midnight Tue & Thu)
Greene King Abbot; Sharp's
Own; Tetley Bitter;
Wadworth 6X; guest beer Ⓗ
Renovated old tin mine smithy
offering squash and exercise
facilities, plus some live music.
The emphasis is on restaurant
and bar meals. Children
welcome. ✿ ◑ ▶ ♿ ♠ ♣ P 🚬

Rilla Mill

Manor House Hotel
Off B3254 at Upton Cross
☎ (01579) 62354
12–3, 7 (6.45 Sat)–11
Draught Bass; guest beers Ⓗ
Comfortable, 17th-century inn
and restaurant in the Lynher
Valley. Excellent food. Self-
catering cottages.
Q ✿ 🚗 ◑ ▶ ♿ P

St Agnes

Driftwood Spars
Trevaunance Cove
☎ (01872) 552428
11–11 (midnight Fri & Sat)
Draught Bass; Ind Coope
Burton Ale; St Austell HSD;
Tetley Bitter; guest beers Ⓗ
Nautical theme pub, close to
an old tin mining harbour
(now a surfing beach). A
rambling, 17th-century inn

with a restaurant and
weekend entertainment.
Extensive menu.
🏚 ♋ ✿ 🚗 ◑ ▶ P

St Austell

Carlyon Arms
Sandy Hill (1 mile E of town
on Bethel road)
☎ (01726) 72129
11–3, 5–11
St Austell XXXX Mild,
Tinners, HSD Ⓗ
Friendly local serving good,
home-cooked food. Eve meals
Tue–Sat. Live music Wed and
Fri eves. 🏚 ✿ 🚗 ◑ ▶ ♣ P

St Breward

Old Inn
☎ (01208) 850711
12–3, 6–11
Draught Bass; John Smith's
Bitter; guest beer Ⓗ
Robust, granite pub on the
edge of Bodmin Moor, dating
from the 11th century, with
slate floors and beamed
ceilings. It is set next to the
highest church in Cornwall
and has a fine selection of
malts. A Sharp's beer is also
stocked.
🏚 ♋ ✿ ◑ ▶ 🍴 ♣ P

St Columb Major

Ring o Bells
Bank Street ☎ (01637) 880259
12 (11 summer)–11
Draught Bass Ⓖ; St Austell
HSD Ⓗ; guest beers Ⓖ
Former coaching inn, long and
narrow. Popular with the
locals, it has a comfortable,
well-furnished lounge and
serves good value food. The
beers constantly change.
🏚 Q ✿ ♠ P

St Just

Star
Fore Street ☎ (01736) 788767
11–3, 5.30–11
St Austell Tinners, HSD Ⓖ
Old, atmospheric bar in a
once-great tin mining area,
where beer from the wood is
served by friendly staff.
🏚 ♋ 🚗 ◑ ▶

St Kew

St Kew Inn
Churchtown ☎ (01208) 841259
11–2.30, 6–11
St Austell Tinners, HSD,
Winter Warmer Ⓖ
Popular, friendly 15th-century
pub, with a worn slate floor
and a large open fire. Well-
known for its food, it also has

a large garden. A listed building. ⚒ Q ❀ ◖ ▶ ⊟ P

St Kew Highway

Red Lion
☎ (01208) 841271
11–3, 6–11
Draught Bass; Exmoor Ale; Morland Old Speckled Hen Ⓗ
17th-century pub, just off the A39; a comfortable lounge, a busy public bar and a games area. ⚒ ☎ ❀ ⚏ ◖ ▶ ⊟ ♠ P

St Stephen

Queen's Head
The Square ☎ (01726) 822407
11–11
St Austell Bosun's, XXXX Mild, HSD Ⓗ**, Winter Warmer** Ⓖ
Old coaching house, a listed building, with a traditional Cornish granite frontage. The interior has been opened out to form a large bar. Friendly village atmosphere (lively on music nights, Fri and Sat). Pool table. ⚒ ❀ ⚏ ◖ ▶ ♠ P

St Teath

White Hart Hotel
☎ (01208) 850281
11–2.30, 6–11
Ruddles County; Ushers Best Bitter Ⓗ
Busy village local, catering for a wide ranging clientele, with a noisy public bar, a small quiet snug and an eating area. Good garden with a children's play area.
⚒ Q ☎ ❀ ⚏ ◖ ▶ ⊟ ♠ P

Saltash

Two Bridges
Albert Road ☎ (01752) 848952
12–11
Courage Best Bitter; Ushers Best Bitter, Founders; guest beer (occasional) Ⓗ
Lively pub with a cosy, country cottage interior. The large garden benefits from river views. Barbecues in summer. ⚒ ❀ ⇌ ♠

Seaton

Olde Smugglers Inn
Tregunnick Lane
☎ (01503) 250646
12–3, 6.30–11 (11–11 summer)
Draught Bass; Wadworth 6X; guest beer Ⓗ
Refurbished pub, with 17th-century origins, lying on the coastal path. The beach is literally a two-minute walk. Home-cooked food. Cider in summer.
⚒ Q ☎ ❀ ◖ ▶ ▲ ⊖ P

Stratton

King's Arms
Howells Road
☎ (01288) 352396
12–3, 6.30–11
Exmoor Ale; Sharp's Own; Whitbread Boddingtons Bitter; guest beers Ⓗ
Delightful, popular, 17th-century village pub with two bars and slate flags. Changing range of guest beers.
⚒ ☎ ❀ ⚏ ◖ ▶ ♠ ⊖ P

Tregrehan

Britannia Inn
On A390 ☎ (01726) 812889
11–11
Bass Worthington BB, Draught Bass; Eldridge Pope Royal Oak; St Austell Tinners; Tetley Bitter; guest beers Ⓗ
Large, 16th-century inn, open all day for food and drink. Safe garden and play area. Separate restaurant.
Q ☎ ❀ ◖ ▶ ⊟ ♿ ▲ P

Treen

Logan Rock Inn
☎ (01736) 810495
10.30–3, 5.30–11
St Austell Tinners, HSD Ⓗ
Good, small pub near Minack Open Air Theatre. The characterful bar offers good food. Try a stiff walk to the cliffs and 'moving' Logan Rock. ⚒ ☎ ❀ ◖ ▶ P

Trematon

Crooked Inn
Off A38 ☎ (01752) 848177
11–3, 6–11
Dartmoor Best Bitter; St Austell XXXX Mild, HSD; guest beer Ⓗ
A good selection of ales and homely bar meals are served in this converted, 18th-century farmhouse. First-class accommodation in a converted stable.
⚒ Q ☎ ❀ ⚏ ◖ ▶ ▲ ⊖ P

Tresillian

Wheel
☎ (01872) 52293
11–3, 6–11 (varies in winter)
Devenish Royal Wessex; Whitbread Flowers Original Ⓗ
14th-century thatched inn, owned by Lord Falmouth. It was General Fairfax's HQ during the Civil War. Popular with locals; good food.
Q ❀ ◖ ▶ P

Truro

City Inn
Pydar Street ☎ (01872) 72623
11–11
Courage Best Bitter, Directors; Ruddles Best Bitter; John Smith's Bitter; Wadworth 6X; Webster's Green Label; guest beers Ⓗ
Lively town pub with a central slate bar, three drinking areas and a large garden. Cornwall CAMRA *Pub of the Year* 1992. Good value food.
❀ ⚏ ◖ ▶ ♠ ⊖ ⊟

Old Ale House
7 Quay Street ☎ (01872) 71122
11–3, 5–11; 11–11 Fri & Sat
Draught Bass; Courage Best Bitter, Directors; John Smith's Bitter; Tetley Bitter; Whitbread Boddingtons Bitter Ⓗ**; guest beers** Ⓖ/Ⓗ
Lively, typical alehouse, hosting live music Mon and Thu. Excellent choice of beers, always changing. Eve meals finish at 7.30 (later in summer). ◖ ▶ ♿

Tywardreath

New Inn
Fore Street ☎ (01726) 813901
11–2.30 (3 Sat), 6–11
Draught Bass Ⓖ**; St Austell XXXX Mild** Ⓗ**, Tinners, Winter Warmer** Ⓖ
Popular village local near the coast, with a large secluded garden and a room for games. In the *Guide* for over 20 years, a classic. Limited parking.
Q ❀ ⊟ ▲ ⇌ (Par) ♠ ⊖ P

Wadebridge

Ship Inn
Gonvena Hill
☎ (01208) 812839
11–11
Draught Bass; Whitbread Boddingtons Bitter, Flowers IPA Ⓗ
Compact, friendly, 16th-century pub, once a coaching inn. A fine leaded window is inset with the pub's name. Folk music. ⚒ ❀ ◖ ▶ ♠ P

Zelah

Hawkins Arms
High Road ☎ (01872) 540339
11–3, 6–11
Ind Coope Burton Ale; Tetley Bitter; guest beers Ⓗ
A homely atmosphere exists in this village pub; worth turning off the bypass for. Good food (dining area for non-smokers); cheap B&B.
⚒ Q ☎ ❀ ⚏ ◖ ▶ ♿ ♠ ⊖ P

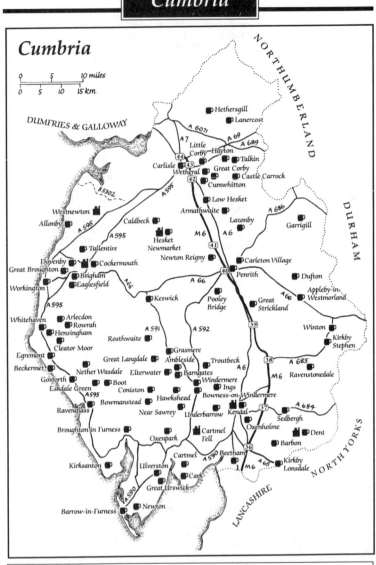

Cumbria

 Cartmel, Kendal; **Dent**, Dent; **Hesket Newmarket**, Hesket Newmarket; **Jennings**, Cockermouth; **Masons Arms**, Cartmel Fell; **Yates**, Westnewton

Allonby

Ship Hotel

Main Street ☎ (01900) 881017
11–3 (not winter Mon & Tue), 7–11;
11–11 Sat (may vary summer)
Yates Bitter, Premium; guest beer Ⓗ
Refurbished hotel on the beautiful Solway Coast; Yates brewery's first pub. Quiet, pleasant surroundings; good food. ♨ Q ⇔ ◑ ♪ ▲ P

Ambleside

Golden Rule

Smithy Brow (100 yds off A591 towards Kirkstone)
☎ (0153 94) 32257
11–11
Robinson's Hatters Mild, Old Stockport Bitter, Hartleys XB, Best Bitter Ⓗ
Traditional drinking pub popular with locals, students and visitors. No jukebox or chips, just lively conversation and good filled rolls. Cumbria's most frequent *Guide* entry. ♨ Q ❀ ♣

Queens Hotel

Market Place
☎ (0153 94) 32206
11–3 (may extend summer), 6–11
Jennings Bitter; S&N Theakston XB; Whitbread Boddingtons Bitter; guest beer Ⓗ
Comfortable, town-centre

hotel with a lounge bar 'upstairs'. The cellar bar 'downstairs' opens at 6.45pm and has lots of nooks and crannies, pool and pizzas till closing time. 🏠 ❀ 🛏 ◖ ▶ P

Appleby-in-Westmorland

Golden Ball

High Wiend ☎ (0176 83) 51493
12–3, 7–11 (may vary)
Jennings Bitter, Cumberland Ale H
Excellent example of a friendly, honest, no frills, town-centre pub. Sandwiches available. 🛏 🍺 ≋ ♣

Royal Oak

Bongate ☎ (0176 83) 51463
11–3, 6–11 (may vary summer)
S&N Theakston Best Bitter; Yates Bitter; Younger Scotch; guest beers H
Pub to the south of the town centre, catering for all tastes. It has a panelled tap room, a lounge bar and a dining room. Up to seven guest beers, plus a house beer brewed by Hesket Newmarket. CAMRA Cumbria *Pub of the Year* 1992.
🏠 Q ❀ 🛏 ◖ ▶ 🍺 ♣

Arlecdon

Sun Inn

☎ (01946) 862011
11.30–2.30, 6–11
Jennings Bitter; Tetley Bitter; guest beers H
Friendly, village local serving good food. Children welcome.
🏠 ◖ ▶ P

Armathwaite

Fox & Pheasant

☎ (0169 74) 72400
11–11
Hesket Newmarket Doris's 90th Birthday Ale; guest beer H
Coaching inn featuring an oak-beamed lounge and a slate-floored stable bar. Good food.
🏠 Q ❀ 🛏 ◖ ▶ ﾖ ≋ ♣ P

Barbon

Barbon Inn

☎ (0152 42) 76233
12–3, 6.30–11
S&N Theakston Best Bitter, Old Peculier H
Village pub with a variety of rooms for drinking plus a dining room. Good value meals. Q ❀ 🛏 ◖ ▶ P ﬞ

Barngates

Drunken Duck

☎ (0153 94) 36347

11.30–3, 6–11
Jennings Bitter; Mitchell's Lancaster Bomber; S&N Theakston Old Peculier; Whitbread Boddingtons Bitter; Yates Bitter H
Isolated but very popular inn with mountain views. No jukebox, machines or TV. Good quality meals include imaginative vegetarian choices. The legend of the name makes amusing reading. A house beer is brewed by Yates.
🏠 Q ❀ 🛏 ◖ ▶ ﾖ ♣ P ﬞ

Barrow-in-Furness

Albion Hotel

29 Dalton Road
☎ (01229) 820089
11–3, 5.30–11; 11–11 Fri & Sat
S&N Matthew Brown Bitter, Theakston Best Bitter; Younger No. 3; guest beer H
Warm, friendly town-centre local, popular with all ages, with two distinctive rooms. Constantly changing guest beers; good quality food. No meals weekends.
❀ 🛏 ◖ 🍺 ≋ ♣

Beckermet

Royal Oak

☎ (01946) 841551
11–3, 5.30–11
Black Sheep Best Bitter; Jennings Bitter, Cumberland Ale H
Cosy, multi-roomed pub, drawing a strong local trade. Popular for food.
🏠 Q ﬞ ❀ 🛏 ◖ ▶ ♣ P

Beetham

Wheatsheaf Hotel

☎ (0153 95) 62123
11–3, 6–11
Thwaites Bitter; Whitbread Boddingtons Bitter H
Comfortable, three-roomed, village hotel with a stone-flagged tap room. Good value meals – home-made pies a speciality. Families welcome till 8.30pm.
🏠 🛏 ◖ ▶ 🍺 ▲ ♣ P

Boot

Burnmoor Inn

Off Hardknott Pass road
☎ (0194 67) 23224
11–2.45, 4.45–11; 12–2.45, 7–10.30 Sun
Jennings Bitter, Cumberland Ale, Cocker Hoop *or* Sneck Lifter H
Charming inn set in a fold in the hills at the foot of Scafell, near the terminus of La'al Ratty. Surrounded by beautiful scenery with masses

---

of things to do, it is perennially popular. The food has an Austrian flavour. Families welcome.
🏠 Q ❀ 🛏 ◖ ▶ ▲ P ﬞ

Bowmanstead

Ship Inn

On A591 just S of Coniston
☎ (0153 94) 41224
12–3, 5.30–11; 12–11 Sat
Robinson's Hartleys XB H
Comfortable old local with a warm welcome. The snug adjoining the bar is used as a family/games room. B&B is popular (book).
🏠 Q ❀ 🛏 ◖ ▶ ▲ ♣ P

Bowness-on-Windermere

Hole in T'wall (New Hall Inn)

Lowside ☎ (0153 94) 43488
11–11
Robinson's Hatters Mild (summer), Old Stockport Bitter, Hartleys XB, Best Bitter, Frederic's, Old Tom H
Former smithy, probably the oldest pub in Bowness. It has a split-level ground floor, a large family/games room upstairs and a sun trap patio. Self-catering flat to let.
🏠 Q ﬞ ❀ 🛏 ◖ ▶ ♣

Brigham

Lime Kiln

Low Road ☎ (01900) 825375
12–2, 6.30–11
Robinson's Hartleys XB H
Village local, popular for meals (not served Mon). Children welcome.
Q ❀ 🛏 ◖ ▶ 🍺 ▲ ♣ P

Broughton in Furness

Manor Arms

☎ (01229) 716286
2 (12 Fri, Sat & summer)–11
Draught Bass; Jennings Cumberland Ale; Taylor Landlord; Yates Bitter; guest beers H
18th-century, traditional, family-run free house. Local CAMRA *Pub of the Year* for the last five years, and a national finalist in 1995. Snacks all day.
🏠 Q ❀ 🛏 ▲ ♣ ﬞ

Caldbeck

Oddfellows Arms

☎ (0169 74) 78227
12–3, 6.30–11
Jennings Bitter, Cumberland Ale; guest beer H
Large pub in one of North

Cumbria

Cumbria's most picturesque villages. The comfortable dining area at the rear serves fine food. The pub has reverted to its original name, after being known as the John Peel. 🏚 Q ❀ ◖ ▶ ♣ P

Cark

Engine Inn
☎ (0153 95) 58341
12–4, 6–11 (12–11 summer)
S&N Theakston Mild, Best Bitter, XB *or* **Old Peculier; Younger Scotch; guest beer** Ⓗ
Comfortable, 18th-century alehouse near the Old Mill House and Holker Hall. Self contained flats to let.
🏚 ❀ 🛏 ◖ ▶ ▲ ⇌ P

Carleton Village

Cross Keys
On A686 ☎ (01768) 66233
11–3, 6–11
Wards Best Bitter Ⓗ
Friendly, 17th-century inn, on the outskirts of Penrith, rumoured to be haunted. Horse brasses adorn the bar, along with other horsey artefacts.
🏚 Q ❀ ◖ ▶ ▲ ♣ 🏳

Carlisle

Caledonian Cask House
Botchergate ☎ (01228) 30460
11–11
Whitbread Boddingtons Bitter; guest beers Ⓗ
The first pub in Carlisle to provide guest beers on a regular basis and now the city's premier cask ale house. Up to five guest beers, changed regularly. Good value, home-cooked food.
◖ ⇌

Carlisle Rugby Club
Warwick Road
☎ (01228) 21300
7 (5.30 Fri, 6 Sat)–11 (12.30–11 Sat during rugby season)
Tetley Bitter; Yates Bitter; guest beer Ⓗ
Welcoming, friendly club with a cosy lounge and a large bar, often crowded when Carlisle Utd are at home. The bar is decorated with rugby memorabilia. Show the *Guide* or CAMRA membership to be signed in. 🏚 ⌛ ❀ ♣ 🏳

Chaplin's
4 Crosby Street
☎ (01228) 29055
11–3, 7–11; 7–10.30 Sun, closed Sun lunch
S&N Theakston Best Bitter; guest beer Ⓗ
Popular and comfortable

city-centre bar. Excellent value food (daily specials). The upstairs restaurant is open eves. Monthly guest beer.
❀ ◖ ⇌

Crown Inn
23 Scotland Road (A6, 1 mile from centre) ☎ (01228) 512789
11–11
S&N Theakston Best Bitter, Newcastle Exhibition Ⓗ
Refurbished ex-State Management pub retaining some of Redfern's superb wood panelling. It stands on the line of Hadrian's Wall, a pleasant walk from the city centre across the River Eden. Good value lunches. ❀ ◖ ♣

Howard Arms
107 Lowther Street
☎ (01228) 32926
11–11
S&N Theakston Best Bitter, XB Ⓗ
Several cubicle-type rooms around one bar make this pub appear smaller than it actually is. Note the unusual tiled frontage. ❀ ◖ ♣

Maltster's Arms
John Street, Caldewgate (A595/B5299 jct, near castle)
☎ (01228) 20499
5.30 (12 Sat)–11
Jennings Cumberland Ale; guest beers Ⓗ
One-roomed pub, recently refurbished, opposite the former State Management Brewery. Guest beers are usually available at weekends.
◖ ▶

Cartmel

Cavendish Arms
Off the square through the arch ☎ (0153 95) 36240
11.30–11
Cartmel Buttermere Bitter, Lakeland Gold, Thoroughbred; guest beers Ⓗ
Olde-worlde country inn: the locals' choice of the village pubs. Renowned for fine food: hog roasts and roast beef cooked on a spit in the dining room (Sun) are its novelty. Guided fell walks by arrangement. Beer festivals Aug.
🏚 Q ❀ 🛏 ◖ ▶ ♿ ♣ ✖

Castle Carrock

Duke of Cumberland
☎ (01228) 70341
12–3, 7–11 (may vary)
Jennings Bitter, Cumberland Ale; Whitbread Boddingtons Bitter Ⓗ
Comfortable pub, in a picturesque fellside village. No meals Mon eve. 🏚 Q ◖ ▶ ♣

Cleator Moor

Crown
Bowthorn Road
☎ (01946) 810136
11–4.30, 7–11; 11–11 Sat
Robinson's Hatters Mild, Hartleys XB, Best Bitter Ⓗ
Good, friendly local at the Whitehaven end of Cleator Moor. 🛏 ◖ ▶ 🏳 ♣

Cockermouth

Swan Inn
Kirkgate ☎ (01900) 822425
11–3 (not Tue), 7–11
Jennings Bitter, Cocker Hoop Ⓗ
Popular pub on a cobbled Georgian square, near the Kirkgate Centre (roadside parking nearby). Ales from the Jennings range may vary; large choice of whiskies. Bustling and friendly. Q ▲ ♣

Trout Hotel
Crown Street
☎ (01900) 823591
11–3, 5.30–11
Jennings Cumberland Ale; Marston's Pedigree; S&N Theakston Best Bitter, XB Ⓗ
Characterful, comfortable hotel in a 300-year-old building with award-winning gardens by the River Derwent (popular for fishing). Wordsworth House and an excellent printing museum are close by. No-smoking area lunchtime. The beer range may vary.
🏚 Q ⌛ ❀ 🛏 ◖ ▶ ▲ P ✖ 🏳

Coniston

Sun Inn
☎ (0153 94) 41248
11–11
Ind Coope Burton Ale; Jennings Bitter; Tetley Bitter Ⓗ
Comfortable, well-appointed 16th-century hotel with a popular public bar. Convenient for Coniston Fells. No meals Jan.
🏚 ❀ 🛏 ◖ ▶ P

Cumwhitton

Pheasant Inn
Off A69 at Warwick Bridge
☎ (01228) 560102
11.30–3, 5.30–11
Marston's Pedigree; Morland Old Speckled Hen; S&N Theakston Best Bitter; Young's Special Ⓗ
Superb country pub dating from 1690, serving excellent food. Many original features have been retained, including

stone floors and beams. The beer range may vary (and increase) in summer.
🏮 Q ❀ 🛏 ◑ ▶ ♿ P

Dent

Sun Inn
Main Street ☎ (0153 96) 25208
11–2.30, 7–11; 11–11 Sat & summer
Dent Bitter, Ramsbottom, T'owd Tup; Younger Scotch Ⓗ
Unspoilt, traditional pub on the cobbled main street of this picturesque village. The jukebox is in the games room. The George & Dragon, almost next door, is the second Dent-owned pub and provides a pleasant alternative. One or both are open 11–11 Mon–Sat.
🏮 Q ❀ 🛏 ◑ ▶ ▲ ♣ P ⊬ 🍴

Dovenby

Ship Inn
On A594 ☎ (01900) 828097
11–3, 5.30–11; 11–11 Sat
Jennings Bitter, Cumberland Ale Ⓗ
Friendly village pub, offering a garden play area for children, plus a free meal for under-tens, Mon–Fri, with each adult main course.
🏮 Q ❀ 🛏 ◑ ▶ ♣ P 🍴

Dufton

Stag Inn
☎ (0176 83) 51608
11–3, 6–11 (11–11 summer)
Whitbread Boddingtons Bitter, Flowers IPA, Castle Eden Ale; guest beers Ⓗ
Welcoming free house in an attractive village on the Pennine Way. Popular with both locals and visitors, it boasts a superb antique kitchen range in the bar.
🏮 ❀ 🛏 ◑ ▶ ▲ ♣ P

Eaglesfield

Black Cock
☎ (01900) 822989
11–3.30, 6–11; 11–11 Sat
Jennings Bitter Ⓗ
Gem of a pub, run by a gem of a landlady; well worth a detour. Unspoilt and unaltered, it stands in a delightful village with interesting historical connections. 🏮 Q ❀ ♣

Egremont

Blue Bell
Market Place ☎ (01946) 820581
11–3, 6–11
Robinson's Hartleys XB, Best Bitter Ⓗ
Light and airy modern decor

---

in an historic building. The long, enclosed garden at the rear is safe for children. A castle ruin stands close by.
🏮 ❀ ♣

Elterwater

Britannia
☎ (0153 94) 37210
11–11
Jennings Bitter; Wadworth 6X; Whitbread Boddingtons Bitter; guest beers Ⓗ
Very popular inn overlooking the village green in probably the finest Lakeland valley. It has a dining room and a small back bar, plus a large, stone-flagged patio.
🏮 Q ❀ 🛏 ◑ ▶ ⊟ ▲ ♣

Eskdale Green

Bower House Inn
4 miles off A595
☎ (0194 67) 23308
11–11; 11–3, 7–10.30 Sun
Courage Directors; Robinson's Hartleys XB; S&N Theakston Best Bitter; Younger Scotch; guest beer (summer) Ⓗ
Set in a beautiful, peaceful area, this 18th-century hotel offers everything from a bar through to a restaurant and conference facilities.
🏮 Q ❀ 🛏 ◑ ▶ P

Garrigill

George & Dragon
☎ (01434) 381293
12–3, 7–11 (12–11 summer, may vary)
McEwan 70/-; S&N Theakston Best Bitter, Newcastle Exhibition, Theakston XB, Old Peculier Ⓗ
Fine old pub in an attractive fellside village. Popular with walkers. 🏮 Q 🛏 ◑ ▶ ▲ ♣

Gosforth

Lion & Lamb
The Square ☎ (0194 67) 25242
12–11
Ruddles Best Bitter; S&N Theakston Best Bitter; John Smith's Bitter; guest beer Ⓗ
Cosy, traditional village pub with a warm welcome.
🏮 ❀ ◑ ▶ ⊟ P

Grasmere

Traveller's Rest
On A591 ½ mile N of village
☎ (0153 94) 35604
11–11
Jennings Bitter, Cumberland Ale, Sneck Lifter Ⓗ
Pub noted for meals. The bar area has a roaring fire and a stone floor. There are also

---

games/family and dining rooms. Handy for Coast to Coast and other walkers. The King's Head, Thirlspot (6 miles N on A591) is in the same ownership and is also recommended.
🏮 ⛵ ❀ 🛏 ◑ ▲ ♣ P

Great Broughton

Punchbowl Inn
19 Main Street
☎ (01900) 824708
11.30–3 (not Mon, except bank hols), 6.30–11 (may vary)
Jennings Bitter Ⓗ
Small, friendly village pub with a cosy atmosphere and a warm welcome. Limited parking. 🏮 Q ♣ P

Great Corby

Queen Inn
☎ (01228) 560731
12–2.30, 5.30–11 (may vary in winter)
Draught Bass; guest beer Ⓗ
Excellent village free house, within ten mins of Wetheral station (across the viaduct). A small garden overlooks the village green. 🏮 Q ❀ ♣ P

Great Langdale

Old Dungeon Ghyll
☎ (0153 94) 37272
11–11
Jennings Cumberland Ale; S&N Theakston XB, Old Peculier; Yates Bitter; guest beers Ⓗ
Pub in a superb setting beneath the Langdale Fells. The climbers' bar is basic, informal and just right for the majority of customers. Live music Fri eve and often at other times. The hotel has a more sedate bar, a lounge and a dining room.
🏮 Q ❀ 🛏 ◑ ⊟ ▲ ♣ ◔ P

Great Strickland

Strickland Arms
Off A6, between M6 jcts 39–40
☎ (01931) 712238
12–3, 6 (6.30 Wed)–11
Bass Worthington BB; Ind Coope Burton Ale; Jennings Bitter; Tetley Bitter Ⓗ
Comfortable, two-roomed pub; no jukebox or machines. Pool and games are played away from the bar.
🏮 ❀ 🛏 ◑ ▶ ♿ ▲ ♣ P 🍴

Great Urswick

Derby Arms
☎ (01229) 586348
12–3, 5.30–11
Robinson's Hatters Mild, Old

Cumbria

Stockport Bitter, Hartleys XB, Frederic's Ⓗ
Comfortable village local. The crack is good and the ale is better! 🏨 🍴 🐾 P

Hawkshead

King's Arms
The Square ☎ (0153 94) 36372
11–11
Greenalls Original; S&N Theakston Best Bitter, Old Peculier; Tetley Bitter Ⓗ
Village-centre pub with a dining room. The beer range may vary in summer. Handy for the Beatrix Potter Museum (NT). Self-catering cottage to let. 🏨 🌼 🛏 🅳 ▶ ▲ 🐾

Hayton

Stone Inn
☎ (01228) 70498
11–3, 5.30–11
Federation Buchanan's Original; Jennings Cumberland Ale; guest beers Ⓗ
Popular village pub, with a fine stone corner bar. No meals, but toasties usually available. Q 🐾 P

Hensingham

Distressed Sailors
Egremont Road
☎ (01946) 692426
12–4, 7–11; 12–11 Sat
Jennings Bitter; Whitbread Boddingtons Bitter; guest beer Ⓗ
Family-run pub with a good atmosphere and friendly regulars; children welcome. Interesting artefacts with a nautical theme.
🌼 🅳 ▶ 🛏 🐾 P

Richmond
Main Street ☎ (01946) 694152
11–3.30, 6–11
S&N Theakston Best Bitter; Whitbread Boddingtons Bitter; guest beer Ⓗ
Modern pub, popular for its home-cooked meals. Splendid hanging baskets make patio drinking a pleasure. Children welcome. The licensees' previous pub nearby was a frequent *Guide* entry.
🌼 🅳 ▶ 🐾 P

Hesket Newmarket

Old Crown
1 mile SE of Caldbeck
OS341386 ☎ (0169 74) 78288
12–3 (not Mon–Fri, except school hols), 5.30–11 (may vary)
Hesket Newmarket Blencathra Bitter, Skiddaw Special, Doris's 90th Birthday Ale, Catbells Pale Ale, Old Carrock Ⓗ

Superb fellside village pub, offering fine home cooking and its own brewery (book for a tour and a meal). Seasonal and special beers are also brewed. 🏨 Q ▶ ▲ 🐾

Hethersgill

Black Lion
Off A6071 ☎ (01228) 75318
11–3, 7–11; 11–11 Sat
Draught Bass; Maclay 60/-; Younger Scotch Ⓗ
Friendly village pub, which doubles as the post office. The Maclay beer may vary. Good value snacks. 🏨 🌼 🐾 P

Ings

Watermill Inn
Off A591 at church
☎ (01539) 821309
12–2, 6–11 (may vary)
Lees Moonraker; S&N Theakston Best Bitter, XB, Old Peculier; guest beers Ⓗ
Family-run, welcoming pub which boasts the widest range of guest beers in Cumbria. No jukebox or machines; good value meals. Three times CAMRA Westmorland *Pub of the Year*. A must for all lovers of traditional ales, surroundings and service.
🏨 Q 🌼 🛏 🅳 ▶ 🐾 ⬠ P ✄

Kendal

Black Swan
8 Allhallows Lane
☎ (01539) 724278
11–3 (not Mon), 6–11 (11–11 Sat in summer)
Draught Bass; guest beers Ⓗ
Cosy pub dating from 1764, popular with more mature conversationalists. Good value bed and (big) breakfast. Meals lunchtime May–Sep, plus Sun; eve meals by arrangement.
🏨 Q 🛏 🐾 P

Burgundy's Wine Bar
19 Lowther Street
☎ (01539) 733803
11–3, 6.30–11; closed Sun lunch & Mon
Courage Directors; guest beers Ⓗ
Pleasant, bistro-style bar with a continental feel, offering a varied choice of home-cooked meals (eve meals by arrangement). Q 🅳 ⬱

Ring-o-Bells
39 Kirkland ☎ (01539) 720326
12–3, 6–11 (may vary in summer)
Vaux Lorimer's Best Scotch, Samson; Wards Best Bitter Ⓗ
Virtually unspoilt pub in the grounds of the parish church. The tiny snug is worth a look

and there's also a cosy front bar, a comfortable lounge and a split-level dining room. Good value B&B. Public car park next door.
🏨 Q 🌼 🛏 🅳 ▶ 🐾 🐾

Keswick

Bank Tavern
Main Street ☎ (0176 87) 72663
11–11
Jennings Mild, Bitter, Cumberland Ale, Sneck Lifter Ⓗ
Popular local in the town centre, but with a village atmosphere.
Q ⬠ 🌼 🛏 🅳 ▶ ▲ 🐾

Kirkby Lonsdale

Red Dragon
Main Street ☎ (0152 42) 71205
11–11
Jennings Bitter, Cumberland Ale, Cocker Hoop, Sneck Lifter Ⓗ
Roomy, family-run pub where an open-plan bar area gives plenty of space for drinkers and diners. The large fireplace is noteworthy. The Jennings beer range may vary.
🏨 🛏 🅳 ▶ 🚹 ▲ 🐾

Kirkby Stephen

White Lion
4 Market Street
☎ (0176 83) 71481
11–3, 6–11 (may vary)
Jennings Bitter, Cumberland Ale, Cocker Hoop Ⓗ
Friendly, two-bar, town-centre local, strong on darts and dominoes. On the Coast to Coast walk. 🅳 ▶ ▲ 🐾

Kirksanton

King William IV
☎ (01229) 772009
11–3, 7–11
Jennings Bitter, Cumberland Ale; guest beer Ⓗ
Popular community local with a friendly atmosphere. The walls are adorned with photos of old Millom and the RAF base. Child portions on the menu. The guest beer varies throughout the year.
🏨 🌼 🅳 ▶ 🚹 🐾 P

Lanercost

Abbey Bridge Inn (Blacksmith's Bar)
2 miles from Brampton, off A69 ☎ (0169 77) 2224
12–2.30, 7–11
Yates Bitter; guest beers Ⓗ
The place to visit, if you are anywhere within 50 miles. Up to three guest beers are usually

Cumbria

available, changing constantly. Superb quality food is served in the restaurant above the bar. The perfect pub, in a beautiful rural setting.
曲 Q ✿ 🏠 🛦 P

Lazonby

Joiners
☎ (01768) 898728
11–11
Draught Bass; Stones Best Bitter; guest beer 🄷
Excellent village pub, with good food and a friendly welcome, very handy for the Settle–Carlisle line. It is run by the former head brewer of Stones brewery.
曲 ✿ 🏠 ◁ ▶ ⇌ ✦ P

Little Corby

Haywain
☎ (01228) 560598
12–3, 7 (6.30 Fri & Sat)–11
Robinson's Old Stockport Bitter, Hartleys XB, Best Bitter, Frederic's 🄷
Superb village local offering a good range of beers and regular live entertainment. Good value food.
Q ✿ ◁ ▶ ✦ P

Low Hesket

Rose & Crown
☎ (0169 74) 73346
12–3, 7–11
Jennings Mild, Bitter, Cumberland Ale 🄷
Comfortable roadside inn, with a spacious bar. Excellent value bar meals.
曲 Q ✿ ◁ ▶ ✦ P

Near Sawrey

Tower Bank Arms
On B5286 ☎ (0153 94) 36334
11–3 (may be later), 5.30 (6 winter)–11
S&N Theakston Mild, Best Bitter, XB; guest beers 🄷
Historic pub immortalised by Beatrix Potter in *The Tale of Jemima Puddleduck*. A part-stone-flagged floor and a real fire in a superb range contribute to the relaxed, friendly atmosphere. Wide range of bottled beers.
曲 Q ✿ 🏠 ◁ ▶ ✦ P

Nether Wasdale

Screes Hotel
☎ (0194 67) 26262
12–3, 6–11 (may vary)
Jennings Bitter; S&N Theakston Best Bitter, Old Peculier; Yates Bitter; guest beers (summer) 🄷
Homely hotel with split-level bars, set in a delightful hamlet in a lovely valley a mile west

of hauntingly beautiful Wastwater; much loved by walkers, climbers and campers. Regular live music; guest ale nights.
曲 Q ♿ ✿ 🏠 ◁ ▶ 🛦 ✦ P

Newton

Farmer's Arms
☎ (01229) 462607
6.30 (12 Sat)–11
Thwaites Best Mild, Bitter; Whitbread Boddingtons Bitter; guest beers (occasional) 🄷
Late 17th-century, beamed pub, popular with locals and visitors. It doubles as the village post office. Families welcome. 曲 ✿ 🏠 ◁ ▶ ✦ P

Newton Reigny

Sun Inn
Off B5288 ☎ (01768) 67055
11.30–3, 6–11; 11–11 Sat
Courage Directors; John Smith's Bitter; Webster's Yorkshire Bitter; guest beer 🄷
Comfortable free house, with a spacious lounge. Popular with students from the nearby college. The forthcoming guest beer is displayed on a blackboard. Good range of whiskies.
曲 ♿ ✿ 🏠 ◁ ▶ 🛦 ✦ P

Oxenholme

Station Inn
☎ (01539) 724094
11–3, 6–11; 11–11 Sat
S&N Theakston Best Bitter; Whitbread Boddingtons Bitter, Flowers Original 🄷
Comfortable, two-roomed local, uphill from the station. A play area and various animals feature in the garden. Guest beers are from the Whitbread Cask Collection.
曲 ✿ 🏠 ◁ ▶ 🛦 ⇌ ✦ P

Oxenpark

Manor House
Leave A590 at Greenodd, right turn after ¼ mile, then 2¾ miles.
☎ (01229) 861345
11–3, 6–11
Robinson's Hatters Mild, Hartleys XB, Best Bitter, Frederic's 🄷
18th-century beamed manor house with spacious dining/bar areas. A comfortable country pub.
曲 Q ✿ 🏠 ◁ ▶ ⅘ 🛦 ✦ P

Penrith

Agricultural
Opp. station ☎ (01768) 862622
11–3.30, 5–11
Jennings Mild, Bitter, Cumberland Ale, Cocker Hoop 🄷

Former Marston's house, unchanged since the Jennings takeover. Numerous clubs meet here. Fine atmosphere.
曲 Q 🏠 ◁ ▶ ⇌ P

Pooley Bridge

Sun Inn
☎ (0176 84) 86205
11–11
Jennings Bitter, Cumberland Ale, Sneck Lifter; guest beer 🄷
Comfortable, wood-panelled, two-bar, former coaching inn. Pool/TV in the lower bar; mainly diners in the lounge, though there is a dining room, too. Cycle hire available.
曲 ✿ 🏠 ◁ ▶ 🍺 🛦 ✦ P

Ravenglass

Ratty Arms
OS096965 ☎ (01229) 717676
11–3, 6–11 (11–11 summer & bank hols)
Jennings Bitter; Ruddles Best Bitter; S&N Theakston Best Bitter; Webster's Yorkshire Bitter; guest beer (summer) 🄷
Cheerful, friendly local, converted from a station, with lots of railway memorabilia. It stands next to the main line and the narrow gauge steam (La'al Ratty) stations (also handy for the Roman bathhouse, Muncaster Castle and a children's playground). Superb food (available all day Sun). Good vegetarian menu.
曲 ♿ ✿ 🏠 ◁ ▶ 🛦 ⇌ P

Ravenstonedale

Black Swan
☎ (0153 96) 23204
11.30–3, 6–11
Jennings Cumberland Ale; S&N Theakston Best Bitter; Tetley Bitter; Younger Scotch; guest beers 🄷
Traditional stone hotel, with a locals' bar, a comfortable lounge and a dining room – all well furnished and decorated. Some bedrooms are adapted for guests with disabilities.
曲 Q ✿ 🏠 ◁ ▶ 🍺 ♿ 🛦 ✦ P

Rosthwaite

Scafell Hotel (Riverside Bar)
☎ (0176 87) 77208
11–11 (12–3, 7–11 Jan)
S&N Theakston Mild (summer), **Best Bitter, XB, Old Peculier; guest beers** 🄷
Refurbished real ale bar at the rear of a country hotel in a beautiful valley. Children (well-behaved), walkers and

75

Cumbria

climbers (boots and all) welcome. Enquire about campers' breakfasts and flask-filling. Live, often impromptu, music.
🏠 ⛺ ❀ 🛏 🍴 ▶ ♿ ♣ P

Rowrah

Stork Hotel
☎ (01946) 861213
11–3, 6–11
Jennings Bitter, Cumberland Ale, Cocker Hoop; Marston's Pedigree H
Family-run local, close to a karting track and the Coast to Coast walk. Limited parking. The beers may vary.
🏠 Q ❀ 🛏 ♿ ♣ P

Sedbergh

Red Lion
Finkle Street
☎ (0153 96) 20433
11–11
Jennings Mild, Bitter, Cumberland Ale H
Popular, town-centre pub used by locals, cyclists, walkers and tourists. Unusual covered patio at the back. Free car park nearby. 🏠 ❀ 🍴 ▶ ♿ ♣

Talkin

Hare & Hounds
From B6413, take village turnoff, not Tarn
☎ (0169 77) 3456
7 (12 Sat)–11 (12–2.30, 7–11 bank hols)
Jennings Cumberland Ale; Whitbread Boddingtons Bitter; guest beers H
Charming, award-winning inn close to the lovely Talkin Tarn: a classic village pub with beams, stone fireplaces, stained-glass and bags of atmosphere. Excellent meals include a vegetarian option and a children's menu.
🏠 Q ❀ 🛏 🍴 ▶ ♿ ♿ ♣ P

Tallentire

Bush Inn
☎ (01900) 823707
12–3 (not Tue), 7–11
S&N Theakston XB; guest beer H
Friendly village local and post office combined (PO hours limited). Note the matchbox collection. No food Tue.
🏠 Q ❀ 🍴 ▶ ♣ P

Troutbeck

Queen's Head
Townhead (A592)
☎ (0153 94) 32174
11–11
Mitchell's Lancaster Bomber; Tetley Bitter; Whitbread

Boddingtons Bitter; guest beers H
Popular, roadside pub noted for its high quality meals and the four-poster bed frame which forms part of the bar. Lots of rooms and levels.
🏠 ❀ 🛏 🍴 ▶ ♿ ♣ P

Ulverston

King's Head Hotel
Queen Street ☎ (01229) 582892
10.30–11
S&N Theakston Best Bitter, XB; Whitbread Boddingtons Bitter; guest beers H
Cosy, old town-centre local offering regularly changing guest beers. Bowling green at the rear. Very friendly, but it can get busy at weekends.
🏠 ❀ 🛏 🚆

Stan Laurel
The Ellers (off A590, towards Barrow) ☎ (01229) 582814
12–3, 7–11; 12–11 Thu–Sat
Jennings Bitter, Cumberland Ale; Tetley Bitter; guest beer H
Friendly local near the old Hartleys brewery. Lots of Stan Laurel memorabilia features. Not far from the Stan Laurel Museum (he was born in the town). Q ⛺ ❀ 🍴 ▶ ♿ P

Underbarrow

Punchbowl
☎ (0153 95) 68234
12–3, 6–11 (may vary)
Draught Bass; Whitbread Boddingtons Bitter H
Unspoilt, multi-room, village pub with lots of character. Handy for travellers on the Westmorland Way; camping in the grounds. Last food orders 8pm.
🏠 Q ❀ 🍴 ▶ ♿ P

Wetheral

Wheatsheaf
☎ (01228) 560686
12–3, 6–11; 11–11 Sat
Greenalls Bitter, Original H
Comfortable and friendly village pub. Excellent home-cooked food from an interesting and varied menu (no lunches winter Mon).
🏠 Q ❀ 🍴 ▶ 🚆 ♣ P

Whitehaven

Golden Fleece
Chapel Street ☎ (01946) 63194
11–11
Jennings Bitter, Oatmeal Stout, Sneck Lifter H
Lively drinkers' pub offering the best bar prices in town. The Jennings beer range may vary, but there are always three available. ❀ 🚆 ♣

Jubilee Inn (Canteen)
Low Road (½ mile from centre on St Bees road, B5345)
☎ (01946) 692848
11–3, 6.30–11; 11–11 Thu–Sat
Jennings Bitter H
Busy, very friendly local, where games and sports are taken very seriously. There is something happening in the bar every night, but the lounge at the back is quiet. Near the RL ground; the closest BR station is Corkickle (ten mins' walk). Q ❀ 🍴 ▶ 🍺 ♣ P

Windermere

Grey Walls Hotel (Greys Inn)
Elleray Road
☎ (0153 94) 43741
11–11
S&N Theakston Mild, Best Bitter, XB, Old Peculier; guest beers H
Turn of the century, former doctor's house and surgery, now a pleasant hotel. The adjoining Greys Inn is noted for its guest beers and exceptionally good value meals (served all day Sat). Unobtrusive pool table and TV. The paved patio is well away from the road.
🏠 ⛺ ❀ 🛏 🍴 ▶ 🚆 ♣ P

Winton

Bay Horse
☎ (0176 83) 71451
12–2 (not Mon–Tue in winter), 7–11 (12–11 summer, may vary)
Jennings Bitter; S&N Theakston Best Bitter; Younger Scotch; guest beers H
Traditional village local overlooking the green. It has a stone floor in the bar (dogs allowed), a lounge and a games room. Food always available. Children's certificate.
🏠 Q ❀ 🛏 🍴 ▶ 🍺 ♣ P

Workington

Commercial Inn
Market Place ☎ (01900) 603981
12–5, 6.30–11
Jennings Mild, Bitter H
Quiet, friendly pub just out of the town centre. ♣

George IV
29 Stanley Street (near harbour, behind station)
☎ (01900) 602266
11–3, 7–11
Jennings Bitter H
Cosy, end-of-terrace, quiet local, on probably the oldest street in town. Convenient for football, RL and greyhound stadia. Children welcome. Next to an attractive harbour development. 🏠 Q ⛺ 🚆 ♣

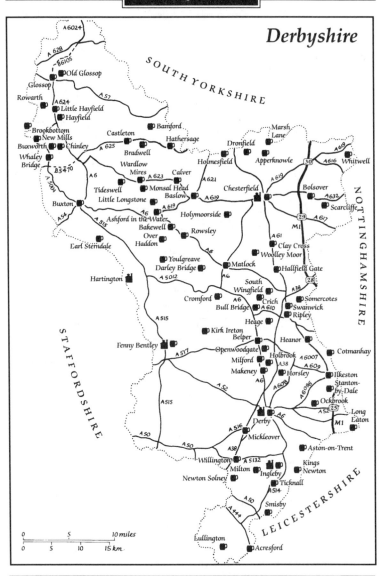

Derbyshire

Black Bull, *Fenny Bentley;* **Brunswick,** *Derby;* **John Thompson Inn/Lloyds,** *Ingleby;* **Leatherbritches,** *Fenny Bentley;* **Townes,** *Chesterfield;* **Whim,** *Hartington*

Acresford

Cricketts Inn
Burton Road ☎ (01283) 760359
11–3, 6.30–11; 12–2.30, 7–10.30 Sun
Draught Bass; Marston's Pedigree; guest beer Ⓗ
18th-century former coaching inn: a tidy, basic bar and smart lounge. Its name means a 'wooded copse'. Good reputation for food. Petanque court.
🏩 ❀ ◑ ▶ ⊞ ♣ P

Apperknowle

Yellow Lion
High Street ☎ (01246) 413181
12–3, 5–11
Draught Bass; Greene King Abbot; Stones Best Bitter; guest beers Ⓗ
Busy, stone-built village free house, with a comfortable lounge and a no-smoking restaurant. The extensive menu includes vegetarian dishes. Winner of CAMRA awards.
Q ❀ 🛏 ◑ ▶ P

Derbyshire

Ashford in the Water

Bull's Head
Church Street
☎ (01629) 812931
11.30–3, 6.30–11
Robinson's Old Stockport Bitter, Best Bitter Ⓗ
Unspoilt country pub where the comfortable main bar has an original oak-beamed ceiling. Very popular with villagers and walkers; busy at weekends. Good variety of bar lunches.
🏚 Q ❀ ◐ ⊞ & ▲ ♣ P

Aston-on-Trent

Malt Shovel
The Green ☎ (01332) 792256
11.30–4, 5.30–11
Marston's Pedigree; Tetley Bitter; guest beer Ⓗ
Victorian pub: a friendly lounge and a panelled bar with bar billiards. Secluded off the main road in an unspoilt village. Q ❀ ◐ ▶ ⊞ ♣ P ⌦

Bakewell

Queen's Arms Hotel
Bridge Street ☎ (01629) 814586
11–11
Burtonwood Mild, Bitter Ⓗ
Stone-built local, near the market. Book eve meals in winter. 🏚 ◐ ▶ &

Wheatsheaf Hotel
Bridge Street ☎ (01629) 812985
11–11
Mansfield Riding Bitter, Bitter, Old Baily Ⓗ
Large, multi-roomed, stone, town-centre pub. ❀ ◐ ▶ ⊞ &

Bamford

Derwent
Main Road ☎ (01433) 651395
11–11
Marston's Bitter, Pedigree; Stones Best Bitter Ⓗ; **guest beer**
Unspoilt Peak District hotel dating from 1890, with a tap room, two lounge areas and a dining room serving reasonably-priced home-cooking.
☎ ❀ 🏚 ◐ ▶ ⊞ ▲ ≉ ♣ P

Baslow

Robin Hood Inn
Chesterfield Road
(A619/B6050 jct)
☎ (01246) 583186
11.30–3.30, 6.30–11; 11–11 Sat
Mansfield Riding Bitter, Bitter, Old Baily Ⓗ

Country pub catering for motorists as well as hikers. No-smoking area lunchtime. Note: a cask breather may be used on Riding Mild in winter.
🏚 ❀ ◐ ▶ ⊞ & ▲ ♣ P ⌦ ⊟

Belper

Lord Nelson
Bridge Street (A6)
☎ (01773) 824465
2.30 (11 Fri & Sat)–11
Marston's Pedigree; guest beers Ⓗ
Two-roomed town tavern served by a central bar. Busy at weekends, but more relaxed in the week. Cider in summer.
❀ ◐ ⊞ ▲ ≉ ♣ ⌒ P

Bolsover

Black Bull
3 Hilltop (A632/B6419 jct)
11–3.30, 7–11
Burtonwood Forshaw's, Top Hat Ⓗ
Friendly, olde-worlde pub near historic Bolsover Castle. Book Sun lunch. ◐ ▶ ♣ P ⊟

Bradwell

Valley Lodge
Church Street
☎ (01433) 620427
12–3 (not Mon–Fri in winter), 7–11
Stones Best Bitter; Wards Best Bitter; Whitbread Boddingtons Bitter; guest beers Ⓗ
Large, lively three-roomed pub in a scenic Peak District village. The tap room has a pool table and is separated from the comfortable lounge by a small foyer bar.
🏚 ❀ 🏚 ◐ ▶ ⊞ ▲ ♣ P

Brookbottom

Fox Inn
Brookbottom Road
☎ (0161) 427 1634
11.30–3, 7 (5.30 summer)–11
Robinson's Hatters Mild, Best Bitter Ⓗ
Old whitewashed pub in a quiet hamlet a mile from New Mills centre: a comfortable beamed lounge with original features and a basic games room. Access on foot from Strines station is along part of the Goyt Way. Families catered for until early eve.
🏚 ☎ ❀ ◐ ▶ ▲ ♣ P

Bull Bridge

Lord Nelson
☎ (01773) 852037
11–3, 6–11
Mansfield Riding Mild, Bitter, Old Baily Ⓗ

Popular, two-roomed local in a small hamlet, one mile SE of Crich. Busy with food trade at lunchtime. Mansfield's seasonal ales. ❀ ◐ ♣ P ⊟

Buxton

Baker's Arms
26 West Road ☎ (01298) 24404
12–3, 6–11
Ind Coope Burton Ale; Marston's Pedigree; Tetley Bitter Ⓗ
Cosy, two-roomed pub with an ivy-clad exterior, just behind the market place.
Q ❀ & ▲ ≉ ♣ P

Sun Inn
33 High Street
☎ (01298) 23452
1.30 (12 Sat)–11
Bateman Mild; Marston's Bitter, Pedigree Ⓗ
Comfortable, two-roomed pub close to the market (Tue and Sat), attracting the more mature drinker. Marston's Head Brewer's Choice sold.
Q ❀ ≉ P

Swan Inn
40 High Street
☎ (01298) 23278
11.30–3; 11–11 Fri & Sat
Mansfield Bitter; Morland Old Speckled Hen; Tetley Bitter Ⓗ; **guest beers**
Nicely presented pub with three rooms around a central bar. Over 60 whiskies; varying guest beers, often from local microbreweries.
🏚 Q ◐ ≉ ♣ P

Buxworth

Navigation Inn
Canal Basin, 100 yds off B6062
☎ (01663) 732072
11–11
Marston's Pedigree; Taylor Landlord; Webster's Yorkshire Bitter; guest beers Ⓗ
Excellent stone, multi-roomed pub with a restaurant area, alongside the only remaining canal tramway interchange in the UK. Food at all times including all day Sun. 🏚 ☎
❀ 🏚 ◐ ▶ ⊞ & ♣ ⌒ P

Calver

Bridge Inn
Calver Bridge (A623)
☎ (01433) 630415
11.30–3 (4.30 Sat), 5.30 (6 Sat)–11
Hardys & Hansons Best Bitter, Kimberley Classic Ⓗ
Unspoilt, traditional village local with two rooms. The spacious tap room has a games area. Eve meals Tue–Sat.
🏚 Q ❀ ◐ ▶ ⊞ & ▲ ♣ P ⌦

Castleton

Bull's Head
Cross Street ☎ (01433) 620256
12–3, 6–11 (12–11 summer)
Robinson's Best Bitter, Old Tom Ⓗ
Friendly local in a major tourist village. The large lounge features an aquarium. There is also a pool room and a restaurant (book eve meals).
❀ 🛏 ◑ ▮ ♣ P

Chesterfield

Chesterfield Bowl
Storforth Lane, Birdholm (off A61) ☎ (01246) 550092
11–11
Hardys & Hansons Best Bitter, Kimberley Classic Ⓗ
16-lane bowling centre bar open to the public. ♿ P

Derby Tup
387 Sheffield Road, Whittington Moor
☎ (01246) 454316
11.30–3, 5 (6 Sat)–11
Exmoor Gold; Marston's Pedigree; S&N Theakston Old Peculier; Taylor Landlord; Tetley Bitter; guest beers Ⓗ
Superb, unspoilt, corner free house with three rooms, offering 15 guest beers a week (one mild). Eve meals till 7.30.
Q ◑ ▮ 🍴 ♿ ♣

Market Hotel
95 New Square
☎ (01246) 273641
11–11
Ind Coope Burton Ale; Marston's Pedigree; Tetley Bitter; guest beers Ⓗ
Tetley Festival Alehouse, open-plan with a stone and wood floor, exposed brick and wood panelling. Wide choice of guest beers. ❀ ◑

Royal Oak
43 Chatsworth Road (A617, opp. B&Q) ☎ (01246) 277854
11.30–11
Bateman XB; S&N Theakston Best Bitter, XB, Old Peculier; Townes Best Lockoford; guest beers Ⓗ
Friendly local hosting beer festivals and live music, serving seven ales, 30 bottle-conditioned continental beers and 80 whiskies.
🍴 ❀ 🍴 🍴 ♣ ♡ P 🍴

Rutland Arms
16 Stephenson Place
11–11; 7–10.30 Sun, closed Sun lunch
Marston's Pedigree; Whitbread Boddingtons Bitter, Castle Eden Ale; guest beers Ⓗ

One of the town's oldest beer houses, next to the crooked spire: a family-run pub, particularly popular lunchtimes and weekends. No food Sun. ◑ ▮ 🍴 ♣

Chinley

Squirrels
Green Lane ☎ (01663) 751200
12–3, 7–11
Wards Best Bitter; Whitbread Boddingtons Bitter; guest beer Ⓗ
Former railway hotel with a spacious and functional bar area and an extensive menu. Snooker table. 🛏 ◑ ▮ 🍴 ♣

Clay Cross

Prince of Wales
8 Thanet Street
☎ (01246) 865698
12–4 (4.30 Sat), 7–11
Bass Mild, Worthington BB; Stones Best Bitter Ⓗ
Comfortable, small village pub with a lounge and a public bar. No gimmicks. ❀ 🍴 ♣

Cotmanhay

Bridge Inn
Bridge Street ☎ (0115) 9322589
11–11
Hardys & Hansons Best Mild, Best Bitter Ⓔ
Traditional village local by the Erewash Canal, frequented by locals, fishermen and boaters. A rare find. Q ❀ 🍴 ♣ P

Crich

Cliff Inn
Town End, Cromford Road
☎ (01773) 852444
11–3, 6–11
Hardys & Hansons Best Mild, Best Bitter, Kimberley Classic Ⓗ
Friendly, popular stone local with two rooms, close to the National Tramway Museum.
❀ ◑ ▮ 🍴 P

Cromford

Bell Inn
27 The Hill (A6 jct)
☎ (01629) 822102
12–3 (not winter), 7–11
Hardys & Hansons Best Mild, Best Bitter Ⓗ
Three-roomed, 18th-century, basic local built to serve mill workers. The very old snug has a warm atmosphere; the popular public bar fields games teams. Q ❀ ♿ ♣

Darley Bridge

Three Stags' Heads
Main Road

12–3, 6–11; 12–11 Sat
Hardys & Hansons Best Mild, Best Bitter Ⓗ
250-year-old village pub with a smart lounge, plus a bar and a pool room. Good outside drinking area.
🍴 Q ❀ 🍴 ♣ P

Derby

Alexandra Hotel
Siddals Road
☎ (01332) 293993
11–2.30, 4.30 (6 Sat)–11
Draught Bass; Bateman Mild, XB; Marston's Pedigree; Younger No.3; guest beers Ⓗ
Award-winning pub featuring two rooms, subtle decor and wooden floors. Bottled beer collection and railway memorabilia in the bar. Six changing guest beers.
Q ❀ ◑ 🍴 ♿ 🍴 ♡ P

Brunswick Inn
Railway Terrace
☎ (01332) 290677
11–11
Brunswick Recession, First Brew; Marston's Pedigree; Taylor Landlord Ⓗ**; guest beers** Ⓗ/Ⓖ
The oldest purpose-built railwayman's pub, where 14 handpumps serve beer from all around the country as well as its own brewery. Several rooms with stone-flagged floors. Beer festivals held.
Q 🍴 ❀ 🍴 🍴 ♣ ♡ 🍴

Flower Pot
King Street ☎ (01332) 204955
11–11
Draught Bass; Marston's Pedigree; Taylor Landlord Ⓗ**; guest beers** Ⓗ/Ⓖ
Bustling, friendly, extended pub serving ten beers. Mini-beer festivals and brewery theme weekends are held. Meals finish early.
Q ❀ ◑ ▮ ♿ ♣

Furnace Inn
9 Duke Street
☎ (01332) 331563
11–11
Hardy & Hansons Best Mild, Best Bitter, Kimberley Classic Ⓗ
Traditional local off St Mary's Bridge, near the historic Bridge Chapel. The open-plan interior features piano nights Sat and Sun. ❀ 🍴 ♣

Peacock Inn
87 Nottingham Road
☎ (01332) 340712
11–3 (3.30 Sat), 6.30–11; 11–11 Fri
Marston's Pedigree Ⓗ
Stone coaching house on a former main road, now a lively local: a long front bar, with a lower room at the rear.
🍴 ❀ 🍴 ♣

Derbyshire

Royal Standard
Derwent Street
☎ (01332) 299332
11–11
Exmoor Gold; Mansfield Riding Mild, Riding Bitter, Bitter, Old Baily; guest beer ℍ
Imposing, handsomely-fronted corner house acquired by Mansfield and transformed into an excellent ale house; seasonal brews are available. The small front bar hosts a games night Thu. ◑ ◱ ♣

York Tavern
23 York Street
☎ (01332) 362849
12–3, 6–11; 12–11 Fri & Sat
Marston's Pedigree; guest beer ℍ
Thriving terraced boozer with tremendous character. ✿ ◑ ♣

Dronfield

Old Sidings
91 Chesterfield Road
☎ (01246) 410023
12–11
Bass Mild, Worthington BB, Draught Bass; Stones Best Bitter ℍ
Lively pub with an L-shaped lounge on two levels (railway theme). Restaurant in the basement. ✿ ◑ ▶ ⇌ ♣ P

Victoria
5 Stubley Lane
☎ (01246) 412117
12–11
Banks's Mild, Bitter; Marston's Pedigree; guest beer ℍ
Genuine local with a comfortable, L-shaped lounge. Darts area at one end. ✿ ◑ ♣

Earl Sterndale

Quiet Woman Inn
Off A515 ☎ (01298) 83211
11–3, 6–11
Bateman Mild; Marston's Bitter, Pedigree, Owd Rodger ℍ
Classic, unspoilt, village inn, a haven for walkers with superb countryside in all directions. Local cheese and eggs for sale. In every edition of the *Guide*. ✌ Q ☎ ✿ ◱ ▲ ♣ P

Fenny Bentley

Bentley Brook Inn
At Buxton/Bakewell Road jct
11–11
Leatherbritches Belter, Bespoke; Marston's Pedigree; Tetley Bitter; guest beers ℍ
Imposing country house, home of Leatherbritches Brewery. Seven ales; beer festivals in summer.
✌ Q ✿ ⊠ ◑ ▶ ▲ P

Glossop

Crown Inn
142 Victoria Street
☎ (01457) 862824
11.30–11
Samuel Smith OBB, Museum (winter) ℍ
Friendly local with two small, comfortable snugs, an active games room and an attractive central bar. The cheapest pub pint in town.
✌ Q ✿ ♿ ⇌ ♣ ✄

Friendship Inn
Edward Street
☎ (01457) 855277
12–3 (4 Sat; not Thu), 5 (7 Sat)–11
Robinson's Hatters Mild, Best Bitter ℍ
Warm pub with an attractive, wood-panelled, lounge interior. Games room at the rear. ✌ ✿ ♿ ⇌

Prince of Wales
Milltown (off A57)
☎ (01457) 864679
11.30–3, 5–11; 11–11 Sat
Banks's Mild; Marston's Bitter, Pedigree ℍ
Cosy, characterful, stone, terraced pub, just off the High Street. Marston's Head Brewer's Choice sold. Eve meals Fri–Sat. ✌ ✿ ◑ ▶ ◱ ♿ ⇌ ♣ P

Whiteley Nab
1 Charlestown (A624)
☎ (01457) 852886
12–11
Vaux Lorimer's Best Scotch, Double Maxim; guest beer ℍ
Welcoming pub, a 15-min walk from the centre. Collection of saucy postcards and old local photos. Good reputation for food. The guest beer comes from the Vaux group. ✿ ◑ ▶ P

Hallfield Gate

Shoulder of Mutton
Near Shirland
12 (7 Tue)–11
Mansfield Bitter; guest beers ℍ
16th-century, old-fashioned country pub. ✿ ♿

Hathersage

Scotsman's Pack
School Lane ☎ (01433) 650253
12–3, 6–11; 12–11 Sat

Burtonwood Mild, Bitter, Forshaw's ℍ
Comfortable village pub with three lounge areas served by a central bar. A feature is 'Little John's Chair', made for a giant, but perhaps not the one buried in the churchyard. ✌
Q ☎ ✿ ⊠ ◑ ▶ ♿ ▲ ♣ P

Hayfield

Royal Hotel
Market Street
☎ (01663) 742721
12–3, 6–11; 12–11 Sat
Marston's Pedigree; John Smith's Bitter; Webster's Yorkshire Bitter; guest beers ℍ
Centrally located pub next to the river and cricket ground. A former vicarage, it boasts original oak panels and pews. Regular live music. ✌ Q ☎
✿ ⊠ ◑ ▶ ♿ ▲ ♣ P

Heage

Black Boy
Old Road (set back from B6013) ☎ (01773) 856799
12–3 (not Mon), 6.30–11
Mansfield Riding Mild, Riding Bitter, Bitter, Old Baily ℍ
Friendly, large, open-plan, stone pub and restaurant. Mansfield seasonal ales stocked. ✌ ✿ ◑ ▶ ♣ P

Heanor

Derby Arms
High Street ☎ (01773) 713508
11–4, 7–11; 12–2, 7–10.30 Sun
Home Mild, Bitter ⒠
Traditional, two-roomed, drinkers' pub; small and friendly. TV in the bar; very popular for games. ✿ ◱ ♣

Holbrook

Wheel Inn
Chapel Street
☎ (01332) 880006
11.30–3.30, 6.30–11
Mansfield Riding Mild ℍ; Taylor Landlord ⒢; Vaux Extra Special; Wards Thorne Best Bitter ℍ; guest beers ⒢
Friendly, country pub with beamed rooms. The garden has ponds and a rockery. Good value home-cooking.
✌ ☎ ✿ ◑ ▶

Holmesfield

Traveller's Rest
Main Road ☎ (0114) 2890446
12–11
Home Bitter; Stones Best Bitter; Younger No.3 ℍ
Pleasant pub with a pool table in the tap room and a spacious lounge. ✿ ◱ ♣ P

80

Holymoorside

Lamb Inn
Loads Road ☎ (01246) 566167
12–3 (not Mon–Thu), 7–11
Draught Bass; Home Bitter; S&N Theakston XB; guest beers Ⓗ
Cosy village pub offering up to four guest beers. Local CAMRA *Pub of the Year 1994.*
🏚 Q ⊛ ❧ ♣ P

Horsley

Coach & Horses
47 Church Street
☎ (01332) 880581
11.30–3, 6–11
Banks's Mild; Marston's Bitter, Pedigree Ⓗ
Popular, open-plan village pub with a beamed ceiling, conservatory and a large garden. Home-cooked food (eve meals 6–8). Marston's Head Brewer's Choice sold.
🏚 ⛵ ⊛ ◑ ▶ ❧ ♣ P

Ilkeston

Dewdrop Inn
Station Street (off A6096)
☎ (0115) 9329684
11.30–3, 7–11
Kelham Island Pale Rider; Springhead Roaring Meg; Vaux Extra Special; Wards Best Bitter Ⓗ**; guest beers** Ⓖ/Ⓗ
Old, unchanged, Victorian boozer (formerly the Middleton Hotel) with a high-ceilinged lounge, a bar, passageway and an intimate snug. Occasional cider.
🏚 Q ⛵ ⊛ ◑ ▶ ♣ ⊖

Spring Cottage
i Fulwood Street
☎ (0115) 9323153
11–3 (4 Fri, 5 Sat), 6 (7 Sat)–11
Draught Bass; guest beers Ⓗ
Friendly, well-established, back-street local.
🏚 ⛵ ◑ ❧ ♣ P

Ingleby

John Thompson Inn
Off A514 ☎ (01332) 862469
10.30–2.30, 7–11
Draught Bass; JTS XXX Ⓗ
Upmarket brew pub converted from a farmhouse in 1969. The interior has a wealth of oak and displays antiques and paintings. 🏚 ⛵ ⊛ ◑ ❧ ♣ P

Kings Newton

Pack Horse Inn
Packhorse Road
☎ (01332) 862767
11.30–2.30, 6–11
Burtonwood Forshaw's, Top Hat Ⓗ

Renovated old pub in market garden country, catering for diners but with a top bar and a two-level lounge.
🏚 ⊛ ◑ ▶ ❧ P

Kirk Ireton

Barley Mow
Main Street ☎ (01335) 370306
12–2, 7–11; 12–2 Sun, closed Sun eve
Marston's Pedigree; S&N Theakston Old Peculier; Taylor Landlord; guest beers Ⓖ
Jacobean gem, a tall, gabled building of several rooms with low-beamed ceilings, mullioned windows, slate tables and well-worn woodwork. 🏚 Q ⊛ ❧ ♣ P

Little Hayfield

Lantern Pike
Glossop Road
☎ (01663) 747590
12–3, 7–11
Taylor Landlord; Whitbread Boddingtons Bitter, Flowers IPA Ⓗ
Picturesque, stone pub in a hamlet surrounded by excellent walking country. The comfortable country interior features a collection of beer jugs. ⊛ 🏨 ◑ ▶ P

Little Longstone

Packhorse
Main Street ☎ (01629) 640471
11–3, 5 (6 Sat)–11
Marston's Bitter, Pedigree Ⓗ
Unspoilt village local, a pub since 1787; three rooms, one doubling as a dining room. Ramblers are welcome in the tap room. Excellent meals.
🏚 Q ⊛ ◑ ▶ ❧ ♣

Long Eaton

Hole in the Wall
Regent Street (off Market Place) ☎ (0115) 9734920
11–3, 6–11; 11–11 Mon, Fri & Sat
Bass Worthington BB, Draught Bass; guest beers Ⓗ
Excellent, two-roomed local: a bar with Sky TV and pool, a pleasant lounge, plus an off-sales hatch. The nice back garden has a skittle alley and barbecue. The guest beers are changed weekly. Beware the Scrumpy Jack cider on a fake handpump. ⊛ ◑ ❧ ♣

Lullington

Colvile Arms
Coton Road ☎ (01827) 373212
7–11; 12–3, 7–11 Sat
Draught Bass, Marston's Pedigree; guest beer (weekend) Ⓗ

18th-century village free house; a basic, wood-panelled bar, a smart lounge, plus a second lounge/function room. Bowling green in the garden.
🏚 Q ⊛ ❧ P

Makeney

Holly Bush
Holly Bush Lane
☎ (01332) 841729
12–3, 6–11; 12–11 Sat
Marston's Pedigree, Owd Rodger; Ruddles County; Taylor Landlord; guest beers Ⓖ
Old pub of exceptional character, a Grade II listed building. The beer is brought up from the cellar in jugs. The snug sits between two bar rooms. Occasional cider.
🏚 Q ⛵ ⊛ ◑ ❧ ♣ ⊖ P

Marsh Lane

Fox & Hounds
Main Road ☎ (01246) 432974
12–3, 7 (6 summer)–11
Burtonwood Bitter, Forshaw's Ⓗ
Pub with a comfortable lounge and a tap room, plus a large garden and play area. Good selection of meals.
Q ⊛ ◑ ▶ ❧ ♣ P

Matlock

Boat House
Dale Road ☎ (01629) 583776
11.30–11
Hardys & Hansons Best Mild, Best Bitter, Kimberley Classic Ⓗ
Basic, three-roomed, friendly pub.
🏚 ⛵ ⊛ 🏨 ◑ ▶ ❧ ⇌ ♣ P

Gate
72 Smedley Street
☎ (01629) 580818
12–3, 7 (6.30 Fri & Sat)–11
Home Bitter; Marston's Pedigree; S&N Theakston XB; guest beer Ⓗ
Comfortably refurbished, 150-year-old former livery stables catering for office workers and locals.
🏚 ⊛ ◑ ❧ ♣ P

Thorntree
48 Jackson Road
☎ (01629) 582923
11.30–3 (not Mon or Tue), 7–11
Draught Bass; Mansfield Bitter, Old Baily; guest beer Ⓗ
Friendly, mid-19th-century pub with superb views. Its two cosy rooms are deservedly popular. Q ⊛ ◑ ❧ ♣

Mickleover

Honeycomb
Ladybank Road
☎ (01332) 515600

81

Derbyshire

11.30–2.30 (3 Sat), 6.30–11
Everards Beacon, Tiger, Old Original; Shepherd Neame Bishops Finger Ⓗ
Two-level estate pub; its interior design incorporates interlocking hexagons. Pool and darts on the lower level. No meals Sun. ✲ ◑ ⊞ ♣ P

Vine Inn
Uttoxeter Road (A516)
☎ (01332) 513956
11.30–3, 6.30–11
Ind Coope Burton Ale; Tetley Bitter; guest beers Ⓗ
Village local in what is now a suburb. The small back bar boasts wooden settles; a long lounge is down a passageway. Many guest ales have been served.
Q ⛳ ✲ ◑ ⊞ ₰ ♣ ◠

Milford

King William IV
The Bridge (A6)
☎ (01332) 840842
12–2, 6–11
Fuller's London Pride; Marston's Pedigree; guest beer (weekend) Ⓗ
Traditional one-roomed country pub with stone walls and a beamed ceiling, sheltered under wooded cliffs by the River Derwent. Parking can be difficult. No meals Sun eve or Mon lunch. ⋈ ◑ ▶

Milton

Swan Inn
Main Street ☎ (01283) 703188
12–2.30, 7–11
Marston's Pedigree Ⓗ
Popular and friendly village pub with a smart lounge and a locals' bar. Handy for Repton and Foremark Reservoir. No food Mon (except bank hols).
♨ ✲ ◑ ▶ ⊞ ♣ P

Monsal Head

Monsal Head Hotel
☎ (01629) 640250
11–11
Marston's Pedigree; Ruddles Best Bitter; S&N Theakston Old Peculier; John Smith's Bitter Ⓗ; **guest beers** Ⓖ
150-year-old country hotel with an elegant lounge. Most of the ales are in the Stable Bar, retaining stall seating, a manger and an inglenook.
♨ Q ✲ ⋈ ◑ ▶ Å ♣ P

New Mills

Beehive
Albion Road
11–3, 5.30–11
Whitbread Boddingtons Bitter, Flowers IPA; guest beers Ⓗ

Unusual, triangular pub with a large vault, a smaller cosy lounge and a small restaurant. A former toll house, moved and rebuilt on its current site.
⇌ (Newtown) ♣

Newton Solney

Unicorn Inn
Repton Road ☎ (01283) 703324
11–3, 5–11; 11–11 Sat
Draught Bass; Marston's Pedigree; guest beer Ⓗ
Busy village free house with a bar created from original smaller rooms, plus a lounge/meeting room. No meals Sun. Q ✲ ⋈ ◑ ▶ ♣ P

Ockbrook

Royal Oak
Green Lane ☎ (01332) 662378
11.30–2.30, 7–11; 12–2.30, 7–10.30 Sun
Draught Bass; guest beer Ⓗ
17th-century village pub with a cobbled yard and a cottage garden. Several small rooms and a larger function room.
♨ Q ✲ ◑ ⊞ ◐ ♣ P

Old Glossop

Bull's Head
102 Church Street
☎ (01457) 853291
12–11
Robinson's Old Stockport Bitter, Best Bitter, Old Tom Ⓗ
Listed, 16th-century inn, with a friendly village atmosphere at the foot of the Pennines; popular with hikers. Renowned for its Indian/Balti cuisine.
⛳ ✲ ◑ Å ⇌ (Glossop) ♣

Openwoodgate

Bull's Head
2 Kilburn Lane (A60)
☎ (01773) 822669
11–2.30, 6.30–11
Hardys & Hansons Best Mild, Best Bitter, Kimberley Classic Ⓗ
Exceptionally well-run, hospitable village local on the crest of a hill, high above Belper. A smart lounge and a locals' bar. No food Mon.
♨ ✲ ◑ ▶ ♣ P

Over Haddon

Lathkil Hotel
½ mile S of B5055
☎ (01629) 812501
11.30–3, 6.30–11
Wards Mild, Thorne Best Bitter, Best Bitter Ⓗ
Free house in an idyllic setting enjoying a panoramic view of Lathkil Dale. A fine oak-

panelled bar with traditional furnishings. Excellent food (not served Sun eve). Family room lunchtime.
♨ Q ⛳ ⋈ ◑ ▶ Å P ⊟

Ripley

Prince of Wales
Butterly Hill ☎ (01773) 743499
12–3, 7–11 (may vary)
Marston's Bitter, Pedigree; guest beer Ⓗ
Popular, friendly local with changing guest beers. ♣ P

Three Horseshoes
Market Place ☎ (01773) 743113
11–3 (4 Sat), 5 (7 Sat)–11
Vaux Samson; guest beer Ⓗ
Two-roomed town local with a pool table. ◑ ♣ P ⊟

Rowarth

Little Mill Inn
Signed off Siloh Road, off Mellor Road ☎ (01663) 743178
11–11
Banks's Bitter; Camerons Strongarm; guest beer Ⓗ
Large, multi-roomed pub of character boasting huge log fires and a working water wheel. Adventure playground outside for children. Good meals.
♨ Q ✲ ⋈ ◑ ▶ ◐ Å P ⊟

Rowsley

Grouse & Claret
Main Road ☎ (01629) 733233
11–11
Mansfield Riding Bitter, Bitter, Old Baily Ⓗ
Over 100 years old, an imposing stone pub, comfortably refurbished but retaining original features and a tap room (hikers welcome). Wide range of home-cooked meals (open Sun afternoon for food). Family room in summer and on winter eves. Seasonal beers sold. ♨ ⛳ ✲ ⋈ ◑ ▶
◐ Å ♣ P ⧗

Scarcliffe

Elm Tree
Station Road ☎ (01246) 823213
12–3, 7–11; 12–2.30, 7–10.30 Sun
Bass Worthington BB; Mansfield Bitter; Stones Best Bitter; guest beer Ⓗ
Attractive, two-bar village pub, popular in summer. Home-cooking.
✲ ◑ ⊞ ♣ P ⊟

Smisby

Smisby Arms
Main Street ☎ (01530) 412677

82

Bovey Tracey

Old Thatch Inn
Station Road ☎ (01626) 833421
11.30–3, 6–11
Ind Coope Burton Ale; Teignworthy Reel Ale; Tetley Bitter; Wadworth 6X Ⓗ
One-bar pub split into three rooms: a main bar, pool area and dining area. A low ceiling and a natural brick wall are features. Near the Gateway to the Moor. Q ❀ ◗ ◗ ♣ P

Bradninch

Castle Inn
Fore Street ☎ (01392) 881378
11.30–2.30, 6.30–11
Oakhill Best Bitter; guest beers Ⓗ
Friendly, popular pub at the centre of town. Good value, home-made meals. Note: the Burton Ale is kept under a cask breather. ◗ ◗ ♿ ♣ P

Branscombe

Fountain Head
☎ (01297) 680359
11–2.30, 6.30–10.30 (11 summer)
Branscombe Vale Branoc, Old Stoker Ⓗ
14th-century pub with huge log fires, wood-panelled walls and a stone-flagged floor. The lounge bar was formerly the village blacksmith's. The forge now forms the central fireplace. Good, wholesome food. The accommodation is self-catering.
🍴 Q ❀ 🛏 ◗ ◗ 🍴 ▲ ♣ ◠ P

Braunton

Mariner's Arms
South Street ☎ (01271) 813160
11–2.30, 6–11
Courage Best Bitter, Directors; Exmoor Ale Ⓗ
Busy local whose landlord has a miraculous memory for faces and their favourite tipple. Low prices. ◗ ◗ ▲ ♣

Bridestowe

Foxhounds
On A386 ☎ (01822) 820206
11–11
Whitbread Boddingtons Bitter, Flowers IPA Ⓗ
Externally traditional pub, with a semi-modern interior. A good local trade is supplemented by Dartmoor hikers. 🍴 🛏 ◗

Brixham

Blue Anchor
Fore Street ☎ (01803) 859373
11

Blackawton Headstrong; Dartmoor Strong; guest beer Ⓗ
Historic, 16th-century harbourside pub, where the food is very reasonably priced. The building used to be a sail loft, and its nautical character survives. Live music. Popular with tourists. 🍴 Q ◗ ♣

Broadhembury

Drewe Arms
☎ (01404) 841267
11–2.30, 6–11; 12–2.30, 7–10.30 Sun
Otter Bitter, Ale, Head; guest beers Ⓖ
Characterful inn with a picturesque exterior and an old-fashioned interior. This largely unspoilt village pub stands amongst thatched, whitewashed cottages. No meals Sun eve.
🍴 ❀ ◗ ◗ 🍴 ♣ ◠ P

Broadhempston

Monk's Retreat
The Square ☎ (01803) 812203
12–3, 6.30–11.30
Draught Bass; Teignworthy Reel Ale; guest beers Ⓗ
Cosy pub with a warm atmosphere, in the middle of a quiet village. Very large menu; no food Mon. Q 🛏 ◗

Buckland Monachorum

Drake Manor Inn
☎ (01822) 853892
11.30–2.30 (3 Sat), 6.30–11
Ushers Best Bitter, Founders Ⓗ
16th-century local in a picturesque village. Ushers seasonal ales are stocked.
🍴 Q ❀ 🛏 ◗ ♣ P

Butterleigh

Butterleigh Inn
Near M5 jct 28
☎ (01884) 855407
12–2.30, 6 (5 Fri)–11; 12–2.30, 7–10.30 Sun
Cotleigh Tawny, Barn Owl, Old Buzzard; guest beers (occasional) Ⓗ
Friendly village inn serving good quality and value food.
🍴 Q ❀ 🛏 ◗ ◗ ♣ P

Chagford

Globe
High Street ☎ (01647) 433485
11–3, 7–11 (11–11 winter Sat)
Courage Best Bitter, Directors; guest beers Ⓗ
Friendly, 16th-century, two-bar coaching inn in the centre of a delightful country town. Cider in summer.
🍴 🍴 🛏 ◗ ◗ ▲ ◠

Chipshop

Chipshop Inn
Off A384, W of Tavistock
OS437751 ☎ (01822) 832322
12–2.30 (3 Sat), 5–11
Draught Bass; Exmoor Ale; Sharp's Own; guest beer Ⓗ
Welcoming, one-bar pub on a remote crossroads. Skittle alley. 🍴 Q ❀ ◗ ◗ ♿ ♣ P

Chittlehamholt

Exeter Inn
☎ (01769) 540281
11.30–3, 6–11
Ind Coope Burton Ale; Tetley Bitter Ⓗ**; guest beers** Ⓖ
16th-century thatched inn on the edge of Exmoor. This friendly pub, used by locals and tourists, has a homely atmosphere.
🍴 Q ❀ 🛏 ◗ ◗ ◠ P

Clayhidon

Half Moon Inn
☎ (01823) 680291
12–2.30, 7–11
Draught Bass; Cotleigh Tawny, Old Buzzard; guest beers (occasional) Ⓗ
Popular pub on the edge of the village, offering good value, home-made meals in comfortable surroundings. Handy for the breath-taking Blackdown Hills.
🍴 Q ❀ 🛏 ◗ ◗ ▲ ♣ ◠ P

Cockington

Drum Inn
☎ (01803) 605143
11–2.30 (3 Sat & summer), 7 (6 summer)–11 (11–11 school summer hols)
Dartmoor Best Bitter, Legend Ⓗ
Large, friendly family pub with extensive gardens, in a picturesque, thatched village. Skittles played. Cider in summer.
🍴 Q 🛏 ❀ 🛏 ◗ ◗ ♣ ◠ P ⚲

Colaton Raleigh

Otter Inn
Exmouth Road
☎ (01395) 568434
11–2.30 (3 summer), 6 (5.30 summer)–11; 12–2.30 (3 summer), 7–10.30 Sun
Dartmoor Best Bitter, Legend; Greene King Abbot; John Smith's Bitter Ⓗ
Large, tenanted country pub which has had free brewery owners in recent years. Locals recently banned the disgust of its patrons. Excellent, home-produced meals. Cider in summer.
Q 🍴 🛏 ❀ ◗ ◗ ♣ ◠

11.30–3, 6 (5.30 Fri, 7 Sat)–11
Greene King Abbot; Marston's Pedigree; Morland Old Speckled Hen; guest beers Ⓗ
17th-century village pub, well renovated and extended. The cosy original bar has bench seats and steps up to a large lounge. No meals Sun eve.
🍴 Q 🛏 ❀ 🛏 ◗ P

Somercotes

Horse & Jockey
47 Leabrooks Road
☎ (01773) 602179
11–3, 6–11
Home Mild, Bitter; S&N Theakston Mild, XB; guest beer Ⓗ
Bustling, deservedly popular, multi-roomed local, one of the oldest in the area. Two skittle alleys. ❀ 🛏 ♣

South Wingfield

Old Yew Tree Inn
Manor Road ☎ (01773) 833763
12–3 (not Mon, except bank hols), 7–11
Marston's Pedigree; guest beers Ⓗ
Excellent, popular pub near Wingfield Manor, with oak panelling, a roaring fire and good food. Three guest ales.
🍴 Q ◗ ◗ ♿ ▲ P

Stanton-by-Dale

Chequers
Dale Road ☎ (0115) 9320946
11–2.30 (3 Thu–Sat), 7–11
Draught Bass Ⓔ
Delightful, cottage-style inn; a compact single bar where an old water pump takes pride of place. Home-made lunches of the highest quality. No meals Sun. Q ❀ ◗ ♣ P

Swanwick

Boot & Slipper
The Green ☎ (01773) 606052
12–3, 7–11
Mansfield Riding Bitter, Bitter, Old Baily Ⓗ
Friendly, one-roomed local. A collection of plates reflects the area's mining heritage. Pool and a TV room upstairs; skittles outside. 🍴 ❀ ♣ P 🍴

Gate Inn
The Delves ☎ (01773) 602039
11.30–3, 7–11
Courage Directors; Marston's Pedigree; John Smith's Bitter Ⓗ
Smart, open-plan pub with a bar, lounge and eating areas (meals Thu–Sat).
❀ ◗ ◗ ♣ P 🍴

Ticknall

Chequers
Ashby Road ☎ (01332) 864392
12–2.30, 6–11
Marston's Pedigree; Ruddles Best Bitter, County Ⓗ
Small, two-roomed local, with an inglenook, dating from the 16th century. Many games.
🍴 Q ❀ ♣ P

Staff of Life
Ashby Road ☎ (01332) 862479
11.30–2.30, 6 (7 winter)–11
Everards Tiger, Old Original; Fuller's ESB; Marston's Pedigree, Owd Rodger; S&N Theakston Old Peculier Ⓗ**; guest beers** Ⓗ
17th-century former bakehouse, originally called the Loaf of Bread; now a food-oriented pub. ❀ ◗ ◗

Tideswell

George
Commercial Road
☎ (01298) 871382
11–3, 7–11
Hardys & Hansons Best Mild, Best Bitter, Kimberley Classic Ⓗ
Substantial, stone hotel next to the parish church – 'the Cathedral of the Peak' – now with an enlarged lounge, a snug and a tap room.
🍴 Q ◗ 🛏 ♣ P

Horse & Jockey
Main Road ☎ (01298) 871597
11.30–3, 7 (6 Fri)–11
Courage Directors; John Smith's Bitter; Tetley Bitter Ⓗ
Friendly, two-roomed village pub with a distinctly local atmosphere. Excellent home-cooking. Q ❀ ◗ 🛏 ♣

Wardlow Mires

Three Stags' Heads
At A623/B6465 jct
☎ (01298) 872268
7 (11 Sat, summer & bank hols)–11
Hoskins & Oldfield Old Navigation; Kelham Island Fat Cat, Pale Rider; Springhead Bitter; guest beer Ⓗ
Carefully restored, two-roomed, 17th-century farmhouse pub of character. The stone-flagged bar is heated by an ancient range.
🍴 Q ❀ ◗ ▲ ◠ P

Whaley Bridge

Shepherd's Arms
7 Old Road (off old A6)
☎ (01663) 732384

11.30–3, 7.30–11
Banks's Mild; Marston's Bitter; Pedigree Ⓗ
Ageless local, overlooking the main street. The lounge is softly lit and quiet, in contrast to the excellent, lively vault with its flagged floor.
🍴 Q ◗ 🛏 ≉ ♣ P

White Horse
1 Lower Macclesfield Road (old A6/B5470 jct)
☎ (01663) 732617
1.45 (12 Sat)–11; 1.45–5, 7–11 Wed
Whitbread Boddingtons Mild, Bitter; guest beers Ⓗ
Sociable, lounge-style, Victorian pub, built in local stone and offering a rare mild.
🛏 ❀ ≉ ♣ P

Whitwell

Jug & Glass
Portland Street
☎ (01909) 720289
11–3, 6.30–11
John Smith's Bitter, Magnet Ⓗ
Unspoilt, two-roomed stone local with a timber bar and matching fireplace – a listed building in a mining community. 🍴 ❀ 🛏 ♣ P

Willington

Green Dragon
The Green ☎ (01283) 702327
11–3, 6–11
Ind Coope Burton Ale; Marston's Pedigree; Tetley Bitter; guest beers Ⓗ
Intimate pub set back from the road, between the Trent and Mersey Canal and the railway; popular with diners.
❀ ◗ ◗ ≉ P

Woolley Moor

White Horse Inn
Off B6014 ☎ (01246) 590319
11–2.30 (3 Sat), 6.30 (6 Sat)–11
Draught Bass; guest beers Ⓗ
Pub almost legendary for its ale and food, set in excellent walking country with views of the Derbyshire hills. Inventive menu (no food Sun eve).
Q ❀ ◗ ◗ ▲ ◠ P

Youlgreave

Bull's Head Hotel
Fountain Square, Church Street ☎ (01629) 636307
11–3, 6.30–11
Marston's Bitter, Pedigree Ⓗ
Welcoming pub in a picturesque Peak District village. Marston's Head Brewer's Choice. Varied menu.
Q 🛏 ❀ 🛏 ◗ ◗ 🛏 ▲ ♣ P

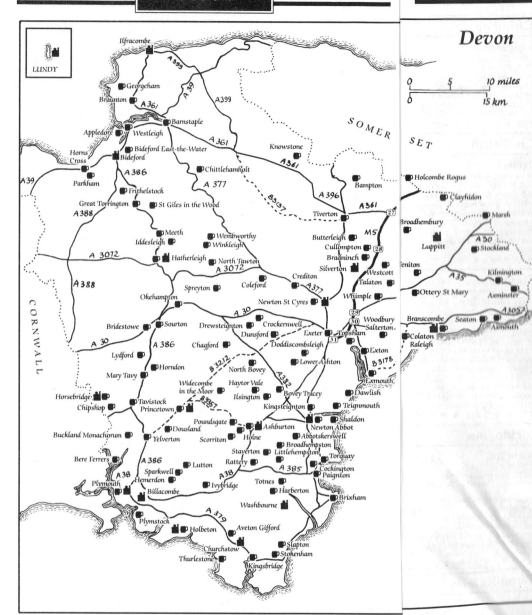

SOMER SET

CORNWALL

LUNDY

Devon

0 — 5 — 10 miles
0 — 15 km

Appledore

Champion of Wales
Meeting Street
☎ (01237) 424500
11–11
Oakhill Best Bitter, Yeoman Ⓗ
Convivial back-street local in an attractive fishing village; frequented by fishermen and named after a 17th-century boat. 🏚 ⅙ &

Royal George
Irsha Street ☎ (01237) 474335
11–3, 6–11
Draught Bass; guest beer Ⓗ
Well-preserved, 17th-century pub in a magnificent position overlooking the Taw and Torridge estuary. Fine reputation for food, especially fish. Q ⅙ 🏚 ◗ ▸ &

Ashburton

London Inn
11 West Street
☎ (01364) 652478
11–2.30 (3 Sat), 5.30–11
Thompson's Best Bitter, IPA, Man of War, Figurehead Ⓗ
15th-century coaching inn, home of Thompson's Brewery for 14 years and in the *Guide* consecutively for 15. Large restaurant. Not all Thompson's beers may be available.
🏚 ⅙ 🏚 ◗ ▸ ♣ ⌂

Aveton Gifford

Taverners
Fore Street ☎ (01548) 550316
12–3 (5 Thu & Fri), 7–11; 12–11 Sat
Courage Best Bitter; Ushers Best Bitter, Founders Ⓗ
Friendly village pub, popular with the locals for its games and skittle alley. The walled garden features a fountain, aviary and pets corner. Note the unusual handpumps. Ushers seasonal beers stocked.
🏚 ⅙ 🏚 ◗ ♣

Axminster

Axminster Inn
Silver Street ☎ (01297) 34947
11–11
Palmers BB, IPA, Tally Ho!, 200 (occasional) Ⓗ
Basic drinkers' pub in the town. 🏚 ⅙ 🏚 ⟷ ♣ ⌂

Axmouth

Ship Inn
☎ (01297) 21838
11–2 (2.30 Sat), 6–11
Devenish Royal Wessex; Whitbread Flowers IPA Ⓗ

Well-known pub serving excellent food in a large dining area. Convalescing owls make unusual drinking companions. Cider available, and family room open, in summer. 🏚 Q
⅙ 🏚 ◗ 🏚 & ▲ ♣ ⌂ P

Bampton

Exeter Inn
Tiverton Road
☎ (01398) 331345
11–2.30, 6–11
Draught Bass; Drinklink Parson's Nose; Exmoor Ale; guest beers Ⓗ
Friendly pub with a good local atmosphere. Cider in summer.
🏚 Q ⅙ 🏚 🏚 ◗ ▸ ♣
⌂ P 🏚

Barnstaple

Corner House
108 Boutport Street
☎ (01271) 43528
11–2.30, 6–11
Draught Bass Ⓗ/Ⓖ**; guest beer** Ⓗ
Genuine town alehouse, with an unspoilt interior. Convivial conversational atmosphere.
Q ⅙

Rolle Quay
Rolle's Quay ☎ (01271) 45182
11–11
Cotleigh Barn Owl, Old Buzzard Ⓗ/Ⓖ**; Ushers Best Bitter; guest beers** Ⓗ
Welcoming, town-centre pub known for its range of real ales (76 different ones in 1994) and extensive, well-priced food menu. Summer beer festival.
Q ⅙ 🏚 ◗ 🏚 & ▲ ♣ ⌂

Bere Ferrers

Old Plough
☎ (01822) 840358
12–3, 7–11
Draught Bass Ⓖ**; Whitbread Boddingtons Bitter, Flowers IPA** Ⓗ**; guest beers** Ⓖ
16th-century village inn, by the River Tavy in an area of outstanding beauty. Cider in summer. 🏚 🏚 ◗ ▸ ⟷ ☀

Bideford East-the-Water

Ship on Launch
14 Barnstaple Street
☎ (01237) 472426
11–11
Beer choice varies Ⓗ
Pub with an unspoilt [interior] featuring old ships' [...] legacy of Bideford's [...] past. Frequented by [...] drinking locals. Ha[...] cyclists and walker[s...] Tarka Trail. One b[...]
🏚 ⅙ Q 🏚 ◗ ▸ &

Abbotskerswell

Two Mile Oak
On A381 ☎ (01803) 812411
11–2.30, 5–11; 11–11 Sat & summer
Draught Bass Ⓖ**; Whitbread Flowers IPA; guest beers** Ⓗ
15th-century coaching house, with two bars and a restaurant. The lounge has ales. Can get busy in summer.
🏚 🏚 ◗ ▸ ▲ ♣ P

Coleford

New Inn

☎ (01363) 84242
11.30–2.30, 6–11
Hall & Woodhouse Badger BB; Otter Ale; Wadworth 6X ⊞
Large, well-appointed pub/restaurant with one bar. This 13th-century, Grade II-listed building has a splendid thatched roof. Though rather expensive it is still worth a visit.
🏚 Q ❀ 🛏 ◖ ▶ ♣ P

Crediton

Crediton Inn

28a Mill Street
☎ (01363) 772882
11–11
Draught Bass; guest beers ⊞
Friendly local with a good atmosphere. ◖ ▶ ⇌ ♣ P

Crockernwell

Crow's Nest

On old A30 ☎ (01647) 281267
11–11
Bass Worthington BB, Draught Bass; Greene King Abbot ⊞
Modern(ish) pub boasting splendid views over northern Dartmoor. Good quality, basic food, at reasonable prices, is served all day.
🏚 Q ❀ ◖ ▶ 🍺 ▲ ♣ ⌂ P

Cullompton

White Hart

19 Fore Street ☎ (01884) 33260
11–11 (may vary)
Courage Best Bitter, Directors; John Smith's Bitter ⊞
Modernised town-centre pub serving good value food.
🏚 🛏 ◖ ▶ & P

Dawlish

Marine Tavern

Marine Parade
☎ (01626) 865245
11–11
Draught Bass; Dartmoor Best Bitter; guest beers (summer) ⊞
Modern smart, seafront hotel/pub. ⛵ ❀ 🛏 ◖ ▶ ⇌

Doddiscombsleigh

Nobody Inn

☎ (01647) 252394
12–2.30, 7 (6 summer)–11
Draught Bass; guest beer Ⓖ
16th-century inn with many original features, Grade II-listed. Renowned for its food and immense range of whiskies (240) and wines (700), it was also the winner of a *Cheese Pub of 1994* award. The house beer comes from Branscombe Vale. No-smoking area lunchtime.
🏚 Q ❀ 🛏 ◖ ▶ ⌂ ⌀

Dousland

Burrator Inn

☎ (01822) 853121
11–11
Draught Bass; Wadworth 6X; Whitbread Flowers Original; guest beers ⊞
Victorian country inn, near Burrator Reservoir in Dartmoor National Park; ideally situated for walking the moors. Large restaurant.
🏚 ⛵ ❀ 🛏 ◖ ▶ & ♣ P

Drewsteignton

Drewe Arms

The Square ☎ (01647) 21224
11–3, 6–11; 11–11 Sat (varies in summer)
Whitbread Flowers IPA Ⓖ
Traditional, thatched, village pub, untouched for about a century; home of 'Aunt Mabel' Mudge, Britain's oldest and longest serving licensee until her recent retirement. The pub is now run by villagers who propose to buy it.
🏚 Q ❀ 🛏 ◖ ▶ ▲ ♣ ⌂

Dunsford

Royal Oak

☎ (01647) 252256
11.30 (12 Mon)–2.30 (3 Fri & Sat), 6.30 (7 Mon, 6 Fri & Sat)–11
Draught Bass; Brains Bitter; Morland Old Speckled Hen; guest beers ⊞
Popular local in a small village with a well-decorated Victorian interior. Beer festivals in March and Nov.
🏚 Q ❀ 🛏 ◖ ▶ ▲ ⌂ P

Exeter

Brook Green

Well Street (near football ground) ☎ (01392) 496370
12–2 (11–3 Sat), 6–11
Otter Ale; guest beers ⊞
Comfortable, back-street pub. Note: the Whitbread beers and Whitbread supplied guests are kept under nitrogen. ◖ ⊟ ⇌ (St James's Park) ♣ P

Cowick Barton

Cowick Lane, St Thomas
☎ (01392) 70411
11–2.30, 6.30–11
Draught Bass; Courage Best Bitter; Ruddles County; guest beer ⊞
Friendly, cosy, 'country pub in the city'. Courage Directors is sold as Old Priory Ale. Good choice of country wines.
❀ ◖ ▶ ⊟ P

Double Locks Hotel

Canal Banks, Marsh Barton (follow lane next to incinerator over canal) ☎ (01392) 56947
11–11
Adnams Broadside Ⓖ; **Everards Old Original** ⊞; **Smiles Bitter, Best Bitter, Exhibition; guest beers** Ⓖ
Recently acquired by Smiles brewery, this pub has lost some of its former charm but is still all-round good value. Varied menu at reasonable prices; frequent live music. The public bar is open in summer. Wheelchair WC.
🏚 ❀ ◖ ▶ ⊟ & ▲ ♣ ⌂ P

Exeter & Devon Arts Centre

Bradninch Place
☎ (01392) 219741
11–11; closed Sun
Branscombe Vale Branoc; Dartmoor Legend; Wadworth 6X ⊞
Pleasant, friendly bar popular with all ages. Events are held most lunchtimes and eves. Eve meals finish at 7.
◖ ▶ & ⇌ (Central) ⌀

Great Western Hotel

St David's Station Approach
☎ (01392) 74039
11–11
Draught Bass; Stones Best Bitter; guest beers ⊞
Friendly, two-bar hotel with a pub atmosphere and a railway theme. 🛏 ◖ ▶ ⊟ ⇌ (St David's) P

Hour Glass

Melbourne Street, St Leonards
☎ (01392) 58722
12–11
Brains Bitter; Greene King Abbot; Wadworth 6X ⊞
Cosy, friendly pub above the quay with a nautical theme. Good bottled beer selection.
❀ ◖ ▶ ⊟ ⇌ (St Thomas)

Jolly Porter

St David's Hill
☎ (01392) 54848
11–11
Courage Best Bitter, Directors; John Smith's Bitter; guest beers ⊞
Popular, friendly pub close to the university and St David's station. Jazz Wed eve. Good value food. ◖ ▶ ⇌ (St David's) ♣

Mill-on-the-Exe

Bonhay Road
☎ (01392) 214464
11–11

Devon

St Austell XXXX Mild, Tinners, HSD H
Smart riverside pub, recently acquired by St Austell Brewery. The only permanent mild outlet in Exeter.
🌐 ◖ ▶ ᕕ ≠ (St David's) P

Well House
Cathedral Yard
☎ (01392) 58464
11–11; 7–10.30 Sun, closed Sun lunch
Draught Bass; guest beers H
Popular pub on the cathedral close with a Roman cellar. Five guest beers usually include several local small-brewery beers. ᕙ ◖ ≠ (Central)

Exmouth

Country House Inn
176 Withycombe Village Road
☎ (01395) 263444
10.30–2.30, 5–11
Devenish Royal Wessex; Whitbread Boddingtons Bitter, Castle Eden Ale, Flowers Original H
One-time blacksmith's shop now a village-style local with an aviary in the garden. Barbecues by a stream in the summer. Good, home-made food (booking advised). Eve meals Fri and Sat; no food Sun. 🌐 ◖ ▶ ᕕ ♣ ᗡ

Grove
Esplanade ☎ (01395) 272101
11–3, 5.30–11 (varies in summer)
Brakspear Special; Branscombe Vale Branoc; Greene King Abbot; Whitbread Boddingtons Bitter, Flowers Original; guest beers H
Friendly seafront pub with a timbered traditional bar. Good, home-cooked food. 'Beer Nights' on the last Sat of the month, Sept–May. Live music Fri. ᗷ 🌐 ◖ ▶ ᕕ P

Exton

Puffing Billy
Station Road ☎ (01392) 873152
12–3, 6–11
Draught Bass; Branscombe Vale Branoc H
16th-century pub with two bars. The menu specialises in fish dishes. Branoc is replaced by a house beer from Branscombe in summer.
ᕙ 🌐 ◖ ▶ ᕗ ᕕ ♣ P

Feniton

Nog Inn
Ottery Road (opp. station)
☎ (01404) 850210
11–3, 6–11
Cotleigh Tawny; guest beers H
Lively village local with a

---

friendly atmosphere and a good range of mostly local beers. Ratcatcher Ale is brewed by Branscombe Vale. The pub has a squash court.
ᕙ ᗷ 🌐 ᕗ ≠ ♣ P

Frithelstock

Clinton Arms
☎ (01805) 623279
12–2.30, 5.30–11
Draught Bass; guest beer H
Village pub on a green with mature oaks. Note the monastic priory ruins opposite. Fascinating menu.
Q ᗷ 🌐 ◖ ▶ ᕕ ♣ P

Georgeham

King's Arms
Chapel Street
☎ (01271) 890240
12 (12.30 winter)–3.30, 6–11 (midnight Fri & Sat)
Draught Bass; Fuller's Chiswick H; **Marston's Pedigree; guest beers** G
Lovely village pub, with friendly locals. Occasional live jazz weekend eves.
ᕙ 🌐 ◖ ▶ ᗷ ♣ ᗡ

Rock
Rock Hill ☎ (01271) 890322
11–2.30, 6–11; 11–11 Sat
Marston's Pedigree; St Austell HSD; Tetley Bitter; Ushers Best Bitter; Wadworth 6X; guest beers H
An absolute gem, with eight real ales always available plus cider in summer: a charming, 16th-century inn with a friendly atmosphere. Local CAMRA *Pub of the Year* 1994 and 95.
ᕙ ᗷ 🌐 ᕗ ◖ ▶ ᕕ ♣ ᗡ P

Great Torrington

Black Horse Inn
The Square ☎ (01805) 622121
11–3, 6–11
Courage Directors; John Smith's Bitter; Ushers Best Bitter; Wadworth 6X; guest beers H
14th-century, half-timbered coaching inn, used as HQ by General Fairfax in the Civil War. A friendly pub with well-prepared food (not served Sun eve).
ᕙ ᗷ ᕗ ◖ ▶ ♣

Hunters Inn
Well Street ☎ (01805) 623832
11–11
Wadworth 6X; Whitbread Flowers Original H
18th-century, olde-worlde, one-bar pub with a function room. Popular with the younger set. Limited parking.
ᕙ ᕗ ◖ ♣ ᗡ P

New Market Inn
South Street ☎ (01805) 622289
11–11
Whitbread Boddingtons Bitter, Fuggles IPA; guest beers H
Recently refurbished old pub with a dining area. Live music at weekends.
ᕙ 🌐 ᕗ ◖ ▶ ♣ P

Torridge Inn
Mill Street ☎ (01805) 623654
11–11
Adnams Broadside; Draught Bass E; **Whitbread Flowers IPA, Castle Eden Ale** H
Built in 1650, this thatched inn near the bank of the River Torridge has one comfortable, friendly bar. Occasional live folk music. Easy access to the commons and the Tarka Trail.
ᗷ 🌐 ◖ ▶ ᗷ ♣

Harberton

Church House Inn
☎ (01803) 863707
12–3, 6–11
Draught Bass; Courage Best Bitter; guest beers H
Beautiful, 12th-century pub with a friendly atmosphere: a long, one-roomed bar with a small family room hidden behind a medieval oak screen. The guest beers change daily.
ᕙ Q ᕘ 🌐 ◖ ▶ ᗷ ♣ ᗡ P

Hatherleigh

Tally Ho
14 Market Street (A386)
☎ (01837) 810306
11–3, 6–11
Tally Ho Potboiler's Brew, Tarka's Tipple, Nutters, Thurgia, Janni Jollop H
Not-to-be-missed brew pub with a great atmosphere and good food.
ᕙ Q 🌐 ᕗ ◖ ▶ ♣

Haytor Vale

Rock Inn
☎ (01364) 661305
11–3, 6.30–11
Draught Bass; Dartmoor Best Bitter; Eldridge Pope Hardy Country, Royal Oak H
200-year-old village inn serving excellent food in a pleasant atmosphere.
ᕙ Q ᗷ 🌐 ᕗ ◖ ▶ ᕕ ᗷ P ⌧

Hemerdon

Miners Arms
On Plympton–Cornwood road
☎ (01752) 343232
11.30–2.30 (3 Sat), 5.30–11
Draught Bass; guest beers G/H
Former tin miners' pub on a

hill overlooking Plympton. Good facilities for children.
🏰 Q 🐴 ❀ ◐ ♿ ♣ P

Holbeton

Dartmoor Union
Fore Street ☎ (01752) 830288
11.30–3, 6–11
Summerskills Best Bitter; Wadworth 6X H
Homely, well-laid-out pub offering a good varied menu.
🏰 🐴 ❀ ◐ ◑ ♿ ⛀ P 🚂

Mildmay Colours
Off A379 ☎ (01752) 830248
11–3, 6–11
Mildmay Colours Best, SP, 50/1, Old Horse Whip G/H; **guest beers** H
Picturesque old manor house with a brewery at the rear. The public bar is entirely gravity-fed.
🏰 Q ❀ 🛏 ◐ ◑ ⊟ ♣ ⛀ P

Holcombe Rogus

Prince of Wales
☎ (01823) 672070
11.30–3 (not Tue), 6.30–11
Cotleigh Tawny, Old Buzzard; Otter Bitter; Wadworth 6X; guest beers H
Pleasant country pub with cash register handpumps. The restaurant serves excellent food. Beer festivals every bank hol. Cider in summer.
🏰 Q 🐴 ❀ ◐ ◑ ♿ ▲ ♣ ⛀ P

Holne

Church House Inn
3½ miles from Buckfast
☎ (01364) 631208
12–2.30, 7–10.30 (11 Fri & Sat) (11.30–3, 6.30–11 summer)
Blackawton Bitter; Dartmoor Best Bitter; Morland Old Speckled Hen; Palmers IPA; Wadworth 6X H
Traditional, 14th-century village inn in Dartmoor National Park. No background music or games machines. Good food, using fresh local produce, served daily (restaurant bookings advisable). Bar skittles. 🏰 Q 🐴 ❀ 🛏 ◐ ◑ ⊟ ▲ ⛀ P

Horndon

Elephant's Nest
Off A386, 1½ miles E of Mary Tavy ☎ (01822) 810273
11.30–2.30, 6.30–11; 12–2.30, 7–10.30 Sun
Exmoor Gold; Palmers IPA; St Austell HSD; Whitbread Boddingtons Bitter; guest beer H
Picturesque, 16th-century moorland pub with a relaxed atmosphere. The bar food is good value and varied.
🏰 Q 🐴 ❀ ◐ ◑ ♿ ⛀ P

Horns Cross

Hoops Inn
On A39 ☎ (01237) 451222
11–11
Butcombe Bitter; Marston's Pedigree; guest beers H
Thatched coaching inn of character with log fires. It stages occasional beer festivals, plus folk and jazz eves. Close to the North Devon Coast Path.
🏰 Q 🐴 ❀ 🛏 ◐ ◑ ♣ P

Horsebridge

Royal Inn
☎ (01822) 870214
12–2.30, 7–11; 12–2.30, 7–10.30 Sun
Draught Bass; Royal Inn, Tamar, Horsebridge Best, Right Royal, Heller; Sharp's Own H
15th-century country pub and brewery, once a nunnery. No food Sun eve.
🏰 Q ❀ ◐ ◑ ⊟ ♿ ♣ P

Iddesleigh

Duke of York
On B3217 ☎ (01837) 810253
11.30–3 (not Mon–Wed), 6.30–11 (11.30–11 summer)
Adnams Extra; Cotleigh Tawny G
Totally unspoilt, 15th-century village inn with a rocking chair by the log fire. Ideal for walkers on the Tarka Trail. Good views of Dartmoor.
🏰 Q ❀ 🛏 ◐ ◑ ▲

Ilsington

Carpenter's Arms
☎ (01364) 661215
11–2.30, 6–11
Whitbread Flowers IPA G
Farmers' and villagers' local, run at a leisurely pace in a small village on the edge of Dartmoor. 🏰 Q ❀ ◐ ◑ ⛀

Ivybridge

Imperial
28 Western Road (off A38)
☎ (01752) 892269
11–11
Courage Best Bitter; Ruddles County; Wadworth 6X; guest beer H
Old-fashioned pub with a homely, parlour feel. Noted for its food (formidable mixed grill). Cider in summer.
🏰 🐴 ❀ ◐ ◑ ♿ ♣ ⛀ P

Kilmington

New Inn
The Hill ☎ (01297) 33376
10.30–3, 6–11 (11–11 summer)
Palmers BB, IPA E
Traditional country pub in every edition of the *Guide*. The most westerly Palmers tied house. 🏰 🐴 ❀ ◐ ◑ ⊟ ▲ P

Kingsbridge

Ship & Plough
The Quay ☎ (01548) 852485
11–11
Blewitts Nose, Best, Head Off; guest beer H
Splendid, oak-beamed pub with friendly locals; the former Blewitts brew pub, now relegated to a brewery tap. Other Blewitts brews may replace the regulars. No food Sun eve, otherwise great value meals. 🐴 ❀ ◐ ◑

Kingsteignton

Old Rydon
Rydon Lane ☎ (01626) 54626
11–2.30, 6–11; 12–2.30, 7–10.30 Sun
Draught Bass; Wadworth 6X; guest beer H
Very old, friendly pub/restaurant with a conservatory. Excellent food.
🏰 Q ❀ ◐ ◑ P

Knowstone

Mason's Arms
Off A361 ☎ (01398) 341231
11–3, 5.30–11
Cotleigh Tawny; Hall & Woodhouse Badger BB H
Classic, traditional, Devonshire pub: a thatched inn dating from the 13th century. 🏰 Q 🐴 ◐ ◑

Littlehempston

Tally Ho! Inn
☎ (01803) 862316
12–2.30, 6–11
Dartmoor Best Bitter; Teignworthy Reel Ale; Wadworth 6X H
14th-century house, beside the main railway line in an otherwise peaceful village. Curios cover the natural stonework. Most tables are for diners. 🏰 Q ❀ ◐ ◑ ♿ P

Lower Ashton

Manor Inn
Just off B3193, over bridge
☎ (01647) 252304
12–2.30, 6 (7 Sat)–11; 12–2.30, 7–10.30 Sun; closed Mon
Draught Bass; S&N Theakston XB; Teignworthy Reel Ale H; **Wadworth 6X** G; **guest beer** H
CAMRA SW *Pub of the Year* 1993, renowned for its real fires, real food and real ale. A

Devon

late Victorian, two-bar country pub, small but welcoming, in a quiet stretch of the Teign Valley. Beer mats display guest beers to date (over 600).
🏃 Q ⊛ ◖ ▶ 🍴 ▲ ♣ ☍ P

Lutton

Mountain Inn
Off A38 at Plympton
☎ (01752) 837247
11–3, 7 (6.30 June–Oct)–11
Dartmoor Best Bitter, Legend; Wadworth 6X; guest beers Ⓗ
Exposed cob walls and a large fireplace make this a pub worth visiting. Families are very welcome (high chair provided). Cider in summer.
🏃 Q ⛾ ⊛ ◖ ▲ ♣ ☍ P

Lydford

Castle Inn
☎ (01822) 82242
11.30–3, 6–11
Dartmoor Best Bitter Ⓗ; **Palmers IPA; Wadworth 6X; guest beers** Ⓖ
Cosy, 16th-century inn, next to the castle, featuring low ceilings, slate floors, large stone fireplaces and curios.
🏃 Q ⛾ ⊛ 🛏 ◖ ▶ 🛆 ♣ P

Mucky Duck
In Lydford Gorge
☎ (01822) 82208
12 (11 Sat & summer)–11; closed Mon lunch in winter
Draught Bass; Smiles Bitter; guest beers Ⓗ
Accommodating inn, with slate floors, exposed stone walls and two large family rooms. Live music Wed and Sun nights. Cider in summer.
🏃 Q ⛾ ⊛ 🛏 ◖ ▲ ♣ ☍ P

Marsh

Flintlock Inn
Off A303 ☎ (01460) 234403
11–2.30, 6.30–11
Dartmoor Best Bitter; Fuller's London Pride; guest beer Ⓗ
17th-century inn with rustic ceiling timbers and exposed stonework. The inglenook features a baker's oven.
🏃 ◖ ▶ 🛆 A P ⅄

Mary Tavy

Mary Tavy Inn
Lane Head (A386)
☎ (01822) 810326
11.30 (11 summer)–3, 6–11
Draught Bass; St Austell XXXX Mild, HSD; guest beers Ⓗ
Welcoming 16th-century inn on the western edge of Dartmoor, with good value food and accommodation.
🏃 Q ⛾ ⊛ 🛏 ◖ ▶ ▲ ♣ P

Meeth

Bull & Dragon
On A386 ☎ (01837) 810325
12–3 (not winter Mon), 7–11 (11–5, 6–11 summer)
Butcombe Bitter; Dartmoor Best Bitter; guest beer (occasional) Ⓗ
Welcoming 16th-century thatched village inn with a small bar. The main emphasis is on good food. Children are welcome in the games room (the Bull Pen). 🏃 ⊛ ◖ ▶ ♣ P

Newton Abbot

Dartmouth Inn
63 East Street (opp. hospital)
☎ (01626) 53451
11–11
Draught Bass; guest beers Ⓗ
Reported to be the oldest pub in the town, specialising in guest beers (over 1,100 tried so far, resulting in a vast pumpclip collection). CAMRA S Devon *Pub of the Year* 1992, 1994 and 1995. No food Sun.
🏃 Q ⛾ ⊛ ◖ ⇌ ♣ ☍

Newton St Cyres

Beer Engine
By station ☎ (01392) 851282
11.30–2.30, 6–11; 11–11 Sat & bank hols
Beer Engine Rail Ale, Piston Bitter, Sleeper Heavy Ⓗ
Friendly and popular brew pub on the Barnstaple railway line. The downstairs bar is open at weekends (with live music) and the brewery can be viewed from there.
🏃 Q ⊛ ◖ ▶ ▲ ⇌ P

North Bovey

Ring of Bells
☎ (01647) 40375
11–3, 6–11 (11–11 summer)
Dartmoor Best Bitter; Ind Coope Burton Ale; Wadworth 6X; guest beer (summer) Ⓗ
Rambling, low-beamed, 13th-century, thatched pub in an attractive Dartmoor village. Good food.
🏃 Q ⛾ ⊛ 🛏 ◖ ▶ ☍

North Tawton

Railway Inn
Whiddon Down Road
☎ (01837) 52789
12–2, 6–11
Wadworth 6X; guest beers Ⓗ
Free house next to a disused railway station: a locals' pub where meals include daily specials. Old railway photographs decorate the walls. 🏃 Q ⛾ ⊛ 🛏 ◖ ▶ 🛆 ▲ ♣ ☍ P

Okehampton

Plymouth Inn
26 West Street ☎ (01837) 53633
11–2.30, 7–11; 11–11 Sat
Marston's Pedigree; guest beers Ⓖ
Old coaching inn with a cosy bar, and a good restaurant.
Q ⛾ ⊛ ◖ ▶ 🛆 ♣

Ottery St Mary

King's Arms
Gold Street ☎ (01404) 812486
10.30–2.30, 5.30–11; 10.30–11 Sat
Branscombe Vale Olde Stoker; Morland Old Speckled Hen; Shepherd Neame Spitfire; John Smith's Bitter; Wadworth 6X Ⓗ
Busy town local, popular with young and old. Eve meals at weekends. Oversized glasses used for John Smith's.
⛾ 🛏 ◖ ▶ 🛆 ♣ ☍ P ⅄ 🍴

Paignton

Devonport Arms
42 Elmbank Road (near zoo)
☎ (01803) 558322
11–11
Courage Best Bitter; Morland Old Speckled Hen; John Smith's Bitter Ⓗ; **guest beers** Ⓗ/Ⓖ
Back-street local, well worth finding, with friendly locals.
🏃 Q ⛾ ⊛ ◖ ▲ ♣

Polsham Arms
35 Lower Polsham Road
☎ (01803) 558360
11–11
Gale's HSB; Wadworth 6X; Whitbread Boddingtons Bitter; guest beers Ⓗ
Two-bar pub, featuring pool, skittles and music in one bar, with a quieter lounge bar. Up to ten guest ales; mini-festivals throughout the year. Bikers welcome. Eve meals finish at 6.
Q ⊛ ◖ ▶ ⇌ ♣ P

Parkham

Bell Inn
☎ (01237) 451201
12–3, 6.30–11
Draught Bass Ⓖ; **Whitbread Flowers IPA** Ⓗ; **guest beer**
13th-century thatched cottages, internally modernised. Good food and atmosphere make this a pub not to miss. ⊛ ◖ ▶ ♣ P

Plymouth

Brasserie
Ocean Quay, Richmond Walk, Devonport ☎ (01752) 500008

Devon

11–3, 5.30 (7 Nov–Mar)–11 (11–11 June–Aug)
Summerskills Best Bitter H
Pub in the Mayflower Marina, where visitors' moorings are available. Wide range of high quality food from a light snack to full à la carte dining (seafood a speciality). Families welcome. ✿ ◖ ▶ ♿ P

Clifton Hotel

35 Clifton Street, Greenbank
☎ (01752) 266563
5 (11.30 Fri)–11; 11.30–3, 7–11 Sat
Draught Bass H; **Greene King Abbot; Ind Coope Burton Ale; Summerskills Indiana's Bones** G; **Whitbread Boddingtons Bitter** H; **guest beers**
Warm, friendly pub fielding numerous teams. The guest beers are unusual for Plymouth. Summerskills house beer. ♿ ⚏ ♣

Dolphin Hotel

14 The Barbican
☎ (01752) 660876
10–11
Draught Bass; M&B Highgate Dark; guest beers H
The only pub on the Barbican untouched by brewery developers, opposite the old fish market. The Tolpuddle Martyrs stayed here on their return to the UK. The only gravity dispense in the area.
🏚 Q ♣

Fareham

6 Commercial Road, Coxside
☎ (01752) 260433
11–11
St Austell HSD; Summerskills Best Bitter H
Small, cosy pub near Queen Anne's Battery Marina. A big welcome for all. ◖ ♿ ♣

King's Head

21 Bretonside (by main bus station) ☎ (01752) 665619
11–11
Courage Directors; King's Head BSB; Marston's Pedigree; Morland Old Speckled Hen; Wadworth 6X; guest beers H
Plymouth's oldest pub and brew pub, close to the historic Barbican. Student-oriented, it has traditional gas lighting. Ask for a brewery tour – no charge. ✿ ◖ ♿

Kitty O'Hanlons

5 St Andrew's Street
☎ (01752) 661624
10 (11 Sat)–11
Bass Worthington BB, Draught Bass; Whitbread Boddingtons Bitter H
Irish theme pub, formerly known as the Abbey, in the city centre. ◖

Notte Inn

Notte Street (near Barbican)
☎ (01752) 254883
11–11; 11–3, 5–11 Mon; 7–10.30 Sun, closed Sun lunch
Draught Bass; Morland Old Speckled Hen; Wadworth 6X; Whitbread Boddingtons Bitter; guest beer H
Pub offering a friendly atmosphere and good food cooked to order (real chips and generous portions). Over 20 malt whiskies. Q ◖ ▶

Prince Maurice

3 Church Hill, Eggbuckland
☎ (01752) 771515
11–3, 7 (6 Fri)–11; 11–11 Sat
Draught Bass; Eldridge Pope Royal Oak; Hall & Woodhouse Tanglefoot; Summerskills Best Bitter, Indiana's Bones; guest beers H
Plymouth CAMRA *Pub of the Year* 1994/95: a small, two-bar house near a 16th-century church. Ten regular beers.
🏚 ✿ ⊞ ♣ P ☖

Royal Albert Bridge Inn

930 Wolseley Rd, St Budeaux
☎ (01752) 361108
11–11
Draught Bass; Courage Best Bitter H
Friendly, riverside local in the shadow of Brunel's bridge, with picturesque views across the River Tamar to Cornwall.
✿ ◖ ▶ ⊞ ♣

Shipwright's Arms

13 Sutton Road, Coxside
☎ (01752) 665804
11–3, 6 (5.30 Fri)–11
Courage Best Bitter, Directors H
Cosy, compact, one-room pub with many loyal regulars. No food Sun. 🏚 ✿ ◖ ♿ ♣ P

Plymstock

Boringdon Arms

13 Boringdon Terrace, Turnchapel ☎ (01752) 402053
11–11
Draught Bass; Butcombe Bitter; Summerskills Best Bitter; Whitbread Boddingtons Bitter; guest beers H
Welcoming village local, offering eight beers; frequent beer festivals with 12 more. Good value food and B&B.
🏚 ☗ ✿ ⌂ ◖ ♣ ☖

New Inn

Boringdon Road, Turnchapel
☎ (01752) 402765
11–11
Draught Bass; Marston's Pedigree; Whitbread

Boddingtons Bitter; guest beers H
Recently refurbished village local with a very welcoming atmosphere. 🏚 ◖ ♣

Poundsgate

Tavistock Inn

☎ (01364) 631251
11–2.30, 6–11
Courage Best Bitter; Ushers Best Bitter, Founders H
700-year-old, unspoilt pub in a small Dartmoor village, with a cosy front bar. Very popular in summer.
🏚 Q ☗ ✿ ◖ ▶ ☖ P

Princetown

Plume of Feathers

Two Bridges Road
☎ (01822) 890240
11–11
Draught Bass; St Austell HSD; guest beers H
Princetown's oldest building, with slate floors, exposed beams and granite walls. Used by walkers (campsite and hostel accommodation).
🏚 ☗ ✿ ⌂ ◖ ♿ ▲ ☖ P

Rattery

Church House Inn

☎ (01364) 642220
11–2.30, 6–11
Dartmoor Best Bitter, Legend; guest beers H
One of England's most historic inns, dating from 1028. A large fireplace and a grandfather clock enhance the bar area. Good range of home-cooked food. 🏚 Q ✿ ◖ ▶ ▲ P

St Giles in the Wood

Cranford Inn

Cranford (B3227)
☎ (01805) 623309
11–2.30, 6–11
Draught Bass; Morland Old Speckled Hen; Tetley Bitter; guest beers H
Pub converted from old farm buildings. Popular for meals. Great atmosphere.
🏚 Q ✿ ⌂ ◖ ▶ P

Scorriton

Tradesman's Arms

OS704685 ☎ (01364) 631206
12–2, 7–11
Bass Worthington BB, Draught Bass; guest beers H
300-year-old pub built to serve the tin miners from the moor. A quiet, friendly pub with a good atmosphere. No meals Mon eve. 🏚 Q ☗ ✿ ⌂ ◖
▶ ▲ ♣ ☖ P ⊬

Devon

Seaton

Hook & Parrot

The Esplanade
☎ (01297) 20222
11–11
Draught Bass; Whitbread Flowers Original Ⓗ
Seafront pub with a terrace and a cellar bar (open eves). The former coffee bar area is being converted to a restaurant. Occasional guest beers are stocked in summer.
Q ✿ ◖ ▲ ♣

Shaldon

Clifford Arms

34 Fore Street
☎ (01626) 872311
11–2.30, 5–11; 11–11 Sat
Draught Bass; Palmers IPA; guest beers Ⓗ
Pub with a horseshoe-shaped bar with more room at the back; popular with locals in winter and visitors in summer. Cider in summer. Excellent menu. ➰ ✿ ◖ ▲ ᕙ

Slapton

Queen's Arms

☎ (01548) 580800
11.30–3, 6–11
Draught Bass; Exmoor Ale; Palmers IPA Ⓗ
14th-century pub in the centre of this South Hams village. The decor features items of local interest. The food menu offers a wide choice at reasonable prices.
➿ Q ✿ ◖ ▲ ♣ ᕙ P

Sourton

Bearslake Inn

On A386 ☎ (01837) 861334
12 (11.30 summer)–3, 7 (6.30 summer)–11
Dartmoor Best Bitter; Wadworth 6X Ⓗ
Quiet, traditional Devon inn: stone floors and walls with pictures of the old county.
Q ▤ ◖ ▶ P

Sparkwell

Treby Arms

Off A38 at Plympton (follow Cornwood road)
☎ (01752) 837363
11–3, 6.30–11
Draught Bass; M&B Brew XI; Wadworth 6X; guest beers Ⓗ
Pub dating from around 1750, next to Dartmoor Wildlife Park. Compact and cosy, it also has a restaurant.
➿ Q ✿ ◖ ▲ ♣ P 🍺

Spreyton

Tom Cobley Tavern

☎ (01847) 231314

12–2.30 (not Mon, except bank hols), 6 (7 Mon)–11
Cotleigh Tawny; Exe Valley Dob's Best Bitter; guest beers Ⓗ
Genuine village pub. The function room has a superb indoor barbecue. Parties can book it. All food is home-made, good, honest English fare (not served Mon). Good B&B. ➰ Q ✿ ▤ ◖ ▶ ♣ P

Staverton

Sea Trout Inn

☎ (01803) 762274
11–3, 6–11
Draught Bass Ⓖ**; Dartmoor Best Bitter; Wadworth 6X; guest beer** Ⓗ
Three 16th-century cottages have been converted into this beamed pub, named after a large fish caught by a landlord. Warm atmosphere.
➰ Q ✿ ▤ ◖ ▶ ♣
⇌ (summer only) ♣ ᕙ P

Stockland

King's Arms

☎ (01404) 881361
12–3, 6.30–11
Exmoor Ale; Hall & Woodhouse Badger BB; Ruddles County; John Smith's Bitter Ⓗ
17th-century coaching inn on the old Plymouth–London route. Popular with locals and tourists alike. No lunches Sun.
➰ ➿ ✿ ▤ ◖ ▶ 🛏 & ♣ P

Stokenham

Tradesman's Arms

N of A379 ☎ (01548) 580313
12–2.30, 6 (7 summer)–11 (closed Mon–Thu eves in winter)
Adnams Bitter; Draught Bass; guest beers Ⓗ
Elegant, 15th-century free house, nestling in the South Hams. It offers an interesting menu and an extensive selection of whiskies. The Madras curry on Sun lunch is a speciality. Cider and interesting guest beers in summer.
➰ Q ✿ ◖ ▶ & ▲ ᕙ P

Talaton

Talaton Inn

☎ (01404) 822214
12–2.30, 7–11
Otter Bitter; Wadworth 6X; guest beer Ⓗ
Popular village local offering a range of fresh, home-made food in both the bar and the 16th-century, beamed lounge. Skittle alley available for functions.
➰ ➿ ✿ ▤ ◖ ▶ ♣ P

Tavistock

Tavistock Inn

Brook Street ☎ (01822) 612661
11.30–3, 5.30–11; 11.30–11 Fri & Sat; 12.30–3, 7–10.30 Sun
Courage Best Bitter; Ushers Best Bitter, Founders Ⓗ
Friendly town local next to the former site of the Tavistock Brewery: a single bar with pool and dining areas. Ushers seasonal ales stocked. ➰ ◖ ▶

Teignmouth

Blue Anchor

Teign Street ☎ (01626) 772741
11–11
Adnams Broadside; Marston's Pedigree; S&N Theakston Old Peculier; Whitbread Boddingtons Bitter; guest beers Ⓗ
One-bar, quayside pub dominated by a pool table and a jukebox. Always seven real ales available. Breakfasts 9–2. No meals Mon or Sun.
➰ ✿ ◖ ▶ ⇌ ♣ ᕙ

Golden Lion

85 Bitton Park Road
☎ (01626) 776442
12–4, 6–11
Beer range varies Ⓗ
Two-bar free house, selling a constantly changing range of two or three ales, from national and local breweries.
✿ 🍺 ⇌ ♣ ᕙ P

Thurlestone

Village Inn

☎ (01548) 560382
11.30–2.30, 6–11
Draught Bass; Palmers IPA; Wadworth 6X; guest beer (summer) Ⓗ
Cosy village inn, featuring oak beams from the Spanish Armada fleet. The bar offers an extensive range of meals. Cider in summer.
Q ➿ ✿ ◖ ▶ & ᕙ P

Tiverton

Racehorse

Wellbrook Street
☎ (01884) 252606
11–11
Courage Directors; John Smith's Bitter; Ushers Best Bitter; Webster's Yorkshire Bitter Ⓗ
Popular local with a friendly atmosphere. A large function room-cum-skittle alley stands at the rear. The children's garden has play equipment and pets. Barbecues on summer Suns.
➰ ➿ ✿ ◖ & ♣ ᕙ P

White Horse
Gold Street ☎ (01884) 252022
11–11
Bass Worthington BB, Draught Bass Ⓗ
Small, friendly, town-centre pub serving good value food.
♘ ❀ ⌂ ◖ ♣

Topsham

Bridge Inn
Bridge Hill
☎ (01392) 873862
12–2, 6–10.30 (11 Fri & Sat); 12–2, 7–10.30 Sun
Adnams Broadside; Draught Bass; Branscombe Vale Branoc; Exe Valley Devon Glory; Robinson's Old Tom; Wadworth 6X Ⓖ
Well-known, 18th-century Grade II-listed pub, unchanged for many years, and in the same family for generations. Up to 12 ales.
♔ Q ❀ ⇌ P

Globe Hotel
34 Fore Street
☎ (01392) 873471
11–11
Bass Worthington BB, Draught Bass; Hancock's HB; Ushers Best Bitter Ⓗ
Family-run, 16th-century, coaching inn, Grade II-listed with many original beams intact. Excellent food. No meals Sun.
Q ♘ ⌂ ◖ ◗ ♿ ⇌ ♣ P

Torquay

Crown & Sceptre
2 Petitor Road, St Marychurch
☎ (01803) 328290
11–3, 5.30–11; 11–11 Sat
Courage Best Bitter, Directors; Marston's Pedigree; Morland Old Speckled Hen; Ruddles County; John Smith's Bitter; guest beer Ⓗ
200-year-old stone coaching inn. The ceiling is hung with chamber pots. No food Sun.
♔ Q ♘ ❀ ◖ ▣ ♿ ♣ P

Devon Dumpling
108 Shiphay Lane, Shiphay (near Torbay hospital)
☎ (01803) 613465
11–2.30 (3 Fri), 5.30–11; 11–11 Sat
Courage Best Bitter; Morland Old Speckled Hen; Ruddles County; John Smith's Bitter; Wadworth 6X Ⓗ
16th-century converted farmhouse, reputedly haunted. The family room is upstairs. Popular with locals.
♔ Q ♘ ❀ ◖ ◗ ♿ ▲ ♣ P

Wig & Pen
168–170 Union Street
☎ (01803) 213848
11–11
Courage Best Bitter, Directors; Morland Old Speckled Hen; John Smith's Bitter; guest beer Ⓗ
Busy, town-centre pub, popular with the business community lunchtimes and a younger clientele eves.
◖ ⇌ (Torre) ♣

Totnes

Kingsbridge Inn
9 Leechwell Street (near Leech Wells) ☎ (01803) 863324
11 (12 winter)–2.30, 5.30–11
Draught Bass; Courage Best Bitter; Dartmoor Best Bitter; S&N Theakston Old Peculier; guest beer Ⓗ
Friendly pub with a comfortable, lowlit bar, an eating area, many alcoves and a low ceiling. Car park eves only. Q ♘ ❀ ◖ ◗ ▲ ♣ ⊂ ⊘

Rumours
30 High Street
☎ (01803) 864632
10–11
Draught Bass; Dartmoor Best Bitter; guest beers Ⓗ
Bare-floorboarded, café-style pub with a continental atmosphere. No music makes this ideal for conversation. Open early for breakfast. Cider in summer. Q ◖ ◗ ▲ ⇌ ⊂

Wembworthy

Lymington Arms
Lama Cross (1 mile from A377, via Eggesford station)
☎ (01837) 83572
12–3, 6–11.30
Marston's Pedigree; Whitbread Boddingtons Bitter, Flowers IPA; guest beer Ⓗ
Old coaching inn, built by Lord Portsmouth for entertaining his friends.
♘ ❀ ⌂ ◖ ◗ ♣ ⊂ P

Westcott

Merry Harriers
On B3181 ☎ (01392) 881254
12–2.30, 7–11; 12–2, 7–10.30 Sun
Draught Bass Ⓗ
Friendly pub serving possibly the best Bass in the area. Good food in the restaurant and bar (not served Sun). Skittle alley.
♔ ❀ ◖ ◗ ♿ ♣ P

Westleigh

Westleigh Inn
Off B3233 ☎ (01271) 860867
11.30–2.30, 6–11
Ruddles County; Ushers Best Bitter; guest beer Ⓗ
Well run, by a landlord of 16 years' residence, this popular 15th-century pub lies in a picturesque village. Plenty to occupy children in summer.
♔ Q ❀ ◖ ◗ ♿ P

Whimple

New Fountain Inn
Church Road
☎ (01404) 822350
11–3, 6–11
Oakhill Best Bitter; Shepherd Neame Spitfire; guest beers Ⓗ
Village local popular with all ages, serving an interesting menu of home-made meals every day. Children welcome.
♔ ❀ ◖ ◗ ▣ ⇌ ♣ ⊂ P

Widecombe in the Moor

Rugglestone Inn
½mile S of village OS721766
☎ (01364) 621327
11.30–2.30 (11–3 Sat), 7 (6 summer)–11
Draught Bass; Butcombe Bitter Ⓖ
Unspoilt Dartmoor pub, popular with walkers.
♔ Q ❀ ◖ ◗ ♿ ♣ ⊂ P

Winkleigh

King's Arms
The Square ☎ (01837) 83384
11–3, 6–11 (11–11 summer)
Princetown Jail Ale, Best Bitter; Wadworth 6X Ⓗ
Old traditional alehouse featuring original beams and an interesting carved bar.
♔ Q ❀ ◖ ◗ ♣ ⊂

Woodbury Salterton

Diggers Rest
☎ (01395) 232375
11–2.30, 6.30–11
Draught Bass; Dartmoor Best Bitter; Tetley Bitter Ⓗ
14th-century, thatched pub, well known for its food. Beers are dispensed via unusual handpumps. Large games room at the rear. The family room is also the skittle alley.
♔ Q ❀ ◖ ◗ ▣ ▲ ♣ ⊂ P

Yelverton

Rock Inn
On Princetown road, near roundabout ☎ (01822) 852022
11–11
Draught Bass; Fuller's London Pride; St Austell HSD; Whitbread Boddingtons Bitter; guest beers Ⓗ
Pub which incorporates the oldest building in Yelverton, dating back to the 16th-century: three bars plus a family room with videos.
♔ ♘ ❀ ◖ ◗ ♣ P

Dorset

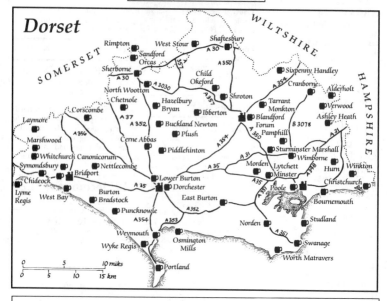

 Eldridge Pope, Goldfinch, Dorchester; **Hall & Woodhouse,** Blandford Forum; **Palmers,** Bridport; **Poole,** Poole

Alderholt

Churchill Arms
Daggons Road
☎ (01425) 652147
11–3, 6–11
Hall & Woodhouse Badger BB H
Convivial and comfortable village pub featuring a wood-panelled front bar with a pool room, plus a skittle alley.
🏠 ⛲ ❀ ◗ ▶ P

Ashley Heath

Struan Hotel
Horton Road (½ mile N of A31/A338)
☎ (01425) 473553
11–3, 6–11
Hall & Woodhouse Badger BB, Tanglefoot; Wells Eagle H
1920s manor house licensed in 1954. A friendly atmosphere prevails in the smart lounge bar and a jazz band plays every Thu eve. Wells Eagle is sold as Struan Bitter.
🏠 ❀ 🛏 ◗ ▶ P

Blandford Forum

Damory Oak
Damory Court Street (B3082)
☎ (01258) 452791
11–11
Hall & Woodhouse Badger BB H

Situated on the fringe of town, this Hall & Woodhouse pub has a friendly, comfortable two-roomed bar. 🏠 ❀ ❀ P

King's Arms
Whitecliff Mill Street
☎ (01258) 452163
11–11
Bass Worthington BB, Draught Bass; Ringwood Best Bitter H
Historic Georgian hotel, the starting place of the Great Fire of Blandford, and at that time a chandler's shop. It was also the site of the JL Marsh Brewery. Parking and eve meals for residents.
🏠 ❀ 🛏 ❀ ❀

Stour Inn
5 Dorchester Road, Blandford St Mary ☎ (01258) 451276
11–2.30 (3 Sat), 6–11
Hall & Woodhouse Badger BB H
Cosy, friendly, one-bar pub, set back from the road in an attractive row of terraced houses. Hall & Woodhouse Brewery is just around the corner. Q ❀ ◗ ❀

Bournemouth

Cottonwood Hotel
81 Grove Road
☎ (01202) 553183
11–3, 5–11

Draught Bass; Ringwood Best Bitter; guest beer (winter) H
Hotel bar, open to non-residents, on the East Clifftop with views across Poole Bay to the Purbeck Hills.
Q 🛒 ❀ 🛏 ◗ ▶ P 🍴

Dean Court Supporters' Club
King's Park
☎ (01202) 398313
11–3, 7–11
Bass Worthington BB; M&B Highgate Dark; Wadworth 6X; guest beer H
Large, two-roomed club adjoining AFC Bournemouth football ground, with an interesting guest beer list. Show this guide or CAMRA membership to be signed in (no admittance on matchdays to non-club members).
♿ ❀ P

Moon in the Square
4–8 Exeter Road
☎ (01202) 314940
10.30–11
Courage Directors; S&N Theakston Best Bitter, XB; Wadworth 6X; guest beers H
Superb, comfortable, Wetherspoon pub on two levels (no-smoking upstairs), offering a fine range of ales and good value food. Only half a mile from the beach, but amongst the big stores.
Q ◗ ▶ 🚭 🍴

94

Porterhouse

113 Poole Road, Westbourne
☎ (01202) 768586
11–11
**Ringwood Best Bitter, XXXX
Porter, Fortyniner, Old
Thumper; guest beers** H
E Dorset CAMRA *Pub of the
Year* 1994; the best example of
a proper pub in Bournemouth,
with reasonable prices. ◗ ◗

Punch & Judy

31 Poole Hill ☎ (01202) 290016
11–3, 5–11
**Marston's Bitter, Pedigree,
Owd Rodger** H
Pub close to the town centre
and popular with all ages.
Good value food. ◗ ₲

Bridport

George Hotel

South Street ☎ (01308) 423187
11–11; 11–3, 7–11 Sun
**Palmers BB, IPA, Tally Ho!,
200** H
Unspoilt, oak-panelled pub at
the town centre, with a mixed
clientele. It can get very busy
at weekends. Pricey beer; basic
family room.
ﯹ ﯹ ﯹ ◗ ◗ ▲ ♣

Woodman

61 South Street
☎ (01308) 456455
11–3, 7–11
**Draught Bass; Fuller's
London Pride; guest beer** H
Welcoming local on the south
side of town. Excellent value
carvery at weekends. Some
interesting guest beers.
◗ ◗ ₲ ▲ ♣

Buckland Newton

Gaggle of Geese

☎ (01300) 345249
12–2.30, 6.30–11
**Draught Bass; Butcombe
Bitter; Fuller's London Pride;
Hall & Woodhouse Badger
BB; Wadworth 6X** H
Large country pub with a
friendly atmosphere. A goose
auction is held here in May.
Good value meals. Wheelchair
access is via the kitchen.
ﯹ ﯹ ﯹ ◗ ◗ ₲ ▲ ♣ P

Burton Bradstock

Dove Inn

Southover (off B3157 E of
village) ☎ (01308) 897897
11–2.30, 7–11
**Teignworthy Reel Ale;
Wadworth 6X; guest beers** H
Attractive, three-bar
smugglers' inn near the sea.
Up to five ales are available at
any one time in summer.
Popular with campers.
ﯹ ﯹ ◗ ◗ ₲ ▲ ♣ ◔ P

Three Horseshoes

Mill Street ☎ (01308) 897259
11–2.30, 6–11
**Palmers BB, IPA, Tally Ho!
200** H
Pretty inn with a popular
restaurant, in a picturesque
village, close to the coast. Busy
in summer when families are
welcome.
ﯹ ﯹ ﯹ ﯹ ◗ ◗ ₲ ▲ ♣ P ↙

Cerne Abbas

Red Lion

Long Street ☎ (01300) 341441
11.30–2.30, 6.30–11.30
**Wadworth IPA, 6X; guest
beer** H
Victorian-fronted pub in a
popular, pretty village below
the famous giant. Very good
food. ﯹ Q ﯹ ◗ ▲ ♣

Chetnole

Chetnole Inn

☎ (01935) 872337
11–2.30 (4 Sat), 6.30–11
Palmers IPA; guest beers H
Popular village pub opposite
the church in unspoilt
countryside. Excellent range of
guest beers; good food. Cider
in summer. ﯹ Q ﯹ ◗ ◗
₲ ▲ ⇌ ♣ ◔ P

Chideock

George

On A35 ☎ (01297) 89419
11–11
**Palmers BB, IPA, Tally Ho!,
200** H
Thriving, thatched village
local; its cosy bars are built
around an attractive
horseshoe-shaped bar.
ﯹ ﯹ ﯹ ﯹ ◗ ◗
▲ ♣ P ↙ ◻

Child Okeford

Saxon Inn

Gold Hill (end of narrow lane,
N end of village)
☎ (01258) 860310
11–2.30, 7–11
**Draught Bass; Butcombe
Bitter; guest beer** H
Pub converted from two
cottages in 1949, but which
looks older. The garden has
plenty of wildlife. No meals
Tue or Sun eves.
ﯹ ﯹ ﯹ ◗ ◗ ▲ ♣ P

Christchurch

Olde George Inn

2A Castle Street
☎ (01202) 479383
10.30–2.30 (3 Sat), 6 (7 Sat)–11
**Ringwood Fortyniner;
Whitbread Strong Country,
Flowers Original; guest
beer** H

Centrally located Tudor
coaching inn with two low-
ceilinged bars and a pleasant
courtyard. The music room
hosts a folk and blues night
Wed and jazz on Thu. Friendly
welcome. ﯹ ◗ P

Corscombe

Fox Inn

☎ (01935) 891330
12–2.30, 7–11; 12–11 Sat
Exmoor Ale G; **Fuller's
London Pride; Palmers BB** H
Real two-bar village pub in
ramblers' countryside. Lovely
stone flags, a slate bar and
fresh food are features.
ﯹ Q ﯹ ◗ ◗ ₲ ▲ ♣ ◔

Cranborne

Sheaf of Arrows

The Square ☎ (01725) 517456
11.30–3, 6–11; 11.30–11 Thu–Sat
**Hampshire Lionheart;
Ringwood Best Bitter; guest
beer** H
Thriving, traditional local with
two contrasting bars: a large
lively locals' public and a
small, quiet lounge, plus a
skittle alley. Occasional cider;
beer festivals held.
Q ﯹ ₲ ◗ ◗ ▲ ♣ ◔

Dorchester

Tom Brown's

47 High East Street
☎ (01305) 264020
11–3, 6–11; 11–11 Fri
**Goldfinch Tom Brown's,
Flashman's Clout, Midnight
Blinder** H
Popular, drinker's brew pub
selling award-winning ale (no
keg beer). W Dorset CAMRA
Pub of the Year 1994. ₲ ◗ ♣

East Burton

Seven Stars

East Burton Road
☎ (01929) 462292
11–2.30, 6 (6.30 winter)–11
**Tetley Bitter; Whitbread
Castle Eden Ale; guest
beers** H
Large, urban-looking pub on
the edge of the village; cosy
inside. Popular for its good
value food.
ﯹ ﯹ ◗ ◗ ₲ ▲ ♣ P

Hazelbury Bryan

Antelope

Pidney (off B3143) OS745091
☎ (01258) 817295
11–3, 5.30–11; 11–11 Sat
**Hall & Woodhouse Badger
BB, Hard Tackle** G
Remote country pub with real
character. The simply

Dorset

furnished single bar has changed little over the years, reflecting local Dorset life.
🏚 Q ❀ 🏠 🚻 ♣ 🕭 P

Hurn

Avon Causeway
Off B3073 ☎ (01202) 482714
11–11
Ringwood Old Thumper E; **Wadworth IPA, 6X, Farmer's Glory, Old Timer; guest beers** H
Family pub converted from the old Hurn railway station (closed 1935). The large bar area features rail memorabilia and two full-sized carriages are parked by the platform.
🚼 ❀ 🕭 🚻 P

Ibberton

Crown Inn
Church Lane (4 miles SW of A357 from Shillingstone)
OS788077 ☎ (01258) 817448
11–3, 7 (5.30 summer)–11
Draught Bass; Wadworth 6X; guest beer H
Idyllic country inn with a flagstone floor and a large inglenook. Well off the beaten track, nestling below Bulbarrow Hill.
🏚 Q 🚼 ❀ 🕭 🚻 ♣ 🕭 P

Laymore

Squirrel Inn
800 yds from B3165 jct
OS387048 ☎ (01460) 30298
11.30–2.30, 6–11
Cotleigh Harrier; Oakhill Yeoman; guest beers H
Unexpected red-brick pub in the middle of nowhere, offering a good selection of guest beers (beer festival in June).
🏚 Q ❀ 🏠 🕭 🚻 ♣ 🕭 P

Lower Burton

Sun
½mile N of Dorchester on old Sherborne road
☎ (01305) 250445
11–3, 5.30–11
Fuller's London Pride; Smiles Bitter; guest beers H
Friendly, popular pub serving good value food.
🏚 Q 🕭 🚻 🚻 ♣ 🕭 P

Lyme Regis

Angel
Mill Green, Monmouth Street (off High St) ☎ (01297) 443267
11–3, 7–11
Palmers BB, IPA, 200 (summer) G
Unspoilt, back-street local with a 1950s feel. 🏠 🍺 🚻 🚻 ♣ P

Royal Standard
Marine Parade, The Cobb
☎ (01297) 442637
11–3, 7–11 (11–11 summer)
Palmers BB, IPA, Tally Ho!, 200 H
Pricey but popular (especially in the tourist season), 400-year-old pub on the beach.
🏚 🚼 ❀ 🏠 🕭 🚻 🚻 ☀

Lytchett Minster

St Peter's Finger Inn
Dorchester Road (B3067)
☎ (01202) 622275
11–2.30 (3 summer), 6 (5 summer)–11
Hall & Woodhouse Badger BB, Hard Tackle, Tanglefoot; Wells Eagle H
Busy village local with a large function room, a games bar and a collection of regimental drums in the lounge. The garden has an adventure playground. Family room in summer.
🏚 Q 🚼 ❀ 🕭 🚻 🚻 ♣ P

Marshwood

Bottle Inn
☎ (01297) 678254
11–2.30, 6–11
Exmoor Ale; Wadworth 6X; guest beer (summer) H
Rethatched, 400-year-old pub. The unspoilt interior features a low ceiling and wooden pews. Handy for walks – maps are available.
🏚 Q ❀ 🏠 🕭 🚻 🚻 ♣ P

Morden

Cock & Bottle
On B3075 ☎ (01929) 459238
11–2.30, 6–11
Hall & Woodhouse Badger BB, Hard Tackle (summer), **Tanglefoot; Wells Eagle** H
Friendly, village pub in a rural setting. A restaurant has been built on, but is in keeping with the character of this 400-year-old inn. 🏚 ❀ 🕭 🚻 🚻 ♣ P

Nettlecombe

Marquis of Lorne
OS956517 ☎ (01308) 485236
11–2.30, 6–11
Palmers BB, IPA H, **Tally Ho!** or **200** G
Large, welcoming, 16th-century inn, nestling beneath Eggardon Hill, offering an extensive range of good value food. The children's play area boasts scenic views. Cider in summer. 🏚 🚼 ❀ 🏠 🕭 🚻 ♣ 🕭 P ☀

Norden

Halfway Inn
Wareham Road (A351)

☎ (01929) 480402
11–2.30, 6–11
Ringwood Best Bitter, Old Thumper G; **Whitbread Strong Country, Flowers Original** H
Thatched Purbeck-style pub with low-ceilinged rooms. An unusual menu of Greek Cypriot dishes makes this pub popular with diners.
❀ 🕭 🚻 🚻 P

North Wootton

Three Elms
☎ (01935) 812881
11–2.30, 6.30 (6 Fri & Sat)–11
Butcombe Bitter; Fuller's London Pride; Hop Back Summer Lightning; Shepherd Neame Spitfire; Whitbread Boddingtons Bitter; guest beers H
Popular country inn famed for its food (especially vegetarian). 1000 model vehicles on show. Nine real ales; the house beer is Ash Vine Bitter.
🏚 Q ❀ 🏠 🕭 🚻 P ☀

Osmington Mills

Smugglers Inn
1 mile off A353
☎ (01305) 833125
11–2.30 (3 Sat), 6.30–11 (11–11 summer)
Courage Best Bitter; Ruddles County; Wadworth 6X; guest beers H
Spacious, beamed pub close to the clifftop, on the coastal path. It can get crowded in summer. Good restaurant. 🏚 Q ❀ 🕭 🚻 🚻 ♣ 🕭 P

Pamphill

Vine Inn
Off B3082
☎ (01202) 882259
11–2.30, 7–11
Whitbread Strong Country; guest beer H
Split-level country pub with two small bars and a nice outdoor drinking area. Handy for the NT Kingston Lacy estate and house.
❀ 🍺 ♣ 🕭 🚻

Piddlehinton

Thimble
☎ (01300) 348270
12–2.30, 7–11
Eldridge Pope Hardy Country; Hall & Woodhouse Badger BB, Hard Tackle; Ringwood XXXX Porter, Old Thumper H
Enlarged country pub with part of the bar straddling the River Piddle.
🏚 ❀ 🕭 🚻 🚻 ♣ 🕭 P

Plush

Brace of Pheasants

☎ (01300) 348357
12 (11.30 summer)–2.30, 7–11
Butcombe Bitter; Wadworth 6X; guest beers (summer) [H]
Traditional, warm village pub offering good food.
⛰ Q ♞ ❀ ◖ ◗ ♿ ♣ P

Poole

Albion Hotel

470 Ringwood Road, Parkstone ☎ (01202) 732197
11–3, 5–11; 11–11 Sat
Hall & Woodhouse Badger BB, Tanglefoot [H]
Large, two-bar pub on the main road into Poole. The comfortable lounge has a homely feel and the basic public bar a pool table. No eve meals Sun. ❀ ◖ ◗ ⊞ ♣ P

Blue Boar

29 Market Close
☎ (01202) 682247
11–3, 5 (6 Sat)–11
Courage Best Bitter, Directors; John Smith's Bitter; Webster's Green Label; guest beer [H]
Former wine merchant's house built circa 1750 in old Poole town: a plush lounge and food bar at street level, plus a more basic cellar bar (open eve only) which has regular live music. No lunches Sun. The beer range may vary. ◖ ⊞ ♣

Branksome Railway Hotel

429 Poole Road, Branksome
☎ (01202) 769555
11–11
Hampshire King Alfred's; Wadworth 6X; Whitbread Boddingtons Bitter [H]
Large, one-bar pub, opposite Branksome station, built in Victorian railway style with railway pictures and high ceilings. No lunches Sun. The beer range may vary.
◖ ⇌ (Branksome) ♣ P

Inn in the Park

26 Pinewood Road
☎ (01202) 761318
11–2.30 (3 Sat), 5.30 (6 Sat)–11
Draught Bass; Wadworth IPA, 6X [H]
Plush inn in an exclusive residential area near Branksome beach. A comfortable bar has an adjoining restaurant which welcomes children at lunchtime. ⛰ Q ❀ 🛏 ◖ ◗ P

Tudor Bars

3 Banks Road, Sandbanks
☎ (01202) 707244
11–3, 6–11
Hampshire King Alfred's; Ringwood Best Bitter; Wadworth 6X; guest beers [H]
Spacious, long bar with pool tables, 100 yards from Shore Road beach, overlooking Brownsea Island.
♞ ◖ ◗ ♣ P

Portland

Corner House

49 Straits, Easton
☎ (01305) 822526
11–3, 6–11
Eldridge Pope Dorchester, Hardy Country, Royal Oak; guest beer [E]
Basic but welcoming corner local with a games area. Winner of Eldridge Pope's *Cellar Supremo* award. The guest beer comes from their Brewer's Choice range. Cider in August. ❀ 🛏 ♣

Puncknowle

Crown Inn

Church Street
☎ (01308) 897711
11–2.30, 7–11
Palmers BB, IPA, Tally Ho!, 200 [H]
Attractive, thatched inn with an extensive menu, including vegetarian dishes. Two comfortable bars. ⛰ Q ♞ ❀ 🛏 ◖ ◗ ⊞ ♿ ▲ ♣ ⌓ P

Rimpton

White Post Inn

On B3148
☎ (01935) 850717
12–3, 6.30–11
Draught Bass [G]**; Butcombe Bitter; Oakhill Yeoman; guest beers** [H]
Genuine free house straddling the Somerset/Dorset border. Excellent value food; pleasant views. Q ❀ ◖ ◗ ♣ ⌓ P

Sandford Orcas

Mitre Inn

☎ (01963) 220271
11.30–2.30, 7–11
Morland Old Speckled Hen; John Smith's Bitter; Wadworth 6X [H]
Flagstone-floored, rural 18th-century local. Good value home cooking (no meals Mon eve). Sandford cider.
⛰ Q ❀ 🛏 ◖ ◗ ♿ ♣ ⌓ P

Shaftesbury

Fountain Inn

Breach Lane, Enmore Green
☎ (01747) 52062
11–3, 6.30–11; 11–11 Sat
Butcombe Bitter; Smiles Best Bitter; Wadworth 6X; Young's Special; guest beer [H]
Comfortable, split-level bar patronised by the young, plus a skittle alley and a large games room. ❀ ◖ ◗ ♣ ⌓ P

Olde Two Brewers

St James Street
☎ (01747) 54211
11–3, 6–11
Courage Best Bitter, Directors; Wadworth 6X; guest beers [H]
Popular, well-run pub below the town, easily reached via Gold Hill (made famous by the Hovis advert). It has many different drinking areas and a secluded garden with superb views. Excellent, home-cooked food. ❀ ◖ ◗ P

Sherborne

Digby Tap

Cooks Lane ☎ (01935) 813148
11–2.30, 5.30–11
Beer range varies [H]
Basic, traditional town drinking house in a side-street, the former tap room of an old hotel. Stone-flagged floors, panelling and old photos add to the atmosphere. Twenty beers a week. No food Sun.
⛰ ♞ ◖ ⇌ ♣ ⌓

Skippers

Horsecastles (A352)
☎ (01935) 812753
11–3, 5.30–11
Adnams Bitter; Draught Bass; Wadworth IPA, 6X [H]
A Dorset rarity – a Wadworth tied house; formerly an end of terrace cider house. Note the many artefacts. Regular food events. Q ❀ ◖ ◗ ♣ P

Shroton

Cricketers

W of A350 ☎ (01258) 860421
11–3, 7–11
Beer range varies [H]
Well-run village inn with an excellent restaurant. Handy for walkers enjoying the glorious scenery from the iron age hill fort on Hambledon Hill.
⛰ Q ❀ ◖ ◗ ♣ P

Sixpenny Handley

Roebuck

High Street ☎ (01725) 552002
11–2.30, 6.30–11
Ringwood Best Bitter, XXXX Porter, Fortyniner; guest beer (occasional) [H]
Upmarket, L-shaped bar with a cosy fireside. The beer is often brought from the cellar in a jug. No food Mon.
⛰ Q ♞ ❀ ◖ ◗ ♣ P

Dorset

Studland

Bankes Arms
Manor Road ☎ (01929) 450225
11–3, 6–11 (may vary; 11–11 Easter–Oct)
Poole Bosun Bitter; guest beers Ⓗ
Lovely NT building in Purbeck stone, overlooking the sea, near the popular Studland beaches. Home-made food.
🏚 ⛲ 🚗 ◗ ● P

Sturminster Marshall

Red Lion
Church Street (1 mile E of A350) ☎ (01258) 857319
11–2.30, 7 (5.30 summer)–11
Hall & Woodhouse Badger BB, Hard Tackle Ⓗ
Large, one-bar village pub with a skittle alley doubling as a children's room. It draws trade from a large area for food. 🏚 ⛲ ⛲ ◗ ● ♣ P

Swanage

Red Lion
High Street ☎ (01929) 423533
11–11
Ringwood Fortyniner; Whitbread Strong Country, Flowers Original Ⓖ
Popular, down-to-earth, two-bar town pub. The public bar adjoins the cellar from where the beers and cider are dispensed by gravity. A lounge with a pool table leads to a garden and children's room. Eve meals Fri–Sat.
⛲ ⛲ ◗ ● ♣ ♣ ● P

Symondsbury

Ilchester Arms
☎ (01308) 422600
11–3, 7–11
Palmers BB, IPA, Tally Ho!, 200 (summer) Ⓗ
Stone-flagged, village pub in an attractive location, offering excellent home-cooked meals. Separate skittle alley.
🏚 ⛲ ◗ ● ♣ ⚓ ♣ ● P

Tarrant Monkton

Langton Arms
Near A354 ☎ (01258) 830225
11.30–3, 6–11; 11.30–11 Sat
Beer range varies Ⓗ/Ⓖ
Traditional, 17th-century country pub with four changing ales in the lounge bar and on request in the public bar. It also boasts extensive children's play areas, a skittle alley and a local and varied menu.
🏚 Q ⛲ ⛲ ⛲ ◗ ● ♣ ⚓ ♣ P

Verwood

Albion
Station Road (B3081, W side of town) ☎ (01202) 825267
11–2.30, 5 (6 Sat)–11
Gibbs Mew Salisbury, Deacon, Bishop's Tipple Ⓗ
Built in 1866, this was once the Verwood railway station. Today it is a superb cosy pub serving good value, varied food. Local CAMRA *Pub of the Year* 1993. ⛲ ◗ ● P

West Bay

George
George Street ☎ (01308) 423191
11–2.30, 5.30 (7 winter)–11
Palmers BB, IPA, 200 Ⓗ
Imposing pub, facing the harbour. The restaurant is popular in the tourist season.
Q ⛲ ⛲ ⛲ ◗ ● ⚓ ♣ P

West Stour

Ship Inn
☎ (01747) 838640
11–3.30, 6–11
Draught Bass; Oakhill Best Bitter; guest beers Ⓗ
18th-century coaching inn on the A30: an unspoilt bar with snugs. Good local food.
🏚 Q ⛲ ⛲ ◗ ● ♣ ⚓ ♣ P 🍴

Weymouth

Dorset Brewers Ale House
33 Hope Street (far side of harbour) ☎ (01305) 786940
11–11
Draught Bass; Courage Directors; Eldridge Pope Dorchester; Hall & Woodhouse Badger BB; Ringwood Old Thumper Ⓗ
Very pleasant pub opposite the old Devenish Brewery, with a basic, wooden-floored type of decor. 🏚 ⛲ ● ♣ ●

Weatherbury Hotel
7 Carlton Road North (off Dorchester Rd) ☎ (01305) 786040
11–2.30, 5–11; 11–11 Fri & Sat
Draught Bass; guest beers Ⓗ
The best range of beers (four guests) in Weymouth is served in this large, modern lounge bar set in a residential part of town. Prices are a little high.
⛲ ⛲ ⛲ ◗ ● ⇌ ♣ P

Whitchurch Canonicorum

Five Bells
☎ (01297) 489262
12–3, 6–11

Palmers BB, IPA, 200 (summer) Ⓗ
Pub built in 1904 after the original building burnt down. Excellent views from the garden. Families welcome.
🏚 ⛲ ◗ ● ♣ ⚓ ♣ ● P

Wimborne

Crown & Anchor
Wimborne Road, Walford (B3078, N of town)
☎ (01202) 841405
10.30–2.30, 6–11
Hall & Woodhouse Badger BB Ⓗ
Pleasant local by the River Allen. Nearby walks and a craft centre at Walford Mill add to its appeal. No food winter Sun.
🏚 Q ⛲ ◗ ⚓ P

Winkton

Fisherman's Haunt
Salisbury Road ☎ (01202) 484071
10.30–2.30, 6–11
Draught Bass; Ringwood Best Bitter, Fortyniner; Wadworth 6X Ⓗ
17th-century, Avon Valley hotel, ideal for country-lovers and walkers. Good value food. Children welcome in one lounge.
🏚 Q ⛲ ⛲ ◗ ● ♣ P

Worth Matravers

Square & Compass
Off B3069
☎ (01929) 439229
11–3, 6–11; 11–11 Sat
Ringwood Fortyniner; Whitbread Strong Country; guest beers Ⓖ
Stone sculptures, fossils and beachcombing finds decorate this fine, traditional Purbeck building which has sea views. Run by the Newman family since 1904 and ever present in this guide. Ring to camp.
🏚 Q ⛲ ⚓ ● P ⚋

Wyke Regis

Wyke Smugglers
76 Portland Road
☎ (01305) 760010
11–2.30, 6–11
Courage Directors; Ringwood Old Thumper; Whitbread Boddingtons Bitter, Flowers Original; guest beers Ⓗ
100 years-old in 1995, a popular local fielding many games teams. The Courage and Ringwood beers vary through the range. Lunches served summer weekdays.
⛲ ⛲ ◗ ♣ ♣ P

Durham

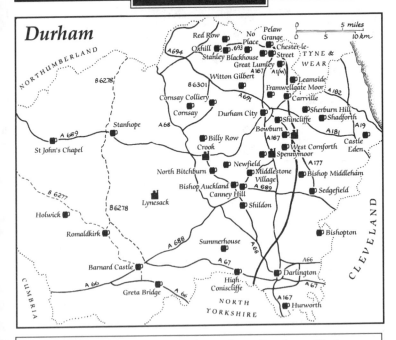

Durham

Butterknowle, Lynesack; **Durham**, Bowburn; **Hodges**, Crook; **Whitworth Hall**, Spennymoor

Barnard Castle

King's Head
14 Market Place
☎ (01833) 690333
11–3, 7–11; 11–11 Sat
Butterknowle Conciliation Ale; Ind Coope Burton Ale; John Smith's Bitter; Tetley Bitter Ⓗ
Imposing one-time hotel, now a pub with a nursing home above and a coffee shop attached. Dickens stayed here in 1838 while researching *Nicholas Nickleby*. Two large, oak-panelled lounge bars. ◑ P

Try also: Three Horseshoes, Galgate (Bass)

Billy Row

Dun Cow (Cow's Tail)
Old White Lea (leave Billy Row village by the Royal George – unsigned road)
☎ (01388) 762714
7–11
Butterknowle Banner, Conciliation Ale Ⓗ
Unspoilt gem, well off the beaten track but worth seeking out. It has been in the same family since 1830 and the present landlord is only the fifth. Two small rooms give a very relaxed atmosphere. Folk

night one Fri per month. Note: closed lunchtimes.
🏚 Q ❀ ▲ ♣ P

Bishop Auckland

Tap & Spile
13 Cockton Hill Road (opp. General Hospital)
☎ (01388) 602550
11–3, 6–11; 11–11 Fri & Sat
Butterknowle Banner, Conciliation Ale; guest beers Ⓗ
Two-roomed pub: a bar/games room with a lounge attached. Plenty of traditional games, e.g. shove-ha'penny, skittles, darts, Toad in the Hole, chess and cards. Six guest beers. No food Sun.
🏚 ❀ ◑ ♦ ♿ ⇌ ♣ ⌂ P

Bishop Middleham

Olde Fleece Inn
Bank Top
☎ (01740) 652392
12–3, 4.30–11
Draught Bass; Whitbread Boddingtons Bitter, Castle Eden Ale; guest beers Ⓗ
Popular pub in a quiet, picturesque village, serving excellent meals. Live music Mon eves. Happy hour 4.30–7 weekdays. No meals Mon.
🏚 ◑ ♦ P ⊟

Bishopton

Talbot
The Green
☎ (01740) 630371
11–3, 6–11
Bass Worthington BB; Camerons Strongarm; Ind Coope Burton Ale Ⓗ
Pleasant village local with a growing emphasis on meals. In the *Guide* for 22 consecutive editions, with the same landlord behind the bar all that time.
🏚 Q ❀ ◑ ♦ P

Blackhouse

Charlaw Inn
On B6532
☎ (01207) 232085
11–3, 6–11
S&N Theakston Best Bitter, XB; Whitbread Boddingtons Bitter Ⓗ
There are five rooms in this large pub including a restaurant and a conservatory for families. The outside play area has swings. Soccer memorabilia features in the bar; lively bar games. Excellent meals.
Q ☻ ❀ ◑ ♦ ⊟ ♿ ♣ P ⊬

Try also: Wardles Bridge, Holmside (Free)

Durham

Bowburn

Cooperage
Durham Road (200 yds from A1(M)/A177 jct)
☎ (0191) 377 9473
11–11; 7–10.30 Sun, closed Sun lunch
S&N Theakston Best Bitter, Newcastle Exhibition, Theakston XB; guest beers Ⓗ
Open-plan pub, with plenty of games. ⌂ ◖ ◗ ♣ P

Canney Hill

Sportsman Inn
4 Canney Hill (A689, ½ mile E of Bishop Auckland)
☎ (01388) 603847
12–3, 7–11 (may close Mon & Tue in winter)
Draught Bass; Camerons Bitter, Strongarm; Taylor Landlord; guest beers Ⓗ
On the edge of town, a pub with a small snug. Quiet weekday lunchtimes, but the bar and lounge are lively in the eve. Popular for Sun lunches. Large vegetarian menu. ⌂ ◖ ◗ ♣ P ⊟

Carrville

Ramside Hall Hotel
☎ (0191) 386 5282
11–3, 5–11.30 (midnight Sat)
McEwan 80/-; S&N Theakston Best Bitter, Newcastle Exhibition, Theakston XB; guest beers Ⓗ
Large four-star hotel with a 27-hole golf course, plus a ghost known as the Grey Lady. NB: hotel beer prices.
❀ ⌂ ◖ ◗ Ⅻ ♣ P ⊬ ⊟

Try also: **Blacksmith Arms**, Low Pittington (Vaux); **Hallgarth Manor Hotel**, Pittingdon (Free)

Castle Eden

Castle Eden Inn
☎ (01429) 836250
11–11
Whitbread Eden Bitter, Castle Eden Ale; guest beers Ⓗ
Real ale oasis on the east coast with very friendly staff. It can get very busy at mealtimes (good value meals). Guest beers are usually from Castle Eden Brewery. Mini-beer festivals. ❀ ⌂ ◖ ◗ P

Chester-le-Street

Butcher's Arms
Middle Chare (off Front St)
☎ (0191) 388 3606
11–3, 6.30–11
Camerons Bitter, Strongarm; guest beer Ⓗ
Comfortable, single-roomed

---

pub with a fine array of porcelain jugs and plates. The staff and clientele are friendly, in what is reputed to be the oldest hostelry in the town.
❀ ⌖ ◖ ≈ ♣

Market Tavern
South Burns ☎ (0191) 388 4749
11–11
Whitbread Boddingtons Bitter, Castle Eden Ale; guest beers Ⓗ
Two-roomed, town-centre pub opposite the market. It can get very lively at weekends. No food Sun. ◖ ≈ ♣

Cornsay

Blackhorse Inn
Main Street (2 miles W of B6301, Cornsay Colliery road)
☎ (0191) 373 4211
7–11; 12–2.30, 7–10.30 Sun
Bass Worthington BB, Draught Bass; Stones Best Bitter; guest beer (weekends) Ⓗ
Remote, West Durham village pub with a picturesque view of Gladdow Valley. It has a main bar and a large dining area (Sun lunches served – closed other lunchtimes). Outside drinking is on the village green. Q ❀ ◗ ♣ P

Cornsay Colliery

Firtree (Monkey)
Hedley Hill Lane Ends (B3601, ½ mile S of village)
☎ (0191) 373 3212
7–11; 12–2, 7–10.30 Sun; closed Tue
Vaux Lorimer's Best Scotch Ⓗ
Century-old, basic country pub with a small bar and a separate family room. Coal fires add to the warm and friendly atmosphere. Closed lunchtimes except Sun.
⌂ Q ⌖ ♣ P ⊟

Darlington

Britannia
Archer Street
☎ (01325) 463787
11.30–3 (may extend), 5.30–11
Camerons Strongarm; Tetley Bitter, Imperial Ⓗ
Relaxed, uncomplicated old local, on the fringe of the town centre but a million miles from the hectic weekend 'circuit'. A bastion of cask beer for 130 years, still recognisable as the private house it originally was. Q ♣ P

Central Borough
Hopetown Lane (off A167)
☎ (01325) 468490
11–11
Camerons Strongarm Ⓗ
Small street-corner local in an area of terraced housing. Run by the same landlady since

---

1956 and with a justifiably loyal clientele, it stands near the Railway Museum, which is housed in one of the world's oldest stations, on the original Stockton & Darlington Railway. ⌖ ≈ (North Rd) ♣

Cricketers Hotel
53 Parkgate ☎ (01325) 384444
11.30–3, 5.30–11
Black Sheep Best Bitter; John Smith's Magnet Ⓗ
Small, town-centre pub/hotel with a comfortable public bar. Close to the Civic Theatre.
⌂ ◖ ◗ ≈ P

Glittering Star
Stonebridge ☎ (01325) 351251
11.30–3.30, 5.30–11; 11–11 Fri & Sat
Samuel Smith OBB Ⓗ
Renovated, town-centre local, remodelled faithfully on traditional pub design principles with not a hint of pastiche or gimmickry. It is hard to believe it was a boarded-up empty shell for five years until Sam Smith's revived its interest in 1993.
◖ ⌖ ≈ ♣

Pennyweight
Bakehouse Hill, Market Place
☎ (01325) 464244
11–11
Vaux Samson, Double Maxim, Waggle Dance; Wards Best Bitter; guest beers Ⓗ
Busy, one-room market place pub with a modern layout but many traditional features in the furnishings. It can be noisy and pricey at weekends but has an adventurous range of beers for a Vaux tied house.
◖ ≈

Railway Tavern
8 High Northgate (A167)
☎ (01325) 464963
11–11
Whitbread Boddingtons Bitter; Cains Bitter; Wadworth 6X; guest beers Ⓗ
Possibly the first 'Railway' pub in the world, taking its name from the nearby 1825 Stockton & Darlington line. A buoyant, well-run, two-roomer with usually six cask ales, it offers good value (and varied) meals. Equally expansive 'menu' of board games. No lunches Sat or eve meals Tue.
❀ ◖ ◗ ♣

Tap & Spile
99 Bondgate ☎ (01325) 381679
11.30–11
Beer range varies Ⓗ
Popular, town-centre pub, after the style of a Victorian ale house – if you ignore the machines, TV, taped music and live rock bands. It offers up to eight real beers and

regular farmhouse ciders. The house beer is brewed by Hadrian. 🍺 ♣ ⌂ ⅏

Traveller's Rest

West Auckland Road,
Cockerton (A68,
1 mile W of centre)
☎ (01325) 468177
11.30–11
**John Smith's Bitter,
Magnet** Ⓗ
Attractive, 1920s, two-roomed local in a now-urbanised village: a comfortable music-free lounge and a bustling public bar. Built for the long-defunct Haughton Road Brewery Co. Q 🍺 🍴 ♣

Try also: Number Twenty 2, Conniscliffe Rd (Free)

Durham City

Brewer & Firkin

58 Saddler Street
☎ (0191) 386 4134
11 (may be 12)–11 (may close afternoons)
**Whitbread Boddingtons
Bitter, Castle Eden Ale; guest
beers** Ⓗ
Formerly the Buffalo Head, this pub is now decorated in a jazz style and entertainment is staged most eves. Popular with students, locals and tourists. Drinks discount for CAMRA members. 🍺 ⌂

Dun Cow

37 Old Elvet
☎ (0191) 386 9219
11–11
**Whitbread Boddingtons
Bitter, Castle Eden Ale; guest
beer** Ⓗ
Two-roomed homely pub, where the beer is still cheaper in the public bar. The guest beer is from the Whitbread range, changing fortnightly. Traditionally sporty, the pub is popular with players, fans, students and locals.
Q 🍺 🍴 ⅙

Garden House

North Road ☎ (0191) 384 0273
11–3, 5.30 (6 Sat)–11
**Vaux Samson; Wards Best
Bitter; guest beer** Ⓗ
Cosy, traditional, popular pub on the edge of the city centre, with a warm atmosphere. Home-cooked food includes a traditional Sun lunch and special monthly theme nights. No food Sun eve. Karaoke and quiz nights. Large conservatory.
Q ❀ 🍴 ♿ ⇆ ♣ P 🍽

Half Moon Inn

New Elvet ☎ (0191) 386 4528
11–11; 12–3, 7–10.30 Sun
**Bass Worthington BB,
Draught Bass; guest beer** Ⓗ

A *Guide* regular, featuring a split-level, semi-circular bar. Guest beers are from the Bass guest range. This warm, friendly pub may be extended in the next year. Sky TV.
Q ♣ 🍽

Try also: Elm Tree, Crossgate (Vaux); **Victoria Hotel,** Hallgarth St (Free)

Framwellgate Moor

Tap & Spile

27 Front Street
☎ (0191) 386 5451
11.30–3, 6 (5 Fri)–11
**Village White Boar; guest
beers** Ⓗ
The third pub in the Tap & Spile chain, recently refurbished but unaltered: three rooms and a partitioned family/games area. Converted in 1988, it still attracts visitors from a wide area. Up to eight guest beers and Weston's Old Rosie cider served.
Q 🛏 🍺 ♣ ⌂ ⅏

Try also: Marquis of Granby, Front St (Samuel Smith)

Great Lumley

Old England

Front Street ☎ (0191) 388 5257
11–11
**Bass Worthington BB; guest
beers** Ⓗ
Warm, friendly pub with a good atmosphere in its comfortable lounge and noisy bar. Popular with the locals. No food Mon–Thu lunch, nor Sun eve. Q 🍴 🍺 ♣ P

Greta Bridge

Morritt Arms Hotel

Off A66 ☎ (01833) 627392
11–11 (Sir Walter Scott bar opens 8.30pm)
**Butterknowle Conciliation
Ale; S&N Theakston Best
Bitter; Taylor Landlord;
Tetley Bitter** Ⓗ
Two very different hostelries exist here, side by side, in a fine setting secluded from the nearby A66. The main bar, in the magnificently traditional country house hotel, has bow-tied barmen and hotel prices. The detached Sir Walter Scott bar serves the local trade with a smaller beer range at lower prices.
🛏 Q ❀ 🛏 🍴 🍺 ♣ ⌂ P

High Coniscliffe

Duke of Wellington

On A68 ☎ (01325) 374283
11–2.30, 6–11
**Camerons Strongarm; S&N
Theakston Best Bitter, XB** Ⓗ

Traditional, one-roomed village local, opposite a popular riverside beauty spot. Quoits played.
🛏 ❀ 🍺 ♿ ♣ P

Holwick

Strathmore Arms

Off B6277 OS909268
☎ (01833) 640362
12–11
**Courage Directors; Ruddles
Best Bitter; John Smith's
Bitter** Ⓗ
Isolated, but welcoming stone-built hostelry, three miles along a cul-de-sac near the south bank of the Upper Tees. Worth the journey, it is just off the Pennine Way. The bar is cosy and warm, arranged in part around an open hearth. Superb home-made meals (Tue–Sun). Resident ghosts.
🛏 Q ❀ 🍺 🍴 🍴 ♣ P

Hurworth

Bay Horse

45 The Green
☎ (01325) 720663
11–11
**John Smith's Bitter,
Magnet** Ⓗ
Attractive village pub in 18th-century cottages: a plain bar, a cosier lounge and a small conservatory restaurant at the rear. The central archway beneath the sundial (dated 1738) leads to a small car park and garden. No eve meals Sun.
🛏 Q ❀ 🍴 🍴 🍺 ♣ P 🍽

Leamside

Three Horse Shoes

Pithouse Lane (off A690)
☎ (0191) 584 2394
12–2 (not Mon–Wed), 7–11
**S&N Theakston Best Bitter;
Whitbread Boddingtons
Bitter; guest beers** Ⓗ
Friendly country inn comprising a large bar with a lounge at one end and a family room off the other. Regular charity nights. The beer range includes one from Vaux.
🛏 ❀ 🍴 🍴 P

Middlestone Village

Ship Inn

Low Road ☎ (01388) 814092
12–3, 7–11
**Vaux Samson, Waggle Dance;
Wards Best Bitter** Ⓗ
Traditional village pub from the early 1700s, reputedly haunted. Generally quiet afternoons, busy at weekends. Bar skittles played. Good food and accommodation.
🛏 Q 🛏 ❀ 🛏 🍴 🍴 ♣ P 🍽

Durham

Newfield

Fox & Hounds
1A Stonebank Terrace
(follow signs for Binchester
Roman fort)
☎ (01388) 662787
12–3 (5 Fri & Sat), 7–11
**Hodges Original; Tetley
Imperial** ⊞
Friendly, easy-going old local
in an ex-mining village with
extensive views. Exposed
beams, two open stone
fireplaces and bric-a-brac
feature. Said to be haunted.
Quiz nights and traditional
music eves.
🏠 ☎ 🌡 ◑ & ♣ P ⊟

No Place

Beamish Mary Inn
Off A693
☎ (0191) 370 0237
12–3, 6–11; 12–11 Fri & Sat
**McEwan 80/; S&N Theakston
Best Bitter, XB, Old Peculier;
guest beers** ⊞
Extremely popular, this former
CAMRA *National Pub of the
Year* in an ex-mining
community, offers excellent
food. Rock and blues music in
converted stables Thu and Sat;
folk club Wed. Annual beer
festival. No Place BSB is
brewed by Big Lamp. 🏠 Q ☀
🛏 ◑ & ♠ ♣ ⌂ P

Try also: Sun Inn, Beamish
Museum, Beamish (S&N)

North Bitchburn

Red Lion
North Bitchburn Terrace
☎ (01388) 763561
12–3, 7–11
**Courage Directors; John
Smith's Bitter, Magnet; guest
beer** ⊞
Friendly, traditional village
pub with a bar, pool room and
a dining area. Very popular for
its wide range of excellent
value meals. A regular guest
beer is the pub's own Mane
Brew, brewed by Hambleton.
Local CAMRA *Pub of the Year*
1994. 🏠 Q ☀ ◑ ♣ P ⊟

Oxhill

Ox Inn
☎ (01207) 233626
6 (12 Fri)–11; 12–5, 7–11 Sat
Draught Bass; guest beer ⊞
Large, high-ceilinged pub,
with a conservatory leading on
to a patio and garden/play
area, just off a busy main road.
Live music at weekends draws
large crowds.
Q ☎ ☀ ◑ ◑ & ▲ ♣ P

Pelaw Grange

Wheatsheaf
Durham Road
☎ (0191) 388 3104
11–11
**Bass Worthington BB,
Draught Bass; Stones Best
Bitter; guest beers** ⊞
Traditional, 16th-century
coaching inn with horse-
mounting steps outside. A
traditional bar and quieter
lounge, with an emphasis on
food (no meals Sun eve);
families welcome. Reputedly
haunted by a friendly ghost.
Adjacent to Sustrans
Cycleway. Regular folk nights.
☎ ☀ ◑ ◑ ⊞ & ♣ P

Red Row

Black Horse
Off A6076 ☎ (01207) 232569
12 (11 Sat)–3, 7 (6 Sat)–11
**Vaux Waggle Dance; Wards
Best Bitter** ⊞
Traditional alehouse, dating
from the 17th-century, with an
unusually large collection of
matchboxes. 🏠 Q ☀ ♣ P

Romaldkirk

Kirk Inn
The Green ☎ (01833) 650260
12–2.30, 6–11
**Black Sheep Best Bitter;
Butterknowle Bitter;
Whitbread Boddingtons
Bitter, Castle Eden Ale; guest
beers** ⊞
Charming, single-room pub,
with a warm and welcoming
atmosphere. Situated on the
village green, it doubles as a
part-time post office.
🏠 Q ☀ ◑ ◑ ♣

St John's Chapel

Golden Lion
Market Place (A689)
☎ (01388) 537231
11–3, 7–11 (11–11 summer Sat)
**John Smith's Bitter; guest
beers** ⊞
Rambling, E-shaped country
pub with three very different
areas catering for all tastes.
Eve meals are very popular.
Three guest beers stocked.
🏠 ☀ ◑ ▲ P ⊟

Sedgefield

Dun Cow
43 Front Street
☎ (01740) 620894
11–3, 6–11
**S&N Theakston Best Bitter,
XB; guest beers** ⊞
Well-established, country-style
pub in a popular village,
well-liked by the locals. The
bar, lounge and restaurant
have beamed ceilings and a
very cosy atmosphere. Close to
the racecourse.
Q 🛏 ◑ ◑ P ⊟

Nag's Head
8 West End ☎ (01740) 620324
11–3, 6–11
**Vaux Samson, Double
Maxim; Wards Thorne Best
Bitter, Best Bitter** ⊞
Pleasant, cosy little three-
roomer, whose decor reflects
an equine interest.
Q ☎ ◑ ◑ ♣ P ⊟

Shadforth

Plough
South Side ☎ (0191) 372 0375
6.30 (11 Sat)–11; 12–2, 7–10.30 Sun
**Draught Bass; Stones Best
Bitter; guest beers** ⊞
Traditional, old-fashioned pub
with a touch of class.
Frequented by village locals
and visitors, it offers good
quality food (local fish a
speciality).
🏠 Q ☀ ◑ ◑ ⊞ ♣ P

Sherburn Hill

Burley Lodge
Front Street ☎ (0191) 372 2334
11–2 (4 Sat), 7–11
**S&N Theakston Best Bitter;
guest beer** ⊞
Attractive, two-bar pub,
popular with all ages, who
enjoy the traditional games
and bar food. ◑ ♣ P ⊟

Moor Edge
Front Street ☎ (0191) 372 1618
12–4, 7–11
**Vaux Lorimer's Best Scotch,
Double Maxim; Wards Best
Bitter** ⊞
Friendly, traditional village
drinking establishment: a cosy
bar and lounge enhanced by
coal fires. Quality and price
are of paramount importance
here. Quoits played.
🏠 Q ☎ ☀ ⊞ ♣ P ⊟

Shildon

Timothy Hackworth
107 Main Street (B6282 jct)
☎ (01388) 772525
12–11
**Camerons Bitter,
Strongarm** ⊞
Friendly village local named
after a famous steam engine
builder, opposite the world's
first railway passenger station.
The decor features pictures of
old Shildon and steam engines
built by Timothy Hackworth
at the nearby Soho works.
Q ♣ P

Try also: New Masons,
Byerley Rd (Free)

Shincliffe

Seven Stars
On A177
☎ (0191) 384 8454
11.30–3.30, 6.30–11
**Vaux Samson, Waggle Dance;
Wards Best Bitter** Ⓗ
Smart, quiet village
pub drawing an upmarket
clientele to its very
comfortable lounge and
restaurant area; small bar.
Very popular for meals.
Q ⚑ 🏠 ◖ ▶ ⊟

Spennymoor

Frog & Ferret
Coulson Street, Low
Spennymoor (between A167
and town centre)
☎ (01388) 818312
11–11; 11–4, 7–11 Sat
**Courage Directors; S&N
Theakston XB; Samuel Smith
OBB; Whitbread Boddingtons
Bitter; guest beers** Ⓗ
Small, warm and welcoming
pub. The guest beers change
frequently. Friendly and
efficient bar staff. Note the
original sign above the front
door. ⊟

Hillingdon
Clyde Terrace
☎ (01388) 814425
11–3, 6–11; 11–11 Sat
**Bass Worthington BB,
Draught Bass; guest beers** Ⓗ
Friendly pub which tries to
accommodate everybody's
tastes; plenty of mirrors and
tubular steel furniture
feature. It can be a bit loud
at times but is definitely
worth a visit. Quiet,
traditional lounge. ❀ P ⊟

Try also: Ash Tree, Carr Lane
(Vaux)

Stanhope

Queen's Head
89 Front Street (A689)
☎ (01388) 528160
12–3 (5 Sat & summer Fri), 7–11
**S&N Theakston Best Bitter,
Newcastle Exhibition,
Theakston XB; guest beers** Ⓗ
Small, friendly, two-roomed
local near the market place,
recently refurbished after a fire
but retaining its character.
It can get busy Sun
lunchtimes. ⚑ ◖ ▶
⇌ (limited service) ♣

Stanley

Blue Boar Tavern
Front Street (300 yds off A693)
☎ (01207) 231167
11–3, 7–11; 11–11 Thu–Sat
**Bass Worthington BB,
Draught Bass; Stones Best
Bitter; guest beers** Ⓗ
Very popular old pub at the
top of the main street: a former
coaching inn which gets busy
at lunchtimes. A rear entrance
leads to the busy (Fri and Sat)
entertainment room. Guest
ales change weekly, usually
three at a time.
🔥 ❀ ◖ ▶ ♿ ▲ P

Summerhouse

Raby Hunt
On B6279
☎ (01325) 374604
11.30–3, 6.30–11
**Marston's Bitter; Village Old
Raby; guest beers**
(occasional) Ⓗ
Neat, welcoming old stone
free house in a pretty whitewashed hamlet; a homely
lounge and a busy locals' bar.
Good, home-cooked lunches
(not served Sun). Raby Castle

is worth a visit, just five miles
away. 🔥 ❀ ◖ ⊟ ♣ P

West Cornforth

Square & Compass
Slake Terrace
☎ (01740) 650975
7–11; 12–5, 6.30–11 Sat
**S&N Theakston XB; Stones
Best Bitter** Ⓗ
Friendly village pub with a
warm welcome from behind
the bar. Note the photographic
history of the village. ❀ ♣ P

Witton Gilbert

Glendenning Arms
Front Street (A691)
☎ (0191) 371 0316
12–4, 7–11; 11–11 Sat
**Vaux Samson; Wards Best
Bitter; guest beer** Ⓗ
Friendly village local, 20 years
in the *Guide*: two rooms
include a comfortable lounge.
An unspoilt pub with racing
mementoes displayed in the
bar. Outside drinking in the
rear car park. Guest beers are
from the Vaux range.
🔥 Q ❀ ⊟ ♣ P

Traveller's Rest
Front Street (A691)
☎ (0191) 371 0458
11–3, 6–11
**McEwan 80/-; S&N Theakston
Best Bitter, XB, Old Peculier;
Younger Scotch, No.3; guest
beer** Ⓗ
Attractive village inn, very
popular with visitors, serving
a huge variety of meals. The
rear conservatory is ideal for
children and is pleasant in
summer. There is also a
restaurant. Petanque pitch at
the bottom of the rear car park
with seating. ◖ ▶ ♣ P ⌿
🔥 Q 🧒 ❀ ◖ ▶ ♣ P ⌿

THE SYMBOLS

🔥	real fire	♿	easy wheelchair access
Q	quiet (no music or electronic distractions in at least one bar)	▲	camping at or near the pub
🧒	indoor family room	⇌	near railway station
❀	outdoor drinking area	⊖	near underground station or tram stop
⚑	accommodation	♣	pub games
◖	lunchtime meals	⌂	real cider
▶	evening meals	P	car park
⊟	public bar	⌿	no-smoking room or area

⊟ oversized, lined glasses used

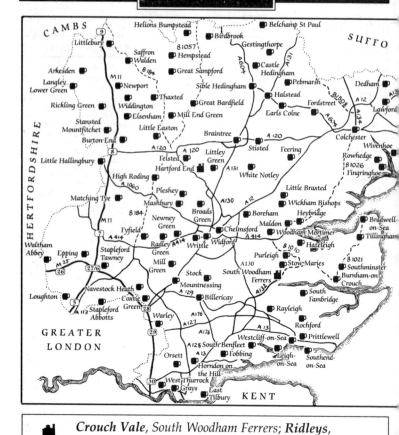

Crouch Vale, *South Woodham Ferrers*; **Ridleys**, *Hartford End*

Aingers Green

Royal Fusilier
Aingers Green Road (S from Gt Bentley village green, then left, straight on at crossroads) OS119204 ☎ (01255) 250001
11–2.30, 6.30–11
Adnams Bitter; guest beer Ⓗ
Free house whose cosy interior features beams and bricks.
🏰 Q ⛵ ❀ P

Arkesden

Axe & Compasses
OS483344 ☎ (01799) 550272
11.30–2.30, 6–11
Greene King IPA, Abbot Ⓗ
Superb, 17th-century, friendly traditional local with a thriving food trade.
🏰 Q ❀ ◑ ▶ ⊟ ♣ P

Belchamp St Paul

Cherry Tree Inn
Knowl Green OS784413
☎ (01787) 237263

12–3, 7–11; 12–11 Sat; closed Tue
Adnams Bitter; Greene King IPA; guest beer Ⓗ
Cosy, friendly, isolated 16th-century pub, comfortably refurbished. Good value beer and food, plus a play area.
🏰 Q ❀ 🛏 ◑ ▶ ▲ ♣ P

Billericay

Coach & Horses
36 Chapel Street (near B1007)
☎ (01277) 622873
10–4, 5.30–11; 11–11 Fri & Sat (and other days if busy)
Greene King XX Mild, IPA, Abbot; guest beers (occasional) Ⓗ
Traditional one-bar local on the site of the former Crown brewery tap, with a friendly, longstanding landlord. Good value meals (no food Sun).
Q ❀ ◑ ▶ ♿ ⇌ P

Birdbrook

Plough
The Street (1 mile off B1054)

11–2.30, 6–11
Adnams Bitter; Greene King IPA; guest beer Ⓗ
Friendly village local. No food Sun eve; good value snacks.
🏰 Q ❀ ◑ ▶ ⊟ ♣ P

Boreham

Queen's Head
Church Road
☎ (01245) 467298
10–3, 5–11
Greene King IPA, Abbot Ⓗ
Excellent, friendly, village local with two contrasting bars. Good value in every way. No meals Sun eve.
Q ❀ ◑ ▶ ⊟ ♣ P

Bradwell-on-Sea

Green Man Inn
Waterside (B1021)
☎ (01621) 776226
11.30–4, 6.30–11 (11–11 summer)
Adnams Bitter; Ridleys IPA, ESX; guest beer Ⓗ
Traditional, 15th-century, riverside inn, formerly used by

L K

Harwich

Little Oakley

A 120

Little Bentley

A 133

Aingers Green

Walton-on-the-Naze

Brightlingsea

Great Clacton

St Osyth Heath

St Osyth

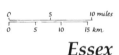

0   5   10 miles

0   5   10   15 km

Essex

local smugglers. A superb fireplace graces the unspoilt public bar. Sit at the Undertaker's Table and try to work out the meaning of the sign above the fireplace.
🍴 Q ❀ 🍴 ◖ 🍴 ♣ A ♣ P

Braintree

King William IV
114 London Road (near A131/A120 jct)
☎ (01376) 330088
11–3, 6–11; 11–11 Sat
Ridleys IPA Ⓖ
Cosy, two-bar local with a very friendly atmosphere. Lunchtime snacks.
🍴 Q 🍴 ♣ P

Wagon & Horses
53 South Street (B1256)
☎ (01376) 553356
11–3 (4 Sat), 5.30 (6 Sat)–11
Greene King IPA, Abbot Ⓗ
Comfortable pub with a large lounge, a raised dining area and a friendly snug. Look for the well. Greene King seasonal beers sold. ❀ ◖ ▶ ≢ ♣ P

Brightlingsea

Railway Tavern
58 Station Road (near B1029)
☎ (01206) 302581

5 (12 Fri & Sat)–11
Mauldons Best Bitter; guest beers
Two-bar pub popular with early eve drinking locals (closed lunchtime Mon–Thu). Railway mementoes adorn the walls. Five guest beers.
🍴 Q ☙ ❀ 🍴 ♿ A ♣ ♢

Broads Green

Walnut Tree
☎ (01245) 360222
11.30–2.30, 6.30–11; 12–2.30, 7–10.30 Sun
Ridleys IPA Ⓗ/Ⓖ
Friendly, three-bar Victorian local on the village green, with a comfortable lounge and an unspoilt public bar, both accessed through a central snug. Home-cooked snacks (not served Thu eve).
🍴 Q ❀ 🍴 P

Burnham-on-Crouch

Olde White Harte
The Quay (near B1010)
☎ (01621) 782106
11–3, 6–11; 11–11 Sat
Adnams Bitter; Tolly Cobbold Bitter Ⓗ
Attractive, old riverside pub, frequented by locals and yachtsmen; bustling on summer eves, particularly weekends. Enjoy a pint on the private jetty.
🍴 Q ❀ 🍴 ◖ ▶ A P

Burton End

Ash
Airport road from M11 jct 8, then signed OS532237
☎ (01279) 814481
11.30–2.30, 5.30–11
Greene King IPA, Rayments Special, Abbot Ⓗ
15th-century thatched pub in a tiny hamlet near Stansted Airport, with a quiet, rural atmosphere. It has been extended to provide a lounge bar/dining room, but the public bar retains character. Good value, wholesome food. No food winter Sun eve. Greene King seasonal beers sold. 🍴 ❀ ◖ ▶ 🍴 ♿ ♣ P

Castle Hedingham

Bell Inn
10 St James Street (B1058)
☎ (01787) 460350
11.30–3, 6–11
Greene King IPA, Abbot Ⓖ
Excellent, genuine-timbered, many-roomed pub with casks behind the bar. Occasional live music; good value food (not served Mon eve except bank hols).
🍴 Q ☙ ❀ 🍴 ◖ ▶ 🍴 A ♣ P ⅟

Chelmsford

Bird in Hand
New Writtle Street
☎ (01245) 259101
11–3, 5–11; 11–11 Sat
Ridleys IPA, ESX Ⓗ
Comfortable, back-street local with a friendly landlord. Handy for the football and county cricket grounds. No food Sun. ❀ ◖ 🍴 ♣ P

Endeavour
351 Springfield Road (A1113, 1 mile NE of centre)
☎ (01245) 257717
11–11; 12–2, 7–10.30 Sun
Greene King XX Mild, IPA, Abbot; guest beer (occasional) Ⓗ
Quiet, three-roomed suburban pub, popular with locals. No-smoking dining area (no food Sun). 🍴 Q ◖ ▶ 🍴 ♣

Partners
30 Lower Anchor Street (near B1007) ☎ (01245) 265181
11–3, 5.30–11; 11–11 Sat
Crouch Vale Best Bitter; Greene King IPA; guest beers Ⓗ
Friendly, often busy, street-corner local, near the football and cricket grounds. Family meeting room at the rear; pool room. Four guest beers, often from small breweries. No food Sat or Sun. ☙ ❀ ◖ ♣ P

Prince of Orange
7 Hall Street (near A138)
☎ (01245) 281695
11–11
Courage Best Bitter, Directors; Gibbs Mew Bishop's Tipple; Greene King IPA; Wadworth 6X; guest beer Ⓗ
Basic, back-street local with varied live music Thu. Rave music upstairs at weekends. No food Sun. 🍴 ❀ ◖ 🍴

Red Lion
147 New London Road (B1007)
☎ (01245) 354092
10.30–11
Ridleys IPA, ESX Ⓗ
Popular, traditional, street-corner pub, with a comfortable lounge and a long, basic public bar. ❀ ◖ ▶ 🍴 ♣

White Horse
25 Townfield Street (behind station) ☎ (01245) 269556
11–3, 5.30 (7 Sat)–11
S&N Theakston Best Bitter; guest beers Ⓗ
Roomy, friendly pub with a good range of games, but no pool or jukebox. Over 500 guest beers have been offered in the last year (up to six at a

time). Essex CAMRA *Pub of the Year* 1992. ⇌ ♣

Colchester

Boadicea
1a St John's Street
☎ (01206) 560545
11–3, 6–11
Beer range varies [H]
17th-century listed building close to the town centre, brought back to life by the present landlord. Pleasant, relaxed atmosphere; pool in the main bar. ⇌ (Town) P

British Grenadier
67 Military Road
☎ (01206) 791647
11–2.30 (3 Fri & Sat), 6–11
Adnams Mild, Bitter; guest beer [H]
Popular workingman's pub with a pool table in the back bar. Happy hour 6–7pm.
Q ⇌ (Town) ♣

King's Arms/ Hogshead
61–63 Crouch Street
☎ (01206) 572886
11–11
Whitbread Boddingtons Bitter, Flowers Original [H]**; guest beers** [H]/[G]
Spacious, single-bar local, popular with young and old alike. The walls are festooned with local memorabilia. Bar food includes a Sun roast; eve meals 5.30–7 Mon–Thu. At least six guest beers, but Boddingtons Mild is kept under an aspirator.
🔥 ❀ ◖ ◗ ♿ ⌓ P

Leather Bottle
Shrub End Road/Straight Road (B1022)
☎ (01206) 766018
11–2.30, 5.30–11; 11–11 Sat
Adnams Bitter; Ansells Mild; Tetley Bitter; guest beer [H]
Attractive pub with a large fire in the centre of the lounge and a public bar with games.
❀ ◖ ⊞ ♿ ♣ P

Odd One Out
28 Mersea Road (B1025)
☎ (01206) 578140
4.30 (11 Fri & Sat)–11
Archers Best Bitter; Ridleys IPA; guest beers [H]
Excellent, friendly pub, drawing a mixed crowd to its cosy lounge and basic public bar. Always four guest beers, one a mild.
🔥 Q ⇌ (Town) ⌓ ⚔

Rose & Crown Hotel
51 East Street
☎ (01206) 866677
11–3, 6.30–11
Adnams Broadside; Tetley Bitter; Tolly Cobbold Original [H]
One of Colchester's oldest buildings, a former coach house with an old prison cell downstairs; now a very comfy pub. Q 🛏 ◖ ◗ ♿ P

Stockwell Arms
18 West Stockwell Street (near A1124) ☎ (01206) 575560
11–11; 10.30–3.30, 6.30–11 Sat
Marston's Pedigree; Nethergate Bitter; Ruddles Best Bitter; Wadworth 6X; Webster's Yorkshire Bitter [H]
Old, timber-framed pub in the Dutch quarter, popular with all. The landlord organises regular walks through local countryside.
❀ ◖ ⇌ (North/Town) ⊟

Tap & Spile
123–125 Crouch Street (near A1124) ☎ (01206) 573572
11–2.30, 5.30–11; 11–11 Sat
Adnams Bitter; Marston's Pedigree; Nethergate Bitter; S&N Theakston Best Bitter; guest beers [H]
Pleasant single-bar pub just outside the town centre. Five guest beers. ❀ ◖ ♣ ⌓

Coxtie Green

White Horse
173 Coxtie Green Road (1 mile W of A128) OS563959
☎ (01277) 372410
11.30–3, 5.30–11; 12–4, 7–11 Sat
Beer range varies [H]
Fairly small, pleasant and comfortable pub serving up to six beers, usually including local independents. Beer festival second weekend in June. No food Sun.
❀ ◖ ◗ ⊞ ♣ P

Dedham

Sun Hotel
High Street ☎ (01206) 323351
11–3, 6–11
Adnams Bitter; John Smith's Bitter; guest beer [H]
15th-century hotel in a picturesque village. Very spacious, with a huge beer garden, it is supposedly haunted by the last witch to be burnt in this country. Regular food specials.
🔥 ❀ 🛏 ◖ ◗ ♿ ♣ P

Earls Colne

Bird in Hand
Coggeshall Road (B1024)
☎ (01787) 222557
12–2.30, 6–11; 12–2.30, 7–10.30 Sun
Ridleys Mild [G]**, IPA** [H]**, ESX, Witchfinder Porter, Winter Ale** [G]
Oyster-like: a drab exterior conceals a pearl of a quiet, traditional, two-bar pub.
🔥 Q ❀ ◖ ◗ ⊞ ♿ ♣ P

Castle
High Street ☎ (01787) 222694
12–11
Greene King XX Mild, IPA, Abbot [H]
Beamed pub with log fires. No meals Sun eve or Mon.
🔥 Q ❀ ◖ ◗ ♣ P

East Tilbury

Ship
Princess Margaret Road
☎ (01375) 843041
11–3, 6–11; 11–11 Sat (may vary winter)
Courage Directors [H]**; Crouch Vale Millennium Gold** (summer) [H]/[G]**; Greene King IPA; guest beers** [H]
Former Courage tied house, now free: the saloon bar has a nautical theme. Food at all sessions; vegetarians catered for. Q ❀ ◖ ◗ ⊞ ♣ P ⊟

Elsenham

Crown
High Street (B1051)
☎ (01279) 812827
10–2.30, 6–11; 12–2.30, 7–10.30 Sun
Crouch Vale Millennium Gold; Tetley Bitter; guest beers [H]
Deservedly popular, friendly village pub with a pargetted exterior and a good reputation for food (but only bread and cheese Sun). Guest beers come from independents.
🔥 ❀ ◖ ◗ ♣ P

Epping

Forest Gate
Bell Common (just off B1393, Ivy Chimneys road) OS451011
☎ (01992) 572312
10–2.30, 5.30–11
Adnams Bitter [H]**, Broadside; Greene King Abbot** [G]**; Ridleys IPA** [H]**; guest beer** [G]
On the edge of Epping Forest, a traditionally-decorated pub with a small bar which can get very busy.
🔥 Q ❀ ◖ ♣ ⌓ P

Feering

Sun Inn
3 Feering Hill (B1024, near Blackwater Bridge)
☎ (01376) 570442
11–2.30, 3–11; 11–11 Sat
Wadworth 6X; guest beers [H]
Timbered pub with exposed beams and open fireplaces. The bistro-style English and Mediterranean food is all home-cooked. Families welcome. Four guest beers.

Phone first to camp. 🏕 ❀ ◖ ▶ & ▲ ⇌ (Kelvedon) ✚ P

Felsted

Chequers

Braintree Road (B1417)
☎ (01371) 820226
11–2.30, 6–11; 11–11 Fri, Sat & summer
Ridleys IPA, ESX Ⓗ
Solid Victorian pub in a sleepy village. A sporting atmosphere spills over from the nearby public school. The landlord has presided now for 40 years. Good value food; weekend barbecues in summer.
🏕 Q ⓢ ❀ ◖ ▶ ⊞ & ✚ P

Fingringhoe

Whalebone

Chapel Road ☎ (01206) 729307
11–3, 6–11
Adnams Bitter; Greene King IPA; Mauldons Bitter, White Adder Ⓗ
Friendly country local in pleasant village surroundings. Families are welcome (fenced-off children's area). Vegetarian and vegan food only, all home-cooked. Close to the Essex Wildlife Trust nature reserve.
🏕 Q ⓢ ❀ ◖ ▶ & P ⑂

Fobbing

White Lion

Lion Hill (B1420, 1 mile S of A13) ☎ (01375) 673281
11–2.30 (4 Sat), 6–11
Ind Coope Benskins BB, Burton Ale; Tetley Bitter; guest beer Ⓗ
Friendly, unspoilt coaching inn which feels like a country pub, despite the proximity of Basildon and the A13. It enjoys a pleasant position on the brow of a hill, overlooking a fine church. No food Sun, or Sat eve. 🏕 Q ❀ ◖ ▶ P

Fordstreet

Cooper's Arms

On A604 ☎ (01206) 241177
12–3, 5 (7 Sat)–11
Greene King IPA; guest beers Ⓗ
Cosy, single-bar village pub boasting a grandfather clock and unusual but comfortable seating. ❀ ◖ ▶ ✚ P

Old Queen's Head

On A604 ☎ (01206) 241584
11–2.30, 6–11 (11–11 summer)
Adnams Bitter; John Smith's Bitter; guest beers Ⓗ
Friendly, 17th-century coaching house-type building, well restored. Timber beams and flagstone floors feature.
🏕 Q ❀ ◖ ▶ & ✚ P

Fyfield

Queen's Head

Queen's Street (off B184)
☎ (01277) 899231
11–3, 6–11; 11–11 Sat
Adnams Bitter; Greene King IPA; Whitbread Boddingtons Bitter; guest beers Ⓗ
Genuine free house, the focal point of the village, popular with all ages. Its long bar has spacious alcoves. Regularly changing guest beers (at least two) always come from independents. The garden looks on to the River Roding. No food Sat eve. ❀ ◖ ▶ ✚ P

Gestingthorpe

Pheasant

Audley End ☎ (01787) 61196
11–3, 6–11
Adnams Bitter, Broadside; Greene King IPA; Nethergate Bitter; guest beers Ⓗ
Multi-roomed pub traditionally furnished, with a friendly local atmosphere. Excellent value food is cooked on the premises, including an extensive vegetarian menu (book weekends). Local cider.
🏕 ⓢ ❀ ◖ ▶ ▲ ✚ ⊂ P

Grays

Bricklayer's Arms

48 Bridge Road (next to football ground)
☎ (01375) 372265
11–3 (may be later), 5–11
Draught Bass; Fuller's London Pride; Hancock's HB Ⓗ
Street-corner, community local: a comfortable saloon and a traditional public. A modern conservatory leads to a pleasant, secure garden with rabbits and an aviary (families welcome in these areas). Food Mon–Fri. ⓢ ❀ ◖ ⊞ ⇌ ✚ P

Theobald Arms

141 Argent Street/King's Walk (near A126) ☎ (01375) 372253
10.30–3, 5.30–11; 10.30–11 Fri & Sat
Courage Best Bitter; Directors; Crouch Vale Millennium Gold Ⓗ
Traditional, family-run, two-bar pub, close to the river. An unusual revolving pool table is housed in the public bar. Good value food.
❀ ◖ ▶ ⊞ & ⇌ ✚ P

Great Bardfield

Vine

Vine Street ☎ (01371) 810355
11–3, 6–11
Ridleys IPA, Mild, Witchfinder Porter Ⓗ
Friendly family pub in an historic and beautiful village. Good value food in large portions. Play area for children. ❀ ◖ ▶ ⊞ ✚ P

Great Clacton

Robin Hood

211 London Road (old A133)
☎ (01255) 421519
12–11
Draught Bass; Hancock's HB; guest beers Ⓗ
A sure shot in Clacton – the best in the area: a large, low-ceilinged pub with an emphasis on food and service.
🏕 Q ◖ ▶ & P ⑂

Great Sampford

Red Lion Inn

Finchingfield Road (B1053)
☎ (01799) 586325
12–3, 5.30–11 (may vary if busy)
Ridleys IPA, ESX, Witchfinder Porter (winter) Ⓗ
Friendly local with a games room and a no-smoking restaurant.
🏕 ❀ ⇱ ◖ ▶ ✚ P

Halstead

Dog Inn

37 Hedingham Road (A604)
☎ (01787) 477774
12–2.30, 6–11
Adnams Bitter; Nethergate Bitter; guest beer Ⓗ
Friendly, 18th-century local, with reasonably-priced accommodation, close to the town centre. Families welcome.
🏕 Q ❀ ⇱ ◖ ▶ ✚ ⊂ P

Harwich

Alma Inn

25 King's Head Street (off the quay) ☎ (01255) 503474
11–3 (later summer), 7 (6 Fri)–11
Greene King IPA; Tolly Cobbold Mild; guest beer Ⓗ
One large bar with a tiny private bar alongside in a pub built in Elizabethan times and refronted by the Georgians. The house beer is brewed by Tolly Cobbold.
🏕 Q ❀ ◖ ⇌ (Town) ✚

Hanover Inn

65 Church Street
☎ (01255) 502927
10.30–3 (later if busy), 6.30–11
Tolly Cobbold Mild, Old Strong Ⓗ
Cosy, timbered fisherman's pub with Admiralty charts displayed in the front bar. The fire burns coal trawled from the sea. Pool and darts in the back bar. Two other Tolly beers are usually available,

including a house beer.
🏚 ⊞ ⇌ (Town) ♣

Hazeleigh

Royal Oak
Fambridge Road (B1018)
☎ (01621) 853249
11–4, 6–11
Greene King XX Mild, IPA Ⓗ
Simple Gray's pub with a
good reputation. ✿ ◑ ▶ ⊞

Helions Bumpstead

Three Horseshoes
Water Lane OS650414
☎ (01440) 730298
11.45–2.30, 7–11; 12–2.30, 7–10.30
Sun
Greene King IPA, Abbot Ⓗ
Fine, friendly, remote old pub
boasting superb award-
winning gardens. No food
Mon/Tue eves or Sun. Greene
King seasonal beers sold.
🏚 Q ✿ ◑ ▶ ⊞ ▲ ♣ P

Hempstead

Blue Bell Inn
High Street ☎ (01799) 599486
11.30–3, 6.30–11; closed Mon
Greene King IPA, Rayments
Special; guest beer Ⓗ
Excellent, welcoming, 16th-
century, listed building in a
delightful village. The dining
area offers a comprehensive
range of good value food (not
served Sun eve). The
birthplace of Dick Turpin.
🏚 Q ⛄ ✿ ◑ ▶ ♣ P

Heybridge

Maltster's Arms
Hall Road (near B1022)
☎ (01621) 853880
11–3, 6–11
Greene King IPA, Abbot Ⓖ
Intimate local, enjoying a good
lunchtime trade. Q ♣

High Roding

Black Lion
The Street (B184)
☎ (01279) 872847
10.30–3, 6–11
Ridleys IPA, ESX Ⓖ
15th-century pub with a
timber-framed interior. The
landlord's cottage garden at
the rear supplies fresh
vegetables for cooking. Ridleys
seasonal ales sold.
🏚 Q ✿ ◑ ▶ ♣ P

Horndon on the Hill

Bell
High Road ☎ (01375) 672451

11–2.30 (3 Sat), 6–11
Bass Charrington IPA Ⓗ,
Draught Bass Ⓖ; Fuller's
London Pride; guest beers Ⓗ
Popular, 15th-century
coaching inn in a picturesque
village, with a 95-year-old hot
cross bun collection! Quality
food is served in the pub and
restaurant. Good views from
the patio. Occasional beer
festivals; the guest beers
change regularly.
🏚 Q ✿ 🛏 ◑ ▶ P

Langley Lower Green

Bull
OS436345 ☎ (01279) 777307
12–2.30, 6–11
Adnams Bitter, Broadside;
Greene King IPA Ⓗ
Classic, rural Victorian local in
one of the smallest Essex
villages. A pitch-penny game
is concealed under a bench in
the saloon. 🏚 Q ✿ ⊞ ♣ P

Lawford

Station Buffet
Manningtree Station (near
A137) ☎ (01206) 391114
10.30–11
Adnams Bitter; Exmoor Stag;
Ridleys IPA, Witchfinder
Porter Ⓗ
Classic station buffet famous
for its excellent, home-cooked
food (book Sun lunch), served
in a tiny, four-person dining
area. Small patio.
Q ✿ ◑ 🔔 ⇌ P

Leigh-on-Sea

Broker
213–217 Leigh Road
☎ (01702) 471932
11–3, 6–11
Crouch Vale Woodham IPA;
Shepherd Neame Master
Brew Bitter, Spitfire; guest
beers Ⓗ
Friendly, family-run local
serving good quality,
traditional, home-cooked food
in the bar and restaurant
(steaks a speciality). ✿ ◑

Crooked Billet
51 High Street, Old Leigh
☎ (01702) 714854
11.30–11
Adnams Bitter; Ind Coope
Burton Ale; Tetley Bitter Ⓗ;
guest beers Ⓗ/Ⓖ
Friendly, listed, 16th-century
pub with estuary views,
formerly the haunt of
smugglers, in an old fishing
town. This Taylor Walker
Heritage pub offers an
extensive fish menu, home-
made pub fare and vegetarian

dishes (no food Sun). At least
three guest beers.
🏚 Q ✿ ◑ ⊞ ⇌

Elms
1060 London Road (A13)
☎ (01702) 74687
10–11
Courage Directors; Greene
King Abbot; S&N Theakston
Best Bitter, XB; Younger
Scotch; guest beers Ⓗ
After three years' disuse,
Wetherspoon's conversion of
this pub is welcome in the
area. The large single bar
features historical photographs
of Leigh. Weekends are busy.
Food served all day.
Q ✿ ◑ ⅙ P ⧖

Little Bentley

Bricklayer's Arms
Rectory Road (near A120)
☎ (01206) 250405
12 (11.30 Sat)–3.30, 6.30–11
Greene King IPA Ⓗ;
Mauldons Squires Ⓖ
Small country pub, family-run
and proud of its food. Popular
with the locals. Q ✿ ◑ ▶ P

Little Braxted

Green Man
Kelvedon Road (1½ miles SE of
village) OS849130
☎ (01621) 891659
11.30–3, 6–11
Ridleys IPA, ESX Ⓗ
Traditional pub in an idyllic
setting with a pleasant garden.
🏚 Q ✿ ◑ ▶ ⊞ ♣ P

Littlebury

Queen's Head
High Street ☎ (01799) 522251
12–11
Draught Bass; Courage
Directors; John Smith's Bitter;
Younger IPA; guest beers Ⓗ
600-year-old village local with
traditional features and good
accommodation. The landlord
is an accomplished chef. It
offered over 140 guest beers in
1994; Easter beer festival. No
food Sun eve.
🏚 ✿ 🛏 ◑ ⅙ ♣ P

Little Easton

Stag
Duck Street (1 mile W of B184)
☎ (01371) 870214
11–2.30 (later if busy), 6–11
Ridleys IPA Ⓗ
Refurbished village local,
enjoying a friendly
atmosphere and fine views
over the Chelmer Valley from
its large garden (which has an
excellent children's play area).
🏚 ✿ ◑ ▶ ⊞ ▲ ♣ P

Little Hallingbury

Sutton Arms
Bishops Stortford Road, Hall Green (A1060)
☎ (01279) 730460
11–2.30, 6–11; 12–3, 5–11 Sat
B&T Shefford Bitter; Ind Coope Burton Ale; Tetley Bitter; guest beer Ⓗ
Attractive pub with a deserved reputation for its wide choice of food. One section retains a 'village local' atmosphere. Book to camp (limited space).
🏚 ❀ ◑ ▶ ▲ ♣ P

Little Oakley

Olde Cherry Tree
Clacton Road (B1414)
☎ (01255) 880333
11–2.30, 7–11
Adnams Bitter, Broadside Ⓗ
Pub where a log fire heats both bars in winter. Occasional gravity-dispensed ales add further interest to the beer range. Lunches at weekends.
🏚 ◑ P

Littley Green

Compasses
Off B1417 opp. Ridleys Brewery OS699172
☎ (01245) 362308
11–3, 6–11
Ridleys IPA, Mild, ESX, Witchfinder Porter, Winter Ale Ⓖ
Victorian, cottage-style pub, the Ridleys brewery tap; difficult to find, but worth the effort. Local CAMRA *Pub of the Year* 1994 (for the fourth time). The bar food speciality is the Essex Huffer (a very large bap).
🏚 Q ☻ ❀ ◑ ▶ ♣ P

Loughton

Wheatsheaf
15 York Hill (off A121, N end of High St) ☎ (0181) 508 9656
11–11
Bass Charrington IPA, Draught Bass; Fuller's London Pride; Hancock's HB Ⓗ
Suburban London pub with an extended bar, popular with the locals. The garden is on the opposite side of the road. The beer list may alter slightly (beer is a bit pricey).
❀ ◑ ♣ P

Maldon

Blue Boar
Silver Street
☎ (01621) 852681
11–2.30 (3 Fri & Sat), 6–11
Adnams Bitter Ⓖ
Friendly, old coaching inn in the town centre, full of character, with a wealth of exposed beams. A classic.
🏚 Q ❀ 🛏 ◑ ▶ ⊟ P

Jolly Sailor
Church Street, The Hythe
☎ (01621) 853463
11–3, 6–11
Courage Directors; Morland Old Speckled Hen; Ruddles Best Bitter Ⓗ
Traditional quayside pub in a superb position overlooking the estuary, giving fine views of Thames barges. Enjoy a stroll along the prom. Limited parking. ❀ 🛏 ◑ ▶ P

Queen's Head
The Hythe ☎ (01621) 854112
10.30–11
Greene King IPA, Abbot Ⓗ
Three-bar pub with a strong nautical atmosphere, overlooking the busy quayside. 🏚 Q ❀ ◑ ⊟ ♣ P

Mashbury

Fox
Fox Road OS650127
☎ (01245) 231573
12–2, 6.30–11
Ridleys IPA, ESX Ⓖ
Friendly, 350-year-old, cosy, country pub with a good value menu (book Sun lunch). Casks are on stillage behind the bar. Hard to find, but worth the effort. 🏚 Q ❀ ◑ ▶ ♣ P

Matching Tye

Fox Inn
The Green OS516113
☎ (01279) 731335
12–3, 7–11
Draught Bass; Fuller's London Pride; guest beers Ⓗ
Three-roomed pub, catering for over-18s only in the left side; the right side is for food. The extensive garden has a petanque area. Normally two guest beers.
🏚 Q ❀ ◑ ▶ ♿ ♣ P

Mill End Green

Green Man
E of B184 OS619260
☎ (01371) 870286
11.30–3, 6–11
Adnams Bitter; Greene King IPA; Ridleys IPA Ⓗ
Friendly, 15th-century, oak-studded, low-beamed country pub, featured in TV's *Lovejoy*. Superb gardens, and an outdoor drinking area for families. Good value food (not served Sun eve).
🏚 Q ❀ 🛏 ◑ ▶ ▲ ♣ P

Mill Green

Viper
Mill Green Road (2 miles NW of Ingatestone) OS641019
☎ (01277) 352010
11–2.30 (3 Sat), 6–11
Beer range varies Ⓗ
Unspoilt country pub in a picturesque woodland setting.
🏚 ❀ ◑ ♣ P

Mountnessing

Prince of Wales
199 Roman Road (B1002)
☎ (01277) 353445
11–3, 6–11
Ridleys IPA, Mild, ESX, Witchfinder Porter Ⓗ
Old, timber-beamed, roadside pub with two distinct drinking areas. 🏚 ❀ ◑ ▶ P

Navestock Heath

Plough Inn
Sabines Road OS538970
☎ (01277) 372296
11–3.30, 6–11
Brains Dark; Cotleigh Tawny; Taylor Landlord; guest beers Ⓗ
Excellent, friendly pub usually stocking 11 ales, always including a mild. Real cider is not on the bar – ask. Local CAMRA *Pub of the Year* 1992–1995. Good value food and beer.
🏚 ☻ ❀ ▶ ♿ ♣ ◔ P

Newney Green

Duck Inn
Near A414; between Writtle and Ongar OS651070
☎ (01245) 421894
11–3, 6–11
S&N Theakston Best Bitter, Old Peculier; Younger IPA; guest beers Ⓗ
Remote, skilfully-modernised farmhouse in a tiny hamlet, now a fine country pub/restaurant. The large garden has a pond. Fine, home-cooked food. The cosy bar has a resident ghost.
❀ ◑ ▶ P

Newport

Coach & Horses
Cambridge Road (B1383)
☎ (01799) 540292
11–3, 6–11
Draught Bass; Whitbread Boddingtons Bitter, Flowers IPA, Original Ⓗ
Warm, welcoming, 16th-century coaching inn offering excellent restaurant and bar food.
🏚 Q ❀ ◑ ▶ ▲ 🚃 ♣ P ✗

109

Essex

Orsett

Foxhound
High Road (B188)
☎ (01375) 891295
12–3.30, 6–11; 11–11 Sat
Courage Best Bitter, Directors; Truman IPA Ⓗ
Traditional village local, an ideal retreat from industrial South Essex. Foxhound memorabilia adorns the saloon while the public bar retains a rustic feel. The Fox's Den restaurant has a good local reputation. Q ⌂ ⓓ ▶ ⏏ ♣ P

Pebmarsh

King's Head
The Street OS851335
☎ (01787) 269306
11–2.30, 6–11
Beer range varies Ⓗ
A real ale drinkers' paradise, with a constantly changing line-up of at least four beers. Hot food available most of the time; cider in summer.
Q ⌂ ⓓ ▶ ⌂ ⌂ P

Pleshey

White Horse
The Street ☎ (01245) 237281
11–3, 7–11
Beer range varies Ⓗ
Pleasant old pub in an historic village, full of nooks and crannies. Families welcome. Wide range of home-cooked food. Ask about the pub ghosts. ᴁ Q ⌂ ⓓ ▶ ⌂ P

Prittlewell

Spread Eagle
267 Victoria Avenue (A127, near Southend Utd FC)
☎ (01702) 348383
11.30–3, 5–11; 11.30–11 Thu & Fri; 11–4, 7–11 Sat
Bass Charrington IPA; Hancock's HB; M&B Highgate Dark; Wadworth 6X; guest beers Ⓗ
Traditional-style alehouse, holding beer festivals most bank hols, with about 50 guest beers, ciders, and a barbecue. Music club Fri night.
Q ⌂ ⓓ ▶ ⌂ ⌂ ⏏ ♣

Purleigh

Bell
The Street (near B1010)
OS842020 ☎ (01621) 828348
11–3, 6–11
Adnams Bitter; Greene King IPA; Ind Coope Benskins BB; Marston's Pedigree Ⓗ
Traditional country pub commanding the high ground in the village; spacious, comfortable and popular.

Good value food (not served Fri eve). Q ⌂ ⓓ ▶ P

Radley Green

Cuckoo
500 yds from A414 between Writtle and Norton Heath OS622054 ☎ (01245) 248356
12–2.30, 6–11
Ridleys IPA, Mild (summer), **Witchfinder Porter** (winter), **ESX** Ⓗ, **Winter Ale** Ⓖ
Secluded, friendly, one-bar local with a large caravan and camping area. Snacks only Sun lunchtime.
ᴁ Q ⌂ ⓓ ▶ ⌂ ♣ P

Rayleigh

Old White Horse
39–41 High Street (A129)
☎ (01268) 777622
10–11
Bass Charrington IPA, Worthington BB, Draught Bass; Fuller's London Pride; guest beers Ⓗ
Single-bar, town-centre pub popular with shoppers. Sport-oriented, its three TV screens regularly feature events. Breakfast daily from 8am (except Sun – no food).
ᴁ ⌂ ⓓ ⌂ ⏏ ♣ P

Rickling Green

Cricketer's Arms
½ mile W of B1383, near Quendon OS511298
☎ (01799) 543210
12–3, 6–11
Whitbread Flowers IPA; guest beers Ⓖ
Enlarged old pub in an idyllic setting overlooking the cricket green. Guest beers always include a mild, or a dark beer, and a strong ale. Excellent and imaginative food; restaurant open 12–7 on Sun.
ᴁ ⌂ ⌂ ⌂ ⌂ ⓓ ▶ ⌂ ♣ P

Rochford

Golden Lion
35 North Street
☎ (01702) 545487
12–11 (may close 3–5 if not busy)
Fuller's London Pride; Greene King Abbot; guest beers Ⓗ
300-year-old ex-tailor's shop; compact, with a good atmosphere. A good variety of guest beers includes a mild. Local CAMRA *Pub of the Year* awards displayed.
⌂ ⌂ ⓓ ⏏ ♣ ⌂

Milestone
Union Lane (off B1013)
☎ (01702) 544229
10–11
Greene King Rayments Special, Abbot; guest beers Ⓗ
Traditional-style pub conversion in a cul-de-sac near

the hospital. Upstairs games room. ⌂ ⓓ ⌂ ⏏ ♣

Rowhedge

Walnut Tree
Fringringhoe Road (1 mile E of B1025) ☎ (01206) 728149
7.30–11; 12–3, 7–11 Sat; closed Mon
Maclay 80/-; guest beers Ⓗ
Lively, rural pub on the outskirts of Colchester, with a rock jukebox. The beer range varies, one is usually cheap. Cheese club Fri eve from 9pm. Lunches Sat/Sun (closed Mon-Fri lunchtime).
⌂ ⓓ ⌂ ♣ P

St Osyth

White Hart
71 Mill Street (W of village)
☎ (01255) 820318
12–3, 7–11
Adnams Bitter; guest beers Ⓗ
Essex CAMRA *Pub of the Year* 1995. Mini-beer festivals are held on bank hols at this family-run pub with a commitment to guest beers. Mellow, mock-Tudor interior.
ᴁ ⌂ ⌂ ⓓ ▶ ⌂ P

St Osyth Heath

Beehive
Heath Road, Chisbon Heath OS139185 ☎ (01255) 830396
11–3, 7–11
Adnams Bitter; Greene King IPA; Tetley Bitter Ⓗ
Pub built in 1993, partly on the site of the burnt-out original. The open-plan lounge around a central bar has a period feel. Young clientele.
ᴁ Q ⌂ ⌂ ♣ P

Saffron Walden

Cross Keys
32 High Street (B184)
☎ (01799) 522207
10.30–11
Ind Coope Benskins BB, Burton Ale Ⓔ; **Tetley Bitter** Ⓗ; **guest beers** Ⓔ
Dated 1450, this single-bar (plus pool room) pub has a good lunchtime trade and can be busy in the eve and weekends. The landlord is a member of the *Guild of Master Cellarmen*. ⌂ ⌂ ⓓ ▶ ⌂ P

Eight Bells
18 Bridge Street
☎ (01799) 522790
11–3, 6–11
Adnams Bitter; Ind Coope Friary Meux BB, Burton Ale; Tetley Bitter; guest beers Ⓗ
16th-century, oak-beamed inn: a single bar with a family room off; the rest of the pub is given over to food. Wide range of good, reasonably-

priced meals. Busy at weekends. ☆ ❀ ◖ ▶ P

Sible Hedingham

Sugar Loaves
175 Swan Street (A604)
☎ (01787) 462720
12–11
Greene King IPA; Whitbread Boddingtons Bitter, Flowers IPA; guest beers Ⓗ
Recently restored, 15th-century, oak-beamed inn; a friendly local with two bars. Live music weekly. Thai food is a speciality. The house bitter is brewed by Mauldons.
🏚 ☆ ❀ ◖ ▶ ⊟ ♿ ♣ P

South Benfleet

Half Crown
27 High Street (B1014)
☎ (01268) 792027
12–11
Draught Bass; Fuller's London Pride; Hancock's HB; M&B Brew XI; guest beer Ⓗ
Thoughtfully renovated family pub. The cellar is below sea level. Regular beer festivals are a feature. Eve meals Mon–Thu.
❀ ◖ ▶ ⇌ ♣ P

Southend-on-Sea

Baker's Bar
Royals Court, 15–17 Alexandra Street (off High St)
☎ (01702) 390403
12–3.30, 5.30–midnight (1am Fri & Sat); 7–10.30 Sun, closed Sun lunch
Adnams Broadside Ⓖ**; Courage Directors; Ridleys IPA; Shepherd Neame Master Brew Bitter** Ⓗ**, Bishops Finger; guest beers** Ⓖ
Authentic, lively former Victorian bakehouse, now an extended cellar bar. Large range of gravity ales and two ciders. Relaxed ambience with music; jazz Sun. No food Sun. Expensive.
❀ ◖ ▶ ⇌ (Central) ⌂

Cork & Cheese
10 Talza Way, Victoria Circus (near A13/A127)
☎ (01702) 616914
11–11; closed Sun
Beer range varies Ⓗ
An oasis in a concrete desert, namely Victoria Circus shopping centre. Ever-changing range of independent brewers' beers. 1994–1995 local CAMRA *Pub of the Year*. Lunches Mon–Fri.
❀ ◖ ⇌ (Victoria) ♣ ⌂

Liberty Belle
10–12 Marine Parade
☎ (01702) 466936
10–11
Courage Best Bitter, Directors; Truman IPA; guest beers Ⓗ

The black sheep of the seafront; it serves a strong regular trade with ales from independent brewers as well as Courage. Darts and pool; rock disco at weekends.
☆ ❀ 🚐 ◖ ⇌ (Central) ♣ ⌂

South Fambridge

Anchor Hotel
Fambridge Road
☎ (01702) 203535
11–3, 6–11; 11–11 Sat
Adnams Bitter; Crouch Vale IPA; Greene King Abbot; guest beers Ⓗ
Traditional, two-bar pub dating back to 1900, close to the River Crouch. Excellent food in a friendly atmosphere. Cider in summer.
❀ ◖ ▶ ♣ ⌂ P

Southminster

Station Arms
39 Station Road
☎ (01621) 772225
12–3, 5.30–11; 12–11 Sat
Crouch Vale Best Bitter; guest beers Ⓗ
Weather-boarded, high street pub offering varied guest beers on a regular basis. Friendly and informal. Regular beer festivals. No eve meals Sun or Wed.
🏚 Q ☆ ❀ ◖ ▶ ⇌ ⌂

Stansted Mountfitchet

Dog & Duck
58 Lower Street (B1351, near B1051 jct) ☎ (01279) 812047
10–2.30, 5.30–11
Greene King IPA, Rayments Special, Abbot Ⓗ
400-year-old, typical weather-boarded and timbered Essex village local offering a genuinely friendly welcome. Snacks Mon–Sat lunchtime.
Q ❀ ⊟ ⇌ ♣ P

Stapleford Abbotts

Rabbits
Stapleford Road (B175)
☎ (01708) 688203
11–2.30 (3 Sat), 6–11
Adnams Bitter; Ind Coope Benskins BB, Burton Ale Ⓗ
Friendly local with a children's play area in the garden. No meals Sun eve.
🏚 Q ❀ ◖ ▶ P

Stapleford Tawney

Moletrap
Tawney Common (single track road, 1 mile W of Toot Hill) OS502014 ☎ (01992) 522394

12–3, 7–11 (may open earlier summer)
McMullen AK, Country; guest beer (summer) Ⓗ
Isolated free house, a farming community pub popular with all ages, in rolling countryside. 400 years old, it was once owned by an inventor of an unusual moletrap.
🏚 Q ❀ ◖ P

Stisted

Dolphin
Coggeshall Road (A120)
☎ (01376) 321143
11–3, 6–11
Ridleys IPA, ESX Ⓖ
Traditional, beamed pub with two bars, one retaining a public bar atmosphere. Good value food (not served Tue or Sun eves). 🏚 Q ❀ ◖ ▶ ⊟ P

Stock

Hoop
High Street ☎ (01277) 841137
11–11
Adnams Mild, Bitter; Jennings Cocker Hoop; Mitchell's Lancaster Bomber; Nethergate Umbel Magna; guest beers Ⓗ
Very popular small bar which holds an annual beer festival in May. Good range of reasonably priced food; at least six guest ales (polypin off-sales). Large garden.
Q ❀ ◖ ▶ ♣ ⌂

Stow Maries

Prince of Wales
Woodham Road OS830993
☎ (01621) 828971
11–11
Fuller's Chiswick; guest beers Ⓗ
Beautifully restored rural gem with a working Victorian bakery and a changing range of five or six esoteric ales (always a mild and a stout or porter). The flagship of Big Ears beer agency, it was CAMRA's East Anglian *Pub of the Year* 1994. Excellent food featuring local produce.
🏚 Q ☆ ❀ ◖ ▶ ▲ ♣ ⌂ P

Thaxted

Rose & Crown Inn
31 Mill End (near B184)
☎ (01371) 831152
11 (12 winter)–2.30, 6–11
Ridleys IPA; guest beers Ⓗ
Friendly, well-run local in an historic town with a magnificent church, Guildhall and windmill. It is believed to have been built on the site of a monks' hostelry. The cosy dining area offers excellent,

home-cooked food.
⊛ ⇔ ◖ ⋈ ◓ ▲ ♣ P

Star

Mill End (B184)
☎ (01371) 830368
11–3 (may vary), 5.30–11 (11–11 summer)
Adnams Mild, Bitter, Broadside; guest beers Ⓗ
Popular local with a keen darts following. Exposed beams and vast brick fireplaces feature in both bars. Safe children's play area. Good value food.
⋈ ⊛ ◖ ◓ ♣ P

Tillingham

Cap & Feathers

8 South Street (B1021)
☎ (01621) 779212
11.30–3, 6–11
Crouch Vale IPA, Best Bitter, Essex Porter; guest beers Ⓗ
Unspoilt, 15th-century pub offering good, home-cooked food, traditional games and a welcoming atmosphere.
⋈ Q ⅀ ⊛ ⇔ ◖ ♣ ⌂ P

Waltham Abbey

Old Spotted Cow

Fountain Place
☎ (01992) 711345
11–11; 12–2, 7–10.30 Sun
McMullen AK, Stronghart Ⓗ
Popular, suburban local with two bars, close to the market square and abbey. No food Sun. ⊛ ◖ ◓ ♣ P

Walton-on-the-Naze

Royal Marine

3 Old Pier Street (near B1034)
☎ (01255) 674000
11–11
Adnams Bitter, Broadside; Marston's Pedigree; Whitbread Boddingtons Bitter Ⓖ
Ex-wine bar, and it still appears so from the outside. Inside, however, is a superb, three-bar pub. Q ⅄ ▲ ⇌

Warley

Brave Nelson

138 Woodman Road (off B186)
☎ (01277) 211690
12–3, 5.30–11; 12–11 Sat
Courage Directors *or* **guest beer; Nethergate Bitter; Ruddles Best Bitter; Webster's Yorkshire Bitter** Ⓗ
Comfortable, pleasant local with wood panelling in both bar areas and many nautical

artefacts. A rare outlet for Nethergate in this area. No food Sun. ⊛ ◖ ♣ P

Westcliff-on-Sea

Hamlet

54 Hamlet Court Road
☎ (01702) 391752
11–11
Adnams Bitter; Greene King Abbot; John Smith's Bitter; Younger IPA; guest beers Ⓗ
Former bank now a one-bar pub offering table service. Popular with young people and often crowded at weekends. Very reasonably priced for the area. ◖ ◗ ⇌

Palace Theatre Centre

430 London Road (A13/West Rd jct) ☎ (01702) 347816
12–2.30 (3 Sat), 6–11
Beer range varies Ⓗ
Foyer bar adjoining an early 1900s theatre. A bistro is incorporated (no food Sun lunchtime). Live bands Sun eve. Q ⊛ ◖ ◗ ⅄ ✍

West Thurrock

Fox & Goose

584 London Road (A126, near Lakeside Shopping Centre)
☎ (01708) 866026
11–11 (may close afternoons if quiet)
Greene King IPA; Tetley Bitter; Wadworth 6X Ⓗ
Traditionally re-styled local; a place to relax after shopping at Lakeside! ⊛ ◖ ◗ ◓ ⅄ P

White Notley

Cross Keys

1 The Street ☎ (01376) 583297
11–3, 6.30–11
Ridleys Mild, IPA, ESX Ⓗ
Unspoilt, 14th-century village local, formerly owned by Chappells Brewery. Eve meals Fri and Sat; no lunches Tue. Ridleys seasonal ales sold.
⋈ ⊛ ◖ ◗ ◓ ♣ P

Wickham Bishops

Mitre

2 The Street ☎ (01621) 891378
11–3.30, 5.30–11; 11–11 Sat
Ridleys IPA, ESX Ⓗ
Lively village local staging regular social events. Busy restaurant.
⋈ Q ⊛ ◖ ◗ ◓ ♣ P

Widdington

Fleur de Lys

High Street ☎ (01799) 540659

12–3, 6–11
Adnams Bitter; Draught Bass; Wadworth IPA, 6X; Whitbread Flowers Original; guest beers Ⓗ
Friendly, well-run village local, offering a good choice of ales and an extensive range of good value, home-cooked dishes. Live folk music Fri eve. Basic but comfortable family room.
⋈ Q ⅀ ⊛ ◖ ◗ ⅄ ▲ ♣ P

Widford

Sir Evelyn Wood

56 Widford Road (near A414)
☎ (01245) 269239
11–3, 6–11
Greene King IPA, Abbot; guest beers Ⓗ
Basic, two-bar local with a games/meeting room.
⊛ ◖ ◗ ◓ ♣

Wivenhoe

Horse & Groom

55 The Cross (B1028, outskirts of village) ☎ (01206) 824928
10.30–3, 5.30–11
Adnams Mild, Bitter, Old; guest beer Ⓗ
Adnams house in a pretty sailing village which always tries to offer Adnams seasonal beers, and interesting guests. Q ⊛ ◖ ⅄ ♣ P

Woodham Mortimer

Hurdlemaker's Arms

Post Office Road (between A414 and B1010)
☎ (01245) 225169
11–3, 6–11
Greene King IPA, Abbot Ⓗ
Run to the highest standards, this superb Gray's outlet has olde-worlde charm and fine gardens. Barbecues Sun lunchtimes are far removed from the burger and bun variety. No food Fri eve.
⋈ Q ⊛ ◖ ◗ ◓ ⅄ ♣ P

Writtle

Wheatsheaf

70 The Green (A122)
☎ (01245) 420695
11–2.30 (3 Fri, 4 Sat), 5.30–11
Greene King XX Mild, IPA, Abbot Ⓗ
Small, friendly village local with traditional decor, but also a Watney's Red Barrel on the bar! Q ⊛ ◓ ♣ P ⊟

Do you care about your pub and your pint? Join CAMRA and help us protect your pleasure.

Gloucestershire

Berkeley, *Berkeley*; **Donnington**, *Stow-on-the-Wold*; **Farmers Arms**, *Apperley*; **Freeminer**, *Sling*; **Goff's**, *Winchcombe*; **Stanway**, *Stanway*; **Uley**, *Uley*

Amberley

Black Horse
N end of village
☎ (01453) 872556
12–3, 6–11; 11–11 Sat
Archers Best Bitter; Hook Norton Best Bitter; Tetley Bitter; guest beers Ⓗ
Lively village local in the middle of Minchinhampton Common. A conservatory-style extension to the bar overlooks the valley.
🍴 Q ⛄ ❀ ◖ ▶ ♣ ⅟

Apperley

Coal House Inn
Gabb Lane (off B4213)
☎ (01452) 780211
12–2.30 (3 summer), 7 (6 summer)–11
Draught Bass; Wadworth 6X; guest beers Ⓗ
Originally a coal wharf, now a welcoming local on the bank of the Severn (moorings), half a mile from the village

centre. The approach road can flood in winter.
🍴 ❀ ◖ ▶ ⊞ ▲ ♣ P

Arlingham

Red Lion
The Cross ☎ (01452) 740269
12–3, 7–11; 11–11 Sat
Butcombe Bitter; Hook Norton Best Bitter; Whitbread Boddingtons Bitter; guest beers Ⓗ
Part-16th-century, large, two-bar village pub. Home-cooking; up to six ales. Cider in summer.
🍴 ❀ ◖ ▶ ⊞ ▲ ♣ ⅁ P

Ashleworth

Boat Inn
The Quay (beyond Tithe Barn)
OS819251 ☎ (01452) 700272
11–2.30, 6–11
Arkell's 3B; Oakhill Yeoman; Smiles Best Bitter; guest beers Ⓖ
Delightful old pub beside the

Severn, a small miracle of survival, owned by the same family for over 400 years. The interior has hardly changed in a century. Lunchtime snacks. Moorings available.
Q ❀ ♣ ⅁ P

Berry Hill

King's Head
28 Grove Road (B4228)
☎ (01594) 810550
11–2.30, 6.30–11
Draught Bass; Greene King Abbot; Marston's Pedigree; S&N Theakston Best Bitter; Wadworth 6X; guest beers Ⓗ
Friendly free house used by locals and visitors. ◖ ▶ ▲ P

Blaisdon

Red Hart
Off A48/A40
☎ (01452) 830477
12.30–3, 7–11
Ind Coope Burton Ale; S&N Theakston Best Bitter; Tetley Bitter; guest beers Ⓗ

Welcoming, beamed and stone-floored village pub with adventurous guest beers. CAMRA regional *Pub of the Year* 1994. Large outdoor area.
🏠 Q ❀ ◗ ◗ ♿ ▲ ♣ ⊂ P

Bledington

King's Head

On B4450 ☎ (01608) 658365
11–2.30, 6–11; 12–2.30, 7–10.30 Sun
Hook Norton Best Bitter; Wadworth 6X; guest beers Ⓗ
Delightful, 16th-century, stone inn overlooking the village green. It specialises in food (book at weekends). Monthly changing guest beers; cider in summer.
🏠 ♉ ❀ 🛏 ◗ ◗ 🏢
⇌ (Kingham) ♣ ⊂ P

Box

Halfway House

OS857003 ☎ (01453) 832631
11–2.30, 6 (5.30 Fri & Sat)–11
Adnams Bitter; Fuller's London Pride; Marston's Bitter, Pedigree; guest beers Ⓗ
Friendly and relaxing pub on the edge of the common, offering an enterprising range of guest beers. A centre for local activities. Q ◗ ◗ ▲ ♣ P

Brimscombe

King's Arms

Bourne Lane (N of A419)
OS874023 ☎ (01453) 882552
12–3, 6.30–11
Dartmoor Best Bitter; Ind Coope Burton Ale; S&N Theakston Best Bitter; guest beers Ⓗ
The public bar forms the lower section of this split-level pub; the upper saloon is comfortable and has a piano. No food Sun, or Mon–Thu eve.
Q ◗ ◗ 🏢 ♣

Broad Campden

Bakers Arms

Off B4081 ☎ (01386) 840515
11.30–3, 5.30 (6 winter)–11
Donnington BB; Hook Norton Best Bitter; Stanway Stanney Bitter; Wickwar Brand Oak; guest beers Ⓗ
Fine old country pub boasting Cotswold stone walls and oak beams. 🏠 Q ❀ ◗ ◗ ♣ ⊂ P

Brockweir

Brockweir Country Inn

Off A466 ☎ (01291) 689548
12–2.30 (3 Sat), 6–11
Freeminer Bitter; Hook Norton Best Bitter; guest beer Ⓗ
Lovely, unspoilt country pub by the River Wye. Its oak beams come from a ship which was built in Brockweir many years ago. Home-cooked food in generous portions. 🏠 Q
♉ ❀ 🛏 ◗ ◗ 🏢 ▲ ♣ ⊂ P

Cheltenham

Adam & Eve

8 Townsend Street
☎ (01242) 525452
10.30–3, 5–11; 10.30–11 Sat
Arkell's 2B, 3B Ⓗ
Friendly, two-bar pub on a side street ten minutes' walk from the town centre.
Q 🏢 ♣

Bayshill Inn

92 St George's Place
☎ (01242) 524388
11–3, 5–11; 11–11 Sat
Hall & Woodhouse Tanglefoot; Wadworth IPA, 6X Ⓗ**, Old Timer** Ⓖ**; guest beer** Ⓗ
Very popular, no-frills town-centre pub near the bus station. Good value lunches; changing guest beers. ◗ ♣ ⊂

Beaufort Arms

184 London Road (A40)
☎ (01242) 526038
11–2.30, 6–11
Hall & Woodhouse Tanglefoot; Wadworth IPA, 6X, Farmer's Glory; guest beers Ⓗ
Excellent local serving interesting food. No food Sun eve, Tue eve in winter, or Thu eve in summer. Q ◗ ◗ ♣ P

Suffolk Arms

Suffolk Road
☎ (01242) 524713
11.30–11
Morland Old Speckled Hen; John Smith's Bitter; Whitbread Boddingtons Bitter, Flowers Original; guest beer (occasional) Ⓗ
Friendly, single-bar local on the outer ring road; formerly a hotel. Popular with office workers lunchtime. ◗ ◗ ♣ ⊂

Whole Hog

Montpellier Walk
☎ (01242) 523431
11–11
Goff's Jouster Ⓗ**; Hook Norton Old Hooky** Ⓖ**; Morland Old Speckled Hen** Ⓗ**; Stanway Stanney Bitter** Ⓖ**; Taylor Landlord; Uley Bitter; guest beers** Ⓗ
Renovated pub with a scrubbed-wood furniture look downstairs and a collection of wall portraits and risqué epigrams. No under-21s. Guest beers change frequently. Food all day Sat/Sun. ◗ ◗ 🏢 ♣ ⊂

Chipping Campden

Volunteer

Lower High Street
☎ (01386) 840688
11.30–3, 7–11
Draught Bass; Hook Norton Best Bitter; S&N Theakston XB; John Smith's Bitter; Stanway Stanney Bitter; Wood Parish; guest beers Ⓗ
Stone pub just away from the village centre. Its name dates from the 1840s but the pub is from 1709. Special monthly food nights. Cider in summer.
🏠 Q 🛏 ◗ ◗ 🏢 ♿ ▲ ♣ ⊂

Cirencester

Corinium Court Hotel

12 Gloucester Street
☎ (01285) 659711
11–3, 6–11
Hook Norton Best Bitter Ⓗ**, Old Hooky** Ⓖ**; Wadworth 6X; guest beers** (occasional) Ⓗ
16th-century hotel with a charming courtyard entrance and a superb, small flagstoned bar opening to a smart lounge. Ideal for conversation. Attractive garden.
🏠 Q ♉ ❀ 🛏 ◗ ◗ ♿ ▲ P

Drillman's Arms

34 Gloucester Road, Stratton (A417) ☎ (01285) 653892
11–3, 5.30–11; 11–11 Sat
Archers Village, Best Bitter; Wadworth 6X; Whitbread Boddingtons Bitter; guest beers Ⓗ
Popular Georgian inn with a small convivial lounge, a public bar and a skittle alley (where families are welcome). Mini-beer festival Aug Bank Hol. 🏠 ♉ ❀ ◗ ◗ 🏢 ▲ ♣ P

Golden Cross

20 Blackjack Street (near Corinium Museum)
☎ (01285) 652137
11–3, 6–11
Arkell's 2B, 3B Ⓗ
Gimmick-free pub relying on friendly and efficient service and good company, and appealing to all ages. Arkell's seasonal beers also sold. Full-size snooker table. Families welcome in the skittle alley if it is not in use.
🏠 ❀ 🛏 ◗ ♿ ▲ ♣

Oddfellows' Arms

10–14 Chester Street
☎ (01285) 641540
11 (11.30 Sat)–3, 5.30 (7 Sat)–11
Ruddles County; Wadworth 6X; guest beers Ⓗ
Sensitively refurbished back-street pub, now moved upmarket with a good range of food and three changing guest beers. Large garden; good family room.
🏠 ♉ ◗ ◗ ▲ ♣

Clearwell

Lamb
The Cross, High Street
☎ (01594) 835441
12–3, 7 (6.30 Fri & Sat)–11
Eldridge Pope Best Bitter ℍ;
Freeminer Bitter ⒼG,
Speculation Ale; Fuller's
London Pride; Marston's
Pedigree; S&N Theakston
Best Bitter; guest beers ℍ
Former iron miners' pub, over
200 years old. The lounge is a
former British Legion room;
the cosy bar has a settle and a
log fire.
♨ Q ◗ ▣ ▲ ♣ ➾ P

Cleeve Hill

High Roost
On B4632
☎ (01242) 672010
11–3, 7–11
Hook Norton Best Bitter, Old
Hooky; guest beers ℍ
Pub set on the highest hill in
the county, with views
through large bay windows
across the Vale of Severn.
Children allowed in for meals
until 8pm (no eve meals Tue).
❀ ⇔ ◗ ▲ ♣ P

Coln St Aldwyns

New Inn
☎ (01285) 750651
11–3, 5.30–11; 11–11 Sat
Courage Best Bitter; Hook
Norton Best Bitter; Ruddles
Best Bitter; Wadworth 6X;
Webster's Yorkshire Bitter;
guest beers ℍ
Friendly, 16th-century
coaching inn, built around a
courtyard and recently saved
from re-development after a
long campaign. Large menu.
♨ Q ☎ ❀ ⇔ ◗ ▲ ♣ P

Dursley

Old Spot Inn
Hill Road
☎ (01453) 542870
11–11
Bass Worthington BB,
Draught Bass; Uley Old Ric,
Old Spot; guest beers ℍ
Built in 1776 as a farm cottage,
this is now a superb watering
hole on the Cotswold Way,
offering some live folk and
blues music. Doorstep
sandwiches, filled pittas and
baguettes served at all times.
♨ Q ❀ ◗ ♣ ✂

Elkstone

Highwayman Inn
Beech Pike (A417)
☎ (01285) 821221
11–2.30, 6–11
Arkell's 2B, 3B, Kingsdown ℍ

Comfortable roadhouse of
16th-century origins: a long
bar, a restaurant and a family
room. Good selection of food.
♨ Q ☎ ❀ ◗ ▲ ▲ ♣ P

Ewen

Wild Duck Inn
Drakes Island OS007977
☎ (01285) 770310
11–11
Fuller's London Pride; S&N
Theakston Best Bitter, XB,
Old Peculier; Wadworth 6X;
guest beers ℍ
Superb country hotel with
beautiful gardens. Built in
1563, it retains a slightly rustic
feel, with panelling, settles, old
paintings and an imposing
Elizabethan fireplace.
Duckpond Bitter is from Hook
Norton. ♨ ❀ ⇔ ◗ ◗
≋ (Kemble) ♣ ○ P

Ford

Plough Inn
On B4077 ☎ (01386) 584215
11–11
Donnington BB, SBA ℍ
Splendid, unspoilt country
pub where the cellar used to
be a gaol. Racing theme;
wooden fort in the children's
area. Note the rhyme on the
front wall. No eve meals Sun
in winter. ♨ ❀ ⇔ ◗ ◗ ♣ P

Foss Cross

Hare & Hounds
The Stump (A429)
☎ (01285) 720288
11–3, 6–11
Everards Tiger; Hook Norton
Best Bitter; Shepherd Neame
Spitfire; Wadworth 6X; guest
beers ℍ
Comfortable, 400-year-old,
stone pub with an L-shaped
bar, licensed since at least
1772. Snacks, children's and
vegetarian meals served in the
bar and separate restaurant.
Adjacent caravan site.
♨ Q ❀ ◗ ◗ ▲ ▲ ♣ P

Gloucester

Black Swan Inn
68–70 Southgate Street (200
yds S of The Cross)
☎ (01452) 523642
11–11; 11–2.30, 6–11 Sat
Arkell's 2B; Donnington SBA;
Fuller's London Pride; Uley
Old Spot ℍ
Very reasonably priced hotel,
recently refurbished
throughout. The two-roomed
bar is decorated in neo-
colonial style, with pictures to
reflect the landlord's love of
the horses. Q ⇔ ◗ ≋ P

Linden Tree
73–75 Bristol Road (A430,
¾ mile S of centre)
☎ (01452) 527869
11–2.30, 5.30 (6 Sat)–11
Hall & Woodhouse
Tanglefoot; Hook Norton Best
Bitter; Smiles Exhibition;
Wadworth IPA, 6X; guest
beers ℍ
Excellent pub in a Grade
II-listed building. Good food
(no meals Sun eve) and fine
accommodation. Tiny car park.
♨ ⇔ ◗ ◗ ♣ P

Prince of Wales
25 Station Road
☎ (01452) 524390
11.30–2.30 (3 Fri & Sat), 5.30–11
Morland Old Speckled Hen;
Whitbread Boddingtons
Bitter, Castle Eden Ale; guest
beers ℍ
Smart, three-storey, Victorian
pub close to rail and coach
stations. Seasonal and guest
ales available, some on gravity
dispense. Bargain
accommodation.
Q ❀ ⇔ ◗ ≋ ♣ P

Raglan Arms
50 Regent Street (one street E
of the park) ☎ (01452) 528864
11–3, 7–11; 11–11 Thu–Sat
Marston's Bitter, Pedigree ℍ
Rather neglected former M&B
house with original Victorian
fittings in its public bar.
Quality ales at bargain prices,
but no food. Q ▣ ♣ P

Whitesmith's Arms
81 Southgate Street
☎ (01452) 414770
11–3, 5–11; 11–11 Sat
Arkell's 2B, 3B, Kingsdown ℍ
Named after maritime metal-
workers, this recently enlarged
pub stands opposite the
historic docks and the
National Waterways Museum.
Maritime decor features;
Arkell's seasonal ales sold.
♨ Q ◗ ◗ ▲ ≋ ♣

Great Barrington

Fox Inn
1 mile N of A40 OS204131
☎ (01451) 844385
11–11
Donnington BB, XXX
(summer), SBA ℍ
Excellent, stone pub
beautifully set by the River
Windrush; popular with
walkers and locals. A rare
outlet for XXX Mild. Riverside
barbecues in summer.
♨ Q ⇔ ◗ ◗ ♣ P

Joyford

Dog & Muffler
Off B4228 OS578133
☎ (01594) 832444

Gloucestershire

10–4, 6 (7 winter)–11
**Fuller's London Pride;
Ruddles County; John
Smith's Bitter; Samuel Smith
OBB** Ⓗ
Out of the way pub. The
restaurant at the front
overlooks a large outdoor
drinking area. Children's
assault course.
🌼 🛏 ◖ ▶ ⊞ ▵ Å ✦ P

Lechlade

New Inn
The Square ☎ (01367) 252296
11–3, 6–11
**Arkell's 3B; Draught Bass;
Morland Bitter; guest beers** Ⓗ
Friendly, town-centre hotel
with large fireplaces. A large
garden extends down to the
Thames (moorings).
🏚 🌼 🛏 ◖ ▶ Å ✦ P

Longborough

Coach & Horses
Off A424 ☎ (01451) 830325
11–2.30, 7–11 (11–11 bank hols)
Donnington BB, XXX (winter),
SBA (summer) Ⓗ
Friendly, one-bar pub in a
quiet village with morris
dancing connections.
Firefighting mementoes reflect
the proximity of the Fire
Services College. Parking can
be difficult. 🏚 Q 🌼 ▶ ✦

Longford

Queen's Head
84 Tewkesbury Road (A38)
☎ (01452) 301882
11–2.30 (3 Sat), 6–11
**Fuller's London Pride;
Marston's Pedigree; Morland
Old Speckled Hen; Wadworth
6X; Whitbread WCPA;
Flowers Original; guest
beers** Ⓗ
18th-century inn with original
beams and a stone-flagged
public bar area. Good selection
of bar meals. Colourful flower
baskets outside (in summer)
reflect the warm welcome
inside. 🌼 ◖ ▶ ⊞ P

May Hill

Glasshouse Inn
Off A40 W of Huntley
OS710213 ☎ (01452) 830529
11.30–2.30, 6–11; 12–2, 7–10.30 Sun
**Butcombe Bitter; Fuller's
London Pride; Whitbread
WCPA; guest beers** Ⓖ
Unspoilt country pub with an
original quarry tiled floor. The
outdoor drinking area has an
old cider press and a bench
canopied by a yew bridge.
Quoits played.
🏚 Q 🌼 ◖ ▶ Å ✦ P

Moreton-in-Marsh

Black Bear
High Street ☎ (01608) 50705
11–3 (10.30–4 Tue), 6–11
Donnington BB, XXX, SBA Ⓗ
Busy, two-bar, town-centre
pub, partly dating back 300
years. An active poltergeist
called Fred is a resident. Paved
courtyard; Aunt Sally played.
Good, home-made food.
🌼 🛏 ◖ ▶ ⊞ Å ≈ ✦ P

Newland

Ostrich
On B4231 ☎ (01594) 833260
12–2.30, 6.30–11
**Exmoor Gold; Freeminer
Speculation Ale; Marston's
Pedigree; Ringwood Old
Thumper; Shepherd Neame
Spitfire; guest beers** Ⓗ
Friendly, charming and
unspoilt pub always serving
eight real ales plus a wide
range of good food.
🏚 Q 🌼 🛏 ◖ ▶ Å ⌂

Newnham

Railway
Station Road (opp. clock
tower) ☎ (01594) 516317
5 (11 Sat)–11
**Draught Bass; Smiles Best
Bitter; guest beers** Ⓗ
Warm, friendly, traditional
pub. No meals Tue. Closed
lunchtime Mon–Fri.
🏚 Q 🌼 ▶ ⊞ Å ✦ ⌂

North Cerney

Bathurst Arms
On A435 ☎ (01285) 831281
11–3, 6–11
**Archers Village; Hook Norton
Best Bitter; Tetley Bitter;
Wadworth 6X; Whitbread
Boddingtons Bitter; guest
beers** Ⓗ
Attractive, 17th-century village
pub with flagstone floors,
settles and a stove in an
inglenook. The tiny River
Churn runs through the
garden. 🏚 Q ▿ 🌼 🛏 ◖ ▶
⊞ Å ✦ P

Northleach

Red Lion
Market Square
☎ (01451) 860251
11–3.30, 6–11
**Courage Best Bitter; John
Smith's Bitter; Ushers
Founders; guest beers** Ⓗ
This old coaching inn doubles
as the local Job Centre!
Welcoming atmosphere;
friendly landlord.
🏚 Q 🌼 🛏 ◖ ▶ ⊞ Å ✦ ⌂ P

Oakridge Lynch

Butcher's Arms
N edge of village
☎ (01285) 760371
12–3, 6–11
**Archers Best Bitter; Draught
Bass; Goff's Jouster; Ruddles
County; S&N Theakston Best
Bitter; Tetley Bitter** Ⓗ
Popular village pub, an
18th-century building formerly
a butcher's shop. Three bars
and a restaurant serve food
Wed–Sat eve and every
lunchtime.
🏚 Q ▿ 🌼 ◖ ▶ ⊞ Å ✦ P

Parkend

Fountain
Off B4234
☎ (01594) 562189
11.30–3, 6–11; 11.30–11 Sat
**Draught Bass; Freeminer
Bitter; guest beers** Ⓗ
Large, popular pub in the
heart of the Forest of Dean,
crammed with interesting
artefacts. Good
accommodation and food
(especially curry).
🏚 Q 🛏 ◖ ▶ ⊞ Å ✦ P

Pope's Hill

Greyhound
On A4151
☎ (01452) 760344
11–3.30, 5.30–11
**Gale's HSB; S&N Theakston
Best Bitter; Tetley Bitter;
guest beers** Ⓗ
Pub filled with beams, brasses
and montages made out of
clock/watch parts.
🏚 ▿ ◖ ▶ Å ✦ ⌂ P

Prestbury

Royal Oak
The Burgage
☎ (01242) 522344
11–2.30 (3 Fri & Sat), 6–11
**Archers Best Bitter; Brains
Bitter; Wadworth 6X;
Whitbread WCPA; guest
beers** Ⓗ
Two-bar pub serving home-
made lunches (no meals Sun).
Hops hang from a beam in the
lounge; pictures of racehorses
and cricket teams are
displayed. Q 🌼 ◖ ⊞ ✦ P

Ruspidge

New Inn
On B4227 ☎ (01594) 824508
7 (12 Sat)–11
**Archers Golden; Wye Valley
Bitter** Ⓗ
Fairly basic village pub open
eves only during the week. A
separate room houses an
interesting selection of games.
🏚 Q 🌼 ✦ ⌂ P

Sapperton

Daneway Inn
Daneway OS939034
☎ (01285) 760297
11–2.30 (3 Sat), 6.30–11
Archers Best Bitter E /H;
Draught Bass H; **Wadworth**
6X; guest beers G
Superb old inn idyllically set
near the western end of the
disused Sapperton canal
tunnel. A magnificent Dutch-
carved fireplace stands in the
lounge. No-smoking family
room, plus a large garden. The
house beer is from Archers.
🏛 Q ♨ ❀ ◖ ▶ ⊟ ♣ ⟲ P ⅏

Slad

Woolpack
On B4070 ☎ (01452) 813429
12 (11 summer)–3, 6–11
Draught Bass; Uley Old Spot,
Pig's Ear; Wadworth 6X;
Whitbread Boddingtons
Bitter H
Authentic, 16th-century pub
clinging to the side of the Slad
Valley, offering splendid
views. It was made famous by
Laurie Lee in *Cider with Rosie*
(autographed copies and the
author can still be found here).
🏛 Q ♨ ❀ ◖ ▶ ⊟ ♣ ⟲ P ⅏

Sling

Miner's Arms
On B4228 ☎ (01594) 836632
11–11
Freeminer Bitter, Speculation
Ale; guest beers H
Basic, no-frills, one-bar pub,
Freeminer's first tied house.
Large selection of imported
bottled beers; 28 whiskies.
Huge sandwiches.
🏛 ❀ ◖ ▶ ♣ Å ♣ ⟲ P

Stonehouse

Spa Inn
Oldends Lane (off B4008)
☎ (01453) 822327
12–3, 7 (6.30 summer)–11
Wadworth IPA, 6X; guest
beers H
Cosy pub adjoining a factory
estate (popular at lunchtime).
Quoits and outdoor skittles
played. ❀ ◖ ▶ ⊟ Å ♣ ⟲ P

Stow-on-the-Wold

Queen's Head
Off main square
☎ (01451) 830563
11–2.30 (3 Sat), 6–11
Donnington BB, SBA H
Deservedly popular, fine old
Cotswold pub: the only pub in
the county in every *Good Beer*
Guide to date. No food Sun or
Mon eve (or some winter

eves). Park in the square.
Cider in summer.
Q ❀ ◖ ▶ ⊟ Å ♣ ⟲

Stroud

Duke of York
22 Nelson Street
☎ (01453) 758715
12 (11.30 Fri & Sat)–3 (4 Fri, 6 Sat),
7–11
Draught Bass; Butcombe
Bitter; Uley Old Spot;
Wells Eagle; guest beers H
Friendly, modest, one-bar pub
at the top end of town.
Q ◖ ⬌

Pelican
Union Street (London Road)
☎ (01453) 763817
11.30–11
Courage Georges BA,
Directors; Marston's Pedigree;
Morland Old Speckled Hen;
Ruddles Best Bitter;
Wadworth 6X; guest beers H
Popular pub close to the
covered market. It runs
its own 50-seat theatre
(available for hire); live music
twice a week. One long,
split-level main bar plus a
Courtyard Bar (open only
Fri/Sat eves). Tiny car park.
🏛 ❀ ◖ ⬌ ♣ ⟲ P

Tetbury

Crown
Gumstool Hill (by car park)
☎ (01666) 502469
11–3, 5.30–11; 11–11 Fri & Sat
Whitbread Boddingtons
Bitter, Flowers IPA, Original;
guest beers H
Busy town pub with a lounge
and conservatory.
🏛 Q ❀ ❀ ◖ ▶ P

Tewkesbury

Berkeley Arms
8 Church Street
☎ (01684) 293034
11–11
Hall & Woodhouse
Tanglefoot (summer);
Wadworth IPA, 6X, Farmer's
Glory, Old Timer H
Ancient pub of character
where access to the lounge and
barn restaurant is through an
unusual alleyway. Children
catered for in summer.
Q ⋈ ◖ ▶ ⊟ ♣

White Bear
Bredon Road
☎ (01684) 296614
11–3, 6.30–11; 11–11 Sat
Wye Valley Bitter, HPA;
guest beers H
Basic one-bar pub off the north
end of the high street.
⊟ ♿ Å ♣ ⟲ P

Todenham

Farrier's Arms
☎ (01608) 50901
12–3, 7–11 (closed Tue eve Nov–Feb)
Hook Norton Best Bitter;
guest beers H
Village pub next to the
blacksmith's shop and the
church, formerly an iron
foundry. 🏛 Q ❀ ◖ ▶ ♣ P

Uley

Old Crown
The Green ☎ (01453) 860502
11.30–2.30 (3 Sat), 7–11
Uley Bitter, Old Spot, Pig's
Ear; Whitbread WCPA,
Boddingtons Bitter H
Single-bar village pub, built in
1638 as farm cottages and
recently improved internally.
Close to the Cotswold Way.
❀ ⋈ ◖ ▶ ♣ P

Waterley Bottom

New Inn
Signed from Stinchcombe or N
Nibley OS758964
☎ (01453) 543659
12–2.30, 7–11
Cotleigh Tawny; Greene King
Abbot H; **S&N Theakston**
Old Peculier G; **Smiles Best**
Bitter; guest beers H
Large, friendly free house
beautifully set amongst steep
hills. The house beer (Cotleigh
WB) is a variation of Harrier
SPA. CAMRA regional *Pub of*
the Year 1993.
🏛 Q ⋈ ◖ ▶ ⊟ ♣ ⟲ P

Winchcombe

Bell Inn
Gretton Road
☎ (01242) 602205
11–11
Draught Bass; Coach House
Coachman's; Donnington BB;
Eldridge Pope Hardy
Country; Shepherd Neame
Spitfire; Wickwar Brand
Oak H
Local where the beer range is
continually reviewed.
🏛 Q ❀ ❀ ◖ Å ♣ ⟲ P

Woodchester

Ram
Station Road ☎ (01453) 873329
11–3, 5.30–11; 11–11 Sat
Archers Best Bitter; Ruddles
Best Bitter; Uley Bitter, Old
Spot; Whitbread Boddingtons
Bitter; guest beers H
Busy, but comfortable, stone-
built, beamed free house
looking across Nailsworth
Valley. Good food is served at
most times. 🏛 ❀ ◖ ▶ ♣ P

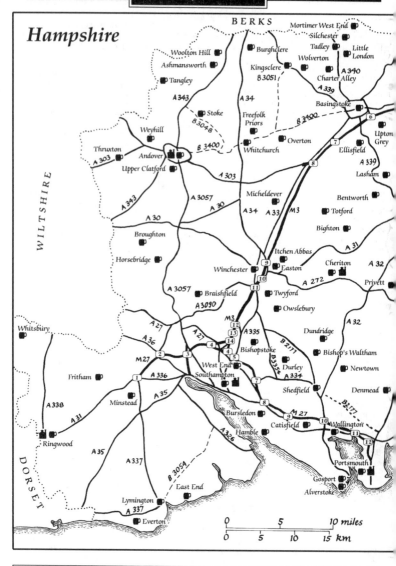

Hampshire

Cheriton, Cheriton; **Gale's,** Horndean; **Hampshire,**
Andover; **Hedgehog & Hogshead,** Southampton;
Newale, Andover; **Ringwood,** Ringwood; **Spikes,**
Portsmouth; **Worldham,** East Worldham

Aldershot

Garden Gate
4 Church Lane East
☎ (01252) 21051
11.30–3, 5.30–11; 11–11 Sat &
summer
**Greene King IPA, Rayments
Special, Abbot** Ⓗ
Two-roomed haven from the
bustling town centre,
behind the railway station. Eve
meals till 7.30. Greene King
seasonal beers sold.
🍴 ⚘ 🛏 ◑ ▶ ⇌ ♣ P

Red Lion
Ash Road
☎ (01252) 23050
11–11

**Courage Best Bitter; Gale's
HSB; Wadworth 6X**
(occasional)**; guest beer** Ⓗ
One-bar pub where music is
rarely heard above the chat.
No pool table or jukebox; TV
at one side of the pub. A
keen promoter of milds and
porters. Ten mins from
Aldershot BR.
🛏 Q ⚘ ◑ ▶ ♣ P

Alton

Eight Bells
33 Church Street
☎ (01420) 82417
12–3, 6–11; 11–11 Fri & Sat
**Fuller's London Pride;
Ringwood Fortyniner;
Wadworth 6X; guest beers** Ⓗ
Cosy pub with a large
collection of chamberpots
hanging from the low, beamed
ceiling. It retains a rural charm
but is only five minutes from
the town centre. Six real ales
include Marston's Head
Brewer's Choice beers. ◖ ◗

Railway Hotel
Anstey Road ☎ (01420) 84208
11–3.30, 5–11
**Courage Best Bitter; Ushers
Best Bitter, Founders** Ⓗ
Good town pub which also
sells Ushers seasonal ales.
Q ◲ ⇌ ♣ P ⊟

Alverstoke

Alverbank Hotel
Stokes Bay Road
☎ (01705) 510005
11–11
Beer range varies Ⓗ
Pleasant historic hotel set back
from the seafront, overlooking
Stokes Bay. A relaxing
atmosphere and two regularly
changing guest beers have
attracted a growing clientele.
⇔ Q ⚘ ◖ ◗ ♣ P

Andover

Lamb Inn
21 Winchester Street (near
police station)
☎ (01264) 323961
11–3, 6 (5 Fri, 7 Sat)–11
Wadworth 6X; guest beers Ⓗ
Welcoming, three-roomed pub
on the edge of the town centre.
The top room (lounge) has a
particularly quiet and cosy
atmosphere, plus cheaper beer.
There are also happy hours.
Beware: the Bass may be kept
under a cask breather. Eve
meals on request.
⇔ Q ⚘ ◖ ◗ ◲ & ♣

Ashmansworth

Plough
Off A343 ☎ (01635) 253047
12–2.30 (not Mon or Tue; 12–3 Sat),
6–11
**Archers Village, Best Bitter,
Golden; guest beers** Ⓖ
At 770 ft above sea level, this
is Hampshire's highest pub
and one of its most unspoilt.
Casks are kept on stillage
behind the bar. Handy for
Highclere Castle.
⇔ Q ⚘ ◖ ▲ ♣ P

Basingstoke

Bounty Inn
81 Bounty Road
☎ (01256) 20071
11–3, 5.30–11; 11–11 Fri & Sat
**Courage Best Bitter; Ushers
Best Bitter, Founders** Ⓗ
Friendly, two-bar local full of
character and characters. The
sports bar has Sky TV; the
lounge bar is for those who
enjoy a more peaceful
atmosphere. Ushers seasonal
beers.
⇔ Q ⥾ ⚘ ◖ ◗ ◲ ♣ P

Hop Leaf
21 Church Street
☎ (01256) 465538
10.30–11
**Bass Worthington BB,
Draught Bass** Ⓗ
Traditional, town-centre pub
which caters for the older
crowd: a haven among the
loud youngsters' pubs in the
eve but also popular weekday
lunchtimes. No meals Sun eve.
⇔ ⚘ ◖ ◗

Queen's Arms
Bunnian Place (by station car
park) ☎ (01256) 465488
11–3, 5–11; 11–11 Fri & Sat
**Courage Best Bitter,
Directors** Ⓗ**; Fuller's London
Pride** Ⓖ**; John Smith's Bitter;
Wadworth 6X** Ⓗ
Pleasant, busy town pub
enjoying good local and
business trades. A typical
Victorian pub, seconds from
the railway station. ◖ ⇌ ♣

Bentworth

Sun
Sun Hill (off A339 down
narrow lane) OS661401
☎ (01420) 562338
12–3, 6–11
**Cheriton Diggers Gold;
Courage Best Bitter;
Marston's Pedigree;
Ringwood Best Bitter;
Wadworth 6X** Ⓗ
Traditional country pub with a
good food reputation, but not
to the cost of beer drinkers. Its
own house beer is brewed by
Hampshire Brewery.
⇔ Q ⥾ ⚘ ◱ ◖ ◗ & ♣ P

Bighton

Three Horseshoes
Off A31/B3047
☎ (01962) 732859
11–2.30, 6–11; 12–2.30, 7–10.30 Sun
Gale's BBB, 5X, HSB Ⓗ
Friendly, traditional, two-bar
local, where the art of good
conversation is still practised.
A pub since 1615, it has a
quiet, relaxing lounge, whilst

Royal Staff
37a Mount Pleasant Road
(top of Waterloo Rd)
☎ (01252) 22932
12–3, 5–11; 12–11 Sat
**Fuller's Chiswick, London
Pride, ESB** Ⓗ
Beautifully refurbished
in Victorian style, this
back-street local has a
very comfortable and lively
single bar with a strong
community atmosphere. Good
children's garden. No food
weekends. Fuller's seasonal
ales sold.
⚘ ◖ ⇌ ♣

Hampshire

the bar houses a country crafts collection and the old pub sign. Handy for the mid-Hants railway (Ropley station two miles). No food Mon.
🏠 Q ⊛ ◖ 🍴 ♿ ♣ P

Bishopstoke

Forester Arms
1 Stoke Common Road
☎ (01703) 620287
11–3, 6–11
Gibbs Mew Overlord, Salisbury, Wake Ale, Deacon, Bishop's Tipple; guest beer Ⓗ
Thriving, reputedly haunted local enjoying a good following. It has a team for everything and everyone. The public bar has a pool annexe; the lounge has a log fire. Lunch by arrangement.
🏠 Q ⊛ ◖ ♣ ◡ P ⊟

Bishop's Waltham

Bunch of Grapes
St Peter's Street
☎ (01489) 892935
10–2 (2.30 Sat), 6–11; 12–2, 7–10.30 Sun
Courage Best Bitter Ⓖ
Situated in a narrow street leading to the parish church, this small one-bar pub has been unaltered for many years and run by the same family for over 80 years. It has a golf society, hence the clubs and balls for sale. Courage Best is rather expensive but Ushers seasonal ales are also sold.
Q ⊛ ♣

Braishfield

Newport Inn
Newport Lane
(lane opp. the phone box)
☎ (01794) 368225
10–2.30, 6–11; 12–2.30, 7–10.30 Sun
Gale's BBB, Best Bitter, 5X, HSB Ⓗ
A gem in a time-warp, worth a detour. Customers come from miles around for the famous door-step sandwiches. Be ready to join in the singing around the piano Sun eve. Large, rambling garden.
🏠 Q ⊛ 🍴 ♣ P

Broughton

Tally Ho!
High Street ☎ (01794) 301280
11–3, 6–11
Cheriton Pots Ale, Best Bitter, Diggers Gold Ⓖ
Once a Georgian doctor's house, now Cheriton's second pub: a haven for beer-drinking, cosmopolitan conversationalists. Very simple food lunchtimes and eves – soup, ploughmans, etc. – but

good quality; no food Tue. The cheapest beer for miles.
🏠 Q ⊛ 🍴 ♣

Burghclere

Queen
Harts Lane (1 mile E of A34)
☎ (01635) 278350
11–3, 6–11
Adnams Bitter, Broadside; Arkell's 3B Ⓗ
Wholesome, homely village free house with a welcome for all. One simple bar with lots of nooks and crannies and a plethora of pub games. Twice local CAMRA *Pub of the Season*. Strong racing following. A difficult pub to drag yourself away from. No food Sun. Q ⊛ 🍴 ♣ P

Buriton

Five Bells
48 High Street
☎ (01730) 263584
11–2.30 (3 Sat), 5.30–11
Ballard's Best Bitter; Ind Coope Friary Meux BB, Burton Ale; Ringwood XXXX Porter, Old Thumper; Tetley Bitter Ⓗ
Traditional, old, beamed free house: a two-bar pub with imposing fireplaces. Excellent range of food, including fresh fish and game in season. Family room weekdays.
🏠 Q ⬮ ⊛ 🍴 ◖ ♦ ♣ P

Bursledon

Jolly Sailor
Land's End Road, Old Bursledon ☎ (01703) 405557
11–2.30, 6–11; 11–11 Sat
Gale's HSB; Hall & Woodhouse Badger BB, Tanglefoot; Wadworth 6X; guest beer Ⓗ
16th-century riverside inn of *Howards' Way* fame, with a beamed ceiling, flagstone floor and a restaurant area offering an extensive menu. Access is difficult – beer arrives by its own cliff railway! The house beer is Gribble Ale.
🏠 ⊛ ◖ ▶ 🍴 ⇌

Linden Tree
School Road (A27/A3025)
☎ (01703) 402356
11–2.30 (3 Sat), 6 (5 Fri)–11
Draught Bass; Wadworth IPA, 6X, Farmer's Glory (summer), **Old Timer** Ⓗ
Excellent, comfortable, one-bar pub with no obtrusive gaming machines. A children's play area and pergola make it ideal for summer; a blazing log fire extends a warm welcome in winter. High-quality, home-cooked lunches (not served Sun). Very friendly.
🏠 ⊛ ◖ ♣ P

Catisfield

Limes at Catisfield
34 Catisfield Lane (off A27)
☎ (01329) 842926
12–2.30, 5–11; 11–3, 7–11 Sat
Gale's HSB; Gibbs Mew Salisbury, Bishop's Tipple; Ringwood Fortyniner Ⓗ, **Old Thumper; guest beer** Ⓖ
Large Victorian building converted to a pub. The public bar has unusual panelling and can get very busy, but the lounge has a more relaxed atmosphere. The petanque terrain in the garden justifies bar extensions in summer.
Q ⊛ ◖ ▶ 🍴 ♣ P

Chalton

Red Lion
OS731161
☎ (01705) 592246
11–3, 6–11
Gale's BBB, Best Bitter, Gold, 5X, HSB; guest beers Ⓗ
Reputedly the oldest pub in Hampshire, this building was constructed at the same time as the church opposite. The original building has a thatched roof, but unfortunately the modern extension does not blend in. Large inglenook in the bar. No meals Sun eve.
🏠 ⬮ ⊛ ◖ ▶ 🍴 P

Charter Alley

White Hart
White Hart Lane (off A340)
☎ (01256) 850048
12–2.30 (3 Sat; may extend in summer), 7–11
Brakspear Bitter; Fuller's London Pride; Harveys BB Ⓗ; **Ringwood Fortyniner** Ⓖ; **guest beers** Ⓗ
Friendly village local, recently altered to include new dining areas and a no-smoking lounge. The front bar features a wood-burning stove; the back lounge incorporates a skittle alley. Guest beers change weekly. Cider in summer. No food Mon eve.
🏠 Q ⊛ ◖ ▶ 🍴 ♣ ◡ P ⚥

Cheriton

Flower Pots Inn
W off B3046/N of A272
☎ (01962) 771318
11.30–2.30, 6–11
Cheriton Pots Ale, Best Bitter, Diggers Gold Ⓖ
Quality, unpretentious, village beer-drinkers' pub with its own brewery across the car park: a public bar and a homely lounge. CAMRA

regional *Pub of the Year* 1995. Occasional one-off brews. No food Sun eve in winter. 🏚 Q
🌳 ✿ 🛏 ◑ ▶ 🏴 ៬ ♣ P

Cove

Thatched Cottage

122 Prospect Road
☎ (01252) 543145
11.30–2.30, 6–11; 12–11 Sat
Courage Best Bitter, Directors; Ruddles County; S&N Theakston Best Bitter, XB; Wadworth 6X Ⓗ
16th-century thatched building (only a pub since 1964) with two beamed bars. The quieter over-25s lounge, with attendant bric-a-brac, contrasts with the more music-oriented bar. Bouncy castle and swings in the garden in summer. No food weekends.
✿ ◑ ♣ P

Crondall

Castle

Croft Lane (off A287 into Pankridge St, then left into Church St)
☎ (01252) 850892
11.30–2.30 (3 Sat), 6–11
Fuller's Chiswick, London Pride, ESB Ⓗ
Proper village local, serving excellent food (no eve food Sun or Mon). A skittle alley is available for hire. Drink to the accompaniment of church bells. Fuller's seasonal beers served.
🏚 Q ✿ ◑ ▶ ♣ P

Denmead

Forest of Bere

Hambledon Road (B2150 S of centre) ☎ (01705) 263145
10.30–2.30 (3 Fri), 6–11 Sat
Hampshire King Alfred's; Ind Coope Friary Meux BB, Burton Ale; Ringwood Best Bitter Ⓗ
Large, friendly old local with a pleasing flint exterior, two bars and a good atmosphere. No lunches Sun.
🏚 Q ✿ ◑ ▣ ♣ P

Harvest Home

Southwick Road (off B2150 in village) ☎ (01705) 255086
11–2.30, 6–11
Gale's BBB, Gold, HSB Ⓗ
Large, single-bar pub on the edge of the village, with a separate dining area. It can be very busy at times. Good value for money.
🏚 ✿ ◑ 🏴 P

Try also: Fox & Hounds, School Lane (Free)

Dundridge

Hampshire Bowman

Dundridge Lane (1 mile off B3035) OS578185
☎ (01489) 892940
11 (12 Mon)–2.30 (3 Sat), 6–11
Archers Village, Golden; Ringwood Best Bitter, XXXX Porter, Fortyniner; guest beers (occasional) Ⓖ
Excellent country pub along a winding country lane. The beers are served from casks stillaged behind the brick-floored bar, which is heated by a log burner. Well regarded food (not served Mon, or Sun eve). 🏚 Q ✿ ◑ ▶ 🏴 ♣ P

Durley

Robin Hood Inn

Wintershill, Durley Street (off B2177) ☎ (01489) 860229
11–2.30, 6–11; 11–11 Sat
Banks's Mild; Marston's Bitter, Pedigree Ⓗ
17th-century ex-coaching inn with two bars and a large garden with a play area. The imaginative menu includes kangaroo steaks. Many events staged. Marston's Head Brewer's Choice also sold.
🏚 Q ✿ ◑ ▶ ▣ P

East End

East End Arms

Lymington Road (3 miles E of IoW ferry) OS362968
☎ (01590) 626223
11.30–3, 6–11
Ringwood Best Bitter Ⓗ, **Fortyniner, Old Thumper; Shepherd Neame Bishops Finger** *or* **Adnams Broadside** Ⓖ
Popular country pub used mainly by locals; rather remote but worth finding. A basic public contrasts with a comfortable lounge. Traditional country game pies served. Busy at weekends.
🏚 ✿ ◑ ▶ ▣ 🏴 ♣ ⌂ P

Easton

Cricketers Inn

Off B3047 ☎ (01962) 779353
11–2.30, 6–11
Cheriton Best Bitter *or* **Digger's Gold; Ringwood Best Bitter, Old Thumper; guest beers** Ⓗ
L-shaped village pub – a former Strong's house now liberated from Whitbread and offering an ever-changing selection of guest beers from small brewers. The interior is well decorated, with various knick-knacks and old pictures of the pub. 🛏 ◑ ♣ P

Ellisfield

Fox

Green Lane ☎ (01256) 381210
11.30–2.30, 6.30–11
Fuller's London Pride; Gale's HSB; Hall & Woodhouse Tanglefoot; Hampshire King Alfred's; Marston's Pedigree; S&N Theakston Old Peculier Ⓗ
16th-century, two-bar country pub with open fires and wood panelling; close to Basingstoke but hard to find. Good food (no meals Mon eve).
🏚 Q ✿ ◑ ▶ ♣ P

Everton

Crown Inn

Old Christchurch Road
☎ (01590) 642655
11–2.30 (3 Sat), 6–11
Draught Bass; Fuller's London Pride; Whitbread Strong Country, Flowers Original; guest beers (summer) Ⓗ
19th-century, traditional village inn, with two bars offering a good selection of home-cooked fare. The lively and friendly public bar has an excellent jukebox. Prize-winning floral displays in summer. No food Sun eve in winter.
🏚 Q ✿ ◑ ▶ ▣ ៬ 🏴 ♣ ⌂ P

Ewshot

Queen's Arms

Warren Corner (A287)
☎ (01252) 850341
11–3, 6–11
Courage Best Bitter; Fuller's London Pride; Hampshire King Alfred's Ⓗ
Roadside pub with an ever-growing reputation for food. A warm, comfortable place far from nearby Fleet's minimal excesses. No food Sun eve.
🏚 Q ✿ ◑ ▶ P

Farnborough

Prince of Wales

184 Rectory Road
☎ (01252) 545578
11.30–2.30, 5.30–11
Brakspear Bitter; Fuller's London Pride; Hall & Woodhouse Badger BB, Tanglefoot; Hogs Back TEA; Ringwood Fortyniner; guest beers Ⓗ
The best free house for miles, offering a wide range of guest beers in a convivial, traditional atmosphere. Invariably busy, it stages occasional small brewery promotions. Friendly staff; excellent lunches (not served Sun).
Q ✿ ◑ ⇌ (North Camp) P

121

Hampshire

Farringdon

Rose & Crown
Crows Lane ☎ (01420) 588231
11–3, 6–11
Beer range varies Ⓗ
Attractive village free house
with a separate restaurant area
(no food Sun eve). Five beers.
🏨 Q ⚘ ◖ ▶ P

Freefolk Priors

Watership Down
Off B3400, ½ mile E of
Whitchurch ☎ (01256) 892254
11–3, 6–11
**Archers Best Bitter; Brakspear
Bitter; guest beers** Ⓗ
Renamed after Richard
Adams's novel, this happy
pub enjoys a pretty location,
with a large garden
overlooking the River Test.
The three guests always
include a mild.
🏨 ⚘ ◖ ▶ P 🛏

Fritham

Royal Oak
1 mile S of B3078 OS232141
☎ (01703) 812606
11–2.30 (3 summer), 6–11
**Ringwood Best Bitter;
Whitbread Strong Country** Ⓖ
In a class of its own – a tiny,
unspoilt, thatched pub in the
heart of the New Forest with a
small front bar and an even
smaller snug. Strong support
for all country sports and
activities. A third beer may be
on offer. 🏨 Q ⚘ ▲ ♣

Froxfield

Trooper
Alton OS727273
☎ (01730) 827293
12–3, 5.30–11
**Draught Bass; Cheriton Best
Bitter; Fuller's London Pride;
guest beer** Ⓗ
Interesting, unusual and
atmospheric, candle-lit local in
an isolated setting. Small but
varied, home-cooked food
menu. 🏨 Q ⛌ ⚘ ◖ ▶ P

Golden Pot

Golden Pot
Old Odiham Road (B3349)
☎ (01420) 84130
11–3.30, 5.30–11
**Draught Bass; Morland IPA,
Bitter, Tanner's Jack, Old
Speckled Hen** Ⓗ
Friendly, rural roadside pub
with a family welcome and a
children's garden. Formerly
drovers' lodgings, it now has a
skittle alley, and camping and
caravanning facilities. Named
after a Roman treasure found
nearby. 🏨 Q ⚘ ◖ ▶ ▲ ♣ P

Gosport

Queen's Hotel
143 Queens Road
☎ (01705) 582645
11.30–2.30, 7–11; 11–11 Sat
**Archers Village; Palmers IPA;
Ringwood Fortyniner; guest
beers** Ⓗ
Beer drinkers' haven hidden
away in the back streets; a
winner of many local CAMRA
awards, including *Pub of the
Year* 1993. Two regularly
changing guest beers plus a
cider. 🏨 ♣ ⏚

White Swan
36 Forton Road (A32)
☎ (01705) 584138
11–11
**Courage Best Bitter; Ushers
Best Bitter, Founders** Ⓗ
Basic local featuring darts and
pool. Seasonal beers from
Ushers are often available.
Meals Fri and Sat lunchtime
only. ◖ ♣

Windsor Castle
33 St Thomas's Road
☎ (01705) 511000
11–3, 6–11; 11–11 Fri & Sat
Gale's 5X, HSB, Festival Mild
(summer) Ⓖ
Recently renovated pub with a
traditional bare-boarded floor
and bar, and beer served
straight from the cask.
Extensive range of whiskies.
⚘ ♿ ♣ P

Hamble

King & Queen
High Street ☎ (01703) 454247
11–11
**Draught Bass; Wadworth 6X;
Whitbread Strong Country;
guest beer** Ⓗ
Friendly, single-bar pub near
the waterfront, with a separate
bistro and laundry! Famous
the world over among the
yachting community.
🏨 ⚘ ◖ ♣ P

Hammer Vale

Prince of Wales
Hammer Lane (off A3 S,
signed Bulmer Hill, right at
T-junction) OS867326
☎ (01428) 652600
11–3, 6–11
**Gale's BBB, Best Bitter, 5X,
HSB, Festival Mild** Ⓖ
Impressive, isolated, classic
1920s roadhouse. Largely
unchanged, its one, long bar
has jacketed casks on stillage
and serves three drinking
areas. Stained-glass windows
in the locals' bar advertise
Amey's Petersfield Brewery.
No food Sun eve.
🏨 Q ⚘ ◖ ▶ ♣ P

Hartley Wintney

Waggon & Horses
High Street ☎ (01252) 842119
11–11
Courage Best Bitter Ⓗ**,
Directors; Gale's HSB;
Wadworth 6X; guest beer** Ⓖ
Friendly, traditional, two-bar
pub in the centre of the village
with a cosy, small lounge but a
livelier public bar.
🏨 Q ⚘ ◖ ♣

Havant

Old House at Home
2 South Street
☎ (01705) 483464
11–11
**Gale's BBB, Best Bitter, Gold,
5X, HSB; guest beers** Ⓗ
Half-timbered, 16th-century
building (despite the date 1339
outside), originally five
cottages used as the vicarage
for the adjacent church. It
became a pub and bakery in
the 1800s and is now a
pleasant, two-bar pub in a
quiet corner of town.
🏨 ⚘ ◖ 🍴 ⇌

Robin Hood
6 Homewell ☎ (01705) 482779
11–11
**Gale's BBB, Best Bitter, 5X,
HSB** Ⓖ
Excellent old pub of unspoilt
character, neatly tucked away
opposite the town graveyard.
Busy lunchtimes. Note the
original flagstones.
🏨 ⛌ ⚘ ◖ ♿ ⇌ ♣ P

Wheelwright's Arms
27 Emsworth Road (E of
centre) ☎ (01705) 483365
11–3, 5.30–11
**Bass Worthington BB,
Draught Bass; Ind Coope
Burton Ale** Ⓗ
Pleasant pub with a central
bar. Children welcome in the
restaurant at weekends. Eve
meals Fri/Sat only.
⚘ ◖ ▶ ⇌ ♣ P

Hawkley

Hawkley Inn
Pococks Lane OS747292
☎ (01730) 827205
12–2.30 (3 Sat), 6–11
**Ballard's Trotton, Best Bitter;
Cheriton Pots Ale; Ringwood
Fortyniner; guest beers** Ⓗ
Busy village free house
attracting a varied clientele,
including walkers. It is
furnished in a very individual
style; the decor includes a
moose head. The beers may
vary. Two beer festivals a year.
No food Sun eve. Cider in
summer.
🏨 Q ⚘ ◖ ▶ ♣ ⏚ 🍴

Horndean

Brewer's Arms
1 Fiveheads Road (off old A3)
☎ (01705) 591325
12–3, 6–11
**Bass Worthington BB;
Whitbread Castle Eden Ale,
Flowers Original; guest
beers** Ⓗ
Friendly, traditional, two-bar
local. ✤ ▲ ♣ P

Ship & Bell Hotel
6 London Road
(by Gale's brewery)
☎ (01705) 592107
10–11
**Gale's BBB, Best Bitter, Gold,
HSB, Festival Mild** Ⓗ
The Gale's brewery tap, built
on the site of the original
brewhouse: a spacious 300-
year-old hotel with two
contrasting bars. Gale's guest
beers also sold.
🚪 ◑ ◗ ⊞ ▲ ♣ P ✦

Horsebridge

John o' Gaunt
½ mile W of A3057,
S of King's Somborne
☎ (01794) 388394
11.30–2.30 (11–3 Sat), 6–11
**Palmers IPA; Ringwood
Fortyniner; guest beer** Ⓗ
Fine village pub in the lovely
Test Valley – superb walking
country. The guest beer is
often an Adnams, and all beers
are good value. Shove-
ha'penny is taken seriously.
No eve meals Tue.
🏚 Q ✤ ◑ ◗ ♣ P

Itchen Abbas

Trout Inn
Main Road ☎ (01962) 779537
11–3, 6 (5.30 summer)–11
Marston's Bitter, Pedigree Ⓗ
Smart, lively country inn in
the lovely Itchen Valley. The
two bars are adorned with
breweriana and local views.
The lounge bar forms part of
the restaurant, whilst the bar
has a separate games area (bar
billiards). Marston's Head
Brewer's Choice also sold.
🏚 Q ✤ 🚪 ◑ ◗ ⊞ ❧ ♣ P

Kingsclere

Swan Hotel
Swan Street ☎ (01635) 298314
11.30–3, 5.30 (6 Sat)–11
**S&N Theakston XB; Tetley
Bitter; guest beers** Ⓗ
Large, friendly traditional inn
with beamed ceilings; parts
date back to the 15th-century.
A good mix of locals and
visitors.
🏚 Q ✤ 🚪 ◑ ◗ ♣ P

Lasham

Royal Oak
☎ (01256) 381213
11–2.30 (3 Sat), 6–11
**Hampshire King Alfred's;
Ringwood Best Bitter** Ⓗ
Cosy, welcoming country pub
with two contrasting bars and
a fine family garden.
Imaginative selection of guest
beers. The good value food is
also recommended. An airfield
and gliding centre are close by.
🏚 Q ✤ ◑ ⊞ ♣ ⌂ P

Little London

Plough
Silchester Road (1 mile E of
A340) ☎ (01256) 850628
12–3, 6–11
**Greene King Abbot;
Ringwood Best Bitter, XXXX
Porter; Whitbread Wethered
Bitter; guest beer** (summer) Ⓗ
Unspoilt village local, with a
quarry-tiled floor and a large
open fire in the bar area. Very
much a community centre,
though visitors are assured of
a welcome. The small lounge
doubles as a TV room, if
required. No food Sun. Cider
in summer.
🏚 Q ✤ ◑ ◗ ♣ ⌂ P

Long Sutton

Four Horseshoes
The Street ☎ (01256) 862488
11–2.30, 6–11
**Gale's BBB, Best Bitter,
HSB** Ⓗ
Isolated country pub with a
friendly, relaxed atmosphere.
A good blend of locals and
foodies, who travel miles for
the beer and food. The
enclosed verandah is used as a
family room. Camping in an
adjacent field.
🏚 Q ✿ ✤ ◑ ◗ ▲ ♣ P

Lymington (Pennington)

Musketeer
26 North Street
☎ (01590) 676527
12 (11.30 Sat)–3, 5.30–11
**Brakspear Bitter; Gale's HSB;
Ringwood Best Bitter; guest
beer** Ⓗ
Traditional, friendly village-
centre local. The lunchtime
menu includes unusual
home-made specials; eve
menu Sat only (booking
required). 🏚 ✿ ✤ ◑ ♣ P

Micheldever

Dever Arms
Winchester Road (off A33)
OS517389 ☎ (01962) 774339

11.30–3, 6–11
**Cheriton Pots Ale; Hall &
Woodhouse Badger BB; Hop
Back Summer Lightning;
Ringwood Best Bitter; guest
beers** Ⓗ
Popular village pub with
wooden beams and a friendly
atmosphere: one large, open
bar with a non-smoking
restaurant and two open fires.
High quality food, particularly
at weekends. No food Sun eve.
Worth the short detour from
the M3. 🏚 Q ✿ ✤ ◑ ◗ ❧ ▲
♣ ⌂ P

Minstead

Trusty Servant
Off A337 ☎ (01703) 812137
11–3, 6–11 (11–11 summer)
**Hook Norton Best Bitter;
Wadworth 6X; guest beers** Ⓗ
Attractive village pub in the
New Forest, with an
interesting pub sign featuring
picture and verse. Excellent
food in the lounge and
restaurant. Sir Arthur Conan
Doyle is buried in the local
churchyard. Beer festival in
the barn in summer.
🏚 Q ✿ 🚪 ◑ ◗ ⊞ ♣ P

Mortimer West End

Turner's Arms
West End Road (Mortimer–
Aldermaston road) OS645644
☎ (01734) 322961
11–2.30 (3 Sat), 6–11
**Brakspear Mild, Bitter,
Special** Ⓗ
Imposing, but comfortable,
Victorian pub dating from
1863, with a bar and a
restaurant area. Good
atmosphere; children welcome
in the restaurant. Extensive
food menu. 🏚 Q ✿ ◑ ◗ P

Newtown

Traveller's Rest
Church Road OS613123
☎ (01329) 833263
11–3, 6–11
**Gibbs Mew Salisbury,
Deacon, Bishop's Tipple** Ⓗ
Picturesque, converted,
18th-century cottage in a
pastoral setting. A relaxing
unspoilt lounge has a low,
matchboard ceiling and there
is a popular public bar.
Camping and caravan site in
the grounds.
🏚 Q ✿ ◑ ◗ ▲ ♣ P

North Camp

Old Ford
Lynchford Road OS517389
☎ (01252) 544840
11–11

Hampshire

Courage Best Bitter,
Directors; Hogs Back TEA;
John Smith's Bitter;
Wadworth 6X Ⓗ
Built in the 1850s and
architecturally part of
North Camp station. The
sympathetically refurbished
interior has a dining room, a
pool room and a family room.
Summer barbecues are held in
the riverside garden which has
a play area and pets corner.
ॐ ⊛ ◖ ▶ ≢ ♣ P

Overton

Old House at Home
Station Road (100 yds N of
B3400) ☎ (01256) 770335
11–3, 5.30–11; 11–11 Sat
Courage Best Bitter; John
Smith's Bitter; Ushers
Founders Ⓗ
Fine community local just out
of the village centre; a recent
internal extension has given
more space. Traditional games
enthusiastically played. Good
family garden with playthings.
No food Sun. Ushers seasonal
ales may displace the John
Smith's.
▦ ⊛ ◖ ◖ ≢ ♣ P ⊟

Owslebury

Ship Inn
Off B2177, 1½ miles N of
Marwell Zoo ☎ (01962) 777358
11–3, 6–11; 11–11 Sat
Bateman Mild; Marston's
Bitter, Pedigree Ⓗ
Lively, 300-year-old village
pub. The comfortable main bar
has nautical and cricket
memorabilia, and a large open
fireplace. A recently enlarged
second bar has a family area.
Good food. Marston's Head
Brewer's Choice sold.
▦ Q ॐ ⊛ ◖ ▶ ♣ P

Petersfield

Good Intent
40 College Street (near old
A3/A272 jct) ☎ (01730) 263838
11–3, 6–11
Gale's BBB, Best Bitter, HSB,
Festival Mild Ⓗ
Friendly, traditional 16th-
century local. Occasional live
music and food theme nights.
Gale's guest ales sold.
▦ Q ॐ ⊛ ◖ ▶ ♣ ♣ P

Old Drum
16 Chappel Street (just off
town square)
☎ (01730) 264159
11–2.30, 5.30–11; 10.30–4, 7–11 Sat
Bass Charrington IPA,
Worthington BB, Draught
Bass Ⓗ
Relaxed, town-centre pub
catering for senior citizens and
office workers lunchtimes.
Taped jazz/blues music in the

eve. No meals Sun or bank
hols. Q ⊛ ◖ ≢ ♣ ♣ P ⊬

Portsmouth

Apsley House
13 Auckland Road West,
Southsea (W of seafront)
☎ (01705) 821294
12–3, 6–11
Greene King Abbot; Ind
Coope Burton Ale; Tetley
Bitter; Wadworth 6X; guest
beer Ⓗ
Back-street pub hidden away
near Southsea shopping
centre. It is named after the
Duke of Wellington's London
home, hence it is also billed as
No.1 Portsmouth on the pub
sign. Meals in summer only
(till 8pm). ▦ ⊛ ◖ ▶ ♣ ◌

Artillery Arms
Hester Road, Milton, Southsea
☎ (01705) 733610
11–3, 6–11
Beer range varies Ⓗ
Ever-popular, back-street,
family-run, free house which
has two bars: a lively public
bar, with pool and darts, and a
quieter lounge. There is also a
family room with an
interesting one-penny, one-
armed bandit. Still one of the
cheapest pubs in the city.
ॐ ◖ ⊞ ♣ P

Connaught Arms
117 Guildford Road, Fratton
☎ (01705) 646455
11.30–2.30, 6–11; 11.30–11 Fri & Sat
Marston's Pedigree;
Wadworth 6X; guest beers Ⓗ
Portsmouth's pastie pub,
serving numerous types at
lunchtime. Handy for Fratton
Rd shopping area. Constantly
changing guest beers from
independent breweries.
⊛ ◖ ≢ ≢ (Fratton) ◌

Dolphin
41 High Street, Old
Portsmouth ☎ (01705) 823595
11–11
Fuller's London Pride; Gale's
HSB; Marston's Pedigree;
Whitbread Boddingtons
Bitter, Flowers Original Ⓗ;
guest beers Ⓖ & Ⓗ
One of the oldest pubs in the
city, situated opposite the
Anglican cathedral and its
lawns. The first in the series of
Hogshead pubs, often serving
14 beers and two ciders.
Handy for the sites of historic
Portsmouth. ▦ Q ⊛ ◖ ▶
≢ (Harbour) ♣ ◌

Dorchester Arms
9 Market Way, Landport
☎ (01705) 825950
11–2.30, 6–11; 11–11 Thu–Sat
Eldridge Pope Dorchester,
Royal Oak; guest beer Ⓗ

Single-bar pub in the shadow
of one of Britain's ugliest
buildings. Handy for
Commercial Rd shops and a
cinema. ◖ ▶ ≢ ♣ ⊬

Eldon Arms
11–17 Eldon Street, Southsea
☎ (01705) 851778
11–2.30 (3 Sat), 5 (6 Sat)–11 (11–11 Fri
& Sat in summer)
Eldridge Pope Dorchester,
Hardy Country, Royal Oak;
Tetley Bitter; guest beers Ⓗ
Friendly, cosmopolitan
alehouse with interesting and
regularly changing guest
beers. Traditional games and
good food make this a pub for
all tastes. Q ⊛ ◖ ▶ ≢ ♣

Fifth Hampshire
Volunteer Arms
74 Albert Road, Southsea
☎ (01705) 827161
12 (11 Sat)–11
Gale's BBB, Best Bitter, Gold,
5X, HSB Ⓗ
Popular, two-bar local, only
200 yds from the King's
Theatre. The birthplace of the
local CAMRA branch
(commemorated by a brass
plaque). TV in the public bar.
No food Sun. Gale's guest ales
sold. Q ◖ ⊞ ♣

Florist
324 Fratton Road, Fratton
☎ (01705) 820289
11–3, 6–11; 11–11 Sat
Wadworth IPA, 6X, Farmer's
Glory, Old Timer Ⓗ
Attractive, two-bar local with
a brewers' Tudor exterior and
a witch's hat tower. The
lounge bar at the rear is the
quiet one; the public bar has
darts, pool, a jukebox and a
TV. Q ⊛ ⊞ ≢ (Fratton)

Golden Eagle
1 Delemere Road, Southsea
☎ (01705) 821658
11–11
Gale's BBB, Best Bitter, 5X,
HSB Ⓗ
Two-bar pub on the corner of
'old' Fawcett Rd. The saloon
doubles as a pool room,
making the larger public bar
more like a saloon! Gale's
guest ales sold.
⊞ ≢ (Fratton) ♣

Old Oyster House
291 Locksway Road, Milton,
Southsea ☎ (01705) 827456
12–3, 6–11; 11–11 Sat
Fuller's London Pride;
Hardington Bitter; Whitbread
Boddingtons Bitter; guest
beers Ⓗ
Pub with a large, single bar
with a nautical theme; the
lounge bar is now the family
room, with pool and table
football. Next to the only

visible remains of the Portsea Canal. A rare outlet for real mild in the city. Two ciders.

🏃 ✳ ♣ ○ P

Red White & Blue

150 Fawcett Road, Southsea
☎ (01705) 780013
11–11
Gale's BBB, Best Bitter, HSB Ⓗ
Popular, compact local which can be crowded on darts or dominos eves. It has recently won its battle to keep its patriotic pub sign. Moose milk is served on the Sat closest to Canada Day (1st July). Gale's Festival Mild makes occasional appearances, as do Gale's guest beers.
◖ ≢ (Fratton) ♣

Sir Loin of Beef

152 Highland Road, Eastney
☎ (01705) 820115
11–11
Draught Bass; M&B Highgate Dark; Ringwood Fortyniner; Old Thumper; Taylor Landlord; Tetley Bitter; Wadworth 6X; guest beers Ⓗ
Genuine free house in the centre of Eastney, handy for the Royal Marines Museum and seafront. As well as the main bar, there is a snug and a no-smoking room. Eight ales, plus two ciders. Live music Sun night. ○ ⛶

Tap

17 London Road, North End
☎ (01705) 614861
10.30–11
Courage Directors; Gale's HSB; Gibbs Mew Bishop's Tipple; Hall & Woodhouse Tanglefoot; Ringwood Old Thumper; Ruddles County; guest beers Ⓗ
Pub opened in 1985 as a brewery tap to the now defunct Southsea Brewery: an enterprising and successful, genuine free house offering a good choice of ten ales, usually a mild, plus a cider and occasionally a perry. Local CAMRA *Pub of the Year* 1992.
Q ✳ ◖ ♣ ○

Wellington

62 High Street, Old Portsmouth (Broad St jct)
☎ (01705) 818965
11–11
Nethergate IPA or Bitter; guest beers Ⓗ
Much improved pub in a popular tourist area, close to the round tower. Plenty of parking nearby. A rare local outlet for Nethergate beers and reasonably priced for the area. Guest beers change frequently.
✳ ≢ (Harbour) ♣

Priors Dean

White Horse (Pub With No Name)

400 yds off main road, signed E Tisted OS714290
☎ (01420) 588387
11–2.30 (3 Sat), 6–11
Ballard's Best Bitter; Gale's BBB, HSB, Festival Mild; Ringwood Fortyniner; S&N Theakston Old Peculier; guest beers Ⓗ
Famous old pub, hidden down a gravel track in a field (the pub sign is missing). Now owned by Gale's, it offers ten ales, two being house beers (the stronger one brewed by Ringwood, the other by Gale's). 🏚 Q ✳ ◖ ▲ P

Privett

Pig & Whistle

Gosport Road (A32)
☎ (01730) 828421
11–11
Fuller's London Pride; Ringwood Best Bitter, Fortyniner, Old Thumper; guest beer Ⓗ
Large roadside hostelry, part of the Lawns Hotel complex. The single spacious bar has a games area and food is served all day. The disco bar is open until 2am Fri/Sat (real ale from the main bar): £3 entry.
🏚 ◖ ♣ P ⛶

Ringwood

Inn on the Furlong

12 Meeting House Lane
☎ (01425) 475139
11–3, 5–11; 11–11 Sat
Ringwood Best Bitter, XXXX Porter, Fortyniner, Old Thumper; guest beers Ⓗ
Ringwood Brewery pub opposite a large car park in this market town. A single bar serves several rooms with flagstone floors. Smoking is discouraged in the conservatory. 🏚 🏃 ✳ ◖ ⛶

Rotherwick

Falcon

The Street ☎ (01256) 762586
12–3, 5.30–11
Brakspear Bitter; Gale's HSB; Hampshire Pendragon; Hogs Back TEA; Ringwood Best Bitter; guest beers Ⓗ
Wonderful, two-bar village local, popular with villagers and visitors: a local CAMRA *Pub of the Season* and an example of how renovation need not ruin a pub. Reasonably priced food (no meals Sun/Mon eves). Cider in summer.
🏚 Q ✳ ◖ ▶ ♿ ▲ ♣ ○ P

Selborne

Selborne Arms

High Street ☎ (01420) 511247
11–3, 5.30–11 (11–11 summer Sat)
Courage Best Bitter; Ruddles County; Wadworth 6X; guest beer Ⓗ
Largely unspoilt and friendly pub in the historic Gilbert White village. An excellent children's garden includes animals and an aviary. No meals Sun eve.
🏚 Q ✳ ◖ ▶ ⊟ ♣ P

Queens Hotel

High Street ☎ (01420) 511454
10–11
Courage Best Bitter; Ushers Best Bitter, Founders Ⓗ
Village pub with a spartan but characterful public bar. The contrasting lounge has sink-into chairs and homely bric-a-brac. The large restaurant serves vegetarian options and good value Sun lunches (no food Sun eve). Ushers seasonal beers sold.
🏚 ✳ 🛏 ◖ ▶ ⊟ ♣ P

Shedfield

Sam's Hotel

Upper Church Road (off B2177) ☎ (01329) 832213
11.30–2.30 (3.30 Sat), 4.30 (6.30 Sat)–11
Banks's Mild; Marston's Bitter, Pedigree Ⓗ
Unspoilt, traditional country inn with three bars: the cosy, quiet lounge has a real fire, the other bars have darts and bar billiards. It is reputed to be the birthplace of British petanque and hosts many tournaments. Marston's Head Brewer's Choice served.
🏚 Q ✳ ⊟ ♣ P

Silchester

Calleva Arms

☎ (01734) 700305
11–3, 5–11; 11–11 Sat
Gale's BBB, Best Bitter, Gold, 5X, HSB Ⓗ
Overlooking the village green, this two-bar country pub has been extended by the addition of a large, no-smoking conservatory. A good centre for exploring Roman Silchester, after which the pub is named (formerly the Crown). No meals Sun lunchtime. Gale's guest beers in summer.
🏚 Q 🏃 ✳ ◖ ▶ ⊟ ▲ ♣ P ⛶

Southampton

Bosun's Locker

Castle Square, Upper Bugle Street ☎ (01703) 333364

11–3, 6 (7 Sat)–11; 11–11 Fri
**Draught Bass; Fuller's
London Pride; Whitbread
Boddingtons Bitter; guest
beer** H
Friendly, nautically-themed
pub close to the city centre
which serves a varied range of
home-cooked food. Inspired
choice of guest beer from
small independents. Tall
people risk being netted!
🏨 🛏 ◖ ▶ ♣

Freemantle Arms

33 Albany Road, Freemantle
☎ (01703) 320759
10–3, 6–11; 10–11 Sat
**Banks's Mild; Marston's
Bitter, Pedigree** H
Friendly, two-bar local in a
quiet cul-de-sac, featuring a
popular, colourful garden and
patio. The venue for the
annual Freemantle leek and
vegetable show (first Sat in
Sept). A good boozer also
stocking Marston's Head
Brewer's Choice. ❀ 🍴 ♣

Gate

138–140 Burgess Road, Bassett
☎ (01703) 678250
11–3, 5.30 (7 Sat)–11
**Eldridge Pope Dorchester,
Hardy Country, Royal Oak;
guest beers** H
Large, recently refurbished
pub near the University. Used
by students but still a regular's
haunt, it is popular at night for
Sky TV, pool and darts. Eve
meals end at 8; no food
Sat/Sun eves. Two changing
guest beers. ❀ 🍴 ♣ P

Guide Dog

38 Earls Road, Bevois Valley
(off Bevois Valley Rd)
11–3, 6–11
**Wadworth IPA, 6X; guest
beer** H
Side-street local; the smallest
pub in Southampton. Note the
display of dolls and
caricatures of the regulars.
Good value. ▶ ♣

Hobbit

134 Bevois Valley Road
☎ (01703) 232591
6–11 (midnight Thu); 5–1am Fri;
1–1am Sat
**Hop Back Special, Wheat
Beer; Whitbread Boddingtons
Bitter, Best Bitter, Flowers
Original; guest beer** H
Multi-levelled pub popular
with students, so it can be very
busy some eves. Live music in
the downstairs bar, or on an
outdoor stage in summer.
❀ ⇌ (St Denys) ♣

Marsh

42 Canute Road (under A3025,
Itchen Bridge)
☎ (01703) 635540
11–11

**Banks's Mild; Marston's
Bitter, Pedigree** H
Characteristic docklands pub,
once a lighthouse, hence the
semi-circular bars. A brisk
lunchtime trade comes from
the nearby Ocean Village and
local businesses. Pool room.
Marston's Head Brewer's
Choice stocked. ❀ 🍴 ▶ 🍴 ♣

Miller's Pond

2 Middle Road, Sholing
(Station Rd jct)
☎ (01703) 444755
11–11
**Wadworth IPA, 6X, Old
Timer; guest beer** H
Pleasant, one-bar local in a
residential area. Run by the
same family for 23 years, it has
a relaxed, friendly atmosphere.
Live music Sat night.
❀ 🍴 ⇌ (Sholing) P

New Inn

16 Bevois Valley Road
☎ (01703) 228437
12–3, 6.45–11
**Gale's BBB, Best Bitter, 5X,
HSB** H
Small but welcoming local,
popular with students. Its
good selection of continental
beers, superb malt whisky
range and excellent lunches
(vegetarians catered for) help
make it a veritable jewel in the
valley. Gale's guest beers.
🍴 ♿ ♣

Park Inn

37 Carlisle Road, Shirley
☎ (01703) 787835
11–3 (3.30 Sat), 5 (6.30 Sat)–11
**Hall & Woodhouse
Tanglefoot; Wadworth IPA,
6X, Farmer's Glory, Old
Timer; guest beer** H
Popular, friendly local, close to
the shops. It maintains a
two-bar feel and has some
interesting mirrors. Slightly
more upmarket than most
side-street pubs. ❀ 🍴 ♣

Richmond Inn

108 Portswood Road,
Portswood ☎ (01703) 554523
11–11
**Banks's Mild; Marston's
Bitter, Pedigree** H
Friendly, two-bar pub in a
busy suburb: a basic public
and a more comfortable
lounge. The old LSD cash
register provides welcome
nostalgia. Excellent whisky
selection. Live Irish music
Thu. Marston's Head Brewer's
Choice available. ❀ 🍴 ♣

Waterloo Arms

101 Waterloo Road,
Freemantle ☎ (01703) 220022
12–2.30, 7–11; 12–11 Fri & Sat
**Hop Back GFB, Special,
Stout, Summer Lightning,
Wheat Beer** H

Popular one-bar local. The
walls are festooned with
awards for the Summer
Lightning. A solid boozer
which doesn't subscribe to
gimmicks. ❀ 🍴
⇌ (Millbrook) ♣

Standford

Robin Hood

Standford Lane (B3004 S of
village) ☎ (01428) 751508
11–11; 11–2.30, 5–11 Mon
**Draught Bass; Gibbs Mew
Overlord, Deacon, Bishop's
Tipple** H
Dating from 1904, this is one
of three pubs built for a Royal
Military Review of Bordon
Camp, although a pub has
been on this site for 400 years.
It was once paired with a pub
called the Little John on the
other side of the ford. No eve
meals Sun. Q ❀ 🍴 ▶ P

Stoke

White Hart

Off B3048 ☎ (01264) 738355
12–3 (11.30–4 Sat), 6.30–11
Brakspear Bitter G**; Fuller's
London Pride; Hampshire
King Alfred's** H**, Lionheart,
Pendragon** G**; Whitbread
Strong Country** H
Traditional village amenity
saved from near extinction to
provide all that is expected
from a country pub. Skittle
alley. Interesting menu.
🏨 ♿ ❀ 🍴 ♿ ♣ P

Tadley

Treacle Mine Hotel

Silchester Road (½mile from
traffic lights) ☎ (01734) 814857
11–11
**Fuller's London Pride;
Morrells Bitter; Wadworth 6X;
guest beer** H
Pleasant, welcoming, one-bar
pub on the edge of Tadley
Common. The name is
connected to local folklore.
Busy early eve meals. Eve
meals for residents.
Q ❀ 🛏 🍴 ♿ ♣ P

Tangley

Cricketer's Arms

☎ (01264) 730283
11–3, 6–11
**Draught Bass; Cheriton Pots
Ale, Diggers Gold** H
Remote, 18th-century drovers'
inn where the bar area enjoys
the warm atmosphere of a
typical village pub. The
large back bar is now a
family/dining room. The field
at the rear is Caravan Club
listed.
🏨 Q ♿ ❀ 🍴 ▶ ♿ ▲ ♣ P

Hampshire

Thruxton

White Horse
Off A303 eastbound
11–3, 6–11
Fuller's London Pride; Smiles Bitter, Best Bitter Ⓗ
Charming old thatched pub which is not spoilt by its proximity to the A303. Beware the low ceilings. Children are allowed in the dining room. No food Sun/Mon eves.
🏚 Q ♿ ⊛ ◑ ▶ ♣ P

Totford

Woolpack
On B3046 S of Brown Candover
☎ (01962) 732101
11.30–3, 6–11
Cheriton Pots Ale; Eldridge Pope Hardy Country; Gale's HSB; Palmers IPA Ⓗ
16th-century, flint-stone country inn and restaurant. The large, pleasant garden has a duck pond.
🏚 Q ⊛ 🛏 ◑ ▶ ♣ P

Twyford

Phoenix
High Street ☎ (01962) 713322
11.30–2.30 (3 Sat), 6–11
Marston's Bitter, Pedigree Ⓗ
Busy, friendly village inn serving good value food. Skittle alley/function room; live music Wed eve. Accommodation is available in nearby village houses. Marston's Head Brewer's Choice available.
🏚 ⊛ ◑ ♣ P

Upper Clatford

Crook & Shears
Off A343 ☎ (01264) 361543
11.30–3.30, 6–11; 11–11 Sat
Fuller's Chiswick, London Pride; Ringwood Fortyniner; Whitbread Flowers Original; guest beers Ⓗ
Homely, 17th-century village pub with low ceilings. The huge fireplace was originally a baker's oven. A skittle alley stands at the rear, with a pleasant garden. No food Sun eve. Try the speciality sausages bought locally.
🏚 Q ⊛ ◑ ▶ 🍴 ♣

Upton Grey

Hoddington Arms
☎ (01256) 862371
11 (11.30 Sat)–2.30, 6 (7 Sat)–11; 12–2.30, 7–10.30 Sun
Draught Bass; Morland IPA, Tanner's Jack, Old Speckled Hen Ⓗ

18th-century, listed building in a pretty village, serving good quality food. Good-sized family room; note the unusual lattice-work ceiling in the bar billiards room. Genuinely friendly.
🏚 ♿ ⊛ ◑ ▶ ♣ P

Wallington

White Horse
44 North Wallington
☎ (01329) 235197
11–2.30, 5–11; 11–11 Sat; 12–2.30, 7–10.30 Sun
Draught Bass; M&B Brew XI; guest beers Ⓗ
Pub by the River Wallington, with a patio garden. Well renovated, its two bars each have a different character, with fresh flowers on the tables. The restaurant serves as a family room Sun lunchtime. No food Sun, or Mon eve.
🏚 Q ⊛ ◑ ▶ ⊟

West End

Master Builder
Swaythling Road (A27)
☎ (01703) 472426
11–2.30, 6 (5 Fri)–11; 11–11 Sat
Draught Bass; guest beers Ⓗ
Large, comfortable roadside pub with many drinking areas, two of which are non-smoking. Five regularly changing guest beers from large and small breweries sold. The pub carries a *Heartbeat* award and the menu includes children's and vegetarian choices. No eve meals Sun/Mon.
⊛ ◑ ▶ P 🍴

Weyhill

Weyhill Fair
On A342 1½ miles from A303 jct
☎ (01264) 773631
11–2.30, 6 (5 Fri, 6.30 Sat)–11
Morrells Bitter, Varsity, Graduate; guest beers Ⓗ
Very popular free house with the Morrells range well supplemented by three rapidly changing guest beers. Excellent food at modest prices (not served Sun eve). The family area is also a no-smoking zone.
🏚 Q ⊛ ◑ ▶ ♿ P 🍴 ⊟

Whitchurch

Prince Regent
104 London Road
☎ (01256) 892179
11–11
Archers Best Bitter, Golden; Hop Back GFB Ⓗ
Unpretentious, genuine local with a view over the Test Valley. Well worth the walk uphill from the village centre. Food served all day. A cellar bar is available for functions.
🏚 ⊛ ◑ ▶ ♣ 🍽 P

Whitsbury

Cartwheel Inn
Whitsbury Road
(signed from A338)
☎ (01725) 518362
11–2.30 (3 Sat), 6–11
Beer range varies Ⓗ
Remote but thriving free house with a games area and a dining room. Six ales are usually available (excellent selection). Formerly a barn, bakery and wheelwright's, hence the name. An imaginative and varied menu features some local produce. No food Tue eve in winter.
🏚 Q ⊛ ◑ ▲ ♣ P

Winchester

Crown & Anchor
168 High Street
☎ (01962) 854897
10 (10.30 Sat)–11
Marston's Bitter, Pedigree Ⓗ
Large, single-bar pub overlooked by King Alfred's statue: two minutes' walk from the bus station. Live jazz Mon night. Marston's Head Brewer's Choice sold. ⊛ ◑ ▲

Eagle Hotel
1 Andover Road
(opp. station)
☎ (01962) 853108
11–3 (may extend Sat), 5–11
Cheriton Pots Ale; Hop Back Summer Lightning; Ringwood Best Bitter; guest beers Ⓗ
Single-bar pub with a function room. Lunches served each day but advance notice needed for eve meals. Annual beer festival May. A beer bus is run to rural pubs each Fri, April–Dec.
🏚 Q 🛏 ◑ ▶ ▲ 🚆 P

Hyde Tavern
57 Hyde Street
☎ (01962) 862592
11–3, 5.30 (6 Sat)–11
Marston's Bitter, Pedigree; guest beer (autumn/winter) Ⓗ
Small, low, 15th-century pub with an uneven floor and two bars. Warm and friendly, but mind your head on the beams.
Q ⊟ ▲ 🚆 ♣

St James Tavern
3 Romsey Road
☎ (01962) 861288
11.30–3 (3.30 Sat), 5.30 (6.30 Sat)–11
Hall & Woodhouse Badger BB, Tanglefoot; Wadworth IPA, 6X; guest beers Ⓗ
Small, single-bar pub up from the Gurkha Museum. Good sandwiches lunchtime (try the bacon and avocado). Crib night Tue; quiz Wed and Sun.
Q ⊛ ◑ ▶ 🚆

Hampshire

Wykeham Arms

75 Kingsgate Street
☎ (01962) 853834
11–11

**Eldridge Pope Dorchester,
Hardy Country, Royal Oak** Ⓗ
Large, busy, attractive pub
with two bars and several
cosy rooms heated only by
log fires. Customers can sit
at old school desks to
enjoy high quality local
specialities. Located near
Winchester Cathedral and
College. No smoking in
the main bar Fri and Sat.
🏚 Q ⊛ 🛏 ◑ ▶ P

Winchfield

Woody's
Station Hill ☎ (01252) 842129
12–2.30, 5.30–11

Beer range varies Ⓗ
An unassuming frontage
belies the interior of this pub
which takes ale from Gale's,
Greene King and Cheriton.
The garden is a joy in summer.
No meals Sat/Sun.
⊛ ◑ ▶ 🏚 ⇌ ⌂ P

Wolverton

George & Dragon
Off A339 ☎ (01635) 298292
12–3, 5.30–11

**Brakspear Special; Fuller's
London Pride; Hampshire
King Alfred's; Wadworth
IPA, 6X** Ⓗ
Open-plan country inn with a
games area to the side of the
bar. Subdued candlelight adds
character. Separate skittle
alley. 🏚 ⊛ ◑ ▶ P

Woolton Hill

Rampant Cat
Broad Layings (off A343 then
road opp. 'The Stores' in
village centre)
☎ (01635) 253474
11.30–2.30, 5.30–11

**Archers Best Bitter;
Arkell's 3B, Kingsdown;
guest beer** Ⓗ
Lovely country pub with a
large, L-shaped bar. The
separate restaurant at the
rear overlooks a patio and
garden with a play area.
Friendly locals and
resident labrador. No food
Mon eve.
🏚 Q ⊛ ◑ ▶ & ♣ P 🍴

Try also: Coopers Arms,
(Ushers)

GUEST BEERS OR GATECRASHERS?

The 1st May 1990 seemed like the dawn of a new age to drinkers and small brewers alike. For on this particular Mayday the guest beer law came into force.

Following the Monopolies and Mergers Commission review of the UK brewing industry in 1989, the Government accepted that more competition was needed in the pub trade and introduced legislation to allow guest beers into some pubs controlled by the national breweries. Only the tenanted or leased side of their pub businesses was affected; managed houses were not obliged to sell a guest beer. The other main condition of the law was that the guest beer had to be a cask-conditioned (real) ale.

Typically, the big brewers rushed to soften the impact of 'outsiders' on their profits. In a variety of measures (some more legitimate than others), they aimed to control the guest beer market in their pubs. By offering to provide their tenants and lessees with a limited choice of other brewers' beers, they immediately assumed control of supply. By acting as middle men, they also added a mark up, resulting in guest beer prices often being substantially higher than those of the pub's regular brews and considerably dearer than if bought in the guest beers' native territory.

The law has since been clarified to make it clear that tenants and lessees can, in fact, take a guest beer in addition to any guest supplied by the controlling brewery, but there's no doubt that many publicans opt for an easy life and just take what their governors offer. This interference in the right of a publican to choose his own guest beer has worked against the spirit of the law. It also means that the same guest beers keep popping up time and again. That's good news for the likes of Wadworth 6X, Marston's Pedigree and Morland Old Speckled Hen, but what about giving some of the smaller breweries a chance? As the breweries section of this book demonstrates, there is no lack of variety out there now.

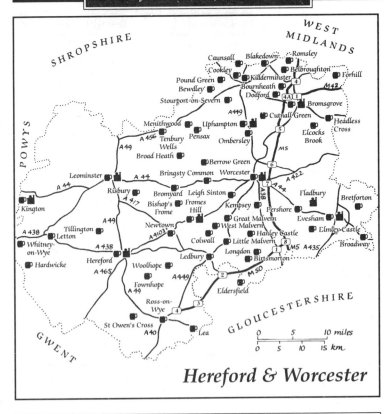

Hereford & Worcester

 Cannon Royall, *Uphampton;* **Evesham,** *Evesham;* **Fromes Hill,** *Fromes Hill;* **Jolly Roger,** *Worcester;* **Marches,** *Leominster;* **Red Cross,** *Bromsgrove;* **Wye Valley,** *Hereford;* **Wyre Piddle,** *Fladbury*

Belbroughton

Holly Bush
Stourbridge Road (A491)
☎ (01562) 730207
11–3, 6–11 (11–11 bank hols)
Ansells Mild; HP&D Bitter, Entire; guest beer H
Traditional roadside inn. A single bar serves three distinct areas, one of which is a dining room. Live piano Wed, Fri and Sat eves. No eve meals Sun.
♨ Q ✿ ◑ ▯ & P

Olde Horseshoe
High Street ☎ (01562) 730233
11–3 (4 Sat), 5.30 (6 Sat)–11
S&N Theakston Mild, Best Bitter, XB, Old Peculier; guest beer H
Old, village-centre pub with a very small lounge, busy with diners. The larger bar has a pool table. Excellent menu; wide range of vegetarian

meals. No meals Mon eve.
✿ ◑ ▯ ⊞ & ♣ ⌂ P

Queens
Queens Hill (B4188)
☎ (01562) 730276
11.30–3, 5.30 (6 Sat)–11
Bateman Mild; Marston's Bitter, Pedigree H
Smart village inn, popular with diners and regulars. Three lounge areas; good range of food (not served Sun eve). A very pretty brook runs by the car park.
Q ⑤ ✿ ◑ ▯ & P

Berrow Green

Admiral Rodney
On B4197 ☎ (01886) 21375
12–3 (not winter Mon; may extend summer), 7–11
Hook Norton Best Bitter; Wye Valley Bitter; guest beers H
Large, rambling country pub with a nautical theme and separate areas for the bar, and

lounge and pool. Skittle alley. No meals Mon eve.
♨ Q ✿ ◑ ▯ ▲ ♣ P

Bewdley

Black Boy
50 Wyre Hill (follow Sandy Bank, off B4194 at Welch Gate)
☎ (01299) 403523
11–3, 7–11
Banks's Mild, Bitter E**; Camerons Strongarm; Marston's Pedigree** H
Not to be confused with the Black Boy Hotel, this 400-year-old pub is a short but steep climb from the town centre. A guest beer sometimes replaces the Camerons. Well-behaved children may be allowed in the games room when it is not in use. ♨ Q ✿ ⊞ ♣ ☐

Cock & Magpie
Severnside North
☎ (01299) 403748

129

11–3, 6–11; 11–11 Sat & summer
Banks's Mild, Bitter E
Popular, traditional, two-bar
riverside local. Severnside
North was once Coles Quay,
busy with river trade before
the canal era. Occasional
flooding! Q ⊞ ≢ ♣ ⊟

George Hotel

Load Street ☎ (01299) 402117
11–3, 5.30–11
**Ind Coope Burton Ale; Tetley
Bitter; guest beer** H
Hotel with a thriving pub
trade. Access is via the
passageway at the side. There
is a cosy, often busy, bar to the
rear, and a larger, generally
quiet, hotel bar at the front.
🏨 ⊛ 🛏 ◁ ▶ ⎕
≢ (SVR) P

Try also: Rising Sun,
Kidderminster Rd (Banks's)

Birtsmorton

Farmer's Arms

Birts Street ☎ (01684) 833308
11–2.30, 6–11
**Hook Norton Best Bitter, Old
Hooky; guest beer** H
Black-and-white pub, tucked
away down a country lane: a
small lounge with a very low
beamed ceiling, and a basic
bar with darts. The garden has
swings and a fine view of the
Malvern Hills.
🏨 Q ⊛ ◁ ▶ ♣ P

Bishop's Frome

Chase Inn

On B4214 ☎ (01885) 490234
12–3.30, 5.30–11 (may be 11–11
summer); 12–11 Sat
**Hook Norton Best Bitter; Wye
Valley Bitter** H
Uncomplicated, welcoming
pub opposite the village green.
Two comfortable bars offer a
good selection of value food
and beer. The landlord will
read your Tarot cards on
request. Buxom Bitter is a
blend supplied by Wye Valley.
Ideal for a peaceful B&B stop.
🏨 Q ⊛ 🛏 ◁ ▶ ▲ ♣ P

Green Dragon

Off B4214 ☎ (01885) 490607
12–2.30, 5–11; 11–11 Sat
**Robinson's Old Tom; Taylor
Golden Best, Landlord; Ram
Tam; Tetley Bitter; guest
beers** H
Multi-roomed, old village inn
that once had a cult following.
It is still popular for its good
value food and six-plus beers.
Original flagstones and an
inglenook in the bar;
contrasting small, but tidy,
restaurant and an often noisy
games room. 🏨 ⊛ ◁ ▶ ♣ P

Blakedown

Old House at Home

26 Birmingham Road
☎ (01562) 700507
11–2.30 (3 Sat), 5–11
**Ansells Bitter; Ind Coope
Burton Ale; Tetley Bitter;
guest beer** H
Refurbished village pub on the
main Birmingham–
Kidderminster road.
🏨 ☃ ◁ ▶ ◇ ≢ ♣ P ⊬

Bournheath

Gate

Dodford Road (off B4551)
☎ (01527) 878169
11–2.30, 6–10.30 (11 Fri & Sat)
**Smiles Best Bitter, Exhibition;
Whitbread Boddingtons
Bitter; guest beer** H
Stylish, converted nailer's
cottage with an added
restaurant and conservatory.
The emphasis is on the
excellent, wide range of food
with Mexican/Cajun
specialities. Balti night Mon.
🏨 ⊛ ◁ ▶ ♣ P

Bretforton

Fleece

The Cross (100 yards S of
B4035) ☎ (01386) 831173
11–2.30, 6–11; 12–2.30, 7–10.30 Sun
**Greene King Abbot; Hobsons
Best Bitter; Hook Norton Best
Bitter; M&B Brew XI; Uley
Old Spot** H
Famous old pub, owned by
the NT. The interior has
remained untouched for many
years and includes inglenooks,
antiques and a world-famous
pewter collection. The no-
smoking family room offers
the same fine old
accommodation as the rest of
the pub. No crisps! 🏨 Q ☃
⊛ ◁ ▶ ▲ ♣ ◇ ⊬ ⊟

Bringsty Common

Live & Let Live

Off A44; at pub sign follow
right-hand track onto common
OS699547 ☎ (01886) 21462
12–3 (not Tue), 6–11; 11–11 Sat
**Draught Bass; Wye Valley
HPA** H
A compass and four-wheel
drive are needed to track
down this splendid cottage-
cum-inn on the common: a
wonderful throwback, with
many charming features and
no frills. Great views towards
the Malverns. Snuff sold; Wye
Valley seasonal beers. A must!
🏨 Q ⊛ ⊞ ▲ ♣ ◇ ⊬ P

Broad Heath

Fox Inn

On B4204 ☎ (01886) 853219
12–3, 6–11
**Batham Best Bitter; Marston's
Pedigree; guest beer** H
Pub with a large lounge bar
retaining some beams from the
16th century. The public bar
has pool and darts. Do not
confuse with Broadheath near
Worcester – this one is near
Tenbury Wells.
🏨 ⊛ ◁ ▶ ⊞ ♣ P

Broadway

Crown & Trumpet

Church Street
☎ (01386) 853202
11–3, 5–11; 11–11 Sat
**Morland Old Speckled Hen;
Stanway Stanney Bitter;
Wadworth 6X; Whitbread
Boddingtons Bitter, Flowers
IPA, Original** H
Fine, 17th-century Cotswold
stone inn, complete with oak
beams and log fires. Food for
walking parties by
arrangement.
🏨 ⊛ 🛏 ◁ ▶ ▲ ♣ ◇

Bromsgrove

Golden Cross Hotel

20 High Street
☎ (01527) 870005
11–11
**Courage Directors; S&N
Theakston Mild, Best Bitter;
Wadworth 6X; Younger
Scotch; guest beer** H
Smart Wetherspoon's town
pub: a long bar, complete with
21 handpumps, spans over
half the length of the open-
plan single room which
features railway carriage
snugs. One beer is sold at a
low price. No music/children
policy. ⊛ ◁ ▶ ◇ ⊬

Hop Pole

78 Birmingham Road
☎ (01527) 870100
12–2.30, 5.30–11; 12–3, 7–11 Sat
**M&B Brew XI; Red Cross
Nailers OBJ** H
Excellent, street-corner local
opposite the Rovers football
ground: an L-shaped bar and a
comfortable lounge, serving
good value lunches (no meals
Sun). HQ of Bromsgrove Folk
Club and many local societies.
OBJ is brewed by the licensee.
Beware the keg cider on a fake
handpump. Q ⊛ ◁ ⊞

Bromyard

Crown & Sceptre

7 Sherford Street
☎ (01885) 482441

11.30–2.30 (3 Fri, 3.30 Sat), 6.30–11
**Banks's Bitter; Hook Norton
Best Bitter; S&N Theakston
Best Bitter; guest beer** Ⓗ
Two plain, but comfortable
drinking areas and a dining
room allow this popular
pub to cater for all;
pleasantly decorated with old
maps and adverts.
🏠 ❀ 🛏 ◖ ▶ ♣ P

Caunsall

Anchor Inn
Cookley Road
☎ (01562) 850254
12–4, 7–11
**Draught Bass; M&B Mild;
Stones Best Bitter** Ⓗ
Pleasant, two-roomed pub in a
small village, a short walk
from the Staffs & Worcs Canal.
Q ⛄ ❀ ◡ P

Colwall

Chase Inn
Chase Road, Upper Colwall
(200 yds off Walwyn Rd,
B4218, signed 'British Camp')
☎ (01684) 540276
12–2.30 (not Tue), 6–11; 12–2.30,
7–10.30 Sun
**Donnington BB, SBA; Wye
Valley HPA, Supreme** Ⓗ
Quiet, cosy, two-bar free
house, tucked away in
a wooded backwater
of the Malvern Hills. A
limited, but very wholesome
menu is served Mon–Sat.
Probably the finest pub
garden in the county.
❀ ◖ 🍽 ♣ P

Cookley

Bull's Head Hotel
Bridge Road ☎ (01562) 850242
11.30–3, 6–11; 11–11 Sat
Banks's Mild, Bitter Ⓔ;
Marston's Pedigree Ⓗ
Large village local, situated
over Cookley canal tunnel.
The garden has a play area.
Access to the canal is down a
steep, twisting path. Good
value food.
⛄ ❀ ◖ ▶ 🍽 ♣ P ⅄

Cutnall Green

New Inn
Kidderminster Road (A442)
☎ (01299) 851202
12–3, 5.30 (6 Sat)–11
**Banks's Mild; Marston's
Bitter, Pedigree** Ⓗ
Small, friendly village local
serving reasonably priced
lunches (vegetarian meals
available). Marston's Head
Brewer's Choice sold.
🏠 Q ❀ 🛏 ◖ ▶ P

Dodford

Dodford Inn
Whinfield Road (off A448,
near Bournheath)
☎ (01527) 832470
12–3, 6 (7 winter)–11 (11–11 summer
Sat)
**Greenalls Mild, Bitter,
Original; guest beers** Ⓗ
Difficult to find, cottagey
village local set in beautiful
countryside. A single room is
split into three areas. Good
pub grub. Popular with local
farmers and ramblers. Families
welcome – good play area for
children. 🏠 Q ❀ ◖ ▶ ♣ P

Elcocks Brook

Brook
Sillins Lane (off Windmill
Lane, Headless Cross)
☎ (01527) 543209
12–2.30, 5–11; 12–11 Sat
**Banks's Mild; Marston's
Bitter, Pedigree** Ⓗ
Popular, friendly country pub
with a spacious, well-
appointed, single lounge bar.
Wide variety of home-cooked
food lunchtime. Pleasant
outside drinking area.
🏠 ❀ ◖ P

Eldersfield

Greyhound
Lime Street (N from
B4211/B4213 jct, signed Lime
Street) OS814305
☎ (01452) 840381
11.30–3.30, 6–11; 11.30–11 Mon & Tue
**Butcombe Bitter; Wadworth
6X; guest beer** Ⓖ
Traditionally furnished pub
with many unusual features:
gravity dispensed beers, quoits
and a garden full of animals.
Camping in the grounds
(including caravans).
Occasional cider in summer.
🏠 Q ⛄ ❀ ▲ ♣ ◡ P

Elmley Castle

Queen Elizabeth
West Side, Main Street
☎ (01386) 710209
12–3, 7–11
Marston's Bitter, Pedigree Ⓗ
Visited by its namesake in
1575, this traditional village
inn has remained unchanged
under the present landlord for
over 30 years. Handy for
walkers on Bredon Hill. It can
get rather smoky.
🏠 Q ❀ ▲ ♣ P

Evesham

Green Dragon
Oat Street (just off High St)
☎ (01386) 446337

11–3, 7–11 (midnight Thu–Sat)
**Courage Directors; Evesham
Asum Ale, Asum Gold;
Ruddles County** or **Draught
Bass** Ⓗ
A cosy lounge, an extensive
bar and a large function room
make up this lively town pub,
complete with its own
brewery. Q ❀ ◖ 🛏 ▲ ⇌ ♣

Trumpet Inn
Merstow Green (just off High
St) ☎ (01386) 446227
11–11
**Draught Bass; Robinson's
Frederic's; Ruddles County** Ⓗ
Convivial, town-centre local
with welcoming bar staff. Fri
and Sat eves can be noisy.
Beware the keg cider on a fake
handpump. ❀ ◖ ▲ ⇌ ♣ ⅄

Try also: Red Horse Inn, Vine
St; **Talbot**, Port St (both M&B)

Forhill

Peacock Inn
Icknield Street (2 miles from
A441/Redhill Rd jct, towards
Wythall) ☎ (01564) 823232
12–11
**Banks's Mild, Bitter;
Camerons Strongarm; Enville
Bitter; Judges Gavel Bender;
Marston's Pedigree; guest
beers** Ⓗ
Excellent country pub with
oak beams throughout. One
bar serves three areas, one
no-smoking. Another bar has
old bar billiards; large lounge.
Daily changing blackboard
menu; Sun lunches served
12–8.
🏠 ⛄ ❀ ◖ ▶ 🛏 ₺ ♣ P ⅄

Fownhope

Green Man Inn
On B4224 ☎ (01432) 860423
11–2.30, 6–11
**Courage Directors; Hook
Norton Best Bitter; Marston's
Pedigree; Samuel Smith OBB;
Whitbread Boddingtons
Bitter** Ⓗ
Classic, 500-year-old, black-
and-white coaching inn,
popular with drinkers and
out-of-town diners from
Hereford, and enjoying a
reputation for good value.
Guests have fishing rights on
the Wye. The longest-running
Guide entry for the county.
🏠 ❀ 🛏 ◖ ▶ 🛏 P

Fromes Hill

Wheatsheaf Inn
On A4103 ☎ (01531) 640888
5 (11 Sat)–11
**Fromes Hill Buckswood
Dingle, Overture, IDK** Ⓗ
One-bar pub owned by
Fromes Hill brewery. Its

Hereford & Worcester

attributes include the cheapest beer in the county. The quality interior deserves a better atmosphere, but often the TV/radio dominates.
🏠 �˜… ⚓ P

Great Malvern

Foley Arms Hotel

14 Worcester Road
☎ (01684) 573397
12–2.30, 5.30–11; 12–11 Sat
Draught Bass; guest beers 🅷
Popular, enlarged 1810 coaching inn. Magnificent views across the Severn Valley can be enjoyed from the bar and terrace. Two imaginative guest beers are available – one low gravity, one high.
Q 🛏 🌴 🏠 🍴 ▮ ⇥ ♣ P ⚲

Hanley Castle

Three Kings

Church End (signed off B4211)
☎ (01684) 592686
11–3, 7–11
Thwaites Bitter; Butcombe Bitter; guest beers 🅷
Superlative, unspoilt pub, 80 years in the same family: a lounge and two other rooms. CAMRA national *Country Pub of the Year* 1993. No food Sun eve. 🏠 Q 🛏 🌴 🏠 🍴 ▮ ♣ ◔

Hardwicke

Royal Oak

On B4348 ☎ (01497) 831248
12–2.30 (not winter Tue), 7–11
Draught Bass; Wye Valley Bitter 🅷
Beautifully situated country inn, handy for Hay book shops. It boasts a number of timbered and wood-panelled bars with benches. Great for balmy summer eves, but dogs are not welcome. Camping by advance arrangement.
🏠 Q 🛏 🍴 ▮ ⚓ ♣ P

Headless Cross

Gate Hangs Well

98 Evesham Road
☎ (01527) 401293
12–3, 5.30–11; 12–11 Sat
Ansells Mild, Bitter; HP&D Entire 🅷
Friendly, one-bar, main road local. Popular with young drinkers, it can get lively in the eve. 🏠 🌴 🍴

Try also: Seven Stars, Birchfield Rd (Free)

Hereford

Barrels

69 St Owen Street
☎ (01432) 274968
11–11

Wye Valley Bitter, HPA, Supreme, Brew 69; guest beers 🅷
Brash, lively and one of the last multi-roomed drinking houses left in Hereford; home to the Wye Valley brewery whose seasonal beers are also stocked. Good mix of locals; and popular with students towards the weekend. A charity beer festival is held Aug. 🌴 🗗 🔥 ♣ ◔

Lancaster

1 St Martins Street
☎ (01432) 275480
11.30–3, 6–11
Beer range varies 🅷
Proudly unpretentious, two-bar riverside free house. The main bar has a small, but loyal, local following; the back bar is usually quiet. Always three beers available (one from Wye Valley; none from the 'Big Boys'). Parking can be tricky. Q 🌴 🍴 ▮ 🔥 ♣ ◔

Three Elms Inn

1 Canon Pyon Road
☎ (01432) 273338
11–11
Marston's Pedigree; Whitbread Boddingtons Bitter, Pompey Royal, Flowers Original; guest beers 🅷
A typical Whitbread managed house when one enters; however the range and quality of beers (always six) suggest this is no ordinary pub. Run with imagination; great for families. An oasis in an area poor for pubs. Wheelchair WC. 🛏 🌴 🍴 ▮ 🔥 ♣ P

Treacle Mine

83–85 St Martins Street
☎ (01432) 266022
11–4, 6–11; 11–11 Fri & Sat
Banks's Mild, Bitter 🅴; **Greene King Abbot; guest beer** 🅷
Popular, refurbished, single-bar pub on the south bank of the river. Old and new meet in a mix of satellite TV and old beams and brickwork. Parking can be a problem. 🌴

Victory

88 St Owen Street
☎ (01432) 274998
11–11
Wye Valley Bitter, HPA, Supreme; guest beers 🅷
Busy pub with an unusual galleon and maritime theme, part of the very successful Wye Valley stable. Seasonal ales are also stocked, as is the best range of guests in Hereford. Good value food. Live music.
🏠 🌴 🍴 ▮ 🔥 ♣ ◔

Try also: Castle Pool Hotel, Castle St (Free)

Kempsey

Walter de Cantelupe Inn

Main Road (A38)
☎ (01905) 820572
12–2.30 (not Mon), 6–11; 12–2.30, 7–10.30 Sun
Marston's Bitter, Pedigree; guest beers 🅷
Sophisticated pub offering quality food. Beer discounts for CAMRA members (show card). Named after the Bishop of Worcester (1235–66) who lived in the village. Eve meals Tue–Sat.
🏠 🌴 🍴 ▮ 🔥 ⚓ P

Kidderminster

Hare & Hounds

Stourbridge Road, Broadwaters (A449, Wolverhampton road)
☎ (01562) 751819
12–3.30, 6–11; 11–11 Sat
Batham Mild, Best Bitter 🅷
Completely refurbished by the brewery: a very pleasant, two-level lounge, a comfortable bar, plus a pool room. 🛏 🌴 🍴 ▮ 🗗 🔥 ♣ P

King & Castle

SVR Station, Comberton Hill
☎ (01562) 747505
11–3 (4 Sat), 5 (6 Sat)–11 (11–11 when SVR trains run, except Sun)
Draught Bass; Batham Best Bitter; M&B Highgate Dark; guest beers 🅷
Station bar, part of the Severn Valley Railway's southern terminus. Children allowed in until 9pm. Full station facilities (e.g. wheelchair toilets) available when trains are operating. No eve meals Mon–Wed.
🏠 🍴 ▮ 🔥 ⇥ ♣ P

Red Man

192 Blackwell Street
☎ (01562) 67555
10–11
Ansells Bitter; HP&D Mild, Entire; Ind Coope Burton Ale; Marston's Pedigree; Tetley Bitter; guest beer 🅷
On the edge of the town centre, just inside the ring road, this pub has a two-roomed lounge with a bar and a pool room to the rear. A recently opened, spacious family conservatory leads to a large garden and play area.
🛏 🌴 🍴 ▮ 🗗 🔥 ♣ P

Station Inn

Farfield
☎ (01562) 822764
12–3, 6–11; 12–11 Fri & Sat
Greenalls Davenports Bitter, Original; Tetley Bitter 🅷
Hidden in a quiet street, just

above Kidderminster railway stations: a welcoming pub with a public bar and a comfortable lounge, plus a pleasant, safe garden. No lunches Sun.
Q ❀ ◖ ▶ ⊟ ⇌ P

Kington

Olde Tavern
22 Victoria Road
☎ (01544) 231384
11–2.30 (not Mon–Fri), 7.30–11; 12–2.30, 7–10.30 Sun
Ansells Bitter Ⓗ
An outstanding relic of old Kington – a must for all connoisseurs of the English pub. Two bars complete with settles, benches and curios hide behind an ornate Victorian facade. Local CAMRA *Pub of the Year* 1993.
Q ⊟ ♣

Old Fogey
37 High Street
☎ (01544) 230685
11.30–3 (not Mon–Fri), 7–11
Fuller's London Pride; Wood Special; Wye Valley Bitter Ⓗ
A reincarnation of the Wine Vaults: a one-bar pub with a wonderfully snug and unspoilt interior. Interesting bar furniture. The friendly locals and cracking atmosphere make a visit a treat. Q ♣

Lea

Crown Inn
Gloucester Road (A40)
☎ (01989) 750407
12–3, 6 (5 summer)–11
Adnams Broadside; RCH Pitchfork; John Smith's Bitter; guest beers Ⓗ
15th-century pub with a half-timbered room recently opened without disturbing the resident ghost. Excellent, enterprising menu.
🏨 Q ❀ ◖ ▶ ♣ P

Ledbury

Horseshoe
Homend ☎ (01531) 632770
12–11
Ansells Bitter; Wye Valley Bitter; guest beers Ⓗ
A steep flight of steps leads to the door of this single-bar, old town pub. With low ceilings and a fireplace, it still has charm, despite its carpets and modern mixed crowd. No food Sun. A ten-min walk from the station.
🏨 ❀ 🏨 ◖ ▶ ♣

Prince of Wales
Church Lane ☎ (01531) 632250
11–3, 7–11

Banks's Hanson's Mild, Bitter; Camerons Strongarm Ⓗ
Two-bar, 16th-century inn in a medieval cobbled street. Its interior retains much of the traditional character of a market town pub, with an easy-going, friendly atmosphere. Folk club Wed.
❀ ◖ ♣ ◠ 🍺

Try also: Brewery Inn, Bye St (Marston's)

Leigh Sinton

Royal Oak
Malvern Road (A4103/B4503 jct) ☎ (01886) 832664
11–3, 6.30–11
Marston's Bitter, Pedigree Ⓗ
Friendly, two-roomed, cosy village local with low beams and an impressive collection of implements and brasses.
🏨 Q ❀ ◖ ⊟ ♣ P

Leominster

Black Horse
74 South Street
☎ (01568) 611946
11–2.30, 6–11; 11–11 Sat
Courage Directors; Marches Best Bitter; Wadworth 6X; guest beers Ⓗ
Once a coaching inn, this free house has the best selection of beers for miles and is also the 'tap' for Marches Brewery. A lively public contrasts with a smaller lounge and restaurant. No eve meals Sun.
❀ ◖ ▶ ⊟ ♿ ♣ P

Grapes Vaults
4 Broad Street
☎ (01568) 611404
11–2.30 (3.30 Sat), 5 (6 Sat)–11
Banks's Mild; Marston's Bitter, Pedigree; guest beer Ⓗ
A plain facade conceals a brilliantly restored town pub. Wood screens, etched-glass and settles, with a lovely snug, make it a must. Adventurous guest beer. Parking tricky.
🏨 Q ◖ ▶

Letton

Swan Inn
On A438 ☎ (01544) 327304
11–11 (11–3, 6–11 winter Mon & Tue)
Beer choice varies Ⓗ
Standard roadside pub that is aspiring to greater things. Value for money, a friendly welcome and food at all hours are the norm. Two main bar areas: a public and a restaurant. A good starting point for Wye Valley rambles. The house beer is brewed by Mansfield.
🏨 Q ❀ ◖ ▶ ⊟ ▲ ♣ P

Little Malvern

Malvern Hills Hotel
British Camp (A449/B4232 jct)
☎ (01684) 540237
11–11
Draught Bass; Hobsons Best Bitter; Morland Old Speckled Hen *or* **Otter Ale** Ⓗ
Comfortable lounge bar in an upmarket weekend retreat on the ridge of the Malvern Hills. Walkers are welcome but are requested to remove muddy boots. The restaurant offers an à la carte menu but no chips.
🏨 Q ❀ 🏨 ◖ ▶ P

Longdon

Plough Inn
On B4211 ☎ (01684) 833767
12–3, 6.30–11
Draught Bass; Hardington Best Bitter; Hook Norton Best Bitter; Tetley Bitter Ⓗ
Large, open, rambling country pub with a games room and skittle alley. Good value food (no meals Sun eve).
🏨 ☕ ❀ ◖ ▶ ♣ P

Menithwood

Cross Keys Inn
Between A443 and B4202 (signed) OS709690
☎ (01584) 881425
10.30–3.30, 6–11
Marston's Bitter, Pedigree; guest beer Ⓗ
Welcoming pub with different drinking areas around a main bar. Justifiably popular. 🏨 Q
☕ ❀ 🏨 ◖ ▶ ♿ ▲ ♣ P

Newtown

Newtown Inn
Newtown Cross (A4103/A417 jct) ☎ (01531) 670423
11–3, 7–11
Banks's Bitter; guest beer Ⓗ
Small, two-bar roadside pub. Its unpretentious exterior belies a pleasant and comfortable interior. Popular, but small restaurant – booking advised. No food Sun eve.
❀ 🏨 ◖ ▶ ⊟ ♣ P

Ombersley

Cross Keys
Kidderminster Road
☎ (01905) 620588
11–3, 6–11
Fuller's London Pride; Marston's Bitter, Pedigree; guest beer Ⓗ
Cosy country pub with a homely atmosphere and a real fire in the front lounge; two other areas plus a restaurant and a small games room. A

good range of reasonably priced food is served. Note the unusual pub sign; the reverse depicts a pig and a parrot!
♨ Q ❀ ◖ ♠ ♣ P

Crown & Sandys Arms

Main Road ☎ (01905) 620252
11–3, 5.30–11
Hook Norton Best Bitter Ⓗ,
Old Hooky Ⓖ; **guest beers** Ⓗ
Smart, olde-worlde, spacious pub with a good range of home-made food, including vegetarian meals; restaurant booking is advisable.
♨ Q ❀ ⇖ ◖ ♠ P ⤢

Pensax

Bell

On B4202 ☎ (01299) 896677
12–3, 6.30–11
Hook Norton Best Bitter;
Taylor Landlord; guest beers Ⓗ
Pub normally serving five ales, including three guest beers – an impressive and growing variety.
♨ Q ⚲ ❀ ◖ ♠ ♣ ⤷ P

Pershore

Brandy Cask

25 Bridge Street
☎ (01386) 552602
11.30–2.30 (may extend summer), 7–11
Courage Best Bitter; Ruddles
Best Bitter, County; guest beers Ⓗ
Convivial town-centre free house, with a large riverside garden, offering two changing guest beers, bar meals and a restaurant. Live music eves; annual beer festival (Aug Bank Hol). Worcester CAMRA *Pub of the Year 1994.* ♨ ❀ ◖ ♠ ♣

Miller's Arms

8 Bridge Street
☎ (01386) 553864
11–3.30 (5 Sat), 7–11 (may extend in summer)
Hall & Woodhouse
Tanglefoot; Wadworth IPA,
6X, Farmer's Glory or **Old**
Timer; guest beer Ⓗ
Busy, town-centre pub of character. The most northerly outpost of Wadworth's chain, it is popular with the young. Fortnightly guest beer; monthly folk and quiz nights. Eve meals in summer.
❀ ◖ ♠ ♣

Pound Green

New Inn

Off B4194 at Buttonoak; 1 mile uphill from Arley station (SVR) ☎ (01299) 401271
12–3 (not Mon–Fri), 7–11
Banks's Mild; Draught Bass;
guest beers Ⓗ

One-bar pub with several distinctly different drinking areas and a restaurant. Up to five ales in summer.
♨ ⚲ ❀ ◖ ♠ ♣ ⤷ P

Risbury

Hop Pole Inn (Bert's)

½mile E of village on Pencombe road OS554549
11–5, 6–11
Wood Parish or **Special** Ⓖ
Very remote and very unusual. The only concession made to the industrial age is electricity in this basic one-bar pub which has been in the landlord's family for over a century. Knock to get in!
♨ Q ❀ ♣ P

Romsley

Manchester Inn

Bromsgrove Road (B4551)
☎ (01562) 710242
11–3, 5–11
Draught Bass; Enville Ale;
M&B Mild, Brew XI Ⓗ/Ⓔ;
guest beer Ⓗ
Roadside pub, by the North Worcestershire Path, and popular with walkers: a public bar and a comfortable, busy lounge. Well priced menu (especially lunchtime). The garden is popular with families in summer.
♨ ❀ ◖ ♠ ♣ P

Ross-on-Wye

Crown & Sceptre

Market Place ☎ (01989) 562765
11–3, 6–11; 11–11 Fri, Sat & summer
Archers Best Bitter; Brakspear
Special; Greene King Abbot;
Morland Old Speckled Hen;
guest beers Ⓗ
The real ale pub in Ross. This comfortable town pub is still on the up and is very popular, especially at weekends. Excellent food. Herefordshire CAMRA Pub of the Year 1994. Beer festival Easter. ❀ ◖ ♠ ⤷

St Owen's Cross

New Inn

At A4137/B4521 jct
☎ (01989) 730274
12–3, 6–11
Draught Bass; Hook Norton
Old Hooky; Smiles Best
Bitter; Tetley Bitter;
Wadworth 6X Ⓗ
18th-century gem covered with hanging baskets in summer. The interior boasts fine fireplaces and period furnishings going back to the 16th century. Good balance between ale and food. Try the doorstop sandwiches.
♨ Q ❀ ⇖ ◖ ♠ ♣ P

Stourport-on-Severn

Angel Hotel

Severnside (off Mart Lane)
☎ (01299) 822661
11–11
Banks's Mild, Bitter Ⓔ
Friendly, two-room riverside pub, a few minutes' walk from the town centre and close to the canal basin (moorings outside). Eve meals in summer. ♨ ⚲ ❀ ⇖ ◖ ◩
♠ ♣ ⤷ P ▯

Wheatsheaf

39 High Street
☎ (01299) 822613
10.30–11
Banks's Hanson's Mild, Mild,
Bitter Ⓔ
Two-room, town-centre pub on the main street, a few minutes' walk from the river and canal. ❀ ◖ ◩ ♠ ♣ P ▯

Tenbury Wells

Ship Inn

65 Teme Street
☎ (01584) 810269
11–3, 7–11
Ansells Bitter; guest beer Ⓗ
Well-to-do market town pub with a comfortable lounge and a restaurant. A bar in an outbuilding is open at weekends. Large garden.
❀ ⇖ ◖ ♠ ♣

Tillington

Bell Inn

Tillington Road
☎ (01432) 760395
11–3, 6–11; 11–11 Sat
Draught Bass; Whitbread
WCPA, Boddingtons Bitter;
Wye Valley Bitter; guest
beer Ⓗ
Competently refurbished pub and restaurant at the heart of the village. A lively public offers pool and a jukebox; the mellow lounge divides into two areas – one cosy, the other for summer with patio-style windows. No food winter Sun eve. ♨ ❀ ◖ ♠ ♣ ⤷ P

Uphampton

Fruiterer's Arms

Uphampton Lane (off A449)
OS839649 ☎ (01905) 620305
12–2.30 (3 Sat), 7–11
Cannon Royall Mild,
Arrowhead, Buckshot, Olde
Merrie; John Smith's Bitter Ⓗ
Rural pub, off the beaten track but worth a visit: a plain bar and a cosy lounge. The Cannon Royall brewery is at the rear. No food Sun.
♨ Q ❀ ◖ ◩ ♠ ♣ ⤷ P

West Malvern

Brewer's Arms
Lower Dingle (signed off B4232) ☎ (01684) 568147
12–3, 7 (6 summer Sat)–11
Marston's Bitter, Pedigree Ⓗ
Sympathetically refurbished, small, friendly pub divided into two areas, one no-smoking; conveniently situated for walkers mid-way along the Malvern Hills. Folk music Tue eve. Marston's Head Brewer's Choice sold. No lunches winter Mon.
Q ᴥ ⊛ ◖ ▮ ⊞ ♣ ⌂ ⌿

Whitney-on-Wye

Rhydspence Inn
On A438, 1½ miles W of village ☎ (01497) 831262
11–2.30, 7–11
Draught Bass; Marston's Pedigree; Robinson's Best Bitter Ⓗ
Plush, refined 14th-century inn that straddles the Welsh border. It retains many fine original features and a public bar. Good food; extensive wine list. A la carte restaurant.
🚗 Q ᴥ ⊛ 🛏 ◖ ▮ ⊞ ▲ ♣ ⌂ P

Woolhope

Crown Inn
☎ (01432) 860468
12–2.30, 7 (6.30 summer Fri & Sat)–11; 12–2.30, 7–10.30 Sun
Hook Norton Best Bitter; Smiles Best Bitter; Tetley Bitter; guest beer (summer) Ⓗ
Unashamedly successful pub that specialises in food. Very popular with out-of-town diners, it also encourages a discerning beer trade – an area of the bar being set aside. Very welcoming.
🚗 Q ⊛ ◖ ▮ ♣ ⌂ P

Worcester

Alma Tavern
74 Droitwich Road
☎ (01905) 28103
11.30–2.30 (11–3 Fri & Sat), 6–11
Ansells Mild, Bitter; Tetley Bitter; guest beer Ⓗ
Cosy local with not a swan neck in sight. Basic good value menu, spiced with Baltis. The guest is nearly always from a small independent brewer. No food Sun eve. 🚗 ⊛ ◖ ▮ ♣ P

Berkeley Arms
School Road, St John's
☎ (01905) 421427
11.30–3, 5.30–11; 11–11 Sat
Banks's Hanson's Mild, Mild, Bitter Ⓔ
Friendly local tucked away in the back streets of a residential area: a smart lounge and a more basic public bar, plus a family games room. The Hanson's is hidden in the public bar. ᴥ ⊛ ⊞ ♣ P ⊟

Brewery Tap
50 Lowesmoor
☎ (01905) 21540
11.30–11
Jolly Roger Quaff, Shipwrecked, Severn Bore, Flagship, Old Lowesmoor Ⓗ
The early home of the Jolly Roger brewery whose beers are now brewed at the Cardinal's Hat. As the name implies, this no-nonsense pub has a nautical theme with appropriate pirate decor. Live entertainment. ◖ ≋ (Shrub Hill) ♣ ⌂ P

Cardinal's Hat
31–33 Friar Street
☎ (01905) 21890
11.30–11
Jolly Roger Ale, Shipwrecked, Flagship; guest beers Ⓗ
Historic pub, home to the Jolly Roger Brewery, boasting front and back bars with a quieter side room. Good choice of guest ales (a bit pricey for the area). Lunches served until 6 Sat; eve meals in summer.
⊛ ◖ ▮ ⌂

Crown & Anchor
233 Hylton Road
☎ (01905) 421481
12–3, 5–11; 12–11 Wed, Fri & Sat
Banks's Mild; Marston's Bitter, Pedigree Ⓗ
Friendly town pub well refurbished in 1994. Very popular with students but in no way exclusive. Excellent skittle alley. Marston's Head Brewer's Choice sold. No food Sun eve. ⊛ ◖ ▮ ▲ ♣

Dragon Inn
51 The Tything
☎ (01905) 25845

11–11; 7–10.30 Sun, closed Sun lunch
Marston's Bitter; S&N Theakston XB; guest beers Ⓗ
One-room town pub with a wide range of customers. Join in the folk sessions Wed nights. The bands every Sun prove popular. Marston's Head Brewer's Choice sold.
⊛ ◖ ≋ (Foregate St) ⌂

Farriers Arms
9 Fish Street (off High St)
☎ (01905) 27569
10.30–11
Courage Best Bitter, Directors; guest beers Ⓗ
Period Grade II-listed building: a comfortable, small lounge and a bar with a jukebox, adorned with knick-knacks and paintings advertising the Wychwood Brewery that has acquired the lease. Usually two Wychwood beers available.
⊛ ◖ ⊞ ≋ (Foregate St)

Plumbers Arms
76 Wylds Lane
☎ (01905) 767592
11.30–2.30, 5.30–11; 11.30–11 Fri & Sat
Draught Bass; M&B Brew XI; guest beers Ⓗ
Welcoming, Victorian terraced local, completely refurbished. Discos and quiz nights; a TV is by the bar but there is a quiet area. ⊛ ◖ ▮ ♣

Swan With Two Nicks
28 New Street
☎ (01905) 28190
11–11
Whitbread Boddingtons Bitter; guest beers Ⓗ
Historic, city-centre pub. Eye-catching features include leaded windows and low beams. The bar area has a pinball machine. King Charles II reputedly hid next door.
◖ ≋ (Foregate St) ♣

Virgin Tavern
Tolladine Road
☎ (01905) 23988
11–3, 5.30–11
Marston's Bitter, Pedigree Ⓗ
Popular, one-room Marston's pub, 1½ miles from the centre. A large garden with play equipment attracts families, as does the good value menu. Summer weekend barbecues. No meals Sun eve. Marston's Head Brewer's Choice sold.
⊛ ◖ ▮ ♣ P

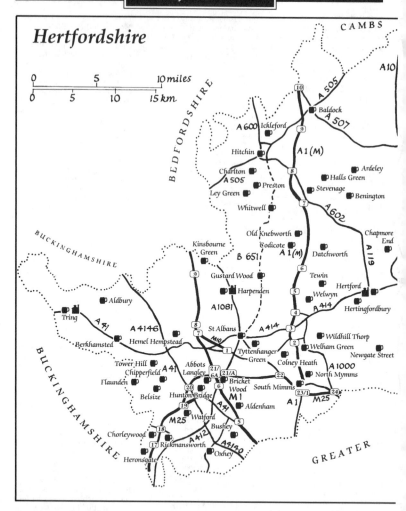

Hertfordshire

CAMBS

BEDFORDSHIRE

BUCKINGHAMSHIRE

BUCKINGHAMSHIRE

GREATER

0 — 5 — 10 miles
0 — 5 — 10 — 15 km

A10

Baldock
A 507
A 505

Ickleford
A 600

Hitchin
A 1 (M)

Charlton
A 505
Preston
Ley Green
Whitwell

Ardeley
Halls Green
Stevenage
Benington
A 602

Old Knebworth
Codicote
A 1 (M)
Datchworth

Chapmore End
A 119

Kinsbourne Green
B 651

Gustard Wood
Harpenden
A 1081

Tewin
Hertford
Welwyn
Hertingfordbury
A 414

Aldbury
Tring
A 41
A 4146
Hemel Hempstead
Berkhamsted

St Albans
M10
A 414

Wildhill Thorp
Welham Green
Newgate Street
A 1000

Tower Hill
Chipperfield
Flaunden
A 41
Abbots Langley
Bricket Wood
Belsize
Hunton Bridge
Watford
Chorleywood
Rickmansworth
Heronsgate
Oxhey

Tyttenhanger Green
Colney Heath
North Mymms
South Mimms
Aldenham
Bushey
M25
M1
A 1
M25

Dark Horse, Hertford; **Fox & Hounds,** Barley; **Harpenden,** Harpenden; **McMullen,** Hertford; **Tring,** Tring

Abbots Langley

Compasses
95 Tibbs Hill Road
☎ (01923) 262870
11–11
Courage Best Bitter, Directors; Ruddles County; guest beer H
A strong food emphasis has not spoiled this pub, which is still popular with locals.
Over 100 whiskies.
❀ ◑ ▶ ঌ ♣ P

Aldbury

Greyhound
19 Stocks Road
☎ (01442) 851228
10.30–11
Tetley Bitter; Tring Ridgeway; guest beers H
Attractive village pub with a traditional, unspoilt front bar dominated by a huge fireplace.
Cider in summer.
⇔ ❀ ⇦ ◑ ▶
🍺 ঌ ▲ ♣ ⌂

Aldenham

Roundbush
Just off B462 OS145985
☎ (01923) 857165
11–11
Ind Coope Benskins BB, Burton Ale; Tetley Bitter; guest beer H
Genuine country pub, circa 1800, with two distinctly separate drinking areas catering for all. Home-cooked food (no meals Sun eve).
⇔ ❀ ◑ ▶ ♣ P

Morland Old Speckled Hen;
Taylor Landlord; Wadworth
6X; Whitbread Boddingtons
Bitter; guest beers Ⓗ/Ⓖ
Former coaching inn on the
old Great North Road.
Recently extended, it usually
has 12 beers. Mini-beer
festivals and barbecues held.
Jamaican cuisine available
(book eve meals).
🚼 ❀ ⓓ 🌓 ➿ ♠ P

White Hart

21 Hitchin Street
☎ (01462) 893247
11–11; 11–4, 7–11 Sat
Greene King XX Mild, IPA,
Abbot Ⓗ
Popular, one-bar town pub
displaying a large Simpson's
Brewery sign inside.
Customers may bring their
own sandwiches to this
genuine drinker's pub. A cask
breather is used on the mild
on rare occasions and a sign is
displayed to notify customers.
❀ ➿ ♠

Belsize

Plough

Dunny Lane OS034008
☎ (01923) 262800
11–3, 5.30–11
Draught Bass; Greene King
IPA; Hancock's HB Ⓗ
Attractive, welcoming brick
and flint pub, popular for its
food and garden. No eve
meals Sun/Mon.
🚼 ❀ ⓓ 🌓 ♠ P

Benington

Bell

4 Town Lane ☎ (01438) 869270
11.30–2.30 (12–3 Sat), 6.30–11
Greene King XX Mild, IPA,
Abbot Ⓗ
14th-century building near the
village green. Note the 17th-
century mural above the
fireplace. Eve meals Thu–Sat.
🚼 ❀ ⓓ 🌓 ♠ P

Lordship Arms

42 Whempstead Road
☎ (01438) 869665
11–3, 6–11
Fuller's ESB; McMullen AK;
Young's Special; guest beer Ⓗ
Smartly renovated country
local at the top end of the
village, serving a changing
range of interesting guest
beers and home-cooked food.
Telephone memorabilia is
featured. 🚼 ❀ ⓓ ♠ ○ P

Berkhamsted

Boat

Gravel Path, Ravens Lane, (off
A41 by canal bridge)
☎ (01442) 877152

11–3, 5.30–11
Fuller's Chiswick, London
Pride, ESB Ⓗ
Smart pub with an excellent
food menu. The patio
overlooks the canal.
No meals winter Sun.
❀ ⓓ ♿ ➿ ♠ P

Bishop's Stortford

Tap & Spile

31 North Street
☎ (01279) 654978
11–3, 5.30–11
Adnams Bitter; Marston's
Pedigree; Nethergate Bitter;
S&N Theakston Best Bitter;
guest beers Ⓗ
Wooden-floored, two-bar pub
on split levels, in keeping with
a turn of the
century building. Four guest
beers are changed regularly.
No food Sun.
🚼 Q ⓓ ♠ ○ P

Bricket Wood

Gate

Station Road ☎ (01923) 672470
12–3 (not Mon), 5.30–11
Fuller's London Pride;
Marston's Owd Rodger;
Morland Old Speckled Hen;
Robinson's Best Bitter; Tring
Ridgeway, Old Icknield Ale;
guest beers Ⓗ
Recently extended pub
offering up to nine beers plus
fruit wines, raspberry or
cherry beers and steam beer.
🚼 ❀ ⓓ 🌓 ➿ ♠ ○ P

Moor Mill

Smug Oak Lane (off A5183 by
M25 bridge) ☎ (01727) 875557
11–11
Draught Bass; Brakspear
Bitter; Courage Directors;
Gale's Best Bitter; S&N
Theakston Best Bitter;
Young's Special Ⓗ; guest
beers Ⓗ/Ⓖ
Restored Anglo-Saxon mill
mentioned in the *Domesday
Book*. A revolving mill wheel
run by the River Ver is its
centrepiece. Book for meals in
the Granary dining room. Four
guest beers, plus occasional
beer festivals. 🚼 Q ❀ ⓓ 🌓 P

Buntingford

Crown

17 High Street
☎ (01763) 271422
12–3, 5.30–11; 12–11 Sat
Courage Best Bitter,
Directors; Mauldons Best
Bitter; guest beer Ⓗ
Popular, friendly pub
featuring a basic locals' bar at
the front. Folk music Mon eve.
Children welcome in the
function room. 🚼 Q ⓓ 🌓

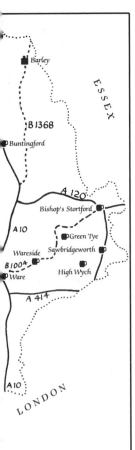

Ardeley

Jolly Waggoner

Off B1037, 1¼ miles E of Cromer
OS310272 ☎ (01438) 861350
12–2 (3 Sat; not Mon), 6.30–11
Greene King IPA Ⓖ, Abbot Ⓗ
Picturesque, 16th-century,
pink-washed former cottages
in a charming village setting
with one recently enlarged bar
and a restaurant. Impressive
row of casks behind the
counter. Good quality food (no
meals Sun eve or Mon).
🚼 Q ❀ ⓓ 🌓 ♠ P 🎱

Baldock

Old White Horse

1 Station Road (A507/A505 jct)
☎ (01462) 893168
11–3, 5.30–11; 11–11 Sat
Fuller's London Pride;

Hertfordshire

Bushey

Swan
25 Park Road (off A411)
☎ (0181) 950 2256
11–11
Ind Coope Benskins BB, Burton Ale H
Justifiably popular public bar pub, worth searching out if you like the traditional. ⚲ ♣

Chapmore End

Woodman
30 Chapmore End (off B158, near A602 jct)
☎ (01920) 463143
12–3, 6–11 (12–11 summer Sat)
Greene King IPA, Abbot G
Gem of a traditional pub in a rural setting. All real ale is on gravity from the cellar behind the public bar. Bar food includes pizza and Balti. Large garden with animals.
⚲ Q ❀ ◖ ▶ ⊞ ♣ P

Charlton

Windmill
Charlton Road
☎ (01462) 432096
10.30–2.30, 5–11
Adnams Broadside H; **Mansfield Riding Mild** G; **Wells Eagle, Bombardier, Fargo** H
Pleasant, friendly village pub, just outside Hitchin. The garden runs down to the River Hiz, with resident ducks. Good quality, home-cooking (no meals Sun).
Q ❀ ◖ ▶ ♣ P

Chipperfield

Royal Oak
1 The Street ☎ (01923) 266537
12–3, 6–11
Bass Worthington BB, Draught Bass; Ind Coope Burton Ale; M&B Highgate Dark; guest beer H
Smart, friendly pub where highly polished wood and brass abound. Sandwiches only Sun. ⚲ Q ⏚ ❀ ◖ ▶ ⊞ & ▲ ♣ P

Chorleywood

Black Horse
Dog Kennel Lane (off A404, W of M25 jct 18)
☎ (01923) 282252
11–11
Adnams Bitter; Greenalls Bitter, Original; Wadworth 6X; guest beer H
Country-style pub on the edge of the common. Good, home-made food (no meals Sun eve). Dogs welcome. ⚲ ❀ ◖ ▶ P

Codicote

Goat
77 High Street (B656)
☎ (01438) 820475
12–11
Greene King IPA; Ind Coope Benskins BB; Tetley Bitter; Wadworth 6X H
Traditional, oak-beamed, timber-framed building built in 1590, with a 17th-century barn now used as a function room. A frequent venue for morris dancers. No food Sun eve. Q ❀ ◖ ▶ ♣ P

Colney Heath

Crooked Billet
High Street ☎ (01727) 822128
11–2.30, 5–11; 11–11 Sat
Brakspear Bitter; Greene King Abbot; S&N Theakston Best Bitter; Young's Special; guest beers H
300-year-old, cottage-style pub: two bars offering good, home-cooked food (eve meals Thu–Sat). The large garden has a children's adventure play area. ⚲ ❀ ◖ ▶ ♣ P

Datchworth

Tilbury
1 Watton Road
☎ (01438) 812496
11–3, 5–11; 11–11 Thu–Sat
Draught Bass; Palmers IPA; guest beer H
Large, friendly two-room pub with a dining area and a large garden. A changing range of nine beers includes a mild; unusual beers are a speciality. Wide range of home-cooked food. Q ❀ ◖ ▶ ⊞ ▲ ♣ ⏁ P

Flaunden

Bricklayer's Arms
Hogpits Bottom
☎ (01442) 833322
11–2.30 (3 Sat), 6–11
Chiltern Beechwood; Marston's Pedigree; guest beers H
Smart country pub serving a good range of ales, usually including mild, sometimes on gravity. Separate restaurant.
⚲ Q ❀ ◖ ▶ ♣ P

Green Dragon
OS014007 ☎ (01442) 832269
11.30–2.30, 6–11; 11.30–11 Sat
Greene King IPA; Marston's Pedigree; Wells Bombardier; Whitbread Boddingtons Bitter; guest beers H
Thriving country pub which, although much extended, retains its original public bar and small serving hatch.

Children welcome in the restaurant.
⚲ ❀ ◖ ▶ ⊞ & ♣ ⏁ P

Green Tye

Prince of Wales
Off B1004 ☎ (01279) 842517
11.30–3, 5.30–11; 11.30–11 Sat
McMullen AK; Whitbread Flowers IPA; guest beers H
Traditional country pub in a picturesque village. The garden is the venue for occasional beer festivals. The guest beer rotates monthly. Popular with ramblers.
⚲ ❀ ◖ ♣ P ⊟

Gustard Wood

Cross Keys
Ballslough Lane (off B651)
OS176165 ☎ (01582) 832165
11–3, 5.30–11 (dining licence Sun)
Draught Bass; Fuller's London Pride; Greene King IPA; Marston's Bitter, Pedigree H; **guest beers** H/G
Interesting 17th-century pub, where only one of the clocks shows the correct time! Good, very reasonably priced meals (no eve meals Sun/Mon).
⚲ Q ♋ ❀ ⚲ ◖ ▶ ♣ P

Halls Green

Rising Sun
Weston Road (minor road from Weston to Cromer)
OS275287 ☎ (01462) 790487
11–2.30, 6–11
Draught Bass; Courage Directors; McMullen AK, Country; guest beer H
Beautiful, one bar-pub in the country. The enormous garden has children's play equipment. The conservatory acts as a restaurant Sun lunch and a family room otherwise. Unusual range of Polish flavoured vodkas.
⚲ Q ♋ ❀ ◖ ▶ ♣ P

Harpenden

Carpenter's Arms
14 Cravell's Road (off A1081)
☎ (01582) 460311
11–3, 5.30–11
Courage Best Bitter; Ruddles County; Webster's Yorkshire Bitter; guest beers H
Immensely welcoming old local; small, cosy and full of charm. Devotees of classic cars will enjoy the memorabilia. No meals Sun.
⚲ Q ❀ ◖ & ⇌ ♣ P

Gibraltar Castle
Lower Luton Road, Batford
☎ (01582) 460005
11–3, 5.30 (6.30 winter)–11

Fuller's Chiswick, London Pride, ESB H
Fans of militaria will love the Gibraltar. The walls are covered with weaponry and medals. Weekly folk music eves and a good food choice (no meals Tue eve).
🏛 ❀ ◖ ▶ ♣ P

Red Cow

171 Westfield Road (off B653)
☎ (01582) 460156
11.30–11
Harpenden Special; Marston's Pedigree; Ruddles County; Webster's Yorkshire Bitter H
Grade II-listed, 16th-century building, housing possibly the smallest pub brewery in the country. Note the 80 plaques carrying drinking quotations and rhymes. Popular with a mixed clientele. No food weekends; eve meals 6–8.
🏛 ❀ ◖ ▶ P

Hemel Hempstead

Post Office Arms

46 Puller Road, Boxmoor
☎ (01442) 61235
11–11
Fuller's London Pride, ESB H
Friendly, back-street local, often busy, with a public bar and a larger, extended lounge.
🏛 ❀ ◖ ▶ ♣

Heronsgate

Land of Liberty, Peace & Plenty

Long Lane (off M25 jct 17)
OS023949 ☎ (01923) 282226
12–11
Courage Best Bitter; Young's Special; guest beers H
Pub built in the 1840s, just outside the Chartist settlement of O'Connorville which was teetotal. The four guest beers come from micro-breweries rare to the area. Six draught Belgian beers, too.
❀ ◖ ▶ ♣ ⌂ P

Hertford

Millstream

88 Port Vale (car access via A119, Worth Rd, and Beane Rd) ☎ (01992) 582755
12–3.30, 5.30–11; 11.30–4.30, 7–11 Sat
Courage Directors; McMullen AK, Country, Gladstone; guest beers H
Lively, one-bar local with a friendly welcome. Attractive garden for children.
❀ ⇌ (North) ♣ P

Sportsman

117 Fore Street
☎ (01992) 551621
12–3, 5.30–11; 12–11 Fri & Sat
Courage Directors; Marston's Pedigree; Morland Old Speckled Hen; Ruddles Best Bitter; Wadworth 6X; guest beers H
Refurbished town-centre pub, formerly known as the Blue Coat Boy after the local school, and once the brewery tap for Young's of Hertford. Regular blues and soul nights. No meals Sun eve.
◖ ▶ ⇌ (East)

White Horse

33 Castle Street
☎ (01992) 501950
12–2.30 (3 Sat), 5.30 (7 Sat)–11
Dark Horse Sun Runner G; **Fuller's London Pride; Hook Norton Best Bitter** H; **guest beers** H/G
Home of the Dark Horse brewery, brewing real ales, plus wheat and fruit beers. The upper floor of this old, timber-framed house is now a non-smoking area where children are welcome. Lunches weekdays. 🏛 Q ❀ ◖ ▶
⇌ (East/North) ♣ ⌂ ⌕

Hertingfordbury

Prince of Wales

244 Hertingfordbury Road (400 yds from A414)
☎ (01992) 581149
11–2.30 (3 Sat), 5.30 (6 Sat)–11
Fuller's London Pride; McMullen AK; Wadworth 6X; Younger IPA; guest beer H
Welcoming, one-bar village pub, offering a limited range of guest beers. The patio is busy in summer. No food Sun eve. 🏛 ❀ 🛏 ◖ ▶ ♣ P

High Wych

Rising Sun

☎ (01279) 724099
12–2.30 (3 Fri & Sat), 5–11
Courage Best Bitter, Directors; guest beer G
Classic, small village pub, which reverted to a genuine free house a few years ago. A *Guide* regular; local CAMRA *Pub of the Year 1994*. A guest beer is always available at weekends in this pub for conversation.
🏛 Q 🛏 ❀ ♣ P

Hitchin

Radcliffe Arms

31 Walsworth Road
☎ (01462) 432615
11–2.30, 5–11
Whitbread Flowers IPA, Original H
Pub with a comfortable, panelled lounge and a basic bar. The patio features lots of plants. ❀ ◖ 🛏 ⇌ ♣ P

Victoria

1 Ickleford Road
☎ (01462) 432682
12–3, 5.30–11
Greene King IPA, Abbot H
Welcoming corner local between the station and the town centre, with a split-level interior. Home-cooked food (eve meals 5–7; no meals Sun).
❀ ◖ ▶ ⇌ ♣ P

Hunton Bridge

King's Head

Bridge Road (off A41, S of M25 jct 20) ☎ (01923) 262307
11–4, 5–11
Ind Coope Benskins BB, Burton Ale; Tetley Bitter; guest beer H
Old pub with one rambling bar. The old canal stables now house a family room and a fold-down skittle alley (summer), whilst the large canalside garden offers games. Good value meals (no food Sun eve). Guest beers from the Carlsberg-Tetley range.
🏛 Q 🛏 ❀ ◖ ♣ P

Ickleford

Cricketers

107 Arlesey Road (off A600, far end of village)
☎ (01462) 432629
11–3, 6–11 Sat
Draught Bass; Fuller's London Pride; Ruddles Best Bitter; Taylor Landlord; Tetley Bitter; guest beer H/G
Very friendly, lively village pub which attracts custom from near and far. Usually ten beers on sale. Local CAMRA *Pub of the Year 1994.*
Q ❀ 🛏 ◖ ▶ ♣ ⌂ P 🍴

Kinsbourne Green

Fox

469 Luton Road (A1081, 2 miles N of Harpenden)
☎ (01582) 713817
11–2.30, 5.30–11
Ind Coope Benskins BB, Burton Ale; Eldridge Pope Hardy Country, Royal Oak; Marston's Pedigree; Tetley Bitter H
Two-bar, traditional pub boasting three real fires. No music; good, home-made food; occasional beer festivals and always a friendly welcome.
🏛 Q ❀ ◖ ▶ 🍴 ♣ P

Ley Green

Plough

Plough Lane (off Gt Offley–Preston road) OS162243
☎ (01438) 871394
11–4, 5.30–11; 11–11 Fri & Sat

Hertfordshire

Greene King IPA, Abbot ⓗ
Country local overlooking
rolling farmland and woods.
Enormous gardens contain a
children's field with play
equipment and livestock.
🏾 Q ☸ ❀ ❍ ▶ ♣ P

Newgate Street

Coach & Horses
61 Newgate Street Village
☎ (01707) 872326
11–11; 12–3, 7.30–10.30 Sun
**Ansells Bitter; Draught Bass;
Ind Coope ABC Best Bitter;
Tetley Bitter** ⓗ
Old, ivy-covered pub next to
the church; a venue for
motorbike, winemaking and
riding clubs. No-smoking
family/function room.
🏾 Q ☸ ❀ ❍ ▶ ♣ P ⊬

North Mymms

Old Maypole
43 Warrengate Road, Water
End (off B197) OS230042
☎ (01707) 642119
11–2.30, 5.30–11
Greene King IPA, Abbot ⓗ
16th-century, split-level pub.
Supervised children are
welcome in the small no-
smoking room. Greene King
seasonal ales also sold.
🏾 Q ☸ ❀ ❍ P ⊬

Old Knebworth

Lytton Arms
Park Lane ☎ (01438) 812312
11–3, 5–11; 11–11 Fri & Sat
**Draught Bass; Fuller's
London Pride; S&N
Theakston Best Bitter;
Wadworth 6X; Woodforde's
Wherry; guest beer** ⓗ
Large, 19th-century, Lutyens-
designed building on the edge
of Knebworth Park, with a
new conservatory at the rear.
The 12 beers always include
one mild; wide selection of
bottled beers; guest ciders and
perry. Regular beer festivals.
🏾 Q ☸ ❍ ▶ ❀ ❑ P ⊬

Oxhey

Victoria
39 Chalk Hill
☎ (01923) 227993
11–3, 5.30–11
**Ind Coope Benskins BB;
guest beer** ⓗ
Unusual, split-level, two-bar
pub in a good drinking area.
❀ ❍ ⇌ (Bushey) ♣

Villiers Arms
108 Villiers Road
☎ (01923) 221556
12–4 (5 Sat), 5.30 (7 Sat)–11
**Greene King IPA; Marston's
Pedigree; guest beer** ⓗ

Friendly, street-corner pub
with a large collection of
knick-knacks, including
brewery items.
❀ ❍ ⇌ (Bushey) ♣

Preston

Red Lion
The Green ☎ (01462) 459585
12–3, 5.30–11; 12–11 Sat
**Greene King IPA; Hall &
Woodhouse Tanglefoot; S&N
Theakston Best Bitter;
Wadworth 6X; guest beers** ⓗ
Attractive, Georgian-style
house collectively owned by
villagers for more than a
decade. Good, home-cooked
food. 🏾 ❀ ❍ ▶ ♣ P

Rickmansworth

Fox & Hounds
High Street ☎ (01923) 441119
11–11
**Courage Best Bitter,
Directors; guest beer** ⓗ
Comfortable, two-bar local
with a rotating guest beer
choice which includes the only
Mole's for miles. Look out for
the amusing pub sign. Local
CAMRA *Pub of the Year* 1994.
No food Sun.
🏾 ❀ ❍ ❑ ⇌ ⊖ ♣ P

St Albans

Farriers Arms
32–34 Lower Dagnall Street
☎ (01727) 851025
12–2.30, 5.30–11; 12–11 Sat (may
vary)
**Draught Bass; McMullen AK,
Country, Gladstone; guest
beer** ⓗ
A perennial entry in the *Guide*:
a good back-street local with
many sporting interests.
Parking is tricky. Q ❀ ♣

Garibaldi
61 Albert Street
☎ (01727) 855046
11–11
**Fuller's Chiswick, London
Pride, ESB** ⓗ
Friendly, popular, back-street
local with a varied clientele.
Renowned for its varied range
of good value, home-made
meals. Seasonal Fuller's beers
also available. Families
welcome. ❀ ❍ ▶ ⇌ (Abbey)
♣ ⊬

Lower Red Lion
34–36 Fishpool Street
☎ (01727) 855669
12–2.30 (3 Sat), 5.30–11
**Adnams Bitter; Fuller's
London Pride; Greene King
IPA, Abbot; guest beers** ⓗ
17th-century free house in a
conservation area. Varied
range of up to four guest
beers; beer festivals. No food
Sun. 🏾 Q ❀ ⛩ ❍ P

Tap & Spile
110 Holywell Hill
☎ (01727) 858982
12–3, 6–11; 12–11 Sat
**Ind Coope Burton Ale; guest
beers** ⓗ
Formerly the Duke of
Marlborough, this small,
two-bar pub stocks eight beers
plus real cider. No food Sun.
Limited parking. 🏾 ❀ ❍ ❑
⇌ (Abbey) ♣ ⊙ P

Sawbridgeworth

Gate Inn
81 London Road (A1184)
☎ (01279) 722313
11.30–2.30, 5.30 (5 Fri, 7 Sat)–11
**Whitbread Boddingtons
Bitter, Castle Eden Ale,
Pompey Royal, Flowers
Original; guest beers** ⓗ
Pub dating from Napoleonic
times, on the site of the town's
Parsonage Gate. Regularly
changing guest beers (from all
over the UK) include a mild.
No food Sun. Q ❍ ♣ ⊙ P

South Mimms

Black Horse
65 Blackhorse Lane (200 yds
from B556) ☎ (01707) 642174
11–3, 5.30–11; 12–11 Sat
**Greene King XX Mild, IPA,
Abbot** ⓗ
Lively local with a genuine,
friendly welcome. Darts in the
bar; comfortable lounge. No
meals Sun.
🏾 Q ❀ ❍ ❑ ♣ P

Stevenage

Marquis of Lorne
132 High Street, Old Town
☎ (01438) 729154
11–11
**Greene King XX Mild, IPA,
Abbot** ⓗ
Friendly and often crowded
pub where sports cartoons
festoon the walls.
🏾 ❀ ❍ ▶ ❑ ⇌ ♣

Woodman's Arms
Chadwell Road, Norton Green
(signed off Gunnels Wood Rd)
☎ (01438) 351599
11 (12 Sat)–3, 5.30 (7 Sat)–11
Greene King IPA, Abbot ⓗ
Former cottage pub with a
modern extension, recently
converted to a single bar.
Separated from most of the
town by an industrial area and
the A1. No food Mon.
🏾 ❀ ❍ ▶ ♣ P

Tewin

Plume of Feathers
57 Upper Green Road
(Burnham Green side of
village) ☎ (01438) 717265
11–2.30 (3 Sat), 6–11

Adnams Bitter; Draught Bass; Morland Old Speckled Hen; Whitbread Boddingtons Bitter; guest beers Ⓗ
One of the county's oldest licence holders: a timber-framed building, sympathetically opened out to one bar with separate areas. Very popular with the business crowd, it offers bar or restaurant meals. Good choice of guest beers (up to four) . No food Sun eve.
⚊ Q ✿ ◖ ▶ ♿ P

Tower Hill

Boot
On Bovingdon–Chipperfield road ☎ (01442) 833155
11.30–11
Adnams Bitter; Ind Coope Benskins BB; Tetley Bitter; Tring Old Icknield Ale; Wadworth 6X; guest beer Ⓗ
Smart old pub inside and out, with various outdoor drinking areas, including a children's play area. Spot the tank! Cider in summer. Good value home-cooking.
⚊ ✿ ◖ ▮ ♣ ひ P

Tring

King's Arms
King Street (near Natural History Museum)
☎ (01442) 823318
11.30–2.30 (11–3 Sat), 7–11
Brakspear Special; Wadworth 6X; guest beers Ⓗ
Back-street local, very busy at all times. Hard to find, but impossible to miss, with always a good and varied selection of ales. No-smoking area lunchtime.
⚊ Q ✿ ◖ ▮ ♣ ひ ✂

Robin Hood Inn
1 Brook Street
☎ (01442) 824912
11–2.30 (3 Sat), 5.30 (6.30 Sat)–11
Fuller's Chiswick, London Pride, ESB Ⓗ
Friendly olde-worlde pub on a street corner; the interior is bedecked with breweriana. Good seafood menu, plus Fuller's seasonal beers.
⚊ Q ✿ ◖ ▶ ♿ ▲ ♣

Tyttenhanger Green

Plough
Off A414, via Highfield Lane
☎ (01727) 857777
11.30–2.30 (3 Sat), 6–11; 12–2.30, 7–10.30 Sun
Fuller's London Pride, ESB; Greene King IPA, Abbot; Morland Old Speckled Hen; Taylor Landlord; Tring Ridgeway Ⓗ
Popular free house offering good value lunches (no food bank hols) and a large collection of bottled beers. Children's play equipment in the garden. ⚊ ✿ ◖ P

Ware

New Rose & Crown
35 Watton Road
☎ (01920) 462572
11.30–2.30, 5–11; 11–11 Fri & Sat
Greene King XX Mild, IPA, Abbot Ⓗ
Friendly, one-bar pub, popular with residents and the local business crowd. Due for alteration and enlargement which should not change its character. Greene King seasonal ales also sold. No food Sun. ◖ ⇌ ♣ P

Wareside

Chequers
On B1004 ☎ (01920) 467010
12–2.30, 6–11
Adnams Bitter, Extra; Bateman XB; Taylor Landlord; Woodforde's Wherry; Young's Special Ⓗ
Inviting cottage pub with real fires and excellent, home-cooked food. The guest beer is normally the *Champion Beer of Britain*. A popular stop-off point for ramblers. No food Sun eve. ⚊ Q ⌂ ◖ ▮ ♣ P

Watford

Bedford Arms
26 Langley Road
☎ (01923) 440047
11–11
Tetley Bitter; guest beers Ⓗ
Popular pub with TV and a

pool table; refurbished since last in the *Guide*. No food Sun.
✿ ◖ ⇌ (Junction) ♣

Welham Green

Hope & Anchor
Station Road ☎ (01707) 262935
11–2.30, 5–11; 11–11 Sat
Courage Best Bitter, Directors; John Smith's Bitter Ⓗ
18th-century village local with two contrasting bars, a large children's play area and well laid-out gardens.
✿ ◖ ▮ ♿ ⇌ ♣ P

Welwyn

Baron
11 Mill Lane ☎ (01438) 714739
12–3, 5–11; 12–11 Sat
Draught Bass; Butcombe Bitter; Fuller's London Pride; S&N Theakston Best Bitter; Whitbread Boddingtons Bitter Ⓗ
Recently-opened free house on the site of an old butcher's shop and slaughterhouse. Formerly the Baron of Beef. Tiny garden. ⚊ ✿ ◖ ▤ ♣

Whitwell

Maiden's Head
High Street ☎ (01438) 871392
11.30–2.30, 5–11
Draught Bass; McMullen AK, Country, Gladstone; guest beer Ⓗ
Timbered pub of character at the heart of the village. Good, home-cooked food. One of the best McMullen outlets.
⚊ ✿ ◖ ▮ ▤ ♣ P

Wildhill Thorp

Woodman
45 Wild Hill Lane, near Essendon (between A1000 and B158) OS265068
☎ (01707) 642618
11.30–2.30, 5.30–11; 12–2.30, 7–10.30 Sun
Greene King IPA, Abbot; McMullen AK; guest beers Ⓗ
Welcoming local serving good, chip-free lunches (no meals Sun). Sky TV in the snug/music room.
Q ✿ ◖ ♣ P

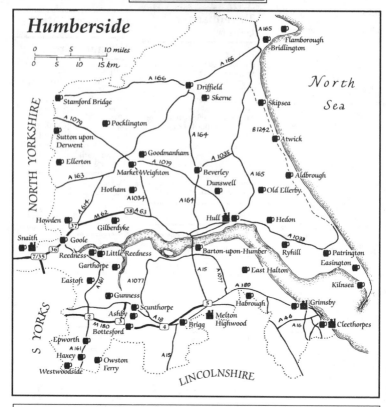

Humberside

Highwood, Melton Highwood; **Hull**, Hull; **Leaking Boot**, Grimsby; **Old Mill**, Snaith; **Willy's**, Cleethorpes

---

Aldbrough

Elm Tree
High Street
☎ (01964) 527568
7–11; 12–2.30, 7–11 Fri & summer;
11–11 Sat
**Bass Worthington BB,
Draught Bass; Stones Best
Bitter** Ⓗ
Quiet, two-bar village local.
Photos in the lounge show old
Aldbrough which has
disappeared into the
North Sea.
🏚 🏵 🍺 ♣ P

Ashby

Malt Shovel
219 Ashby High Street
☎ (01724) 843318
11–11
**S&N Theakston Old Peculier;
John Smith's Bitter;
Whitbread Boddingtons
Bitter; guest beer** Ⓗ
Attractive conversion of a
former snooker hall with
wooden beams and floral

furnishings. Good value
meals. Snooker facilities next
door. 🏚 🍺 🍺

Queen Bess
Derwent Road
☎ (01724) 840827
11.30–3.30 (4 Sat), 6–11
Samuel Smith OBB Ⓗ
Well-appointed estate pub
with three separate rooms and
a large function room. Active
sports and social club.
🏚 🏵 🍺 ♣ P

Atwick

Black Horse
The Green
☎ (01964) 532691
11.30–4, 6–11; 11.30–11 Sat
**John Smith's Bitter; guest
beers** Ⓗ
Comfortable, village local
overlooking the green and
dating from 1750. Three
drinking areas. Food is highly
recommended. Two regularly
changing guest beers.
🏵 🍺 🍺 ♿ ▲ ♣ P

Barton-upon-Humber

Old Mill
Market Lane ☎ (01652) 660333
11–3, 6–11
**Bateman Mild; Marston's
Bitter, Pedigree** Ⓗ
Built on an old Saxon burial
ground, this mill has been
rebuilt, leaving its old
workings visible throughout.
One large room, but plenty
of nooks and crannies.
Marston's Head Brewer's
Choice beers also sold.
🏚 🏵 🍺 ♿ ⇌ P

Volunteer Arms
13 Whitecross Street
☎ (01652) 632309
11–3, 6.45–11
**Burtonwood Mild, Bitter, Top
Hat** Ⓗ
Friendly, two-roomed pub
with a comfortable lounge,
and Sky TV and pool in the
bar. Lunches Thu–Sat.
Q 🍺 🍺 ⇌

Wheatsheaf Hotel

1 Holydyke ☎ (01652) 663175
11–3, 6–11
Wards Mild, Thorne Best Bitter, Best Bitter Ⓗ
Friendly, quiet, two-roomed pub in the centre of Barton.
🏠 Q ✿ ◖ ▶ ≒ P

Beverley

Grovehill

183 Holme Church Lane
(1 mile E of centre)
☎ (01482) 867409
11.30–2, 7–11; 11–11 Sat
Bateman Mild; Marston's Bitter, Pedigree Ⓗ
Former Moors & Robson's pub, built in the 1920s: a plain bar and a well-furnished lounge, popular with pigeon fanciers, model enthusiasts, motorcyclists, and darts and domino players.
♿ ✿ ⊞ ♣ P

Queen's Head

Wednesday Market
☎ (01482) 867363
11–3, 5–11; 11–11 Fri & Sat
Wards Thorne Best Bitter; guest beer Ⓗ
Compact brewer's Tudor pub overlooking Beverley's smaller market place. Refurbished and extended to the rear, where families are catered for. No eve meals Sun. ◖ ▶ ≒

Rose & Crown

North Bar Without
☎ (01482) 862532
11–3, 5–11
Vaux Waggle Dance, Extra Special; Wards Thorne Best Bitter, Best Bitter; guest beer Ⓗ
Substantial brewer's Tudor pub next to the historic North Bar, Westwood and racecourse. Popular for home-cooked food in the comfortable lounge and smoke room. Q ✿ ◖ ▶ ♣ P

Royal Standard Inn

30 North Bar Within
☎ (01482) 882434
11.30–4, 6.30–11
Vaux Double Maxim; Wards Thorne Best Bitter Ⓗ
Two-roomed town local with original 1920s bentwood seating in the front bar (with its etched Darley's window), and a well-furnished lounge at the rear. ✿ ⊞

Tap & Spile (Sun Inn)

1 Flemingate ☎ (01482) 881547
11–11
Beer range varies Ⓗ
Sympathetic restoration of a medieval, timber-framed building, Beverley's oldest pub, set opposite the Minster.

The eight, changing guest beers have transformed the local drinking scene. Eve meals end at 8pm; no food Sat/Sun eves. ✿ ◖ ▶ ♨ ≒

White Horse Inn (Nellie's)

22 Hengate ☎ (01482) 861973
11–11
Samuel Smith OBB, Museum Ⓗ
One of Beverley's landmarks, this historic inn offers a multi-roomed interior with gas lighting, stone-flagged floors, coal fires and home cooking. Folk, jazz and blues eves upstairs. No food Mon.
🏠 ✿ ◖ ▶ ⊞ ♣ P ♨

Bottesford

Black Beauty

Keddington Road
☎ (01724) 867628
11–11
Mansfield Riding Mild, Riding Bitter, Bitter, Old Baily Ⓗ
Popular estate pub with three separate rooms. The lounge bar has live music at weekends and a large TV screen (Sky). The family room has a children's play area and access to an outside playground.
♿ ✿ ⊞ ♣ P

Bridlington

Bull & Sun

11 Baylegate ☎ (01262) 676105
2 (11 Fri & Sat)–11
Vaux Mild, Samson; Wards Thorne Best Bitter Ⓗ
Former millinery shop, near the historic Baylegate and priory in Bridlington old town. Refurbishment may see the basic front room and small rear lounge knocked into one.
♿ ✿ ◖ ▶ ⅙ ♠ ♣

New Crown

158 Quay Road
☎ (01262) 604370
11–11
Wards Best Bitter Ⓗ
Substantial Victorian pub between the old town and the harbour. The large bar/games room with its wooden floor is popular with all ages; spacious, comfortable lounge.
✿ ⋈ ≒ ♣

Old Ship Inn

90 St John Street
☎ (01262) 670466
11–11
Vaux Samson; Wards Thorne Best Bitter; guest beers Ⓗ
Thriving local by the old town, with a traditional atmosphere and comfortable, separate drinking areas with a pool

table in the large bar. Outdoor play area for children.
Q ✿ ♣

Pack Horse Inn

7 Market Place
☎ (01262) 675701
11–3 (may extend summer), 7–11
Burtonwood Bitter, Top Hat Ⓗ
Listed building thought to be 300 years old. The upper windows give an impression of three storeys but the pub is in fact only two (a relic from Daylight Tax days). Inside are a comfortable, open-plan lounge and a pool room.
🏠 ✿ ◖ ♣

Seabirds

6 Fortyfoot ☎ (01262) 674174
11–11
Camerons Bitter, Strongarm; guest beer Ⓗ
Large, attractively extended pub with a comfortable, separate bar with a pool area, and a well-furnished lounge with a conservatory and sailing items for decor. Children's play area outside.
✿ ◖ ▶ ⊞ ♣ P ⊟

Brigg

Brocklesby Ox Inn

Bridge Street (A15/A18)
☎ (01652) 650292
12–3, 6–11
Burtonwood Bitter, Top Hat (occasional) Ⓗ
Smallish, 200-year-old pub, extensively renovated, with much real wood, stained-glass and framed pictures on view. The lounge contains a small dining area where children are welcome (no lunches Mon; no eve meals Sun-Tue or Thu), and the bar has a pool table. Caravans allowed overnight on Sat. ✿ ◖ ▶ ⊞ ≒ (Sat only) ♣ P

Cleethorpes

Crow's Nest

Balmoral Road
☎ (01472) 698867
11.30–3.30 (4 Sat), 6.30 (7 Sat)–11
Samuel Smith OBB Ⓗ
Good-sized, 1950s estate pub with contrasting bar and lounge. Entertainment in the bar Fri eve.
♿ ✿ ⋈ ◖ ▶ ♣ P

Nottingham House

7 Seaview Street (just off sea front) ☎ (01472) 694368
12 (11 Sat)–11
Tetley Mild, Bitter Ⓗ
Town drinking pub with a superb facade. Unusually for the area, there are three separate rooms, including a snug. Highly recommended.
Q ♿ ≒ ♣

Humberside

Smugglers

12–14 High Cliff Road
☎ (01472) 696200
11–11
McEwan 80/-; S&N Theakston
XB, Old Peculier; Younger
Scotch, No. 3; guest beer Ⓗ
Friendly, wood-beamed
basement pub close to the
seafront. Popular with both
locals and tourists. No meals
Sun eve. ✿ ⫞ ⟋ ≒ ♣

Willy's Pub & Brewery

17 High Cliff Road
☎ (01472) 602145
11–11
Bateman XB; Willy's Original;
guest beers Ⓗ
Deservedly popular seafront
pub where the attached
brewery can be viewed from
the bar. It can get very busy,
especially at weekends. Beer
festival Nov. ✿ ⟋ ≒

Driffield

Bell Hotel

Market Place ☎ (01377) 256661
10–2.30, 6–11; 10–11 Thu
Younger Scotch; guest
beers Ⓗ
Historic coaching inn with a
wood-panelled bar serving up
to three guest beers and 170
malt whiskies. Leather seating,
substantial fireplaces and
antiques lend a quality feel.
Separate hotel accommodation
and restaurant.
Q ⫞ ⟋ ♠ ♣ P

Mariner's Arms

47 Eastgate (near cattle
market) ☎ (01377) 253708
3 (11.45 Sat)–11
Burtonwood Mild, Bitter,
Forshaw's Ⓗ
Traditional, street-corner,
two-roomed local. Note the
display of beer bottles in the
bar. ✿ ⊟ ≒ ♣ P

Dunswell

Ship Inn

Beverley Road (A1174)
☎ (01482) 859160
11–11
Hull Mild; Ind Coope Burton
Ale; Stones Best Bitter; guest
beer Ⓗ
Welcoming pub where two log
fires warm the interior, part of
which is given over to a
restaurant area, with church
pew seating. Tasty, home-
cooked food served 11–7.
🏠 ✿ ⟋ ♣ P

Easington

Granby Inn

North Church Side
☎ (01964) 650294
11.30–2.30, 7–11; 11–11 Fri & Sat

Draught Bass; S&N
Theakston Best Bitter; guest
beer Ⓗ
Pub dating from the early
1800s but modernised into a
single L-shaped room. Pool
table in its own alcove. No
food Sun eve.
✿ ⫞ ⟋ ♠ Ⓐ ♣ P

East Halton

Black Bull

Townside (main street)
☎ (01469) 540207
12–11
Marston's Bitter, Pedigree Ⓗ
Deservedly popular village
local with a good-sized bar
and a comfortable lounge. No
food Sat. 🏠 Q ✿ ⟋ ⊟ ♣ P

Eastoft

River Don Tavern

Sampson Street (A161)
☎ (01724) 798225
12–2.30, 7–11
John Smith's Bitter Ⓗ
250-year-old village pub
offering excellent value food
(no meals Tue eve) and a
warm welcome.
Comprehensive vegetarian
menu. Large games room.
🏠 Q ⧖ ✿ ⟋ ♣ P

Ellerton

Boot & Shoe

Main Street ☎ (01757) 288346
6–11; 12–3, 6–11 Sat
Old Mill Bitter; John Smith's
Bitter Ⓗ
Dating back 400 years, this
popular village pub serves
excellent food. Three separate
drinking areas plus a
restaurant. Authentic low
beams add to the cosy
atmosphere. A real gem.
🏠 Q ✿ ⟋ ♣ P

Epworth

Red Lion Hotel

Market Place ☎ (01427) 872208
10.30–11
Ind Coope Burton Ale; Tetley
Bitter; guest beer Ⓗ
Lively and popular, well-
appointed hotel with a varied
menu (sizzling steaks a
speciality) and a separate
restaurant.
🏠 Q ✿ ⫞ ⟋ ♣ P

Flamborough

Rose & Crown

High Street ☎ (01262) 850455
11–3 (may extend summer), 7–11
Camerons Bitter; Tetley
Bitter Ⓗ
Pub frequented by local

fishermen where the L-shaped
room has beamed ceilings and
walls decorated with local
scenes. Comfortable
atmosphere: the pool table is
tucked away. Meals in
summer only. ⟋ Ⓐ ♣ P

Garthorpe

Bay Horse

Shore Road ☎ (01724) 798306
12–3, 7.30–11; 12–11 Sat
Mansfield Riding Bitter, Old
Baily Ⓗ
Comfortable, traditional pub
with a small entrance bar, a
public bar, a games room and
a large lounge. Frequent live
entertainment. Lunches
Wed–Sun; eve meals Wed–Sat.
Close to Blacktoft Sands RSPB
reserve. 🏠 ⟋ ⊟ ♣ P

Gilberdyke

Cross Keys Inn

Main Road ☎ (01430) 440310
12–11
John Smith's Bitter; Tetley
Bitter; Whitbread
Boddingtons Bitter; guest
beers Ⓗ
Traditional village pub still in
its original form. Strong local
following from all ages who
appreciate the emphasis on
traditional beer and games.
Always three rotating guest
beers. 🏠 ✿ ♠ ≒ ♣ P

Goodmanham

Goodmanham Arms

Main Street ☎ (01430) 873849
7–11; 12–3, 7–11 Fri & Sat
Black Sheep Best Bitter; S&N
Theakston Best Bitter; guest
beer Ⓗ
Homely rural pub with no
music or machines, just a
pleasant welcome. Situated on
the Wolds Way footpath, it has
a small but comfortable lounge
and a separate snug. No
cooked food, but fresh
sandwiches to order.
🏠 Q ⧖ ✿ ⟋ Ⓐ ♣ P

Goole

North Eastern

70 Boothferry Road
☎ (01405) 763705
11–11
Old Mill Bitter; Vaux
Samson, Waggle Dance;
Wards Thorne Best Bitter Ⓗ
Recently refurbished pub
named after the erstwhile
owners of the adjacent railway
station. The small, plush
lounge and games-oriented
public bar (three dartboards)
are both lively. The only outlet
for Old Mill in Goole.
✿ ⟋ ⊟ ♠ ≒ ♣

Old George
Market Square
☎ (01405) 763147
11–3, 7–11
**Bass Worthington BB,
Draught Bass; Stones Best
Bitter** Ⓗ
Small, lively, town-centre pub
with idiosyncratic decor.
Lunchtime food (not Sun)
draws office workers and
shoppers; eves see a younger
age group. ❀ Ⓓ ⇌ ♣ P

Grimsby

Corporation
88 Freeman Street
☎ (01472) 356651
11–11
**Bass Mild, Worthington BB,
Draught Bass**
Traditional, three-roomed pub,
the last of its type in the area.
Don't miss the panelled back
room. 🏵 ⇌ (Docks) ♣

Royal Oak
190 Victoria Street
☎ (01472) 354562
11–11; 11–4.30, 7–11 Sat
**Bass Mild, Worthington BB,
Draught Bass; Stones Best
Bitter** Ⓗ
Basic, two-roomed pub, close
to the town centre and the
award-winning National
Fishing Heritage Centre. A
folk club meets here.
Q 🏵 ⇌ (Town) ♣

Spider's Web
180 Carr Lane
☎ (01472) 692065
12 (11 Sat)–11
**Courage Directors; John
Smith's Bitter; Wilson's
Mild** Ⓗ
Pub where a boisterous bar
contrasts with a peaceful
lounge, which has paintings
for sale. The function room
hosts good quality bands. Not
all the beers are dispensed
from any one bar but are
available on request.
Q ❀ 🏵 ♣ P

Swigs
21 Osborne Street
☎ (01472) 354773
11–11; 7–10.30 Sun, closed Sun lunch
**Bateman XB; Willy's Original;
guest beers** Ⓗ
Cosmopolitan, narrow,
town-centre café bar, popular
with office workers and
shoppers at lunchtimes. Quiet
during the afternoon and early
eve; noisier later. The second
outlet for Willy's brewery.
Ⓓ ⇌ (Town)

Tap & Spile
Garth Lane ☎ (01472) 357493
11.30–4, 7–11; 11.30–11, Fri & Sat
Beer range varies Ⓗ & Ⓖ

Large, one-roomed, open-plan
former flour mill, retaining old
stone, brick and woodwork.
Well used, particularly eves,
with a good atmosphere and
up to nine real ales. Local
CAMRA *Pub of the Year* 1995.
No meals Sun.
❀ Ⓓ & ⇌ (Town) ♣ ⏎

Wine Pipe
178 Freeman Street
☎ (01472) 354184
11–11
**Tetley Bitter; Younger IPA,
No.3; guest beer** Ⓗ
Cosy bar and lounge, opened
as a memorial to Grimsby's
fish market – the Pontoon.
Spot the faces of regulars on
the mural. Eve entertainment,
except Mon/Tue. Ⓓ 🍴 & ♣

Gunness

Jolly Sailor
Station Road (A18)
☎ (01724) 782423
12–11
**Courage Directors; John
Smith's Bitter** Ⓗ
Friendly 1930s pub, renovated
but retaining its original style.
Separate function room. Live
music Sat eve.
🏚 Ⓓ 🍴 ⇌ (Althorpe) ♣ P

Habrough

Horse & Hounds
Station Road ☎ (01469) 576940
11–11 (may close 3–7)
**S&N Theakston XB, Old
Peculier; Younger IPA, No.3;
Young's Special; guest beer** Ⓗ
Tastefully converted former
farmhouse/rectory adjoining
the Habrough Hotel, offering a
wide range of beers at
reasonable prices. Excellent
food; good local trade.
🏚 Q ❀ 🛏 Ⓓ ▶ ⇌ ♣ P

Haxey

Loco
31–33 Church Street
☎ (01302) 752879
6.30–11
**Courage Directors; John
Smith's Bitter** Ⓗ
Pub converted from the village
Co-op and fish and chip shop,
a must for railway enthusiasts,
packed with railwayana. Sun
lunches served.
🏚 Q 🛏 ❀ 🍴 ♣ P

Hedon

Shakespeare Inn
9 Baxtergate ☎ (01482) 898371
11–11
**Vaux Samson, Waggle Dance,
Extra Special; Wards Mild,
Thorne Best Bitter, Best
Bitter** Ⓗ

The town's own village pub,
popular with locals and
visitors alike and noted for its
food, snuff box collection and
large range of malt whiskies.
No eve meals Sat/Sun; other
eves till 7.30. 🏚 ❀ Ⓓ ▶ ♣ P

Hotham

Hotham Arms
Main Street ☎ (01430) 422939
11.30–4, 6.30–11; 11.30–11 Fri & Sat
**Black Sheep Best Bitter;
Tetley Bitter; Whitbread
Boddingtons Mild, Bitter** Ⓗ
Estate village pub dating from
1760; extended and altered in
1994 to provide a restaurant in
a conservatory. Separate bar
and games room. Situated on
the Wolds Way footpath.
❀ Ⓓ ▶ A P

Howden

White Horse Inn
Market Place ☎ (01430) 430326
11–3, 6–11; 11 Thu–Sat
**Marston's Pedigree;
Whitbread Boddingtons Mild,
Bitter** Ⓗ
Market town inn dating from
the 14th-century. The original
cellar was used as a dungeon
by Cromwell. A strong
supporter of local darts and
pool leagues. Ⓓ & ♣ P

Hull

Bay Horse
113 Wincolmlee (400 yds N of
N bridge on W bank of River
Hull) ☎ (01482) 329227
11.30–11
**Bateman Mild, XB, Salem
Porter, XXXB, Victory Ale;
Marston's Pedigree; guest
beers** Ⓗ
Spectacular corner pub in an
old industrial area: Bateman's
only tied house north of the
Humber. The bar's wood-
panelled walls display rugby
league memorabilia; lofty
stable bar. Beer festivals in
spring and autumn. Eve meals
till 7. 🏚 Ⓓ ▶ 🏵 & ♣ P

Duke of Wellington
104 Peel Street (N of Spring
Bank, NW of centre)
☎ (01482) 329603
12–3, 7–11; 12–11 Sat
**Taylor Landlord; Tetley
Bitter; guest beers** Ⓗ
Back-street, re-styled Victorian
corner pub, popular with
students and locals. Occasional
beer festivals. ❀ & ♣ P

East Riding
37 Cannon Street
☎ (01482) 329134
12–5, 7–11
Tetley Mild, Bitter Ⓗ

Humberside

Small, street-corner, two-roomed industrial pub to the north of the city centre. The no-nonsense bar features rugby league memorabilia; cosy, wood-panelled lounge. 🍺 ♣

Gardener's Arms

35 Cottingham Road
☎ (01482) 342396
11–11
Ind Coope Burton Ale; Marston's Pedigree; Tetley Mild, Bitter; guest beers 🅷
Tetley Festival Alehouse close to the university. The front room is popular with locals and students, with its dark wood, bare brick walls and original matchboard ceiling. Mr Q's games room behind. ❀ ◑ ♦ P

Grapes Inn

Sykes Street ☎ (01482) 324424
12–4, 7–11
Tetley Mild, Bitter; guest beers 🅷
Friendly local just off the northern section of the central orbital road, near the registry office. Built in the 1930s, it has two distinct areas and features live music Fri, Sat and Mon. Darts is popular. ♠ ♣

Haworth Arms

449 Beverley Road
☎ (01482) 346873
11–11
Bass Mild, Draught Bass; guest beer 🅷
Large, mock Tudor structure at the junction of Cottingham Rd, with an array of rooms/areas. An interesting glass dome features in the ceiling of the main bar; wood panelling throughout. Eve meals till 7; no meals Sun. Families welcome 3–7.
Q ⛄ ◑ ▶ 🍺 ♣

Linnet & Lark

30–32 Princes Avenue
☎ (01482) 441126
11–11
Mansfield Riding Mild, Riding Bitter, Bitter, Old Baily 🅷
A superb stone-flag floor and old furniture give this former car showroom a cosy pub feel (it was converted in 1994 to give Princes Ave its first, much needed, pub). Mansfield seasonal beers are usually available. Free bus Fri and Sat eves to Spring Bank Tavern. ❀ ◑ ♦ P

New Clarence

77 Charles Street
☎ (01482) 320327
11–11
Marston's Pedigree; Tetley Mild, Bitter; guest beers 🅷
Tetley Festival Alehouse off

Kingston Square, near the New Theatre: a large one-roomer run on traditional lines. Regular beer festivals. Hull CAMRA *Pub of the Year* 1994. Live Irish music Thu eve. Eve meals till 7.30; no food Sun eve. ◑ ▶ ♣ ⌂

Old Blue Bell

Market Place (down alley next to indoor market)
☎ (01482) 324382
11–11; 11–3, 7–11 Mon & Wed
Samuel Smith OBB, Museum 🅷
Historic town pub with its original layout of snug, corridor and long, narrow bar. A courtyard connects to the covered market. Large collection of bells. Pool room upstairs. ❀ ◑ 🍺

Olde Black Boy

150 High Street, Old Town
☎ (01482) 326516
12–3, 7–11; 11–11 Fri & Sat
Beer range varies 🅷
Pub dating from 1331 and now the first Tap & Spile Charterhouse. See the display in the bar about local MP William Wilberforce's role in the abolition of slavery. Two upstairs rooms. Hull CAMRA *Pub of the Year* 1993. Ten beers sold, changing daily.
♠ Q ◑ 🍺 ♣ ⌂

Olde White Harte

25 Silver Street
☎ (01482) 326363
11–11
S&N Newcastle Exhibition, Theakston XB, Old Peculier; Younger IPA, No.3; guest beer 🅷
16th-century, courtyard pub, once a residence where the Governor of Hull resolved to deny Charles I entry to the city. Superb woodwork, sit-in fireplaces and stained-glass feature. Varied lunch menu in the bar and the upstairs dining room. Family room lunchtime only. Q ⛄ ❀ ◑ ♣

Spring Bank Tavern

29 Spring Bank
☎ (01482) 581879
11–11
Mansfield Riding Mild, Riding Bitter, Bitter, Old Baily; guest beers 🅷
Mansfield's first cask alehouse, sympathetically refurbished as a street-corner local on the western edge of the city centre. The guest beers (usually four) tend to be expensive.
◑ ≢ (Paragon)

Tap & Spile (Eagle)

169–171 Spring Bank (500 yds from centre) ☎ (01482) 323518
12–11

Beer range varies 🅷
1994 conversion of a street-corner local into a large alehouse, serving 12 cask ales and two ciders. The high quality refurbishment and the beer range make up for the sad loss of the Eagle. Folk music Sun nights. Eve meals end at 7. ❀ ◑ ♦ ♣ ⌂ P ✄

Whalebone Inn

165 Wincolmlee
☎ (01482) 327980
12–11
Tetley Mild, Bitter 🅷
Popular, no-frills drinkers' local on the west side of the River Hull between Scott St and Sculcoates bridges. The old industrial area nearby used to include whale processing plants, which gave this pub its name. ♣

Kilnsea

Crown & Anchor

Main Street ☎ (01964) 650276
11–11
Bass Mild, Draught Bass; Tetley Bitter 🅷
Pub almost on Spurn peninsula, overlooking the busy Humber Estuary. The four rooms (including a restaurant and a family room) house brasses, china and household utensils. The lounge has a Victorian range. Popular for food (breakfasts from 6am).
♠ ⛄ ❀ 🏠 ◑ ▶ ♦ ♠ ♣ P

Little Reedness

Ferry House Inn

Main Street ☎ (01405) 704303
12–2.30 (not Mon), 8–11
Mansfield Riding Bitter, Bitter, Old Baily 🅷
Spacious, welcoming, 500-year-old village local overlooking the River Ouse, near Blacktoft Sands RSPB reserve. Huge log fire. Eve meals Wed–Sat.
♠ ❀ 🏠 ◑ ▶ ♣ P

Market Weighton

Carpenter's Arms

56 Southgate (A1034)
☎ (01430) 873446
12–4, 7–11; 11–11 Sat
Vaux Mild; Wards Thorne Best Bitter 🅷
Unspoilt, welcoming street-corner local with a log fire, an ornate wooden bar and matchboarded walls. Sash windows provide views of the town centre. Large games room. ♠ 🍺 ♣ P

Half Moon Inn

39 High Street
☎ (01430) 872247
7 (3 Fri, 12 Sat)–11

Burtonwood Mild, Bitter Ⓗ
Market town pub with a
friendly welcome. The lounge
area at the front has views of
the church. The bar area at the
rear has a pool table. Popular
with all ages. ❀ ♣ P

Old Ellerby

Blue Bell
Crabtree Lane (old Hornsea
road from Hull)
☎ (01964) 562364
7–11; 12–4, 7–11 Sat (12–3, 7–11 Thu
& Fri in summer)
**Ind Coope Burton Ale;
Morland Old Speckled Hen;
Tetley Mild, Bitter; guest
beer** Ⓗ
Unassuming, white-painted
village pub, reputedly dating
back to the *Domesday Book*. The
tasteful interior has a tiled
floor, low beams and brasses.
Regularly changing guest beer.
No food, but summer
barbecues on the patio.
ﷺ ❀ ▲ ♣ P

Owston Ferry

Crooked Billet
Silver Street ☎ (01427) 728264
11–3 (not Mon, except bank hols),
7–11
**Wards Thorne Best Bitter,
Best Bitter** Ⓗ
Friendly local beside the River
Trent, with its own amateur
boxing club. Weekend sing-
alongs. ﷺ Q ▭ ❀ ◑ ♪ ♣ P

Patrington

Hildyard Arms
1 Market Place
☎ (01964) 630234
12–11
**Tetley Dark Mild, Bitter;
guest beer** Ⓗ
Former Georgian coaching inn
which also served as a corn
exchange for local farmers.
Guest beers are changed on a
regular basis. The Dark Mild (from Tetley
Walker) is unusual for the
area. ﷺ Q ❀ ◑ ♪ ♪ ♣ P

Pocklington

Wellington Oak
York Road (A1079)
☎ (01759) 303854
11.30–2.30, 7–11
Tetley Bitter Ⓗ
Busy, friendly, roadside pub
popular for food. Its semi-
open-plan layout has two
separate drinking areas and a
restaurant. ﷺ ❀ ◑ ♪ P

Reedness

Half Moon
Main Street ☎ (01405) 704484
12–3, 7–11
**Marston's Pedigree;
Whitbread Boddingtons
Bitter, Castle Eden Ale; guest
beer** Ⓗ
Traditional, very clean and
polished local with a caravan
and campsite behind and
Blacktoft Sands RSPB reserve
nearby. Whitbread collection
guest beer. ﷺ ◑ ♪ ▲ ♣ P

Ryhill

Crooked Billet
Pitt Lane (400 yds from A1033)
☎ (01964) 622303
12–4 (not Wed), 7–11; 12–11 Fri & Sat
Burtonwood Mild, Bitter Ⓗ
Busy village pub with an
attractive, beamed ceiling. The
lounge has a stone-floored
lower level. Interesting display
of old cameras.
ﷺ ◑ ♪ ♣ P

Scunthorpe

Riveter
50 Henderson Avenue
☎ (01724) 862701
11–3, 5.30–11; 11–11 Sat
**Old Mill Mild, Bitter,
Bullion** Ⓗ
Pub converted from a
workingmen's club; noisy and
crowded in the eve. Large
games area. Parking limited.
The first Old Mill tied pub.
♣ P

Skerne

Eagle
Wansford Road
☎ (01377) 252178
7–11; 12–2, 7–11 Sat
Camerons Bitter Ⓗ
Classic, unspoilt village local
with a basic bar and a front
parlour. Drinks are served to
your table from a small cellar
off the entrance corridor. Beer
is dispensed from a Victorian
cash register beer engine.
Outside toilets.
ﷺ Q ❀ ⊞ ♣ P

Skipsea

Board Inn
Back Street ☎ (01262) 468342
12–3, 7–11
**Burtonwood Bitter,
Forshaw's** Ⓗ

Village local dating back to the
17th century. The snug has a
painted wooden bar, whilst
the tap room reflects a horse
racing theme. Restaurant and
children's room to the rear.
ﷺ ☟ ❀ ◑ ♪ ⊞ ♿ ▲ ♣
P ⚬

Snaith

Downe Arms
Market Place ☎ (01405) 860544
11.30–11
Mansfield Riding Bitter Ⓗ,
Bitter Ⓔ
Historic, listed building in the
centre of Snaith, popular with
locals and visitors. Function
room and meeting room.
Mansfield seasonal beers also
sold. ﷺ ❀ ◑ ♪ ♿
♒ (limited service) ♣ P

Stamford Bridge

Swordsman
☎ (01759) 371307
11–11; 11–3, 5.30–11 Tue & Wed
Samuel Smith OBB Ⓗ
Old coaching inn overlooking
the River Derwent, offering a
snug, family room, tap room
and garden. Fishing at the rear
for patrons.
ﷺ ☟ ❀ ◑ ♿ ♣ P

Sutton upon Derwent

St Vincent Arms
Main Street ☎ (01904) 608349
11.30–3, 6–11
**Adnams Extra; Fuller's
London Pride; Mansfield
Riding Bitter; Wells
Bombardier; Whitbread
Boddingtons Bitter; guest
beers** Ⓗ
Traditional, cosy, two-roomed
village inn, which is often
busy. Deservedly popular for
its keenly-priced ales and its
home-cooked meals.
ﷺ Q ❀ ◑ ♪ ▲ P ⊟

Westwoodside

Park Drain
400 yds off B1396 OS726988
☎ (01427) 752255
11–11
**Mansfield Riding Bitter; John
Smith's Bitter; Wilson's Mild;
guest beers** Ⓗ
Unusual, remote, Victorian
pub, built to serve the mining
community of a pit that was
never sunk. Comfortable
lounge and excellent
restaurant. Meals all day Sun.
ﷺ ❀ ◑ ♪ ⊞ ▲ P

For further information about the beers listed in the above entries,
check the breweries section at the rear of the book.

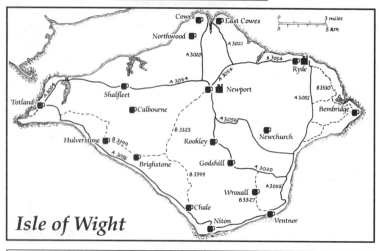

Isle of Wight

Isle of Wight

 Burts, *Newport*; **Goddard's** *Ryde*

Bembridge

Rowbarge
☎ (01983) 872874
12–4, 6–11
**Alloa Arrol's 80/-; Draught
Bass; Courage Directors;
HP&D Entire; Marston's
Pedigree** H
Lively, popular pub with a
nautical theme. Good food
(pizzas a speciality).
🛏 ᖙ ❀ ◖▮ ➾ P

Brighstone

Countryman
Limerstone Road (B3399)
☎ (01983) 740616
11–3, 7–11 (11–11 summer)
**Hall & Woodhouse Badger
BB, Tanglefoot; Hampshire
King Alfred's; guest beers** H
Spacious single-bar pub
enjoying a reputation for fine
food, situated near downland
and unspoilt beaches.
🛏 Q ᖙ ❀ ◖▮ ♣ P ⊬

Calbourne

Blacksmith's Arms
Calbourne Road (B3401, 2
miles W of Newport)
☎ (01983) 529263
11–3, 6–11 (11–11 summer)
Beer range varies H
Friendly, country pub
reputedly haunted by a
murdered barmaid; a cosy
front bar and a larger rear bar
with a dining area.
Imaginative menu. German
draught lager and light and
dark Weissbiers complement
the three or four real ales.
Q ❀ ◖▮ P 🍺

Chale

Wight Mouse
Newport Road (B3399)
☎ (01983) 730431
11–11
**Marston's Pedigree; Morland
Old Speckled Hen; Wadworth
6X; Whitbread Boddingtons
Bitter, Strong Country, Castle
Eden Ale** H
Very busy, old stone pub with
an adjoining hotel, near
Blackgang Chine Theme Park.
An award-winning family and
whisky pub, it has a garden
play area and three family
rooms. Food all day; live
music every night.
🛏 ᖙ ❀ 🛏 ◖▮ ▲ P

Cowes

Anchor Inn
1 High Street
☎ (01983) 292823
11–11
**Greene King Abbot;
Whitbread Boddingtons
Bitter, Flowers Original;
Wadworth 6X; guest beers** H
Ancient town pub of character,
with low, beamed ceilings and
flagstone floors. Good range of
beers, but not cheap.
🛏 ᖙ ❀ ◖▮ ♣ ➾

Union Inn
Watchouse Lane
☎ (01983) 293163
11–2.30, 6–11 (11–11 summer)
**Gale's BBB, Best Bitter, HSB;
guest beer** H
Cosy, single-bar town pub
within 50 yards of the seafront.
The guest beer may be a Gale's

seasonal brew. Eve meals
in summer.
🛏 Q ᖙ 🛏 ▮ ⅃ &

Try also: Pier View, High St
(Whitbread)

East Cowes

Ship & Castle
21 Castle Street (opp. Red
Funnel Ferry terminal
entrance) ☎ (01983) 290522
11–11
**Hall & Woodhouse Badger
BB; S&N Theakston Old
Peculier; guest beers**
(summer) H
Small, single-bar pub with a
good local trade. ◖▮ ♣

Victoria Tavern
62 Clarence Road
☎ (01983) 295961
11–3, 7–11
**Goddard's Special; Marston's
Pedigree; John Smith's Bitter;
guest beer** H
Much modernised, early
Victorian town pub featuring
an unusual clinker-built boat
bar. ◖▮ ♣ ⊟

Godshill

Taverner's Inn
High Street
☎ (01983) 840707
11–3, 6.30–11 (11–11 summer)
**Courage Directors; Marston's
Pedigree; Morland Old
Speckled Hen; John Smith's
Bitter; Wadworth 6X; guest
beer** H
Families are welcome at this
busy village pub. The garden
has a play area and is popular
in summer. Changing guest

Isle of Wight

ale in summer.
🏠 Q ❄ ⚘ ◖ ◗ ♣ ⅄

Try also: Griffin, High St (Whitbread)

Hulverstone

Old Sun Inn
On B3399, 2 miles W of Brighstone
☎ (01983) 740403
11–3, 6–11 (11–11 summer)
Gale's Best Bitter Ⓖ, **Gold, HSB, Festival Mild; guest beers** (summer) Ⓗ
Genuine village local brought alive by the present licensees; popular with locals and holidaymakers. The varied menu puts the emphasis on home-cooked meals. Cider in summer.
🏠 ⚘ ▲ ♣ ⅃ P 🏠

Newchurch

Pointer Inn
High Street
☎ (01983) 865202
11–4, 6–11; 11–11 Sat
Gale's Best Bitter, HSB Ⓗ
Perfect village pub with a warm welcome, frequented by ramblers as well as locals. Family room in summer. Good food. Q ❄ ⚘ ◖ ◗ ▲ ♣ P

Newport

Prince of Wales
36 South Street (opp. bus station) ☎ (01983) 525026
10.30–11
Ushers Best Bitter, Founders Ⓗ
Town-centre pub attracting a cross-section of drinkers. Food includes home-made specials made with real ale. Ushers seasonal ales stocked.
🏠 Q ◖ ♣ ⅃

Railway Medina
1 Sea Street
☎ (01983) 528303
11–11
Gale's BBB, Gold (summer), **5X, HSB** Ⓗ
Delightful, back-street, corner pub with plenty of atmosphere and a good collection of railway memorabilia.
🏠 Q ⚘ ◖ ◗ 🏠 ♣

Niton

Buddle
St Catherine's Road (follow signs for St Catherine's Point)
☎ (01983) 730243
11–11 (11–3, 6–11 winter)
Whitbread Boddingtons Bitter, Flowers IPA, Original; guest beers Ⓗ
Ancient stone pub with strong smuggling connections. Three

guest beers, plus locally produced cider. Try the seafood.
🏠 ❄ ⚘ ◖ ◗ ▲ ♣ ⅃ P

White Lion
High Street
☎ (01983) 730293
11–3, 7–11 (11–11 summer)
Greene King Abbot; Marston's Pedigree; Whitbread Castle Eden Ale; guest beers Ⓗ
Comfortable village pub, well-refurbished, with several rooms.
Q ❄ ⚘ 🏠 ◖ ◗ ▲ ♣ P ⅄

Northwood

Traveller's Joy
Pallance Road (off A3020)
☎ (01983) 298024
11–3, 6–11
Ansells Mild; Courage Directors; Ringwood Old Thumper; S&N Theakston Old Peculier; Wadworth 6X; guest beers Ⓗ
Three times local CAMRA *Pub of the Year*, this pub offers nine cask ales, with at least one mild or porter, from all over the country.
⚘ ◖ ◗ ▲ ♣ ⅃ P 🏠

Rookley

Chequers
Off A3020
☎ (01983) 840314
11–11
Courage Best Bitter, Directors; Morland Old Speckled Hen; John Smith's Bitter; guest beer Ⓗ
Extensively renovated, characterful country pub at the heart of the island. It has a large lounge bar, a flagstone public bar, a quiet area, plus a restaurant and a family room.
🏠 Q ❄ ⚘ ◖ ◗ 🏠 ▲ ♣ P

Ramblers
Rookley Country Park, Main Road
☎ (01983) 721800
11–11 (closed weekday lunchtime in winter)
Hall & Woodhouse Badger BB, Tanglefoot; guest beer Ⓗ
Modern pub set in a 22-acre park with facilities for the whole family. Lively entertainment in summer. Superb, home-cooked food with a worldwide menu and an approved vegan selection.
⚘ 🏠 ◖ ◗ ▲ ♣ P

Ryde

Lake Superior
59 Marlborough Road, Elmfield (1 mile from seafront on Sandown road, A3055)
☎ (01983) 563519

11 (12 winter)–3, 5.30–11; 11–11 Fri & Sat
Adnams Bitter; Draught Bass; Goddard's Special; Hop Back Summer Lightning; Tetley Bitter Ⓗ
Corner local, welcoming and comfortable with attractive decor. A spacious serving area joins two rooms.
🏠 ❄ ⚘ 🏠 ♣ P 🏠

Shalfleet

New Inn
Mill Road
☎ (01983) 531314
11–11 (11–3, 6–11 winter)
Draught Bass; Whitbread Flowers Original; guest beer Ⓗ
Very old, stone-flagged inn by a creek leading to Newtown River. Renowned for seafood.
🏠 Q ❄ ⚘ ◖ ◗ 🏠 ▲ P

Totland

Highdown Inn
Highdown Lane (2 miles E of Alum Bay)
☎ (01983) 752450
11–3, 5 (7 winter)–11.45
Ushers Best Bitter, Founders Ⓗ
Delightful, unusual and very rural pub, with a friendly, relaxed atmosphere. Delicious meals and bar snacks of enormous variety. 🏠 Q ⚘
🏠 ◖ ◗ 🏠 ▲ ♣ P 🏠

Ventnor

Volunteer
30 Victoria Street
☎ (01983) 852537
11–3, 6–11; 11–11 Fri & Sat
Everards Old Original; Hall & Woodhouse Badger BB; Wells Eagle; guest beers Ⓗ
Former Burts town local, well renovated, small and friendly. A popular rings game is played. Guest beers include one from Burts. UK finalists in a Tetley Cask Bitter quality competition. ♣

Wroxall

Star Inn
Clarence Road
☎ (01983) 854701
11–3 (extends in summer), 7–11
Burts Nipper, VPA, Old Vectis Venom; Freetraders Twelve Bore; Ringwood Best Bitter; Whitbread Boddingtons Bitter; guest beers Ⓗ
Old Burts local, destroyed by fire in 1980, but rebuilt in a homely style. Always a warm welcome. Cider in summer.
Q ⚘ ◖ ◗ 🏠 ▲ ♣ ⅃ P 🏠

149

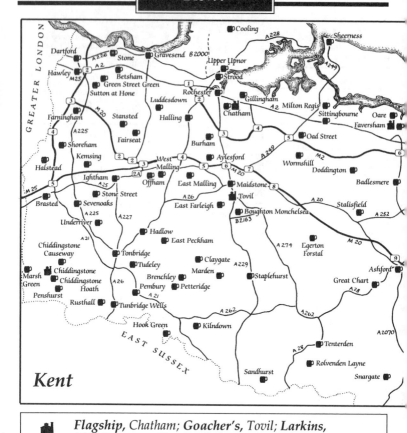

Kent

Flagship, *Chatham;* **Goacher's,** *Tovil;* **Larkins,**
Chiddingstone; **Shepherd Neame,** *Faversham*

Ashford

Beaver Inn
322 Beaver Road
☎ (01233) 620264
11.30–3, 7–11
**Shepherd Neame Master
Brew Bitter, Spitfire**
(occasional) Ⓗ
Very friendly local where
photographs of old Ashford
enhance the timbered decor.
No food Sun or Wed.
Q ❀ ◗ ♣ P

Beaver Road
Off-Licence
36 Beaver Road
☎ (01233) 622904
11–10.30
Beer range varies Ⓖ
Off-licence offering at least
three beers during the week,
and four at weekends, 20–30%
cheaper than pub prices.
Sample before you buy.
Usually three ciders. ⇌ ⌂

Aylesford

Little Gem
High Street ☎ (01622) 717510
11–3, 6–11; 11–11 Sat
**Draught Bass; Fuller's
London Pride** Ⓗ**, ESB** Ⓖ**;
Harveys BB** Ⓗ**; Wadworth
6X** Ⓖ
Claimed to be Kent's smallest
pub: a former bakery, now a
low-beamed Tudor pub with a
small gallery-style upstairs
drinking area. Often busy.
Changing guest beers. No food
Sat/Sun eves. ◗ ▶ ⇌

Badlesmere

Red Lion
Ashford Road
☎ (01233) 740320
11.30–2.30 (4 Fri), 6–11; 11.30–11 Sat
**Fuller's London Pride; Greene
King XX Mild, Abbot;
Shepherd Neame Master
Brew Bitter; guest beers** Ⓗ

16th-century village pub with
gas lights in the bar. A rare
outlet for cask-conditioned
mild and cider. Eve meals
Thu–Sat.
🛏 ❀ ◗ ▶ ▲ ♣ ⌂ P

Barfreston

Yew Tree Inn
☎ (01304) 831619
11–3, 7–11
**Greene King XX Mild, IPA;
Mauldons Black Adder** Ⓗ**;
Otter Ale** Ⓖ**; Taylor Best
Bitter** Ⓗ**; guest beers** Ⓖ
Lively, traditional village-
centre pub, alongside the
church. About 1½ miles from
Shepherds Well station.
🛏 Q ❀ ◗ ▶ ♣ P 🍴

Betsham

Colyer Arms
Station Road (B262, 1 mile S of
A2) ☎ (01474) 832392
11.30–11; 11.30–4.30, 7–11 Sat

Kent

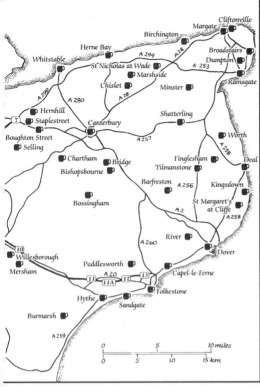

Courage Best Bitter; Ruddles
County; Shepherd Neame
Master Brew Bitter;
Wadworth 6X; guest beers Ⓗ
Village-centre pub named after
a local WWI VC hero. This
friendly, popular local offers
darts, bat and trap, petanque
and sports clubs. Good food in
the restaurant or conservatory,
(not Sun or Mon eves). Large
garden with children's play
area. ♣ ◑ ▶ ⊟ & ♣ P

Birchington

Seaview Hotel
Station Road ☎ (01843) 841702
11–11
**Shepherd Neame Master
Brew Bitter, Best Bitter,
Spitfire** *or* **Bishops Finger** Ⓗ
Built in 1865 to cater for
travellers on the newly-built
London, Chatham and Dover
Railway: a one-bar pub
boasting a friendly
atmosphere.
♣ ❀ ⊨ ◑ ▶ ⇌ ♣ P

Bishopsbourne

Mermaid
800 yds off A2
☎ (01227) 830581
11–3, 6–11

Shepherd Neame Master
Brew Bitter, Porter Ⓗ
Small and attractive pub set in
a typically Kentish village,
former home of author Joseph
Conrad. Other Shepherd
Neame beers are sometimes
available. ♣ Q ❀ ◑ ⊟ ♣

Bossingham

Hop Pocket
☎ (01227) 709866
12–2.30, 7–11
**Fuller's London Pride;
Shepherd Neame Spitfire;
Taylor Landlord** Ⓗ
Candlelit, 19th-century pub; its
ceiling is thatched with hop
bines in Kentish style. Many
special events, including an
annual beer festival, with
camping allowed in the
grounds. A mild is often
available. Bat and trap played.
♣ Q ❀ ◑ ▶ & ♣ ⌂ P

Boughton Monchelsea

Red House
Hermitage Lane (S off B2163,
down Wierton Rd and East
Hall Hill) ☎ (01622) 743986
12–3, 7–11; 12–11 Sat and bank hols
Fuller's London Pride; Greene

King XX Mild, IPA, Abbot;
Hampshire Lionheart; Otter
Ale; guest beers Ⓗ
The seventh consecutive year
in the *Guide* for this popular
country pub offering an
excellent choice of changing
guest beers and an extensive
range of imported beers. Good
selection of fruit beers and
fruit wines. May beer festival.
♣ Q ⛁ ❀ ◑ ▶ ▲ ♣ ⌂ P

Boughton Street

Queen's Head
111 The Street
☎ (01227) 751369
11–3, 6–11; 11–11 Sat
**Shepherd Neame Master
Brew Bitter, Spitfire** Ⓗ
Unpretentious, 16th-century
inn with good value food and
accommodation: a lively
public bar and a wood-
panelled saloon. Wheelchair
WC.
Q ❀ ⊨ ◑ ▶ ⊟ & ▲ ♣ P

Brasted

Bull Inn
High Street (A25)
☎ (01959) 562551
10.30–2.30 (may extend), 5.30–11;
10.30–11 Sat and bank hols
**Shepherd Neame Master
Brew Bitter, Spitfire, Bishops
Finger** Ⓗ
Very friendly pub catering for
both local and passing trade,
in the centre of a village of
antique shops, near Chartwell.
Occasional live folk music.
❀ ◑ ▶ ♣ P

Brenchley

Bull Inn
High Street ☎ (01892) 722701
11–3, 5–11
**Greene King IPA, Abbot;
Shepherd Neame Best Bitter;
guest beer** Ⓗ
Friendly, single-bar, 19th-
century pub with quite a long
bar area and two real fires.
Local photographs abound.
♣ ❀ ⊨ ◑ ▶ ♣ P

Bridge

Plough & Harrow
86 High Street
☎ (01227) 830455
11–3, 6–11
**Shepherd Neame Master
Brew Bitter** Ⓗ
Friendly village local, good for
games. Orginally a maltings
and brewery, it is over 300
years old. ♣ Q & ♣ P

Broadstairs

Albion Hotel
Albion Street
☎ (01843) 868071

151

11-3, 6.30-11
Courage Directors; Shepherd Neame Master Brew Bitter; Webster's Yorkshire Bitter Ⓗ
Hotel bar open to the public. Its large garden boasts views over Viking Bay. Convenient for all the local seaside attractions.
❀ ⛟ ≉

Neptune's Hall
1-3 Harbour Street
☎ (01843) 861400
11-11
Shepherd Neame Master Brew Bitter, Spitfire *or* **Porter** Ⓗ
Busy three-bar, old-fashioned alehouse, the type of pub becoming rarer by the year. Close to the harbour and Dickens's Bleak House, it hosts events during folk week (Aug). ⌂ Q ❀ ◐ ♣

Burham

Toastmaster's Inn
65-67 Church Street
☎ (01634) 861299
11.45-3.30, 5.30-11; 11.45-11 Thu-Sat
Greene King IPA; S&N Theakston Old Peculier; Young's Special; guest beers Ⓗ
180-year-old pub in a rural village setting with a warm, family atmosphere. The restaurant serves authentic Indian dishes.
⌂ Q ☺ ❀ ◐ ◑ ⌓ P

Windmill
292 Rochester Road
☎ (01634) 861919
11.30-3, 7-11
Bass Worthington BB; Fuller's London Pride; guest beer Ⓗ
Friendly, village local with two bars and a restaurant.
❀ ◐ ◑ ⊟ ♣ P

Burmarsh

Shepherd & Crook Inn
Shearway OS101320
☎ (01303) 872336
11.30-3, 7-11
Adnams Bitter; Ind Coope Benskins BB; guest beers Ⓗ
Friendly pub on the east of Romney Marsh, festooned with firearms, copperware, china and many other oddities. Ring the Bull in the saloon. Eve meals Tue-Sat.
⌂ Q ❀ ◐ ◑ ⊟ ▲ ♣ P

Canterbury

Bell & Crown
10-11 Palace Street
☎ (01227) 462459
11-11
Fuller's London Pride Ⓗ**; guest beers**
1950s-style, popular, city-centre local near the Cathedral, featuring WW II memorabilia. Occasional cider in summer.
⌂ ❀ ◐ ◑ ♣ ⌓

Bishops Finger
13 St Dunstans Street (by the Westgate Towers)
☎ (01227) 768915
11-11
Shepherd Neame Master Brew Bitter, Bishops Finger, Spitfire Ⓗ
Small, two-bar, welcoming local with occasional live music.
Q ☺ ❀ ◐ ◑ ♿ ≉ (West) ⊟

Canterbury Tales
12 The Friars (opp. Marlowe Theatre) ☎ (01227) 768594
11-11
Goacher's Light; Shepherd Neame Master Brew Bitter; guest beers Ⓗ
Enterprising, attractive pub and restaurant with ever-changing guest beers, mini-festivals, special promotions and theme nights. Meals all day Sun. ◐ ◑ ♿

New Inn
19 Havelock Street
☎ (01227) 464584
11-3 (3.30 Fri & Sat), 6-11
Beer range varies Ⓗ
One of a row of terraced houses: well known to students, but no inn sign! Its reputation is sufficient. Excellent value meals.
❀ ◐ ◑ ♣ ⊟

Try also: Olive Branch, Burgate (Carlsberg-Tetley)

Capel-le-Ferne

Royal Oak
New Dover Road (B2011)
☎ (01303) 244787
11.30-3 (4 Sat), 6 (7 Sat)-11 (may vary summer)
Shepherd Neame Master Brew Bitter; guest beers Ⓗ
Split-level, two-bar pub dating from the 17th century. Nearby panoramic views along and across the Channel. Games and TV are kept separate from the main bar area.
⌂ ❀ ◐ ◑ ▲ ♣ P

Chartham

Cross Keys
Bolts Hill
☎ (01227) 738216
11-11; 11-2.30, 6-11 Tue
Adnams Bitter; Shepherd Neame Spitfire; John Smith's Bitter; guest beers Ⓗ
Village local dating from the late 18th century. Good quality bar snacks lunchtime.
⌂ ❀ ▲ ♣ ⌓ P ⊟

Chatham

Alexandra
43 Railway Street
☎ (01634) 843959
11-3 (4 Sat), 5 (7 Sat)-11; 11-11 Fri
Shepherd Neame Master Brew Bitter, Spitfire, Porter Ⓗ
Impressive Victorian building, very near the station. Noted for its dog in the window.
❀ ≉ ♣

Chiddingstone Causeway

Little Brown Jug
On B2027, opp. Penshurst station ☎ (01892) 870318
11.30-3, 6-11
Harveys BB; guest beers Ⓗ
Busy, friendly, family-run free house offering three ever-changing guest beers – many unusual. Excellent range of good food. Spacious garden.
⌂ Q ❀ ⛟ ◐ ◑ ♿
≉ (Penshurst) P

Chiddingstone Hoath

Rock
OS498433 ☎ (01892) 870296
11.30-3, 5.30-11
Larkins Bitter *or* **Best Bitter; Shepherd Neame Master Brew Bitter** Ⓗ
16th-century rural pub in an isolated setting. A worn, red-brick floor features in the main bar, which is heated by a wood-burning stove. The unusual hexagonal wooden pump handles dispense Larkins ales, brewed just down the road. Hook the Bull game. No food Mon.
⌂ Q ❀ ◐ ◑ ⊟ ♣ P

Chislet

Six Bells
Church Lane (off A28 and A299) ☎ (01227) 860373
12-3, 6.30 (6 Sat)-11
Adnams Bitter, Broadside Ⓗ**; guest beers**
Spacious, traditionally-appointed free house, with an open log fire and a large garden. It hosts occasional international food nights and a beer festival (July). Bat and trap and boules played. Eve meals Tue-Sat.
⌂ Q ❀ ◐ ◑ ▲ ♣ ⌓ P

Claygate

White Hart
On B2162 ☎ (01892) 730313
11-3, 6-11
Goacher's Light; Shepherd Neame Master Brew Bitter; Wadworth 6X Ⓗ

Splendid country pub set among orchards and hop gardens. En suite bedrooms; restaurant open daily. Wheelchair WC. ⌂ Q ❀ ⊨ ◖ ◗ ♿ ▲ ♣ ⌓ P ⊟

Cliftonville

Olde Charles
382 Northdown Road
☎ (01843) 221817
11–3, 5.30–11; 11–11 Fri & Sat
Draught Bass; Whitbread Castle Eden Ale; guest beers [H]
Not as old as it may appear, this pub is Edwardian. Its interior, though spacious, still manages to be cosy. The large garden has pot-bellied pigs. Good restaurant (booking advisable weekends).
⌂ ❀ ◖ ◗ ♣ P

Cooling

Horseshoe & Castle
Main Road ☎ (01634) 221691
11.30–3, 7 (5 Fri)–11
Beer range varies [H]
Nestled in the sleepy village of Cooling, which has Dickensian connections, this pub reputedly has a haunted cellar. Three constantly changing beers. Cider also varies but is available in winter only.
⌂ ❀ ◖ ◗ ⌓ P ⊬

Try also: Victoria Inn, Cliffe (Shepherd Neame)

Dartford

Tiger
28 Saint Albans Road (off A226) ☎ (01322) 293688
11–11
Courage Best Bitter; Everards Tiger; Shepherd Neame Master Brew Bitter; John Smith's Bitter [H]
L-shaped bar with a 'quiet end'. This busy, back-street pub tends to have a local trade eves and weekends. Several teams fielded. ◖ ♣

Wat Tyler
80 High Street
☎ (01322) 272546
10–11
Courage Best Bitter; Elgood's Cambridge Bitter; S&N Theakston Old Peculier; Young's Special; guest beer [H]
Historic, 14th-century, town-centre free house with a friendly, conversational atmosphere. Q ◖ ≹ ⌓

Try also: Paper Moon, 55 High Street (Wetherspoon's)

Deal

Saracen's Head
11 Alfred Square
10.30–11 (may vary)
Shepherd Neame Master Brew Bitter, Spitfire, Bishops Finger [H], **Porter** [G]
Large, single-bar, corner pub in an historic part of the old town. The range of Shepherd Neame beers may vary.
⌂ ⊨ ◖ ♣

Ship Inn
141 Middle Street (parallel to seafront) ☎ (01304) 372222
11–11
Bass Worthington BB, Draught Bass; Fuller's ESB; Greene King Abbot; Shepherd Neame Master Brew Bitter; guest beers [H]
Cosy pub in an old part of town. Royal Navy prints and memorabilia feature in the front bar; old beer signs in the back bar. Live music – including a pub piano. ⌂ ◖

Try also: Prince Albert, Alfred Sq (Free)

Doddington

Chequers
The Street
11–4, 7–11; 11–11 Fri & Sat
Shepherd Neame Master Brew Bitter, Bishops Finger, Spitfire (occasional) [H]
Traditional village local with two contrasting bars. It hosts motorcycle clubs and is now more popular than ever. Four friendly ghosts!
⌂ Q ☋ ❀ ◖ ⊕ ♣ P

Dover

Eagle Hotel
London Road
☎ (01304) 201543
10–11
Courage Best Bitter, Directors; John Smith's Bitter [H]
Large, two-bar, corner pub surmounted by a golden eagle statue. Large games area; occasional live music. ⊕ ♣

Old Endeavour
124 London Road
☎ (01304) 204417
11–11
Shepherd Neame Master Brew Bitter [H]
This lively town pub, hosting regular live music, backs on to the River Dour. A friendly pub, attracting a mixed clientele. Large games/meeting room. ❀ ♣

Dumpton

Brown Jug
204 Ramsgate Road
☎ (01843) 862788
11–3, 6–11
Whitbread Fremlins Bitter; guest beer [H]
Flint-walled pub of real character, reputedly a billet for officers in the Napoleonic Wars. Look for the water clock in the rear bar. The guest beer is supplied by either Bass or Whitbread. Petanque played.
⌂ Q ❀ ⊕ ≹ (Dumpton Pk)

East Farleigh

Bull Inn
Lower Road ☎ (01622) 726282
11–11
Wadworth 6X; Whitbread Fremlins Bitter; guest beers [H]
Turn-of-century pub, rebuilt following a fire. The well-used function hall is the only remaining original part. Two gardens – one has a mini-zoo.
⌂ ❀ ◖ ◗ ♿ ▲ ≹ ♣ P

East Malling

Rising Sun
125 Mill Street
☎ (01732) 843284
12–11
Goacher's Light; Harveys BB; Shepherd Neame Master Brew Bitter; Younger No.3; guest beer [H]
Family-run free house, a regular entry in the *Guide*. This terraced village pub serves a range of keenly priced beers and good value lunches.
❀ ◖ ♿ ≹

East Peckham

Harp
Hale Street ☎ (01622) 872334
11–11
Adnams Broadside; Fuller's London Pride; Harveys BB [H]
The growing display of plates, horse brasses and kettles makes this an Aladdin's cave worthy of a visit. Family-run, friendly and popular with both visitors and locals.
⌂ ❀ ◖ ◗ ♿ ▲ ≹ ♣ P

Try also: Bush, Blackbird & Thrush, Peckham Bush (Shepherd Neame)

Egerton Forstal

Queen's Arms
OS893464 ☎ (01233) 756386
11–3, 6–11
Adnams Bitter; Rother Valley Level Best; Wells Bombardier; guest beers [H]
Quiet village local, offering a range of beers from micros and independents. Dating back 150 years, the pub has two bars with beamed ceilings. Wells Bombardier is named after the landlady's father, Bombardier Billy Wells. Try

the all day breakfasts. No
lunches Tue.
🏠 Q ✿ ◑ ▌ 🍴 ♣ 🕭 P

Fairseat

Vigo Inn

Gravesend Road (A227, 1 mile
N of A20) ☎ (01732) 822547
12–3 (not Mon, except bank hols),
6–11
**Harveys XX Mild, BB;
Young's Bitter, Special; guest
beers** 🅷
Haven for ale drinkers, often
serving two milds and always
a Goacher's beer: an ancient
drovers' inn named in honour
of a local resident who fought
in the famous battle. The buzz
of conversation is only
interrupted when the
Daddlums table is used.
🏠 Q ✿ ▲ ♣ P ⅄ 🕇

Farningham

Chequers

High Street (off A20)
☎ (01322) 865222
11–11
**Fuller's London Pride, ESB;
Morland Old Speckled Hen;
Taylor Landlord; guest
beers** 🅷
Convivial, popular corner local
in a picturesque village,
offering an enterprising and
varied range of beers
(although rather pricey). Well
worth finding. Eve meals
Sun–Thu. ✿ ◑ ▌ ♣

Faversham

Crown & Anchor

41 The Mall (50 yds from A2)
☎ (01795) 532812
10.30–3 (4 Sat), 5.30 (6 Sat)–11
**Shepherd Neame Master
Brew Bitter** 🅷
Friendly pub, famous for its
doorstep sandwiches and
Hungarian goulash.
🏖 ✿ ◑ ▌ ⇌ ♣

Shipwright's Arms

Hollowshore (left at end of
Ham Road, first right)
OS017636 ☎ (01795) 590088
11–3, 7–11; 11–11 Sat
**Shepherd Neame Master
Brew Bitter, Spitfire** 🅶
Pleasantly located, 17th-
century pub at the junction of
Oare and Faversham Creeks,
popular with locals and
visiting boatsmen. No mains
water or electricity. The only
regular pub outlet for Pawley
Farm cider. Always one
Goacher's beer.
🏠 Q ✿ ◑ ▌ ♣ 🕭 P ⅄

Finglesham

Crown Inn

The Street ☎ (01304) 612555
11–3, 6–11

Courage Directors; Morland
Old Speckled Hen; Ruddles
County; Shepherd Neame
Master Brew Bitter 🅷
Popular village local with a
restaurant. A friendly,
welcoming, award-winning
pub. ✿ ◑ ▌ P

Folkestone

Clifton Hotel

Langhorne Gardens (clifftop)
☎ (01303) 851231
10.30–3, 5.45–11
**Draught Bass; Courage
Directors** 🅷
Long-standing Mecca for
Bass drinkers: a popular,
comfortable, quiet bar
and a plush lounge
overlooking the English
Channel.
Q ⅖ ✿ 🚐 ◑ ▌ ⇌ (Central)

Harvey's Wine Bar

10 Langhorne Gardens
☎ (01303) 253758
11.30–11
**Bass Worthington BB,
Draught Bass; guest beers** 🅷
Basement bar, under
Langhorne Garden Hotel, with
lots of nooks and crannies.
Biddenden cider.
🏠 ✿ ◑ ⇌ (Central) 🕭

Lifeboat

42 North Street
☎ (01303) 243958
11–3 (5 Fri), 6–11; 11–11 Sat
**Fuller's London Pride; Hall &
Woodhouse Badger BB;
Harveys Old; Ruddles
County; Wadworth 6X;
Young's Special** 🅷
Basic, single-room pub,
attracting a mixed clientele.
Regular games nights;
occasional Irish folk band.
✿ ◑ ▌ ♣

Gillingham

Barge

63 Layfield Road
☎ (01634) 850485
12–4, 7–11; 12–11 Sat
Wadworth 6X; guest beers 🅷
Candlelit pub offering
panoramic views of the River
Medway; lots of naval
artefacts hung in the bar. Mon
night is folk night. Charity
mini-beer festival in summer.
✿ ◑ ▌ ♣

King George V

1 Prospect Row, Brompton
☎ (01634) 842418
11–3, 6–11; 12–11 Sat
Draught Bass; guest beers 🅷
Friendly house in an area with
naval and military
connections, close to Fort
Amherst, the Historic
Dockyard and the Royal
Engineers' Museum. Three

guest beers. No food Sun.
Q ✿ 🚐 ◑

Will Adams

73 Saxton Street
☎ (01634) 575902
11–3, 7–11
**Fuller's London Pride; guest
beers** 🅷
Friendly, early Victorian pub
featuring some original glass;
named after Gillingham's
famous adventurer of *Shogun*
fame. Good value food.
✿ ◑ ⇌ ♣

Try also: **Falcon**, Marlborough
Rd (Free); **Mackland Arms**,
Station Rd, Rainham; **Rose
Inn**, High St, Rainham (both
Shepherd Neame)

Gravesend

Jolly Drayman

1 Love Lane, Wellington Street
(off A226) ☎ (01474) 352355
11 (12 Sat)–3, 6 (7 Sat)–11
**Bass Worthington BB,
Draught Bass; guest beers** 🅷
The only pub in Kent to have
been in every edition of the
Guide, housed in what was
originally a brewery. The
ceilings are very low – take
care. Comfortable seating and
a friendly atmosphere. Known
locally as the Coke Oven.
Lunches Mon–Fri.
✿ ◑ ♣ P

Prince Albert

26 Wrotham Road
☎ (01474) 352432
11–11
**Shepherd Neame Master
Brew Bitter, Spitfire, Porter** 🅷
Classic, two-bar, town-centre
local near the station, with a
friendly, bustling atmosphere.
🏠 ✿ ⇌ P

Somerset Arms

10 Darnley Road (one-way
system, near station)
☎ (01474) 533837
11–3.30, 5–11; 11–11 Fri & Sat
Beer range varies 🅷
Large, town-centre hostelry
furnished with church pews
and a wealth of brass pots and
tankards. Quiet lunchtime and
most early eves, but with
discos Thu–Sun. Eve meals
Mon–Thu. ◑ ▌ ⇌ ⅄

Windmill Tavern

45 Shrubbery Road, Windmill
Hill ☎ (01474) 352242
11–11; 12–3, 7.30–10.30 Sun
**Ruddles Best Bitter, County;
Webster's Yorkshire Bitter;
guest beers** 🅷
Three-bar pub in a conservation area. The garden is a
picture in summer and has a
play area for children. Truly a
country pub in the town,
pleasant both inside and out.

No Sun lunches in winter.
🏮 ◑ ▶ 🍴 ⅃ 🚭 ♣ P

Try also: New Inn, 1 Milton Rd (Whitbread)

Great Chart

Hooden Horse
The Street ☎ (01233) 625583
11–2.30, 6–11
Goacher's Light; Hook Norton Old Hooky; Hop Back Summer Lightning; S&N Theakston Old Peculier; guest beers ⒣
Hop-strewn ceilings and candelit tables feature in this tiled- and timber-floored pub. Extensive range of home cooked food of a very high standard. Live music weekly. A must if you are in the area. The first pub of four in the group. 🏮 ◑ ▶ ⌂

Green Street Green

Ship
Green Street Green Road (B260), 1½ miles E of Longfield)
☎ (01474) 702279
11–2.30, 6–11
Courage Best Bitter; Wadworth 6X; Young's Bitter, Winter Warmer; guest beers ⒣
Impressive, 17th-century building, set back on a green from the main road. Regular gourmet and speciality eves. Families welcome in the converted stables (TV and central heating). 🚶 🐕 🏮 ◑ ⅃ ♣ P

Hadlow

Fiddling Monkey
Maidstone Road (A26)
☎ (01732) 850267
11–3, 6–11; 11–11 Fri & Sat
Larkins Bitter; John Smith's Bitter; guest beers ⒣
Large, welcoming, one-bar pub with both locals and visitors. Bat and trap played. 🚶 🏮 ◑ ⅃ ♣ P

Halling

Homeward Bound
72 High Street
☎ (01634) 240743
12–3, 7–11
Shepherd Neame Master Brew Bitter, Porter ⒣
Friendly, relaxed pub in the village centre, renowned for its charity exploits. Good value lunches. No food Sun. 🚶 ◑ 🍴 ♣ P

Halstead

Rose & Crown
Otford Lane ☎ (01959) 523120
11–2.30, 4.30–11

Courage Best Bitter; Harveys Armada; Larkins Bitter; guest beer ⒣
200-year-old village local in a row of terraced cottages; a Grade II listed building. Beware: the Scrumpy Jack cider is keg. 🚶 Q 🏮 ◑ ⅃ P

Try also: Harrow Inn, Old London Road, Knockholt (Shepherd Neame)

Hawley

Papermaker's Arms
Hawley Road (A225)
☎ (01322) 224212
11–11
Fuller's London Pride; Marston's Pedigree; Morland Old Speckled Hen; Whitbread Flowers WCPA, IPA ⒣
Spacious roadhouse where the large bar is festooned with brass pots, pans, kettles, etc. Unobtrusive background music. The restaurant area can be partitioned off. Eve meals Wed–Sat. 🏮 ◑ ▶ 🅰 P

Herne Bay

Prince of Wales
173 Mortimer Street
☎ (01227) 374205
10–11
Shepherd Neame Master Brew Bitter, Bishops Finger, Porter (occasional) ⒣
Traditional back-street pub, a *Guide* regular; the previous landlord retired in 1994, and thankfully the pub has remained the same. Some good woodwork and old glass windows feature. Q 🐕 🚶 🚭 ♣

Share & Coulter
Thornden Wood Road, Greenhill (1 mile S of Greenhill roundabout, A299)
☎ (01227) 374877
11–3, 6–11
Shepherd Neame Master Brew Bitter, Bishops Finger ⒣
400-year-old cottage buildings in a country location by camping grounds. Mixed clientele; friendly surroundings. Bat & trap pitch. No food Sun. 🚶 Q 🏮 ◑ ⅃ 🚭 🅰 ♣ P

Hernhill

Red Lion
The Village Green (½ mile S of A299) ☎ (01227) 751207
11–3, 6–11; 11–11 Sat
Fuller's London Pride; Morland Old Speckled Hen; S&N Theakston Old Peculier; Shepherd Neame Master Brew Bitter; Whitbread Boddingtons Mild, Bitter ⒣
14th-century hall house, adjacent to the village green. Occasional mini-beer festivals; live jazz summer Sun. A rare outlet for mild. 🏮 ◑ ▶ 🅰 ♣ P

Hook Green

Elephant's Head
Furnace Lane (B2169)
OS655358 ☎ (01892) 890279
11 (12 Sat)–3, 5.30 (6 Sat)–11 (11–11 summer Sat)
Harveys XX Mild, Pale Ale, BB, Old, Armada ⒣
15th-century pub, almost astride the Kent/Sussex border. One of only a handful of Harvey's pubs to sell the entire range, including seasonal brews. Home-cooked food is available in both the bar and restaurant. Large garden. 🚶 Q 🏮 ◑ ▶ P

Hythe

Duke's Head
9 Dymchurch Road
☎ (01303) 266229
11–11
Draught Bass; Greene King IPA, Abbot; guest beers ⒣
Pub between the canal and Hythe Green, serving good food in large helpings. The clientele is a friendly mix of all ages. Reputedly haunted by a ghost called George. 🚶 🏮 ◑ ♣

Ightham

Old House
Redwell Lane (⅓ mile SE of village, between A25 and A227) OS590559
☎ (01732) 882383
7–11 (9 Tue); 7–11 Sat
Brakspear Bitter ⒢; **Whitbread Flowers IPA** ⒣; **guest beers** ⒢
Difficult to find pub, as there is no sign: an unspoilt part of a 16th-century house, with a large open fireplace, caught in a timewarp. At least two beers are served direct from the cask. 🚶 Q 🅰 ♣

Kemsing

Rising Sun
Cotmans Ash Lane OS563599
☎ (01959) 522683
11–3, 6–11
Morland Old Speckled Hen; Whitbread Boddingtons Mild, Fremlins Bitter, Flowers Original; guest beers ⒣
Pub whose main bar area is a converted hunting lodge, offering a step back in time. Occasional beer festivals. An ideal country pub for the family in summer, with its lovely outdoor area. Hikers

Kent

are always welcomed.
🏠 Q 🍴 🐕 ⑧ ◖ ▶ 🅰 🌲 ⌂ P

Kilndown

Globe & Rainbow
SW of Lamberhurst, off A21
OS700253 ☎ (01892) 890283
11–2.30, 6–11
**Harveys BB; Whitbread
Fremlins Bitter, Flowers IPA,
Original; Young's Special** Ⓗ
Large, traditional pub with
extensive gardens, serving
excellent home-cooked food in
the bar and restaurant (book
restaurant). A games room
with a full-length skittle alley
can be hired. Excellent range
of whiskies.
🏠 Q 🍴 ⑧ ◖ ▶ 🌲 ⌂ P

Kingsdown

King's Head
Upper Street ☎ (01304) 373915
11–2.30, 7–11; 12–2.30, 7–10.30 Sun
**Bass Worthington BB,
Draught Bass; Hancock's
HB** Ⓗ
Popular, two-bar village local,
friendly and welcoming. Meals
Wed–Sat (booking advised).
⑧ ◖ ▶ 🔄 🅰

Luddesdown

Cock Inn
Gold Street, Henley Street
OS664672 ☎ (01474) 814208
12–2.30, 5–11; 12–11 Fri & Sat
**Adnams Bitter; Ansells Mild;
Ind Coope Burton Ale** Ⓗ;
guest beers Ⓗ/Ⓖ
Deservedly well-frequented,
two-bar downland house in an
isolated downland location, although
accessible by public footpath
from Sole Street station
(1 mile). Undoubtedly one of
the best pubs in Kent. Free
scheduled bus service to
villages. No food Sun; eve
meals finish at 8.
🏠 Q ⑧ ◖ ▶ 🌲 ⌂ P

Maidstone

Greyhound
77 Wheeler Street
☎ (01622) 754032
11–3, 6–11
**Shepherd Neame Master
Brew Bitter** Ⓗ
Friendly, traditional, street-
corner pub serving Shepherd
Neame at its best (one other of
Shep's beers is also on). Live
jazz Sun lunchtime. No food
Sun. Q ⑧ ◖ 🚂 (East) 🌲 P

Hare & Hounds
45–47 Lower Boxley Road
(A229) ☎ (01622) 678388
11–3 (3.30 Fri), 5.30–11; 11.30–5, 7–11
Sat
Marston's Pedigree;

**Wadworth 6X; Whitbread
Flowers IPA; guest beer** Ⓗ
Welcoming, often busy, town
pub opposite the prison. Patio
area at the rear where
barbecues may be held. Eve
meals finish at 7. No food Sat
eve or Sun.
⑧ ◖ ▶ 🚂 (East) 🌲

Hogshead
24 Earl Street
☎ (01622) 758516
11–11
**Wadworth 6X; Whitbread
Boddingtons Bitter, Flowers
Original; Young's Special** Ⓗ;
guest beers Ⓗ/Ⓖ
Popular, busy, town-centre
pub, formerly the Druids, now
a Whitbread alehouse. Five
regular beers, plus up to four
ever-changing guest ales. No
food Sun.
🏠 ⑧ ◖ 🚂 (East) ⌂

Pilot
23–25 Upper Stone Street
(A229) ☎ (01622) 691162
11–3, 6 (7 Sat)–11
**Harveys XX Mild, BB, Old,
Armada** Ⓗ
Historic pub, a favourite for
many years. Harveys beers are
a welcome variation in the
area. Excellent selection of
home-made meals (not served
Sun); good value.
🏠 ⑧ ◖ ▶ 🌲

Wheelers Arms
1 Perry Street (off A229)
☎ (01622) 752229
12–3, 6–11; 11–11 Sat
**Shepherd Neame Master
Brew Bitter, Spitfire, Bishops
Finger, Porter** Ⓗ
Cosy, corner local, which
satisfies all tastes, with good
beer, food and company, plus
musical eves. Friendly
landlord and bar staff. No
food Mon.
⑧ ◖ ▶ 🚂 (East) 🌲

Marden

Stilebridge Inn
Staplehurst Road (A229)
☎ (01622) 831236
11–3, 6–11; 11–11 Sat
Beer range varies Ⓗ
Comfortable cocktail-style
lounge with a piano player on
Fri and Sat nights. Note the
growing collection of
pumpclips. Q ⑧ ◖ ▶ P

Margate

Everyone's Inn
Addington Street
☎ (01843) 223907
11–11
Younger IPA; guest beer Ⓗ
Friendly free house a couple of
minutes' walk from the

town centre, next to the
Theatre Royal. Formerly
known as the London Tavern,
it gained its present name on
becoming a free house.
Regular music nights.
🏠 🐕 ◖

Princess of Wales
20 Tivoli Road
☎ (01843) 223944
11–3, 6–11; 11–11 Sat
**Shepherd Neame Master
Brew Bitter, Spitfire** Ⓗ
Two-bar, corner local,
converted in the mid 1800s
from three cottages. During its
recent refurbishment the
under-used children's room
was opened out to give more
seating in one of the bars, but
it still retains its local feel.
⑧ 🌲

Quart in a Pint Pot
28 Charlotte Square
☎ (01843) 223672
11.30–3, 5.30–11; 11–11 Sat
**Draught Bass; M&B Brew XI;
guest beers** Ⓗ
A short walk from the High
Street, and away from the
busy seafront, this cosy,
expanded, back-street pub has
a pepperpot folly on the roof.
⑧ ◖

Spread Eagle
25 Victoria Road
☎ (01843) 293396
11.30–3, 5.30–11; 11–11 Fri & Sat
**Fuller's London Pride; Greene
King IPA; Young's Special;
guest beers** Ⓗ
A Victorian frontage to
Georgian premises leads into
this excellent two-bar pub,
which is busy, with a
welcoming atmosphere.
Twelve times in the *Guide*.
⑧ ◖ 🌲

Marsh Green

Wheatsheaf Inn
On B2028 ☎ (01732) 864091
11–3, 5.30–11; 11–11 Sat
**Adnams Bitter; Harveys BB;
Larkins Bitter; guest beers** Ⓗ
Popular, friendly, multi-bar
pub with a conservatory,
varied beers and disabled
facilities. Picturesque view
from the garden. 🏠 Q 🐕
⑧ ◖ ▶ 🌲 ⌂ P ♿

Marshside

Gate Inn
Boyden Gate ☎ (01227) 860498
11–2.30 (3 Sat), 6–11
**Shepherd Neame Master
Brew Bitter, Spitfire, Bishops
Finger, Porter** Ⓖ
Splendid country pub with the
same landlord for 20 years,
featuring apple trees, ducks,

quizzes, cricket, rugby, a pub
pianist, jazz and folk eves.
Beer festival Aug; Mummers
at Christmas. Accommodation
is new. Excellent food. ♨ Q
⌂ ❀ ⌑ ◑ ♿ ▲ ♣ P

Mersham

Farriers Arms
Flood Street ☎ (01233) 624218
11–2 (3.30 Sat), 6.30–11
**Ind Coope Friary Meux BB;
guest beers** Ⓗ
Popular village local with two
bars, a restaurant and a
conservatory. The garden has
a mill stream running through
it. Note the oak beams and
low doors. ♨ ⌂ ❀ ⌑ ◑ ♣ P ✄

Royal Oak
The Street ☎ (01233) 720444
11–2.30, 6–11
**Shepherd Neame Master
Brew Bitter, Spitfire** Ⓗ
Three-bar village local with a
tie collection in the saloon and
a charity collection in the
gents'. Friendly clientele of all
ages. No food Tue eve.
♨ Q ⌂ ❀ ◑ ◗ ⊞ ♣ P

Milton Regis

Three Hats
93 High Street
☎ (01795) 425016
11–3, 5.30–11; 11–11 Sat
**John Smith's Bitter; Young's
Special** Ⓗ
16th-century pub near
Sittingbourne and Kemsley
Light Railway Station. ❀ ♣

Minster (Thanet)

Saddler
7 Monkton Road
☎ (01843) 821331
10.30–2.30, 6–11; 11–11 Sat
**Shepherd Neame Master
Brew Bitter, Spitfire, Bishops
Finger, Porter** Ⓗ
Excellent, two-bar Victorian
village local giving a warm
welcome to casual visitors. Bat
and trap played. The stronger
beers rotate. Q ❀ ◑ ▲ ⇋ ♣

Oad Street

Plough & Harrow
☎ (01795) 843351
11–11
**Greene King IPA; Shepherd
Neame Master Brew Bitter;
Tetley Bitter; guest beers** Ⓗ
Popular free house with a
constantly changing range of
beers (six guests). Excellent
public bar. Cider in summer.
Camping in the car park by
arrangement.
♨ ❀ ◑ ⊞ ▲ ♣ ⌓ P

Oare

Three Mariners
2 Church Road
☎ (01795) 533633
10.30 (11 winter)–4, 6–11; 10.30 (11
winter)–11 Sat
**Shepherd Neame Master
Brew Bitter, Spitfire** Ⓗ
Rambling pub at the village
centre. The decor reflects
nautical associations with the
nearby creek.
♨ ⌂ ❀ ◑ ◗ ♣ P

Windmill
Oare Road ☎ (01795) 534291
11–3, 6–11
**Shepherd Neame Master
Brew Bitter** Ⓗ
Situated in front of a sailless
windmill, this friendly pub
welcomes visitors on the road
from Faversham. Good value
food. ❀ ◑ ♣ P

Offham

King's Arms
The Green (⅛ mile from A20)
☎ (01732) 845208
11–2.30, 6–11; 11–11 Fri & Sat
**Courage Best Bitter; Young's
Special; guest beer** Ⓗ
This splendid, low-beamed
country pub near the village
green has a reputation for
good food (not served Sun;
eve meals Tue–Fri).
♨ ❀ ◑ ♿ ▲ P

Paddlesworth

Cat & Custard Pot
OS196398 ☎ (01303) 892205
12–2.30, 7–11
**Shepherd Neame Master
Brew Bitter** Ⓗ
Rural pub filled with
memorabilia from the Battle of
Britain, including a model
aircraft hanging from the
ceiling. Beware: other Sheps
beers are kept under a cask
breather. ⌂ ❀ ◑ ♣ P

Pembury

Black Horse
High Street ☎ (01892) 822141
11–11
**Harveys BB; King & Barnes
Sussex; Wadworth 6X;
Young's Special** Ⓗ
Busy but friendly pub in the
village centre: a single large
bar with an eating area. Black
Horse Bitter is another beer
renamed (probably a national
brand). ♨ Q ❀ ◑ ♣

Penshurst

Spotted Dog
Smarts Hill (towards
Fordcombe, 2nd right, 1st left)
☎ (01892) 870253

11–2.30, 6–11
**King & Barnes Sussex;
Wadworth 6X; guest beer** Ⓗ
1520 peg-tiled, listed building,
nestling in the hillside with
one of the best views in Kent.
Built in Tonbridge, it was
floated up the river and
brought up the hill by oxen.
Inside are low oak beams, a
red tiled floor and a large
inglenook. ♨ ⌂ ❀ ◑ ◗ P

Petteridge

Hopbine
Petteridge Lane (½ mile S of
Brenchley) OS668413
☎ (01892) 722561
12 (11 Sat)–2.30, 6–11
**King & Barnes Mild, Sussex,
Broadwood, Festive** Ⓗ
Unspoilt, one-bar, warm pub
stocking the full seasonal
range of King & Barnes beers.
The many regulars include a
visiting folk group, plus other
musicians some eves. No food
Wed eve. ♨ ❀ ◑ ◗ ⌓ P

Ramsgate

Addington Arms
45 Ashburnham Road (50 yds
off A253) ☎ (01843) 591489
11–11
**Courage Directors; John
Smith's Bitter; Wadworth
6X** Ⓗ
Large, busy, back-street free
house, formerly known as the
Australian Arms, recently
refurbished. A conservatory
houses a children's room. Sky
TV. ⌂ ❀ ◑ ♣

Churchill Tavern
19–22 The Paragon
☎ (01843) 587862
11.30–11
**Courage Directors; Fuller's
London Pride; Ringwood Old
Thumper; S&N Theakston
Old Peculier; Taylor
Landlord; guest beers** Ⓗ
Beautifully restored, former
hotel bar, overlooking the
harbour; rebuilt to resemble a
country pub using old timbers
and church pews. The best
selection of beers in Thanet.
Annual beer festival. ♨ ♣

Hotel de Ville
45 Grange Road (100 yds from
B2054) ☎ (01843) 592289
4.30 (11 Fri & Sat)–11
**S&N Theakston XB;
Whitbread Boddingtons
Bitter; Younger IPA** Ⓗ
Free house on the outskirts of
town, popular with all ages. Its
name (French for town hall) is
not as incongruous as it seems:
Ramsgate was formerly
known as the 'Ville of
Ramsgate'. ⌑ ♣

Kent

Wheatsheaf

17 High Street, St Lawrence
☎ (01843) 597937
11–11
**Courage Directors; guest
beers** (occasional) H
Games-oriented pub where
standards of pool and darts
are high. This sturdy oak
beamed pub, dates from 1883,
and can get very busy.
🅰 ≢ ♣

River

Royal Oak

36 Lower Road
☎ (01304) 822073
11–11 (may close afternoons)
**Shepherd Neame Master
Brew Bitter** H
Open-plan pub created from
an original flint building and
the next door cottage; set in an
attractive residential area near
Dover. Other Shepherd Neame
beers are sometimes stocked.
◖ ≢ (Kearsney) ♣ P

Rochester

Granville Arms

83 Maidstone Road
☎ (01634) 845243
11–11
Greene King IPA, Abbot H
Unusual-shaped pub with an
inviting atmosphere and a
small, square bar. Five
minutes' walk from the castle,
cathedral and Dickensian High
Street. No food Sun.
🏚 ◖ ♣ P

Greyhound

68 Rochester Avenue
☎ (01634) 844120
10–3, 6–11; 10–11 Sat
**Shepherd Neame Master
Brew Bitter** H
Excellent, back-street local
which also sells bottle-
conditioned Spitfire. The
lounge features chaises-
longues and a kitchen range.
🏚 ♣

Man of Kent

6–8 John Street
☎ (01634) 818771
12–11
Beer range varies H
Style & Winch tile-fronted pub
with five ever-changing beers.
Goacher's beers often sold.
🏚 ❀ ≢ ♣ ○

Ship Inn

347 High Street
☎ (01634) 844264
11–11
**Courage Best Bitter; guest
beers** H
Lively, two-bar pub renowned
for its Sun lunch jazz sessions.
Live music in the theatre

lounge most eves. Once the
Lion Brewery tap – the
brewer's old house can still be
seen next door, albeit with a
modern lower storey added.
No food Sun. ❀ ◖ ≢ P

Star Inn

Star Hill ☎ (01634) 826811
11–11; closed Sun eve in winter
Beer range varies H
One-bar pub, with seven
handpumps, handy for the
station and historic Rochester
High Street. Collection of
bottled beers. ◖ ≢

Rolvenden Layne

Another Hooden Horse

26 Maytham Road (follow
signs from Tenterden to
Rolvenden, left at church)
☎ (01580) 241837
11–2.30, 6–11
**Goacher's Light; Hook
Norton Old Hooky; Hop Back
Summer Lightning; S&N
Theakston Old Peculier; guest
beers** H
Out-of-the-way village pub
consisting of one beamed bar
adorned with hops and
brewery memorabilia. Plain
wooden seating and floors.
Price premium on half pints.
❀ ◖ ▶ ○

Rusthall

Toad Rock Retreat

1 Upper Street (off A264,
1 mile W of Tunbridge Wells)
☎ (01892) 520818
11–3, 6–11; 11–11 Sat
**Adnams Bitter; Fuller's
London Pride; Greene King
IPA; Harveys BB; Whitbread
Boddingtons Mild** H; **guest
beers** G/H
Friendly, two-bar pub, dating
from the 16th century,
opposite a local landmark,
Toad Rock. Good value food,
including vegetarian dishes, is
always available. Ever-
changing selection of guest
ales. 🏚 Q ❀ ◖ ▶ ♣ P

St Margaret's at Cliffe

Cliffe Tavern

High Street ☎ (01304) 852400
10.30–11
**Greene King Abbot; Judges
Old Gavel Bender; Shepherd
Neame Master Brew Bitter,
Bishops Finger; Wadworth
6X** H
Smart pub/hotel/restaurant,
where locals and tourists are
welcomed. Live music in the
back bar/restaurant (electric
piano). 🏚 ❀ ◖ ▶ 🍴 🅰 P

Hope Inn

High Street ☎ (01304) 852444
10.30–11
**Shepherd Neame Master
Brew Bitter, Spitfire** H
18th-century pub, well
refurbished and modernised.
Popular with locals and the
tourist trade.
🏚 ❀ ◖ ▶ 🅰 ♣ P

St Nicholas at Wade

Bell

The Street (400 yds from
A28/A299 jct)
☎ (01843) 847250
11.30–3, 6.30–11
**Draught Bass; M&B Highgate
Dark; Whitbread Flowers
IPA; guest beers** H
Country pub, dating from
Tudor times, with a post-war
extension to the rear. The large
number of small rooms helps
preserve an intimate
atmosphere. The only regular
outlet for handpumped mild
in Thanet. Excellent food
(book Sat/Sun).
🏚 ❀ ◖ ▶ 🍴 ♣ P

Sandgate

Ship Inn

65 High Street (A259)
☎ (01303) 248525
11–3, 6–11
**Courage Directors; Greene
King IPA, Abbot; Whitbread
Castle Eden Ale** G
Two-bar pub backing onto the
sea and reputedly haunted by
two ghosts. Portraits of
regulars, past and present,
hang in the back bar. Good
cheap food. Casks on wooden
stillage. Q ❀ ◖ ▶ 🍴 ○

Sandhurst

New Swan

Queen Street (A268)
☎ (01580) 850260
11–3, 5 (6 Sat)–11
**Greene King XX Mild, IPA,
Harveys BB; guest beers** H
The village's only remaining
pub, enjoying a new lease of
life. Do not be put off by the
plain (mid 1950s) exterior – a
warm welcome awaits in the
one large room with a central
bar and a pool table at one end
(simply furnished at the
other). A local once again.
🏚 🐾 ❀ ◖ ▶ ♣ P

Selling

Sondes Arms

Station Road ☎ (01227) 752246
12–4.30, 7–11 (11–11 summer Sat)
**Shepherd Neame Master
Brew Bitter** H

Village local by the station, catering for all. Large garden with animals; games room. Limited parking.
🏚 ❀ ◖ ⇥ ♣ P

Sevenoaks

Halfway House

London Road (200 yds from station) ☎ (01732) 457108
11–2.30, 6 (7 Sat)–11
Greene King IPA, Rayments Special, Abbot Ⓗ
Cosy, welcoming pub dating from the 16th century. Thriving quiz teams. No-smoking restaurant area; no eve meals Sun or Mon. Greene King's seasonal ales stocked.
🏚 ❀ ◖ ◗ ⇥ ♣ P

Shatterling

Green Man

Pedding Hill (A257, Ash–Wingham road)
☎ (01304) 812525
11.15–2.30 (3 Sat), 6.30 (4.30 Sat)–11; 12–3 Sun, closed Sun eve
Shepherd Neame Master Brew Bitter; Young's Bitter Ⓗ
Isolated pub in a very attractive, rural setting, drawing local, passing and tourist trades. Pub games' histories and explanations are displayed. Bat and trap in the garden. ❀ 🏚 ◖ ◗ ▲ ♣ P

Sheerness

Blacksmith's Arms

55 Clyde Street
☎ (01795) 662611
11–11
Shepherd Neame Spitfire or **Bishops Finger** (summer) or **Porter** Ⓗ
Friendly, quiet, back-street terraced local. Pool and darts played; regular quiz nights.
❀ ⛟ ♣

Red Lion

61 High Street, Bluetown
☎ (01795) 663165
12–3, 6 (8 Sat)–11; 12–3, 8–10.30 Sun
Greene King Abbot; guest beers Ⓗ
Welcoming unspoilt, quiet, two-bar pub. Good value snacks Mon–Fri lunch. The house beer is brewed by Greene King. Q ⊞ ⇥

Ship on Shore

155 Marine Parade
☎ (01795) 662880
12–3, 7–11
Draught Bass; Whitbread Boddingtons Bitter; guest beers Ⓗ
Popular pub with locals and passing trade; always a mixed clientele. Good food selection.

Note the unusual grotto in the car park. 🏚 ❀ ◖ ◗ P

Shoreham

Royal Oak

2 High Street
☎ (01959) 522319
10.30–3, 6–11
Adnams Bitter, Broadside; Brakspear Bitter; Whitbread Fremlins Bitter; guest beers Ⓗ
Highly recommended, two-bar pub in the centre of an attractive country village. The hub of local life; cartoons of local characters are displayed on the walls. Ramblers and other visitors welcomed. Unusual games include Toad in the Hole and Tripletell. Guest beers usually include a mild.
🏚 Q ❀ ◖ ◗ ⊞ ⇥ ♣ ⛀

Sittingbourne

King's Head

38 London Road
☎ (01795) 423177
11.30–2.30, 5–11; 11–11 Sat
Webster's Yorkshire Bitter; guest beers Ⓗ
Enterprising free house on the western edge of town. Theobolds cider, plus six guest ales, most from independent brewers, including Goacher's.
❀ ⇥ ⛀ P

Old Oak

68 East Street
☎ (01795) 472685
10.30–2.30, 7–11
Whitbread Flowers IPA; guest beer Ⓗ
Friendly, unspoilt local near the town centre, offering an ever-changing guest ale.
❀ ◖ ⇥

Ship Inn

22 East Street
☎ (01795) 425087
11–3 (4 Fri & Sat), 6.30–11
Courage Best Bitter; John Smith's Bitter; guest beer Ⓗ
Popular, town pub retaining two bars. The guest beer is usually sold at an attractive lower price. Keen local community spirit.
◖ ⊞ ⇥ P

Snargate

Red Lion

On B2080 ☎ (01797) 344648
11–3, 7–11
Bateman XB; Harveys Old; guest beers Ⓖ
Very unusual drinkers' pub with a surprise in every corner. The large garden has animals and many flowers. A must if in the area.
🏚 Q ⛟ ❀ ♣ ⛀ P

Stalisfield

Bowl

Egg Hill Road, Charing
OS950514 ☎ (01233) 712256
12–3 (not Sept–May), 6–11; 12–11 Fri & Sat
King & Barnes Sussex; guest beers Ⓗ
Remote, 16th-century inn with a large inglenook. CAMRA Kent (joint) *Pub of the Year* 1994. Constantly changing range of guest ales.
🏚 ❀ ▲ ♣ P

Stansted

Black Horse

Tumblefield Road (1 mile NE of A20) ☎ (01732) 822355
11–2.30, 6 (7 winter)–11
Larkins Bitter; Whitbread Fremlins Bitter; guest beers Ⓗ
Regular *Guide* entry with long-standing licensees. The centre of village life, also acting as the post office. An excellent base for walkers (several paths converge here). A timeless rural retreat.
🏚 Q ❀ ◖ ◗ ▲ ♣ ⛀ P

Staplehurst

Lord Raglan

Chart Hill Road (⅓ mile N of A229 at Cross-at-Hand)
OS786472 ☎ (01622) 843747
12–3, 6–11
Brakspear Special; Goacher's Light or **Dark; Harveys BB; Whitbread Fremlins Bitter; guest beers** Ⓗ
Unspoilt, rural, beamed pub, well worth finding. The bar area is decorated with hops. Good range of beers; the guest is usually strong. Good food at reasonable prices (not served Sun eve). Children welcome. Cider in summer.
🏚 Q ❀ ◖ ◗ ♿ ⛀ P

Staplestreet

Three Horseshoes

☎ (01227) 750842
11–3 (4.30 Sat), 5–11; 11–11 Fri
Shepherd Neame Master Brew Bitter Ⓖ
Unspoilt Kentish pub with a list of landlords dating back to 1690. Good for games. Eve meals end early.
🏚 Q ❀ ◖ ◗ ▲ ♣ P

Stone

Bricklayer's Arms

62 London Road (A226)
☎ (01322) 284552
11–11
Beer range varies Ⓗ
Small, welcoming, terraced

pub on the eastern fringe of Dartford, serving three regularly changing beers of different strengths. Live music most Sat eves. Younger/ family clientele eves.
🏠 ◑ ♣

Stone Street

Padwell Arms
1 mile S of A25, between Seal and Ightham OS569551
☎ (01732) 761532
12–3, 6–11
Hall & Woodhouse Badger BB, Tanglefoot; Hook Norton Old Hooky; guest beers Ⓗ
Warm and welcoming old pub overlooking an apple orchard. Its large range of beers contributed to its awards, Kent CAMRA *Pub of the Year* 1994, and joint *Pub of the Year* 1995. Convenient for Ightham Mote. Eve meals Thu and Fri.
🏠 🏵 ◑ ▶ ♣ 🍽 P

Strood

Riverside Tavern
8 Canal Road (off A2, opp. Civic Centre)
☎ (01634) 719949
11–11
Caledonian 80/-; guest beers Ⓗ
Pub affectionately known as the Red Brick, boasting panoramic views of Rochester Castle and Cathedral across the river. Four constantly changing beers.
🏵 ◑ ▶ 🍺 ⇌ ♣

Sutton At Hone

Ship
218 Main Road
☎ (01322) 863387
11–3, 5–11; 11–11 Sat
Courage Best Bitter; guest beers Ⓗ
Comfortable village pub with a spacious bar, divided into a boisterous public bar area (focusing on pool and darts) and a quieter saloon bar for the conversational drinker and quiz teams.
🏠 🏵 ⇌ (Farnham Rd) ♣

Tenterden

White Lion Hotel
High Street
☎ (01580) 765077
11–11
Draught Bass; Harveys BB, Old Ⓗ
Large, former coaching inn, now part of a chain. Comfortable front bar. Opposite Kent and East Sussex Steam Railway station.
🏠 🚲 🏵 🏠 ◑ ▶ P

Tilmanstone

Ravens Inn
Upper Street ☎ (01304) 617337
11–2.30, 7–11
Hancock's HB; Whitbread Boddingtons Bitter; guest beers Ⓗ
Refurbished and extended village local, popular with the farming community. Skittle alley. Book eve meals.
🏠 🏵 ◑ ▶ ♣ P

Try also: Plough & Harrow, Sandwich Rd (Free)

Tonbridge

Stag's Head
9 Stafford Road
☎ (01732) 352017
12–3, 6–11; 11–11 Sat
Butcombe Bitter; Taylor Best Bitter; Whitbread Flowers IPA Ⓗ
Friendly, single-bar, back-street pub by Tonbridge Castle. A pool table and other games are available. Note the interesting collection of clocks. The music is sometimes loud.
🏵 ⇌ ♣ P

Try also: Royal Oak, Lower Haysden (Free)

Tudeley

George & Dragon
Five Oak Green Road (B2161, W of Five Oak Green)
☎ (01892) 832521
11–3, 6–11
Greene King IPA, Rayments Special, Abbot Ⓗ
Active, two-bar pub, held up by beams believed to be from a sister ship of the *Mary Rose*. It fields many teams, including crib and bat and trap. New children's play area to the rear; colourful aviary. No food Mon eve. 🏠 🏵 ◑ ▶ 🍺 P

Tunbridge Wells

Bedford Hotel
2 High Street
☎ (01892) 526580
11–11; closed Sun
Greene King IPA, Rayments Special, Abbot Ⓗ
Single-bar, corner pub, opposite the station and close to the Pantiles. Popular with both office workers and shoppers alike during the day, and commuters and regulars eves. Greene King seasonal beers stocked. Note the mild is kept under gas. ◑ ⇌ ♣

Crystal Palace
69 Camden Road
☎ (01892) 548412
11–3 (4 Sat), 7–11

Harveys XX Mild, Pale Ale, BB, Old, Armada (summer) Ⓗ
The only Harveys tied pub in Tunbridge Wells, this Victorian pub is popular with office workers at lunchtime and regulars eves. No food Sun. 🏠 🏵 ♣

Try also: Grapevine, 8 Chapel Place (Free)

Underriver

White Rock
Carters Hill ☎ (01732) 833112
12–3, 6–11
Harveys BB; Marston's Pedigree; guest beers Ⓗ
Attractive, two-bar pub in a quaint village: a cosy saloon with a no-smoking restaurant attached, plus a games room/public bar.
🏠 Q 🏵 ◑ ▶ ♣ P

Upper Upnor

Tudor Rose
29 High Street
☎ (01634) 715305
12–3, 7–11
Young's Bitter, Special; guest beers Ⓗ
Friendly, multi-roomed pub, near Upnor Castle and overlooking the River Medway. Use the village car park. No food Sun.
🏠 🚲 🏵 ◑ ♣

West Malling

Five Pointed Star
100 High Street (off A20/A228) ☎ (01732) 842192
11–11
Greene King XX Mild, IPA, Rayments Special, Abbot Ⓗ
Spacious country town pub where recent renovations have revealed concealed internal features. Food is available from 9am to 10pm Mon–Sat, plus Sun during licensed hours. A comprehensive menu offers good value meals with nothing too pretentious.
🏠 🏵 ◑ ⇌ P

Joiner's Arms
64 High Street
☎ (01732) 840723
11–3, 5–11; 11–11 Fri & Sat
Shepherd Neame Master Brew Bitter, Bishops Finger Ⓗ
Log fires in both the small but cosy bars make this a friendly, warming port of call in an unspoilt town. No food Sun.
🏠 🏵 ◑ ⇌ ♣

Whitstable

Alberres
Sea Street ☎ (01227) 273400
11.30–4, 7–11; 11.30–11 Fri & Sat

Ind Coope Burton Ale; Tetley Bitter; guest beer Ⓗ
A true local. Note the Tomson & Wotton etched windows, also the level to which the sea has penetrated the bar. Friendly and welcoming.
♣

Noah's Ark
83 Canterbury Road (A290)
☎ (01227) 272332
11–3, 6–11
Shepherd Neame Master Brew Bitter Ⓗ
Basic, two-bar pub run by the same landlord for over 30 years.
⊛ ◑ 🍴 🚆 ♣

Tankerton Arms
Marine Parade, Tower Hill
☎ (01227) 272024
12–11
Fuller's London Pride; Shepherd Neame Master Brew Bitter; guest beers Ⓗ
Circa 1900 former hotel, overlooking Tankerton Slopes with panoramic views of the Thames Estuary. Its pleasant,

family atmosphere appeals to local and holiday trades. Note the carvings in the second bar.
🏨 Q 🛇 ⊛ ◑ 🍴 & ♣

Try also: Marine Hotel, Marine Parade (Shepherd Neame)

Willesborough

Hooden Horse on the Hill
Silver Hill Road (Hythe road from Ashford, left at windmill)
☎ (01233) 662226
11–2.30, 6–11
Goacher's Light; Hook Norton Old Hooky; Hop Back Summer Lightning; S&N Theakston Old Peculier; guest beers Ⓗ
Basically furnished, stone-floored, candlelit pub with several areas, all festooned in hop bines. Mexican influenced blackboard menu. Two ever-changing guest beers from independents and micros. Large garden.
⊛ ◑ 🍴 ⇲ P

Wormshill

Blacksmith's Arms
The Street (B2163 from Sittingbourne)
☎ (01622) 884386
12–2.30 (3 summer; not winter Wed & Thu), 7 (6 summer)–11
Fuller's London Pride; Shepherd Neame Master Brew Bitter; guest beer Ⓗ
Traditional country pub dating from the 16th century. Note the Watney's Red Barrel sign. No eve meals Tue or Sun.
🏨 ⊛ ◑ 🍴 A P

Worth

St Crispin
The Street (off A258)
☎ (01304) 612081
11–2.30, 6–11
Beer range varies Ⓗ/Ⓖ
Popular old village local, carefully refurbished and extended. The restaurant is popular. Accommodation is in chalets. 🏨 Q ⊛ 🛏 ◑ 🍴 ♣ P

Try also: Blue Pigeons, The Street (Free)

MAKE MINE MILD

Every May CAMRA activists don their flat caps, take their whippets for a walk to the pub and sit quietly in the corner sipping a half of mild.

Well that's how the satirists would no doubt put it. For May is Mild Month in CAMRA; the time of year when the Campaign seeks to raise the profile of a much maligned type of ale.

The aim of this annual celebration is to rubbish the old-man, cloth-cap silly stereotype of a mild drinker and to promote instead the positive qualities of this classic beer style. Mild, contrary to common perception, is not always a dark beer. There are light milds, too. The 'mildness' referred to in the name reflects the lower hop rate and consequently lower bitterness offered by these beers. Most milds are also lower in alcohol than standard bitters, though some powerful, heavy milds have come to the fore in recent years. These have included Sarah Hughes Original Dark Ruby Mild and Gale's Festival Mild.

It seems that some brewers have themselves been put off by the name 'mild' and its daft connotations. McMullen changed the name of AK Mild to Original AK a few years back, Guernsey LBA Mild is now known as Braye Ale, M&B Highgate Mild is today paraded as High-gate Dark and Banks's Mild, one of the country's most successful examples, is now marketed simply as Banks's.

But this quest for street cred should not detract from the real quality of such beers themselves. Drinkers looking for a refreshing, tasty and not overpowering drink could do a lot worse, as its fans in the mild hotbeds of the Midlands and the North-West already know.

Don't be put off by the name: make yours mild, too.

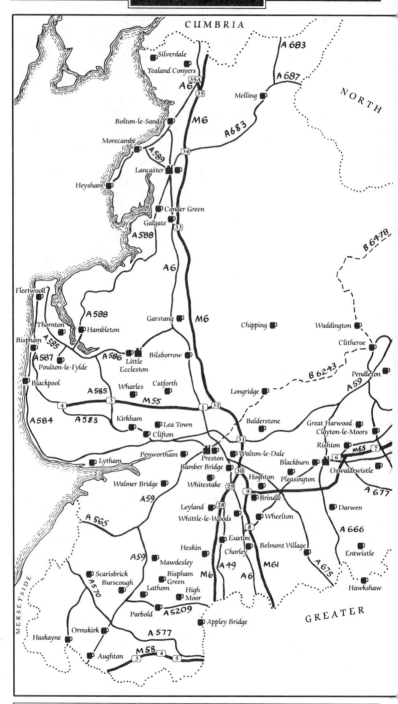

Lancashire

CUMBRIA

Silverdale
Yealand Conyers
A6
35A
35
Melling
A 683
A 687
NORTH
Bolton-le-Sands
M6
A 683
Morecambe
34
A 589
Lancaster
Heysham
Conder Green
Galgate
33
A 588
A6
M6
Garstang
Chipping
Waddington
B 6478
Fleetwood
A 588
Clitheroe
Thornton
Hambleton
Bispham
A 595
A 586
Bilsborrow
Little
Eccleston
B 6243
Pendleton
A 587
Poulton-le-Fylde
Catforth
Longridge
A 59
Blackpool
Wharles
A 585
M 55
Balderstone
Great Harwood
Clayton-le-Moors
4
3
1
32
Rishton
M 65
7
A 584
A 583
Kirkham
Lea Town
Clifton
6
Penwortham
Walton-le-Dale
Blackburn
Oswaldtwistle
Lytham
Preston
Bamber Bridge
31
A 677
Walmer Bridge
Whitestake
30
Hoghton
Pleasington
A 59
Leyland
29
Brindle
9
Darwen
Whittle-le-Woods
28
Wheelton
A 666
Heskin
8
Euxton
Belmont Village
Entwistle
A 59
Mawdesley
Chorley
M 61
A 675
Scarisbrick
Bispham
Green
M6
A 49
A6
Hawkshaw
Burscough
Lathom
High
Moor
A 570
Parbold
A 5209
GREATER
Haskayne
Ormskirk
Appley Bridge
A 577
MERSEYSIDE
Aughton
M 58
3
4
5

Hart, Little Eccleston; **Little Avenham,** Preston; **Mitchell's,** Lancaster; **Moorhouse's,** Burnley; **Porter,** Haslingden; **Thwaites,** Blackburn

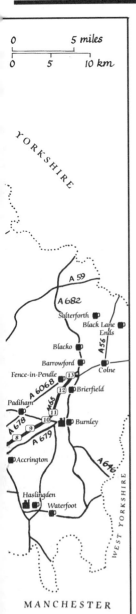

0 — 5 miles
0 — 5 — 10 km

YORKSHIRE

A 59

A 682

Salterforth

Black Lane Ends

Blacko

Barrowford

Fence-in-Pendle

A 6068

Brierfield

Padiham

A 678

Burnley

A 679

Accrington

A 646

Haslingden

Waterfoot

WEST YORKSHIRE

MANCHESTER

Lancashire

Accrington

George Hotel
185 Blackburn Road (A677)
☎ (01254) 383441
12–11
**Ruddles Best Bitter;
Webster's Yorkshire Bitter;
guest beers** Ⓗ
Open-plan, friendly local near
the college, with a bistro and a
conservatory (food all day
Sun). Seven changing beers.
✿ ⌂ ◖ ▶ ⇌ ⌓

King's Arms
26 Lee Street ☎ (01254) 234030
11–11
**John Smith's Bitter; guest
beer** Ⓗ
Modernised, friendly, one-
roomed town-centre pub.
✿ ⇌ ♣

Nag's Head
78 Blackburn Road
☎ (01254) 233965
11–11
Thwaites Best Mild, Bitter Ⓗ
Small, three-roomed local with
a varied clientele. Thwaites
seasonal beers sold. ✿ ⇌ ♣

Appley Bridge

Wheatsheaf
287 Miles Lane
☎ (01257) 252302
12–3.30, 5.30–11
Greenalls Mild, Bitter Ⓗ
Comfortable pub in a semi-
rural area. Mugs and jugs
adorn the ceiling. Excellent
value food. ✿ ◖ ▶ ⊟ ⇌ P

Aughton

Dog & Gun
223 Long Lane
☎ (01695) 423303
5–11; 12–3, 5–11 Sat; 12–2, 7–10.30
Sun
**Burtonwood Mild, Bitter,
Forshaw's** Ⓗ
Excellent village local: a pub
for a quiet pint and
conversation. A central bar
serves two lounges. Bowling
green at the rear.
🏨 Q ✿ ⇌ (Aughton Pk)
♣ P

Royal Oak
134 Liverpool Road (A59)
☎ (01695) 422121
11.30–3.30, 5–11
**Ind Coope Burton Ale; Tetley
Walker Mild, Bitter** Ⓗ
Attractive, popular local
where comfortable drinking
areas surround a central bar.
The original stained-glass
windows are well preserved.
Bowling green to the rear.
Varied lunch menu.
🏨 ✿ ◖ ⊟ ♿ ⇌ (Aughton
Pk) ♣ P

Balderstone

Myerscough
Whalley Road (A59)
☎ (01254) 812222
11.30–3, 5.30–11
**Robinson's Hatters Mild, Best
Bitter** Ⓗ
Pleasant country inn which
relies on passing trade: a cosy,
wood-panelled lounge and
another small room. Eve meals
finish at 8.30. One other
Robinson's beer is stocked.
🏨 Q ✿ ⌂ ◖ ▶ P

Bamber Bridge

Olde Original Withy
Trees
157 Station Road
☎ (01772) 30396
11–11
Burtonwood Bitter Ⓗ
Locals' pub which can get
busy. A recently refurbished,
former farmhouse, it has a
strong darts following.
Q ⪧ ✿ ◖ ⇌ P

Barrowford

Old Bridge Inn
146 Gisburn Road
☎ (01282) 613983
3 (7 Tue, 2 Fri)–11; 11–11 Sat
**Robinson's Old Stockport
Bitter, Best Bitter** Ⓗ
Cosy, welcoming village pub.
The Hartley & Bell windows
are of historic interest.
🏨 ✿ ♿ ♣ P

White Bear
Gisburn Road
☎ (01282) 615646
11–3, 5.30–11; 11–11 Sat
**Bass Special, Worthington
BB; guest beer** Ⓗ
The datestone on the front
reads 1607, but records show
this comfortable pub was built
in 1667. Good home-made
food (restaurant). Q ◖ ▶ ♣ P

Belmont Village

Black Dog
2 Church Street
☎ (01204) 811218
12–4 (3 Tue & Wed), 7–11
Holt Mild, Bitter Ⓗ
Popular, homely, moorland
village pub on the old
Preston–Bolton road: multi-
roomed and well decorated
with antiques, with no
jukebox. The only Holt's in
Lancs. Eve meals Mon and
Tue for residents only.
🏨 Q ⪧ ✿ ⌂ ◖ ▶ ♣ P

Bilsborrow

White Bull
Garstang Road (A6)
☎ (01995) 640324

Lancashire

12 (3 winter)–11
S&N Matthew Brown Mild, Theakston Best Bitter; guest beer H
Unspoilt, quiet pub by the Lancaster Canal.
🏠 Q ✿ ♣ P ❒

Bispham

Bispham Hotel
Red Bank Road (by Sainsbury's) ☎ (01253) 351752
11–3 (4 Sat), 6 (7 Sat)–11
Samuel Smith OBB H
Ornate, old-fashioned pub staging live entertainment. Its thriving social club has over 400 members. No food Mon.
Q ◖ ⊖ (Red Bank Rd)

Old England
226 Red Bank Road (off A587) ☎ (01253) 591006
11–11
Tetley Walker Mild, Bitter; Whitbread Boddingtons Bitter H
Popular local offering baby-changing facilities. A pleasant, airy pub with plenty of standing room.
👶 ✿ ◖ ⊞ ♣ P

Bispham Green

Eagle & Child
Malt Kiln Lane ☎ (01257) 462297
12–3, 5.30–11
S&N Theakston Best Bitter; Whitbread Boddingtons Bitter; guest beers H
Fine village local with a good reputation for food.
🏠 Q ✿ ◖ ▶ P

Blackburn

Florence Hotel
149 Moss Street (opp. new TA barracks) ☎ (01254) 53100
11–2, 5 (6 Mon)–11; 11–11 Fri & Sat
Thwaites Best Mild, Bitter, Craftsman H
Popular pub recently refurbished to provide a games area, a concert area and a semi-open-plan bar room. A Thwaites *Best Beer Garden* award-winner. No food Sun eve. Thwaites seasonal brews stocked. ✿ ◖ ▶ ♣

Navigation Inn
Canal Street, Mill Hill ☎ (01254) 53230
10.30–11
Thwaites Best Mild, Bitter H
Well-patronised, traditional local, next to the Leeds & Liverpool Canal. Cheap beer.
⊞ ≋ (Mill Hill) ♣

Wellington Inn
362 Livesey Branch Road ☎ (01254) 201436

2 (12 Sat)–11
Whitbread Boddingtons Bitter, Flowers IPA, Winter Royal or **Morland Old Speckled Hen** H
Well-designed, corner pub where the emphasis is on entertainment; thrice-weekly sing-alongs. 🏠 ✿ ⊞ ♣

Black Lane Ends

Hare & Hounds
Skipton Old Road (3 miles from Colne centre, past the Golf Club) OS928432 ☎ (01282) 863070
12–3 (not Tue or Thu), 7–11
Taylor Mild, Golden Best, Landlord H
Cosy, friendly inn on the Pennines. Good value home-cooked food (no meals Tue eve). Book to camp.
🏠 Q ✿ ◖ ▶ ▲ ♣ P

Blacko

Cross Gaits
Beverley Road (down side of school) ☎ (01282) 616312
12–3 (not Mon–Wed), 5.30 (6 Sat)–11
Burtonwood Mild, Bitter, Top Hat H
Perfect example of an unspoilt, traditional country pub; warm and comfortable.
🏠 Q ✿ ◖ ▶ ♣ P

Blackpool

Counting House
10 Talbot Square (opp. North Pier) ☎ (01253) 290879
10.30–11
Cains Bitter; Whitbread Boddingtons Bitter; guest beers H
Converted from a former bank, a very busy pub at weekends. Food served until 7.45 daily and all day Sun. The family room closes at 8.
👶 ◖ ▶ ♿ ≋ (North) ✄

Empress Hotel
59 Exchange Street ☎ (01253) 751347
11–11 (1am Fri & Sat in summer)
Thwaites Best Mild, Bitter H
Spacious, Victorian, old-fashioned, basic hotel with a large games room, dance floor and Wurlitzer organ. Lancashire's only ever-present *Guide* entry.
👶 🛏 ⊞ ♿ ≋ (North) ♣

Hogshead
139 Church Street (near Winter Gardens) ☎ (01253) 26582
11–11
Whitbread Boddingtons Bitter, Trophy, Castle Eden Ale H; **guest beers** H/G
Basic popular Whitbread ale house, full of Blackpool FC

memorabilia. Wholesome food. Up to 13 guest beers. Difficult parking.
🏠 ◖ ≋ (North) ♺

Pump & Truncheon
13 Bonny Street (behind Promenade) ☎ (01253) 21869
11–11
Whitbread Boddingtons Mild, Bitter; guest beers H
Pub near the Central Pier where tourists are as welcome as locals. Ever-changing range of beers. 🏠 ◖ ♣

Raikes Hall
Liverpool Road (off Church St) ☎ (01253) 294372
11 (10.30 summer)–11
Bass Mild, Worthington BB, Draught Bass; Stones Best Bitter; guest beer H
Built in 1750 as part of the Raikes Hall Estate, and once a Catholic convent, this large elegantly furnished pub is home to bowls tournaments. One of Blackpool's finest. Popular games room; resident jazz club. Meals till 7.30; children welcome.
✿ ◖ ▶ ⊞ ♿ ♣ P

Ramsden Arms Hotel
204 Talbot Road (A586, by station) ☎ (01253) 23215
10.30–11
Cains Bitter; Ind Coope Burton Ale; Jennings Bitter; Tetley Walker Dark Mild, Bitter; guest beers H
Large, black and white-fronted, award-winning gem with a fine display of tankards and other memorabilia. Four ever-changing guest beers.
👶 🛏 ◖ ⊞ ≋ (North) ♣ P ✄

Saddle Inn
286 Whitegate Drive (A583/Preston old road jct) ☎ (01253) 798900
12 (11.30 Fri & Sat)–11
Bass Mild, Worthington BB, Draught Bass; guest beers H
Small, but cosy, three-roomed, popular local; the oldest continuously licensed house in Blackpool (1776). Excellent value food.
🏠 Q ✿ ◖ P ✄ ❒

Wheatsheaf
192 Talbot Road (A856, opp. station) ☎ (01253) 25062
10.30–11
S&N Theakston Mild, Best Bitter, XB, Old Peculier; guest beer H
Lively, friendly corner local, with a touch of sophistication – a chandelier in the lounge. Simple bar snacks of sandwiches and jacket spuds baked on a log fire.
🏠 ≋ (North) ♣

Bolton-le-Sands

Royal

Main Road (A6)
☎ (01524) 732057
11–11
Mitchell's Original, Lancaster Bomber Ⓗ
1902 building completely knocked through in the mid-1980s but retaining separate dining, lounge and games areas around a central bar. A local most of the year; influx from nearby caravan sites in summer. ⊛ ◖ ▶ ♣ P

Brierfield

Poultry Fanciers' WMC

39 Railway View
☎ (01282) 612404
7.30 (8 Sat)–11
Burtonwood Bitter; Moorhouse's Premier Ⓗ
Fine example of a well-run CIU club. Show the *Guide* or a CAMRA membership card to gain entry. ৬ ⇌ ♣ P

Waggon & Horses

Colne Road (off M65 jct 12)
☎ (01282) 613962
11.30–2.30, 5–11; 11.30–11 Fri & Sat
Thwaites Best Mild, Bitter Ⓗ
Multi-roomed, traditional local, a former CAMRA *Best Refurbished Pub* award-winner. It boasts an antique Italian marble fireplace in the library room. ᴍ Q ⊛ ◖ ▶ ৬ ⇌ ♣ P

Brindle

Cavendish Arms

Sandy Lane ☎ (01254) 852912
11–3, 5.30–11
Burtonwood Bitter Ⓗ
Outstanding traditional village pub displaying stained-glass and wood carving installed in the 1930s. Close to Hoghton Towers. Children welcome at mealtimes. ᴍ Q ъ ⊛ ◖ ▶ ৬ ♣ P

Burnley

Mechanics (Shuttle Bar)

Mechanics Institute, Manchester Road
☎ (01282) 30055
11–3, 5.30 (6.30 Fri & Sat)–11; closed Mon
Moorhouse's Pendle Witches Brew; John Smith's Bitter; Thwaites Bitter; guest beers Ⓗ
Popular town-centre bar in an arts centre. Most guest beers come from micros. Good mix of clientele.
৬ ⇌ (Manchester Rd) P

Sparrow Hawk Hotel

Church Street
☎ (01282) 421551
11–3, 6–11; 11–11 Sat
Moorhouse's Premier, Pendle Witches Brew; S&N Theakston Best Bitter; guest beers Ⓗ
Excellent, well-run hotel bar with a coaching inn atmosphere. Good range of home-cooked meals. Guest beer from independent breweries; house beer from Moorhouse's.
ᴍ ⇔ ◖ ▶ ⇌ (North) ♣ P

Tim Bobbin

319 Padiham Road (100 yds from M65 jct 10)
☎ (01282) 424165
11–11
Samuel Smith OBB Ⓗ
Large, thriving, main road pub, hosting entertainment Wed night. An active social club organises regular outings. Games room. ⊛ ৬ ♣ P

Wheatsheaf

112 Colne Road
☎ (01282) 421120
12–5, 7–11
Moorhouse's Premier; John Smith's Bitter Ⓗ
Small, single-room main road pub – a 'drinkers' boozer'. ♣

Burscough

Martin Inn

Martin Lane, Drummersdale (¾ mile from B5242, near Bescar Village) ☎ (01704) 892302
11.30–3, 5.30–11
Draught Bass; Tetley Walker Dark Mild, Bitter; Walker Best Bitter; Whitbread Boddingtons Bitter; guest beers Ⓗ
Remote, welcoming inn, near Martin Mere Wildfowl Trust and the Leeds & Liverpool Canal, with a large, stone-floored bar area. Good choice of food; adjoining restaurant.
ᴍ ⊛ ⇔ ◖ ▶ ⚘ P

Catforth

Running Pump

Catforth Road (off B5269)
☎ (01772) 690265
11.30–3, 6–11; 11–11 Sat
Robinson's Hatters Mild, Hartleys XB, Best Bitter Ⓗ, **Old Tom** (winter) Ⓖ
Charming country pub of character, serving excellent, home-cooked food (new restaurant). One of the oldest pubs in rural Fylde.
ᴍ Q ⊛ ◖ ▶ ৬ ♣ P

Chipping

Sun Inn

Windy Street ☎ (01995) 61206

11–11
Whitbread Boddingtons Mild, Bitter Ⓗ
Refurbished stone pub in the centre of a cheese-making village: a base for local football and cricket teams. Food served all day until late. Public car park nearby.
ᴍ Q ⊛ ◖ ▶ ৬ ♣

Chorley

Malt 'n' Hops

50–52 Friday Street (200 yds from station)
☎ (01257) 260967
12–11
Wilson's Mild, Webster's Yorkshire Bitter; Whitbread Boddingtons Bitter; guest beers Ⓗ
Single-bar pub of character, furnished with finds from Lancashire's antique dealers. The bar counter was constructed from church pews. The exterior design is unusual for the area. Five guest beers.
⇌

Railway

20–22 Steeley Lane
☎ (01257) 266962
12–11
Draught Bass; S&N Theakston Best Bitter; Stones Best Bitter; guest beers Ⓗ
Lively local decorated in mock Edwardian style with a single bar and large alcoves. A local CAMRA award-winner. Regularly changing guest mild. ᴍ ⇌ ♣

Shepherd's Arms

38 Eaves Lane (1 mile E of centre) ☎ (01257) 275659
12–11
S&N Matthew Brown Mild, Bitter, Theakston Best Bitter; Younger No.3 Ⓗ
Recently renovated, impressive, brick local with a main bar and alcoves. Betting shop at the rear. Close to Leeds & Liverpool Canal Bridge 66. Renowned for its mild.
Q ♣

Tut 'n' Shive

Market Street (opp. Town Hall) ☎ (01257) 262858
11–11
Whitbread Boddingtons Bitter, Castle Eden Ale, Flowers Original; guest beers Ⓗ
Formerly the Royal Oak; the name of the original owners, Chester's, can still be seen in the external tilework. Inside is a split-level bar with a downstairs bar open at weekends. Six regular guests, often including unusual independent beers (can be pricey). ◖ ⇌ ♣

Lancashire

White Bull

135 Market Street
☎ (01257) 275300
11–11
S&N Matthew Brown Mild, Bitter, Theakston Best Bitter; guest beer (weekends) Ⓗ
Well-renovated town-centre pub: a wood panelled, L-shaped seating area and a games alcove. Note the Lion Ales window in the bar. Busy weekends.
❀ ◖ ≢ ♠

Clayton-le-Moors

Wellington Hotel

Barnes Square
☎ (01254) 235762
2 (12 Sat)–11
Thwaites Best Mild, Bitter Ⓗ
Large, multi-roomed local; semi open-plan, with a tap room. ♠

Clifton

Windmill Tavern

Station Road (off A583, close to BNFL works)
☎ (01772) 687203
11–3, 6.30–11; 11–11 Sat (12–3, 7–11 Mon–Sat in winter)
Mitchell's Original, Lancaster Bomber Ⓗ
Based on one of rural Fylde's many old windmills; over 300 years old, but only a pub since 1974. The lounge was once the grain store. The games room is part of the original mill. Good value brews sold.
♨ ⏱ ❀ ◖ ♣ P

Clitheroe

New Inn

Parson Lane (B6243)
☎ (01200) 23212
11–11
Moorhouse's Black Cat Mild, Premier; guest beers Ⓗ
Friendly, multi-roomed, comfortable local, opposite the castle. Folk Fri; jam sessions Sun. The house beer is Flowers IPA.
♨ Q ⏱ ❀ ◖ ▶ ⚘ ≢ ♠

Colne

Golden Ball

Burnley Road
☎ (01282) 861862
12–11
Tetley Walker Mild, Bitter; guest beers Ⓗ
Popular roadside inn offering high quality, value for money food. The well maintained garden incorporates a children's zoo. Open Sun afternoon for meals.
⏱ ❀ ◖ ▶ ⚘ ♣ P

Conder Green

Stork

On A588 ☎ (01524) 751234
11–11
Tetley Walker Bitter; Whitbread Boddingtons Bitter; guest beers Ⓗ
This long, panelled and beamed building has a large restaurant, a plush lounge, a snug (children welcome), and a pool room. Handy for the Lune Estuary path. Meals all day Sun. ♨ ❀ ⏘ ◖ ▶ P

Darwen

Golden Cup

610 Blackburn Road
☎ (01254) 702337
12–3, 5.30–11
Thwaites Mild, Bitter, Craftsman Ⓗ
The oldest pub in town; three small, cosy rooms with low ceilings and an attractive cobbled forecourt. Good value lunches. ♨ Q ❀ ◖ ⚘ P

Greenfield

Lower Barn Street
☎ (01254) 703945
12–3, 5.30–11; 12–11 Fri & Sat
Taylor Landlord; Thwaites Best Mild, Bitter; Whitbread Boddingtons Bitter; guest beers Ⓗ
Open-plan pub, next to the railway line, serving good value food (all day Sun; no eve meals Tue). Three guest beers change regularly, always including a porter. Q ❀ ◖ ▶

Punch Hotel

Chapels ☎ (01254) 702510
12–11
Whitbread Chester's Best Mild, Trophy; guest beers Ⓗ
Large, multi-roomed, friendly games pub. The only outlet in town serving real cider. Whitbread's seasonal beers stocked.
❀ ⏘ ◖ ▶ ⚘ ♣ ⏚ P

Sunnyhurst Hotel

Tockholes Road
☎ (01254) 873035
12–3 (4 Sat), 7–11
Thwaites Mild, Best Bitter Ⓗ
Welcoming pub with a pictorial history of the town on its walls. Next to Sunnyhurst Woods and just on the moors, it is handy for walkers.
Q ❀ ♠

Entwistle

Strawbury Duck

Overshaws Road (signed on the Edgworth–Darwen Roman road) OS727178
☎ (01204) 852013

12–3 (not Mon), 7–11; 12–11 Sat
Marston's Pedigree; Morland Old Speckled Hen; Taylor Best Bitter, Landlord; Whitbread Boddingtons Bitter; guest beers Ⓗ
Old, isolated, but busy, country pub next to the station. A good base for walks in the hill country. Children welcome till 8.30pm.
♨ ⏱ ❀ ⏘ ◖ ▶ ≢ ♠ P ⚹

Euxton

Euxton Mills

Wigan Road (A49/A581 jct)
☎ (01257) 264002
11.30–3, 5.30 (6.15 Sat)–11
Burtonwood Mild, Bitter, Forshaw's Ⓗ
Cosy, comfortable pub with a split-level lounge and a front vault. Children allowed in a rear room for excellent meals.
⏱ ❀ ◖ ▶ ⏚ P

Fence-in-Pendle

Harpers Inn

Harpers Lane
☎ (01282) 616249
11.30–3, 7–11
Thwaites Best Mild, Bitter, Craftsman; Whitbread Boddingtons Bitter; guest beer Ⓗ
Rural pub with a restaurant on the upper level, also serving a large range of good value bar meals (dining licence Sun). Families welcome.
Q ❀ ◖ ▶ ♠ P

Fleetwood

Mount

The Esplanade
☎ (01253) 874619
11–11 (11–3, 6–11 Oct–March)
S&N Theakston Best Bitter; Whitbread Boddingtons Bitter, Flowers Original Ⓗ; **guest beers** (summer) Ⓗ
Named after a local landmark, this large, modernised, Victorian building is close to the beach. The public bar has a loyal clientele; separate pool and darts room.
⏱ ❀ ◖ ⏚ ♠

North Euston Hotel

The Esplanade
☎ (01253) 876525
11–11
Draught Bass; Ruddles County; Webster's Yorkshire Bitter, Wilson's Mild, Bitter; guest beers Ⓗ
Large, Victorian, stone-fronted building overlooking the River Wyre and Morecambe Bay, near bus and tram termini. Spacious rooms; the family room closes at 7. Busy at weekends.
Q ⏱ ⏘ ◖ ⏚ ⊖ P ⚹

Wyre Lounge Bar

Marine Hall, The Esplanade
☎ (01253) 771141
11–4.30 (12–4 winter), 7–11 summer
Courage Directors; Ⓗ
Moorhouse's Premier, Ⓗ
**Pendle Witches Brew; guest
beers** Ⓗ
Part of the attractive Marine
Hall and Gardens complex,
twice a local CAMRA *Pub of
the Year.* Famous throughout
the Fylde coast for its excellent
choice of guest beers.
Q ✿ & P

Galgate

Plough

Main Street ☎ (01524) 751337
11–11
**John Smith's Bitter;
Whitbread Boddingtons
Bitter; guest beer** Ⓗ
Pub at the southern end of the
village, modernised and
open-plan but with a distinct,
cosy 'lounge' end and a games
area. Artefacts on display
include soccer pennants.
Robust, masculine
atmosphere. Handy for the
canal. ♨ ✿ ◑ ♣ P

Garstang

Royal Oak

Market Place ☎ (01995) 603318
11–3 (4 Thu), 7–11; 11–11 Fri & Sat
**Robinson's Hatters Mild,
Hartleys XB, Best Bitter,
Frederic's** Ⓗ
Some parts date from a 1480
farmhouse but this is mostly a
1670 coaching inn,
thoughtfully renovated in
1993, with intimate drinking
areas. Meals extension
until 4pm Sun.
✿ ⊨ ◑ ♣ P

Great Harwood

Merrie England

56 St Hubert's Road
☎ (01254) 888358
12–5, 7–11; 12–11 Fri; 11.30–11 Sat
**Marston's Pedigree;
Whitbread Boddingtons
Bitter, Trophy; guest beers** Ⓗ
Friendly corner local, popular
with all; very well run, with
the beer range and prices well
displayed. Smart, comfortable
lounge. ◑ ⊞ ▲

Royal Hotel

Station Road ☎ (01254) 883541
12–1.30 (3 Sat; not Mon & Tue), 7–11
Beer range varies Ⓗ
Cosy, open-plan pub, free
from loud music. Four guest
beers plus a wide selection of
continental bottles. A CAMRA
regional *Pub of the Year.*
Q ✿ ⊨ ◑ ▶ ▲ ♣ ⊟

Hambleton

Shard Bridge Inn

Old Bridge Lane
☎ (01253) 700208
12–3, 6–11 (11–11 summer)
**Ind Coope Burton Ale; Tetley
Walker Bitter; guest beers** Ⓗ
Originally the Ferry Boat Inn,
dating back to at least 1786,
overlooking the River Wyre by
the new Shard Bridge: a
comfortable, relaxing lounge
and a games room (families
welcome). Watch the water
sports from the outdoor
drinking area. Good, home-
made meals (12–9 Sun).
✿ ◑ ▶ ⊞ ♣ P ⊬

Haskayne

Ship Inn

6 Rosemary Lane (300 yds
from A5147 at Downholland)
☎ (01704) 840572
11–3, 6–11
Tetley Walker Mild, Bitter Ⓗ
Rural canalside pub with a
reputation for good food. It
caters for everyone, with a
family room, children's
playground and a garden:
local CAMRA *Summer Pub of
the Year 1994.* ▱ ✿ ◑ ▶ P

Haslingden

Griffin Inn

86 Hud Rake (off A680)
☎ (01706) 214021
12–11
**Porter Mild, Bitter, Sunshine,
Porter** Ⓗ
Open-plan pub with views
over the surrounding valley.
Great for conversation. Drink
the local CAMRA award-
winning ales, brewed by
landlord David Porter;
occasional ales also brewed.
No food Mon. ♨ Q ◑ ♣

Hawkshaw

Red Lion

91 Ramsbottom Road (A676)
☎ (01204) 852539
12–3 (not Mon), 6.30–11
**Taylor Golden Best, Best
Bitter, Landlord; guest beer** Ⓗ
Set in a picturesque area, a
pub completely rebuilt in 1990,
with a single comfortable bar
and a restaurant. ⊨ ◑ ▶ P

Heskin

Farmer's Arms

Wood Lane (B5250)
☎ (01257) 451276
11–11
**Marston's Pedigree;
Robinson's Hartleys XB;
Whitbread Chester's Mild,**

**Boddingtons Bitter, Castle
Eden Ale; guest beer** Ⓗ
Pub with a comfortable and
attractive, split-level lounge,
popular for food, and a
well-appointed public bar.
Large play area in the garden.
The house beer is brewed at
Castle Eden. Open 12–10.30
Sun for meals.
Q ✿ ◑ ▶ ⊞ P ⊬

Heysham

Royal

Main Street ☎ (01524) 859298
11–3, 5.45–11; 11–11 Thu–Sat
**Bateman Mild; Mitchell's
Original** Ⓗ
Old, four-roomed, low-
ceilinged pub near St Patrick's
Chapel and rock-hewn graves.
Busy local trade; packed with
holidaymakers in summer.
Children admitted to the
games room until 7.30. Other
Mitchell's beers sometimes
stocked. ♨ ✿ ◑ ♣ P

High Moor

Rigbye Arms

2 Whittle Lane
☎ (01257) 462354
12–3, 5.30–11 (12–11 Thu–Sat in
summer)
**Ind Coope Burton Ale; Tetley
Walker Dark Mild, Mild,
Bitter** Ⓗ
Remote, homely rural pub
popular with ramblers, with a
reputation for food (restaurant
open Fri and Sat; meals all day
Sun). Own bowling green. Not
to be missed. ♨ ✿ ◑ ▶ ⊞ P

Hoghton

Black Horse

Gregson Lane (off A675 at
Higher Walton)
☎ (01254) 852541
11.30–11
**S&N Matthew Brown Bitter,
Theakston Mild, Best Bitter,
XB; guest beer** Ⓗ
Large, friendly open-plan
village pub with a games area.
Children allowed in for food.
◑ ▶ P

Royal Oak

Riley Green (A675/A6061 jct)
☎ (01254) 201445
11.30–3, 5.30–11
Thwaites Best Mild, Bitter, Ⓗ
Craftsman; guest beer Ⓗ
Old, low-ceilinged pub formed
from a row of cottages; several
cosy drinking areas. Popular
for food (children allowed in
for meals). Monthly guest
beer. ♨ Q ◑ ▶ & P

Sirloin

Station Road (500 yds off
A675) ☎ (01254) 852293

Lancashire

12-3, 5-11
**Ruddles County; Webster's
Yorkshire Bitter** Ⓗ
Old stone pub, by the former
station: a single bar with a
stone and wood-panelled
interior. The name derives
from an incident in 1617 when
King James I knighted a loin of
beef at nearby Hoghton
Towers. 🏚 🍽 ❀ ◖ P

Kirkham

Queen's Arms
7 Poulton Street (opp. Market
Place) ☎ (01772) 686705
12 (11.30 Thu-Sat)-11
**S&N Theakston Best Bitter,
XB, Old Peculier; guest
beer** Ⓗ
Excellent, well-run, lively
town-centre local, full of
character. Children welcome
in a designated area. Excellent
garden (barbecues in summer);
pool room; wheelchair WC.
❀ ♿ ♣

Swan Hotel
115 Poulton Street
☎ (01772) 682078
12-11
**McEwan 80/-; S&N Matthew
Brown Mild, Bitter,
Theakston Best Bitter; guest
beers** Ⓗ
Good value, homely pub. Look
for the whacky statements on
the chalkboard outside.
Q ❀ 🍽 🍺 ♿ ♣ P

Lancaster

Golden Lion
Moor Lane ☎ (01524) 63198
12-3, 7-11
**S&N Theakston Best Bitter,
XB, Old Peculier; Whitbread
Boddingtons Bitter** Ⓗ
A pub since at least 1612: an
L-shaped bar with an
adjoining games room (bar
billiards and skittles). The
no-smoking 'Heritage' room
displays Lancaster
memorabilia. 🏚 ♣ ✂

John o' Gaunt
55 Market Street
☎ (01524) 65356
11-3 (5 Sat), 6 (7 Sat)-11; 11-11 Fri
**Ind Coope Burton Ale;
Jennings Bitter; Tetley
Walker Bitter; Whitbread
Boddingtons Bitter; guest
beers** Ⓗ
Pub with a handsome original
frontage; small and often
packed. Find the garden. No
food Sun. ❀ ◖ ⇌

Priory
36 Cable Street
☎ (01524) 32606
11-11 (may close afternoons)
**Mitchell's Original, Lancaster
Bomber** Ⓗ

Large, unprepossessing bar,
but improvements are
promised. Popular with
students; most Mitchell's beers
stocked. Handy for the bus
station. ▭

Royal
Thornham Street
☎ (01524) 65007
11.30-3, 7-11
**Thwaites Best Mild, Bitter,
Craftsman** Ⓗ
Pub knocked through in 1992
to make a single large bar with
lots of corners. Daytime trade
comes from the nearby civic
buildings. ❀ ◖ P

Three Mariners
32 Bridge Lane
☎ (01524) 64877
11-11
**Mitchell's Original, Lancaster
Bomber** Ⓗ
Reputedly Lancaster's oldest
pub – 13th century – at least
the beams are of such an age.
Mitchell's seasonal beers
stocked. 🏚 ❀ ◖ ▶ ♣ P

Wagon & Horses
27 St George's Quay
☎ (01524) 65602
11-11
**Robinson's Hatters Mild,
Hartleys XB, Best Bitter, Old
Tom** Ⓗ
Two houses knocked together
– one fitted out in vault style,
the other as a lounge – close to
the Maritime Museum.
🏚 ❀ ◖ ♣

Lathom

Railway Tavern
Hoscar Moss Road, Hoscar
Moss
12-3, 5-11; 12-11 Sat
**Jennings Bitter; Tetley
Walker Dark Mild, Mild,
Bitter; guest beers** Ⓗ
Refurbished but unspoilt
village local next to a rural
station. Friendly service and
good, home-cooked food (not
served Mon lunch). Popular
with cyclists. Children
welcome until 8.30. 🏚 Q ▭
❀ ◖ ▶ 🍺 ⇌ (Hoscar) ♣ P

Ship Inn
Wheat Lane (off B5209, near
Burscough, over canal swing
bridge) ☎ (01704) 893117
12-3, 5.30 (7 Sat)-11
**Moorhouse's Pendle Witches
Brew; S&N Theakston Mild,
Best Bitter, XB; guest beers** Ⓗ
Rural canalside pub, regional
CAMRA *Pub of the Year* 1994:
the gem of the area. An
excellent family-run free house
with nine handpumps and five
changing guest beers. Good
value lunches. No meals Sun.
Q 🍽 ❀ ◖ ♣ P ✂

Lea Town

Smiths Arms (Slip)
Lea Lane (opp. BNFL East
Gate) OS476312
☎ (01772) 726906
11.30-3, 6-11
Thwaites Best Mild, Bitter Ⓗ
Superb old farmhouse pub,
known as the Slip from when
Fylde farmers walked cattle
past and slipped in for a drink.
Well-behaved children
welcome for food (not served
Tue eve). 🏚 Q ❀ ◖ ▶ ♣ P

Leyland

Dunkirk Hall
Dunkirk Lane (B5248/B5253)
☎ (01772) 422102
11-3, 5-11 Fri & Sat
**Courage Directors; John
Smith's Bitter; Webster's
Green Label** Ⓗ
17th-century converted
farmhouse, now a listed
building with flag floors,
panelled walls and beams. No
meals Mon eve. ❀ ◖ ▶ P

George IV
Towngate ☎ (01772) 422165
11-11
**Greenalls Bitter, Original;
guest beers** Ⓗ
Attractive, town-centre pub
near the new shopping centre.
Two guest beers. Meals served
12-7 Sun. ◖ 🍺 ♣ P

Little Eccleston

Cartford Country Inn
& Hotel
Cartford Lane (by toll bridge,
½ mile off A586)
☎ (01995) 670166
12-3, 7 (6.30 summer)-11
Beer range varies Ⓗ
Delightfully situated free
house by the River Wyre
(fishing rights). An extensive
bar menu also offers children's
meals. Four changing guest
beers. 1991/1994 local
CAMRA *Pub of the Year*. Hart
Brewery is at the rear.
🏚 ❀ 🍽 ◖ ▶ ♿ ♣ P ✂

Longridge

Alston Arms
Inglewhite Road
☎ (01772) 783331
11.30-11
**S&N Matthew Brown Mild,
Bitter, Theakston Best Bitter;
guest beers** Ⓗ
Comfortable, friendly pub on
the outskirts of town, on the
way to Chipping or Beacon
Fell. Popular with families; the
large garden/play area boasts
a double decker bus and
animals. 🏚 Q ❀ ◖ ▶ ▲ ♣ P

Lancashire

Forrest Arms

2 Derby Road
☎ (01772) 782610
12–3 (2 Tue; not Wed), 7 (5.30 Mon)–11; 12–11 Fri & Sat
Whitbread Boddingtons Bitter; guest beers Ⓗ
Down-to-earth, three-roomed drinkers' pub near the town centre. Popular with all; video games attract a young set. Two guest beers. Ⓖ ♣

White Bull

1a Higher Road
☎ (01772) 783198
12–11
S&N Matthew Brown Mild, Bitter, Theakston Best Bitter, guest beer Ⓗ
Deservedly popular large pub, catering for all. The pool room features two tables, bar football and bar billiards and gives excellent views of the Ribble Valley. No meals Sun eve. 🏠 ❀ Ⓖ Ⓓ ⊞ ▲ ♣ P

Lytham

Hole in One

Forest Drive (off B5261)
☎ (01253) 730598
11–3, 6–11; 11–11 Fri & Sat
Thwaites Bitter Ⓗ
Busy, friendly, modern local by Fairhaven golf course; full of golfing memorabilia. It features a large games room, plus good, home-made food (extensive menu). Wheelchair WC. Q ❀ Ⓖ ⊞ ♣ P

Queen's Hotel

Central Beach
☎ (01253) 737316
11–3, 5–11; 11–11 Fri, Sat & summer
S&N Theakston Best Bitter, XB; guest beer Ⓗ
Characterful, authentic Victorian pub in the town centre, overlooking the green and estuary. Good reputation for food. Car park opposite. 🏠 ❀ 🛏 Ⓓ ⊞ ♣ ⇌ ♣

Taps

Henry Street (off Lytham Sq)
☎ (01253) 736226
11–11
Beer range varies Ⓗ
Friendly, basic alehouse, serving a wide choice of changing guest beers; very popular and often crowded. Wheelchair WC. Parking difficult. 🏠 ❀ Ⓖ ▲ ⇌ ♣

Mawdesley

Black Bull

Hall Lane OS499151
☎ (01704) 822202
12–11
Greenalls Bitter, Original; guest beers Ⓗ
Rambling, 700-year-old country pub; a central bar serves the lounge and an open area. Games room. 🏠 🛏 ❀ 🛏 Ⓓ Ⓖ ♣ P

Melling

Melling Hall

☎ (01524) 221298
12–2.30 (not Wed), 6–11; 12–2, 7–10.30 Sun
Taylor Landlord; Tetley Walker Bitter; Whitbread Boddingtons Bitter Ⓗ
17th-century manor house converted in the 1940s to a hotel with a friendly locals' bar. Garden play area. 🏠 ❀ 🛏 Ⓓ Ⓖ ♣ P

Morecambe

New Inn

2 Poulton Square
☎ (01524) 831120
11–11
John Smith's Bitter; Whitbread Boddingtons Bitter; guest beers (occasional) Ⓗ
Down-to-earth pub at the centre of the old village of Poulton-le-Sands. Due for a re-vamp that should retain the two small bars and games room. ❀ ⊞ ♣ P

Smugglers' Den

56 Poulton Road
☎ (01524) 421684
11–3, 7–11; 11–11 Fri & Sat (11–11 Tue–Thu in summer)
Jennings Bitter; Tetley Walker Bitter; Whitbread Boddingtons Bitter; guest beer Ⓗ
The smugglers have long since gone but the stained-glass and nautical knick-knacks remind customers of this low-beamed, stone-floored pub's past. Busy in summer, when food is available. 🏠 ❀ Ⓖ ♣ P

Ormskirk

Greyhound

100 Aughton Street
☎ (01695) 576701
11–11
Tetley Walker Mild, Bitter, Winter Warmer Ⓗ
Characterful market town local with a public bar, a snug, a large lounge with nooks and crannies and a games room. A central bar serves all areas including a corridor serving hatch. 🏠 Q ⊞ ⇌ ♣

Hayfield

County Road (A59)
☎ (01695) 571157
12–3, 5.30–11; 12–11 Sat
Courage Directors; John Smith's Bitter; Webster's Yorkshire Bitter; guest beers Ⓗ

Once derelict, now a thriving free house, with good wheelchair access, furnished with a comfortable mixture of new and old. Top quality food. Up to five changing guest beers. Children welcome until 8.30. 🛏 ❀ Ⓓ Ⓖ ⇌ P 🍴

Prince Albert

109 Wigan Road, Westhead
☎ (01695) 573656
12–3 (5 Sat), 5 (7 Sat)–11
Tetley Walker Dark Mild, Bitter; guest beers Ⓗ
A Tetley *Golden Huntsman* award-winner which continues to maintain its excellent standards. A comfortable and friendly village pub enjoying local support. Good value lunches. 🏠 Q ❀ 🛏 Ⓖ ♣ P

Yew Tree

Grimshaw Lane
☎ (01695) 573381
12–3.30, 5–11.30
Cains Mild, Bitter; guest beers Ⓗ
Modern pub with a spacious lounge, a well-patronised public bar and a genuine snug. Good value food (not served Sun). Worth the short walk from the town centre (towards Southport). Q ❀ Ⓖ ⇌ ♣ P

Oswaldtwistle

Royal Oak Inn

334 Union Road
☎ (01254) 236367
12–4 (4.30 Sat), 7–11
Thwaites Best Mild, Bitter Ⓗ
Open-plan pub with a small games area. ⇌ (Church & Oswaldtwistle) ♣

Stop & Rest

Fielding Lane
☎ (01254) 231951
11–11
Whitbread Boddingtons Mild, Trophy; guest beers Ⓗ
Two-room, six-pump local with a spacious lounge. Charity events; occasional beer festivals. Ⓖ ♣ P

Padiham

Hand & Shuttle

1 Eccleshill Street
☎ (01282) 771795
11.30–4, 6–11; 11–11 Fri & Sat
Thwaites Best Mild, Bitter Ⓗ
Friendly, town-centre local. The open-plan refurbishment has not affected its character. 🏠 ♣ P

Parbold

Railway Hotel

Station Road ☎ (01257) 462917
11–11

169

Lancashire

Burtonwood Mild, Bitter, Top Hat Ⓗ
Popular village pub filled with railway memorabilia.
🏛 ❀ ◖ ⅋ ⟗ ⇌ P

Pendleton

Swan With Two Necks
Off A59 ☎ (01200) 23112
12–3 (not Mon), 7–11 (may vary summer)
Bass Worthington BB; Marston's Pedigree; Tetley Walker Bitter Ⓗ
Popular village pub which closes Mon lunch to serve the village as a post office.
🏛 Q ⚲ ❀ ◖ ⅋ ♣ P

Penwortham

St Teresa's Parish Centre
Queensway ☎ (01772) 743523
12–4 (not Mon–Fri), 7–11
Burtonwood Mild, Bitter, Forshaw's; Ind Coope Burton Ale; Tetley Walker Mild, Bitter; guest beers Ⓗ
Thriving, three-bar Catholic club: a comfortable lounge, games room and a concert room. Three guest beers. A former CAMRA *Club of the Year*. Entry restrictions: CAMRA members anytime, others six times a year (50p).
⚲ ⅋ ⅋ P

Pleasington

Railway Hotel
Pleasington Lane (by station)
☎ (01254) 201520
12–3, 6.30–11; 11–11 Sat
Whitbread Boddingtons Bitter; Wilson's Mild, Bitter Ⓗ
Attractive family pub with no jukebox, catering mainly for mature people (own bowling green). Home-cooked local dishes (not served Sun or Mon eves).
🏛 Q ⚲ ❀ ◖ ⅋ ⇌ ♣ P

Poulton-le-Fylde

Thatched House
Ball Street ☎ (01253) 891063
11–11
Whitbread Boddingtons Bitter; guest beer Ⓗ
Popular pub tucked in a corner of St Chad's Norman churchyard. No music, no intrusive games – just a hubbub of conversation in the three busy rooms.
🏛 Q ⅋ Å ⇌

Preston

Adelphi
43 Fylde Street
☎ (01772) 252171
11.30–11; 11–3, 7–11 Sat

Bass Worthington BB; Draught Bass; Stones Best Bitter; guest beers Ⓗ
Large pub, recently expanded into a former shop: two spacious rooms: one for games, popular with students; an upstairs function room hosts live entertainment. Reasonable value food.
❀ ◖ ⅋ ⅋ ♣ P

Dog & Partridge
45 Friargate ☎ (01772) 252217
11–3, 6–11
Bass Worthington BB; Courage Directors; M&B Highgate Dark, Old; guest beer Ⓗ
One roomed, friendly pub, popular with students and bikers. Good value food (not served Sun). DJ Sun/Thu nights. ◖ ⇌ ♣

Fox & Grapes
15 Fox Street ☎ (01772) 252448
10.30–11
S&N Theakston Best Bitter, Newcastle Exhibition, Theakston XB, Old Peculier, Younger IPA, No. 3; guest beer Ⓗ
Popular, town-centre pub attracting all ages; refurbished in a traditional alehouse style. No food Sun. ◖ ⇌

Lamb & Packet
91a Friargate ☎ (01772) 251857
11.30–11; 11.30–3.30, 6.30–11 Sat
Thwaites Best Mild, Bitter, Craftsman Ⓗ
Busy one-roomer near the University. The good value food attracts students and office workers (meals all weekdays until 7pm). ◖ ⅋

Mitre Tavern
90–91 Moor Lane
☎ (01772) 251918
12–3, 5.30–11; 12–11 Sat
Vaux Samson; Wards Thorne Best Bitter, Best Bitter; guest beer Ⓗ
Friendly pub, just out of the town centre: a comfortable lounge and a good vault with pool and darts. Families welcome Sun lunch. Vaux guest beer. ❀ ◖ ⅋ ⅋ ♣ P

Moorbrook Inn
370 North Road
☎ (01772) 201127
4 (12 Fri & Sat)–11
Thwaites Best Mild, Bitter Ⓗ
Convivial pub with small rooms off a main bar: ideal for conversation. Q ❀ ♣

New Britannia
6 Heatley Street
☎ (01772) 253424
11–3 (4 Fri & Sat), 6–11; 7–10.30 Sun, closed Sun lunch

Marston's Pedigree; Whitbread Trophy, Castle Eden Ale, Flowers Original; guest beer Ⓗ
Small, one-bar pub near the University and town centre.
◖ ⅋ ⇌ ♣ ○

Old Black Bull
35 Friargate ☎ (01772) 254402
10.30–11
Whitbread Boddingtons Bitter; guest beers Ⓗ
Tudor-fronted popular pub with a large lounge, a tiny vault and three changing guest beers. Lunches Mon–Fri.
◖ ⅋ ⇌ ♣ ○

Olde Blue Bell
114 Church Street
☎ (01772) 251280
11–3 (4 Sat), 6 (7 Sat)–11
Samuel Smith OBB Ⓗ
A country pub in the town, the oldest in Preston, good for conversation, but it can be packed Fri and Sat nights. Good value food. 🏛 ❀ ◖ P

Plungington Tavern
85 Plungington Road
12.30 (11 Sat)–11
Bass Worthington BB; M&B Highgate Dark; Stones Best Bitter; Webster's Green Label; guest beer (occasional) Ⓗ
Well-maintained, drinkers' pub, serving the community. Fine red brick exterior. ⅋ ♣

Real Ale Shop
47 Lovat Road (off A6, near Moor Park) ☎ (01772) 201591
11–2, 5–10; 12–2, 7–10 Sun
Beer range varies Ⓗ/Ⓖ
Splendid off-licence with up to four beers at a time. Wide range of bottled beers and wines. ○

Ribble Pilot
Mariners Way, Ashton
☎ (01772) 760673
11–11
Banks's Mild, Bitter Ⓔ; **Camerons Strongarm** Ⓗ
Commendable new pub with excellent, split-level drinking and dining facilities; part of Preston's Docklands redevelopment.
❀ ◖ ⅋ ⅋ ⟗ ⊟

Sherwood
Sherwood Way, Fulwood
☎ (01772) 712896
11–11
Bass Worthington BB; Ruddles County; Stones Best Bitter; guest beers Ⓗ
Spacious, open-plan pub with a games area, serving the Sherwood housing estate. Full at weekends. ❀ ◖ ⅋ ⅋ ♣ P

Sumners
Watling Street Road, Fulwood
(B6241) ☎ (01772) 705626
11.30–11

Whitbread Boddingtons Mild, Bitter; guest beers Ⓗ
Large, busy, modern pub, handy for the football ground. The snug has now been incorporated into a large lounge; games room. The guest beer comes from the Whitbread list. Eve meals finish at 8. ❀ ◐ ◗ ⊞ ♿ ♣ P

Wall Street
1 Fishergate ☎ (01772) 823323
11–11
Greenalls Bitter, Original Ⓗ
Large, multi-level, American-styled theme bar, converted from a bank. The main feature is a revolving bank of video screens in the form of a cube. Busy weekend eves (when dress restrictions apply). Eve meals finish at 8. ◐ ◗ ♿ ⇌

Rishton

Rishton Arms
Station Road ☎ (01254) 886396
7 (11 Sat)–11
Thwaites Best Mild, Bitter, Craftsman Ⓗ
Pleasant, two-roomed pub next to the station. Note the grandfather clock in the lounge. ⇌ ♣ P

Salterforth

Anchor Inn
Salterforth Lane
☎ (01282) 813186
12–11
Bass Mild, Special, Worthington BB, Draught Bass; guest beers Ⓗ
Impressive rural watering hole overlooking the Leeds & Liverpool Canal; a popular eating establishment. Semi-open plan, it dates back to 1655. Stalagmites and stalagtites can be viewed in the cellar, on request.
♨ Q ⛑ ❀ ◐ ◗ ♿ ▲ ♣ P

Scarisbrick

Heatons Bridge Inn
2 Heatons Bridge Road (B5242, by Leeds & Liverpool Canal)
☎ (01704) 840549
11.30–11
Tetley Walker Mild; Walker Best Bitter Ⓗ
Popular canalside inn, tastefully extended, and offering excellent value lunches (not served Sun).
♨ Q ❀ ◐ ♣ P

Silverdale

Royal
15 Emesgate Lane
☎ (01524) 701266
11–3 (not winter Mon–Fri), 7–11
Marston's Pedigree (summer); **John Smith's Bitter** Ⓗ
Local with a large bar, entered via the verandah, plus a dining room and a large games room. The garden has a play area. Birdwatchers and walkers are regulars.
❀ ◐ ♣ P

Thornton

Burn Naze
1 Gamble Road (off B5268)
☎ (01253) 852954
11–11
Moorhouse's Premier; Tetley Walker Bitter; guest beer Ⓗ
Unspoilt, popular local, difficult to find. Weekend entertainment. ⛟ ◐ ◗ ♣ P

Waddington

Buck Inn (Lower)
Church Road ☎ (01200) 28705
11–3, 6–11; 11–11 Thu–Sat
Ruddles County; Taylor Best Bitter; Tetley Walker Bitter Ⓗ
Coaching house dating from 1760 and retaining many original features.
♨ Q ⛑ ❀ ⛟ ◐ ◗ ♿ ▲ ♣ P

Walmer Bridge

Longton Arms
2 Liverpool Old Road
☎ (01772) 612335
2 (12 Sat)–11
Greenalls Mild, Bitter Ⓗ
Small, friendly, terraced, village local: a tiny public bar at the front; a cosy lounge with armchairs to the rear.
♨ Q ⊞ ♣

Walton-le-Dale

Yew Tree
100 Victoria Road (A6/A675 jct) ☎ (01772) 555103
11.30–3, 6–11
Whitbread Boddingtons Bitter; guest beers Ⓗ
Large, roadside pub with the emphasis on meals but enjoying a local following for its three guest beers.
⛑ ❀ ◐ ◗ ♿ ♣ P

Waterfoot

Jolly Sailor
Booth Road ☎ (01706) 214863
12–3, 5.30–11; 11–11 Fri & Sat
S&N Theakston Best Bitter; Whitbread Boddingtons Mild, Bitter, Flowers IPA; guest beers Ⓗ
Attractive, open-plan pub catering for a mainly local trade. Q ❀ ⛟ ◐ ♿ ♣

Wharles

Eagle & Child
Church Road ☎ (01772) 690312
7–11; 12–3, 7–11 Sat
Whitbread Boddingtons Bitter; guest beers Ⓗ
Rural, thatched, 17th-century free house, beautifully preserved and housing decorative mirrors and many antiques. Caravan Club site open all year. The house beer is brewed by Commercial.
♨ Q ❀ ▲ P

Wheelton

Red Lion
196 Blackburn Road, Lower Wheelton (off A674)
☎ (01254) 830378
12–11
S&N Theakston Best Bitter; Whitbread Boddingtons Bitter; guest beers Ⓗ
Popular village-centre pub with a split-level interior: a comfortable bar and a games room. A short walk from the Leeds & Liverpool Canal. No food Tue; eve meals until 8.
♨ ❀ ◐ ◗ ♣ P

Whitestake

Farmer's Arms
Wham Lane (½ mile W of A582)
☎ (01772) 613210
11–11
Marston's Pedigree; Whitbread Boddingtons Bitter, Castle Eden Ale; guest beers Ⓗ
Extended Brewer's Fayre pub between New Longton and Lostock Hall. The real ale bar serves five guest beers. Children's play area. Occasional cider.
♨ Q ⛑ ❀ ◐ ◗ ♿ ♣ ⌓ P

Whittle-le-Woods

Royal Oak
216 Chorley Old Road
☎ (01254) 76485
2.30–11
S&N Matthew Brown Mild, Bitter, Theakston Best Bitter; Young's Special; guest beers Ⓗ
Atmospheric, small, terraced local with a cosy front room and a games room. Note the Nuttalls windows.
♨ Q ❀ ⊞ ♣

Yealand Conyers

New Inn
40 Yealand Road
☎ (01524) 732938
11–3, 5.30–11 (11–11 Sat & summer)
Robinson's Hatters Mild, Hartleys XB, Best Bitter, Frederic's, Old Tom Ⓗ
Old village inn, popular for food. The conversion of the adjacent barn to a restaurant should soon free the bar for drinking. ♨ Q ❀ ◐ ◗ ♣ P

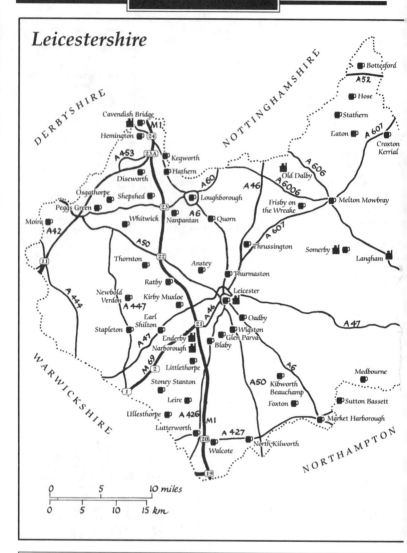

Leicestershire

[Map of Leicestershire showing towns, roads, and brewery locations including: Bottesford, Hose, Stathern, Eaton, Croxton Kerrial, Cavendish Bridge, Hemington, Kegworth, Hathern, Old Dalby, Melton Mowbray, Diseworth, Loughborough, Frisby on the Wreake, Osgathorpe, Shepshed, Somerby, Langham, Peggs Green, Whitwick, Nanpantan, Quorn, Thrussington, Moira, Thornton, Anstey, Thurmaston, Ratby, Leicester, Newbold Verdon, Kirby Muxloe, Oadby, Stapleton, Earl Shilton, Wigston, Glen Parva, Enderby, Blaby, Narborough, Littlethorpe, Medbourne, Stoney Stanton, Kibworth Beauchamp, Leire, Foxton, Sutton Bassett, Ullesthorpe, Lutterworth, Market Harborough, Walcote, North Kilworth. Surrounding counties: Derbyshire, Nottinghamshire, Warwickshire, Northampton]

Belvoir, *Old Dalby*; **Everards**, *Narborough*;
Featherstone, *Enderby*; **Hoskins, Hoskins & Oldfield**,
Leicester; **Oakham**, *Oakham*; **Parish**, *Somerby*;
Ruddles, *Langham*; **Shardlow**, *Cavendish Bridge*

Anstey

Old Hare & Hounds
34 Bradgate Road
☎ (0116) 2362496
11–3.30, 6.30–11; 11–11 Fri & Sat
Marston's Bitter, Pedigree ⊞
Split-level pub with three
rooms and one central bar.
A popular local.
⊛ ♣ P

Barrowden

Exeter Arms
Main Street
☎ (01572) 747247
12–3, 6–11
**Marston's Bitter, Pedigree;
guest beers** ⊞
Reopened stone pub on a
village green opposite a duck
pond; decorated with farm

implements. Always a mild or
porter sold. ♨ ⊛ ◑ ♣ P ✗

Blaby

Baker's Arms
The Green
☎ (0116) 2771166
11–2.30, 6 (6.30 Sat)–11
**Ruddles Best Bitter; S&N
Theakston Best Bitter, XB;
Webster's Yorkshire Bitter** ⊞

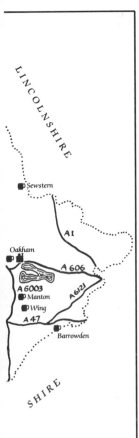

Cosy, low-beamed, thatched, 15th-century village pub with a museum bakery. Petanque piste in summer. No eve meals Tue. Q ❀ ◖ ▮

Bottesford

Rutland Arms
High Street ☎ (01949) 843031
11.30–2.30, 5.30–11; 11.30–11 Sat
Greenalls Shipstone's Bitter; Tetley Bitter Ⓗ
U-shaped bar, half devoted to pool, games machines and TV. The lounge area is comfortable, with an open fire. Luxurious restaurant. Beware: Greenalls Original and all guests are kept under gas.
🏚 ❀ ◖ ▮ ⅋ ≢ P

Cavendish Bridge

Old Crown
Off A6, by Trent Bridge
☎ (01332) 792392
11.30–3, 5–11
Draught Bass; Marston's Pedigree; guest beers Ⓗ
Riverside village pub, decorated with breweriana and old advertisements. Good range of guest beers; popular for food. 🏚 ❀ ◖ ▮ P

Croxton Kerrial

Peacock
1 School Lane (A607)
11.30–2.30, 6.30–11 (varies summer)
Morland Old Speckled Hen; Whitbread Boddingtons Bitter, Flowers IPA; guest beers Ⓗ
Large, comfortable pub with a 300-year history. Good, home-cooked food. Children's certificate. Cider in summer.
🏚 ❀ ❀ ◖ ▮ ⅋ ♣ ⌂ P ⊟

Diseworth

Plough
33 Hall Gate ☎ (01332) 810333
11–2.30, 5 (6 Sat)–11; 12–2.30, 7–10.30 Sun
Draught Bass; M&B Highgate Dark; guest beers Ⓗ
Comfortable village pub, close to E Midlands Airport. Eve meals Mon–Fri.
🏚 ❀ ◖ ▮ ⅋ ♣ P

Earl Shilton

Red Lion
168 High Street (A47)
☎ (01455) 840829
11–2.30 (3 Sat), 5.30 (6 Sat)–11
Draught Bass; M&B Mild Ⓗ
Basic beer drinkers' pub with three rooms and one central bar. ❀ P

Eaton

Castle Inn
33 Vicarage Lane
☎ (01476) 870949
12–3, 7–11
Mansfield Riding Bitter, Bitter, Old Baily Ⓗ
Friendly village local in beautiful countryside near Belvoir Castle; extended to include a skittle alley and pool room. ❀ ❀ ◖ ▮ ⅋ ♣ P

Foxton

Black Horse
Main Street ☎ (01858) 545250
11–11
Marston's Bitter, Pedigree Ⓗ
Large village pub close to the Grand Union Canal. Two rooms plus a conservatory dining area (no-smoking). Marston's Head Brewer's Choice beers sold. 🏚 ❀ 🖂 ◖ ▮ ⅋ ♣ ♣ P ⅋

Frisby on the Wreake

Bell Inn
Main Street ☎ (01664) 434237
12–2.30, 6–11; 12–2.30, 7–10.30 Sun
Ansells Bitter; Draught Bass; Bateman Mild, XXXB; Marston's Pedigree; Tetley Bitter; guest beers Ⓗ
Large, friendly village local dating from 1759 but since extended. Popular with diners and for its guest beers.
🏚 ❀ ❀ ◖ ▮ ♣ P

Glen Parva

Glen Parva Manor
The Ford, Little Glen Road
☎ (0116) 2477604
11.30–2.30, 6–11
Mansfield Riding Mild, Riding Bitter, Bitter, Old Baily Ⓗ
16th-century, extended manor house, refurbished in 1994 into a spacious pub. Families are particularly welcome (indoor and outdoor play areas). Close to the Grand Union Canal. Mansfield's seasonal beers sold. ❀ ❀ ◖ ▮ ⅋ P ⅋

Hathern

Three Crowns
Wide Lane ☎ (01509) 842233
12–2.30, 5.30–11; 11–11 Sat
Bass Worthington BB, Draught Bass; M&B Mild, Highgate Dark Ⓗ
Lively village local with three drinking areas. Skittle alley.
🏚 ❀ ♣ P ⊟

Hemington

Jolly Sailor
Main Street ☎ (01332) 810448
11–11
Draught Bass, M&B Mild; guest beers Ⓗ
Popular village local close to E Midlands Airport.
🏚 ❀ ⅋ ▮ ♣ ⌂ P

Hose

Black Horse
21 Bolton Lane
☎ (01949) 860336
12–2.30 (3 Sat), 6.30 (7 Sat)–11
Home Mild, Bitter; John Smith's Bitter; guest beers Ⓗ
Traditional pub at the heart of village life, sympathetically refurbished. Pleasant garden; good choice of food (book eve meals).
🏚 Q ❀ ❀ ◖ ▮ ⅋ ⅋ ♣ P

Leicestershire

Rose & Crown
Bolton Lane ☎ (01949) 860424
12–2.30, 7–11; 12–2.30, 7–10.30 Sun
Beer range varies ℍ
Village pub where the
emphasis is on good food: one
large bar with eating and
drinking areas. Q ◖ ▶ ㄫ P

Kegworth

Red Lion
High Street ☎ (01509) 672466
11–3, 5–11
**Draught Bass; M&B Mild;
Marston's Pedigree; S&N
Theakston Best Bitter;
Whitbread Boddingtons
Bitter; guest beers** ℍ
Busy, old-fashioned local
known for reasonable prices.
Good menu until 8.30 (not
served Sun). Children's play
area. ㅿ Q ㆍ ㊉ ◖ ▶ ▲ ♣ P

Kibworth Beauchamp

Coach & Horses
2 Leicester Road
☎ (0116) 2792247
11.30–2.30, 5–11; 11–11 Sat
**Ansells Mild, Bitter; Draught
Bass; Tetley Bitter** ℍ
Cosy, old coaching inn with
coin-filled beams and brasses.
Traditional home-cooking.
ㅿ ◖ ▶ ♣ P

Kirby Muxloe

Royal Oak
Main Street ☎ (0116) 2393166
11–2.30, 6.30–11
**Adnams Bitter; Everards
Mild, Beacon, Tiger, Old
Original; guest beer** ℍ
A modern exterior conceals a
comfortable, traditionally-
styled lounge/bar with a
restaurant, popular with
business folk and locals. The
guest beer is supplied by
Everards. ㊉ ◖ ▶ P

Leicester

Black Horse
1 Foxon Street, Braunstone
Gate ☎ (0116) 2540030
12–2.30 (3 Thu–Sat), 5.30 (6 Sat)–11
**Everards Beacon, Tiger; guest
beers** ℍ
Friendly, 120-year-old
drinkers' pub near the city
centre, popular with students
and untouched by
refurbishment. Guest beers
come from Everards' Old
English Ale Club. ㊉

Clarendon
West Avenue, Clarendon Park
(near A6) ☎ (0116) 2707530
11.30–11
**Draught Bass; M&B Mild;
guest beers** ℍ

Two-roomed corner pub in a
terraced residential area,
popular with students eves.
㊉ ㉓ ⚹

Fuzzock & Firkin
203 Welford Road (A50)
☎ (0116) 2708141
12–11
**Firkin Fuzzock, Ass,
Dogbolter** ℍ
Basically furnished pub, the
Stork's Head until 1993. Firkin
beers come from the Phantom
& Firkin in Loughborough.
Popular with the young eves.
Meals served 12–6. ㊉ ◖ P

Hat & Beaver
60 Highcross Street (off High
St) ☎ (0116) 2622157
11–3, 6–11
**Hardys & Hansons Best Mild,
Best Bitter, Kimberley
Classic** ℇ
Basic, relaxed two-roomed
local, formerly a Bass house.
TV in the bar. Well-filled cobs.
Close to the Shires shopping
centre. ㊉ ㉓ ♣

Northbridge Tavern
1 Frog Island (A50)
☎ (0116) 2512508
11–11
**Hoskins & Oldfield HOB
Bitter; Marston's Pedigree;
Tetley Bitter; Whitbread
Boddingtons Bitter** ℍ
Wood-panelled free house, a
former Leicester Brewing &
Maltings house; the city's only
canalside pub. Busy lunchtimes; food all day. ㊉ ◖ ▶ ♣

Red Lion
19 Highcross Street (off High
St) ☎ (0116) 2620368
12 (11.30 Sat)–2.30, 5 (6 Sat)–11;
12–2.30 Sun, closed Sun eve
**Burtonwood Bitter,
Forshaw's, Top Hat** ℍ
Typical town local, with a
small bar (dominated by pool)
and a refurbished, comfortable
lounge; acquired by
Burtonwood from Allied in
1993. ㉓ ♣

Salmon
19 Butt Close Lane
☎ (0116) 2532301
11–11
Banks's Mild, Bitter ℇ
Small pub, refurbished in
typical Banks's style: one
U-shaped room serves a
varied clientele. Near St
Margaret's bus station. ㊉ ◖ ㅂ

Tudor
100 Tudor Road
☎ (0116) 2620087
11–2.30 (3 Sat), 6–11
**Everards Mild, Beacon, Tiger,
Old Original** ℍ
Corner pub in a terraced area
with a Victorian exterior. It
retains two rooms, plus an
upstairs games room. ㊉ ♣

Victoria Jubilee
112 Leire Street (off A46)
11–2.30 (3.30 Sat), 6–11
Marston's Bitter, Pedigree ℍ
Friendly, two-roomed local in
a terraced area; the Full Moon
until the 1887 Jubilee. ㊉ ㉓ ♣

Wilkie's
29 Market Street
☎ (0116) 2556877
12–11; closed Sun
**Adnams Extra; Fuller's
London Pride, Shepherd
Neame Spitfire; Whitbread
Boddingtons Bitter; guest
beers** ℍ
Simply decorated, continental
bar with up to five real ales
plus 120 imported beers, some
on draught. German food. ◖ ㄥ

Leire

Queen's Arms
Main Street ☎ (01455) 209227
12–3, 5.30–11
Marston's Bitter, Pedigree ℍ
Warm, traditional, rural
village pub: one open bar and
a lounge with a beamed
ceiling. Marston's Head
Brewer's Choice sold. Summer
barbecues. ㅿ ㊉ ◖ ▶ P

Littlethorpe

Plough
Station Road ☎ (0116) 2862383
11–2.30 (3 Sat), 6–11
**Everards Mild, Beacon, Tiger,
Old Original; guest beer** ℍ
Friendly, thatched village local
featuring a cosy, unspoilt bar,
a lounge and a dining area.
The guest beer is supplied by
Everards. Long alley skittles
available. Wheelchair access
from the car park. ㊉ ◖ ▶ ㉓ ㄫ
⇌ (Narborough) ♣ P

Loughborough

Gate Inn
Meadow Lane
☎ (01509) 263779
11.30–2.30 (3 Sat), 6–11
**Banks's Mild; Marston's
Pedigree** ℍ
Welcoming, true community
pub. Three cosy drinking
areas, plus the Flight Deck, are
served by a single bar.
ㅿ Q ㊉ ⇌ ♣ P ㅂ

Old Pack Horse
4 Woodgate ☎ (01509) 214590
11.30–2.30, 4–11; 11.30–11 Fri & Sat
**Hardys & Hansons Best Mild,
Best Bitter, Kimberley
Classic** ℍ
Well refurbished coaching inn
retaining many old features
including stables. ㅿ ◖ ▶ ♣ P

Swan in the Rushes
21 The Rushes (A6)
☎ (01509) 217014

11–2.30 (3.30 Sat), 5 (6.30 Sat)–11
Archers Golden; Marston's Pedigree; Whitbread Boddingtons Bitter; guest beers H
Popular town pub. The changing guest beers always include a mild. Imaginative, reasonably priced food.
🏠 Q 🚪 ◁ ▶ 🍴 ⅃ ♿ ⌣ P

Tap & Mallet
36 Nottingham Road
☎ (01509) 210028
11.30–2.30, 5–11; 11–11 Sat
Bateman Mild; Marston's Pedigree; S&N Theakston Best Bitter, XB; guest beers H
Refurbished ex-S&N pub, now a popular free house. A large garden has children's play equipment. Three guest beers.
🏠 ❀ ◁ ♣ ⌣

Three Nuns
30 Churchgate
☎ (01509) 213660
11–11
Everards Tiger, Old Original, Ridleys IPA; guest beers H
Busy pub, recently extended, serving a good range of ales. Open 9am Thu–Sat for good breakfasts. Braille menu. Beware the keg cider on a fake handpump. ❀ ◁ ♿ ⌣ P

Lutterworth

Unicorn
29 Church Street (off A426)
☎ (01455) 552486
10.30–2.30, 5.30–11
Draught Bass; M&B Mild, Brew XI; guest beers H
Quiet, friendly town pub with a large, basic bar and a small, cosy lounge (no jeans).
🏠 Q ◁ ♣ P

Manton

Horse & Jockey
2 St Mary's Road
☎ (01572) 737335
11–2.30, 7–11 (extends in summer)
Mansfield Riding Bitter, Old Baily H
250-year-old, unspoilt, village pub near Rutland Water.
🏠 ❀ ◁ 🚪 ♣ ☗

Market Harborough

Red Cow
58–59 High Street (old A6)
☎ (01858) 463637
11–3 (4 Sat), 6 (7 Sat)–11
Marston's Bitter, Pedigree H
No-frills, town-centre boozer: the single bar is small and unspoilt; games and conversation dominate. Food is limited. Marston's Head Brewer's Choice sold. Q ♣

Medbourne

Nevil Arms
12 Waterfall Way
☎ (01858) 565288
12–2.30, 6–11
Adnams Bitter; Ruddles Best Bitter, County; guest beers H
1876 coaching inn on the village green, next to a stream. A popular venue for families. Two varying guest beers.
🏠 ⅃ ❀ 🚪 ◁ ▶ ▲ ♣ P

Melton Mowbray

Crown
10 Burton Road
☎ (01664) 64682
11–3 (4 Sat), 7–11
Everards Beacon, Tiger, Old Original; guest beer H
Comfortable, two-roomed pub. 🏠 ❀ ◁ 🚂 🚅 ♣

Moira

Rawdon Arms
1 Shortheath Road
☎ (01283) 226788
12–3, 5.30–11; 11–11 Sat
Marston's Pedigree; Morland Old Speckled Hen; S&N Theakston XB, Old Peculier; guest beers H
Welcoming pub where the small back room hosts folk music Thu. The restaurant specialises in French food.
🏠 Q ❀ ◁ ▶ 🚪 ♣ P

Nanpantan

Priory
Nanpantan Road
☎ (01509) 216333
11.30–2.30 (3 Sat), 5.30 (5 Fri, 6 Sat)–11
Home Mild, Bitter; Marston's Pedigree; S&N Theakston XB H
Imposing, turreted pub guarding Nanpantan: a large bar, snug and a lounge-cum-function room. Live jazz Fri. Eve meals 6–8.30, Tue–Sat.
Q ❀ ◁ ▶ 🚪 ♣ P ☗

Newbold Verdon

Jubilee Inn
Main Street ☎ (01455) 822698
11–2.30 (not Wed), 6 (5.30 Thu–Sat)–11; 12–2, 7–10.30 Sun
Marston's Bitter, Pedigree H
Friendly, unspoilt, two-roomed local. 🏠 ❀ ♣ P

North Kilworth

White Lion Inn
Lutterworth Road
☎ (01858) 880260
12–3, 5.30–11; 12–11 Sat
Marston's Bitter, Pedigree H
Former coaching inn near the Grand Union Canal (Bridge 45). The single bar has numerous distinct areas, including a tiled games area. Marston's Head Brewer's Choice sold. No eve meals Mon. 🏠 ❀ ◁ ▶ ♿ P

Oadby

Cow & Plough
Stoughton Farm Park, Gartree Road ☎ (0116) 2720852
5–9
Bateman Mild; Fuller's London Pride; Hoskins & Oldfield HOB; guest beers H
East Midlands CAMRA *Pub of the Year* 1995; part of a leisure park during the day. Its atmospheric vaults are adorned with breweriana. No-smoking family room; guest beers from small breweries.
Q ⅃ ❀ 🚪 ♣ ⌣ ⌥

Oakham

Wheatsheaf
Northgate ☎ (01572) 723458
11.30 (11 Sat)–2.30, 6–11
Adnams Bitter; Everards Beacon, Tiger H
Friendly, 17th-century two-roomed local opposite the church. No food Sun. No-smoking area lunchtime.
🏠 Q ❀ ◁ 🚅 ⌥

White Lion Hotel
30 Melton Road
☎ (01572) 724844
11.30–3, 6–11
Draught Bass; Jennings Bitter; Ruddles Best Bitter H
Split-level pub in a Grade II listed building, reopened in 1989 after closure in 1978. Beware the Scrumpy Jack cider is keg. 🏠 🚪 ◁ ▶ 🚅 P

Osgathorpe

Royal Oak
Main Street ☎ (01530) 222443
7–11; 12–3, 7–11 Sat
M&B Mild; Marston's Pedigree H
Friendly local in a farming area. 🏠 Q ⅃ ❀ 🚪 ▲ ♣ P

Peggs Green

New Inn
Zion Hill (B587)
☎ (01530) 222293
11.30–2.30, 7–11
Draught Bass; M&B Mild H
Excellent country pub with a multitude of cosy corners. The large garden is ideal for families. Monthly folk (Irish) club. 🏠 ⅃ ❀ ♿ ♣ P

Quorn

Apple Tree
Station Road ☎ (01509) 412296

11-2 (3 Sat), 7-11
Draught Bass; M&B Mild [H]
Two-roomed village local, friendly and unassuming.
Q ♣ P

Ratby

Plough
6 Burroughs Road
☎ (0116) 2392103
11.30-3, 5.45 (6 Sat)-11
Bateman Mild; Marston's Bitter, Pedigree [H]
Large refurbished, regulars' pub, also popular with diners. Marston's Head Brewer's Choice sold. ⌂ ♘ ◖ ◗ ♣ P

Sewstern

Blue Dog
Main Street ☎ (01476) 860097
12.30-3 (may vary Sat), 6-11
Beer choice varies [H]
Built in the 1640s, a lively village pub near the Viking Way. Pet-friendly. Beer festivals held. Beware all the Whitbread beers are under gas. ⌂ Q ❀ ◖ ◗ ▲ ♣ P

Shepshed

Railway
160 Charnwood Road
☎ (01509) 503283
11-3, 6-11
Banks's Mild; Marston's Bitter, Pedigree [H]
Very busy local with a good, basic bar. ❀ ♣ P

Richmond Arms
Forest Street ☎ (01509) 503309
11-2, 7-11
Draught Bass; M&B Mild; guest beer [H]
Hospitable local of traditional character, with a sporting emphasis. ❀ ♿ ♣

Somerby

Old Brewery Inn
High Street ☎ (01664) 454866
11.30-2.30, 6-11
Parish Mild, Special, Somerby Premium, Poachers Ale, Porter, Baz's Bonce Blower [H]
A popular choice for a few beers or an excellent meal: the Parish Brewery tap. Beware the keg cider on a fake handpump.
⌂ ❀ ⛝ ◖ ◗ ♿ ▲ ♣ P

Stapleton

Nag's Head
Main Street ☎ (01455) 845056
11-2.30 (11.30-3 Sat), 5.30-11
Marston's Bitter, Pedigree [H]
Typical country pub popular with regulars and passing trade. ❀ ◖ ◗ P

Stathern

Red Lion
Red Lion Street
☎ (01949) 861579
5.45-11; 12-11 Fri, Sat & summer
Marston's Pedigree; Whitbread Boddingtons Bitter; guest beers [H]
Interesting rustic pub with a 400-year history. Acts of Parliament and, it is rumoured, Charles I's death warrant were signed here. Two large, busy rooms.
⌂ ❀ ◖ ◗ ⊞ ▲ ♣ P

Stoney Stanton

Francis Arms
Huncote Road
☎ (01455) 272034
11-2, 5.30-11; 11-11 Sat
Bateman Mild; Marston's Bitter, Pedigree [H]
Basic village pub dominated by beer drinkers. Collection of old rifles on the ceiling. Two rooms with one central bar.
⌂ ❀ ♣ P

Sutton Bassett

Queen's Head Inn
Main Street ☎ (01858) 463630
11.45-2.30, 6.30-11
Adnams Bitter; Tetley Bitter; guest beers [H]
Welcoming village hostelry with two comfortable rooms served from a central bar. Four or more independent guest beers (500 served last year), plus country wines. Beer festival Oct. Restaurant upstairs. ⌂ ❀ ◖ ◗ P ⊟

Thornton

Bricklayer's Arms
Main Street ☎ (01530) 230808
12-3, 7 (6 summer)-11
Everards Mild, Beacon, Tiger, Old Original, Daredevil; guest beers [H]
Unspoilt, traditional village local, partly dating from the 16th century. A basic stone-floored bar and a cosy lounge. Guest beers are supplied by Everards. ⌂ Q ♘ ◖ ◗ ♣ P

Thrussington

Blue Lion
Rearsby Road
☎ (01664) 424266
12-3, 6-11
Marston's Bitter, Pedigree [H]
Welcoming, large village pub where the landlord has historic links with its previous owners, Sileby Brewery. Bizarre collection of teapots; agricultural artefacts. Marston's Head Brewer's Choice sold. ❀ ◖ ◗ P

Thurmaston

Unicorn & Star
796 Melton Road
☎ (0116) 2692849
11-3, 6-11
Greenalls Shipstone's Mild, Shipstone's Bitter [H]
Basic beer drinker's bar with no frills, but a comfortable lounge. ⌂ ❀ ♣ P

Walcote

Black Horse
Main Street ☎ (01455) 552684
12-2 (not Mon & Tue), 6.30-11; 12-2.30, 7-10.30 Sun
Hook Norton Best Bitter, Old Hooky; Hoskins & Oldfield HOB; Taylor Landlord; guest beers [H]
Single-bar free house, close to M1 jct 20. Excellent Thai food; independent guest beers. Occasional ciders.
⌂ Q ◖ ◗ ⇆ P

Whitwick

Three Horseshoes
11 Leicester Road
☎ (01530) 837311
11-3, 6.30-11
Draught Bass; M&B Mild [H]
Traditional, two-roomed pub with a welcoming public bar.
⌂ Q ❀ ⊞ ♿ ♣ P

Wigston

Horse & Trumpet
Bull Head Street (A50)
☎ (0116) 2886290
11-2.30, 5 (6 Sat)-11
Everards Beacon, Tiger, Old Original [H]
Old coaching inn with a comfortable, modernised lounge, popular for business lunches (no food Sat).
❀ ◖ ♿ ♣ P

Meadowbank
Kelmarsh Avenue (300 yards from A50) ☎ (0116) 2811926
12 (11.30 Sat)-2.30, 6-11
Banks's Mild, Bitter [E]; **Marston's Pedigree** [H]
Modern estate pub with a basic bar and a comfortable lounge. Eve meals Wed.
❀ ◖ ⊞ ♣ P ⊟

Wing

Cuckoo
Top Street ☎ (01572) 737340
11.30-3, 6.30-11
Draught Bass; Marston's Pedigree; guest beers [H]
Whitewashed, unspoilt, thatched village local. Beer festival and steam rally in summer. No lunches Tue.
⌂ ❀ ◖ ◗ ▲ ♣ P ⊟

Lincolnshire

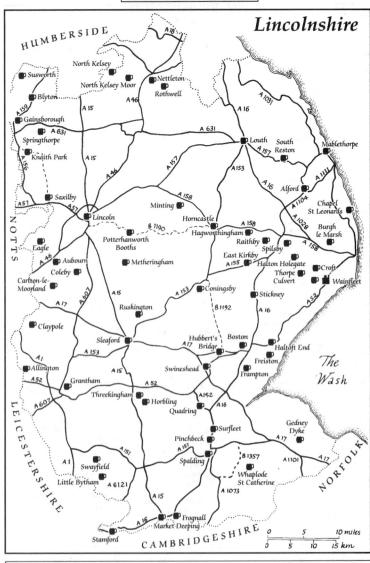

Lincolnshire

 Bateman, Wainfleet

Alford

Half Moon

West Street ☎ (01507) 463477
10–11 (1am Fri & Sat)
**Bass Worthington BB,
Draught Bass; Vaux
Samson** ⓗ**; guest beers**
Welcoming, ever-expanding
pub with a restaurant, in a
craft-oriented market town, an
ideal base for exploring
the Wolds and Tennyson
Country.
☻ ❀ ◑ ◗ ⊟ ♣ P

Allington

Welby Arms

The Green ☎ (01400) 281361
12–2.30 (3 Sat), 5.30 (6.30 Sat)–11
**Draught Bass; Oak Wobbly
Bob; John Smith's Bitter;
Taylor landlord; guest
beers** ⓗ
A regular *Guide* entry,
boasting over 60 guest ales a
year. The dining area serves
good home cooking, including
Sun lunches (no Sun eve
meals). ♨ Q ❀ ◑ ◗ ఉ ♣ P

Aubourn

Royal Oak

Royal Oak Lane
☎ (01522) 788291
12–2.30, 7–11; 12–2.30, 7–10.30 Sun
**Bateman XB, XXXB; Samuel
Smith OBB; guest
beers** ⓗ
Welcoming village local.
Brasses and pumpclips
adorn the lounge. The bar
has an early Space Invaders
machine.
♨ ❀ ◑ ◗ ⊟ ♣ P

177

Lincolnshire

Blyton

Black Horse
93 High Street
☎ (01427) 628277
12–3.30, 5 (7 winter)–11 (closed winter Mon)
Bass Special; guest beer Ⓗ
Cosy village local; a lounge with a linked bar and a dining room. Families welcomed; small garden with a children's play area. Wide range of guest beers, plus a cider in summer.
🏰 ✿ ◐ ♣ ⌂ P

Boston

Ball House
Wainfleet Road (A52, 1 mile from town) ☎ (01205) 364478
11–3, 6.30–11; 11–11 Sat & summer
Draught Bass; Bateman Mild, XB Ⓗ
Friendly mock Tudor pub with a large roaring fire in winter. The home-cooked food (with daily specials) is popular. Its unusual name derives from its situation on a former cannon ball store.
🏰 ✿ ◐ & ♠ ♣ P

Eagle
144 West Street
☎ (01205) 361116
11–2.30, 6 (5 Thu & Fri)–11; 11–11 Sat
Adnams Broadside; Marston's Pedigree; Taylor Landlord Ⓗ; **guest beers**
Traditional town pub always offering six ales with ever-changing guest beers, one always low-priced. Folk club (alternate Mon).
✿ ⊟ ≠ ♣ ⌂

Golden Lion
46 High Street
☎ (01205) 352745
11.30–3, 7–11; 11–11 Sat
Hardys & Hansons Best Mild, Best Bitter, Kimberley Classic Ⓗ
Cosy, friendly pub within easy walking distance of the town centre, overlooking the River Witham. Pictures of boats once using the local port adorn the walls. ✿ & ≠ ♣

Olde Magnet Tavern
South Square
☎ (01205) 369186
11–4, 5.30–11; 11–11 Fri & Sat
Bass Mild, Worthington BB, Draught Bass; S&N Theakston Old Peculier; Stones Best Bitter; Taylor Landlord Ⓗ
Friendly riverside pub amongst warehouses that have been converted to an arts centre and for residential use. Opposite the historic Guildhall Museum.
🏰 ✿ ⊯ ◐ ▶ ⊟ & ≠ ♣ P

Ship Tavern
Custom House Lane
☎ (01205) 358156
11–3, 7–11
Draught Bass; Bateman Mild, XB; Whitbread Boddingtons Bitter Ⓗ
Friendly, town-centre pub, refurbished in a traditional style. Convenient for the Wed/Sat markets.
🏰 Q ◐ ⊟ & ≠ ♣

Burgh le Marsh

Olde Burgh Inn
High Street ☎ (01754) 810204
11.30–2.30, 7–11
Bateman XB; Marston's Pedigree; S&N Theakston Best Bitter, XB; guest beer Ⓗ
This Grade II-listed building, which houses an authentic beam dated 1699, first became a pub shortly after the Battle of Waterloo. A very busy establishment which serves fine food. Games room.
Q ✿ ⊯ ◐ ▶ & ▲ ♣ P ⊟

Red Lion
Storeys Lane ☎ (01754) 810582
11–11
Bateman XB; Vaux Samson Ⓗ
Welcoming, traditional country pub; the only no-food pub in this large village. Fine collection of brassware and stuffed fauna. The pool and games room and sports area at the rear are popular with all ages. 🏰 Q & ▲ ♣ P

Carlton-le-Moorland

White Hart
12 Church Street
☎ (01522) 788863
11–3, 7–11
Marston's Pedigree; Ruddles Best Bitter; John Smith's Bitter; guest beer Ⓗ
Friendly pub with a central bar surrounded by comfortable nooks and crannies. Brasses and brewery symbols adorn the walls. Book to camp. 🏰 ✿ ◐ ▶ & ▲ ♣ P

Chapel St Leonards

Ship
Sea Lane ☎ (01754) 872640
11–3.30, 7–11
Bateman Mild, XB, Valiant, Salem Porter, XXXB Ⓗ
Recently refurbished, welcoming, busy local, away from the hustle and bustle of the resort. The cosy bar/lounge features two real fires and the full range of beers from the local brewery. Meals in summer.
🏰 Q ✿ ◐ ▲ ♣ P

Claypole

Woolpack
Main Street ☎ (01636) 626274
11–11
Marston's Bitter, Pedigree; guest beer Ⓗ
Low-beamed pub where a flagstoned public bar (games) leads onto a small lounge with a real fire. Bottled beers decorate the shelves. Quality food served in the small lounge. 🏰 ✿ ◐ ▶ ♣ ⌂ P

Coleby

Tempest Arms
Hill Rise ☎ (01522) 810287
11.30–2.30, 6.30–11
Bateman XB; Courage Directors; Marston's Pedigree; Webster's Yorkshire Bitter; guest beer Ⓗ
Welcoming village local, perched on Lincoln Edge with fine views towards Newark. The scene of frequent crazy stunts and pranks. Good display of pump clips.
✿ ◐ ▶ & ♣ P

Coningsby

Ratty's
43 High Street
☎ (01526) 344609
12–3, 6.30–11 (supper licence)
Courage Directors; John Smith's Bitter; guest beers Ⓗ
This expanding pub with a riverside garden, overlooked by the church with its one-handed clock, is becoming increasingly popular with families and young people. Handy for the RAF Battle of Britain Memorial Flight.
🏰 ✿ ◐ ▶ & ♣ P

Croft

Old Chequers Inn
Lymn Bank OS503611
☎ (01754) 880320
11–3, 7–11
Bateman Mild, XB Ⓗ
Small, rural watering-hole, reputed to be the oldest pub in Lincolnshire; well off the beaten track. Sit by the roaring open fire in the snug bar, which is adorned with old agricultural implements, or sit outside and watch the world idle by. 🏰 Q ✿ ◐ ▶ & ♣

Eagle

Struggler
42 High Street
☎ (01522) 868676
12–11
John Smith's Bitter, Magnet; guest beer Ⓗ

Traditional village pub with oak-beamed ceilings and open fireplaces: a comfortable lounge for a quiet pint and good conversation with the friendly locals, plus a lively bar and a popular games room.
🏚 Q ॐ ⊛ ⊟ ▲ ♣ P ⊟

East Kirkby

Red Lion
Main Road ☎ (01790) 763406
11–3, 7–11
Bateman XB; John Smith's Bitter; guest beers ℍ
An extensive breweriana collection adorns every available space within and without this popular rural pub which maintains links with aircrews once stationed at the nearby wartime airfield (now an air museum).
🏚 ॐ ⊛ ◑ ▶ ▲ ♣ P

Frampton

Moore's Arms
Church End ☎ (01205) 722408
10–11
Draught Bass; Bateman XB; guest beers ℍ
Popular village local with a deserved reputation for meals.
⊛ ◑ ▶

Freiston

King's Head
Church Road
☎ (01205) 760368
11.30–3, 7–11; 11.30–11 Sat
Draught Bass; Bateman Mild, XB ℍ
15th-century, traditional village pub with a 'Lancaster' restaurant (book). Popular lunchtimes and at weekends. Fine selection of home-cooked food; excellent value.
🏚 Q ◑ ♣ P

Frognall

Goat
155 Spalding Road
☎ (01778) 347629
11–2.30 (3 Sat), 6–11
Adnams Bitter; Draught Bass ℍ/ℊ**; guest beers** ℍ/ℊ
Well-run country pub set back from the A16. A new extension has added facilities for families and meetings. 237 guest beers, mainly from independents and micros, offered in 1994. Excellent food.
🏚 Q ॐ ⊛ ◑ ▶ ▲ ♣ P

Gainsborough

Eight Jolly Brewers
Ship Court, Silver Street
☎ (01427) 677128

11–3, 7–11
Bateman Mild, XB; South Yorkshire Barnsley Bitter; guest beers ℍ
Real ale haven serving eight beers at all times, specialising in smaller brewers' products: a small bar and a lounge area upstairs. The adjacent car park is pay and display until 6pm.
Q ◑ ⊟ ♣ ○

Gedney Dyke

Chequers
☎ (01406) 362666
11–3, 7–11
Adnams Bitter; Draught Bass; Bateman XXXB; Greene King Abbot; Morland Old Speckled Hen ℍ
Attractive country pub and restaurant in a quiet village setting, dating back to circa 1795. It can be very busy, but is worth seeking out, especially if hungry as well as thirsty. 🏚 ⊛ ◑ ▶ ♣ P

Grantham

Angel & Royal Hotel (Angel Bar)
High Street ☎ (01476) 65816
12–2.30 (3 Fri; not Mon–Wed), 6–11; 11–4, 7–11 Sat
Draught Bass; Courage Directors; guest beers ℍ
Reputedly England's oldest coaching inn, established in the 13th century and commissioned by the Knights Templar. 🏚 Q ⊛ ⊯ ◑ ▶ P

Beehive Inn
10–11 Castlegate
☎ (01476) 67794
11–3, 7–11
Adnams Broadside; Whitbread Boddingtons Bitter; guest beers ℍ
Renowned as the only pub in England with a living sign. Popular with young people and biker friendly. ⊛ ◑ ⇌

Blue Bull
64 Westgate ☎ (01476) 70929
11–3 (4 Sat), 7–11
Wadworth 6X; Whitbread Boddingtons Bitter; guest beers ℍ
A welcoming, lively atmosphere prevails at the local CAMRA *Pub of the Year* 1995. An 1850s pub and restaurant, it serves good, home-cooked food (not Sun eve), plus a wide range of guest beers and occasional ciders. Q ◑ ▶ ⇌ ♣ ○ P

Blue Pig
9 Vine Street ☎ (01476) 63704
11–11
Draught Bass; Wadworth 6X; Whitbread Boddingtons Bitter, Castle Eden Ale,

Flowers Original; guest beers ℍ
Tudor building which survived the Grantham Fire of 1660. A popular drinking place for all ages. Good value lunches. 🏚 ◑ ○

Chequers
25 Market Place
☎ (01476) 76383
12–3 (not Mon–Wed), 5–11; 12–11 Fri; 11–4, 7–11 Sat
Beer range varies ℍ
Thriving popular free house, local CAMRA *Pub of the Year* 1993. The beer range is always changing (usually seven guest beers; over 350 sold in 1994). ◑

Odd House
4 Fletcher Street
☎ (01476) 65293
11–11
Courage Directors; John Smith's Bitter; Vaux Extra Special; guest beers ℍ
Friendly, two-room, terraced pub, popular with all ages.
🏚 Q ⊛ ⇌ ♣

Hagworthingham

George & Dragon
Main Road ☎ (01507) 588255
11–11 (closes Mon & Tue afternoons in winter)
Courage Directors; John Smith's Bitter; guest beers ℍ
Large, comfortable, village pub close to the Tennyson-Twenty Ramblers Trail, in the picturesque Wolds. Very busy and popular. Home-cooked fish and chips a speciality Fri; take-aways available.
Q ⊛ ◑ ▶ ⊟ ▲ ♣ P

Haltoft End

Castle Inn
☎ (01205) 760393
11–3, 7–11
Bateman Mild, XB ℍ
Friendly, roadside local which can be very busy summer weekends. A keen darts and domino pub with an excellent adventure playground for children. 🏚 ⊛ ⇌ ◑ ♣ P

Halton Holegate

Bell
Firsby Road ☎ (01790) 753242
11–3, 7–11
Draught Bass; Bateman XB; Whitbread Boddingtons Bitter ℍ
The pub sign depicts a Lancaster from a nearby wartime airfield and a railway sleeper serves as a mantlepiece, in this unpretentious, hospitable inn. Interesting food.
🏚 Q ⊛ ◑ ▶ ♣ P

Lincolnshire

Horbling

Plough Inn
4 Spring Lane
☎ (01529) 240263
11–3, 6.30–11
Greene King IPA; guest beers Ⓗ
Late 17th-century building owned by the parish council. Fred, the resident ghost, wanders the premises after time searching for a late drink. Speciality eves in the restaurant.
🏚 🍴 ❀ ◖ ▶ 😄 ᵬ ♣ P ⊟

Horncastle

Red Lion
Bullring ☎ (01507) 523338
11–3, 7–11
Greenalls Shipstone's Mild, Bitter, Davenports Bitter; Tetley Bitter Ⓗ
Pleasant, friendly pub, a meeting place for clubs and societies. It also supports a flourishing theatre in the converted stables.
🏚 Q 🍴 🚗 ◖ ᵬ ♣ P

King's Head (Thatch)
Bullring ☎ (01507) 523360
11–3 (4 Sat), 7–11
Bateman Mild, XB, Valiant, Salem Porter Ⓗ
Cosy, diminutive pub which, with its award-winning outdoor floral display, affords a warm welcome. The walls are adorned with horse-racing pictures and decorative plates, and shelves are filled with pot plants. 🏚 Q ◖ ▶ ♣

Hubbert's Bridge

Wheatsheaf
Station Road ☎ (01205) 290347
11–3, 5–11; 11–11 Mon & Sat
Vaux Samson, Extra Special; Wards Thorne Best Bitter Ⓗ
Family-run, bankside pub, ideal for fishing and near good golfing facilities. Excellent food is served in both the bar and restaurant; ever-changing specials and imaginative vegetarian dishes available.
🏚 ❀ 🚗 ◖ ▶ ▲ ➤ ♣ P

Knaith Park

Stag's Head
Willingham Road (B1241)
☎ (01427) 612917
12–3 (not Mon), 7–11; 12–11 Sat
Marston's Pedigree; Tetley Bitter; Wards Best Bitter; Willy's Bitter Ⓗ
Small village pub, a base for local cricketers. The home-made pies are highly recommended (no meals Mon). 🏚 Q ❀ ◖ ▶ 😄 ♣ P

Lincoln

Dog & Bone
10 John Street (off Monks Rd, near N Lincs College)
☎ (01522) 522403
12–3, 7 (5 Fri & Sat)–11
Draught Bass; Bateman XB, Valiant, XXXB, Salem Porter; Marston's Pedigree; guest beer Ⓗ
Friendly, one-roomer, formerly known as the Gay Dog, boasting an array of old relics with a touch of humour. Popular with students; occasional fun nights. One guest beer. 🏚 ❀ ᵬ ➤ ♣ P

Golden Eagle
21 High Street
☎ (01522) 521058
11–3, 5.30–11; 11–11 Sat
Bateman XB; Fuller's London Pride; Gale's Best Bitter; Hop Back Summer Lightning; guest beers Ⓗ
Friendly pub half a mile from the city centre, mainly frequented by locals but strangers are made welcome. Photos of bygone Lincoln adorn the walls. Regularly changing guest beers and a guest cider feature (it hosts Lincoln's annual cider festival). Q ❀ ◖ 😄 ♣ ⊃ P

Jolly Brewer
26 Broadgate ☎ (01522) 528583
11–11
Draught Bass; Everards Tiger; S&N Theakston XB; Younger Scotch, No. 3; guest beers Ⓗ
Very popular city-centre pub, attracting a wide range of customers; previously known as the Unity. Families welcome lunchtimes. No food Sun.
🏚 ❀ ◖ ➤ ♣ ⊃ P

Peacock Inn
23 Wragby Road
☎ (01522) 524703
11.30–2.30, 7–11; 11–11 Sat
Hardys & Hansons Best Mild, Best Bitter, Kimberley Classic Ⓗ
Popular local, not far from the cathedral and castle. Dominoes and darts are popular. No food Sun.
🏚 ❀ ◖ 😄 ♣ P

Portland Arms
50 Portland Street
☎ (01522) 513912
11–11
Draught Bass; Courage Directors; John Smith's Bitter, Magnet; Thwaites Bitter; Wilson's Mild; guest beers Ⓗ
Simple, clean, friendly town pub with no ties. Five guest beers from near and far are served in a lively tap room and a cosy, quiet, best room. A traditional gem.
Q 😄 ➤ ♣ ⊃ P

Queen in the West
12–14 Moor Street
☎ (01522) 526169
11.30–3, 5.30–11; 11.30–11 Fri & Sat
Bateman XB; Courage Directors; Morland Old Speckled Hen; S&N Theakston XB, Old Peculier; Taylor Landlord Ⓗ
Traditional pub with a comfortable lounge and a public bar housing various games. Eight cask ales are normally available. Popular with local workers for weekday lunches and with residents eves. ◖ 😄 ♣

Sippers
26 Melville Street
☎ (01522) 527612
11–3, 5 (4 Fri, 7 Sat)–11; 7–10.30 Sun, closed Sun lunch
Bateman XXXB; Courage Directors; Marston's Pedigree; Morland Old Speckled Hen; John Smith's Bitter; Wilson's Mild Ⓗ
Friendly, street-corner local near the station; busy with workers lunchtime; quieter eves. Wide range of interesting and varied guest beers. Eve meals Mon-Fri. ◖ ▶ ➤ ♣

Small Beer Off-Licence
91 Newland Street West
☎ (01522) 528628
10.30–10.30
Bateman XXXB; Everards Beacon; Taylor Landlord; guest beers Ⓗ
Pleasant, back-street off-licence serving many different guest beers, together with British and foreign bottled beers. ⊃

Strugglers
83 Westgate ☎ (01522) 524702
11–3, 5.30–11; 11–11 Fri & Sat
Bass Mild, Draught Bass Ⓗ
Basic, two-roomed gem with a hatch serving the old smoke room. The cask mild has returned at the request of the mixed clientele. Strong on darts and dominoes; frequented by footballers at weekends. Q ❀ 😄 ♣

Tap & Spile
21 Hungate ☎ (01522) 534015
11–11
Draught Bass; guest beers Ⓗ
Now part of the pub chain, the former White Horse always offers a wide selection of ales. The open-plan bar is divided into distinct drinking areas.
🏚 Q ❀ ◖ ➤ ♣ ⊃ ✂

Victoria
6 Union Road
☎ (01522) 536048
11–11

Bateman XB; Everards Old Original; Taylor Landlord; guest beers Ⓗ
Noted (uphill) free house with a constantly changing range of up to six guest beers, usually including a mild. Regular brewery feature nights, plus festivals at Xmas and in summer. Q ❀ ◐ ⊞ ⌓

Woodcocks
Burton Lane End (off A57, between Lincoln and Saxilby)
☎ (01522) 703460
11–11
Bateman Mild; Marston's Bitter, Pedigree Ⓗ
Large, family-oriented pub in its own grounds on the banks of the Fosdyke Canal, with children's play areas indoors and out. Marston's Head Brewer's Choice ales sold.
❀ ◐ ◑ ♿ P

Little Bytham

Willoughby Arms
On B1176 opp. the old station
☎ (01780) 410276
6–11; 12–3, 6–11 Sat
Ruddles County; guest beers Ⓗ
Cosy, welcoming village pub, with splendid views over rolling fields from the back room bar. Two guest beers; good home cooking every eve, and weekend lunchtime.
Q ❀ ◐ ◑ ♿ ♣ P

Louth

Mason's Arms
Cornmarket ☎ (01507) 609525
11–11
Draught Bass; Bateman Mild, XB, Salem Porter, XXXB; Marston's Pedigree; guest beer Ⓗ
Old posting inn from the 18th century, splendidly restored by the present owners and providing all the facilities of a small country hotel. Food available throughout the day; the home-made dishes are highly praised.
Q ❀ ◐ ◑ ♣

Wheatsheaf
62 Westgate ☎ (01507) 605262
11–3, 5–11; 11–11 Sat
Draught Bass; Morland Old Speckled Hen; Whitbread Boddingtons Bitter, Bentley's Yorkshire Bitter, Flowers Original; guest beers Ⓗ
Attractive old inn dated 1612, sited in a Georgian terrace. Popular and comfortable. Lunches served weekdays. Beware the keg cider on a fake handpump. Q ❀ ◐ P

Woodman Inn
134 Eastgate ☎ (01507) 602100
11–3 (4 Wed & Fri), 7–11; 11–11 Sat
John Smith's Bitter, Magnet, *or* **Courage Directors; guest beer** Ⓗ
Large, comfortable one-roomer. No food Sun.
❀ ◐ ♣

Mablethorpe

Montalt Arms
George Street (off High St)
☎ (01507) 472794
11.30–3, 7–11
Draught Bass; Bateman XB; Stones Best Bitter; guest beer Ⓗ
Welcoming pub named in honour of a 13th-century knight, Robert de Montalt, offering a pleasant, L-shaped lounge bar and a well-appointed restaurant. No meals winter Mon. An oasis in a beer desert. Beware the keg cider on a fake handpump.
❀ ◐ ◑

Market Deeping

Vine
19 Church Street
☎ (01778) 342387
11–2, 5.30–11
Wells Eagle, Bombardier, Fargo; guest beers Ⓗ
Former 1870s prep school, now a friendly local with a small lounge and a larger busy bar. Many social nights hosted. Ask to see the model train set.
Q ❀ ♿ ▲ ♣ P

Metheringham

White Hart
High Street ☎ (01526) 320496
11–4, 6.30–11; 11–11 Thu–Sat
Mansfield Riding Mild, Riding Bitter, Bitter, Old Baily Ⓗ
Friendly village local with a warm welcome. Internal alterations are expected, but these should not affect the character. Mansfield's seasonal ales stocked. ❀ ◐ ◑ ⊞ ♣

Minting

Sebastapol Inn
Church Lane ☎ (01507) 578688
12–3, 7–10.30; closed Mon
Draught Bass; Bateman Mild; guest beers Ⓗ
Comfortable, 16th-century, village local, offering excellent food in pleasant surroundings. Note the 100-year-old bar billiards table. Q ❀ ◐ ◑ ⊞ ♿ ♣ P

Nettleton

Salutation Inn
Church Street (A46 jct)
☎ (01472) 851228
12–3, 6–11; 12–11 Sat
Fuller's London Pride; Morland Old Speckled Hen; Whitbread Boddingtons Mild, Bitter, Flowers Original; guest beer Ⓗ
Traditional 19th-century coaching inn, renovated with care. The large garden has a children's play area and a menagerie. Close to the Viking Way, it is popular with locals, diners and walkers. Speciality food nights and beer festivals.
Q ❀ ◐ ◑ ♿ P

North Kelsey

Royal Oak
High Street ☎ (01652) 678544
12–3, 7–11
Draught Bass; Vaux Samson; Wards Best Bitter; guest beer Ⓗ
Fine, friendly, old village pub. The lounge bar has two real fires. There is also a games room and a snug. Popular for meals. ◐ ◑ ♣ P

North Kelsey Moor

Queen's Head
Station Road (near the disused N Kelsey station) OS070018
☎ (01652) 678055
12–3, 7–11
S&N Theakston Best Bitter; Tetley Bitter; guest beer Ⓗ
Friendly, three-roomed free house; a bit out of the way but worth finding. Eve meals Tue–Sat.
Q ❀ ◐ ◑ ⊞ ♿ ▲ ♣ P

Pinchbeck

Packing Shed
Glenside South ($1\frac{1}{2}$miles W of A16, S side of River Glen)
☎ (01775) 640355
12–3, 7–11
Ansells Bitter; Draught Bass; Ind Coope Burton Ale; Tetley Bitter Ⓗ
Large, deservedly popular free house with a warm welcome. Having grown out of a small restaurant and bar, it retains a good name for food.
Q ❀ ◐ ◑ ⌓ P

Potterhanworth Booths

Plough
Plough Hill (B1201/B1190 jct)
☎ (01522) 794798
12–3, 7–11
Marston's Pedigree; Morland Old Speckled Hen; Ruddles County; John Smith's Bitter; guest beer Ⓗ
Large, welcoming rural pub with a good children's play area. Good choice of guest beers. ❀ ◐ ◑ ▲ ♣ P

Lincolnshire

Quadring

White Hart
Town Drove (50 yds W of A152) ☎ (01775) 821135
12–3 (not Mon), 7–11
Bateman Mild, XB; Whitbread Boddingtons Bitter Ⓗ
Friendly, popular village pub with a lively atmosphere. Darts and pool played. Wheelchair access is from the car park at the rear.
🏨 ❀ ♿ ♣ P

Raithby

Red Lion
Main Street ☎ (01790) 753727
11–3 (not Mon–Fri, except bank hols), 7–11
Home Bitter; S&N Theakston XB; Tetley Bitter Ⓗ
Inviting and friendly pub in an attractive Wolds village, serving excellent cuisine (intimate restaurant open Wed-Sat eve). Freshly-made pizzas and bistro-style bar food. Comfortable accommodation.
🏨 Q ❀ 🍴 🍺 ♣ ♻ P

Rothwell

Nickerson Arms
Hillrise (off A46)
☎ (01472) 371300
12–2, 7 (5 Mon & Fri)–11
Bateman XB, XXXB; Fuller's London Pride; Marston's Pedigree; Shepherd Neame Spitfire; Taylor Landlord Ⓗ; **guest beers** Ⓗ/Ⓖ
Pub situated in a lovely Wolds village offering ten real ales, Belgian classics, unpasteurised continental lagers, ciders, malt whiskies and a wine list for the connoisseur, to accompany proper food: a formula to suit all tastes. Live jazz most Sun eves. Families welcome.
🏨 Q ❀ 🍴 ♻ P ⚥

Ruskington

Black Bull
10 Rectory Road
☎ (01526) 832270
11.30–2.30 (3 Fri, 3.30 Sat), 6.30–11
Draught Bass; Bateman XB Ⓗ
Comfortable local in a large village. Its mock-Tudor frontage is graced with interesting sculptures of two monkeys. Part of the public bar was once used as stables. No meals Sun eve.
❀ 🍴 🍺 ♿ 🍺 ♣ P

Saxilby

Ship Inn
21 Bridge Street
☎ (01522) 702259

11.30–2.30 (3 Fri & Sat), 7 (5.30 summer)–11
Courage Directors; John Smith's Bitter Ⓗ
Friendly pub in a pleasant village; very popular with sportsmen and canal boaters. Good food at reasonable prices (eve meals to order). Camping and caravanning site at the rear of the pub by prior arrangement.
❀ 🍴 ▲ 🍺 ♣ P

Sleaford

Carre Arms Hotel
Mareham Lane
☎ (01529) 303156
11–3, 7–11
Draught Bass; Stones Best Bitter Ⓗ
Comfortable hotel with a large bar that manages to be snug and cosy. The lounge has a brasserie and can get busy. Separate restaurant.
🍴 🍺 P

Nag's Head
64 Southgate ☎ (01529) 413916
11–3, 7–11; 11–11 Fri & Sat
Draught Bass; Bateman XB, XXXB; guest beers Ⓗ
Down-to-earth local with live music most weekends.
🍺 ♣ P

Rose & Crown
4 Watergate ☎ (01529) 303350
11–3, 7–11
Mansfield Riding Bitter, Bitter, Old Baily Ⓗ
Welcoming, town-centre pub with friendly staff and a large games area. A ghost in the cellar turns off the keg beer gas! No meals weekends.
❀ 🍴 ♣ P

South Reston

Waggon & Horses
Main Road ☎ (01507) 450364
11–3, 7–11; 11–11 Sat
Bass Worthington BB, Draught Bass; guest beers Ⓗ
Comfortable, quiet inn on the Louth to Mablethorpe road. Popular with diners; meals are served in the bar and dining room. Beware the keg cider on a fake handpump.
🏨 ❀ 🍴 ▲ ♣ P

Spalding

Lincoln Arms
4 Bridge Street
☎ (01775) 722691
11–3, 6.30–11
Mansfield Riding Mild, Riding Bitter, Bitter, Old Baily; guest beers Ⓗ
18th-century riverside pub, close to the town centre; unpretentious and cosy, with a

friendly welcome. Mansfield seasonal beers sold.
❀ 🍴 🍺 ♣

Red Lion Hotel
Market Place ☎ (01775) 722869
11–11
Bass Worthington BB, Draught Bass; Marston's Pedigree; guest beers Ⓗ
Busy, town-centre hotel bar, popular with locals and visitors to this historic town. Home to Spalding Blues & Jazz Club. Q 🍴 🍺 🍴 ♿ 🍺

Spilsby

Nelson Butt
10 Market Street
☎ (01790) 752258
10.30–3, 7–11
Bateman XB; Marston's Pedigree Ⓗ
Basic, friendly, no-frills, small market town pub. Q ❀ ♣ P

Springthorpe

New Inn
Hill Road ☎ (01427) 83254
12–2, 7–11; closed Mon eve
Bateman XXXB; Marston's Pedigree Ⓗ
Friendly village local renowned for its cheerful singing landlord and excellent food.
🏨 Q ❀ 🍴 🍺 ♣ P ⚥ ⊟

Stamford

Daniel Lambert
20 St Leonard's Street
☎ (01780) 55991
11.30–3, 6–11
Adnams Bitter; Courage Directors; John Smith's Bitter; Taylor Landlord; guest beer Ⓗ
Named after a 52-stone man, buried in Stamford; a 200-year-old, traditional single-room pub with a recently added cellar restaurant. Meals served Wed-Sat eve, plus Sun lunch.
🏨 🍴 🍺 ♣

Dolphin
60 East Street ☎ (01780) 55494
11–3, 7–11
Adnams Broadside; Hall & Woodhouse Tanglefoot; Wells Eagle, Bombardier, Fargo; guest beer Ⓗ
Pub dating back to 1714, divided into small, intimate rooms. Note the collection of old Stamford prints. Beer festival July. Wheelchair WC.
Q 🍴 🍴 🍺 ♿ 🍺 ♣

St Peter's Inn
11 St Peter's Street (300 yds from bus station)
☎ (01780) 63298
11–2.30 (not Mon), 5.30–11; 12–11 Fri & Sat

Lincolnshire

Marston's Bitter, Pedigree; guest beers Ⓗ/Ⓖ
Friendly pub on the edge of town, in a 200-year-old stone building. Beers on handpull in the lounge bar and gravity in the downstairs 'Cloister' bar. Local CAMRA *Pub of the Year* 1993. Guests include Marston's Head Brewer's Choice. Meals Thu–Sat eve, plus Sun lunch.
❀) ≠ P

White Swan
21 Scotgate ☎ (01780) 52834
11–3, 5 (6 Sat)–11
Bateman Mild, XB, XXXB, Victory Ⓗ
18th-century, stone building, a pub since 1836. This friendly, ex-Mann's house is strong on games. ⚌ Q ≠ ♣

Stickney

Plough & Dove
Main Road ☎ (01205) 480965
11–3.30, 6.30–11
Bateman XB; Courage Directors; John Smith's Bitter; guest beers (occasional) Ⓗ
Lively village pub, reputedly frequented by Arthur Lucan (Old Mother Riley) during his travels. Occasional entertainment and theme nights.
⚌ ⛛ ❀ ◖) ⊞ & ♠ ♣ P ⊟

Surfleet

Mermaid Inn
2 Gosberton Road (A16)
☎ (01775) 680275
11.30–3, 6.30–11
Adnams Broadside; S&N Theakston Best Bitter, XB; John Smith's Bitter; guest beers Ⓗ
Former brewery situated by the River Glen. Recently refurbished, it has a relaxing, friendly atmosphere and is renowned for meals. The large garden has a play area.
⚌ Q ❀ ⊨ ◖) & P

Susworth

Jenny Wren
Main Street ☎ (01724) 783441

11–3, 7–11
John Smith's Bitter; Webster's Yorkshire Bitter; guest beer Ⓗ
Superb, 18th-century, country pub close to the River Trent: a large ground-floor drinking area with many nooks and crannies and an upstairs restaurant with a reputation for fine food. Wheelchair WC.
⚌ ❀ ⊨ ◖) & ♠ P ⊬

Swayfield

Royal Oak Inn
High Street
☎ (01476) 550247
11.30–2.30, 6–11
Draught Bass; Oakham Old Tosspot; Tetley Bitter Ⓗ
Delightful, stone village inn with a spacious but cosy interior. Its beamed ceiling is just high enough to clear the grandfather clock. Worth seeking out for its food as well as the beer.
⚌ ❀ ⊨ ◖) & ♣ P ⊟

Swineshead

Wheatsheaf Hotel
Market Place
☎ (01205) 820349
12–2.30, 6–11; 12–11 Sat
Draught Bass; Bateman XB; Marston's Pedigree; guest beers Ⓗ
Traditional village pub with a good selection of bar and restaurant meals (no bar food Tue or Sun). Trad. jazz live alternate Thu.
⚌ ❀ ⊨ ◖) ♣ P

Thorpe Culvert

Three Tuns
Culvert Road OS471603
☎ (01754) 880495
11–3, 7–11
Tetley Bitter; guest beers Ⓗ
Small, 250-year-old riverside pub with a large garden area, tranquil for fishermen. The intimate restaurant is busy at weekends (book). Sun lunch served.
⚌ Q) ≠ ♣ P

Threekingham

Three Kings Inn
Salters Way ☎ (01529) 340249
11–3 (may extend in summer), 7–11
Bass Worthington BB; Draught Bass; Stones Best Bitter; guest beers (occasional) Ⓗ
This pub and the village take their names from three Danish chieftains who were killed in the 9th century battle of nearby Stow Green.
⚌ ❀ ◖) ♠ ♣ P

Wainfleet

Jolly Sailor Inn
19 St John Street
☎ (01754) 880275
11–11
Draught Bass; Bateman Mild, XB Ⓗ
Welcoming, cosy street-corner local. Note the table made from old ship timbers in the bar. ⚌ ◖) ≠ ♣

Royal Oak
73 High Street
☎ (01754) 880328
11–3 (later summer), 7–11
Bateman Mild, XB, Valiant; guest beers (summer) Ⓗ
Cheerful little pub; apparently the building once belonged to Bethleham Hospital for the insane. The detailed model of *HMS Vanguard* on display took two years to build.
⚌ ❀ ⊨ ◖) ♠ ≠ ♣ P

Whaplode St Catherine

Blue Bell Inn
Cranesgate ☎ (01406) 540300
7–11; 11–3, 7–11 Sat
Vaux Samson; guest beers Ⓗ
Lively village local with a friendly and enthusiastic landlord; built in the 17th century and in the same ownership for over 25 years. A new restaurant is planned. Camping and caravanning in the grounds.
⚌ Q ❀) ♠ ♣ P

GOOD PUB FOOD

For many pub enthusiasts, a good meal is as important as a good pint. In recognition of this, CAMRA launched its own guide to *Good Pub Food* some seven years ago. Compiled by award-winning food writer Susan Nowak, this influential guide has now been released in its fourth edition. It features around 500 pubs serving the finest pub cooking, with not a microwaved lasagne in sight. Priced £9.99, it is available in bookshops or post-free from CAMRA (cheques made payable to CAMRA), at 230 Hatfield Road, St Albans, Hertfordshire AL1 4LW. Credit card orders are taken on (01727) 867201. Discounts are available for CAMRA members.

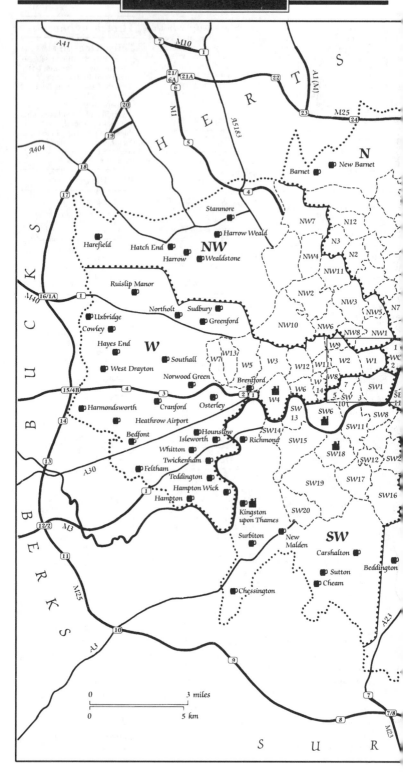

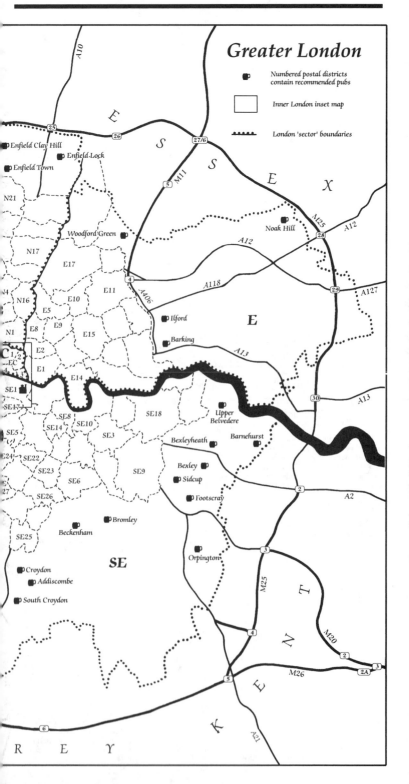

Greater London

■ Numbered postal districts contain recommended pubs

▭ Inner London inset map

••••• London 'sector' boundaries

185

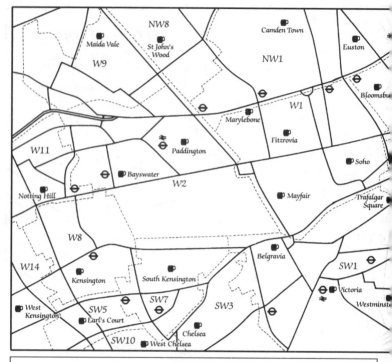

Bishops, *Borough Market, SE1;* **Flamingo**, *Kingston upon Thames;* **Freedom**, *Fulham, SW6;* **Fuller's**, *Chiswick, W4;* **Young's**, *Wandsworth, SW18*

NB: Pubs within Greater London are divided into seven geographical sectors: Central, East, North, North-West, South-East, South-West and West, reflecting London postal boundaries (see Greater London map on previous pages). Look under Central London for postal districts EC1 to EC4, and WC1 and WC2. For each of the surrounding sectors, postal districts are listed in numerical order (E1, E2, etc.), followed in alphabetical order by the outlying areas which do not have London postal numbers (Barking, Ilford, etc.). The Inner London map, above, shows the area roughly covered by the Circle Line and outlines regions of London (Bloomsbury, Holborn, etc.) which have featured pubs. Some regions straddle more than one postal district.

Central London

EC1: Clerkenwell

Artillery Arms
102 Bunhill Row
☎ (0171) 253 4683
11–11
Fuller's Chiswick, London
Pride, ESB Ⓗ
Tiny corner pub with a happy mixture of office and local clientele. Fuller's seasonal beers also stocked.
Ⓓ ≈ (Old St) ⊖ ♣

Sekforde Arms
34 Sekforde Street
☎ (0171) 253 3231
11–11; 12–3 Sun, closed Sun eve
Young's Bitter, Special, Winter Warmer Ⓗ
Small, attractive, corner pub

with an upstairs restaurant.
Q Ⓓ ♪ ≈ (Farringdon) ⊖ ♣

EC1: Holborn

Melton Mowbray
18 Holborn ☎ (0171) 405 7077
11–11; closed Sat & Sun
Fuller's Chiswick, London
Pride, ESB Ⓗ
Popular pub, once a camping and climbing shop, now a fine, traditional, multi-level bar. A recently opened downstairs bar doubles as a function room eves. Fuller's seasonal beers served. Q ✿ Ⓓ ♪ &
≈ (Farringdon) ⊖ (Chancery Lane)

EC1: Old Street

Sutton Arms
15 Great Sutton Street
☎ (0171) 253 3251

11–11 (4 Sat); closed Sun
Everards Tiger; Whitbread Boddingtons Bitter, Flowers Original; Young's Special; guest beers Ⓗ
Bustling side-street pub where the beer range may vary. It can be loud Fri eves.
Ⓓ ≈ (Barbican) ⊖

EC1: Smithfield

Bishops Finger
9–10 West Smithfield
☎ (0171) 248 2341
11–11; closed Sat & Sun
Shepherd Neame Master Brew Bitter, Best Bitter, Spitfire, Bishops Finger; guest beer Ⓗ
Popular, small, single bar that usually has the full Shep's range of beers, including seasonal brews. Beware the fake handpump for keg cider.
Ⓓ ≈ (Farringdon) ⊖ ♣

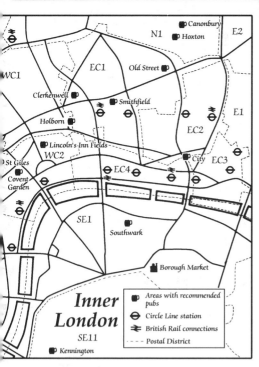

Inner London
SE11

- Areas with recommended pubs
- ⊖ Circle Line station
- ⇌ British Rail connections
- - - - Postal District

Map labels: Canonbury, Hoxton, N1, E2, Old Street, EC1, WC1, Clerkenwell, Smithfield, E1, Holborn, EC2, Lincoln's Inn Fields, WC2, St Giles, City, EC3, Covent Garden, EC4, SE1, Southwark, Borough Market, Kennington

EC2: City

Fleetwood
36 Wilson Street
☎ (0171) 247 2242
11–9.30 (3 Sat); closed Sun
Fuller's Chiswick, London Pride, ESB; guest beers H
Busy city venue within the Broadgate development offering quick service from friendly staff. High quality food; free bar snacks most eves. Beware the keg cider on a fake handpump. Fuller's seasonal beers sold. ✿ ◖ ▶ ⇌ (Liverpool St) ⊖ (Moorgate)

EC3: City

Elephant
Fenchurch Street
☎ (0171) 623 8970
11–10.30 (may close earlier); closed Sat & Sun
Young's Bitter, Special, Winter Warmer H
Ex-Finch's pub run by a landlord who was at the nearby East India Arms for 21 years: a small, basic upstairs bar and a large lounge bar downstairs. Q ✿ ◖ 🍴 ⎕ ⇌ (Fenchurch St) ⊖ (Aldgate) ♣

Lamb Tavern
10–12 Leadenhall Market
☎ (0171) 626 2454
11–9; closed Sat & Sun
Young's Bitter, Special H
Large, two-bar pub in Leadenhall Market, popular with Lloyds underwriters. Q ◖ ⇌ (Liverpool St) ⊖

Swan
Ship Tavern Passage, 77–80 Gracechurch Street
☎ (0171) 283 7712
11–9; closed Sat & Sun
Fuller's Chiswick, London Pride, ESB H
Traditional bar at ground level, with a larger bar upstairs. Watch the steps to the gents'. Fuller's seasonal beers also stocked. Q ⊖ (Bank)

Three Lords
27 Minories
11–11 (may close earlier); closed Sat & Sun
Young's Bitter, Special H
Pub whose name appears to commemorate the Jacobite Rebellion in 1745. Q ◖ ▶ ⇌ (Fenchurch St) ⊖ (Aldgate) ⊠

Wine Lodge
145 Fenchurch Street
☎ (0171) 626 0918
11–10 (ground floor closes 7.30); closed Sat & Sun

Young's Bitter, Special, Winter Warmer H
Basic pub with wooden floors which was privately owned until taken over by Young's. The ground floor is a no-smoking bar lunchtimes. Q ⇌ (Fenchurch St) ⊖ (Monument) ⊠

EC4: City

Banker
Cousin Lane
☎ (0171) 283 5206
11–9; closed Sat & Sun
Fuller's Chiswick, London Pride, ESB H
Pub built in railway arches under Cannon St station, with views of the Thames from the raised drinking area and patio. ✿ ◖ ⇌ (Cannon St) ⊖

City Retreat
74 Shoe Lane
☎ (0171) 353 7904
11–9 (11 Fri; may vary); closed Sat & Sun
Young's Bitter, Special, Winter Warmer H
Small, cosy, single bar with local character, unusual for a City pub. Q ◖ ⇌ (City) ⊖ (Farringdon) ♣

WC1: Bloomsbury

Calthorpe Arms
252 Grays Inn Road
☎ (0171) 278 4732
11–3, 5.30–11; 11–11 Thu-Sat
Young's Bitter, Special, Winter Warmer H
Relaxed, welcoming single bar local, popular with staff from nearby ITN. The upstairs dining room is open lunchtimes. Q ✿ ◖ ▶ ♿ ⊖ (Russell Sq)

Queen's Head
66 Acton Street
☎ (0171) 837 4491
11–11
Draught Bass; Fuller's London Pride; Hook Norton Best Bitter; Stones Best Bitter H
One-bar, Victorian pub with some original fittings including a tiled wall and floor. Sky TV. Cider occasionally in summer. ✿ ◖ ▶ (King's Cross) ⊖ ♣ ⎕

Rugby Tavern
19 Great James Street
☎ (0171) 405 1384
11–11; closed Sat & Sun
Fuller's Chiswick, London Pride, ESB H
Popular pub frequented by locals and office workers alike, serving a good range of beer (Fuller's seasonal beers stocked) and excellent food.

No-smoking lunchtime in the function room. Q ✿ ◖ ▶
⊖ (Russell Sq) ⊬

WC1: Holborn

Three Cups
21–22 Sandland Street
☎ (0171) 831 4302
11–11; closed Sat & Sun
Young's Bitter, Special, Winter Warmer Ⓗ
Busy, back-street, single-bar pub catering for the office trade. Q ✿ ◖ ▶ ⊖

WC2: Covent Garden

Hogshead Ale House
21 Drury Lane
☎ (0171) 240 2489
11–11
Brakspear Bitter; Fuller's London Pride; Whitbread Boddingtons Bitter Ⓗ; guest beers Ⓗ/Ⓖ
Small, cosy pub opposite the New London Theatre, offering frequent, interesting guest beers. ◖ ⊖

Marquess of Anglesey
39 Bow Street
☎ (0171) 240 3216
11–11
Young's Bitter, Special, Winter Warmer Ⓗ
Busy, corner pub handy for all the attractions around Covent Garden. A restaurant and bar are housed on the first floor. ◖ ▶ ⊖

Nag's Head
10 James Street
☎ (0171) 836 4678
11–11
Draught Bass; McMullen AK, Country; guest beers Ⓗ
Comfortable pub, popular with tourists and opera-goers; due for refurbishment. ◖ ▶ ⊖

Roundhouse
1 Garrick Street
☎ (0171) 836 9838
11–11
Marston's Pedigree; S&N Theakston Best Bitter, Old Peculier; Younger IPA; guest beers Ⓗ
Wedge-shaped pub on the corner of Garrick St and New Row. ◖ ▶ ⊖ ⌣

Sugar Loaf
40 Great Queen Street
☎ (0171) 405 0592
11.30 (12 Sat)–11; closed Sun & bank hols
Draught Bass; Hancock's HB Ⓗ
Two-bar pub opposite the Freemasons Hall and the Connaught Rooms. ◖ ▶ ⊖

WC2: Lincoln's Inn Fields

Seven Stars
53 Carey Street
☎ (0171) 242 8521
11–9; closed Sat & Sun
Courage Best Bitter, Directors Ⓗ
Olde-worlde pub built in 1602, popular with members of the legal profession from the nearby law courts.
Q ◖ ▶ ⊖ (Temple)

WC2: St Giles

Angel
61 St Giles High Street
11 (12 Sat)–11; closed Sun
Courage Best Bitter, Directors; S&N Theakston Best Bitter, XB; guest beer Ⓗ
Reputedly haunted pub near Centrepoint. No food Sat.
◖ ⊖ (Tottenham Ct Rd) ♣

East London

E1: Stepney

Hollands
Brayforde Square
☎ (0171) 790 3057
11–11
Young's Bitter, Special Ⓗ
Treasure house of Victorian breweriana and press cuttings in a Grade II-listed interior.
⇌ (Limehouse)
⊖ (Whitechapel)

E1: Whitechapel

Lord Rodney's Head
285 Whitechapel Road
11–11
B&T Shefford Mild, Bitter, SOS, SOD, Black Bat Ⓗ
Narrow, one-bar pub housing dozens of clocks. Popular with staff and students from the London Hospital opposite. Regular live bands. ⊖ ♣

E2: Bethnal Green

Camden's Head
456 Bethnal Green Road
☎ (0171) 613 4263
11–11
Courage Directors; Greene King IPA; S&N Theakston Best Bitter, XB; Younger Scotch; guest beers Ⓗ
An oasis in a large keg area. Regular beer festivals/promotions are held. Weston's Old Rosie cider sold.
Q ✿ ◖ ▶ ⇌ ⊖ ⊬

E2: Shoreditch

Owl & Pussycat
34 Redchurch Street
☎ (0171) 739 2808

11 (5 Sat)–11
Beer range varies Ⓗ
Popular, roomy, free house offering varying beers and a convivial atmosphere in a Grade II-listed building. The upstairs restaurant and bar can be booked for functions. Music Sat night (jazz). ✿ ◖ ▶

E5: Clapton

Anchor & Hope
High Hill Ferry
☎ (0181) 806 1730
11–3, 5.30 (6 Sat)–11
Fuller's London Pride, ESB Ⓗ
Small, one-bar riverside pub noted for its charity collections. ✿ ♣

Prince of Wales
146 Lea Bridge Road
☎ (0181) 533 3463
11–11
Young's Bitter, Special, Winter Warmer Ⓗ
Large, popular, riverside pub.
Q ✿ ◖ ▶ ⊟ P

E8: Hackney

Lady Diana
95 Forest Road
☎ (0171) 254 3439
11.30–11; 11.30–3.30, 7–11 Sat
Fuller's Chiswick, London Pride; Greene King Abbot; guest beers Ⓗ
Comfortable pub with a paved garden at the rear. Friendly atmosphere; a superb local.
✿ ◖ ▶ ♣

E9: Hackney

Falcon & Firkin
360 Victoria Park Road
☎ (0181) 985 0693
12–11
Firkin Mild Ⓖ/Ⓗ, Falcon Bitter, Hackney Bitter, Dogbolter Ⓗ
One of Firkin's main breweries/brew pubs. The large outside drinking area is pleasant in summer. ☎ ✿ ◖ ▶ ⅋ (Hackney Wick) ⇌ ⌣

E9: Victoria Park

Royal Standard
84 Victoria Park Road
☎ (0181) 985 3224
12–11
Adnams Extra; Courage Best Bitter, Directors; Marston's Pedigree Ⓗ
Small, two-bar pub where bottled Imperial Russian Stout is also sold. ◖ ♣

E10: Leyton

Drum
557 Lea Bridge Road
☎ (0181) 539 6577
11–11

Courage Directors; Greene King Abbot; S&N Theakston Best Bitter, XB, Old Peculier; Younger Scotch; guest beer Ⓗ
The fourth oldest Wetherspoon pub, with a more local flavour than some of the company's more recent developments. At least one guest beer is usually on sale. Q ❀ ◑ ▶ ≋ (Walthamstow Central) ⊖ ⇗ ✢

Hollybush
32 Grange Road
☎ (0181) 539 3709
11.45 (11 Sat)–3, 7–11
Greene King IPA, Abbot Ⓗ
Pub with a well-modernised interior in a Victorian structure; near Leyton Orient FC. ❀ ≋ ⊖ ♣

E11: Leytonstone

Birkbeck Tavern
45 Langthorne Road
☎ (0181) 539 2584
11–11
Draught Bass; Courage Directors; Fuller's London Pride; guest beers Ⓗ
Everyone deserves a local like this sympathetically refurbished, friendly pub. ❀ ⊞ ⊖ (Leyton) ♣

E11: Wanstead

Duke of Edinburgh
Nightingale Lane
☎ (0181) 989 0014
12–11
Tetley Bitter; Young's Bitter; guest beer Ⓗ
Well-run back-street local, which has regained the popularity it lost after its change from a tenancy. Live jazz every other Sun lunchtime. No food Sun. ❀ ◑ ⊖ (Snaresbrook) ♣

George
High Street
11–11
Courage Directors; Greene King IPA; Abbot; S&N Theakston Best Bitter, XB; Younger Scotch; guest beers Ⓗ
Large corner pub, popular with all ages. It features pictures of famous 'Georges', and memorabilia about Wanstead in its heyday. One or two guest beers are usually available, mostly at weekends. Q ❀ ◑ ⊖ ⇗ P ✢

E14: Isle of Dogs

Cat & Canary
Fishermans Walk, Canary Wharf ☎ (0171) 512 9187
11–9; 12–3 Sat & Sun, closed Sat & Sun eves

Fuller's Chiswick, London Pride, ESB Ⓗ
Although this pub is situated in the office complex of Canary Wharf, it has a real traditional atmosphere. The interior decor was rescued from a church in France! Weekday lunches. Fuller's seasonal beers sold. ❀ ◑ ⊖ (DLR Canary Wharf) ♣ ✢

E14: Stepney

Queen's Head
8 Flamborough Street
11–2.30, 5.30 (7.30 Sat)–11
Young's Bitter, Special, Winter Warmer Ⓗ
Friendly local in a conservation area. Note the London 'Fives' dartboard. A plaque on the bar and photographs celebrate the Queen Mother's famous visit. Lunches Mon–Fri. ◑
≋ (Limehouse) ⊖ (DLR) ♣

E15: Stratford

Goldengrove
146–148 The Grove
☎ (0181) 519 0750
11–11
Courage Directors; S&N Theakston Best Bitter, XB; Wadworth 6X; Younger Scotch; guest beer Ⓗ
Former shop premises, transformed into a friendly and deservedly popular pub with a name derived from a poem by Gerard Manley Hopkins. Photos and prints commemorate former local industries and the nearby Theatre Royal. Q ❀ ◑ ◖ ⅋
≋ (Stratford) ⊖ ⇗ ✢

Try also: Theatre Royal Bar, Gerry Raffles Sq (Free)

E17: Walthamstow

College Arms
807–809 Forest Road
☎ (0181) 531 8001
11–11
Courage Best Bitter, Directors; Gale's HSB; Greene King IPA; Young's Special; Whitbread Boddingtons Bitter Ⓗ
Former Wetherspoon house serving up to six handpumped beers and up to four on gravity (the range may vary). Occasional live music. ◑ ▶ ⅋ ♣

Copper Mill
205 Coppermill Lane
☎ (0181) 520 3709
11–11
Fuller's London Pride, ESB; Greene King IPA; Tetley Bitter; Wadworth 6X;

Whitbread Boddingtons Bitter Ⓗ
Small local appealing to all ages, converted a few years ago from an off-licence. ❀ ≋ (St James's St) ⊖ (Blackhorse Rd)

Barking

Britannia
1 Church Road (near A123)
☎ (0181) 594 1305
11–3, 5–11; 11–11 Sat
Young's Bitter, Special, Winter Warmer Ⓗ
Two-bar pub with a roomy, comfortable lounge and a more basic public: Young's most easterly tied pub. Note the caryatids on the exterior – an example of Victorian architecture at one time commonplace in East London. No meals Fri eve or weekends. Q ❀ ◑ ▶ ⊞ ≋ ⊖ ♣ P

Ilford

Prince of Wales
63 Green Lane (A1083)
☎ (0181) 478 1326
11–3, 5.30–11; 11–11 Fri & Sat
Ind Coope Burton Ale; Tetley Bitter Ⓗ
Pleasant pub with three distinct drinking areas, including a snug. The small, split-level garden is the best place to spend an all too rare hot summer lunchtime in Ilford. Lunches Mon–Fri. ❀ ◑ ⊞ ♣ P

Rose & Crown
16 Ilford Hill (A118 near A406)
☎ (0181) 478 7104
11–11
Ind Coope Burton Ale; Tetley Bitter; guest beers Ⓗ
Large, comfortable, friendly, one-bar pub offering at least two guest beers. Still one of the best pubs in Ilford despite increasing competition. ◑ ≋ ⇗

Try also: General Havelock, High Rd (Taylor Walker)

Noak Hill

Bear
Noak Hill Road
☎ (01708) 381935
11–11
Bass Worthington BB, Draught Bass; Fuller's London Pride; Greene King IPA Ⓗ
Large, comfortable, one-bar pub with a huge garden, safe for children. The beer range may vary. Occasional beer festivals. No food Sun; eve meals Tue–Thu. ⇘ ❀ ◑ ▶ ♿ P

Greater London

Woodford Green

Cricketers
299–301 High Road (A11)
☎ (0181) 504 2734
11–3, 5.30–11; 11–11 Sat
Draught Bass; McMullen AK, Country; guest beer Ⓗ
Pleasant, two-bar pub with a saloon and a more basic public. Occasional food theme eves, otherwise no eve meals are served. McMullen's seasonal beers (including Stronghart) sold when available. No food Sun.
Q Ⓓ ⊞ ♣ P

Traveller's Friend
496–498 High Road (A104)
☎ (0181) 504 2435
11–11
Courage Best Bitter, Directors; Ridleys IPA; guest beers Ⓗ
Excellent little drinkers' pub with panelled walls and snob screens; a warm, friendly atmosphere. It usually stocks six ales and has never sold keg bitter. No food Sun. Function room upstairs. Q ⊛ Ⓓ & P

North London

N1: Canonbury

Earl of Radnor
106 Mildmay Grove
☎ (0181) 241 0318
11–11
Fuller's London Pride, ESB Ⓗ
Lovingly restored Victorian pub offering good, home-cooked food (not served Sat). No fruit machines or jukebox but occasional taped music. An all too rare Fuller's house for this side of town. Seasonal beers sold. ⊛ Ⓓ & ⇌

Marquess Tavern
32 Canonbury Street
☎ (0171) 354 2975
11–11
Young's Bitter, Special, Winter Warmer Ⓗ
Good example of mid-19th century architecture; a building with a warm, friendly atmosphere. Home-cooked food. ⌂ Q ⊛ Ⓓ
⇌ (Essex Rd) ⊖ (Highbury & Islington) ♣

N1: Hoxton

George & Vulture
63 Pitfield Street
☎ (0171) 253 3988
11–11
Fuller's London Pride, ESB Ⓗ
Traditional pub, well run by experienced tenants. Clients include 'suits' at lunchtimes

and locals and college students at night. ⊛ Ⓓ ⊞ &
⇌ (Old St) ⊖ ♣

Wenlock Arms
26 Wenlock Road (off A501)
☎ (0171) 608 3406
11–11
Ansells Mild; Tetley Bitter; guest beers Ⓗ
Carefully restored corner local; off the beaten track, but worth a detour for its constantly changing range of real ales and ciders. Regular live music (usually jazz). Adjacent to the site of the former Wenlock Brewery.
⌂ ⇌ (Old St) ♣ ⌀ ⊟

N1: Islington

Crown
116 Cloudesley Road
☎ (0171) 837 7107
11–11
Fuller's Chiswick, London Pride, ESB Ⓗ
Popular pub, serving a fine range of beers (including Fuller's seasonal ales) in ornate and sumptuous Victorian surroundings. It has a central island bar and an eating area. ⌂ Q ⊛ Ⓓ
⇌ (Highbury & Islington)
⊖ (Angel)

N2: East Finchley

Welch's Ale House
130 High Road
☎ (0181) 444 7444
11–11
Fuller's London Pride; Greene King Abbot; Ruddles County; Wadworth 6X; Webster's Yorkshire Bitter; guest beers Ⓗ
Early shop conversion where 12 handpumps dispense an ever-changing range of guest beers. Country wines are also available. No food Sun.
Ⓓ ⊖ ♣ ⌀

N3: Finchley Central

Catcher in the Rye
317 Regent's Park Road
☎ (0181) 343 4369
11–11
Draught Bass; Brakspear Bitter; S&N Theakston XB; guest beers Ⓗ
Tasteful conversion of former shop premises in an under-pubbed area. Occasional beer festivals. The origin of the house beer is not declared. No food Sun eve. ⊛ Ⓓ ⊖ ♣

N4: Crouch Hill

Tap & Spile
29 Crouch Hill
☎ (0171) 272 7748
11–11

Nethergate Bitter; guest beers Ⓗ
Small corner pub in alehouse style; revitalized after a management change. Usually eight beers available; the lower gravity beers mostly offer good value for the area.
⊛ Ⓓ & ⇌ ♣ ⌀

N7: Holloway

Admiral Mann
9 Hargrave Place
☎ (0171) 485 4739
11–3, 6–11; 11–11 Mon, Fri & Sat
McMullen AK, Country, Stronghart Ⓗ
Small, cosy, two-bar pub, well off the beaten track, which continues to water one of North London's beer deserts. No food weekends.
⊛ Ⓓ ⊞ & ⇌ (Camden Rd) ♣

N12: North Finchley

Tally Ho
749 High Road
☎ (0181) 445 4390
11–11
Courage Directors; Greene King Abbot; S&N Theakston Best Bitter, XB; guest beer Ⓗ
Imposing landmark pub on two floors, renovated in Wetherspoon style. Photos of old Finchley decorate the walls. Q Ⓓ ⌀ ⊬

N16: Stoke Newington

Rochester Castle
145 Stoke Newington High Street ☎ (0171) 249 6016
11–11
Courage Directors; Greene King Abbot; S&N Theakston Best Bitter, XB; Wadworth 6X; Younger Scotch; guest beer Ⓗ/Ⓖ
Cavernous single bar, refurbished to a high standard, utilizing lots of natural light; always popular with its varied local clientele. Formerly called the Tanner's Hall.
Q ⊛ Ⓓ ⇌ ♣ ⌀ ⊬

N17: Tottenham

Elbow Room
503–505 High Road
☎ (0181) 801 8769
11–11
Courage Directors; Greene King IPA, Abbot; S&N Theakston XB; Younger Scotch; guest beers Ⓗ
Standard Wetherspoon shop conversion beneath a station. A full menu is served until 10pm (including vegetarian

meals); roast lunch Sun. Tiny, non-segregated, no-smoking area. ◖ ◗
≢ (Bruce Grove) ♣ ⊁

N21: Winchmore Hill

Dog & Duck
74 Hoppers Road
☎ (0181) 886 1987
12–11
Brakspear Bitter; Whitbread Boddingtons Bitter, Flowers Original; guest beer Ⓗ
Tucked away local with a loyal clientele. The beer range may vary. ⋈ ❀ ≢ (Palmers Green) ♣

Half Moon
749 Green Lanes
☎ (0181) 360 5410
11–11
Courage Directors; Greene King IPA, Abbot; S&N Theakston Best Bitter, XB; guest beers Ⓗ
Wetherspoon conversion of a former shop: comfortable and popular, with all the expected facilities. Q ◖ ◗ ≢ ◌ ⊁

Orange Tree
18 Highfield Road
☎ (0181) 360 4853
11–11
Adnams Bitter; Greene King IPA; guest beer Ⓗ
Down-to-earth, back-street local offering a changing guest beer. Under-21s may not be admitted. Eve meals finish at 7pm. ❀ ◖ ◗ ≢ ♣

Barnet

Moon Under Water
148 High Street
☎ (0181) 441 9476
11–11
Courage Directors; Greene King IPA, Abbot; Morland Old Speckled Hen; S&N Theakston XB; guest beers Ⓗ
One long bar opens into an expanded rear drinking area in this popular Wetherspoon house which is the local CAMRA *Pub of the Year*. Q ◖ ◗ ⊖ (High Barnet) ◌ ⊁

Olde Mitre
58 High Street
☎ (0181) 449 6582
11–11; 11–3, 7–11 Sat
Ind Coope Friary Meux BB *or* Benskins BB, Burton Ale; Tetley Bitter; guest beer Ⓗ
Traditional coaching inn, now an ale house which can get very crowded, especially at weekends. Pleasant ambience – in contrast to some neighbouring pubs, No food Sun. Q ◖
⊖ (High Barnet) ♣ P

White Lion
50 St Albans Road
☎ (0181) 449 4560
11–3, 5 (6 Sat)–11
Eldridge Pope Royal Oak; Freetraders Twelve Bore; Wadworth 6X; guest beer Ⓗ
Revitalised and refurbished free house on the edge of town, with three distinct drinking areas. Noted for its home-cooked lunches.
❀ ◖ ♣ P

Enfield Clay Hill

Fallow Buck
Clay Hill
☎ (0181) 363 9467
11–3, 6 (5.30 Fri)–11
Ind Coope Burton Ale; Marston's Pedigree; Tetley Bitter; guest beer Ⓗ
Located in rural Enfield, this pub partly dates from the 16th century. The largest bar contains several distinct drinking areas. Children welcome in the restaurant area. Note the hitching rail for horses in the car park. Live jazz Thu. ❀ ◖ ◗ ⊞ P

Enfield Lock

Greyhound
425 Ordnance Road
☎ (01992) 764612
11–2.30 (3 Fri & Sat), 6.30 (7 Sat)–11
McMullen AK, Country, Gladstone; guest beer Ⓗ
Unspoilt, two-bar oasis on the River Lea Navigation, opposite the now derelict Royal Small Arms Factory. The guest beer alternates with McMullen's seasonal beers. ⋈ ❀ ◖ ⊞
≢ (not Sat/Sun) ♣ P

Enfield Town

Old Wheatsheaf
3 Windmill Hill
☎ (0181) 363 0516
11–3, 5–11; 11–11 Fri & Sat
Adnams Bitter; Ind Coope Benskins BB, Burton Ale; Tetley Bitter; guest beer Ⓗ
Two-bar, Edwardian pub near the town centre. A former London CAMRA *Pub of the Year*, it continues to maintain high standards. Impressive exterior floral displays in summer. No food Sun. ❀ ◖
≢ (Enfield Chase) ♣ P

New Barnet

Builders Arms
3 Albert Road
☎ (0181) 441 1215
11–3, 5.30–11
Greene King IPA, Abbot Ⓗ
Tucked away local, full of character, attracting loyal

custom from near and far. Other Greene King beers are sometimes available. No food Sun.
Q ❀ ◖ ⊞ ≢ ♣

NW1: Camden Town

Spread Eagle
141 Albert Street
☎ (0171) 264 1410
11–11
Young's Bitter, Special, Winter Warmer Ⓗ
Multi-roomed pub built in 1858 and expanded into two adjoining premises in the 1930s and 1963. Lots of wood features. Very friendly staff and clientele.
❀ ◖ ◗ ⊞
≢ (Camden Rd) ⊖

NW1: Euston

Nelson's Head
48 Stanhope Street
☎ (0171) 387 1147
11–11
Draught Bass; Fuller's London Pride; Young's Bitter Ⓗ
Narrow, one-bar pub house, rebuilt in 1899. The bar is decorated with scenes of Nelson's famous battles, including Trafalgar. It is famous for its doorstep sandwiches and serves food until 4pm Mon–Fri (but may cook at other times if asked).
❀ ◖ ≢ (Warren St) ⊖ ♣

Neptune
51 Werrington Street
☎ (0171) 380 1390
11–11
Wells Eagle, Bombardier; guest beer Ⓗ
Single-bar corner pub, very much a local and a regular *Guide* entry. Seen on TV in the *Real McCoy* programme.
Q ◖ ≢ ⊖ ♣

NW1: Marylebone

Perseverance
11 Shroton Street
☎ (0171) 723 7469
11–11
Adnams Mild, Old; Draught Bass; Fuller's London Pride Ⓗ
Very well presented public house with a friendly atmosphere and enthusiastic staff who serve a large bar area. A regular *Guide* entry with a licensee of 20 years' standing. Formerly a 19th-century coaching house. Eve meals weekdays.
Q ❀ ◖ ◗ ⅙ ≢ ⊖ ⊟

Greater London

NW2: Cricklewood

Beaten Docket
50–56 Cricklewood Broadway
☎ (0181) 450 2972
11–11
Courage Directors; Greene
King IPA, Abbot; S&N
Theakston XB; Younger
Scotch; guest beer
(weekends) Ⓗ
Large Wetherspoon pub
housed in a former car
showroom, in an area not
known for good beer. It can
get busy at weekends.
❀ ◖ ▶ ✂

NW3: Belsize Park

Washington
50 Englands Lane
☎ (0171) 722 6118
11–11
Ind Coope Burton Ale;
Marston's Pedigree; Tetley
Bitter; Young's Bitter; guest
beer Ⓗ
Victorian corner pub with a
central bar, built in 1865 by D
Tidey, possibly a distant
relative of today's landlord.
Lots of original wooden
fittings and an etched-glass
feature. Home of Hampstead
Comedy Club (book), it can be
very busy. ◖ ▶ ⊖ ♣

NW3: Hampstead

Duke of Hamilton
23–25 New End
☎ (0171) 794 0258
11–11; 12–2.30, 7–10.30 Sun
Fuller's Chiswick, London
Pride, ESB; guest beer Ⓗ
Unusually for Hampstead, this
pub is not famous and thus
relies on local trade, drawing a
good mix of customers and
offering a warm welcome to
everyone. ❀ ◖ ▶ ⊖

Flask
14 Flask Walk
☎ (0171) 435 4580
11–11
Young's Bitter, Special,
Winter Warmer Ⓗ
Famous Hampstead hostelry
attracting the famous and the
unknown alike. It has a
genuine public bar where the
beer is cheaper: a rarity for the
area. Q ❀ ◖ ▶ ⊟ ﯺ ⊖ ♣

Holly Bush
22 Holly Mount
☎ (0171) 435 2892
11–3, 5.30–11
Ind Coope Benskins BB,
Burton Ale; Tetley Bitter;
guest beer Ⓗ
Very pleasant, secluded
Hampstead local, first
established as a pub in 1896.

The traditional interior is
gas-lit; the rear bar was
formerly the stables. Regular
live music. 🕮 Q ◖ ▶ ⊖ ♣

NW4: Hendon

Chequers
20 Church End
☎ (0181) 203 5658
12–11
Courage Best Bitter,
Directors; S&N Theakston
Best Bitter Ⓗ
An island bar serves two
distinct drinking areas in this
popular local near Church
Farm House Museum.
❀ ◖ ▶ ♣ P

NW5: Kentish Town

Pineapple
51 Leverton Street
☎ (0171) 485 6422
12 (11 Sat)–11
Brakspear Bitter; Marston's
Pedigree; Whitbread
Boddingtons Bitter Ⓗ
Cosy, friendly, back-street
local with a passionate
following. Local artists'
paintings are for sale. Note the
magnificent Bass brewery
mirrors. ⇌ ⊖ ♣

NW6: Kilburn

Queen's Arms
1 Kilburn High Road
☎ (0171) 624 5735
11–11
Young's Bitter, Special,
Winter Warmer Ⓗ
Corner pub with separate
areas, built in 1958 after the
original pub (1839) was
destroyed by a bomb in 1940.
Lots of wood panelling and
framed prints provide decor.
Unusual roof garden. Small
car park. 🕮 Q ❀ ◖ ▶ ⊟
⇌ (Kilburn High Rd)
⊖ (Kilburn Pk) ♣ P

NW7: Mill Hill

Rising Sun
137 Marsh Lane
☎ (0181) 959 3755
12 (11 Sat)–3, 5.30–11
Ind Coope Burton Ale; Tetley
Bitter; Young's Bitter Ⓗ
Historic country pub with a
tiny bar and an unusual raised
snug. An additional lounge is
open at busy times. Children
welcome until 9pm.
Q ⛊ ❀ ◖ ♣ P

NW8: St John's Wood

Clifton
☎ (0171) 624 5233
11–11

Adnams Bitter; Nicholson's
Best Bitter; Tetley Bitter;
Wadworth 6X; guest beer Ⓗ
Victorian villa, split into three
sections with a conservatory
dining area. Good menu;
open for diners Sun afternoon
until 6pm. No food Sun eve.
Upmarket and expensive
for the area.
🕮 Q ❀ ◖ ▶ ♣

New Inn
2 Allitsen Road
☎ (0171) 722 0728
11–11
Greene King IPA, Rayments
Special, Abbot Ⓗ
Traditionally renovated,
friendly, one-bar pub in a side
road. Good value bar meals
until 9pm in the dining area.
❀ ◖ ▶ ⊖

NW10: Harlesden

Coliseum
2 Manor Park Road
☎ (0181) 961 6570
11–11
Courage Directors; S&N
Theakston Best Bitter, XB;
Younger Scotch; guest
beers Ⓗ
Former cinema, now part of
the Wetherspoon chain and a
welcome addition to the area.
Note the large mural of Gary
Cooper and Merle Oberon,
plus the film posters and
articles about the area.
Q ❀ ◖ ▶ ﯺ
⇌ (Willesden Jct) ⊖ ✂

Grand Junction Arms
Acton Lane
☎ (0181) 965 5670
11–11
Young's Bitter, Special,
Winter Warmer Ⓗ
Large, comfortable, three-bar
pub with moorings on the
Grand Union Canal. The
garden offers children's play
equipment and barbecues in
summer. Good value food is
served all day. Not all bars
may be open. Children
welcome in the smaller lounge
until 9pm.
Q ⛊ ❀ ◖ ▶ ⊟ ﯺ ⇌ ⊖ ♣ P

NW11: Golders Green

White Swan
243 Golders Green Road
☎ (0181) 458 2036
11–11
Ind Coope Burton Ale; Tetley
Bitter; Young's Bitter Ⓗ
Lively local in an
underpubbed area. The large,
attractive garden hosts
summer barbecues. Home-
cooked bar meals.
❀ ◖ ▶ ⊟ ⊖ (Brent Cross)

Harefield

Plough
Hill End Road
☎ (01895) 822129
11–3, 6–11
**Brakspear Special; Fuller's
London Pride; Ruddles Best
Bitter; Taylor Landlord;
Wadworth 6X; guest beers** Ⓗ
Excellent, single-bar free house
near the hospital; often very
busy in summer. Good value
food (not served Sun).
Q ❀ ◖ ▮ P

White Horse
Church Hill ☎ (01895) 822144
11–3, 6–11
**Greenalls Bitter, Shipstone's
Bitter, Original; Tetley Bitter;
Wadworth 6X; guest beer** Ⓗ
Excellent, lively, traditional
local on the south side of the
village; a Grade II-listed
building, dating from the 17th
century. ♨ Q ❀ ◖ ▮ ♣ P ⊁

Harrow

JJ Moon's
3 Shaftesbury Parade
☎ (0181) 423 5056
11–11
**Courage Directors; Greene
King IPA, Abbot; S&N
Theakston XB; Younger
Scotch; guest beers** Ⓗ
Small, friendly Wetherspoon
pub in a former bakery.
Q ◖ ▮ ⊁

Harrow Weald

Seven Bells
749 Kenton Lane
☎ (0181) 954 0261
11–11
**Eldridge Pope Hardy
Country; Ind Coope ABC Best
Bitter; Tetley Bitter; guest
beers** Ⓗ
A good mixture of locals and
passing trade helps create a
pleasant atmosphere in this
250-year-old, two-bar pub.
There's not much to attract the
younger drinker, though.
Occasional beer festivals. No
food Sun eve.
❀ ◖ ▮ ♣ P ⊁

Hatch End

Moon & Sixpence
250 Uxbridge Road
☎ (0181) 420 2074
11–11
**Courage Directors; Greene
King IPA, Abbot; S&N
Theakston XB; Younger
Scotch** Ⓗ
Popular, often crowded, pub
that attracts all walks of life.
One of Wetherspoon's smaller
pubs, hence its better

atmosphere. Pleasant garden.
Q ❀ ◖ ▮ ⇌ ⊁

Stanmore

Malthouse
7 Stanmore Hill
11–11
Beer range varies Ⓗ/Ⓖ
Former wine bar, now an
enterprising free house,
serving up to six real ales,
many rare for the area.
Frequent beer festivals.
◖ ▮ ⊖ ⌣

Vine
154 Stanmore Hill
☎ (0181) 954 4676
11–3, 5–11
**Ind Coope Benskins BB,
Burton Ale; Tetley Bitter;
guest beers** Ⓗ
Old, single-bar, former
coaching inn retaining
separate drinking areas. Part
of the original bar can be seen
in the rear room. ❀ ♣ P

Wealdstone

Royal Oak
60 Peel Road
11–11
**Ind Coope Burton Ale; Tetley
Bitter; guest beers** Ⓗ
Imposing pub built in 1932,
with a pleasant conservatory.
The lounge is split into various
drinking areas. Limited
parking. The house beer, Oak
Bitter, is currently brewed by
Eldridge Pope. Q ⛟ ❀ ◖ ▤
⇌ (Harrow & Wealdstone)
⊖ ♣ P

**South-East
London**

SE1: Southwark

Abbey
94 Webber Street
☎ (0171) 928 4480
11–11
**Shepherd Neame Master
Brew Bitter, Spitfire; guest
beer** (occasional) Ⓗ
Two-bar, back-street free
house serving lunches Mon–
Fri. Beware the fake
handpump for keg cider.
◖ ▤ ♣

Founders Arms
Bankside, 52 Hopton Street
(below Blackfriars Bridge)
☎ (0171) 928 1899
11–11
**Young's Bitter, Special,
Winter Warmer** Ⓗ
Built in 1979, this pub has
excellent views over the
Thames and is popular with
tourists. The only pub in the
area open all weekend and

with food available at all
times. Pleasant riverside
terrace. ❀ ◖ ▮
⇌ (Blackfriars) ⊖

Trinity Arms
29 Swan Street
11–11
Beer range varies Ⓗ
Two-bar pub, built circa 1850
and now used by postal
workers. Live jazz and blues
Wed and Thu. Pool played.
Small garden. Beware the fake
handpump for keg cider. ❀

SE3: Blackheath

Bitter Experience
129 Lee Road
11 (10 Sat)–9.30 (10 Fri & Sat); 12–3,
7–9 Sun
Beer range varies Ⓖ
Outstanding off-licence
offering a wide range of real
ales, foreign and British
bottle-conditioned beers and
real ciders. ⇌ (Lee) ⌣

SE5: Camberwell

Duke of Clarence
181 Camberwell Road
☎ (0171) 703 4007
11–11
**Draught Bass; M&B Highgate
Dark; guest beer** Ⓗ
Excellent local, with a bar on
the main road, a comfortable
saloon at the back and a snug
in between. The guest beer
varies and mild is usually
available. ◖
⇌ (Denmark Hill) ♣

Fox on the Hill
149 Denmark Hill
☎ (0171) 738 4756
11–11
**Courage Directors; S&N
Theakston Best Bitter, XB,
Old Peculier; Wadworth 6X;
Younger Scotch; guest beer** Ⓗ
Imposing roadhouse furnished
to Wetherspoon's usual
standard. Always one guest
beer available. Excellent
facilities for disabled visitors
(wheelchair WC). Open all day
Sun for meals (restaurant
licence). Q ❀ ◖ ▮ ⅙
⇌ (Denmark Hill) ⌣ P ⊁

SE6: Catford

Tiger's Head
350 Bromley Road
☎ (0181) 698 8645
11–11
**Courage Directors; S&N
Theakston Best Bitter, XB;
Wadworth 6X; Younger
Scotch; guest beers** Ⓗ
Popular, large Wetherspoon
pub which has been extended
to the rear. Guest beers at all
times and even more at the
occasional beer festivals.
Q ❀ ◖ ▮ ⅙ P ⊁

Greater London

SE8: Deptford

Crystal Palace Tavern
105 Tanner's Hill
☎ (0181) 692 1536
3–midnight (1am Fri); 12–1am Sat
Beer range varies H
Popular pub where the beer
range changes weekly and
includes many beers not
normally available in the area:
wheat beers and real ciders are
often featured. Regular live
music (with late night
extension); barbecues in
summer. ❀ ⇌ (St John's/
New Cross) ⊖ (New Cross
Gate) ⏍

Dog & Bell
116 Prince Street
☎ (0181) 692 5664
11–11
**Fuller's London Pride, ESB;
guest beers** H
Well-hidden gem, well worth
seeking out for its regularly
changing choice of beers and
wide range of malt whiskies.
The drinking area has recently
been extended to accommodate
trade generated by the pub's
growing reputation. No meals
Sun eve. Q ❀ ⟨ ▶ ⇌ ♣

Old Manor House
58 Bush Road
☎ (0171) 394 1796
12 (11 Fri & Sat)–11
**Young's Bitter, Special; guest
beers** H
Recently refurbished, one-bar
pub; an oasis in a real ale
desert. Meals available
occasionally.
⊖ (Surrey Quays) ♣

SE9: Eltham

Banker's Draft
80 High Street
☎ (0181) 294 2578
11–11
**Courage Directors; S&N
Theakston Best Bitter, XB;
Wadworth 6X; Younger
Scotch; guest beers** H
This former bank is one of
Wetherspoon's smallest
outlets. Memorabilia relating
to the late Frankie Howerd,
born locally, adorns the walls.
Q ⟨ ▶ ♿ ⇌ ✄

Porcupine
24 Mottingham Road
☎ (0181) 857 6901
11–11
**Courage Best Bitter; S&N
Theakston Best Bitter, XB;
John Smith's Bitter** H
Large, three-bar pub with a
mock Tudor interior. The
spacious garden contains an
aviary and a small zoo.
Families welcomed in the
conservatory. ❀ ⟨
⇌ (Mottingham) ♣ P

SE10: Greenwich

Ashburnham Arms
25 Ashburnham Grove
☎ (0181) 692 2007
12–3, 6–11
**Shepherd Neame Master
Brew Bitter, Best Bitter,
Spitfire** H
Friendly local; CAMRA
London *Pub of the Year* 1994.
Vegetarian meals available; no
eve meals Mon or Tue. Note:
the Porter (winter) and
Bishops Finger (summer) are
kept under cask breathers.
❀ ⟨ ▶ ⇌ ♣ ⊟

Richard I
52 Royal Hill
☎ (0181) 692 2996
11–11
**Young's Bitter, Special,
Winter Warmer** H
Classic pub with two bars and
a garden (where summer
barbecues are held). The
traditional-style public bar
features old photos of pub
outings. No food Sun.
Q ❀ ⟨ ⇌ ♣

SE11: Kennington

Greyhound
336 Kennington Park Road
☎ (0171) 735 2590
11–11
**Courage Best Bitter,
Directors; Wadworth 6X;
guest beer** H
Popular, long, narrow pub
with a raised area at the rear.
Good food (Mon–Sat).
⟨ ⊖ (Oval)

Mansion House
46 Kennington Park Road
☎ (0171) 735 2291
11–11
**Greene King Abbot;
Marston's Pedigree; Morland
Old Speckled Hen; Young's
Special; guest beers** H
Pub offering outside drinking
at pavement benches.
Weekday lunches are home-
cooked and good value.
❀ ⟨ ⊖

SE14: New Cross

Rose Inn
272 New Cross Road
☎ (0181) 692 3193
11–4, 5.30–11
**Courage Best Bitter,
Directors; Young's Special** H
One-bar, family pub almost
opposite New Cross Gate
station. The bar is divided into
discrete alcoves by screens.
Aviary in the garden.
❀ ⟨ ♿ ⇌ (New Cross Gate)
⊖ ♣

SE17: Walworth

Beehive
60–62 Carter Street
☎ (0171) 703 4992
11–11
**Bishops Cathedral; Courage
Best Bitter, Directors; Fuller's
London Pride; Wadworth 6X;
guest beer** H
A gem; tucked away from the
busy Walworth Road, it serves
a wide range of meals until
10pm every day. Extensive
range of malts and wines. Well
worth searching for in an area
which is a beer desert. ❀ ⟨ ▶

SE18: Shooters Hill

Bull Hotel
151 Shooters Hill
☎ (0181) 856 0691
11–3, 5.30 (7 Sat)–11
**Courage Best Bitter,
Directors** H
Near the top of Shooters Hill,
this is one of the few unspoilt
Courage pubs in an area
dominated by pubs acquired
by the company from the
former Beasley Brewery. No
food Sun. Q ❀ ⟨ ♣

SE18: Woolwich

Prince Albert (Rose's)
49 Hare Street
☎ (0181) 854 1538
11–11; 12–3 Sun, closed Sun eve
Beer range varies H
Town-centre pub serving an
excellent range of beers – three
ales always available from a
regularly changing list of at
least 14. ⇌ (Woolwich
Arsenal) ♣

SE22: East Dulwich

Clockhouse
196a Peckham Rye
☎ (0181) 693 2901
11–11
**Young's Bitter, Special,
Winter Warmer** H
Comfortable pub facing
Peckham Rye Common. Note
the collection of timepieces
and old beer bottle labels.
Despite not having a real
garden – just a large patio –
the pub has won Young's
Garden Display competition for
the last three years. Barbecues
in summer. ❀ ⟨ ▶

SE23: Forest Hill

Bird in Hand
35 Dartmouth Road
☎ (0181) 699 7417
11–11
**Courage Directors; S&N
Theakston Best Bitter, XB;
Wadworth 6X; Younger
Scotch; guest beers** H

An original Victorian exterior contains a completely 'Wetherspoonized' interior: one of the group's smaller premises. It enjoys a busy local trade, especially from pensioners exploiting the cheap beers lunchtime. Historic photographs of the area are on display. Three or four beer festivals a year.

Q ❀ ◖ ▮ ⇌ ⇔ ⋌

Railway Telegraph
112 Stanstead Road
☎ (0181) 699 6644
11–3, 5.30–11; 11–11 Fri & Sat
Shepherd Neame Master Brew Bitter, Best Bitter, Spitfire, Bishops Finger, Porter Ⓗ
Busy and popular; despite being prominently placed on the South Circular, this pub remains very much a meeting place for the community. Local sea-fishing and motorbikers' clubs supported. No food Sun. Beware the keg cider on a fake handpump.

ᕦ ❀ ◖ ⛁ ⇌ ♣ P

SE24: Herne Hill

Lord Stanley
31 Hinton Road
12–11
Fuller's London Pride; guest beers Ⓗ
Genuine free house offering a wide selection of guest beers. The two large bars are decorated with enamel advertising signs and American car plates. Note the original Charrington, Toby and Taplow leaded windows. Reasonably priced extensive menu available at all times.

❀ ◖ ▮ ⇌ (Loughborough Jct) ♣

SE25: South Norwood

Alliance
91 High Street (A213)
☎ (0181) 653 3604
11–11
Courage Best Bitter, Directors; Marston's Pedigree; Morland Old Speckled Hen; Wadworth 6X; guest beer Ⓗ
Corner pub with an unspoilt exterior, close to the station and shops: one L-shaped bar. Fast changing guest beers come from small independent breweries. Imperial Russian Stout is also stocked. Good food (not served Sun).

◖ ⇌ (Norwood Jct) ♣

Clifton Arms
21 Clifton Road
☎ (0181) 771 2443
11–11

Fuller's London Pride; Ind Coope Burton Ale; Tetley Bitter; guest beer Ⓗ
Friendly, one-bar back-street local near Selhurst Park. It can be busy before, and closed after, some football matches. The two guest beers generally come from independent regional brewers. No food Sun.

◖ ⇌ (Selhurst) ♣

Port Manor
1 Portland Road (A215)
☎ (0181) 655 1308
11–11
Fuller's London Pride; Greene King Abbot; Young's Special; guest beer Ⓗ
Lively, comfortable one-bar pub with an extra serving area on the balcony in summer. Popular with all ages, it can be rather crowded eves. Always six beers on offer at competitive prices, with guests generally from small breweries. No food Sun.

◖ ▮ ⇌ (Norwood Jct)

SE26: Upper Sydenham

Dulwich Wood House
39 Sydenham Hill
☎ (0181) 693 5666
11–11
Young's Bitter, Special, Winter Warmer Ⓗ
Always busy, with a mixed clientele: a country-style pub in suburbia with a large garden which has petanque, its own bar (electric pumps), a barbecue daily in summer and a children's play area with entertainment (clowns, etc.) on alternate summer Suns. Sun lunches are popular.

🍴 Q ❀ ◖ ⛁ ▲ ♣ P

SE27: West Norwood

Hope
49 Norwood High Street,
☎ (0181) 670 2035
11–11
Young's Bitter, Special, Winter Warmer Ⓗ
Small, but busy, one-bar local with a strong community spirit. Every May regulars organise a charity walk from Brighton to London in aid of MS. This and other events raise up to £15,000 a year.

❀ ◖ ⇌ ♣

Addiscombe

Builder's Arms
65 Leslie Park Road (off A222)
☎ (0181) 654 1803
11.30–3, 5 (6.30 Sat)–11; 11.30–11 Fri

Fuller's Chiswick, London Pride, ESB Ⓗ
Extremely popular, back-street pub with almost a country pub atmosphere. Its two cosy bars are warmly decorated, with plenty of woodwork and comfortable seating. Good food (not served Fri–Sun eves). The excellent garden is popular with families (access through the bar). Fuller's seasonal beers sold.

Q ❀ ◖ ▮ ⇌

Claret Free House
5a Bingham Corner, Lower Addiscombe Road (A222)
☎ (0181) 656 7452
11.30 (11 Sat)–11
Eldridge Pope Royal Oak; Palmers IPA; guest beer Ⓗ
Small, cosy bar in a shopping parade which attracts a loyal local following. Three regularly changing guest beers come from all over the country. Lunches Mon–Fri.

◖ ⇌

Barnehurst

Red Barn
Barnehurst Road
☎ (01322) 332361
11–3, 6–11
Bass Charrington IPA; Fuller's London Pride; Greene King IPA; Hancock's HB; guest beer Ⓗ
Three bars at ground level, with a fourth downstairs, (used for functions). A plaque declares this pub to be the birthplace of British trad. jazz.

❀ ⇌ ♣

Beckenham

George Inn
High Street
☎ (0181) 650 2293
11–11
Draught Bass; Fuller's London Pride; Hancock's HB; guest beer Ⓗ
17th-century, historic inn, in the centre of town, used by the local community and shoppers. A warm, cosy halt for good food and a selection of cask beers.

❀ ◖ ⇌ (Beckenham Jct) P

Jolly Woodman
9 Chancery Lane
☎ (0181) 650 3664
11–11
Bass Charrington IPA, Draught Bass; Fuller's London Pride; guest beers Ⓗ
Popular back-street local with a friendly village feel: a good beer house with no music or loud gaming machines. Lunches Mon–Sat.

❀ ◖ ⇌ (Beckenham Jct) ♣

Greater London

Beddington

Plough
Croydon Road (A232/B272 jct)
☎ (0181) 647 1122
11–3, 5.30–11; 11–11 Fri & Sat
Young's Bitter, Special, Winter Warmer Ⓗ
Imposing, Tudor-style, single-bar building opened in 1897 to replace an 18th-century pub. The original coachhouse still stands in the old stable yard, now used for outdoor drinking. Popular with a wide range of clientele. Good lunches, Mon–Fri.
🏨 ❀ ◖ & ♣ P

Bexley

Black Horse
63 Albert Road
☎ (01322) 52337
11–3, 6.30–11; 11–11 Fri; 12.30–3, 7–10.30 Sun
Courage Best Bitter; S&N Theakston XB; Younger Scotch Ⓗ
Back-street local that supports a football team. A real cracker, well worth a visit. ⇌

Bexleyheath

Robin Hood & Little John
Lion Road ☎ (0181) 303 1128
11–2.30, 6–11
Courage Best Bitter, Directors; John Smith's Bitter; Wadworth 6X; guest beer Ⓗ
Friendly, Grade II-listed building dated early 1800. The tables are made from sewing machine treadles. Home-made meals and hot bar snacks served (except Sun).
ⴵ ❀ ◖ ♣

Rose
179 Broadway
☎ (0181) 303 3846
11–11
Greene King IPA; Ind Coope Burton Ale; Tetley Bitter; guest beer Ⓗ
One-room, horseshoe-shaped pub; the surroundings are plush and comfortable, but the atmosphere is friendly. Busy with shoppers and workers daytime; like a back-street local eves. Home-made lunches. ❀ ◖ ⇌ P

Royal Oak (Polly Clean Stairs)
Mount Road (off A227)
11–3, 6–11
Courage Best Bitter; John Smith's Bitter; Wadworth 6X; guest beers Ⓗ
Historic, village-style local surviving in the midst of suburbia. A gem. Q ❀ P

Bromley

Bitter End
139 Masons Hill
☎ (0181) 466 6083
12–3 (not Mon), 5–10 (9 Mon); 7–9 Sun
Beer range varies Ⓖ
Interesting off-licence selling an ever-changing range of beers; containers available.

Croydon

Arkwright's Wheel
151 North End
☎ (0181) 649 8638
11–11; 12–3 Sun, closed Sun eve
Adnams Bitter; Ind Coope Burton Ale; Tetley Bitter; Young's Bitter; guest beer Ⓗ
Large, single-bar, Victorian-style alehouse converted from a former hotel. Guest beers are mainly from the Carlsberg-Tetley list. Popular with a transient crowd. No food Sun.
Q ◖ ▶ & ⇌ (West)

Cricketer's Arms
23 Southbridge Place
(near A232)
☎ (0181) 688 4103
11–11; 11–3, 6–11 Sat
Bass Worthington BB; Fuller's London Pride; Harveys BB; guest beer Ⓗ
Quiet, one-bar pub offering a country atmosphere despite its position close to the old town flyover (western end).
◖ ▶ ♣ P

Dog & Bull
24–25 Surrey Street
(off A235)
☎ (0181) 688 3664
11–11
Young's Bitter, Special, Winter Warmer Ⓗ
Traditional, 18th-century, Grade II-listed building in the market street; modernised and extended into next door premises, without loss of character. Excellent garden in the old yard. Greater London CAMRA *Pub of the Year* 1994. Weekday lunches.
Q ❀ ◖ ⇌ (East/West) ♣

Porter & Sorter
Station Road (off A22, between post office and E Croydon station)
☎ (0181) 688 4296
11–11; 11–3, 7–11 Sat; 12–3 Sun, closed Sun eve
Courage Best Bitter, Directors; Everards Tiger; Ruddles County; Wadworth 6X; guest beer Ⓗ
The only surviving building of character in an area of glass and concrete blocks: a pub with a comfortable, welcoming interior and efficient, friendly service – even when crowded

with commuters or local office workers. Lunches Mon–Fri. Limited parking.
❀ ◖ ⇌ (East) ♣ P

Princess Royal
22 Longley Road
☎ (0181) 684 4056
11–3, 5.30 (7 Sat)–11
Greene King XX Mild, IPA, Rayments Special, Abbot Ⓗ
Small, cosy pub offering a friendly welcome and the full range of Greene King ales, plus seasonal changes. The bar was recently extended but is still cosy. Known locally as the Glue Pot (see reverse of pub sign). No meals Sun.
🏨 ❀ ◖ ▶ ♣

Royal Standard
1 Sheldon Street (off the high street)
☎ (0181) 688 9749
11.30–3, 5–11; 11–11 Fri & Sat
Fuller's Chiswick, London Pride, ESB Ⓗ
Quiet, friendly, back-street local, traditional and very popular. Recently extended and refurbished without loss of character, it still has fine etched-glass windows and a small serving hatch in the rear bar. The garden is across the street. No food Sun. Fuller's seasonal beers sold.
Q ❀ ◖ ♣

Footscray

Seven Stars
Foots Cray High Street
☎ (0181) 300 2057
11.30–3.30, 5–11
Bass Charrington IPA, Draught Bass Ⓗ
16th-century pub, retaining many original features.
❀ ◖ ♣

Orpington

Cricketers
93 Chislehurst Road
☎ (01689) 820164
11–3, 5–11; 11–11 Sat
Courage Best Bitter, Directors; guest beers Ⓗ
Cosy pub on Broomhill Common, serving a good range of food and ales. Guest beers change regularly.
❀ ◖ ▶ ♣ P

Sidcup

Alma
Alma Road
11–2.30, 5.30 (7 Sat)–11
Courage Best Bitter; Young's Bitter, Special Ⓗ
Deservedly popular, back-street local retaining some of its Victorian-style interior.
❀ & ⇌ ♣

Greater London

South Croydon

Stag & Hounds
26 Selsdon Road (B275, near
A235 jct) ☎ (0181) 688 1908
11–11
**Fuller's London Pride;
Harveys BB; guest beer**
(occasional) Ⓗ
Popular pub, busy at
weekends with the
football/rugby fraternity. It
features an island bar, wood-
panelled walls, old
photographs and a tie
collection. No food Sun.
🏵 ◖ � ♣ P

Upper Belvedere

Royal Standard
39 Nuxley Road
☎ (01322) 432774
11–11
**Draught Bass; Belhaven 80/;
Fuller's London Pride; Greene
King IPA Ⓗ; M&B Highgate
Dark Ⓖ; guest beers Ⓗ**
Centrally located pub offering
regularly changing guest
beers. Two beer festivals a
year, one specialising in
Scottish beers.
🌣 🏵 ◖& ♣ P

Try also: **Victoria**, Victoria St
(Free)

South-West London

SW1: Belgravia

Fox & Hounds
29 Passmore Street
11–3, 5.30–11; 12–2, 7–10.30 Sun
**Bass Charrington IPA,
Draught Bass; Greene King
IPA; Hancock's HB Ⓗ**
Small, friendly pub with a beer
and wine licence only. A real
gem. ◖ ⊖ (Sloane Sq)

Star Tavern
6 Belgrave Mews West
☎ (0171) 234 2806
11.30–3, 5 (6.30 Sat)–11; 11.30–11 Fri
**Fuller's Chiswick, London
Pride, ESB Ⓗ**
Unchanging and unspoilt: a
mews pub in the heart of
Belgravia. Weekday lunches.
🏮 ◖ ▮ ⊖ (Hyde Pk Crnr)

Turk's Head
10 Motcomb Street
☎ (0171) 235 7850
11–11
**Bass Worthington BB,
Draught Bass; guest beers Ⓗ**
Pleasant, friendly, corner pub
near Knightsbridge and Hyde
Park Corner.
🏮 Q ◖ ▮ ⊖ (Hyde Pk Crnr)

SW1: Trafalgar Square

Old Shades
37 Whitehall
☎ (0171) 930 4019
11–11
**Bass Worthington BB,
Draught Bass; Fuller's
London Pride Ⓗ**
Long, narrow, wood-panelled
pub. In common with other
pubs in this area, its licence is
granted by Buckingham
Palace.
🏮 ◖ ▮ 🚞 (Charing Cross) ⊖

SW1: Victoria

Wetherspoon's
Victoria Island, Victoria
Station ☎ (0171) 931 0445
11–11
**Courage Directors; S&N
Theakston Best Bitter, XB;
Younger Scotch; guest beer Ⓗ**
A must for thirsty travellers
with a train to catch; you can
watch the departure board
while you drink.
◖ ▮ & 🚞 ⊖ ⊂ ⌦

SW1: Westminster

Buckingham Arms
62 Petty France
☎ (0171) 222 3386
11–11; 11–3, 5.30–11 Sat
**Young's Bitter, Special,
Winter Warmer Ⓗ**
Popular pub near the passport
office, with a corridor drinking
area behind the bar.
◖ ▮ 🚞 (Victoria)
⊖ (St James's Pk)

Cardinal
23 Francis Street
11–11; 11–3, 8–11 Sat
**Bass Worthington BB,
Draught Bass; Fuller's
London Pride; guest beer Ⓗ**
Large pub with a wine and
food bar at the rear and a
restaurant upstairs. Regular
beer festivals.
◖ 🚞 (Victoria) ⊖

Westminster Arms
9 Storeys Gate
11–11; 12–3 Sun, closed Sun eve
**Draught Bass; Brakspear
Bitter; Wadworth 6X; guest
beer Ⓗ**
Pleasant haven, handy for
Westminster Abbey and the
Houses of Parliament. Meals
(lunchtime and eve) are served
in the wine bar on the lower
floor. ⊖ (St James's Pk)

SW2: Brixton

Crown & Sceptre
2 Streatham Hill
☎ (0181) 671 0843
11–11

**Courage Directors; Greene
King IPA, Abbot; S&N
Theakston Best Bitter, XB;
Younger Scotch; guest beer Ⓗ**
Large Wetherspoon pub by a
crossroads, featuring yellow
walls, a dark blue ceiling,
shelves of books, prints, 'arty'
objects and a marble-topped
bar. Often crowded at
weekends. A chess club,
charity events and beer
festivals are all hosted.
Q 🏵 ◖ ▮ ⊂ P ⌦

Hope & Anchor
123 Acre Lane
☎ (0171) 274 1787
11–11
**Young's Bitter, Special,
Winter Warmer Ⓗ**
CAMRA SW London *Pub of the
Year 1993*. The garden is a
delight in summer. A family
room is open Sun lunchtime.
Excellent food in huge
portions. 🏮 Q 🏵 ◖ ▮
⊖ (Clapham North) ♣

SW3: Chelsea

Builder's Arms
13 Britten Street
☎ (0171) 352 6660
11–11
**Brakspear Bitter; Marston's
Pedigree; Whitbread
Boddingtons Bitter Ⓗ**
Two-bar pub with interesting
frieze, depicting Chelsea and
the pub itself. ◖ ⊕

Cooper's Arms
87 Flood Street
11–11
**Young's Bitter, Special,
Winter Warmer Ⓗ**
Busy, café-bar-style pub. Q ◖

Crown
153 Dovehouse Street
☎ (0171) 352 9505
11–11
**Brakspear Bitter; Fuller's
London Pride; Whitbread
Flowers Original; guest
beers Ⓗ**
Much improved, small corner
pub behind Brompton
Hospital. Beware the keg cider
on a fake handpump.
◖ ⊖ (S Kensington)

Surprise
6 Christchurch Terrace
☎ (0171) 352 4699
11–11
**Draught Bass; Hancock's HB;
Taylor Landlord Ⓗ**
Popular pub with an
interesting frieze around the
top of the bar. ◖ ♣

SW5: Earl's Court

Blackbird
209 Earl's Court Road
☎ (0171) 835 1855
11–11

Greater London

Fuller's Chiswick, London Pride, ESB Ⓗ
Fuller's Ale and Pie House in a converted bank, opposite Earl's Court station. Fuller's seasonal beers stocked. ◖ 🕩 ⊖

SW6: Fulham

White Horse
1 Parsons Green
☎ (0171) 736 2115
11–3, 5 (7 Sat)–11
Draught Bass; M&B Highgate Dark, Old; guest beers Ⓗ
Large, busy pub facing Parsons Green, with a terrace for outside drinking. It hosts regular beer festivals, and a large selection of Trappist beers is stocked.
🏚 ◖ 🕩 ⊖ (Parsons Green)

SW7: South Kensington

Anglesea Arms
15 Selwood Terrace
11–3, 5.30–11
Adnams Bitter; Brakspear Special; Fuller's London Pride; Greene King Abbot; guest beer Ⓗ
Notable pub: one of the first free houses to sell a range of real ales. Charles Dickens and D H Lawrence lived nearby.
Q ◖ 🕩

SW8: Battersea

Old Red House
133 Battersea Park Road (opp. Dogs' Home)
☎ (0171) 622 1664
11–11
Courage Best Bitter, Directors; Wadworth 6X; Wells Bombardier; Young's Bitter Ⓗ
Family house hosting darts and quizzes through the week and Wed night karaoke. Live music weekends and Sun lunchtime.
🏵 ◖ 🕩 ⇌ (Battersea Pk) ♣ P

SW8: Stockwell

Priory Arms
83 Lansdowne Way
☎ (0171) 622 1884
11–11
Marston's Pedigree; Young's Bitter, Special; guest beers Ⓗ
Friendly, popular local, CAMRA SW London *Pub of the Year* 1992 and 1994. The four guest beers change daily. Home-cooked, good value food served Mon–Fri, 12–5; snacks Sat. 🏵 ◖ 🕹 ⊖ ♣ ♨

Surprise
16 Southville
☎ (0171) 622 4623
11–11

Young's Bitter, Special, Winter Warmer Ⓗ
Charming, friendly, back-street local with outside seating (petanque played), adjacent to Larkhall Park. It enjoys an excellent reputation for home-cooked food.
🏚 Q 🏵 ◖ ♣

SW10: West Brompton

Fox & Pheasant
1 Billing Road
☎ (0171) 352 2943
12–3, 5.30–11
Greene King IPA, Rayments Special, Abbot Ⓗ
Small, two-bar local, just off Fulham Rd, near Chelsea FC. Billing Rd is private, so parking is difficult. 🏵 ◖

SW10: West Chelsea

Finch's
190 Fulham Road
☎ (0171) 351 5043
11–11
Young's Bitter, Special, Winter Warmer Ⓗ
Busy pub with much original wood- and tilework, plus a circular window declaring 'Stout, Burton and Bitter, 2d a glass'. Originally the King's Arms, it was always known as Finch's, and was eventually renamed. ◖ 🕩

SW11: Battersea

Beehive
197 St John's Hill (opp. St John's Hospital)
☎ (0171) 207 1273
11–11
Fuller's Chiswick, London Pride, ESB Ⓗ
Small, one-bar pub on a main bus route; twice voted CAMRA SW London *Pub of the Year*. No meals Sun. Fuller's seasonal beers sold.
🏵 ◖ 🕩 & ⇌ (Clapham Jct)

Castle
115 Battersea High Street
☎ (0171) 228 8181
11–11
Young's Bitter, Special, Winter Warmer Ⓗ
Very traditional, relaxed and informal pub where the main feature is a wide, open fireplace with a spit roast. No meals Sun eve. Near Clapham Jct. 🏚 Q 🏵 ◖ ♣ P

Eagle Ale House
104 Chatham Road
☎ (0171) 228 2328
11–11

Fuller's London Pride; Marston's Pedigree; Whitbread Boddingtons Bitter, Flowers Original Ⓗ
Very small, charity-conscious back-street pub with plenty of local trade and a friendly atmosphere. Freshly-cooked, cheap meals. 🏵 ◖ ♣

Try also: Duke of Cambridge, Battersea Park Rd (Young's)

SW12: Balham

Grove Hotel
39 Oldridge Road (off the High Road)
☎ (0181) 673 6531
11–11
Young's Bitter, Special, Winter Warmer Ⓗ
Large Victorian local: a friendly and lively public bar with a separate darts room, plus a comfortable, but under-used saloon bar, good for discreet meetings. Limited food menu. ◖ ♣

Nightingale
97 Nightingale Lane
☎ (0181) 673 1637
11–3, 5.30–11; 11–11 Fri & Sat
Young's Bitter, Special, Winter Warmer Ⓗ
Small Victorian local, changing as the area has changed. Good service even at busy times. It is well-known for its prize-winning charity efforts, especially an annual 35-mile sponsored walk. The enclosed garden is suitable for children. No food Sun. Q 🏵 ◖ 🕩 & ♣

SW13: Barnes

Coach & Horses
27 Barnes High Street
☎ (0181) 876 2695
11–11
Young's Bitter, Special, Winter Warmer Ⓗ
Very cosy, welcoming, conversational, one-bar local with a huge log fire. There is a garden play area, plus a 'Paddock Room' for children, functions and barbecues. No food in the bar Sun, but barbecues Sun in summer.
🏚 Q 🏖 ◖
⇌ (Barnes Bridge)

Red Lion
2 Castelnau ☎ (0181) 748 2984
11–11
Fuller's Chiswick, London Pride, ESB Ⓗ
Large, refurbished Georgian-fronted pub, close to Barnes Common and pond, which creates a village atmosphere. A wide selection of meals is available until 9.30. Children welcome in the dining area and garden. Fuller's seasonal beers sold.
🏚 🏵 ◖ 🕩 ⇌ ♣ P

SW14: Mortlake

Hare & Hounds
216 Upper Richmond Road, East Sheen ☎ (0181) 876 4304
11–11
Young's Bitter, Special, Winter Warmer Ⓗ
Comfortable, roomy pub. The oak-panelled lounge has a pleasant atmosphere, part of the bar is set aside for snooker, and a large, walled garden provides a children's play area and hosts barbecues. Wide choice of good value food. Live music Sun eve.
⛰ Q ❀ ◖ ◗ ⇌

SW15: Putney

Railway
202 Upper Richmond Road
☎ (0181) 788 8190
11–11
Courage Directors; S&N Theakston Best Bitter, XB; Younger Scotch; guest beers Ⓗ
Comfortable, typical Wetherspoon renovation back to a traditional pub. A model train runs around the main bar, whilst the upstairs bar displays historic photographs of Putney and the history of the local railway. This may have a different range of guest beers to the main bar.
Q ◖ ◗ ♿ ⇌ ⌓ ⅟

SW16: Streatham

Pied Bull
498 Streatham High Road
11–11
Young's Bitter, Special, Winter Warmer Ⓗ
Pub opposite the common. It has had its ups and downs over the years but is now doing well under a new landlord. Eve meals finish at 8.30. ⛰ Q ❀ ◖ ◗ ⊞
⇌ (Streatham Common) P

SW17: Tooting

Castle
38 Tooting High Street
☎ (0181) 672 7018
11–11
Young's Bitter, Special, Winter Warmer Ⓗ
Large, friendly, comfortable Young's pub opposite the tube and handy for the shops. Children allowed in if eating. Cricket club in summer.
⛰ ❀ ◖ ♿ ⊖ (Broadway)
♣ P

SW18: Earlsfield

Country House
2 Groton Road
☎ (0181) 874 2715
12–11
Courage Best Bitter, Directors; John Smith's Bitter; Young's Bitter Ⓗ
Quiet, almost rural, pub next to the railway line. Worth seeking out. ◖ ◗ ⊞ ⇌ ♣

SW18: Wandsworth

County Arms
345 Trinity Road (Wandsworth Common) ☎ (0181) 874 8532
11–11
Young's Bitter, Special, Winter Warmer Ⓗ
Very well-run, comfortable, main road pub which has been extensively refurbished but has kept its original character. The emphasis is on food which is highly recommended (not served Sun eve).
⛰ Q ❀ ◖ ◗ P ⅟

Grapes
39 Fairfield Street
☎ (0181) 874 8681
11–11; 12–3, 7.30–10.30 Sun
Young's Bitter, Special, Winter Warmer Ⓗ
Small, one-bar pub on a notorious one-way system. The horseshoe-shaped bar has recently been redecorated. Weekday lunches.
❀ ◖ ⇌ (Town) ♣

Old Sergeant
104 Garratt Lane
☎ (0181) 874 4099
11–11; 11–3, 5–11 Tue & Wed
Young's Bitter, Special, Winter Warmer Ⓗ
Young's pub near Sainsbury's; an old coaching house with many prints, plates and brass objects on its walls. It fields darts, football, quiz and basketball teams. A traditional, friendly family pub which does lots of charity work.
⛰ ❀ ◖ ⊞ ♣

Queen Adelaide
35 Putney Bridge Road
☎ (0181) 874 9165
11–11
Young's Bitter, Special, Winter Warmer Ⓗ
Large pub just off the notorious Wandsworth one-way system. The large garden hosts barbecues in summer. Special roast lunches Sun; no food Sat. ⛰ ❀ ◖ ♣

SW19: Merton

Prince of Wales
98 Morden Road
☎ (0181) 542 0573
11–3, 5–11; 11–11 Fri & Sat
Young's Bitter, Special, Winter Warmer Ⓗ
Unspoilt, mid-Victorian pub with a lively, young clientele. A wood partition separates the small public bar (with darts), from the spacious saloon, which has a back door to the patio. No meals Sun eve.
Q ᵷ ❀ ◖ ◗ ⊞
⇌ (Morden Rd)
⊖ (S Wimbledon) ♣ P

Princess Royal
25 Abbey Road
☎ (0181) 542 3273
11–3.30, 5.30–11
Courage Best Bitter, Directors; Fuller's London Pride; Marston's Pedigree *or* **Wadworth 6X; Morland Old Speckled Hen** Ⓗ
Warm and welcoming, two-bar, 200-year-old corner house with low ceilings and diverse decorations. Good food is a bonus. No meals Sun eve. Beware the keg cider on a fake handpump. ❀ ◖ ◗ ⊞
⊖ (Collier's Wood) ♣

SW19: South Wimbledon

Sultan
78 Norman Road
☎ (0181) 542 4532
12–11
Hop Back Mild, GFB, Special *or* **Wilt, Stout, Summer Lightning, Wheat Beer** Ⓗ
Original features of this late 1950s building have been cherished. It reopened in 1994 as the third pub of Hop Back Brewery, serving its full range of beers. A lively, cheerful atmosphere in two bars.
Q ❀ ◖ ♿ ♣ ⊟

SW19: Wimbledon Common

Crooked Billet
Crooked Billet
☎ (0181) 946 4942
11–11
Young's Bitter, Special, Winter Warmer Ⓗ
Large, convivial, bare-brick-walled pub, with a converted barn-type eating area to the rear. The clientele is slightly more mature than at the neighbouring Hand in Hand. Just off Wimbledon Common.
⛰ Q ❀ ◖ ◗ ⅟

Hand in Hand
Crooked Billet
☎ (0181) 946 5720
11–11
Young's Bitter, Special, Winter Warmer Ⓗ
Large, mixed period pub with an unusual layout, attracting a young, professional clientele, but retaining a village atmosphere. Very busy Sun lunchtimes and popular with walkers from the adjacent Common. Q ᵷ ❀ ◖

Greater London

SW20: Raynes Park

Cavern
100 Coombe Lane
☎ (0181) 944 8211
11–11
Fuller's London Pride; S&N Newcastle Exhibition; Theakston XB; Whitbread Boddingtons Bitter; Young's Bitter Ⓗ
Open since 1990, a friendly one-roomer, attractively laid out with Beatles/1960s rock 'n' roll posters and photographs. A good jukebox and an authentic red telephone box are in use. An asset to the area. No meals at weekends.
⊛ ◖ ⇌

Carshalton

Racehorse
17 West Street
(off A232)
☎ (0181) 647 6818
11–11
Courage Best Bitter, Directors; King & Barnes Sussex; guest beer Ⓗ
Smart, two-bar pub offering a formal eating area in the lounge (excellent menu) and good bar meals. Guest beers come from micro-breweries, with at least two every week. The enterprising tenant also leases the Windsor Castle. No food Sun eve.
Q ⊛ ◖ ▮ ⊞ ⇌ ♣ P

Windsor Castle
378 Carshalton Road
☎ (0181) 669 1191
11–11
Bass Worthington BB, Draught Bass; Fuller's London Pride; Hancock's HB; guest beer Ⓗ
Large, one-bar pub at the main crossroads. It stocks a good range of guest beers and offers excellent food in the restaurant or bar (no meals Sun eve). Popular with retired folk, especially lunchtime.
⊛ ◖ ▮ ⇌ ♣ P

Cheam

Railway
32 Station Way
(off A217/A213)
☎ (0181) 642 7416
11–11
Courage Best Bitter; S&N Theakston Best Bitter, XB Ⓗ
Detached, 19th-century building formerly owned by Courage and now part of the Southern Inns (S&N) estate. A definite local, with the emphasis on beer and conversation. No music.
Q ◖ ▮ ⇌

Chessington

North Star
271 Hook Road, Hook (A243)
☎ (0181) 397 4223
12 (11 Sat)–11
Bass Charrington IPA, Draught Bass; Hancock's HB; M&B Highgate Dark; guest beer Ⓗ
Pub on the main road, with a large garden; ten years in the *Guide* and one of the first outlets for Highgate Dark in London. No meals Tue or Sun.
Q ⅏ ⊛ ◖ ▮ ♣ P

Kingston upon Thames

Bricklayer's Arms
53 Hawks Road (off A2043)
☎ (0181) 546 0393
11–11
Morland Bitter, Old Masters, Tanner's Jack, Old Speckled Hen Ⓗ
Genuine local noted for its excellent food in generous portions. The nearest decent pub to Kingstonian FC. Background music (generally blues/soul/jazz). No food Sun eve. Limited parking.
⅏ ⊛ ◖ ▮ ♣ P

Cocoanut
16 Mill Street
☎ (0181) 546 3978
11–3, 5.30–11; 11–11 Sat
Fuller's London Pride, ESB Ⓗ
CAMRA London *Pub of the Year* 1992. Fuller's seasonal beers sold as available. No food Sun.
⅏ ⊛ ◖

Park Tavern
19 New Road
10.30–11
Brakspear Special; Whitbread Boddingtons Bitter; Young's Bitter, Special; guest beers Ⓗ
Friendly local close to the Kingston Gate of Richmond Park. Parking can be difficult.
🏰 ⊛

Wych Elm
93 Elm Road
☎ (0181) 546 3271
11–3, 5–11; 11–11 Sat
Fuller's Chiswick, London Pride, ESB Ⓗ
Friendly pub with a good regular following for its smart lounge and basic, but tidy, public bar. Attractive garden with impressive floral displays. No food Sun. Fuller's seasonal beers sold.
⊛ ◖ ⊞ ♣

New Malden

Royal Oak
90 Coombe Road (B283)
☎ (0181) 942 0837
11–11
Ind Coope Benskins BB, Burton Ale; Tetley Bitter; Young's Bitter; guest beer Ⓗ
Imposing pub on the main road; winner of the local authority's *Prettiest Pub* award. Occasional live music.
⊛ ◖ ⅏ ⇌ ♣ P ⼂

Woodie's
Thetford Road (W end of road off South Lane)
☎ (0181) 949 5824
11–11
Courage Directors; Fuller's London Pride; Whitbread Boddingtons Bitter, Flowers Original; Young's Bitter, Special Ⓗ
Ex-cricket pavilion decorated with hundreds of sporting photos: a fairly quiet but popular pub. Quite unique and well worth a visit.
🏰 Q ⊛ ◖ ♣ P

Richmond

Coach & Horses
8 Kew Green (A205)
☎ (0181) 940 1208
11–11
Young's Bitter, Special, Winter Warmer Ⓗ
Large, traditional, edge-of-town coaching inn with many preserved features from the 19th century; popular with local families and visitors to Kew. The large garden hosts occasional jazz sessions. The new dining area is renowned for its generous food portions. No meals Sun eve. 🏰 Q ⊛ ⍾ ◖ ▮
⇌ (Kew Bridge)
⊖ (Kew Gdns) ♣ P

Orange Tree
45 Kew Road
☎ (0181) 940 0944
11–11
Young's Bitter, Special, Winter Warmer Ⓗ
Fine, popular pub in a large Victorian building, with a fringe theatre upstairs and a bistro/wine bar downstairs. A good variety of meals is served from a counter in the lounge (no food Sun eve). Live jazz in the wine bar Sun eve.
🏰 Q ⊛ ◖ ▮ ⇌ ⊖

Triple Crown
15 Kew Foot Road
☎ (0181) 940 3805
11–11
Beer range varies Ⓗ
Popular pub close to Richmond Athletic, home of London Scottish Rugby Club. Local CAMRA *Pub of the Year* 1994, it serves a large range of malt whiskies and a constantly changing selection of beers from a list of over 100.
⊛ ◖ ⇌ ⊖

Waterman's Arms

12 Water Lane
☎ (0181) 940 2893
11–3, 5.30–11; 11–11 Sat
Young's Bitter, Special, Winter Warmer Ⓗ
Small Victorian pub in a cobbled stone lane leading to the river, with an attractive bar in its cosy, two-room layout. Simple, home-made meals (soups, casseroles and a wide range of cheeses).
🏚 Q 🌣 ❦ ◗ ♣

White Cross Hotel

Water Lane
☎ (0181) 940 6844
11–11
Young's Bitter, Special, Winter Warmer Ⓗ
Extremely popular, Thames-side pub in a splendid, picturesque setting, offering excellent bar food and service. The riverside terrace bar is open in summer. Local CAMRA *Pub of the Year* 1992.
🏚 Q ❀ ◗ ◗

Surbiton

Waggon & Horses

1 Surbiton Hill Road (A240)
11–3, 5–11; 11–11 Sat
Young's Bitter, Special, Winter Warmer Ⓗ
The landlord is now in his 28th year at this pub which is noted for its charity collections. The only Young's pub in the Royal Borough with a public bar. No meals weekends. Q ❀ ◗ 🍺 ♣

Sutton

Moon on the Hill

9 Hill Road
☎ (0181) 643 1202
11–11
Courage Directors; Marston's Pedigree; S&N Theakston Best Bitter, XB; Younger Scotch; guest beer Ⓗ
Large Wetherspoon house in a former department store in the town square. A double staircase leads to a no-smoking area and a terrace garden at the rear. Regular price promotions and beer festivals. Guest ales come from micro-breweries.
Q ❀ ◗ ♦ ♿ 🍺 ♡ ✄

New Town

7 Lind Road (off A232)
☎ (0181) 642 0567
11–3, 5–11; 11–11 Sat
Young's Bitter, Special, Winter Warmer Ⓗ
Large, busy and friendly, two-bar, street-corner pub in the New Town area. The carpeted public bar has an adjoining games room. There's also an unusual, three-level saloon bar. Occasional jazz

sessions. No meals Sun eve.
Q ❀ ◗ ◗ 🍺 🚆 ♣

W1: Fitzrovia

Bricklayer's Arms

31 Gresse Street
☎ (0171) 636 5593
11–11
Samuel Smith OBB Ⓗ
Small, busy pub on two floors; food is served in the upper bar. A former winner of CAMRA's refurbishment award. ◗ ▸
Ө (Tottenham Ct Rd) ♣

Duke of York

47 Rathbone Street
11–11
Greene King IPA, Rayments Special, Abbot Ⓗ
Local at the end of a pedestrian street. It also sells Greene King's seasonal beers.
◗ ▸ Ө (Goodge St) ♣

One Tun

58–60 Goodge Street
☎ (0171) 436 4667
11–11
Young's Bitter, Special, Winter Warmer Ⓗ
Busy, one-bar pub with an island bar; an ex-Finch's house. Live music monthly.
◗ Ө (Goodge St) ♣

Rising Sun

46 Tottenham Court Road
☎ (0171) 636 6530
11–11
Courage Best Bitter, Directors; S&N Theakston Best Bitter, XB, Old Peculier; guest beers Ⓗ
Much improved pub: formerly Presley's, it has now reverted to its original name.
Q ◗ ▸ Ө (Goodge St) ♡

W1: Marylebone

Beehive

7 Homer Street
11–3, 5.30 (7 Sat)–11; 11–11 Fri
Fuller's London Pride; Whitbread Boddingtons Bitter Ⓗ
Small, friendly, back-street pub of a type now becoming rare. ◗ 🚆 Ө

Golden Eagle

59 Marylebone Lane
11–11; 11–3, 5.30–11 Sat
Draught Bass; Brakspear Bitter; Fuller's London Pride Ⓗ
Tiny corner pub featuring a piano player at weekends.
Ө (Bond St)

Turner's Arms

26 Crawford Street
11–11

Shepherd Neame Master Brew Bitter, Bishops Finger Ⓗ

Pub where the customers like the Christmas decorations so much that they stay up all year. Unusual brewer for the area. ◗ ▸ 🚆 Ө

Westmoreland Arms

34 George Street
☎ (0171) 935 4753
11–11; 12–3 Sun, closed Sun eve
Bateman XB; Jennings Bitter; Marston's Pedigree; Whitbread Boddingtons Bitter Ⓗ
Airy, corner pub with a large collection of water jugs.
◗ Ө (Baker St)

Worcester Arms

39 George Street
11 (12 Sat)–11
Draught Bass; Brakspear Bitter; S&N Theakston XB Ⓗ
Small, friendly pub boasting a Courage Alton Brewery mirror. ◗

W1: Mayfair

Guinea

30 Bruton Place
☎ (0171) 409 1728
11–11; 11–3, 7–11 Sat; closed Sun
Young's Bitter, Special, Winter Warmer Ⓗ
Small, intimate mews pub with an exclusive restaurant at the rear. The manager has won numerous awards for pub food (the latest for steak and kidney pudding). ◗ ▸

Windmill

6 Mill Street ☎ (0171) 491 8050
11–11 (3 Sat); closed Sun
Young's Bitter, Special, Winter Warmer Ⓗ
Split-level pub opposite the Rolls Royce showroom.
◗ ▸ Ө (Oxford Circus)

W1: Soho

Burlington Bertie

Shaftesbury Avenue
☎ (0171) 437 0847
11–11
Draught Bass; Brakspear Bitter; S&N Theakston Old Peculier; guest beers Ⓗ
New pub in former shop premises; two bars, one on the first floor balcony. Live piano. The beer range may vary.
◗ ▸ Ө (Piccadilly Circus)

Pillars of Hercules

7 Greek Street
☎ (0171) 437 1179
11–11
McEwan 80/-; Marston's Pedigree; S&N Theakston Best Bitter, Old Peculier; guest beers Ⓗ

Greater London

Warm, friendly pub just off Soho Square. Very busy at times. No food Sun.
◖ ✈ (Tottenham Ct Rd)

W2: Bayswater

Leinster Arms
17 Leinster Terrace
☎ (0171) 723 5757
11–11
Ind Coope Burton Ale; Nicholson's Best Bitter; Tetley Bitter Ⓗ
Friendly pub, just off Bayswater Rd. The licensee won the Ind Coope *Grandmaster Cellarman* award for 1993. Eve meals finish at 8. A gem. ◖ ▶ ✈ (Paddington) ✈ (Bayswater) ♣

W2: Paddington

Archery Tavern
4 Bathurst Street
☎ (0171) 402 4916
11–11
Hall & Woodhouse Badger BB, Tanglefoot; Wells Eagle; guest beers Ⓗ
Wood-panelled pub next to a working stable. It sometimes offers beers from the Gribble Inn at Oving, Sussex.
◖ ▶ ✈ ✈ (Lancaster Gate) ♣

Victoria
10a Strathearn Place
☎ (0171) 724 1191
11–11
Fuller's Chiswick, London Pride, ESB Ⓗ
Victorian pub with plenty of original woodwork and mirrors, and an interesting model of an old royal yacht. Its name is allegedly derived from Queen Victoria's rest here on her way to opening Paddington Station. Fuller's seasonal beers sold. ◖ ✈ ✈

W3: Acton

Castle
140 Victoria Road
☎ (0181) 992 2027
11–11
Fuller's Chiswick, London Pride, ESB Ⓗ
Large, welcoming refuge on the edge of North Acton industrial estate. The comfortable lounge is adorned with pictures celebrating the BBC Radio era. Fuller's seasonal ales stocked.
❀ ◖ ▶ ⬚ ✈ (North) ♣ P

Duke of York
86 Steyne Road
☎ (0181) 992 0463
11–11
Courage Best Bitter; Morland Old Speckled Hen; Wadworth 6X; Webster's Green Label,

---

Yorkshire Bitter; Young's Special Ⓗ
Fine example of a town pub which affords welcome shelter from a busy high street. The garden has won numerous local awards.
⬚ ❀ ◖ ▶ ✈ (Central) ♣

King's Head
214 High Street
☎ (0181) 992 0282
11–11
Fuller's Chiswick, London Pride, ESB Ⓗ
Large, single-bar, corner pub with separate drinking areas. A haven of tranquility in a rather boisterous area of town. No-smoking area lunchtime. Chat to Jasper, the parrot.
Q ❀ ◖ ✈ (Central)
✈ (Town) ♣ ✄

W4: Chiswick

Bell & Crown
72 Strand on the Green
☎ (0181) 994 4164
11–11
Fuller's Chiswick, London Pride, ESB Ⓗ
Pleasant pub with a conservatory overlooking the Thames. Fuller's seasonal ales sold. ◖ ▶ ✈ (Kew Bridge)

Crown & Anchor
374 Chiswick High Road
☎ (0181) 995 2607
11–11
Young's Bitter, Special, Winter Warmer Ⓗ
Corner pub, with a tiled frontage, facing Turnham Green. ◖ ✈ (Chiswick Pk) ♣

Duke of York
107 Devonshire Road
☎ (0181) 994 2118
Fuller's Chiswick, London Pride, ESB Ⓗ
Corner pub, south of Chiswick High Rd. Ask for real Chiswick as the keg version is also sold. Fuller's seasonal ales available. ◖ ✈ (Turnham Green) ♣

George & Devonshire
8 Burlington Lane
☎ (0181) 994 1859
11–11
Fuller's Chiswick, London Pride, ESB Ⓗ
Large, two-bar pub facing the notorious Hogarth Roundabout, near Hogarth's house. Beware the keg cider on a fake handpump. Handy for Fuller's Brewery. Seasonal ales sold. ❀ ◖ ▶ ⬚

George IV
184 Chiswick High Road
☎ (0181) 994 4624
11–11

Fuller's Chiswick, London Pride, ESB Ⓗ
Large, two-bar pub with a lounge broken up into intimate alcoves. Guest beers may be available. Beware the keg cider on a fake handpump.
❀ ◖ ▶ ✈ (Turnham Green)

W5: Ealing

Duffy's
124 Pitshanger Lane
☎ (0181) 998 6810
11–3 (4 Fri & Sat), 5.30–11
Draught Bass; Brakspear Bitter; Fuller's London Pride; Gale's HSB Ⓗ
Pub formerly a shop, which it still resembles, at least from the outside. There are two distinct drinking areas plus a restaurant area at the rear. Regency Bitter is a house beer (not brewed here). ◖ ▶

Fox & Goose
Hanger Lane
☎ (0181) 997 2441
11–11
Fuller's Chiswick, London Pride, ESB Ⓗ**; guest beers** Ⓗ/Ⓖ
Pub where a tiny public bar, a large, comfortable saloon and a very pleasant garden at the rear combine to offer a welcome refuge from the nearby infamous Hanger Lane gyratory system.
◖ ⬚ ✈ (Hanger Lane) P

Red Lion
13 St Mary's Road
☎ (0181) 567 2541
11–11
Fuller's Chiswick, London Pride, ESB Ⓗ
A gem of a pub opposite Ealing Film Studios, hence its alternative name of 'Stage 6'. The walls sport studio-related pictures and the many certificates won by the landlord, not least for the garden at the rear, very pleasant in summer.
Q ❀ ✈ (Broadway)
✈ (South)

Wheatsheaf
41 Haven Lane
☎ (0181) 997 5240
11–11
Fuller's Chiswick, London Pride, ESB Ⓗ
Deceptively large, two-bar pub to the north of Ealing town centre. An extensive refurbishment in 1993 introduced much wood and exposed brickwork but also a separate public bar. Live music Sun, and occasionally other, nights.
◖ ▶ ⬚ ✈ (Broadway)
✈ ♣

W6: Hammersmith

Andover Arms
57 Aldensley Road
☎ (0181) 741 9794
11–11
Fuller's Chiswick, London Pride, ESB Ⓗ
Pleasant, back-street local (difficult to find without a map) in Brackenbury Village. No meals Sun, or Sat lunch. Thai food a speciality.
❀ ◖ ◗ ⊖ (Ravenscourt Pk)

Cross Keys
57 Black Lion Lane
☎ (0181) 748 3541
11–11
Fuller's Chiswick, London Pride, ESB Ⓗ
Popular pub between King St and the river, a meeting place for London Cornish RUFC. Upmarket food. ❀ ◖ ◗

Dove
19 Upper Mall
☎ (0181) 748 5405
11–11
Fuller's London Pride, ESB Ⓗ
Famous riverside pub dating back to the 17th century. It is claimed that Charles II and Nell Gwynne drank here. The public bar has been listed in the *Guinness Book of Records* as the smallest in London. Thai food available Mon–Fri eves.
Q ❀ ◖ ◗ ⊞ ⊖

Salutation
154 King Street
☎ (0181) 748 3660
11–11
Fuller's Chiswick, London Pride, ESB Ⓗ
Former coaching house with an interesting tiled frontage.
❀ ◖ ⊖

Thatched House
115 Dalling Road
☎ (0181) 748 6174
11–11
Young's Bitter, Special, Winter Warmer Ⓗ
Triangular-shaped pub, many years in the *Guide*. Patio drinking area.
🚪 ❀ ◖ ⊖ (Ravenscourt Pk)

W7: Hanwell

Fox
Green Lane ☎ (0181) 567 3912
11–3, 5.30–11; 11–11 Sat
Courage Best Bitter, Directors; Marston's Pedigree Ⓗ
Unspoilt local serving good food and beer at the confluence of the River Brent and the Grand Union Canal. Popular with boaters preparing to ascend the nearby flight of 12 locks. Open until 4 Sun for meals. Q ◖

W8: Kensington

Britannia
1 Allen Street
☎ (0171) 937 1864
11–11
Young's Bitter, Special, Winter Warmer Ⓗ
Deservedly popular pub with a comfortable, wood-panelled saloon and a small public bar. The conservatory serves as a no-smoking area at lunchtime. Handy for Kensington High St shopping. ◖ ⊞ ⊖ (High St)

Churchill Arms
119 Kensington Church Street
11–11
Fuller's Chiswick, London Pride, ESB Ⓗ
Extremely busy pub with a large collection of bric-a-brac. Thai food a speciality. Fuller's seasonal ales served.
◖ ◗ ⊖ (Notting Hill Gate)

W9: Maida Vale

Truscott Arms
55 Shirland Road
☎ (0171) 286 0310
11–11
Draught Bass; Courage Directors; Whitbread Boddingtons Bitter, Flowers Original Ⓗ
Large, single-bar pub with an impressive bank of handpumps. Occasional barbecues in the garden. ❀ ◖ ⊖ (Warwick Ave)

Warrington Hotel
93 Warrington Crescent
☎ (0171) 286 2929
11–11
Brakspear Special; Fuller's London Pride, ESB; Marston's Pedigree; Young's Special; guest beer Ⓗ
Large, florid, 'gin palace'-type pub, with a semi-circular, marble-topped bar. Thai restaurant upstairs.
◖ ⊞ ⊖ (Warwick Ave)

Warwick Castle
6 Warwick Place
11–11
Bass Worthington BB, Draught Bass; Fuller's London Pride; Wadworth 6X Ⓗ
Quiet pub near Regent's Canal Paddington Basin. Note the print of Paddington Station over the fireplace.
🚪 ◖ ⊖ (Warwick Ave)

W11: Notting Hill

Portobello Star
171 Portobello Road
☎ (0171) 229 8016
11–11

Whitbread Castle Eden Ale, Flowers Original Ⓗ
Small, basic market pub.
⊖ (Ladbroke Grove)

W12: Shepherd's Bush

Crown & Sceptre
57 Melina Road
☎ (0181) 743 6414
11–11
Fuller's London Pride, ESB Ⓗ
Back-street, two-bar pub; an oasis in a beer desert, displaying much QPR FC memorabilia. ◖ ◗ ♣

W13: West Ealing

Kent
2 Scotch Common
11–11
Fuller's London Pride, ESB Ⓗ
Large pub next to the park: a small public bar and a large, split-level lounge with much polished woodwork and cut glass, leading to a spacious garden.
❀ ◖ ⊞ ⇌ (Castlebar) P

W14: West Kensington

Seven Stars
253 North End Road
☎ (0171) 385 3571
11–11
Fuller's London Pride, ESB Ⓗ
Large, comfortable, two-bar pub rebuilt in 1938 in Art Deco style. Eve meals finish at 8; no food Sun.
❀ ◖ ◗ ⊞ ⊖

Warwick Arms
160 Warwick Road
☎ (0171) 603 3560
11–11
Fuller's Chiswick, London Pride, ESB Ⓗ
Traditional local built in 1828 and boasting attractive Wedgwood handpumps. Fuller's seasonal beers sold. Handy for Earl's Court and Olympia. No food Sun eve.
🚪 Q ◖ ◗ ⇌ (Olympia) ⊖

Bedfont

Beehive
333 Staines Road
☎ (0181) 890 8086
11–11
Fuller's London Pride, ESB Ⓗ
Excellent pub with a friendly atmosphere, an attractive lounge and a well-kept garden. Good value meals from a Thai and a traditional menu (not served Sat lunch or Sun); barbecues in summer.
❀ ◖ ◗ P

Greater London

Brentford

Brewery Tap
47 Catherine Wheel Road
☎ (0181) 560 5200
11–11
Fuller's London Pride, ESB Ⓗ
Cosy, lively, Victorian local, with three elevated bars, off the High St and by the Grand Union Canal. Live trad. jazz Tue and Thu, blues Fri and a piano player Sat. Good value, home-cooked food (not served Sun eve); meals finish at 8 other eves. Fuller's seasonal ales. ❀ ◖ ▶ ⊞ ⇌ ♠

Royal Oak
38 New Road
☎ (0181) 568 7876
11–11
Courage Best Bitter; Fuller's London Pride Ⓗ
Comfortable, welcoming local, retaining its public bar. Football dominates the conversation in the same way that Brentford's ground dominates the pub. Very busy on match days (home supporters only please). Beware the keg cider on a fake handpump. ❀ ◖ ⊞ ⇌ ♠

Cowley

Coachman's Inn
High Street ☎ (01895) 234786
11–11
Fuller's London Pride; John Smith's Bitter; Webster's Yorkshire Bitter; guest beers Ⓗ
Very unusually-shaped building of interconnected, weatherboarded octagons. The two rooms are on split-levels, the lower used as a restaurant. Beware the keg cider on a fake handpump. Q ❀ ◖ ▶ P ⌇

Cranford

Queen's Head
123 High Street
☎ (0181) 897 0722
11–11
Fuller's Chiswick, London Pride, ESB Ⓗ
Large, Tudor-style pub: one bar but two distinct drinking areas. The lounge (without a bar) is mainly used for dining (home-cooked food; not served weekend eves). Award-winning garden.
⚲ Q ⍣ ❀ ◖ ▶ ♠ P

Feltham

General Roy
Poplar Way ☎ (0181) 893 2977
11–11
Bass Worthington BB, Draught Bass; Fuller's London Pride; guest beers Ⓗ
Popular pub, opened in 1992 on a new residential/business estate, with a large L-shaped bar. Good food (not served Sun eve). Occasional ale festivals. ❀ ◖ ▶ ⅋ P

Greenford

Black Horse
425 Oldfield Lane
☎ (0181) 578 1384
11–11
Fuller's Chiswick, London Pride, ESB Ⓗ
Canalside pub on the Grand Union's Paddington arm; a busy, friendly pub set in the middle of the Greenford industrial area. Large garden.
❀ ◖ ⇌ ⊖ ♠ P

Hampton

White Hart
70 High Street
☎ (0181) 979 5352
11–3, 5.30–11; 11–11 Fri & Sat
Whitbread Boddingtons Bitter, Flowers Original; guest beers Ⓗ
Genuine free house where eight handpumps serve a selection of beers that change constantly. Friendly atmosphere; large log fire. The new cycle rack is useful.
⚲ Q ❀ ◖ ♠

Hampton Wick

White Hart
1 High Street
☎ (0181) 977 1786
11–3, 5–11; 11–11 Thu–Sat
Fuller's Chiswick, London Pride, ESB; guest beers Ⓗ
Large, mock Tudor pub with a spacious, oak-panelled lounge. Good, home-cooked food (not served Sun eve). ⚲ ◖ ▶ ⇌ P

Harmondsworth

Crown
High Street ☎ (0181) 759 1007
11–11
Brakspear Bitter; Courage Best Bitter, Directors; Harveys BB; Marston's Pedigree; John Smith's Bitter Ⓗ
Despite its proximity to Heathrow Airport, this is still a true village local, convivial, characterful and occasionally lively. Local newspapers and enamel signs feature. Coaches welcome.
⚲ Q ❀ ⚲ ◖ ▶ ♠ ⊟

Hayes End

Moon & Sixpence
1250–1256 Uxbridge Road
☎ (0181) 561 3541
11–11
Courage Directors; S&N Theakston Best Bitter, XB; Wadworth 6X; Younger Scotch; guest beers Ⓗ
Typical Wetherspoon

conversion of a former bank. Old photos of Hayes are among the decorations. Popular with all ages.
❀ ◖ ▶ ⅋ ⌇

Heathrow Airport

Tap & Spile
Upper Concourse, Terminal 1
☎ (0181) 897 3696
11–11
Marston's Pedigree; guest beers Ⓗ
Busy airport bar providing a wide choice of beers for the thirsty traveller, most of which change regularly and usually include Marston's Head Brewer's Choice. It opens at 9am for continental breakfasts.
Q ⍣ ⊖ ⌂ P

Hounslow

Cross Lances
236 Hanworth Road (A314)
☎ (0181) 570 4174
11–11
Fuller's London Pride, ESB Ⓗ
Early Victorian, traditional local with popular public bar. The saloon has a large, welcoming fire. Wholesome meals served at all times. Fuller's seasonal beers sold.
⚲ Q ❀ ◖ ▶ ⊞ ⇌ ♠ P

Jolly Farmer
177 Lampton Road (100 yds S of A4) ☎ (0181) 570 1276
11–11
Courage Best Bitter, Directors; Wadworth 6X Ⓗ
Popular, cosy local where the friendly licensees offer very good weekday lunches.
❀ ◖ ⊞ ⊖ (Central) ♠ P

Isleworth

Bridge Inn
457 London Road
☎ (0181) 568 0088
11–11
Marston's Pedigree; John Smith's Bitter; Wadworth 6X Ⓗ
Pub built in the 1870s by Farnell, to provide sustenance for workers on the iron bridge. A friendly pub, it now incorporates an excellent Thai restaurant. No food Sun.
⚲ ◖ ▶ ⇌

Castle
18 Upper Square, Old Isleworth ☎ (0181) 560 3615
11–11
Young's Bitter, Special, Winter Warmer Ⓗ
Prominent pub, a long-standing *Guide* entry, housing a large and comfortable bar, plus a games room. Families are welcome in the conservatory. Near Syon Park and the Thames.
⚲ Q ⍣ ❀ ◖ ⊞ ♠ P

Victoria Tavern

56 Worple Road
☎ (0181) 892 3536
11–11
Ansells Mild; Eldridge Pope Dorchester; Whitbread Flowers IPA; guest beers Ⓗ
Compact, popular, traditionally refurbished, street-corner pub in a quiet area of the town, catering for local and family trade. A small conservatory and a well-designed patio area, with a pond, fountain and rabbits, are features. Renowned for keenly priced beer and snacks. No food Sun; eve meals finish at 7.
❀ ◑ ▶ ⊟ ♣

Northolt

Plough

Mandeville Road
☎ (0181) 845 1750
11–11
Fuller's London Pride, ESB Ⓗ
Very attractive, thatched pub built in the 1940s on the edge of Northolt village.
❀ ◑ ⊖ ♣ P

Norwood Green

Plough

Tentelow Lane
☎ (0181) 574 1945
11–11
Fuller's Chiswick, London Pride, ESB Ⓗ
Historic inn, Fuller's oldest and mainly a locals' pub. It often appears crowded because of the surprisingly large space devoted to the bar servery. A former function room acts as an overspill area. No food Sun. ♨ Q ❀ ◑ ♣ P

Osterley

Hare & Hounds

Wyke Green, Windmill Lane
☎ (0181) 560 5438
11–11
Fuller's London Pride, ESB Ⓗ
Despite being surrounded by parkland, and a golf course, relative isolation does not prevent this pub being very busy at times. Although the car-borne trade predominates, walkers are also attracted. The menu offers hot meals at all times. ♨ Q ❀ ◑ ▶ P

Ruislip Manor

JJ Moon's

12 Victoria Road
☎ (01895) 622373
11–11
Courage Directors; Greene King Abbot; S&N Theakston Best Bitter, XB; Younger Scotch; guest beers Ⓗ
Traditional-style, mock Victorian alehouse, converted from an old Woolworth's store. Very popular with all ages. Q ❀ ◑ ▶ ♿ ⊖ (Ruislip Manor) ➚ ⊁

Southall

Hambrough Tavern

The Broadway
☎ (0181) 574 9008
11–11
Beer range varies Ⓗ
Along with many other pubs in the town, this owes its existence to the building of the canal at the turn of the 18th century. However, the current building dates from only 1982. It offers a constantly changing range of four real ales in the often lively saloon bar.
❀ ⊟ ♣ P

Sudbury

Black Horse

1018 Harrow Road, Wembley (A4005) ☎ (0181) 904 1013
11–3, 5.30–11; 12–11 Sat
Ind Coope Burton Ale; Tetley Bitter; Young's Bitter; guest beers Ⓗ
Very popular, busy pub providing good service. Children welcome in the conservatory. Occasional beer festivals. No meals Sun.
Q ❀ ◑ ♣ P

Teddington

Hogarth

58 Broad Street
☎ (0181) 977 3846
11–11
Fuller's Chiswick, London Pride Ⓗ
Popular pub, right in the town centre. Recent structural alterations have made it much roomier and there is great emphasis on food. Open at 9.30 for breakfast. No eve meals Sun. No-smoking area at the rear. Fuller's seasonal ales stocked. ♨ ❀ ◑ ▶ ⇌ ⊁

Queen Dowager

49 North Lane
☎ (0181) 943 3474
11–11
Young's Bitter, Special, Winter Warmer Ⓗ
Friendly, comfortable pub, just off the main street, with a first class garden; named after Queen Adelaide, widow of William IV. Local CAMRA *Pub of the Year* 1993. No meals Sun.
Q ❀ ◑ ⊟ ⇌ ♣

Twickenham

Prince Albert

30 Hampton Road (A311)
☎ (0181) 894 3963
11–11

Fuller's Chiswick, London Pride, ESB Ⓗ
Friendly Victorian local where the pleasant decor includes wood panelling. The carvery Sun lunches are highly recommended. Occasional live blues music. Fuller's seasonal beers stocked. ♨ Q ❀ ◑ ▶

Prince Blucher

124 The Green
☎ (0181) 894 1824
11–11
Fuller's Chiswick, London Pride, ESB Ⓗ
Large, comfortable, old, one-bar pub which, although modernised, still shows great character. Some snacks available. Fuller's seasonal beers sold. ♨ ❀ P

Uxbridge

Load of Hay

33 Villiers Street
☎ (01895) 234676
11–3, 5.30 (7 Sat)–11
Beer range varies Ⓗ
Cosy local originally built as Elthorne Light Militia Officers' Mess. The small front bar opens as a restaurant Sat eve and is highly recommended. No eve meals Mon or Sun. Cider in summer. Close to Brunel University.
Q ❀ ◑ ▶ ➚ P ⊁ ⊟

West Drayton

De Burgh Arms

Station Approach
11–11
Eldridge Pope Best Bitter, Hardy Country; Ind Coope Burton Ale; Tetley Bitter; guest beer Ⓗ
Comfortable, island-bar pub by the station, recently refurbished and converted to a 'Salmon & Hare' house by Allied. The guest beer is from the company's Tapster's Choice list.
Q ❀ ◑ ▶ ♿ ⇌ P ⊁

Whitton

White Hart

123 Kneller Road
☎ (0181) 893 3646
11–11
Marston's Pedigree; Smiles Best Bitter; John Smith's Bitter; Wadworth 6X Ⓗ
17th-century coaching inn purchased as a free house in 1991 after closure in 1989 following a fire; sympathetically restored. Excellent food (not served Sun). The huge, pleasant garden is popular with families and has a safe play area for children. No food Sun.
❀ 🏠 ◑ ⇌ ♣ P ⊟

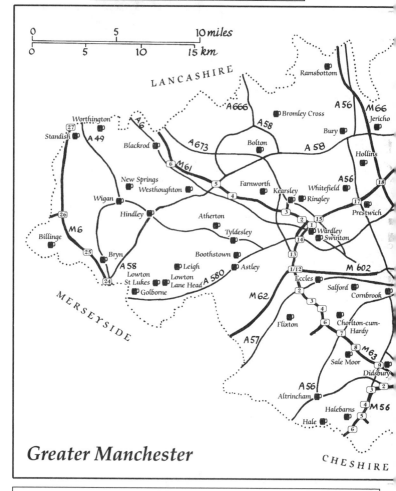

Greater Manchester

Holt, *Cheetham;* **Hydes' Anvil,** *Manchester;* **Lees,**
Middleton Junction; **Thomas McGuinness,** *Rochdale;*
Millgate, *Failsworth;* **Oak,** *Heywood;* **Robinson's,**
Stockport

Altrincham

Hogshead Ale House
Old Market Place
☎ (0161) 972 7062
11–11
Beer range varies Ⓗ
Once the town hall: it's
rumoured Bonnie Prince
Charlie once called at this old
coaching inn, now a successful
Hogshead conversion.
🏚 🍺 ❀ ◑ ▮ ⇌ ⊖ ⏴ ⅄

Malt Shovels
68 Stamford Street
☎ (0161) 928 2053
12–3, 5–11; 12–11 Fri & Sat

Samuel Smith OBB Ⓗ
Friendly town-centre pub with
live jazz most nights. Pool
room upstairs. No food Sun.
❀ ◑ ⇌ ⊖ ⏴

Orange Tree
Old Market Place
☎ (0161) 928 2600
11–11
**Courage Directors; Marston's
Pedigree; Morland Old
Speckled Hen; Wilson's
Bitter; guest beer** Ⓗ
Once the smallest pub in
Altrincham, where, in 1823, a
man sold his wife for 1/6d.
The present building dates
from 1880. Note the old photos

showing local pubs now gone
and the pub under restoration.
A former local CAMRA *Pub of
the Year*. Q 🏚 ◑ ▮ ⇌ ⊖ ⅄

Tatton Arms
3–5 Tipping Street
☎ (0161) 941 2502
11.30–11
**Whitbread Boddingtons
Bitter; guest beers** Ⓗ
Thriving two-roomed local
where pictures reflect the
long-serving landlord's
nautical background and the
locals' interest in the two
Manchester football clubs. No
food Sun.
🏚 ❀ ◑ ⊟ ⇌ ⊖ ⏴ P

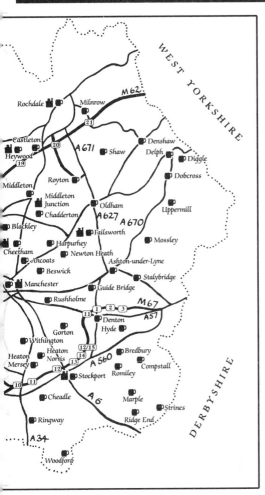

many guest beers. Cider in summer; regular beer festivals.
❀ ◖ ⇌ ⏃

Witchwood

152 Old Street
☎ (0161) 344 0321
12–11
Courage Directors; Marston's Pedigree; S&N Theakston Best Bitter, XB; John Smith's Bitter; guest beers Ⓗ
Enterprising free house with a good reputation for live music. A Coach House house beer is another regular; three guest beers. Extension to midnight in the Venue Bar Thu–Sat. Occasional cider in summer.
◖ ⇌ ⏃

Astley

Cart & Horses

221 Manchester Road
☎ (01942) 870751
12–11
Holt Mild, Bitter Ⓗ
Large roadside local sat awkwardly on the A572 (there is a story why): a large lounge, a separate no-smoking area and a very popular tap room.
🍽 ♣ P ✲

Atherton

Pendle Witch

2–4 Warburton Place (alley off Market St)
5 (12 Thu–Sat)–11
Moorhouse's Black Cat Mild, Premier, Pendle Witches Brew; guest beers Ⓗ
Moorhouse's only pub in the area, providing a good range of beers in a friendly atmosphere. Formally two town houses, then a 'fun' pub, it is now a one-room pub with a split-level floor. ❀ ♣

Spinners Arms

76 Bolton Road
☎ (01942) 882498
7 (12 Fri & Sat)–11; 12–4, 7–11 Wed & Thu
Taylor Landlord; Tetley Walker Dark Mild, Bitter; guest beers Ⓗ
Another of Atherton's growing gems, this pub has a long lounge with a raised area, and a tap room for bar football, pinball and pool. Clay pipes available filled. Large, cobbled car park at the front; garden at the rear.
❀ 🍽 ⇌ ♣ P

Billinge

Hare & Hounds

142 Upholland Road
☎ (01744) 892843
12–3, 7–11; 12–11 Fri & Sat
Taylor Landlord; Tetley

Ancoats

Mitchell Arms

215 Every Street (off A665, near A662 jct)
☎ (0161) 273 3097
12–3, 7–11; 12–11 Fri & Sat
Banks's Mild, Bitter Ⓔ
Community local, run by a no-nonsense licensee. Currently under threat from the proposed route of a Metrolink extension. 🍽 ♣ ⊟

Ashton-under-Lyne

Dog & Pheasant

528 Oldham Road
☎ (0161) 330 4894
12–5, 7.30–11
Banks's Mild; Marston's Bitter, Pedigree Ⓗ
Popular and friendly pub close to Daisy Nook Country Park. Good value food lunchtime and Tue and Thu eve.

Marston's Head Brewer's Choice sold. 🍽 ◖ ♣ P

Oddfellows

King's Road ☎ (0161) 330 6356
12–11
Robinson's Hatters Mild, Best Bitter Ⓗ
Popular, many-roomed local, a long-time regular in the *Guide*. It boasts many traditional features, not least a splendid bar. A no-smoking room is a welcome addition. Other Robinson's beers are sometimes sold. ❀ ♣ ✲

Station

2 Warrington Street (by bypass) ☎ (0161) 330 6776
11.30–11; 12–3 (4 summer), 7–11 Sat
Marston's Pedigree; Whitbread Chester's Mild, Boddingtons Bitter; guest beers Ⓗ
Long-established, enterprising free house close to the town centre. Five handpumps serve

Walker Dark Mild Ⓗ, Mild, Bitter; guest beers Ⓗ
Popular, large redbrick pub with two rooms. The lounge is free from distractions.
Q ⊞ ♣ P

Sandbrook Arms

78 Sandbrook Road, Tontine (off B5206) ☎ (01695) 625775
6–11 (12–3, 6–11 summer); 12–11 Fri & Sat
Ind Coope Burton Ale; Taylor Landlord; Tetley Walker Mild, Bitter; guest beers Ⓗ
Large, open-plan, nicely decorated pub with an eating area. Frequented by Orrell RUFC. Lunches in summer.
◖ ▶ & P

Blackley

Pleasant Inn

370 Chapel Lane (off A6104, at bottom of Crab Lane)
☎ (0161) 740 3391
1 (12 Sat)–11
Robinson's Hatters Mild, Best Bitter Ⓗ
Small, three-roomed community pub in an ancient urban village. The lively vault, golf society room and lounge attract a loyal local clientele in this fairly remote location. Family room till 8.
Q ⭢ ⊛ ⊞ ♣

Try also: Old House at Home, Bottomley Side (Courage)

Blackrod

Gallagher's

38 Little Scotland (½ mile from A6) ☎ (01942) 833101
12–11
Tetley Walker Mild, Bitter; Walker Best Bitter; Whitbread Boddingtons Bitter; guest beers Ⓗ
18th-century coaching inn on the Bolton/Wigan border. Its excellent restaurant is well known and also serves real ale. ⊛ ◖ & ▲ P

Bolton

Bob's Smithy Inn

1448 Chorley Old Road (B6226) ☎ (01204) 842622
12–4 (not Mon), 5–11
Taylor Best Bitter; Tetley Walker Mild; Walker Bitter; Whitbread Boddingtons Bitter; guest beers Ⓗ
Popular pub on the fringes of the moors, with panoramic views of Bolton. Named after the local blacksmith who frequented it. ⭤ ⊛ ◖ ♣ P

Clifton Arms

94 Newport Street
☎ (01204) 392738

11–11; 11–3, 7–11 Sat; 12–2, 7–10.30 Sun
Jennings Bitter; Moorhouse's Premier; Tetley Walker Mild, Bitter; guest beers Ⓗ
Popular pub convenient for the bus/rail interchange. Mini-beer festivals held. No food Sun. ◖ ⇌ ♣

Crofter's Arms

494 Halliwell Road (A6099)
☎ (01204) 849695
12–3.30 (4.30 Sat), 7–11
Greenalls Bitter, Original; Tetley Walker Bitter; guest beers Ⓗ
Large, corner-terrace pub with a spacious lounge and vault.
⊞ ♣

Lodge Bank Tavern

260 Bridgeman Street, Great Lever ☎ (01204) 531946
11–5.30, 7.30–11; 11–11 Fri, Sat & summer
Lees GB Mild, Bitter Ⓗ
Comfortable, welcoming local near Bobbyheywood Park; one of the last pubs in Bolton to be granted a spirits licence.
⊛ ⇌ ♣ P

Lord Clyde

107 Folds Road (A676)
☎ (01204) 521705
11–11
Hydes' Anvil Mild, Light, Bitter Ⓔ
Friendly, traditional, multi-roomed local near the town centre: a small, L-shaped tap room, a small room at the rear and a large lounge. Eve meals served when Bolton FC are at home. ⊛ ◖ ⊞ ♣ P 🍴

Park

259 Bridgeman Street, Great Lever ☎ (01204) 399486
3 (11 Thu–Sat & summer)–11
Holt Bitter; Tetley Walker Mild, Bitter Ⓗ
Large pub next to Bobbyheywood Park; multi-roomed with a strong sports influence. No lunches Sun.
Q ⊛ ◖ ⊞ ⇌ ♣

Pilkington Arms

154 Derby Street (A579)
☎ (01204) 527960
11–11
Mitchell's Original; Tetley Walker Bitter Ⓗ
Unpretentious local with an excellent domino vault; run by the same family for the last 25 years. ⊞ ♣

Sweet Green Tavern

127 Crook Street
☎ (01204) 392258
11.30–3, 6.30 (7 Sat)–11; 11.30–11 Thu & Fri
Tetley Walker Mild, Bitter; guest beers Ⓗ
Multi-roomed, deceptively large pub across from the

bus-rail interchange. Three changing guest beers. Bolton CAMRA *Pub of the Year* 1992/1993. Home fans only on Bolton FC match days.
⭤ Q ⊛ ◖ ⇌ ♣ P

Boothstown

Royal Oak

20 Leigh Road (A572, near A577 jct) ☎ (0161) 790 3502
12–3 (4 Fri & Sat), 7–11
Holt Bitter; John Smith's Bitter; Wilson's Mild Ⓗ
Basic, but welcoming, three-room village local which runs a golf society and a football team. ⊞ ♣

Bredbury

Arden Arms

Ashton Road
☎ (0161) 430 2589
11.30–11 (11.30–3, 5.30–11 winter Mon & Tue)
Robinson's Hatters Mild, Best Bitter Ⓔ
Unspoilt, traditional, small-roomed pub in a semi-rural area, popular on summer weekends. Good value food (no meals Mon–Fri eves).
Q ⊛ ◖ ♣ P

Horsfield Arms

Ashton Road
☎ (0161) 430 6930
11.45–11; 11.45–3, 7–11 Sat
Robinson's Hatters Mild, Best Bitter Ⓔ
Unglamorously situated in front of Robinson's bottling plant, this pub's unassuming exterior hides a comfortable and welcoming interior. Loyal clientele. Q ⊛ ◖ P

Bromley Cross

Flag Inn

50 Hardmans Lane (near B6472) ☎ (01204) 302236
11–11
Whitbread Boddingtons Bitter; guest beers Ⓗ
Whitbread cask ale house with an enterprising landlord, serving a wide range of beers. It can be very busy eves. Local CAMRA *Pub of the Year* 1994. The cellar is visible from the pub. Good selection of games.
⭤ ♣ ⌂

Bryn

Bath Springs

455 Wigan Road
☎ (01942) 202716
11–11
Ind Coope Burton Ale; Tetley Walker Dark Mild, Bitter; guest beers Ⓗ
Formidable redbrick building named after Bath Springs

Brewery of Ormskirk.
Excellent value, home-cooked
lunches (Mon–Fri). Smart
function room upstairs.
◑ ☖ ⇌ ♣

Bury

Blue Bell

840 Manchester Road (A56
near Blackford Bridge)
☎ (0161) 766 2496
12–11
Holt Mild, Bitter Ⓗ
Large, three-roomed pub with
a traditional vault and a
friendly host, popular with
mature Man. Utd supporters.
The large, comfortable lounge
is patronized by friendly
locals. Pool room. Q ❀ ♣ P

Dusty Miller

87 Crostons Road
(B6213/B6214 jct)
☎ (0161) 764 1124
12–11; 12–4, 7–11 Sat
**Moorhouse's Black Cat Mild,
Premier, Pendle Witches
Brew; guest beers** Ⓗ
One of only a handful of
Moorhouse's tied pubs, this is
well worth the short walk
from the town centre. Situated
at a busy junction (note the old
stone fingerpost outside), this
two-roomer has a central bar
and an enclosed courtyard to
the rear. No food Wed.
❀ ♣

Old Blue Bell

2 Bell Lane (B6221/B6222 jct)
☎ (0161) 761 3674
12–11
Holt Mild, Bitter Ⓗ
Large, brick building at a busy
road junction. The spacious
lounge offers live music Thu
eve; the traditional vault is
popular for dominoes.
Separate bar area for people
who just want to chat.
☳ ♿ ♣

Tap & Spile

36 Manchester Old Road (off
A56) ☎ (0161) 763 7483
12–3, 5–11; 11–11 Fri & Sat
Beer range varies Ⓗ
Small, friendly, end-of-terrace
local with a varied clientele.
Two house beers: Special
(brewed by Hadrian) and
Premium (Ushers). No jukebox
or pool table – a beer drinker's
paradise! The home-made
kormas are recommended (no
food Sun). ◑ ♿ ❀ ♣ ◡ ⌁

Try also: Bridge Inn,
Manchester Rd (Free)

Castleton

Blue Pits Inn

842 Manchester Road (A664)
☎ (01706) 32151

12–4 (5 Fri & Sat), 7.30–11
Lees GB Mild, Bitter Ⓗ
Welcoming and friendly local
in a former railway building,
reputedly once used as a
mortuary. Three distinct
drinking areas and a large
upstairs function room now
provide a much more cheerful
note. ⇌ P

Try also: New Inn,
Manchester Rd (Robinson's)

Chadderton

Horton Arms

Streetbridge (B6195, almost
under A627M)
☎ (0161) 624 7793
11.30–11
Lees GB Mild, Bitter Ⓗ
Comfortable pub which has a
country feel, despite its easy
access to town. It is neatly laid
out in distinct drinking areas,
with one quiet room.
Deservedly popular. No food
Sun. ❀ ◑ P

Try also: Rifle Range Inn,
Burnley Lane (Lees)

Cheadle

Queen's Arms

177 Stockport Road (A560)
☎ (0161) 428 3081
12–11
**Robinson's Hatters Mild, Old
Stockport Bitter, Best Bitter** Ⓗ
Welcoming, community local
which encourages families
(swing and slide on the old
bowling green; family room
till 7.30). No food at weekends.
☳ ☷ ◑ ♣ P ⌁

Cheetham

Queen's Arms

4–6 Honey Street (off A665,
Cheetham Hill Rd)
☎ (0161) 834 4239
12–11; 12–4, 7–11 Sat
**Bateman Dark Mild, XXXB;
S&N Theakston Old Peculier;
Taylor Best Bitter, Landlord;
guest beers** Ⓗ
Pub with a lovely example of
an Empress Brewery tiled
facade. Extended into next
door, it has doubled in size.
The back garden, with
children's play area, overlooks
Irk Valley and the city centre.
Ever-changing range of guest
beers. Noted for food
including many ethnic dishes.
☳ ❀ ◗ ⇌ (Victoria)
✆ ♣ ◡

Chorlton-cum-
Hardy

Beech Inn

72 Beech Road
☎ (0161) 881 1180

11–11
**Marston's Pedigree; Morland
Old Speckled Hen; Taylor
Best Bitter, Landlord;
Wadworth 6X; Whitbread
Chester's Mild, Flowers
Original; guest beers** Ⓗ
Thriving, popular, three-room
pub just off the village green –
no food, no music, no
gimmicks; popular with all
ages. Q ❀ ☖ ♣

Compstall

Andrew Arms

George Street
☎ (0161) 427 2281
11–11
**Robinson's Hatters Mild, Best
Bitter** Ⓗ
Pub which pleases all who
visit, with an open fire in the
comfortable lounge and a
vault for TV fans and card
players. ☳ ❀ ◑ ♣ P

Cornbrook

Hope Inn

459 Chester Road (A56)
☎ (0161) 848 0038
11–4, 7–11
Hydes' Anvil Light, Bitter Ⓔ
Basic, two-roomed, street-
corner local in an area which
once boasted a multitude of
pubs and breweries. A lone
handpump stands on the bar
in case of powercuts! ♣

Delph

Royal Oak
(Th' Heights)

Broad Lane, Heights (1 mile
above Denshaw Rd) OS982090
☎ (01457) 874460
7–11
**Whitbread Boddingtons
Bitter; guest beers** Ⓗ
Isolated, 250-year-old, stone
pub on an historic packhorse
route overlooking the Tame
Valley: a cosy bar and three
rooms. Good, home-cooked
food (eve meals Fri–Sun).
☳ Q ❀ ◗ P

Denshaw

Black Horse Inn

2 The Culvert, Oldham Road
(A672) ☎ (01457) 874375
12–3, 6–11
**Banks's Mild, Bitter; guest
beer** Ⓗ
Attractive, 17th-century stone
pub in a row of terraced
cottages: a cosy, L-shaped bar
area and two separate rooms –
one available for party
bookings. It plans to develop
its already wide range of food.
☳ ❀ ◑ ♿ P

Try also: Junction, Rochdale
Rd (Lees)

Greater Manchester

Denton

Chapel House
145 Stockport Road
☎ (0161) 336 3058
11–11
Holt Mild, Bitter ℍ
Large, imposing, redbrick
building with a comfortable
lounge and a traditional vault.
Q ◁ ♣ P

Jolly Hatters
67 Stockport Road
☎ (0161) 336 3682
11–11
Hydes' Anvil Light, Bitter 🄴
No-nonsense local, often busy,
with a strong accent on games.
◁ ♣

Didsbury

Royal Oak Hotel
729 Wilmslow Road (B5093)
☎ (0161) 445 3152
11–11
**Bateman Mild; Marston's
Bitter, Pedigree** ℍ
Devastated by fire and rebuilt
in 1994, this is now restored to
glory as the central pub in
Didsbury Village. Its central
bar serves two rooms; mini-
bar in the front lounge. Look
out for the splendid ceramic
spirit barrel collection.
Legendary cheese lunches.
Marston's Head Brewer's
Choice served. Q ◁

Station
682 Wilmslow Road (B5093)
☎ (0161) 445 9761
11–11
**Bateman Mild; Marston's
Bitter, Pedigree** ℍ
One of the few remaining
traditional locals in the village:
a quiet pub filled with the
noise of conversation. Note the
photos of old Didsbury. Floral
displays in summer. Marston's
Head Brewer's Choice sold.
Q ❄ 🍴 ♣

Diggle

Diggle Hotel
Station Houses (off A670 via
Huddersfield Rd) OS011081
☎ (01457) 872741
12–3, 5–11; 11–11 Sat
**Taylor Golden Best,
Landlord; Whitbread OB
Mild, Boddingtons Bitter, OB
Bitter** ℍ
18th-century, stone pub in a
small hamlet; popular and
busy, especially in summer.
Good food. ❄ 🛏 ◁ ▶ P

Dobcross

Navigation Inn
Wool Road (A670)
☎ (01457) 872418

11.30–3, 5 (6 Sat)–11
**Banks's Hanson's Mild,
Bitter; Camerons Strongarm;
Marston's Pedigree; guest
beer** (occasional) ℍ
Next to the Huddersfield
Narrow Canal; a stone pub
built in 1806 to slake the thirst
of navvies cutting the
Standedge Tunnel under the
Pennines. The open-plan
lounge is a shrine to brass
band music. Popular
with visitors and locals.
Eve meals finish early; no
eve meals Sun.
❄ ◁ ▶ 🍴 ♣ P 🚃

Eccles

Crown & Volunteer
171 Church Street
☎ (0161) 789 3866
11.30–11; 11.30–5, 7–11 Sat
Holt Mild, Bitter ℍ
Popular community pub
with splendid 1930s decor.
Note the wooden panelling
in the lounge.
🍴 ⇌ ♣ P

Grapes Hotel
439 Liverpool Road, Peel
Green (A57, near M63 jct 2)
☎ (0161) 789 6971
11–11; 11–4.30, 7–11 Sat
Holt Mild, Bitter ℍ
Listed Edwardian building
with much original polished
wood and etched-glass in its
five rooms. Two pool tables in
the billiards room.
🛏 🍴 ♿ ⇌ (Patricroft) ♣ P

Lamb Hotel
33 Regent Street (A57, opp.
bus station)
☎ (0161) 789 3882
11.30–11; 11.30–5, 7–11 Sat
Holt Mild, Bitter ℍ
Four-roomed, Edwardian
listed pub. A splendid
mahogany bar and much
original woodwork and ornate
etched-glass remain intact. The
purpose-built billiards room,
with its full-size table, is still
much used. Q 🍴 ⇌ ♣ P

Failsworth

Millgate
Ashton Road, West Failsworth
(off A62) ☎ (0161) 688 4910
11.30–11
**Holt Mild, Bitter; Millgate
Bitter, Willy Booth's;
Whitbread Boddingtons
Bitter; guest beers** ℍ
Large, low-level pub, a
recently completely revamped
British Legion club. Extensive
restaurant menu (meals all day
Sun). Brewing began in 1995.
🛏 ❄ ◁ ▶ 🍴 ♿ P

Try also: Cotton Tree, Ashton
Rd East (Marston's)

Farnworth

Market Hotel
11–13 Brackley Street
☎ (01204) 72888
11–3, 7–11; 11–11 Fri & Sat
**Walker Mild, Bitter; guest
beer** ℍ
Town-centre pub with a large
public bar and a vault for
games. An ideal stop-off on
market days (Mon, Fri and
Sat). No food Sun.
❄ ◁ 🍴 ⇌ ♣

Flixton

Church Inn
34 Church Road (B5213, 100
yds from B5158 jct)
☎ (0161) 748 2158
11–3.30, 5–11; 11–11 Fri & Sat
**Greenalls Mild, Bitter,
Original; guest beer** ℍ
Former schoolhouse and
courtrooms, licensed for 120
years and comfortably
furnished, with separate
seating areas. Well-behaved
children welcome till 8pm.
❄ ◁ ♿ ⇌ ♣ P

Golborne

Millstone Inn
52 Harvey Lane (½ mile from
centre) ☎ (01942) 728031
12–4, 7–11; 12–11 Fri & Sat
**Greenalls Mild, Bitter; Stones
Best Bitter** ℍ
Popular local with a keen
sporting tap room and two
lounges. At the Haydock end
of the town, close to the
racecourse. ❄ ♣ P

Railway Hotel
131 High Street
☎ (01942) 728202
12 (11 Sat)–11
**S&N Theakston Mild, Best
Bitter; guest beers** ℍ
Welcome first entry for this
friendly, popular local where a
central bijou bar serves both a
long, smart lounge and a
vault. Note the guest beer
pump clips. Occasional live
music. A beer club runs trips
to breweries and festivals.
❄ 🛏 🍴 ♣ P

Gorton

Coach & Horses
227 Belle Vue Street (A57)
5.30 (12 Sat)–11
**Robinson's Hatters Mild, Best
Bitter, Old Tom** (winter) ℍ
Classic, two-roomed
community local where a loyal
band of regulars mingles
happily with cinemagoers
from the multi-screen
opposite, introducing them to
arguably the most consistently

good Robinson's you're likely to find. Thanks to CAMRA, it's safe from a road scheme!
⬚ ⇌ (Belle Vue) ♣ P

Friendship
786 Hyde Road (A57, W of B6167 jct) ☎ (0161) 223 3762
12–3.30, 6–11; 12–11 Sat
Banks's Mild; Bateman Mild; Marston's Bitter Ⓗ
Well-named local offering two draught milds, three-nights-a-week sing-along-style entertainment, four separate rooms (including the lobby), and a five-star community atmosphere. Q ⬚ ♣

Traveller's Call
521 Hyde Road (A6010/A57 jct) ☎ (0161) 223 1722
11–11
Hydes' Anvil Mild, Bitter Ⓗ
Splendid, old-style, no-frills Manchester boozer, surviving another year as the road widening scheme is rethought yet again. The main room is the narrow front vault (with TV often dominant), but don't miss the charming rear lounge (not always open) through a sliding door. ⬚ ♣

Vale Cottage
1 Croft Bank (off Hyde Rd, A57, by footpath at side of Lord Nelson pub) ☎ (0161) 223 2477
11.45–3, 5.30–11
Taylor Landlord; Webster's Yorkshire Bitter, Wilson's Bitter Ⓗ
Classy but unstuffy pub set in rural surroundings, entirely untypical of the area. Most of the pub is devoted to quiet social drinking (and eating), but a small corner maintains a public bar atmosphere, with TV coverage of big football matches. Eve meals till 7.30, Mon–Fri. No lunches Sat.
🌼 ◖ ▶

Waggon & Horses
738 Hyde Road (A57) ☎ (0161) 223 6262
11–11
Holt Mild, Bitter Ⓗ
Large, modernised, main road pub, with linked drinking areas of distinct character, including one for darts and pool; well appointed in the brewery's functional but attractive style. Holt's other hallmark – low prices – help make it still very busy despite competition. ♣ P

Guide Bridge

Boundary
2 Audenshaw Road ☎ (0161) 330 1679
11–11

John Smith's Bitter; Wilson's Bitter; guest beers Ⓗ
Comfortable local handy for Guide Bridge railway station.
◖ ▶ ⇌ ♣

Hale

Railway
128 Ashley Road (opp. station) ☎ (0161) 941 5367
11–11
Robinson's Hatters Mild, Old Stockport Bitter, Hartleys XB, Best Bitter Ⓗ
Unspoilt, 1930s style, multi-roomed pub retaining plenty of wood panelling. Patio at the rear. Families welcome till 8.30. No food Sun.
Q ❄ ❀ ◖ ⬚ ♿ ⇌ ♣

Halebarns

Unicorn Hotel
329 Hale Road (A538, 1 mile from M56 jct 6) ☎ (0161) 980 4347
11.30–3 (3.30 Sat), 5.30–11
Hydes' Anvil Mild, Bitter Ⓔ
Smart, comfortable roadside pub with a separate dining area (children welcome here). No meals Sun eve.
Q ❀ 🛏 ◖ ⬚ ♿ ♣ P ⊟

Harpurhey

Junction
Hendham Vale (A6010, near A664 jct) ☎ (0161) 203 4723
11.30–11
Holt Bitter; Lees Bitter; Whitbread Boddingtons Bitter Ⓗ
Serious drinkers' pub with an unusual curved frontage, a very deep, double-level cellar and a traditional vault. Irish music dominates the jukebox.
🎵 🛏 ⬚ ⊖ (Woodlands Rd) ♣

Heaton Mersey

Crown Inn
6 Vale Close, Didsbury Road (A5145) ☎ (0161) 442 4531
11–11
Robinson's Hatters Mild, Best Bitter Ⓗ
Traditional building claiming to be the oldest pub in Stockport. Very busy, with two bars, it has recently been opened out, but pleasing divisions remain. The award-winning food is never allowed to detract from the atmospheric village pub feel. Eve meals Tue–Thu. ❀ ◖ ▶ P

Heaton Norris

Moss Rose
63 Didsbury Road (A5145) ☎ (0161) 442 9510

11.30–3 (4 Sat), 5.30 (7 Sat)–11; 11.30–11 Mon & Fri
Hydes' Anvil Light, Bitter Ⓔ
An unpromising early 1970s exterior conceals a comfortable, welcoming local with a traditional feel and a good contrast between the lounge and vault. No food Sun. ◖ ⬚ ♣ P ⊟

Nursery
Green Lane (off A6) ☎ (0161) 432 2044
11.30–3, 5.30–11; 11.30–11 Sat & bank hols
Hydes' Anvil Mild, Bitter Ⓔ
Comfortable, unspoilt 1930s pub with its own bowling green, well-hidden in a pleasant suburb. A good choice of rooms includes a lounge with fine wood panelling. Excellent food (set lunches only) Sun. Children welcome if dining.
Q ❀ ◖ ⬚ ♣ P ⊟

Heywood

Engineer's Arms
11–13 Aspinall Street (just off A58) ☎ (01706) 368365
11–3, 7–11; 11–11 Fri & Sat
Samuel Smith OBB Ⓗ
Friendly local just outside the town centre. Many original features of the bar area have survived thanks to thoughtful renovation. ❀ ♣ P

Wishing Well
89 York Street (A58) ☎ (01706) 620923
11–11
Moorhouse's Premier, Pendle Witches Brew; Taylor Landlord; Thwaites Craftsman; guest beer Ⓗ
Pub recently given a new lease of life by enthusiastic owners. Two house beers are sold, Wigwam from Oak and Millersbrook from Moorhouse's. Home-produced lunches. 🛏 ◖ ♣

Try also: Starkey Arms, Manchester Rd (Holt)

Hindley

Cumberland Arms
39 Chapel Green Road (off A58) ☎ (01942) 255117
12–4.30, 7–11
Tetley Walker Dark Mild, Bitter Ⓗ
Traditional end-terrace local that has been in the same family for 40 years. One of the last of a dying breed. 🎵 ⬚

Edington Arms
186 Ladies Lane (by station) ☎ (01942) 259229
12–11
Holt Mild, Bitter; John

Greater Manchester

Smith's Magnet; Whitbread Flowers IPA, Boddingtons Bitter; guest beers Ⓗ
Ten real ales at very keen prices are normally on sale at this very popular pub. There are two large, comfortable rooms plus an upstairs function room that doubles as a piano bar Sat eve. Children welcome early eves. ⇌ ♣

Minstrel
174 Wigan Road
☎ (01942) 242010
11–11
Beer range varies Ⓗ
Welcoming, small but lively local where six beers are always on sale. Food is served all day, including Sun. Children welcome. ☀ ◖ ▶ ♣

Wiganer
44 Wigan Road
☎ (01942) 208884
12–11
Whitbread Flowers IPA, Boddingtons Bitter; guest beers Ⓗ
Large, single-room bar whose walls are bedecked with photos, drawings, shirts and balls depicting Wigan RLFC's past and present glories. Good value lunches. ◖ P

Hollins

Hollins Bush Inn
257 Hollins Lane (off A56 at Blackford Bridge)
☎ (0161) 766 5692
12–3, 6–11; 12–11 Fri & Sat
Lees GB Mild, Bitter Ⓔ
Friendly, three-roomed, 200-year-old village local with a welcoming atmosphere. Very popular with families at weekends. Good selection of bar snacks (no food Sun).
◖ ♣ P

Try also: Bridge Inn, Blackford Bridge (Free)

Hyde

Oddfellows
33 Ridling Lane
☎ (0161) 351 1725
12–4, 7–11; 11–11 Fri & Sat
Vaux Mild, Bitter, Samson Ⓗ
Unassuming, friendly pub just outside the town centre, now attracting a strong local following. Genuine German Hefeweiss beer available, served in correct glasses.
⇌ (Newton)

Werneth
151 Stockport Road, Gee Cross
☎ (0161) 368 5501
11–11
Whitbread OB Mild, Boddingtons Bitter Ⓗ
Solidly traditional, Victorian

pub at the bottom of a steep hill. The original tap room enjoys a committed local following. ☀ ⊞ ♣ P

Jericho

Famous Gamecock Inn
455 Rochdale Old Road (B6222 opp. Fairfield Hospital)
☎ (0161) 764 4784
12–4, 6–11
Banks's Mild; Moorhouse's Premier; guest beers Ⓗ
Originally a beer house and once a blacksmith's, this pub built in 1824 retains three separate rooms. The house beer, Gamecock Strong Ale, is brewed by Oak.
♨ Q ⌂ ☀ ◖ ▶ ⊞ ♣ P ⅍

Kearsley

Clock Face
63–65 Old Hall Street (just off A666) ☎ (01204) 71912
11.30–11
Holt Bitter; Tetley Walker Mild, Bitter Ⓗ
Traditional local deriving its name from a large working clock on the facade. Children welcome. Q ☀ ♣

Leigh

Musketeer
15 Lord Street
☎ (01942) 701143
11–11
Whitbread Boddingtons Mild, Bitter; guest beers Ⓗ
Smart, town-centre local featuring a lounge divided into two separate rooms with a standing area in front of the bar and a small, cosy alcove at the side. The bright, sporting tap room offers vault prices. Eve meals end at 8. ◖ ▶ ⊞ ♣

Red Brick Inn
94 Twist Lane
☎ (01942) 671698
12–11
Hydes' Anvil Light, Bitter; Tetley Walker Mild, Bitter Ⓗ
As the name implies, a large, redbrick inn with a central bar serving a pleasant, large lounge, a vault and pool room at the rear, and a small eating area. One of two Hydes' outlets in the area.
♨ ◖ ⊞ ♣ P

Try also: Victoria, Kirkhall Lane (Tetley Walker)

Lowton Lane Head

Red Lion
324 Newton Road
12–3.30, 5.30–11; 12–11 Sat
Greenalls Mild, Bitter, Davenports Bitter, Original;

Tetley Walker Bitter; guest beers Ⓗ
Large, friendly pub with a restaurant. The lounge is served by the main bar, with a smaller room leading to a garden and bowling green. Pool room. Food all day Sun. Popular with all ages.
☀ ♨ ◖ ▶ ⊞ ♣ P

Lowton St Lukes

Hare & Hounds
1 Golborne Road
☎ (01942) 728387
12–11
Tetley Walker Dark Mild, Bitter; guest beers Ⓗ
Large, open-plan local with four distinctive lounge and bar areas, catering for all ages. A sizeable garden features a children's play area. Regular beer festivals.
♨ ☀ ◖ ▶ ⊞ ♣ P

Manchester City Centre

Beerhouse
Angel Street (off A664, near A665 jct) ☎ (0161) 839 7019
11.30–11
Burtonwood Bitter; Moorhouse's Pendle Witches Brew; S&N Theakston Best Bitter, XB, Old Peculier; guest beers Ⓗ
Popular, basic free house with an extensive menu of beers and ciders shown on a blackboard. Special offers on food at certain times. Eve meals Thu and Fri only, 5–7.
☀ ◖ ▶ ⇌ (Victoria) ⊖ ⌂ P

Briton's Protection
50 Great Bridgewater Street (by New Hallé concert hall)
☎ (0161) 236 5895
11.30–3, 5–11; 11.30–11 Fri; 5–11 Sat; 7–10.30 Sun
Jennings Bitter; Robinson's Best Bitter; Tetley Walker Bitter; guest beer Ⓗ
Pub retaining much original character, with glazed tiling and leaded windows. The long bar separates the front bar (always popular) and two small rooms to the rear, served through a serving hatch door. Popular lunchtime food; eve meals to order. Q ⌂ ☀ ◖ ▶ ⇌ (Deansgate/Oxford Rd) ⊖ (G Mex)

Castle
66 Oldham Street (near Piccadilly Gardens)
☎ (0161) 236 2945
11.30–5.30, 7.30–11
Robinson's Hatters Mild, Old Stockport Bitter, Best Bitter, Old Tom Ⓗ
Robinson's only city-centre pub. A tiled facade leads into

the front bar, with a cosy snug behind and a large pool room at the rear, also used for live music. Family room lunchtime. Q ⛄ 🍴 🍺 (Victoria/Piccadilly) ⊖ (Market St) ♣

Circus Tavern
86 Portland Street (A62)
☎ (0161) 236 5818
11–11 (varies at weekends)
Tetley Walker Bitter Ⓗ
The city's smallest pub, where a one-person bar serves only one draught beer. It was nominated as a Heritage pub by Tetley in 1994. No music; no lager; just a superb atmosphere in a timeless gem. 🏚 Q 🍺 (Piccadilly) ⊖ (Piccadilly Gdns)

Crown Inn
321 Deansgate
☎ (0161) 834 7301
11–11
Vaux Mild, Samson Ⓗ
Former Wilson's pub on the corner of Trafford St in the Castlefield area. Its one bar manages to capture the feel of a vault in one part and a comfortable lounge in the other. Good value, home-cooked food (no meals Sat or Sun) and recommended accommodation. The doors may close early. 🏨 🍺 🍺 (Deansgate) ⊖ (G Mex) ♣ ✄

Hare & Hounds
46 Shudehill (near Arndale bus station) ☎ (0161) 832 4737
11–11
Cains Mild, Bitter; Tetley Walker Bitter; guest beers Ⓗ
Well-run, traditional local featuring extensive tiling and leaded glass: a front bar, a lobby, a comfortable back room and a function room upstairs. Home-made food (eves on request). 🏚 Q 🍺 🍺 🍺 (Victoria) ⊖ (High St/Market St) ♣

Harp & Shamrock
36 New Mount Street (off Rochdale Rd, A664, between Angel St and Gould St)
☎ (0161) 834 8597
11–11
Marston's Bitter, Pedigree Ⓗ
Friendly, basic, street-corner local gradually being restored to its former glory. It has the smallest gents' in the city. 🏚 🍺 🍺 🍺 (Victoria) ⊖ ♣ P

HR Fletcher's
2–10 St Mary's Street (off Deansgate) ☎ (0161) 835 1567
12–11; closed Sun
Bass Worthington BB, Draught Bass; M&B Highgate Dark; Ruddles County; guest beers Ⓗ

Formerly known as the Gemstone, this former jeweller's shop boasts eight handpumps. 🍺 ✄

Sinclair's Oyster Bar
Shambles Square (behind Marks & Spencer)
☎ (0161) 834 0430
11–11
Samuel Smith OBB, Museum Ⓗ
Ancient building, partially rebuilt in the original style and incongruous amidst 1970s development. The upstairs bar has two rooms; many small, lively rooms downstairs. Lunches a speciality (food all day Sun). The only Sam's tied house in the city. 🏚 🍺 🍺 (Victoria) ⊖

Smithfield Hotel
37 Swan Street (A665, between A62 and A664)
☎ (0161) 839 4424
11–11
Bateman Dark Mild; Fuller's London Pride; guest beers Ⓗ
Previously Walker's, and originally Smithfield Vaults (when the Smithfield Market was just at the rear), this is now a comfortable, one-room pub with a dining room at the back. Good value. Eve meals till 8.30. 🏨 🍺 🍺 🍺 (Victoria) ⊖ ♣

Unicorn
26 Church Street (opp. outdoor market) ☎ (0161) 832 7938
11.30–11; 11.30–3, 5.30–11 Sat
Bass Light, Worthington BB, Draught Bass; Stones Best Bitter Ⓗ
Pub where several drinking areas surround a central bar, featuring much oak panelling and etched-glass. 🍺 ⊖ 🍺

Vine Inn
42–46 Kennedy Street
☎ (0161) 236 3943
11.30–11; 11.30–3, 7–11 Sat; 12–3 Sun, closed Sun eve
Courage Directors; John Smith's Bitter; Whitbread Boddingtons Bitter Ⓗ
Former small, two-roomed bar, extended into the building next door to create a multi-level pub catering for business types at lunchtime and couples eves. Lunches Mon–Fri. Note the listed tiled frontage. 🍺 🍺 (Oxford Rd) ⊖ (St Peter's Sq) ♣

White House
122 Great Ancoats Street (A665, Laystall St jct)
☎ (0161) 228 3231
12–4, 8–11; 12–11 Fri & Sat
Cains Bitter; Holt Bitter; guest beer (occasional) Ⓗ
Friendly two-roomer adjacent to the new superstores

complex and the Rochdale–Ashton Canal. The lounge walls are adorned with photographs of old film stars. 🏚 🍺 🍺 (Piccadilly) ⊖ ♣

White Lion
43 Liverpool Road (opp. Air and Space Museum)
☎ (0161) 832 7373
11–11
Marston's Pedigree; Morland Old Speckled Hen; Taylor Landlord; Whitbread Boddingtons Bitter; guest beers Ⓗ
Pub at the heart of the Castlefield area, close to the canal basin. Old city photographs adorn the walls. Interesting, good value, home-cooked food; no eve meals Sat or Sun. 🏚 🍺 🍺 (Deansgate) ⊖ (G Mex) ♣

Marple

Pineapple
Market Street
☎ (0161) 427 3935
11–11
Robinson's Hatters Mild, Hartleys XB, Best Bitter, Frederic's Ⓗ
Enterprising, comfortable and welcoming, redbrick pub in the centre of Marple, built in 1892. Inventive, good value food (breakfasts Sat). 🏚 Q 🏨 🍺 🍺 ♣ P

Middleton

Crown Inn
52 Rochdale Road (A664)
☎ (0161) 654 9174
11.30–11
Lees GB Mild, Bitter Ⓔ
Very popular, end-terrace pub with a small snug and a larger, brass-hung lounge. It still uses the 'electric pillar' type of dispense which is becoming rare. ♣ P

Lancashire Fold
77 Kirkway, Alkrington (½ mile off A664)
☎ (0161) 643 4198
11.30–11
Lees GB Mild, Bitter Ⓗ, **Moonraker** Ⓔ
Exceptionally popular and busy, modern estate-style pub. The comfortable and spacious lounge and bustling public bar dispense copious amounts of ale. No food Sun. 🍺 🍺 ♣ P

Try also: **Britannia**, Middleton Gardens (Lees)

Milnrow

Free Trade Tavern
115 Newhey Road (B6225)
☎ (01706) 847056

12–3, 5–11
Lees GB Mild, Bitter Ⓗ
Friendly pub on the edge of
town. ♿ ⊛ ♣ P

Waggon Inn
Butterworth Hall (off Newhey
Rd, B6225) ☎ (01706) 48313
11–11
Burtonwood Mild, Bitter Ⓗ
Friendly and popular, 18th-
century local retaining a
multi-roomed layout.
♿ ⊛ ▲ ♣ P

Try also: Gallows, Wildhouse
Lane (Free)

Mossley
Tollemache Arms
Manchester Road
☎ (0145 783) 2354
11.30–3, 5–11
**Robinson's Hatters Mild, Best
Bitter** Ⓗ
Popular, cosy and sociable
stone local next to the
Huddersfield Narrow Canal,
which is overlooked by the
small garden. Compact
oak-panelled rooms and a
polished bar feature. In the
same building since 1959.
♨ Q ⊛ ♣ P

New Springs
Collier's Arms
192 Wigan Road
☎ (01942) 831171
1.30–11; 7–11, 7.30–11
Burtonwood Mild, Bitter Ⓗ
18th-century, canalside
pub close to Haigh Country
Park. Warm welcome.
♨ Q ♣

Kirkless
Albion Way ☎ (01942) 242821
11.30–3.30, 7–11; 11.30–11 Fri & Sat
**Burtonwood Mild, Bitter,
Forshaw's, Top Hat** Ⓗ
Pub situated on the Leeds &
Liverpool Canal. Excellent
food. ⊛ ◖ ▶ ⊟ P

Newton Heath
Railway Hotel
82 Dean Lane (just off A62, by
station) ☎ (0161) 681 8199
11–11; 11–4, 7–11 Sat
Holt Mild, Bitter Ⓔ
Imposing, very popular,
Victorian pub with a well-used
vault. Steam locomotives
feature in the etched windows.
⊟ ⇌ (Dean Lane) ♣

Oldham
Beer Emporium
92–94 Union Street (by library)
☎ (0161) 628 7887
12–11; 12–4, 7–11 Sat

**Marston's Pedigree; S&N
Theakston Best Bitter, Old
Peculier; Whitbread OB
Bitter; guest beers** Ⓗ
Popular town-centre free
house with four regular and
four guest beers (often a mild).
Its clientele varies from
students to solicitors but it is
often smoky and noisy when
busy at nights and weekends.
Function room. No food Sun.
Occasional cider.
◖ ⇌ (Mumps)

Dog & Partridge
376 Roundthorn Road (off
B6194)
☎ (0161) 624 3335
7 (11 Fri)–11; 11.30–3, 7–11 Sat
Lees GB Mild, Bitter Ⓗ
Popular, comfortably
furnished, detached pub in a
semi-rural setting, with
low-beamed ceilings.
♨ ⊛ ♣ P

Hark to Topper
5 Bow Street
☎ (0161) 624 7950
11.30–3, 7–11; 11.30–11 Fri & Sat
Samuel Smith OBB Ⓗ
Detached, town-centre pub (a
former Rochdale and Manor
Brewery pub known as the
Manor Inn), with an
impressive brick exterior,
dating from 1835. Just off the
high street, its pleasant,
open-plan interior has a
central bar and etched-
glass windows.
♨ ◖ ⇌ (Mumps)

Hogshead
36 Union Street (near Spindles
shopping centre)
☎ (0161) 628 0301
11–11
**Whitbread Chester's Mild,
Boddingtons Bitter, Castle
Eden Ale; guest beers** Ⓗ
Recently refurbished
Whitbread cask alehouse
providing a varied choice of
guest beers through its ten
handpumps. Excellent
lunchtime food (not
weekends), together with
special events and a function
room, caters for all tastes.
Occasional cider.
◖ ⇌ (Mumps) P

Try also: Falconer's Arms,
Hollins Rd (Lees)

Prestwich
Royal Oak
23 Whittaker Lane (just off
A665)
☎ (0161) 773 8663
11–11; 11–5, 7–11 Sat
Hydes' Anvil Mild, Bitter Ⓔ
Comfortable, friendly local just
off Bury Old Rd: the only
Hydes' outlet in the area,

offering a lounge, a traditional
vault and a news room.
Q ⊖ (Heaton Pk) P ⊟

Ramsbottom
Royal Oak
39 Bridge Street
☎ (01706) 822786
12–11
**Thwaites Best Mild, Bitter,
Craftsman** Ⓗ
Friendly, three-roomed,
village-centre pub in a
conservation area; popular
with weekend visitors to the
nearby E Lancs Railway. The
only local Thwaites outlet to
offer bar lunches Wed–Sun.
♿ ◖ ♣

Try also: Old Dun Horse,
Bolton St (Thwaites)

Ridge End
Romper
Ridge End Road
☎ (0161) 427 1354
12–2.30 (3 Sat), 6–11
**Coach House Coachman's;
Marston's Pedigree; S&N
Theakston Old Peculier;
Whitbread Boddingtons
Bitter, Flowers IPA** Ⓗ
Longtime haunt of the
Cheshire set, now giving beer
the same prominence as food.
Tucked on a bend, it has the
Dark Peak on one side and the
Cheshire plain on the other.
⊛ ◖ ▶ P

Ringley
Lord Nelson
Kearsley Hall Road (off A667)
☎ (01204) 79456
12–3 (4 Sat), 7–11 (may open all day
in summer)
Thwaites Mild, Bitter Ⓗ
Traditional, large, multi-
roomed village pub in a scenic
spot next to the river. Look out
for the Railway Room. Folk
nights Tue and Thu. The
garden has a children's play
area. ♨ Q ⊛ ⇌ (Kearsley)
♣ P

Ringway
Romper
Wilmslow Road (off A538, 200
yds from M56 jct 6, towards
Wilmslow) ☎ (0161) 980 6806
11.30–11; 11.30–3, 5.30–11 Sat
**Draught Bass; S&N
Theakston Best Bitter;
Whitbread Boddingtons Mild,
Bitter; guest beer** Ⓗ
Multi-roomed, low-ceilinged
country pub featuring original
fireplaces and stone floors.
World War II aeroplanes
feature in pictures on the
walls. ♨ Q ⊛ ◖ ⊟ ♣ P

Rochdale

Albert
62 Spotland Road (A608)
☎ (01706) 45666
11–11
Burtonwood Mild, Bitter Ⓗ
Popular local with a good
early eve atmosphere in the
open-plan bar. Separate TV,
games and pool rooms; free
oldies jukebox. ♨ ♣

Cask & Feather
1 Oldham Road (Drake St jct)
☎ (01706) 711476
11–11
**Thomas McGuinness Mild,
Best Bitter, Special Reserve,
Tommy Todd Porter; guest
beers** Ⓗ
Distinctive, castle-style,
stone-fronted pub on a main
shopping street close to the
town centre; home of the
Thomas McGuinness brewery,
well-appointed and spacious.
No food Sun. ◖ ⇌

Eagle
59 Oldham Road (A671/Wood
St jct) ☎ (01706) 47222
12–3, 5–11; 11–11 Fri
Samuel Smith OBB Ⓗ
Lively and popular, stone-
fronted pub on the edge of the
town centre. Tastefully
decorated, it retains many
interesting period features and
artefacts. ⇌ ♣

Healey Hotel
172 Shawclough Road, Healey
(B6377) ☎ (01706) 45453
12–3, 5–11
**Robinson's Hatters Mild, Best
Bitter, Old Tom** Ⓗ
Friendly and popular pub
retaining a traditional feel,
separate rooms and a
splendid, tiled interior. Healey
Dell Nature Reserve is
opposite. Lunches Mon–Fri;
eve meals Wed and Thu only.
Q ♨ ◖ ▶

Merry Monk
234 College Road (near
A6060/B6222 jct)
☎ (01706) 46919
12–11
**Bateman Mild; Marston's
Bitter, Pedigree; guest beers** Ⓗ
Friendly, unpretentious local
serving up to three guest
beers. Unusual Ring the Bull
game; free jukebox. ♣ P

Success to the Plough
179 Bolton Road, Marland
(A58) ☎ (01706) 33270
12–11
Lees GB Mild, Bitter Ⓗ
Imposing, detached redbrick
pub displaying its name in
glazed tiles on a gable wall.
The extensive interior is

sub-divided into separate
areas. Home of the John Willie
Lees Crown Green Bowls
Classic. No food Sat or Sun.
♨ ◖ ⊞ ♣ P

Try also: Flying Horse, Town
Hall Sq (Free)

Romiley

Duke of York
Stockport Road
☎ (0161) 430 2806
11.30–11
**Courage Directors; John
Smith's Bitter; guest beers** Ⓗ
Long, low pub of harmonious
proportions, just as pleasing
inside, with its beamed lounge
and vault. Close to the Peak
Forest Canal.
♨ ◖ ◗ ♿ ⇌ ♣ P

Royton

Marston Tavern
83 Rochdale Road (near Town
Hall) ☎ (0161) 628 0569
12–3, 7–11
**Bateman Mild; Marston's
Bitter, Pedigree; guest beer** Ⓗ
Detached, town-centre pub
with two distinct drinking
areas. A former Rothwell
house called the Radcliffe
Arms, it was acquired by
Marston's in 1961, who
changed its name after
refurbishment in 1976. Good,
friendly atmosphere. No food
Sat or Sun. ◖ ♣

Puckersley Inn
22 Narrowgate Brow (off A671
via Dogford Rd)
☎ (0161) 624 4973
5 (12 Sat)–11
Lees GB Mild, Bitter Ⓗ
Popular, detached, stone-
fronted pub with extensive
views over Royton and
Oldham. The lounge is
attractively and artistically
furnished, while the separate
vault is lively and more basic.
Q ⊞ ♣ P

Try also: Railway, Oldham Rd
(Lees)

Rusholme

Albert
5 Walmer Street (off B5177 at
Shere Khan) ☎ (0161) 224 2287
11–11
Hydes' Anvil Bitter Ⓔ
Friendly, two-roomed local
with a strong Irish
atmosphere. Traditional music
sessions Sun eve.
Q ⊞ ♿ ♣ ⊟

Sale Moor

Legh Arms
178 Northenden Road
(A6144/B5166 jct)

12 (11 Apr–Oct)–11
Holt Mild, Bitter Ⓗ
Large, Edwardian, redbrick
pub, recently refurbished with
the loss of its revolving door.
It does still retain an island bar
serving a lively vault (which is
now accessible from the rear
lounge), a snug, a lobby and a
smoke room. 1 mile E of
Brooklands Metrolink station.
Q ♨ ⊞ ♣ P

Salford

Crescent
20 Crescent (A6, near
University) ☎ (0161) 736 5600
12–11; 7–10.30 Sat
Beer range varies Ⓗ
Rambling, three-roomed house
popular with students. Old
furniture, including an
unplayed piano, features and
guest beers change regularly.
Good whisky selection. Note
the friendly cats.
♨ ♨ ◖ ⇌ (Crescent) ⌂ P

Eagle
19 Collier Street (off Trinity
Way, near A6041 jct)
☎ (0161) 834 8957
11–11
Holt Mild, Bitter Ⓗ
Small, friendly, back-street
local in an area of old terraced
housing and modern car
showrooms, dissected by a
new dual carriageway.
Q ⊞ ⇌ (Victoria) ⊖ ♣ P

Egerton Arms
Gore Street (off A34, near A6
jct) ☎ (0161) 834 3182
11–11; 12–3 Sun, closed Sun eve
**Holt Mild, Bitter; Marston's
Bitter, Pedigree** Ⓗ
Exuberant and flamboyant
pub, with chandeliers and art
nouveau lamps. A cracking
pub with class.
♨ ⊨ ◖ ⊞ ⇌ (Central) ♣

King's Arms
11 Bloom Street (just off A6,
opp. A34 jct)
☎ (0161) 839 4338
12–11
**S&N Theakston Best Bitter;
Taylor Landlord; Whitbread
OB Bitter; guest beers** Ⓗ
Friendly and popular, three-
room Boddington Pub Co. 'ale
house': 11 real ales and bottled
foreign beers. Live music Sun
eve. ◖ ♿ ⇌ (Central) ♣ ⌂

Olde Nelson
285 Chapel Street (opp.
cathedral) ☎ (0161) 832 6189
11–3.30 (4 Sat), 6.30 (7 Sat)–11
**Whitbread Chester's Mild,
Boddingtons Bitter, Trophy** Ⓗ
Multi-roomed Victorian gem
featuring a sliding door to the
vault and lots of etched-glass.
The demolition threat seems to
be on hold. Q ⏴ ⇌

Greater Manchester

Union Tavern
105 Liverpool Street (between A5063 and A5066)
☎ (0161) 736 2885
11–11
Holt Mild, Bitter Ⓗ
Welcoming local in an area of industrial blight and depopulation. Exceptional brown tiled exterior. Q ⬦ ♣

Welcome
Robert Hall Street (off A5066)
☎ (0161) 872 6040
11.45–4, 7–11
Lees GB Mild, Bitter Ⓔ
The very best of Ordsall's handful of surviving pubs, presided over by the doyenne of Salford licensees. New housing is being built around the pub, which always lives up to its name and offers a function room as well as a lounge and a games room. The 'handpumps' work electric pumps. Q ⬦ ♣ P

Shaw

Black Horse
203a Rochdale Road (B6194)
☎ (01706) 847173
2 (12 Sat)–11
Lees GB Mild, Bitter Ⓗ
Friendly, stone roadside pub, ten mins' walk from Shaw station; a cosy, timber-framed lounge and a separate vault.
⬥ ⬦ ♣ P

Try also: **Blue Bell**, Market St (Robinson's)

Stalybridge

Q
3 Market Street
☎ (0161) 303 9157
5–11; 12–3, 7–11 Sat
Marston's Bitter Ⓗ
Eves-only pub, reminiscent of a Dutch brown bar. It has a *Guinness Book of Records* entry for the shortest British pub name. Cocktail and foreign bottled beer bars are housed upstairs. Up to four guest beers. Lunches served Sun.
⇌ P

Rose & Crown
7 Market Street
☎ (0161) 303 7098
11–11
Vaux Mild, Bitter, Samson, Waggle Dance *or* Extra Special Ⓗ
Comfortable, town-centre pub with a friendly atmosphere. Multi-roomed, with unpretentious fittings, it is deservedly popular with regulars and casual visitors.
⇌ ♣ P

White House
1 Water Street
☎ (0161) 303 2288

11–11
Bateman Mild; Marston's Bitter; Thwaites Bitter; guest beers Ⓗ
Friendly, popular, four-roomed establishment serving breakfast from 9am. Over 50 whiskies and a range of foreign bottled beers are also sold. Folk club Thu. ◖ ⇌ P

Standish

Dog & Partridge
School Lane ☎ (01257) 401218
11–11
Tetley Walker Dark Mild, Mild, Bitter; Walker Best Bitter; Whitbread Boddingtons Bitter Ⓗ
Modern, open-plan pub. The weekend's Wigan rugby video is shown Tue eve. ⛐ ⬥ P

Stockport

Arden Arms
23 Millgate (behind Asda, off Market Place)
☎ (0161) 480 2185
11.45–11; 12.30–3, 7–10.30 Sun
Robinson's Hatters Mild, Best Bitter, Old Tom Ⓗ
Classic, multi-roomed pub where the snug is accessed through the bar. This listed gem is well looked after and well liked. Not to be missed.
Q ⬥ ⬂ ◖ ♣ P

Armoury
Greek Street, Shaw Heath (off A6) ☎ (0161) 480 5055
11–11; 11–4, 7.30–11 Sat
Robinson's Hatters Mild, Best Bitter Ⓔ
Pub where a plain exterior conceals a fine 1920s interior, with much evidence of its former Bell's ownership. A central bar serves a bright, comfortable lounge, a back darts room, a lobby and a superb vault. Public parking nearby. Handy for Edgeley Park. Q ⬦ ⇌ ⛿

Blossoms
2 Buxton Road, Heaviley (A5102/A6 jct)
☎ (0161) 480 2246
12–3, 5.30–11; 12–11 Fri & Sat
Robinson's Hatters Mild, Best Bitter, Frederic's, Old Tom Ⓗ
Classic, multi-roomed local with a welcome for all. Three rooms and a lobby lead off a central bar – the rear smoke room is particularly fine. Long-established folk club Sat eve. A rare local outlet for Frederic's. Q ⬂ ◖ ▷ ♣ P

Crown Inn
154 Heaton Lane (150 yards W of A6, under viaduct)

☎ (0161) 429 0549
12–11
Lees Bitter; Whitbread Boddingtons Bitter; guest beers Ⓗ
Partially opened out, this ten-ale house retains the true feel of a multi-room, town-centre pub. Attractively furnished, its no-smoking room is possibly the best. Very atmospheric, with a very varied clientele.
⬥ ⇌ ⬤ ⛿

Greyhound
27 Bowden Street, Edgeley (behind Blue Bell, at top of station approach)
☎ (0161) 480 5699
12–11
S&N Theakston Best Bitter; Whitbread Boddingtons Mild, Bitter; guest beers Ⓗ
An estate pub exterior conceals a friendly local, an increasingly rare outlet for cask Boddingtons Mild. Open 11am when Stockport County are at home.
⬥ ⬦ ⇌ ♣ P

Manchester Arms
25 Wellington Road, South Stockport (A6)
☎ (0161) 480 2852
11–11
Robinson's Hatters Mild, Best Bitter, Old Tom Ⓗ
The term 'basic boozer' could have been coined for the 'MA', but it's none the worse for that. Customers range from businessmen to bikers at this lively and friendly pub where a corner bar serves a plain vault, a boisterous pool room and a rear 'lounge'.
⛐ ◖ ⬦ ⇌ ♣

Queen's Head (Turner's Vaults)
12 Underbank (down steps from market)
☎ (0161) 480 1545
11.30–11; 7–10.30 Sun, closed Sun lunch
Samuel Smith OBB, Museum Ⓗ
Originally a tasting room for the Wine Vaults, this small three-roomed pub was magnificently restored in 1990 to much acclaim. The spirit taps on the bar, the world's smallest gents' and the delightfully atmospheric snug are key features. Local CAMRA *Pub of the Year* 1994.
Q ◖ ▷ ⛿

Woolpack
70 Brinksway (A560)
☎ (0161) 429 8821
11.30–3, 5.30 (7 Sat)–11; 11–11 Fri
Marston's Pedigree; S&N Theakston Best Bitter; Tetley

Walker Bitter; Thwaites Best Mild; guest beers H
Cosy and lively, open-plan local, with three distinct rooms. One varied guest beer is always available. Located next to the Pyramid and the motorway, but with little else nearby, it remains extremely popular.
◖ ᵬ P

Strines

Sportsman's Arms
105 Strines Road (1 mile from Marple on New Mills road)
☎ (0161) 427 2888
11.30–3, 5.30–11
Bateman Mild; Mitchell's Original; guest beers H
Welcoming country pub with two rooms: a vault and a lounge/dining room; pleasant garden. Guest beers change regularly. Good views over the valley.
Q ✿ ◖ ▶ ᵬ ♣ P

Swinton

Cricketers' Arms
227 Manchester Road (A6 near A572 jct)
☎ (0161) 794 2008
11.45–11; 11.45–4, 7–11 Sat
Holt Mild, Bitter E
Thriving, two-roomed local, popular with older customers. Sing-along Wed and Sat eves.
⊟ ♣

Farmers' Arms
156 Manchester Road (A6, 400 yds E of A572 jct)
☎ (0161) 794 5599
11–11
S&N Theakston Best Bitter, Old Peculier; Whitbread Boddingtons Bitter; guest beer H
Comfortable, low-ceilinged pub with several distinct areas in its lounge and separate bar. Notable for breakfasts served daily, including Sun, from 9.30am. Eve meals end at 7.
✿ ◖ ▶ ⊟ ♣ P

Tyldesley

Half Moon Inn
115–117 Elliot Street
☎ (01942) 873206
11–4 (4.30 Sat), 7–11
Holt Mild, Bitter; guest beers H
Town-centre pub popular with all ages: one main room with nooks and crannies, and a separate pool room. Situated halfway along the Monkey Run (ask at the bar).
✿ ♣

Try also: Black Horse, Elliot St (Tetley Walker)

Uppermill

Cross Keys
Off Running Hill Gate, A670, up Church Rd
☎ (01457) 874626
11–3, 5.30–11; 11–11 Sat & summer
Lees GB Mild, Bitter H
Attractive, 18th-century, stone building overlooking Saddleworth Church. The public bar has a stone-flagged floor and a Yorkshire range. The hub of many local activities, including mountain rescue and clay pigeon shooting. Folk nights Wed. Eve meals till 7.30.
🏨 Q ✿ ◖ ▶ ⊟ ᵬ ♠ ♣ P

Try also: Waggon Inn, High St (Robinson's)

Wardley

Morning Star
520 Manchester Road (A6, near M61/M62 – no access)
☎ (0161) 794 4927
12–11
Holt Mild, Bitter H
Friendly community pub on the outskirts of town with a thriving vault. Entertainment at weekends. Excellent lunches, Mon–Fri.
✿ ◖ ⊟ ⇌ (Moorside) ♣ P

Westhoughton

White Lion
2 Market Street (B5235)
☎ (01204) 811991
11–11
Holt Mild, Bitter H
Good, town-centre local with distinctive Holt character. Its tiles and woodwork have now been restored to their former glories. No meals Sat or Sun.
✿ ◖ ♣ P

Whitefield

Coach & Horses
71 Bury Old Road (A665)
☎ (0161) 798 8897
11.30–11; 11.30–5, 7–11 Sat
Holt Mild, Bitter H
1830s roadside pub that has been included in the *Guide* for many years. A good stop on a Metrolink crawl!
Q ⊖ (Besses O' Th' Barn) ♣ P

Eagle & Child
Higher Lane (A667)
☎ (0161) 766 3024
11–11
Holt Mild, Bitter H
Large, roadside hostelry with a relaxing atmosphere; one of few pubs left with its own bowling green. Varied and interesting selection of home-produced lunches.
⛺ ✿ ◖ ♣ P

Try also: Church Inn, Bury New Rd (Holt)

Wigan

Beer Engine
69 Poolstock (B5238, off A49)
☎ (01942) 321820
11–11
Marston's Pedigree; John Smith's Bitter; guest beers H
True free house: a comfortable lounge and a large concert room, offering a wide range of events, including annual beer, pie and music festivals. Well-kept bowling green.
✿ ◖ P

Bird I' Th' Hand (Th' en 'ole)
102 Gidlow Lane (off B5375)
☎ (01942) 241004
12–11
S&N Theakston Best Bitter; Tetley Walker Mild, Bitter; guest beers (occasional) H
Tiny, comfortable locals' pub with impressive mosaic work above the door.
✿ ◖ ▶ ᵬ ♣ P

Gems
15 Upper Dicconson Street
☎ (01942) 826588
11–11
Holt Bitter; Tetley Walker Mild, Bitter; Walker Best Bitter; Whitbread Boddingtons Bitter H
Busy, modern, one-roomed bar popular with office workers lunchtime and crowded at weekends. The TV is constantly tuned to sport.
✿ ◖

Old Pear Tree
44 Frog Lane
☎ (01942) 243677
11–11; 11–4, 7–11 Sat
Burtonwood Mild, Bitter, Forshaw's, Top Hat H
Excellent town-centre pub near the bus station. Relaxing atmosphere in the lounge; lively vault (the haunt of darts and dominoes devotees). Good value food (till 7.30; no eve meals Fri). ✿ ◖ ▶ ⇌

Orwell
Wallgate ☎ (01942) 323034
11–11
Greenalls Original; Tetley Walker Bitter; Whitbread Boddingtons Bitter; guest beers H
Large, open-plan pub at the heart of the Wigan Pier complex. Food is available all afternoon in summer, when it is busy with tourists. Eves are quieter. Children welcome.
✿ ◖ ᵬ ⇌ (NW/Wallgate)

Greater Manchester

Seven Stars
262 Wallgate (A49, near Pier)
☎ (01942) 243126
12–5, 7–11
Thwaites Mild, Bitter Ⓗ
Excellent former Magee Marshall's pub next to the canal, with an unusual horseshoe bar. Warm welcome. ◑ ⊟ ♣ P

Withington

Orion
8 Burton Road
☎ (0161) 445 6910
11–11
Holt Mild, Bitter Ⓗ
Thriving local with a separate lounge and vault served by a connecting L-shaped bar. A recent acquisition by Holt.
❀ ⊟ ♣

Red Lion
Wilmslow Road (B5093)

11–11
Banks's Mild; Marston's Bitter, Pedigree, Owd Rodger Ⓗ
Busy, cosmopolitan pub on the main road, one of the oldest in Manchester. The vault and other front rooms exude character; waves of extensions at the rear, including a conservatory. Well-regarded food; eve meals Mon–Thu, 5.30–8. ❀ ◑ ▶ ⊟ P

Woodford

Davenport Arms (Thief's Neck)
550 Chester Road (A5102)
☎ (0161) 439 2435
11–3.30, 5.15 (5.30 Sat)–11
Robinson's Hatters Mild, Old Stockport Bitter, Best Bitter Ⓗ**, Old Tom** Ⓔ
Superb, unspoilt country pub on the edge of suburbia. Its

multi-roomed layout includes a no-smoking snug where children are admitted lunchtimes. Large, attractive garden at the rear. In the same family for over 60 years.
▨ Q ㋡ ❀ ◑ ⊟ ♣ P ⊬

Worthington

White Crow
Chorley Road (A5106)
☎ (01257) 474344
12–11
Greenalls Mild, Bitter, Original; Stones Best Bitter; Tetley Walker Bitter; guest beers Ⓗ
Large pub famed for its food (from a sandwich to a steak). Meals all day Sun till 8.30. Close to Worthington Lakes.
▨ ㋡ ❀ ◑ ♿ P

Try also: Crown Hotel, Platt Lane (Free)

SUNDAY BEST

August 6, 1995, was a day to remember.

At 3pm, CAMRA members all around Britain strolled up to the bar and ordered a pint. What's new about that?, one might wonder. The answer is that August 6 was a *Sunday* and for the first time on a Sunday pub users were able to buy themselves an alcoholic drink at any time in the afternoon.

Previously, standard Sunday hours in England and Wales were 12–3, 7–10.30 (with slight variations in Scotland and Northern Ireland). CAMRA had for many years called for greater flexibility in licensing hours and, having won significant concessions at the end of the 1980s with 11–11 weekday opening, had stepped up its campaign for more sensible Sunday hours.

As it stood, the law made no sense. Restaurants, pizza parlours and pubs which served food on Sunday afternoons could also sell alcoholic drinks to their dining customers. But an alcoholic drink by itself was forbidden. Finally sense prevailed and it was with some pleasure that the CAMRA drinkers raised their 3 o'clock pints in celebration and drank to the campaign's success.

On the down side, the Government's move came too late for us to change the Sunday hours declared for pubs in this year's *Good Beer Guide*, so readers should check directly with pubs what their new Sunday opening times are.

What is needed now is more flexibility with evening hours, not just on Sunday but throughout the week. Overseas visitors are shocked to find that 11pm is the latest they can normally buy themselves a drink. At the very least it is ironic that quiet, well-behaved social drinkers in a rural village inn have to drink up so early, but buoyed up nightclubbers in town can pour it back until the small hours.

Publicans and even police officers have been vocal in their support for less stringent closing times and see a more relaxed approached to licensing hours as a means of easing conflict late at night. Turning hundreds of drinkers out onto the streets at just after 11pm is a recipe for trouble in congested town centres. The introduction of staggered closing times in Scotland has proved successful and now CAMRA wants to see the same law applied throughout the UK.

Campaigners may have to stay up late to celebrate this victory when it comes, but it will be all the more enjoyable for that!

THE NEW BREWERIES

The 1996 *Good Beer Guide* introduces no less than 57 new independently owned breweries and brew pubs. Full details can be found in the breweries section, beginning on page 410, but here is a county by county checklist of the new producers.

ENGLAND

Bedfordshire: Stag, Stotfold

Berkshire: Butts, Great Shefford; Greenwood's, Wokingham; Hop Leaf, Reading

Buckinghamshire: Vale, Haddenham

Cheshire: Beartown, Congleton

Cumbria: Cartmel, Kendal

Derbyshire: Leatherbritches, Fenny Bentley

Devon: Combe, Ilfracombe; Jollyboat, Bideford; Princetown, Princetown

Durham: Durham, Bowburn; Hodges, Crook

Gloucestershire: Berkeley, Berkeley; Goff's, Winchcombe

Hampshire: Spikes, Portsmouth

Hereford & Worcester: Marches, Leominster; Wyre Piddle, Fladbury

Hertfordshire: Dark Horse, Hertford; Harpenden, Harpenden

Humberside: Highwood, Melton Highwood; Leaking Boot, Grimsby

Kent: Flagship, Chatham

Lancashire: Hart, Little Eccleston

Leicestershire: Belvoir, Old Dalby

Greater London: Freedom, Fulham

Greater Manchester: Millgate, Failsworth

Norfolk: Iceni, Ickburgh

Northamptonshire: Frog Island, Northampton

Nottinghamshire: Maypole, Eakring

Oxfordshire: Edgcote, Banbury

Shropshire: Crown Inn, Munslow; Davenports Arms, Worfield

Somerset: Henstridge, Henstridge; Juwards, Wellington

Staffordshire: Eccleshall, Eccleshall

Suffolk: Old Chimneys, Market Weston

East Sussex: Cuckmere Haven, Exceat Bridge; Old Forge, Pett; Skinner's, Brighton; White, Bexhill

Tyne & Wear: Darwin, Sunderland; Mordue, North Shields

Warwickshire: Bull's Head, Alcester

West Midlands: Britannia, Upper Gornal; Rainbow, Coventry

Wiltshire: Tisbury, Tisbury

West Yorkshire: Blackmoor, Batley; Merrimans, Leeds; Old Court, Huddersfield; Rat & Ratchet, Huddersfield; Wild's, Slaithwaite

WALES

Gwent: Newport, Newport

SCOTLAND

Fife: Fyfe, Kirkcaldy

Grampian: Aberdeenshire, Ellon

Strathclyde: Glaschu, Glasgow; Heather, Glasgow

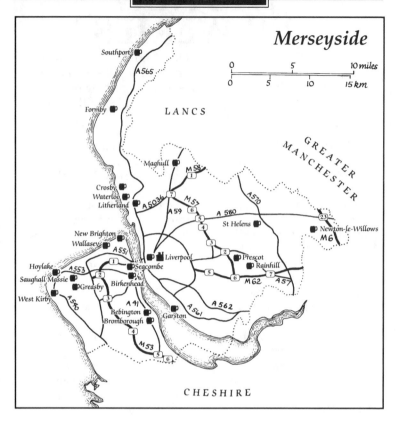

Merseyside

🏠 *Black Horse & Rainbow, Cains, Passageway, Liverpool*

Bebington

Cleveland
31 Bebington Road,
New Ferry
☎ (0151) 645 2847
11.30–11
Thwaites Best Mild, Bitter, Craftsman Ⓗ
Ever-popular, open-plan local in a pedestrian area.
≒ ♣ P

Rose & Crown
57 The Village
☎ (0151) 643 1312
11.30–3, 5.30–11; 11.30–11 Fri & Sat
Thwaites Best Mild, Bitter, Craftsman Ⓗ
Bustling, friendly, multi-room local, popular with office workers and shoppers at lunchtime, and with local residents at night.
No food Sun.
Q Ⓓ ⊕ ≒ ♣

Birkenhead

Chester Arms
20 Chester Street (near Woodside Ferry terminal)
☎ (0151) 650 0676
11–11
Marston's Bitter; Morland Old Speckled Hen; Robinson's Best Bitter; guest beer Ⓗ
A tiny frontage disguises a long, carpeted, friendly bar with good food and extensive happy hours. The guest beer is usually a mild. Marston's Head Brewer's Choice sold.
❀ Ⓓ ▶ ≒ (Hamilton Sq)

Claughton Cask
50 Upton Road
☎ (0151) 652 2056
11–11
Cains Bitter; Whitbread Boddingtons Mild, Bitter, Bentley's Yorkshire Bitter; guest beers Ⓗ
Unusually, a Whitbread pub where the licensee has a free choice of guest beers (most from micro-breweries). Sport-orientated, the pub has a big screen in the lounge. Comfortable nooks and crannies provide escape. Eve meals till 8. Ⓓ ▶ ♣ ⌂

Crown & Cushion
60 Market Street
☎ (0151) 647 8870
11–11
Bass Worthington BB; M&B Highgate Dark; guest beers Ⓗ
Refurbished, two-room, back-street pub. Friendly licensee and staff. Live entertainment weekends.
Ⓓ ▶ ⊕ ≒ ♣

Lord Napier
St Paul's Road, Rock Ferry (off A41) ☎ (0151) 645 3659
11–11
Cains Mild; Whitbread Boddingtons Bitter Ⓗ

Friendly, comfortable, two-roomed pub with a family atmosphere. Keen darts and bowls teams.
🍺 ≠ (Rock Ferry) ♠

Bromborough

Archers
149 Mark Rake
☎ (0151) 334 3406
11–11
Cains Bitter; Jennings Bitter; Tetley Walker Mild, Bitter Ⓗ
Large two-roomed pub attracting all ages. Live music Thu–Sun. The Jennings may be displaced by guest beers.
≠ (Bromborough Rake) ♠ P

Crosby

Crow's Nest
63 Victoria Road (close to Crosby village)
☎ (0151) 931 5081
11.30–11
Cains Bitter, FA Ⓗ
Popular, refurbished pub, with lounge, snug and public bars. The exterior sign advertises what it doesn't have – no food, no music, no pool, no machines – but traditional beer and conversation!
Q 🍺 ≠ (Blundellsands) P

Formby

Freshfield Hotel
Massams Lane, Freshfield (N of centre, ½ mile from B5424)
☎ (01704) 874871
11.30–11
Whitbread Boddingtons Mild, Bitter, Flowers IPA, Trophy, Castle Eden Ale; guest beers Ⓗ
Suburban pub converted to a Hogshead alehouse, with a large bar serving 12 ales. Bar lunches Mon–Fri (sausages a speciality). The TV and games area has a stone-flagged floor.
❀ ◑ ≠ (Freshfield) P

Garston

King Street Vaults
74–76 King Street
☎ (0151) 427 5850
11–11
Walker Mild, Bitter Ⓗ
Popular darts-oriented pub in Garston dockland. Wheelchair toilet available. Cable television. 🍺 ♿ ♠

Swan Inn
6 James Street
☎ (0151) 427 2032
12–11
Tetley Walker Mild, Bitter Ⓗ
Small, side-street local just off the shopping street; known as the Duck. Cable TV. 🍺 ≠ ♠

Greasby

Irby Mill
Mill Lane ☎ (0151) 604 0194
11.30–3, 5–11; 11.30–11 Sat
Cains Mild, Bitter; Jennings Bitter; S&N Theakston Best Bitter; Tetley Walker Bitter; guest beers Ⓗ
Excellent, unspoilt country pub where the licensee maintains the best pub traditions. CAMRA regional *Pub of the Year* 1995. Q ❀ ◑ P

Hoylake

Green Lodge
2 Stanley Road (300 yds from Hoylake roundabout)
☎ (0151) 632 2321
11–11
Burtonwood Bitter, Forshaw's Ⓗ
Large hotel refurbished into a smart, split-level lounge bar and a restaurant (open Sun). Near the beach, it has a large front garden, popular with families. Quizzes and other events. No bar meals Sun.
🚼 ❀ 🛏 ◑ ≠ P

Litherland

Priory
64 Sefton Road (200 yds off A5036 via School Lane)
☎ (0151) 928 1110
11.30–11
Ind Coope Burton Ale; Walker Mild, Bitter, Best Bitter; guest beers Ⓗ
Comfortable family pub in a residential area; a large lounge and a smaller public bar. Eve meals end at 7; no eve meals Sun. ❀ ◑ ▶ 🍺 ♿ ♠ P

Liverpool: *City Centre*

Anderson's Piano Bar
26 Exchange Street East, L2
☎ (0151) 236 0649
11–8 (11 Fri); closed Sat & Sun
Cains Mild, Bitter; S&N Theakston Best Bitter; guest beers Ⓗ
Surprising pub hidden in a business area: the city's only piano bar. A good range of lunches includes Chinese dishes. German weissbiers a speciality. ◑ ⊖ (Moorfields)

Cambridge Hotel
Mulberry Street, L7 (near university)
11.30–11
Burtonwood Mild, Bitter, Forshaw's, Top Hat; guest beer Ⓗ
Pub popular with students and nurses. Frequent events and quizzes. No food Sat.
❀ ◑ ♠

Carnarvon Castle
5 Tarleton Street, L2
11–11 (8 Tue & Wed); closed Sun
Draught Bass; Cains Mild, Bitter Ⓗ
Small, attractive, two-roomed pub in the shopping area. It can be very busy lunchtime and early eve (toasties lunchtime). Interesting model collection. Q ⊖ (Central)

Cracke
13 Rice Street, L1 (off Hope St)
☎ (0151) 709 4171
11.30–11
Cains Bitter; Marston's Pedigree; Oak Best Bitter, Wobbly Bob; guest beer Ⓗ
Characterful, back-street pub with interesting nooks, enjoying a strong local trade, but also popular with students. Excellent, good value lunches. ❀ ◑ ♠

Everyman Bistro
9 Hope Street, L1
☎ (0151) 708 9545
12–midnight; closed Sun
Cains Bitter; guest beers Ⓗ
Theatre basement bar and bistro now extended to include a bar in the foyer. Up to four guest beers. Very busy after 11pm and popular with both diners and drinkers (extensive, varied food range).
Q ◑ ▶ ⬡

Flying Picket
24 Hardman Street, L1 (behind Trade Union Resource Centre)
☎ (0151) 709 3995
12–11; closed Sun
Coach House Coachman's, Gunpowder Mild; guest beers Ⓗ
Bar housed in the Union Resource Centre, but open to anyone. Keen anti-sexist and anti-racist policy. The only outlet for Coach House beers in the city. Wheelchair WC. ◑ ♿ P

Globe
17 Cases Street, L1 (opp. Central station)
11–11
Draught Bass; Cains Mild, Bitter Ⓗ
Central local, a favourite for its Cains beers. Note the roof-top globe outside. A slope in the bar floor tests your sobriety. Small back lounge.
≠ (Lime St) ⊖ (Central)

Peter Kavanagh's
2–6 Egerton Street, L8 (off Catharine St)
☎ (0151) 709 3443
11–11
Cains Bitter; Ind Coope Burton Ale; Tetley Walker Mild, Bitter; guest beers Ⓗ
Characterful pub with characterful customers.

Merseyside

Bric-a-brac abounds in the unusually shaped bars.
Q ◖ ✠

Pig & Whistle
12 Covent Garden, L2
☎ (0151) 236 4760
11.30–11 (may vary Mon–Wed); 12–9 Sat; closed Sun
Walker Mild, Bitter, Best Bitter; guest beer Ⓗ
Comfortable, traditional pub in the business area, with a convivial atmosphere. The upstairs bar opens lunchtime. Good value food Mon–Fri.
◖ ⊖ (Moorfields/James St)

Poste House
23 Cumberland Street, L1
☎ (0151) 236 4760
11–11
Cains Mild, Bitter Ⓗ
Friendly, two-roomed, historic pub in the business area. Good value lunches. No food Sat or Sun. Additional seating upstairs. ◖ ⊖ (Moorfields)

Railway
18 Tithebarn Street, L2
☎ (0151) 236 7210
11–11
Cains Mild, Bitter; Tetley Walker Bitter Ⓗ
Pub close to the remains of Exchange station, used by white collar workers lunchtime and locals at night. Good value lunches. Breakfast served from 9.15. No food Sun.
◖ ⊖ (Moorfields) ♣

Roscoe Head
Roscoe Street, L1 (opp. bombed out church)
11.30 (12 Sat)–11
Ind Coope Burton Ale; Jennings Bitter; Tetley Walker Mild, Bitter Ⓗ
A bar, a snug, a back lounge and a side lounge off a small main bar make up this friendly gem. No music or electronic invaders. An ever-present in the *Guide*, lacking wall space to hang its many deserved awards. No food weekends.
Q ◖ ⇌ (Lime St) ⊖ (Central)

Ship & Mitre
133 Dale Street, L2 (near Birkenhead Tunnel entrance)
☎ (0151) 236 0859
11 (12.30 Sat)–11; closed Sun
Cains Mild, Bitter; Holt Bitter; guest beers Ⓗ
Local CAMRA *Pub of the Year* 1994, Liverpool's foremost free house, subject to a potential change of ownership. Up to eight guest beers and two ciders. The best value lunches in town. ◖ ⇌ (Lime St)
⊖ (Moorfields) ⌂ 🗗

Swan
86 Wood Street, L1
☎ (0151) 709 5281
11.30–11

Cains Mild, Bitter; Marston's Pedigree; Oak Wobbly Bob; guest beers Ⓗ
Excellent, back-street free house with the best rock jukebox in town. It celebrated its centenary as the Swan in 1995. Good, home-cooked lunches. ◖ ⊖ (Central) ⌂

United Powers
66–68 Tithebarn Street, L2
☎ (0151) 236 5205
11–11; closed Sun
Courage Directors; Ruddles County; guest beers Ⓗ
Friendly, well-run pub on the edge of the business area, serving good value lunches (no meals Sat). Note the impressive old station clock.
◖ ⊖ (Moorfields) ♣

White Star (Quinn's)
2–4 Rainford Gardens, L2
☎ (0151) 236 4572
11–11
Draught Bass; Cains Bitter; Stones Best Bitter; guest beers Ⓗ
Pub near the site of the Cavern, of Beatles fame, catering for shoppers, business people and regulars. Bass maintain the pub sympathetically and supply the guest beers.
⇌ (Lime St) ⊖ (Moorfields)

Liverpool: *East*

Albany
40–42 Albany Road, L13
☎ (0151) 228 8597
11–11
Cains Mild, Bitter Ⓗ
Lively, friendly local in a backstreet terrace. No food weekends. ◖ ♣

Clock
110 High Street, L15
☎ (0151) 733 7980
2 (12 Mon & Sat)–11
Cains Bitter Ⓗ
Pub close to Picton Clock, a local landmark. Good wheelchair facilities inside but ask for access via the rear. Happy hours until 7pm. ♿ ♣

Clubmoor
119 Townsend Lane, Anfield, L6 ☎ (0151) 263 4220
11–11
Cains Mild, Bitter Ⓗ
Handsome, detached main road pub with a bar (Sky TV) and a large lounge. Near Everton and Liverpool FCs.
❀ 🍺 ♣

Edinburgh
4 Sandown Lane, L15
12–11
Cains Bitter; Walker Mild, Bitter Ⓗ
Tiny local hidden away from the busy Wavertree High St.

A small lounge, an even smaller bar, but a big welcome. 🍺

Halton Castle
86 Mill Lane, L12
☎ (0151) 270 2013
11.30–11
Cains Mild, Bitter Ⓗ
Multi-roomed village local with busy public bar.
Q ❀ 🍺 ♣ P

Kensington
109 Kensington, L7
☎ (0151) 263 9975
12–11
Cains Mild, Bitter Ⓗ
Popular, two-roomed, street-corner local close to shops.
🍺 ♣

Lord Nelson
146 East Prescot Road, L14
(A57) ☎ (0151) 220 1894
11.30–11
Cains Bitter Ⓗ
Friendly local on a main road, with a small bar and a back lounge; formerly Joseph Jones Knotty Ash Brewery tap.
❀ ♣ P

Mount Vernon
1 Irvine Street, L7
☎ (0151) 709 9432
12–11
Cains Bitter; guest beers Ⓗ
Attractive, small, round-house, pub with a beautiful interior. Popular with students. The manager has fought hard to keep his guest beers, following the pub's sale to Paramount.
⇌ (Edge Hill) ♣ P

Rocket
2 Bowring Park Road, L14
☎ (0151) 220 8821
11–11
Cains Bitter Ⓗ
Modern pub, named after the famous loco, which is depicted in relief on the side. No food Sat.
❀ ◖ ⇌ (Broad Green)

Wheatsheaf
186 East Prescot Road, L14
(A57) ☎ (0151) 228 5080
11.30–11
Cains Bitter; guest beer Ⓗ
Popular, traditional pub, offering waitress service in the two lounges, plus a busy bar. Quiz night Mon.
Q 🍺 P

Liverpool: *North*

Bull
2 Dublin Street, L3
☎ (0151) 207 1422
11–11
Tetley Walker Mild, Bitter Ⓗ
Street-corner local where a warm welcome is guaranteed.
🍺

Liverpool: *South*

Anglesea Arms
34 Beresford Road, L8 (off
Park Rd) ☎ (0151) 727 4874
11.30 (11 Sat)–11
**Tetley Walker Dark Mild,
Bitter** Ⓗ
Lively, friendly, wood-
panelled pub near a busy
shopping area. Two rooms are
split by a central bar. ⊞ ♣

Brewery Tap
35 Stanhope Street, L8 (off
Parliament St, by Cains
brewery) ☎ (0151) 709 2129
11–11
**Cains Mild, Bitter, Stout, FA;
guest beers** Ⓗ
Deserved winner of the
CAMRA national *Pub
Refurbishment* award 1994.
Original beer labels and
posters adorn the walls. Three
guest beers, plus Danish and
German bottled beers.
Q ✿ ◑ P

Falstaff
110 Gateacre Park Drive, L25
☎ (0151) 428 5116
11–11
**Greenalls Original; Tetley
Walker Mild, Bitter; guest
beer** Ⓗ
Pub recently renovated to
provide eating and no-
smoking areas, but retaining
its traditional bar. The guest
beer is from the Allied list.
◑ ▶ ⊞ ♿ ♣ P ⤫

Masonic
19 Lodge Lane, L8
☎ (0151) 734 2271
11–11
Tetley Walker Mild, Bitter Ⓗ
Small, friendly, characterful
local on the edge of the
Toxteth area. Reasonable
prices. ⛟ ⊞ ⇌ (Edge Hill)

Royal George
99 Park Road, L8
☎ (0151) 708 9277
11–11
**Tetley Walker Dark Mild,
Bitter; guest beer** Ⓗ
Popular pub known locally as
Blacks, featuring happy hours
Mon–Fri, 5–8pm. One
changing guest beer, the
cheapest in the city (all guests
are the same price). Regular
live music. ⊞ ♣

Willowbank
329 Smithdown Road, L15
11–11
**Ind Coope Burton Ale;
Walker Mild, Bitter, Winter
Warmer** Ⓗ
Comfortable pub, popular
with students in the eve. The
traditional public bar caters for
locals. ✿ ⊞ ♣ P

Maghull

Red House
31 Foxhouse Lane
☎ (0151) 526 1376
11–11
Tetley Walker Bitter, Imperial
(summer); **Walker Mild, Best
Bitter, Winter Warmer** Ⓗ
Friendly, suburban local with
a reputation for modestly
priced lunches. An oasis in
Maghull for lovers of real
pubs. Liverpool buses stop
outside. No food Sun.
✿ ◑ ⊞ ⇌ ♣ P

New Brighton

Commercial Hotel
Hope Street (off Victoria Rd)
☎ (0151) 639 2105
11.30–11
**Cains FA; Walker Mild,
Bitter, Best Bitter, Winter
Warmer** Ⓗ
Traditional, two-roomed,
street-corner local with a basic
bar and a cosy lounge (table
service). A peaceful haven for
older people.
Q ⊞ ⇌ ♣

Stanley's Cask
212 Rake Lane
☎ (0151) 691 1093
11.30–11
**McEwan 70/-; S&N Theakston
Best Bitter, XB, Old Peculier;
Younger IPA; guest beers** Ⓗ
Small, popular, dark pub with
a TV room. Frequently
changing guest beers at
reasonable prices. ✿ ◑ ♣

Newton-le-Willows

Bull's Head
Southworth Road (A572 at
Golborne/Winwick jct)
☎ (01925) 221480
11.30–3, 5–11; 11.30–11 Sat
**Ind Coope Burton Ale; Tetley
Walker Bitter; guest beers** Ⓗ
Tastefully refurbished pub.
The layout is open-plan but
with partitions to separate the
comfortable drinking and
dining areas. Children's
adventure playground.
(Children allowed in till 8pm.)
✿ ◑ ▶ P

Old Crow Inn
248 Crow Lane East (A572, 1
mile from centre)
☎ (01925) 225332
12–3.30, 7–11; 12–11 Fri & Sat
**Tetley Walker Dark Mild,
Bitter; guest beers**
(occasional) Ⓗ
Roadside local with a large,
comfortable lounge,
refurbished in early 1995.
Well-used tap room. Ask for
eve meals. ✿ ◑ ⊞ ♣ P

Prescot

Clock Face
54 Derby Street
☎ (0151) 430 0701
11–11
Thwaites Bitter, Craftsman Ⓗ
Attractive, old sandstone
mansion converted to a pub in
the 1980s. An oasis of pleasant
relaxation. Q ✿ ◑ P

Hare & Hounds
(Tommy Hall's)
10 Warrington Road
12–11
**Cains Mild, Bitter; guest
beers** Ⓗ
Small, old ex-Joseph Jones pub
which was badly altered in the
1970s but still retains a good
atmosphere. Guest beers
mostly come from Whitbread.
⇌

Rainhill

Commercial
Station Road (just off A57)
☎ (0151) 426 6446
12–11
**Cains Mild, Bitter; S&N
Theakston Best Bitter** Ⓗ
Victorian pub which has been
sympathetically altered but
still has three distinct
drinking areas.
✿ ⊞ ⇌ ♣ P

St Helens

Brown Edge
299 Nutgrove Road
☎ (0151) 426 4156
12–11
**Burtonwood Bitter,
Forshaw's** Ⓗ
Three-roomed pub with an
unusual bar, a cosy lounge
and a garden lounge suitable
for children, overlooking a
bowling green and play area.
Book Sun lunch. ⛟ ✿ ◑ ⊞
⇌ (Thatto Heath) ♣ P ⌷

Hope & Anchor
194 City Road
☎ (01744) 24199
12–11
Tetley Walker Mild, Bitter Ⓗ
Busy pub hosting lots of
events. The disco is loud. ⊞

Phoenix
Canal Street
☎ (01744) 21953
11–11
Taylor Landlord; guest beer Ⓗ
Popular alehouse (especially
with students at weekends).
The bar is home to serious
rugby league fans and walls
are adorned with pictures of
past touring sides. Lunchtime
snacks. ⊞ ⇌ (Central) ♣ ⌷

Merseyside

Royal Alfred

Shaw Street ☎ (01744) 26786
11–11
Cains Bitter; guest beer Ⓗ
Busy, cosmopolitan, town-centre pub, offering some live music. ⍩ ◖ ⊟
⇌ (Central) ♣ P ⊟

Turk's Head

49–51 Morley Street
☎ (01744) 26949
11–11
Cains Mild, Bitter; Holt Bitter; Tetley Walker Bitter; guest beer Ⓗ
Unusual, half-timbered pub in an inner town area: the epitome of a true community local, with a kiddies' club, pensioners' club and a racing club. Book for meals Sun.
⍩ ❀ ◖ ⊟ ♣

Wheatsheaf

Westfield Street
☎ (01744) 37453
12–11
Tetley Walker Dark Mild, Bitter; guest beers Ⓗ
Busy, town-centre local with a variety of customers.
⇌ (Central) ♣

Saughall Massie

Saughall Hotel

Saughall Road (400 yds off Holylake Rd)
☎ (0151) 677 2854
12 (11 Sat)–11
Thwaites Bitter Ⓗ
Pleasant, ex-Whitbread country pub, refurbished to provide comfortable, wood-panelled drinking areas around a central bar. Summer barbecues in the garden.
Q ❀ ◖ ⅋ P

Seacombe

Prince Alfred

3 Church Road
☎ (0151) 638 1674
11–11
Cains Bitter; Whitbread Boddingtons Mild, Bitter; guest beers Ⓗ
The area's best choice of beers in the area's best pub: small, comfortable and friendly. Just up the road from Seacombe ferry terminal. Good value guest ales. ❀ ⅋ ♣ ⊟

Southport

Berkeley Hotel

19 Queens Road (near Holy Trinity church)

☎ (01704) 530163
12–11
Courage Directors; Moorhouse's Black Cat Mild, Pendle Witches Brew; Ruddles Best Bitter; guest beers Ⓗ
Family-run hotel just north of the town centre. Berkeley Bitter is brewed by Moorhouse's. Good food.
❀ ⍩ ◖ ⇌ P

Cheshire Lines

81 King Street
(near A565, just S of centre)
☎ (01704) 532178
11.30–11
Robinson's Best Bitter; Walker Mild, Bitter, Best Bitter; guest beers (occasional) Ⓗ
Half-timbered hostelry in one of the guest house areas, featuring old stone from the original Cheshire Lines railway station (closed 1952).
⍩ ❀ ⇌ ♣ P

Lakeside Inn

Marine Lake, Promenade (Seabank Rd jct)
☎ (01704) 530173
11–11
Fuller's London Pride; Marston's Pedigree Ⓗ
Tiny one-room bar, adjacent to the Floral Hall and tourism offices. Listed in the *Guinness Book of Records* as Britain's smallest pub. Theatre entertainers are regulars.
Q ❀

Upsteps Hotel

20 Upper Aughton Road, Birkdale (off A5267, Eastbourne Rd)
☎ (01704) 569245
11.30–11
S&N Matthew Brown Bitter, Theakston Mild, Best Bitter, XB; guest beers (occasional) Ⓗ
Cosy, friendly, traditional pub, home of various teams. The name comes from the front entrance.
❀ ⅋ ⇌ (Birkdale) ♣ P

Zetland Hotel

53 Zetland Street
☎ (01704) 544541
11.30–11
Burtonwood Mild, Bitter, Forshaw's, Top Hat Ⓗ
Large, refurbished, Victorian pub with its own bowling green. It retains separate rooms. The family room is open until 8.30pm.
⍩ ⚲ ❀ ◖ ⅋ ♣ P

Wallasey

Cheshire Cheese

2 Wallasey Village
☎ (0151) 638 3152
12–11
Cains Mild, Bitter; S&N Theakston Best Bitter Ⓗ
Wallasey's oldest licensed premises, rebuilt in 1884. Beer has been sold on this site for more than 500 years. Separate public, lounge and snug bars serve all ages. No music.
❀ ◖ ⅋ ♣

Farmer's Arms

225 Wallasey Village, Wirral
☎ (0151) 638 2110
11.30–11
Cains Bitter; S&N Theakston Best Bitter; Tetley Walker Bitter; guest beer Ⓗ
Former local CAMRA *Pub of the Year*, which remains popular: a front bar, side snug and back lounge with no jukebox. The guest pump is in the bar. No meals weekends.
◖ ⅋ ⚲ ⇌ (Grove Rd)

Primrose Hotel

11 Withens Lane, Liscard (off Manor Rd) ☎ (0151) 637 1340
12–11
Cains Bitter; S&N Theakston Best Bitter; guest beers Ⓗ
Unmistakable, half-timbered pub with wood-panelled walls, an ornate ceiling and a mixed clientele. ❀ ♣ P

Waterloo

Volunteer Canteen

45 East Street
☎ (0151) 928 6594
12–11
Cains Bitter; S&N Theakston Best Bitter Ⓗ
Refurbished, traditional, corner local: a bar and a cosy lounge with waitress service. No music, food or machines.
⍩ Q ❀ ⅋ ⇌ ♣

West Kirby

Hilbre Court

Banks Road ☎ (0151) 625 7811
11–11
Tetley Walker Dark Mild, Bitter; guest beers Ⓗ
Popular, friendly pub with a restaurant. The lounge bar is open-plan but with distinct drinking areas. Try the excellent lunches. Close to the promenade and Wirral Way.
❀ ◖ ◗ ⇌ ♣ P

Can't remember who brews what? Check the Beers Index at the back of this book for an instant answer.

224

BEER FESTIVAL CALENDAR 1996

CAMRA beer festivals provide wonderful opportunities for sampling beers not normally found in the locality. Festivals are staffed by CAMRA members on a voluntary basis and offer a wide range of interesting real ales from breweries all over the country, plus live entertainment and much more. The major event is the Great British Beer Festival in August, where over 400 different beers can be enjoyed. For further details of this and the regional events outlined below, together with precise dates and venues, contact CAMRA on (01727) 867201, or see your local press.

JANUARY
Atherton
Exeter
Merseyside
York

FEBRUARY
Basingstoke
Battersea
Bradford
Dorchester
Dover
Durham
Fleetwood
Liverpool
Llandudno
Plymouth
Sussex
Truro

MARCH
Camden (London Drinker)
Darlaston
Darlington
Dukeries (N Notts)
Ealing
Eastleigh
Gosport
Leeds
Rugby
Wigan

APRIL
Castle Point
Chippenham
Coventry
Dunstable
Farnham
Mansfield
Newcastle upon Tyne
Oldham
Swansea

MAY
Alloa
Cambridge
Chester
Cleethorpes
Colchester

Dewsbury
Dudley
Frodsham
Lincoln
Milton Keynes
Northampton
Ongar
Rhyl
Ripon
Sudbury
Wolverhampton
Woodchurch
Yapton

JUNE
Barnsley
Bury St Edmunds
Catford
Doncaster
Exeter
Larling
Leighton Buzzard
St Ives (Cambs)
Salisbury
Stockport
Surrey
Thurrock (Grays)

JULY
Ardingly
Canterbury
Chelmsford
Cotswolds
Derby
Grantham
Tameside Canals
Woodcote

AUGUST
Great Bntish Beer Festival
Peterborough
Portsmouth
Truro

SEPTEMBER
Bangor (Wales)
Belfast
Birmingham
Burton upon Trent

Carmarthen
Chappel (Essex)
Chichester
Durham
Feltham
Harbury
Ipswich
Maidstone
Newton Abbot
Northampton
Northwich
Sheffield
Shrewsbury

OCTOBER
Alloa
Bath
Bedford
Cardiff
Darlington
Denbigh
East Lancs
Eastleigh
Edinburgh
Guernsey
Holmfirth
Keighley
Loughborough
Middlesbrough
Norwich
Nottingham
Overton
Scunthorpe
Stoke-on-Trent
Swindon
Wakefield

NOVEMBER
Aberdeen
Bury
Dudley
Hitchin
Jersey
Luton
Mid Wales
Rochford
Woking

DECEMBER
London (Pig's Ear)

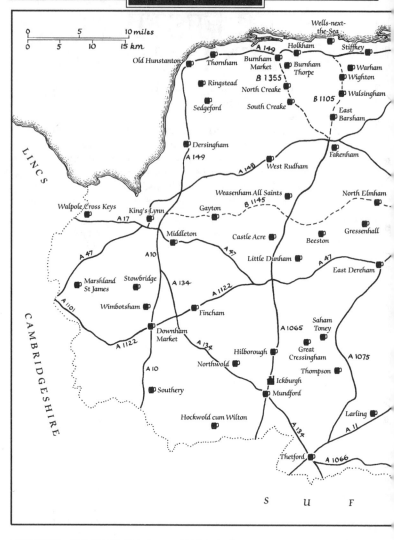

 Buffy's, *Tivetshall St Mary*; **Chalk Hill**, *Norwich*; **Iceni**, *Ickburgh*; **Reepham**, *Reepham*; **Woodforde's**, *Woodbastwick*

Attleborough

Griffin
Church Street
☎ (01953) 452149
11–3, 5.30–11
Greene King Abbot; King & Barnes Sussex; Wells Bombardier; Whitbread Wethered Bitter; guest beer Ⓗ
16th-century coaching inn, well restored. Quality food.
🏠 Q 🐴 ❀ 🛏 ◑ ▶ ⇌ P

Banningham

Crown
Church Road
☎ (01263) 733534
12–2.30, 7–11
Greene King IPA, Abbot; Whitbread Flowers IPA Ⓗ
Comfortable village pub with a large bar divided into three sections. Children welcome.
🏠 Q ❀ ◑ ▶ ♣ P

Beeston

Ploughshare
The Street ☎ (01328) 701845
12–2.30, 6–11; 12–11 Sat
Greene King IPA, Rayments Special, Abbot; guest beer Ⓗ
Although the building is 17th century, there has been a pub on this site since circa 1420. A friendly village pub where families are welcome. Monthly folk music. Cider in summer.
🏠 ❀ ◑ ▶ ♣ ⌂ P

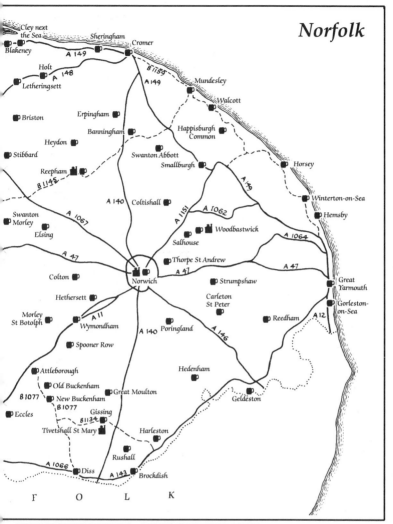

Norfolk

(map of Norfolk showing locations including Cley next the Sea, Sheringham, Cromer, Blakeney, Holt, Letheringsett, Briston, Erpingham, Mundesley, Walcott, Heydon, Banningham, Happisburgh Common, Stibbard, Swanton Abbott, Smallburgh, Horsey, Reepham, Coltishall, Winterton-on-Sea, Hemsby, Swanton Morley, Elsing, Salhouse, Woodbastwick, Colton, Norwich, Thorpe St Andrew, Great Yarmouth, Hethersett, Strumpshaw, Carleton St Peter, Gorleston-on-Sea, Morley St Botolph, Wymondham, Poringland, Reedham, Spooner Row, Hedenham, Attleborough, Old Buckenham, Great Moulton, Geldeston, New Buckenham, Eccles, Gissing, Tivetshall St Mary, Harleston, Rushall, Diss, Brockdish; F O L K)

Blakeney

Manor Hotel
Coast Road ☎ (01263) 740376
10.30–2.30, 6–11
Adnams Mild, Bitter, Extra Ⓗ
Pub with a comfortable bar
overlooking the marshes.
Adjoining rooms lead to an
enclosed garden. Well-
appointed restaurant.
Q ☻ ❀ 🍴 ◑ ▶ P

White Horse
High Street ☎ (01263) 740574
11–3, 6–11
**Adnams Bitter; Whitbread
Boddingtons Bitter, Flowers
Original; guest beer** Ⓗ
Popular, village pub with a
long through-bar. Good wine
cellar.
Q ☻ ❀ 🍴 ◑ ▶ ⚓ ♣ P

Briston

Green Man
Hall Street ☎ (01263) 861449
11–11
**Greene King IPA, Abbot;
guest beer** Ⓗ
A large inglenook features in
this 200-year-old building with
genuine beams. Friendly local
atmosphere. No food Sun eve.
🍺 ☻ ❀ ◑ ▶ ♿ ▲ ♣ P

Brockdish

Greyhound
The Street (A143)
☎ (01379) 668775
12–2 (not normally Mon–Thu, but
check), 7–11; 12–2, 7–10.30 Sun
**Woodforde's Wherry; guest
beer** Ⓖ

Homely, one-bar, 17th-century
village inn serving award-
winning home cooking in a
friendly atmosphere. The
house beers are brewed by
Buffy's.
🍺 Q 🍴 ◑ ▶ P ⚥ 🚪

Burnham Market

Hoste Arms
The Green ☎ (01328) 738257
11–11
**Ruddles County; Webster's
Yorkshire Bitter;** Ⓗ
**Woodforde's Wherry; guest
beer** Ⓖ
17th-century, multi-roomed
inn with an excellent
reputation for food. Jazz and
blues bands play weekly.
Occasional cider. 🍺 Q ☻
❀ 🍴 ◑ ▶ ▲ ⌂ P ⚥

Norfolk

Burnham Thorpe

Lord Nelson
Walsingham Road (off A149)
☎ (01328) 738241
11–3, 6–11 (11–11 summer)
**Greene King IPA, Abbot;
Woodforde's Nelson's
Revenge; guest beer**
(winter) G
Built in 1650; Nelson would
have known this as the Plough
when he held a party here in
1793. The facilities are being
improved and there are now
three bars, but still no bar
counter. High back settles and
table service are other features.
A rare gem. Blanket pressure
is used on the Mild.
🏚 Q ◖ ▶ ♣ P ⌿

Carleton St Peter

Beauchamp Arms
Buckenham Ferry OS350043
☎ (01508) 480247
11.30–3 (not Mon–Fri in winter), 6–11;
11–11 Sat
**Adnams Bitter; Woodforde's
Wherry; guest beers** H
Large multi-roomed free
house in a quiet location on
the south bank of the Yare.
Plenty of moorings; a good
area for walking.
🏚 Q ⛅ ⛱ ◖ ▶ ▲ ♣ P

Castle Acre

Ostrich
Stocks Green ☎ (01760) 755398
12–3, 7–11
**Greene King XX Mild, IPA,
Abbot** H
Coaching inn on the village
green, near a beautiful priory.
Good food. Q ◖ ▶ ♣ P

Cley next the Sea

George & Dragon
High Street ☎ (01263) 740652
11.30 (11 summer)–2.30, 7 (6.30
summer)–11; 12–2, 7–10.30 Sun
**Greene King IPA, Abbot;
guest beer** H
Two bars plus a room for
diners and families; a place
where ale and bird watching
meet, there being a scrape just
over the sea wall.
🏚 ⛱ ⛅ ⛱ ◖ ▶ P

Coltishall

Red Lion
Church Street
☎ (01603) 737402
11–3, 5–11
**Adnams Bitter; Greene King
Abbot; Morland Old
Speckled Hen; Whitbread
Boddingtons Bitter, Flowers
Original; guest beer** H

16th-century, two-bar pub
with a restaurant area and a
comfortable and friendly
atmosphere. Good playground
next to the car park.
⛅ ◖ ▶ ⛁ ♣ P

Colton

Ugly Bug Inn
High House Farm Lane
(signed from A47)
☎ (01603) 880794
12–3, 5.30–11
**Adnams Bitter; Greene King
IPA, Abbot; guest beer** H
Originally a barn converted to
a house, then extended to a
pub. The walls are adorned
with pre-war advertisements.
Local beers feature as guests
(four per week).
Q ⛱ ⛅ ⛱ ◖ ▶ ⛦ P

Cromer

Bath House Hotel
The Promenade
☎ (01263) 514260
11–3, 6.30–11 (11–11 summer; closed
Jan & Feb)
**Eldridge Pope Best Bitter;
Ridleys IPA; guest beers** H
Seafront pub with a good
outside drinking area
overlooking the beach. The
dining area is very popular
with holidaymakers; locally
caught fish features on the
menu. Q ⛅ ⛱ ◖ ▶ ▲ ⇌

Dersingham

Feathers Hotel
Manor Road ☎ (01485) 540207
11–2.30, 5.30–11
**Adnams Bitter; Draught Bass;
guest beers** H
Large stone-built hotel, near
Sandringham House, featuring
wood panelled bars. Good
food in the bars and
restaurant. The games bar is in
the old stable block.
🏚 ⛅ ⛱ ◖ ▶ ▲ ♣ P

Diss

White Horse
Market Place ☎ (01379) 642913
11–11
**Adnams Bitter; Mansfield Old
Baily** H
Small, single-bar local, split
into separate areas. ⇌ ♣

Downham Market

Crown Hotel
Bridge Street ☎ (01366) 382322
11–2.30, 5.30–11; 11–11 Fri & Sat
**Bateman XB; Ruddles
County; John Smith's Bitter;
Wadworth 6X; guest beer** H
17th-century coaching inn at
the town centre. Occasional
live music. 🏚 ⛅ ⛱ ◖ ▶ P

East Barsham

White Horse
Fakenham Road
☎ (01328) 820645
11–3, 7 (6 summer)–11
**Greene King Abbot;
Whitbread Boddingtons
Bitter; Woodforde's Wherry;
guest beer** H
Genuine, old beamed building
set in lovely countryside. Two
restaurant areas are separate
from the bar, which has a large
inglenook. Beware the keg
cider on a fake handpump.
🏚 ⛅ ⛱ ◖ ▶ ♣ P

East Dereham

George Hotel
Swaffham Road
☎ (01362) 696801
10.30–2.30, 5–11
**Draught Bass; Fuller's
London Pride; Woodforde's
Wherry** H
Comfortable, wood-panelled
hotel bar in a former coaching
inn. Cask breathers may be
used on handpumped beers
not listed above. ⛅ ⛱ ◖ ▶

Eccles

Old Railway Tavern
(Eccles Tap)
Station Road
12 (1 Wed)–2.30, 5.30–11
Adnams Bitter G**; Greene
King IPA** H**, Abbot; guest
beer** G
Unchanging, amiable pub
where customers and ale are
treated with equal care.
🏚 Q ⛅ ⇌ (Eccles Rd)
♣ ⌂ P ⛁

Elsing

Mermaid
Church Street
☎ (01362) 637640
12–3, 7–11
**Adnams Bitter, Broadside;
Woodforde's Wherry; guest
beer** H
Old village local: a single bar
retaining many original
features, with pool at one end
and a real fire at the other.
There is also a restaurant and
gardens. Children welcome.
🏚 Q ⛅ ◖ ▶ ♣ P ⛁

Erpingham

Spread Eagle
Eagle Street ☎ (01263) 761591
11–3, 6.30–11
**Woodforde's Mardler's Mild,
Wherry, Gt Eastern, Norfolk
Nog, Headcracker** H
16th-century country inn, the
former site of Woodforde's

brewery, offering a games room, family room and a large main bar. The house beer is from Woodforde's.

🏠 Q 🕿 🏵 ◗ ▲ ♣ P

Fakenham

Bull

Bridge Street ☎ (01328) 862560
11–3, 7–11; 11–11 Thu–Sat
John Smith's Bitter; Webster's Yorkshire Bitter; Woodforde's Wherry Ⓗ
Three-roomed pub in the town centre: a lounge, a public bar with games and a restaurant area. Relaxed atmosphere. Eve meals in summer. ◗ ▶ ⊟ ♣

Fincham

Swan

High Street ☎ (01366) 347765
11.30–3, 6.30–11
Greene King IPA; guest beers Ⓗ
Comfortably refurbished village pub with good, reasonably priced food (no-smoking eating area).
🏠 🏵 🏕 ◗ ▶ ♣ P

Gayton

Crown

Lynn Road ☎ (01553) 636252
11–3, 6–11
Greene King XX Mild, IPA, Rayments Special, Abbot Ⓗ
A roaring fire provides a warm welcome and travellers are well provided for with a family room and a restaurant, but this pub is still the centre of village life.
🏠 🕿 🏵 ◗ ▶ ♣ P

Geldeston

Wherry

The Street ☎ (01508) 518371
11–3, 7 (6 summer)–11
Adnams Bitter, Old, Broadside Ⓗ, **Tally Ho** Ⓖ
Friendly pub which retains the charm of a small village inn, with its original old bar. An extension provides plenty of drinking room and a restaurant.
🏠 Q 🕿 🏵 ◗ ▶ ▲ ♣ P

Gissing

Crown

Lower Street ☎ (01379) 677718
11.30–2.30, 6.30–11
Adnams Bitter; Greene King Abbot; guest beer Ⓗ
Difficult to find, but this local is well worth seeking out: a single bar with separate pool, drinking and (no-smoking) dining areas. Friendly landlord. Q 🕿 🏵 ◗ ▶ & P

Gorleston-on-Sea

Dock Tavern

Dock Tavern Lane
☎ (01493) 442255
11–11
Adnams Broadside; Draught Bass; Greene King IPA; guest beers Ⓗ
Welcoming local near the river, with a collection of maritime artefacts. An outdoor menagerie includes a pot-bellied pig. Note the 1953 flood mark by the door. 🏵 ◗

Short Blue

47 High Street
☎ (01493) 602192
10.30–11
Beer range varies Ⓗ
Cosy, wood-panelled single bar with much stained-glass and local memorabilia. The front entrance is in the main street; the rear entrance, from the riverside, is up steep steps. Beware the keg cider on a fake handpump. Eve meals 6–8.30 Mon–Fri. 🏵 ◗ ▶

Great Cressingham

Windmill Inn

Water End (A1065)
☎ (01760) 756232
11–2.30, 6.30–11; 12–2.30, 7–10.30 Sun
Adnams Bitter, Broadside; Bass Charrington IPA, Draught Bass; Samuel Smith OBB; guest beers Ⓗ
Crammed full of bits and bobs, this inviting pub on the edge of the village offers good quality food, six drinking areas, olde-worlde charm and a large garden. 🏠 Q 🕿 🏵 ◗ ▶ & ▲ ♣ P

Great Moulton

Fox & Hounds

Frith Way ☎ (01379) 77506
11–3, 7–11
Adnams Bitter; Whitbread Boddingtons Bitter; guest beers Ⓗ
15th-century, single-bar pub and restaurant. A low ceiling with exposed beams gives a very comfortable feel. No food Mon. 🏠 🏵 ◗ ▶ & ♣ P

Great Yarmouth

Clipper Schooner

19 Friars Lane (E bank of river)
☎ (01493) 854926
11–11
Adnams Mild, Bitter, Broadside; guest beers Ⓗ
Comfortable, large and welcoming, single-bar estate pub with a varied clientele.
🕿 🏵 ◗ ▶ ♣ ⊖ P

Mariner's Tavern

69 Howard Street South (near Town Hall) ☎ (01493) 332299
11–4, 8–11 (not Mon–Wed eves); closed Sun
Bass Worthington BB, Draught Bass; M&B Highgate Dark; guest beers Ⓗ
Ex-Lacons 1950s pub with a noted porch gable and wood panelling throughout the bar, plus a lounge/restaurant (children welcome).
Q 🏵 ◗ ▶ ⇌ ♣ P ⊬

Gressenhall

Swan

The Green ☎ (01362) 860340
12–2.30, 6–11 (11–11 summer)
Greene King IPA, Abbot; guest beers (summer) Ⓗ
Comfortable, single-bar local, handy for the Norfolk Rural Life Museum. Good value food in the dining area. No food Sun eve.
🏠 Q 🏵 ◗ ▶ & ♣ P

Happisburgh Common

Victoria

Off B1159 ☎ (01692) 650228
11.30–2.30, 7–11 (11–3, 5.30–11 summer); 11–11 Sat
Courage Directors; John Smith's Bitter; Woodforde's Wherry Ⓗ
Difficult to find rural pub with camping facilities. A good base for visiting the coast.
Q 🕿 🏵 ◗ ▲ ♣ P ⊟

Harleston

Cherry Tree

74 London Road (B1134)
☎ (01379) 852345
11.30–2.30, 6–11
Adnams Mild, Bitter, Old, Extra (summer), **Broadside** Ⓗ
Friendly, unspoilt, two-roomed, timber-framed local with an impressive cast iron range. Petanque played.
🏠 Q 🏵 ◗ ⊟ & ♣ P

Hedenham

Mermaid

Norwich Road
☎ (01508) 482480
11–3, 6 (7 Sat)–11
Adnams Bitter; Draught Bass; Greene King IPA Ⓗ
Comfortable, refurbished country pub, which has retained much of its original character. A large open fire offers a warm welcome.
🏠 Q 🏵 ◗ ▲ ♣ P

Hemsby

King's Head

North Road ☎ (01493) 730568

11–11
Greene King IPA; John Smith's Bitter; Woodforde's Gt Eastern H**; guest beers** (summer) G
Pleasant, 18th-century village pub with oak beams in the bar, a (no-smoking) dining room and a very friendly atmosphere. The Asian board game of Carrom is played.
ꬉ ✿ ◖ ▶ ▲ ♣ P

Hethersett

King's Head
36 Old Norwich Road
☎ (01603) 810206
11–2.30, 5.30 (6 Sat)–11
Courage Directors; Marston's Pedigree; Morland Old Speckled Hen; John Smith's Bitter; Wadworth 6X; Woodforde's Wherry H
Classic, friendly old pub: the public bar has a clay tiled floor and timber beams. The dining area is off the lounge bar. Good bus service from Norwich and Wymondham (including Sun). No eve meals Sun, Mon or Thu.
ꬉ Q ✿ ◖ ▶ ⊞ ♣ P

Heydon

Earle Arms
The Street ☎ (01263) 587376
12–3, 7–11
Morland Old Speckled Hen; Woodforde's Wherry; guest beer H
Unspoilt, three-roomed pub on the village green with a conservatory at the rear (children welcome). Good food. ꬉ Q ✿ ◖ ▶
⊞ ₺ ▲ ♱ ○ ✠

Hilborough

Swan
On A1065 ☎ (01760) 756380
11–2.30, 5.30–11; 12–2.30, 7.30–10.30 Sun
Draught Bass; Greene King IPA, Abbot H**; Tolly Cobbold Mild** G**; guest beers** H
Superb roadside free house which boasts no keg bitter. Warm welcome; good food.
ꬉ Q ◖ ▶ P

Hockwold cum Wilton

New Inn
Station Road ☎ (01842) 828668
11–3, 6–11; 11–11 Sat
Greene King IPA; Whitbread Boddingtons Bitter; guest beers H
16th-century, part-flint, welcoming coaching inn, active in local charities. Good food includes home-cooked specials.
ꬉ Q ✿ ⍾ ◖ ▶ ♣ P

Holkham

Victoria
Park Road (by Holkham Hall)
☎ (01328) 710469
11–3, 6–11 (11–11 summer)
Greene King IPA; guest beers H
Families are welcome in this two-bar, circa 1820 pub on the edge of the Holkham Estate. Popular with tourists, the restaurant has a fine view over the marshes. ꬉ Q ➹ ✿ ⍾
◖ ▶ ⊞ ₺ ♣ P

Holt

White Lion
8 White Lion Street
☎ (01263) 712259
11–3, 6 (6.30 winter)–11
Woodforde's Wherry, Norfolk Nog; guest beer (summer) H
300-year-old pub with a cosy cottage atmosphere and an unspoilt interior. No eve meals Sun–Wed in winter. A cask breather is used on the Nelson's Revenge.
ꬉ ✿ ⍾ ◖ ▶ ⊞ ₺ ♣ P

Horsey

Nelson's Head
The Street (just off B1159)
☎ (01493) 593378
11–2.30 (3 Sat), 7 (6 summer)–11
Woodforde's Wherry, Nelson's Revenge (summer) H
Friendly, one-bar country pub with nautical artefacts; handy for the marshes and Horsey Mill, and within walking distance of the Broads and the beach. Austrian food is a speciality. ꬉ Q ➹ ✿ ◖ ▶ P

King's Lynn

Duke's Head Hotel (Lynn Bar)
Tuesday Market Place
☎ (01553) 774996
11–2.30 (3 Tue), 6–11
Adnams Bitter; Draught Bass; Greene King Abbot; guest beer H
Behind the elegant Georgian facade of the Duke's Head is the small, comfortable, wood-panelled Lynn Bar, an oasis of calm in the market place.
Q ⍾ ◖ ▶ P

London Porterhouse
78 London Road
☎ (01553) 766842
12–3, 6–11; 11–11 Sat
Greene King IPA, Abbot G
A long, but very narrow, wood-panelled bar and gravity dispense help to give real character to this tiny local, near the historic South Gates.
Q ✿ ♣

Seven Sisters
3 Extons Road
12–3, 7–11
S&N Theakston Old Peculier; John Smith's Bitter; Younger IPA; guest beer H
Street-corner local close to the football ground, with a (no-smoking) restaurant. Live music every Fri. No food Wed.
✿ ◖ ▶ ♣ ⊟

White Horse
9 Wootton Road, Gaywood
☎ (01553) 763258
11–3 (3.30 Sat), 5.30 (6 Sat)–11
Greene King IPA; Morland Old Speckled Hen; John Smith's Bitter; guest beer H
Busy, two-roomed pub close to Gaywood Clock. A locals' pub with lots of activities and many games teams. Interesting guest beers.
⊞ ♣ ⊟

Larling

Angel
On A11 ☎ (01953) 717963
11–3 (may extend), 5–11; 11–11 Fri & Sat
Adnams Bitter; Tetley Bitter; guest beers H
Pub recently returned to a free house and restored structurally in keeping with its reputation as an excellent local, where travellers are also at ease. Many varied guest ales. Phone to camp.
ꬉ Q ✿ ⍾ ◖ ▶ ⊞ ▲ ♣ P

Letheringsett

King's Head
Holt Road (A148)
☎ (01263) 712691
11–3, 5.30–11
Adnams Bitter; Draught Bass; Greene King IPA, Abbot H
300-year-old, beamed building where a marquee in the beautiful gardens features live music in summer. A good village local, also catering well for visitors.
ꬉ ➹ ✿ ◖ ▶ ₺ ♣ P

Little Dunham

Black Swan
The Street ☎ (01760) 722200
12–2, 7–11 (supper licence)
Beer range varies H
Families are welcome in this friendly village local which has genuine beams. Built in 1735, it was at one time owned by Nelson. Two real ales.
ꬉ ➹ ✿ ◖ ▶ ♣ P

Marshland St James

England's Hope
School Road ☎ (01945) 430319

Norfolk

5.30 (5 Fri, 4 Sat)–11
Draught Bass; guest beers Ⓗ
A rarity: a re-opened, well-renovated Fenland local, small, cosy and welcoming, with an open fire in the brick hearth. Free nibbles on Sun; basket meals eves.
🏠 ❀ & ♠ P

Middleton

Gate Inn
Hill Road, Fair Green (N of A47) ☎ (01553) 840518
12–3, 7 (5 Fri)–11
Draught Bass; Whitbread Boddingtons Bitter Ⓗ
Small, but recently extended village pub, offering good food in pleasant surroundings, enhanced by award-winning floral displays. 🏠 ❀ ◑ ♣

Morley St Botolph

Buck
Deopham Road (signed off A11) ☎ (01953) 604483
12–3, 6–11; 12–11 Fri & Sat
Whitbread Boddingtons Bitter, Flowers IPA; guest beer Ⓗ
Friendly, welcoming single-bar country pub. The dining area has a library of second hand books. No food Tue.
🏠 Q ❀ ◑ ♦ ♠ P

Mundesley

Royal Hotel
30 Paston Road (B1159, coast road) ☎ (01263) 720096
11–3, 6–11
Adnams Bitter; Greene King IPA, Abbot; guest beer Ⓗ
Very old, historic inn of great character. It is said that Lord Nelson stayed here as a boy. The oak-panelled bar is packed with Nelson memorabilia.
🏠 Q ⛺ ❀ 🏠 ◑ ♦ ♠ P

Mundford

Crown
Crown Street (village green) ☎ (01842) 878233
11–11
Iceni Boadicea Chariot; Marston's Pedigree; Samuel Smith OBB; Woodforde's Wherry, Nelson's Revenge; guest beer Ⓗ
Attractive, two-bar, 16th-century village inn, popular with walkers. A great supporter of local micro-breweries.
🏠 🏠 ◑ ⛽ ♠ P 🍺

New Buckenham

King's Head
Market Place ☎ (01953) 860487

11.30–2.30, 7–11
Adnams Bitter; guest beers Ⓗ
Simple, two-roomed pub on the village green, handy for the annual fair. Traditional home-cooked food (no meals Mon). 🏠 Q ❀ ◑ ♦ &

North Creake

Jolly Farmers
Burnham Road
☎ (01328) 738185
11.30–2.30 (3 Sat), 6.30–11
Greene King IPA Ⓗ**, Abbot; Ind Coope Burton Ale** Ⓖ**; guest beers** (summer)
Unpretentious pub at the centre of a pretty, unspoilt village, in easy reach of the North Norfolk coast. Good food and at least two beers on gravity; the beer range increases in summer. No eve meals winter Mon.
🏠 Q ◑ ♦ P 🍺

North Elmham

Railway
Station Road ☎ (01362) 668300
11–2, 7–11
Ansells Bitter; Tetley Bitter; guest beers Ⓗ
Single-bar, drinkers' pub with a genuine pre-1930s feel. Close to the Mid-Norfolk Railway Museum. 🏠 ❀ & ♠ ♣ P 🍺

Northwold

Crown Inn
High Street ☎ (01366) 727317
12–3, 6–11; 12–11 Sat
Greene King IPA, Abbot; guest beers Ⓗ
Well-restored example of a chalk lump inn with a good local atmosphere. Good food.
🏠 Q ❀ ◑ ♦ P 🍺

Norwich

Alexandra Tavern
16 Stafford Street (corner of Gladstone St)
☎ (01603) 627772
11–11
Chalk Hill Tap Bitter; Courage Best Bitter; Marston's Pedigree; Morland Old Speckled Hen Ⓗ
Jolly Victorian corner pub with a relaxed, friendly atmosphere.
❀ 🏠 & ⟳

Billy Bluelight
27 Hall Road ☎ (01603) 623768
11–2.30, 5.30–11; 11–11 Fri & Sat
Woodforde's Wherry, Gt Eastern Ⓗ**; guest beers** Ⓖ
Busy bar in a good drinking area, a recent addition to the Woodforde's estate, stocking the full range of Woodforde's beers (including house beers).
🏠 ◑ ♦

Champion
101 Chapelfield Road (near St Stephen's roundabout)
11–3, 7–11 (not Tue eve)
Adnams Bitter, Old, Extra; Wadworth 6X (summer) Ⓗ
Cosy, city-centre pub with three rooms off a central bar. Note the Lacons windows.
Q ♣

Coach & Horses
82 Thorpe Road
☎ (01603) 620704
11–11
Chalk Hill Tap Bitter, CHB, Dreadnought, Old Tackle; guest beers Ⓗ
Busy pub, home of the Chalk Hill Brewery. A drinkers' pub with entertainment Sat eve.
🏠 ❀ ◑ ⟳ ⟳ ⟳ P

Eaton Cottage
75 Mount Pleasant
☎ (01603) 453048
11–11
Adnams Bitter; Marston's Pedigree; John Smith's Bitter; guest beers Ⓗ
Truly traditional and unspoilt corner local, celebrating its centenary in 1995. It frequently has a beer from Scott's Brewery. ❀ 🏠 & ♣

Fat Cat
49 West End Street (corner of Nelson St) ☎ (01603) 624364
12 (10.30 Sat)–11
Adnams Bitter; Fuller's London Pride Ⓗ**; Hop Back Summer Lightning; Kelham Island Pale Rider** Ⓖ**; Woodforde's Nelson's Revenge** Ⓗ
Traditional Victorian pub serving a wide range of popular and unusual beers, many from the adjoining tap room. ❀ & ♣ ⟳

Horse & Dray
137 Ber Street
☎ (01603) 624741
11–11
Adnams Mild, Bitter, Old, Extra, Broadside; guest beers Ⓗ
Comfortable pub near the city centre shopping area; popular at lunchtimes. 🏠 ⛺ ◑ &

Mustard Pot
101 Thorpe Road
☎ (01603) 32393
12–3, 5.30–11; 12–11 Fri & Sat
Adnams Bitter, Old; Marston's Pedigree; guest beers Ⓗ
Comfortable pub, a mile from Thorpe Station. No food Sun eve. ❀ ◑ ♦ P

Plasterer's
43 Cowgate (off Magdalen St)
10.30–11
Adnams Mild, Bitter, Old,

231

Broadside; Ind Coope Burton Ale; Tetley Bitter Ⓗ
Dark, cosy pub, with many knick-knacks. Good quality lunches Mon–Sat. Q Ⓖ

Reindeer
10 Dereham Road (near inner ring road) ☎ (01603) 666821
11–11
Beer range varies Ⓗ
Cosmopolitan city pub where six guest beers are always available alongside the Reindeer's own brews (some of which are kept under gas). Very popular at weekends.
✿ Ⓖ ▶ & ♣ ⌂ ✄

Ribs of Beef
24 Wensum Street
☎ (01603) 619517
10.30–11
Adnams Bitter; Marston's Pedigree; Reepham Rapier; Whitbread Boddingtons Bitter, Flowers IPA; Woodforde's Wherry Ⓗ
Comfortable pub overlooking the River Wensum. The downstairs room is no-smoking (children welcome).
Q ⌕ Ⓖ ♣ ⌂ ✄

Rosary
95 Rosary Road (near the yacht station) ☎ (01603) 666287
11–11
Adnams Bitter; Draught Bass; Woodforde's Wherry; guest beers Ⓗ
Friendly drinkers' pub with a good selection of games. The house beer comes from Woodforde's.
Q ⌕ Ⓖ ⇌ (Thorpe) ♣ P

St Andrew's Tavern
4 St Andrew's Street
☎ (01603) 614858
11–11; closed Sun Oct–March
Beer range varies Ⓗ
Popular city venue which can be busy at lunchtimes. The cellar bar is open Fri and Sat lunchtimes. Adnams Beers, plus three guests, are usually sold. ✿ Ⓖ

Steam Packet
39 Crown Road (behind Anglia TV) ☎ (01603) 615533
11–11; closed Sun
Draught Bass; Fuller's London Pride; Woodforde's Wherry; guest beer Ⓗ
Triangular-shaped city-centre ale house; formerly the Market Tavern. ✿ Ⓖ ⇌ 🍽

Trafford Arms
61 Grove Road (behind Sainsbury's) ☎ (01603) 628466
11–11
Adnams Bitter; Tetley Bitter; Whitbread Boddingtons Bitter; guest beers Ⓗ
A 1950s exterior belies the comfortable interior of this popular pub. Beware the keg cider on a fake handpump.
Ⓖ ▶ & ♣ P

Vine
7 Dove Street
☎ (01603) 629258
10.30–11
Adnams Mild, Bitter, Extra, Broadside; guest beer Ⓗ
Probably the smallest pub in Norwich; close to the market place and Guildhall. Live folk music Wed. Ask for oversized glasses. 🍽

Old Buckenham

Ox & Plough
The Green ☎ (01953) 860004
12–2, 6.30–11; 11–11 Sat & summer
Adnams Bitter; Bass Worthington BB; guest beers Ⓗ
Friendly local, recently extended, overlooking the green in a pleasant village. No food Wed. ✿ ✿ Ⓖ ▶ & ♣ P

Old Hunstanton

Ancient Mariner
Golf Course Road (off A149)
☎ (01485) 534411
11–3, 6–11; 11–11 Sat & summer
Adnams Bitter, Broadside; Draught Bass; guest beer Ⓗ
Pub attached to the Le Strange Arms Hotel, featuring a nautical atmosphere, low beams and many different drinking areas. Two family rooms and views of the sea.
✿ ⌕ ✿ 🍽 Ⓖ ▶ & ♣ P ✄

Poringland

Dove
Bungay Road (B1332)
☎ (01508) 494312
11–3.30 (may close earlier), 6–11; 11–11 Sat
Greene King IPA; Tetley Bitter; Whitbread Boddingtons Bitter, Flowers Original Ⓗ
Roadside pub refurbished to reveal much of the original beams and brickwork; bare boards in one bar. The modern conservatory houses the restaurant (children welcome). The garden has some farmyard animals.
✿ ✿ Ⓖ ▶ ▲ ♣ P

Reedham

Railway
17 The Havaker
☎ (01493) 700340
12–3.30, 6.30–11; 12–11 Fri & Sat
Beer range varies Ⓗ/Ⓖ
Friendly Victorian free house overlooking the station: a keg-free zone. Plenty of games

available (old and new); summertime barbecues in the courtyard garden. Extensive range of malt whiskies; cider in summer. ✿ ✿ 🚃 Ⓖ ▶ ▲
⇌ ♣ ⌂ P ✄ 🍽

Reepham

King's Arms
Market Place ☎ (01603) 870345
11.30–3, 5.30–11; 11–11 Sat
Adnams Bitter, Broadside; Draught Bass; Fuller's London Pride; Woodforde's Wherry; guest beer Ⓗ
Restored old coaching inn with lots of wooden beams and red brick, plus three large fireplaces. A single bar links the family room and public bar; steps down to the lounge and restaurant.
✿ Q ⌕ ✿ Ⓖ ▶ ♣

Ringstead

Gin Trap
High Street ☎ (01485) 525264
11.30–2.30, 7 (6 summer)–11
Adnams Bitter; Draught Bass; Greene King Abbot; Woodforde's Norfolk Nog Ⓗ
Village pub with a split-level bar, a small restaurant and a large garden. Good food, regular music and a fine display of animal traps. The house beer is from Woodforde's.
✿ ✿ Ⓖ ▶ ♣ P 🍽

Rushall

Half Moon
☎ (01379) 740793
11–3, 6–11
Adnams Bitter; guest beers (summer) Ⓗ
16th-century, former coaching inn, recently modernised, adding a conservatory dining extension (food all day Sun). The house beer comes from Woodforde's.
✿ ✿ 🍽 Ⓖ ▶ ▲

Saham Toney

Bell
Bell Lane ☎ (01953) 884934
11.30–3, 6–11 (12–2.30, 7–11 winter)
Beer range varies Ⓗ
Pub recently restored to its original (1798) state with exposed brickwork and wooden floors. Good quality, home-made food. The hub of village life, catering for all.
✿ ⌕ ✿ Ⓖ ▶ ♣ P

Salhouse

Bell
3 Lower Street
☎ (01603) 721141
11–3, 7 (6 summer)–11; 11–11 Sat

Morland Old Speckled Hen;
Webster's Yorkshire Bitter;
Whitbread Flowers IPA Ⓗ
Two-bar village local retaining
some original features. Beware
the keg cider on a fake handpump. 🏮 Q 🕯 ◖ ▶ ⊟ ♣ P

Sedgeford

King William IV

Heacham Road
☎ (01485) 71765
11–3, 6.30–11
Draught Bass; Thwaites Best
Mild; guest beers Ⓗ
Outstanding village local close
to the Peddars Way footpath.
Interesting guest beers; regular
entertainment. Popular for
good value food.
🕯 ◖ ▶ ⊟ ▲ ♣ P

Sheringham

Windham Arms

15–17 Wyndham Street
☎ (01263) 822609
11–11
Draught Bass; John Smith's
Bitter; Woodforde's Mardler's
Mild, Wherry, Nelson's
Revenge, Norfolk Nog
Brick and flint, two-bar pub,
popular with locals and
visitors for its good range of
beers and extensive bar menu.
The dining area is off the
lounge bar. Large outdoor
drinking area.
🏮 Q 🕯 ◖ ▶ ⊟ ▲ ⇌ ♣ P

Smallburgh

Crown

On A149 ☎ (01692) 536314
12–3 (4 Sat), 5.30 (7 Sat)–11 (closed
Sun eve in winter)
Greene King IPA, Abbot;
Tetley Bitter; Tolly Cobbold
Mild; guest beer Ⓗ
Comfortable, two-bar pub and
restaurant in a 15th-century
thatched and beamed village
building. The games room
opens onto a lovely garden.
🏮 🕯 ⋈ ◖ ▶ ♣ P

South Creake

Ostrich Inn

Fakenham Road
☎ (01328) 823320
12–2.30, 6.30–11
Woodforde's Wherry Ⓗ
Pub with a large, single bar
featuring a pool table at one
end and a low ceiling with
exposed beams, divided into
areas by high-backed seating.
🏮 🕯 ◖ ▶ P

Southery

Jolly Farmers

60 Feltwell Road
☎ (01366) 377327
11–2.30, 6–11

Adnams Bitter; Greene King
IPA, Abbot; guest beers Ⓗ
Well-run, friendly 1960s pub,
worth driving the infamous
road from Feltwell to get here!
Popular for good value food
(no-smoking dining area).
◖ ▶ P

Spooner Row

Three Boars

Bunwell Road
☎ (01953) 605851
11.30–2.30, 5.30–11
Tetley Bitter; Whitbread
Flowers Original Ⓗ
Excellent example of a turn-of-
the-century pub. The very
large garden has animals to
entertain children. 🏮 Q 🕯
◖ ▶ ⊟ ▲ ⇌ (limited service)
♣ P

Stibbard

Ordnance Arms

Guist Bottom (A1067)
☎ (01328) 829471
11–3, 5.30–11
Greene King IPA; guest
beers Ⓗ
Traditional old pub with an
open fire in the front bar, plus
two more drinking areas.
Popular with locals, it has a
comfortable, friendly
atmosphere. A Thai restaurant
at the rear is open Tue–Sat
eves. 🏮 Q 🐴 🕯 ▶ P

Stiffkey

Red Lion

44 Wells Road
☎ (01328) 830552
11.30 (11 summer)–2.30, 6.45 (6
summer)–11
Greene King IPA, Abbot Ⓗ;
Woodforde's Wherry; guest
beers Ⓖ / Ⓗ
Old-fashioned pub, re-opened
in 1990, with open fires and a
restaurant (providing
excellent, home-cooked food).
The unspoilt village is in an
area popular with walkers.
🏮 Q 🐴 🕯 ◖ ▶ ▲ ♣ P

Stowbridge

Heron

Station Road (off A10)
☎ (01336) 384147
11–3, 7–11
Adnams Bitter; Draught Bass;
Greene King IPA, Abbot;
guest beers Ⓗ
Friendly pub by the Ouse,
with two cosy bars and a
wealth of bric-a-brac.
🏮 Q 🐴 🕯 ⋈ ◖ ▶ ♣ P

Strumpshaw

Shoulder of Mutton

Norwich Road
☎ (01603) 712274

11–11
Adnams Bitter, Old, Extra;
Ridleys IPA; guest beer
(summer) Ⓗ
Friendly, unpretentious,
one-bar village pub with an
eating area and plenty of space
for outdoor drinking
(barbecues in summer). No
food Sun eve. 🏮 🕯 ◖ ▶ ♣ P

Swanton Abbott

Jolly Farmers

Aylsham Road
☎ (01692) 538542
11–11
Greene King IPA, Rayments
Special, Abbot; guest beers Ⓗ
400-year-old pub which retains
many of its original
characteristics. A good,
friendly local, it often features
unusual guest beers.
Q 🐴 🕯 ◖ ▶ ⅙ ♣ P ⊬

Swanton Morley

Darbys

112 Elsing Road
☎ (01362) 637647
11–2.30, 6 (7 Sat)–11
Adnams Bitter, Broadside;
Woodforde's Mardler's Mild,
Wherry; guest beers Ⓗ
Single-bar pub, with a dining
area converted from two
cottages but retaining original
features: beams, fireplace and
a range. Large adventure play
area. 🏮 🐴 🕯 ◖ ▶ ▲ P 🍴

Papermakers

Town Street ☎ (01362) 637785
11–3.30, 7–11
Greene King Abbot; guest
beers Ⓗ
Single-bar local, with a real
fire at each end, opposite the
village church and the bowling
green. Children welcome. No
food Sun eve.
🏮 🕯 ◖ ▶ ⅙ ▲ ♣ ⌕ P

Thetford

Albion

93–95 Castle Street
☎ (01842) 752796
11–2.30, 6–11; 11–11 Fri & summer;
12–2, 7–10.30 Sun
Greene King IPA, Abbot Ⓗ
With the present landlord
chalking up more than 25
years' service, this small,
flint-faced local remains
pleasantly unspoilt and
generally quiet. Seasonal
specials from Greene King
sold. Q 🕯 ♣ P

Thompson

Chequers Inn

Griston Road (from Thetford,
left off A1075 at Griston)
OS923969 ☎ (01953) 483360

11–3, 6–11
**Adnams Bitter; Burton Bridge
Bitter; Eldridge Pope Royal
Oak; Tetley Bitter; guest
beers** H
Friendly, 16th-century
thatched pub, originally three
cottages, serving a good choice
of ales and excellent food. Low
oak-beamed ceilings, quarry
tiles and horse brasses give
plenty of character. A
ramblers' favourite.
Q ❧ ❀ ◑ ▯ ⅃ ⌂ P

Thornham

Chequers Inn
High Street
☎ (01485) 512229
12–2.30, 7–11 (11–3, 6–11 summer)
**Adnams Bitter; Greene King
IPA; Marston's Pedigree;
guest beer** H
Friendly, 18th-century inn on
the main coast road.
🚶 Q ❧ ❀ ⛴ ◑ ▯ ▲ ♣ P

Thorpe St Andrew

Gordon
88 Gordon Avenue (at
Heartsease roundabout, take
Harvey Lane then 1st left)
☎ (01603) 34658
11–2.30, 7–11
**Ind Coope Burton Ale; Tetley
Bitter; Whitbread
Boddingtons Bitter** H
Large, friendly, neo-Tudor
suburban building dating from
1934. Q ❀ ♣ P

Walcott

Lighthouse
Coast Road (B1159)
☎ (01692) 650371
11–3, 6.30–11; 11–11 Sat
**Adnams Bitter; Tetley Bitter;
Wadworth 6X; guest beer** H
Large, friendly pub and
restaurant, very popular with
locals and visitors. Open for
food all day Sun.
🚶 ❧ ❀ ◑ ▯ ▲ ♣ P

Walpole Cross Keys

Woolpack Inn
Sutton Road ☎ (01553) 828327
12–3, 7–11
**Adnams Bitter, Broadside;
guest beer** H
On the old A17; a pleasant
country inn with picturesque
gardens in summer. No eve
food Mon/Tue.
🚶 Q ❧ ❀ ◑ ▯ P

Walsingham

Bull
Common Place, Shirehall Plain
☎ (01328) 820333

11–3, 6–11 (11–11 Sat in summer)
**Ind Coope Burton Ale; Tolly
Cobbold Original; Whitbread
Boddingtons Bitter; guest
beers** H
15th-century inn, with one
wall originally part of a nearby
priory. The lounge contains
original beams, which are still
charred after a fire. Note the
400 priests' calling cards. Eve
meals in summer.
🚶 Q ❀ ⛴ ◑ ▯

Warham

Three Horseshoes
69 The Street
☎ (01328) 710547
11–2.30 (3 summer), 6–11
Greene King IPA H**, Abbot** G**;
Woodforde's Mardler's
Mild** H**, Wherry** G**; guest
beers** (summer)
Old village pub with basic
decor and some unusual
artefacts, including a 1921
electric pianola. Excellent,
home-cooked food (local
produce). 🚶 Q ❧ ❀ ⛴ ◑ ▯
▲ ♣ P ⅟

Weasenham All Saints

Ostrich
On A1065 ☎ (01388) 838221
11–2.30 (3 Sat & summer), 7–11
Adnams Bitter; guest beer
(occasional) H
Real pub with a fire and a
welcome to match; totally
unspoilt. 🚶 Q ❀ ▲ ♣ P

Wells-next-the-Sea

Crown Hotel
The Buttlands
☎ (01328) 710209
11–2.30, 6–11
**Adnams Bitter; Marston's
Pedigree; S&N Theakston
Old Peculier** H
Comfortable hotel bar. A large
restaurant serves à la carte
meals; children are catered for
in a south-facing sun lounge.
Imposing Georgian facade.
🚶 ❧ ❀ ⛴ ◑ ▯

West Rudham

Duke's Head
Lynn Road ☎ (01485) 528540
11–3, 6.30–11; 12–2.30, 7–10.30 Sun
**Adnams Bitter; Woodforde's
Wherry; guest beer** H
Roadside pub offering good
food and a library of old
cricket books.
🚶 Q ❀ ◑ ▯ ⅃ ⌂ ♣ P

Wighton

Sandpiper
High Street ☎ (01328) 820752

11–2.30, 6–11 (11–11 summer)
**Adnams Broadside; Elgood's
Cambridge Bitter** (summer)**;
Woodforde's Broadsman**
(summer)**; guest beers**
(summer) H
Pub where a central fireplace,
with a brick chimney,
separates the bar from the
family room. The beer range
includes a house bitter.
🚶 Q ❧ ❀ ⛴ ◑ ▯ ▲ ♣ P

Wimbotsham

Chequers
7 Church Road
☎ (01366) 387704
11.45–3, 6.30–11; 11.45–11 Sat
**Greene King XX Mild, IPA,
Abbot** H
Lively local overlooking the
village green.
Q ❀ ◑ ▯ ♣ P

Winterton-on-Sea

Fisherman's Return
The Lane
☎ (01493) 393305
11–2.30, 7 (6 summer)–11
(11–11 summer Sat)
**Adnams Bitter; Draught
Bass; Elgood's Cambridge
Bitter; M&B Highgate Dark;
John Smith's Bitter; guest
beers** H
Popular, two-bar local near the
beach. The lounge bar has a
cosy feel with its beams and
fishing photos. Family room
open in summer. Beware the
keg cider on a fake
handpump.
🚶 Q ❧ ❀ ⛴ ◑ ▯ ⅃ ♣ P

Woodbastwick

Fur & Feather
Slab Lane
☎ (01603) 720003
11–2.30, 6–11
**Woodforde's Mardler's
Mild, Broadsman, Wherry,
Nelson's Revenge, Norfolk
Nog** G
Pub converted from two
cottages, next door to
Woodforde's Brewery. Food-
oriented; tables may have to
be booked.
Q ❀ ◑ ▯ ⌂ P ⅟ ▤

Wymondham

Feathers
Town Green
☎ (01953) 605675
11–2.30, 7 (6 Fri)–11
**Adnams Bitter; Greene King
Abbot; Marston's Pedigree;
guest beers** H
Large, single-room bar,
comfortably furnished: a
popular local.
Q ❀ ◑ ▯ ♣ ⌂ P

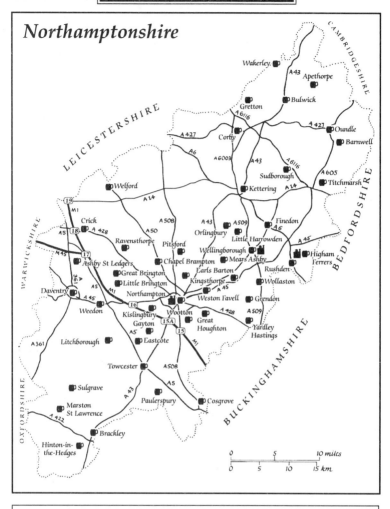

Northamptonshire

(Map showing locations including Wakerley, Apethorpe, Bulwick, Gretton, Corby, Oundle, Barnwell, Sudborough, Titchmarsh, Kettering, Welford, Crick, Ravensthorpe, Pitsford, Orlingbury, Little Harrowden, Finedon, Wellingborough, Mears Ashby, Higham Ferrers, Ashby St Ledgers, Chapel Brampton, Great Brington, Earls Barton, Rushden, Wollaston, Little Brington, Kingsthorpe, Daventry, Northampton, Weston Favell, Grendon, Weedon, Kislingbury, Wootton, Gayton, Great Houghton, Yardley Hastings, Eastcote, Litchborough, Towcester, Sulgrave, Paulerspury, Cosgrove, Marston St Lawrence, Brackley, Hinton-in-the-Hedges, surrounded by Leicestershire, Cambridgeshire, Bedfordshire, Buckinghamshire, Oxfordshire, Warwickshire)

 Cannon, *Wellingborough;* **Frog Island**, *Northampton;* **Nene Valley**, *Higham Ferrers*

Apethorpe

King's Head
King's Cliffe Road
☎ (01780) 470627
11–2.30, 6–11
Fuller's London Pride; Marston's Bitter; Wadworth 6X; guest beer (occasional) ⊞
Attractive, stone country pub in an historic village, originally built for estate workers. The public bar has been decorated by customers with bar towels and football shirts from around the world. Plush lounge; restaurant with an extensive menu.
🏚 ❀ ◑ ▮ ⊞ ♣ P

Ashby St Ledgers

Old Coach House Inn
Main Street (off A361)
☎ (01788) 890349
12–2.30, 6–11; 12–11 Sat; 12–2.30, 7–10.30 Sun
Everards Old Original; Whitbread Boddingtons Bitter, Flowers Original; guest beers ⊞
Classic country pub which offers real fires and wood panels for the winter and a large garden for the summer. It now has a house beer, St Ledger Special. Award-winning food and up to four

guest beers. Beer festivals in March and Oct.
🏚 ❀ 🚲 ◑ ▮ ⊞ & ⌂ P ⊟

Barnwell

Montagu Arms
☎ (01832) 273726
11–3, 7–11 (11–11 summer Sat)
Courage Directors; Hook Norton Old Hooky; Ruddles County; John Smith's Bitter; guest beer ⊞
Reputedly haunted, 16th-century, stone-built inn: two bars with low, beamed ceilings. The house beer is brewed by Tolly Cobbold. Good food menu (not served Mon eve). Caravan and

235

camping area.
📷 Q ⊛ 🚐 ◁ ▷ 👤 ♿ ♣ P ⊟

Brackley

Greyhound Inn
101 High Street
☎ (01280) 703331
12–2.30, 7–11
**Ruddles Best Bitter; Tetley
Bitter; guest beers** Ⓗ
Pub with an L-shaped bar,
plus a snug room, games room
and a restaurant where
Mexican dishes are a
speciality. Forty malt whiskies.
Family room and real cider in
summer. 📷 ♨ ◁ ▷ ⌚

Red Lion
11 Market Place
☎ (01280) 702228
11–11
**Wells Eagle, Bombardier,
Fargo** Ⓗ
16th-century, stone-built pub.
The public bar has a pool
table, the lounge bar an
inglenook. Regular music
events in the barn bar in the
garden. 📷 Q ⊛ 🚐 ◁ ▷ ♣

Bulwick

Queen's Head
Main Street ☎ (01780) 450272
11–3, 6–11
**Bateman XXXB; Greene King
Abbot; guest beers** Ⓗ
Built in 1675 and named after
the wife of Charles II; a quiet,
cosy, idyllic country pub in a
pretty village. Food is always
available in the bar and
restaurant. Note the collection
of international bank notes.
📷 ⊛ ◁ ▷ ♣ P

Chapel Brampton

Brampton Halt
Brampton Halt, Pitsford Road
(between A508 & A50)
☎ (01604) 842676
11–3, 5–11
**Adnams Bitter, Broadside;
Everards Tiger, Old
Original** Ⓗ
Old station master's house,
now an unusual and attractive
pub: a single cosy room with
an L-shaped bar, large gardens
and lawns. Northampton and
Lamport Preservation Railway
is open to visitors Sun and
holidays. Q ⊛ ◁ ▷ P

Corby

Knight's Lodge
Tower Hill Road
☎ (01536) 742602
12–3 (4 Fri & Sat), 6 (6.30 Sat)–11
**Everards Beacon, Tiger, Old
Original; guest beer** Ⓗ
Early 17th-century pub on the
site of a 12th-century knights'

lodgings, in what was a
clearing in the forest. Now
wholly surrounded by modern
housing, it is an oasis in an
ex-steel town. Eight ghosts;
graffiti dated 1860 features on
a staircase window. Upstairs
restaurant (no food Sun eve).
📷 ⊛ ◁ ▷ P

Cosgrove

Navigation Inn
Thrupp Wharf (signed from
A508 N of village)
☎ (01908) 543156
11–3.30, 6.30–11
**Courage Best Bitter; Hook
Norton Best Bitter; Morland
Old Speckled Hen; guest
beers** Ⓗ
Stone pub set in attractive
countryside by the Grand
Union Canal. A spacious
balcony offers views of boats
and summer sunsets. A
restaurant, boasting two
pianos, offers excellent food.
📷 ⊛ ◁ ▷ ♣ P

Crick

Royal Oak
22 Church Street
☎ (01788) 822340
7 (12 Sat)–11
**Marston's Bitter, Pedigree;
guest beer** Ⓗ
Unusual, three-roomed pub
hosting monthly folk music in
winter and serving varied
guest beers all year.
📷 Q ⊛ ♣

Daventry

Coach & Horses
Warwick Street
☎ (01327) 76692
11–2.30, 5 (4.30 Fri)–11; 12–3, 7–11 Sat
**Ind Coope Burton Ale;
Marston's Pedigree; Tetley
Bitter; guest beers** Ⓗ
Open fires, boarded floors and
stone walls give a warm feel to
this town-centre pub. The
stables across the coaching
yard host a jazz night alternate
Thus. Fortnightly changing
guest beers. No food Sun.
📷 Q ⊛ ◁ ♣

Try also: Dun Cow, Brook St
(Carlsberg-Tetley)

Earls Barton

Stag's Head
25 High Street
☎ (01604) 810520
11–3 (4 Sat), 6–11; 12.30–3, 7–10.30
Sun
**Home Bitter; S&N Theakston
Best Bitter, XB, Old Peculier;
guest beer** Ⓗ
Grade II-listed, olde-worlde
village pub. Its central beam is
reputed to be a ship's timber,

possibly floated up the River
Nene. No meals Sun.
📷 Q ⊛ ◁ ♣ P

Eastcote

Eastcote Arms
6 Gayton Road
☎ (01327) 830731
12–2.30 (3 Sat; not Mon), 6–11
**Draught Bass; Fuller's
London Pride; Jennings
Bitter; Samuel Smith OBB,
guest beer** Ⓗ
Lively, unspoilt country local
almost lost through building
development. Now it is back
as vibrant as ever. A small,
no-smoking dining room
through the snug serves
home-cooked food (eve meals
Thu–Sat). Garden for families.
📷 Q ⊛ ◁ ▷ P

Finedon

Bell
Bell Hill ☎ (01933) 680332
11.30–2.30, 5.30 (6 Sat)–11
**Ruddles Best Bitter, County;
Vaux Samson; Wards Best
Bitter; guest beers** Ⓗ
The oldest pub in Northants
(AD 1042), and reputedly the
third oldest in the country, this
is an historian's dream: local
memorabilia features in many
of the stone rooms. A warm
welcome is guaranteed.
📷 Q ⊛ ◁ ▷ ♣ P

Gayton

Eykyn Arms
20 High Street
☎ (01604) 858361
12–2, 7 (5.30 summer)–11
**S&N Theakston XB; Wells
Eagle, Fargo; guest beers** Ⓗ
Unspoilt, friendly local
fielding active skittles and
darts teams. The bar has a key
ring collection and the quiet
lounge is decorated with ships
and planes. A flower-covered
patio leads to a pool room at
the rear. A genuine free house.
📷 Q ⌚ ⊛ ◁ ▷ ⊞ ♣ P

Great Brington

Fox & Hounds
Althorpe Coaching Inn (off
A428) ☎ (01604) 770651
11.30–3, 5.30–11; 11–11 Sat
**S&N Theakston Best Bitter,
XB, Old Peculier; guest
beers** Ⓗ
350-year-old coaching inn with
flagstone floors, original
beams and some wood
panelling. The olde-worlde
interior is split into three areas
of character. Log fires create a
welcoming atmosphere. Six
guest beers (pricey though).
📷 ⊛ ◁ ▷ P

Great Houghton

Old Cherry Tree
Cherry Tree Lane (turn by White Hart) ☎ (01604) 761399
12–2.30, 6 (7.30 Sat)–11; 12–2.30, 7–10.30 Sun
Wells Eagle, Bombardier, Fargo H
Listed pub hidden down a dead-end lane, featuring exposed stonework, low ceilings, cosy inglenooks and a real fire in the bar. Popular for lunches with local businessmen. No lunches Sat or Sun. ♨ Q ❀ ◑ ❑ ♣ P

Grendon

Half Moon
42 Main Road
12–2.30 (3.30 Sat), 6 (6.30 Sat)–11
Wells Eagle, Fargo; guest beer H
Thatched, friendly village local with a warm atmosphere and lots of original beams and brass. Games are kept to one end of the large bar, plus a small adjoining area for darts. No meals Sun eve.
♨ ❀ ◑ ◗ & ♣ P

Gretton

Talbot
33 High Street
☎ (01536) 771609
11.30–2.30, 7–11
Everards Beacon, Tiger; guest beer H
Good, honest village local in what was a 17th-century farmhouse. English country wines sold. Strong pub teams, including for Northants skittles, fielded. Guest beers tend to be strong.
♨ ❀ ⊨ ◑ & ♠ ♣ P

Higham Ferrers

Green Dragon Hotel
4 College Street
☎ (01933) 312088
11–11
Shepherd Neame Spitfire; Tetley Bitter; guest beers H
17th-century coaching inn, a very popular drinking and eating house, offering excellent value food and a good range of ales. The large gardens have a children's adventure playground. Two beer festivals a year.
♨ Q ❄ ❀ ⊨ ◑ ◗ & P

Hinton-in-the-Hedges

Crewe Arms
Off A43 ☎ (01280) 703314
12–2.30, 7 (6.30 Fri & Sat)–11

Hook Norton Best Bitter; Marston's Pedigree; Morland Old Speckled Hen; guest beers H
Hidden away in a small village, this old, stone pub has three different bars to cater for various tastes, plus two gardens and an à la carte restaurant. Good selection of country wines.
♨ Q ◑ ◗ ♣ P

Kettering

Three Cocks
Lower Street ☎ (01536) 512569
10.30–3, 5–11
Banks's Mild; Marston's Bitter, Pedigree H
19th-century pub with an attractive painted frontage, near the town centre. Marston's Head Brewer's Choice is also available. ◑ ♣

Try also: Old Market Inn, Market Place (S&N); **Talbot**, Meadow Rd (Marston's)

Kingsthorpe

Queen Adelaide
50 Manor Road
☎ (01604) 714524
11–2.30 (3 Sat), 5.30–11
Banks's Bitter; Morland Old Speckled Hen; Wadworth 6X; Webster's Yorkshire Bitter H
Busy local in old Kingsthorpe village, a Grade II-listed building dating back to 1640. The public bar retains its original ceiling, panelling and old photographs of Kingsthorpe. Northants skittles room. Home-cooked lunches Mon–Sat.
Q ❀ ◑ ❑ ♣ ⊟

Kislingbury

Sun Inn
6 Mill Road (off A45, 2nd right) ☎ (01604) 830594
11.30–3, 5.30–11
Beer range varies H
400-year-old, well-preserved village pub boasting an unusual collection of Toby jugs. This highly attractive inn hosts an outdoor beer festival annually. The house beer (Sun Ale) is Jennings Bitter.
❀ & ♣ P

Litchborough

Red Lion
4 Banbury Road
☎ (01327) 830250
11.30–2.30 (not Mon), 6.30–11
Banks's Bitter Ⓔ; **Marston's Pedigree** H
Impressive ironstone local: a cosy bar with a large inglenook and two adjoining

rooms (a pool table in one and Northants skittles in the other). Always a warm welcome; good value food (Tue–Sat). Good range of English country wines. Families welcome.
♨ Q ❀ ◑ ◗ ❑ ♣ P ⊟

Little Brington

Saracen's Head
High Street ☎ (01604) 770640
11–3, 5.30–11; 11–11 Sat
Fuller's London Pride; Morland Old Speckled Hen; Wadworth 6X; Whitbread Flowers Original; guest beers H
300-year-old village pub with a cosy log fire, recently refurbished to enhance its character. It hosts games eves and offers special rates for pensioners' meals Wed lunch in the dining area.
♨ ❄ ❀ ◑ ◗ & ♣ P

Little Harrowden

Lamb
Orlingbury Road
☎ (01604) 673300
11–3, 7–11
Adnams Broadside; Morland Old Speckled Hen; Wells Eagle, Bombardier, Fargo; guest beer H
Pleasant village local with oak beams in the lounge and a traditional bar with Northants skittles. Booking is recommended for the popular Sun lunches (wild boar a speciality). No food Sun eve. Live music.
♨ Q ❄ ❀ ◑ ❑ ♣ P

Marston St Lawrence

Marston Inn
1½ miles off B4525
☎ (01295) 711906
12–2 (not Mon), 7–11
Hook Norton Best Bitter, Old Hooky H, **Twelve Days; guest beers** G
Village local, with a single bar, catering mainly for drinkers, with at least one beer direct from the cask and, unusually for the area, one cider. The pub is known for its excellent home cooking. No food Mon or Sun eve.
♨ Q ❀ ◑ ◗ ⌂ P ✗

Mears Ashby

Griffin's Head
Wilby Lane ☎ (01604) 812945
11.30–2.30 (3 Sat), 5.30–11
Wadworth IPA, 6X; Wells Eagle; guest beers H
Characterful pub with a specialist skittles and darts

area in the back bar. The solid wooden bar serves a comfortable lounge and a restaurant. ♨ ✿ ◗ ▶ P

Northampton

Crown & Cushion
276 Wellingborough Road (A4500) ☎ (01604) 33937
11–11
Banks's Bitter; Ruddles Best Bitter; John Smith's Bitter Ⓗ
Extremely well-run pub, popular with carriers of hods and briefcases alike. The large bar has a central servery; the busy games area features a well-used jukebox. Well-kept garden with safe play equipment. ✿ ♣

Try also: **Victoria**, Poole St (Free)

Orlingbury

Queen's Arms
11 Isham Road ☎ (01933) 678258
11–2.30, 5.30–11
Fuller's London Pride; Marston's Pedigree; Morland Old Speckled Hen; S&N Theakston Best Bitter; guest beers Ⓗ
Recently refurbished rural pub, dating back to the 1750s. A real beer drinkers' local, it was Northants CAMRA *Pub of the Year* 1994. Over 300 different real ales stocked so far. No food weekends. ♨ Q ✿ ◗ P

Oundle

Black Horse
52 Benefield Road ☎ (01832) 272575
11.30–2.30, 6.30–11
Draught Bass; John Smith's Bitter; guest beer Ⓗ
Stone pub, restored in 1990: a large bar with a games area, a lounge serving popular food, and an attractive patio garden with a children's play area. The pub is easily spotted by the large, black wooden horse at the front.
♨ Q ✿ ◗ ▶ P ⊟

Paulerspury

Barley Mow
53 High Street ☎ (01327) 33260
12–3, 7–11
Everards Tiger; Marston's Pedigree; John Smith's Magnet; Webster's Yorkshire Bitter Ⓗ
Open-plan pub with an L-shaped bar, plus a restaurant in the old maltings at the rear. Sit in the large inglenook. The pub's ghost,

Rebecca, is said to appear occasionally. ♨ ✿ ◗ ▶ ♣ P

Pitsford

Griffin
25 High Street ☎ (01604) 880346
12–2.30, 6–11 (12–11 winter Sat)
S&N Theakston Best Bitter, XB, Old Peculier; guest beers Ⓗ
Listed, stone village pub with a warm welcome. The lounge is split into two cosy areas and there's a traditional front bar. The griffin was the heraldic emblem of the Earls of Strafford – Lords of the Manors of Boughton and Pitsford. Football, darts and golf groups meet regularly. Q ✿ ◗ ⊞ ♣ P

Ravensthorpe

Chequers
Church Lane ☎ (01604) 770379
11–3, 6–11; 11–11 Sat
Fuller's London Pride; Samuel Smith OBB; Thwaites Bitter; guest beers Ⓗ
One of the county's few free houses, set in rolling countryside and well worth finding. A beamed, single, L-shaped bar is adorned with bric-a-brac, creating a warm, cosy atmosphere. Excellent value food and beer. The family room is across the courtyard. Q ⊠ ✿ ◗ ▶ ♣ P

Rushden

Rushden Historical Transport Society
Station Approach (A6, N end of town, on one-way system) ☎ (01933) 318988
7.30–11; 12–2.30, 7.30–10.30 Sun
Fuller's London Pride; guest beers Ⓗ
Midland railway station building saved by locals after the 1962 branch line closure. The gas-lit bar is packed with transport memorabilia. Activities extend into a carriage parked at the platform edge. 50p daily membership. ♨ Q ✿ P ⊟

Unicorn
29 Grove Road ☎ (01933) 413457
12–3, 6–11; 11–11 Fri & Sat
Beer range varies Ⓗ
Re-opened in 1994, this pub has a happy, friendly family atmosphere and caters for the ale enthusiast with seven regularly changed guest beers. ♨ ⊠ ✿ ♣ ⊬

Try also: **Feathers**, High St (Wells)

Sudborough

Vane Arms
Main Street ☎ (01832) 733223
11.30–3 (not Mon), 5.30 (6 Sat)–11
Beer range varies Ⓗ
Outstanding free house of great character in a thatched village, with a small upstairs restaurant. It stocks nine real ales, 21 country wines and even draught Kriek and Frambozen. En suite accommodation (special weekend rates); no food Sun or Mon eves. Mexican dishes are a speciality.
♨ Q ✿ ⊨ ◗ ▶ ♿ ♣ ⌂ P

Sulgrave

Star
Manor Road (off B4525; follow Sulgrave Manor signs) ☎ (01295) 760389
11–2.30, 6–11
Hook Norton Best Bitter, Old Hooky, Twelve Days; guest beers Ⓗ
Popular village local with a big tourist trade, due to nearby Sulgrave Manor, the ancestral home of George Washington. The single bar has a large fireplace with a resident customer – George the skeleton. ♨ Q ✿ ⊨ ◗ ▶ P

Titchmarsh

Dog & Partridge
6 High Street ☎ (01832) 732546
12–2 (4.30 Sat), 6 (6.30 Sat)–11
Adnams Broadside; Morland Old Speckled Hen; Wells Eagle, Bombardier Ⓗ
18th-century pub in a peaceful village off the A605. One large bar incorporates quiet and games areas. A good, welcoming local.
♨ Q ✿ ♣ P ⊟

Try also: **Red Lion**, Clopton (Free)

Towcester

Plough
Market Square, Watling Street (A5) ☎ (01327) 50738
11–11
Adnams Broadside; Wells Eagle, Bombardier; guest beer Ⓗ
Pub fronting the small market square. A small bar at the front leads to a larger seating area at the rear. Take-away food available. ♨ ◗ ▶ P

Wakerley

Exeter Arms
Main Street ☎ (01572) 747817
12–2.30, 6–11
Bateman XB; Marston's Pedigree; guest beer Ⓗ

17th-century, stone pub; the comfortable lounge has a wood-burning stove. Annual firework display. No food Mon. 🏚 🏵 ᶜ ▸ ⊞ ▲ ♣ P

Weedon

Globe Hotel
High Street (A5/A45 jct)
☎ (01327) 40336
11–11
Marston's Bitter, Pedigree;
Webster's Yorkshire Bitter;
guest beers Ⓗ
Very professional establishment: while still maintaining a pub feel in the bar, much effort is made to ensure complete satisfaction in all areas. High quality food. Ideal for a weekend break or a quick drink while passing.
🏚 Q ⌕ 🏚 ᶜ ▸ ᵹ P

Try also: **Wheatsheaf**, High St (Banks's)

Welford

Shoulder of Mutton
12 High Street (A50)
☎ (01858) 575375
12–2.30, 7–11
Bass Worthington BB,
Draught Bass; guest beer Ⓗ
Welcoming, 17th-century local with a single bar divided by arches. The games room doubles as a family room when weather prevents use of the extensive play facilities in the garden. The good value menu caters for children's and vegetarian tastes (no meals Thu). 🏚 ⌕ 🏵 ᶜ ▸ ♣ P

Wellingborough

Cannon
Cannon Street
☎ (01933) 279629

11–11
Cannon Light Brigade, Pride,
Florrie Night-in-Ale, Fodder;
guest beers Ⓗ
Brew pub on the edge of the town centre; a popular local offering bar billiards, card games and lunchtime snacks.
🏚 🏵 ♣ P

Vivian Arms
153 Knox Road
(side street, between station and town centre)
☎ (01933) 223660
11–2.30 (3 Sat), 6 (7 Sat)–11
Hall & Woodhouse
Tanglefoot; Wells Eagle,
Fargo Ⓗ
A rare surviving Northamptonshire street-corner local; a calm wood-panelled bar, a cosy, cosmopolitan lounge and a large games room. Peace in two of the three bars and not a diner in sight!
🏚 🏵 🏚 ⇌ ♣ P

Weston Favell

Bold Dragoon
48 High Street
☎ (01604) 401221
11–3, 6–11; 11–11 Sat
Banks's Bitter; Wadworth 6X;
Whitbread Boddingtons
Bitter, Flowers IPA; guest
beers Ⓗ
Pub on the edge of Northampton, which retains its village atmosphere. The front bar has games and the rear lounge a central fire. Two constantly changing guest beers. 🏵 ♣ P

Wollaston

Boot
35 High Street

☎ (01604) 664270
11–2.30, 6–11
Draught Bass; Marston's
Pedigree; Tetley Bitter Ⓗ
Unspoilt local, a whitewashed, thatched, listed pub. Two front rooms act as the bar; the back rooms house Northants skittles. Well worth finding.
🏚 Q 🏵 🏚 ♣ P

Wootton

Wootton Workingmen's Club
23 High Street
☎ (01604) 761863
12–2 (2.30 Fri & Sat), 7–11; 12–2.30, 7–10.30 Sun
Draught Bass; Wells Eagle;
guest beers
East Midlands CAMRA *Club of the Year* 1993 and deservedly so, with one of the best selections of real ales in the county (four guests). The lounge area is more like a pub and the concert room offers live entertainment at weekends. CIU entry restrictions apply.
♣ P

Yardley Hastings

Red Lion
89 High Street (off Bedford Rd)
☎ (01604) 696210
11–2.30 (3 Sat), 6–11
Adnams Broadside; Wells
Eagle Ⓗ
Superb village pub with a welcoming atmosphere in its low-beamed lounge and its public bar with an adjoining Northants skittle room (formerly the gents' loo). A *Guide* entry for the past 12 years. Excellent food (not served Sun).
🏚 Q 🏵 🏚 ᵹ ♣ P

WHY JOIN CAMRA?

I do my bit. I drink real ale and never touch keg or lager. What do I gain from joining CAMRA?

Well, apart from supporting our researchers, organisers, lobbyists and active campaigners around the country, you can actually have a say in what CAMRA should or shouldn't be doing, on a national and local level. You can also help choose pubs for the *Good Beer Guide*, enjoy social outings like brewery trips and take advantage of big discounts on CAMRA products such as the *Good Beer Guide* and on entrance fees to CAMRA beer festivals. You also receive *What's Brewing*, the award-winning monthly newspaper (no mere newsletter), which provides up to the minute news about breweries, beers and all the ups and downs in the world of beer and pubs.

For just £12 a year (somewhere between six and a dozen pints, depending on where you live), it's a real bargain.

Northumberland

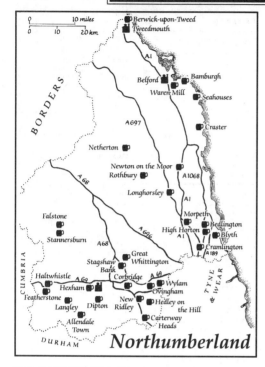

Northumberland

BORDERS

CUMBRIA

DURHAM

TYNE & WEAR

Berwick-upon-Tweed
Tweedmouth

A1

Belford
Bamburgh
Waren Mill
Seahouses

A697

Craster

Netherton

Newton on the Moor
Rothbury
A1068

Longhorsley

A1

Morpeth
Bedlington
High Horton
Blyth
A696
Cramlington
A189

Falstone

Stannersburn
A68

Stagshaw
Bank
Great
Whittington

Haltwhistle
A69
Corbridge
Wylam

Hexham
Ovingham

Featherstone
New
Hedley on
the Hill

Langley
Dipton
Ridley

Allendale
Carterway
Town
Heads

Border, *Tweedmouth;*
Hexhamshire, *Hexham;*
Longstone, *Belford*

Allendale Town

King's Head
Market Square
☎ (01434) 683681
11–11
**Butterknowle Bitter;
S&N Theakston Best
Bitter, XB, Old Peculier;
guest beers** Ⓗ
Welcoming pub in a
friendly town, high up
in the Pennines. A fine
selection of ales in
pleasant surroundings.
🏠 Q 🚪 ◖ ▶ P

Bamburgh

Victoria Hotel
Front Street ☎ (01668) 214431
11–11
Tetley Bitter; guest beers Ⓗ
An aristocrat amongst
pubs: excellent food and
accommodation in an
imposing hotel
frequented by a cross-
section of northern
Northumberland
society.
Q ♿ 🚪 ◖ ▶ ▲ ♣

Bedlington

Northumberland Arms
Front Street East
☎ (01670) 822754
11–3, 7–11; 11–11 Wed–Sat
Beer range varies Ⓗ
Long-established real ale
outlet in an old
Northumbrian market
town. Three ever-
changing beers in a
comfortable atmosphere.
Very busy at weekends.
◖ ♣

Try also: Grapes, Front St
(Bass)

Berwick-upon-Tweed

Auld Brewers Arms
119 Marygate
☎ (01289) 302641
11–11
Border Old Kiln Ale Ⓗ
Pleasant, olde-worlde pub
with its original bar fittings
still intact. Pleasant,
welcoming atmosphere.
🐚 ◖ 🚲

Free Trade
Castlegate ☎ (01289) 306498
12–2, 7–11 (may vary)
Vaux Lorimer's Best Scotch Ⓗ
Wonderfully preserved
Borders boozer serving
possibly the best pint of
Lorimer's Scotch in the
country. This Victorian pub
features a screen at the
entrance and basic furnishings.
Unpredictable opening hours.
Q 🚪 🚲

Blyth

Flying Horse
78 Waterloo Road
☎ (01670) 353314
11–11
**Ruddles County; Webster's
Yorkshire Bitter; guest
beers** Ⓗ
Small, comfortable pub, very
much a locals' pub, but offering
a warm welcome to all. ◖

Oddfellows Arms
91 Bridge Street
☎ (01670) 356535
11–3, 6–11; 11–11 Fri & Sat
Stones Best Bitter Ⓗ
Snug and cosy pub near the
river. A loyal band of regulars
contributes to the warm
welcome. 🏠

Top House
Marlowe Street
☎ (01670) 356731
11–11
**S&N Theakston Best Bitter,
Newcastle Exhibition,
Theakston XB** Ⓗ
Slightly out of the town centre,
but well worth seeking out,
this comfortable, cosy pub has
some interesting old gaming
machines. 🏠

Carterway Heads

Manor House Inn
Shotley Bridge (A68, 6 miles S
of Corbridge)
☎ (01207) 255268
12–3, 6–11
**Big Lamp Bitter;
Butterknowle Bitter; guest
beers** Ⓗ
A warm welcome awaits at
this charming country inn
which has splendid views over
the Derwent Valley. There is
usually a guest stout or porter
available, plus guest ciders,
and this pub is also noted for
its good, varied food.
🏠 Q 🚪 ◖ ▶ ⌂ P

Corbridge

Dyvells
Station Road ☎ (01434) 633566
7–11 (may vary in summer)
**Draught Bass; Stones Best
Bitter; guest beers** Ⓗ

An ideal base for exploring the Roman Wall, a pub with a warm welcome from both the landlord and his customers. Biddenden Cider is usually available.
🏚 Q ❀ 🍴 🚂 ♨

Wheatsheaf

St Helen's Street
☎ (01434) 632020
11–11
Wards Thorne Best Bitter; guest beers Ⓗ
Excellent country hotel and restaurant; warm and welcoming.
Q ❀ 🍴 ◖▶ ⊞ ♣ P

Cramlington

Blagdon Arms

Village Square
☎ (01670) 731162
12–11
Wards Best Bitter; guest beer Ⓗ
Much extended, village-centre pub with a small cosy bar and a large lounge divided into several areas.
❀ ◖ ⊞ 🚂

Brockwell Seam

Brockwell Centre, Northumbrian Road
☎ (01670) 732071
11–11
Bass Worthington BB, Draught Bass; guest beer Ⓗ
Newly-built pub, away from the town centre; the name reflects the area's mining history. Events and live entertainment most eves. The manager is qualified in sign language. No food Sun eve. ❀ ◖▶ ⊞ & ♣ P

Plough

Middle Farm Buildings
☎ (01670) 737633
11–3, 6–11; 11–11 Fri & Sat
S&N Theakston XB; guest beers Ⓗ
In the old village, a fine and sympathetic conversion of former farm buildings into a traditional pub catering for a wide cross-section of visitors. Architecturally interesting; always a good selection of guest beers.
❀ ◖ ⊞ 🚂 P

Craster

Jolly Fisherman

Haven Hill ☎ (01665) 576218
12–3, 6–11; 11–11 Sat
Vaux Lorimer's Best Scotch; Wards Best Bitter Ⓗ
Welcoming pub in a tiny village, famous for its seafood (try the crab sandwiches). Marvellous sea views.
◖▶ ♣ P

Dipton

Dipton Mill Inn

Dipton Mill Road (off B6306, 2 miles S of Hexham)
☎ (01434) 606577
12–2.30, 6–11
Hexhamshire Shire Bitter, Devil's Water, Whapweasel; guest beers Ⓗ
An excellent advertisement for Hexhamshire brewery; cosy and welcoming, with coal fires throughout. It is noted for its home-cooked food. The family room is basic.
🏚 Q 👃 ❀ ◖▶ A ♣ P ⊟

Falstone

Blackcock Inn

☎ (01434) 240200
11–3, 6–11; 11–11 Fri & Sat
Federation Buchanan's Best Bitter; Whitbread Boddingtons Bitter, Castle Eden Ale; guest beers Ⓗ
Historic pub near Kielder Water. Popular with water-sports enthusiasts and walkers, it is always friendly and cosy. Very good food.
🏚 Q 👃 🍴 ◖▶ & A ♣ ♨ P ⊟

Featherstone

Wallace Arms

☎ (01434) 321872
12 (4 Mon & Tue)–11
Hexhamshire Low Quarter Ale, Shire Bitter, Devil's Water, Whapweasel; S&N Newcastle Exhibition Ⓗ
Welcoming country inn, the second Northumberland pub to sell Hexhamshire beers. Music sessions Sun lunchtime.
🏚 Q ❀ P ⊟

Great Whittington

Queen's Head

☎ (01434) 672267
12–2, 6–11
Hambleton Bitter; guest beers Ⓗ
One of the county's oldest inns, dating back to the 15th century and set in lovely countryside close to Hadrian's Wall. A house beer, brewed by Hadrian Brewery, is available, along with changing guest beers and good quality food.
🏚 Q ◖▶ P

Haltwhistle

Grey Bull Hotel

Wapping ☎ (01434) 321991
11–11
John Smith's Bitter, Magnet; Stones Best Bitter; Webster's Yorkshire Bitter; guest beers Ⓗ

Basic town pub, popular with locals, but visitors are always made welcome. The front bar is always busy; the back bar, with wood panelling, is usually quieter. Quoits played.
🏚 Q 👃 ❀ 🍴 ◖▶ ⊞ & A 🚂 ♣ P

Spotted Cow

Castle Hill ☎ (01434) 320327
12–3, 6.30–11
Courage Directors; Webster's Yorkshire Bitter; Whitbread Boddingtons Bitter; guest beers Ⓗ
Traditional, low-ceilinged pub with its bar mounted on barrels. A couple of spotted cow jugs sit on the shelves alongside a large range of malt whiskies.
❀ 🍴 ◖▶ ⊞ A 🚂 ♣ P

Hedley on the Hill

Feathers Inn

☎ (01661) 843607
6–11; 12–3, 6–11 Sat
Jennings Cumberland Ale; Whitbread Boddingtons Bitter; guest beers Ⓗ
Friendly hilltop pub with an excellent atmosphere. Lunch and eve meals served Sat; closed Mon–Fri lunchtimes.
🏚 Q P

Hexham

Tap & Spile

Battle Hill ☎ (01434) 602039
11–11
Beer range varies Ⓗ
Busy, two-roomed, market town pub with a changing range of ales from far and wide. Popular with customers connected with agriculture and other trades at lunchtimes. Live music Mon eve. ◖ 🚂

Try also: Globe Inn, Battle Hill (S&N)

High Horton

Three Horseshoes

Hathery Lane
☎ (01670) 822410
11–11
Draught Bass; Ind Coope Burton Ale; Tetley Bitter; guest beers Ⓗ
Large, friendly, 18th-century coaching inn with six handpumps and a good selection of malt whiskies. Twice-yearly beer festivals. Children welcome in the large conservatory. No meals Sun eve. ❀ ◖▶ P

Langley

Carts Bog Inn

On A686 ☎ (01434) 684338

Northumberland

12–3 (not Mon, except bank hols), 7–11
Marston's Pedigree; S&N Theakston Best Bitter; guest beers ⑭
Isolated pub on the moor edge, built in 1730 on a site where brewing had taken place since 1521. Local musicians play on the second Thu of each month, and spontaneously on other summer eves. Quoits and camping in the grounds.
🏚 Q ⛺ ⑭ ▶ ▲ ♣ P

Longhorsley

Linden Pub
Linden Hall Hotel (in grounds of the hotel, on A697)
☎ (01670) 516611
11–3, 6–11
Beer range varies ⑭
Secluded country pub in an attractive converted granary. Summer barbecues are held in the courtyard; also giant chess. Children are always welcome.
⛺ ❀ ⑭ ♣ P

Morpeth

Joiners
6 Wansbeck Street
☎ (01670) 513540
11–11
Draught Bass; S&N Newcastle Exhibition, Theakston XB; guest beers ⑭
Large, two-roomed pub. A wheelchair ramp is available on request. ⑭ ≼

Tap & Spile
Manchester Street
☎ (01670) 513540
12–2.30, 4.30–11; 11–11 Fri & Sat
Beer range varies ⑭
Welcoming, two-roomed, town pub offering an excellent range of beers, plus Weston's Old Rosie cider. Music Sun lunchtime. Local CAMRA *Pub of the Year.* ⑭ 🍺 ♣ ◖

Netherton

Star Inn
On B634 ☎ (01669) 630238
12–1.30, 7–11 (may vary in winter)
Whitbread Castle Eden Ale Ⓖ
Remote, unspoilt, marvellous pub set in beautiful countryside, popular with walkers. Time has stood still here; the beer is served by gravity direct from the cellar. Note the disused cockfighting pit opposite. 🏚 Q ❀

New Ridley

Dr Syntax
☎ (01661) 842383
12–3, 6–11
Jennings Cumberland Ale; Morland Old Speckled Hen; S&N Theakston Best Bitter; Whitbread Castle Eden Ale; guest beers ⑭
This warm and welcoming inn stands in the heart of Northumberland countryside with fine views over the Tyne Valley. Outside drinking in front of the pub (no garden).
Q ❀ 🍺 ♣ P 🍴

Newton on the Moor

Cook & Barker
½ mile off A1 ☎ (01665) 575234
11–11
S&N Theakston Best Bitter; Whitbread Castle Eden Ale; guest beers ⑭
Friendly, large, multi-roomed pub and restaurant with a welcoming atmosphere. Displays of foreign bank notes abound.
🏚 Q ❀ 🍺 ⑭ ▶ P 🍴

Ovingham

Bridge End
West Road ☎ (01661) 832219
11–11
Taylor Landlord; Tetley Mild, Bitter; guest beers ⑭
Cosy, open-plan pub, converted from two stone, terraced cottages, preserving their original beams and fireplace. Lounge/restaurant at the rear. ❀ 🍺 ⑭ ▶ P

Rothbury

Turk's Head
High Street ☎ (01669) 20434
11–11
Wards Best Bitter ⑭
Basic, multi-roomed pub, popular with the locals.
🏚 ⑭ ▶ 🍺

Seahouses

Olde Ship Hotel
Main Street ☎ (01665) 720200
11–3, 6–11
Longstone Bitter; Morland Old Speckled Hen; S&N Theakston Best Bitter; guest beers ⑭

Cosy local bar full of maritime memorabilia, within easy reach of Seahouses harbour (boat trips to the Farne Islands). A quiet and comfortable haven in a growing resort. 🏚 Q ⑭ ▶ P

Stagshaw Bank

Fox & Hounds
On A68, 2 Miles N of Corbridge ☎ (01434) 633024
11–11
McEwan 80/-; S&N Theakston Best Bitter; guest beers ⑭
Old stone building offering a warm welcome. The large conservatory extension serves as a restaurant.
🏚 ❀ 🍺 ⑭ ▶ ♣ P

Stannersburn

Pheasant Inn
On minor road near Falstone, 1 mile from Kielder Water
☎ (01434) 240382
11–3, 6–11
Ind Coope Burton Ale; Tetley Bitter; guest beers ⑭
Originally a farm, this building is 400 years old, with stone walls and low beams. The bars feature many old farm implements and pictures of the valley, together with antique copper and brassware.
🏚 Q ❀ 🍺 ⑭ ▶ ▲ P 🍴

Waren Mill

Burnside
☎ (01668) 214544
12–3 (not winter weekdays), 7–11
Longstone Bitter; guest beers ⑭
Modern, open-plan pub with a thriving summertime trade from the adjacent campsite. Two miles from Longstone Brewery, this is effectively the brewery tap. Close to scenic Budle Bay. ⑭ ▶ ▲ P

Wylam

Boat House
Station Road ☎ (01661) 853431
12–3, 6–11; 12–11 Fri & Sat
Butterknowle Conciliation Ale; McEwan 80/-; S&N Theakston Best Bitter; Taylor Landlord; Younger No.3; guest beers ⑭
Two-roomed pub next to the station and Wylam Bridge. A warm welcome is assured. Biddenden Cider. 🏚 Q ❀
⑭ ▶ 🍺 ≼ ♣ ◖ P 🍴

CAMRA membership costs less than a pint a month and is terrific value. Join now!

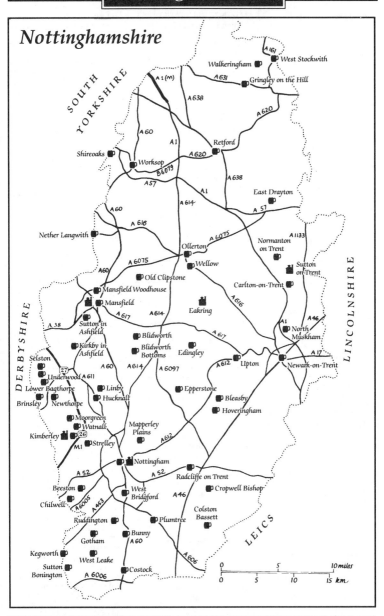

Nottinghamshire

Fellows, Morton & Clayton, Nottingham; *Hardys & Hansons*, Kimberley; *Mansfield*, Mansfield; *Maypole*, Eakring; *Springhead*, Sutton on Trent

---

Beeston

Commercial Inn
19 Wollaton Road
☎ (0115) 9254480
11–3, 5.30–11; 11–11 Fri & Sat

Hardys & Hansons Best Mild, Best Bitter E, Kimberley Classic H
Refurbished and extended, popular local, decorated with pictures of old Beeston. Skittle alley. Q ❀ ◗ ⊞ ♣ P

Victoria Hotel

Dovecote Lane
☎ (0115) 9254049
11–3, 5 (6 Sat)–11
Bateman XB; Courage Directors; Marston's Pedigree; Samuel Smith OBB;

Nottinghamshire

guest beers H
Since being taken over by the
Tynemill Pub Company, this
pub has improved beyond
belief. It now offers a wide
range of guest beers, real cider
and over 140 whiskies. Eve
meals finish at 8.
🏚 Q ✿ ◖▮ ➓ ♣ ↺ P ⊬

Bleasby

Wagon & Horses
Gypsy Lane ☎ (01636) 830283
11–3 (not Mon), 6–11
**Home Bitter; Marston's
Pedigree; S&N Theakston XB;
guest beers** H
200-year-old country pub,
originally a farmhouse; two
comfortable rooms plus a pool
area. Outside are a barbecue
site and playground. Eve
meals 6–8; no food Mon.
🏚 ✿ ◖▮ 🍴 ▲ P

Blidworth

Bird in Hand
Main Street ☎ (01623) 792356
11–3, 6–11; 11–11 Fri & Sat
**Mansfield Riding Bitter,
Bitter, Old Baily** H
Traditional, ex-agricultural
and mining village pub: a
large, comfortable bar with an
open fire. Panoramic views
over countryside. Reliable,
English home-cooked food
and some more adventurous
dishes (not served Sun eve).
🏚 ✿ ◖▮ ♣ P

Blidworth Bottoms

Fox & Hounds
Between A60 and A614
12–3, 6–11
**Hardy & Hansons Best Mild,
Best Bitter** H
Comfortable pub in a hamlet
one mile south of Blidworth.
Excellent reputation for
home-cooked English food;
renowned for Sun lunches,
including vegetarian.
🏚 Q 🍴 ✿ ◖▮ 🍴 ♣ P 🖿

Brinsley

Robin Hood
Hall Lane ☎ (01773) 713604
12–2 (3 summer), 7–11
**Hardys & Hansons Best Mild,
Best Bitter** H
Characterful pub in DH
Lawrence country; rumoured
to be haunted by a previous
licensee. Singers on Sat. Two
skittle alleys.
🏚 Q ✿ 🍴 ♣ P

Bunny

Rancliffe Arms
139 Loughborough Road
☎ (0115) 9844727
11.30–2.30 (not Mon), 6 (7 Mon)–11

**Mansfield Riding Mild,
Riding Bitter, Old Baily** H
Imposing, former 17th-century
coaching inn: two bars and a
restaurant. Piano sing-alongs
Sat nights. Beware: the car
park is on a bend. No food
Sun or Mon eves.
🏚 Q ✿ ◖▮ ▲ P

Carlton-on-Trent

Great Northern
Ossington Road (off A1)
☎ (01636) 821348
12–2.30, 5.30–11
**Mansfield Riding Bitter;
Springhead Bitter; guest
beers** H
Pub adjacent to the main East
Coast railway line and popular
with train spotters; the bar has
railway artefacts. The large
family room is stocked with
games. Play area outdoors.
🏚 🍴 ✿ ◖▮ & ♣ P 🖿 🖬

Chilwell

Cadland Inn
High Road ☎ (0115) 9251769
11–3, 6–11; 11–11 Thu–Sat
Draught Bass; guest beers
(weekend) H
Friendly, multi-roomed pub
with a horse racing theme,
popular with young and old.
No lunches Sun. Q ✿ ◖▮ P

Colston Bassett

Martins Arms
School Lane ☎ (01949) 81361
12–2.30 (3 summer), 6–11
**Draught Bass; Bateman XB,
XXXB; Marston's Bitter,
Pedigree; guest beers** H
Charming village free house,
full of character. Original, high
quality menu in both the bar
and restaurant (no food Sun or
Mon eves).
🏚 Q 🍴 ✿ ◖▮ ♣ P

Costock

Generous Briton
14 Main Street
11.30–2.30, 6.30–11; 12–2.30, 7–10.30
Sun
**Mansfield Riding Bitter,
Bitter, Old Baily** H
Friendly, two-roomed village
local. Games and conversation
in the bar. Food is traditional.
Flowered courtyard.
🏚 Q ◖▮ ♣ P

Cropwell Bishop

Wheatsheaf
11 Nottingham Road
☎ (0115) 9892247
12–3, 6–11; 11–11 Sat
**Mansfield Riding Mild,
Riding Bitter, Bitter, Old
Baily** H
Village local with a public bar

and a new U-shaped lounge.
Parts date back over 500 years
and are reputedly haunted.
Superb Chinese banquets in an
upstairs room for parties
(book). 🏚 🍴 ✿ ◖▮ 🍴 ♣ P

East Drayton

Bluebell
Low Street ☎ (01777) 248322
12–11
**Mansfield Riding Bitter,
Bitter, Old Baily; guest
beers** H
Friendly, 200-year-old pub
sympathetically decorated.
Good, home-cooked food.
Q 🍴 ✿ 🏚 ◖▮ ♣ P

Edingley

Old Reindeer
Main Street ☎ (01623) 882253
12–3, 6–11; 12–11 Sat
**Mansfield Riding Mild,
Riding Bitter, Bitter, Old
Baily** H
Delightful, family-run, 18th-
century, rural local with two
comfortable rooms; the tap
room houses a collection of
chamber pots. Barbecues in
summer. Mansfield's seasonal
beers. 🏚 ✿ ◖▮ 🍴 ▲ ♣ P

Epperstone

Cross Keys
Main Street ☎ (0115) 9663033
11.45–2.30 (not Mon), 6–11; 12–2.30,
7–10.30 Sun
**Hardys & Hansons Best Mild,
Best Bitter** E**, Kimberley
Classic** H
Splendid village pub in a rural
setting. Three rooms include a
simply-furnished bar and an
attractive lounge displaying
CAMRA accolades. Excellent
award-winning food (not
served Mon, or Sun eve).
🏚 Q 🍴 ✿ ◖▮ 🍴 ♣ P 🖬

Gotham

Sun Inn
The Square ☎ (0115) 9830484
12–3, 6–11
**Everards Mild, Beacon, Tiger,
Old Original; guest beer** H
Comfortable, friendly local.
Food is served in the lounge;
the bar is reserved for games
and conversation.
Q 🍴 ✿ ◖ 🍴 ♣

Gringley on the Hill

Blue Bell Inn
High Street ☎ (01777) 817406
6.30 (12 Sat)–11
**Draught Bass; Stones Best
Bitter; guest beers** H
Low-ceilinged, village pub.
Mind the step.
🏚 Q ✿ 🍴 ▲ ♣ 🖬

Nottinghamshire

Hoveringham

Reindeer Inn
Main Street ☎ (0115) 9663629
12–3 (not Mon), 5–10 (5.30–11 Sat & Mon)
Marston's Bitter, Pedigree; guest beers Ⓗ
Attractive country pub with a clear view of the cricket pitch. The bar is for drinkers during the eve with meals taken in the restaurant. No food Sun or Mon eves. ♨ ❀ ◐ ♣ P

Hucknall

Nabb Inn
Nabb Lane (near Hucknall Town FC) ☎ (0115) 9630297
11–2.30 (3 Fri & Sat), 6–11
Hardys & Hansons Best Mild, Best Bitter, Kimberley Classic Ⓗ
Located on the Watnall side of Hucknall, this popular pub caters for all ages. The large, comfortable lounge has a pool table in a secluded area. Sky TV. No meals Sun lunch; eve meals on request. ❀ ◐ ♣ P

Kegworth

Station Hotel
Station Road (towards Sutton Bonington) ☎ (01509) 672252
11.30–2.30, 6–11; 11.30–11 Sat
Draught Bass; M&B Mild; guest beers Ⓗ
Built in 1847 as a hotel for the now-closed station, a pub now owned by Enterprise Inns. Guest beers from national brewers. Pleasant, traditional decor; home-cooked food. The large garden has a fine view. Three rooms plus a restaurant. ♨ Q ❀ ♨ ◐ ◗ ♣ P

Kimberley

Nelson & Railway
Station Road ☎ (0115) 9382177
11–3, 5–11; 11–11 Thu–Sat
Hardys & Hansons Best Mild Ⓔ, **Best Bitter** Ⓗ/ Ⓔ, **Kimberley Classic** Ⓗ
Originally two separate inns; now a splendid, two-roomed, Victorian alehouse. Good value, home-cooked food (not served Sun eve).
❀ ♨ ◐ ◗ ♨ ♣ P

Kirkby in Ashfield

Countryman
Park Road ☎ (01623) 752314
12–3, 7–11
S&N Theakston Best Bitter, XB, Old Peculier; guest beers Ⓗ
18th-century inn with beamed alcoves. It was decorated by a wandering sculptor in the late

---

1970s; his work can be admired in the bar. Irish folk band Fri nights. ❀ ◐ ◗ ♿ P

Linby

Horse & Groom
Main Street ☎ (0115) 9632219
11.30–3, 6–11
Home Mild, Bitter; S&N Theakston XB Ⓗ
Charming village pub: three intimate lounge bars and a traditional, drinkers' bar with an authentic fireplace. Extensive garden and large children's play area. Eve meals Fri and Sat in summer till 8.30. ♨ Q ♣ ❀ ◐ ◗ ♨ ♣ P

Lower Bagthorpe

Dixie's Arms
School Road (off B600 at Underwood) ☎ (01773) 810505
12–3, 7–11
Home Mild, Bitter; guest beer Ⓗ
250-year-old country pub with a tap room, lounge and a snug. The guest beer changes twice a week. ♨ ♣ ❀ ◗ ▲ ♣ P

Mansfield

Bleak House Club
117 Sutton Road (25 yds from A38/Skegby Lane jct)
☎ (01623) 659850
11–3 (not Mon–Wed), 7–11
Draught Bass; Mansfield Bitter; guest beers Ⓗ
Established in 1926 as a men-only club, now much more accommodating: a homely beamed lounge and a games room. ♨ ♿ ♣ ☗

Plough
180 Nottingham Road (A60, 1 mile from centre)
☎ (01623) 23031
11–11
Whitbread Boddingtons Bitter; guest beers Ⓗ
Large, friendly one-roomed pub serving eight ales. Live music Thu. Good value food. Handy for the football ground. ❀ ◐ ◗ P

Tap & Spile
29 Leeming Street
☎ (01623) 21327
11.30–3, 5.30–11
Beer range varies Ⓗ
Two-roomed town pub sympathetically renovated. Traditional games in the back room; children welcome in the snug. ♣ ♿ ♣ ◖ P

Mansfield Woodhouse

Greyhound
High Street ☎ (01623) 643005
12–4, 7–11

Home Mild, Bitter; S&N Theakston Best Bitter, XB; guest beers Ⓗ
Village local popular with all ages: a lounge bar and a tap room. ❀ ♨ ≠ ♣ P

Mapperley Plains

Traveller's Rest
Plains Road (B684)
☎ (0115) 9264412
11–11
Home Bitter; S&N Theakston Mild, Best Bitter, XB, Old Peculier; guest beers Ⓗ
Comfortable roadhouse, not far from the highest point in the county, affording good views towards the Trent Valley. Excellent home cooking includes children's specials. No food Sun or Mon eves. ♨ ♣ ❀ ◐ ▲ ♣ P

Moorgreen

Horse & Groom
On B600 ☎ (01773) 713417
11–2.30, 5–11; 11–11 Sat
Hardys & Hansons Best Mild, Best Bitter, Kimberley Classic Ⓗ
Popular roadside pub: one large bar, a well-equipped garden, and a function room. A good starting point for walks. ♨ ❀ ◐ ◗ ♣ P

Nether Langwith

Jug & Glass
Queen's Walk
☎ (01623) 742283
11.30–4, 7–11
Hardys & Hansons Best Bitter Ⓔ, **Kimberley Classic** Ⓗ
Unspoilt, 15th-century inn by the village stream. ♨ Q ❀ ♨ ◐ ◗ ♨ ♣ P ☗

Newark-on-Trent

Mail Coach
13 London Road
☎ (01636) 605164
11–2.30 (3 Wed & Fri, 4 Sat), 5.30 (7 Sat)–11
Ind Coope Burton Ale; Tetley Bitter; Thwaites Bitter; guest beers Ⓗ
Busy pub in the shadow of the former Hole's brewery, drawing a mixed clientele. Live music at weekends; relaxed atmosphere for lunches. No meals Sun. ♨ ❀ ♨ ◐ ◗ P

Newcastle Arms
George Street
12–2.30 (3 Fri), 7–11
Home Mild, Bitter; S&N Theakston XB; Wells Bombardier; guest beer Ⓗ
Since 1841 this two-roomed pub has served mainly a local

trade and rail travellers. The bar echoes to the sound of dominoes and lively chatter; comfortable lounge. Beware: occasional use of an aspirator on slow-selling guest beers.
❀ ➿ (Northgate) ♣ ᛤ

Old Malt Shovel

25 Northgate ☎ (01636) 702036
11.30–3, 7 (5 Fri)–11
Taylor Landlord; guest beers Ⓗ
Single-roomer at the end of a pleasant stroll along the river past the castle. Excellent Mediterranean/Mexican restaurant. No food Tue eve. Occasional ciders.
ᛤ ❀ ᛰ ♪ & ♣ ᗕ

Wheatsheaf

Slaughterhouse Lane (opp. Morrison's supermarket)
☎ (01636) 702709
11–3, 7–11; 11–11 Fri & Sat
Mansfield Riding Mild, Riding Bitter, Bitter, Old Baily Ⓗ
Pub styled on a 1940s tap room and frequented by students and sportsmen. Pool and table skittles are popular, as are the summer barbecues. Mansfield seasonal beers.
❀ ♣

Wing Tavern

13 Bridge Street
☎ (01636) 702689
11–3 (2.30 Tue & Thu), 7–11
S&N Theakston Best Bitter, XB, Old Peculier Ⓗ
Formerly an 18th century 'food emporium' which had a licence to serve port in its vaults; today, a three-room retreat for market traders, shoppers and those seeking quiet games. ᛤ ❀ ♣ ᗕ

Newthorpe

Ram Inn

Beauvale Road (B6010)
☎ (01773) 713312
11–4, 5.30–11; 11–11 Sat
Hardys & Hansons Best Mild, Best Bitter Ⓔ**, Kimberley Classic** Ⓗ
Community local in a 1960s building. Good value food (no meals Sun eve).
ᛥ Q ❀ ᛰ ♪ ᛓ ♣ P

Normanton on Trent

Square & Compass

Eastgate ☎ (01636) 821439
12–3, 6–11; 12–11 Sat
Adnams Bitter; Stones Best Bitter; guest beers Ⓗ
Popular, low-beamed pub on the edge of the village. Good home-cooked food in the bar or the small restaurant.
ᛥ ᛤ ❀ ᛘ ᛰ ♪ ᛓ & ▲ ♣ P ᛤ

North Muskham

Crown

Main Street ☎ (01636) 640316
12–3, 7–11
Mansfield Riding Bitter, Bitter Ⓗ
A true hub of village life, this comfortable two-room pub is handy for the River Trent. A large passage has been furnished with stools and a TV for kids. Mansfield's seasonal beers. ❀ ᛰ ▲ ♣ P

Nottingham

Bell Inn

18 Angel Row, Old Market Square ☎ (0115) 9475241
10.30–11; 10.30–2.30, 5.30–11 Sat
Draught Bass; Black Sheep Special; Eldridge Pope Hardy Country; Jennings Mild; Cumberland Ale; Marston's Pedigree; guest beers Ⓗ
Popular, timber-framed, 15th-century inn; owned by the Jackson family since 1898. Cellar tours by appointment. Jazz Sun lunch and Sun–Tue eves. Guest beers are in the back room. The regular beers may vary. Q ❀ ᛰ

Canal Tavern

2 Canal Street
☎ (0115) 9240235
11–11
Mansfield Riding Mild, Riding Bitter, Bitter, Old Baily; guest beers Ⓗ
Small, single-bar alehouse, just south of the city centre, renovated with an original tiled wall as a main feature and much canal memorabilia. No meals Sun eve. Q ᛰ ➿

Castle

Lower Parliament Street (by ice stadium) ☎ (0115) 9504601
11.30–2.30, 5.30–11; 12–2.30, 7–10.30 Sun
Ansells Bitter; Ind Coope Burton Ale; Tetley Bitter Ⓗ
Pub offering one large room with alcoves and split-level areas, and a summerhouse built half-in and half-out. Eve meals finish early. ❀ ᛰ ♪ ♣

Cooper's Arms

3 Porchester Road, Thorney-wood ☎ (0115) 9502433
11–3, 6 (5.30 Fri)–11
Home Mild, Bitter Ⓔ**; S&N Theakston XB** Ⓗ
Large, Victorian local featuring a comfortable lounge, a bar, a darts room and a tiny family room. Covered skittle alley outside. ᛥ ᛓ ♣ P

Hole in the Wall

63 North Sherwood Street
☎ (0115) 9472833

11–3, 6–11 (11–11 during university terms)
Mansfield Riding Bitter, Bitter, Old Baily; guest beers Ⓗ
Traditionally-themed, one-room alehouse boasting 15 handpumps. Tue eve jazz; summer barbecues. Mansfield seasonal beers. ❀ ᛰ ♪

Limelight

Wellington Circus (part of Nottingham Playhouse complex) ☎ (0115) 9418467
11–11
Adnams Bitter; Courage Directors; Marston's Pedigree; S&N Theakston XB; Whitbread Boddingtons Bitter; guest beers Ⓗ
Traditional, pleasing interior in a 1960s building: a welcome retreat from the city centre. 'Brewery weeks' feature a range of breweries. Good food (not served Sun). Eve meals until 8. Occasional cider.
Q ❀ ᛰ ♪ ᗕ ᛢ

Lincolnshire Poacher

161–163 Mansfield Road (600 yds N of Victoria Centre)
☎ (0115) 9411584
11–3, 5 (6 Sat)–11
Bateman Mild, XB, Valiant, XXXB, Victory; Marston's Pedigree; guest beers Ⓗ
The city's leading real ale house, inspiring a sea-change in attitudes to beer in recent years. Over 80 whiskies.
Q ❀ ᛰ ♪ ♣ ᗕ

Magpies

Meadow Lane
☎ (0115) 9863851
11–2.30, 5–11
Home Mild, Bitter Ⓔ**; Marston's Pedigree; S&N Theakston XB** Ⓗ
On the city's eastern edge, handy for the sports grounds. The drinkers' bar has Sky TV and pool. No meals Sat or Sun; eve meals finish at 8.30.
❀ ᛰ ♪ ᛓ ♣ P ᛤ

March Hare

248 Carlton Road, Sneinton
☎ (0115) 9504328
11.30–2.30, 6–11
Courage Directors; John Smith's Bitter Ⓗ
Good, two-roomed local run by Nottingham's longest-serving licensee since its opening in 1958. Remarkable value lunches. ᛰ ᛓ ♣ P

Nag's Head

140 Mansfield Road (600 yds N of Victoria Centre)
☎ (0115) 9505209
10.30–11
Draught Bass; Stones Best Bitter Ⓗ
16th-century coaching house, a last stop for men condemned

to the gallows. One refused the customary pint and was hanged three minutes before the arrival of a reprieve! Comfortable front lounge; bar to the back. Q ❀ ◖ ⊞ ♣

Navigation Inn

6 Wilford Street
☎ (0115) 9417139
11.30–2.30, 5–11; 11.30–11 Fri & Sat
Banks's Bitter ⓔ; Camerons Strongarm; Marston's Pedigree Ⓗ
Canalside pub next to the locks displaying plenty of canal memorabilia. One split-level bar, popular with students at weekends. Other Banks's beers occasionally available. ❀ ◖ ⇌ ♣ ⊟

Norfolk Hotel

68 London Road
☎ (0115) 9520333
10.30–11; 10.30–3, 7–11 Sat
Home Mild, Bitter Ⓗ/ⓔ; S&N Theakston XB Ⓗ
Large town pub on the main road south: a lively bar and a more sedate lounge. Popular with games players. Handy for football grounds. ❀ ⇌ ♣ P

Portland Arms

24 Portland Road (off A610)
☎ (0115) 9782429
11.30–3, 7–11
Hardys & Hansons Best Mild, Best Bitter Ⓗ
Friendly local on the north side; open-plan but retaining a traditional atmosphere. Good value snacks. ❀ ♣

Raven Inn

19 Rawson Street, New Basford ☎ (0115) 9424052
10.30–11
Home Mild, Bitter; guest beers Ⓗ
Basic, back-street local with a friendly welcome. Pool room; disco Fri and Sat. ☼ ❀ ♣

Red Lion

21 Alfreton Road (A610)
☎ (0115) 9705645
11–3, 5–11; 11–11 Fri & Sat
Marston's Pedigree; Morland Old Speckled Hen; Whitbread Boddingtons Bitter, Flowers Original; Wadworth 6X; guest beers Ⓗ
Enterprising, well-run pub just north of the city centre: one open-plan room with well-defined areas. Ever-changing beers. No meals Sat; eve meals Tue only (till 7.30); Sun brunches from 11. House beer from Coach House. ❀ ◖ ◗

Tom Hoskins

12–14 Queens Bridge Road, The Meadows
☎ (0115) 9850611
11.30–2.30 (3 Sat), 5 (6 Sat, except match days)–11; 11.30–11 Fri

Hoskins Beaumanor Bitter, Penn's Ale, Old Nigel; guest beers Ⓗ
Friendly pub: one L-shaped bar decorated with brewery artefacts. Curry nights and curry parties by arrangement. No meals Sun or non-football Sats. ❀ ◖ ⇌ ♣ P

Tottle Brook

Glaisdale Drive West, Wollaton ☎ (0115) 9296224
11.30–2.30 (3 Fri), 6–11; 11–11 Sat
Banks's Mild, Bitter ⓔ; Camerons Strongarm Ⓗ
Modern, friendly pub with a drinkers' bar and a pleasant lounge. Reasonably-priced ale plus a good value menu.
❀ ◖ ◗ ⊞ ♣ P ⏃ ⊟

Trip to Jerusalem

1 Brewhouse Yard, Castle Road ☎ (0115) 9473171
11–11; 12–2.30, 7–10.30 Sun
Hardys & Hansons Best Mild, Best Bitter, Kimberley Classic; Marston's Pedigree Ⓗ
One of the oldest inns in England: the back rooms are cut out of the sandstone cliff below Nottingham Castle. The flagged floor and smoke-blackened beams add to the atmosphere. ⌂ Q ❀ ◖ ♣

White Lion

43 Carlton Road
☎ (0115) 9580296
11–3, 5.30–11
Banks's Mild, Bitter; Camerons Strongarm Ⓗ
1930s-style, two-bar, corner pub; a recent Banks's acquisition. Q ❀ ◖ ⊞ ♣

Old Clipstone

Dog & Duck

Main Road ☎ (01623) 822138
11–3, 6.30–11
Home Bitter; S&N Theakston XB; guest beers Ⓗ
Friendly village local enjoying passing trade from Centre Parcs and Sherwood Forest.
⌂ Q ☼ ❀ ◖ ◗ ▲ ♣ P

Ollerton

White Hart

Station Road ☎ (01623) 822410
11.30–4, 7–11
Samuel Smith OBB Ⓗ
Pub in an old village, popular with locals and tourists.
❀ ◖ ◗ ⊞ ♣ P ⊟

Plumtree

Griffin Inn

Main Road ☎ (0115) 9375743
11–2.30, 5.30–11; 12–2, 7–10.30 Sun
Hardys & Hansons Best Mild, Best Bitter ⓔ, Kimberley Classic Ⓗ
Substantial Victorian, brick pub where an open interior

envelops a central bar. Good selection of food (no meals Sun lunch). Garden play area.
⌂ Q ❀ ◖ ◗ ♣ P ⏃ ⊟

Radcliffe on Trent

Royal Oak

Main Road ☎ (0115) 9333798
11–11
Marston's Pedigree; Morland Old Speckled Hen; Taylor Landlord; Whitbread Boddingtons Bitter, Castle Eden Ale; guest beers Ⓗ
Village local with a cosy lounge and a boisterous public. At least nine ales. No meals Sun eve.
◖ ◗ ⊞ ⇌ ♣ P

Retford

Clinton Arms

24 Albert Road (S of centre, off A638) ☎ (01777) 702703
11–11
Courage Directors; John Smith's Bitter; Webster's Green Label; guest beers Ⓗ
Refurbished pub with a quiet lounge, a bustling bar and a games room. Live music (rock) Thu. Cider in summer. Q ☼
❀ ◖ ◗ ⬟ & ❀ ⏃ ◠ P ⊟

Market Hotel

West Carr Road, Ordsall
☎ (01777) 703278
11–3, 6–11; 11–11 Sat
Draught Bass; Marston's Pedigree; Morland Old Speckled Hen; S&N Theakston Best Bitter, XB; Whitbread Boddingtons Bitter; guest beers Ⓗ
Pub with a restaurant and large function room, offering 12 beers. ❀ ◖ ⇌ P ⊟

Turk's Head

Grove Street (off Town Sq)
☎ (01777) 702742
11–3, 7–11
Vaux Samson; Wards Best Bitter Ⓗ
Attractive pub, built in 1936.
⌂ Q ❀ ❀ ◖ & ♣ P ⊟

Ruddington

Three Crowns

23 Easthorpe Street
☎ (0115) 9213226
11.30–3, 6–11
Mansfield Riding Bitter, Bitter, Old Baily; Tetley Bitter; Whitbread Boddingtons Bitter; guest beers Ⓗ
Known as the Top House, this quiet and friendly village local is handy for the Great Central Railway Walk. Q ❀ ◖

Selston

Horse & Jockey

Church Lane ☎ (01773) 863022

Nottinghamshire

11–11
Adnams Broadside; Draught Bass; Bateman XB; Courage Directors; Hook Norton Old Hooky; Wells Bombardier; guest beers G
Small friendly village pub dating from 1664: three rooms with low beamed ceilings. Home-cooked food.
🏨 ⅃ ❀ ◖ ▮ ⅄ ♣ P 🍴

Shireoaks

Hewitt Arms

Shireoaks Park, Thorpe Lane
☎ (01909) 500979
12–3, 6.30–11
Bateman XB, XXXB; Marston's Bitter, Pedigree; Morland Old Speckled Hen; guest beers H
Converted 18th-century coach house in the grounds of Shireoaks Hall.
🏨 Q ❀ ◖ ⅃ ▮ ⅄ ≠ ⌂ P

Strelley

Broad Oak Inn

Main Street ☎ (0115) 9293340
11–11
Hardys & Hansons Best Mild, Best Bitter, Kimberley Classic H
Refurbished and extended, 17th-century, listed building in a rural setting. ❀ ◖ ▮ P

Sutton Bonington

Anchor Inn

Bollards Lane
☎ (01509) 673648
7 (11 Sat)–11
Marston's Pedigree H
Welcoming, family-run village local: a split-level single room reputed to be haunted. Beware: the Banks's mild is kept under gas. 🏨 ❀ ♣ P

Sutton in Ashfield

Mason's Arms

Unwin Road (B6021)
☎ (01623) 552024
11–3, 7–11 (11–11 summer Sat)
Draught Bass; Marston's Pedigree; S&N Theakston Best Bitter, *or* **XB,** *or* **Old Peculier; guest beers** H
Stone-built, two-bar pub with a natural stone cellar. A pub has been on this site since the 1400s. Q ❀ 🛏 ⅃

Underwood

Red Lion

Church Lane, Bagthorpe (off B600) ☎ (01773) 810482
12–3, 6–11 (12–11 summer Sat)
Marston's Pedigree;

Whitbread Boddingtons Bitter, Pompey Royal, Flowers Original; guest beers H
300-year-old, beamed, friendly village pub with an eating area where children are welcome. Large garden and children's play area; barbecues in summer. Independent guest beers. ❀ ◖ ▮ P

Upton

Cross Keys

Main Street ☎ (01636) 813269
11.30–2.30, 5.30 (6 Sat)–11; 12–2.30, 7–10.30 Sun
Bateman XXXB; Marston's Pedigree; Springhead Bitter; Whitbread Boddingtons Bitter; guest beer H
Attractive, 17th-century pub with a split-level single bar. Excellent food in the bar and restaurant. Beer festival just before Easter. Folk music most Sun eves. 🏨 ❀ ◖ ▮ ♣ P

Walkeringham

Three Horseshoes

High Street ☎ (01427) 890959
11.30–3, 7–11
Bass Worthington BB, Draught Bass; Stones Best Bitter H
Large village local attracting clientele from a wide area to its restaurant. Lunches Tue–Sat. ❀ ◖ ▮ ⅄ ♣ P 🍴

Watnall

Queen's Head

Main Road ☎ (0115) 9383148
11–2.30 (3 Sat), 5.30–11
Home Mild, Bitter; S&N Theakston XB, Old Peculier; guest beer H
17th-century village local, a wonderful example of how to renovate a historic pub: a splendid, wood-panelled bar and a small, intimate snug. No meals Sat or Sun eves; other eves till 8. 🏨 Q ❀ ◖ ▮ ♣ P

Royal Oak

Main Road ☎ (0115) 9383110
11–11
Hardys & Hansons Best Mild, Best Bitter, Kimberley Classic H/E
Traditional, olde-worlde pub with a lounge upstairs. Happy hour 5.30–8, Mon–Fri. No lunches Sun.
Q ⅃ ❀ ◖ 🛏 ♣ P

Wellow

Durham Ox

Newark Road
☎ (01623) 861026

11–3, 6–11
Marston's Pedigree; Ruddles Best Bitter; John Smith's Bitter; guest beers H
Popular village local with games and good food.
❀ ◖ ▮ ♣ P 🍴

West Bridgford

Bridgford Wines

116 Melton Road
☎ (0115) 9816181
5 (7 Mon, 3 Thu & Fri, 11 Sat)–11, 12–2, 7–10 Sun & bank hols
Oakham JHB; guest beers G
Off-licence for the ale and cider enthusiast: three guest beers, plus, in summer, Budweiser Budvar. Interesting ciders and bottled beers from around the world. ⅄ ⌂ P

West Leake

Star Inn (Pit House)

Melton Lane (Sutton Bonington road) ☎ (01509) 852233
11–3, 6–11
Draught Bass; S&N Theakston XB; guest beer H
Fine, old coaching inn: a half-panelled lounge with a flag-tiled bar, and a recently opened additional room. Large garden. 🏨 Q ❀ ◖ ▮ 🛏 P

West Stockwith

Waterfront Inn

Canal Lane ☎ (01427) 891223
12–3, 7–11; 12–11 Sat
Vaux Samson, Extra Special; Wards Best Bitter; guest beers H
Village pub and restaurant, opposite the marina. Popular in summer. Vegetarian meals a speciality. Q ❀ ◖ ▮ ⅄ ♣ P

Worksop

Greendale Oak

Norfolk Street (off Westgate)
☎ (01909) 489680
12–11; 12–4, 7–11 Mon
Tetley Bitter; Stones Best Bitter H
Mid-terraced, small, two-roomed cosy pub, gas-lit. Darts and fishing teams. Friendly clientele. Eve meals 5–7.30. ❀ ◖ ▮ ⅄ ≠ ♣ P

Top House

Sparken Hill ☎ (01909) 478125
11.30–3.30, 5–11
Adnams Bitter, Broadside; Mansfield Riding Bitter; Morland Old Speckled Hen; guest beers H
Old pub: four low-ceilinged rooms and a conservatory. Mansfield seasonal brews.
Q ⅃ ❀ ◖ ▮ ⅄ P

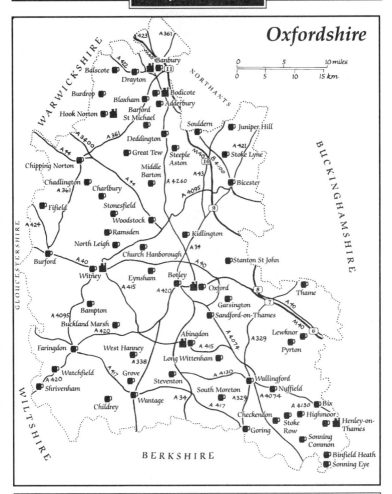

Oxfordshire

Brakspear, Henley-on-Thames; **Edgcote**, Banbury; **Hook Norton**, Hook Norton; **Morland**, Abingdon; **Morrells**, Oxford; **Plough Inn**, Bodicote; **Wychwood**, Witney

Abingdon

Brewery Tap
Ock Street ☎ (01235) 521655
11–11
Morland IPA, Bitter, Old Masters, Tanner's Jack, Old Speckled Hen Ⓗ
Listed ex-Morland brewery offices, once threatened with demolition. Genuine home-cooking. ❀ ◑ ⅏ ♣ P

Adderbury

White Hart
Tanners Lane, West Adderbury (off Horn Hill Rd)
☎ (01295) 810406
11–2.30, 5–11
Whitbread Boddingtons Bitter; guest beers Ⓗ
Idyllic, unassuming back of village local. Small, cosy and friendly.
🚪 Q ❀ 🛏 ◑ ▶ ♣ P

Balscote

Butcher's Arms
Shutford Road
☎ (01295) 730750
12–3, 6–11
Hook Norton Best Bitter Ⓗ
Classic one-roomed village pub popular with hikers and locals. Conversation rules!
🚪 Q ❀ ♣ P

Bampton

Romany
Bridge Street ☎ (01993) 850237
11–11
Archers Village; Hook Norton Best Bitter; Morland Bitter Ⓗ; **guest beers** Ⓗ/Ⓖ
Lovely village pub famous for its excellent value food: one large bar with a restaurant area. 🚪 ❀ 🛏 ◑ ⅏ ♣

Banbury

Coach & Horses
4 Butcher's Row (between Town Hall and Banbury Cross) ☎ (01295) 273552

Oxfordshire

10.30–3, 7–11
**Hook Norton Mild, Best
Bitter, Old Hooky** H
Pub with a village atmosphere
in the town centre: plenty of
conversation; no machines.
Hook Norton seasonal beers.
Q ❀ ⌘ ≠ ♣

Reindeer Inn

47 Parsons Street (off North
Bar St) ☎ (01295) 264031
11–2.30, 5 (7 Sat)–11; closed Sun
**Hook Norton Mild, Best
Bitter, Old Hooky; guest
beers** H
Superbly restored, 15th-
century former coaching inn,
with a relaxed atmosphere
(tidy dress – no under-21s).
Note the Jacobean, panelled
back room.
🚪 Q ❀ ◑ ≠ ⌂ P

Barford St Michael

George Inn

Lower Street ☎ (01869) 338226
12–2.30, 6–11; 11–11 Sat
**Adnams Bitter; S&N
Theakston Best Bitter;
Wadworth 6X; guest beers** H
300-year-old, stone and thatch
pub with beamed ceilings and
open fires, set in the Swere
Valley. Camping in the
garden. No meals Sun eve.
🚪 ⏷ ❀ ◑ ▲ ♣ P

Bicester

Littlebury Hotel

Kings End ☎ (01869) 252595
11–3, 5–11
Marston's Pedigree H
Pleasant, welcoming hotel
noted for functions and
receptions. Home-cooked
meals. Children welcome.
Q ❀ 🚪 ◑ ▷ ⚅ P

Binfield Heath

Bottle & Glass

Harpsden Road (off A4155, ½
mile NE of centre)
☎ (01491) 575755
11–3, 6–11
Brakspear Bitter H/E**, Old** H**,
Special** H/E
Thatched, beamed, 17th-
century, country pub with a
flagstoned floor in its larger
bar. Excellent, home-cooked
food, including vegetarian
options (no meals Sun eve).
Large garden. Handpump-
operated electric pumps may
be used in summer.
Q ❀ ◑ ▷ P

Bix

Fox at Bix

Oxford Road (A4130)
☎ (01491) 574134
11–3, 7–11

Brakspear Bitter, Old or
Special H
Large, comfortable, virginia
creeper- and ivy-clad, two-bar,
roadside pub with panelled
rooms. Two log fires; lots of
brass. Good, home-cooked
food (not served Mon eve).
The large garden has lovely
views. 🚪 Q ❀ ◑ ▷ ⚅ ♣ P

Bloxham

Red Lion Inn

High Street ☎ (01295) 720352
11.30–2.30, 7–11
**Adnams Bitter; Wadworth 6X;
guest beers** H
Welcoming, two-bar pub with
a large garden and an
extended lounge/dining area.
Good mix of customers.
🚪 Q ❀ ◑ ▷ ⚅ ⚅ ▲ ♣ P

Bodicote

Plough

High Street ☎ (01295) 262327
11–3, 5.45–11
**Bodicote Bitter, No. 9,
Porter** H
14th-century, two-room brew
pub. Home-cooked food is
served in the lounge/diner.
Meals cooked to order Sun.
❀ ◑ ▷ ♣

Botley

Fair Rosamund

Chestnut Road
☎ (01865) 243376
12–3, 7–11
Marston's Bitter, Pedigree H
Friendly, 1950s estate pub,
pleasantly refurbished: a large,
L-shaped bar and a very
comfortable lounge. Keen beer
prices for the area.
Q ❀ ⚅ ♣ P

Buckland Marsh

Trout

Tadpole Bridge (off A420,
towards Bampton) OS334004
☎ (01367) 870382
12–2.30, 5.30–11 (11.30–11 summer)
**Archers Village; Gibbs Mew
Bishop's Tipple; Morland
Bitter** H
18th-century, Grade II-listed
pub. The large garden has a
marquee, a camping/
caravanning site and fishing.
Q ⏷ ❀ ◑ ▷ ▲ ♣ P ⊟

Burdrop

Bishop Blaize

Between Sibford Ferris and
Sibford Gower
☎ (01295) 780323
12–2.30 (not Mon), 6–11 (12–3, 6–11
Bank Hol Mon)
Hook Norton Best Bitter;

**S&N Theakston XB; guest
beers** H
Friendly, 17th-century village
inn where the large garden has
stunning views. Quizzes, darts
and crib. 🚪 ❀ ◑ ▷ ♣ P

Burford

Lamb Inn

Sheep Street ☎ (01993) 823155
11–2.30, 6–11
Wadworth IPA, 6X H**, Old
Timer** G
Pleasant locals' bar in a smart
hotel. The floor in front of the
bar is flagstoned; comfortable
seating area behind. A gem.
🚪 Q 🚪 ◑ ▷ ⚅

Chadlington

Tite Inn

Mill End ☎ (01608) 676475
12–2.30, 6.30 (7 winter)–11; closed
Mon except bank hols
**Archers Village, Old
Cobleigh's; guest beers** H
16th-century free house and
restaurant with no jukebox,
machines or pool. The lovely
garden has country views.
No-smoking garden room in
summer. Children welcome.
🚪 Q ❀ ◑ ▷ ⚅ ♣ P ⤬

Charlbury

Rose & Crown

Market Street
☎ (01608) 810103
12–3, 5.30–11; 12–11 Fri & Sat
**Archers Village, Best Bitter;
guest beers** H **&** G
Popular, one-room, town-
centre pub with a small
garden. Excellent rotation of
guest beers. 🚪 ❀ ≠ ♣

Checkendon

Black Horse

Off A4074; towards Stoke
Row, left up a narrow lane
OS667841 ☎ (01491) 680418
12–2.30, 7–11
**Brakspear Bitter; Old Luxters
Barn Ale** G
Pub in the same family for
generations, hidden away in
the woods next to a farm.
Tasty filled rolls. No music, no
indoor gents', difficult to find,
but worth the effort. A classic.
🚪 Q ⏷ ❀ ▲ ♣ P

Childrey

Hatchet

High Street ☎ (01235) 751213
12–3, 7–11
**Brains Dark; Morland Bitter;
guest beers** H
Friendly village local with an
impressive array of guest ales.
❀ ◑ ▷ ♣ P

Chipping Norton

Chequers
Goddards Lane
☎ (01608) 644717
11–2.30, 5.30 (6 Sat)–11
Fuller's Chiswick, London Pride, ESB Ⓗ
Friendly, traditional pub next to the theatre. Fuller's *Best Pub* 1995. Seasonal beers sold.
🏚 Q ✿ ◖ ▶ ♣

Church Hanborough

Hand & Shears
Church Road
☎ (01993) 883337
12–2.30, 6.30–11
Exmoor Ale; Taylor Landlord; guest beers Ⓗ
Pleasant and comfortable pub in a lovely stone village. Interesting food; changing guest beers. 🏚 ☡ ◖ ▶ P ☷

Deddington

Crown & Tuns
New Street ☎ (01869) 337371
11–3, 6–11
Hook Norton Mild, Best Bitter, Old Hooky; guest beer Ⓗ
Small, basic, one-bar, 16th-century inn, noted for sports. Large garden; welcoming landlord. In every edition of the *Guide*. 🏚 ✿ ♣

Drayton

Roebuck Inn
Stratford Road (A422)
☎ (01295) 730542
11–2.30, 6–11
Fuller's London Pride; Hook Norton Best Bitter; Marston's Pedigree; Ruddles County; Whitbread Boddingtons Bitter; guest beers (occasional) Ⓗ
17th-century, picturesque village pub noted for good food. 🏚 Q ✿ ◖ ▶ ₲ P

Eynsham

Queen's Head
Queen Street ☎ (01865) 881229
12–2.30, 6.30–11
Morland Bitter, Tanner's Jack; guest beers Ⓗ
Friendly, 18th-century, two-bar village local. Always ask which beers are available.
🏚 Q ✿ 🍴 ▣ ♣

Faringdon

Folly
54 London Street
☎ (01367) 240620
10.30–2.30, 5.30–11
Morrells Bitter, Varsity Ⓗ

Charming, homely little town pub with no frills; at the foot of Faringdon Folly. A public bar and two lounges. Mild may be kept under CO_2.
🏚 Q ✿ ▣ ♣

Fifield

Merrymouth Inn
Stow Road (A424)
☎ (01993) 831652
11–2.30, 6–11
Banks's Bitter; Donnington BB, SBA; Marston's Pedigree; guest beers Ⓗ
13th-century Cotswold inn with a beamed bar and a stone floor; mentioned in the *Domesday Book*. Home-cooking.
🏚 Q ☡ ✿ 🍴 ◖ ▶ ♣ P ☷

Garsington

Three Horseshoes
The Green ☎ (01865) 361395
11–11
Draught Bass; Morrells Bitter, Mild, Varsity, Graduate Ⓗ
Popular village pub with a large garden and outdoor children's area. No-smoking conservatory restaurant. Good food. 🏚 Q ✿ ◖ ▶ ▣ ᕷ 🅰 P

Goring

Catherine Wheel
Station Road (off B4009)
☎ (01491) 872379
11–2.30 (3 Sat), 6–11
Brakspear Mild, Bitter, Old, Special, OBJ Ⓗ
Over 500-year-old pub, extended into a former blacksmith's shop. The bar is split-level and L-shaped, with a 'public bar' end. Children allowed in the 'pit' and restaurant area. Extensive menu; no meals Sun eve.
🏚 Q ✿ ◖ ▶ 🚆 ♣

John Barleycorn
Manor Road (off B4009 at Miller of Mansfield pub)
☎ (01491) 872509
10–2.30, 6–11
Brakspear Bitter, Special Ⓗ
16th-century, low-beamed inn with a cosy lounge. Extensive, good-value menu (daily specials). Children allowed in the lounge/restaurant. Close to the Thames and the Ridgeway footpath.
Q ✿ ◖ ▶ ▣ 🚆 ♣

Great Tew

Falkland Arms
Off B4022 ☎ (01608) 683653
11.30–2.30 (not Mon), 6–11; 12–2, 7–10.30 Sun
Donnington BB; Hall & Woodhouse Tanglefoot; Hook Norton Best Bitter; Wadworth 6X Ⓗ**; guest beers** Ⓗ **&** ₲

Classic, thatched, 16th-century inn in a preserved village, featuring oak panels, oil lamps, settles, flagstoned floors, malt whiskies and fruit wines – a gem! No food Sun.
🏚 Q ✿ 🍴 ◖ 🅰 ♣ ☖

Grove

Volunteer
Station Road (A338)
☎ (01235) 769557
11–11
Archers Village; Fuller's London Pride; Morland Bitter; Wadworth 6X; Whitbread Boddingtons Bitter; guest beers Ⓗ
Early Victorian, friendly pub with a large garden. Food all day. A mini-bus picks up/takes home from/to Wantage every day.
✿ ◖ ▶ ♣ P

Henley-on-Thames

Bird in Hand
61 Greys Road (off A4155, near Market Place car park)
☎ (01491) 575775
11–3, 5–11; 11–11 Sat
Adnams Broadside; Draught Bass; Fuller's London Pride; Morland IPA Ⓗ**; guest beer** (occasional) ₲
Comfortable, welcoming, one-bar, town local. The only real ale free house (but loan-tied to Morland) in Henley. Safe garden for children. No meals Sun. Q ✿ ◖ 🅰 🚆 (not winter Sun) ♣

Highmoor

Dog & Duck
On B481 ☎ (01491) 641261
11–2.30, 6–11
Brakspear Mild, Bitter, Special Ⓗ
Cosy, three-roomed, roadside pub in Chiltern woodland. The large, enclosed garden hosts barbecues on summer weekends. Restaurant quality, home-made food (includes vegetarian); reasonable prices; generous portions. No meals Mon. 🏚 Q ✿ ◖ ▶ ♣ P

Hook Norton

Pear Tree Inn
Scotland End (near brewery)
☎ (01608) 737482
12–2.30 (3 Sat), 6–11
Hook Norton Mild, Best Bitter, Old Hooky Ⓗ
Charming, 18th-century, one-room, brick-faced pub. Log fires and beams feature. Large garden (with games) for children. Good food. No eve meals Tue or Sun. Hook Norton seasonal beers.
🏚 Q ✿ 🍴 ◖ ▶ 🅰 ♣ P

Oxfordshire

Juniper Hill

Fox
Just E of A43 ☎ (01869) 810616
12–2, 7–11
Hook Norton Best Bitter Ⓗ,
Old Hooky Ⓖ
Friendly pub in the centre of a hamlet. It appeared as the Waggon & Horses in *Lark Rise to Candleford*. 🍴 Q ✿ ♣ P

Kidlington

King's Arms
4 The Moors, Old Kidlington (bottom of High St)
☎ (01865) 373004
11–3, 6–11
Ind Coope ABC Best Bitter, Burton Ale; guest beers Ⓗ
Small, but very attractive and friendly village local, an ex-coaching inn. Both the bar and lounge are small and can get crowded. Thatched toilets. Good public transport to Oxford. ✿ ◖ 🍺 ♣ P

Lewknor

Olde Leathern Bottel
1 High Street (off B4009, near M40 jct 6) ☎ (01844) 351482
11–2.30, 6–11
Brakspear Bitter, Old, Special Ⓗ
Comfortable, inviting, family-run village pub with a large, well-kept garden. The food is good quality, home-made and reasonably priced (vegetarian options).
🍴 ⛺ ✿ ◖ ▶ 🍺 ♿ ♣ P

Long Wittenham

Machine Man Inn
Fieldside (off A415, follow signs) ☎ (01865) 407835
11–3, 6–11
Black Sheep Best Bitter; Eldridge Pope Hardy Country, Royal Oak; guest beers Ⓗ
Basic, friendly village local. Its name comes from the machine mender who used to own it. Good value, home-made food (including vegetarian). Book Sun eve. ETB-approved accommodation. Four changing guest beers.
🍴 ⛺ ✿ 🛏 ◖ ▶ ♿ ♣ P

Middle Barton

Fox
27 Enstone Road (½mile off A4260) ☎ (01869) 40338
12–2.30, 6–11
Samuel Smith OBB; S&N Theakston XB; Wychwood Best; guest beers Ⓗ
Small, 15th-century, Cotswold stone pub featuring beams, a flagstone floor and a good atmosphere. Noted for good food in the bar or restaurant. Summer beer festival.
🍴 Q ⛺ ✿ ◖ ▶ ▲ ♣ P

North Leigh

Woodman Inn
New Yatt Road (off A4095)
☎ (01993) 881790
12–3 (4 Sat), 6–11
Hook Norton Best Bitter; Wadworth 6X; Wychwood Shires; guest beers Ⓗ
Small village pub offering home-made food. The large, terraced garden hosts twice-yearly beer festivals.
🍴 ✿ 🛏 ◖ ▶ ♣ P

Nuffield

Crown
Gangsdown Hill (A4130)
☎ (01491) 641335
11–2.30, 6–11
Brakspear Bitter, Old *or* **OBJ, Special** Ⓗ
Early 17th-century, beamed, cosy, waggoners' inn with three rooms; two have inglenooks. Large garden. Excellent range of good value, home-made food with a frequently changing menu. Children welcome in the dining area lunchtime.
🍴 Q ✿ ◖ ▶ ▲ ♣ P

Oxford

Black Boy
91 Old High Street, Headington (off A420)
☎ (01865) 63234
11–3, 6–11; 11–11 Sat
Morrells Bitter, Mild, Varsity, Graduate, College; guest beer (occasional) Ⓗ
Popular 1930s pub with an award-winning garden. The comfortable saloon displays interesting local history items. Good food (no meals Sun eve).
Q ✿ ◖ 🍺 ♣ P

Bookbinder's Arms
17–18 Victor Street, Jericho
☎ (01865) 53549
10.30–3, 6–11; 11–11 Sat
Morrells Bitter, Mild Ⓗ
Thriving, street-corner local: a single bar with two distinct drinking areas. Popular for games. ◖ ♣

Butcher's Arms
5 Wilberforce St, Headington
☎ (01865) 61252
11.30–2.30, 5.30–11
Fuller's Chiswick, London Pride, ESB Ⓗ
Lively, welcoming back-street local. Good food. Seasonal beers sold. 🍴 ✿ ◖ ♿ ♣

Cricketer's Arms
43 Iffley Road (A4158)
☎ (01865) 726264
12–3, 6–11 (midnight Fri);
12–midnight Sat
Morland IPA, Bitter, Old Masters, Old Speckled Hen; guest beer Ⓗ
Friendly, refurbished East Oxford local, now having only one room. Regular live music, including jazz Tue eve and blues Sun lunchtime. No meals Sun eve (other eves till 8).
✿ ◖ ♣

Fir Tree Tavern
163 Iffley Road (A4158)
☎ (01865) 247373
12–3, 5.30–11; 12–11 Sat
Morrells Bitter, Mild, Varsity, Graduate Ⓗ, **College** Ⓖ; **guest beer** Ⓗ
Small, split-level, Victorian pub. Piano player Wed and Sun eve; jam session Tue eve. Freshly made pizzas a speciality. Food all day Sat. Cider in summer.
✿ ◖ ▶ ♣ ⏺

King's Arms
40 Holywell Street
☎ (01865) 242369
10.30–11
Morland Bitter; Wadworth 6X; Younger No.3; Young's Bitter, Special, Winter Warmer Ⓗ
Big, busy and boisterous, city-centre pub – an Oxford institution. Six different drinking areas: the atmospheric Don's Bar at the rear is worth seeking out. Open 10.30am Sun for snacks.
🍴 Q ⛺ ✿ ◖ ▶ ♣ ✂

Marsh Harrier
40 Marsh Road, Cowley (off B480)
☎ (01865) 775937
12–2.30, 6–11; 12–11 Fri & Sat
Fuller's London Pride, ESB Ⓗ
Small, friendly, two-bar pub with an attractive, cosy lounge. An oasis in a part of the city not renowned for good beer. Seasonal beers sold.
🍴 ✿ 🍺 ♿ ♣

Old Tom
101 St Aldates (A420)
☎ (01865) 243034
10.30–11
Morrells Bitter, Varsity; guest beer (occasional) Ⓗ
Small, lively, 17th-century, city-centre pub adorned with cricketing memorabilia. Popular with all types, it takes its name from the bell at Christ Church College. Eve meals finish early (no eve meals Sun). No-smoking area lunchtime.
Q ✿ ◖ ▶ ⇌ ✂

Oxfordshire

Prince of Wales
73 Church Way, Iffley
☎ (01865) 778543
11–3, 6–11
**Adnams Extra; Hall &
Woodhouse Badger BB,
Tanglefoot; Wadworth IPA,
6X, Farmer's Glory; guest
beers** Ⓗ
Attractively refurbished
Wadworth pub in a pleasant
riverside village, a short walk
from Iffley Lock. Wide range
of guest beers; beer festival
last weekend of each month.
🏚 Q ✿ ◑ ▶ P

Red Lion
Godstow Road, Wolvercote
☎ (01865) 52722
11–2.30, 5.30–11; 11–11 Fri & Sat
**Shepherd Neame Spitfire;
Wychwood Best; guest
beers** Ⓗ
Welcoming, two-bar pub on
the main road through the
village. An ex-Halls pub, it is
now a true free house, so the
two guest beers can be a
genuine surprise. Popular
lunchtimes, especially Sun
(good value Sun lunches).
✿ ◑ ▶ 🍺 ♣ P

Three Goats' Heads
3–5 St Michael's Street
☎ (01865) 721523
11–11
**Samuel Smith OBB,
Museum** Ⓗ
Cosy city-centre pub on two
levels, next to the Oxford
Union. Well refurbished, with
much wood and tiling in
evidence, it has been
commended in CAMRA's Pub
Preservation awards. The only
Sam Smith's for miles. ◑ ▶ ⇌

Victoria Arms
Mill Lane, Old Marston
(¼ mile down drive, W off Mill
Lane) ☎ (01865) 241382
11.30–3, 6–11 (11–11 summer)
**Hall & Woodhouse
Tanglefoot; Wadworth IPA,
6X, Farmer's Glory, Old
Timer; guest beer** Ⓗ
Popular riverside pub serving
good food and the full range
of Wadworth beers. Crowded
in summer, but it has a large
garden, a patio and a
children's play area.
🏚 ⴲ ✿ ◑ ▷ ⅋ ▲ P

Pyrton

Plough
Knightsbridge Lane (off B4009)
☎ (01491) 612003
11.30–2.30, 6 (7 Tue)–11; closed Mon
eve
**Adnams Bitter; Brakspear
Bitter; Fuller's London
Pride** Ⓗ
Attractive, 17th-century,
thatched pub in a quiet village.

Popular for its extensive menu
of home-made food, served in
the bar and restaurant.
Families welcome in the
restaurant lunchtime. The beer
range may vary.
🏚 ✿ ◑ ▶ ▲ ♣ P

Ramsden

Royal Oak
High Street ☎ (01993) 86213
11.30–2.30, 6.30–11
**Archers Golden; Banks's
Bitter; Hook Norton Best
Bitter, Old Hooky; guest
beers** Ⓗ
Friendly, 17th-century former
coaching inn with a courtyard.
The restaurant serves high
quality local produce.
🏚 Q ✿ 🍴 ◑ ▶ ⅋ P 🏨

Sandford-on-Thames

Fox
25 Henley Road (off A423)
☎ (01865) 777803
12–2.30, 7–11
Morrells Bitter Ⓖ/Ⓗ**, Mild**
(winter) Ⓗ**, Varsity**
(summer) Ⓖ
Village local serving the
cheapest Morrells beer in
Oxfordshire. In the same
family for 76 years; 18 years in
the *Guide*. 🏚 Q ✿ ⅋ ♣ P

Shrivenham

Prince of Wales
High Street ☎ (01793) 782268
11.30–3, 6–11
**Hall & Woodhouse
Tanglefoot; Wadworth IPA,
6X; guest beer** Ⓗ
17th-century, stone coaching
inn with a comfortable,
beamed interior. No meals Sun
eve. 🏚 Q ✿ ◑ ▶ ♣ P

Sonning Common

Bird in Hand
Peppard Road (B481, S of
village) ☎ (01734) 723230
11–2.30, 6–11
**Courage Best Bitter; Fuller's
London Pride; Ruddles
County** Ⓗ
Friendly, 16th-century pub,
with beams and an inglenook.
Good value food in the bar
and restaurant. Vegetarian
options. No meals Sun eve.
The attractive garden backs
onto woodland. Q ✿ ◑ ▶ P

Sonning Eye

Flowing Spring
On A4155, 2 miles E of
Caversham ☎ (01734) 693207
11.30–3, 5–11 (11–11 summer)

Fuller's Chiswick, London
Pride, ESB Ⓗ
Traditional alehouse with a
piano. It hosts friendly sports
teams and stages events in the
huge garden. The good quality
food is all home-cooked with
nothing frozen (no food Sun
eve). Fuller's seasonal beers
sold. 🏚 Q ✿ ◑ ▶ ♣ ⌂ P

Souldern

Fox
Fox Lane (off B4100)
☎ (01869) 245284
11.30–3, 5 (6 Sat)–11
**Draught Bass; Fuller's
London Pride; Hook Norton
Best Bitter; guest beers** Ⓗ
Friendly, Cotswold stone pub
in the village centre, noted for
its food, served in the bar and
restaurant (not Sun eve).
🏚 Q ✿ 🍴 ◑ ▶ ♣ P

South Moreton

Crown
High Street (off A4130 and
A417) ☎ (01235) 812262
11–3, 5.30–11
**Adnams Bitter; Hall &
Woodhouse Tanglefoot;
Wadworth IPA** Ⓗ**, 6X; guest
beer** Ⓖ
Enthusiastically run village
local, deservedly popular for
meals, including vegetarian.
Families welcome throughout
the pub. Water coolers are
used on casks behind the bar.
🏚 Q ⴲ ✿ ◑ ▶ ♣ P

Stanton St John

Star Inn
Middle Road (100 yds off
B4027) ☎ (01865) 351277
11–2.30, 6.30–11; 12–2.30, 7–10.30
Sun
**Hall & Woodhouse
Tanglefoot; Wadworth IPA,
6X, Farmer's Glory, Old
Timer** Ⓗ
17th-century inn retaining
original features. Tasty,
home-cooked food, with
vegetarian dishes, is served at
reasonable prices. Popular
no-smoking family room.
🏚 ⴲ ✿ ◑ ▶ 🍺 ♣ P ⊬

Steeple Aston

Red Lion
South Street (off A4260)
☎ (01869) 340225
11–3, 6–11
**Hall & Woodhouse
Tanglefoot; Hook Norton Best
Bitter; Wadworth 6X** Ⓗ
Friendly adult retreat with a
floral summer terrace and a
library. Bar lunches, except
Sun. The dining room serves
eve meals, Tue–Sat.
🏚 Q ✿ ◑ P

253

Oxfordshire

Steventon

Cherry Tree

High Street ☎ (01235) 831222
11.30–2.30, 6 (6.30 Sat)–11
Brakspear Bitter; Wadworth IPA, 6X, Farmer's Glory, Old Timer; guest beer H
Comfortable, inviting tavern of character with a good layout. Good quality, inventive menu (well-used by businesses for lunch). ⌂ ❀ ◗ ▶ ♣ P ⚲

Stoke Lyne

Peyton Arms

Off B4100 ☎ (01869) 345285
11–2.30 (not Mon), 5.30–11
Hook Norton Mild, Best Bitter, Old Hooky G
Small, basic village local unchanged by time – a rural gem! Aunt Sally played.
⌂ Q ❀ ♣ P

Stoke Row

Cherry Tree

Off B481 at Highmoor
☎ (01491) 680430
11–3, 6–11
Brakspear Mild, Bitter, Special, OBJ G
Low-beamed, attractive village local close to the famous Maharajah's Well. Families are welcome in the lounge and the games room. The garden has swings and a slide. Snacks available (rolls only Mon).
⌂ ⛲ ❀ ◗ ⊞ ♣ P

Stonesfield

Black Horse

Church Street (off A44)
☎ (01993) 891616
10.30–2.30, 5.30–11
Courage Best Bitter; John Smith's Bitter; guest beers H
Basic local with an hospitable atmosphere. ⌂ ❀ ⊞ ♣ P

Thame

Rising Sun

26 High Street
☎ (01844) 214206
11–2.30, 6–11
Hook Norton Best Bitter; Wadworth 6X; guest beers H
Attractive, 16th-century, beamed building with low ceilings. Lots of board games played. Excellent, home-cooked menu. ⌂ ❀ ◗ ▶ ♣

Six Bells

44 Lower High Street
☎ (01844) 212088
11–3, 6–11
Fuller's Chiswick, London Pride, ESB H
Comfortable, old, two-bar pub

with some original 16th-century ship's timbers. The lounge bar ceiling has straps to assist perpendicular drinkers. Food is recommended (not served Sun eve). Fuller's seasonal beers.
Q ⛲ ❀ ◗ ▶ ♣ P

Swan Hotel

9 Upper High Street
☎ (01844) 261211
11–11
Brakspear Bitter; Hook Norton Best Bitter; guest beers H
Popular inn overlooking the market place, with many unusual fittings (spot the boar's head). Excellent restaurant and bar meals (including vegetarian and children's). ⌂ ⛲ ⊭ ◗ ▶ ♿

Wallingford

Coach & Horses

12 Kinecroft (off High St, 400 yds W of A329/A4130 jct)
☎ (01491) 825054
11–2.30 (3 Fri & Sat), 6–11
Fuller's Chiswick, London Pride H, **ESB** G
Cosy, two-bar pub overlooking the Kinecroft common (which acts as its garden). Good value food (not served Sun or Mon eves). The landlord is a steam rally enthusiast. Fuller's seasonal beers. ⌂ ❀ ◗ ⊞ ♣

Kings Head

2 St Martin's Street (A329, near A4130 jct) ☎ (01491) 838309
11–11
Brakspear Bitter H
Lively town-centre pub, popular with locals. Families welcome until 4pm. ♣ P

Wantage

Royal Oak

Newbury Street (A338)
☎ (01235) 763129
12–2.30 (not Mon–Thu), 5.30 (7 Sat)–11; 12–2.30, 7–10.30 Sun
Draught Bass; Fuller's London Pride; Hall & Woodhouse Badger BB, Tanglefoot; Wadworth 6X H; **guest beers** G/H
Boisterous pub with two large bars. Poets and peasants, hoi-polloi and hooray Henries all enjoy a convivial camaraderie. No food Sun. Guest beers change frequently.
⊭ ◗ ⊞ ♣

Watchfield

Royal Oak

Oak Road (off Shrivenham Rd)
☎ (01793) 782668
12–2.30, 6.30–11
Ushers Best Bitter, Founders; guest beer H

Friendly, ivy-covered, cottage pub, a low-ceilinged village local dating back to the 18th century. ⌂ ❀ ◗ ▶ ♿ ♣ P 🏠

West Hanney

Lamb Inn

School Road (off A338)
☎ (01235) 868917
11–2.30, 6.30–11
Draught Bass; Morland Bitter; Shepherd Neame Spitfire; Whitbread Flowers Original; guest beers H
Very friendly pub serving good food.
Q ⛲ ❀ ◗ ▶ ♿ ♣ P

Witney

Carpenter's Arms

132 Newland
☎ (01993) 702206
12–3, 6–11
Morrells Bitter, Varsity H
Very comfortable and friendly pub on the main road from Oxford: one large bar with a small pool room. Good bus service from Oxford.
❀ ◗ ▶ ♣ P

House of Windsor

31 West End ☎ (01993) 704277
12–3.30 (not Mon), 6 (7 Sat)–11
Hook Norton Best Bitter; Marston's Pedigree; Wadworth 6X; guest beers H
Popular town free house with varied, well-chosen guest beers. Pleasant single bar at the front; small eating area at the rear. Beware the proximity of the doors to the bar when entering. ⌂ ◗ ♣

Woodstock

Black Prince

2 Manor Road (A44)
☎ (01993) 811530
12–2.30, 6.30–11
Archers Village; S&N Theakston XB, Old Peculier; guest beer H
Characterful, 16th-century pub on the main road, with a pleasant garden on the River Glyme. A superb suit of armour stands in the bar. Mexican food is a speciality.
⌂ ❀ ◗ ▶ P

Queen's Own

59 Oxford Street
☎ (01993) 812414
11–3, 6 (5 Fri & Sat)–11
Hampshire Lionheart; Hook Norton Best Bitter, Old Hooky; guest beers H
Formally a Hook Norton tied house, re-opened as a free house: a very attractive stone building that is quite narrow at the front, but opens out into a pleasant seating area at the rear. ◗

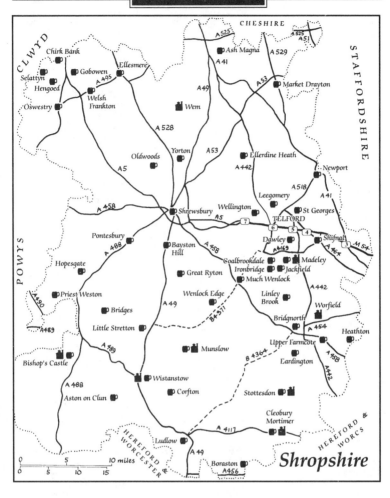

All Nations, Madeley; **Crown Inn**, Munslow; **Davenports Arms**, Worfield; **Fox & Hounds**, Stottesdon; **Hanby**, Wem; **Hobsons**, Cleobury Mortimer; **Three Tuns**, Bishop's Castle; **Wood**, Wistanstow

Ash Magna

White Lion
East of, and off, Whitchurch A525 bypass ☎ (01948) 663153
12–2 (2.30 Sat; not Mon), 6–11
Bass Worthington BB, Draught Bass; M&B Highgate Dark; guest beers H
Pub where two rooms are separated by the bar. Many real ale mementoes are displayed in the public bar; hickory-handled golf clubs feature in the lounge. Along with bar billiards and skittles, there's also a bowling green. No food Sun.
🏨 Q ❀ ◖ ▶ ❦ ♣ 🖰

Aston on Clun

Kangaroo Inn
☎ (01588) 660263
12–3, 7–11
Draught Bass, Bass Worthington BB; M&B Highgate Dark; guest beer (summer) H
Pub offering a large public bar, a lounge and a dining area.

The spacious grounds allow camping. The village holds an ancient tree dressing ceremony in May.
🏨 ◖ ▶ Å ⇌ (Broome Halt)
♣ P

Try also: Engine & Tender, Broome (Free)

Bayston Hill

Compasses
Hereford Road
☎ (01743) 722921
12–3, 5–11; 12–11 Fri & Sat; closed winter

Shropshire

M&B Highgate Dark, Brew XI; guest beer Ⓗ
Set on a rise as the A49 passes through the village, this pub has a snug and an extended bar, boasting a huge collection of carved wooden elephants and other mementoes.
Q ♪ ⊞ ♿ ♣

Bishop's Castle

Castle Hotel
Market Square
☎ (01588) 638403
12–3, 6.30–11
Bass Worthington BB, Draught Bass; guest beer Ⓗ
Fine country town hotel. The front entrance leads to a snug bar with much original woodwork. There is a larger room off and a public bar at the rear. Good selection of games; popular with the locals. Large garden.
🏚 Q ✤ ⊯ ◖♪ ♣ P

Boraston

Peacock Inn
Worcester Road (A456)
☎ (01584) 810506
11.30–3, 6–11
Draught Bass; Ind Coope Burton Ale; Tetley Bitter Ⓗ
Grade II-listed building, licensed since 1830 when it had stabling for six horses. The panelled rooms have south facing windows. Good blackboard selection of imaginative food, but the emphasis remains on pub, not restaurant, matters.
🏚 ✤ ◖♪ ⊞ ♣ P

Bridges

Horseshoe Inn
OS394964 ☎ (01588) 650260
12–3 (not Mon, or Tue–Thu in winter), 6–11
Adnams Bitter, Extra; Shepherd Neame Spitfire; guest beers Ⓗ
Attractively situated in a quiet valley by the River Onny: an excellent local, appreciated by walkers from the Long Mynd and Stiperstones hills. Local CAMRA *Pub of the Year* 1995. Two guest beers.
🏚 Q ⛺ ✤ ◖♪ ♣ ♨ P

Bridgnorth

Bear Inn
Northgate ☎ (01746) 763250
11–2.30 (10.30–3 Fri & Sat), 5.15 (6 Sat)–11; 12.30–2.30, 7.30–10.30 Sun
Batham Mild, Best Bitter; Ruddles Best Bitter; Whitbread Boddingtons Bitter; guest beer Ⓗ
Grade II-listed pub, near the historic Northgate: two

---

characterful bars with a guest beer changing daily. Good quality food; gourmet eve every Thu (book). No food Sun.
🏚 Q ✤ ⊯ ◖♪ ⊞ ♣ P

Black Boy
58 Cartway ☎ (01746) 764691
12–2.30 (3 Sat), 6.30–11
Banks's Mild, Bitter; Marston's Pedigree Ⓗ
17th-century inn in an area of outstanding beauty, overlooking the River Severn. Open fires in winter; flower-decked patio in summer.
Q ✤ ⊯ ◖♪ ⊞ ♿ ⚉ (SVR)

Railwayman's Arms
SVR Station, Hollybush Road (off B4364) ☎ (01746) 764361
11–4 (12–2 winter), 7–11; 11–11 Sat
Bass Worthington BB; Batham Best Bitter; M&B Highgate Dark; Wood Special; guest beers Ⓗ
Bar located on the platform of a Victorian station, with an interesting collection of railwayana. The Severn Valley Railway runs throughout the summer. Good range of guest beers, hot snacks and locomotives available. 🏚 ✤
♿ ⚉ ≋ (SVR) ♣ ♨ P

Chirk Bank

Bridge
☎ (01691) 773213
11–3, 6–11
Banks's Mild, Bitter Ⓔ; **Camerons Strongarm** (summer) Ⓗ
Traditional, two-bar local, 50 yards from the Welsh border in the Ceiriog Valley, below the Llangollen Canal. Chirk station is a ten-minute walk along the canal.
Q ✤ ⊯ ◖♪ ⊞ ♣ P ⊟

Cleobury Mortimer

King's Arms Hotel
Church Street
☎ (01299) 270252
11.30–11
Hobsons Best Bitter; Hook Norton Best Bitter; Taylor Landlord; Wye Valley HPA; guest beers Ⓗ
Comfortable pub with three distinctive areas, one for eating and two for drinking. The classical music is very popular as a background.
🏚 ✤ ⊯ ◖♪

Corfton

Sun Inn
On B4368 ☎ (01584) 861239
11–2.30, 6–11
Whitbread Boddingtons Mild, Flowers IPA; guest beers Ⓗ

17th-century inn, family-run, with impressive beer, food and facilities; the dining area is off the lounge. A large garden boasts views of Clee Hill. Children's certificate. 🏚 Q ✤
◖♪ ⊞ ♿ ▲ ♣ P ⚉ ⊟

Eardington

Halfway House
Cleobury Road (B4363)
☎ (01746) 762670
6–11; 12–3, 6–11 Sat
Whitbread Boddingtons Bitter, Flowers Original Ⓗ
Extensively and well refurbished country inn. Note the fine 1620 wall painting and the old phones. Caravan site at the rear; letting cottages alongside. No-smoking family conservatory.
🏚 ✤ ⊯ ♣ P ⚉

Ellerdine Heath

Royal Oak
1 mile off A53 OS603226
☎ (01939) 250300
11–3, 5–11; 11–11 Sat
Brains Dark, SA; Hanby Drawwell; Wood Parish; guest beers Ⓗ
Nicknamed the Tiddly, because of its small size: a friendly one-bar pub extended to include a pool room without spoiling the ambience. Frequented by all ages. Good value pub grub (not served Mon eve/Tue lunch).
🏚 Q ✤ ◖♪ ▲ ♣ ♨ P

Ellesmere

White Hart
Birch Road ☎ (01691) 622333
12–3 (not winter), 7–11
Bateman Mild; Marston's Bitter, Pedigree Ⓗ
Tucked away from the town centre, this Grade III-listed pub is in Shropshire's Lake District and near the Llangollen Canal.
Q ✤ ⊞ ♿ ♣ P

Gobowen

Cross Foxes
The Cross
☎ (01691) 670827
11–11
Banks's Mild; Marston's Bitter, Pedigree Ⓗ
Traditional, welcoming village local by the station. Marston's Head Brewer's Choice stocked.
Q ✤ ⊞ ♿ ▲ ≋ ♣ P ⊟

Great Ryton

Fox
E off A49 at Dorrington
OS490032 ☎ (01743) 718499

12–3, 7–11
Draught Bass; guest beers H
Pub in a slightly elevated
position, giving expansive
views south toward the hills of
South Shropshire: one main
L-shaped bar and a restaurant
(supper licence).
❀ ◑ ▶ P

Heathton

Old Gate Inn
Between Bobbington and
Claverley OS813924
☎ (01746) 710431
12–3, 7–11
**Blackbeard Stairway to
Heaven; Enville Ale; HP&D
Entire; Tetley Bitter; guest
beers** H
16th-century characterful,
beamed, country pub; family
oriented, friendly, and
popular. Excellent selection of
home-produced food. The
attractive gardens feature a
barbecue and a children's play
area. The only HP&D inn in
Shropshire. ♨ ❀ ◑ ▶ ⊞ P

Hengoed

Last Inn
3 miles N of Oswestry on
B4579 (Weston Rhyn road)
☎ (01691) 659747
7–11
**Draught Bass; Whitbread
Boddingtons Bitter; guest
beers** H
Busy rural pub near the Welsh
border, with family and games
rooms. No meals Tue eve; Sun
lunch served. Fourteen years
in the *Guide*.
♨ Q ➹ ▶ ⅋ ⌂ P

Hopesgate

Stables Inn
Off A488 at Hope
☎ (01743) 891344
11.30–2.30, 7–11; closed Mon
**Tetley Bitter; Wood Special;
guest beer** H
Outstanding pub enjoying
lovely views of surrounding
hills and a welcoming
atmosphere. Excellent, home-
cooked cuisine is served in the
dining room (lunches Tue–
Sun; eve meals Wed–Sat).
Attractively furnished bar;
massive log fire.
♨ Q ❀ ♣ P

Linley Brook

Pheasant Inn
Britons Lane (off B4373,
Bridgnorth–Broseley road)
☎ (01746) 762260
12–2.30, 6.30–11
Beer range varies H
Two-roomed pub in an
attractive rural setting. Well

worth finding for its cosy
lounge with two real fires.
Ever-changing guest beers
from three handpulls.
♨ Q ❀ ◑ ▶ ⅋ ♣ P

Little Stretton

Green Dragon
☎ (01694) 722925
11–3 (later summer weekends), 6–11
**Wadworth 6X; Whitbread
Boddingtons Mild, Bitter;
Wood Parish** H
Main bar with a dining area,
set at the beginning of Ashes
Hollow, a valley leading on to
the Long Mynd, one of the
many nearby walking areas.
The beer range may vary.
♨ Q ❀ ◑ ▶ ▲ P

Ludlow

Bull Hotel
14 Bull Ring ☎ (01584) 873611
11–11
**Bateman Mild; Marston's
Bitter, Pedigree** H
The plain front of this classic
coaching inn hides the Tudor
half-timbering seen through
the arch (the original facade
was destroyed by fire in 1795).
Its one long bar, with various
corners and levels, is host to
the Ludlow Fringe Festival.
Marston's Head Brewer's
Choice stocked. ♨ ❀ ◑ ▶ ⇌

Church Inn
Buttercross ☎ (01584) 872174
11–11
**Ruddles County; Webster's
Yorkshire Bitter; guest beer
(summer)** H
Tucked away in Ludlow's
pedestrian area, on one of the
town's most ancient sites, this
upmarket inn stands near the
church of St Lawrence, the
largest and most majestic in
Shropshire. Q ⋈ ◑ ▶ ⇌

Old Bull Ring Tavern
44 Bull Ring ☎ (01584) 872311
11–11
**Ansells Mild, Bitter; Tetley
Bitter; guest beer** H
Cosy, two-roomer, dating back
650 years and popular with all
ages. Quoits played. No eve
meals Sun. ♨ ◑ ▶ ⅋ ⇌ ♣

Market Drayton

Star
Stafford Street
☎ (01630) 652530
10.30–3, 6.30–11; 10.30–11 Wed, Fri &
Sat
**Federation Buchanan's
Special; Hanby Black Magic
Mild, Drawwell,
Nutcracker** H
Hanby's first tavern, where a
basic, open-plan bar caters for
locals of all ages. ❀ ♣ P

Much Wenlock

George & Dragon Inn
2 High Street (off A458/
A4169) ☎ (01952) 727312
11–2.30, 6–11
**Hook Norton Best Bitter;
guest beers** H
Step back in time into this
atmospheric, small pub. A
large collection of jugs hangs
from the beams, while
ephemera decorate all walls.
Discreet music emanates from
vintage equipment. No eve
meals Sun. ◑ ▶

Munslow

Crown Inn
☎ (01584) 841205
12–2.30, 7–11
**M&B Mild; Munslow Boys
Pale Ale, Ale; Wadworth 6X;
guest beers** (occasional) H
Interesting roadside inn
brewing its own beers, and
serving meals prepared by an
award-winning chef.
Specialities include Thai and
French dishes. The brew house
is visible from the bar.
♨ ❀ ◑ ▶ ⅋ ♣ ⌂ P

Newport

Shakespeare
Upper Bar ☎ (01952) 811924
11–11
**Banks's Mild; Draught Bass;
S&N Theakston Best Bitter,
XB, Old Peculier** (winter);
guest beers H
Old, one-bar town pub which
is frequented by all ages, but
packed Fri and Sat eves.
Excellent floral displays
❀ ⅊ ▲ ♣ P ⊟

Oldwoods

Romping Cat
☎ (01939) 290273
12–3 (not Fri), 7–11; 12–2, 7–10.30 Sun
**Whitbread Castle Eden Ale;
guest beers** H
Genuine, no-frills country pub,
a tremendous supporter of
local charities. Four guest
beers weekly.
Q ❀ ♣ ⊟

Oswestry

Oak Inn
47 Church Street
☎ (01691) 652304
11–3, 6–11
**Draught Bass; M&B Brew XI;
guest beers** H
Long-established, genuine
local opposite the parish
church. The pub has had only
three licensees in 73 years!
Q ❀ ⅋ ⅊ ♣

Shropshire

Pontesbury

Horseshoes Inn
Minsterley Road (A488)
☎ (01743) 790278
12–3, 6–11
**Fuller's London Pride;
Whitbread Boddingtons
Bitter; guest beers** ⊞
Busy local in a large village,
convenient for walking in the
South Shropshire hills.
❀ ◑ ▶ ♣ P

Priest Weston

Miner's Arms
OS293913 ☎ (01938) 561352
11–3, 6–11
**Bass Worthington BB,
Draught Bass** ⊞
Remote, classic country pub,
still largely unspoilt, drawing
walkers visiting a nearby stone
circle. The well can be viewed.
Monthly folk singing; annual
folk festival. ₥ ◑ ▶ ♣ P

Selattyn

Cross Keys
On B4579 ☎ (01691) 650247
6–11
Banks's Mild, Bitter ⊞
17th-century superb example
of a small village pub; an
unspoilt interior of various
rooms, including a skittle
alley. Close to Offa's Dyke
footpath. Phone for lunchtime
hours. Holiday flat to let.
₥ Q ☎ ❀ ⋈ & ▲ ♣ P

Shifnal

Old Bell
Church Street
☎ (01952) 417777
12–3, 5–11
Draught Bass; guest beers ⊞
Old coaching inn featuring
two, oak-beamed bar areas
and a noted dining room with
an extensive menu of home-
cooked meals. Good value
accommodation.
Q ❀ ⋈ ◑ ▶ & ≋ ♣ P

Wheatsheaf Tap House
61 Broadway
☎ (01952) 460938
11–11
**Banks's Mild, Bitter;
Camerons Strongarm; guest
beers** ⊞
Refurbished Banks's ale house
theme pub, with real coal fires
in two of the three rooms. The
house mild is Hanson's, the
bitter Camerons.
₥ Q ❀ ◑ ▶ ⊞ ≋ ♣ P ⊟

White Hart
High Street ☎ (01952) 461161
12–3, 6–11; 12–11 Fri & Sat

**Ansells Bitter; Enville
Simpkiss Bitter, Ale; Ind
Coope Burton Ale; guest
beers** ⊞
Reputedly haunted, highly
regarded black-and-white,
16th-century coaching inn.
Cosy and friendly, it boasts
seven handpumps, offering
two guest beers. Good food
selection (not served Sun).
Q ❀ ◑ ⊞ ≋ ♣ P

Shrewsbury

Castle Vaults
16 Castle Gates
☎ (01743) 358807
11.30–3 (4 Sat), 6–11; 7–10.30 Sun,
closed Sun lunch
**Marston's Pedigree; Ruddles
Best Bitter; guest beers** ⊞
Free house with a roof garden,
in the shadow of the castle,
specialising in home-cooked
Mexican food served in an
open bar area (no meals Sun).
Up to six guest beers,
constantly changing.
₥ Q ❀ ⋈ ◑ ▶ ≋ ○

Coach & Horses
Swan Hill
☎ (01743) 365661
10.30–11
Draught Bass; guest beers ⊞
Unspoilt, Victorian pub in a
quiet part of town attracting a
mixed clientele. The bar is
wood panelled with a
partitioned area at the side; the
lounge is used as a restaurant,
12–3 daily. Two changing
guest beers Q ❀ ◑ ⊞ ≋

Dolphin
48 St Michael's Street
☎ (01743) 350419
5 (3 Fri & Sat)–11
Beer range varies ⊞
Early Victorian gas-lit drinking
house with a porticoed
entrance. Up to six hand-
pulled beers; no lager, not
even in bottles.
Q ⊞ ≋ ♣ ⊟

Loggerheads
1 Church Street
☎ (01743) 355457
10.30–11
**Draught Bass; M&B Mild;
Stones Best Bitter; guest
beer** ⊞
Cosy, side-street pub with four
rooms; one has a shove-
ha'penny board and strong
sporting links. Don't miss the
room on the left with its
scrubbed-top tables and high
backed settles, formerly for
men only. No food Sun.
Q ◑ ⊞ ≋ ♣

Nag's Head
22 Wyle Cop
☎ (01743) 362455
11–11
Beer range varies ⊞

Often lively, reputedly
haunted, historic house of
considerable architectural
interest, including lots of
wood mouldings. Three or
four beers from Carlsberg-
Tetley. ❀ ≋ ♣

Proud Salopian
Smithfield Road (50 yds from
Welsh Bridge)
☎ (01743) 236887
11–11; 7–10.30 Sun, closed Sun lunch
**Draught Bass; Whitbread
Boddingtons Bitter, Fuggles
IPA; guest beers** ⊞
Pub across a busy road from
the River Severn; the cellar is
prone to flooding. Thomas
Southam, the Shrewsbury
brewer, was the Proud
Salopian. Three guest beers
include a mild. ◑ & ≋ ♣

Three Fishes
4 Fish Street ☎ (01743) 344793
11.30–11
**Taylor Landlord; Wadworth
6X; Whitbread Boddingtons
Bitter, Flowers Original,
Fuggles IPA; guest beer** ⊞
Single-roomed, timber-framed
no-smoking pub: one of the
few pubs nationally where
smoking is not allowed
anywhere. It stands amongst
other buildings of the same era
in a narrow side street.
◑ ≋ ⌀

Stottesdon

Fox & Hounds
High Street
☎ (01746) 718222
7–11; 12–3, 7–11 Sat
**Woody Woodward's Wust
Bitter, Bostin, Wild Mild,
Gobstopper** ⊞
Traditional, unspoilt village
local serving home-brewed
ales from a small brewery
on the premises. The beers
are brewed by the landlord
and his son. Gobstopper
winter ale is now available on
a more regular basis. Skittle
alley for hire.
₥ Q ❀ ◑ ▶ ▲ ♣ P

Telford: Coalbrookdale

Coalbrookdale Inn
12 Wellington Road
☎ (01952) 433953
12–3, 6–11
**Courage Directors; Enville
Mild; guest beers** ⊞
Warm and friendly, 18th-
century inn near the Museum
of Iron. Five guest beers are
always available at this, the
1995 CAMRA national *Pub of
the Year*. Eve meals finish at 8;
no food Sun.
₥ Q ❀ ◑ ▶ ♣ ○ P

Dawley

Three Crowns Inn
Hinkshay Road (off B4373 at
Finger Rd Garage)
☎ (01952) 590868
11–3 (4 Sat), 6.30–11
Marston's Bitter, Pedigree H
Small, friendly, well-
decorated, open-plan,
neighbourhood local; an outlet
for Marston's Head Brewer's
Choice. ❀ ◖ ♣ P

Ironbridge

Golden Ball
1 Newbridge Road (off A4169,
Madeley Hill, at Jockey Bank)
☎ (01952) 432179
12–3, 6–11 (12–11 summer Sat)
**Draught Bass; Courage
Directors; Ruddles Best
Bitter; John Smith's Bitter;
guest beers** H
Multi-roomed pub dating from
the early 18th century and
retaining a period feel. A
varied food menu offers
traditional and international
fare. The landlord's
cellarmanship skills have won
awards. ⚬ ❀ 🛏 ◖ ▶ ♣ P

Horse & Jockey
15 Jockey Bank (set back from
A4169, Madeley Hill)
☎ (01952) 433798
12–3, 6.30–11
**Draught Bass; M&B Highgate
Dark; guest beers** H
Two-roomed pub with a small
bar and a large lounge which
caters for diners, though not
exclusively. A recent
runner-up in a national steak
& kidney pie competition.
❀ ◖ ▶ ◖ ♣ P

Old Vaults Wine Bar
29 High Street
☎ (01952) 432716
11–11 (12–3, 6.30–11 winter)
**Adnams Broadside; guest
beers** H
Food-oriented wine bar in a
splendid location; the terrace
overlooks the famous
Ironbridge. Good local food,
plus a Spanish Tapas menu.
Always one Shropshire guest
beer is sold, plus Belgian La
Trappe Blond and foreign
bottles. The beer is at wine
bar prices.
⚬ ❀ 🛏 ◖ ▶ ⌣

Jackfield

Black Swan
Lloyds Head ☎ (01952) 882471
11–11
**Bass Worthington BB;
Hobsons Best Bitter; M&B
Highgate Dark** H
Attractive, one-room pub

dating from 1750, with original
oak beams. Note the 100-year-
old school clock above the
piano. Food is served all day.
The house beer is produced by
Coach House. ❀ ◖ ▶ ▲ ♣ P

Leegomery

Malt Shovel Inn
Hadley Park Road (off A442,
at Leegomery roundabout)
☎ (01952) 242963
11.30–2.30 (3 Sat), 5–11
**Banks's Mild; Marston's
Bitter, Pedigree, Owd
Rodger** H
Welcoming, two-roomed pub;
very homely, with horse
brasses and open fires: an
outlet for Marston's Head
Brewer's Choice. Weekday
lunches. ⚬ ◖ ◖ ♣ P

Madeley

All Nations
20 Coalport Road
☎ (01952) 585747
12–3, 7–11
All Nations Pale Ale H
One-bar pub overlooking
Blists Hill Museum, one of the
four brew pubs left before the
modern resurgence. Always
popular, not least because of
its prices, it serves no other
draught products. Accessed by
the road opposite the museum.
❀ ▲ ♣ P

St Georges

Albion Inn
Station Hill ☎ (01952) 614193
12–2.45 (4.30 Sat), 5 (7 Sat)–11
**Banks's Mild; Marston's
Bitter, Pedigree** H
Refurbished to a comfortable
standard, a friendly,
welcoming, neighbourhood
pub serving good, home-
cooked food. Marston's Head
Brewer's Choice sold. ❀ 🛏 ◖
▶ ⇌ (Oakengates) ♣ P 🔔

Wellington

Plough
King Street ☎ (01952) 255981
12–3, 5.30–11; 12–11 Sat
**Draught Bass; M&B Highgate
Dark, Brew XI; Tetley
Bitter** H
Large, 18th-century pub with a
central bar which serves all
areas. The lounge is at the
front with a bar/games room
behind. ❀ ◖ ▶ ◖ ⇌ (Telford
West) ♣ P

Upper Farmcote

Lion O'Morfe
Off Bridgnorth–Stourbridge
road, follow Claverley sign
☎ (01746) 710678

11.30 (12 Mon & Sat)–2.30 (5 Sat),
7–11
Banks's Mild, Bitter E;
Draught Bass; guest beer H
Extended Georgian
farmhouse: a traditional bar, a
games room, a lounge and a
conservatory (families
welcome). Floodlit boules. Its
name is derived from 'Morfa'
– Welsh for 'Marsh'. No food
Fri/Sat eves or Sun.
⚬ Q ⍭ ❀ ◖ ▶ ◖ ♣ P ⚥ 🔔

Welsh Frankton

Narrow Boat Inn
Ellesmere Road
☎ (01691) 661051
11–3, 7–11
Tetley Bitter; guest beers H
Welcoming pub beside the
Shropshire Union (Llangollen)
Canal. Three guest beers.
❀ ◖ ▶ ▲ P

Wenlock Edge

Wenlock Edge Inn
Hill Top (B4371)
☎ (01746) 785403
12–2.30 (not Mon), 7–11
**Hobsons Best Bitter, Town
Crier; Webster's Yorkshire
Bitter** H
Welcoming, family-run pub on
top of Wenlock Edge,
attracting a mostly mature
clientele. All meals are home-
cooked (good but limited
menu). No food Mon (story-
telling nights).
⚬ Q ❀ 🛏 ◖ ▶ ◖ P

Wistanstow

Plough
¼ mile from A49/A489 jct
☎ (01588) 673251
12–2.30, 7–11
**Wood Parish, Special,
Wonderful, Christmas
Cracker; guest beers** H
The Wood Brewery tap: a
village local with a good food
reputation. Two bars: the
public is split into snug and
games areas. Ramblers and
cyclists are welcomed. No
food Sun eve/Mon lunch.
⚬ Q ⍭ ◖ ▶ ◖ ♿ ♣ ⌣ P

Yorton

Railway
OS505239 ☎ (01939) 220240
11.30–3, 6–11
**Draught Bass; Wadworth 6X;
Whitbread Castle Eden Ale;
Wood Parish, Special** H
Pub owned by the same family
for many years, reflected in its
unchanging atmosphere. A
friendly, simple bar and a
large lounge. One of the beers
may be on gravity to
accommodate a guest. ⚬ Q
❀ ⇌ (request) ♣ P

Somerset

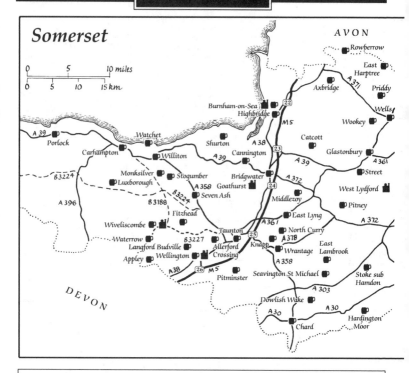

Ash Vine, *Trudoxhill*; **Berrow**, *Burnham-on-Sea*;
Bridgwater, *Goathurst*; **Cotleigh**, *Wiveliscombe*;
Cottage, *West Lydford*; **Exmoor**, *Wiveliscombe*;
Henstridge, *Henstridge*; **Juwards**, *Wellington*;
Oakhill, *Oakhill*

Allerford Crossing

Victory Inn

½ mile S of B3227 OS182249
☎ (01823) 461282
11–3, 6–11
**Cotleigh Tawny; Morland
Old Speckled Hen; Ringwood
Fortyniner; Taylor Landlord;
guest beers** H
Large, multi-roomed pub
which caters for all, especially
families. Up to 11 real ales but
beware the Boddingtons and
John Smith's (aspirated.) Good
value food in the bar and
restaurant. Two gardens; the
family one now features a
full-size train and bouncy
castle in summer. Cider in
summer.
🏚 🐄 ❀ ◑ ▶ 🍴 ᴴ ♣ ⌂ P ⚲

Appley

Globe Inn

2½ miles N of A38 at White Ball
Hill OS071215
☎ (01823) 672327

11–3 (not Mon), 6.30–11
**Cotleigh Tawny, Barn Owl;
Dartmoor Best Bitter**
(occasional) H
Lovely old village inn, deep in
the countryside. The bar is a
simple hatchway in a
flagstoned corridor, with
several cosy rooms leading off.
Pretty garden with some
children's play equipment.
Good quality, good value food
always available. Well worth
the journey down the winding
lanes.
🏚 Q 🐄 ❀ ◑ ▶ ▲ ♣ ⌂ P

Axbridge

Lamb Inn

The Square ☎ (01934) 732253
11.30–2.30 (3 Sat), 6.30–11
**Draught Bass; Butcombe
Bitter; Wadworth 6X; guest
beers** H
Rambling old pub, now
owned by Butcombe, opposite
King John's hunting lodge.
Large, terraced garden. The
unusual bar is made of bottles.
Q ❀ 🛏 ◑ ▶ 🍴 ᴴ ♣

Bridgwater

Commercial Inn

Redgate Street (off A372)
☎ (01278) 426989
11–2.30 (3 Sat), 7–11; 11–2.30, 7–10.30
Sun
**Butcombe Bitter; Whitbread
Flowers IPA; guest beers** H
Popular local next to the
station. It has a bar area with a
pool table, plus a lounge area,
skittle alley and garden.
❀ ◑ ᴴ ♣ 🚲 ♣ P

Fountain Inn

West Quay
☎ (01278) 424115
11.30–3, 6.30–11; 11–11 Fri & Sat
**Butcombe Bitter; Hall &
Woodhouse Tanglefoot;
Wadworth 6X; guest
beers** H
Single-roomed pub on the
river, providing a friendly,
local feel in the town centre.
Mixed clientele. Guest
beers come from Wadworth's
list. No food Sun.
Q ◑ ᴴ 🚲 🚲

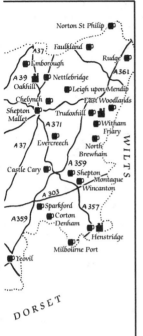

Burnham-on-Sea

Royal Clarence Hotel
31 The Esplanade
☎ (01278) 783138
11–11
RCH PG Steam, Pitchfork, Slug Porter, East Street Cream, Firebox; guest beers Ⓗ
The RCH brewery tap: a large seafront hotel catering for a wide range of customers. It hosts two large beer festivals a year (Feb and Oct) and stocks the full range of RCH beers, plus a good selection of bottled beers. The Addlestones cider is under gas; try the Crossmans or Wilkins Traditional.
Q ⚲ ⛺ ◗ ᗡ ᴕ ⓓ Ⓐ ⌂ ⚲

Cannington

Malt Shovel Inn
Blackmoor Lane (off A39)
☎ (01278) 653432
11.30–2.30 (3 Sat), 7–11
Butcombe Bitter; John Smith's Bitter; guest beer Ⓗ
Family-run free house overlooking the Quantocks. Rich's and Lanes cider available. No meals Sun eve.
⚲ Q ⛺ ❀ ⛺ ◗ ᗡ ᗡ ⌂ P

Carhampton

Butcher's Arms
Main Road (A39)
☎ (01643) 821333
11–3, 6–11; 11–11 Sat
Cotleigh Tawny; Smiles Bitter; Whitbread Flowers Original; guest beers (occasional) Ⓗ
Village local, home of the cricket team and host to other rural pastimes; one of the last pubs to carry on the tradition of wassailing the cider orchard. Recommended for families. Rich's cider available.
⚲ ⚲ ❀ ⛺ ◗ ᗡ Ⓐ ⇌ (West Somerset Railway) ᴕ ⌂

Castle Cary

George Hotel
Market Place ☎ (01963) 350761
10.30–3, 6–11; 12–2.30, 7–10.30 Sun
Draught Bass; Butcombe Bitter Ⓗ
Thatched, Grade II-listed coaching inn (1470), on the Leyland Trail (walkers welcome): a privately-owned hotel with a reputation for good food. ⚲ Q ⛺ ◗ ᗡ ⓓ P

Try also: Horse Pond, The Triangle (Free)

Catcott

King William Inn
Off A39 ☎ (01278) 722374
11.30–3, 6–11
Eldridge Pope Dorchester, Hardy Country, Royal Oak; Palmers IPA Ⓗ
Old village pub with a modern restaurant extension, a small public bar with a dartboard, and a traditional lounge bar with a glass-covered old well in the centre (discovered when an extension was added to the family room and skittle alley).
Q ❀ ◗ ᗡ ⓓ ⓓ ᴕ ⌂ P

Chard

Bell & Crown
Combe Street, Crimchard
☎ (01460) 62470
11–3 (not Mon), 7–11
Shepherd Neame Best Bitter, Spitfire; Smiles Bitter; guest beer Ⓗ
Some ten minutes' walk from the town centre and popular with locals, this pub still has gas lighting. Good value food (not served Sun/Mon eves). Regular beer festivals.
Q ❀ ◗ ᗡ ᴕ P

Chelynch

Poacher's Pocket
☎ (01749) 880220
11.30 (12 Mon)–2.30, 6–11

Butcombe Bitter; Oakhill Best Bitter; Wadworth 6X; guest beer Ⓗ
Part-14th-century pub in a small village, half a mile north of the A361. It is mostly given over to food, but remains popular as a locals' drinking pub. The large garden is well-patronised on summer weekends. Wilkins cider.
⚲ Q ❀ ◗ ᗡ ᴕ ⌂ P

Corton Denham

Queen's Arms Inn
3 miles S of A303
☎ (01963) 220317
11.30–3, 6.30–11
Exmoor Ale; RCH PG Steam; guest beers Ⓗ
Comfortable, rural pub in superb walking country. Guest ales of the month are featured on a chalkboard. Good choice of specials on the food menu. Taunton and Inch's cider.
⚲ Q ❀ ⛺ ◗ ᗡ ⓓ ⓓ Ⓐ ᴕ ⌂ P ⚲

Dowlish Wake

New Inn
☎ (01460) 52413
11–3, 6–11
Butcombe Bitter; S&N Theakston Old Peculier; Wadworth 6X Ⓗ
Popular village pub with two bars and a good-sized garden which caters for families. A range of home-cooked food includes Swiss specialities. Near Perry's cider farm. ⚲ Q ⚲ ❀ ⛺ ◗ ᗡ ⓓ ᴕ ⌂ P

East Harptree

Castle of Comfort
On B3134 ½ mile N of B3135
☎ (01761) 221321
12–2.30, 7–11
Draught Bass; Butcombe Bitter; guest beers Ⓗ
Stone-built coaching inn on the old Roman road. Two bars serve up to four ales, with guest beers usually available at weekends (over 350 beers to date). Ask the landlord about the real ale ghost. Good value food. ❀ ◗ ᗡ ᴕ P

East Lambrook

Rose & Crown
Silver Street (off A303)
☎ (01460) 240433
11.30–2.30 (3 Sat), 7–11
Bass Worthington BB; M&B Highgate Dark; Otter Ale; guest beers Ⓗ
Cosy, oak-beamed, traditional, two-bar village pub, one of the few in Somerset to stock a permanent traditional mild.

Somerset

Good value food. Burrow Hill cider. Children's certificate. 🏮 ⌂ ✿ ◖ ▸ ⊟ ⅋ ▲ ♣ ⌂ P ⅋ ⊟

East Lyng

Rose & Crown
☎ (01823) 698235
11–2.30, 6.30–11
Butcombe Bitter; Eldridge Pope Hardy Country, Royal Oak Ⓗ
Comfortable, civilised village pub, popular with locals and visitors alike. It features a large stone fireplace, beams and antique furniture. A small restaurant area leads off the main bar. The food is good and the garden pleasant.
🏮 Q ✿ 🚪 ◖ ▸ ♣ P

East Woodlands

Horse & Groom
1 mile SE of A361/B3092 jct
☎ (01373) 462802
11.30 (12 Mon)–2.30, 6.30–11
Bateman XB; Wadworth 6X; guest beer Ⓖ
17th-century inn on the western edge of Longleat estate. A cosy bar with an open fireplace and a flagstone floor, plus a small dining room. A new extension has been completed as a family room. Seafood is a speciality (no food Sun eve or Mon). Cider in summer.
🏮 Q ✿ 🚪 ◖ ▸ ♣ ⌂ P

Emborough

Old Down Inn
At A37/B3139 crossroads
☎ (01761) 232398
11.30–3, 7–11
Draught Bass Ⓗ
Atmospheric coaching inn circa 1640, with a variety of rooms and old furniture. It burnt down in 1886. No food Sun. Camp opposite.
🏮 Q 🚪 ◖ ▸ ▲ ♣ P

Evercreech

Bell Inn
Bruton Road (B3081)
☎ (01749) 830287
11.30–3, 6.30 (5.30 Fri)–11
Butcombe Bitter; Courage Directors; John Smith's Bitter; guest beers Ⓗ
17th-century inn with roaring fires: one bar, with a restaurant area and a games room. 🏮 Q ◖ ▸ ⊟ ♣ P

Faulkland

Tucker's Grave Inn
On A366, 1 mile E of village
☎ (01373) 834230
11–3, 6–11

Draught Bass; Butcombe Bitter Ⓖ
Former cottage that has doubled as an inn for over 200 years. Three old-fashioned rooms; no bar counter. The burial site of a suicide in 1747; the story of the unfortunate Edward Tucker can be found above the parlour fireplace. Cheddar Valley cider.
🏮 Q ✿ ⊟ ▲ ♣ ⌂ P

Fitzhead

Fitzhead Inn
Off B3227 ☎ (01823) 400667
12–3, 7–11
Cotleigh Tawny; guest beers Ⓗ
Cosy village pub with a reputation for good quality, good value food (booking recommended). Three guest beers are always available, plus Bollhayes cider.
🏮 Q ✿ ✿ ◖ ▸ ▲ ♣ ⌂

Glastonbury

Beckets Inn
43 High Street
☎ (01458) 832928
12–11
Hall & Woodhouse Tanglefoot; Wadworth IPA, 6X, Old Timer; guest beer Ⓗ
Basic, town-centre pub with three rooms and a central bar.
🏮 ✿ ✿ ▲

Who'd A Thought It
17 North-Load Street
☎ (01458) 834460
11–2.30, 6–11
Draught Bass; Eldridge Pope Hardy Country, Blackdown Porter; Palmers IPA; guest beers (occasional) Ⓗ
Attractive town pub featuring numerous collections and war-time posters. It has its own phonebox inside, along with a well. Regional *Loo of the Year* winner (wheelchair toilet).
🏮 Q ✿ ✿ 🚪 ◖ ▸ ▲ P ⅋

Hardington Moor

Royal Oak
Moor Lane (off Yeovil-Crewkerne road)
☎ (01935) 862354
12–3 (not Mon), 7–11
Butcombe Bitter; Hardington Bitter; Hook Norton Old Hooky; guest beer Ⓗ
Former farmhouse offering a warm and friendly atmosphere, and a good choice of snacks and meals (not served Mon lunch). Three ciders are usually available. Skittle alley for functions. Camping by arrangement.
🏮 Q ✿ ◖ ▸ ▲ ♣ ⌂ P

Henstridge

Bird in Hand
Ash Walk ☎ (01963) 362255
11–2.30, 5.30–11; 11–11 Sat
Draught Bass; Smiles Bitter; guest beer Ⓗ
Classic village pub with wooden beams. A low roof and suitable lighting create a pleasant atmosphere. Taunton cider.
⌂ ✿ ◖ ⊟ ⅋ ▲ ♣ ⌂ P

Highbridge

Cooper's Arms
Market Street
☎ (01278) 783562
11–3, 5.15–11
Palmers IPA; guest beers Ⓔ
Large, long-roomed pub with two lounges and a bar skittle alley. A large blackboard displays the ever-changing guest beers (at least four plus two house beers – usually from big brewers). The station is on the doorstep. No food.
✿ ▲ ⇌ P

Knapp

Rising Sun
Off A361, then follow signs
OS301254 ☎ (01823) 490436
11–2.30, 6.30–11
Draught Bass; Exmoor Ale; Whitbread Boddingtons Bitter Ⓗ
15th-century inn: a fine example of a Somerset longhouse with many original features, including two inglenooks. Winner of many national awards for its extensive fish menu, it has a busy weekend food trade (eve meals also in the restaurant). Local farm cider in summer.
🏮 Q ✿ ✿ 🚪 ◖ ▲ ⌂ P

Langford Budville

Martlett Inn
½ mile off B3187
☎ (01823) 400262
12–3, 7–11
Cotleigh Tawny, Barn Owl; Exmoor Ale Ⓗ
Old, multi-roomed, village local, part-flagstoned, with low beams and two roaring fires in winter. Good food served. Large garden.
🏮 Q ✿ ✿ ◖ ▸ ⊟ ▲ ♣ P

Leigh upon Mendip

Bell
High Street ☎ (01373) 812316
12–3, 7–11
Draught Bass; Butcombe Bitter; Wadworth 6X Ⓗ

Much altered and extended village inn, now comfortably furnished with the emphasis on food (served in the restaurant and throughout the pub). Friendly local atmosphere at the bar.
🏚 ❀ ◖▶ P

Luxborough

Royal Oak
☎ (01984) 40319
11–2.30, 6–11
Cotleigh Tawny; Exmoor Ale G; Whitbread Flowers IPA H; guest beers
Unspoilt, rural village pub in the heart of the Brendon Hills (superb walking country). The pub is known locally as the Blazing Stump and is noted for home-cooked food. Folk club Fri. The car park is 50 yds from the pub. Rich's and Cheddar Valley cider.
🏚 Q ☞ ❀ 🏚 ◖▶ ▲ ♣ P

Middlezoy

George Inn
☎ (01823) 698215
12–3, (not Mon) 7–11
Butcombe Bitter; Courage Best Bitter; guest beers H
Thriving village local now owned by a local couple. Old beams and a flagged floor enhance the main bar; there is also a dining room and large skittle alley with a bar. Good quality food (not served Sun eve or Mon). Cider in summer.
🏚 ☞ ❀ 🏚 ◖▶ 🍴 ♣ ▲ ♣ ⌂ P 🍴

Milbourne Port

Queen's Head
High Street (A30)
☎ (01963) 250314
11–11
Butcombe Bitter; Ringwood Fortyniner; Whitbread Flowers Original; guest beers H
Busy village pub with a restaurant and a skittle alley. Excellent food and guest beers (four). 🏚 Q ☞ ❀ 🏚 ◖▶ 🍴 ♣ ⌂ P

Monksilver

Notley Arms
☎ (01984) 656217
11.30–2.30, 6.30–11; 12–2.30, 7–10.30 Sun
Exmoor Ale; Morland Old Speckled Hen; Ushers Best Bitter; Wadworth 6X H
Country inn at the village centre, an ideal base for walking in the Brendon Hills. Noted for its award-winning food, it has a large, child-

friendly garden and a family room. Beware the Addlestones cider is kept under gas.
🏚 Q ☞ ❀ ◖▶ ♣ P

Nettlebridge

Nettlebridge Inn
On A367, 1 mile N of Oakhill
☎ (01749) 841360
11.30–2.30, 6–11
Oakhill Best Bitter, Black Magic, Yeoman H
Big roadside pub in a pretty valley on the edge of the Mendips: the 'tap' for nearby Oakhill Brewery. Priority is given to good value food in the single, large main bar.
❀ 🏚 ◖▶ P

North Brewham

Old Red Lion
On Maiden Bradley–Bruton road OS722368
☎ (01749) 850287
12–3, 6–11
Butcombe Bitter; guest beer H
Stone-built, former farmhouse in an isolated rural setting. The bar is in the old dairy, with flagged floors. Two regular guest beers, one usually a mild; Thatcher's cider. 🏚 Q ❀ ◖▶ ♣ ⌂ P

North Curry

Bird in Hand
Queen Square
☎ (01823) 490248
12–2.30, 7–11
Butcombe Bitter; Hall & Woodhouse Tanglefoot; Wadworth 6X; guest beers H
Superbly renovated village local with low beams and ever-changing guest ales. The pub runs many special eves and produces a 'what's on' newsheet for the village. Rich's Farmhouse cider. 🏚 Q ☞ ❀ ◖▶ 🍴 ▲ ♣ ⌂ P ✕

Norton St Philip

Fleur de Lys
High Street (B3110)
☎ (01373) 834333
10–3, 5–11; 10–11 Sat
Bass Charrington IPA, Draught Bass; Oakhill Best Bitter; Wadworth 6X H
Ancient stone building, partly dating from the 13th century, which has undergone an extensive, but mainly sympathetic refurbishment. Unfortunately, the resited bar now blocks the old passageway through which the pub ghost was said to pass on his way to the gallows.
🏚 Q ❀ ◖▶ ♣ P

Pitminster

Queen's Arms
Off B3170 at Corfe
☎ (01823) 421529
11–3, 5–11
Brains SA; Cotleigh Tawny; Greene King Abbot; guest beers H
Popular, cosy village pub and restaurant, also serving interesting bar meals. Usually four guest beers. The bar area is effectively divided in half by an old black iron stove, great to warm by after a walk on the Blackdown Hills. Cider in summer.
🏚 Q ❀ 🏚 ◖▶ 🍴 ▲ ♣ ⌂ P

Pitney

Halfway House
☎ (01458) 252513
11.30–2.30, 5.30–11
Bridgwater Sunbeam; Butcombe Bitter; Cotleigh Tawny; Oakhill Best Bitter; Teignworthy Reel Ale; guest beers G
Old village pub featuring real fires, flagstone floors and rudimentary wooden furniture. It always has six–nine beers available, mostly from South-West micros. Try the home-cooked curries (no food Sun). A real gem; Somerset CAMRA *Pub of the Year*.
🏚 Q ☞ ❀ ◖▶ ▲ ♣ P

Try also: Rose & Crown, Huish Episcopi (Free)

Porlock

Ship Inn
High Street ☎ (01643) 862507
10.30–3, 5.30–11
Draught Bass; Cotleigh Old Buzzard; Courage Best Bitter; guest beer H
Old, traditional inn mentioned in *Lorna Doone*. A superb bar area attracts the locals; the restaurant specialises in local food cooked on an Aga. Perry's cider available. Good for families. 🏚 Q ❀ 🏚 ◖ ▶ 🍴 ▲ ♣ ⌂ P

Priddy

New Inn
☎ (01749) 676465
11.30 (12 Mon)–2.30, 7–11; 12–2.30, 7–10.30 Sun
Draught Bass; Eldridge Pope Hardy Country; Wadworth 6X H
15th-century farmhouse on the village green, with flagstoned bars. Warm and friendly, it enjoys a reputation for good food, including a choice of vegetarian meals. Popular at weekends. Wilkins cider. 🏚 Q ❀ 🏚 ◖▶ 🍴 ▲ ♣ ⌂ P

Somerset

Rowberrow

Swan Inn
☎ (01934) 852371
12–3, 6–11; 12–2.30, 7–10.30 Sun
Draught Bass; Butcombe Bitter; Wadworth 6X; guest beers Ⓗ
Former cider house, converted from three stone cottages and now housing two bars with fake beams and a large fireplace. No food Sun.
🏨 Q ❀ ◖ ▶ P

Rudge

Full Moon
1 mile N of A36 bypass at Standerwick OS829518
☎ (01373) 830936
12–3, 6–11
Draught Bass; Butcombe Bitter; Wadworth 6X Ⓗ
Splendid, 300-year-old building, greatly extended in 1991, but retaining most of its original features, including the stone floors. The emphasis is on the food trade, skittle alley, families and accommodation. C&W music Sun eves.
🏨 Q ❀ 🏨 ◖ ▶ ⌑ ▲ ♣ ⌂ P

Seavington St Michael

Volunteer
On old A303 ☎ (01460) 240126
12–2.30 (not Mon), 5.30–11; 12–11 Sat
Oakhill Best Bitter; guest beers Ⓗ
Roadside pub: a small public bar and a large lounge with low beams and wood-panelled walls. Good pub food. Scalextric car racing Mon nights, when no food is served. 🏨 Q ◖ ▶ ♣ P

Seven Ash

Quantock Cottage Inn
On A358 ☎ (01823) 432467
12–2.30, 6–11
Bridgwater Coppernob; Cotleigh Tawny; guest beer Ⓗ
Comfortable, family-run pub on the busy road to Minehead. Good family facilities (family room in summer). Lanes cider also in summer. Food served Wed–Sun. 🏨 Q ☎ ❀ 🏨 ◖ ▶ & ▲ ♣ ⌂ P

Shepton Mallet

Horseshoe Inn
Bowlish (A371, ½ mile W of centre) ☎ (01749) 342209
12–2.30, 6–11
Draught Bass; guest beer Ⓗ
Unpretentious local on the edge of town. The lounge bar is mainly used as a dining area. For the more down-to-earth pub-goer, there is a popular and splendidly well-equipped public bar. No food Sun eve or Mon.
🏨 ❀ ◖ ▶ 🏨 ♣

King's Arms
Leg Square ☎ (01749) 343781
11.30–2.30, 6–11
Ansells Bitter; Eldridge Pope Hardy Country; Ind Coope Burton Ale Ⓗ
Originally 17th-century, but much altered; a pub of some character. The large games room has a skittle alley; there is also a cosy snug, and a large main bar where food predominates. The conservatory looks on to an open courtyard.
❀ 🏨 ◖ ▶ 🏨 ♣ P

Shepton Montague

Montague Inn
Off A359, S of Bruton OS675316 ☎ (01749) 813213
12–3 (not Mon–Fri), 5.30–11
Butcombe Bitter; Marston's Pedigree; guest beer Ⓖ
Remote but convivial country pub. Thatcher's cider served.
🏨 Q ❀ ⌂ P

Shurton

Shurton Inn
Follow signs to Hinkley Point power station
☎ (01278) 732695
11–2.30, 6–11
Exmoor Ale; Morland Old Speckled Hen; John Smith's Bitter Ⓗ
Village pub hosting various music eves and a flea market in the skittle alley every Sun lunch. Lanes cider. 🏨 Q ❀ ◖ ▶ 🏨 & ▲ ♣ ⌂ P 🏨

Sparkford

Sparkford Inn
Off A303 ☎ (01963) 440218
11–2.30, 6.30–11
Worthington BB, Draught Bass; Wadworth 6X; guest beers Ⓗ
15th-century coaching inn, retaining many of its original features, including several rooms and corridors, catering for all the family. Regular music eves and Sun car boot events. Cider in summer. 🏨 Q ☎ ❀ 🏨 ◖ ▶ & ▲ ♣ ⌂ P

Stogumber

White Horse
The Square ☎ (01984) 656277
11–2.30, 6–11
Cotleigh Tawny; Exmoor Ale Ⓗ
Traditional pub in an historic village. Accommodation and a restaurant are housed in the adjoining market house. Look out for memorabilia of the long-gone Stogumber Brewery. Sheppy's cider in summer. Limited parking.
🏨 Q 🏨 ◖ ▶ 🏨 ♣ ⌂ P

Stoke sub Hamdon

Half Moon Inn
Off A303, below Ham Hill
☎ (01935) 824890
12–2.30, 6.30–11
Oakhill Best Bitter; Whitbread Best Bitter, Flowers Original; guest beers Ⓗ
Popular village local which concentrates on real ales (always four guests). Live bands most Sat eves; regular folk club and jazz music. East Chinnock cider.
❀ 🏨 ▲ ♣ ⌂ P

Street

Two Brewers
38 Leigh Road
☎ (01458) 442421
11–3, 6–11
Courage Best Bitter, Directors; Wadworth 6X; guest beers Ⓗ
Recently refurbished, open-plan pub with a large, central bar. Two ever-changing guest ales come from all over the country. Good food.
Q ☎ ◖ ▶ ▲ ♣ P

Taunton

Mason's Arms
Magdalene Street
☎ (01823) 288916
10–3, 5 (6 Sat)–11
Draught Bass; Exe Valley Dob's Best Bitter; guest beers Ⓗ
Comfortable, one-bar pub with a relaxing atmosphere, situated off the main streets. Fresh food is always available.
Q 🏨 ◖ ▶ 🍽 ♣

Minstrel's (Castle Hotel)
Castle Bow ☎ (01823) 337780
11–3, 7–11; 11–11 Thu–Sat
Draught Bass; Eldridge Pope Hardy Country; guest beer Ⓗ
Popular, town-centre bar, part of the well-known Castle Hotel, but run separately. It features high ceilings and wood panelling. Live music three nights a week. Popular at lunchtimes with shoppers (no-smoking area lunchtime).
🏨 ◖ ▶ 🍽 ⌀

Wood Street Inn

Wood Street
☎ (01823) 333011
11–11 (may close afternoons if quiet)
Beer range varies Ⓗ
Basic back-street local, popular
with all ages. The three
changing beers tend to be from
local independent breweries.
Live music at weekends. Large
public car park opposite.
🏶 🛏 ይ 🚲 ♣

Trudoxhill

White Hart

½ mile S of A361 at Nunney
Catch OS749438
☎ (01373) 836324
12–3, 7 (6.30 Fri & Sat)–11
Ash Vine Bitter, Challenger,
Black Bess Porter, Hop &
Glory; guest beer Ⓗ
Comfortable, open-plan village
pub with exposed beams and a
large fireplace. Ash Vine
brewery is at the rear. Ash
Vine's monthly special brews
also served, plus Thatcher's
cider. 🏚 🏶 ◖ ▶ ⊂ P

Watchet

West Somerset Hotel

Swain Street
☎ (01984) 634434
11–11
Courage Directors; John
Smith's Bitter; guest beers Ⓗ
Lively local; a former coaching
inn at an historic port.
Accommodation and matches
are arranged for touring
cricket teams. Good value
food.
ㅎ 🏶 🛏 ◖ ▶ 🖵 ይ 🛦 ♣ 🖵

Waterrow

Rock Inn

On B3227 ☎ (01984) 623293
11–2.30, 6–11
Cotleigh Tawny; Exmoor
Gold; John Smith's Bitter Ⓗ
Interesting old inn, set against
a rockface, which forms the
rear wall of part of the bar
area (public-style at one end
with a lounge and restaurant
at the other). Sheppy's cider in
summer.
🏚 Q 🛏 ◖ ይ 🛦 ♣ ⊂ P

Wellington

Cottage Inn

31 Champford Lane
☎ (01823) 664650
11–3, 6–11
Cotleigh Tawny; John Smith's
Bitter; guest beers Ⓗ
Cosy town local, handy for the
cinema. Always at least two

guest beers on. Popular with
the locals, it serves good value
bar lunches. 🏶 ◖ ♣ P

Try also: **Ship Inn**, Mantle St
(Gibbs Mew)

Wells

Britannia Inn

Bath Road (B3139)
☎ (01749) 672033
12–2.30, 5–11; 11–11 Sat
Butcombe Bitter; John
Smith's Bitter; Ushers Best
Bitter Ⓗ
'Top of the town' local serving
housing estates at the north
end of the city. Eve meals at
weekends. Q ㅎ ◖ ▶ P

Try also: **Rose & Crown**, St
John's St (Ushers)

Williton

Forester's Arms

55 Long Street
☎ (01984) 632508
11–11
Cotleigh Tawny; John Smith's
Bitter; guest beers Ⓗ
17th-century inn, close to the
West Somerset Railway
station; an ideal base for
walking the Quantock Hills.
Reputed to be haunted by the
ghost of a 14-year-old girl
from the neighbouring old
workhouse.
🏚 🏶 🛏 ◖ ▶ ይ 🚲 ♣ P

Wincanton

Bear Inn

12 Market Place
☎ (01963) 32581
11–2.30, 5.30–11
Draught Bass; Fuller's
London Pride; guest beers Ⓗ
Large former coaching inn
with several drinking areas
and a substantial games room.
Weekly archery in the skittle
alley. Guest beers always
include a session, as well as a
stronger, beer.
🏚 Q 🛏 ◖ ▶ ♣ P

Red Lion Inn

Market Place ☎ (01963) 33095
11–11
Draught Bass; Oakhill Best
Bitter; Young's Special Ⓗ
Welcoming, one-bar, town-
centre pub with a congenial
atmosphere. Popular with the
locals. ◖ ♣ ⊂

Witham Friary

Seymour Arms

On minor road off B3092, by
old railway station OS745410
☎ (01749) 850742
11–3, 6–11

Ushers Best Bitter Ⓗ
Old village local, unspoilt by
progress. It boasts a central
serving hatch and a fine
garden. Rich's cider on
gravity. 🏚 Q 🏶 ⊞ 🛦 ♣ ⊂

Wiveliscombe

Courtyard Hotel

10–12 High Street
☎ (01984) 623737
11.30–3, 7–11
Cotleigh Tawny; Oakhill Best
Bitter; Teignworthy Reel
Ale Ⓗ**; guest beers** Ⓗ/ Ⓖ
Pub with a small, quiet bar
featuring household
furnishings, plus a new
underground cellar bar which
offers beers on gravity
dispense. Usually four guests
available, plus Thatcher's
cider. Q 🛏 ◖ ⊂

Wookey

Burcott Inn

☎ (01749) 673874
11–2.30 (3 Sat), 6–11
Cotleigh Tawny; guest
beers Ⓗ
Popular roadside pub with a
friendly atmosphere. The
L-shaped bar has a copper
serving top. There is also a
small games room and a
good-sized garden, featuring
an old cider press. Good food
(no meals Sun eve in winter).
🏚 Q ㅎ 🏶 ◖ ▶ ♣ P

Wrantage

Canal Inn

On A372 ☎ (01823) 480210
12–3, 7–11
Exmoor Ale; Whitbread
Flowers Original; guest
beer Ⓗ
Friendly local offering good
food and an outdoor children's
play area. Skittles and darts
are played. Lanes local cider.
🏚 Q 🏶 ◖ ▶ 🛦 ♣ ⊂ P

Yeovil

Armoury

1 The Park ☎ (01935) 71047
12–2.30, 6 (6.30 Mon–Tue)–11; 11–11
Fri & Sat
Adnams Broadside; Butcombe
Bitter; Wadworth 6X, Farmer's
Glory; guest beer Ⓗ
Lively, simply furnished, town
pub, formerly (as its name
suggests) an armoury. Snacks
and salads are available
lunchtimes (not Sun). Live
bands play every other Sat
eve. Taunton cider.
Q 🏶 ◖ ይ ♣ ⊂ P

Taste the exotic! Visit a CAMRA beer festival (see page 225 for details).

Staffordshire

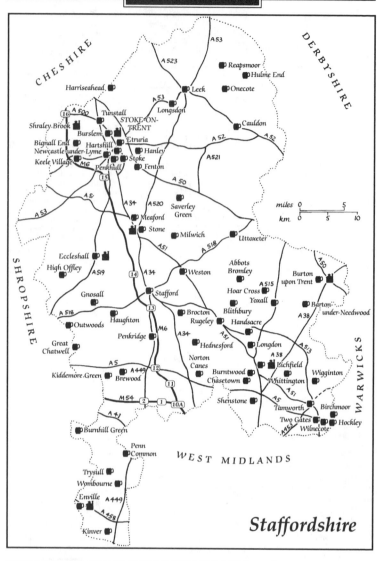

Staffordshire

Burton Bridge, *Burton upon Trent*; **Eccleshall**, *Eccleshall*; **Enville**, *Enville*; **Lichfield**, *Lichfield*; **Marston's**, *Burton upon Trent*; **Rising Sun**, *Shraley Brook*; **Titanic**, *Burslem*

Abbots Bromley

Bagot Arms
Bagot Street (B5234)
☎ (01283) 840371
11–2.30, 5.30–11
Marston's Pedigree Ⓗ
18th-century coaching inn specialising in good food. Close to Blithfield Reservoir.

Marston's Head Brewer's Choice stocked. Q ❋ ◖ ▶ ♣ P

Barton-under-Needwood

Top Bell
52 Barton Gate (B5016)
☎ (01283) 712510
12–3, 6–11

Burtonwood Bitter, Forshaw's, Top Hat Ⓗ
Typical, beamed country pub. Live music is encouraged.
🏧 ❋ ◖ ▶ & ▲ ♣ P

Bignall End

Plough
Ravens Lane (B5500)
☎ (01782) 720469

266

Staffordshire

12–3, 7–11; 12–11 Fri & Sat
**Banks's Bitter; Camerons
Strongarm; Marston's
Pedigree; guest beers** H
Welcoming, roadside hostelry,
catering for local and passing
trade in two rooms, with a
split-level lounge. Good value
meals; constantly changing
guest beers. ❀ ◖ ▶ ♣ P

Birchmoor

Gamecock Inn
☎ (01827) 331254
11–3, 6–11
Draught Bass; M&B Mild H
Old mining village pub with
several rooms and plenty of
character.
🚪 Q 🛏 ❀ ◖ ▶ ᕼ ♣ P

Blithbury

Bull & Spectacles
Uttoxeter Road (B5014)
☎ (01889) 504201
12–3, 6–11
**Ind Coope Burton Ale;
Marston's Pedigree** H
15th-century country pub near
Blithfield Reservoir.
❀ ◖ ▶ ♣ P

Brewood

Swan
15 Market Square
☎ (01902) 850330
11–3, 7–11
**Draught Bass; S&N
Theakston XB; Younger
Scotch; guest beer** H
One-roomed lounge pub with
mostly original beams and two
snug areas. Skittle alley
upstairs. 🚪 ◖ ♣ P

Brocton

Chetwynd Arms
Cannock Road (A34)
☎ (01785) 661089
11.30–3, 5.45–11; 11–11 Sat
**Banks's Mild, Bitter;
Camerons Strongarm;
Marston's Pedigree** H
Bustling main road pub at the
north-west boundary of
Cannock Chase. No meals Sat
eve or Sun. ❀ ◖ ▶ ᕼ ᕒ ♣ P

Burnhill Green

Dartmouth Arms
Snowdon Road OS787006
☎ (01746) 783268
12–3, 7–11
**Ansells Mild, Bitter; Ind
Coope ABC Best Bitter,
Burton Ale; guest beer** H
Popular village pub, renowned
for home-made bar meals
served in the small restaurant
area (book at busy times).
Children's meals are served in
the garden only. Carlsberg-

Tetley 'guest' beer. No meals
Sun eve or Mon lunch.
🚪 ❀ ◖ ▶ P

Burntwood

Drill
Spindlestyche Lane (off
Rugeley Rd) ☎ (01543) 682393
11–11
**Everards Tiger; Tetley
Bitter** H
Lively country pub close to
Cannock Chase. Live
entertainment. Open for Sun
breakfast. The house bitter
(Brill) is Lichfield Inspired.
❀ ◖ ▶ P

Burton upon Trent

Beacon Hotel
227 Tutbury Road (A50)
☎ (01283) 568968
11–3, 6–11
**Draught Bass; Ruddles
County; guest beer or Ind
Coope Burton Ale** E
Large, comfortable, three-
roomed hotel on the outskirts
of Burton, with a purpose-
built family room. Good value
meals. The landlord is a
Burton *Master Cellarman*.
Q 🛏 ❀ ◖ ▶ ᕼ ᕒ ♣ P ᕲ

Boathouse Inn
The Dingle, Stapenhill (off
Ferry St) ☎ (01283) 538831
12–3 (not Mon–Thu), 7–11
**Draught Bass; Greene King
Abbot; Marston's Pedigree;
Morland Old Speckled Hen;
Ruddles County; Wadworth
6X** H
Pub on a bank of the Trent
beside the ferry bridge, with a
garden play area for children,
and an upstairs restaurant.
Jazz Thu eve. Q ❀ ◖ ▶ P

Burton Bridge Inn
24 Bridge Street (A50, by Trent
Bridge) ☎ (01283) 536596
11.30–2.15, 5.30–11; 12–2, 7–10.30
Sun
**Burton Bridge Summer Ale,
XL, Bridge Bitter, Porter, Top
Dog Stout, Festival; guest
beer** (Sun) H
Cheery brewery tap with
wooden pews and award-
covered walls. Regular
seasonal and commemorative
brews; good range of whiskies
and country wines. Easter beer
festival. No food Sun. Q ◖ ♣

Cooper's Tavern
Cross Street (off Station Street)
☎ (01283) 532551
12–2.30, 5 (7 Sat)–11
**Draught Bass; Hardys &
Hansons Best Mild** G**, Best
Bitter** H**, Kimberley Classic** G**;
Marston's Pedigree** H
Truly traditional alehouse
with a renowned tap room:
note the stillaged casks, barrel
tables and 'top bench' seat.

Basic, good value food (no
meals Sun). Coaches welcome.
Staffordshire CAMRA *Pub of
the Year 1994.* Q ◖ ᕒ ⇌ ♣

Roebuck Hotel
Station Street
☎ (01283) 568660
11–11; 11–3, 6–11.30 Sat
**Ansells Mild, Bitter; Ind
Coope Burton Ale; Marston's
Pedigree; S&N Theakston XB;
guest beer** H
Ind Coope's busy, one-room
tap, just across the road from
the brewery. One guest beer
from the 'Tapster's Choice' list
is available; over 350 different
guest beers have been served.
Busy at weekends. Eve meals
end at 8pm. Beware the keg
cider on a fake handpump.
❀ 🚪 ◖ ▶ ⇌ ♣

Thomas Sykes
Heritage Brewery, Anglesey
Road ☎ (01283) 510246
11.30–3, 5 (7 Sat)–11; 11.30–11 Fri
**Draught Bass; Heritage Dark
Amber; Marston's Pedigree;
guest beers** H
Classic alehouse, in the former
stables and wagon sheds of the
old Thomas Sykes brewery.
Stone cobbled floors, high
ceilings and breweriana create
a traditional atmosphere. A
Burton Bridge beer is always
available. Q 🛏 ❀ ♣ P

Cauldon

Yew Tree
Off A52/A523
☎ (01538) 308348
11–3, 6–11
**Draught Bass; Burton Bridge
Bridge Bitter; M&B Mild** H
One of the finest pubs in the
country, dating back to the
17th century. Its superb
collection of antiques includes
working polyphonia, a
pianola, grandfather clocks
and sundry Victoriana. Look
for the 'Acme' dog carrier and
the huge old oak tree.
Q ❀ Å ♣ P

Chasetown

Uxbridge Arms
2 Church Street (off High St)
☎ (01543) 674853
12–3, 6–11; 12–11 Sat
**Bass Worthington BB,
Draught Bass; M&B Highgate
Dark; guest beers** H
Popular town pub with a
lounge and a restaurant area, a
large bar and a pool room.
Changing guest beers. No
meals Sun eve. ❀ ◖ ▶ ᕼ P

Eccleshall

George Hotel
Castle Street ☎ (01785) 850300
11–11

267

Staffordshire

Slaters Best, Premium; guest
beers Ⓗ
Originally a coaching inn, this
town-centre hotel now has ten
excellent bedrooms and a
bistro. Eccleshall's first
brewery for over a century
opened here in 1995.
🛏 ☎ 🍴 🌙 🍴 Å P

Enville

Cat
Bridgnorth Road (A458)
☎ (01384) 872209
12–3, 7–11; closed Sun
Draught Bass; Enville Ale,
Gothic; S&N Theakston XB;
guest beers Ⓗ
Part-16th-century inn with a
defunct brewery at the rear:
four different beamed rooms
with real fires. The upstairs
restaurant (open Wed–Sat)
serves local game. Enville
brewery is 1½ miles away. No
meals Sun.
🛏 Q ❀ 🍴 🌙 ♣ P

Gnosall

Boat
Wharf Road
☎ (01785) 822208
11 (11.30 winter)–11
Marston's Bitter,
Pedigree Ⓗ
Popular pub next to Bridge 34
on the Shropshire Union
Canal. Meals served Easter–
end Sept (except Sun).
🛏 🍴 🌙 & ♣ P ⊟

Great Chatwell

Red Lion
2 miles E of A41 OS792143
☎ (01952) 691366
12–3 (not Mon), 6 (7 winter)–11 (12–11
summer Sat)
Bass Worthington BB,
Draught Bass; S&N
Theakston Best Bitter; guest
beers Ⓗ
Friendly, family-run country
pub with a range of guest
beers. Excellent children's
play area in the garden. Good
value food in the bar and
restaurant.
🛏 ☎ ❀ 🍴 🌙 🍴 Å ♣ P

Handsacre

Crown
24 The Green (A513)
☎ (01543) 490239
11.30 (11 Thu–Sat)–3, 6–11
Bass Worthington BB,
Draught Bass; M&B Highgate
Dark Ⓔ
Characterful, canalside,
two-roomed local,
incorporating a games room
where children are welcome.
No food Sun.
Q ☎ ❀ 🍴 🍴 ♣ P

Harriseahead

Royal Oak
42 High Street
☎ (01782) 513362
7–11; 12–3, 7–11 Sat
Courage Directors; John
Smith's Bitter; guest beers Ⓗ
Busy, genuine free house in a
semi-rural location on the
Kidsgrove side of Mow Cop
Folly (NT): a smallish bar and
larger lounge. Weekly guest
beers (the best choice in the
area). Occasional mini-beer
festivals. ❀ 🍴 ♣ P ⊟

Haughton

Bell
Newport Road (A518)
☎ (01785) 780301
11.30–3, 6–11
Mansfield Riding Mild;
Marston's Pedigree;
Whitbread Boddingtons
Bitter; guest beer Ⓗ
One-roomed village free
house. 🛏 ❀ 🍴 🌙 Å ♣ P

Hednesford

Queen's Arms
Hill Street ☎ (01543) 878437
12–3, 6.30 (7 Sat)–11
Bass Worthington BB,
Draught Bass; M&B Highgate
Dark Ⓔ
Welcoming, two-roomed pub
of traditional nature, well
supported by locals. Excellent,
home-made food, well priced.
🛏 Q ❀ 🍴 🍴 ➔ ♣ P

High Offley

Anchor
Old Lea (By Bridge 42 of the
Shropshire Union Canal)
OS775256 ☎ (01785) 284569
11–3, 6–11 (12–3 (Sat only), 7–11
(Thu–Sat only) winter)
Marston's Pedigree, Owd
Rodger; Wadworth 6X Ⓖ/Ⓗ
Built during the Crimean War
and originally called the
Sebastopol Inn, this classic
two-bar, canalside pub is not
easily found by road. Gift shop
behind for canalware. The
Marston's beers are available
in summer only.
🛏 Q ❀ 🍴 Å ♣ ⌂ P

Hoar Cross

Meynell Ingram Arms
1 mile W of A515 at
Newchurch OS133234
☎ (01283) 575202
12–3, 6–11; 12–11 Sat
Marston's Pedigree;
Whitbread Boddingtons
Bitter Ⓗ
Extended, former estate pub in

rural surroundings with
hunting memorabilia. No food
Sun eve. 🛏 Q ❀ 🍴 🌙 ♣ P

Hockley

Prince of Wales
Hockley Road, Wilnecote
☎ (01827) 280013
12–3, 7–11
S&N Theakston Mild, Best
Bitter, XB; guest beer Ⓗ
Traditional, welcoming local.
Local sports supported.
Q 🍴 & ⇌ (Wilnecote) ♣ P

Hulme End

Manifold Hotel
On B5054 ☎ (01298) 84537
11.30–3, 6–11
Wards Mild, Thorne Best
Bitter, Best Bitter; guest beers
(summer) Ⓗ
Formerly known as the Light
Railway, this impressive stone
hotel is set in picturesque open
countryside by the River
Manifold.
🛏 Q 🍴 🌙 & Å P ⊟

Keele Village

Sneyd Arms
1 The Village (off A525)
☎ (01782) 614533
12–3, 7–11
HP&D Entire; Ind Coope
Burton Ale; Tetley Bitter;
guest beers Ⓗ
Built in 1852, this friendly
village pub is used by students
and staff from the University
of Keele. Built of solid stone
on the old Sneyd estate, it
offers a wide range of food
daily. Q 🍴 🌙 🍴 ♣ P

Kiddemore Green

New Inns
Between Brewood and Bishops
Wood OS859088
☎ (01902) 850614
12–3, 7–11
Burtonwood Mild, Best Bitter,
Forshaw's, Top Hat Ⓗ
Pleasant, isolated rural inn,
with much brass and oak
beams. Burtonwood beers are
new to the area. Barbecue
summer Sun. 🛏 ❀ 🍴 ♣ P ⌀

Kinver

Crown & Anchor
Enville Road ☎ (01384) 872567
11.30–3, 7–11
Banks's Mild, Bitter Ⓔ;
Marston's Pedigree Ⓗ
Opened as a beer house in
1853, a former Bass pub, now
tied to Banks's. An island front
bar and a rear pool room draw
a mixed clientele. 🛏 ❀ ♣ P

Plough & Harrow
High Street
☎ (01384) 872659
12–3 (not winter Mon–Thu), 7–11
Batham Mild, Best Bitter, XXX Ⓗ
Popular pub known as the Steps. Its three rooms are on different levels. Movie star pictures decorate the lounge walls.
🏚 🐂 ❀ ◖ ▶ ♣ ⏏ P

Whittington Inn
On A449, S of A458 jct
☎ (01384) 872110
11–2.30 (3 Sat), 5.30–11 (11–11 summer)
Banks's Mild, Bitter; Camerons Strongarm; Marston's Pedigree Ⓗ
Converted, 16th-century manor house visited by Charles II after the Battle of Worcester. It boasts panelled walls, ornate moulded ceilings, with low beams, and a walled Tudor garden.
🏚 Q ❀ ◖ ▶ P ⊟

Leek

Abbey Inn
Abbey Green Road (1 mile from Leek, off A523)
☎ (01538) 382865
12–3, 7–11
Draught Bass; guest beer Ⓗ
Large, stone establishment with two rooms and a central bar. Good atmosphere. Local pianist Sat.
Q ❀ 🛏 ◖ ▶ ⊟ P

Swan
2 St Edward Street
☎ (01538) 382081
11–3, 7–11
Bass Worthington BB, Draught Bass; M&B Highgate Dark; guest beer Ⓗ
Three-roomed, 16th-century coaching inn opposite St Edward's church. The comfortable lounge is mainly given over to non-smoking diners lunchtime. Changing guest beer; range of malt whiskies. The function room hosts a folk club and mini-beer festivals. Eve meals in summer.
❀ ◖ ▶ ⊟ ♣

Wilke's Head
16 St Edward Street
☎ (01538) 383616
12–3, 7–11; 11–11 Sat
Whim Magic Mushroom Mild, Hartington Bitter, Old Izaak, Black Christmas; guest beers Ⓗ
Whim Brewery's only tied outlet, bringing choice to Leek for the discerning drinker: a basic, lively two-roomer. ♣

Lichfield

Earl of Lichfield Arms
10 Conduit Street (opp. Market Sq) ☎ (01543) 251020
11–11; 11–4, 7–11 Sat
Banks's Mild; Marston's Bitter, Pedigree Ⓗ
Popular, city-centre bar, known locally as the Drum. Meals served Mon–Sat. Marston's Head Brewer's Choice stocked.
❀ ◖ ⇌ (City)

George & Dragon
28 Beacon Street
☎ (01543) 263554
12–11
Banks's Mild, Bitter Ⓔ**; Marston's Pedigree** Ⓗ
Traditional, large bar and a cosy lounge. ❀ ♣ P ⊟

Greyhound
Upper St John Street
☎ (01543) 262303
11.45–3, 5–11; 11.30–11 Fri & Sat
Ansells Bitter; Draught Bass; guest beers Ⓗ
Busy local with an extended lounge, serving rotating premium bitters.
🐂 ◖ ⇌ (City) ♣ P

Queen's Head
14 Queen Street
☎ (01543) 410932
11–11
Adnams Bitter; Marston's Pedigree; guest beers Ⓗ
Marston's first ale house; a two-room local converted into a busy one-roomed pub with changing guest beers. It attracts all ages. Eve meals finish at 8.30.
Q ◖ ▶ ⇌ (City) ♣

Scales
24 Market Street
☎ (01543) 410653
11–11; 11–4, 7–11 Sat
Bass Worthington BB, Draught Bass; Lichfield Steeplejack; M&B Highgate Dark; guest beers Ⓗ
Very busy, city-centre pub: one room with an impressive long bar and an array of handpulls. An example of Bass's Ale Shrine concept.
❀ ◖ ♿ ⇌ (City) ♣

Longdon

Swan With Two Necks
40 Brook End (off A51)
☎ (01543) 490251
12–2.30, 7–11; 12–2, 7–10.30 Sun
Ansells Mild, Bitter; Burton Bridge Bridge Bitter; Ind Coope Burton Ale; guest beers Ⓗ
400-year-old, beamed village pub with a stone-flagged bar, a comfortable lounge and a restaurant. No food Sun.
🏚 Q ❀ ◖ ▶ ⊟ P

Longsdon

New Inn
Leek Road (A53)
☎ (01538) 385356
11.30–2.30, 7–11
Banks's Mild; Marston's Bitter, Pedigree Ⓗ
Close to the main road, this popular village pub has one main room. Good atmosphere.
🏚 ◖ ♣ P ⊟

Meaford

George & Dragon
The Highway (100 yds S of A34 Meaford roundabout)
☎ (01785) 818497
12–3, 6–11
Burtonwood Bitter, Forshaw's, Top Hat Ⓗ
Large, main road hostelry with a spacious, wood-panelled lounge bar. The ex-Beefeater restaurant on the first floor caters for parties.
🏚 ❀ ◖ ♣ P

Milwich

Green Man
Sandon Lane (B5027)
☎ (01889) 505310
12–2, 5.30–11; 12–11 Sat
Bass Worthington BB, Draught Bass; guest beers Ⓗ
Welcoming village pub near a tiny 1833 schoolhouse. A list of landlords since 1792 is displayed in the bar. Large selection of whiskies. No meals Sun eve or Tue; other eves till 8pm.
🏚 ❀ ◖ ▲ ♣ P

Newcastle-under-Lyme

Albert Inn
1 Brindley Street (near Sainsbury's) ☎ (01782) 615525
12–3, 7–11
Burtonwood Bitter, Forshaw's Ⓗ
Small, backstreet local, recently refurbished and displaying a collection of old clay pipes over the entrance door. Q ♣

Albion
99 High Street
☎ (01782) 617589
12–4, 7–11
Marston's Pedigree Ⓗ
Rock theme pub, built in the 1830s. Note the unusual guitar arm handpumps and the cartoon murals on a baseball theme. A friendly pub, which caters for a particular clientele.
🐂 ❀ ♣

Staffordshire

Bull's Vaults

Hassel Street (near bus station)
☎ (01782) 616555
11–11; 12–2.30, 7–10.30 Sun
Banks's Mild, Bitter Ⓔ;
Camerons Strongarm;
Marston's Pedigree Ⓗ
Popular, town-centre pub
catering for all ages in one
room with three different
areas. No meals Sun ◖ ♣ ⊟

Castle Mona

4 Victoria Street (off A34 S)
☎ (01782) 612849
11–4 (not Mon–Thu), 7–11
Greenalls Mild, Davenports
Bitter, Original Ⓗ
Popular, street-corner local,
outside the town centre, built
in 1876. Three rooms: a basic
bar, a comfortable lounge and
a pool room. ❀ ⊞ ♣

Crossways

Nelson Place
☎ (01782) 616953
11–11; 11–4, 7–11 Sat
Courage Directors; Vaux
Samson; Wards Mild; guest
beer Ⓗ
Large corner pub, opposite the
Queen's Gardens, offering up
to six ales. A haunt of
crossword fans: two rooms
with a bar-cum-games room.
🚪 ◖ ♣

Old Brown Jug

41 Bridge Street (behind Kwik
Save) ☎ (01782) 711393
12–3 (4 Sat), 7–11 (may vary)
Marston's Bitter, Pedigree Ⓗ
Town-centre local dating from
1790, which attracts a varied
clientele. Two distinct areas: a
bar with bare floorboards and
a lounge off. Extensive home-
cooked menu; Marston's Head
Brewer's Choice beers. Beware
the keg cider on a fake
handpump. ❀ ◖ ♣ P

Victoria

King Street
☎ (01782) 615569
11–3, 6.30–11; 11–11 Sat
Bass Worthington BB,
Draught Bass; Whitbread
Boddingtons Bitter Ⓗ
Popular, two-roomed
Victorian pub, convenient for
the New Victoria Theatre. A
comfortable lounge and a busy
bar. Beware the keg cider on a
fake handpump.
Q ❀ ◖ ♣

Norton Canes

Railway Tavern

Norton Green Lane
☎ (01543) 279579
12–2 (3 Sat), 7–11
Ansells Mild, Bitter; Ind
Coope Burton Ale; Tetley
Bitter Ⓗ
Friendly village pub with a
bowling green and an

enthusiastic following. Cosy
bar. ❀ ♣ P

Onecote

Jervis Arms

On B5053 ☎ (01538) 304206
12–3, 7–11
Draught Bass; Marston's
Pedigree; Ruddles County;
S&N Theakston Mild, Best
Bitter, XB, Old Peculier Ⓗ
Free house in a superb country
setting beside the River
Hamps, with an emphasis on
good quality food. Family-
oriented (good play area). It
takes its name from a former
aide of Lord Nelson, Admiral
Jervis. Q ☎ ❀ ◖ ▲ P

Outwoods

Village Tavern

Signed from A518 (1 mile)
OS788182 ☎ (01952) 691216
12–3 (12–2 Sat & Sun only winter), 6
(7.30 winter)–11
Enville Ale; Whitbread
Boddingtons Bitter; guest
beers Ⓗ
Friendly country inn in a small
village, frequented by walkers
and cyclists. Good value food;
families are made welcome.
Wildmans, the house beer, is
brewed by Enville.
🚪 Q ❀ ◖ ▲ ♣ P

Penkridge

Boat

Cannock Road (by Bridge 86
of Staffs & Worcs Canal)
☎ (01785) 714178
12–3, 6.30–11
Ansells Bitter; HP&D Entire;
Ind Coope Burton Ale;
Marston's Pedigree; Tetley
Bitter Ⓗ
Comfortable, homely,
canalside pub with plenty of
brass on display. Bar skittles in
the corridor. No meals Sun
eve, except in summer.
❀ ◖ ♣ P

Cross Keys

Filance Lane (by Bridge 84 of
Staffs & Worcs Canal)
OS925134 ☎ (01785) 712826
11–3 (4 Sat), 6.30 (5 Fri)–11
Banks's Mild; Bass
Worthington BB Ⓔ**, Draught**
Bass Ⓗ**; M&B Highgate**
Dark Ⓔ
Canalside pub, busiest in the
holiday season. Barbecue in
the garden. No meals Sun eve.
❀ ◖ ♣ P

Littleton Arms

St Michael's Square (A449)
☎ (01785) 712287
12 (11 Wed & Sat)–11
Bass Worthington BB,
Draught Bass; M&B Highgate
Dark; guest beers Ⓗ

Large, town-centre hotel with
several linked lounge areas
and a restaurant. Beer festivals
held in the Grade II-listed
stables on some bank hol
weekends.
❀ 🚪 ◖ ▶ ៃ ⇌ P ⎰

Penn Common

Barley Mow

Pennwood Lane (off Wakeley
Hill) OS949902
☎ (01902) 333510
12–2.30, 6.30–11; 11–11 Sat
Holden's Mild; HP&D Entire;
Ind Coope Burton Ale;
Marston's Pedigree; guest
beer Ⓗ
Hidden gem, circa 1630, near
Penn golf course. The garden
is very popular in summer.
The guest beer is a 'best' from
Ind Coope. 🚪 ❀ ◖ ▶ ៃ P

Reapsmoor

Butcher's Arms

Off B5053 ☎ (01298) 84477
12–3, 7–11
Marston's Pedigree; guest
beer Ⓗ
Basic rural pub, popular with
the local farming community,
but sometimes isolated in
winter. 🚪 Q ▲ P

Rugeley

Red Lion

Market Street
☎ (01889) 570328
11–4, 6–11; 11–11 Fri & Sat
Banks's Mild, Bitter Ⓔ
Small, three-roomed pub with
bags of atmosphere. Pool and
darts rooms, and a cosy bar.
❀ ♣ P

Saverley Green

Hunter

Sandon Road
☎ (01782) 392067
12–3, 7–11
Burtonwood Mild, Bitter,
Forshaw's, Top Hat; guest
beers Ⓗ
Cosy, country pub offering
great hospitality. Occasional
beer festivals.
🚪 ☎ ❀ ◖ ▲ ♣ P

Shenstone

Railway

Main Street ☎ (01543) 480503
12–3, 5–11; 12–11 Fri & Sat
Bateman Mild; Marston's
Bitter, Pedigree, Owd Rodger
(winter) Ⓗ
Village pub, built to serve the
Birmingham–Lichfield railway
in the 1800s; previously a
butcher's shop and an old
chapel. The lounge and bar are

frequented by locals. Winner of a *Best Garden* competition three years running. Marston's Head Brewer's Choice beers.
🌳 ◖ ▶ ⊟ ᕟ ⇌ ♣ P

Stafford

Bird in Hand
Mill Street ☎ (01785) 52198
11–11; 11–5, 7–11 Sat
Bass Worthington BB; Courage Best Bitter, Directors; John Smith's Bitter; guest beers Ⓗ
Popular, enterprising town-centre pub with a bar, snug, games room and recently extended lounge. No meals Sun. 🏨 🌳 ◖ ⊟ ⇌ ♣

Forester & Firkin
3 Eastgate Street
☎ (01785) 223742
11–11
Firkin Chopper, Forester, Pecker, Dogbolter; guest beer Ⓗ
Brew pub refurbished in Firkin style, enjoying greater trade than in earlier incarnations. Business folk lunchtime; students eves. Stafford's first brewery since Dawson's closed in 1952. 🌳 ◖ ♣ P

Stafford Arms
Railway Street
☎ (01785) 53313
12–11
Titanic Best Bitter, Lifeboat, Premium, Stout, Captain Smith's, Wreckage; guest beers Ⓗ
Local CAMRA *Pub of the Year* 1994. Titanic Inns' second pub selling the full Titanic range and four guests from independents. Two beer festivals a year. Games include corridor skittles in summer. Good basic food (no food Sun, or Sat eve; other eves till 8).
🌳 ◖ ▶ ⇌ ♣ ⌂ P

Tap & Spile
59 Peel Terrace (just off B5066, 1 mile from centre)
☎ (01785) 223563
11.30–11
Beer range varies Ⓗ
This sympathetic conversion to a Tap & Spile has greatly increased choice in North Stafford. Eight changing guest beers mean an excellent choice every day, with 300 ales sold in the first year. Regular quizzes and folk music.
♿ 🌳 ◖ ⊟ ♣ ⌂ ✕

Telegraph
Wolverhampton Road (A449)
☎ (01785) 58858
11–2.30, 4.30–11; 11–11 Fri & Sat
Bass Worthington BB, Draught Bass; M&B Highgate Dark; guest beers Ⓗ
Good, honest local, with a

lounge and bar, not far from the town centre. Good value meals. ◖ ▶ ⊟ ♣ P

Stoke on Trent: *Burslem*

Bull's Head
14 St John's Square
☎ (01782) 834153
12–2.30, 5–11; 12–11 Fri; 12–3, 6.30–11 Sat (may vary)
Titanic Lifeboat, Best Bitter, Premium, Stout, Captain Smith's; guest beers Ⓗ
Two-roomed, town-centre pub owned by Titanic. Besides its own range of 'good quality beers' it serves changing guest beers. Beer festivals June and Sept. 🏨 Q 🌳 ⊟ ♣ ⌂

George Hotel
Swan Square ☎ (01782) 577544
11.30–2.30, 5.30–11
Marston's Bitter, Pedigree; Morland Old Speckled Hen Ⓗ
Fine, pseudo-Georgian building, circa 1928. The bar is open to non-residents, but smart casual dress is required. Special rates on accommodation for CAMRA members. Both the restaurant and bar meals are recommended.
Q 🏨 ◖ ▶ P

Etruria

Plough
147 Etruria Road (near Festival Park entrance)
☎ (01782) 269445
12–3, 6 (5 Fri, 7 Sat)–11
Robinson's Hatters Mild (occasional), **Old Stockport Bitter, Hartleys XB, Best Bitter, Frederic's** Ⓗ, **Old Tom** Ⓖ
The only Robinson's pub in the city: always a friendly welcome. Excellent, home-made meals. Old Tom is only served in half pints. ◖ ▶

Fenton

Malt 'n' Hops
295 King Street (A50)
☎ (01782) 313406
12–3, 7–11
Beer range varies Ⓗ
Welcoming, well-run pub where at least 15 changing guests are sold each week. Bursley Bitter (Burtonwood), Turners Tipple and Old Arnold (Hardington) are house beers, others are planned. Crowded at weekends. ⇌ (Longton)

Hanley

Coachmaker's
65 Lichfield Street (next to bus station) ☎ (01782) 262158
11.30–11

Bass Worthington BB, Draught Bass Ⓗ
Fine example of a Potteries town-centre pub. Mid-terraced, it comprises three small rooms and a beer corridor, served from a tiny bar. An unpretentious, drinkers' pub. 🏨 Q ⊟ ♣

Golden Cup
65 Old Town Road
☎ (01782) 212405
11–11
Draught Bass; Ruddles County Ⓗ
Friendly local, boasting splendid bar fittings. Its ornate Edwardian exterior proudly-proclaims 'Bass only'. The last beer house in Hanley to obtain a liquor licence, it is now famous for its 'Big Breakfast'. Beware the keg cider on a fake handpump. 🌳 ◖ ♿ ♣

Hartshill

Jolly Potters
296 Hartshill Road
☎ (01782) 45254
11–3 (4 Sat), 6 (7 Sat)–11; 11–11 Fri
Draught Bass; M&B Mild Ⓗ
An increasingly rare example of a typical Potteries town-centre pub. Situated in a conservation area, it has four small rooms and a central corridor. Q 🌳 ⊟ ♿ ♣

Penkhull

Marquis of Granby
51 St Thomas's Place
☎ (01782) 47025
11–3 (4 Thu–Sat), 6.30–11
Banks's Mild; Marston's Bitter, Pedigree Ⓗ
Red-brick pub opposite the village church: a large, comfortable lounge and a public bar, popular for games. Marston's Head Brewer's Choice beers sold. 🌳 ◖ ⊟ ♣ P

Stoke

Glebe
Glebe Street ☎ (01782) 44600
12–11
Banks's Mild, Bitter; Camerons Strongarm; Marston's Pedigree Ⓗ
Large, recently refurbished, corner pub surrounded by the civic offices. Popular with town hall staff and students from the nearby university.
◖ ♿ ⇌ 🍺

Tunstall

White Hart
43 Roundwell Street
☎ (01782) 835817
11–5, 7–11; 11–11 Fri & Sat
Banks's Mild; Marston's Bitter, Pedigree Ⓗ

Staffordshire

Compact, split-room, corner pub on the edge of the town centre. Friendly, characterful and unpretentious, the only Marston's pub in town. Park in side streets. ❀ ◖ ♣

Stone

Pheasant
Old Road ☎ (01785) 814603
11.30–4, 6–11; 11–11 Fri & Sat
Banks's Mild; Marston's Bitter, Pedigree Ⓗ
Friendly local, immaculately maintained and extended to provide a dining room (no meals Mon–Thu eve or Sun).
❀ ◖ ◗ Ⓔ ⇌ ♣

Star Inn
21 Stafford Street (A520, by Trent & Mersey Canal)
☎ (01785) 813096
11–3, 5.30–11; 11–11 Fri, Sat and summer
Banks's Mild, Bitter; Camerons Strongarm; Marston's Pedigree; guest beers Ⓗ
The oldest canalside pub, dating from 1568, located on 13 different floor levels. Very busy in summer. No meals Sun eve.
🏚 Q ⛄ ❀ ◖ ◗ Ⓔ ♣ P Ⓗ

Tamworth

Boot Inn
Lichfield Street
☎ (01827) 68024
11–11
Bateman Mild; Marston's Pedigree, Owd Rodger Ⓗ
Town-centre pub, attracting a varied clientele. Marston's Head Brewer's Choice beers sold. ◖ ♿ ⇌ P

Hamlet's Real Ale Bar
Lower Gungate
☎ (01827) 52277
10.30–3, 7 (6.30 Fri)–11; 10.30–11 Sat
Marston's Pedigree; Samuel Smith OBB; guest beers Ⓗ
Town-centre free house with up to three guest beers changing regularly. Good atmosphere, but it can be busy at weekends. Snacks served. A must. ⇌

White Lion
Aldergate (next to council offices) ☎ (01827) 64630
11–3, 5 (5 Thu)–11; 11–11 Fri & Sat
Banks's Mild, Bitter; Marston's Pedigree Ⓗ
Basic, three-roomed corner pub, including a restaurant area. Banks's Brewer's Choice beers sold. Varied clientele.
◖ ⇌ ♣ P

Trysull

Bell
Wombourne Road
☎ (01902) 892871

11.30–2.30, 5.30–11
Batham Best Bitter; Holden's Mild, Bitter, Special Ⓗ
Holden's only pub in the county: a comfortable village local with a restaurant. No meals Sun/Mon eves.
🏚 Q ❀ ◖ ◗ ♣ P Ⓗ

Two Gates

Bull's Head
Watling Street (A5/A51 jct)
☎ (01827) 287820
12–2.30 (3 Sat), 7–11
Banks's Mild; Marston's Pedigree Ⓗ
Busy, friendly local where darts, dominoes and football are all supported. Marston's Head Brewer's Choice beers sold. Q ❀ ◖ ◗ Ⓔ
⇌ (Wilnecote) ♣ P Ⓗ

Uttoxeter

Black Swan
Market Street
☎ (01889) 564657
11–3.30, 6–11; 11–11 Wed, Fri & Sat
Bass Worthington BB, Draught Bass Ⓗ
17th-century, listed building of great character. Visitors are made welcome by the locals and the Scottish landlord.
Ⓔ ⇌ ♣ P

Vaults
Market Place ☎ (01889) 562997
11–3, 5.30 (7 Fri & Sat)–11
Bass Worthington BB, Draught Bass; M&B Highgate Dark Ⓗ
Friendly, unspoilt, three-roomer with a large bottle collection. Ⓔ ⇌ ♣

Weston

Saracen's Head
Stafford Road (A518)
☎ (01889) 270286
11.30–11
Bass Worthington BB, Draught Bass Ⓔ; **guest beer** Ⓗ
Open-plan, country pub below Weston Bank. It runs a courtesy bus for regulars and parties of six or more diners.
🏚 ❀ ◖ ◗ ♣ P Ⓗ

Woolpack
The Green ☎ (01889) 270238
11.30–3, 6–11; 11.30–11 Fri & Sat
Marston's Bitter, Pedigree; guest beer Ⓗ
This 17th-century 'Inn on the Green' has been carefully extended, retaining separate drinking and dining areas. Good selection of quality, home-cooked food at sensible prices. No meals Sun eve.
🏚 ❀ ◖ ◗ Ⓔ ♣ P

Whittington

Bell Inn
Main Street ☎ (01543) 432377

12 (11.30 Sat)–3, 6–11
Draught Bass; Ind Coope Burton Ale; Tetley Bitter Ⓗ
Traditional, beamed, village local with a large garden to the rear and a children's play area. Popular summer weekends.
🏚 Q ⛄ ❀ ◖ ◗ ♣ P

Dog Inn
Main Street
☎ (01543) 432252
11–3, 5–11
Ansells Mild, Bitter; Draught Bass; Ind Coope Burton Ale; Tetley Bitter Ⓗ
Refurbished, 17th-century coaching inn and restaurant with dominoes and crib teams. Families welcome.
❀ 🏚 ◖ ◗ ♿ ♣ P

Wigginton

Old Crown
Main Road
11–3, 6–11
S&N Theakston Mild, Best Bitter, XB, Old Peculier; guest beer Ⓗ
Excellent, two-roomed village pub, with a recently refurbished and extended lounge. Local CAMRA *Pub of the Year* 1993 and 1994. Changing guest beers at reasonable prices.
Q ❀ ◖ Ⓔ ♣ P

Wilnecote

Globe
91 Watling Street (A5)
☎ (01827) 280885
1 (12 Sat)–3.30, 7–11
Marston's Bitter, Pedigree Ⓗ
Excellent, traditional local, serving Marston's Head Brewer's Choice beers.
Q ❀ Ⓔ ⇌ ♣

Wombourne

Red Lion
Old Stourbridge Road (set back from A449)
☎ (01902) 892270
11.30–11
Bass Worthington BB, Draught Bass; Ruddles County; guest beers Ⓗ
17th-century coaching inn on the old main road. The lounge is geared towards food (special pensioners' meals); split-level bar. 🏚 ❀ ◖ ◗ ♣ P

Yoxall

Crown Inn
Main Street ☎ (01543) 472551
11.30–3, 5.30–11
Marston's Pedigree Ⓗ
Attractive village pub with a conservatory area suitable for families. No food Sun.
⛄ ❀ ◖ ◗ ♿ ♣ P

BEERS OF THE YEAR

Chosen by CAMRA tasting panels, by votes from the general public at beer festivals and through a poll of CAMRA members, these are the *Good Beer Guide Beers of the Year*. Each was found to be consistently outstanding in its category and took its place in the *Champion Beer of Britain* contest at the Great British Beer Festival at Olympia in August 1995. These beers have also been awarded a tankard symbol in the breweries section of this book.

DARK AND LIGHT MILDS

Bateman Dark Mild
Cains Dark Mild
Crown Buckley Dark Mild
Hoskins & Oldfield Best Mild
King & Barnes Mild Ale
Ridleys Mild
S&N Theakston Mild Ale

OLD ALES AND STRONG MILDS

Adnams Old Ale
Cotleigh Old Buzzard
Sarah Hughes Original Dark
    Ruby Mild
King & Barnes Old Ale
Orkney Dark Island
S&N Theakston Old Peculier

BITTERS

Caledonian Deuchars IPA
Cheriton Pots Ale
Cotleigh Tawny Bitter
Everards Beacon Bitter
Oakham JHB
Plassey Bitter
South Yorkshire Barnsley Bitter

BARLEY WINES

Dyffryn Clwyd De Laceys
Cottage Norman's Conquest
Hoskins & Oldfield Old
    Navigation Ale
Pilgrim Conqueror
Robinson's Old Tom
Woodforde's Headcracker

BEST BITTERS

Buffy's Polly's Folly
Butterknowle Conciliation Ale
Dyffryn Clwyd Cwrw Castell
Fuller's London Pride
Hogs Back TEA
Otter Ale
Springhead Leveller

PORTERS AND STOUTS

Bateman Salem Porter
Cropton Scoresby Stout
Harveys 1859 Porter
Hop Back Entire Stout
Nethergate Old Growler
RCH Old Slug Porter

STRONG BITTERS

Bullmastiff Son of a Bitch
Dyffryn Clwyd Pedwar Bawd
Fuller's ESB
Goddard's Fuggle-Dee-Dum
Hadrian Centurion Best Bitter
Hop Back Summer Lightning
Springhead Roaring Meg

BOTTLE-CONDITIONED BEERS

Bass Worthington White Shield
Burton Bridge Burton Porter
Courage Imperial Russian Stout
Eldridge Pope Thomas
    Hardy's Ale
Gale's Prize Old Ale
King & Barnes Festive
Shepherd Neame Spitfire

273

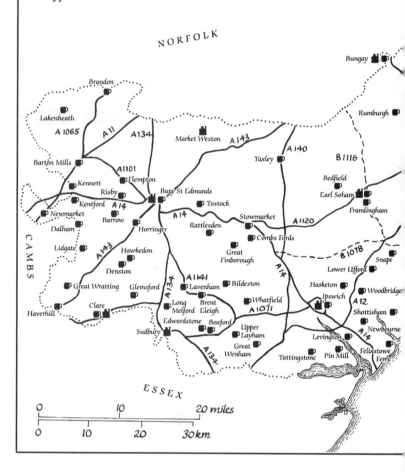

Suffolk

Aldeburgh

White Hart
High Street
☎ (01728) 453205
11–3, 6–11; 11–11 Sat
Adnams Bitter, Old, Extra, Broadside H
Popular, welcoming one-bar pub adorned with nautical pictures.
♨ ❀ 🏠 ♠ ♣

Barrow

Weeping Willow
39 Bury Road
☎ (01284) 810492
11–3.30, 6–11
Greene King XX Mild, IPA, Abbot H
One of the oldest buildings in the village. The beamed lounge has an inglenook.
♨ ❀ ◁ ▶ ♠ P

Barton Mills

Bull Inn
The Street
☎ (01638) 712238
11–11
Adnams Bitter; Draught Bass; Greene King IPA; guest beer H
Imposing old coaching inn near the A11. A family-run pub and hotel. ❀ 🏠 ◁ ▶ P

Cider in summer.
🌳 ❀ 🛏 🍴 ◖ ▲ ♣ 👜 P 🚽

Blaxhall

Ship
☎ (01728) 688316
11–3, 7–11
**Adnams Bitter; Tolly
Cobbold Mild** Ⓗ
Traditional bar with both a
pool table and a piano. The
dining area offers a good value
menu. ❀ 🛏 ◖ ▶ ▲ P

Boxford

White Hart
Broad Street ☎ (01787) 211071
12–3, 6 (6.30 Mon–Fri winter)–11
Adnams Extra *or* **Broadside;
Greene King IPA; guest
beers** Ⓗ
Timber-framed pub in a
central village, riverside
location, now enjoying a new
lease of life. Around 100 guest
ales a year. Beware the keg
cider on a fake handpump.
🏚 ❀ ◖ ▶ ♣ P 🚽

Bramfield

Bell
The Street ☎ (01986) 784395
11–2.30, 6.30–11
**Adnams Mild, Bitter; guest
beers** Ⓖ
Two-bar local with no frills.
Ring the Bull played.
Q ❀ 🍴 ♣ P

Brandon

Duke of Wellington
Thetford Road
☎ (01842) 810219
11–3, 6.30–11; 11–11 Sat
**Greene King XX Mild, IPA,
Abbot** Ⓗ
Super town local, previously
two flint cottages. Warm,
homely and games-oriented.
❀ ⇌ ♣

Brent Eleigh

Cock
Lavenham Road
☎ (01787) 247371
12–3, 6–11; closed Tue
Greene King XX Mild, IPA Ⓗ;
Nethergate Old Growler Ⓖ
An absolute gem! Thatched,
unspoilt, and at peace with the
world. A cask breather is used
on the Abbot Ale. 🏚 Q ❀ 👜

Bungay

Chequers
23 Bridge Street
☎ (01986) 893579
11–3.30, 5–11; 11–11 Sat
Adnams Bitter; Bass

**Charrington IPA, Draught
Bass; guest beers** Ⓗ
Friendly local with ever-
changing guest beers, in a
busy little town. A covered
area at the rear hosts excellent
barbecues. No food Sat.
❀ ◖ ▲ ♣ P

Green Dragon
29 Broad Street
☎ (01986) 892681
11–3, 5–11 (may vary); 11–11 Fri & Sat
**Adnams Bitter; Green Dragon
Chaucer, Bridge Street,
Dragon** Ⓗ
Lively two-bar brew pub on
the edge of town. A third
room can provide a quiet area
if needed. Watch for one off
and seasonal brews.
🏚 Q 🌳 ❀ ◖ ▶ 👜 ▲ ♣ P

Bury St Edmunds

Black Boy
69 Guildhall Street
☎ (01284) 752723
11–3, 5–11
**Greene King XX Mild, IPA,
Abbot** Ⓗ
15th-century pub near the
town centre. Popular at
lunchtime for good food.
Occasional pub theatre
upstairs. Q ◖ ▶ 👜 ♣ P

Fleetwoods
25 Abbeygate Street
☎ (01284) 705703
11–3, 5–11; 11–11 Fri & Sat
Beer range varies Ⓗ
Unpretentious bar, near the
Abbey Gardens, offering an
ever changing selection of ales.
Wide choice of good value
lunches. Popular with the
young at weekends. The
entrance is in lower Baxter St.
◖ P

Flying Fortress
Mount Road, Great Barton (2
miles from centre, off Thurston
Rd) ☎ (01284) 787665
12–3, 5 (6 Sat)–11
**Adnams Bitter; Bass
Worthington BB; Whitbread
Flowers IPA; guest beers** Ⓔ
Friendly pub with displays
and photos connected with the
former local WWII airfield.
❀ ◖ ▶ 👜 ♣ P

Ipswich Arms
1 Tayfen Road
☎ (01284) 703623
12–2, 6.30–11
**Greene King XX Mild, IPA,
Abbot** Ⓗ
Interesting, semi-circular,
19th-century, light brick pub
on a busy corner. The early
photograph (1871) in the
lounge was taken from the
top of a nearby church spire.
Good value food.
◖ ▶ ⇌ P

Bedfield

Crown
Church Lane ☎ (01728) 628431
11.30–3, 6–11; 11–11 Sat
**Greene King IPA; guest
beer** Ⓗ
Village local with a friendly
welcome. 🏚 ❀ ◖ ▶ ♣ P

Bildeston

King's Head
132 High Street
☎ (01449) 741434
12–2.30, 5–11; 11–11 Sat
**Greene King IPA; Mauldons
Bitter; guest beers** Ⓗ
Large, lively pub retaining
many original features.
Regular live music weekends,
plus other entertainments. A
cask breather is used on Tolly
Cobbold Mild occasionally.

Suffolk

Queen's Head
39 Churchgate Street
☎ (01284) 761554
11–11
**Courage Directors; Mauldons
White Adder; Nethergate
Umbel Magna; Whitbread
Boddingtons Bitter; guest
beers** Ⓗ
White brick, 18th-century
coaching inn with plenty of
history beneath a Victorian-
style refurbishment. Busy with
a young trade at weekends.
🏵 ◖ ▶ ➾

Rising Sun
Risbygate Street
☎ (01284) 701460
11–11
**Greene King XX Mild, IPA,
Abbot** Ⓗ
16th-century pub offering live
music Fri and Sat eves. No
food Sun. 🏵 ◖ ▶ P

Rose & Crown
48 Whiting Street
☎ (01284) 755934
11–11; 11–3, 7–11 Sat; 12–2.30,
7–10.30 Sun
**Greene King XX Mild, IPA,
Abbot** Ⓗ
Unspoilt, family-run town
local, near the brewery, and
frequented by its staff. The
mild outsells the bitter. No
food Sun. Q ◖ ⌻

Butley

Oyster
☎ (01394) 450790
11–3, 5–11; 11–11 Sat
**Adnams Mild, Bitter, Old,
Broadside** Ⓗ
Ancient village inn,
modernised in recent times.
Excellent folk night every Sun,
when no food is served. Pets
in the garden, plus camping. A
good base for visiting this
rural area. 🏠 🏵 🛏 ◖ ▶ ▲

Carlton

Poacher's Pocket
Rosemary Lane (off A12)
☎ (01728) 602174
11.30–3, 6–11; closed Mon
Adnams Bitter; guest beers Ⓗ
Small free house, refurbished
in a country cottage style. No
food Sun. Guest ales include
many micro-brewery beers.
Q 🏵 ◖ ▶ ▲
➾ (Saxmundham) P

Clare

Bell Hotel
Market Hill ☎ (01787) 277741
11–11
**Greene King IPA; Nethergate
IPA, Bitter, Umbel Ale, Old
Growler** Ⓗ
Timber-framed, 16th-century

hotel full of character. A cosy
bar, comfortable lounge and
two restaurant areas. Friendly
atmosphere. Families
welcome.
🏠 Q 🏵 🛏 ◖ ▶ ⌻ ♣ P

Combs Fords

Gladstone Arms
1 mile from Stowmarket on
Needham road
☎ (01449) 612339
11–2.30, 5–11
**Adnams Bitter, Old,
Broadside; guest beer** Ⓗ
Adnams tied house with areas
to suit all tastes. A good games
venue. 🏠 🏵 ♣ P

Dalham

Affleck Arms
☎ (01638) 500306
11–2.30, 6.30–11
Greene King IPA, Abbot Ⓗ
Elizabethan thatched pub by
the River Kennett, used by
walkers at weekends.
🏠 Q 🏵 ◖ ▶ ⌻ P

Denston

Plumber's Arms
Wickham Street
☎ (01440) 820350
11–2.30, 5–11
**Greene King IPA, Rayments
Special, Abbot** Ⓗ
Large country pub dating back
to the 1700s, an original
stopping place for horse
traffic. Book eve meals. A cask
breather is used on the mild.
🏠 Q 🏵 ◖ ▶ ⌻ ♣ P

Earl Soham

Victoria
By A1120 ☎ (01728) 685758
11–2.30, 5.30–11
**Earl Soham Gannet, Victoria,
Albert Ale, Jolabrugg** Ⓗ
Characterful pub, the home of,
and only regular outlet for,
Earl Soham Brewery. Simple,
but effective, wooden
furnishings. Excellent value
food. 🏠 Q 🏵 ◖ ▶ ♣ P

Edwardstone

White Horse
Mill Green ☎ (01787) 211211
12–3, 6.30–11
**Greene King XX Mild, IPA,
Abbot** Ⓗ
Excellent village local offering
numerous old games. Note the
enamel signs in the public bar.
Book Sun lunch.
🏠 🏵 ◖ ▶ ⌻ ▲ ♣ ⌒ P

Felixstowe Ferry

Victoria
North of town, near mouth of
River Deben ☎ (01394) 271636

11–3, 6–11; 11–11 Sat & summer
**Adnams Bitter; Tolly
Cobbold Mild; guest beers** Ⓗ
Pub re-opened in 1994, almost
150 years after it originally
opened. A new storm porch
protects visitors from the
winds off the North Sea, just
yards away. Eve meals end at
8.30. 🏠 Q 🐾 🏵 ◖ ▶ ♿ P

Flempton

Greyhound
The Green (off A1101)
☎ (01284) 728400
11–2.30, 5–11; 11–11 Sat
Greene King IPA, Abbot Ⓗ
Traditional village local
behind the church. The public
bar has a tiled floor, and there
is a smart lounge and a large,
enclosed garden. Cask
breather used on the mild.
🏠 Q 🏵 ◖ ▶ ⌻ ♣ P

Framlingham

Railway
9 Station Road
☎ (01728) 723693
12–2.30, 5.30–11; 11–3, 6–11 Sat
**Adnams Mild (summer),
Bitter, Old, Broadside** Ⓗ
Friendly but basic public bar, a
fine setting for the excellent
local ales. The lounge, with its
Victorian fireplace, offers a
comfortable contrast.
🏠 Q 🐾 🏵 ◖ ⌻ ♣ P

Glemsford

Angel
Egremont Street
☎ (01787) 218671
12–2.30, 5–11
Greene King IPA, Abbot Ⓖ
Quiet, traditional pub, the
oldest house in the village and
once home of Wolsey's
secretary John Cavendish.
Q 🏵 ⌻ ♣ P

Great Finborough

Chestnut Horse
High Road ☎ (01449) 612298
11–3, 6–11
**Greene King XX Mild, IPA,
Abbot** Ⓗ
Friendly village local where
sewing machine table bases
are a feature. No eve meals
Tue or Sun. 🏠 🏵 ◖ ▶ ▲ ♣ P

Great Wenham

Queen's Head
On Capel St Mary road
☎ (01473) 310590
12–2.30, 6.30–11
**Adnams Bitter; Greene King
IPA, Abbot; guest beers** Ⓗ
Victorian, cottage-style,
one-bar house with a small,

no-smoking dining room (Indian and English food). Wide range of games (no pool!). 🏠 🛡 ◑ ▶ ▲ ♣ P 🎴

Great Wratting

Red Lion

School Road ☎ (01440) 783237
11–2.30, 5–11; 11–11 Fri & Sat
Adnams Mild, Bitter, Old, Extra Ⓗ
Picturesque village pub with a whalebone arch over the front door. Good, genuine home-cooked food.
🏠 Q 🛡 ◑ ▶ 🍴 ♣ P

Hasketon

Turk's Head

Low Road ☎ (01394) 382584
12–3, 6–11
Tolly Cobbold Mild, Original, Tollyshooter; guest beer Ⓗ
Converted into a pub in the 17th-century, this small, quiet house is packed with curios. Two bars, plus a large barn for functions. Huge garden; eve meals in summer.
🏠 Q 🛡 ◑ ▶ 🍴 ▲ ♣ P

Haverhill

Queen's Head

Queen Street ☎ (01440) 702026
11–11
Courage Best Bitter, Directors; Nethergate Bitter, Umbel Magna Ⓗ
15th-century, Grade II-listed, genuine free house of three rooms with a welcoming atmosphere.
Q ◑ ▶ ♣ 🍴 P 🎴

Hawkedon

Queen's Head

Rede Road ☎ (01284) 89218
12–3, 5–11; 12–11 Sat
Greene King IPA; Mauldons Bitter; Woodforde's Wherry; guest beer Ⓗ
Classic village pub near the church, dating in part from the 14th-century with low ceilings, heavy beams and a large inglenook. Home-made meals from a menu which changes regularly. 🏠 🛡 ◑ ▶ P

Horringer

Six Bells

The Street ☎ (01284) 735551
11.30–2.30, 6 (6.30 Sat)–11
Greene King XX Mild, IPA Ⓗ, **Abbot** Ⓖ
Welcoming, traditional local, in a picturesque village near Ickworth Park (NT). Renowned for its range of home-made, good value pies.

Greene King seasonal ales.
🏠 Q 🛡 ◑ ▶ 🍴 ♣ P

Ipswich

County Hotel

24 St Helen's Street (opp County Hall)
☎ (01473) 255153
11–11; 11–2.30, 5–11 Sat
Adnams Mild, Bitter, Old, Extra, Broadside, Tally Ho; guest beer Ⓗ
Two-bar pub, offering good value good quality food. Eve meals finish at 8.30 (not served Sun). Popular with students lunchtimes. ◑ ▶ 🍴

Golden Lion Hotel (Vaults Bar)

Cornhill (by Town Hall)
☎ (01473) 233211
11–3, 5–11; closed Sun
Adnams Bitter, Extra; Whitbread Boddingtons Bitter; guest beers Ⓗ
Part of an 18th-century extension to a 16th-century hotel in the town centre. A quiet bar during the week, but busy at weekends. 🛥 🖂 ◑ ▶

Grand Old Duke of York

212 Woodbridge Road
☎ (01473) 257115
11–3, 5–11
Adnams Bitter, Old, Broadside; Wadworth 6X; Whitbread Boddingtons Bitter; guest beer Ⓗ
Popular pub: a single, large room with an L-shaped bar. The Duke of York reputedly slept here. No meals Sun eve. Wheelchair WC.
Q 🛡 ◑ ▶ 🦽 P

Greyhound

9 Henley Road
☎ (01473) 252105
11–2.30, 5–11; 11–11 Sat
Adnams Mild, Bitter, Old, Extra, Broadside; guest beers Ⓗ
Attractive and busy two-roomed pub. Food is popular (no eve meals Sun).
Q 🛡 ◑ ▶ 🍴 ♣ P

Plough

2 Dog's Head Street
☎ (01473) 288005
11–3, 5–11; 11–11 Fri & Sat
Adnams Bitter; Marston's Bitter, Pedigree; Nethergate Old Growler; guest beers Ⓗ
Good conversation is assured in this prominent, large (but friendly) town-centre pub which offers an impressive beer range (ten handpumps). Lunches Mon–Fri.
Q 🛥 ◑ 🍴 ♣ 🖂

Tap & Spile (Dove)

76 St Helen's Street
☎ (01473) 211270

11–3, 5–11; 11–11 Thu–Sat
Beer range varies Ⓗ
Many features of the original structure remain in this popular, three-roomed pub, where a covered back yard now offers more space. Over 400 different ales served in its first two years (beer flavoured sausages, too!). No food Sun.
Q 🛥 🛡 ◑ ▶ 🦽 ♣ 🖂 P

Kennett

Bell Inn

Bury Road ☎ (01638) 750286
11–2.30, 6.30–11.30
Greene King IPA, Abbot; Marston's Pedigree; guest beers Ⓗ
Heavily beamed, welcoming pub, c15th-century. Well known for food, it also draws local customers.
🏠 Q 🛡 🖂 ◑ ▶ 🍴 ⇌ P

Kentford

Cock

Bury Road ☎ (01638) 750360
11–3 (not Mon), 5–30–11; 11–11 Sat
Greene King IPA, Rayments Special, Abbot Ⓗ
Large country pub, dating partly from the 1600s, with three bars. Welcoming landlady. Good for families (large garden and play area).
🏠 Q 🛡 ◑ ▶ 🦽 ♣ P 🎴

Lakenheath

Plough

Mill Road ☎ (01842) 860285
11–2.30, 6–11
Greene King IPA Ⓗ
Popular pub in a busy village. Its fine flint exterior, typical of the region, conceals a spacious bar and a pool room. A cask breather is used on the mild.
🛡 ♣ P

Lavenham

Angel

Market Place ☎ (01787) 247388
11–11
Adnams Bitter; Mauldons White Adder; Nethergate Bitter; Webster's Yorkshire Bitter Ⓗ
Impressive 14th-century coaching inn, overlooking the Guildhall. Pick a quiet time and ask to see the medieval vaulted cellars. Very relaxed atmosphere. Quality menu and accommodation.
🏠 Q 🛡 🖂 ◑ ▶

Cock

Church Street
☎ (01787) 247407
11–11
Draught Bass (summer)**; Greene King XX Mild, IPA;**

Suffolk

S&N Theakston Old Peculier H
Traditional, three roomer opposite an impressive church: a beamed bar with stone floor, a lounge and a garden room (licensed for families). Large gardens include a play area. Mauldons' occasional brews also sold. ⚔ Q ⌛ ❀ ◑ ▶ ⊞ & ♣ ♻ P ✄

Levington

Ship
Church Lane ☎ (01473) 659573
11.30–3, 6–11
Greene King IPA; Ind Coope Burton Ale G; **Tetley Bitter** H; **Tolly Cobbold Mild; Whitbread Flowers Original** G
Old thatched, beamed inn, once a place for smugglers, now catering for walkers, birdwatchers and sailors. Home-cooked menu lunchtime and Wed–Sat eves.
⚔ Q ❀ ◑ ▶ & ▲ P ✄

Lidgate

Star
The Street ☎ (01638) 500275
11–3, 5 (6 Sat)–11
Greene King XX Mild (occasional), **IPA, Abbot** H
Busy, friendly 400-year-old village pub, noted for its Mediterranean food.
⚔ Q ❀ ◑ ▶ ⊞ ♣ P ⊟

Long Melford

George & Dragon
Hall Street ☎ (01787) 371285
11–11
Greene King IPA, Rayments Special, Abbot H
Family-run, former coaching inn with a lounge-style single bar and a restaurant with an interesting menu. Still a good drinking pub with live music (folk and blues) every Wed eve. ❀ ⚔ ◑ ▶ P

Lower Ufford

White Lion
The Street ☎ (01394) 460770
11.30–2.30, 6–11
Tolly Cobbold Mild, Bitter, Old Strong; Whitbread Flowers Original (winter) G
Delightful, one-bar pub with a large fireplace, dominating and dividing the area. Popular and interesting food menu (no food Mon).
⚔ Q ⌛ ❀ ◑ ▶ ▲ ♣ P

Lowestoft

Factory Arms
214 Raglan Street
☎ (01502) 574523

10.30–11
Courage Directors; Scott's Golden; Wells Eagle; Woodforde's Gt Eastern; guest beers H
Lively, single-bar, back-street local near the town centre. No pretensions: a friendly pub to seek out. & ⇌ ♣ ◌

Triangle
29 St Peter's Street
☎ (01502) 582711
11–11
Green Jack Bitter, Best Bitter, Golden Sickle, Norfolk Wolf Porter, Lurcher; guest beers H
Excellent pub, now owned by the Green Jack Brewery, overlooking the old market place. ⚔ ⊞ ♣ ◌

Welcome
182 London Road
☎ (01502) 585500
10.30–4, 7.30–11
Adnams Bitter, Old; Bass Worthington BB; Greene King IPA, Abbot H
Small, town-centre local which welcomes newcomers.
◑ ⇌ ♣

Middleton

Bell
The Street ☎ (01728) 648286
11–3.30, 6.30–11
Adnams Mild, Bitter, Old, Broadside G
15th-century, part thatched pub with low ceilings and two inglenooks. A family pub just off the beaten track, near Minsmere RSPB reserve. Adnams seasonal beers served.
Q ⌛ ❀ ◑ ▶ ⊞ ▲ ♣ P

Newbourne

Fox
The Street ☎ (01473) 736307
11–4, 6–11; 11–11 Fri & summer
Greene King IPA; Ind Coope Burton Ale; Tolly Cobbold Bitter; Whitbread Flowers IPA, Original; guest beers G
Characterful, timber-framed inn with two bars and beers served from a tiny stillage. Excellent home-cooked food. Popular skittle alley outside in summer.
⚔ Q ⌛ ❀ ◑ ▶ ▲ P

Newmarket

Five Bells
16 St Mary's Square
☎ (01638) 664961
11–3.30, 6–11; 11–11 Fri & Sat
Greene King XX Mild, IPA, Abbot H
Traditional, comfortable one-bar local. Many team games played; children's

---

amusements in the garden.
⚔ ❀ & ♣ P

Waggon & Horses
High Street ☎ (01638) 662479
11–11
Adnams Broadside; Fuller's London Pride; Morland Old Speckled Hen; Whitbread Boddingtons Bitter, Castle Eden Ale H; **guest beers** G/H
16th-century coaching inn, in a busy location, drawing a strong lunchtime custom. Beer descriptions and prices are well displayed. Some guest beers are racked behind the bar. Petanque played.
⚔ ❀ ◑ ▶ ◌ P

Pin Mill

Butt & Oyster
The Quay ☎ (01473) 780764
11–3, 7–11 (11–11 summer)
Tolly Cobbold Mild, Bitter H / G, **Original, Tollyshooter; guest beers** H
Classic riverside pub featured in just about everything from Arthur Ransome's books to the BBC's *Lovejoy*. CAMRA Regional *Pub of the Year* 1992. A perennial *Guide* entry.
⚔ Q ⌛ ❀ ◑ ▶ ♣ P ✄

Rattlesden

Five Bells
High Street ☎ (01449) 737373
11–11
Adnams Bitter; Ridleys IPA; Wadworth 6X; guest beer H
Small, relaxed, one-bar pub, next to the church and overlooking the village. Petanque pitch. ⚔ Q ❀ ♣

Risby

White Horse
On A14 Risby slip road
☎ (01284) 810686
12–3, 6–11
Courage Best Bitter; Morland Old Speckled Hen; John Smith's Bitter; guest beers H
18th-century inn offering an informal, relaxing atmosphere. Families welcome.
⚔ Q ❀ ⛝ ◑ ▶ ♣ P

Rumburgh

Buck
Mill Road ☎ (01986) 785257
11–2.30, 5.30–11
Adnams Bitter, Old; guest beer H
Historic inn, said to have been the guest house of the local priory. Refurbishment and extensions have added a number of interlinked areas around the original core.
⚔ ❀ ◑ ▶ ♣ P

Shottisham

Sorrel Horse
☎ (01394) 411617
11.30–3 (2.30 winter), 6.30 (7 winter)–11
Tolly Cobbold Mild (summer), **Bitter, Old Strong; guest beers** (summer) Ⓖ
Traditional, 15th-century smugglers' inn with beams, settles and agricultural artefacts. Bar billiards in the public bar. Guest ales come from the Pubmaster range.
🏨 Q ❀ ◑ ▶ ⊞ ▲ ✦ P

Sibton

White Horse
Halesworth Road (off A1120 at Peasenhall Garage)
☎ (01728) 879337
11.30–2.30, 7–11
Adnams Bitter, Broadside Ⓗ
16th-century, heavily beamed inn; the single bar has a raised gallery area. Pleasant dining room and a large garden with play equipment. Well behaved children welcome. No food Sun eve. 🏨 ❀ 🚲 ◑ ▶ ✦ P

Southwold

Lord Nelson
East Street
☎ (01502) 722079
10.30–11
Adnams Mild, Bitter, Old, Extra, Broadside, Tally Ho Ⓗ
Busy, friendly pub in a popular seaside town. Adnams seasonal beers also sold.
🏨 🚲 ❀ ◑ ▶ ▲ ✦

Red Lion
South Green
☎ (01502) 722385
11–11
Adnams Mild, Bitter, Old, Extra, Broadside Ⓗ
Three-room pub, near the sea. The bar has panelled walls and a flagstoned floor. The dining room has a real fire; local fish is a favourite. Often busy in summer.
🏨 🚲 🏠 🚲 ◑ ▶ ▲ ✦

Snape

Golden Key
Priory Road
☎ (01728) 688510
11–3, 6–11
Adnams Bitter, Broadside (summer), **Old, Tally Ho** Ⓗ
Small 17th-century pub with a restaurant extension. Low ceilings and huge fireplaces feature in the main bar. Good, home-cooked food. Adnams seasonal beers served.
🏨 Q 🚲 ❀ 🏠 ◑ ▶ ▲ P

Stowmarket

Royal William
Union Street (up Stowupland St from station)
☎ (01449) 674553
11–3, 6–11
Greene King XX Mild, IPA, Abbot, Winter Ale Ⓖ
Good example of a small-town, back-street pub which still serves the beer from a back room. ❀ ◑ ▶ ⇌ ✦

Tattingstone

White Horse
White Horse Hill
☎ (01473) 328060
11–3, 6–11
Greene King IPA; Tetley Bitter; Tolly Cobbold Mild; Whitbread Boddingtons Bitter Ⓗ
Roomy, timber-framed, 17th-century house with no fruit machines; instead the art of conversation is encouraged. Regular folk nights Sun. Popular with ramblers.
🏨 Q 🚲 ❀ ◑ ▶ ⊞ ▲ ✦ P

Tostock

Gardener's Arms
Church Road (off village green) ☎ (01359) 74060
11.30–2.30, 7–11
Greene King IPA, Abbot Ⓗ
Old building with original beams. The basic public bar has church pews, a tiled stone floor and pool. The comfortable lounge has a large fireplace. Good value home-made food (no meals Sun lunch or Mon/Tue eves).
🏨 ❀ ◑ ▶ ⊞ ✦ P

Upper Layham

Marquis of Cornwallis
☎ (01473) 822051
11–3, 6–11
Adnams Bitter; guest beer Ⓗ
Large, timber-framed, 16th-century roadside inn with character. The fireplace dominates the bar area, but quiet drinking and eating areas give ample space. Ask for oversized glasses.
🏨 Q 🚲 ❀ 🏠 ◑ ▶ ▲ ✦ P ⊟

Wangford

Wangford Plough
London Road
☎ (01502) 578239
11–2.30, 7–11
Adnams Bitter Ⓖ, **Old** Ⓗ, **Extra** Ⓖ
Friendly, roadside local with a comfy snug and small dining room. The beer is served from cooling cabinets.
🏨 ❀ ◑ ▶ & ✦ P

Wenhaston

Star
Hall Road ☎ (01502) 478240
11–2.30, 6–11
Adnams Bitter, Old Ⓖ
Three-roomed village local with a large garden. Adnams seasonal ales also sold.
🏨 🚲 ❀ ◑ ✦ P

Whatfield

Four Horseshoes
The Street ☎ (01473) 827971
11.30–3 (not Mon–Thu), 7–11
Adnams Bitter, Broadside; guest beer Ⓗ
Two-bar, rural pub packed with character. Local artefacts and militaria adorn the walls. A popular venue with war gamers. The guest ale is usually from a local brewer, but a cask breather may be used on Greene King IPA. Eve meals Sat and Sun.
🏨 ❀ ◑ ▶ ⊞ ▲ ✦ P

Woodbridge

King's Head
Market Square
☎ (01394) 387750
Adnams Mild, Bitter Ⓗ, **Old** Ⓖ, **Extra, Broadside** Ⓗ, **Tally Ho** Ⓖ; **Whitbread Boddingtons Bitter** Ⓗ
Very busy, 14th-century, town-centre pub of character. Renovations have provided a patio area, modern toilets and a small, cosy restaurant. Varied, high quality food.
🏨 Q ❀ ◑ ▶ ⇌ P

Seckford Arms
Seckford Street
☎ (01394) 384446
11–11
Adnams Bitter; Draught Bass; Greene King IPA; Scott's Dark Oast Ⓗ
Busy, two-bar pub; a family-run free house, specialising in South American food.
Q 🚲 ❀ ◑ ▶ ⇌

Yaxley

Bull
Ipswich Road (A140)
☎ (01379) 783604
11–3, 5–11; 11–11 Fri & Sat
Adnams Bitter; guest beers Ⓗ
16th-century genuine free house, with lots of character beneath its beams. Remarkably relaxed and rural for a house on a busy road. Home-made food. Q ❀ 🏠 ◑ ▶ ▲ ✦ P

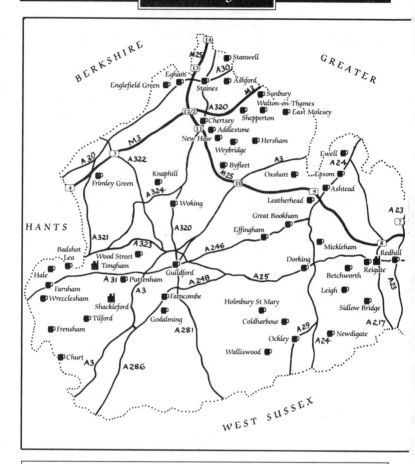

Cyder House, *Shackleford*; **Hogs Back**, *Tongham*;
Pilgrim, *Reigate*

Addlestone

Magnet
21 Station Road (B3121)
☎ (01932) 847908
11–11
**Greene King XX Mild, IPA,
Abbot** Ⓗ
Small and cosy local, first
licensed around 1869, much
improved in recent years. The
name originally referred to a
magnet (drawing in custom).
Today's sign shows the old
boys' comic of the same name.
🏚 ❀ ◐ ➷ ♣

Ashford

District Arms
180 Woodthorpe Road
☎ (01784) 252160
11–11

**Courage Best Bitter,
Directors; John Smith's Bitter;
guest beers** Ⓗ
Welcoming, single-bar local
serving excellent lunches. A
mild is offered occasionally.
Large function room.
🏚 Q ❀ ◐ &

Ashtead

Brewery Inn
15 The Street (A24)
☎ (01372) 272405
11–3, 5.30–11
**Ind Coope Friary Meux BB,
Burton Ale; King & Barnes
Sussex; Marston's Pedigree;
Tetley Bitter; guest beer** Ⓗ
Large pub on the site of
George Sayer's Ashtead
brewery. Busy round the bar
but the raised area offers room
for a quiet pint.
❀ ◐ ◗ & ♣ P

Badshot Lea

Crown Inn
Pine View Close (off A324)
☎ (01252) 20453
10.30–11
Fuller's London Pride, ESB Ⓗ
Attractive, traditional pub
from 1860, which sits among
modern housing. Cosy,
low-ceilinged interiors. Good
value food. Fuller's seasonal
brews also sold.
Q ❀ ◐ ◗ ♣ P

Betchworth

Dolphin Inn
The Street ☎ (01737) 842288
11–3, 5.30–11
**Young's Bitter, Special,
Winter Warmer** Ⓗ
Attractive, 16th-century inn by
the church, featuring stone

Surrey

Surrey

flags and inglenooks. Popular with ramblers. Good food.
🍺 Q ❀ ◖ ❱ ♣ P

Bletchingley

William IV
Little Common Lane (off A25 N of village) ☎ (01883) 743278
11–3, 6–11
Bass Charrington IPA, Draught Bass; Fuller's London Pride; Harveys BB; Pilgrim Progress; guest beer Ⓗ
Traditional inn away from the village centre, with two tiny bars and a dining room (known locally for its food). The guest beer is brewery supplied. Q ❀ ◖ ❱ ⬚ P

Byfleet

Plough
104 High Road (off A245) ☎ (01932) 353257
11–3, 5.30–11
Courage Best Bitter; guest beers Ⓗ

Wonderful pub offering interesting beers, good food, a warm welcome and frequent beer festivals. Eve meals Wed only. 🍺 Q ❀ ◖ ❱ ♣ P

Caterham

King & Queen
34 High Street (B2030) ☎ (01883) 345438
11–3, 5–11; 11–11 Sat
Fuller's Chiswick, London Pride, ESB Ⓗ
400-year-old building, originally three cottages but converted to a pub in the 1840s. Recent refurbishment has retained the several linked drinking areas. Up to five Fuller's beers. Eve meals end at 8.45. No meals Sun.
🍺 Q ❀ ◖ ❱ ♣ P ⚬

Chertsey

Coach & Horses
14 St Ann's Road (B375) ☎ (01932) 563085
11–11
Fuller's Chiswick, London Pride, ESB Ⓗ
Interesting, tile-hung corner building dating from 1860. Refurbishment has left the pub unrecognisable from its former self but the polished wood and deep green interior is not displeasing.
Q ❀ ⛺ ◖ ❱ ▲ ♣ P

Vine
5 Bridge Road (B375) ☎ (01932) 563010
11–3, 5–11; 11–11 Sat
Courage Best Bitter; King & Barnes Sussex; Wadworth 6X Ⓗ
Popular, well-run local dating back 400 years and adorned with cameras, mugs, old records and stuffed birds. The garden has an aviary and swings. Q ❀ ◖ ❱ ▲ ♣ P

Churt

Crossways
Crossways Road (A287) ☎ (01428) 714323
11–3, 6 (5.30 summer)–11
Hogs Back TEA; Ringwood Fortyniner, Old Thumper; guest beers Ⓗ
First class village local with two, good contrasting bars and a strong following for its five different beers each week. Many pub games played.
Q ❀ ◖ ⛉ ♣ P

Coldharbour

Plough Inn
Coldharbour Lane (road to Leith Hill from Dorking) OS152441 ☎ (01306) 711793
11.30–3, 6 (7 winter)–11

Adnams Old, Broadside; Gibbs Mew Bishop's Tipple; Hall & Woodhouse Badger BB; Pilgrim Porter, Talisman Ⓗ
Ten real ales await a weary walker or mountain cyclist at this friendly, family-run pub. Children welcome weekends and summer lunchtimes.
🍺 ⛺ ❀ ⛉ ◖ ❱ ♣ ⚬

Dorking

Bush
10 Horsham Road (A2003, 400 yds S of one-way system) ☎ (01306) 889830
12–2.30 (3 Sat), 6–11
Brakspear Bitter; Fuller's London Pride; Harveys BB; Thwaites Bitter Ⓗ
Friendly, well-run local with its own marbles ring. Occasional barbecues in summer. The beer range may vary. Eve meals Tue–Sat.
❀ ◖ ❱ ♣

Cricketers
81 South Street (A25, one-way system) ☎ (01306) 889938
11.30–11
Fuller's Chiswick, London Pride, ESB Ⓗ
One-bar pub with bare brick walls and a large, etched mirror depicting a cricketer. Pleasant, sheltered patio garden. Other Fuller's beers usually available. No lunches Sun; eve meals Mon–Thu.
❀ ◖ ❱ ♣

King's Arms
45 West Street (A25, one-way system) ☎ (01306) 883361
11–11
King & Barnes Sussex; Marston's Pedigree; Ringwood Best Bitter; Tetley Bitter; Wadworth 6X; guest beer Ⓗ
Converted from three cottages in the 16th-century, this pub has several linked drinking areas. Live music on Sun eve. The changing guest beer is always from an independent brewery. Beware of the fake handpump for keg cider. No eve meals Sun/Mon. No-smoking area lunchtime.
❀ ◖ ❱ ♣ P ⚬

Dormansland

Old House at Home
63–65 West Street ☎ (01342) 832117
12–3.30, 6–11 (11–11 summer)
Shepherd Neame Master Brew Bitter, Spitfire, Bishops Finger or **Porter** Ⓗ
Lively pub away from the village centre. 🍺 ❀ ◖ ❱ ♣ P

281

Surrey

East Molesey

Europa
171 Walton Road (B369)
☎ (0181) 979 5183
11–11
**Courage Best Bitter,
Directors; King & Barnes
Sussex; John Smith's Bitter** Ⓗ
Pub with three distinctive
bars: a lively public, a quiet
snug and a comfortable
lounge. Wheelchair access is
via the back bar.
Q ✿ ◖ ◨ ⅋ ♣ ⊟

Effingham

Plough
Orestan Lane OS115538
☎ (01372) 458121
11–2.45, 6–11
**Young's Bitter, Special,
Winter Warmer** Ⓗ
Quality and efficiency
dominate in both beer and
food at one of Young's finest
pubs, a *Pub of the Year*. Off the
beaten track, it requires
imaginative public transport
arrangements.
Q ✿ ◖ ▶ ⅋ P ⅄

Egham

Crown
38 High Street
☎ (01784) 432608
11–3, 5.30–11
**S&N Theakston Best Bitter,
XB, Old Peculier; Young's
Special; guest beers** Ⓗ
Warm, friendly inter-war pub
with an attractive and
secluded garden. It attracts all
ages and offers live music
most Sun lunchtimes. No
meals Sun. Guest beers are
supplied by S&N.
✿ ◖ ⇌ ♣ P

Englefield Green

Beehive
34 Middle Hill (off A30)
☎ (01784) 431621
12–2.30 (2.30 Sat), 5.30 (6 Sat)–11
**Brakspear Special; Gale's Best
Bitter, HSB; Greene King
Abbot; guest beer** Ⓗ
Very small and friendly village
pub (large parties phone
ahead). Beer festivals in the
garden late May and August
Bank Hol weekends; cider
festival Halloween weekend.
Summer barbecues.
♨ Q ✿ ◖ ♣ ◔ P

Epsom

Barley Mow
12 Pikes Hill (off Upper High
St, A2022) ☎ (01372) 721044
11–3.30, 5.30–11
**Fuller's Chiswick, London
Pride, ESB** Ⓗ
Popular local attracting all

types. The rear conservatory
backs onto a large, pleasant
garden. No food Sun eve.
✿ ◖ ▶ ⅋ ♣

King's Arms
144 East Street (A24)
☎ (01372) 723892
11–3, 5–11; 11–11 Sat
**Young's Bitter, Special,
Winter Warmer** Ⓗ
Large, Victorian inn with a
lively public bar and a
comfortable lounge. Pleasant,
landscaped garden. No food
Sun. Q ✿ ◖ ▶ ◨ ♣ P

Ewell

King William IV
19 High Street (B2200)
☎ (0181) 393 2063
**Ind Coope Friary Meux BB,
Burton Ale; Tetley Bitter** Ⓗ
Genuine local recently saved
from conversion to a pool bar.
Live music Thu and Sat nights;
summer barbecues in the
garden, which has pets to
amuse children. No lunches
Sun. ✿ ◖ ◨ ⅋ ⇌ P

Farncombe

Cricketers
37 Nightingale Road
☎ (01483) 420273
12–3, 5–11
**Fuller's Chiswick, London
Pride, ESB** Ⓗ
Splendid, friendly local with
several drinking areas. Usually
crowded, especially with
photos of cricketers, and
customers of varying ages and
types. Q ✿ ◖ ⇌ ♣

Three Lions
55 Meadrow (A3100)
☎ (01483) 417880
12–3, 5.30–11; 11–11 Sat
**Shepherd Neame Master
Brew Bitter, Best Bitter,
Spitfire, Bishops Finger** Ⓗ
Deceptively ancient (1630)
former coaching inn, known
locally as Scratchers. One
large, rambling bar with
separate areas and pool. Live
rock music at weekends. No
food Sun. Beware of the keg
cider from a fake handpump.
♨ ✿ ◖ ⇌ ♣ P

Farnham

Bricklayers
36 Weydon Lane (off
A31/A325) ☎ (01252) 726214
11–2.30, 7–11; 11–11 Fri & Sat
**Courage Best Bitter; guest
beers** Ⓗ
Spacious but cosy, two-bar
estate pub with an
enterprising guest beer policy.
The friendly management has
built a thriving trade. Live
music weekends.
♨ ✿ ◖ ▶ ◨ ⅋ ♣ P

Hop Blossom
Long Garden Walk,
Castle Street
☎ (01252) 710770
12–2.30, 4.45–11; 11–11 Fri & Sat
Fuller's London Pride, ESB Ⓗ
Busy pub, tucked behind the
main street, offering
idiosyncratic decor and jazz
and classical music. ◖ ⇌ ♣

Queen's Head
9 The Borough (A325)
☎ (01252) 726524
11–11
**Gale's BBB, Best Bitter, 5X,
HSB, Festival Mild** (summer);
guest beer Ⓗ
Classic pub in the centre of
town, bustling with a good
mix of customers in the
contrasting bars. Gale's
seasonal beers, plus a guest,
are often featured. No food
Sun. ♨ ◖ ⅋ ♣

Shepherd & Flock
22 Moor Park Lane (A31
Bourne Mill roundabout)
☎ (01252) 716675
11–3, 5.30–11; 11–11 Sat
**Courage Best Bitter; Fuller's
London Pride; Greene King
IPA; Hogs Back TEA; guest
beers** Ⓗ
Cottage-like pub which
maintains a range of up to
eight ales. Popular with
drinkers and diners (no meals
Sun eve) and, although set on
a major roundabout, it has a
peaceful air and a safe outdoor
children's area. ✿ ◖ ▶ ♣ P

Frensham

Holly Bush
Shortfield Common (off A287)
☎ (01252) 793593
11–2.30 (3 Sat), 6–11
**Morland IPA, Tanner's Jack;
Wells Bombardier** Ⓗ
Two-bar village pub, with
Surrey slats, dating from the
turn of the century. Thriving
pool, darts and quiz teams.
Frensham Ponds are nearby.
Children's play area in the
garden. No meals Sun eve.
✿ ◖ ▶ ◨ ♣ P

Frimley Green

Old Wheatsheaf
205 Frimley Green Road
(A321)
☎ (01252) 835074
11–3, 5–11; 11–11 Sat
**Morland Bitter, Tanner's Jack,
Old Speckled Hen; guest
beer** Ⓗ
100-year-old village local, now
refurbished into a single bar
with panelled alcoves. Good
lunch trade. The bookable
skittle alley becomes a family
room Sun lunchtime. No food
Sun. ✿ ◖ ♣ P

Godalming

Red Lion

Mill Lane ☎ (01483) 415207
11–11; 11–2.30, 6.30–11 Sat
**Courage Best Bitter;
Wadworth 6X; guest beers** Ⓗ
Two-bar pub located by the
town's 'Pepperpot'. The
high-ceilinged public was
formerly an Oddfellows Hall;
the quieter lounge houses a
25-ft grand piano-shaped bar.
Copper, brass and ceramics
also feature. Imaginative guest
beer policy. No eve meals Sun.
❀ ◑ ▶ ♴ ≠ ♠

Great Bookham

Anchor

161 Lower Road (off A246 via
Eastwick Rd)
☎ (01372) 452429
11–3, 5.30–11
**Courage Best Bitter,
Directors; guest beer** Ⓗ
500-year-old local with oak
beams, exposed brickwork and
a large inglenook. The feel is
rustic despite the surrounding
suburbia. No food Sun.
♨ Q ❀ ◑ ♣ P

Guildford

King's Head

27 Kings Road (A320)
☎ (01483) 68957
11–3, 5–11
**Fuller's Chiswick, London
Pride, IPA, ESB** Ⓗ
Extended and refurbished,
multi-roomed pub on the edge
of town, featuring bare board
flooring, and no-smoking
dining areas. Friendly, local
atmosphere; good value beer
and food. Busy lunchtime with
students.
♨ ◑ ▶ ≠ (London Rd) ♣ ⊬

Plough

16 Park Street (one-way
system) ☎ (01483) 570167
11–11
**Harveys BB; Ind Coope
Burton Ale; Tetley Bitter** Ⓗ
Small, single-bar pub by the
main station. Interesting
photos of old Guildford are
displayed. ◑ ≠

Sanford Arms

58 Epsom Road (A246)
☎ (01483) 572551
11–2.40, 5.30–11; 11.30–3.10, 6–11 Sat
**Courage Best Bitter;
Wadworth 6X; guest beer** Ⓗ
Friendly, wood-panelled local
with well-separated bars, a
garden with an aviary and a
small conservatory. The guest
beer (from independent
breweries) is changed
regularly. No food Thu eve.
Q ❀ ◑ ▶ ♴
≠ (London Rd) ♣

White House

8 High Street
☎ (01483) 302006
11–11
**Fuller's Chiswick, London
Pride, ESB** Ⓗ
Recently-opened, riverside
pub in former offices. A large
downstairs bar leads to a patio
overlooking the River Wey; a
smaller drinking area upstairs
(no-smoking lunchtime) is
available for meetings. No
meals Sun eve.
♿ ❀ ◑ ▶ ♴ ≠ ⊬

Hale

Ball & Wicket

104 Upper Hale Road (A3106)
☎ (01252) 735278
4 (11 Sat)–11
Wadworth 6X; guest beers Ⓗ
Attractive, half-tiled pub
opposite the cricket green.
Welcoming atmosphere; horse
brasses and beams feature. The
beer range changes regularly.
♨ ♣ ⟲ P

Wellington's

Folly Hill (A287)
☎ (01252) 715549
11.30–2.30, 5–11; 11–11 Sat
Beer range varies Ⓗ
Spacious, 1930s roadhouse
with a pleasant atmosphere.
The selection of four guest
beers changes regularly.
❀ ⊨ ◑ ▶ ♣ P

Hersham

Bricklayer's Arms

6 Queens Road (off A317)
☎ (01932) 220936
11–11
**Brakspear Bitter; Fuller's
London Pride; Hall &
Woodhouse Tanglefoot;
Whitbread Boddingtons
Bitter, Flowers IPA** Ⓗ
Friendly, two-bar, Victorian
pub, with spectacular floral
displays in summer. No food
Sat/Sun eves.
❀ ⊨ ◑ ▶ ♴ ♴ ♣

Holmbury St Mary

King's Head

Pitland Street (off B2126,
follow signs to MSSL)
☎ (01306) 730282
11–3, 6–11; 11–11 Sat
**Ringwood Best Bitter, Old
Thumper; guest beers** Ⓗ
Very good village local with
unusual church-arched doors,
wooden pews and an
imaginative layout (adjoining
games/TV area). Changing
range of five beers. Large
garden with lovely views. No
meals Sun eve.
♨ ❀ ◑ ▶ ♴ ♠ ♣ ⟲ P

Knaphill

Garibaldi

136 High Street (off A322)
☎ (01483) 473374
11–3, 5–11
**Fuller's London Pride;
Harveys BB; guest beers** Ⓗ
An oasis within a desert of
blandness and lack of choice: a
one-bar pub retaining two
separate identities. The small
lounge is often crowded with
drinkers, whilst the public
offers more space for inner
contemplation! Q ❀ ◑ ▶ P

Robin Hood

88 Robin Hood Road
☎ (01483) 472173
11–3, 5–11
Beer range varies Ⓗ
An excellent retreat from the
Goldsworth Park jungle,
which it overlooks, this pub
often offers unusual beers for
the area. Good garden (events
in the summer). ♿ ❀ ◑ ♴ P

Leatherhead

Plough

93 Kingston Road
☎ (01372) 377608
11–3, 5.30–11; 11–11 Sat
**Hogs Back TEA; Tetley Bitter;
guest beers** Ⓗ
Pleasant, two-bar pub with a
restaurant in a conservatory.
Good vegetarian selection. No
food Sun, or Mon eve. Varied
guest beers. ❀ ◑ ▶ ♴ ♣ P

Leigh

Plough

Church Road
☎ (01306) 611348
11–2.30 (3 Sat), 5–11
**King & Barnes Sussex,
Broadwood, Old, Festive** Ⓗ
Village green pub with two
contrasting bars: the 15th-
century lounge has an
attached restaurant; the
Victorian public houses many
traditional games. See the
separate 'menu' for details.
❀ ◑ ▶ ♴ ♣ P

Mickleham

King William IV

Byttom Hill (off A24
southbound) ☎ (01372) 372590
11–3, 6–11
**Adnams Bitter; Hall &
Woodhouse Badger BB; Hogs
Back TEA; Whitbread
Boddingtons Bitter; guest
beer** Ⓗ
Pub perched precariously on a
hillside where the popular
garden offers views across to
Norbury Park. The extensive
menu (no food Mon eve)

Surrey

includes five vegetarian dishes. 🏠 Q ❀ ◖ ▶

Newdigate

Surrey Oaks
Parkgate Road, Parkgate
OS205436 ☎ (01306) 631200
11.30–2.30 (3 Sat), 5.30 (6 Sat)–11
Greene King Abbot; Young's Bitter; guest beers ⊞
Fine, 16th-century pub with stone-flagged floors, a large inglenook, and a large, pleasant garden. Adventurous guest beer policy. Separate restaurant and games room. No meals Sun/Mon.
🏠 ❀ ◖ ▶ ♣ P

New Haw

White Hart
New Haw Road (A318)
☎ (01932) 842964
11.30–3, 5.30 (5 Sat)–11
Courage Best Bitter, Directors; John Smith's Bitter ⊞
Friendly pub from the 1850s, on the banks of the Wey Navigation. Sup in the comfortable bar or in the pleasant, canalside garden.
Q ❀ ◖ ♣ P

Ockley

Cricketer's Arms
Stane Street (A29)
☎ (01306) 627205
11–3, 6–11
Fuller's London Pride; Ringwood Best Bitter; Wadworth 6X; guest beer (occasional) ⊞
16th-century pub featuring local flagstones on both the floor and the roof.
🏠 ❀ ◖ ▶ ♣ P

Outwood

Dog & Duck
Prince of Wales Road
OS313460 ☎ (01342) 842964
11–11
Hall & Woodhouse Badger BB, Tanglefoot; Gribble Ale; Wadworth 6X ⊞
Friendly, rural pub offering good food (separate restaurant). Ring the Bull played. 🏠 ❀ ◖ ▶ ♿ ♣ P

Oxshott

Bear
Leatherhead Road (A244)
☎ (01372) 842747
11–3, 5.30–11
Young's Bitter, Special, Winter Warmer ⊞
Comfortable, open-plan pub with a large conservatory (children welcome). Extensive menu of home-cooked food.

No meals Sun eve in winter.
🏠 Q ❀ ◖ ▶ ♣ P

Oxted

George Inn
52 High Street, Old Oxted (off A25) ☎ (01883) 713453
11–11
Adnams Bitter; Draught Bass; Fuller's London Pride; Harveys BB; Morland Old Speckled Hen; Wadworth 6X; Whitbread Boddingtons Bitter ⊞
Very well-run, 15th-century inn which serves excellent food in both the comfortable bar and the separate restaurant. 🏠 Q ❀ ◖ ▶ P

Puttenham

Good Intent
62 The Street (off B3000, near church) ☎ (01483) 810387
11–2.30, 6–11; 11–11 Sat
Courage Best Bitter; Morland Old Speckled Hen; Wadworth 6X; guest beers ⊞
Pleasant 16th-century former coaching inn offering interesting guest beers and bar meals. Popular with locals, diners and walkers. Eve meals Tue–Sat.
🏠 Q ❀ ◖ ▶ ♣ ♿ P

Redhill

Garland
5 Brighton Road (A23)
☎ (01737) 760377
11–11
Harveys XX Mild, Pale Ale, BB, Armada ⊞
1860s corner local with a keen darts following; usually busy. Harveys seasonal beers also sold. No eve meals Tue in winter. ❀ ◖ ▶ ≢ ♣ P

Home Cottage
3 Redstone Hill (A25)
☎ (01737) 762771
10.30–11
Young's Bitter, Special, Winter Warmer ⊞
Victorian pub behind the station. Note the ancient bank of handpumps in the front bar. Children welcome in the conservatory.
🏠 ❀ ◖ ▶ ≢ ♣ P

Reigate

Bull's Head
55 High Street (A25 westbound) ☎ (01737) 249429
11–11
Fuller's London Pride; Gale's HSB; Ind Coope Burton Ale; Young's Bitter, Special ⊞
One of Reigate's oldest pubs, featuring plenty of brass around a large open fire. It can be busy lunchtime and early

---

eve. No meals weekends.
🏠 ❀ ◖ ≢

Nutley Hall
8 Nutley Lane (one-way road behind northern car park)
☎ (01737) 241741
11–11
King & Barnes Mild, Sussex, Broadwood, Old, Festive ⊞
Two-bar house with a busy front bar (active games teams). It can be very busy over the weekend. Eve meals Fri–Sat only. K&B seasonal ales are kept. ❀ ◖ ≢ ♣ ♿ P

Yew Tree
99 Reigate Hill (A217)
☎ (01737) 244944
11–11
Courage Best Bitter, Directors; Wadworth 6X; Young's Bitter ⊞
Wood-panelled lounge bar halfway up Reigate Hill. Often full of people 'working late in the office'. 🏠 ❀ ◖ ▶ ♣ P 🏳

Shepperton

Barley Mow
67 Watersplash Road (off B376 at Shepperton Green)
☎ (01932) 225580
11–11
Adnams Broadside; Courage Best Bitter; guest beers ⊞
Convivial, one-bar pub with several drinking areas. Popular with the locals, including those from Shepperton Studios. Accommodation is in an adjoining cottage.
🏠 ❀ 🛏 ◖ ▶ P

Sidlow Bridge

Three Horseshoes
Ironsbottom (off A217)
☎ (01293) 862315
12–3, 5.30–11
Fuller's London Pride, ESB; Harveys BB; guest beers ⊞
Rural free house, once a coaching inn. The many devoted regulars imbibe a prodigious amount of London Pride. Summer barbecues in the large garden. Two guest beers, one strong. ❀ ◖ ♣ P

Staffhurst Wood

Royal Oak
Caterfield Lane (2½ miles S of A25 at Limpsfield) OS407485
☎ (01883) 722207
11–3, 5.30–11; 11–11 Sat
Adnams Bitter, Broadside; Larkins Bitter ⊞
Pub offering good food in two eating areas off the main bar, and summer barbecues in the garden, which has views towards Kent and Sussex. No food Sun eve or Mon.
🏠 ❀ ◖ ▶ P

Staines

Beehive
35 Edgell Road
☎ (01784) 452663
11–11
Courage Best Bitter; Pilgrim Surrey, Porter, Progress; guest beers Ⓗ
Busy and friendly pub on the south side of town, close to the river, offering an interesting selection of guest beers, and the choice of public bar, lounge or games room.
🍴 Q ❀ 🚃 ◖ ▶ ⊟ ≠ ♣ ♨

Hobgoblin
14 Church Street
☎ (01784) 452012
11–11
Wychwood Shires, Best, Dr Thirsty's Draught, Hobgoblin; guest beers Ⓗ
Popular, single-bar pub in the town centre, always providing Wychwood and ever-changing guest beers. The landlord operates a 'child-free zone' policy. However, the youthful eve clientele demand decibels with their drinks. 🍴 ◖ ♿

Stanwell

Wheatsheaf
Town Lane (B328)
☎ (01784) 253372
11–11; 11–4, 7–11 Sat
Courage Best Bitter, Directors; Marston's Pedigree Ⓗ
Two-bar, one-price village local which supports games and sports clubs. Meals Mon–Sat (eves till 8pm).
❀ ◖ ▶ ⊟ ♣ P

Sunbury

Grey Horse
63 Staines Road East (A308)
☎ (01932) 782981
11–2.30, 5.30–11; 11–11 Fri & Sat
Courage Best Bitter, Directors; Young's Special Ⓗ
Lively, one-bar pub, popular with office workers at lunchtime. Small garden at the rear. Limited parking. No meals Sat/Sun. 🍴 ❀ ◖ ≠

Tilford

Duke of Cambridge
Tilford Road ☎ (01252) 792236
11–11
Courage Best Bitter; Greene King IPA; Hall & Woodhouse Tanglefoot; guest beers Ⓗ

Friendly, roadside free house which has sold over 180 different guest beers to date (five usually available). The large garden offers a children's play area and summer barbecues. ❀ ◖ ▶ ▲ ♣ P

Walliswood

Scarlett Arms
Walliswood Green Road
☎ (01306) 627243
11–2.30, 5.30–11
King & Barnes Mild, Sussex, Broadwood, Old, Festive Ⓗ
This low-beamed, classic country inn started life as two cottages in 1620, becoming a pub in 1907. Marvellous ambience; large inglenook; good food. K&B seasonal ales also kept. 🍴 Q ❀ ◖ ▶ ♣ P

Walton-on-Thames

Regent
19 Church Street (A3050)
☎ (01932) 243980
11–11
Courage Directors; S&N Theakston Best Bitter, XB; Wadworth 6X; Younger Scotch; guest beer Ⓗ
Former cinema, tastefully refurbished with old photographs depicting the history of Walton. Popular with students. Q ◖ ▶ ♿ ⊙ ✍

Warlingham

White Lion
3 Farleigh Road (B269)
☎ (01883) 624106
11–11
Bass Charrington IPA, Draught Bass; Fuller's London Pride; guest beer Ⓗ
15th-century building with several rooms off a central bar. The inglenook is surrounded by high-backed settles. Low beams and a stained-glass window give extra character.
🍴 Q ❀ ◖ ▶ ♣ P

Weybridge

Old Crown
83 Thames Street (off A317)
☎ (01932) 842844
11–11
Courage Best Bitter, Directors; guest beers Ⓗ
16th-century, Grade-II listed pub with a weatherboarded facade and several rooms with differing atmospheres. Home-cooked food includes daily specials. Two changing guest beers. Children's certificate.
Q ⊙ ❀ ◖ ▶ ♣ P

Prince of Wales
11 Cross Road, Oatlands (off A3050 via Anderson Rd)
☎ (01932) 852082
11–11
Adnams Bitter; Courage Best Bitter; Fuller's London Pride; Tetley Bitter; Wadworth 6X; Whitbread Boddingtons Bitter Ⓗ
Friendly, cosy pub with traditional decor. The restaurant is used for bar lunches, and for a full menu in the eve (not Sun eve). Good value food. Limited parking.
Q ❀ ◖ ▶ P

Woking

Star
Wych Hill, Hook Heath
☎ (01483) 760526
12–11
Ansells Mild; Ind Coope Friary Meux BB; Tetley Bitter; Young's Special; guest beer Ⓗ
Welcoming and lively pub, tucked away in suburbia and attracting a happy mix of age groups: one large single bar with an adjoining restaurant. Although by the roadside, it can be difficult to find.
Q ❀ ◖ ▶ P

Wood Street

White Hart
White Hart Lane
☎ (01483) 235939
11–3, 5.30–11
Gibbs Mew Salisbury, Deacon, Bishop's Tipple; guest beers Ⓗ
Picturesque village pub on the green, with a beamed interior and a resident ghost. One large square bar (serving seven beers) and an adjacent restaurant. No eve meals Sun.
Q ❀ ◖ ▶ ♣ P

Wrecclesham

Sandrock
Sandrock Hill Road
☎ (01252) 715865
11–11
Batham Mild, Best Bitter; Brakspear Bitter; guest beers Ⓗ
Superb, no-frills suburban pub serving a changing selection of beers, plus a good range of whiskies. Customers come from near and far. A former regional CAMRA *Pub of the Year*. No meals Sun.
🍴 Q ❀ ◖ ♣

Try also: Bat & Ball, Bat & Ball Lane (Free)

CAMRA speaks for you! Join up now!

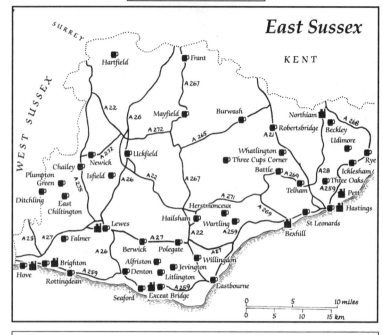

East Sussex

Cuckmere Haven, Exceat Bridge; *First In, Last Out*, Hastings; *Harveys*, Lewes; *Hedgehog & Hogshead*, Hove; *Kemptown*, Brighton; *Old Forge*, Pett; *Rother Valley*, Northiam; *Skinner's*, Brighton; *White*, Bexhill

---

Alfriston

Market Cross (Smugglers)

Waterloo Square
☎ (01323) 870241
11–2.30 (3 Sat), 6–11
Courage Best Bitter, Directors; Harveys BB, Old Ⓗ
In the centre of one of the area's prettiest villages, and therefore busy with tourists at times, this pub has an excellent atmosphere, a large inglenook and a collection of kitchen implements. Two names and two ghosts.
Q ✿ ◖ ▮

Battle

King's Head

37 Mount Street (just off High St) ☎ (01424) 772317
10.30–3, 5.30–11
Archers Village; Courage Best Bitter, Directors; Harveys BB; John Smith's Bitter Ⓗ
15th-century inn at the top end of town, featuring award-winning floral displays in summer, a lovely inglenook and a low beamed ceiling. Friendly, welcoming and

characteristically right for this ancient town. No food Sun eve in winter.
🚪 ✿ 🛏 ◖ ▮ ♣

Squirrel

North Trade Road (A271, 1¼ miles from village)
☎ (01424) 772717
11–3, 5–11; 11–11 Sat; closed winter Mon
Beer range varies Ⓗ
Pub with a friendly atmosphere, a very keen landlord who favours independent brewers and always a good range of beers (usually nine). Good food; separate restaurant. Pool/family room; large garden.
🚪 ☾ ✿ ◖ ▮ ☖ ▲ ♣ P ✗

1066

High Street
☎ (01424) 773224
11–3, 5–11; 10–11 Fri, Sat & summer
Wadworth 6X; Whitbread Boddingtons Mild, Bitter, Fremlins Bitter, Flowers Original; guest beers Ⓗ
Popular and busy pub near the abbey. The large function rooms upstairs often feature live music.
🚪 ✿ ◖ ▮ ▲ ☀ ♣

Beckley

Rose & Crown

Northiam Road (B2088 opp. B2165 jct) ☎ (01797) 252161
11–3, 5–11; 11–11 Sat
Adnams Bitter; Greene King Abbot; Harveys Pale Ale, BB; Whitbread Fremlins Bitter; guest beers Ⓗ
Spacious, welcoming family pub half a mile west of the village, with fine views from the garden. Up to seven beers available. Camping by permission of the landlord.
🚪 Q ☾ ✿ 🛏 ◖ ▮
☖ ▲ ♣ P

Berwick

Cricketer's Arms

In side road 100 yds W of Drusillas roundabout
☎ (01323) 870469
11–3, 6–11
Harveys BB, Old Ⓖ
Time has stopped here! Obviously once cottages, this is truly a special pub. Beer comes from the cask and a stone-floored public bar means walkers are welcome. No eve meals Sun–Wed in winter.

Harveys seasonal brews
served. 🍴 Q ✿ ◑ ▶ 🖰 ♿ P

Brighton

Albion

28 Albion Hill, up hill behind
old Tamplin's Brewery
☎ (01273) 604439
11–11
**Whitbread Boddingtons Mild,
Bitter; guest beers** Ⓗ
Back-street, corner house with
a friendly welcome and a
strong accent on bar billiards
(no pool). Guest beers usually
come from independent
breweries. Some enlargement
is planned. ✿ ♣ 🖰

Basketmaker's Arms

12 Gloucester Road (300 yds
SE of station)
☎ (01273) 689006
11–3, 5.30–11; 11–11 Fri & Sat
**Gale's BBB, 5X, HSB, Festival
Mild; guest beer** Ⓗ
Often-busy, back-street pub,
with an interesting collection
of old tins for decor. Excellent
food, with roasts (and a veggie
option) on Sun and a good
menu all week. The guest beer
is from the Gale's Beer Club.
◑ ≋

Bugle

24 St Martin's Street (N of The
Level, off Lewes Rd)
☎ (01273) 607753
11–3, 6–11; 11–11 Fri & Sat
**Courage Best Bitter,
Directors; Harveys BB;
Young's Special; guest
beers** Ⓗ
Traditional, unspoilt Irish
local: one main bar with
sub-sections allowing for
privacy. ✿

Dover Castle

43 Southover Street
☎ (01273) 605492
11–11
**Shepherd Neame Best Bitter,
Spitfire** Ⓗ
Street-corner pub with a
strong local trade. Although
the bar billiard table is situated
in the main bar, the pool table
is discreetly tucked away in a
side area. Darts and other
traditional games remain
highly popular. Canned music
played at a low level. ♣ 🖰

Evening Star

56 Surrey Street (200 yds S of
station) ☎ (01273) 328931
12 (11 Sat)–11
Beer range varies Ⓗ
Billed as Brighton's permanent
real ale festival: nine pumps
offer a constantly changing
range of independent brewers'
beers, plus ales from a
brewery in the pub cellar.
Over 1200 different beers have

been sold since the pub
opened in March 1992,
including exclusive one-offs.
◑ ≋ ⟲

Grey's

105 Southover Street (up steep
hill E of The Level)
☎ (01273) 680734
11–3, 5.30–11; 11–11 Sat
**Fuller's London Pride;
Whitbread Flowers Original;
guest beer** Ⓗ
Pub where the small, cosy bar
enjoys a 'front room'
atmosphere. Live music Mon
eve. Food, which includes
vegetarian, is recommended
(no meals Sun lunchtime; eve
meals Tue/Wed only). Small
selection of bottled Belgian
beers. The guest beer usually
comes from Brewery on Sea.
◑ ▶

Hand in Hand

33 Upper St James's Street
☎ (01273) 602521
11–11
**Kemptown Budget Bitter,
Best Bitter, Celebrated
Staggering Ale, SID, Old
Grumpy** Ⓗ
The home of the Kemptown
brewery is a very compact,
usually crowded, one-bar pub
with unique decor. The beer
range varies according to the
brewer's whim. Occasional
cider. ◑ ▶ ⟲

Lamb & Flag

9 Cranbourne Street (by
Churchill Sq)
☎ (01273) 326415
10.30–11; closed Sun
**Fuller's London Pride;
Kemptown Budget Bitter** Ⓗ
Friendly town-centre bar,
popular with shoppers and
office staff. Close to the clock
tower. Q ◑ ≋

Pump House

46 Market Street (near town
hall, in the Lanes)
☎ (01273) 326864
11–11
**Bass Worthington BB,
Draught Bass; Fuller's
London Pride; Harveys BB;
guest beers** Ⓗ
Pub built in 1766 on the site of
the original town pump house.
The upper part dates from the
18th-century and the cellars
from medieval times. Shop-
like frontage; wooden panels
within. No meals Sun eve. ◑ ▶

Sir Charles Napier

50 Southover Street
☎ (01273) 601413
11–3, 6–11; 11–11 Sat
**Gale's BBB, Best Bitter, HSB;
guest beer** (Mar–Oct) Ⓗ
Wooden panels help to retain
atmosphere in this corner
house where many forms of

breweriana are displayed. A
small back room and the
garden may be used by
well-behaved children (till
8pm). The guest beer is from
Gale's Beer Club.
☗ ✿ ◑ ♣ ⟲

Sussex Yeoman

7 Guildford Road (50 yards W
of station) ☎ (01273) 327985
11–3, 5–11; 11–11 Fri & Sat
**Arundel Best Bitter; Bateman
XB; Hall & Woodhouse
Tanglefoot; Harveys BB;
guest beers** Ⓗ
Welcoming free house holding
two beer festivals every year.
Food is available every day
and features a speciality
sausage menu (the pub has an
entry in the *Good Sausage
Guide*). Music includes blues,
and live jazz on Sun. ◑ ▶ ≋

Walmer Castle

45 Queens Park Road
☎ (01273) 682466
5.30–11; 12–3, 5.30–11 Sat
**King & Barnes Sussex,
Broadwood, Festive, Old** Ⓗ
Corner pub, typical of the
area. The interior is wood
panelled, with all manner of
hanging oddities. Regular live
entertainment (poets' night
Tue). Pizzas and Balti-style
food are specialities. Family
room till 9pm.
☗ ✿ ◑ ♣ ⟲

Burwash

Bell Inn

High Street ☎ (01435) 882304
11–3.30, 6–11
**Harveys BB, Old; guest
beer** Ⓗ
Superb old pub now owned by
Beards of Sussex. It has been
in the *Guide* every year since
1974. The house ale is Bateman
XB, offering a subtle link to
Rudyard Kipling's home
which stands nearby
(Batemans, NT). 🍴 ◑ ♿ P

Chailey

Horns Lodge

South Street, South Chailey
(A275) ☎ (01273) 400422
11–3, 6–11
**Courage Directors; Harveys
BB; Wadworth 6X; guest
beer** Ⓗ
Single-bar pub with separate
family and dining areas. The
large garden has a marbles
ring. A proud winner of many
pub trophies. No meals
Sun eve. 🍴 ☗ ✿ ◑ ♣ P

Denton

Flying Fish

42 Denton Road
☎ (01273) 515440

East Sussex

11–3, 6 (5 Fri & Sat)–11
Harveys XX Mild, BB H
Originally a 16th-century barn,
but now a pub of many years
standing, with two bars and a
pool room. A pleasant 'rural'
pub but check the tide tables,
as it can flood at high water
(hence the interesting stillage
arrangement built into the
bar!). No food Sun.
🏨 ❀ ◗ ▶ ♣ P

Ditchling

White Horse
16 West Street
☎ (01273) 842006
11–11
**Harveys BB; Taylor Landlord;
guest beers** H
Welcoming, single-bar village
pub, close to Anne of Cleves's
house. Real cider is now
available in all but the
coldest months. A good range
of food includes vegetarian
options. The cellar is reputedly
haunted.
🏨 ❀ ◗ ▶ ♣ ○

Eastbourne

Alexandra Arms
453 Seaside (A259, E of centre)
☎ (01323) 72913
11–3, 5.30–11
**Butcombe Bitter; Fuller's
London Pride; Harveys BB;
S&N Theakston Old Peculier;
Smiles Best Bitter; guest
beers** H
Two-bar local with a friendly
welcome. Good food includes
daily specials. One bar is filled
with reading books. Quiz Sun
night. *Evening Argus Sussex
Pub of the Year.*
🏨 ❀ ◗ ▯ ♣ P

Hogshead
South Street (opp. station)
☎ (01323) 723107
11–11
Harveys BB G/H**; Marston's
Pedigree; Wadworth 6X** H**;
Whitbread Boddingtons
Bitter** G/H**, Flowers
Original** H**; guest beers** G/H
Large, boisterous, youngsters'
pub in the theme mould. Jugs
available at discounted prices
on selected beers. ◗ ⇌ ○

Hurst Arms
76 Willingdon Road (A22 1½
miles N of centre)
☎ (01323) 721762
11–11
**Harveys Pale Ale, BB,
Armada** H
This large Victorian building
incorporates a huge public bar
and a cosy lounge. Its name is
derived from old local
landowners. Harveys seasonal
beers also sold. Q ❀ ◗

Lamb
High Street, Old Town (A259
Seaford road, W of centre)
☎ (01323) 720545
11–3, 5.30–11
**Harveys XX Mild, Pale Ale,
BB, Armada** H
A Harveys show house with
three distinctively different bar
areas – each on a separate
level. Beams aplenty; parts
date from 1290. Occasional
gravity dispense in the lower
youngsters' bar Fri–Sat nights.
Cellar tours by arrangement.
Family room lunchtimes.
Harveys seasonal brews
served. Q ⛺ ❀ ◗ ▶ ▯ P

East Chiltington

Jolly Sportsman
Chapel Lane (off B2116)
OS372153 ☎ (01273) 890400
11.30–2.30, 6 (7 winter)–11; closed
Mon
**King & Barnes Sussex; John
Smith's Bitter; guest beers** H
Nestled under the South
Downs, this community pub is
located close to a 13th-century
church and commands good
views across the Sussex
Weald. The bar is small, but
there are separate rooms for
dining and pool. Bookable
Sun lunches Nov–Apr. No eve
meals Tue or Sun.
❀ ◗ ▶ ♣ P

Exceat Bridge

Golden Galleon
Off A259, on the River
Cuckmere ☎ (01323) 892247
11–2.30, 6–11 (10.30 Mon–Thu in
winter)
**Cuckmere Haven Best
Bitter** H**; guest beers** H/G
Brew pub with a large bar
divided into drinking and
food areas; originally a tea
room, converted in the 1970s.
A large garden overlooks the
river. Popular with walkers.
Four guest ales plus three
other beers from Cuckmere
Haven. Four-pint jugs and
take-aways available.
🏨 ⛺ ❀ ◗ ▶ ▲ ♣ ○ P

Falmer

Swan
Middle Street, North Falmer
☎ (01273) 681842
11–2.30, 6–11
**Gibbs Mew Premium,
Bishop's Tipple; Palmers IPA;
Shepherd Neame Bishops
Finger; guest beer** H
The same family has run this
village local since 1903. Three
bars, one no-smoking. Note
the pictures and mementoes of
village life.
🏨 ⛺ ❀ ◗ ▯ ⇌ P ✂

Frant

Abergavenny Arms
Frant Road (A207)
☎ (01892) 750233
11–3, 6–11
Harveys BB H**; Rother Valley
Level Best** G**; guest
beers** G/H
Large, two-bar country pub
originating from the 15th
century and featuring many
genuine beams. The lounge
was used as a courtroom in
the 18th century, with cells in
the cellar. The large beer range
has been recently extended.
Quality food at a reasonable
price (no meals Sun eve).
🏨 Q ❀ ◗ ▶ ▲ ♣ P ⊟

Hailsham

Grenadier
High Street (N end)
☎ (01323) 842152
11–11
**Harveys XX Mild, BB, Old,
Armada** H
Popular, two-bar town pub: an
imposing building with a
tastefully renovated interior
(spot the original gas lamp
fittings). In the same family for
over 40 years and close to the
Cuckoo Trail foot and cycle
path. Harveys seasonal beers
sold. ❀ ◗ ▯ & ♣

Hartfield

Anchor Inn
Church Street (B2110)
☎ (01892) 770424
11–11
**Harveys BB; Marston's
Pedigree; Wadworth 6X;
Whitbread Boddingtons
Bitter, Fremlins Bitter** H
Near Ashdown Forest and the
famous Pooh Bridge: a 15th-
century farmhouse which still
retains its oak beams and old
world feel. Wooden
panelling
continues the country theme.
Can you find the four-leaf
clovers in the garden?
🏨 Q ⛺ ❀ ▱ ◗ ▲ ♣ P

Hastings

First In, Last Out
14 High Street
☎ (01424) 425079
11–11
**FILO Crofter, Cardinal; guest
beer** H
Home of the FILO brewery:
a pub in the historic old
town, featuring alcove seating
and an impressive, open
central fireplace. Busy
eves and weekends.
Lunches Tue–Sat.
🏨 Q ❀ ◗ & ▲ ♣ ○

288

Stag

All Saints' Street (off the Bourne, Old Town)
☎ (01424) 425734
12–3, 6–11; 11–11 Sat
Shepherd Neame Master Brew Bitter, Best Bitter, Spitfire, Bishops Finger *or* **Porter** Ⓗ
Ancient smugglers' pub in the picturesque Old Town. Features include its own game, Loggits, and a collection of mummified cats. Annual mini-beer festival. No meals Sun-Mon.
🏚 🌣 🌢 🌣 🌣 🌢 🌢 🌢 🌢

Herstmonceux

Brewer's Arms

Gardner Street (A271)
☎ (01323) 832226
11–2.30, 6–11; 12–2.30, 7–10.30 Sun
Adnams Broadside; Harveys BB; guest beers Ⓗ
Traditional country village pub with an old world atmosphere and many antiques. This Beards house specialises in beers from independent breweries (usually a choice of five). No food Tue eve.
🏚 🌣 🌢 🌢 🌢 🌢 P 🌢

Welcome Stranger

Chapel Row (100 yds S of A271 on road to church)
☎ (01323) 832119
7–11; 12–2, 7–11 Sat; 12–2, 7–10.30 Sun
Harveys BB, Old Ⓗ
Fine example of an unspoilt country alehouse, the last in Sussex to obtain a full licence. Known locally as the Kicking Donkey, the pub has been in the same family since 1908. Beer is served through a hatch into the small bar room. Note: closed lunchtime Mon–Fri.
🏚 Q 🌣 🌢 P 🌢

Hove

Farm Tavern

13 Farm Road (off Western Rd) ☎ (01273) 325902
11–11
Bateman XB; Harveys BB; guest beers Ⓗ
Small, cosy, welcoming pub, just off the beaten track. Clean and well-kept, it's a credit to the Beards pub chain. The only pub in the area to serve ale in oversized glasses. The TV is only turned up for major sporting occasions. Q 🌢 🌢 🌢

Grenadier

200 Hangleton Road (off A27, towards Devil's Dyke)
☎ (01273) 735901
11–11
Draught Bass; Fuller's London Pride; guest beers Ⓗ

Large but homely estate pub with two bars; often busy. The managers make full use of the guest beer list available to them, with many independent brews passing through the pumps. Beware: the cider is not the real thing. No lunches Sun. 🌣 🌢 🌢 🌢 🌢 P

Icklesham

Queen's Head

Parsonage Lane (off A259 opp. church) ☎ (01424) 814552
11–3, 6–11; 11–11 Sat & summer
Beer range varies Ⓗ
Tile-hung country pub in a rural setting with superb views from the garden. Magnificent mahogany bar; warm, friendly atmosphere. Ever-changing range of interesting beer; excellent food. Camping by prior permission.
🏚 Q 🌢 🌢 🌢 🌢 🌢 P 🌢

Isfield

Laughing Fish

Station Road (½mile W of A26)
☎ (01825) 750349
11–3, 6–11
Harveys Pale Ale, BB, Old; guest beer Ⓗ
Friendly village pub next to the Lavender Line restored railway station, two miles from Bentley Wildfowl Park and motor museum. An underground stream cools the cellar. The porch was built by the Canadian Army.
🏚 🌣 🌢 🌢 🌢 🌢 P

Jevington

Eight Bells

High Street ☎ (01323) 484442
11–3, 6–11
Adnams Broadside; Butcombe Bitter; Courage Best Bitter; Harveys BB; guest beers Ⓗ
Country pub with contrasting drinking areas. One has an inglenook and an antique cash register. The more modern side has local paintings for sale and sometimes local produce. Just off the South Downs bridleway.
🏚 Q 🌣 🌢 🌢 🌢 P

Lewes

Black Horse

55 Western Road
☎ (01273) 473653
11–2.30, 5.30 (6 Sat)–11
Brakspear Bitter; Harveys BB; Smiles Best Bitter; guest beer Ⓗ
Popular, two-bar local, originally built as a coaching inn in 1810. Note the pictures

---

of pubs in old Lewes.
Q 🌣 🌢 🌢 🌢 🌢

Brewer's Arms

91 High Street
☎ (01273) 479475
11–11
Hancock's HB; Harveys BB; guest beers Ⓗ
Traditional, quiet pub, popular with locals. The public bar has a pool table and holds discos Fri night. No lunches Sun. Cider in summer.
🌢 🌢 🌢 🌢 🌢

Dorset Arms

22 Malling Street
☎ (01273) 477110
11–3, 6–11
Harveys Pale Ale, BB, Armada Ⓗ
The Harveys brewery tap (spot the occasional director): a smart, two-bar pub with a restaurant. No meals Sun. Harveys seasonal beers also sold. 🌢 🌣 🌢 🌢 🌢

Gardener's Arms

46 Cliffe High Street
☎ (01273) 474808
11–3, 5.30–11; 11–11 Thu–Sat
Beer range varies Ⓗ
Unpretentious, friendly, two-bar pub, near the Harveys brewery. A true free house; up to eight ales from independent brewers are available at any one time. A must. No meals Sun. 🌢 🌢 🌢 🌢

Snowdrop

119 South Street
☎ (01273) 471018
11–11
Harveys BB; Hop Back Summer Lightning Ⓗ
Lively, two-bar, two-storey pub aimed at the Lewes youth. Avalanche by Brewery on Sea is a house beer exclusive to the pub. Situated by the edge of a 19th-century landslide disaster site. Note the 1960s decor.
🌣 🌢 🌢 🌢

Litlington

Plough & Harrow

On Exceat–Wilmington road
☎ (01323) 870632
11–2.30 (3 summer), 6.30–11
Hall & Woodhouse Badger BB, Hard Tackle, Tanglefoot; Harveys BB; Wells Eagle, Bombardier Ⓗ
Attractive pub which caters for a varied clientele. It features a very busy restaurant (particularly Sun lunchtimes) but has a proper bar section too – often with live music – decorated with models and railway memorabilia. Well-situated for walkers. The beer range may vary.
Q 🌣 🌢 🌢 P

East Sussex

Mayfield

Rose & Crown
Fletching Street
☎ (01435) 872200
11–3, 5–11 (11–11 summer)
**Draught Bass; Harveys BB;
Whitbread Boddingtons
Bitter; guest beers** Ⓗ
Country inn with various
rooms, odd corners and loads
of character. Welcoming log
fire in the inglenook in winter.
Excellent quality menu (AA
rosette) although prices are to
match. Smaller portions are
available for children. Usually
five beers available.
🏚 Q ♿ ❀ 🏚 ◖ ▶ ♣ P

Newick

Crown Inn
Church Road (S off A272)
☎ (01825) 723293
11–11
**Adnams Bitter; Courage
Directors; Greene King
Abbot; Harveys BB; guest
beers** Ⓗ
One-bar village local, popular
with the rugby club. Regular
games and quizzes. An old
archway retained from its
coaching days leads to a
suntrap courtyard.
No lunches Sun.
🏚 ❀ ◖ ♣ P

Plumpton Green

Fountain
Station Road ☎ (01273) 890294
10.30–2.30, 6–11 (may vary)
**Young's Bitter, Special,
Winter Warmer** Ⓗ
The most southerly tied house
owned by Young's, and
originally a bakehouse, is now
a popular single-bar pub
which has appeared in every
Good Beer Guide. Over half of
all sales (including spirits, etc.)
are for draught bitter. A
mobile fish and chip van visits
Tue eve. 🏚 ❀ ♣ P

Polegate

Junction Tavern
99 Station Road (A27 just E of
centre) ☎ (01323) 482010
11–11 (11–3, 5–11 winter)
**Adnams Bitter; Harveys BB;
S&N Theakston Old Peculier;
guest beers** Ⓗ
A country pub in town: a
run-down Courage house
extensively restored by Beards.
The separate, uncarpeted
public bar, with two coal fires
and lots of reading material, is
now known locally as the
Library! Park opposite.
🏚 Q ❀ ◖ ▶ 🏚 & ⇌
♣ ⚥ 🖫

Robertsbridge

Ostrich
Station Road ☎ (01580) 881737
11–11
**Harveys BB, Old; King &
Barnes Sussex; Rother Valley
Level Best; Shepherd Neame
Master Brew Bitter, Spitfire** Ⓗ
Former station hotel tastefully
restored to its former glory,
maintaining classic internal
architectural features. It now
functions as an excellent local,
as well as a haven for visitors.
🏚 🏠 ◖ ▶ 🏚 & ⇌
♣ ◌ P

Seven Stars
High Street ☎ (01580) 880333
11–3, 5.30–11; 11–11 Fri & Sat
**Belhaven St Andrew's Ale;
Courage Best Bitter,
Directors; Greene King
Abbot; Harveys BB; guest
beers** Ⓗ
Warm, oak-beamed pub in the
village centre, home of the
famous Red Monk ghost; a
pub since 1500. Seven to ten
beers served, plus good food.
Live music once a week.
🏚 Q ❀ 🏠 ◖ ▶ ⇌ ♣ P

Rottingdean

Black Horse
65 High Street
☎ (01273) 302581
10.30–2.30, 6–11
Harveys BB; guest beers Ⓗ
Traditional, two-bar village
local, offering a good range of
five guest beers. The snug,
which is the oldest part of the
pub, allows in children. ◖ 🏚

Try also: **Plough**, High St
(Bass)

Rye

Ypres Castle
Gun Garden (down steps to
rear of Ypres Tower)
☎ (01797) 223248
11–11
**Hook Norton Best Bitter;
King & Barnes Sussex; guest
beers** Ⓗ
Not immediately obvious, this
unspoilt pub is well worth
seeking out (access on foot
only). Superb views of the
harbour; safe garden; near
Rye's picturesque areas,
familiar from a dozen films.
Good food (fresh fish a
speciality). Guest beers include
a mild. 🏚 Q ♿ ❀ ◖ ▶ ♣

St Leonards

North Star
Clarence Road (20 yards off
A21, Bohemia Rd, behind
shops) ☎ (01424) 436576
11–3, 5.30–11; 11–11 Sat

**Fuller's London Pride;
Harveys BB; guest beer** Ⓗ
Basic, two-bar, back-street
local. Excellent choice of guest
beers. ◖ ♣

Seaford

White Lion Hotel
74 Claremont Road (A259,
W of centre)
☎ (01323) 892473
11–2.30 (3 Sat), 6–11
**Fuller's London Pride;
Harveys BB, Old; Shepherd
Neame Bishops Finger** Ⓗ
Hotel with spacious bars,
including a games bar. The
range of bar food is extensive
and there is also a separate
restaurant. A good base for
walkers on the South Downs.
❀ 🏚 ◖ ▶ ▲ ⇌ ♣ P

Try also: **Wellington**, Steyne
Rd (Free)

Telham

Black Horse
Hastings Road (A2100)
☎ (01424) 773109
11–3, 5.30–11
**Shepherd Neame Master
Brew Bitter, Best Bitter,
Spitfire, Bishops Finger** Ⓗ
A good stopping off point
between Battle and Hastings: a
pub with an unusual skittle
alley in the attic. Boules
played in summer. Music
weekend every Spring Bank
Hol. Special beers are often
brewed for the event.
Occasional folk music in the
bar. 🏚 ❀ ◖ ▶ ▲ ♣ P

Three Cups Corner

Three Cups Inn
On B2096 ☎ (01435) 830252
11–3, 6.30–11
**Arkell's 3B; Harveys BB;
guest beers** Ⓗ
Old country pub with an
inglenook and a cosy interior,
popular with the locals. Pub
game addicts will not be
disappointed. Selection of
snuffs available. Usually five
beers, invariably from
independent breweries.
Caravans welcome. 🏚 Q ♿
❀ ◖ & ▲ ♣ P ⚥

Three Oaks

Three Oaks
Butchers Lane (near A259)
☎ (01424) 813303
12–3, 7–11
**Rother Valley Level Best;
guest beers** Ⓗ
Pleasant country pub with
atmosphere. Pool table;
home-cooked food. Adjacent
to the railway station. Good
local walks.
🏚 Q ❀ ◖ ▶ ▲ ⇌ ♣ P 🖫

Uckfield

Alma Arms

Framfield Road (B2102 E of centre) ☎ (01825) 762232
11–2.30, 6–11; 12–2, 7–10.30 Sun
Harveys XX Mild, Pale Ale, BB, Old, Armada H
Traditional pub with a comfortable saloon bar and family room in a poor town for drinking. Run by the same family for generations. A rare opportunity to sample the full range of Harveys beers. Small garden area.
Q ☎ ⊛ ◖ 🛏 ⅋ ⩾ ♣ P ⅄

Udimore

King's Head

Udimore Road (B2089 W of village) ☎ (01424) 882049
11–4, 5.30–11
Rother Valley Level Best; guest beer H
Dating from 1535, a traditional village ale house with no cellar. Beams, two open fires

and a wood floor are features. Home-cooked food. Family room and skittle room; boules also played.
🍺 Q ☎ ⊛ ◖ 🛏 ♣ ⅄

Wartling

Lamb at Wartling

On minor road N from Pevensey roundabout (A27)
OS658092 ☎ (01323) 832116
11–2.30 (3 Sat & summer), 7 (6 Sat & summer)–11
Bass Charrington IPA, Draught Bass; Fuller's London Pride H
Village local next to the church, offering a small, comfy bar and a little lounge. Separate restaurant but bar food is available most sessions. Two roaring fires in winter.
🍺 Q ☎ ⊛ ◖ 🛏 ♣ P

Whatlington

Royal Oak

On A21 ☎ (01424) 870492
12–2.30, 7 (6 Sat)–11; closed Tue

Harvey's Pale Ale; Marston's Pedigree; Morland Old Speckled Hen; Young's Special H
Splendid example of a rural pub, complete with a 15th-century interior, including a mock baronial hall and an 80-ft indoor well. Warm atmosphere and good food.
🍺 Q ◖ 🛏 P

Willingdon

Red Lion

99 Wish Hill (just off A22)
☎ (01323) 502062
11–2.30, 5.30–11
King & Barnes Sussex, Broadwood, Old, Festive H
Unassuming, popular village local at the foot of the South Downs. Busy lunchtimes and weekends, with good value food available Mon–Sat. K&B seasonal beers also sold.
⊛ ◖ 🛏 ♣ P ⅄

Try also: Wheatsheaf (Inntrepreneur)

IN CIDER DEALING

Cider, just like beer, comes in various forms. There are sweet and dry ciders. Some are strong, others are stronger. And just like beer, some are 'real', others are 'keg'. Keg beer, as discussed elsewhere in this book, is a beer which has been filtered, pasteurised and stored in pressurised containers before being pumped to the bar with lots of gas. Keg cider undergoes a similar fate. Nearly all the well-advertised brands are keg: Strongbow, Woodpecker, Dry Blackthorn, Old English, Red Rock and, yes, despite the name, Scrumpy Jack.

You could almost hear the marketing men thinking aloud when Scrumpy Jack was conceived. Everyone knows 'scrumpy' is a term for recklessly strong cider, traditionally brewed on small farms in the time-honoured fashion. By building it into the name of a powerful keg cider, though neither traditional nor farm-produced, it helped to attract the young and easily led. Then the brand managers went a step further in their quest for the 'traditional' look. They created a keg tap which looked like a handpump. Anyone duped into thinking this cider was 'real' was soon disappointed when the landlord pulled back the tall handle and the cider fizzed out just like any other keg product.

Sadly, other cider manufacturers have followed suit. CAMRA believes this less than honest practice should stop. Scrumpy Jack clearly has its followers and the Campaign takes no issue with that. But unsuspecting drinkers should not be conned by these fake handpumps and the specious 'cellarmanship' certificates which form part of the marketing package. Other dispense systems are already available for Scrumpy Jack, and, in an effort to preserve the integrity of the handpump – the recognised symbol of tradition in the brewing trade – the Campaign is actively urging publicans to request one of these normal keg fonts if selling this cider.

On a positive note, in the last year Bulmers has introduced Scrumpy Jack Old Hazy. This *is* a real cider and should indeed be served by handpump, just like real ale.

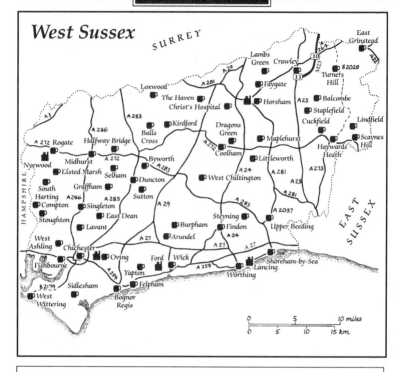

West Sussex

 Arundel, Ford; *Ballard's*, Nyewood; *Brewery on Sea*, Lancing; *Gribble*, Oving; *King & Barnes*, Horsham

Arundel

Swan Hotel
27 High Street
☎ (01903) 882314
11–11
Arundel Best Bitter, Gold, Stronghold, Old Knucker; guest beer Ⓗ
Centrally located, close to the castle, this former *Guide* regular has been sympathetically restored as Arundel Brewery's first tied house. The framed but ageing picture of a swan in the bar is actually the previous pub sign, made of beaten brass and dating from 1850.
🏚 ☕ ⌂ ◑ ▶

Balcombe

Cowdray Arms
London Road (B2036/B2110 jct) ☎ (01444) 811280
11–3, 5.30–11 (11–11 Sat in summer)
Harveys BB Ⓗ **; guest beers** Ⓗ & Ⓖ
Popular roadhouse with ample parking and a good selection of guest ales (500 in the last four years). Beer festival April. The conservatory is a

no-smoking eating area. Children's certificate.
Balcombe Best Bitter is a house beer. Q ☕ ❀ ◑ ▶ ♣ ⌂ P

Balls Cross

Stag
Kirdford Road (2 miles NE of Petworth, off A283) OS987263
☎ (01403) 820241
11–3, 6–11
King & Barnes Sussex, Festive Ⓗ
16th-century pub with original stone floors and an inglenook. Sited on an old coaching route, it has always been a pub. K&B seasonal beers also sold.
🏚 Q ☕ ❀ ◑ ▶ 🍴 ♣ P

Bognor Regis

Lamb
Steyne Street (off High St)
☎ (01243) 868215
11–11
Arundel Best Bitter; Fuller's London Pride; Whitbread Flowers IPA, Original Ⓗ
Busy, friendly and popular, two-bar pub close to the town centre. No eve meals
Sun/Mon.
🏚 ❀ ◑ ▶ 🍴 ≈ ♣

Burpham

George & Dragon
☎ (01903) 883131
11–3, 6–11
Arundel Best Bitter; Courage Directors; guest beers Ⓗ
Popular free house in a pleasant village two miles from Arundel, offering regular changes to the beer and menu. The village is accessed by a cul-de-sac nearly opposite Arundel station. A good base for walking.
🏚 Q ❀ ◑ ▶ & P

Byworth

Black Horse Inn
Off A283 ☎ (01798) 342424
11–3, 6–11
Fuller's London Pride; Gale's HSB; Young's Bitter; guest beer (summer) Ⓗ
Traditional, welcoming pub with original wood panelling, exposed beams and floorboards. Families welcome in the separate eating areas. The menu features fresh local produce (no meals Sun eve, Jan/Feb). The garden overlooks Shimmings Valley.

Elizabethan function room upstairs. ♨ Q ❀ ◑ ▶ ♣ P

Chichester

Chequers Inn

203 Oving Road (200 yds W of A27) ☎ (01243) 786427
11–11
Fuller's London Pride; Ringwood Best Bitter; Whitbread WCPA, Boddingtons Bitter; guest beers H
Popular and genuine local on the edge of town, with more of an appearance of a country inn. Busy front bar and games room; quieter lounge.
Q ♿ ❀ ◑ ▣ ➔ ⌂ P

Hogshead

50 South Street
☎ (01243) 785753
11–11
Fuller's London Pride H; **Gibbs Mew Bishop's Tipple; Ringwood Old Thumper** G; **Whitbread Boddingtons Bitter, Flowers Original** H; **guest beers** H & G
A welcome oasis in a city awash with bland national brews, this Georgian building (an inn since 1740) has been revamped in the functional Hogshead style. Welcoming log fire, good value food (eves till 7pm; no meals Sun eve) and 11 ales.
♨ Q ❀ ◑ ▶ ⇌ ⌂

Christ's Hospital

Bax Castle

Two Mile Ash Road (road from Southwater to Christ's Hospital) OS148273
☎ (01403) 730369
11.30–2.30 (3 Fri & Sat), 6–11
Ansells Bitter; Draught Bass; Fuller's London Pride; John Smith's Bitter; guest beer H
Small, one-bar pub which is difficult to find (situated behind a former railway bridge on a T-junction to Barns Green and Christ's Hospital). The old railway line is now part of the Downs Link, popular with cyclists and walkers. Large, safe garden for children.
♨ Q ♿ ❀ ◑ ▶ ♣ P ⌯

Compton

Coach & Horses

On B2146 near Hants border
☎ (01705) 631228
11–2.30, 6–11
Fuller's ESB; guest beers H
15th-century coaching inn well situated for good walking and cycling. A separate restaurant offers an imaginative range of dishes. Four guest beers.
♨ Q ◑ ▶ ♿ ♣ P

Coolham

Selsey Arms

Coolham Cross Roads (A272)
☎ (01403) 741537
11–3, 5.30–11
King & Barnes Sussex; Wadworth 6X; Whitbread Strong Country; guest beer H
Basic, one-bar pub with three separate rooms, each with its own fire. Sociable mix from surrounding villages.
♨ Q ❀ ◈ ◑ ▶ ♣ P

Crawley

Maid of Sussex

89 Gales Drive, Three Bridges
☎ (01293) 525404
11–11
Courage Best Bitter, Directors; S&N Theakston Best Bitter; Webster's Yorkshire Bitter H
Large, friendly, well-run estate pub, about ten minutes' walk from Three Bridges station.
♿ ❀ ◑ ▶ ▣ ♣ P

Plough

Ifield Street, Ifield
☎ (01293) 524292
11–3 (4 Fri & Sat), 6–11
King & Barnes Sussex, Broadwood, Old, Festive H
Traditional village local now on the edge of town, next to the church and Ifield Barn Theatre (ten minutes from Ifield station). No lunches Sun. K&B seasonal beers also sold.
◑ ▶ ▣ ♣

White Hart

High Street ☎ (01293) 520033
10–11
Harveys BB, Armada H
Popular, two-bar, town-centre pub offering occasional live music. All Harveys seasonal beers sold as available. No meals Sat/Sun.
♨ ◑ ⇌ ♣ P

Cuckfield

White Harte

South Street ☎ (01444) 413454
11–3, 6–11
King & Barnes Sussex, Broadwood, Old, Festive H
Two-bar village pub situated on a double bend. Genuine oak beams and an inglenook in the saloon; a more spartan public bar provides contrast. The family room is only open in summer. K&B seasonal beers available.
♨ Q ♿ ❀ ◑ ▣ ♣ P

Dragons Green

George & Dragon

Off A272 ☎ (01403) 741320
11–3, 6.30–11; 11–11 Sat

Coolham

King & Barnes Sussex, Broadwood, Old, Festive H
Very popular, low-beamed country local, where meals are popular. A unique feature is the tombstone in the garden. Dwile Flonking takes place annually in June.
♨ Q ❀ ◑ ▶ ▣ ♣ P

Duncton

Cricketers

Main Road (A283)
☎ (01798) 342473
11–3, 6–11
Hop Back Summer Lightning; Ind Coope Friary Meux BB, Burton Ale; Young's Bitter; guest beer H
Pub where the cosy, friendly bar features a large inglenook. Separate, split-level eating areas; attractive garden (barbecues in summer); skittle alley. No food Sun/Mon eves in winter. Cider in summer.
♨ Q ❀ ◑ ▶ ♣ ⌂ P

East Dean

Hurdlemakers

Main road ☎ (01243) 811318
11–2.30 (3 Sat), 6–11
Ballard's Wassail G; **Ruddles Best Bitter; Ushers Best Bitter; Wadworth 6X** H
Well-run free house which also functions as a village shop. The excellent garden houses old stables now converted to self-contained accommodation (facilities for disabled guests). New family room (walkers welcome). Good range of food.
♨ ♿ ❀ ◈ ◑ ▶ ♿ ♣ ♣ ⌯

East Grinstead

Dunnings Mill

☎ (01342) 326341
11–2.30 (3 Sat), 5.30–11
Harveys XX Mild (summer), **BB, Old, Armada** H
Attractive old pub with beams and drinking areas on three levels. A cellar bar is open eves. Eve meals Wed–Sat.
♨ Q ❀ ◑ ▶ P

Elsted Marsh

Elsted Inn

Off A272 OS834207
☎ (01730) 813662
11–3, 5.30–11
Ballard's Trotton, Best Bitter, Wassail; Brewery on Sea Spinnaker Classic; Fuller's London Pride; guest beers H
Welcoming, tastefully refurbished Victorian pub, the former home of Ballard's brewery. The brewery now houses a picture gallery. Excellent home-cooking.
♨ Q ❀ ◈ ◑ ▶ ♣ P

West Sussex

Faygate

Cherry Tree
Crawley Road (A264)
☎ (01293) 851305
11–3 (3.30 Sat), 6–11
King & Barnes Sussex ⊞
Two cottages built in 1660
which became a pub in 1870.
Two open fires and an
inglenook with original beams;
warm atmosphere and good
value meals. Note: the Old and
Broadwood are kept under
cask breathers.
🛏 Q ⛲ ❀ ◑ ◐ ☕ ♣ P

Felpham

Old Barn
Felpham Road
☎ (01243) 821564
11–11
**Arundel Best Bitter; Fuller's
ESB; Greene King Abbot;
Marston's Pedigree;
Ringwood Best Bitter; guest
beers** ⊞
Single-bar pub equidistant
from the village centre and
Southcoast World (Butlins),
popular with visitors and
locals. Quiz and music nights;
at least two guest ales.
◑ ◐ ☕ P

Findon

Village House Hotel
Horsham Road
☎ (01903) 873350
10.30–11
**Courage Directors; Harveys
BB; Ruddles County; Wadworth
6X; guest beers** ⊞
16th-century village local
where the bar is decorated
with racing silks from local
stables. Two guest ales. Noted
for its curries.
🛏 ❀ 🛏 ◑ ◐ P

Fishbourne

Bull's Head
99 Fishbourne Road (A259)
☎ (01243) 785707
11–3, 5.30–11; 11–11 Sat
**Fuller's London Pride; Gale's
BBB, Best Bitter, 5X, HSB;
guest beer** ⊞
Large, comfortable pub with a
restaurant specialising in fish
in summer and game in winter
– all home-cooked. Function
room/skittle alley. Access to
the car park is off Mill Lane.
Cider in summer.
🛏 ⛲ ❀ ◑ ◐ ♣ ☖ P ⅄

Graffham

Forester's Arms
☎ (01798) 867202

11–2.30, 5.30–11; 12–3, 7.30–10.30
Sun
**Courage Directors; Harveys
XX Mild (summer), Pale Ale,
Old; Morland Old Speckled
Hen; guest beer** (occasional) ⊞
Heavily beamed, 17th-century
inn in good walking country,
close to the South Downs Way.
The restaurant and bar menus
feature English farmhouse fare
with an emphasis on game.
🛏 Q ❀ ◑ ◐ ♿ ♠ P

Halfway Bridge

Halfway Bridge Inn
On A272 ☎ (01798) 861281
11–3, 6–11
**Cheriton Pots Ale; Gale's
HSB; guest beers** ⊞
Early 18th-century coaching
house, retaining much
character in its several
interconnecting rooms, all
with real fires. A roast half
shoulder of lamb often
features on an adventurous
menu. No eve meals in winter.
🛏 Q ❀ ◑ ◐ ♣ P ⅄

The Haven

Blue Ship
Down lane W of minor road
from Bucks Green to Five
Oaks OS084306
☎ (01403) 822709
11–3, 6–11
**King & Barnes Sussex,
Broadwood, Old** Ⓖ
One of the classic pubs of
Britain: a good, basic country
pub with four small rooms, the
front room having a brick floor
and an inglenook. No bar as
such: drinks are served
through a hatch. Very popular
at weekends. No eve meals
Sun/Mon. K&B seasonal beers
served. 🛏 Q ⛲ ❀ ◑ ◐ ♣ P

Haywards Heath

Star
1 The Broadway
☎ (01444) 413267
11–11
**Brakspear Bitter; King &
Barnes Sussex; Morland Old
Speckled Hen; Wadworth 6X;
Whitbread Boddingtons Mild,
Bitter; guest beers** ⊞
Large, L-shaped pub with bare
wood floors and panelling.
One of the Hogshead cask ale
houses: 13 handpumps all
serve a different beer. Large
selection of bottled ales.
Q ❀ ◑ ◐ ◫ ⇌ ♣ ☖ P

Horsham

Bedford Hotel
Station Road ☎ (01403) 253128
11–11; 11–4, 6–11 Sat
Draught Bass; Fuller's

**London Pride; Marston's
Pedigree; Wadworth 6X;
Whitbread Boddingtons
Bitter, Strong Country** ⊞
Large and welcoming, street-
corner pub with two bars in
contrasting styles. Lunches
Mon–Sat. Lined glasses used if
requested.
🛏 ⛲ ❀ ◑ ◐ ⇌ ♠ P ⊟

Dog & Bacon
North Parade (B2237, near A24
roundabout) ☎ (01403) 252176
11–2.30, 6–11
**King & Barnes Sussex,
Broadwood, Old** ⊞
Popular pub in the suburbs of
Horsham, attracting a good
cross-section of the local
populace. No-smoking family
room at the front. Occasional
theme eves. Eve meals Wed–
Sat. K&B seasonal beers sold.
⛲ ❀ ◑ ◐ ◫ ♠ P ⅄

Hornbrook
Brighton Road (A281, 1 mile
from centre) ☎ (01403) 252638
11–3, 5.30–11 (11–11 summer)
**King & Barnes Sussex,
Festive** ⊞
Though known as a family
pub, with facilities for children
and a varied menu, this pub
also offers a friendly
atmosphere for drinkers, with
the option of two bars. Log fire
in winter; barbecue in
summer. Children's certificate
applied for. Note: Broadwood
is kept under a cask breather.
K&B seasonal brews also sold.
🛏 Q ❀ ◑ ◐ ◫ ♿ ♠ P

Stout House
29 Carfax (pedestrianised area
by bandstand)
☎ (01403) 267777
10–4, 7.30–11
**King & Barnes Sussex,
Broadwood** (occasional), **Old,
Festive** ⊞
Popular, friendly, traditional
town-centre pub enjoying its
13th consecutive year in the
Guide. K&B seasonal beers also
sold. ◫ ⇌ ♠

Tanner's Arms
78 Brighton Road
☎ (01403) 250527
11–2.30, 6–11
**King & Barnes Mild, Sussex,
Old** ⊞
Small drinkers' local with an
emphasis on beer rather than
food: a public bar and a small
lounge. Q ❀ ◫ ♠

Kirdford

Forester's Arms
OS016268 ☎ (01403) 820205
12–2.30, 6–11; 11–11 may close
3–5.30 Sat in summer if quiet)
**King & Barnes Mild, Sussex,
Broadwood, Festive** ⊞

Traditional, 15th-century inn with an inglenook and an original flagstone floor, combining a real pub atmosphere with good all-round facilities. Events include jazz and folk eves, and spit roasts in summer. Supper licence. No meals Tue eve.
🏚 Q ❀ 🚪 ◖ ▶ 🍺 ᕦ ♣ ᗕ P ☐

Lambs Green

Lamb Inn

Off A264 at Faygate roundabout ☎ (01293) 871336
11–3, 5.30–11
Wadworth 6X 🅗; Young's Bitter, Special 🅖, Winter Warmer; guest beer 🅗
Extended 15th-century country pub with a separate restaurant. A wide range of home-cooked food includes Sun roasts. Live music Sun eves. 🏚 ❀ ◖ ▶ P

Lavant

Earl of March

Lavant Road (A286 2 miles N of Chichester)
☎ (01243) 774751
10.30–3, 6–11
Ballard's Best Bitter; Ringwood Fortyniner, Old Thumper; S&N Theakston Best Bitter; guest beers 🅗
Spacious pub with a separate public bar, popular with all and often lively. The garden affords splendid views of the Downs. Good food (large home-cooked portions) with game prominent. Live music. The best value pub in the area, with three guest beers. Dogs welcome. ❀ ◖ ▶ ᕦ ♣ ᗕ P

Lindfield

Linden Tree

47 High Street
☎ (01444) 482995
11–3, 6–11
Beer range varies 🅗
Small, friendly free house in the centre of an attractive village. The remains of an old brewery may be seen at the rear. Seven, varying ales. No meals Sun. Wheelchair access is via the back door.
🏚 Q ❀ ◖ ᕦ

Littleworth

Windmill

OS193205 ☎ (01403) 710308
11–3, 5.30 (6 Sat)–11
King & Barnes Sussex 🅗, Old, Festive 🅖
Fine, out of the way local with a comfortable saloon and a public bar with a strong rustic theme. No meals Sun eve.
🏚 Q ❀ ◖ ▶ ᕦ ♣ ᗕ P

Loxwood

Sir Roger Tichbourne

Billingshurst Road, Alfold Bars (B2133) ☎ (01403) 752377
12–2.30, 6–11
King & Barnes Mild (summer), Sussex, Old, Festive 🅗
Pleasant, low-beamed country pub with a quiet saloon on the right and a larger, busier bar with an inglenook on the left. Set back 75 yds from the main road and easily missed in the dark. Eve meals Fri/Sat only.
🏚 Q ❀ ◖ ▶ ▲ ♣ P

Maplehurst

White Horse

Park Lane (between A281 and A272 S of Nuthurst)
☎ (01403) 891208
12–2.30 (3 Sat), 6–11
Brakspear Bitter; Harveys BB; King & Barnes Sussex; guest beers 🅗
The landlord's enthusiasm for real ale ensures at least three and usually five ales are available in this pub which has a comfortable small bar, with a real fire, and a main bar with a very wide bar top. An ideal family lunchtime venue.
🏚 Q ᕁ ❀ ◖ ▶ ♣ ᗕ P

Midhurst

Crown

Edinburgh Square (behind old fire station) ☎ (01730) 813462
11–11
Ballard's Best Bitter 🅗; Cheriton Pots Ale 🅖; Fuller's London Pride, ESB 🅗; Hampshire King Alfred's, 1066; guest beers 🅖
Welcoming, traditional old pub where superb hospitality makes it justifiably popular. An ever-changing range of guest beers is served by gravity from a new cellar. The rear function hall is used by live bands. Two annual beer festivals. 🏚 ❀ 🚪 ◖ ▶ ♣

Swan Inn

Red Lion Street
☎ (01730) 812853
11–2.30, 5.30–11; 11–11 Sat
Harveys Pale Ale, BB, Old 🅗
Outstanding, 15th-century, split-level inn in the middle of the old market square. Note the 16th-century mural in the upper dining area, and the half-timbered toilets.
🏚 Q 🚪 ◖ ▶ ᕦ P

Oving

Gribble Inn

☎ (01243) 786893
11–2.30, 6–11

Gribble Ale, Reg's Tipple, Plucking Pheasant, Pig's Ear; Hall & Woodhouse Badger BB 🅗
Picturesque, 16th-century, thatched village local with a fine garden. Popular home-brewed ales are produced in a compact brewhouse adjoining the skittle alley (view the process). Deceptively spacious, but mind the low beams. Good bar food.
🏚 Q ᕁ ❀ ◖ ▶ ᕦ ♣ ᗕ P

Rogate

Wyndham Arms

North Street (A272)
☎ (01730) 821315
11–3, 6–11
Ballard's Best Bitter, Golden Bine; Cheriton Pots Ale; King & Barnes Sussex; Ringwood Fortyniner; guest beers 🅖
Cosy and friendly, 16th-century inn situated opposite the village church and reputed to be haunted! Note the new window to view the stillage. Fine collection of framed vintage comics. All meals are home-made from fresh produce. Tiny car park.
🏚 Q 🚪 ◖ ▶ ᕦ ♣ P

Scaynes Hill

Sloop Inn

Freshfield Lock (1½ miles off A272 via Church Lane and Sloop Lane) OS384244
☎ (01444) 831219
11–3, 6–11
Harveys BB; guest beer 🅗
Cosy, two-bar riverside inn, close to the Bluebell railway and popular with walkers. Good home-cooked food, lunch and eve (ploughman's at all times). A Beards pub with the same tenant for 11 years.
🏚 ❀ ◖ ▶ 🍺 ᕦ ♣ P

Selham

Three Moles

1 mile S of A272 at Halfway Bridge OS935206
☎ (01798) 861303
11.30–2.30, 5–11; 11–11 Sat
King & Barnes Mild, Sussex, Old, Festive 🅗
Small, isolated country pub, formerly a station hotel. Traditional games and hospitality are features, with no food served. Cider in summer. 1995 CAMRA regional *Pub of the Year*.
Q ❀ ▲ ♣ ᗕ P ☐

Shoreham-by-Sea

Lazy Toad

88A High Street
☎ (01273) 441622

West Sussex

11–2.30, 5.30–11
Greene King Abbot; Hall & Woodhouse Badger BB, Tanglefoot; Young's Winter Warmer G
Fine example of a one-bar free house; well-run with a friendly atmosphere; a haven of gravity dispensed beer (the range may change from time to time). No meals Sun. ◁ ⇌

Marlipins
38 High Street
☎ (01273) 453369
10–4.30, 5.30–11
Bass Worthington BB, Draught Bass; Fuller's London Pride; Harveys BB H
Excellent, low-beamed, 16th-century, one-bar Charrington pub next to the museum. Busy at weekends. Good food. Patio at the rear.
Q ✿ ◁ ▶ ⇌

Red Lion Inn
Old Shoreham Road
(by old tollbridge)
☎ (01273) 453171
11.30–11
Courage Best Bitter, Directors; Wadworth 6X; Young's Special; guest beers H
Former 16th-century coaching inn with a ghost. The Toll Bar used to be a mortuary. Very low beams and an inglenook are features. Good food at all times. Beer festivals; regular live music; friendly atmosphere.
🏠 Q ✿ ◁ ▶ P ⅌

Royal Sovereign
6 Middle Street (turn N by Marlipins museum)
☎ (01273) 453518
11–11
Adnams Bitter; Brakspear Special; Whitbread Castle Eden Ale, Pompey Royal; Young's Special H
Small, single-bar Whitbread pub with a tasteful recent extension. Original United Brewery leaded windows still feature. Always busy, with a flavour of the sea.
Book Sun lunches.
🏠 ◁ ▶ ⇌

Sidlesham

Crab & Lobster
Mill Lane
(off B2145 via Rookery Lane)
☎ (01243) 641233
11–2.30, 6–11
Arundel Stronghold; Gale's BBB, Best Bitter H
Attractive, two-bar country pub next to Pagham Harbour in a good area for bird watching and walking. Pretty garden. No eve meals Wed.
🏠 Q ✿ ◁ ▶ ♿ ▲ ♣ P

Singleton

Horse & Groom
On A286 ☎ (01243) 811455
11–3, 7 (5 summer Fri, 6 summer Sat)–11; closed Tue eve in winter
Ballard's Best Bitter; Cheriton Diggers Gold; Harveys Armada; guest beers H
Friendly village local, an ideal stop for coast-bound traffic; also handy for the Downland Museum and Goodwood. Live folk music Sat eves. The enclosed rear garden has swingboats and a trampoline. Family room lunchtimes. The restaurant features home-cooking. No eve meals Sun–Wed in winter.
🏠 ✿ ▱ ◁ ▶ ▲ ♣ P

South Harting

Ship Inn
☎ (01730) 825302
11–2.30, 5.30–11; 11–11 Sat
Fuller's London Pride, ESB; Palmers IPA; guest beers H
17th-century, low-beamed, friendly pub in the village centre, with a noted restaurant in the saloon bar. No eve meals Sun in winter.
🏠 Q ✿ ◁ ▶ ⊞ ♣ P

Staplefield

Jolly Tanners
Handcross Road
☎ (01444) 400335
11–3, 5.30–11
Fuller's Chiswick, London Pride; Thwaites Best Mild; Wadworth 6X; guest beer H
Very pleasant pub on the edge of the village, not far from the cricket field; a rare example of a free house keeping a regular cask mild. Reputation for high quality meals (separate restaurant for parties).
🏠 Q ✿ ◁ ▶ ⊞ ♣ P

Steyning

Chequer
41 High Street
☎ (01903) 814437
10–2.30, 5–11; 10–11 Wed–Sat
Fuller's London Pride; Gale's HSB; King & Barnes Sussex; Whitbread Boddingtons Mild, Flowers Original; Young's Special H
Splendid, multi-roomed establishment, parts of which date from the early 1400s.
🏠 ◁ ▶ ♣

Stoughton

Hare & Hounds
Off B2146, through Walberton
OS791107 ☎ (01705) 631433
11–3, 6–11

Adnams Broadside; Gale's HSB; Whitbread Boddingtons Bitter; guest beers H
Fine example of a Sussex flint-faced building in a secluded South Downs setting; popular and lively, with a good local trade. Humorous posters advertise the guest beers. Good value food (fresh local seafood and game). Its 21st year in the *Guide*.
🏠 Q ✿ ▱ ◁ ▶ ♣ P

Sutton

White Horse
The Street ☎ (01798) 869221
11–2.30, 6–11
Arundel Best Bitter; Bateman XB; Courage Best Bitter, Directors; Young's Bitter H
Characterful, Georgian village inn. Comfortably furnished saloon; bare boards in the Village Bar. Popular in summer with walkers and with visitors to the Roman villa at nearby Bignor.
🏠 Q ✿ ▱ ◁ ▶ ♣ P

Turners Hill

Red Lion
Lion Lane (off B2028)
☎ (01342) 715416
11–3, 6–11
Harveys XX Mild, Pale Ale, BB, Old H
Unchanging village pub with an interesting collection of bottled beers: its 21st entry in the *Guide*. Pool room upstairs. Jazz day near Midsummer's Day. No food Sun.
🏠 Q ✿ ◁ ♣ P

Upper Beeding

Bridge
High Street ☎ (01903) 812773
11–2.30, 5.30–11
King & Barnes Mild (summer), **Sussex, Old, Festive** H
Traditionally appointed riverside inn with a friendly welcome. ✿ ◁ ⊞ ♣

West Ashling

Richmond Arms
Mill Lane (400 yds W of B2146) ☎ (01243) 575730
11–2.30, 5.30–11; 11–11 summer Sat
Brakspear Bitter; Fuller's Chiswick; Greene King Abbot; Marston's Pedigree; Taylor Landlord; guest beers H
Homely, ten-pump, small village local near the duck pond. Wide selection of home-cooked bar meals; skittle alley. Enjoy a pint under the pagoda in the summer. Cider is also served in summer.
🏠 Q ✿ ◁ ▶ ♣ ⌂ P

West Chiltington

Elephant & Castle
Church Street
☎ (01798) 813307
11–4, 6–11; 11–11 Fri & Sat
King & Barnes Mild, Sussex, Broadwood, Old, Festive H
Pub offering a friendly public bar and a farmhouse lounge with low beams and basic seating. Large garden with sheltered areas.
🏚 ❀ ◖ ▶ ⊞ ♣ ⟲ P

Five Bells
Smock Alley
☎ (01798) 812143
11–3, 6–11
Beer range varies H
Spacious, one-bar pub near the village, with an imaginative selection of five guest ales (298 in the last five years). No eve meals Sun. 🏚 Q ❀ ◖ ▶ ⟲ P

Queen's Head
The Hollows
☎ (01798) 813143
11–3, 6–11
Fuller's London Pride; Greene King Abbot; King & Barnes Sussex; Wadworth 6X; Whitbread Boddingtons Bitter, Flowers Original H
400-year-old, two-bar pub at the village centre, run by a former King & Barnes brewhouse manager. Collections of coins, banknotes, golf balls and bottles, plus clog and morris dancing, feature.
🏚 ❀ ◖ ▶ ⊞ ♣ P

West Wittering

Lamb Inn
Chichester Road (B2179 1 mile NE of centre)
☎ (01243) 511105
11–2.30, 6–11
Ballard's Best Bitter H, **Wassail** G; **Bunces Benchmark, Best Bitter; Ringwood Fortyniner; guest beer** H
Old roadside inn with a convivial atmosphere and an excellent range of beers. Extensive menu; dining area.

No meals Sun eve in winter.
🏚 Q ❀ ◖ ▶ ⚫ ▲ P

Wick

Locomotive
74 Lyminster Road
11–3, 6–11
Adnams Bitter; Ansells Mild; Eldridge Pope Hardy Country, Royal Oak; Marston's Pedigree; guest beer H
Friendly one-bar local offering good food and a well-appointed family room. Patio, children's activity area and two boules pitches outside. Cider in summer.
🏚 ▱ ❀ ◖ ▶ ⚫ ▲ ♣ ⟲ P

Worthing

Alexandra
28 Lyndhurst Road (near hospital) ☎ (01903) 234833
11–11
Draught Bass; Fuller's London Pride; Harveys BB; M&B Highgate Dark H
Friendly, two-bar local with a games room. So far the Alex has avoided being 'improved' out of recognition and the accent remains on service and the quality of the beer rather than gimmicks.
🏚 Q ❀ ⊞ ♣

Coach & Horses
Arundel Road, Clapham (old A27 at western edge of town)
☎ (01903) 264665
11–3, 5.30–11; 10.30–11 Sat
Arundel Best Bitter; Greene King Abbot; Ind Coope Burton Ale; Tetley Bitter H
Former coaching inn on a bypassed loop of the old A27, still welcoming travellers.
🏚 ❀ ◖ ▶ ▲ ♣ P

Cricketers
66 Broadwater Street, West Worthing ☎ (01903) 233369
11–3, 6–11; 11–11 Fri & Sat
Bass Worthington BB, Draught Bass; Fuller's London Pride; Harveys BB; Young's Winter Warmer H
Pub situated on a corner of Broadwater Green and home

to Broadwater cricket club. The eastern end of the L-shaped bar has all the tradition of the public bar it once was; the other end is a comfortable saloon, leading to a dining area. No food Mon or Sun/Tue eves.
Q ▱ ❀ ◖ ▶ ♣

Richard Cobden
2 Cobden Street
☎ (01903) 236856
11–3, 5.30–11; 11–11 Fri & Sat
Wadworth 6X; Whitbread Flowers Original; guest beers H
Friendly, corner local three minutes' walk from the central station. Two guest beers supplement the standard ales.
❀ ◖ ⚫ ⇌ ♣

Vine
27–29 High Street, Tarring
☎ (01903) 202891
11–2.30 (3 Sat), 6–11
Ballard's Best Bitter; Hall & Woodhouse Badger BB; Harveys BB; Hop Back GFB, Summer Lightning H; **guest beers** H & G
Popular local in a well-preserved village street, attracting a wide cross-section of customers; vibrant and often noisy late eves. The former Parsons brewery stands at the rear. Beer festival Oct. House beer from Brewery on Sea. No food Sun.
❀ ◖ ⚫ ⇌ ♣ (West) P

Yapton

Maypole
Maypole Lane (off B2132, ½mile N of B2233 jct)
☎ (01243) 551417
11–2.30 (3 Sat), 5.30–11
Ringwood Best Bitter; Whitbread Flowers Original; Younger IPA; guest beers H
Deservedly popular, two-bar pub with a skittle alley and a continually changing range of guest beers from independent breweries. Regular beer festivals. Meals are excellent value (no eve meals Sun or Tue).
🏚 Q ❀ ◖ ▶ ⊞ ⚫ ♣ P

CAMRA PRODUCTS

T-shirts, sweatshirts, ties, baseball caps, badges, pens, clocks, mirrors, key rings, calendars and diaries: this is just a selection of the numerous items CAMRA produces for sale to its members and the general public. They make wonderful gifts for pub-loving friends, or just treat yourself! And, with all profits channelled into defending Britain's great pub and brewing heritage, you can help preserve your local beers and pubs at the same time. A catalogue of the latest products is available from the Products Secretary at CAMRA, tel. (01727) 867201.

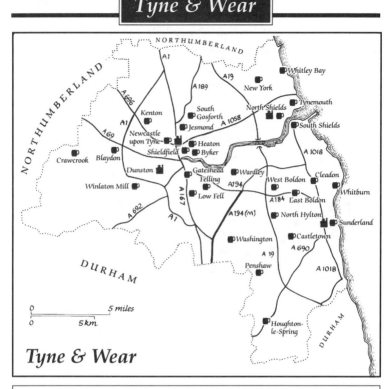

Tyne & Wear

 Big Lamp, *Newcastle upon Tyne;* **Darwin**, *Sunderland;* **Federation**, *Dunston;* **Hadrian**, *Newcastle upon Tyne;* **Mordue**, *North Shields;* **Vaux**, *Sunderland*

Blaydon

Black Bull
Bridge Street
☎ (0191) 414 2846
12 (1 Sat)–11
Draught Bass; Camerons Strongarm; Ind Coope Burton Ale; Whitbread Castle Eden Ale Ⓗ
Basic, friendly local drawing a regular clientele, but visitors are made welcome. Regular music sessions.
🏚 Q ✿ ⇌ ♣ P

Byker

Cumberland Arms
Byker Buildings
☎ (0191) 265 6151
11–11
Beer range varies Ⓖ
Basic pub overlooking Ouseburn Valley. Local morris dancers and bands find a warm welcome here. Up to eight beers at all times help to make every visit a treat. Often live music upstairs. Quieter bar and lounge downstairs.
🍴 ⊖ P

Free Trade Inn
St Lawrence Road
☎ (0191) 265 5764
11–11
Hadrian Emperor; McEwan 80/-; S&N Theakston Best Bitter, Newcastle Exhibition, Theakston XB; Younger No.3; guest beer Ⓗ
Basic, split-level pub offering a splendid view of the river and always a friendly welcome from the staff and customers. Nothing fancy – just well-kept beer and great company.
🏚 ✿

Castletown

Wessington
Wessington Way
☎ (0191) 548 9384
11–11
Whitbread Boddingtons Bitter, Castle Eden Ale; guest beer Ⓗ
Hectic, new, upmarket motel/diner complex on a busy main road, with a strong emphasis on family eating, hence the large restaurant and small bar area. Kids can play in the Charlie Chalk Fun

Factory! Food all day Sun.
🏚 ✿ 🛏 ◑ ▶ ♿ P

Cleadon

Cottage Tavern
North Street
☎ (0191) 536 7883
11–3, 5.30–11
Vaux Samson, Extra Special Ⓗ
Small, well-established local, often busy early eve.
Close to the Cleadon Hills.
✿ ♣ 🍴

Crawcrook

Rising Sun
Bank Top
☎ (0191) 413 3316
11–11
Marston's Pedigree; Whitbread Boddingtons Bitter, Flowers Original guest beers Ⓗ
A warm welcome awaits at this smart, friendly inn. Good, home-cooked food and a family area help create an excellent atmosphere.
Q 🏚 ✿ ◑ ▶ P

East Boldon

Black Bull
98 Front Street
☎ (0191) 536 3969
11–11
Vaux Samson; guest beer Ⓗ
Low-ceilinged, roadside inn,
refurbished in standard
Vaux farmhouse style;
comfortable, friendly and
popular for meals.
❀ ◖ ▸ ≽ ♣ P

Grey Horse
14 Front Street
☎ (0191) 536 4186
11–11
**Vaux Samson, Waggle
Dance** Ⓗ**; guest beer**
Excellent, attractive village
pub with well-trained staff.
The large, food-oriented
lounge has a solid oak bar
top reclaimed from an old
church. There is also a
smaller bar/games room,
plus an upstairs function
room with a bar. No
food Sun eve.
❀ ◖ ▸ ⊞ ≽ ♣ P

Felling

Old Fox
Carlisle Street
☎ (0191) 420 0357
11–4, 6–11; 12–11 Thu–Sat
**Webster's Yorkshire Bitter;
guest beers** Ⓗ
Thriving community pub with
a range of four guest beers
served in a comfortable
environment. Various eve
events offer a change from
the peaceful lunchtime and
early eve scene.
♨ ⇔ ⊖

Wheatsheaf
26 Carlisle Street
☎ (0191) 438 6633
12–3, 7–11; 12–11 Fri & Sat
**Big Lamp Bitter, Prince
Bishop Ale; guest beers** Ⓗ
The brewery tap (across the
river) of the Big Lamp
Brewery, the oldest small
brewery in the North East.
With its warm welcome and
thriving social scene, visitors
will not be disappointed. The
cheapest beer on Tyneside.
♨ ⊖

Gateshead

Borough Arms
80–82 Bensham Road
☎ (0191) 478 1323
12–3 (4 Fri), 6–11; 11–11 Sat
**Draught Bass; S&N
Theakston XB; guest
beers** Ⓗ
Warm, welcoming, town-
centre pub with two rooms.

Good quality lunches at
reasonable prices.
♨ ❀ ◖ ⊖ P

Heaton

Chillingham
Chillingham Road
☎ (0191) 265 5915
11–3, 6–11; 11–11 Sat
**Draught Bass; McEwan 80/-;
S&N Theakston Best Bitter,
XB; Taylor Landlord; guest
beers** Ⓗ
Magnificent, large, two-
roomed roadside pub.
Excellent woodwork and fine
furnishings throughout, and
friendly staff and customers,
ensure that the beers can be
enjoyed in comfort. Well-
attended mini-beer festivals
hosted.
❀ ◖ ⊖ (Chillingham Rd) P

Houghton-le-Spring

Burn Inn
Hetton Road
☎ (0191) 584 2130
11–11
**Camerons Bitter,
Strongarm** Ⓗ
Imposing, roadside pub at a
busy crossroads. An extensive
conservatory caters for
families and diners. No meals
Sun eve.
❀ ◖ ▸ ⊞ ♿ ♣ P ⊬ 目

Jesmond

Legendary Yorkshire Heroes
Archbold Terrace
☎ (0191) 281 3010
11–11
**McEwan 80/-; S&N Theakston
Best Bitter, Old Peculier;
John Smith's Bitter;
Younger No.3; guest
beers** Ⓗ
Twelve handpumps are the
finest features of this modern
pub set on the ground floor of
a 1960s grey concrete office
block. The pub is surprisingly
characterful and comfortable
considering its exterior aspect.
◖ ⊖

Kenton

Crofter's Lodge
Kenton Lane
☎ (0191) 286 9394
11–11
**Vaux Samson, Waggle Dance;
Wards Thorne Best Bitter,
Best Bitter; guest beers** Ⓗ
Pub with a large, modern
lounge with a conservatory
and a traditional public bar.
Families welcome.
❀ ◖ ▸ ⊞ P ⊬

Low Fell

Aletaster
706 Durham Road
☎ (0191) 487 0770
11–11
**Marston's Pedigree; Morland
Old Speckled Hen; S&N
Theakston Best Bitter, XB;
Younger No.3; guest beers** Ⓗ
T&J Bernard's flagship pub
offers a steadily increasing
guest list; the bar boasts 16
handpumps. Warm and
friendly. ❀ ⇔ P

Newcastle upon Tyne

Armstrong Hydraulic Crane
903–907 Scotswood Road
☎ (0191) 272 3261
11–11
**Courage Directors; John
Smith's Bitter; Webster's
Yorkshire Bitter; guest
beers** Ⓗ
The last of the legendary
Scotswood Road pubs, this
fine house offers three distinct
areas. Many mementoes of the
industrial history of this part
of Newcastle are displayed.
The panelled lounge has a
mirrored ceiling. Eve meals
finish at 8.30; not served Sun.
❀ ⇔ ◖ ▸ P

Bacchus
High Bridge ☎ (0191) 232 6451
11.30–11; 7–10.30 Sun, closed Sun
lunch
**S&N Theakston XB; Stones
Best Bitter; Tetley Bitter;
guest beers** Ⓗ
Large, two-roomer at the heart
of the thriving city fashion
area. Beautifully furnished
throughout, it has a fine
selection of woodwork and
mirrors to delight the eyes. No
food Sun. ◖ ≽ (Central)
⊖ (Monument)

Broken Doll
Blenheim Street
☎ (0191) 232 1047
11–11
**S&N Theakston Best Bitter,
XB, Old Peculier; guest
beers** Ⓗ
Once again this pub has
cheated the bulldozers!
Newcastle Planning
Department would still like to
convert this popular and
historic pub, a centre of live
art and entertainment, into a
tree-lined boulevard!
❀ ◖ ≽ (Central) ⊖

Chapel Park
Hartburn Drive
☎ (0191) 267 6887
12–3.30, 6–11; 12–11 Fri & Sat

Camerons Bitter, Crown
Special, Strongarm Ⓗ
Large, open-plan, modern pub
in the middle of a 25-year-old
estate, with games and quiet
areas off the main bar. ♣ P ⊟

Cooperage
32 The Close, Quayside
☎ (0191) 232 8286
11–11
Ind Coope Burton Ale;
Marston's Owd Rodger;
Tetley Bitter; guest beers Ⓗ
In one of the oldest buildings
on Newcastle's quayside, this
bustling bar is always worth a
visit. Huge wooden beams and
exposed stone walls help
create a wonderful
atmosphere. Modifications
include access and facilities for
disabled visitors.
◖ & ⇌ (Central) ⊖

Crown Posada
31 The Side ☎ (0191) 232 1269
11 (12 Sat)–11
Draught Bass; Butterknowle
Conciliation Ale; Jennings
Bitter; S&N Theakston Best
Bitter; Whitbread
Boddingtons Bitter; guest
beers Ⓗ
An architectural gem, this pub
is always worth visiting. The
bar can be very busy, but on
quiet days customers can
delight in the beautiful stained
glass windows and unusual
ceiling. An ideal spot from
which to explore Quayside.
Q ⇌ (Central) ⊖

Tap & Spile
1 Nun Street
☎ (0191) 232 0026
11–11; 7–10.30 Sun, closed Sun lunch
Beer range varies Ⓗ
Busy, city-centre pub, by
Grainger Market. The large bar
boasts eight handpumps; the
downstairs bar with four
further handpumps is open
eves and weekends and offers
live music. ◖ ⊖ (Monument)
ⓒ

Tilley's Bar
Westgate Road
☎ (0191) 232 0692
12–11; 7–10.30 Sun, closed Sun lunch
Jennings Bitter, Cumberland
Ale, Cocker Hoop, Sneck
Lifter; S&N Newcastle
Exhibition Ⓗ
Very comfortable two-roomer
near the Tyne Theatre. The
small lounge has a raised
seating area lined with
mirrors. The large bar is
popular with students, theatre-
goers and actors. The
theatrical theme incorporates
old photographs of bygone
stars. Meals Mon–Fri.
⋈ ◖ ⇌ (Central) ⊖

Try also: Quayside Beefeater,
Quayside (Vaux)

New York

Shiremoor House Farm
Middle Engine Lane
☎ (0191) 257 6302
11–11
Butterknowle Conciliation
Ale; S&N Theakston Best
Bitter, XB; Stones Best Bitter;
guest beers Ⓗ
CAMRA award-winning, very
popular pub renowned for its
beer and food. Mini-beer
festivals held. Q ❀ ◖ ▶ P

North Hylton

Shipwrights
Ferryboat Lane
☎ (0191) 549 5139
11–3.30, 5–11
Vaux Samson; Waggle Dance,
Extra Special Ⓗ
Old, rambling riverside inn on
a quiet back road under the
main A19 bridge. Extensive
range of bar meals; families
most welcome. Nineteen
consecutive years in the *Guide*.
Accommodation is planned.
⋈ ◖ ▶ P

North Shields

Bell & Bucket
37 Norfolk Street
☎ (0191) 257 4634
11–11
Camerons Strongarm;
Marston's Pedigree; guest
beers Ⓗ
Comfortable, two-tier pub in
an old fire station. A warm
welcome from the licensee and
staff ensures an enjoyable visit.
The jukebox plays unobtrusive
music. Good range of
whiskies. ◖ ⊖ ⊟

Chainlocker
Duke Street, New Quay (opp.
ferry landing)
☎ (0191) 258 0147
12–4, 6–11; 11–11 Fri & Sat
Marston's Pedigree; Taylor
Landlord; Tetley Bitter; guest
beers Ⓗ
Classic, friendly pub on a
bustling riverfront, offering a
warm welcome and good
food. Folk night Fri. ◖ ▶

Magnesia Bank
1 Camden Street
☎ (0191) 257 4831
11–11
Butterknowle Conciliation
Ale; Ind Coope Burton Ale;
Longstone Bitter; Taylor
Landlord; Tetley Bitter; guest
beers Ⓗ
An excellent find, this pub
(local CAMRA *Pub of the Year*)
sells a good range of beers,
including from several north-

eastern independents. Live
music and excellent food.
⋈ ❀ ◖ ▶ ⊟

Porthole
11 New Quay
☎ (0191) 257 6645
11–11
Jennings Cumberland Ale;
Village White Boar;
Whitbread Boddingtons
Bitter; guest beers Ⓗ
1834 original pub on the banks
of the Tyne, offering changing
guest beers. A nautical theme
runs throughout, with plenty
of memorabilia. Live music
eves. ◖ P

Tap & Spile
184 Tynemouth Road
☎ (0191) 257 2523
11–11
Beer range varies Ⓗ
There is always a warm
welcome and an excellent
choice of beers on 11
handpumps at this busy, lively
Tap & Spile. ◖ ▶ ⓒ

Try also: Prince of Wales, Bell
St (Samuel Smith)

Penshaw

Grey Horse
Village Green, Old Penshaw
☎ (0191) 584 4882
11–3.30 (4.30 Sat), 6–11
Tetley Bitter Ⓗ
Village pub, difficult to find
but worth seeking out, in the
shadow of a local landmark,
Penshaw Monument. Friendly
welcome. A *Guide* regular for
15 years. No food Sun. Tiny
car park. ◖ P

Try also: Prospect, Victoria
Tce (Vaux)

Shieldfield

Globe Inn
Wesley Street (next to tallest
block of flats in the area)
☎ (0191) 232 0901
11–11
Draught Bass; Stones Best
Bitter; guest beers Ⓗ
A large, traditional bar and a
smaller lounge make this pub
worth the effort of finding. A
wide range of customers
ensures that there are always
friendly regulars to chat to.
❀ ⊞ ⊖ (Jesmond/Manors)
P

South Gosforth

Brandling Villa
Station Road
☎ (0191) 285 6410
11–11; 11–3.30, 7.30–11 Sat
McEwan 80/-; S&N Theakston
Best Bitter, XB; guest beers Ⓗ

Small, cosy bar and a large, comfortable lounge in an out-of-town pub with a traditional feel. Situated between two busy roads, it can be crowded at times, but strangers are always made welcome. Good quality home cooking. 🍴 🍺 ⊖

South Shields

Alum House

Ferry Street (by ferry landing)
☎ (0191) 427 7245
11–11
Banks's Bitter; Camerons Bitter, Strongarm; Marston's Pedigree; guest beers ⊞
Popular riverside pub, ideal if you've missed the ferry. A cellar bar opens at weekends, catering for live music. ⊖ 🍺

Bamburgh

175 Bamburgh Avenue
☎ (0191) 454 1899
11–11
Whitbread Boddingtons Bitter, Castle Eden Ale, Flowers Original; Morland Old Speckled Hen; guest beers ⊞
Large, open-plan pub at the finish of the Great North Run route with terrific views over the North Sea. Guest ales come from the Whitbread stable. Annual beer festival. No lunches Sun. 🌸 🍴 ▶ ⛰

Chichester Arms

Laygate (A194/B1298 jct)
☎ (0191) 420 0127
11–3, 5.30–11; 11–11 Sat
Ind Coope Burton Ale; Tetley Bitter; guest beers ⊞
Street-corner local at a busy bus and metro interchange, with a brash, bright interior.
🍴 🍺 ⊖ (Chichester) 🍺

Dolly Peel

137 Commercial Road
☎ (0191) 427 1441
11–11
Courage Directors; S&N Theakston XB; Taylor Landlord; Younger No.3; guest beers ⊞
Pioneering free house, largely responsible for the South Tyneside real ale revival. Small, and therefore always busy, it stocks a large range of malt whiskies and two ever-changing guest ales. Q 🍺 P

Holborn Rose & Crown

East Holborn (opp. Middle Dock gate) ☎ (0191) 455 2379
11–11
Draught Bass; S&N Theakston XB; Younger No.3; guest beers ⊞
Classic, 19th-century pub, just out of the town centre, which retains many of its original

features. Local bric-a-brac adorns the walls and bar. Guest ales change constantly.
🌸 🍺

Riverside

3 Commercial Road
☎ (0191) 455 2328
12–11
Taylor Landlord; Whitbread Boddingtons Bitter, Castle Eden Ale; guest beers ⊞
Compact bar near the riverside and Customs House arts complex. Comfortable and friendly, it offers a good range of ever-changing guest ales.
Q ⊖

Try also: Steamboat, Mill Dam (Vaux)

Sunderland: *North*

Harbour View

Harbour View
☎ (0191) 567 1402
11–11
Bass Worthington BB, Draught Bass; guest beers ⊞
Popular, seafront local, overlooking the new marina complex. Fixed price guest ales. Extremely busy on match days. 🌸

Smugglers

Marine Walk
☎ (0191) 514 3844
11–11
Butterknowle Banner; Vaux Double Maxim *or* Samson; guest beer ⊞
Cosy nautical pub on the edge of the beach, popular for its meals and sea views. Warm welcome for families; it hosts a 'Junior Pirates' club on Fri eve. Occasional beach barbecues at bank hols. No meals Sun eve. Handy for Roker Park.
🏨 🌸 🍴 ▶

Sunderland: *South*

Borough

1 Vine Place ☎ (0191) 567 7909
11–11; 7–10.30 Sun, closed Sun lunch
Vaux Lorimer's Best Scotch, Samson, Double Maxim, Waggle Dance; guest beer ⊞
Small, but lively, city-centre pub with contrasting bars. Downstairs has an island bar in traditional Victorian style and is popular with students, while upstairs is a noisy, trendy disco bar. Busy at weekends (live entertainment).
🍺 🍺

Brewery Tap

9 Dunning Street
☎ (0191) 567 7472
11–11
Vaux Samson, Double Maxim, Waggle Dance ⊞
Traditional pub attached to the

Vaux brewery, with a warm and cosy atmosphere. Popular with brewery workers, it can be busy Sat afternoons. Walls are adorned with pictures of old Sunderland. Car park available eves and weekends.
🍴 🍺 P

Coopers Tavern

32 Deptford Road
☎ (0191) 567 1886
11–11
Vaux Lorimer's Best Scotch, Samson, Double Maxim, Waggle Dance, Extra Special ⊞
Warm and welcoming, cask-only ale house, just out of the city centre. Off the beaten track, but worth searching out.
🍺

Fitzgerald's

10–12 Green Terrace
☎ (0191) 567 0852
11–11
Bass Worthington BB, Draught Bass; S&N Theakston Best Bitter, XB; guest beers ⊞
Busy, city-centre pub, near the university, comprising a large, open-plan lounge and a more relaxed 'Chart' room. Good selection of independent guest ales. Always packed eves and weekends. Annual beer festival. 🌸 🍴 🍺

Ivy House

6 Worcester Street (behind Park Lane bus station)
☎ (0191) 567 3399
11–11
Vaux Samson; Wards Best Bitter; guest beer ⊞
Loud, brash, city-centre pub with a strong football following, refurbished in the usual Vaux style. Very popular with students, hence always busy. 🍴 🍺 🍺

Saltgrass

36 Ayres Quay, Deptford
☎ (0191) 565 7229
11–3, 6–11; 11–11 Fri & Sat
Vaux Samson, Double Maxim, Waggle Dance, Extra Special; Wards Thorne Best Bitter, Best Bitter ⊞
Well-established, award-winning pub with a warm, friendly atmosphere. Free transport to other local pubs provided at weekends.
🏨 🌸 🍴 🍺 🍺

Tap & Spile

Salem Street, Hendon
☎ (0191) 514 2810
11–11
Beer range varies ⊞
Local CAMRA *Pub of the Year* 1993–96, serving 11 varying ales and three ciders. Popular with students and locals alike,

Tyne & Wear

it is a short walk from the city centre. Live music Mon nights. Annual (Nov) beer festival.
🍴 ◑ 🍺 ♣ ⌂

Try also: Chester's, Chester Rd (Vaux)

Tynemouth

Fitzpatrick's
29 Front Street
☎ (0191) 257 8956
11–11
Beer range varies Ⓗ
Busy, comfortable pub on a main street. This attractive, comfortable Fitzgerald's outlet offers a good range of ever-changing guest beers. Eve meals in summer.
Q ◑ ▶ ⊖

Tynemouth Lodge Hotel
Tynemouth Road
☎ (0191) 257 7565
11–11
Draught Bass; Belhaven 80/-; Black Sheep Best Bitter Ⓗ
18th-century, unspoilt free house where full measures and a warm welcome are assured. No children; no hot food; no dogs; no music and no pub games. 🍴 Q ❀ ⊖ P

Wardley

Green
White Mare Pool
☎ (0191) 495 0171
11–11
S&N Theakston Best Bitter; guest beers Ⓗ
Large roadside pub owned by the local Sir John Fitzgerald pub chain. Adjacent to

Heworth golf course, it is a magnet for diners and local sportsmen on Fri eves. Ever-changing range of guest beers. Mini-beer festivals held.
◑ ▶ 🍺

Washington

Three Horse Shoes
Washington Road, Usworth (opp. Nissan factory)
☎ (0191) 536 4183
12–3, 6.30–11; 12–11 Fri & Sat
Vaux Lorimer's Best Scotch, Samson, Double Maxim; guest beer Ⓗ
Large roadside family pub in Usworth 'village' near the Aircraft Museum. Popular for meals; families are catered for in the large, food-dominated lounge. The bar hosts an annual beer festival. No meals Sun eve.
❀ ◑ ▶ 🍺 ♣ P

Try also: Sandpiper, Easby Rd, Biddick (Whitbread)

West Boldon

Black Horse
Rectory Bank
☎ (0191) 536 1814
11–3, 7–11
Morland Old Speckled Hen; Stones Best Bitter; Taylor Landlord; Whitbread Boddingtons Bitter, Castle Eden Ale; guest beers Ⓗ
Large, whitewashed pub, next to the parish church, with a very popular restaurant and a small bar area, offering a wide selection of ales (usually ten). No food Sun. Limited parking.
❀ ◑ ▶ P

Whitburn

Jolly Sailor
1 East Street ☎ (0191) 529 3221
11–11
Bass Worthington BB, Draught Bass Ⓗ
Reputedly haunted pub in one of Tyne & Wear's most attractive villages. It has several small rooms served from a tiny bar area. Popular for lunchtime meals (not served Sun). 🍴 ➤ ❀ ◑ 🍺 ♣

Whitley Bay

Briar Dene
The Links ☎ (0191) 252 0926
11–11
Draught Bass; Courage Directors; S&N Theakston Best Bitter, XB, Old Peculier; Stones Best Bitter; guest beers Ⓗ
Large, attractive pub with several drinking areas, a splendid bar and sea views. Ever-changing range of guest beers; mini-beer festivals held.
Q ➤ ❀ ◑ ▶ P

Winlaton Mill

Huntley Well
Spa Well Road (A694)
☎ (0191) 414 2731
12–3, 7–11
Ind Coope Burton Ale; Tetley Bitter; guest beers Ⓗ
Early 20th-century building with a friendly Geordie atmosphere; a former social club, built on the site of an old well, near the start of the Derwent Walk, a renowned nature trail. Darts and pool in the bar. ◑ ▶ ♣ P

ALE TODAY – GONE TOMORROW?

After years of denying drinkers choice by enforcing the sale of bland, national brews, it seems the big brewers have at last got the message. Cask-conditioned ale is the in thing and the major breweries have been quick to capitalise on this new interest in real ale. The 'alehouse' has become the latest in the line of theme pubs, thanks largely to the success of Pubmaster's Tap & Spile chain. In pubs across the country, walls have been smashed down, carpets rolled back, old brewery advertisements pinned up and redundant barrels installed as tables. Such wanton destruction of traditional old pubs (and in some cases the loss of historically important pub names) has only been redeemed by the sale of numerous cask ales, many from independent and small breweries (if often at a premium price).

Whitbread has marched ahead with its Tut 'n' Shive chain (sounds familiar?) and Hogshead Ale Houses, S&N has launched T&J Bernard's and Allied has bought and expanded the Firkin brew pub empire. Let's hope the cask ale revival continues, for we know from past experience that today's Cask and Copper is likely to become tomorrow's Jamaican Calypso Bar, if the accountants have their way.

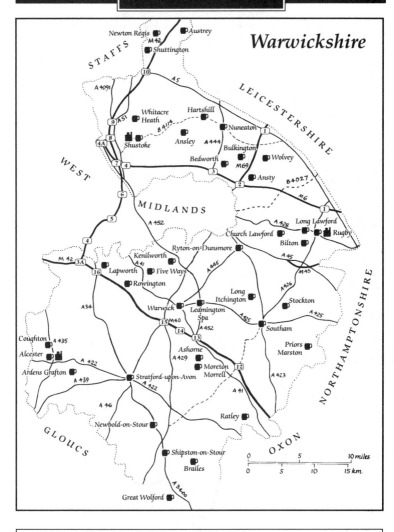

Warwickshire

 Bull's Head, Alcester; **Church End**, Shustoke; *Judges*, Rugby

Alcester

Holly Bush Hotel
Henley Street
☎ (01789) 762482
11–3, 6–11
Adnams Broadside; M&B Mild, Brew XI Ⓗ
Fine, unspoilt, traditional local in an historic market town, run by a long-serving landlord and landlady. Serious dominoes played.
Q ⽕ ⊛ ⊞ ⅄ ♠ ♣

Three Tuns
34 High Street
☎ (01789) 766550
11–11
Batham Best Bitter; Bull's Head Light; Fuller's London Pride; Hobsons Best Bitter; Stanway Stanney Bitter; guest beers Ⓗ
Home of the Bull's Head Brewery, with eight real ales available at most times. It holds occasional independents beer festivals and boasts its own newspaper. Several pub games have been devised by regulars. It was converted back into a real pub after several years as a wine bar.
Q ⅄ ♣

Ansley

Lord Nelson
Birmingham Road (B4114)
☎ (01203) 392305
12–2.30 (3 Sat), 6.30 (6 Sat)–11
Draught Bass; Tetley Bitter; guest beers Ⓗ

Warwickshire

Large roadside pub based on a nautical theme. The public bar features a sloping floor which becomes more noticeable the more you drink.
🍴 ❀ ◖ ▶ 🍺 ♣ P

Ansty

Rose & Castle Inn
Main Road (B4065 off M6 jct 3)
☎ (01203) 612822
11–3, 6 (5.30 summer)–11
Draught Bass; HP&D Entire; Tetley Bitter; guest beer Ⓗ
One room restaurant-cum-bar, on two levels. Popular with diners. The canalside garden (moorings available) has a safe children's activity area. Guest beers come from Carlsberg-Tetley's Tapster's Choice list.
⛵ ❀ ◖ ▶ P

Ardens Grafton

Golden Cross
Wixford Road OS114538
☎ (01789) 772420
11–2.30, 6–11
Draught Bass; M&B Highgate Dark; Tetley Bitter; guest beers Ⓗ
Fine views over the Vale of Evesham to the Cotswolds can be enjoyed from this old, stone pub. Note the doll and teddy collections. Three guest beers change weekly; other milds occasionally on sale. Home to an MG drivers' club and photographic clubs.
Q ❀ ◖ ▶ 🍴 ♣ P ✗

Ashorne

Cottage
☎ (01926) 651410
7–11; 12–3, 7–11 Sat
Ansells Mild, Bitter Ⓗ
Friendly, early Victorian local with old photographs of the village on the walls. Watch out for the steps to the pub. Closed weekday lunchtimes, except bank hols. 🍴 ◖ ▶ ♣

Austrey

Bird in Hand
Church Road
☎ (01827) 830260
12–2.30, 6.30–11
Bateman Mild; Marston's Bitter, Pedigree Ⓗ
Excellent rural village pub and restaurant with a thatched roof. Marston's Head Brewer's Choice beers are stocked. A repeated past winner of CAMRA's local Pub of the Year.
Q ❀ ◖ ▶ 🍴 ♣ P

Bedworth

White Swan
All Saints Square
☎ (01203) 312164

11–11
Mansfield Riding Mild; Wells Eagle, Bombardier Ⓗ
Busy town pub near an open-air market; a large lively lounge bar/games room, now extended into an adjoining shop. No food Sun.
◖ 🍴 ≈ ♣

Try also: British Queen, King St (Ansells)

Bilton

Black Horse
43 The Green, Main Street
☎ (01788) 811473
11–2.30, 5.30–11; 11–11 Fri & Sat
Ansells Mild, Bitter; Ind Coope Burton Ale Ⓗ
Friendly village pub with a large, comfortable lounge and a traditional bar. No food Sun.
❀ ◖ 🍴 ♣ P

George Inn
2 The Green ☎ (01788) 522693
11–3, 5–11; 11–11 Fri & Sat
Ansells Mild, Bitter; Judges Barristers; Tetley Bitter Ⓗ
Comfortable, open-plan pub that appeals to all ages. One of the few regular outlets for Judges in the area.
◖ 🍴 ♣ P

Brailes

Gate Inn
Upper Brailes (B4035)
☎ (01608) 685212
12–2.30, 7 (6 Fri)–11
Hook Norton Best Bitter, Old Hooky Ⓗ
Friendly, old village local where children are always welcome; next to the site of the former Brailes Brewery. Aunt Sally played. Hook Norton seasonal beers sold.
🍴 ❀ ◖ ▶ 🍺 🍴 🥄 ♣ P

Try also: George, Lower Brailes (Hook Norton)

Bulkington

Weavers Arms
12 Long Street, Ryton (off Wolvey Rd) ☎ (01203) 314415
12–3.30, 6–11
Draught Bass; M&B Mild, Brew XI; guest beers Ⓗ
Relax and take time to enjoy this friendly village pub which is popular with locals and visitors alike. No food Sun.
🍴 Q ❀ ◖ 🍺 ♣

Church Lawford

Old Smithy
Green Lane ☎ (01203) 542333
11–3, 5.30–11; 11–11 Sat
Ansells Mild, Bitter; Greenalls Shipstone's Bitter;

Judges Old Gavel Bender; Tetley Bitter Ⓗ
Smart, friendly village pub, popular with diners. A recently added conservatory/eating area gives more room in the lounge for drinkers. There is also a games room. Local CAMRA *Pub of the Year 1994*.
🍴 ❀ ◖ ▶ ♣ P

Coughton

Throckmorton Arms
Coughton Hill (A435)
☎ (01789) 762879
11–3, 5–11
Banks's Bitter; Draught Bass; M&B Brew XI Ⓗ
Spacious, main road pub close to the NT's Coughton Court. Three comfortable, air-conditioned lounges and a dining room give this pub a fresh smoke-free atmosphere whilst retaining a traditional pub look. Extensive range of home-cooked food.
🍴 Q ❀ 🛏 ◖ ▶ 🥄 ♣ P

Try also: Little Lark, Studley (Free)

Five Ways (Haseley Knob)

Case is Altered
Case Lane (off A4177/A4141 island, towards Rowington) OS225701 ☎ (01926) 484206
11–2.30, 6–11; 12–2, 7–10.30 Sun
Ansells Mild, Bitter Ⓖ; Samuel Smith OBB Ⓗ; Whitbread Flowers Original Ⓖ
Unspoilt country gem with many relics of long-lost Warwickshire breweries. The small bar has a roaring fire in winter. Bar billiards in a lobby. The lounge is only open on Fri/Sat eves and Sun. The 'gravity' beers are served by unusual cask pumps.
🍴 Q ♣ P

Great Wolford

Fox & Hounds
OS247345 ☎ (01608) 674220
12–3, 6–11
Hook Norton Best Bitter; M&B Brew XI; Shepherd Neame Spitfire; Smiles Best Bitter; Thwaites Bitter; Whitbread Boddingtons Bitter; guest beers Ⓗ
Beautiful, atmospheric old place offering an excellent range of beers, an interesting, good value menu and an extensive range of malt whiskies. It can take some finding first time but is well worth the effort.
🍴 ❀ 🛏 ◖ ▶ 🥄 🍴 ♣ 👄 P

Hartshill

Anchor Inn
Mancetter Road (B4111)
☎ (01203) 398839
11–2.30, 6–11
Everards Tiger, Old Original;
Morland Old Speckled Hen;
S&N Theakston Old Peculier;
guest beer ⊞
Pub with a pleasant lounge
bar and a restaurant; always
popular especially in summer.
The downstairs bar opens
Easter to Sept. Situated on the
canal, it has a children's
activity area.
🏾 ❀ ◖ 🌡 ⤵ ☐ P

Try also: Royal Oak Inn,
Oldbury Rd (Wells)

Kenilworth

Clarendon House Hotel
Old High Street (A429/A452
jct) ☎ (01926) 57668
11.30–2.30 (3 Sat), 6–11
Hook Norton Best Bitter;
Whitbread Boddingtons Mild,
Bitter, Flowers IPA,
Original ⊞
Quiet, pleasant bar in an
olde-worlde residential hotel,
serving good value bar meals;
eve meals are served in
Cromwell's Bistro.
Q ❀ 🛏 ◖ 🌡 P

Earl Clarendon
127 Warwick Road (A452)
☎ (01926) 54643
11–11
Marston's Bitter, Pedigree ⊞
Cosy, welcoming pub which is
popular with locals. No food
Sun. Beware the keg cider on a
fake handpump. ❀ ◖

Royal Oak
36 New Street (A429, near
A452 jct) ☎ (01926) 53201
12–2.30, 6–11; 12–11 Sat
Marston's Bitter, Pedigree ⊞
One of the last remaining
locals' bars in the town,
complemented by a small,
cosy lounge. The landlord is
an ex-Coventry City goalie.
Beware the keg cider on a fake
handpump. 🏾 ❀ 🍺 ⤵

Lapworth

Navigation
Old Warwick Road
☎ (01564) 783337
11–2.30, 5.30–11; 11–11 Sat
Draught Bass; M&B Highgate
Dark, Brew XI; guest beers ⊞
Two-roomed canalside pub;
one room has a stone floor. A
large garden area runs
alongside the canal. Pump
clips display beers that really

have been served in the pub.
Solihull CAMRA *Pub of the
Year* 1994 and 1995.
🏾 Q ❀ ◖ 🌡 ⤵ ♣ ☐ P

Leamington Spa

Hope & Anchor
41 Hill Street ☎ (01926) 423031
11–11
Ansells Mild, Bitter; guest
beer ⊞
Thriving street-corner local
with a friendly welcome and a
good atmosphere. ♣

Red House
113 Radford Road
☎ (01926) 881725
11–2.30, 5–11; 11–11 Fri & Sat
Adnams Extra; Bass
Worthington BB, Draught
Bass ⊞
Popular, Victorian pub on the
edge of town with a friendly,
varied clientele, and strong
Irish connections. Note the
wide range of Irish whiskeys
and fine Guinness toucans.
The only local outlet for
Adnams Extra. 🏾 Q ❀ ♣

Somerville Arms
4 Campion Terrace
☎ (01926) 426746
11–2.30 (3 Fri), 5.30–11; 11–11 Sat
Ansells Mild, Bitter; Ind
Coope Burton Ale; Marston's
Pedigree; Tetley Bitter; guest
beer ⊞
Popular, friendly local with a
busy bar at the front and a
cosy lounge at the back. Each
bar has its own drinking motto
'Real ale for your health: you'll
get no better' and 'Abound in
hops all ye who enter here'.
Good humour, great
atmosphere. Q 🍺 ♣

Long Itchington

Harvester
6 Church Road
☎ (01926) 812698
11–3, 6–11
Hook Norton Best Bitter, Old
Hooky; guest beer ⊞
Unchanging, friendly country
pub with an imposing
fishtank. The one ever-
changing guest beer tends to
be a strong premium bitter. A
regular *Guide* entry.
Reasonable prices.
Q ◖ 🌡 🍺 ▲ ♣ P

Long Lawford

Sheaf & Sickle
Coventry Road
☎ (01788) 544622
12–3, 6–11; 11–11 Sat
Ansells Mild, Bitter; guest
beers ⊞
Popular pub, catering for a

variety of tastes with a
comfortable lounge, a bar with
a games area and a restaurant.
The garden overlooks the local
cricket pitch. Good reputation
for food and the ever changing
range of guest beers. Beware:
Tetley Bitter is kept under gas.
❀ ◖ 🌡 🍺 ⚹ ▲ ♣ P

Moreton Morrell

Black Horse
2 miles from M40 jct 12
☎ (01926) 651231
11–3, 7–11
Hook Norton Best Bitter;
Shepherd Neame Bishops
Finger ⊞
Welcoming, friendly village
pub with a games area in the
back bar; popular with locals
and students from the nearby
agricultural college. A peaceful
garden at the rear offers views
over the Warwickshire
countryside. The baps are
recommended. ❀

Newbold-on-Stour

Bird in Hand
Stratford Road (A3400)
☎ (01789) 450253
12–2.30, 6–11; 11–11 Sat
Hook Norton Best Bitter, Old
Hooky; guest beer ⊞
Busy, friendly local
comprising a main bar with an
adjacent games room. The
excellent food includes
seasonal specialities. Regular
special food eves, and a curry
club. Aunt Sally League
Champions 1994. Cider in
summer. Hook Norton
seasonal beers sold.
🏾 ❀ 🛏 ◖ 🌡 🍺 ⚹ ♣ ☐ P

Newton Regis

Queen's Head
Main Road ☎ (01827) 830271
11–3, 5–11; 11–11 Mon, Fri, Sat &
summer
Adnams Broadside; Bass
Worthington BB, Draught
Bass; M&B Highgate Dark,
Brew XI; guest beer ⊞
Spacious, two-roomed pub in
good surroundings. Food is
available at all times (busy Sun
lunchtime). Q ⚹ ❀ ◖ 🌡 🍺 P

Nuneaton

Oddfellows Arms
Upper Abbey Street
☎ (01203) 385437
12–11
M&B Brew XI; Mansfield
Riding Mild; Wells
Bombardier ⊞
Welcoming town pub
featuring a large room with
character, a cosy snug and a
games room at the rear. ❀ ♣

Warwickshire

Priors Marston

Holly Bush Inn
Holly Bush Lane
☎ (01327) 260934
12–3, 5.30–11; 12–11 Sat
Draught Bass; Hook Norton Best Bitter; Marston's Pedigree; S&N Theakston Old Peculier; guest beers Ⓗ
Old stone pub with many individual areas (including a restaurant), once separate rooms. The main part is dominated by a large inglenook. Appealing atmosphere. Traditional bar meals are always available. Families welcome (children's play area).
🏃 Q ❀ 🛏 ◁ ▶ ♣ P

Ratley

Rose & Crown
☎ (01295) 678148
12–3, 6–11
Hall & Woodhouse Tanglefoot; Wells Eagle, Bombardier, Fargo Ⓗ
Gem of a pub, stone-built in a secluded village. This welcoming, family-run local is reputedly haunted by a Roundhead ghost from the nearby battle of Edgehill. Good food; families welcome. Aunt Sally played.
🏃 ❀ ◁ ▶ & Å ♣

Try also: Castle, Edgehill (Hook Norton)

Rowington

Tom O' The Wood
Finwood Road (400 yds off B4439, right at crossroads, 1 mile S of Lapworth)
☎ (01564) 782252
11.30–3, 6.30–11 (11.30–11 summer)
Marston's Pedigree; Morland Old Speckled Hen; S&N Theakston Old Peculier; Wadworth 6X; Whitbread Boddingtons Bitter; guest beers Ⓗ
Well-modernised, 18th-century inn: one large room attractively divided to provide a relaxing atmosphere. Friendly staff offer a welcome to all. Regular live entertainment. Families welcome. ❀ ◁ ▶ ♣ P ⊁

Try also: Fleur de Lys, Lowsonford (Whitbread)

Rugby

Engine Inn
1 Bridget Street (off Lawford Rd) ☎ (01788) 579658
12–11
M&B Highgate Dark, Brew XI Ⓗ

Traditional, Victorian corner local now in the middle of a new housing development. A Grade II-listed building, it has two lounges, a corner bar and a small snug.
🛏 ❀ 🍺 & ♣

Half Moon
28–30 Lawford Road
☎ (01788) 574420
1 (11 Fri, 12 Sat)–11
Ansells Mild, Bitter; Ind Coope Burton Ale; guest beers Ⓗ
Basic, but friendly and welcoming, mid-terrace pub, close to the town centre; always popular.
🏃 & ♣

Quigley's PMC
Albert Street (by Post Office)
☎ (01788) 571315
12–2.30 (not Mon–Thu), 6–11; 11–11 Sat
Vaux Samson; Wards Best Bitter Ⓗ
A little bit of Ireland in Rugby: a traditional-style Irish bar often hosting live entertainment. CAMRA members welcome.
🏃 Q ♣

Raglan Arms
50 Dunchurch Road (off the gyratory system)
☎ (01788) 544441
12–2.30 (3 Mon, Fri & Sat), 7–11
Fuller's London Pride; Greene King Abbot; Marston's Bitter, Pedigree; Robinson's Best Bitter; guest beer Ⓗ
Deceptively large, terraced pub close to Rugby School. A pub to sit and sup in, with beers at very reasonable prices. No food or music. Marston's Head Brewer's Choice sold.
Q ♣ P

Three Horseshoes Hotel
Sheep Street
☎ (01788) 544585
11–3, 5.30–11
Judges Old Gavel Bender; Whitbread Boddingtons Bitter; guest beer Ⓗ
Plush, town-centre hotel. Special accommodation rates for CAMRA members (show card).
🏃 Q 🛏 🛏 ◁ ▶ 🍺 & P 🍴

Victoria Inn
1 Lower Hillmorton Road
☎ (01788) 544374
12–2.30 (4 Sat), 7 (6 Fri)–11
Draught Bass; M&B Highgate Dark, Brew XI; guest beer Ⓗ
Victorian corner pub, with original fittings, near the town centre: a basic bar and a friendly lounge. Trad. jazz Mon eve. Weekday lunches.
◁ 🍺 ⇌ ♣

Ryton-on-Dunsmore

Old Bull & Butcher
Oxford Road (5 miles E of Coventry, on A423)
☎ (01203) 307400
11–11
Ansells Mild; Tetley Bitter; Ind Coope Burton Ale Ⓗ
Fine old pub standing alone on the A423, with original oak beams. The restaurant menu includes 48oz steaks.
🏃 🛏 ❀ ◁ ▶ P

Shipston-on-Stour

Black Horse
Station Road (off A3400)
☎ (01608) 661617
11–3, 6–11
Home Bitter; Ruddles Best Bitter; S&N Theakston XB; Wadworth 6X; Webster's Yorkshire Bitter Ⓗ
Thatched pub dating back to the 12th century; originally a row of cottages for Cotswold sheep farmers, it has an interesting interior. An excellent children's room leads to the garden. Good value food. 🏃 🛏 ❀ ◁ ▶ 🍺 & ♣ P

Try also: Coach & Horses, New St (Free)

Shustoke

Griffin Inn
On B4116, sharp bend between Coleshill and Atherstone
☎ (01675) 481205
12–2.30, 7–11; 12–2.15, 7–10.30 Sun
Beer range varies Ⓗ
Old country village inn, full of charm, with a low-beamed ceiling and open log fires. Very popular with real ale fans; the Church End brewery next door gives off a wonderful aroma on brewing days. Good food lunchtime.
🏃 Q 🛏 ❀ ◁ Å P

Plough Inn
The Green (A447, 2 miles from Coleshill) ☎ (01675) 481557
12–3, 5.30–11
Draught Bass; Marston's Pedigree; M&B Mild, Brew XI Ⓗ
Busy village pub with a friendly atmosphere, due to gain a conservatory. Local CAMRA *Pub of the Year* 1992. Beware the keg cider on a fake handpump. 🏃 ◁ ▶ ♣ P

Shuttington

Wolferstan Arms
Main Road ☎ (01827) 892238
11–2.30, 6–11
Banks's Mild; Marston's Pedigree

Two-roomed village pub and restaurant, on top of a hill, offering panoramic views from the garden. Marston's Head Brewer's Choice beers stocked. Popular for food.
Q 🌢 🍴 🛏 🍴 ♣ P

Southam

Old Mint
Coventry Street
☎ (01926) 812339
12 (11.30 Tue)–2.30, 7 (6.30 Fri)–11
Draught Bass; Hook Norton Best Bitter; Marston's Pedigree; Taylor Landlord; Wadworth 6X; guest beers Ⓗ
15th-century, stone building used as a mint in the Civil War. Friendly and cosy atmosphere.
🔥 Q 🌢 🛏 🍴 🍴 🛏 P

Try also: **Bowling Green**, Coventry St (Greenalls)

Stockton

Crown
High Street ☎ (01926) 812255
12–3, 7–11 (11–11 Fri & Sat in summer)
Ansells Mild, Bitter; guest beers Ⓗ
Comfortable village bar serving up to six guest ales and a select choice of malt whiskies. Pool and petanque played. The function room is in a 300-year-old barn. Home-cooked food is served in the bar and restaurant. Cider in summer. 🔥 🌢 🍴 🍴 ♣ 🍷 P

Stratford-upon-Avon

Queen's Head
Ely Street ☎ (01789) 204914

11.30–11; 12–2.30, 7–10.30 Sun
Draught Bass; Hancock's HB; M&B Brew XI; guest beers Ⓗ
Lively, popular town-centre pub with an L-shaped bar. A house ale is occasionally obtained (named after the dog) and a wide range of guest ales come mainly from small independent breweries. Eve meals Fri and Sat.
🔥 🌢 🍴 🍴 ≠ 🍷

Warwick

Cape of Good Hope
66 Lower Cape (off Cape Rd, ½ mile N of centre)
☎ (01926) 498138
12–2.30 (3 Sat), 6 (7 Sat)–11
Whitbread Boddingtons Bitter Ⓗ**; guest beers** Ⓗ/Ⓖ
True canalside pub – the water is just a few feet from the front door. Built at the same time as the canal, it has a traditional bar at the front and a comfortable lounge to the rear. Good value bar meals. A popular pub with a friendly welcome. Limited parking.
🌢 🍴 🍴 🛏 ♣ P

Old Fourpenny Shop
27 Crompton Street (off Henley Road, near racecourse)
☎ (01926) 491360
12–2.30 (3 Fri & Sat), 5.30 (5 Fri, 6 Sat)–11; 12–2.30, 7–10.30 Sun
M&B Brew XI; guest beers Ⓗ
Do not be surprised if the beer range changes during your visit: five guest beers, one of which is normally a mild or a stout. Try to spot an independent brewery whose beer has not been stocked. The restaurant, with a

high-class menu, opens Tue–Sat lunch and eve. No food Sun. 🛏 🍴 🍴

Samuel's
27 Coten End (A445, towards Leamington)
☎ (01926) 493774
12–2.30, 5–11; 12–11 Sun
RCH PG Steam; Tetley Bitter; guest beers Ⓗ
Popular, single-bar pub with a reputation for unusual guest beers. Oversized lined glasses ensure a full measure, the only pub locally using them.
🌢 ≠ 🍺

Whitacre Heath

Railway
Station Road (between Coleshill and Kingsbury)
☎ (01675) 464227
11.30–3, 5–11
Marston's Pedigree; Morland Old Speckled Hen; Ruddles Best Bitter, County; John Smith's Bitter; guest beers Ⓗ
Friendly old pub, noted for its good range of beers, extensive bar menu, and farmyard animals to amuse the children. There's no longer a station nearby, despite the name.
🔥 🌢 🍴 🍴 🛏 ⚑ ♣ P

Wolvey

Bull's Head
Church Hill (B4065)
☎ (01455) 220383
11.30–3.30, 6–11
Marston's Bitter, Pedigree Ⓗ
Refurbished pub in the heart of the village: a large well-appointed bar and a comfortable lounge with a new conservatory extension.
🌢 🍴 🍴 🛏 ⚑ ♣ P

THE SYMBOLS

🔥	real fire	ⅾ	easy wheelchair access
Q	quiet (no music or electronic distractions in at least one bar)	⚑	camping at or near the pub
🌣	indoor family room	≠	near railway station
🌢	outdoor drinking area	⊖	near underground station or tram stop
🛏	accommodation	♣	pub games
🍴	lunchtime meals	🍷	real cider
🍴	evening meals	P	car park
🛏	public bar	⚲	no-smoking room or area
	🍺	oversized, lined glasses used	

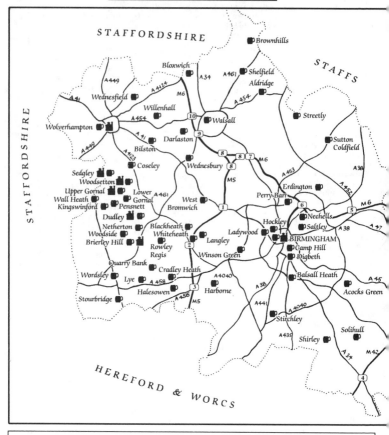

STAFFORDSHIRE

Brownhills

Bloxwich

Shelfield

Aldridge

STAFFS

Wednesfield

Willenhall

Streetly

Wolverhampton

Walsall

Darlaston

Sutton Coldfield

Bilston

Coseley

Wednesbury

Erdington

Sedgley

Woodsetton

Perry Barr

Upper Gornal

Wall Heath

Lower Gornal

West Bromwich

Kingswinford

Pensnett

Hockley

Nechells

Dudley

Netherton

Blackheath

Ladywood

BIRMINGHAM

Woodside

Whiteheath

Langley

Camp Hill

Brierley Hill

Rowley Regis

Winson Green

Digbeth

Quarry Bank

Cradley Heath

Balsall Heath

Acocks Green

Wordsley

Lye

Harborne

Stourbridge

Halesowen

Stirchley

Solihull

Shirley

HEREFORD & WORCS

Banks's, Wolverhampton; **Batham**, *Brierley Hill*;
Britannia, *Upper Gornal*; **British Oak**, *Dudley*;
Holden's, *Woodsetton*; **Sarah Hughes**, *Sedgley*;
Rainbow, *Coventry*

Aldridge

Lazy Hill
196 Walsall Wood Road
(1 mile from centre)
☎ (01922) 52040
12–2.30, 6–11
**Ansells Mild, Bitter; HP&D
Entire; Ind Coope Burton Ale;
Marston's Pedigree; Tetley
Bitter** Ⓗ
Large, 16th-century pub with
three pleasant rooms. Busy at
weekends.
🏰 P

Barston

Bull's Head
Barston Lane
☎ (01675) 442830
11–2.30, 5.30 (6 Sat)–11

**Draught Bass; M&B Brew XI;
Tetley Bitter** Ⓗ
Beamed country pub, the
centre of village life, partly
dating back to 1490. No meals
Wed eve or Sun.
🏰 Q ❀ ◖ ▶ P

Bilston

Spread Eagle
Lichfield Street (A41)
☎ (01902) 403801
11.30–3.30, 7–11
**British Oak Mild, Eve'ill
Bitter, Old Jones; Tetley
Bitter** Ⓗ
Three-roomed urban pub: a
basic bar with wooden
floorboards. The second
British Oak pub (other British
Oak beers are sometimes
available). ◖ ▶ 🏵 ♣ P

White Rose
20 Lichfield Street, Swan Bank
(A41) ☎ (01902) 493474
12 (11 Sat)–3, 7–11
**Banks's Mild; M&B Highgate
Dark, Brew XI** Ⓔ
Friendly pub, where locals will
teach the Indian card game
'Seep' to visitors. 🏵 ♣

Birmingham:
Acocks Green

Bernie's Real Ale
Off-Licence
908 Warwick Road
☎ (0121) 708 1664
12–2 (not Mon or Wed), 5.30–10; 12–2,
7–10 Sun
Beer range varies Ⓗ & Ⓔ
Off-licence serving a
constantly changing range of
ales.

West Midlands

M 42
4A 8
WARWICKSHIRE
7 4
M6
6
A 45
A 444
2
Hampton in Arden
A 4114
A 46
Barston
Coventry
5
A 4141
A 452
A 46
A 423
Knowle
Dorridge
WARWICKSHIRE

Balsall Heath

Old Moseley Arms
53 Tindal Street
☎ (0121) 440 1954
3 (12 Fri & Sat)–11
**Ansells Mild, Bitter; HP&D
Entire; Marston's Pedigree** Ⓗ
Small, two-roomed pub with a
1930s, oak-panelled interior.
Popular with students. ❀ ⊞
♣

Camp Hill

Brewer & Baker
Old Camp Hill
☎ (0121) 772 8185
11–11
**Banks's Mild, Bitter;
Camerons Strongarm** Ⓗ
Pub built on the site of a
former brewery and bakery.
Lots of alcoves; good food.
Packed on Birmingham City
match days. ❀ ♿ ♣ ⊟

City Centre

Flapper & Firkin
Cambrian Wharf, Kingston
Row ☎ (0121) 236 2421

11–11
**Firkin Flapper, Duckarsed,
Dogbolter; Tetley Bitter;
guest beer** Ⓗ
Canalside Firkin pub behind
the Symphony Hall, boasting
upstairs and downstairs bars
where bands regularly play.
Mixed clientele. Skittles played
(Wed). ❀ ◑ ▶ ♣

Gunmaker's Arms
Bath Street
☎ (0121) 236 1201
11 (12 Sat)–3, 5 (7 Sat)–11
**Draught Bass; Hancock's HB;
M&B Mild** Ⓗ
Happy, welcoming pub where
the landlord has won many
awards for cellarmanship.
Q ❀ ◑ ▶ ⊞ ⇌ (Snow Hill)
♣

Keys Club
9 Margaret Street (beneath
Midland Institute)
☎ (0121) 236 6645
11–10 (3 Sat); closed Sun
Beer range varies Ⓗ
Club stocking up to 11
different ales, most from
Enville Brewery (including a
house beer). The bar is
downstairs. Free membership.

Book eve meals.
Q ◑ ▶ ⇌ (Snow Hill/New
St) ♣

Old Contemptibles
176 Edmund Street
☎ (0121) 236 5264
12–10.30 (11 Thu & Fri); 7–11 Sat;
closed Sun
**Draught Bass; M&B Highgate
Dark, Brew XI; guest beers** Ⓗ
Busy, popular pub which
holds beer festivals and draws
a mixed clientele. No food Sat
eve. Q ◑ ▶ ⇌ (Snow Hill)

Prince of Wales
84 Cambridge Street (behind
Symphony Hall)
☎ (0121) 643 9460
11–3, 7–11
**Ansells Mild, Bitter; Ind
Coope Burton Ale; Marston's
Pedigree; Tetley Bitter** Ⓗ
Quiet pub with a friendly
atmosphere. Eve meals end at
8. Q ◑ ▶ ♿

Queen's Arms
150 Newhall Street
☎ (0121) 236 5828
11–11; 12–3 Sun, closed Sun eve
**Draught Bass; M&B Mild;
guest beer** Ⓗ
City bar, next to the Science
Museum. ◑ ▶ ♿ ⇌ (Snow
Hill) ♣

Queens Head Tavern
23 Essex Street
☎ (0121) 622 3491
12–11; 12–2.30, 7–11 Sat
**Courage Best Bitter,
Directors; Marston's Pedigree;
Red Cross Nailers OBJ** Ⓗ
Small, basic pub, popular with
actors and theatregoers.
Beware the keg cider on a fake
handpump.
◑ ▶ ⇌ (New St)

Village
15a Hurst Street
☎ (0121) 622 4742
1–11.30
**Banks's Bitter; Camerons
Strongarm; Marston's
Pedigree** Ⓗ
Vibrant, friendly, gay pub
with excellent accommodation.
🛏 ❀ 🍴 ⇌ (New St) ⊟

Digbeth

Anchor
308 Bradford Street
☎ (0121) 622 4516
11–11
**Ansells Mild; Tetley Bitter;
guest beers** Ⓗ
Old corner pub with a nice
atmosphere, handy for the
coach station.
❀ ◑ ▶ ⊞ ⇌ (Moor St) ♣

Lamp Tavern
157 Barford Street, Highgate
☎ (0121) 622 2599

West Midlands

12–11 (11.30 Sat)
Marston's Pedigree; Stanway
Stanney Bitter; Wadworth 6X;
Whitbread Boddingtons Mild,
Bitter; guest beers Ⓗ
Friendly pub, with a good
choice of ales. The only regular
outlet in Brum for Stanway
beers. Live music. CAMRA
Birmingham *Pub of the Year*
1994–95. ◑ ⇌ (New St/Moor
St)

Erdington

Beer Shop
55 New Street
☎ (0121) 384 3636
6.30 (5 Sat)–10.30; 7–10.30 Sun
Taylor Landlord; guest
beers Ⓗ
Excellent off-licence with a
good choice of guest beers and
a wide range of bottled beers.
⇌

Harborne

Junction
212 High Street
☎ (0121) 426 1838
10.30–11
Draught Bass; M&B Mild,
Brew XI; guest beer Ⓗ
There is something for all in
this busy pub which holds
regular activity nights. Likely
soon to undergo a major
refurbishment and become a
Bass 'Ale Shrine' pub.
◑ ▶ Ⓠ & ♣ P

New Inn
74 Vivian Road
☎ (0121) 427 5062
11–3, 5.30–11; 11–11 Sat
Banks's Mild, Bitter;
Camerons Strongarm Ⓗ
Lively pub serving locals,
business people and students.
The keen bowling team helps
to convey a village-type
atmosphere in a busy suburb.
Banks's seasonal beers sold.
Wheelchair WC.
Ⓠ ❀ ◑ ▶ Ⓠ & ♣ ⊟

Hockley

Black Eagle
16 Factory Road
☎ (0121) 523 4008
11.30 (12 Sat)–3, 5.30 (7 Sat)–11
Ansells Mild, Bitter; HP&D
Entire; Ind Coope Burton Ale;
Marston's Pedigree Ⓗ
A pleasurable pub to visit;
welcoming, with good staff.
🏠 Ⓠ ⛵ ❀ ◑ ▶ Ⓠ

Church Inn
22 Great Hampton Street
☎ (0121) 515 1851
11–11
Ansells Mild; Batham Best
Bitter; HP&D Entire; Tetley
Bitter Ⓗ
Pub with very good food and

a good atmosphere.
⛵ ◑ ▶ ⇌ (New St)

White House
New John Street West (400 yds
off A41) ☎ (0121) 523 0782
10–11
M&B Mild, Brew XI Ⓗ
Typical back-street pub; good,
friendly and welcoming.
Ⓠ ◑ ♣

Woodman
Well Street (off Gt Hampton
St) ☎ (0121) 523 0590
11–11
M&B Mild Ⓗ
Lively, two-roomed local with
an L-shaped bar. ◑

Ladywood

Vine
Rawlins Street (behind Tesco)
☎ (0121) 454 7943
11–3, 5 (7 Sat)–11
Ansells Mild, Bitter; Ind
Coope Burton Ale; Marston's
Pedigree; Tetley Bitter Ⓗ
Bustling, one-roomed pub.
🏠 ◑ & ⇌ (Five Ways) ♣

Nechells

Villa Tavern
307 Nechells Park Road
☎ (0121) 328 9831
11–2.30, 5.30–11; 11–11 Fri & Sat
Ansells Mild, Bitter; HP&D
Entire; Marston's Pedigree;
Tetley Bitter Ⓗ
Locals' pub with a good
welcome. Eve meals Fri–Sun.
Ⓠ ◑ ▶ Ⓠ ⇌ (Aston) ♣ P

Perry Barr

Seventh Trap
81 Regina Drive
☎ (0121) 356 2092
11–11 (11–3, 5.30–11 lounge)
Banks's Mild, Bitter Ⓔ;
Marston's Pedigree Ⓗ
Attractive two-bar house on
the outskirts of the city, next to
a shopping centre. Eve meals
6–8; Sun roast lunch (no meals
Sun eve). Children's menu.
❀ ◑ ▶ Ⓠ & ⇌ ♣ P ⊟

Saltley

Havelock Tavern
28 Havelock Road
☎ (0121) 328 0054
11–11
M&B Mild Ⓗ, Bitter Ⓔ
Two-bar pub; the lounge is
decorated with china. Ⓠ ♣

Stirchley

Hibernian
1063 Pershore Road, Selly Park
☎ (0121) 472 0136

12–11; 12–2.30, 6–11 Sat
Ansells Mild, Bitter; Ind
Coope Burton Ale; Marston's
Pedigree; Tetley Bitter Ⓗ
Large, four-roomed pub with a
semi-circular bar; one room is
set aside for bands. A Burton
Cellarman award-winner.
🏠 ◑ ▶ Ⓠ & P

Three Horseshoes
Pershore Road
☎ (0121) 458 1378
12–3, 5.30–11
Banks's Mild; Greenalls
Davenports Bitter, Original;
Marston's Pedigree; Tetley
Bitter; guest beers Ⓗ
Partly listed, large, brightly-lit,
one-roomed pub that started
life as a Royal Mail sorting
house. ⛵ ◑ ▶

Winson Green

Olde Windmill
84 Dudley Road (A456)
☎ (0121) 455 6907
11–11
M&B Mild, Brew XI; guest
beer Ⓗ
Small, traditional, old pub of
two rooms with a cosy lounge.
Opposite Dudley Road
Hospital. ❀ ◑ Ⓠ ♣ P

Blackheath

Bell & Bear
71 Gorsty Hill Road (A4099)
☎ (0121) 561 2196
11–11, 12–3, 6–11 Sat; 12–2.30,
7–10.30 Sun
HP&D Mild, Bitter, Entire;
Ind Coope Burton Ale; Taylor
Landlord; Tetley Bitter; guest
beers Ⓗ
Comfortable, rambling,
one-room pub catering for
drinkers and diners.
Magnificent views. No food
Sun. ❀ ◑ ▶ P

Shoulder of Mutton
Halesowen Street, Rowley
Regis ☎ (0121) 559 4174
12–11
Burtonwood Bitter, Top
Hat Ⓗ
Lively, one-roomer with
several cosy bays. Book Sun
lunch. 🏠 ❀ ⇌ (Rowley
Regis) ♣ P

Waterfall
132 Waterfall Lane
☎ (0121) 561 3499
12–3, 5–11; 12–11 Fri & Sat
Batham Best Bitter; Enville
Ale; Hook Norton Old
Hooky; Marston's Pedigree;
guest beers Ⓗ
It's worth the uphill walk from
the station, or down from the
town, to sample at least seven
ales here. Beware the keg cider
on a fake handpump.
❀ ◑ ▶ Ⓠ ⇌ (Old Hill) ♣ P

Bloxwich

Knave of Hearts
Lichfield Road
☎ (01922) 405576
12–2.30 (3 Fri & Sat), 6 (5 Thu & Fri, 6.30 Sat)–11
HP&D Mild, Entire; Tetley Bitter Ⓗ
Large, pleasant two-roomed pub with mock Victoriana. Live music, but no food, Sun eve. ❀ ◖ ▮ ♣ P

Romping Cat
Elmore Green Road (off A34)
☎ (01922) 475041
12–11
Banks's Mild, Bitter Ⓔ
Superb street-corner local; a very friendly three-roomed pub with etched windows.
⛾ ❀ ⇌ ♣ 目

Royal Exchange
Stafford Road (A34)
☎ (01922) 479618
11–2.30, 5–11; 11–11 Fri & Sat; 12–2.45, 7–10.30 Sun
Banks's Mild; Marston's Bitter, Pedigree Ⓗ
Pleasant local where the bar has sporting memorabilia and the lounge is comfortable. Marston's Head Brewer's Choice. ❀ ◖ ⇌ ♣ P 目

Sir Robert Peel
Bell Lane (A4124/B4210 jct)
☎ (01922) 405512
12–2.30 (3 Sat), 5 (7 Sat)–11
Bass Worthington BB, Draught Bass; M&B Highgate Dark; Stones Best Bitter Ⓗ
Large, friendly pub with a comfortable bar and a plush lounge. Good food in the bar and restaurant (not served Sun eve). ❀ ◖ ▮ ⇌ ♣

Brierley Hill

Bell
172 Delph Road (B4172)
☎ (01384) 572376
12–3, 5–11; 11–11 Fri & Sat
HP&D Mild, Entire; Tetley Bitter; guest beers Ⓗ
Popular Victorian pub at the bottom of the famous Delph 'Nine' locks. Tapster's Choice guest ales. No food Sun.
⛾ ❀ ◖ ▮ ♣ P

Blue Brick Tap House
153 Dudley Road (A461)
☎ (01384) 78448
11–11
Banks's Mild, Bitter; Camerons Strongarm; Marston's Pedigree; guest beers Ⓗ
Large pub with a number of linked rooms, mostly gaslit. Hanson's Mild and Camerons Bitter are sold as house beers.
⛾ ❀ ◖ ▮ ♣ P 目

Brownhills

Hussey Arms
Chester Road (A452)
☎ (01543) 373198
12–2.30, 6–11; 12–11 Fri & Sat
HP&D Mild, Entire; Tetley Bitter; guest beer Ⓗ
Softly-lit pub, featuring Victoriana, wrought iron tables, ceramic tiles and stained-glass.
❀ ◖ ▮ ▮ ♿ ♣ P ✠

Prince of Wales
98 Watling Street
☎ (01543) 372551
7.30–11; 12–3, 7.30–11 Sat; 12–2.30, 7.30–10.30 Sun
Ansells Bitter; M&B Highgate Dark Ⓗ
Small, homely single-roomed local. ⛾ Q ❀ ♣

Royal Oak
Chester Road, Shire Oak (A452) ☎ (01543) 452089
12–3, 6–11
Ansells Mild, Bitter; Ind Coope Burton Ale; Tetley Bitter; guest beers Ⓗ
Known as the Middle Oak; a good example of an extremely friendly 1930s pub with a small, but splendid bar and a well decorated lounge. Booking advised for Fri/Sat eve meals; no meals Sun eve.
❀ ◖ ▮ ▮ ♿ ♣ P 目

Coseley

White House
1 Daisy Street (B4163)
☎ (01902) 402703
11–3, 6–11
HP&D Mild, Bitter, Entire; guest beers Ⓗ
Popular free house offering good value food and genuine guest beers. On the Dudley–Bilston bus route. No food Sun. ⛾ ◖ ▮ ▮ ⇌ ♣

Coventry

Biggin Hall Hotel
Binley Road, Copsewood (A428, 3 miles E of centre)
☎ (01203) 451046
10.30–11; 10.30–3.30, 6–11 Sat
Banks's Mild; Marston's

Vine (Bull & Bladder)
10 Delph Road (B4172)
☎ (01384) 78293
12–11
Batham Mild, Best Bitter, XXX Ⓗ
Famous Black Country brewery tap on top of the Delph Run: a multi-roomed pub which has undergone a tasteful extension and general refurbishment.
⛾ ❀ ◖ ▮ ♣ P

Bitter, Pedigree, Owd Rodger; guest beers Ⓗ
Built in 1923 in mock-Tudor style; a smart bar and a plush lounge with a large oak central table. The games room doubles as a family room. Good food (no meals Sun).
⛾ Q ⛾ ❀ ◖ ▮ ▮ ♣ P

Black Horse
Spon End (inner ring road jct 7) ☎ (01203) 677360
10–11
Draught Bass; M&B Mild, Brew XI; Tetley Bitter Ⓗ
Traditional drinking pub with separate rooms and attractive panelling in the lounge. Busy at weekends. ⛾ Q ▮ ♣ P

Boat Inn
188 Blackhorse Road, Exhall
☎ (01203) 367438
12–3, 6.30–11
Ansells Mild, Bitter; Tetley Bitter; guest beer Ⓗ
18th-century pub next to a canal boat builder's yard; little altered in recent years.
⛾ ❀ ◖ ▮ ♣ ⌀ P

Broomfield Tavern
14–16 Broomfield Place, Spon End (opp. Sovereign Park)
☎ (01203) 228506
12–11 (12–4, 7–11 Tue & Wed in winter)
Banks's Mild; Marston's Pedigree; Ruddles Best Bitter, County; S&N Theakston XB; guest beers Ⓗ
Friendly local hosting regular folk music. ❀ ◖ ▮ ♿ ♣

Greyhound
118 Much Park Street (near Coventry University)
☎ (01203) 221274
12–11
Mansfield Riding Mild; Wells Eagle, Bombardier; guest beers Ⓗ
Friendly, one-roomed, city-centre pub, offering a well-priced menu (not served Sun). Popular with lawyers and students lunchtimes. Beware the Scrumpy Jack cider is keg.
❀ ◖ ▮ ♣

Malt Shovel
93 Spon End (inner ring road jct 7) ☎ (01203) 220204
12–2.30 (3 Fri & Sat), 7–11
Ansells Mild, Bitter; Tetley Bitter; guest beers Ⓗ
Long-standing *Guide* entry, comfortable and relaxed with three wood-panelled rooms served by a central bar. Lunches Mon–Fri.
⛾ Q ❀ ◖ ▮

New Inn
Bull's Head Lane (1½ miles from centre, off A427)
☎ (01203) 453764

West Midlands

12 (11 Fri & Sat)–11
**Morland Old Speckled Hen;
Ruddles County; guest
beers** H
Pleasant, back-street, two-roomed pub off Binley Rd,
behind the cricket ground. The
lounge is olde-worlde.
❀ 🍴 ♣ P

Newt & Cucumber
Bailey Lane (opp. Cathedral)
11.30–11
**Bass Worthington BB; Greene
King Abbot; S&N Theakston
Best Bitter, XB; guest beers** H
Modern, city-centre pub built
on an old bomb-site. Dress
code at weekends. 🍴 ▶ ♿

Nursery Tavern
38–39 Lord Street, Chapelfields
(¾ mile from inner ring road
jct 7) ☎ (01203) 674530
11–11
**Courage Best Bitter; John
Smith's Bitter; Wadworth 6X;
guest beers** H
Lively, three-roomed pub
offering lots of events and
trips. No food Sun; eve meals
Fri and Sat. Good variety of
guest beers. Children welcome
till 7.30 in the back room.
Q ❀ 🍴 🍴 ♣

Rainbow Inn
Birmingham Road, Allesley
(off A45) ☎ (01203) 402888
11–11
**Courage Best Bitter,
Directors; Rainbow Belchers
Wood, Firecracker, Sley
Alle** H
17th-century coaching inn
retaining the feel of a village
pub even though on the city's
south-western edge: a busy
bar and a quiet lounge for
meals. It started brewing in
1994. No food Sun; eve meals
Tue–Fri until 8.30.
🏨 Q ❀ 🍴 🍴 ♣ P

Royal Oak
22 Earlsdon Street, Earlsdon
☎ (01203) 674140
5–11
**Ansells Mild; Draught Bass;
Ind Coope ABC Best Bitter;
Tetley Bitter; guest beers** H
Popular pub known locally as
the Chapel. One area has table
service. 🏨 Q ❀

Cradley Heath

Plough & Harrow
82 Corngreaves Road
☎ (01384) 560377
11–3, 7–11; 11–11 Fri & Sat
Banks's Mild, Bitter E
Traditional Black Country
town pub with several small
rooms; popular with locals
and factory workers. No
children in the public bar.
🚼 ❀ 🍴 ♣ 🍴

Darlaston

Fallings Heath Tavern
Walsall Road (A4038)
☎ (0121) 526 3403
12–2.30 (3 if busy), 7.30–11
**Ansells Mild, Bitter; Tetley
Bitter; guest beer**
(weekends) H
Friendly local: a busy bar,
quieter lounge and an
extended children's room.
🚼 ❀ 🍴 ♣ P 🍴

Horse & Jockey
88 Walsall Road (A4038)
☎ (0121) 526 4553
11–11
Banks's Mild, Bitter E
Busy local, popular with
games/sports players. The bar
can get busy; the cosy lounge
is quieter. ❀ 🍴 ♣ P 🍴

Dorridge

Railway
Grange Road
☎ (01564) 773531
11–3, 4.30–11; 11–11 Wed, Fri & Sat;
12–2.30, 7–10.30 Sun
**Draught Bass; M&B Mild,
Brew XI** H
Refurbished, open-plan pub,
retaining a separate bar. Good
value beer and food for the
area.
🏨 Q ❀ 🍴 🍴 ♿ 🍴 ♣ P

Dudley

Fellows
Castle Hill, The Broadway
☎ (01384) 237303
11–11
**Draught Bass; Marston's
Pedigree; Whitbread
Boddingtons Bitter, Fuggles
IPA; guest beers** H
Former gatehouse of Dudley
Zoo, converted to a one-roomed Beefeater pub with a
restaurant area.
❀ 🍴 ♿ 🍴 P

Lamp
116 High Street (A459)
☎ (01384) 254129
11–11
**Batham Mild, Best Bitter,
XXX** H
Lively, welcoming local with a
plain, boisterous bar, a
comfortable lounge with an
eating area and new
accommodation (disabled
facilities). The old Matthew
Smith brewery attached is
being upgraded. Eve meals
weekdays until 7.30.
🏨 ❀ 🛏 🍴 🍴 ♿ ♣ P

Halesowen

Fairfield Inn
Fairfield Road, Hurst Green

11–3 (3.30 Sat), 5.30–11
**Banks's Hanson's Mild,
Bitter** E; **Marston's
Pedigree** H
Large roadhouse, with a lively
bar and a smart, busy lounge.
No food Sun.
❀ 🍴 🍴 🚂 (Rowley Regis)
♣ P

Rose & Crown at Hasbury
Hagley Road
☎ (0121) 550 2757
12–2.30 (3 Sat), 5.30 (6 Sat)–11
**HP&D Mild, Entire; Tetley
Bitter** H
Established *Guide* entry:
various drinking areas, with
their own atmospheres, radiate
from a central bar. Excellent
menu (not served Sun).
🏨 🍴 ♣ P

Waggon & Horses
21 Stourbridge Road
☎ (0121) 550 4989
12–11
**Batham Best Bitter; Enville
Simpkiss Bitter, Ale; guest
beers** H
Friendly hostelry attracting
clients from near and far, with
an ever-changing range of
beers from 16 handpumps –
one dispensing a house beer.
♣ 🍴

Whitley
Stourbridge Road
☎ (0121) 550 1056
12–3 (4 Sat), 6–11
**Banks's Mild; Greenalls
Davenports Bitter, Original** H
Two-roomed pub on the main
road, catering for local and
passing trade. Revived by
refurbishment and a greater
stress on ale and food (not
served Sun).
❀ 🍴 🍴 ♣ P 🍴

Hampton in Arden

White Lion
High Street ☎ (01675) 442833
12–11
**Draught Bass; M&B Brew XI;
John Smith's Bitter** H
Small, friendly local with a
restaurant. The public bar has
not changed for 50 years.
Close to the NEC.
🏨 🛏 🍴 🍴 🚂 ♣ P

Kingswinford

Old Courthouse
High Street (A4101)
☎ (01384) 833456
11–2.30 (3 Sat), 5–11; 11–11 Fri
**Banks's Mild; Bass
Worthington BB, Draught
Bass; Batham Best Bitter;
Stones Best Bitter; guest
beers** H
Comfortable one-roomed pub

West Midlands

with many different areas, including a restaurant. Built in the 1770s as a manorial court, this Grade II-listed building has been extended to offer accommodation. Beware the fake handpump for keg cider. No eve meals Sun.
🏚 🛏 ◗ ♿ P

Park Tavern
182 Cot Lane (off A4101/A491)
☎ (01384) 287178
12–11
Ansells Bitter; Batham Best Bitter; Tetley Bitter; guest beer Ⓗ
Friendly local, with a bustling bar and a quieter lounge. Close to the Broadfield House Glass Museum.
🏚 🍴 ♣ P

Union
Water Street
☎ (01384) 830668
12–2.30 (4 Sat), 6 (7 Sat)–11
Banks's Mild, Bitter Ⓔ
Small, traditional, back-street local, in the same family for over 60 years. Note the John Rolinson Brewery window.
🏚 ♣ P

Knowle

Vaults
St John's Close
☎ (01564) 773656
12–2.30, 5–11
Ansells Mild; HP&D Bitter; Ind Coope Burton Ale; Tetley Bitter; guest beers Ⓗ
Three-level pub adjoining a nightclub; the top area offers some seclusion. Solihull CAMRA *Pub of the Year* 1992 and 93. Beware the keg cider on a fake handpump.
◗ ♣ ◔

Langley

Brewery Inn
Station Road
☎ (0121) 544 6467
11.30–2.30, 6–11
HP&D Mild, Bitter, Entire, Deakin's Downfall; guest beers Ⓗ
Pub where the original HP&D brewery can be seen through a viewing panel in the corridor: a basic bar and a Victorian-style lounge. No food Sun. Tapster's Choice guest beers. Near Langley Maltings.
🏚 ◗ 🍴 ≉ (Langley Green) ♣ P

Crosswells
High Street
☎ (0121) 552 2629
11–2.30 (3 Fri & Sat), 5.30 (5 Sat)–11
HP&D Mild, Bitter, Entire, Deakin's Downfall Ⓗ
Typical HP&D pub featuring

original Crosswells Brewery windows. 🏚 Q ◗ 🍴
≉ (Langley Green) ♣

New Navigation
Titford Road (off A4123)
☎ (0121) 552 2525
11.30–3 (3.30 Sat), 6 (7 Sat)–11
HP&D Mild, Entire, Deakin's Downfall; Tetley Bitter; guest beer Ⓗ
Friendly pub near the end of the Titford Canal. The single U-shaped room is divided into several areas. No food Sun. Tapster's Choice guest ales.
🏚 ◗ ♣

Lower Gornal

Fountain Real Ale Bar
8 Temple Street (off A459)
☎ (01384) 834888
12–3 (not Mon–Wed), 7 (6 summer)–11; 12–2.30, 7–10.30 Sun
Adnams Broadside; Blackbeard Stairway to Heaven; Everards Tiger; Hall & Woodhouse Tanglefoot; guest beers Ⓗ
Comfortable free house, until recently the last known brewhouse in Gornal. Seasonal beer festivals; good range of guest beers.
🏚 🏚 ♣ ◔

Lye

Fox
8 Green Lane (off A4036)
☎ (01384) 423665
11–11
Banks's Mild, Bitter Ⓔ
Two-roomed pub up a narrow side street: a bustling public bar, popular with locals, and a quiet, comfortable lounge.
🏚 🍴 ≉ P 🍴

Netherton

Dry Dock
21 Windmill End
☎ (01384) 235369
11–3, 6–11
Ansells Mild; HP&D Entire; guest beer Ⓗ
One of Mad o'Rourke's original Little Pubs. Set at a famous canal junction, the one-roomed pub boasts a narrow boat as its central bar. Irish ambience; frequent live folk music. Well known for food. 🏚 🏚 ◗ ◗ P

Pensnett

Holly Bush Inn
Bell Street (off A4101)
☎ (01384) 78711
12–4 (4.30 Sat), 7–11
Batham Mild, Best Bitter Ⓗ
Basic, one-roomed, estate local where mild outsells bitter.
🏚 ♣ P

Quarry Bank

Sun Inn
218 High Street
☎ (01384) 566254
11.30–3, 6.30–11
Banks's Hanson's Mild, Mild, Bitter Ⓔ
Large roadhouse, popular with locals and shoppers (near the Merry Hill complex). Good value food (not served Sun or Mon). Beware the keg cider on a fake handpump.
🏚 ◗ 🍴 ♣ P 🍴

Rowley Regis

Cock Inn
75 Dudley Road (B4171)
☎ (0121) 561 4273
12–2.30 (3 Fri, 4 Sat), 5 (6 Sat)–11
Banks's Mild; HP&D Bitter, Entire, Deakin's Downfall; Tetley Bitter Ⓗ
Large, one-roomed Victorian-style pub divided into separate areas. 🏚 Q 🏚 ◗ ♣ P

Sir Robert Peel
1 Rowley Village (B4171)
☎ (0121) 559 2835
12–4, 7–11
Ansells Mild, Bitter; M&B Highgate Dark; Tetley Bitter; guest beer Ⓗ
The oldest building in Rowley village, a traditional three-roomed pub, licensed since 1840. One servery is in the entrance passageway. Warm welcome. 🏚 Q 🏚 ≉ ♣

Sedgley

Beacon Hotel
129 Bilston Street (A463)
☎ (01902) 883380
12–2.30, 5.30–10.45 (11 Fri); 11.30–3, 6–11 Sat; 12–2.30, 7–10.30 Sun
Hook Norton Best Bitter; Sarah Hughes Sedgley Surprise, Ruby Mild; guest beers Ⓗ
Multi-roomed brewery tap restored in authentic Victorian style. Q 🏚 ♿ ♣ P

Bull's Head
27 Bilston Street (A463)
☎ (01902) 679606
1–3.30 (12–4 Sat), 6–11; 1–11 Thu & Fri
Holden's Mild, Bitter Ⓔ/Ⓗ, Special Ⓗ
Excellent drinkers' pub. Piano afternoons Thu and Fri.
🏚 🏚 ♿ ♣ ◔ 🍴

Shelfield

Four Crosses
Green Lane (off A461)
☎ (01922) 682518
12–11
Banks's Mild, Bitter Ⓔ;

313

West Midlands

Marston's Pedigree; guest beer H
Saloon bar and a cottage-style lounge in a free house.
✿ ◖ ▶ P

Shirley

Bernie's Real Ale Off-Licence
266 Cranmore Boulevard (off A34) ☎ (0121) 744 2827
12–2 (not Mon), 5.30–10; 12–2, 7–9.45 Sun
Batham Best Bitter; Hook Norton Best Bitter; Titanic Premium; guest beers H
Off-licence serving six changing beers, most from independent breweries. ढ़ ▱

Red Lion
Stratford Road
☎ (0121) 744 1030
11–2.30 (3 Sat), 6.30–11
Ansells Mild, Bitter; HP&D Mild; Ind Coope Burton Ale; Marston's Pedigree; Tetley Bitter; guest beers H
Main road pub forming part of a shopping complex. The large lounge has three distinct areas; pool room at the rear. Two guest beers from the Carlsberg-Tetley range. ◖ ♣

Solihull

Old Colonial
Damson Lane (½ mile from A45, off Damson Parkway)
☎ (0121) 705 9054
11.30–11; 11–3, 6.30–11 Sat
Draught Bass H; M&B Mild, Brew XI E; guest beer H
Modern, single-room pub with seven areas; the central area has a sliding roof and there's also a no-smoking area, a games area and a children's area (until 7).
ढ़ ✿ ◖ ♣ P ✕

Stourbridge

Crown
208 Hagley Road (50 yds from A491/B4187 jct)
☎ (01384) 394777
12–11
Ansells Mild, Bitter; Tetley Bitter; guest beers H
Large, U-shaped bar, always busy, but particularly popular early eve with homeward-bound workers.
🍺 ✿ ◖ ⇌ (Junction) P 🍴

Old White Horse
South Road (A451/B4186 jct)
☎ (01384) 394258
12–3, 5–11
Courage Directors; Marston's Pedigree; Ruddles Best Bitter H
Large pub on a busy junction: one large lounge with many

drinking areas, all served from a large bar. Food in the bar or Harvester restaurant. The beer range may vary. Wheelchair WC. ✿ ◖ ▶ ढ़ ♣ P

Royal Exchange
75 Enville Street
☎ (01384) 396726
12–11
Batham Mild, Best Bitter H
Terrace-fronted pub on a busy road: a basic, lively bar and a small, quiet lounge.
Q ✿ ⟁ ♣

Seven Stars
Brook Road, Oldswinford
☎ (01384) 394483
11–11
Batham Best Bitter; S&N Theakston Best Bitter, XB, Old Peculier; guest beers H
Large, busy roadhouse, full of character. Note the ornate tiling and the magnificent carved wood back-bar fitting. Separate restaurant area.
✿ ◖ ▶ ⇌ (Junction) P

Shrubbery Cottage
28 Heath Lane, Oldswinford
☎ (01384) 377598
12–2.30, 6–11
Holden's Mild, Bitter, Special; guest beers H
Busy drinking house, well-known for its charity fund-raising. Popular with students.
✿ ◖ ⇌ (Junction) P

Unicorn
145 Bridgnorth Road, Wollaston ☎ (01384) 394823
11–3, 6–11; 11–11 Fri & Sat
Batham Mild, Best Bitter H
Batham's ninth pub, a basic drinking house, popular with all ages, and unspoilt by progress. The original brewhouse still stands.
Q ✿ ⟁

Streetly

Farmer John's
Aldridge Road (½ mile off A4041) ☎ (0121) 352 1000
11–11; 11–3, 5.30–11 Sat
Banks's Mild, Bitter E; Camerons Strongarm; Marston's Pedigree H
Large, modern, one-roomed, food-oriented pub with a Victorian theme. Alcoves and partitions create intimate areas. No food Sun eve.
Q ✿ ◖ ▶ ढ़ ♣ ✕ 🍴

Sutton Coldfield

Blake Barn
Blake Street, Four Oaks (by station) ☎ (0121) 308 8421
11–3, 5–11; 11–11 Sat
Banks's Mild, Bitter E; Camerons Strongarm; Marston's Pedigree H
Large, modern estate pub with

typical Banks's rustic decor. Food is a speciality. ✿ ◖ ▶ ढ़
⇌ (Blake St) ♣ P 🍴

Duke
Duke Street ☎ (0121) 355 1767
11.30–3, 5.30–11
Ansells Mild, Bitter; Ind Coope Burton Ale; Tetley Bitter H
Excellent, traditional side-street pub near the town centre, with two rooms and a fine mahogany back bar.
Q ✿ ⟁ ♣ P

Laurel Wines
63 Westwood Road (off A452)
☎ (0121) 353 0399
12–2, 5.30–10.30 (11 Fri & Sat)
Batham Best Bitter; Burton Bridge Festival; Marston's Pedigree; Wadworth 6X; guest beers G
Friendly off-licence with a good choice of real ales. ▱

Upper Gornal

Britannia (Sally's)
109 Kent Street (A459)
☎ (01902) 883253
7.30–11; 7.30–10.30 Sun
Britannia Sally Perry Mild, Wally Williams Bitter; Courage Directors; Morland Old Speckled Hen; Ruddles County; Wye Valley Brew 69; guest beers H
Brew pub built in 1780 which boasts an untouched, late 19th-century tap room where beer is served from handpumps against the wall. The original brewhouse is intact and brewing again.
🍺 Q ✿ ढ़ ♣ P

Wall Heath

Wall Heath Tavern
14 High Street (A449)
☎ (01384) 287319
11–3, 6–11
Ansells Mild; HP&D Entire; Tetley Bitter H
Busy pub on the edge of the village centre. Both the bar and the lounge have a relaxed, friendly atmosphere. Excellent reputation for food.
✿ ◖ ▶ ढ़ ♣ P

Walsall

Hamemaker's Arms
87 Blue Lane West (A454)
☎ (01922) 28083
11.30–3, 6–11; 11–11 Sat
Banks's Mild, Bitter E; Camerons Strongarm H
Pleasantly modernised 1930s pub with a well-laid-out bar and bright, comfortable lounge. The name refers to the brass collar hames worn by carthorses, a bygone local industry. No eve meals Sun.
Q ✿ ◖ ▶ ⟁ ⇌ ♣ P 🍴

Katz
23 Lower Rushall Street
☎ (01922) 725848
12–2.30, 5–11; closed Sun
HP&D Entire; Ind Coope Burton Ale; M&B Highgate Dark; Marston's Pedigree; Tetley Bitter; guest beers Ⓗ
Two-roomed pub, previously called the Victoria.
♨ ❀ ◖ ⇌

King Arthur
Liskeard Road, Park Hall
(2 miles from centre, off A34)
☎ (01922) 31400
12–3, 5.30–11; 12–11 Sat; 12–3, 7.30–10.30 Sun
Courage Best Bitter, Directors; Marston's Pedigree; Ruddles Best Bitter, County; John Smith's Bitter; guest beer Ⓗ
1960s pub, not to everyone's taste, but the food and beer make this difficult to find pub worth a visit. No food Sun eve. Children welcome.
❀ ◖ ◗ ♿ P ⊟

New Fullbrook
West Bromwich Road
☎ (01922) 21761
11.30–11; 11–11 Sat
Banks's Mild; Bass Worthington BB; M&B Highgate Dark, Brew XI Ⓔ
1930s roadhouse with a large bar, a games room and a small, pleasant lounge.
♘ ◖ ⇌ (Bescot Stadium)
♣ P ⊟

Oak Inn
336 Green Lane (A34)
☎ (01922) 645758
12–2.30 (11.30–3 Sat), 7–11; 7–10.30 Sun, closed Sun lunch
Brakspear Bitter; S&N Theakston Mild; guest beers Ⓗ
Popular pub close to the town centre. It has an island bar and a collection of china mugs. No food Sun, or Tue and Sat eves.
♨ ❀ ◖ ◗ ⇌ ♣ P ⊟

Royal Oak
81 Lord Street, Palfrey
☎ (01922) 645913
12–3, 7–11
Banks's Mild; M&B Highgate Dark, Brew XI Ⓔ
Deceptively large, multi-roomed pub which retains its off-licence counter. Children allowed in the homely smoke room. The large lounge has a leaded skylight. No food Sun.
Q ♘ ❀ ◖ ◗ ⊞ ♣

Tap & Spile
5 John Street ☎ (01922) 27660
12.30–3, 5.30–11; 12–11 Thu–Sat
Tetley Mild, Bitter; guest beers Ⓗ
Formerly known as the Pretty Bricks, a welcoming, two-bar pub near the town centre. Walsall CAMRA *Pub of the Year* 1994. No food Sun, or Mon eve. ♨ ◖ ◗ ⊞ ⇌ ♣ P

Wednesbury

Old Blue Ball
19 Hall End (off A462)
☎ (0121) 556 0197
12–3, 5–11; 11.15–4.30, 7–11 Sat
Bass Worthington BB; M&B Highgate Dark; Stones Best Bitter Ⓔ**; guest beers** Ⓗ
Old, back-street local with a tiny, genuinely cosy bar, a smoke room and a larger lounge. Q ♘ ❀ ⊞ ♣ ⊟

Wednesfield

Broadway
Lichfield Road (A4124)
☎ (01922) 405872
12–3, 5 (6 Sat)–11
Ind Coope Burton Ale; Tetley Bitter; guest beer Ⓗ
Pleasant, multi-roomed pub with wood panelling in the lounge; the back lounge features ornate plaster coving and stained-glass partitions. Tapster's Choice guest beer. Eve meals Thu–Sat until 8; no food Sun. ❀ ◖ ◗ ⊞ ♿ ♣ P

Dog & Partridge
High Street ☎ (01902) 723490
11–11
Banks's Mild, Bitter Ⓔ**; Camerons Strongarm** Ⓗ
The oldest house in Wednesfield (pre-1840) with a well in the back room, oak beams, and wattle and daub construction on view. A Grade II-listed building.
♨ ♘ ❀ ◖ ♣ P ⊟

Pyle Cock
Rookery Street (A4124)
☎ (01902) 732125
10.30–11
Banks's Mild, Bitter Ⓔ
Excellent local with lovely etched windows depicting a pyle cock. Q ♘ ❀ ⊞ ♿ ♣ P

Vine
Lichfield Road
☎ (01902) 733529
11–3, 6–11
Whitbread Boddingtons Bitter; John Smith's Bitter Ⓗ**; guest beers** Ⓗ
Revitalised, friendly, multi-roomed pub. Wide range of guest beers, one usually a mild. Good value Sun lunch.
♨ ♘ ❀ ◖ ◗ ⊞ ♣ ⌓ P

West Bromwich

Churchfield Tavern
18 Little Lane (next to Sandwell General Hospital)
☎ (0121) 588 5468
11–11
Banks's Hanson's Mild, Mild, Bitter Ⓔ
Popular, three-roomed local with a children's play area in the garden. ♘ ❀ ◖ ◗ ⊞ ♣

Wheatsheaf
379 High Street
☎ (0121) 553 4221
11–11; 12–2.30, 7–10.30 Sun
Holden's Mild, Bitter, Special, XL Ⓗ
Boisterous, two-roomed terraced pub serving top-notch food lunchtimes and Sat eve (no food Sun).
❀ ◖ ⊞ ♣ ⌓ ⊟

Whiteheath

Whiteheath Tavern
400 Birchfield Lane (A4034, near M5 jct 2)
☎ (0121) 552 3603
12–3 (may vary), 8–11
Ansells Mild, Bitter; Banks's Mild Ⓗ
Friendly local with a comfortable lounge. The bar is popular with darts and card players. ⊞ ♣

Willenhall

Brewer's Droop
44 Wolverhampton Street (behind Lock Museum)
☎ (01902) 607827
12–3, 6–11
Batham Best Bitter; Enville Ale; Hook Norton Old Hooky; S&N Theakston Old Peculier; guest beers Ⓗ
An unusual array of artefacts enhances the appeal of this popular former coaching house. No food Sun; eve meals Fri and Sat only. ◖ ◗ ♿ ♣

Falcon Inn
77 Gomer Street West
☎ (01902) 633378
12–11
Banks's Mild; Greene King Abbot; Samuel Smith OBB; Marston's Pedigree; guest beers Ⓗ
Sports-oriented pub with five changing guest beers; over 400 guests have been featured.
Q ❀ ⊞ ♣ ⊟

Robin Hood
54 The Crescent
☎ (01902) 608006
12–3 (3.30 Fri & Sat), 7 (5.30 Fri)–11; 12–2.30, 7–10.30 Sun
Ansells Mild; Ind Coope Burton Ale; Tetley Bitter; guest beer Ⓗ
Refurbished, but retaining its character; a friendly, extremely welcoming pub. The licensee is a Burton *Cellarman*. ❀ ♣ P

Wolverhampton

Brewery Tap
Dudley Road (½mile from ring road) ☎ (01902) 351417

West Midlands

12–11
HP&D Mild, Entire; Tetley Bitter H
One-bar, multi-alcoved pub where the HP&D brewery is visible from a viewing area: a stylised 1980s Victorian pub in Black Country decor. HP&D seasonal beers sold. No food Sun. ⏴ ◖ P

Clarendon
38 Chapel Ash (A41)
☎ (01902) 20587
11–11
Banks's Mild, Bitter E; **Camerons Strongarm** H
Banks's brewery tap. Recently 'Spoiled by Progress' with the loss of its public and corridor bars. Weekday lunches. Banks's seasonal beers sold.
◖ P ⊟

Combermere Arms
Chapel Ash (A41)
☎ (01902) 21880
11–2.30, 5.30–11
Bass Worthington BB, Draught Bass; M&B Highgate Dark; guest beer H
Cunningly disguised as a terraced house: a small lounge, a smoke room, a games room, verandah and a corridor, all served by one bar.
⏴ ⊛ ◖ ⅋ ♣

Feathers
Molineux Street
☎ (01902) 26924
12–3, 5–11 Fri; 11–11 Sat
Banks's Mild, Bitter E
Small, friendly local, handy for the university and football ground, with an award-winning garden. It closes Sat afternoons when Wolves are at home. Weekday lunches.
⊛ ◖ ⊕ ⇌ ♣

Great Western
Sun Street (off A4124, near railway bridge)
☎ (01902) 351090
11–11; 11–2.30, 5–11 Sat; 12–2.30, 7–10.30 Sun
Batham Best Bitter; Holden's Mild, Bitter, Special H
Revitalised pub with a new lounge, next to the old low level station and featuring rail memorabilia. Excellent value Black Country food. CAMRA national *Pub of the Year* 1991.
⏴ ⊛ ◖ ♣ P

Homestead
Lodge Road (off A449)
☎ (01902) 787357
11–2.30 (3 Sat), 6–11
Ansells Mild, Bitter; HP&D Entire; Marston's Pedigree; guest beer H

Large, pleasant suburban pub with an excellent children's playground, a plush lounge and a basic bar. 'Tapster's Choice' guest beer.
⊛ ⏪ ◖ ◗ ⊕ ♣ P

Horse & Jockey
Robert Wynd
☎ (01902) 884552
12–3, 7–11
Banks's Mild, Bitter E; **Draught Bass; Marston's Pedigree; Tetley Bitter; guest beer** H
Victorian-style, renovated local. No food Sun.
⏴ ◖ ⊕ ♣ P

Lewisham Arms
69 Prosser Street (off A460)
☎ (01902) 53505
11.30–3, 6–11; 11–11 Sat
Banks's Mild, Bitter E
Glorious Victorian alehouse with etched windows and iron balconies. The large, unspoilt bar caters for all. Small smoke room. ⊕ ♣

Mitre
5 Lower Green (off A41)
☎ (01902) 753487
12–2.30, 6–11; 12–11 Sat
Banks's Mild; Bass Worthington BB, Draught Bass; Stones Best Bitter; guest beer H
Pleasant, popular old pub in a conservation area by the village green. Varied rooms.
Q ⊛ ◖ ⊕ ♣

Newhampton Inn
Riches Street (off A41)
☎ (01902) 745773
11–11
Courage Best Bitter, Directors; Marston's Pedigree; Ruddles County; John Smith's Bitter; guest beer H
Busy corner local, attracting a diverse crowd to its four different rooms and large garden (bowling green). The guest beer and cider change daily. ⏴ Q ⊛ ◖ ⊕ ♣ ⌣

Old Stag's Head
Pennwood Lane
☎ (01902) 341023
11.30–2.30, 6–11; 11.30–11 Sat
Banks's Mild, Bitter E
Village local on the edge of Penn Common, a surprisingly large olde-worlde pub.
⊛ ◖ ◗ ⊕ P

Queen's Arms
13 Graisley Row (off A449, Penn Road) ☎ (01902) 26589
11–3, 5.30–11

Burtonwood Mild, Bitter, Forshaw's, Top Hat H
Small, friendly, one-roomed pub in an industrial estate. No food Sun. ⊛ ◖ ◗ ♣ P

Stamford Arms
Lime Street
☎ (01902) 24172
12–3, 6–11; 12–11 Sat
Banks's Mild, Bitter E
Many-roomed Victorian pub with an award-winning garden and notable exterior tiling. A hidden gem.
Q ⧖ ⊛ ⊕ ♣

Swan
Bridgnorth Road
☎ (01902) 754736
11–3, 5–11; 11–11 Sat
Banks's Mild, Bitter E; **Camerons Strongarm** H
Mostly original Victorian pub with a lounge, a bar and a snug, on a busy corner.
⏴ Q ⊛ ⊕ ♣ P ⊟

Woodsetton

Park Inn
George Street (off A457)
☎ (01902) 882843
11–11
Holden's Mild, Bitter, Lucy B, Special, Stout, XL H
Boisterous brewery tap, frequented by all ages. All weather barbecues Fri–Sun in the conservatory.
⏴ ⧖ ⊛ ◖ ◗ ♣ ♣ P

Woodside

Railway
39 Buxton Road (off A4036)
☎ (01384) 573483
11–11; 12–4.30, 7–11 Sat
Banks's Hanson's Mild, Bitter E
Cosy, late-Victorian, one-roomed local; handy for Merry Hill centre.
⊛ ♣ P ⊟

Wordsley

Samson & Lion
140 Brierley Hill Road (B4180)
☎ (01384) 77796
11 (12 winter)–11
Banks's Mild; Marston's Pedigree; guest beers H
Sympathetically restored hostelry next to Stourbridge Canal Lock 4. Facilities for boaters; two skittle alleys. The garden houses a pigsty and an aviary. No meals Sun eve. Marston's Head Brewer's Choice stocked.
⏴ ⧖ ⊛ ⏪ ◖ ♣ ♣ P

Do you care about your pub and your pint?
Join CAMRA and help us protect your pleasure.

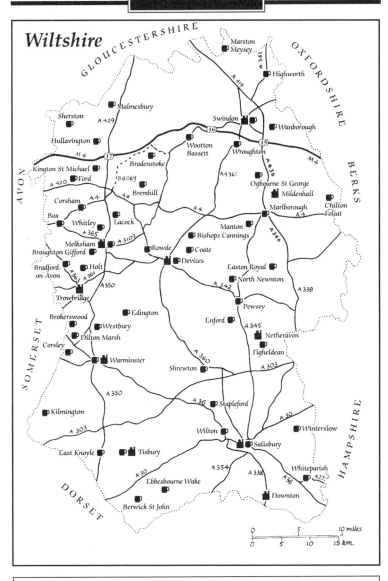

Wiltshire

Archers, Arkell's, Swindon; Bunces, Netheravon; Foxley, Mildenhall; Gibbs Mew, Salisbury; Hop Back, Downton; Mole's, Melksham; Tisbury, Tisbury; Ushers, Trowbridge; Wadworth, Devizes

Berwick St John

Talbot Inn
The Cross ☎ (01747) 828222
11.30–2.30, 7–11; 12–3 Sun, closed Sun eve
Adnams Bitter, Broadside Draught Bass; Wadworth 6X Ⓗ**, Old Timer** Ⓖ
Unspoilt, beamed 400-year-old

building, originally cottages situated down winding lanes. Home-cooked food (not served Sun lunch). 🏰 Q ❀ ◁ ▶ ♠ P

Bishops Cannings

Crown
Chandlers Lane
☎ (01380) 860218
11–3, 7–11

Wadworth 6X, IPA Ⓗ
Handsome pub in an attractive village.
🏰 Q ❀ ◁ ▶ ⊟ ♠ ♣ P

Box

Quarryman's Arms
Box Hill (300 yds S of A4)
OS834693 ☎ (01225) 743569

Wiltshire

11–3, 7–11; 11–11 Thu–Sat
Butcombe Bitter; Wadworth 6X; Wickwar Brand Oak Ⓗ; **guest beer** Ⓖ
Open-plan pub with superb views; hidden in a maze of lanes, yet close to the A4. Phone for directions.
🏨 ☀ ◖ ▶ ♠ 🍴 ⌂ P

Bradenstoke

Cross Keys
Off B4069 ☎ (01249) 890279
12–3 (not Mon–Thu), 7–11
Archers Best Bitter; Dartmoor Best Bitter; Wadworth 6X Ⓗ
Traditional, 200-year-old local in a pretty village. A cosy, quiet lounge and a public bar.
🏨 ☀ ◖ ▶ 🍴 ♠ P

Bradford-on-Avon

Beehive
263 Trowbridge Road
☎ (01225) 863620
12–2.30 (3 summer), 7–11
Beer range varies Ⓗ/Ⓖ
Canalside pub with an excellent and ever-changing range of ales. Warm and friendly; a beer lover's dream. No food Sun eve.
Q ◖ ▶ ♠ ⌂ P

Dandy Lion
35 Market Street
☎ (01225) 863433
11–3, 6–11
Draught Bass; Wadworth 6X, Farmer's Glory (summer), **Old Timer; guest beer** Ⓗ
Comfortable, 18th-century pub with a deep red interior, furnished with antiques.
◖ ▶ ⇌

Bremhill

Dumb Post
Dumb Post Hill (off A4 W of Calne) OS975727
☎ (01249) 813192
12–2.30, 7–11
Archers Best Bitter; Wadworth IPA (summer), **6X** Ⓗ
Pub on a hill outside a village above the Marden Valley. Fine views. 🏨 Q ☀ ◖ ▶ 🍴 ♠ P

Brokerswood

Kicking Donkey
Follow signs to Woodland Park from A36/A350
OS833520☎ (01373) 823250
11.30–2.30, 6 (6.30 Sat)–11
Ash Vine Challenger; Hall & Woodhouse Tanglefoot; S&N Theakston Old Peculier; Wadworth 6X Ⓗ
17th-century country inn with exposed beams and brasses, divided into three drinking areas and a restaurant. The

garden seats 200. No eve meals Sun or Mon, Jan–Feb.
🐾 ☀ ◖ ▶ ♠ ⌂ P

Broughton Gifford

Bell on the Common
The Common
☎ (01225) 782309
11–3, 6.30–11; 11–11 Sat
Wadworth IPA, 6X Old Timer Ⓗ
Handsome old pub by the village common. The large garden is excellent for families.
🏨 ☀ ◖ ▶ 🍺 ♠ P

Chilton Foliat

Wheatsheaf
☎ (01488) 682391
11–2.30 (3 Fri & Sat), 6–11
Everards Tiger; Morland Bitter, Old Masters, Tanner's Jack, Old Speckled Hen; guest beer Ⓗ
Pretty thatched pub and restaurant with stained-glass windows depicting native wild birds. Near Littlecote House. Cider in summer.
🏨 Q ☀ ◖ ▶ 🍺 ♠ ⌂ P

Coate

New Inn
☎ (01380) 860644
11–3, 5.30–11
Wadworth IPA, 6X Ⓖ
A *Guide* regular; the focus of village life. Casks are on stillage behind the bar. Ring to check lunchtime opening.
🏨 Q ☀ 🍺 ♠ P

Corsham

Two Pigs
38 Pickwick ☎ (01249) 712515
7–11
Bunces Pigswill; guest beers Ⓗ
Lively stone pub on the old London–Bath road. It stocks an ever-changing range of at least three guest beers and caters for over-21s only. Twice local CAMRA *Pub of the Year*. Closed lunchtime, except Sun.
☀ ⌂

Corsley

Cross Keys
Lye's Green (½mile N of A362 at Royal Oak)
☎ (01373) 832406
12–3 (not Mon–Tue or Thu–Fri), 6.30 (7 Sat & Mon)–11
Draught Bass; Butcombe Bitter; Mole's Best Bitter; guest beer (occasional) Ⓗ
Welcoming free house of character; a popular, spacious pub with a splendid fireplace.
🏨 ☀ ◖ ▶ ♠ ⌂ P

Devizes

Bell by the Green
Estcourt Street
☎ (01380) 723746
11–2, 6–11
Wadworth IPA, 6X; guest beers Ⓗ
Pub situated opposite the Crammer Pond. The family garden has swings and pets.
☀ 🍺 ◖ ▶ ♠ P

British Lion
9 Estcourt Street
☎ (01380) 720665
11–11
Beer range varies Ⓗ
Basic pub serving a wide range of ales, many not normally found locally. Lion's Pride house beer is brewed by Coach House. ☀ ⌂ 🍺

Hare & Hounds
Hare & Hounds Street
☎ (01380) 723231
11–3, 7–11
Wadworth IPA, 6X, Farmer's Glory Ⓗ
This perennial *Guide* entry continues to serve fine ale in relaxed surroundings. No food Sun. 🏨 Q ☀ ◖ ♠ ♣ P

Lamb
20 St John's Street
☎ (01380) 725426
11–3, 7–11
Wadworth IPA, 6X Ⓗ
A welcome first appearance for this unspoilt, but basic, town pub with many small rooms around the bar area. ♠

Dilton Marsh

Prince of Wales
94 High Street (B3099)
☎ (01373) 865487
11–2.30 (3 Sat), 6.30–11
Draught Bass; Wadworth 6X; guest beer Ⓗ
Simple, well-run, open-plan local. No food Sun. ◖ ♠ P

East Knoyle

Fox & Hounds
The Green (⅛mile S of A303 at Willoughby Hedge, signed)
OS807932 ☎ (01747) 830573
11–2.30 (3 Sat), 6–11
Marston's Pedigree; Smiles Bitter; Wadworth 6X: guest beers Ⓗ
Remote, 14th-century, thatched hillside inn with panoramic views: three cosy bars, a children's room and a skittle alley. Good food.
🏨 Q 🍺 ☀ ◖ ▶ 🍺 ♠ ♣ P

Easton Royal

Bruce Arms
On B3087 ☎ (01672) 810216

318

Wiltshire

11–2.30, 6–11
Wadworth 6X; Whitbread Strong Country Ⓗ
Classic village pub, now reopened. Despite refurbishment, it retains its basic character with brick floor, scrubbed tables and benches. ⚌ Q ⚘ 🅯 Ⓐ ♣ P

Ebbesbourne Wake

Horseshoe Inn
Off A30, via Fovant OS242993
☎ (01722) 780474
11.30–3, 6.30–11
Adnams Broadside; Ringwood Best Bitter; Wadworth 6X; guest beer Ⓖ
Remote, part-17th century inn nestling between old droves. Retaining an excellent village atmosphere, its bars are adorned with country artefacts.
⚌ Q ⛄ ⚘ 🅯 Ⓓ Ⓐ ♣ ⌂ P

Edington

Lamb
Westbury Road (B3098)
☎ (01380) 830263
11–2.30 (3 Sat), 5.30 (6 Sat)–11
Gibbs Mew Overlord, Salisbury Ⓗ
Attractive village pub with low-beamed ceilings, stone fireplaces, two bars and a dining room. No eve meals Tue. ⚌ ⚘ Ⓓ Ⓓ 🅑 ♣ P

Enford

Swan
Longstreet ☎ (01980) 670338
12–3, 7–11
Hop Back Special; guest beers Ⓗ
Cosy, unspoilt, thatched free house with an unusual gantry sign. Children welcome in the small bar. ⚌ ⚘ Ⓓ Ⓓ ♣ ⌂ P

Figheldean

Wheatsheaf
High Street ☎ (01980) 670357
12–3, 7–11
Draught Bass; Hop Back Special; guest beers Ⓗ
Single-bar pub with a large open fire and alcoves, plus a family room and a large garden. No meals Mon.
⚌ ⛄ ⚘ Ⓓ Ⓓ ♣ P

Ford

White Hart
Off A420 ☎ (01249) 782213
11–2.30, 5.30–11
Draught Bass; Hall & Woodhouse Tanglefoot; Marston's Pedigree; Smiles Best Bitter, Exhibition; Wadworth 6X; guest beers Ⓗ

Picturesque inn full of character, with up to ten ales. The cosy and welcoming bar can get busy at weekends, but the outside drinking area is ideal in summer. Award-winning restaurant.
Q ⛄ ⚘ 🅯 Ⓓ Ⓓ ⌂ P

Highworth

Wine Cellar
High Street ☎ (01793) 763828
12–4 (not Mon–Thu), 7–11
Archers Village, Best Bitter; guest beers Ⓖ
Friendly, popular bar housed in a stone-walled, low-ceilinged Georgian cellar. Noted for its range of wines and whiskies. Q ♣ ⌂

Holt

Old Ham Tree
Ham Green (B3107)
☎ (01225) 782581
11.15–3, 6.30–11
Marston's Pedigree; Wadworth 6X; guest beer Ⓗ
18th-century coaching inn of character with a comfortable lounge/restaurant and a simple, friendly locals' bar. Good variety of meals (generous portions).
Q ⚘ 🅯 Ⓓ 🅑 ♣ ⌂ P

Hullavington

Queen's Head
The Street ☎ (01666) 837221
12–2 (11.30–3 Sat), 7–11
Archers Village; Wadworth 6X; guest beers Ⓗ
Homely local with open fires and a skittle alley. No food Sun. Local CAMRA *Pub of the Year 1994.* ⚌ Q ⚘ 🅯 ♣ P

Kilmington

Red Lion
On B3092 ☎ (01985) 844263
11–3, 6.30–11
Butcombe Bitter; Marston's Pedigree; guest beer Ⓗ
Unspoilt NT-owned pub near Stourhead Gardens. The single bar has a curtained-off area. Good choice of hot and cold food; eve meals Fri–Sat.
⚌ Q ⚘ 🅯 Ⓓ Ⓓ ♣ ⌂ P

Kington St Michael

Jolly Huntsman
☎ (01249) 750305
11.30–3, 6.30–11 (11.30–11 summer)
Ind Coope Burton Ale; Mole's Tap; Wadworth 6X; Whitbread Boddingtons Bitter; guest beers Ⓗ
Popular village pub usually offering at least six ales.
⚘ 🅯 Ⓓ Ⓓ ⌂ P 🅱

Lacock

Rising Sun
32 Bowden Hill (1 mile E of Lacock) OS937680
☎ (01249) 704363
11.30–3, 6–11
Mole's Tap, Best Bitter, Landlord's Choice, Brew 97, XB; guest beers Ⓗ
Attractive, single-bar, 17th-century, stone inn, high above the Avon Valley. Spectacular views from the pretty garden. Appetising menu (no food Sun).
⚌ Q ⚘ Ⓓ Ⓓ Ⓐ ♣ ⌂ P

Malmesbury

Red Bull
Sherston Road (B4040, W of town) ☎ (01666) 822108
11–2.30 (3.30 Sat; not Tue), 6.30 (6 summer, 7 Tue)–11
Draught Bass; Whitbread WCPA, Boddingtons Bitter; guest beers Ⓗ
Popular pub. The skittle alley becomes a children's room at weekends.
⚌ ⛄ ⚘ Ⓓ Ⓓ P

Smoking Dog
62 High Street
☎ (01666) 825823
11.30–11
Archers Best Bitter Ⓖ**; Smiles Bitter; Wadworth 6X** Ⓗ**; guest beers** Ⓖ
Lively, friendly, town-centre, beer drinkers' pub. Home-made food (not served Sun eve). Families welcome. Cider in summer.
⚌ ⚘ Ⓓ Ⓓ Ⓐ ♣ ⌂

Whole Hog
Market Cross
☎ (01666) 825845
10–11
Archers Best Bitter; guest beers Ⓗ
Former restaurant, now a popular wine, ale and food house. Three guest beers. Table top games and newspapers provided. Ⓓ Ⓓ

Manton

Oddfellows Arms
High Street ☎ (01672) 512352
12–2.30, 6–11
Wadworth IPA, 6X; guest beer Ⓗ
Small, cosy village local with a secluded garden. Good food (not served Sun eve).
⚌ Q ⚘ Ⓓ Ⓓ ⌂ P

Marlborough

Lamb
The Parade
☎ (01672) 512668
11–11

319

Wiltshire

Wadworth IPA, 6X Ⓖ; guest beer Ⓗ
Popular pub with a cheerful atmosphere and regular live music. ❀ 🚗 ◑ ▶ ♣

Marston Meysey

Old Spotted Cow
Signed from A419
☎ (01285) 810264
11–3, 6–11; 12.30–3, 7–10 Sun
Draught Bass; Hook Norton Best Bitter; Smiles Bitter; Wadworth 6X; guest beer (occasional) Ⓗ
Cotswold stone farmhouse on the edge of an award-winning best-kept village. Two log fires; large gardens. Varied menu.
🚗 Q ❀ 🚗 ◑ ▶ ⅍ ▲ ♣ P ⚹

Melksham

Red Lion
3 The City ☎ (01225) 702960
11–3, 5 (6 Sat)–11; 11–11 Fri
Draught Bass; guest beers Ⓗ
13th-century, stone pub of character, once King John's hunting lodge, and the oldest pub in Wiltshire. A popular, friendly local. One guest ale changes every Fri and a mild is usually sold. Thirty malt whiskies. No food Sun.
Q ❀ ◑ ♣ P

North Newnton

Woodbridge Inn
On A345 ☎ (01980) 630266
11–11
Wadworth IPA, 6X, Farmer's Glory; guest beer Ⓗ
16th-century country inn on the Hampshire Avon, winner of awards for its food and wine. Informal and cosy.
❀ 🚗 ◑ ▶ ▲ ♣ P

Ogbourne St George

Old Crown
Marlborough Road (off A346)
☎ (01672) 841445
11.30–3, 6–11
Wadworth 6X; guest beer Ⓗ
Pub with a single, cosy, carpeted bar. The restaurant features a well. Cider in summer. 🚗 ◑ ▶ ♣ ⌂ P

Pewsey

Cooper's Arms
Ball Road (lane off B3087)
☎ (01672) 562495
12–2, 7–11
Gale's HSB; Ruddles Best Bitter; Wadworth 6X; guest beer Ⓗ
Thatched pub of great character with a low-ceilinged

bar, festooned with farming artefacts. Folk/rock bands Fri.
🚗 🐾 ⅍ ❀ ⊟ ▲ ⇌ ♣ P

Rowde

George & Dragon
High Street ☎ (01380) 723053
12–3, 7–11
Wadworth IPA, 6X Ⓗ
Popular for its top quality food, this pub retains many features of a country inn.
🚗 Q ◑ ▶ ♣ P

Salisbury

Avon Brewery Inn
75 Castle Street (200 yds N of Market Sq) ☎ (01722) 327280
11–11
Eldridge Pope Dorchester, Hardy Country, Royal Oak Ⓗ
Busy Victorian pub near the city centre. The garden boasts a riverside terrace and petanque. Excellent value traditional lunches. ❀ ◑ ▲ ♣

Deacon's Alms
118 Fisherton Street
☎ (01722) 336409
11–3, 6–11
Hop Back GFB, Summer Lightning; Ringwood Old Thumper; Wadworth 6X; Whitbread Boddingtons Bitter Ⓗ
Busy town pub with a small public bar leading to a large drinking area at the rear. Good range of food. 🚗 ◑ ▶ ▲ ⇌

Royal George
17 Bedwin Street
☎ (01722) 327782
11–3 (4 Sat), 6–11
Gibbs Mew Wiltshire, Salisbury, Wake Ale, Deacon, Bishop's Tipple Ⓗ
Comfortable, Grade II-listed pub, off the market place. Low-beamed, with one original beam from the *Royal George*, sister ship of the *Victory*. Trad. jazz alternate Sun. Home-cooked specials.
🐾 ❀ 🚗 ◑ ▲ ♣ P

Village
33 Wilton Road (A36)
☎ (01722) 329707
11–11
Hampshire King Alfred's; Oakhill Best Bitter; Taylor Landlord Ⓗ; guest beers Ⓖ
Neat, friendly, cosy pub, popular with rail buffs. Unusual guest beers from micro breweries are chosen by customers. ▲ ⇌ ♣

Wyndham Arms
27 Estcourt Road (College St jct) ☎ (01722) 328594
4.30 (3 Fri, 12 Sat)–11
Hop Back Mild (winter), GFB,

Special, Wilt (summer), Summer Lightning, Wheat Beer (summer) Ⓗ
Busy pub, ten mins' walk from the city centre. The original home of Hop Back brewery.
Q ▲ ♣

Sherston

Rattlebone Inn
Church Street (B4042)
☎ (01666) 840871
12–3, 6–11
Draught Bass; Smiles Best Bitter; Wadworth 6X; guest beers Ⓗ
Old, friendly pub named after a local hero. Rattlebone SPA is brewed by Archers. Skittles, an unusual six-sided pool table, and boules feature.
🚗 Q ❀ ◑ ▶ ⊟ ⅍ ♣ P

Shrewton

George Inn
London Road (B3806)
☎ (01980) 620341
11–3, 6–11; 11–11 Sat
Ringwood Best Bitter; Ushers Best Bitter; Wadworth 6X; guest beers Ⓗ
17th-century chalk, flint and stone inn, which once housed a brewery. A pitcher of any beer is sold at one standard price. Good value food.
🚗 Q 🐾 ❀ 🚗 ◑ ▶ ♣ P

Stapleford

Pelican
Warminster Road (A36)
☎ (01722) 790241
11–2.30 (3 Sat), 6–11; 12–2.30, 7–10.30 Sun
Otter Bitter; Ringwood Best Bitter, Fortyniner; guest beer Ⓗ
Welcoming, 18th-century coaching inn. Good value food; the restaurant was once a stables and mortuary. The large garden adjoins the River Till. Four-pint pitchers of beer sold. 🚗 Q ❀ ◑ ▶ ♣ P

Swindon

Clifton Inn
Clifton Street
☎ (01793) 523162
11–2.30, 6–11
Arkell's 2B, 3B, Kingsdown Ⓗ
Hard to find, true local serving a quiet area in the old town. Friendly landlord (and ghost). Arkell's seasonal ales. ❀ ◑ P

Glue Pot
Emlyn Square
☎ (01793) 523935
11–11
Archers Village, Best Bitter, Black Jack, Golden, Old Cobleigh's; guest beer Ⓗ

The Archers brewery tap, in Brunel's railway village. A one-room pub, with large tables and high-backed booths. Weekday lunches. ❀ ◖ ⇌ ♣

King's Arms Hotel
Wood Street ☎ (01793) 522156
11–3, 6–11
Arkell's 2B, 3B, Kingsdown [H]
Victorian hotel in the old town area; a large open bar with a quiet area. Arkell's seasonal brews stocked. 🛏 ◖ ◗ ♿ P

Kingsdown
Kingsdown Road, Kingsdown
☎ (01793) 824802
11–2.30, 6–11
Arkell's 2B, 3B, Kingsdown [H]
Arkell's brewery tap, run by a friendly landlord. No food Sun eve. Arkell's seasonal brews stocked. ❀ ◖ ◗ ⊞ ♣ P

Rising Sun
6 Albert Street
☎ (01793) 529916
11–11
Courage Best Bitter; Ushers Best Bitter, Founders [H]
Busy, back-street boozer in the old town. A winner of local CAMRA awards. Ushers seasonal ales stocked.
◖ ◗ ⊞ ♣ ⌓

Steam Railway
14 Newport Street
☎ (01793) 538048
11–11
Draught Bass; Greenalls Original; Marston's Pedigree; Wadworth 6X; Whitbread Boddingtons Bitter, Flowers Original; guest beers [H]
Large, popular pub with a lively main bar. The Ale Bar has more tradition and is quieter. Wheelchair WC.
♨ ❀ ◖ ⊞ ♿ P

Wheatsheaf
32 Newport Street
☎ (01793) 523188
11–2.30, 5.30–11
Adnams Bitter; Wadworth IPA, 6X, Farmer's Glory; guest beer [H]
Refurbished pub with an extended lounge bar; lively at weekends. Eve meals Sun–Thu, till 7.30. ❀ 🛏 ◖ ⊞

Tisbury

Crown Inn
Church Street
☎ (01747) 870221
11–2.30, 7–11
Gibbs Mew Wiltshire, Salisbury, Wake Ale, Deacon (summer) [H]
Friendly, old coaching inn offering good wholesome food (special price lunch for pensioners), a skittle alley and a family room. Wheelchair WC. ♨ ⛀ ❀ ◖ ◗ ♿ ▲ ⇌ ♣ ⌓ P

Wanborough

Black Horse
Callas Hill ☎ (01793) 790305
11–3, 5.30–11; 11–11 Sat
Arkell's 2B, 3B [H]
Homely, genuine village pub: past CAMRA regional *Pub of the Year*. No food Sun. Arkell's seasonal brews. ❀ ◖ ⊞ ▲ P

Plough
High Street ☎ (01793) 790523
12–2.30, 5–11; 11–11 Fri & Sat
Archers Village; Draught Bass; Morland Old Speckled Hen; Wadworth 6X; Whitbread Boddingtons Bitter; guest beer [H]
Ancient, thatched pub with a long, beamed, stone-walled bar. No meals Sat lunch or Sun. ♨ Q ❀ ◖ ◗ ⊞ ♣ P

Warminster

Yew Tree
174 Boreham Road
☎ (01985) 212335
12–2 (11–4 Sat), 6–11
Ringwood Best Bitter, Fortyniner; guest beer [H]
On the outskirts of town, this 18th-century former coaching inn caters mainly for a local trade. ❀ 🛏 ◖ ◗ ♣ P

Westbury

Crown Inn
Market Place ☎ (01373) 822828
11–2.30, 5.30 (6 Sat)–11
Wadworth 6X; guest beer [H]
Welcoming, well-appointed local with a new function room and skittle alley. No food Sun; eve meals Fri and Sat. ❀ ◖ ◗ ⊞ ♣ ⌓ P

Oak Inn
Warminster Road (A350)
☎ (01373) 823169
12–2.30 (not Mon–Wed), 5.30 (6 Sat)–11
Draught Bass; Fuller's London Pride; Ringwood Best Bitter, Fortyniner [H]
A mock-Tudor exterior conceals a 16th-century inn with more recent additions. The old brewery at the rear is now used as offices. Occasional beer festivals in the skittle alley. Eve meals Thu–Sat. ♨ ❀ ◖ ◗ ⊞ ♣ P

Whiteparish

Parish Lantern
Romsey Road
☎ (01794) 884392
11.30–3, 6.30–11
Ringwood Best Bitter; guest beers [H]
Welcoming, one-bar pub just out of the main village.
♨ ❀ ◖ ◗ ♣ P

Whitley

Pear Tree
Top Lane ☎ (01225) 709131
12–2.30, 7–11
Bunces Pigswill; Wadworth 6X; guest beer [H]
Delightful pub in an unspoilt village location. The half-acre garden has a children's play area, animals and barbecues in summer. Upstairs restaurant; skittle alley.
♨ Q ⛀ ❀ ◖ ◗ ♣ P

Wilton

Bear Inn
West Street ☎ (01722) 742398
11–2.30 (3 Sat), 5 (6 Sat)–11
Hall & Woodhouse Badger BB [H]
16th-century roadside inn, a welcoming one-bar pub. Snacks available. ♨ ❀ ♣

Bell
Shaftesbury Road
☎ (01722) 743121
11–2.30, 6–11; 11–11 Sat
Bass Worthington BB, Draught Bass; guest beer [H]
Built in 1610: a traditional pub with a bar and a lounge.
♨ Q ❀ 🛏 ◖ ⊞ P

Winterslow

Lion's Head
The Common
☎ (01980) 862234
12–2.30 (not Mon–Thu), 7–11; 12–2.30, 7–10.30 Sun
Fuller's London Pride; Ringwood Best Bitter; Wadworth 6X; Webster's Yorkshire Bitter; Whitbread Boddingtons Bitter [H]
Friendly, family-run village pub, popular with walkers. Good food at reasonable prices. Q ⛀ ❀ ◖ ◗ ♿ ♣ P

Wootton Bassett

Borough Arms
High Street ☎ (01793) 854833
11–2.30, 6–11; 11–11 Fri & Sat
Arkell's 2B, 3B [H]
Real local partly from the 17th century. ♨ ❀ 🛏 ⊞ ♣

Wroughton

Carter's Rest
High Street ☎ (01793) 812288
11.30–2.30, 5.30–11; 11–11 Sat
Archers Village, Best Bitter, Black Jack, Golden; Morland Old Speckled Hen; guest beers [H]
Archers tenancy serving all its beers, plus four guests. Lively public bar. Cider in summer.
♨ ❀ ◖ ⊞ ♣ ⌓ P

North Yorkshire

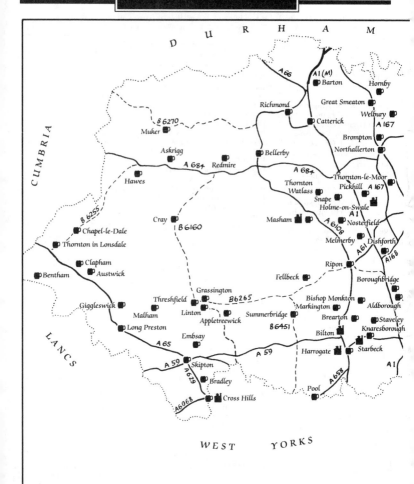

North Yorkshire

Black Sheep, Masham; **Wm. Clark**, Scarborough; **Cropton**, Cropton; **Daleside**, Starbeck; **Franklin's**, Bilton; **Hambleton**, Holme-on-Swale; **Lastingham**, Pickering; **Malton**, Malton; **Marston Moor**, Kirk Hammerton; **Old Bear**, Cross Hills; **Rooster's**, Harrogate; **Rudgate**, Tockwith; **Selby**, Selby; **Samuel Smith**, Tadcaster; **Whitby's**, Whitby

---

Acaster Malbis

Ship Inn
☎ (01904) 705609
11.30–3, 7–11
Taylor Landlord; Tetley Mild, Bitter Ⓗ
17th-century coaching inn on the banks of the River Ouse, popular with boaters and campers.
🛏 ✿ 🚪 ◑ ▶ ▲ ♣ P

Aldborough

Ship Inn
Low Road ☎ (01423) 322749
12–2.30 (3 Sat), 5.30–11
S&N Theakston Best Bitter; John Smith's Bitter; Tetley Bitter; guest beers Ⓗ
Excellent pub in an historic village. Comfortable and relaxing. No meals Sun eve.
Q ✿ 🚪 ◑ ▶ ♿ ♣ P ⊟

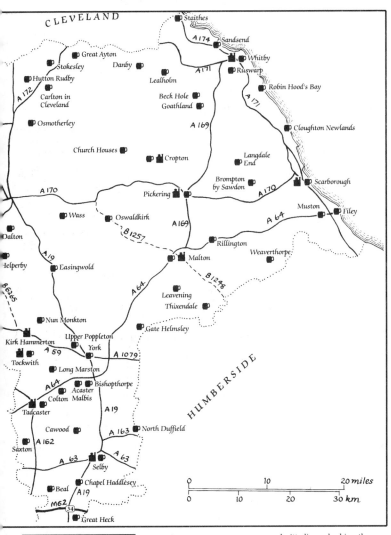

North Yorkshire map

C L E V E L A N D
Staithes
A174 Sandsend
Great Ayton
Stokesley Danby Whitby
Hutton Rudby Lealholm A171 Ruswarp
Carlton in Cleveland Robin Hood's Bay
Beck Hole
Osmotherley Goathland
A169 Cloughton Newlands
Church Houses
Cropton Langdale End
Brompton by Sawdon Scarborough
A170 Pickering A170
Wass Oswaldkirk A169 Muston Filey
B1257 Rillington
Dalton Weaverthorpe
Helperby Easingwold Malton
B1248
Leavening
Thixendale
Nun Monkton Gate Helmsley
Kirk Hammerton Upper Poppleton
York A1079
Tockwith
Long Marston HUMBERSIDE
Bishopthorpe
Acaster Malbis
Colton
Tadcaster A19
Cawood North Duffield
Saxton A162 A163
A63 Selby
Beal Chapel Haddlesey
M62 A19
Great Heck

0   10   20 miles
0   10   20   30 km

Appletreewick

New Inn
☎ (01756) 720252
12–3 (not Mon, except bank hols), 7–11
John Smith's Bitter; Younger No.3; guest beer Ⓗ
Friendly inn with spectacular views of river and moorland: one main, L-shaped room with a separate room across the hall. Large range of foreign beers, including draught Belgian ales. Close to the Dales Way.
♨ ⅍ ❀ ⛢ ◖ ♣ ⌂ P

Askrigg

King's Arms Hotel
☎ (01969) 650258
11–3 (5 Sat), 6.30–11
Dent Bitter, Ramsbottom; McEwan 80/-; Younger No.3 Ⓗ
16th-century racing stables converted to a coaching inn in the early 17th century. It will be recognised as the Drover's Arms from the TV series *All Creatures Great and Small*.
♨ ⅍ ❀ ⛢ ◖ ▶ ♣

Austwick

Game Cock
☎ (0152 42) 51226
11–3, 6.30–11
Thwaites Bitter Ⓗ
Pub with a plainly-furnished little bar, decorated with memorabilia, plus a restaurant and a verandah (children admitted) overlooking the attractive main street. No food Mon; other eves till 8.30.
♨ ❀ ⛢ ◖ ▶ ♣ P

Barton

King William IV
1 Silver Street
☎ (01325) 377256
12–2.30 (not Mon or Tue; 11.30–4 Sat), 6.30–11
John Smith's Bitter, Magnet Ⓗ
Recently extended roadside local with a number of separate spaces clustered around a single serving area. Excellent garden with play equipment. Thai meals a speciality.
♨ ❀ ◖ ▶ ♣ P

North Yorkshire

Beal

King's Head Inn
Main Street ☎ (01977) 673487
7–11; 12–4, 7–11 Sat
John Smith's Bitter; Tetley Bitter; guest beers Ⓗ
Known locally as Fred's, after the current landlord's father, this pub's outstanding feature is its time-warp bar. Virtually all the present day fittings and fixtures appear in a 1940s inventory. ⚶ ✿ ⊟ ♣ P

Beck Hole

Birch Hall Inn
☎ (01947) 896245
11–3, 7.30–11 (11–11 summer)
S&N Theakston Mild, Best Bitter, XB; guest beers Ⓗ
Tiny time-warp pub in a charming village. Cleveland CAMRA *Pub of the Year* 1994. Popular with walkers, the pub also contains a small shop and a tea room. Q ⟷ ✿ ⊟

Bellerby

Cross Keys
On A6108 ☎ (01969) 622256
11.30–2.30 (not Mon in winter), 7–11; 11–11 Fri & Sat
Marston's Pedigree; S&N Theakston Best Bitter; John Smith's Bitter; guest beer (summer) Ⓗ
Village local on the doorstep of Wensleydale and Swaledale. Home-made pies and soup are specialities.
⚶ Q ⟷ ✿ ⋈ ◁ ▷ ▲ ♣ P ⊟

Bentham

Punch Bowl
Low Bentham
☎ (0152 42) 61344
12–2 (not Mon), 6–11
Mitchell's Original Ⓗ
18th-century, old-time village inn, extended ten years ago but the small rooms remain. Restaurant open weekends.
⚶ ✿ ◁ P

Bishop Monkton

Lamb & Flag
Boroughbridge Road
☎ (01765) 677322
11.45–3, 5.30–11
S&N Theakston Best Bitter; Tetley Bitter; guest beers Ⓗ
Very attractive, two-roomed country inn in a pleasant village. ⚶ Q ⟷ ✿ ◁ ♣ P

Bishopthorpe

Ebor
Main Street ☎ (01904) 706190
11–11
Samuel Smith OBB, Museum Ⓗ

Modernised village pub in Sam Smith's 'brassy' style. Horses abound in the pub's decor, as do prize certificates from the *York in Bloom* competition.
Q ⟷ ✿ ◁ ▷ ⊟ ⚷ ▲ ♣ P ⊬

Boroughbridge

Black Bull Inn
6 St James' Square (Market Square) ☎ (01423) 322413
11–11
Black Sheep Best Bitter; Old Mill Bitter; John Smith's Bitter Ⓗ
Attractive, 13th-century inn, extended to the rear in recent years to accommodate a restaurant. It retains a traditional pub atmosphere, with a comfortable lounge and a cosy snug. Popular for quality meals. ⚶ Q ⋈ ◁ ▷

Three Horse Shoes
Bridge Street ☎ (01423) 322314
11–3, 5–11
S&N Theakston Best Bitter Ⓗ; **Vaux Samson** Ⓔ
Welcoming, unspoilt, 1930s hotel with wood panelling and stained-glass windows. The separate rooms have retained a friendly atmosphere. No meals Sun eve (other eves till 8.30). ⚶ Q ⟷ ✿ ◁ ▷ ⊟ P

Bradley

Slaters Arms
Crag Lane (back road to Farnhill) ☎ (01535) 632179
11–3, 6–11
Commercial Alesman; John Smith's Bitter Ⓗ
Pleasant village local dating from 1760, with a fine inglenook and a suntrap rear garden. Popular with boaters from the nearby Leeds & Liverpool Canal.
⚶ Q ◁ ▷ ⚷ ♣ P

Brearton

Malt Shovel
Off B6165 ☎ (01423) 862929
12–3, 6.45–11; closed Mon
Daleside Bitter; Old Mill Bitter; S&N Theakston Best Bitter; guest beers Ⓗ
Friendly, welcoming, 16th-century village pub; unspoilt, with exposed beams and stonework. Renowned for good, home-cooked food. No meals Sun eve.
⚶ Q ⟷ ✿ ◁ ▷ ♣ P

Brompton (Northallerton)

Three Horse Shoes
Station Road ☎ (01609) 773591
12–3, 6–11

Bass Worthington BB; Camerons Strongarm; S&N Theakston XB; guest beers Ⓗ
Pub with a small bar and a larger lounge. Live music upstairs at weekends.
⚶ ◁ ⊟ ♣ ⊟

Brompton by Sawdon

Cayley Arms
Main Street (A170)
☎ (01723) 859372
11.30–3.30 (not Mon), 4.30–11
S&N Theakston Best Bitter; Tetley Bitter; guest beer Ⓗ
Prominent pub offering excellent food and an extensive range of whiskies. It was named after aviation pioneer Sir George Cayley and aircraft memorabilia is featured. Children's play area.
⚶ Q ⟷ ✿ ◁ ▷ ⚷ ▲ P ⊬

Carlton in Cleveland

Blackwell Ox
☎ (01642) 712287
12–3, 6.30–11 (11–11 Sat in summer)
Bass Worthington BB, Draught Bass; guest beers Ⓗ
The only pub in the village: an old local with rooms off a central bar. Popular with walkers and campers. Thai cooking a speciality. A local CAMRA *Pub of the Season* 1994.
⚶ Q ⟷ ✿ ⋈ ◁ ▷ ▲ ♣ P

Catterick

Bay Horse Inn
Low Green ☎ (01748) 811383
12–3 (4 Sat; not Wed or Thu), 7–11
S&N Theakston XB; John Smith's Bitter; Tetley Bitter; guest beers Ⓗ
Comfortably furnished 100-year-old, traditional village pub overlooking the green, a stone's throw from the busy A1.
⚶ Q ⟷ ✿ ♣ P ⊟

Cawood

Ferry
King Street (upstream of swing bridge)
☎ (01757) 268515
12–4, 6.30–11 (12–11 Sat in summer)
Adnams Bitter, Broadside; Mansfield Riding Mild, Riding Bitter, Old Baily; guest beer Ⓗ
Quiet, historic village pub on the west bank of the River Ouse. It is connected with Cardinal Wolsey who lived in Cawood Castle. Low ceilings; friendly family atmosphere.
⚶ Q ⟷ ✿ ⋈ ◁ ▷ ▲ ♣ P

North Yorkshire

Chapel Haddlesey

Jug
Main Street ☎ (01757) 270307
12–3, 7–11; 11–11 Sat
Mansfield Bitter; guest beer H
250-year-old small village inn,
once also a blacksmith's shop,
on the north bank of the River
Aire. Welcoming atmosphere;
friendly ghost. Try the
Desperate Dan Cow Pie.
🏠 Q ❀ ◑ ▶ ⌷ ▲ ♣ P

Church Houses

Feversham Arms
OS669974 ☎ (01751) 433206
12–2.30, 7–11
Tetley Bitter H
Small inn in a remote hamlet
in Upper Farndale. Popular
with walkers, the bar has a
stone-flagged floor and a cast
iron range. Restaurant.
🏠 Q ⏣ ❀ 🛏 ◑ ▶ P

Chapel-le-Dale

Hill Inn
On B6255 ☎ (0152 42) 41256
12–3, 6.30–11; 11.30–11 Sat
**Dent Bitter; S&N Theakston
Best Bitter, XB; Old
Peculier** H
Well-known, isolated pub on
the Three Peaks Walk, with
bare floorboards and exposed
stonework: a cosy bar, a pool
room and a food bar (children
welcome). Music Sat night;
folk Sun lunch.
🏠 ❀ ◑ ▲ ♣ P

Clapham

New Inn
☎ (0152 42) 51203
11.30–3, 7–11; 11–11 Sat
**Courage Directors; Dent
Bitter; S&N Theakston Best
Bitter; Tetley Bitter; guest
beer** H
Large coaching inn dated 1776:
two lounge bars with oak
panelling (1990 vintage), and a
separate restaurant (no-
smoking; children welcome).
🏠 ❀ 🛏 ◑ ▶ ▲ ♣ P

Cloughton Newlands

Bryherstones
☎ (01723) 870744
12–3, 7–11
**S&N Theakston Best Bitter;
Younger Scotch, No.3; guest
beer** H
Busy country pub on three
levels offering a good choice of
whiskies, a children's play
area and an extensive menu.
🏠 Q ⏣ ❀ ◑ ▶ 🛏 ▲
♣ P ⅋

Colton

Sun Inn
☎ (01904) 744261
11.30–3, 7–11
**Draught Bass; John Smith's
Bitter; Stones Best Bitter;
guest beers** (summer) H
17th-century inn, the gem of a
lovely village. Ask about the
resident ghost. The landlady
signs for deaf visitors.
Q ❀ ◑ ▶ 🛏 ♣ P

Cray

White Lion Inn
On B6160
☎ (01756) 760262
11–2.30, 6–11 (11–11 summer)
**Moorhouse's Premier, Pendle
Witches Brew; Tetley Bitter;
guest beer** (occasional) H
Marvellous, traditional, cosy
Dales inn, nestling beneath
Buckden Pike. The beams and
stone flags are original. The
barn has been converted into
excellent accommodation.
Ring the Bull played; home-
cooked meals served.
🏠 Q ⏣ ❀ 🛏 ◑ ▶ ▲ ♣ P

Cropton

New Inn
☎ (01751) 417330
11.30–3, 6.30–11; 11–11 Sat
**Cropton King Billy, Two
Pints, Stout, Special; Tetley
Mild, Bitter** H
An ideal pub to get snowed in
at – a free house with its own
brewery at the top of a very
steep hill. Nearby camp sites
make it popular in summer.
Pleasant and relaxed.
🏠 Q ❀ 🛏 ◑ ▶ ⅊ ▲
♣ P ⅋ 日

Cross Hills

Old White Bear
6 Keighley Road
☎ (01535) 632115
11–11
**Old Bear Bitter, Barnsey;
Whitbread Boddingtons
Bitter, Castle Eden Ale** H
Built in 1735; a cosy, friendly,
multi-roomed pub serving
beers from the Old Bear
Brewery (on the premises).
Popular with all ages.
🏠 Q ⏣ ❀ ◑ ♣ P

Dalton

Jolly Farmers of Olden Times
☎ (01845) 577359
7.30–11; 12–3, 7.30–10.30 Sun; closed
most lunchtimes
**Courage Directors; John
Smith's Bitter; guest beers** H

200-year-old, modernised
village pub with some original
beams retained. Join in the
conversation at the bar.
Lunches served when open.
🏠 Q ❀ 🛏 ▶ ▲ ♣ P

Danby

Duke of Wellington
2 West Lane
☎ (01287) 660351
11–3, 7–11 (11–11 summer)
**Camerons Strongarm;
Marston's Pedigree; Ruddles
Best Bitter; John Smith's
Magnet** H
Village local; a coaching inn
from 1732. Walkers are
welcomed. 🏠 Q ⏣ ❀ 🛏
◑ ▶ ⅊ ▲ ⇌ ♣ ⌷ P ⅋ 日

Dishforth

Crown Inn
Main Street
☎ (01845) 577398
12–3, 6.30–11
Camerons Bitter; guest beer
(weekends) H
Friendly, welcoming village
pub. 🏠 ♣ P

Easingwold

Station
Knott Lane, Raskelf Road
11.30–3, 4.30–11; 11.30–11 Fri & Sat
**Hambleton Bitter; John
Smith's Bitter; Tetley Bitter;
guest beer** H
Historic, Victorian relic of
Britain's shortest standard
gauge railway. Brewery
planned. 🏠 Q ⏣ ❀ 🛏 ◑
▶ ⅊ ⅍ ▲ ♣ P

Embsay

Elm Tree Inn
5 Elm Tree Square
☎ (01756) 790717
11.30–3, 5.30–11
Bateman XB; guest beers H
Village pub popular for both
beer and food: a large, open-
plan beamed main bar, and a
small side room with pew-
type seats. Ever changing
guest beers. Q ❀ ◑ ▶ ♣ P ⅋

Fellbeck

Half Moon
On B6265
☎ (01423) 711560
12–3, 6.30–11
**S&N Theakston Best Bitter;
John Smith's Bitter; Taylor
Landlord; Younger Scotch** H
Good roadside pub close to
Brimham Rocks: a large, sunny
lounge and a small back bar.
Self-catering cottages to let.
🏠 Q ⏣ ❀ 🛏 ◑ ▶ ▲ ♣ P

325

North Yorkshire

Filey

Imperial
20 Hope Street
☎ (01723) 512185
12–11
**Morland Old Speckled Hen;
Whitbread Boddingtons
Bitter, Trophy; guest beers** H
Busy, two-roomed, town-centre pub. Meals till 6pm in summer.
Q ◑ & ▲ ≋ ♣ P ⊟

Gate Helmsley

Duke of York
Main Street ☎ (01759) 372429
11–11
Tetley Bitter H
Best Rural Pub and *Best Food Pub*, in last year's *Yorkshire Evening Press Pub of the Year* contest: a pub catering for both locals and townies eating out.
❀ ◑ ▶ P

Giggleswick

Black Horse
Church Street
☎ (01729) 822506
12–3 (may extend), 6.30–11
**Holt Bitter; S&N Theakston
Best Bitter; Taylor Best Bitter;
Tetley Bitter** H
17th-century, village-centre pub adjoining the church. Smart, stained-glass, mullioned windows and chamfered corners are features. The well-upholstered interior has much woodwork. One room, with an attractive open fireplace.
❀ ❀ ❤ ◑ ▶ ▲ ♣ P

Goathland

Goathland Hotel
☎ (01947) 896203
11–3, 7–11 (longer in summer)
**Camerons Bitter,
Strongarm** H
Old, stone pub, convenient for steam trains at Goathland station. It is also known as *Heartbeat's* Aidensfield Arms.
❀ ☎ ❀ ❤ ◑ ▶ ≋ ♣ P

Grassington

Black Horse Hotel
Garrs Lane ☎ (01756) 752770
11–11
**Black Sheep Best Bitter,
Special Strong; S&N
Theakston Old Peculier; John
Smith's Bitter; Tetley Mild,
Bitter** H
No-nonsense, friendly hotel in the village centre, popular with locals and visitors. Excellent food is served in the dining room; bar meals in the open lounge. ❀ ❀ ❤ ◑ ▶ ♣

Great Ayton

Buck
West Terrace ☎ (01642) 722242
11–11
**Whitbread Boddingtons
Bitter, Trophy, Flowers
Original; guest beers** H
Riverside coaching inn dating from the 1700s, enjoying a friendly atmosphere and strong local patronage. Good for bar meals.
Q ☺ ❀ ◑ ▶ ♣ P

Great Heck

Bay Horse Inn
Main Street ☎ (01977) 661125
12–3, 7–11; 11–11 Fri & Sat
**Tetley Bitter; Whitbread
Boddingtons Bitter; guest
beers** H
Cosy country inn (once three cottages) on the edge of the village, close to the marina on the Aire & Calder Canal. Good value snacks and meals.
◑ ▶ P

Great Smeaton

Bay Horse
On A167 ☎ (01609) 881466
12–3, 6.30–11
**John Smith's Bitter; Ruddles
County; guest beers** H
Small freehouse in the middle of a row of roadside cottages, with two linked rooms: a functional bar and a soft-furnished lounge.
❀ ❀ ◑ ▶ ❤ ♣

Harrogate

Coach & Horses
16 West Park
☎ (01423) 568371
11–11
**Black Sheep Best Bitter; John
Smith's Bitter; Tetley Bitter** H
Pub with a comfortable lounge bar overlooking West Park Stray. Amusing caricatures of locals adorn the walls. Separate dining room. ◑ ▶

Gardener's Arms
Bilton Lane ☎ (01423) 506051
12–3 (not Wed), 6 (7 Sat)–11
Samuel Smith OBB H
Attractive, single-bar stone pub in a rural setting, next to Franklin's Brewery and popular with walkers to Nidd Gorge. Three rooms – two with real fires. No meals winter eves.
❀ Q ❀ ◑ ▶ ▲ ♣ P

Hales Bar
1 Crescent Road
☎ (01423) 569861
11–11
**Bass Worthington BB,
Draught Bass; Stones Best
Bitter** H

Excellent, welcoming, town-centre pub: a front locals' bar and an atmospheric, gas-lit lounge at the rear. Gas cigar lighters, stuffed birds, old barrels and wood panelling all add to the atmosphere. Good, cheap food; no eve meals Sun.
◑ ▶ ❤ & ≋ ♣

Tap & Spile
Tower Street (400 yds from West Park Stray)
☎ (01423) 526785
11–11
Beer range varies H
Comfortable atmospheric alehouse with exposed brick and wood panelling: three inter-connecting rooms around a central bar. ❀ ♣ ◔ P

Hawes

Board Hotel
Market Place
☎ (01969) 667223
11–4.30, 6.30–11; 11–11 Sat
**Ruddles County; S&N
Theakston XB; Tetley Bitter;
Webster's Yorkshire Bitter;
guest beers** (occasional) H
Market pub with a mid-19th-century stone frontage and a recently modernised but unpretentious interior. Cider in summer.
❀ ❀ ❤ ◑ ▶ ▲ ♣ ◔

Helperby

Golden Lion
Main Street ☎ (01423) 360870
6 (12 Sat)–11
**Taylor Best Bitter; Tetley
Bitter; guest beers** H
The home of Helperby beer festivals continues to attract punters from far and wide with the best selection of guest beers for miles. ❀ ❀ ▶ ♣

Hornby

Grange Arms
☎ (01609) 881249
12–3, 7–11; closed Mon, except bank hols
**S&N Theakston XB, Old
Peculier; John Smith's
Magnet; guest beer** H
Pleasant, whitewashed and pantiled village pub with a snug bar and a dining room.
❀ Q ❀ ◑ ▶ ❤ ♣ P ⊟

Hutton Rudby

Station Hotel
49 Enterpen ☎ (01642) 700266
7–11; 12–3, 7–11 Sat
**S&N Theakston Best Bitter;
John Smith's Magnet** H
Traditional pub with a strong local patronage. Darts is popular. ❀ ❀ ♣

North Yorkshire

Knaresborough

Blind Jack's
19 Market Place
☎ (01423) 869148
11.30–3, 6–11; 11.30–11 Wed–Sat
Ind Coope Burton Ale; Tetley Bitter; guest beers Ⓗ
Pub created in 1991 in a Georgian listed building and named after a local hero: an atmospheric, small community alehouse, the CAMRA 1992 *Best New Pub* award-winner. No bar food Mon lunchtimes or Sun eve.
Q ◖ ▮ ⇌ ♣

Half Moon
Abbey Road
☎ (01423) 863022
5.30–11; 12–3, 7.30–11 Sat
Mansfield Riding Bitter, Old Baily Ⓗ
Small and friendly, one-roomed local overlooking the river (it hosts a Boxing Day Tug of War with the pub across the water). Worth the steep walk back up the hill to the town centre.
Å ♣

Marquis of Granby
On A59, 400 yds from centre towards York
☎ (01423) 862207
11.30–3, 5.30–11; 11.30–11 Wed & Sat
Samuel Smith OBB Ⓗ
Fine example of an Edwardian-style, twin-roomed pub. The exterior was recently restored to its original brickwork. No meals Sun.
❀ ◖ ⌂ & Å ♣ P

Langdale End

Moorcock
☎ (01723) 882268
11–2.30 (2 Sat; not Mon–Thu in winter), 8 (7 Fri & Sat)–11
Daleside Bitter; Malton Double Chance; Whitby Wobble; guest beer Ⓗ
Sympathetically renovated, remote pub, often busy in summer. Limited meals service in winter: lunches Sat and Sun; eve meals Thu–Sat.
❀ Q ⛺ ❀ ◖ ▮
& Å ♣ ⌂ P ⅄

Lealholm

Board Inn
Village Green
☎ (01947) 897279
11–2, 7–11 (11–11 summer)
Camerons Bitter, Strongarm Ⓗ
Old village pub with wooden beams in its bar and lounge. Darts, dominoes and quoits are popular.
❀ Q ❀ ⌂ ◖ ▮ Å ⇌ ♣ P

Leavening

Jolly Farmer
Main Street ☎ (01653) 658276
12–3, 7–11
John Smith's Bitter; Tetley Bitter; guest beers Ⓗ
Unspoilt, 17th-century, friendly village local. Guest beers are usually from local independent breweries. Excellent, reasonably-priced food is served in a separate dining room. A must.
❀ ⛺ ❀ ⌂ ♣ P

Linton

Fountaine
☎ (01756) 752210
12–2.30 (may extend in summer), 7–10.30 (11 Fri & Sat)
Black Sheep Best Bitter, Special Strong; S&N Theakston Best Bitter, XB; Younger Scotch Ⓗ
Pub in a superb position next to the village green and beck. Its traditional, low-beamed interior includes a dining area and a partitioned section with high-backed settles around an open fire. Excellent food.
❀ Q ❀ ◖ ♣

Long Marston

Sun Inn
York Road ☎ (01904) 738258
11–3, 5.30–11; 11–11 Sat
Samuel Smith OBB, Museum Ⓗ
Friendly village pub, in Sam Smith's panelled fashion, which serves local community needs, as well as catering for visitors. Q ◖ ▮ ⌂ & P

Long Preston

Maypole
☎ (01729) 840219
11–3, 6–11; 11–11 Sat
Commercial Alesman; Taylor Landlord; Whitbread Boddingtons Bitter, Castle Eden Ale Ⓗ
Welcoming pub facing the village green and maypole: two comfortable rooms, each with an open fire. Meals (comprehensive menu) are usually served in the dining room. Cider in summer. ❀ Q
❀ ⌂ ◖ ▮ ⌂ & ⇌ ♣ ⌂ P

Malham

Lister Arms
Over the bridge on road to Goredale Scar
☎ (01729) 830330
12–3 (2 winter), 7–11
Ind Coope Burton Ale; Younger Scotch; guest beers Ⓗ
Popular village pub dating from 1702, partly opened out into three areas, with a sheltered garden to the rear. Hikers welcome, as are dogs. Two guest beers in winter, three in summer. Liefmans Kriek on tap, plus a large range of bottles and whiskies. Cider in summer.
❀ ❀ ⌂ ◖ ▮ Å ♣ ⌂ P

Malton

Crown Hotel (Suddaby's)
Wheelgate ☎ (01653) 692038
11–3, 5.30–11; 11–11 Fri; 10.30–4, 7–11 Sat
Malton Pale Ale, Double Chance, Pickwick's Porter, Owd Bob; guest beer Ⓗ
Busy town-centre pub with a conservatory eating area. Local horse racing mementos feature. ❀ Q ⛺ ❀ ◖ ▮ &
⇌ ♣ P ☐

King's Head
Market Place ☎ (01653) 692289
10.30–2.30 (may extend in summer), 7–11
Tetley Bitter; Wards Best Bitter; guest beers Ⓗ
Pub whose distinctive, ivy-covered frontage overlooks the market place. Extensive menu. Busy – especially on market days. Q ⛺ ◖ ▮ & ❀ P ⅄ ☐

Markington

Yorkshire Hussars
Main Street ☎ (01765) 677715
12–3 (summer only), 7–11
Black Sheep Best Bitter; John Smith's Bitter; Whitbread Boddingtons Bitter; guest beers Ⓗ
Unspoilt village pub near a well-known equestrian centre.
❀ Q ❀ ⌂ Å ♣ P

Masham

White Bear
Wellgarth ☎ (01765) 689319
11–11
S&N Theakston Mild, Best Bitter, XB, Old Peculier Ⓗ
Two-roomed village local in the courtyard of Theakston's offices and adjacent to Black Sheep Brewery. Excellent meals; live entertainment Sat eves. ❀ ❀ ⌂ ◖ ▮ ⌂ ♣ P

Melmerby

George & Dragon
Main Street
☎ (01765) 640303
11–3, 5–11 (11–11 summer)
Franklin's Bitter; S&N Theakston Best Bitter; guest beers Ⓗ
Traditional, three-room local with log fires in each room. No jukebox or electronic machines. Local independent breweries promoted.
❀ Q ⌂ ◖ ▮ ♣ P

North Yorkshire

Muker

Farmer's Arms
☎ (01748) 886297
11–3, 7–11
Butterknowle Bitter; S&N Theakston Best Bitter, Old Peculier Ⓗ
Village-centre pub, handy for the Pennine Way and coast to coast walks. The interior retains traditional character, with wooden seating and flagged floors.
🏚 Q ☞ ❀ 🍴 ◖ 🌂 ♣ P

Muston

Ship
West Street ☎ (01723) 512722
11–3, 7–11
Camerons Bitter; Ind Coope Burton Ale; Tetley Bitter; Whitbread Castle Eden Ale; guest beer Ⓗ
One-roomed pub with a partitioned dining area (good food). A pleasant village local.
❀ ◖ 🗝 🌂 ♣ P

Northallerton

Tanner Hop
2a Friarage Street (just E of Town Hall roundabout)
☎ (01609) 778482
11–11 (supper licence)
Black Sheep Best Bitter; John Smith's Bitter; guest beers Ⓗ
Former tithe barn, used as a wartime dance hall, hence the name. Wide range of guest ales, from near and far.
◖ 🗝 ⇌ ♣ ◔ 🍴

North Duffield

King's Arms
Main Street ☎ (01757) 288492
12–2 (not Tue–Thu in winter), 4–11
John Smith's Bitter; Tetley Bitter; guest beers Ⓗ
Traditional 18th-century, village free house close to an attractive duck pond. Good facilities for children; constantly changing range of guest ales. Beer festivals held. No eve meals Sun–Tue.
🏚 ❀ ◖ 🌂 ♣ ◔ P

Nosterfield

Freemason's Arms
On main road between A1 and Masham ☎ (01677) 470548
12–3 (not Mon), 7–11
Black Sheep Best Bitter; S&N Theakston Best Bitter; Tetley Bitter; guest beers Ⓗ
Welcoming country inn with a flagstoned bar and an interesting collection of wartime memorabilia. Excellent reputation for meals and often busy.
🏚 Q ◖ P

Nun Monkton

Alice Hawthorn
☎ (01423) 330303
12–2.30, 6.30–11
Camerons Bitter; S&N Theakston XB; Tetley Bitter; Whitbread Castle Eden Ale; guest beers Ⓗ
Warm, welcoming pub in a picturesque village, complete with maypole and duck pond. Great food.
🏚 Q ☞ ❀ ◖ 🗝 🌂 🍴 ♣ P

Osmotherley

Pied Piper Country Inn
Clack Lane End (A684)
☎ (01609) 883436
11–11
Draught Bass; McEwan 80/-; S&N Theakston Best Bitter, XB, Old Peculier Ⓗ
Beamed, olde-worlde pub with coal and log fires: a lounge, a games/family room and a restaurant.
🏚 Q ☞ ❀ 🍴 ◖ 🌂 ♣ P 🍴

Oswaldkirk

Malt Shovel
Main Street
☎ (01439) 788461
11.30–3, 6.30–11
Samuel Smith OBB, Museum Ⓗ
Historic pub, an inn for over 300 years and previously the manor house. It has always been well maintained and occasionally sympathetically restored. 🏚 ☞ ❀ 🍴 ◖ 🌂 P

Pickering

Black Swan
18 Birdgate ☎ (01751) 472286
10.30–3.30, 6–11; 10.30–11 Mon
Courage Directors; Ruddles County; John Smith's Bitter Ⓗ
Former coaching inn: one long bar with distinct drinking areas, popular with locals and visitors alike. Large car park at the rear.
🏚 Q 🍴 ◖ 🌂 ♣ P

Pickhill

Nag's Head
☎ (01845) 567391
11–11
Hambleton Bitter; S&N Theakston Best Bitter, XB, Old Peculier; John Smith's Bitter Ⓗ
Comfortable village pub renowned for its food: a small lounge and a cosy bar, with a large tie collection. Separate restaurant.
🏚 ❀ 🍴 ◖ 🗝 🌂 ♣ P

Pool

Hunter's Inn
Harrogate Road
☎ (0113) 2841090
11–11
Beer range varies Ⓗ
Warm pub with a mixed clientele. Excellent view over Wharfe Valley. 🏚 ❀ ♣ P

Redmire

King's Arms
SW of village green
☎ (01969) 622316
11–3, 5.30–11
Black Sheep Special Strong; S&N Theakston XB; John Smith's Bitter; guest beers Ⓗ
Comfortable, family-run village pub in a scenic location, within walking distance of Castle Bolton. Wensleydale railway is set to re-open nearby. Good value food. 🏚 Q ❀ 🍴 ◖ 🌂 ♣ P

Richmond

Black Lion
12 Finkle Street (off market place) ☎ (01748) 823121
11–11
Camerons Strongarm; Tetley Bitter, Imperial; Whitbread Flowers Original Ⓗ
Old, residential coaching inn. Its traditional bars are popular with locals.
🏚 Q 🍴 ◖ ♣ P ⅄ 🍴

Holly Hill Inn
Holly Hill, Sleegil (Hudswell road, S of centre)
☎ (01748) 822192
12–11
S&N Theakston Mild, Best Bitter, XB, Old Peculier; guest beer Ⓗ
Country pub on the edge of town: a busy public bar with an adjoining games room, plus a quiet lounge. Families welcome. The garden leads to a field with panoramic views over Richmond.
🏚 ❀ ◖ 🌂 ♣ P 🍴

Rillington

Coach & Horses
Scarborough Road (A64)
☎ (01944) 758373
11–3, 5.30–11
S&N Theakston Best Bitter; Tetley Bitter; Younger Scotch Ⓗ
Prominent pub featuring a display of numerous pot cats.
Q ☞ ❀ 🍴 ◖ 🌂 🗝 ♣ P ⅄

Ripon

Golden Lion
69–70 Allhallowgate (3rd left when approaching town from A1) ☎ (01765) 602598

11–3, 7–11
**Black Sheep Best Bitter;
Hambleton Goldfield; S&N
Theakston Best Bitter; John
Smith's Bitter; Tetley Bitter;
guest beer** Ⓗ
Traditional family eating pub
(excellent food). Friendly,
conversational atmosphere.
Popular with locals.
🏾 Q ⏚ ❀ 🛏 ◖ ➍ ☗

One Eyed Rat

51 Allhallowgate (3rd left
when approaching town from
A1) ☎ (01765) 607704
6–11; 12–2, 5.30–11 Fri; 12–3, 6–11 Sat
**Taylor Landlord; Tetley
Bitter; Whitbread
Boddingtons Bitter; guest
beers** Ⓗ
Very popular terraced pub
close to the town centre.
🏾 Q ❀ ➍

Wheatsheaf

Harrogate Road, Quarry Moor
(by new bypass roundabout, S
of centre) ☎ (01765) 602410
12–3, 7–11; 12–11 Sat
**Vaux Samson; Wards Best
Bitter** Ⓗ
Small, friendly pub with a
large sunken garden at the
rear. Note the ornately carved
timbers in this listed building.
Q ❀ ◖ ➍ ▲ P

Robin Hood's Bay

Bay Hotel

The Dock (bottom of the hill,
on sea wall) ☎ (01947) 880278
11–11
**Courage Directors; Ruddles
County; John Smith's Bitter** Ⓗ
Friendly old pub on two
levels, with breathtaking
views over the bay.
🏾 Q ❀ 🛏 ◖ ➍ ❧ ▲ ➍ P

Ruswarp

Bridge

By station ☎ (01947) 602780
12–2 (3 Sat), 7 (6 Fri)–11
**Courage Directors; John
Smith's Bitter, Magnet** Ⓗ
Three-room pub beside the
bridge over the River Esk.
🏾 Q ⏚ ❀ ◖ ➍ ▲ ❧ ➍

Sandsend

Hart

East Row ☎ (01947) 890304
11–3.30 (may extend in summer),
6–11; 12–3, 7.30–10.30 Sun
**Camerons Bitter,
Strongarm** Ⓗ
One-roomed pub with a
separate restaurant. No meals
Mon eve. 🏾 ❀ ◖ ➍ ➍ P

Saxton

Greyhound

Main Street ☎ (01937) 557202

12–3, 5.30–11; 11–11 Sat
Samuel Smith OBB Ⓗ
Country pub that retains its
integrity: values as well as
value remain important, hence
the pub's continuing
popularity. 🏾 Q ⏚ ❀ ➍

Scarborough

Alma Inn

1 Alma Parade (near
Northway traffic lights, behind
Barclay's Bank)
☎ (01723) 375587
11.30–2.30 (3 Thu & Fri, 4.30 Sat),
7–11
**S&N Theakston Best Bitter,
Newcastle Exhibition,
Theakston XB; Tetley Bitter;
Younger Scotch; guest
beers** Ⓗ
Busy pub with a varied
clientele. Local photographs
and interesting bric-a-brac
feature. Excellent choice of
guest beers. Q ❀ ◖ ⊟ ❧

Golden Ball

31 Sandside ☎ (01723) 353899
11–3, 6–11
**Samuel Smith OBB,
Museum** Ⓗ
Unspoilt pub with views over
the harbour and South Bay
from the front bar. Food
served Easter–Oct.
Q ⏚ ❀ ◖ ➍ ⊟

Hole in the Wall

26–32 Vernon Road
☎ (01723) 373746
11.30–2.30 (3 Sat), 7–11
**Malton Double Chance; S&N
Theakston Best Bitter, XB,
Old Peculier; guest beers** Ⓗ
Friendly, busy pub just off the
town centre, towards the Spa.
Excellent guest beers; varied
clientele. Extensive collection
of beer mats behind the bar.
No meals Sun.
Q ◖ ❧ ❧ ➍ ⊙

Jolly Roger

27 Eastborough
☎ (01723) 351426
11–11
**S&N Theakston Best Bitter,
XB, Old Peculier; guest
beer** Ⓗ
Busy pub on the route to the
beach and harbour. The bars
are situated on two levels. Folk
club Mon. Lunches and family
room in summer only.
⏚ 🛏 ◖ ➍

Leeds Arms

26 St Mary's Street (200 yds
from seafront, up from
Princess Sq) ☎ (01723) 361699
11.30–3.30 (4 Sat), 7–11
**Bass Mild, Worthington BB,
Draught Bass; guest beer** Ⓗ
Small, unspoilt, one-roomed
fishing pub in the old town.
Old photographs, many with
fishing and lifeboat

connections, adorn the walls.
Popular with locals and
visitors. 🏾 Q

Prince of Wales

2 Castle Road
☎ (01723) 373517
11–11
**Tetley Mild, Bitter, Imperial;
guest beers** Ⓗ
Small, two-roomed, busy pub,
just off the town centre. Rugby
league memorabilia features in
the bar. Welcoming
atmosphere. 🏾 Q ❧ ➍

Scalby Mills Hotel

Scalby Mills Road (by Sea Life
Centre, follow signs)
☎ (01723) 500449
11–11
**Cropton Two Pints; Tetley
Bitter; guest beers** Ⓗ
Traditional, old pub on the
Cleveland Way, with views
across the bay. Eve meals in
summer only. Q ◖ ➍ ▲ P

Tap & Spile

94 Falsgrave Road
☎ (01723) 363837
11–11
Beer range varies Ⓗ
Sympathetically renovated,
busy old coaching inn with
local memorabilia on its walls:
three rooms; large garden. Eve
meals in summer. 🏾 Q ❀ ❀
➍ ⏚ ❧ ➍ ⊙ P ❧

Selby

Albion Vaults

New Street (town side of A19
swing bridge over River Ouse)
☎ (01757) 213817
11–4.30, 7–11; 11–11 Mon, Fri & Sat
Old Mill Mild, Bitter Ⓗ
Reputed to be the oldest pub
in Selby, with comfortably
furnished bars. The rear bar
has a pool table and TV.
Q ❀ ◖ ⊟ ⏚ ❧ ➍

Cricketer's Arms

Market Place ☎ (01757) 702120
11–11; 11–4, 5.30–11 Tue & Wed
**Samuel Smith OBB,
Museum** Ⓗ
Town pub popular with
younger locals. The drinking
area is partitioned into
alcoves. Wheelchair access via
the rear entrance. ◖ ⏚ ❧ ➍

Skipton

Cock & Bottle

30 Swadford Street
☎ (01756) 794734
11–11
**Marston's Pedigree; Taylor
Landlord; Whitbread
Boddingtons Bitter, Castle
Eden Ale; guest beers** Ⓗ
Early 18th-century coaching
inn, sympathetically
refurbished as a split-level,

one-bar Hogshead alehouse, preserving original beamed ceilings, stone walls and fireplaces. Friendly atmosphere; mixed clientele.
🏠 ✲ ◖ ≉ ♣

Royal Shepherd

Canal Street ☎ (01756) 793178
11–4, 5–11; 11–11 Fri & Sat
Cains Bitter; Marston's Pedigree; Whitbread Boddingtons Bitter, Trophy, Castle Eden Ale H
Quiet, friendly, civilised, three-roomed pub in an attractive canalside location. The main bar has many photos of old Skipton and an unusual canal-themed stained-glass window. The snug is a shrine to Yorkshire cricket and overlooks an award-winning garden. 🏠 Q ◖ ◖ ♣

Snape

Castle Arms Inn

☎ (01677) 470270
12–2, 7–11; 12–2, 7–10.30 Sun
Hambleton Bitter; S&N Theakston Best Bitter; John Smith's Bitter; guest beers H
Cosy, Grade II-listed, 14th-century inn with its own caravan and camping facilities. The function room doubles as a family room.
🏠 ⛺ 🛏 ◖ ▶ ▲ ♣ P

Staithes

Cod & Lobster

Slip End (harbourside)
☎ (01947) 840295
11–11
Camerons Strongarm; Ind Coope Burton Ale; Tetley Imperial H
Pub by the harbour where Captain Cook developed his interest in the sea: one long room with nautical relics. Children are allowed in until early eve. No access for cars.
🏠 ✲ ☖ ♣

Staveley

Royal Oak

Main Street ☎ (01423) 340267
11.30–3, 5.30–11
Rudgate Viking; John Smith's Bitter; Tetley Bitter H
Much improved, old village inn, popular with locals (keen darts team) and visitors alike. Good food Tue–Sat.
🏠 Q ◖ ◖ ☖ ♣ P

Stokesley

White Swan

1 West End (W end of High St)
☎ (01642) 710263
11.30–3, 5.30 (7 Sat)–11
S&N Theakston Best Bitter, XB; Whitbread Castle Eden

Ale; guest beers H
Cosy, traditional pub where the oak-panelled lounge bar has agricultural memorabilia on the walls. No jukebox. Three guest beers. Ploughman's meals, with a wide range of cheeses, till 10pm. 🏠 Q ♣ ◌ 日

Summerbridge

Flying Dutchman

Main Street ☎ (01423) 780321
11.30–2.30, 6–11
Samuel Smith OBB, Museum (occasional) H
Stone-built village inn named after the famous racehorse. The lounge is comfortable. Excellently priced beer. No eve meals Sun in winter.
🏠 ✲ 🛏 ◖ ▶ ▲ ♣ P

Tadcaster

Angel & White Horse

Bridge Street ☎ (01937) 835470
11–2.30, 5 (7 Sat)–11
Samuel Smith OBB, Museum H
Large, yet pleasing, town pub next to Sam Smith's brewery. The oak-panelled walls are minimally decorated with historic photos of the brewery. Cheap beer. 🏠 Q ✲ ◖

Thixendale

Cross Keys

☎ (01377) 88272
12–3 (not winter Mon), 6–11
Jennings Bitter; Tetley Bitter H
Traditional, one-roomed, village inn, in the heart of the Yorkshire wolds. Unspoilt and welcoming, it serves good food at reasonable prices. (No meals between Christmas and New Year.) No children.
🏠 Q ✲ ◖ ▶ ▲ ♣

Thornton in Lonsdale

Marton Arms

☎ (0152 42) 41281
12–3 (not Mon–Fri in winter), 6 (7 winter)–11
Black Sheep Best Bitter; Dent Bitter; Jennings Bitter; S&N Theakston Best Bitter; guest beers H
Pre-turnpike coaching inn, dated 1679, but reputedly older: a large, comfortable, oak-beamed lounge and a restaurant. Up to 15 beers are sold. 🏠 ✲ 🛏 ◖ ▶ ♣ ◌ P

Thornton-le-Moor

Black Swan

☎ (01609) 774117
12–3, 7–11

Hambleton Bitter, Stallion; John Smith's Bitter, Magnet H
Large, village-centre inn with a spacious lounge and a separate (popular) restaurant. The bar has a pool table.
✲ ◖ ▶ ⊞ ▲ ♣ P

Thornton Watlass

Buck Inn

☎ (01677) 422461
11–2.30, 6–11
Black Sheep Best Bitter; S&N Theakston Best Bitter; John Smith's Bitter; Tetley Bitter; guest beers H
Popular pub in a picturesque village green setting, with a bar, lounge, restaurant and function/family room. Very varied menu. Hambleton beers are regular guests.
🏠 Q ⛺ ✲ 🛏 ◖ ▶ ☖ ♣ P

Threshfield

Long Ashes

On caravan site, off B6160
☎ (01756) 752434
11–3, 6.30–11 (11–11 summer)
Moorhouse's Pendle Witches Brew; S&N Theakston Mild, Best Bitter; Tetley Bitter H
Split on three levels, with stone walls and beamed ceilings, this converted lodge has a mischievous female ghost. It stands next to an extensive chalet/caravan park. Full menu. Wheelchair access is via the side door.
🏠 ⛺ ✲ 🛏 ◖ ▶ ☖ ▲ ♣ P

Old Hall Inn

On B6265
☎ (01756) 752441
11.30–3, 6 (5.30 summer)–11
S&N Theakston Best Bitter; Taylor Best Bitter, Landlord; Younger Scotch; guest beers (summer) H
Smart country inn with several rooms. Above the coal-fired range, the blackboard menu displays a selection of unusual dishes. Children can choose from the 'Brats' Board'. No food Sun eve or Mon.
🏠 ⛺ ✲ 🛏 ◖ ▶ ☖ ▲ ♣ P

Tockwith

Spotted Ox

Westfield Road
☎ (01423) 358387
11–3, 6–11; 11–11 Sat
Tetley Bitter; guest beers H
The large number of pump clips adorning the bar surround give an idea of the range of guest beers here. The open-plan layout is broken up by partition walls (watch the low beam!).
✲ ◖ ▶ P

Upper Poppleton

Lord Collingwood
Hodgson Lane
☎ (01904) 794388
11.30–3, 5.30–11
Mansfield Riding Bitter, Bitter, Old Baily Ⓗ
Central pub in a commuter village, specialising in home-cooked food. Daily specials include vegetarian options. Count the hanging jugs and mugs! Mansfield's seasonal ales are also sold. ⚒ ◑ ▶ P

Wass

Wombwell Arms
☎ (01347) 868280
12–2.30, 7–11
Black Sheep Best Bitter; Taylor Landlord; guest beer Ⓗ
18th-century inn on the southern edge of the North Yorkshire Moors. Log fires; good food.
⚒ Q ⛺ ⛢ ◑ ▶ P

Weaverthorpe

Star
☎ (01944) 738273
7–11; 12–4.30, 7–11 Sat
John Smith's Bitter; Tetley Bitter; guest beer Ⓗ
Country pub popular with locals and visitors. Extensive menus offer good value meals. Game specialities in season.
⚒ Q ⛺ ✿ ⛢ ◑ ▶ ⛓ ♣
P ⅍

Welbury

Duke of Wellington
☎ (01609) 882464
12–3 (not Mon or Tue), 7–11
McEwan 80/-; John Smith's Bitter, Magnet Ⓗ
Attractive, friendly pub in a pretty village. It comprises an intimate restaurant, a cosy lounge and bar area, and also a separate bar frequented by darts and domino teams. Families welcome.
⚒ ✿ ◑ ♣ P ⌑

Whitby

Middle Earth Tavern
26 Church Street (right over swing bridge, E of centre)
☎ (01947) 606014
11–3, 6.30–11; 11–11 Sat & summer
S&N Theakston Mild, Best Bitter, XB, Old Peculier Ⓗ
Two-roomed pub – one a games/children's room. Live music most nights.
⚒ ⛺ ✿ ⛢ ◑ ⛓ ⅙ ≷

Tap & Spile
New Quay Road (opp. bus station) ☎ (01947) 603937
11–11
Beer range varies Ⓗ

Large, multi-roomed, red brick pub, formerly known as the Cutty Sark. Meals served 11–7.30.
Q ⛺ ◑ ▶ ⛢ ≷ ♣ ⌑ ⅍

York

Ackhorne
St Martin's Lane
☎ (01904) 629820
11.30–3, 5.30–11; 12–2, 7–10.30 Sun
Beer range varies Ⓗ
Welcoming local, a haven from the Micklegate crawl. This pub concentrates on North Yorkshire beers. Q ◑ ≷

Blue Bell
Fossgate ☎ (01904) 654904
12–11
Vaux Bitter, Samson, Extra Special; Wards Best Bitter; guest beers Ⓗ
Small, but perfectly formed pub, last refurbished at the turn of the century, but none the worse for that. Two cosy rooms with bags of atmosphere. Guest beers come from Vaux. ⛢ ♣

Fox Inn
Holgate Road (at Poppleton Rd/Acomb Rd jct, by carriage works) ☎ (01904) 798341
11–11
Tetley Bitter; guest beers Ⓗ
Four-roomed Victorian heritage pub with a front drinkers' bar and a corridor serving hatch. Its busy times are unusual – early Fri eve and Sun eve (but quiet Sat eve).
⚒ Q ✿ ◑ ⅙ ♣ P

Lighthorseman
124 Fulford Road
☎ (01904) 624818
11.30–2.30, 5.30–11
Thwaites Bitter, Craftsman, Old Dan Ⓗ
This pub's Victorian splendour (unusually light and airy) has recently been officially recognised by the granting of listed building status.
⛺ ◑ ⛢ P

Maltings
Tanners Moat (below Lendal Bridge) ☎ (01904) 655387
11–11
Black Sheep Best Bitter; guest beers Ⓗ
Congested gem – a small, award-winning house full of artefacts which can get busy.
⚒ ◑ ≷

Other Tap & Spile
15 North Street
☎ (01904) 656097
11.30–11
Cropton Two Pints; Hadrian Gladiator; Old Mill Bitter; guest beers Ⓗ
Busy, three-roomed pub offering up to nine beers. No food Sun lunchtime.

No-smoking family room.
⛺ ✿ ◑ ≷ ♣ ⌑ ⅍

Royal Oak
17 Goodramgate
☎ (01904) 653856
11–11
Ind Coope Burton Ale; Tetley Bitter; Whitbread Castle Eden Ale Ⓗ
Great, welcoming town pub, close to the Minster, with good wheelchair access downstairs.
Q ⛺ ◑ ▶ ⅖ ⅍

Waggon & Horses
48 Gillygate
☎ (01904) 654103
11–11
Beer range varies Ⓗ
Popular sporting pub (but don't mention football) run by a keen landlord. A regular outlet for local breweries. Good value, freshly-prepared food.
⛺ ✿ ⛢ ◑ ▶ ⛢ P

Wellington Inn
47 Alma Terrace (off Fulford Rd) ☎ (01904) 654642
11–3, 6 (5.30 Fri)–11; 11–11 Sat
Samuel Smith OBB, Museum Ⓗ
Possibly York's best value beer, in a small, traditional terraced pub. The floral delights of the beer patio are an added attraction.
⚒ ⛺ ✿ ⛢

York Arms
26 High Petergate (by front door of Minster)
☎ (01904) 624508
11–11
Samuel Smith OBB, Museum Ⓗ
Popular pub with locals and tourists – a rare occurrence in the walled city! A sliding door leads to York's smallest bar – a panelled gem.
Q ⛢ ◑ ⛢ ≷

York Beer Shop
Sandringham Street (off A19/Fishergate)
☎ (01904) 647136
11 (4.15 Mon, 10 Sat)–10; 12–2, 7–10 Sun
Old Mill Bitter; Rooster's Yankee; Taylor Landlord; guest beers Ⓗ
Off-licence now ten years old and still looking to improve. Draught beer to take out in any quantity, plus an ever-increasing range of bottles. Mouth-watering cheeses complete the picture. ⌑

Protect your pleasure!
Join CAMRA – see
page 546.

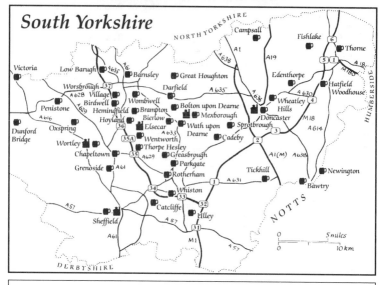

South Yorkshire

 Concertina, *Mexborough*; **Kelham Island**, *Sheffield*; **South Yorkshire**, *Elsecar*; **Stocks**, *Doncaster*; **Wards**, *Sheffield*; **Wortley**, *Wortley*

Barnsley

Shaw Inn
Racecommon Road
☎ (01226) 294021
12–11
**Morland Old Speckled Hen;
John Smith's Bitter; guest
beer** Ⓗ
Proper pub catering for all
ages. Folk club Mon.
☼ ✿ ◑ 🍴 ♣ P

Bawtry

Turnpike
High Street ☎ (01302) 711960
11–3, 6–11
**Stocks Best Bitter, Select, St
Leger Porter; guest beers** Ⓗ
Welcoming pub opposite the
market place. The interior is of
wood, glass and brick with a
flagstone floor. Good value,
varied menu (eve meals
Tue–Thu). Weekly guest beers.
✿ ◑ ◗

Birdwell

Cock Inn
Pilley Hill ☎ (01226) 742155
12–3, 7–11
Draught Bass Ⓗ; **Whitbread
Boddingtons Bitter** Ⓗ
Popular 200-year-old village
local in Yorkshire stone with a
slate floor, a superb fireplace
and much brass. Extensive
garden with play area. Eve
meals Mon–Sat. 🏚 ✿ ◑ P

Bolton upon Dearne

Cross Daggers Inn
Church Street (150 yds off
B6098) ☎ (01709) 892299
12–4, 7–11
**John Smith's Bitter; South
Yorkshire Barnsley Bitter** Ⓗ
Built in 1923 and virtually
unspoiled, a pub with many
rooms, including a games
room with snooker. Corridor
drinking area.
🏚 Q ☼ ✿ ⅍ ⇌ ♣ P

Brampton Bierlow

Brampton Hall
Manor Road ☎ (01709) 877488
11–11
**John Smith's Magnet; South
Yorkshire Barnsley Bitter;
Stones Best Bitter; guest
beer** Ⓗ
Popular converted 15th-
century manor house in a
small village. No eve meals
Sun. 🏚 Q ✿ ◑ ◗ ⅍ P 🏠

Cadeby

Cadeby Inn
Main Street ☎ (01709) 864009
12–3, 5–11; 11–11 Sat
**Courage Directors; John
Smith's Bitter; Samuel Smith OBB; Tetley
Bitter; guest beers** Ⓗ
Converted farmhouse with a
large lounge and a smaller bar.
Pleasant garden, popular with
families. Guest beers from
Tetley. 🏚 ✿ ◑ ◗ ⅍ P ⒴

Campsall

Old Bells
High Street ☎ (01302) 700423
11–3, 5.30–11
**Ruddles County; John
Smith's Bitter; Tetley Bitter;
guest beer** Ⓗ
At over 850 years old, this, the
oldest pub in Doncaster
borough, once served Dick
Turpin and Oliver Cromwell.
A lounge, small smoke room, a
tiny snug and two restaurants.
Q ✿ ◑ ◗ ⅍ ⅍ P

Catcliffe

Waverley
Brinsworth Road
☎ (01709) 360906
12–4 (5 Sat), 6–11
**John Smith's Magnet; guest
beers** Ⓗ
Large, friendly pub with a
good children's/pub menu. A
wide range of ales changes
weekly.
☼ ✿ ◑ ◗ ⅍ ⅍ ♣ P 🏠

Chapeltown

Prince of Wales
80 Burncross Road (near
swimming baths)
☎ (0114) 2467725

11–3 (3.30 Sat), 5.30 (6.30 Sat)–11;
12–2.30, 7–10.30 Sun
Vaux Waggle Dance H; **Wards
Best Bitter** E & H
Welcoming, two-roomed local.
No obtrusive music or
electronic games, just a
traditional tap room and
comfortable lounge.
Q ✿ ◑ ⊞ ⇌ ♣ P

Darfield

Hewer & Brewer

Snapehill Road (off A635)
☎ (01226) 752956
12–3, 7–11
**McEwan 80/-; S&N Theakston
Best Bitter; guest beers** H
Typical roadside pub with
many rooms. The upstairs
function room houses a small
mining museum.
⚒ ⛿ ✿ ♠ A ♣ P

Doncaster

Corporation Brewery Taps

135 Cleveland Street (A630,
near south bus station)
☎ (01302) 363715
12–2 (3 Sat), 7–11
Samuel Smith OBB H
Multi-room, off town centre
pub, which supports live
music and pub games. Sky TV
in the public bar. Bar snacks in
summer. Q ⛿ ✿ ⇌ ♣ ⊬

Leopard

1 West Street ☎ (01302) 363054
11–11
**Marston's Pedigree; John
Smith's Bitter; guest beers** H
Lively, street-corner boozer
with a superb tiled frontage.
The guest beers are selected
from all over the country. Live
music upstairs weekends. No
food Sun. ◑ ⊞ ⇌ ♣ P

Masons Arms

Market Place ☎ (01302) 364391
10.30 (11 Mon, Wed & Thu)–4,
7.30–11; 12–3, 7.30–10.30 Sun
Tetley Bitter H
Tetley Heritage Inn, 200 years
old, displaying photos of old
Doncaster. A perennial entry
in the *Guide*. Q ✿ ⊞ ⇌

Olde Crown

Church Street
☎ (01302) 360096
11–3 (not Mon or Wed in winter),
7–11; 11–11 Sat & summer Fri
**Bass Worthington BB; M&B
Highgate Dark; South
Yorkshire Barnsley Bitter;
guest beer** H
Welcoming oasis in the
shadow of St George's church.
Busy bar; comfortable lounge.
A rare outlet for mild. Folk
night Mon; jazz Thu. An ever
improving pub.
Q ✿ ⇔ ◑ ⊞ ⇌ ♣ P ⊟

Railway

West Street ☎ (01302) 349700
11–11
**John Smith's Bitter, Magnet;
South Yorkshire Barnsley
Bitter** H
Bustling pub with a large bar
and a tiny lounge. Twice
CAMRA's Doncaster *Pub of the
Season*. ◑ ⇌ ♣ ⊟

Salutation

14 South Parade
☎ (01302) 342736
12–11; 12–3, 7–11 Sat
**Ind Coope Burton Ale;
Marston's Pedigree; Tetley
Bitter, Imperial; guest beers** H
The oldest pub in the town
centre, a coaching inn since
1754, refurbished to maintain
this image. Live music Sun.
No food Sat/Sun.
⚒ ✿ ◑ ♣ P

White Swan

34a Frenchgate
☎ (01302) 366573
11–11
**Vaux Waggle Dance; Wards
Thorne Best Bitter, Best
Bitter** H
Friendly, town-centre pub
with a front tap room boasting
the highest bar in Britain and a
comfortable lounge reached
via a tiled passage. Good value
lunches (not served Sun). The
metered Wards is usually real
but check. ◑ ⇌ ♣

Dunford Bridge

Stanhope Arms

Off A628 ☎ (01226) 763104
11–3 (not Mon), 7–11
**Mansfield Riding Mild,
Bitter, Old Baily** H
Large, multi-roomed pub,
originally a shooting lodge, in
a small hamlet by the
Woodhead tunnel. Camp in
the grounds. An alternative
Pennine Way passes nearby.
Q ⛿ ✿ ⇔ ◑ ⊞ ⚒ A
♣ P ⊟

Edenthorpe

Eden Arms

Edenfield Road (by Tesco)
☎ (01302) 890468
11.30–3, 5–11; 11.30–11.30 Sat
Tetley Bitter, Imperial H
Relatively new pub in a
growing estate. One of Tetley's
'Big Steak Houses', popular
lunchtimes and weekends.
Various events help make this
a friendly pub for all,
including families.
✿ ◑ ⚒ P ⊬

Fishlake

Hare & Hounds

Church Street
☎ (01302) 841208
12–3.30, 7–11; 12–2.30, 7–10.30 Sun

**Mansfield Riding Bitter, Old
Baily** H
Pub featuring a spacious,
horse-brassed lounge and a
smaller public bar (pool and
dominoes). The landlord was
Mansfield's *Host of the Year*
1993. ✿ ⊞ ⚒ A ♣ P

Greasbrough

Prince of Wales

9 Potter Hill ☎ (01709) 551358
11–4, 7–11
Beer range varies H
Popular, two-bar village pub
with a constantly changing
beer range, a traditional tap
room and a comfortable
lounge. Its prices are below the
local average. ✿ ⊞ ⚒ ♣ ⊟

Great Houghton

Old Hall Inn

High Street ☎ (01226) 758706
12–3.30 (5 Sat), 7–11
**Hardys & Hansons Best
Bitter** H
Busy, three-roomed pub on the
site of an old coaching inn.
Disco Sat; games knockout
Sun eve. A courtesy coach is
available.
⚒ Q ✿ ⊞ ⚒ ♣ P ⊟

Grenoside

Cow & Calf

Skew Hill Lane
☎ (0114) 2468191
11.30–3, 6–11; 11.30–11 Sat
Samuel Smith OBB, Museum
(occasional) H
Large, converted farmhouse
with several separate drinking
areas; comfortable and
relaxing with old world
charm. No eve meals Sun.
⛿ ✿ ◑ ▶ ♣ P ⊬

Hatfield Woodhouse

Green Tree

Bearswood Green (A18/A614
jct) ☎ (01302) 840305
11–3, 5–11
**Wards Thorne Best Bitter;
guest beers** H
Friendly, welcoming, 17th-
century inn, popular for its
excellent, reasonably priced
food. Guest beers are usually
Vaux products.
⚒ Q ✿ ⚤ ◑ ▶ P

Hemingfield

Lundhill Tavern

Beech House Road (off A633, ½
mile along Lundhill Rd)
☎ (01226) 752283
12–5.30, 7–11
**John Smith's Bitter; South
Yorkshire Barnsley Bitter;
Stones Best Bitter; Taylor
Landlord; guest beers** H

South Yorkshire

Pub off the beaten track, steeped in mining history. Sun lunch served. Q ♣ P

Hoyland

Beggar & Gentleman
Market Street
☎ (01226) 742364
11–11
South Yorkshire Barnsley Bitter; Whitbread Boddingtons Mild, Bitter, Trophy; Wadworth 6X; guest beers Ⓗ
Spacious, town-centre ale house, catering for all ages. The cellar stillage is visible from the games room window. Good value lunches (no meals Sun). ❀ ◑ ♣ P

Furnace Inn
163 Milton Road (off B6097)
☎ (01226) 742000
12–3 (11.30–3.30 Sat), 6.30–11; 12–2.30, 7–10.30 Sun
Vaux Waggle Dance Ⓗ; Wards Thorne Best Bitter Ⓔ, Best Bitter Ⓔ & Ⓗ
Welcoming, stone pub by an old forge pond, holding awards for *Superloo*, *Wards in Bloom* and *Wards Pub of the Year* 1994–5. Q ❀ ⇌ (Elsecar) ♣ P ⊟

Low Barugh

Miller's Inn
Dearne Hall Road
☎ (01226) 382888
11–3, 5.30–11; 11–11 Fri & Sat
John Smith's Bitter; Taylor Landlord; Tetley Bitter; guest beers Ⓗ
Busy free house backing onto the River Dearne, forming part of an attractive row of cottages. Q ❀ ◑ ◗ ♣ P

Mexborough

Concertina Band Club
9a Dolcliffe Road (up hill off Bank St) ☎ (01709) 580841
12–4, 7–10.30 Sun
Concertina Best Bitter; Mansfield Bitter; John Smith's Bitter; Wards Best Bitter; guest beers Ⓗ
CAMRA members are welcome at this small, friendly club which is steeped in local history. Brewing on the premises began in 1992, and the choice of Concertina beers varies. Twice CAMRA *Regional Club of the Year*. ⇌ ♣ ⊟

Falcon
12 Main Street
☎ (01709) 571170
11.30–4 (5.30 Mon, 4.30 Fri, 5 Sat), 7–11
Old Mill Bitter Ⓗ
This lively pub has a large, smart lounge with raised

seating areas (entertainment some eves). The tap room has games. ❀ ⊞ ⇌ ♣

George & Dragon
81 Church Street (off A6023, near river) ☎ (01709) 584375
12–4, 7–11; 12–11 Fri & Sat
Vaux Samson, Double Maxim, Waggle Dance; Wards Best Bitter Ⓗ
Welcoming, cosy pub with a central bar. A new extension provides dining and function facilities. Pleasant garden, popular with families. No lunches Sun. ❀ ◑ ◖ P ⊟

Newington

Ship Inn
Misson Road (200 yds from A614) ☎ (01302) 710334
12–3, 5.30–11
S&N Theakston Best Bitter, XB, Old Peculier Ⓗ
Friendly village local from the 1700s offering an eve carvery and traditional Sun lunches. Children's adventure play area. ❀ ◑ ◗ ⊞ ◖ ▲ ♣ P

Oxspring

Waggon & Horses
Sheffield Road (B6462/B6449 jct) ☎ (01226) 763259
7 (12 Sat)–11
Courage Directors; John Smith's Bitter; Stones Best Bitter Ⓗ
Once a farmhouse, this cosy pub has low, beamed ceilings and nooks and crannies. The venue for the village gala duck race. ⚨ ❀ ◑ ◗ ◖ ♣ P

Parkgate

Station Hotel
Aldwarke Road
☎ (01709) 525469
11–2.30, 5.30 (7 Fri & Sat)–11
John Smith's Magnet; Stones Best Bitter; Whitbread Boddingtons Bitter Ⓗ
Welcoming pub whose exterior has changed little since it was used in the film *Tread Softly Stranger*. 'Two for the price of one' meals most eves. ⇗ ❀ ◑ ◗ ◖ P ⊬ ⊟

Penistone

Cubley Hall
Mortimer Road, Cubley Village (1 mile from Penistone on Stocksbridge road)
☎ (01226) 766086
11–3, 6–11
Marston's Pedigree; Whitbread Boddingtons Bitter, Bentley's Yorkshire Bitter, Trophy; guest beers Ⓗ
Multi-roomed, former gentleman's residence in a country setting. The adjacent

carvery also sells real ale. Extensive grounds include a children's play area. Food all day Sun.
Q ⇗ ❀ ⚨ ◑ ◗ ◖ ▲ ♣ P ⊬

Rotherham

Charter Arms
Eastwood Lane (high level of market) ☎ (01709) 373066
11–11
Mansfield Riding Bitter, Bitter, Old Baily Ⓗ
Friendly modern, refurbished pub offering excellent food, a comfortable lounge, a function room and a games room. Very popular with shoppers.
◑ ⊞ ⇌ ♣

Kingfisher
Mary Street ☎ (01709) 838422
11–11
Old Mill Bitter, Bullion Ⓗ
Pleasant, friendly, single-room pub, very close to the town centre and reputedly haunted. Traditional wooden bar with brass fittings.
❀ ⚨ ◑ ◖ ♣ ⊟

Midland Inn
Midland Road, Masbrough (off A629, near bus depot)
☎ (01709) 560027
11–3, 7–11; 11.30–11 Sat & summer
Whitbread Boddingtons Bitter, Flowers Original Ⓗ
A white marble facade fronts a compact, multi-roomed pub, with a central bar. Various snugs, plus a games room.
⚨ ⇗ ◖ ♣ P ⊟

Moulder's Rest
110–112 Masbrough Street (200 yds from Millmoor soccer ground) ☎ (01709) 560095
12–3, 6 (5 Fri, 7.30 Sat)–11; 12–3, 7.30–10.30 Sun
Stones Best Bitter; guest beer Ⓗ
Large, main road corner pub, featuring a well-patronised tap room, a snug and a through lounge. Big on games. Good value food (not served weekends). ⚨ ◑ ⇌ ♣ P ⊟

Woodman
Midland Road, Masbrough (off A629, by bus depot)
☎ (01709) 561486
12–3, 7–11; 12–2, 7–10.30 Sun
Stones Best Bitter; guest beer Ⓗ
Friendly, former Bentley's pub with a traditional tap room, a snooker room and a snug lounge. It was built as a local in 1853 but the housing has since been demolished. ❀ ⊞

Sheffield: *Central*

Bath Hotel
66 Victoria Street (off Glossop Rd) ☎ (0114) 2729017

South Yorkshire

12–3, 6.30 (5 Fri, 7.30 Sat)–11;
7.30–10.30 Sun, closed Sun lunch
**Ind Coope Burton Ale;
Marston's Pedigree; Tetley
Bitter; Wards Best Bitter;
guest beer** Ⓗ
Tetley Heritage pub converted
from Victorian cottages; a
small, friendly two-roomed
local. The original ground
lease prohibits the use of the
site as an ale house or for
other noxious activities. No
lunches Sat. Ⓓ ♣

Brown Bear
109 Norfolk Street
☎ (0114) 2727744
11–11
**Courage Directors; Marston's
Pedigree; Ruddles County;
John Smith's Bitter, Magnet;
Stones Best Bitter** Ⓗ
Rare for the city centre – a
two-roomed, traditional-style
pub, handy for the Crucible
and Lyceum theatres. Beware
the keg Scrumpy Jack cider on
fake handpump. ⊛ Ⓓ ⇌ ♣

Fagan's
69 Broad Lane
☎ (0114) 2728430
11–3, 5.30–11; 11–11 Fri & Sat
**Marston's Pedigree; Tetley
Bitter** Ⓗ
Lively, popular pub noted for
impromptu folk music
sessions in the back room. It
has a cosy snug by the
entrance to the main bar.
Q ⊛ Ⓓ ♣

Fat Cat
23 Alma Street
☎ (0114) 2728195
12–3, 5.30–11
**Kelham Island Bitter;
Marston's Pedigree; S&N
Theakston Old Peculier;
Taylor Landlord; guest
beers** Ⓗ
Sheffield's first real ale free
house, opened in 1981: two
comfortable rooms (one
non-smoking), a corridor
drinking area and an upstairs
function room. Kelham Island
Brewery is situated in the
grounds. ⍩ Q ⊛ Ⓓ ⌂ ⚥

Harlequin
26 Johnson Street
☎ (0114) 2729864
12–4, 7–11
Wards Best Bitter Ⓔ
Traditional, street-corner pub,
noted for the pot-bellied stove
in the tap room, which leads
through to a comfortable
lounge area. It also has a pool
room, and a corridor drinking
area. ⍩ ⊛ ⇌ (Midland) ♣

Lord Nelson
166 Arundel Street
☎ (0114) 2722650
12–11; 12–5, 7.30–11 Sat

**Hardys & Hansons Best
Bitter, Kimberley Classic** Ⓗ
Comfortable street-corner local
in an area of small workshops
at the edge of the city centre.
Upstairs games/function
room. Ⓓ ⇌ ♣

Red Deer
18 Pitt Street ☎ (0114) 2722890
11.30–11; 12–3, 7–11 Sat; 7–10.30 Sun,
closed Sun lunch
**Alloa Arrol's 80/-; Ind Coope
Burton Ale; Marston's
Pedigree; Tetley Mild, Bitter,
Imperial; Wards Best Bitter;
guest beer** Ⓗ
Friendly local close to the
university, with a central bar
and a gallery extension.
Excellent, home-cooked meals.
The paintings on display are
for sale. No-smoking area at
lunchtime. Q ⊛ Ⓓ ⚥

Red Lion
109 Charles Street
☎ (0114) 2724997
11.30–3, 5.30–11; 7–10.30 Sun, closed
Sun lunch
**Vaux Samson; Wards Best
Bitter; guest beers** Ⓗ
Pub featuring a small tap
room and a large lounge with
raised seating areas. The
conservatory overlooks the
garden. ⊛ Ⓓ 🍴 ⇌

Rutland Arms
86 Brown Street
☎ (0114) 2729003
11.30–3, 5–11; 12–4, 7.30–11 Sat; 12–3,
8–10.30 Sun
**Ind Coope Burton Ale;
Marston's Pedigree; Tetley
Bitter; Younger No. 3** Ⓗ
City-centre gem in a cultural
quarter. A comfortable lounge
hides behind a distinctive
Gilmour's frontage. Eve meals
served 5–7 Mon–Fri.
Q ⊛ ⍩ Ⓓ ▶ ⇌ P

Ship Inn
312 Shalesmoor
☎ (0114) 2720655
12–3, 6 (7 Sat)–11; 11–11 Fri
**Hardys & Hansons Best
Bitter** Ⓗ
Community pub where an
impressive Tomlinson's
frontage opens onto a
comfortable, L-shaped lounge
and pool room. ♣ P ⊟

Tap & Spile
42 Waingate ☎ (0114) 2726270
11.30–3, 5 (7 Sat)–11; 7–10.30 Sun,
closed Sun lunch
Beer range varies Ⓗ
Refurbished, ex-Gilmour's
street-corner pub. The large
bar has exposed brickwork
and bare boards, while a
smaller sideroom has a raised
darts area (no-smoking
lunchtime). Eight beers, plus
two ciders. Ⓓ ⇌ ♣ ⌂ ⚥

Washington
79 Fitzwilliam Street
☎ (0114) 2754937
11.30–3, 6.30–11; 12–2, 7–10.30 Sun
**Ind Coope Burton Ale;
Marston's Pedigree; Tetley
Mild, Bitter** Ⓗ**; guest beer**
Popular meeting place for
groups with two comfortably
furnished rooms. No food
weekends. Q Ⓓ ⊟ ♣

Sheffield: *East*

Carbrook Hall
537 Attercliffe Common
☎ (0114) 2440117
12–3, 5 (7 Sat)–11; 11–11 Fri
**John Smith's Magnet; Stones
Best Bitter; guest beers** Ⓗ
Large, reputedly haunted
three-roomed pub having links
to the Civil War through John
Bright, a Parliamentarian.
Q ⊛ Ⓓ ▶ ⌂ P

Cocked Hat
75 Worksop Road
☎ (0114) 2448332
11–11; 11–3.30, 7–11 Sat
**Marston's Bitter, Pedigree;
guest beer** Ⓗ
Popular, refurbished Victorian
pub next to the Don Valley
Stadium. A popular lunchtime
pub, offering good value
meals. Winner of several local
CAMRA awards. The guest
beers come from the Marston's
range. ⍩ Q ⊛ Ⓓ ♣

Enfield Arms
95 Broughton Lane, Carbrook
☎ (0114) 2425134
11.30 (11 Sat)–11
**Bass Worthington BB; Stones
Best Bitter; Tetley Bitter;
guest beers** Ⓗ
Renovated, good value
street-corner pub with a large
games area, all parts served by
a central bar. Opposite
Sheffield Arena. ⍨ Ⓓ ♣ P

Milestone
12 Peaks Mount, Waterthorpe
☎ (0114) 2471614
11–11
Banks's Mild, Bitter Ⓔ**;
Camerons Strongarm; guest
beers** Ⓗ
Modern but appealing pub
serving Crystal Peaks
Shopping Centre: a large
lounge with a conservatory,
but the beer is considerably
cheaper in the public. Good
value food.
⊛ Ⓓ ⅊ ⊖ ♣ P

Red Lion
145 Duke Street
☎ (0114) 2728296
12–4, 7–11
**Burtonwood Bitter,
Forshaw's** Ⓗ
Largely unspoilt, welcoming,
traditional local with a central
bar and drinking area plus

three separate rooms of varying character. ❀ ⇌ ♣

Sheffield: *North*

Cask & Cutler

1 Henry Street
☎ (0114) 2721487
12–3, 5.30–11; 11–11 Fri & Sat
Beer range varies Ⓗ
A shrine to the independent brewer, serving five changing guest beers. Two main drinking rooms are set around a traditional bar. Home-cooked food finishes at 6.30 eves (not served Sun).
Q ◖ ◗ ⊖ (Shalesmoor) ♣ ⌂ P ⊟

Mill Tavern

2–4 Earsham Street, Burngreave ☎ (0114) 2756461
11–4, 7–11
Old Mill Mild, Bitter Ⓗ
One bar serves all areas of this local, including a pool area. The only regular outlet for Old Mill in Sheffield. ❀ ♣

Morrisey's East House

18 Spital Hill ☎ (0114) 2726916
12–3, 5–11
Taylor Landlord; Whitbread Boddingtons Bitter; guest beers Ⓗ
Long, narrow pub with a single bar, home to climbing and hiking clubs. ♿ ♣

Robin Hood

Greaves Lane, Little Matlock, Stannington (right turn after Pinegrove Country Club)
☎ (0114) 2344565
11.30–3, 7–11
Stones Best Bitter Ⓔ; **guest beer** Ⓗ
Large former coaching inn on a defunct route to Manchester, retaining its tap room complete with wildlife theme. Long-serving licensees. Guest beers from the Bass Caskmaster range. Eve meals Tue–Sat. Quick service.
Q ❀ ◖ ◗ ⊟ ♣ P

Staffordshire Arms

40 Sorby Street
☎ (0114) 2721381
11–11
Stones Best Bitter Ⓔ
Friendly, unspoilt, back-street local: two rooms with a central bar. ♿ ♣

Sheffield: *South*

Byron House

16 Nether Edge Road
☎ (0114) 2551811
11.30–11
Draught Bass; Ruddles Best Bitter; Stones Best Bitter Ⓗ
Friendly, two-roomed suburban local with a plush lounge and a traditional tap room. Q ❀ ⊟ ♣

Earl of Arundel & Surrey

528 Queens Road (Bramall Lane/A61 jct)
☎ (0114) 2551006
11–11
Vaux Waggle Dance; Wards Thorne Best Bitter, Best Bitter Ⓗ/Ⓔ
Imposing, Victorian (1879) red-brick building (part circular), at a busy road junction. Sheffield's only pound house, its stable is still in use. Lofty, split-level lounge; pool room. ◖ ♣ P

Fleur de Lys

Totley Hall Lane
☎ (0114) 2361476
11–11
Bass Worthington BB, Draught Bass; Stones Best Bitter Ⓗ
Large, popular pub on the edge of the city with two oak-panelled rooms, the larger having a dining area. Handy for the Derbyshire moors. No eve meals Sat/Sun.
⌂ Q ☕ ❀ ◖ ◗ ♿ ♣ P

Old Mother Redcap

Prospect Road, Bradway
☎ (0114) 2360179
11.30–3.30, 5.30–11; 11–11 Sat
Samuel Smith OBB Ⓗ
Modern stone building in the style of an old farmhouse. Inside is a single L-shaped room, divided into small areas, with a very friendly atmosphere. Eve meals Thu and Fri. Q ❀ ◖ ◗ ♣ P ⊟

Shakespeare

106 Well Road
☎ (0114) 2553995
12–3.30 (4 Sat), 5.30 (7 Sat)–11
Stones Best Bitter; Tetley Bitter, Imperial; guest beer Ⓗ
Three cosy drinking areas in an imposing pub with a view over Sheffield. Close to Heeley City Farm. ❀ ♣ P

Small Beer Real Ale Off-Licence

57 Archer Road
☎ (0114) 2551356
11 (10.30 Sat)–10; 12–2, 7–10 Sun
Bateman XXXB; Fuller's London Pride; Taylor Landlord; guest beer Ⓗ
Small, but well stocked off-licence, selling a wide range of bottle-conditioned and Belgian beers.

Sheffield: *West*

Banner Cross

971 Ecclesall Road
☎ (0114) 2661479
11–11
Ind Coope Burton Ale; Tetley Bitter; guest beer Ⓗ
Busy local with a panelled lounge, a large, quiet tap room, and an upstairs games room. Q ❀ ◖ ♣

Cherry Tree

2 Carterknowle Avenue
☎ (0114) 2585051
12–11
Bass Worthington BB, Draught Bass; Stones Best Bitter; guest beer Ⓗ
Friendly estate local built in 1961. The single bar has a raised area. Q ❀ ♣ P

Devonshire Arms

118 Ecclesall Road
☎ (0114) 2722202
11–11
Taylor Landlord; Wards Best Bitter; guest beers Ⓗ
Extensively renovated local with several partitioned seating areas and a conservatory. The Wards brewery tap. Q ❀ ♿ P

Hallamshire House

49–51 Commonside
☎ (0114) 2663611
11–11
Taylor Landlord; Vaux Double Maxim, Waggle Dance; Wards Best Bitter Ⓗ
A small frontage, with hanging baskets, hides a large interior: a lounge/music room, a full-size snooker table, a games room and a snug, all of high quality. Q ◖ ♣

Old Grindstone

3 Crookes
☎ (0114) 2660322
11–11
Taylor Landlord; Vaux Samson, Waggle Dance; Wards Best Bitter; guest beer Ⓗ
Spacious, busy pub: the Victorian-design lounge has a raised area and the oak-panelled games room is based on a gentleman's club. Eve meals end at 7.30. ❀ ◖ ◗ ♣

Old Heavygate

114 Matlock Road
☎ (0114) 2340003
2 (12 Sat)–4, 7–11
Hardys & Hansons Best Bitter, Kimberley Classic Ⓗ
Pub dating from 1696, previously a cottage and toll house. ❀ ⊟ ♿ ♣ P ⊟

Star & Garter

82–84 Winter Street (by University Arts Tower)
☎ (0114) 2720695
11.30–11; 12–3, 7–11 Sat
Ind Coope Burton Ale; John Smith's Magnet; Tetley Bitter; guest beer Ⓗ
Pub where a central bar serves an open-plan lounge. Folk music Sun eve. ❀ ◖ ♣

South Yorkshire

Sprotbrough

Boat Inn
Nursery Lane
☎ (01302) 857188
11–3, 6–11 (may extend summer); 11–11 Sat
Courage Directors; John Smith's Bitter, Magnet Ⓗ
17th-century former coaching house where Sir Walter Scott wrote *Ivanhoe*. Reopened in 1985 after use as a farm, it enjoys an attractive setting. No food Sun eve. ✪ ◑ ▶ ⅋ P

Thorne

Canal Tavern
South Parade (next to bridge over canal) ☎ (01405) 813688
11.30–3, 5.30–11; 11.30–11 Sat
Tetley Bitter, Imperial; Whitbread Boddingtons Bitter, Trophy; guest beer Ⓗ
Canalside hostelry, popular with boaters, offering a wide range of beers and food.
⚄ ✪ ◑ ▶ ⅋ ⇌ (South) ♣ P

Green Dragon
Silver Street (market place)
☎ (01405) 812797
11–11
Wards Thorne Best Bitter Ⓗ
Lively, attractive lounge with a video jukebox plus a small, colourful bar providing games.
⅋ ⇌ (South) ♣ P ⊟

Thorpe Hesley

Masons Arms
Thorpe Street
☎ (0114) 2468079
11.30–3, 7–11
S&N Theakston Best Bitter, Old Peculier; John Smith's Bitter; Younger IPA Ⓗ
Welcoming, early 19th-century pub with one bar and three rooms on a split level. No food Sun. ✪ ◑ ▶ ⅋ P

Tickhill

Carpenter's Arms
West Gate ☎ (01302) 742839
11–3.30, 6–11
Vaux Samson, Double Maxim; Wards Best Bitter Ⓗ
Appealing pub with a lounge, a bar and a large, no-smoking family room. No food Sun. Award-winning garden.
➳ ✪ ◑ ⅋ ♣ P ⊟

Royal Oak
Northgate ☎ (01302) 742351
11–3 (4.30 Sat), 6 (5.30 Thu & Fri)–11
John Smith's Bitter; Whitbread Boddingtons Bitter, Trophy; guest beers Ⓗ
Friendly local with a comfortable lounge and bar serving two guest beers. Home-cooking; eve meals

Thu–Sat. Children's menu.
✪ ◑ ▶ ⅋ ♣ P

Scarbrough Arms
Sunderland Street
☎ (01302) 742977
11–3, 6–11
Courage Directors; Ruddles County; John Smith's Magnet; guest beers Ⓗ
Popular local with three rooms of differing character. Guest beers, from independent breweries, vary weekly. Home-made lunches (no food Sun). ⚄ Q ✪ ◑ ⅋ ♣ P ⊟

Ulley

Royal Oak
Turnshaw Road
☎ (0114) 2872464
Samuel Smith OBB Ⓗ
Old-world, friendly village pub of character. Loads of beams and brasses. Excellent food. ➳ ✪ ◑ ▶ P

Victoria

Victoria Inn
On A616 near pipe works
☎ (01484) 682755
12–2 (not Mon–Thu), 7–11; 12–2, 7–10.30 Sun
S&N Theakston Best Bitter; Tetley Bitter Ⓗ
A long standing *Guide* entry, an absolute gem unchanged for almost 40 years. ⚄ Q P

Wath upon Dearne

Staithes
Doncaster Road
☎ (01709) 873546
12–11
John Smith's Bitter; South Yorkshire Barnsley Bitter; Stones Best Bitter; guest beer Ⓗ
Pub taking its name from a loading point for coal onto a canal barge. Look for the replica handpumps around the rooms. Good wholesome meals. ⚄ Q ✪ ◑ ▶ P

Wentworth

Rockingham Arms
Main Street ☎ (01226) 942075
11–11
S&N Theakston Best Bitter, XB, Old Peculier; Younger No. 3; guest beer Ⓗ
200-year-old pub, a former coaching inn, boasting five open fires and a bowling green. Entertainment Thu and Fri in 'The Barn'. Theme nights. ⚄ ➳ ✪ ⅋ ◑ ▶ P

Wheatley Hills

Wheatley Hotel
Thorne Road ☎ (01302) 364092
10.30–11

Marston's Pedigree; Ruddles County; John Smith's Bitter, Magnet Ⓗ
Large, friendly hotel with a comfortable lounge, well-equipped children's room and a large garden. The restaurant (closed Sun eve) serves excellent value home-cooking.
➳ ✪ ⅋ ◑ ▶ P

Whiston

Golden Ball
Turner Lane ☎ (01709) 378200
11.45–3, 5–11; 11.45–11 Fri & Sat
Ind Coope Burton Ale; Taylor Landlord; Tetley Bitter, Imperial; guest beer Ⓗ
Picture postcard pub offering a pleasant outside drinking area. Extensive bar menu and a restaurant. Children's certificate. The landlord is an Ind Coope *Master Cellarman*.
⚄ ✪ ◑ ▶ P ⅋

Wombwell

Royal Oak
13 Church Street
☎ (01226) 210900
11.30–11
John Smith's Bitter; Whitbread Boddingtons Bitter; guest beers Ⓗ
Active town-centre pub displaying Clarkson's Brewery windows. Live music Fri and Sun; a popular meeting place for clubs. Eve meals finish early. The guest beers include a mild. ✪ ⅋ ◑ ▶ ⇌ ♣

Worsbrough Village

Edmunds Arms
25 Worsbrough Village (off A61) ☎ (01226) 206865
11–3, 6–11
Samuel Smith OBB Ⓗ
Splendid inn opposite an historic church and near a working watermill. The restaurant offers good value food (not served Mon eve).
Q ✪ ◑ ▶ ⅋ P

Wortley

Wortley Arms Hotel
Halifax Road
☎ (0114) 2882245
12–2.30, 5.30–11; 12–11 Sat
Stones Best Bitter; Wilson's Mild; Wortley Bitter, Earls Ale; Younger IPA, No.3; guest beers Ⓗ
16th-century coaching house, opposite the church; popular with walkers. Frequent folk nights. Wortley beers are brewed in the cellar.
⚄ Q ➳ ✪ ⅋ ◑ ▶
⅋ ➳ ♣ P ⅋ ⊟

337

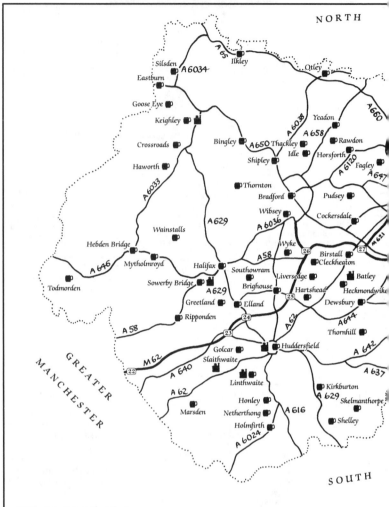

West Yorkshire

 Blackmoor, Batley; **Clark's,** Wakefield; **Commercial, Goose Eye,** Keighley; **Linfit,** Linthwaite; **Merrimans,** Leeds; **Old Court, Rat & Ratchet,** Huddersfield; **Ryburn,** Sowerby Bridge; **Steam Packet,** Knottingley; **Taylor,** Keighley; **Tomlinson's,** Pontefract; **Wild's,** Slaithwaite

---

Bingley

Brown Cow
Ireland Bridge (Harden Road)
☎ (01274) 569482
11.30–3, 5.30–11
Taylor Golden Best, Best Bitter, Landlord, Ram Tam Ⓗ
Wood panelling and stained-glass give a rural feel to this riverside pub where à la carte dining features prominently. Sun eve meals in summer only. ⌘ ❀ ⇔ ◑ 🕩 ⬥ P

Birstall

White Bear
108 High Street
(B6125, 200 yds N of village)
☎ (01924) 476212
12–3 (2.30 Mon), 5.30 (5 Mon)–11;
11–11 Fri & Sat
Tetley Mild, Bitter Ⓗ
Pub offering a large, opened-out lounge, a small, but cosy tap room and good value accommodation.
No eve meals Sat or Sun.
Q ❀ ⇔ ◑ 🕩 🍺 ♣ P

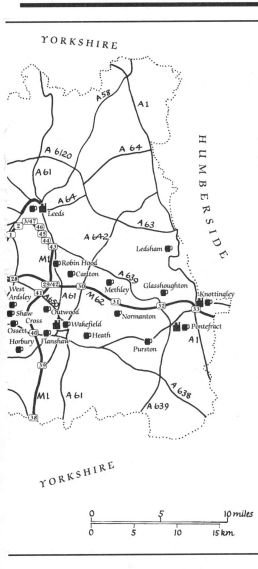

YORKSHIRE

HUMBERSIDE

A58 A1
A6120 A64
A61 A64
Leeds
3/47
2 A63
1 45 A642
44 Ledsham
43
M1 Robin Hood
28 Carlton A639
West 29/42 30 Methley Glasshoughton
Ardsley 41 A61 M62 Knottingley
Shaw A650 31 32 33
Cross Outwood Normanton
Ossett 40 Wakefield Pontefract
Horbury Flanshaw Heath A1
39 Purston
M1 A61
A639
38 A638

YORKSHIRE

```
0         5        10 miles
|----|----|----|----|----|
0      5      10     15 km
```

Bradford

Castle
20 Grattan Road
(off Westgate)
☎ (01274) 393166
11.30–11; closed Sun
**Mansfield Riding Mild,
Riding Bitter, Bitter; guest
beers** H
Built in Yorkshire stone,
in a style appropriate to its
name, this comfortable,
open-plan alehouse offers
beers from independent
brewers. Eve meals Fri and Sat
till 7.30. Car park open eves
and weekends.
◖ ▶ ≠ (Interchange) P

Corn Dolly
110 Bolton Road
☎ (01274) 720219
11.30–11
**Moorhouse's Premier;
S&N Theakston Best Bitter,
XB; Whitbread Boddingtons
Bitter; guest beers** H
Local CAMRA *Pub of the
Year* for the last two years:
up to 12 guest beers every
week, over 800 pumpclips
on display and eight beers
always available.
Comfortable and friendly.
Lunches Mon–Fri;
sandwiches Sat.
🏠 ❋ ◖ & ≠ (Forster Sq)
♣ P

Exchange Ale House
Market Street
☎ (01274) 729102
11–11; closed Sun
**Ruddles County; S&N
Theakston Best Bitter, XB;
John Smith's Magnet;
Webster's Yorkshire Bitter** H
City-centre cellar bar with a
brick barrel-roof, stone floor,
wood panelling and low
lighting. A friendly
atmosphere prevails through
loud rock music. No food
weekends.
◖ ≠ (Interchange/Forster Sq)

Fighting Cock
21–23 Preston Street (between
Thornton and Listerhills
Roads) ☎ (01274) 726907
11.30–11
**Black Sheep Special Strong;
Marston's Pedigree; Old Mill
Bitter; Samuel Smith OBB;
Taylor Landlord; Vaux
Double Maxim; guest beers** H
Down to earth, bare-boarded
drinkers' haven in an
industrial area. Eight regular,
and at least three, guest beers,
plus continental bottled beers.
The menu (not Sun) boasts a
famous chili and docker's
wedge sandwiches. Live
bands. ◖ ⌂

Haigy's Bar
31 Lumb Lane
☎ (01274) 731644
7 (12 Sat)–1am; closed Sun
**Black Sheep Best Bitter;
Tetley Bitter; guest beers** H
Lively pub with a late licence,
situated in a somewhat
notorious area. Nevertheless it
offers a friendly welcome and
is worth a visit for the range of
beers. Handy for Bradford
City FC. Meals served till
12.30am.
❋ ▶ & ♣ P

Idle Cock
1190 Bolton Road (A6176,
2 miles from centre)
☎ (01274) 639491
11.30–11
**Black Sheep Special Strong;
Old Mill Bitter; S&N
Theakston XB; Taylor
Landlord; Tetley Bitter; Vaux
Extra Special; guest beers** H
Excellent, two-roomed free
house undergoing a new
lease of life. Constantly
changing beer range.
❋ ⌂

Mail Coach
32 Huddersfield Road, Odsal
(200 yds from Odsal Stadium)
☎ (01274) 671857
7 (12 Sat)–11
Vaux Bitter, Samson H
Three-roomed pub with an
interesting mix of clientele;
very busy on Northern match
days. 🏠 ♣ P

West Yorkshire

Malt Kiln

129 Idle Road, Undercliffe
☎ (01274) 630035
11–11
**Ind Coope Burton Ale;
Marston's Pedigree; Tetley
Bitter; guest beers** Ⓗ
1930s roadhouse in London
suburban style, now a Tetley
Festival Alehouse. Its one
room is divided into
comfortable seating areas.
Popular, and can be loud at
anytime. ❀ P

Melborn Hotel

104 White Abbey Road
☎ (01274) 726867
11.30–11
**Commercial Alesman;
Mansfield Bitter; Tetley
Bitter; guest beers** Ⓗ
Multi-roomed, down to earth,
very friendly, inter-war pub
with a large tap room. Live
music is staged in the
impressive music room,
adorned with music
memorabilia (concerts
Thu–Sun nights).
❀ ⇔ 曰 ♣ P

New Beehive

171 Westgate
☎ (01274) 721784
11–11 (1am Fri & Sat)
**Commercial Alesman;
Mitchell's Original, Lancaster
Bomber; Moorhouse's Pendle
Witches Brew; Old Mill
Bitter; Taylor Landlord; guest
beers** Ⓗ
Well-preserved, Edwardian
gaslit inn: a multi-roomed,
atmospheric and popular pub.
The large cellar bar has a
skittle alley and stages
concerts.
Ⓜ Q ❀ ⇔ ◖ 曰 ♣ ⇔ P

Prospect of Bradford

527 Bolton Road
☎ (01274) 639835
3–5, 7–11
**S&N Theakston Best Bitter;
Tetley Bitter** Ⓗ
Nearer the city centre than it
would appear: a pub with a
spacious drinking area and
panoramic views over
Bradford (watch City play
free). Accommodation by
arrangement. Ⓜ ♣ P

Queen Ale House

863 Thornton Road,
Fairweather Green
☎ (01274) 542898
12–11
**Whitbread Boddingtons
Bitter, Trophy, Castle Eden
Ale, Flowers Original; guest
beers** Ⓗ
Busy, two-roomed free house
with an ever-changing beer
range. Local stone and slate
flooring adds to the character.
No meals Sun. ❀ ◖ 曰 ♣ P

Ram's Revenge

1–3 Upper Millergate (top of
Ivegate) ☎ (01274) 720283
11.30–11; 11.30–5, 7–11 Sat
**Moorhouse's Pendle Witches
Brew; S&N Theakston XB;
Taylor Best Bitter, Landlord;
Tetley Bitter** Ⓗ
City-centre alehouse with an
adjoining lounge bar which
only opens weekday
lunchtimes and Fri/Sat nights.
◖ ⇌ (Interchange/Forster Sq)
♣

Shoulder of Mutton

28 Kirkgate ☎ (01274) 726038
11–11; 12–2, 7–10.30 Sun
**Samuel Smith OBB,
Museum** Ⓗ
This is the 17th consecutive
Guide entry for this small,
multi-room, city-centre pub
dating from 1825. A cross-
section of clients enjoy the
home-made lunches (not Sun)
and the large, multi-award-
winning suntrap garden.
Q ⍭ ❀ ◖ ⇌ (Interchange/
Forster Sq) ♣

Steve Biko Bar

Bradford University, D Floor,
Richmond Building (off
Great Horton Rd)
☎ (01274) 733466
11 (7 Sat)–11; 7–10.30 Sun, closed
Sun lunch
**Greene King Abbot; John
Smith's Bitter; Taylor
Landlord; Wadworth 6X;
Whitbread Castle Eden Ale,
Flowers Original; guest
beers** Ⓗ
Large, open-plan bar with
plenty of seating. It can get
noisy eves. ▶ ⅙ ⇌
(Interchange) ♣ ⇔ P ✗

Brighouse

Junction

Ogden Lane, Rastrick
☎ (01484) 713089
4.30 (12 Mon, Fri & Sat)–11 (may
close Mon afternoons if quiet)
**Burtonwood Bitter,
Forshaw's, Top Hat** Ⓗ
Former Tetley house, now the
only Burtonwood pub in
Calderdale. It can get a bit
noisy, particularly when
there's live entertainment
(Thu). ⅙ ♣ P

Carlton

Rosebud

Westfield Road
☎ (0113) 2822236
12–2.30 (4 Sat), 5.30 (5 Sat)–11; 12–11
Fri
**John Smith's Bitter; Vaux
Samson** Ⓗ
Friendly two-roomed village
local. The traditional tap room
is home to serious games
teams; good conversation in

the lounge. No meals
weekends (snacks Sat).
Ⓜ Q ❀ ◖ 曰 ♣ P

Cleckheaton

Marsh

28 Bradford Road (A638, 400
yds S of A643 jct)
☎ (01274) 872104
11.45–3, 7–11
**Old Mill Mild, Bitter,
Bullion** Ⓗ
Well-established, friendly local
with a good mix of customers.
A triangular exterior hides an
ingenious internal layout with
games area, quiet dias and an
ubiquitous crinkly brick wall.
❀ ♣ P

Cockersdale

Valley

68 Whitehall Road
☎ (0113) 2852483
12–3, 5.30–11; 12–11 Sat
Samuel Smith OBB, Museum
(occasional) Ⓗ
Traditional, tastefully
furnished, roadside local
offering good value beer and
food: four separate rooms with
a friendly atmosphere.
Wonderful views over SW
Leeds and Cockersdale. Ideal
after a long walk.
Q ⍭ ❀ ◖ ♣ P

Crossroads

Quarry House Inn

Bingley Road, Lees Moor
(½mile from A629/A6033 jct)
☎ (01535) 642239
12–3, 7–11
**Ind Coope Burton Ale; Taylor
Landlord; Tetley Bitter** Ⓗ
Family-run converted
farmhouse in open
countryside with extensive
views. The bar is a former
church pulpit and is set in a
small cosy area. Twice winner
of a local CAMRA *Pub of the
Season* award. Excellent food.
Families welcome.
Ⓜ ❀ ◖ ▶ ⅙ ▲ P

Dewsbury

Market House

8 Church Street (200 yds N of
bus station) ☎ (01924) 457310
11–11
**S&N Theakston Best Bitter;
Tetley Mild, Bitter** Ⓗ
Tetley Heritage pub, with a
beautiful bank of handpumps
in the excellent tap room. The
back lounge is served by a
small serving hatch. The
corridor in between is often
the busiest of the three areas.
Wheelchair access at the rear.
No food Sun.
Ⓜ ❀ ◖ 曰 ⇌ ♣

West Riding Licensed Refreshment Rooms

Railway Station,
Wellington Road
☎ (01924) 459193
11–11
**Bateman Mild, XB, Valiant;
guest beers** Ⓗ
Three-roomed pub, converted
from the waiting room on
Dewsbury station, with wood
floors and real fires. In the
short time it has been open, it
has offered an amazing range
of guest beers from near and
far. Wheelchair WC. Meals
served 12–7 (lunch only Sun).
🏚 Q ♿ ❀ ◑ ♿ ⇌ ♣ ♨
P ⌷

Eastburn

White Bear

Main Road
☎ (01535) 653000
12–11
**Tetley Bitter; Whitbread
Flowers IPA, Original** Ⓗ
Large, roadside pub split into
several areas, with a genuine
tap room. Live music Mon
(folk), Wed (guitar and
singing) and Fri (live band).
Very popular for its authentic
Indian menu.
🏚 ❀ ◑ ▶ ⌻ A ♣ P

Elland

Collier's Arms

66 Park Road (A6025)
☎ (01422) 372007
11.30–3, 5.30–11; 11.30–11 Sat
**Samuel Smith OBB,
Museum** Ⓗ
Two-roomed cottage pub with
a conservatory to the rear
overlooking a canal
(moorings). Attractive small
garden. Eve meals Thu–Sat,
6–8.30. 🏚 ⛱ ❀ ◑ ♣ P

Golden Fleece

Lindley Road, Blackley (1 mile
S of Elland, close to M62 jct 24)
OS106195 ☎ (01422) 372704
12–2.30 (not Sat), 7–11
**Vaux Samson; Wards Thorne
Best Bitter** Ⓗ
Attractive village inn, tucked
away on a quiet road: two
welcoming rooms. Fine views
to the front; cricket pitch to the
rear. 🏚 Q ❀ ◑ P

Fagley

Blue Pig

Fagley Road, Lower Fagley
(narrow road at the end of
Fagley Rd) OS193351
☎ (0113) 2562738
3 (12 Fri & Sat)–11
**S&N Theakston Best Bitter;
Taylor Landlord; Tetley
Bitter; guest beers** Ⓗ

Split-level pub on the Leeds
Country Way, within a slice of
a golf course. Flooding
necessitated the building of
the low front wall and
tortuous entrance route. Quiz
most eves. Excellent family
room. ⛱ ❀ ♣ P

Flanshaw

Flanshaw Hotel

Flanshaw Lane (off A638)
☎ (01924) 290830
11.30 (1 Tue)–11
Beer range varies Ⓗ
Large, friendly community
pub with cheap guest beers
(usually two) served in
oversized glasses. Eve
activities are varied. Close to
M1 jct 40.
❀ ◑ ▶ ⌻ ⅃ ♣ P ⊟

Glasshoughton

Rock Inn

Rock Hill (off Front St, B6136)
☎ (01977) 552985
11–11
**Wards Thorne Best Bitter;
guest beer** Ⓗ
Popular, friendly, traditional
local, comprising a lounge, tap
room and snug, all with open
fires. Upstairs pool room.
Good menu; food served until
7. 🏚 ❀ ◑ ▶ ⌻ ⅃ ♣ P

Golcar

Golcar Lily

Slades Road (follow signs for
Heath House Mill)
☎ (01484) 659277
12–3, 5.30–11; 11–11 Sat
**Mansfield Riding Bitter,
Bitter, Old Baily; guest beer** Ⓗ
Pub built in 1875 as a Co-op
and converted 14 years ago.
The country hillside setting
affords panoramic views over
the Colne Valley. The licensee
is an Ind Coope *Master
Cellarman*. No food Mon
eve (get fit night).
❀ ◑ ▶ ♣ P

Goose Eye

Turkey Inn

Take Oakworth road from
Keighley, right at Fell Lane
then right
☎ (01535) 681339
12–3 (5 Sat; not Mon), 5.30 (7 Sat)–11
**Goose Eye Bitter, Pommie's
Revenge; Ind Coope Burton
Ale; Tetley Bitter** Ⓗ
Attractive, traditional, old pub
in a scenic location, offering
good food in good portions,
although the beer is pricey for
the locale. Busy in summer
and at weekends. No food
Mon. 🏚 ❀ ◑ ▶ ♣ P

Greetland

Greetland Community & Sporting Association

Rochdale Road
(B6113, by church)
☎ (01422) 370140
7 (12 Sat)–11; 12–3, 7–11 Wed
**Taylor Best Bitter; guest
beers** Ⓗ
Club which caters for all ages
with a single friendly bar.
Athletic types sample the wide
variety of guest ales. There
may be a 50p admission
charge for non-members.
♣ P

Star Inn

1 Lindwell (off B6113)
☎ (01422) 373164
12–3, 7–11
**Wards Thorne Best Bitter,
Best Bitter** Ⓗ
Friendly local: a well-lit, busy
tap room and a cosy lounge
with subdued lighting. The
start/finish of the
Calderdale Way is nearby.
❀ ♣

Halifax

Horse & Jockey

301 Warley Road, Highroad
Well (1½ miles W of centre)
☎ (01422) 361992
12–11
**Old Mill Bitter; John Smith's
Bitter; Webster's Yorkshire
Bitter** Ⓗ
Pleasantly decorated,
welcoming, two-roomed pub,
popular with all ages. The tap
room is always busy.
❀ ◑ ⌻ ⅃ P

Lewin's

22–26 Bull Green
☎ (01422) 352043
11–11
**Bass Worthington BB,
Draught Bass; Stones Best
Bitter; Taylor Landlord; guest
beers** Ⓗ
Popular, stone-built, town-
centre pub with three bars
attracting a varied clientele.
🏚 ◑ ⌻ ⇌ ♣

Pump Room

35 New Road (left from
station) ☎ (01422) 381465
11–11
**Black Sheep Special Strong;
Mansfield Riding Bitter,
Bitter; Marston's Pedigree;
Old Mill Bitter; Taylor
Landlord; guest beers** Ⓗ
Long two-bar alehouse, home
to various teams. Mansfield
seasonal brews, plus a house
beer and four or more guest
beers are served. 'Hot
Meal/Cool Pint' specials. No
food Sun. ❀ ◑ ⇌

West Yorkshire

Shears Inn
Paris Gates, Boys Lane (in valley bottom behind flats off Shaw Hill) ☎ (01422) 362936
11.45–11
Taylor Golden Best, Best Bitter, Landlord; Younger Scotch, No. 3; guest beer Ⓗ
Popular, old pub which is home to a number of sports teams. Dwarfed by adjacent mills, it is convenient for the Hebble Trail footpath. No meals weekends.
🅼 ❀ Ⓓ ♣ P

Tap & Spile
1 Clare Road ☎ (01422) 353661
11–11
Big Lamp Bitter; Tetley Bitter; Wells Eagle; guest beers Ⓗ
Mock Tudor extravaganza built in 1931 as Ramsden's brewery tap. Sensitive conversion to a traditional ale house has retained many original fittings in its two drinking areas. Spacious upstairs function room.
Ⓓ ⇌ ♣ ⟲ ⸜

Three Pigeons Ale House
1 Sun Fold, South Parade ☎ (01422) 347001
12–3, 5–11; 11–11 Fri & Sat
Black Sheep Special Strong; Old Mill Bitter; Taylor Landlord; Tetley Bitter; Whitbread Boddingtons Bitter; guest beer Ⓗ
Refurbished, neo-Georgian 1930s pub with an Art Deco interior (an octagonal drinking area with rooms radiating off). The house beer is brewed by Coach House. 🅼 🛏 Ⓓ ⇌ ♣

Woodcock
213 Gibbet Street (½ mile W of centre) ☎ (01422) 359906
11.30–11
Bateman XXXB; Mitchell's Lancaster Bomber; Old Mill Bitter; Taylor Landlord; Wadworth IPA; guest beers Ⓗ
No-frills alehouse offering up to 12 beers and two ciders. Shelves are adorned with pumpclips and bottles. The leaded windows recall days when it was a Ramsden's house. 🅼 Ⓓ ♣ ⟲

Hartshead

New Inn
Prospect Road (B6119) ☎ (01274) 874781
6 (11 Sat)–11; 12–3, 5–11 Fri
Tetley Bitter; Whitbread Boddingtons Bitter; guest beers Ⓗ
Village local saved from closure and enlarged into adjoining cottages with bars on two floors. Many old features have been retained.

Fine views. Usually three guest beers. No food Tue lunchtime or Mon; eve meals end at 8.30. 🅼 ❀ Ⓓ ♠ ♣

Haworth

Haworth Old Hall
Sun Street (opp. park) ☎ (01535) 642709
11–11
Draught Bass; Stones Best Bitter; Taylor Golden Best; Tetley Bitter Ⓗ
Family-friendly, three-roomed, 17th-century building featuring open stonework, beams and mullioned windows. Large garden; à la carte restaurant. Good Sun lunches. 🛏 ❀ 🛏 Ⓓ ♠ Ⓐ
⇌ (KWVLR) P

Royal Oak
2 Mill Hey (opp. station) ☎ (01535) 643257
11.30–3, 7–11; 11.30–11 Sat
Courage Directors; John Smith's Bitter; Webster's Yorkshire Bitter Ⓗ
Formerly the village mortuary and a courthouse, this pub offers a large open lounge and a small family room decorated with railway memorabilia.
🅼 🛏 Ⓓ ⇌ (KWVLR) ♣ P

Heath

King's Arms
Heath Common (A61 then A638 from Wakefield) ☎ (01924) 377527
11.30–3, 5.30–11
Clark's Bitter, Festival Ale; Taylor Landlord; Tetley Bitter Ⓗ
Friendly pub surrounded by 100 acres of common grassland. Superb food.
🅼 🛏 ❀ Ⓓ ♠ ♣ P ⸜ 🗒

Hebden Bridge

Fox & Goose
9 Heptonstall Road (A646) ☎ (01422) 842649
11.30–3, 7–11
Goose Eye Bitter; guest beers Ⓗ
Small, friendly pub serving three independents' guest ales; those you missed are listed above the bar! Foreign bottled beers also stocked. Parking difficult. No meals Tue eve.
Q ❀ Ⓓ ♣

Hare & Hounds
Billy Lane, Chiserley ☎ (01422) 842671
12–3 (not Tue–Thu winter, or Mon all year), 7–11
Taylor Golden Best, Best Bitter, Landlord Ⓗ
Known locally as Lane Ends, this cosy hillside pub is near the Automobilia Transport

---

Museum. Popular bar meals (not served Mon eve in summer or Mon/Tue eves in winter). Hours may vary according to weather conditions and custom. Families welcome.
🅼 Q ❀ Ⓓ ♣ P

Mount Skip Inn
Heights Road, Wadsworth (off Birchcliffe Rd and Wadsworth Lane) OS006272 ☎ (01422) 842765
12–3 (not winter Mon), 7–11; 12–11 Sat
Taylor Golden Best, Best Bitter, Landlord, Ram Tam (winter); Tetley Bitter Ⓗ
Pub set above Hebden Bridge with views along the Calder Valley and Cragg Vale. Home-cooked food includes vegetarian (no lunches Mon). Calderdale Way footpath is at the rear – camping is possible.
🅼 ❀ Ⓓ ♣ P

Heckmondwike

Old Hall
New North Road (400 yards NW of the green) ☎ (01924) 404774
11.30–2.30, 6–11
Samuel Smith OBB Ⓗ
The childhood home of Joseph Priestley, discoverer of Oxygen, this late medieval, timber-framed, aisled house is encased in stone and retains much original work, including a fine 1640s ceiling. Upper gallery function room.
❀ Ⓓ ♠ P

Holmfirth

Rose & Crown (Nook)
Victoria Square (down alley behind Barclay's Bank) ☎ (01484) 683960
11.30–11
Samuel Smith OBB; Stones Best Bitter; Taylor Best Bitter, Landlord, Ram Tam; Tetley Mild; guest beers Ⓗ
Legendary, basic, traditional boozer with an extensive range of beers and a stone floor. Not visible from the road and difficult to find.
🅼 🛏 ❀ ♣

Honley

Railway
1 Woodhead Road (A616/A6024 jct) ☎ (01484) 661309
11.30–3, 5–11; 11.30–11 Fri & Sat
S&N Theakston Best Bitter; Taylor Landlord; Tetley Mild, Bitter; guest beer Ⓗ
Busy village pub in a corner location, bigger than it would first appear. A bottle and plate collection vies with pictures by local artists for wall space.

Swings and slides outside. No lunches Sun.
🏛 🌸 ◁ ⇌ ♣ P

Horbury

Bingley Arms
Bridge Road ☎ (01924) 281331
2 (12 Sat)–11
Tetley Bitter Ⓗ
Imposing stone pub nestling between the River Calder and the adjacent canal, with a well-positioned garden. Food planned after refurbishment.
🌸 ♣ P.

Calder Vale
Millfield Road (400 yds from A642, Southfield Rd)
☎ (01924) 275351
12–3.30, 6.15–11
John Smith's Bitter; guest beers Ⓗ
Comfortable local built by Fernandes Brewery in 1884. Situated in Horbury Junction on the outskirts of town, it can be difficult to find, but the local characters and atmosphere make it worth the journey. Q 🌸 ♣ P

Horsforth

Old King's Arms
The Green ☎ (0113) 2581189
11–11
Marston's Pedigree; Tetley Mild, Bitter; guest beers Ⓗ
Stone-built, Victorian pub, Tetley's first Festival Ale House in Leeds. The tap room remains an oasis of calm, separate from the large main room. Five guest beers.
🌸 ◁ 🍺 ♣ P

Huddersfield

Marsh Liberal Club
Glenfield, 31 New Hey Road (A640, 1 mile from centre)
☎ (01484) 420152
12–2 (not Mon), 7–11; 12–11 Sat
Black Sheep Best Bitter; Samuel Smith OBB; Taylor Best Bitter; Tetley Mild, Bitter; guest beers Ⓗ
Club housed in a Grade II-listed building, usually boasting three guest beers. Bowling green to the rear. Occasional cider. Show this guide or a CAMRA membership card at the bar to be signed in. ⛄ 🌸 ♣ P

Rat & Ratchet
40 Chapel Hill (A616, near ring road jct) ☎ (01484) 516734
12 (3 Mon & Tue)–11
Adnams Bitter; Bateman Mild; Mansfield Old Baily; Marston's Pedigree; Taylor Best Bitter, Landlord; guest beers Ⓗ
Pub offering 14 ales at all times, with an ever changing range of guests. Its own brewery produces special beers. Bi-annual beer festivals. Chilli night Tue; curry day Wed; no eve meals other days. Lunches Wed–Sat.
🌸 ◁ ▶ ⇌ ♣ ⌂ P

Shoulder of Mutton
11 Neale Road, Lockwood (off B6108 near A616 jct, 1 mile S of centre) ☎ (01484) 424835
7 (3 Sat)–11
Taylor Best Bitter, Landlord; Tetley Mild, Bitter; Whitbread Boddingtons Bitter; guest beers Ⓗ
Genuine free house with a traditional atmosphere, at the head of a cobbled street. Over the years, subtle alterations have taken place without destroying the innate charm.
🌸 ⇌ (Lockwood) ♣

Slubber's Arms
1 Halifax Old Road (just off A641, ¾ mile from centre)
☎ (01484) 429032
12–3.30, 6.30 (7 Sat)–11
Marston's Pedigree; Taylor Best Bitter; guest beers Ⓗ
150-year-old beer house which has grown into an odd-shaped pub by absorbing adjoining cottages. It has strong associations with the textile industry, hence the name. Note the black leaded kitchen range in the lounge. Snacks lunchtime. 🏛 Q ♣

Zeneca Club
509 Leeds Road (A62, 3 miles NE of centre)
☎ (01484) 421784
12–11
Taylor Best Bitter; Tetley Mild, Bitter; guest beer Ⓗ
Twice winner of CAMRA's *Club of the Year* award: a large club with three lounges, two bars, eight snooker tables, bowls, tennis, croquet, etc. Show the *Guide* or CAMRA membership to be signed in. Lunches Mon–Fri.
⛄ 🌸 ◁ ♣ P ✗

Idle

Brewery Tap
51 Albion Road
☎ (01274) 613936
11.30–3 (4 Sat), 6.30–11
Tetley Bitter; Whitbread Flowers IPA, Castle Eden Ale; guest beers Ⓗ
Pub converted from a bakery by the now defunct Trough Brewery. Wood panelled walls, a stone-flagged floor and a large central bar are features. Live rock music Tue and Sat nights. 🌸 ♿ ♣

Springfield Hotel
172 Bradford Road
☎ (01274) 612710
12–11

Vaux Samson Ⓗ
Roadside local on the edge of a large housing estate, featuring two small rooms: a lounge with pool and a tap room popular with darts players. Like the car park, it is often not big enough. 🍺 ♣ P

Ilkley

Midland Hotel
9 Station Road
☎ (01943) 607433
11–11
Courage Directors; Goose Eye Bitter; Marston's Pedigree; John Smith's Bitter; Webster's Green Label Ⓗ
Convenient for bus and train stations: a pub with two rooms, one of which is games-oriented. The lounge is warm and comfortable.
Q ◁ 🍺 ⇌ ♣ P

Keighley

Albert Hotel
13 Bridge Street
☎ (01535) 602306
11–3, 5.30–11; 11–11 Fri & Sat
Taylor Golden Best, Best Bitter, Landlord, Ram Tam (winter) Ⓗ
Spacious Victorian pub with a boisterously good humoured atmosphere. Half a motorcycle hangs on the wall and there's a psychedelic 1960s mural. Popular with all sorts. ♣ P

Boltmaker's Arms
117 East Parade
☎ (01535) 661936
11.30–11; 11–4.30, 7–11 Sat
Taylor Golden Best, Best Bitter, Landlord; Tetley Bitter Ⓗ
Small, split-level, one-roomed pub, popular with locals and visitors. At least 18 whiskies.
⇌ (BR/KWVLR) ♣

Cricketer's Arms
Coney Lane
☎ (01535) 669912
11–11
Taylor Golden Best, Best Bitter, Landlord, Ram Tam Ⓗ
Small, comfortable local wedged between mills a short walk from the town centre. Bar snacks lunchtime.
♿ ⇌ ♣

Grinning Rat/Rat Trap
2 Church Street
☎ (01535) 609747
Grinning Rat 11–11; Rat Trap 8–midnight (2am Thu–Sat)
Taylor Landlord; Tetley Bitter; Whitbread Boddingtons Bitter, Castle Eden Ale; guest beers Ⓗ
Centrally-located, popular, large, multi-level alehouse with up to 17 beers available at weekends (one mild). The

Rat Trap is the adjoining night club (two bars). ⓓ ⓖ ⚇ ⓒ

Red Pig

Church Street
☎ (01535) 605383
12–3, 7–11; 12–11 Fri & Sat
Commercial Alesman; Taylor Golden Best, Landlord; guest beers ℍ
Very popular, town-centre pub featuring exposed brickwork and local artists' exhibits: an ex-Trough pub. No dogs.
🏚 ⚇ ♣

Volunteer Arms

Lawkholme Lane (behind the Cavendish pub in Cavendish St) ☎ (01535) 600173
11–11
Taylor Golden Best, Best Bitter ℍ
Compact local with two rooms, the smaller used mainly for games.
⚇ (BR/KWVLR) ♣

Keighley to Oxenhope and Back

Keighley & Worth Valley Buffet Car

Stations at Keighley, Ingrow West, Oakworth, Haworth and Oxenhope
☎ (01535) 645214/talking timetable (01535) 647777
Runs Sat & Sun Mar–Oct
Beer range varies ℍ
Volunteer-run railway buffet car giving changing views of the Worth Valley and serving local independents' beers. Bottle-conditioned beers from Commercial. Q ▲ (Marsh, Oxenhope) ⚇ (Keighley) P (Keighley, Ingrow W, Oxenhope) ⚇ ⊟

Kirkburton

Royal

64 North Road
☎ (01484) 602521
11.30–3 (not Mon), 5–11; 11.30–11 Sat
Ind Coope Burton Ale; Taylor Landlord; Tetley Mild, Bitter, Imperial; guest beers (occasional) ℍ
Welcoming Victorian pub serving excellent quality and value food. Refurbished lounge; separate tap room and upstairs function room. No jukebox. 🏚 ⚇ ⓓ ▶ ⚇ ♣ P

Knottingley

Steam Packet Inn

2 Racca Green (A645)
☎ (01977) 677266
11–11
Steam Packet Gamekeeper, Chatterley, Foxy, Bit o Black, Brown Ale; guest beers ℍ

Large, three-room pub on a canal bank. The beer range may vary and include special brews. 🏚 ⚇ ⚇ ▲ ♣ P ⊟

Ledsham

Chequers

Claypit Lane (off A1)
☎ (01977) 683135
11–3, 5.30–11; 11–11 Sat; closed Sun
S&N Theakston Best Bitter; Younger Scotch, No.3 ℍ
Beautiful, unspoilt village inn, with ivy-covered walls, a maze of small rooms, oak beams, real fires and plenty of conversation. A gem! Restaurant upstairs.
🏚 Q ⚇ ⓓ ▶ ♣ P

Leeds

Beer Exchange

121 Woodhouse Street, Woodhouse ☎ (0113) 2314658
12–3, 5.30–11
Fuller's London Pride; Marston Moor Cromwell; guest beer ℍ
CAMRA regional *Pub of the Year* 1995: three areas around a central bar, with wood panels and exposed brick. No music; large no-smoking area. Regular beer festivals.
Q ⓓ ▶ ⚇ ⓒ ⚇ ⊟

Beer Paradise

Unit 11, Riverside Place, Bridgewater Road, Cross Green (off south accommodation road)
☎ (0113) 2359082
10–6 (8 Thu & Fri); 12–3 Sun
Huge beer emporium specialising in Belgian/foreign beers but with a good range of bottle-conditioned British beers. CAMRA members are automatic members (take your card). ⓖ ⓒ P

Bricklayer's Arms

St Marks Road, Woodhouse
☎ (0113) 2458277
11–3.30, 5–11 (11–11 term time)
Courage Directors; Marston's Pedigree; John Smith's Bitter, Magnet; guest beers ℍ
Buried amidst the university's St Marks flats, this typical corner local comprises a single bar broken up by screens into separate drinking areas. Good cheap food and guest beers.
⚇ ⓓ ♣ P

Chemic Tavern

Johnston Street, Woodhouse
11–3, 5.30–11; 11–11 Sat
Ind Coope Burton Ale; Tetley Bitter; guest beer ℍ
Attractive, two-roomed local with low beams, mirrors and many wallplates. No electronic beeps, just that rare thing – conversation! Q ⚇ ♣ P

City of Mabgate

45 Mabgate (off Regent St)
☎ (0113) 2457789
11–11
Marston's Pedigree; Morland Old Speckled Hen; Whitbread Boddingtons Bitter, Trophy; guest beers ℍ
Former Leeds CAMRA *Pub of the Year*, recovering in the hands of a developments group which has put back the guest beers Whitbread removed. 🏚 ⚇ ⓓ ⚇ ♣

Commercial

Elland Road, Churwell
☎ (0113) 2532776
11.30–3, 6–11
Tetley Mild, Bitter ℍ
Pleasantly refurbished pub retaining separate drinking areas plus a family room; known to locals as 'Top 'Ole'.
⚇ ⚇ ⓓ ♣ P

Duck & Drake

48 Kirkgate ☎ (0113) 2465806
11–11
Old Mill Bitter; S&N Theakston Best Bitter, XB, Old Peculier; Taylor Landlord; Younger No.3; guest beers ℍ
Popular alehouse serving a wide range of ales to a wider range of people. Bare floorboards throughout. The tap room has a rare Yorkshire doubles dartboard.
🏚 ⓓ ⚇ ♣ ⓒ

Eagle Tavern

North Street (A61)
☎ (0113) 2457146
11–3, 5.30–11
Taylor Golden Best, Mild, Best Bitter, Landlord, Ram Tam; guest beers ℍ
Legendary Leeds alehouse, winner of many CAMRA awards, which has hit the 1000-guest beer mark within five years despite having just two guest handpumps. A white Georgian building, it has a large, airy tap room and a comfortable lounge.
Q ⚇ ⚇ ⓓ ♣ ⓒ P

Feast & Firkin

Woodhouse Moor
☎ (0113) 2453669
11–11
Fuzz Bitter, Feast Bitter, Dogbolter; Tetley Bitter ℍ
Opened in 1994, and once a police/fire station and a library, this ornate brew pub is close to the university. Specials brewed occasionally. Food is well priced. Wheelchair WC.
ⓓ ⓖ ⓒ P ⚇

Fox & Newt

Burley Street, Burley
☎ (0113) 2432612
11–11

West Yorkshire

Fox & Newt Cushtie, Black & Amber, Bitch; Whitbread Castle Eden Ale Ⓗ
Formerly the Rutland Hotel, a brew pub with basic bare boards; popular with students. Ⓓ ☍

Grove
Back Row, Holbeck
☎ (0113) 2439254
12–11; 12–4, 7–11 Sat
Draught Bass; Courage Directors; Ruddles Best Bitter, County; John Smith's Bitter, Magnet Ⓗ
Virtually unchanged, inter-war pub boasting four complete rooms and an excellent Yorkshire corridor drinking area. It is often dubbed the home of folk music in Leeds.
❀ Ⓓ ⊞ ≝ (City) ♣

Horse & Trumpet
The Headrow
☎ (0113) 2430338
11–11
Marston's Pedigree; Tetley Mild, Bitter, guest beers Ⓗ
Tetley Festival Alehouse with a fine Victorian facade giving way to an opened out and altered interior. Up to four independent guest beers. Smart dress – checked by doormen – at weekends. No food Sun. Ⓓ ⌣

Londoner
Lovell Park Road
☎ (0113) 2453666
11–11
Tetley Bitter; guest beers Ⓗ
Modern pub just on the edge of the city centre, elevated to Tetley Festival Alehouse status. Open-plan, bare-boarded and dimly lit, it is now a disco-free zone by popular demand. Five changing guest beers.
❀ Ⓓ ▶ ♣ P

Nag's Head
20 Town Street, Chapel Allerton ☎ (0113) 2624938
11–11
Samuel Smith OBB Ⓗ
White-painted, 17th-century pub in Georgian manor house style with a large lounge and a busy tap room. No food Sun.
❀ Ⓓ ⊞ ♣ P

New Inn
Elland Road, Churwell
☎ (0113) 2533468
11–11
Whitbread Boddingtons Bitter, Trophy, Castle Eden Ale; guest beers Ⓗ
This popular roadside pub, known locally as 'Bottom 'Ole', has a stone flagged bar and partitioned drinking areas. Good range of guest beers but beware: some guests

may be kept under an aspirator. Good food at reasonable prices.
❀ Ⓓ ▶ ☍ ♣ P

New Roscoe
Bristol Street, Sheepscar
☎ (0113) 2460778
11–11
Moorhouse's Premier; Tetley Bitter; guest beer Ⓗ
Former club with a large plush lounge, an expansive tap room and a smaller Roscoe room featuring artefacts from the original Roscoe which fell to urban road planners. An Irish atmosphere prevails.
❀ Ⓓ ☍ ♣ P

Old Vic
17 Whitecote Hill, Bramley
☎ (0113) 2561207
11–11 (4 Sat; not Tue), 7–11
Taylor Golden Best, Landlord; Tetley Bitter; guest beer Ⓗ
Formerly a vicarage, this popular free house is set back from the road in its own grounds. Two lounges and a tap/games room are served from a central bar.
♨ Ⓓ ⊞ ☍ ♣ P

Palace
Kirkgate ☎ (0113) 2445882
11–11
Ind Coope Burton Ale; Marston's Pedigree; Tetley Mild, Bitter, guest beers Ⓗ
Recent addition to the Tetley Festival Alehouse group, offering up to six guest beers from independent breweries. The opened-out bar retains character. No eve meals Sun; other eves till 8. ❀ Ⓓ ▶ ⊞ ♣

Prince of Wales
Mill Hill ☎ (0113) 2452434
11–11
Courage Directors; Ruddles County; John Smith's Bitter Ⓗ
Pub with a comfy lounge with brass decorations and a separate pool area. Note the etched windows.
♨ Ⓓ ≝ (City) ♣

Tap & Spile
Merrion Centre
☎ (0113) 2445355
11–3, 5–11; 11–11 Fri; closed Sun
Beer range varies Ⓗ
Conversion to a Tap & Spile has breathed new life into this pub. Popular with shoppers, businessmen and students, it serves a wide range of changing ales. No food Sun.
Ⓓ ☍

Traveller's Alehouse
Hill Top Road, Armley
☎ (0113) 2637096
11–11
S&N Theakston XB; Taylor Landlord; Whitbread

Boddingtons Bitter, Trophy, Castle Eden Ale, Flowers Original; guest beers Ⓗ
Sherwood Inns alehouse, with a wide range of beers (pricey). Great food range, too, with a 'crock pot' stew or chilli available until early eve.
❀ Ⓓ ☍ ♣ P

Whitelocks
Turk's Head Yard (off Briggate) ☎ (0113) 2453950
11–11
S&N Theakston Best Bitter, Newcastle Exhibition; Younger Scotch, IPA, No.3 Ⓗ
A feast of brass and glass, including mirrors of long lost breweries, adorns one of the area's oldest and most attractive pubs. Large outdoor drinking area. Eve meals end at 8 (7.30 Fri and Sat). ❀ Ⓓ ▶

Wrens
61a New Briggate
☎ (0113) 2458888
11–11
Ind Coope Burton Ale; Tetley Mild, Bitter, Imperial Ⓗ
Popular, three-roomed pub opposite the Grand Theatre. Superb hanging baskets outside. The no-smoking room has a theatre theme. Ⓓ ♣ ✂

Linthwaite

Sair Inn
139 Lane Top, Hoyle Ing (off A62) ☎ (01484) 842370
7–11; 12–3, 7–11 Sat
Linfit Mild, Bitter, Special, English Guineas Stout, Old Eli, Leadboiler Ⓗ
19th-century pub which recommenced brewing 14 years ago. It features stone-flagged floors and roaring fires in several rooms. A dozen beers brewed on the premises.
♨ ♖ ♠ ♣ ☍ ✂

Liversedge

Black Bull
37 Halifax Road (A649, 400 yds N of A62)
☎ (01924) 403779
12–4, 5.30–11; 11–11 Sat
Black Sheep Special Strong; Clark's Burglar Bill; Old Mill Bitter; Stones Best Bitter; Tetley Bitter; guest beers Ⓗ
No-nonsense drinkers' local that usually has three guest beers. The front tap room remains although when internal walls have been removed. Great atmosphere.
❀ ♣ P

Marsden

Tunnel End
Reddisher Road (400 yds S of station) ☎ (01484) 844636
7.30–11; 2–5, 7.30–11 Sat

Ind Coope Burton Ale; Tetley Mild, Bitter ⊞
Cosy, three-roomed pub with a friendly atmosphere, close to the Standedge canal tunnel and picnic area. Lunches Sun.
🏚 ⊛ ◖ ♣

Methley

New Bay Horse
Main Street, Mickletown
☎ (01977) 553557
12–4, 6–11
Tetley Bitter; guest beer ⊞
Traditional local, good for families. Planned further expansion (agreed by customers) will only enhance this excellent boozer. Leeds CAMRA *Pub of the Year* 1994–95. No eve meals Sun.
Q 🌣 ⊛ ◖ ▶ ⊟ ♿ ♣ P

Mytholmroyd

Shoulder of Mutton
38 New Road (B6138)
☎ (01422) 883165
11.30–3, 7–11; 11.30–11 Sat
Whitbread Boddingtons Bitter, Flowers IPA, Castle Eden Ale; guest beers ⊞
Popular roadside local with a fine display of Toby jugs and china. Two guest beers. No eve meals Tue.
🏚 ◖ ▶ ⇌ ♣ P

Netherthong

Clothier's Arms
106 School Street
☎ (01484) 683480
12–4 (not Mon), 7–11; 12–11 Fri & Sat
Old Mill Bitter; Taylor Landlord; Tetley Bitter; Whitbread Boddingtons Bitter; guest beers ⊞
Friendly village pub offering a wide selection of beers at reasonable prices. Separate rooms for both darts and pool. The main bar consists of one large room decorated with bottled-conditioned beers. Lunches Tue–Sat.
Q ◖ ♣

Normanton

Junction Inn
Market Street
☎ (01924) 893021
11–4.30, 7–11; 12–2.30, 7–10.30 Sun
John Smith's Bitter; Wards Thorne Best Bitter ⊞
Friendly pub in the centre of town, popular with the locals. It comprises a traditional bar (Sat night sing-alongs) and a spacious lounge, busy at weekends. Good value traditional food (not served Mon).
⊛ ◖ ⊟ ♿ ⇌ ♣ P

Ossett

Brewer's Pride
Low Mill Road (bottom of Healey Road)
☎ (01924) 273865
12–3, 5.30–11; 12–11 Fri & Sat
Beer range varies ⊞
Very popular free house, despite its elusive location, with well-worn but cosy decor and three log fires. Four beers from independents, plus a large selection of Belgian bottles. Home-cooked lunches (not Sun). 🏚 Q ⊛ ◖ ♣ ⌣

George
Bank Street ☎ (01924) 264754
12–3, 7–11; 11.30–11 Fri & Sat
Ind Coope Burton Ale; Taylor Landlord; Tetley Mild, Bitter; guest beer (occasional) ⊞
Deservedly popular town-centre pub next to the new police fortress. Eve meals Mon. ⊛ ◖ ⊟ ♿ ♣ P

Little Bull
99 Teal Street (¼ mile from Queen's Drive)
☎ (01924) 273569
12–3, 6–11
Thwaites Best Mild (occasional), Bitter, Craftsman ⊞
Friendly, quiet and very popular local with a comfortable, L-shaped lounge and a small but lively tap room. Regular games nights. Reasonable prices.
🏚 Q ⊟ ♣ P

Otley

Bay Horse
Market Place ☎ (01943) 461122
11–11
Tetley Mild, Bitter; guest beer ⊞
Tiny pub with stained-glass windows, sandwiched between shops. A hatchway serves the tap room and linked spaces make up the main lounge. Good beef sandwiches.
⊛ ◖ ⊟ ♣

Junction
44 Bondgate ☎ (01943) 463233
11–3, 5.30–11; 11–11 Fri & Sat
S&N Theakston XB, Old Peculier; Taylor Best Bitter, Landlord; Tetley Bitter; guest beers ⊞
Single-roomed, stone-floored pub in a prominent corner position. Lively young atmosphere. Public car park close by. ◖ ♣

Red Lion
33–35 Kirkgate
☎ (01943) 462226
11–11

Outwood

Kirklands Hotel
605 Leeds Road (old A61)
☎ (01924) 826666
11–11
Old Mill Mild, Bitter, Bullion, Porter ⊞
Large, three-star hotel tied to Old Mill brewery (unusual beers in this area). The comfortable and spacious bar areas feature exposed bricks.
⊛ 🛏 ◖ ▶ ⌣

Pontefract

Greyhound
13 Front Street (50 yds N of centre) ☎ (01977) 791571
12–4, 7–11; 11–11 Fri & Sat
Ruddles Best Bitter; S&N Theakston XB; John Smith's Bitter; Tomlinson's Femme Fatale ⊞
Popular pub hosting live music Fri and Sun eves.
🏚 ⇌ (Tanshelf) ♣

Liquorice Bush
8 Market Place
☎ (01977) 703843
11–4, 7–11
Wards Thorne Best Bitter; guest beers ⊞
Town-centre pub, close to the bus station; one large room with a spacious alcove at either end. Popular lunchtime for the wide range of bar meals (no food Sun); lively at weekends. ◖ ♿ ⇌ (Monk Hill/Bag Hill/Tanshelf) ♣

Tap & Spile
28 Horsefair (opp. bus station)
☎ (01977) 793468
12–11
Hambleton Stallion; S&N Theakston Old Peculier; Tomlinson's Sessions; guest beers ⊞
Chain alehouse, with bare brickwork and floorboards in its three separate drinking areas, including one lounge. Nine changing guest beers include one from Cotleigh. Good value, home-cooked food (not Sun). Some guests can be pricey.
◖ ⇌ (Baghill/Monk Hill) ♣ ⌣ P

Pudsey

Butcher's Arms
Church Lane ☎ (0113) 2564313
11–11; 11–3.30, 7–11 Sat

Courage Directors; John Smith's Bitter, Magnet ⊞
Small, well-kept pub near the Market Place; four drinking areas served from one bar. Note the large whisky selection. ◖ ▶

Samuel Smith OBB H
Busy central pub with an open interior and 1980s furniture and decor. Separate dining area. ❀ ◗ ◔ ♣

Mason's Arms

Lowtown
☎ (0113) 2577857
11–11
Whitbread Boddingtons Bitter, Trophy; guest beer H
Fine example of a Victorian pub in the Yorkshire House style. Nice Bentley's windows front an unaltered interior of three rooms. ⊟ ♣ P

Purston

White House

257 Pontefract Road
☎ (01977) 791878
11–4, 7–11
Samuel Smith OBB H
Small, but spacious, open-plan pub, very popular with locals. A vast collection of rugby and football photographs adorns the walls. Nineteenth year in the *Guide*. No food Sun.
❀ ◗ ◔ ♣ P

Rawdon

Emmott Arms

Town Street
☎ (0113) 2506036
11–11
Samuel Smith OBB H
Old pub with a traditional tap room, modern lounge and upstairs restaurant. Dark wood and low ceilings add atmosphere. Friendly, knowledgeable bar staff.
⏣ ◗ ▶ ⊟ ♣ P

Ripponden

Blue Ball Inn

Blue Ball Road, Soyland (off A58, near Baitings Reservoir)
OS011192 ☎ (01422) 823603
12–3 (not Tue), 7–11
Draught Bass; S&N Theakston Old Peculier; Taylor Golden Best, Landlord; guest beers H
Cosy moorland inn dating from 1672, with panoramic views over the upper Ryburn Valley. Regular folk music, sing-alongs and live jazz. Four guest beers.
🛏 Q ⏣ ❀ 🍴 ◗ ▶ ◔ P

Old Bridge Inn

Priest Lane (off A58, near B6113 jct) ☎ (01422) 822595
12–3.30, 5.30–11; 12–11 Sat
Black Sheep Special Strong; Ryburn Best Bitter; Taylor Golden Best, Best Bitter; guest beer (summer) H
Possibly Yorkshire's oldest pub (recorded as early as 1307)

in a picturesque setting by a pack horse bridge, over which the Calderdale Way footpath passes. Home of the local Pie Appreciation Society. No eve meals Sat or Sun.
🛏 Q ❀ ◗ ▶ P

Robin Hood

Angel

55 Wakefield Road, Rothwell Haigh (A639)
☎ (0113) 2822202
11–11
Marston's Pedigree; John Smith's Bitter; Stones Best Bitter; Whitbread Boddingtons Bitter; guest beers H
Tasteful, traditional roadside local with rooms around a central bar. Good, home-cooked food (all day Sun). Eve meals end at 8 (9 Mon). Note the unusual 'bum-rest' in the corridor drinking area. Children's certificate.
◗ ▶ ♣ P

Shaw Cross

Huntsman

1 Walker Cottages, Chidswell Lane (¼ mile NE of A653/B6128 jct) ☎ (01924) 275700
12–3 (not Mon), 7–11
Black Sheep Special Strong; John Smith's Bitter; Stones Best Bitter; Taylor Landlord; guest beers H
Friendly pub converted from two 17th-century cottages surrounded by fields with fine views. Farm artefacts adorn the walls, guns hang from the beams and a Yorkshire range provides warmth. No food Sun. 🛏 ❀ ◗ P

Shelley

Three Acres Inn

Roydhouse (off B116 near Emley Moor mast)
☎ (01484) 602606
11–3, 7–11
Mansfield Riding Bitter, Bitter, Old Baily; Taylor Best Bitter; guest beers H
Attractively set pub with an emphasis on wining and dining. Twenty en suite bedrooms. Resident pianist.
🛏 ◗ ▶

Shipley

Shipley Pride

1 Saltaire Road
☎ (01274) 585341
11.30 (11 Sat)–11
Clark's Festival Ale; Tetley Bitter; guest beer H
Friendly, two-roomed pub popular with locals and passing trade. ◗ ⊟ ⇌ ♣ P

Victoria Hotel

192 Saltaire Road
☎ (01274) 585642
11.30–11
Whitbread Boddingtons Bitter, Trophy; guest beers H
Friendly local with Victorian-style decor (stained-glass and wood). The nearest pub to the historic village of Saltaire.
Q ◗ ◔ ⇌ (Saltaire) P

Silsden

Bridge Inn

Keighley Road
☎ (01535) 653144
11–3, 5–11; 12–11 Fri & Sat
Black Sheep Best Bitter; John Smith's Bitter; guest beer H
Canalside pub which predates the canal, being first recorded in 1660. The original drinking rooms are now the cellar and toilets. The outside drinking area was the original main road. Parking for boats only.
🛏 ❀ ◗ ▶ ♣

Skelmanthorpe

Chartist

74 Commercial Road (B6116)
☎ (01484) 863766
11.30–11
Hardys & Hansons Best Bitter H
The only Hardys & Hansons pub in Kirklees: a busy and friendly roadside local. One large L-shaped room combining both lounge and tap room areas. ❀ ♣ P

Southowram

Shoulder of Mutton

14 Cain Lane ☎ (01422) 361101
12–3 (may extend Sat), 7–11
Marston's Pedigree; Morland Old Speckled Hen; Ruddles County; John Smith's Bitter; guest beers H
Village local with a changing range of guest beers. 🛏 ♣

Sowerby Bridge

Puzzle Hall

21 Hollins Mill Lane (400 yds from A58) ☎ (01422) 835547
12–11
Vaux Samson; Wards Best Bitter; guest beer H
Tiny, two-roomed (former brew) pub, nestling between the canal and river. Live jazz Tue; folk Thu and Sat. Wed is curry night (other eves meals end at 7). Guest Vaux beer.
🛏 Q ❀ ◗ ▶ ⇌ ♣ 🍺 P

Rams Head Inn

26 Wakefield Road
☎ (01422) 835876
7 (6 Fri)–11; 11–11 Sat & bank hols

West Yorkshire

Ryburn Best Bitter, Rydale, Old Stone Troff, Luddite, Stabbers, Coiners H
Ryburn's tied house, ¼ mile up hill from its relocated brewery. Internal remodelling has provided additional room. Sing-alongs Sat/Sun nights.
🏻 Q ❀ ♣ P

Try also: **Navigation Inn**, Chapel Lane (Free)

Thackley

Commercial Inn
61 Park Road
☎ (01274) 616363
1 (3 winter)–11
Whitbread Trophy; guest beers H
Cosy, old-fashioned local, built in the 1840s and tastefully renovated. Near village football and cricket grounds.
Q ❀ 🖰 å ♣ P

Thornhill

Savile Arms
12 Church Lane (B6117)
☎ (01924) 463738
5–11; 12–4, 7–11 Sat
Black Sheep Best Bitter; Old Mill Bitter; Tetley Bitter; guest beers H
Small, cosy, 600-year-old village pub with four rooms; often known as Church House. Friendly and unspoilt thanks to its long-serving licensee. Lunches Sat. Q ❀ 🖰 ♣ P

Thornton

Blue Boar
354 Thornton Road
☎ (01274) 833298
4 (2 Fri, 12 Sat)–11
Taylor Golden Best, Best Bitter, Landlord H
Locals' pub with an open-plan main bar and a separate pool room. ♣

Todmorden

Bramsche Bar
31 Rochdale Road (opp. library) ☎ (01706) 815117
12–11
S&N Theakston Best Bitter, XB, Old Peculier; Taylor Landlord H
Basic, bare-floored pub close to the Rochdale Canal and the town centre. Named after Todmorden's twin town.
❀ 🖰 ➘

Mason's Arms
1 Bacup Road, Gauxholme (A681, near A6033 jct)
☎ (01706) 812180
7 (7.30 Sat)–11; 12–3, 7.30–10.30 Sun
Marston's Pedigree; John Smith's Bitter; Thwaites Bitter H

Almost underneath a railway viaduct and close to the Rochdale Canal, this small, comfortable free house features a snug with scrubbed sycamore tables (reputedly once used for a post-mortem), and photos of the Summit tunnel explosion. Lunches Sun. Q 🖰 å ➘ (Walsden) ♣

Staff of Life
550 Burnley Road, Knotts Bend (A646, 1½ miles N of centre) ☎ (01706) 812929
12–3 (not Mon or Tue in winter), 5 (7 Mon & Tue in winter)–11; 12–11 Sat
Jennings Bitter, Cumberland Ale, Sneck Lifter; guest beers H
Atmospheric pub in a wooded gorge. The overhanging crag has supernatural connections.
🏻 ❀ 🖰 🖰 ➘ P

White Hart
White Hart Fold, Station Road
☎ (01706) 812198
11.30–3.30, 7–11; 11–11 Fri & Sat
Tetley Mild, Bitter; guest beer H
Imposing brewers' Tudor, former Ramsden's pub with a single large lounge, where much original panelling remains. It usually offers a guest beer from Moorhouse's, plus another guest.
❀ 🖰 ➘ ♣ P

Wainstalls

Withens Hotel
Cold Edge Road (by windfarm) OS045307
☎ (01422) 244809
7–11; 12–3, 7–11 Sat (12–2, 7–11 weekdays Easter–Sept)
Taylor Best Bitter, Landlord; guest beer (summer) H
The highest pub in the county, with expansive views over the Calderdale Hills and beyond. Built in 1862 to serve passing quarrymen, it now caters for walkers, motorists, families and viewers of Ovenden Moor windfarm. No meals Sat eve.
🏻 ❀ 🖰 ➘ P

Wakefield

Albion Inn
94 Stanley Road (Peterson Road from Kirkgate roundabout) ☎ (01924) 376206
11–4, 7–11; 11–11 Sat
Samuel Smith OBB H
Impressive, 1930s local at the edge of the town centre. Popular lunchtimes for good value, home-cooked food. Twelve years in the *Guide*.
❀ 🖰 ➘ (Kirkgate) ♣ P

Elephant & Castle
109 Westgate
☎ (01924) 376610
11–11

Courage Directors; John Smith's Bitter; guest beers H
Friendly, old, town-centre local changed only slightly by the opening out of its rooms. Separate pool room in the back. Note the impressive tiled Warwick's of Boroughbridge frontage. Old photos and brewery mirrors add to the interest.
🏻 🖂 🖰 ➘ (Westgate) ♣

Henry Boon's
130 Westgate
☎ (01924) 378126
11–11
Clark's Bitter, Festival Ale; Taylor Landlord; Tetley Bitter; guest beers H
Clark's brewery tap: a popular alehouse with stone-flagged floors, thatched bar and many brewery artefacts. Live music Wed; rock and blues bands Thu and Sun lunch. Two changing guest beers. No food Sun.
🖰 ➘ (Westgate) ♣

Primrose Tavern
Monk Street ☎ (01924) 375847
11–11
Mansfield Riding Bitter, Bitter, Old Baily H
Friendly, old, two-bar local, hosting sporting and quiz nights. Q ❀ å
➘ (Kirkgate) ♣ P

Rainbow Inn
40 Lower Warrengate
☎ (01924) 374433
11–11; 11–3, 5.30–11 Mon & Thu
John Smith's Bitter, Magnet; guest beer H
City-centre pub with a lively tap room and regular guest beers. Very popular lunchtime for good, home-cooked food.
🖰 🖰 å ➘ (Kirkgate/ Westgate) ♣ P 🖰

Redoubt
28 Horbury Road, Westgate (next to St Michael's church)
☎ (01924) 377085
11–11
Tetley Mild, Bitter; guest beers H
Cosy, four-room Heritage pub. The walls are adorned with rugby league photographs. A nice little hideaway.
Q ❀ å ➘ (Westgate) P

Talbot & Falcon
56 Northgate (near bus station)
☎ (01924) 201693
11–11
Marston's Pedigree; S&N Theakston Best Bitter; Tetley Mild, Bitter, Imperial; guest beers H
Long, narrow Tetley Festival Alehouse with a central bar, catering for a very varied clientele. Up to five guest beers. 🖰

Wakefield Labour Club

18 Vicarage Street
(near market hall)
☎ (01924) 371626
7–11; 11–3, 7–11 Sat; 12–2 Sun, closed
Sun eve
Taylor Golden Best; guest beers Ⓗ
Unpretentious and friendly club. Two rotating guest beers from small independent breweries; cosmopolitan clientele. Wakefield CAMRA *Pub(?) of the Year* 1994. The town centre's last true free house. Show the *Guide* or CAMRA membership to be signed in. Q ☎ ❀ ♿
⚲ (Westgate/Kirkgate) P

West Ardsley

British Oak

407 Westerton Road
☎ (0113) 2534792
12–3, 6–11
Whitbread Boddingtons Bitter, Castle Eden Ale, Flowers Original; guest beer Ⓗ
On the outside just a standard estate pub but inside a real

gem. Guest beers almost always come from small independents. An excellent local staging many events.
❀ ◖ ♿ ♣ P

Wibsey

Gaping Goose

5–6 Slack Bottom Road (off Buttershaw Lane)
☎ (01274) 601701
12–3, 7–11
Black Sheep Best Bitter; S&N Theakston Old Peculier; Taylor Landlord; Tetley Bitter; Whitbread Trophy Ⓗ
Intimate, friendly true village local, recently extended to offer much needed extra space. Large collection of brassware in the pleasant lounge.
❀ ♿ ♣ P

Wyke

Junction

459 Huddersfield Road
☎ (01274) 679809
12 (4 Mon)–11
Thwaites Best Mild, Bitter Ⓗ
Quaintly V-shaped building

occupying a prominent position at the top of the village: a traditional, two-roomed pub popular with a broad range of locals. Meals end at 7.30; no food Sun. ◗ ♣

Yeadon

New Inn

Albert Square
☎ (0113) 2503220
11–11
John Smith's Bitter, Magnet; guest beer Ⓗ
Friendly, 18th-century stone pub which, although much altered, has a rustic interior. Guest beers change regularly. No food Sat. ♨ ❀ ◖ 🍴 ♣ P

Tut & Shive

11 The Green
☎ (0113) 2506052
11–11
Whitbread Boddingtons Bitter, Castle Eden Ale; guest beer Ⓗ
Built in 1728, this imposing, stone pub has been refurbished in the Tut & Shive style. 'Crock pot' meals Mon–Thu till 11pm. ◖ ◗ ♣ P

TRAINS AND BEERS AND PLANES

Not so long ago you couldn't do much better than a cold, fizzy can or some insipid keg beer when waiting for a transport connection.

Travel termini seemed to be one of the last bastions of the 'it'll do' standard of catering, and that meant keg or nothing for thirsty travellers. These days, it can be a positive pleasure to check the departures board and discover that your plane or train has been delayed.

Real ale has become the in thing at many UK airports. Heathrow now has at least 11 bars serving cask-conditioned beer, as opposed to just three four years ago. Tap & Spile and Wetherspoon's have each opened two outlets, and Forte's three, somewhat contrived, olde-worlde Shakespeare Ale Houses are all the same a great improvement on the tacky keg pubs they have replaced. Gatwick is also taking off, if you pardon the pun, with Wetherspoon's and Forte grasping the nettle in an airport where Bass already runs two thriving pubs. And regional airports have followed suit. There are Tap & Spiles at Aberdeen and Glasgow, for instance.

Back on terra firma, railway stations have found favour with some of the new pub companies. In place of plasticky bars serving plasticky beer to accompany the infamously plasticky sandwiches, real ale pubs are rising from the ashes of derelict waiting rooms or filling odd corners of bright, modern concourses. Wetherspoon's, Regent Inns and the new Head of Steam company have all cashed in on the enormous customer throughput at major stations and created new train spotter heavens.

Clwyd

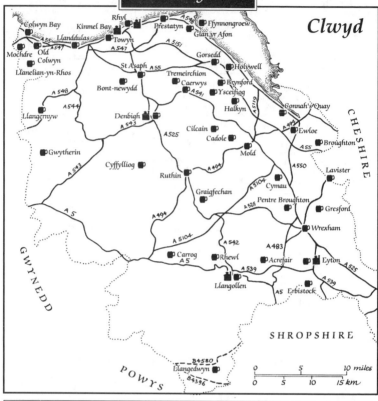

Clwyd

Dyffryn Clwyd, Denbigh; **Plassey**, Eyton

Acrefair

Duke of Wellington
Llangollen Road (A539)
☎ (01978) 820169
7–11; 12–3.30, 7–11 Fri (12–11 Mon–Fri in summer); 11–11 Sat
Bateman Mild; Marston's Bitter, Pedigree Ⓗ
Reputedly haunted 18th-century former coaching inn: two small, cosy areas separated by a central passageway. Artistic old photos; traditional outside toilet. Children's tractor in the garden. Meals in summer only. ⚏ ⊛ ◑ ♣ P

Bont-newydd

Dolben Arms
W of Trefnant OS015705
☎ (01745) 582207
7–11
Dyffryn Clwyd Four Thumbs; S&N Theakston XB Ⓗ
16th-century, remote country inn in a picturesque valley, accessible only by narrow country lanes. One single bar

separates into restaurant, lounge and games areas.
Q ⊛ ◑ ♣ P

Brynford

Llyn y Mawn Inn
Brynford Hill (B5121)
☎ (01352) 714367
12–3 (not Mon), 5.30–11
John Smith's Bitter; guest beers Ⓗ
600-year-old, family-run former coaching inn undergoing sympathetic renovation and extension. Quality is evident throughout. Well worth a slight detour off the A55. Local CAMRA *Pub of the Year* 1995. No lunches Sun. Cider in summer.
⚏ ⊛ ◑ ▶ & ♣ ⌂ P ⊁ ⊟

Cadole

Colomendy Arms
Gwernaffield Road (off A494)
☎ (01352) 810217
7 (12 Fri & Sat)–11
Burtonwood Bitter; Marston's Bitter; guest beers Ⓗ

Excellent village local from which a footpath leads to Loggerheads Country Park. Pets corner.
⚏ ⏚ ⊛ ▲ ♣ P

Caerwys

Piccadilly
North Street (B5122)
☎ (01352) 720284
12–3, 6.30–11
Cains Mild; Whitbread Boddingtons Bitter, Flowers IPA Ⓗ
Recently renovated (following a fire) village local, sympathetically finished.
⚏ Q ⊛ ◑ ▶ ⊞ P

Carrog

Grouse Inn
½ mile off A5 ☎ (01490) 430272
12–3 (4 summer; not Mon/Tue in winter), 7–11
Lees GB Mild (summer), **Bitter** Ⓗ
Village pub overlooking a river, with a cosy lounge and friendly locals.
⚏ Q ⏚ ⊛ ⍁ ◑ ▶ ♣ P

Cilcain

White Horse
2 miles S of A541
☎ (01352) 740142
12–3, 7–11
Marston's Bitter; guest beers Ⓗ
Attractive village pub in a popular walking area close to Moel Fammau Country Park. The split-level lounge is popular for meals; the separate public bar welcomes walkers. Guest beers come from the Marston's list, changing regularly.
🏔 ❀ ◑ ▶ ⊟ ♿ ♣ P

Colwyn Bay

Park Hotel
128 Abergele Road (main road E of centre, near Eirias Park)
☎ (01492) 530661
11–11
Bass Worthington BB; M&B Mild; guest beers Ⓗ
Large, single-room pub popular with locals for its pool table, darts, quizzes, etc. ⇌

Taylor's
Pen-y-Bryn Road, Upper Colwyn Bay (top of King's Rd, 1 mile from centre)
☎ (01492) 533360
11–3, 5.30–11
Tetley Walker Bitter; Marston's Pedigree; guest beers Ⓗ
Free house inn and restaurant, built 15 years ago in old brick, with a plaster and natural wood interior. Panoramic views from the lounge; separate function room; downstairs bar with pool tables. All furnished to a high standard.
🏔 Q ☎ ❀ ◑ ▶ ⊟ ♣ P

Wings Social Club
Imperial Buildings, Princes Drive, Station Square (1st floor of Imperial Hotel)
☎ (01492) 530682
12–3, 7–11; 11–11 Sat
Lees GB Mild, Bitter Ⓗ
Increasingly popular club where families are welcome lunchtimes: a large bar and lounge, plus separate snooker, pool and darts rooms. ⇌ ♣

Connah's Quay

Sir Gawain & The Green Knight
Golftyn Lane
☎ (01244) 812623
12–3, 5.30–11; 12–11 Sat
Samuel Smith OBB Ⓗ
Converted farmhouse with an aviary, close to Dee Estuary Bird Sanctuary. Eve meals till 8.30; no lunches Mon.
❀ ◑ ▶ ♣ P

Cyffylliog

Red Lion
Off B5105 at Llanfwrog OS058578 ☎ (01824) 716664
6.30–11; 11–11 Sat & summer
Lees GB Mild, Bitter Ⓗ
Excellent, unspoilt village pub with several areas, including a very good family room. Situated in a picturesque valley, off the beaten track, but worth finding. Lunches in summer.
🏔 Q ☎ ❀ ⊯ ◑ ▶ ⊟ ♣ P ⊟

Cymau

Talbot Inn
Cymau Lane ☎ (01978) 761410
12–3 (not Mon–Wed), 7–11
Hyde's Anvil Dark Mild, Bitter Ⓔ
Quiet village pub next to Hope Mountain and Country Park. Phone to check the availability of food. Q ❀ ◑ ▶ ⊟ ♣ P ⊟

Denbigh

Bull Hotel
Hall Square ☎ (01745) 812582
11–3, 5.30–11
Bass Worthington BB, Draught Bass; guest beers (occasional) Ⓗ
Town-centre hotel, just off the main street, offering good value meals. The guest beer is usually from Shepherd Neame. Small car park.
🏔 ⊯ ◑ ▶ P

Golden Lion
Back Row ☎ (01745) 812227
12–11
Bateman Mild; Marston's Bitter, Pedigree Ⓗ
Friendly pub just off the High Street. The roof is low, so watch your head. Full of character and characters.
◑ ▶ ⊟ ♣

Erbistock

Cross Foxes
Overton Bridge (A528)
☎ (01978) 780380
12–3, 7–11
Marston's Bitter, Pedigree Ⓗ
Olde-worlde inn with a warm atmosphere. The fish dishes are excellent. Superb views of the River Dee from the garden.
🏔 Q ☎ ❀ ◑ ▶ ⊟ ♣ P

Ewloe

Boar's Head
Holywell Road
☎ (01244) 531065
12–3, 6–11

Greenalls Mild, Bitter Ⓗ
Comfortable, traditional pub with an amazing brass collection. Good value lunches. Q ◑ P

Eyton

Plassey Leisure Park
Off B5426 – follow 'Craft Centre' sign – S of Wrexham
☎ (01978) 780277
7.30–11; 12–2. 7.30–11 Sat & Sun (bar)
Plassey Bitter, Cwrw Tudno, Dragon's Breath Ⓗ
Thriving camping/caravan park with its own brewery, craft centre and golf course. The refurbished Treetops Bar is open Mar–Oct; real ale also in the restaurant (closed Mon). Wheelchair access to the restaurant. Q ☎ ▶ ♿ ▲ P

Ffynnongroew

Railway
Main Road ☎ (01745) 560447
12–4, 7–11; 11–11 Sat
Vaux Mild, Bitter; guest beer (occasional) Ⓗ
Friendly, sporty local.
🏔 ❀ ▲ ♣ P

Glan yr Afon

White Lion
Glan yr Afon Road (W of A548 at Ffynnongroew, 1 mile from A548) OS118817
☎ (01745) 560280
12–2 (4 Sat; not Mon/Tue), 6–11
Ruddles Best Bitter; guest beers Ⓗ
Excellent, prize-winning pub retaining much of its original character. The conservatory is full of plant life. Clay pigeon shooting, with a lamb roast, is held in the interesting grounds for organised parties.
🏔 ❀ ◑ ▶ ⊟ ♣ ⊃ P

Gorsedd

Druid Inn
Just off A5026 OS153767
☎ (01352) 710944
7–11
Marston's Pedigree; Whitbread Boddingtons Bitter; guest beers Ⓗ
Smart country pub opposite a church. A selection of comfortable rooms suit all tastes; separate restaurant. No eve meals Sun or Mon; lunches served Sun only.
🏔 ❀ ▶ ⊟ ▲ ♣ P

Graigfechan

Three Pigeons
On B5429 ☎ (01824) 703178
6.30–11; 12–3, 7–10.30 Sun

Clwyd

Draught Bass Ⓗ & Ⓖ; **guest beers** Ⓖ
There are fine views over the Vale of Clwyd from this popular, 17th-century inn which offers live entertainment at weekends, a skittle alley for pre-booked parties, and a small camp/caravan site at the rear. No meals Mon–Wed.
🏾 Q ⛄ ❀ ◗ 🍴 🖧 Å ♣ P

Gresford

Griffin
The Green ☎ (01978) 852231
1 (12 Sat)–4.30, 7–11
Greenalls Mild, Bitter Ⓗ
Unspoilt village local, near the church. Quiet and unpretentious. 🏾 Q ❀ ♣ P

Gwytherin

Lion Inn
☎ (01745) 860244
12–3, 6–11
Marston's Bitter, Pedigree Ⓗ
Tastefully refurbished traditional village local, perhaps 300 years old with stone walls, oak-beamed ceilings and two fires. A recent convert to cask-conditioned beer.
🏾 Q ❀ 🍴 ◗ 🍴 🖧 Å ♣ P

Halkyn

Britannia Inn
Pentre Road (just off A55)
☎ (01352) 780272
11–3, 5.30–11; 11–11 Sat
Lees GB Mild, Bitter Ⓗ, **Moonraker** Ⓔ
500-year-old stone pub with four rooms and a superb view over the Dee Estuary from the conservatory restaurant. A pub of character with a warm welcome for locals and tourists alike.
🏾 ⛄ ❀ ◗ 🍴 🖧 Å ♣ P

Holywell

Glan yr Afon
Milwr (off old A55) OS196739
☎ (01352) 710052
12–2.30, 7–11
Courage Directors; Ruddles Best Bitter; Webster's Yorkshire Bitter Ⓗ
17th-century inn in a secluded spot, with good views and a deserved reputation for good value food. Separate function room; supper licence till 1am. No eve meals Mon.
⛄ ❀ ◗ 🍴 P

Red Lion
High Street ☎ (01352) 710097
11–11
Ansells Mild; Tetley Walker Bitter; guest beer Ⓗ

Well-established, town-centre local (handy for shops), with an unspoilt, single-bar interior. 🏾 ♣

Lavister

Nag's Head
Old Chester Road (B5445)
☎ (01244) 570486
11.30–3, 5–11
Whitbread Boddingtons Bitter, Flowers IPA; guest beers Ⓗ
Large, comfortable roadside pub in a small village, with a bowling green at the rear.
🏾 ❀ ◗ 🍴 🖧 Å ♣ P

Llanddulas

Valentine Inn
Mill Street ☎ (01492) 518189
12–3, 5.30–11 (may vary); 12–2, 7–10.30 Sun
Bass Worthington BB, Draught Bass; S&N Theakston Mild Ⓗ
Small village pub with a public bar and a comfortable lounge. Eve meals in the tourist season only.
🏾 Q ❀ ◗ 🍴 Å ♣

Llanelian-yn-Rhos

White Lion Inn
☎ (01492) 515807
11–3, 6–11
Ansells Mild; Marston's Pedigree; Tetley Walker Bitter; guest beer Ⓗ
Friendly, olde-worlde village pub, with a tasteful extension for diners (good meals). A bar (stone floor), a tiny snug and a lounge suit all visitors. A true free house, it varies its guest beer and often features local Welsh brews.
🏾 Q 🍴 ◗ 🍴 🖧 Å ♣ P

Llangedwyn

Green Inn
☎ (01691) 828234
11–3, 6–11
Whitbread Boddingtons Bitter; guest beers Ⓗ
Out of the way pub in the picturesque Tanat Valley that always has four guest ales and is popular with families and walkers. The cider alternates between sweet and dry, from March to Oct. Restaurant upstairs. 🏾 ❀ 🍴 ♣ ◖ P

Llangernyw

Stag Inn
☎ (01745) 860213
12–2 (3 Sat), 6–11
M&B Brew XI; guest beer Ⓗ
Classic, 18th-century country inn, in the heart of a beautiful

village. The walls and ceiling are covered in brasses: an horologists' paradise, aptly described as the 'old curiosity shop with fine food and ales'. No-smoking restaurant. 🏾 Q ⛄ ❀ 🍴 ◗ 🖧 Å ♣ P

Llangollen

Cambrian Hotel
Berwyn Street (A5)
1 (12 summer)–3.30, 7–11
Ind Coope Burton Ale; Tetley Walker Bitter Ⓗ
Friendly, family-run hotel. The unspoilt back bar is old-fashioned without being olde-worlde. Meals in summer. Q ⛄ ❀ 🍴 Å ♣ P

Wynnstay Arms
Bridge Street ☎ (01978) 860710
12–3, 7–11 (11–11 summer)
Cains Bitter; Ind Coope Burton Ale Ⓗ
Comfortable, welcoming hotel with a cosy bar and a restaurant. Close to the River Dee, it boasts a large, enclosed garden. The menu caters for children.
🏾 ⛄ ❀ 🍴 ◗ 🍴 Å ♣ P

Mochdre

Mountain View
7 Old Conwy Road
☎ (01492) 544724
11.30–3, 6–11; 11.30–11 Sat
Burtonwood Mild, Bitter, Forshaw's, Top Hat Ⓗ
Friendly village local: a large lounge with a dining area, plus a separate bar with a pool table, full of locals. Pleasant atmosphere; good food.
Q ❀ ◗ 🍴 🖧 Å ♣ P

Mold

Boar's Head
17 Chester Street (A494)
☎ (01352) 758430
11.30–3 (5 Fri & Sat), 7–11
Ind Coope Burton Ale; Tetley Walker Bitter Ⓗ
Supposedly haunted former coaching inn with an attractive black and white exterior and a brown-decored interior. The walls of the U-shaped single bar are cluttered with pictures and paintings. Lively atmosphere at weekends.
❀ ◗ 🍴 ♣ P

Y Pentan
3–5 New Street
☎ (01352) 753772
11–3, 6.30–11; 11–11 Fri & Sat
Bateman Dark Mild; Marston's Bitter, Pedigree Ⓗ
Lively, town-centre pub with a friendly welcome. An outlet for Marston's Head Brewer's

Choice. No lunches Sun; no
eve meals Mon–Wed.
⟨⌂ ▶ ⊞ & ♣

Old Colwyn

Marine Hotel
Abergele Road (main road,
near Police HQ)
☎ (01492) 515484
12 (11.30)–11
**Bass Worthington BB,
Draught Bass; M&B Mild** Ⓗ
Large pub with three bars; the
side bar is popular with locals.
The residents' restaurant also
serves as a function room.
❀ ⌂ ⟨⌂ ♣ P ⊟

Red Lion
385 Abergele Road
☎ (01492) 515042
5 (12 summer)–11
**Bass Worthington BB; Cains
Mild, Bitter; M&B Mild;
Whitbread Boddingtons
Bitter; guest beers** Ⓗ
Popular, traditional town pub
with a bar and two lounges. A
proper meeting place for
locals, where all are made
welcome. ⋈ Q ❀ ⊞ ♣

Pentre Broughton

Cross Foxes
High Street ☎ (01978) 755973
7 (11 Sat)–11
Burtonwood Bitter Ⓗ
Friendly, popular village local
with a coal fire. Live music
Sat. ⋈ Q ⊞ ♣ P

Prestatyn

Nova
Central Beach
☎ (01745) 888021
12–11
**Bass Worthington BB,
Draught Bass** Ⓗ
Modern leisure centre pub by
the main beach, at the
start/end of Offa's Dyke Path.
⅚ ❀ & A P ⊟

Rhewl

Sun Inn
Off B5103 OS178448
☎ (01824) 703163
12–3, 6–11
**Bass Worthington BB; guest
beers** Ⓗ
Old drovers' pub with slate
floors: a centre for fishing,
walking and fell running. One
guest is usually from Dyffryn
Clwyd brewery.
⋈ Q ⅚ ❀ ⟨⌂ ▶ ⊞ ♣ P

Rhyl

White Horse
Bedford Street (near Town
Hall) ☎ (01745) 334927
11–11
**John Smith's Bitter; guest
beers** Ⓗ
Basic, back-street pub with the
largest selection of real ales for
many a mile. Guests include
Marston's Head Brewer's
Choice and at least one Welsh
beer. ❀ ≉ ♣

Ruthin

Wine Vaults
St Peter's Square
☎ (01824) 422067
12–11
Robinson's Best Bitter Ⓗ
Friendly town-centre pub with
two basic rooms.
❀ ⊞ A ♣ P

St Asaph

Red Lion
Gemig Street (High Street)
☎ (01745) 383570
12–2.30, 5.30–11; 11.30–3, 6–11 Sat
**Ind Coope Burton Ale; Tetley
Walker Mild, Bitter; guest
beers** (occasional) Ⓗ
Cosy, multi-level pub with a
large lounge and a public bar
with TV. Children's certificate.
⋈ ⟨⌂ ▶ ⊞ P

Towyn

Morton Arms
Sandbank Road (just off A548)
☎ (01745) 330211
11 (12 winter)–11
**Bass Worthington BB,
Draught Bass; M&B Mild;
guest beer** (summer) Ⓗ
Modern pub in a tourist area
(it can be quite noisy in
summer). Easily reached from
nearby caravan parks.
Separate restaurant.
❀ ⟨⌂ ▶ A ♣ P

Tremeirchion

Salusbury Arms
On old Holywell Road
☎ (01745) 710262
11–11 (12.30am Thu–Sat)
**Marston's Bitter, Pedigree;
guest beers** Ⓗ
Multi-roomed pub with three
separate drinking areas plus a
restaurant and a large garden.
⋈ Q ⅚ ❀ ⟨⌂ ▶ ⊞ & A ♣ ⊟

Wrexham

Albion Hotel
1 Pen-y-Bryn ☎ (01978) 364969
12–4, 7–11
Lees Bitter Ⓗ
Bright and friendly town pub
with a good local following.
The only town centre outlet for
Lees. ⋈ ⊞ ≉ (General)

Black Horse
Yorke Street ☎ (01978) 352474
11.30–11 (midnight Thu–Sat; no
admission after 10.30 Thu–Sat)
**Bateman Mild; Marston's
Bitter, Pedigree** Ⓗ
Recently renovated one
(large)-roomed pub. Disco at
weekends, when dress
restrictions apply. Also busy
lunchtimes, but quiet and
relaxing at other times. Wide
range of good meals.
Marston's Head Brewer's
Choice also sold.
Q ❀ ⟨⌂ ▶ & P

Golden Lion
13 High Street
☎ (01978) 364964
12–11; 12–5, 7.30–11 Fri; 12–4,
7.30–11 Sat
**Bass Worthington BB,
Draught Bass; Stones Best
Bitter; guest beer** Ⓗ
Town-centre pub, very busy at
weekends and popular with
students. ❀ ⟨⌂ ⊟

Horse & Jockey
Hope Street ☎ (01978) 351081
11–11
**Ind Coope Burton Ale; Tetley
Walker Bitter** Ⓗ
Thatched, listed pub serving
good food. Beware the fake
handpump for keg cider.
Q ⟨⌂ ⊞ ▶ ≉ (Central) ♣

Seven Stars Hotel
Chester Street
☎ (01978) 263753
11–11
**Whitbread Boddingtons
Bitter; guest beers** Ⓗ
Busy, refurbished, town-centre
pub, offering a welcome choice
of ale. ⟨⌂

Ysceifiog

Fox
N of A541, W of Mold
OS152715 ☎ (01352) 720241
12–3 (not Wed), 6–11
Felinfoel Bitter; guest beers Ⓗ
Classic, unspoilt village pub,
with a good range of beers; a
centre of village activities.
Three guests include a mild.
⋈ Q ⊞ ♣

CAMRA speaks for you!
Join up now!

Dyfed

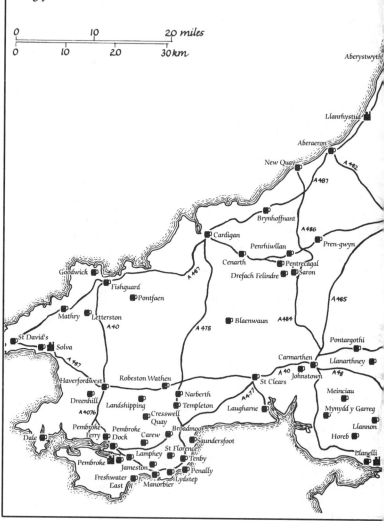

```
0          10              20 miles
0      10       20       30 km
```

Aberystwyth

Llanrhystud

Aberaeron

New Quay

A 482

A 487

Brynhoffnant

A 486

Pren-gwyn

Cardigan

Penrhiwllan

Cenarth

Pentrecagal

Drefach Felindre

Saron

A 485

Goodwick

Fishguard

Pontfaen

A 487

A 484

Blaenwaun

Mathry

Letterston

A 40

A 478

Pontargothi

St David's

Solva

A 487

Carmarthen

Llanarthney

A 48

Haverfordwest

Robeston Wathen

St Clears

A 40

Johnstown

Meinciau

Dreenhill

Narberth

Landshipping

Templeton

Laugharne

Mynydd y Garreg

A 4076

Cresswell Quay

Broadmoor

Llannon

Pembroke Ferry

Pembroke Dock

Carew

Saundersfoot

Horeb

Llanelli

Dale

Lamphey

St Florence

Pembroke

Jameston

Tenby

Freshwater East

Manorbier

Penally

Lydstep

 Aberystwyth, Llanrhystud; **Crown Buckley, Felinfoel**, Llanelli; **Pembroke**, Pembroke; **Solva**, Solva

Aberaeron

Royal Oak
30 North Road (main coast road) ☎ (01545) 570233
11–11
Ind Coope Burton Ale; Tetley Bitter; guest beer Ⓗ
Village green pub, close to a large caravan and camping site. Good choice of food.
♨ Q ◗ ▸ ⊞ & ▲

Aberystwyth

Cambrian Hotel
Alexandra Road
(opp. station)
☎ (01970) 612446
11–11
Draught Bass; Hancock's HB; guest beers Ⓗ
Elegant, 106-year-old hotel, popular with locals, students and visitors: a cocktail lounge

and a separate games room. Families welcome. The beer is reliable, but expensive.
🛏 ◗ ▸ ▲ ⇌ ♣

Mill Inn
Mill Street
☎ (01970) 612306
12–3, 6–11; 12–11 Sat
Aberystwyth Dinas Draught; Ansells Mild; Greenalls Original; Tetley Bitter; guest beers Ⓗ

The longest surviving free house in Aberystwyth; a very popular local, offering live Welsh folk music (Wed), occasional cider, a changing selection of guest beers on six pumps, and a friendly atmosphere. ▲ ⇶ ♣

Blaenwaun

Lamb Inn
OS237271 ☎ (01994) 448440
Hours vary
Young's Bitter; guest beers Ⓗ
Traditional country local in an isolated hamlet. Friendly welcome. ✿ ♣ P

Bow Street

Rhydypennau Inn
On A487
☎ (01970) 828308
11–3, 6–11; 11–11 Sat
Hancock's HB; Whitbread Boddingtons Bitter, Flowers IPA; guest beer Ⓗ
White-painted pub offering a variety of ales from its guest pump. Two bars: the accent is on food in the lounge, which adjoins a large restaurant area. Restaurant meals only Sun lunchtime. Eve meals in winter: Tue–Sat only.
🏚 Q ✿ ◑ ♦ ⊟ ♣ P

Broadmoor

Cross Inn
☎ (01834) 812287
11–11
Bass Worthington BB; guest beers (summer) Ⓗ
Pub with a small public bar and a lounge/dining area, plus a family room and a large outside play area.
🏃 ✿ ◑ ♦ ♣ P ⊟

Brynhoffnant

Brynhoffnant Inn
On A487
☎ (01239) 654413
12 (6 winter)–11
Bass Worthington BB; Crown Buckley Best Bitter; John Smith's Bitter Ⓗ
Large, one-room bar with a games room attached; popular with locals and tourists. A huge log fire burns at one end. Helpful staff.
🏚 ✿ ◑ ♦ ▲ ♣ P

Caio

Brunant Arms
1 mile NE of A482
☎ (01558) 650483
12–3, 7 (6 summer)–11 (may be 12–11 in summer)
Hook Norton Best Bitter; guest beers Ⓗ
Friendly pub, full of character; close to Dolaucothi gold mines.
🏚 ✿ 🚗 ◑ ♦ ▲ ♣ P

Capel Bangor

Tynllidiart Arms
On A44 ☎ (01970) 880248
11–2.30, 6–11; closed winter Sun
Aberystwyth Premium; Flowers Original; guest beers Ⓗ
Cottage pub with two small bars, dating from 1688. The guest beer is usually from an independent brewery. Draught cider in summer. Bottled Belgian beers.
🏚 ◑ ♦ ♣ ⌂ ⊟

Cardigan

Commercial Hotel
Pendre ☎ (01239) 612574
11 (10 Sat)–11; closed Sun
Felinfoel Bitter, Dark, Double Dragon (summer) Ⓗ
Comfortable small-town pub with a friendly landlord and a congenial atmosphere. No food. Beware: the pub will close for a late afternoon break if not busy. 🏚 ✿ ♣

Carew

Carew Inn
On A4075 ☎ (01646) 651267
12–2.30, 4.30–11 (11–11 summer)
Bass Worthington BB; Crown Buckley Rev. James; Pembroke Main Street Ⓗ
Large, rural pub with farmers and tradespeople. Impromptu musical eves.
🏚 ✿ 🚗 ◑ ♦ ♣ P ⊁

Carmarthen

Boar's Head Hotel
Lammas Street
☎ (01267) 222789
11–11
Felinfoel Bitter, Dark, Double Dragon; guest beers Ⓗ
17th-century coaching inn with 1820 extensions; now a fully modernised, family-run hotel. Excellent food.
Q ◑ ♦ ⇶ P

Mansel Arms
1 Mansel Street
☎ (01267) 236385
11–11
Bass Worthington Dark, BB; guest beers Ⓗ
Pub situated alongside the town's provision market; popular with shoppers and other locals. ✿ ◑

Queen's Hotel
Queen's Street
☎ (01267) 231800
11–11
Bass Worthington BB, Draught Bass; guest beers Ⓗ
Popular town-centre pub.
Q ✿ ◑ ♣

Cenarth

Three Horseshoes
☎ (01239) 710119
11–11
Draught Bass Ⓖ; **Crown Buckley Dark, Best Bitter** Ⓗ; **guest beers** Ⓖ/Ⓗ
Busy, traditional, low-beamed pub, close to Cenarth Falls.
🏚 Q 🐶 ✿ ◑ ♣ P

Cresswell Quay

Cresselly Arms
☎ (01646) 621210

Dyfed

11–3, 5–11 (maybe 11–11 summer)
Whitbread Flowers IPA; guest beers (Monday) G
Famous old pub hardly altered since 1900 when boats sailed up to the quay. Beer is served from a jug. Time stands still in this quaint setting.
🏚 Q ✿ ♣ P ⌸

Cwmann

Ram Inn
On A482 ☎ (01570) 422556
11–11
Draught Bass; Fuller's London Pride; guest beer H
Traditional pub with a warm welcome, originally a drovers' hostelry in the 16th century.
🏚 Q ✿ ◑ ♣ P

Dale

Griffin
☎ (01646) 636227
11 (6 winter, may vary)–11;
Bass Worthington BB; Felinfoel Double Dragon; Uley Old Spot; guest beers H
Pub on the edge of the bay, very popular in summer with water sports enthusiasts. One guest beer in winter, two in summer (many from Uley).
🏚 Q ✿ ◑ Å ♣ ⌣

Dreenhill

Denant Mill Inn
Off Dale Road, 2½ miles from Haverfordwest
☎ (01437) 766569
12–3, 6–11 (may vary in winter)
Beer range varies G/H
A pub fast becoming a legend with beer and food connoisseurs, set in an old water mill. A merry-go-round of beers from all over the UK, plus Belgian brews. Excellent food and accommodation, and always good conversation. Voted *Best Heritage Pub* in Pembrokeshire, 1994. 🏚 Q ☻ ✿ 🛏 ◑ Å ♣ P ⅄

Drefach Felindre

Red Lion
☎ (01559) 370780
11 (5 Mon)–11
Bass Worthington BB, Draught Bass; guest beer H
Friendly village pub, recently refurbished.
🏚 ✿ 🛏 ◑ Å ♣ P

Dryslwyn

New Cross Inn
Court Henry (1 mile N of A40)
☎ (01558) 668276
6.30 (11 Sat)–11
Bass Worthington BB *or* **Crown Buckley Best Bitter** G

Family-run pub with a small public bar and a popular, separate restaurant area.
🏚 Q ◑ ♣ 🔔 & Å P

Ffairfach

Torbay
27 Heol Cennen (A483)
☎ (01558) 322029
12–3, 6–11; 11–11 Sat
Crown Buckley Dark, Best Bitter H
Family-run village pub with a strong accent on good, home-cooked food. 🏚 Q ✿ ◑
Å 🔔 (not winter Sun) ♣ P

Fishguard

Coach House
10 High Street
☎ (01348) 873883
11–11
Bass Worthington BB; Whitbread Flowers IPA H
Renovated old town pub, popular with the young. Two restaurants. ✿ ◑ ♣

Foelgastell

Smith's Arms
Off A48 ☎ (01269) 842213
11–11 (supper licence)
Crown Buckley Dark; Whitbread Boddingtons Mild, Flowers Original H
Friendly pub in a quiet village just off the main holiday route.
🏚 Q ✿ 🛏 ◑ 🔔 & Å P

Freshwater East

Freshwater Inn
☎ (01646) 672329
12–3, 7–11 (12–11 summer)
Bass Worthington BB; Greenalls Original; guest beers (summer) H
Pub in a beautiful setting with cliff-top views. Tastefully modernised, with a relaxing atmosphere. Occasional live music. 🏚 Q ☻ 🛏 ◑ ♣ Å
♣ P ⅄ ⌸

Goginan

Druid Inn
On A44 ☎ (01970) 880650
11–3, 5.30–11; closed Sun
Banks's Bitter; Camerons Strongarm; guest beers H
Pub set into the hillside in a former lead-mining village. Selection of Romanian vodkas and bottled Czech lager.
🏚 ✿ ◑ & ♣ P ⌸

Goodwick

Glendower Hotel
Glendower Square
☎ (01348) 872873
11–11
Crown Buckley Dark, Best Bitter H

Pub ideal for ferry passengers, only five minutes' walk from the Ireland terminal and the station. Good food and accommodation. ☻ 🛏 ◑ &
⇌ (Fishguard Harbour) ♣

Haverfordwest

George's
24 Market Street
☎ (01437) 766683
11–3, 7–11
Beer range varies H
Unusual pub in the old part of town which combines a restaurant, a bar and a gift shop. Excellent food.
Q ✿ ◑

King's Arms Hotel
23 Dew Street
☎ (01437) 763726
11–3, 5.30 (7 Sat, maybe earlier)–11
S&N Theakston Best Bitter, XB; guest beers H
Olde-worlde town pub, recently renovated back to life. A log-burner and a flagged floor are featured. Some 150 different ales sold in the last year. A local CAMRA *Best New Pub* award-winner.
🏚 Q ☻ ◑ ♣

Pembroke Yeoman
Hill Street (near St Thomas's Green) ☎ (01437) 762500
11–11
Draught Bass; Ruddles County; guest beers H
Homely, Victorian pub in an old part of town. Three guest beers; varied, large food menu.
🏚 Q ✿ ◑

Horeb

Waunwyllt
Off B4309 at Five Roads
☎ (01269) 860209
12–3, 7–11 (supper licence)
Felinfoel Double Dragon; guest beers H
Friendly pub, worth finding. Families welcome; extensive menu.
🏚 Q ✿ 🛏 ◑ ♣ & P ⌸

Jameston

Tudor Lodge
☎ (01834) 871978
12–11
Bass Worthington BB; guest beer H
Beautiful country manor with a pleasant garden. Popular with holidaymakers and locals. Friendly atmosphere; interesting interior layout.
🏚 ☻ ✿ 🛏 ◑ Å ⇌ P

Johnstown

Friends Arms
St Clears Road
☎ (01267) 234073

11–11
**Ansells Mild; Ind Coope
Burton Ale; Tetley Bitter** Ⓗ
Old village tavern which once
doubled as a blacksmith's.
Very friendly. ☸

Lamphey

Dial Inn

The Ridgeway
☎ (01646) 672426
11–3, 6–11; 11–11 Sat
**Bass Worthington BB;
Draught Bass; Hancock's HB;
guest beer** Ⓗ
Elegant and comfortable
lounge, with a back bar and a
separate restaurant (interesting
menu). Very popular all year.
🚪 Q ⛄ ☸ ◖ ▶ ♿ ⇌ ♣ P
⅄ ☗

Landshipping

Stanley Arms

OS013117 ☎ (01834) 891227
12–3, 6–11
**Bass Worthington BB,
Draught Bass; Tetley Bitter;
guest beer** Ⓗ
Attractive, two-bar pub near
the estuary. Popular with boat
users. Pleasant garden;
excellent food. Live music.
🚪 Q ⛄ ☸ ◖ ▶ A P

Laugharne

Browns Hotel

King Street (A4066)
☎ (01994) 427320
11–11
Crown Buckley Best Bitter Ⓗ
Friendly village pub full of
Dylan Thomas memorabilia.
No-smoking area in summer.
A ♣ ⅄

Letterston

Harp Inn

31 Haverfordwest Road (A40)
☎ (01348) 840061
11–3, 6–11
**Marston's Pedigree;
Whitbread Flowers IPA,
Original** Ⓗ
Modernised country inn and
restaurant with an impressive
menu. Near the coast and the
Preseli Mountains.
🚪 ☸ ◖ ▶ ☗ ♿ P ⅄

Llanarthney

Golden Grove Arms

On B4300 ☎ (01558) 668551
12–2.30 (not Mon), 6–11; 11–11 Sat
**Crown Buckley Rev. James;
Whitbread Boddingtons
Bitter** Ⓗ
Large roadside pub which has
successfully combined good
beer with good food.
🚪 ☸ ⛵ ◖ ▶ ♣ P

Llanbadarn Fawr

Black Lion

☎ (01970) 623448
11.30–3, 6–11
Banks's Mild, Bitter Ⓔ;
**Camerons Strongarm; guest
beer** Ⓗ
Popular, friendly pub,
frequented by locals and
students. Function room with
a bar at the rear; beer garden
at the side. Live music during
the week. ☸ ◖ A ♣ P ☗

Llandeilo

White Horse Inn

125 Rhosmaen Street (A483,
through arch at top of main
street) ☎ (01558) 822424
12–11
**Bass Worthington Dark, BB;
Wadworth 6X; Wells
Bombardier; guest beers** Ⓗ
17th-century coaching inn
with a courtyard. Friendly
atmosphere; renowned for
good food. The bar front is
adorned with caricatures of its
regulars. Large car park at the
rear. Two guest beers, with
plenty of variety. 🚪 Q ⛄ ☸
◖ ▶ ☗ ♿ ⇌ ♣ ♻

Try also: Farmer's Arms,
Rhosmaen St (Free); **Three
Tuns**, Market St (Free)

Llandovery

Red Lion

2 Market Square
11.30–3 (not Wed), 5.30–8; closed Sun
**Crown Buckley Dark, Best
Bitter** Ⓖ
Ancient, eccentric and friendly
pub with one basic drinking
room and no bar. In the same
family for a century. Hard to
find, but well worth the effort
(the sign is not visible from the
road; look for red posts in the
pedestrianised square).
🚪 Q A ⇌

White Swan

47 High Street (A40)
☎ (01550) 20816
12–3.30 (may extend in summer),
7–11
**Ind Coope Burton Ale;
Wadworth 6X; guest beers**
(occasional) Ⓖ
Former coaching inn, first
licensed in 1812. Pleasant
suntrap garden with rural
views. Unrestricted parking
outside. 🚪 Q ☸ ♿ A ♣

Try also: White Hart, Stone St
(Bass)

Llandybie

Red Lion

The Square
☎ (01269) 851202

11–3, 6–11; 12–3 Sun, closed Sun eve
**Draught Bass; Whitbread Best
Bitter** Ⓗ
Attractive pub offering a good
welcome to families and good
food.
🚪 ⛄ ☸ ⛵ ◖ ▶ ⇌ P ⅄

Llanelli

Half Moon

71a Wern Road
☎ (01554) 772626
11.30–3, 6–11; 11.30–11 Fri, Sat &
summer
**Crown Buckley Best Bitter,
Rev. James** Ⓗ
Lively pub offering a good
choice of meals (no eve food
Sun–Tue). Folk music Tue. The
house beer is brewed by
Crown Buckley. Beware the
keg cider on a fake
handpump. ◖ ▶ ♿

Island House

Island Place (roundabout near
Crown Buckley brewery)
☎ (01554) 774724
11.30–3, 6.30–11; 11.30–11
**Bass Worthington Dark, BB,
Draught Bass; guest beers** Ⓗ
Friendly local near the town
centre. Large council car park
nearby. Q ☗ ♿

Thomas Arms Hotel

Thomas Street (A476)
☎ (01554) 772043
11–3, 6–11; 11–11 Fri & Sat
**Crown Buckley Best Bitter,
Rev. James** Ⓗ
Plush showpiece hotel for
Crown Buckley: various
function rooms and a relaxed,
roomy lounge bar.
Q ⛵ ◖ ▶ P

Try also: Greenfield, Erw Rd
(Crown Buckley)

Llannon

Red Lion

3 Heol-y-Plas (A476)
☎ (01269) 841276
5 (12 Sat)–11
Felinfoel Bitter Ⓗ, **Dark** Ⓔ,
Double Dragon Ⓗ
Pub dating back to at least the
17th century and rumoured to
have a secret tunnel leading to
the nearby church. Excellent
food (lunches Sat/Sun only).
🚪 Q ⛄ ☸ ◖ ▶ P

Lydstep

Lydstep Tavern

Hillside ☎ (01834) 871521
12–3, 6.30–11 (may close beginning of
week in winter)
**Bass Worthington BB; Tetley
Bitter** (summer) Ⓗ
Pretty village pub with a very
pleasant interior, good menu
choice and a friendly welcome.
Q ⛄ ☸ ◖ ▶ A ⇌ ♣ P

Dyfed

Manorbier

Castle Inn
☎ (01834) 871268
11–11
S&N Theakston Best Bitter, XB, Old Peculier; guest beer Ⓗ
Friendly pub near the castle and beach; very popular with locals and holidaymakers.
Q ⓫ ⊛ ⟨⟩ ▲ ♣

Mathry

Farmer's Arms
Off A487 ☎ (01348) 831284
11–11
Bass Worthington BB, Draught Bass; Hancock's HB (summer) Ⓗ
Rural pub with a timbered interior: a monks' brewhouse in 1291. Friendly welcome.
⌂ ⊛ ⟨⟩ ⟨⟩ ₺ ▲ ♣ P

Meinciau

Black Horse
On B4309 ☎ (01269) 860247
11–2, 7–11; closed Sun
Crown Buckley Dark, Felinfoel Bitter Ⓖ
Traditional, small-roomed pub on top of a hill. ⌂ Q ⊛ ♣ P

Mynydd y Garreg

Prince of Wales Inn
Heol Meinciau
☎ (01554) 890522
12–3 (not Mon, except bank hols), 5.15–11
Beer range varies Ⓗ
Small pub serving an excellent range of beers. No under-14s. Lunches Tue–Sat.
⌂ Q ⊛ ⟨⟩ ₺ ▲ ♣ P ⊟

Narberth

Angel Hotel
High Street ☎ (01834) 860215
11–3, 5–11
Crown Buckley Rev. James; Everards Tiger; guest beers Ⓗ
Attractive pub offering excellent food and friendly service. Q ⟫ ⊛ ⟨⟩ ⟨⟩ ₺ ▲

Kirkland Arms
St James Street, East Gate
☎ (01834) 860423
11–3, 5–11
Felinfoel Bitter, Double Dragon; guest beer Ⓗ
Genuine local with local beer.
Q ⊛ ⟨⟩ ⊕ ▲ ♣ P

New Quay

Black Lion
Glanmor Terrace (one way system, top of the hill)
☎ (01545) 560209
11–11 (12–3, 6–11 winter, may vary)
Ind Coope Burton Ale; Tetley Bitter Ⓗ
Popular pub with tourists. Quality food; good garden for children.
Q ⟫ ⊛ ⋈ ⟨⟩ ⟨⟩ ₺ ▲ ♣ P

Pembroke

Castle Inn
17 Main Street
☎ (01646) 682883
11–11
Bass Worthington BB, Draught Bass; Tetley Bitter; guest beer Ⓗ
Old pub, full of character and characters of various nationalities and backgrounds. Very busy weekends with young people. ⟫ ⊛ ₺ ⇌ ♣

Old Cross Saws
109 Main Street
☎ (01646) 682475
11–11
Crown Buckley James Buckley Ale, Rev. James Ⓗ
Rugby followers' local; a lively and friendly pub. A good base for sightseeing.
⊛ ⋈ ⟨⟩ ⟨⟩ ₺ ⇌ ♣

Pembroke Dock

Station Inn
Dimond Street
11–3, 6–11 (11–11 summer)
Pembroke Main Street, Golden Hill, Darkling; guest beers Ⓗ
Converted railway station keeping the old building's character, full of railway memorabilia. The Pembroke Brewery tap.
Q ⊛ ⟨⟩ ₺ ⇌ P

Pembroke Ferry

Ferry Inn
Under Cleddau Bridge, Pembroke Dock side
☎ (01646) 682947
11–3, 7 (6.30 Sat)–11 (hours vary in winter)
Draught Bass; Hancock's HB Ⓗ
Well-run, busy pub with a good stock of malts and a naval theme. Good value meals (best to book).
⌂ Q ⊛ ⟨⟩ ▲ ⇌ ♣ P

Penally

Cross Inn
☎ (01834) 844030
11–3, 7–11 (11–11 summer)
Bass Worthington BB; guest beers Ⓗ
Large village pub very close to beaches and a golf course. Very busy in summer. A good base for holidays. ⌂ ⟫ ⊛ ⋈ ⟨⟩ ⟨⟩ ₺ ▲ ⇌ ♣ P ⊟

Penrhiwllan

Penrhiwllan Inn
On A475 ☎ (01559) 370394
11–11; closed Sun
Bass Worthington BB, Draught Bass; guest beer (occasional) Ⓖ
Unspoiled country pub and restaurant with a good welcome and very reasonably priced beer (further reduced by a happy hour each weekday eve). The pub offers a lift service within a five-mile radius.
⌂ ⟫ ⊛ ⟨⟩ ⟨⟩ ♣ P

Pentrecagal

Pensarnau Arms
On A484 ☎ (01559) 370339
11 (4 Mon, 12 Tue–Sat Nov–Easter)–11
Aberystwyth Dinas Draught Ⓗ; Draught Bass Ⓖ; Crown Buckley Rev. James Ⓗ
Small but inviting pub with a very accommodating landlord. Welcoming fire in winter months.
⌂ ⟫ ⟨⟩ ▲ ♣ P

Try also: Bluebell Inn Newcastle Emlyn (Felinfoel)

Pontargothi

Cresselly Arms
On A40 ☎ (01267) 290221
11.30–3.30, 6.30–11
Marston's Pedigree; Whitbread Flowers Original; guest beer Ⓗ
Well-appointed pub with a restaurant and garden overlooking the Cothi river.
⌂ ⊛ ⟨⟩ ⟨⟩ P

Pontfaen

Dyffryn Arms
Off B4313 ☎ (01348) 881305
Hours vary
Draught Bass or Ind Coope Burton Ale Ⓖ
1920s front room where time has stood still. Beer is still served by the jug and conversation is a must. Set in the Gwaun Valley, between the Preseli Mountains and Fishguard. ⌂ Q ⊛ ▲ ♣

Pren-gwyn

Gwarcefel Arms
On A475 ☎ (01559) 362720
11–11; 12–3 Sun, closed Sun eve
Bass Worthington BB; Crown Buckley Best Bitter; guest beer (summer) Ⓗ
Popular pub for meals. Children are welcome in all bars and the restaurant.
⌂ ⊛ ⟨⟩ ⟨⟩ ▲ P

Rhandirmwyn

Royal Oak

☎ (01550) 760201
11–3, 6–11 (may extend)
Fuller's London Pride; Ind Coope Benskins BB, Burton Ale; guest beer (summer) H
Once Earl Cawdor's hunting lodge, now a friendly family-owned pub, popular with locals and visitors alike. Excellent views over the Tywi Valley. A good centre for walkers, campers, cyclists and ornithologists (RSPB reserve nearby).
🏰 ⚜ 🛏 ◖ ▶ Å ♣ P ⊟

Robeston Wathen

Bush Inn

☎ (01834) 860778
11–11
Ind Coope Burton Ale; Tetley Bitter; guest beer H
Roadside pub with a garden and a children's play area. Large car park; good food.
⚜ ◖ ▶ P

St Clears

Corvus Inn

Station Road ☎ (01994) 230965
11–11
Bass Worthington BB; guest beers H
Comfortable pub with a very relaxed lounge bar. Popular with locals and lively. Good food. ◖ ▶ ⊕

St David's

Farmer's Arms

Goat Street ☎ (01437) 720328
11–11
Bass Worthington BB; Whitbread Boddingtons Bitter, Flowers Original H

19th-century, stone-built pub maintaining many old features. Popular with fishermen and farmers. Good, home-cooked meals.
🏰 ⚜ ◖ ▶ ᵍ Å ♣ P ⊟

St Florence

Sun Inn

☎ (01834) 871322
4.30 (11 summer)–11
Hancock's HB; guest beer (summer) H
Friendly village pub, full of character, with brasses and old farming implements. Not over-run with tourists.
🏰 Q ◖ ▶ ᵍ ♣ P

Saron

Llwyndafydd Inn

On A484 ☎ (01559) 371048
11–11
Felinfoel Double Dragon H
Small, traditional country inn with a friendly atmosphere and an unspoilt interior.
🏰 Q ⚜ ◖ ▶ ⊕ ᵍ ♣ P

Saundersfoot

Royal Oak

Wogans Terrace
☎ (01834) 812546
11–11
Bass Worthington BB, Draught Bass; Morland Old Speckled Hen; Whitbread Boddingtons Bitter, Flowers IPA, Original H
Very attractively refurbished old pub with a pleasant patio area, very busy in summer.Friendly atmosphere; excellent food. ⚜ ◖ ▶ ⊕ ⊟

Solva

Ship Inn

Main Street ☎ (01437) 721247

11–11
Bass Worthington BB, Draught Bass; Solva Ramsay Bitter; guest beers (summer) H
Small, 300-year-old pub, popular with holidaymakers, in a pretty fishing village setting. Lunches in summer.
🏰 Q 🛏 ⚜ ◖ ▶ ᵍ ♣

Talybont

Black Lion Hotel

On A487 ☎ (01970) 832335
10.30–11
Ind Coope Burton Ale; Tetley Bitter; guest beer H
Imposing, grey slate country hotel with two bars and a restaurant. Popular with the local farming fraternity.
⚜ 🛏 ◖ ▶ ♣ P

Templeton

Boar's Head

☎ (01834) 860286
11–3, 5.30–11 (11–11 bank hols)
Bass Worthington BB, Draught Bass H
Traditional pub with two bars plus a restaurant, popular with villagers and holidaymakers. Meals served during all opening hours.
🛏 ⚜ ◖ ▶ ᵍ P

Tenby

Hope & Anchor

St Julian Street
11–3, 7–11 (11–11 summer)
Bass Worthington BB; Crown Buckley Rev. James; guest beer H
Cosy, one-room pub with a warm welcome. Very close to the harbour and beach. Meals in summer only.
Q ⚜ ◖ ▶ ᵍ Å ⇌ ♣

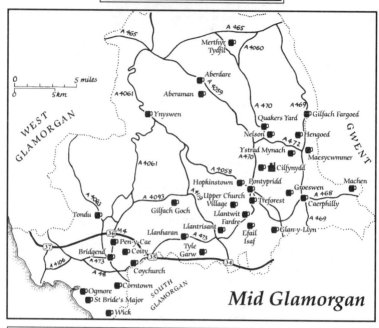

Mid Glamorgan

 Reckless Eric's, Cilfynydd

Aberaman

Temple Bar Vaults
Cardiff Road (B4275)
☎ (01685) 876137
12–4, 6.30–11 (may vary)
**Brains SA; Hancock's HB;
guest beers** Ⓗ
Small, friendly local with
interesting bric-a-brac. In the
same family for 108 years.
♨ Q ♣ ♠ P

Aberdare

Gadlys Arms
26 Bridge Street, Robertstown
(off A4059, opp. Tesco)
☎ (01685) 876055
12–3, 6–11
**Bass Worthington BB,
Draught Bass; Brains Dark;
guest beer** Ⓗ
Comfortable village pub: one
bar plus a popular restaurant.
Extensive bar menu. ❀ ◑ ▶ P

Bridgend

Famous Pen y Bont Inn
Derwen Road
☎ (01656) 652266
11.30–3, 5.30–11; 11–11 Sat &
summer
**Brains SA; Greenalls Bitter;
Marston's Pedigree;
Whitbread Boddingtons
Bitter; guest beer** Ⓗ

Popular, town-centre pub with
a cosy atmosphere and much
railway memorabilia. ◑ ▶ ⇌

Five Bells Inn
Ewenny Road
☎ (01656) 766522
11.30–4, 6–11; 11–11 Sat
**Bass Worthington BB,
Draught Bass** Ⓗ
Spacious, comfortable bar with
an adjoining games area. Quiet
lounge on the upper level.
Q ◑ ⊟ ⇌ ♠ P

Old Castle Inn
90 Nolton Street
☎ (01656) 652305
12–4, 6–11; 12–11 Fri & Sat
**Bass Worthington BB,
Draught Bass or Brains SA** Ⓗ
Warm, friendly local, with
exposed stone walls.
♨ Q ◑ ⊟

Caerphilly

Courthouse
Cardiff Road ☎ (01222) 888120
11–11
**Brains Bitter; Ruddles Best
Bitter; Wadworth 6X** Ⓗ
Traditional, 14th-century long
house with original features.
Its conservatory overlooks the
castle. Caerphilly cheese is
made on the premises. Meals
in the bar or restaurant (not
served Sun). The beer range
may vary. Q ❀ ◑ ▶ ♿ ⇌

Goodrich
Van Road ☎ (01222) 880029
11–11
**Bass Worthington BB,
Draught Bass; Brains Dark,
SA** Ⓗ
Rambling, popular roadside
pub with several rooms,
including a restaurant and a
function room (live music Fri
and Sat). Large public bar
and lounge.
♨ ❀ ⊛ ◑ ▶ ⊟ ⇌

Cilfynydd

Commercial Hotel
On A4054 ☎ (01443) 402486
11–11 (11.45 supper licence)
**Bass Worthington BB;
Hancock's HB** Ⓗ
Large, bustling village pub
offering games (snooker),
live music, comfortable
lounge areas and a
restaurant. No meals Mon
eve. ◑ ▶ ♿ ♠

Coity

Six Bells
120 Heol West Plas
☎ (01656) 653192
12–11
**Bass Worthington BB;
Hancock's HB** Ⓗ
Friendly, comfortable, two-bar
village local, opposite the
ruins of Coity Castle.
Q ❀ ⊟ P

Corntown

Golden Mile
Corntown Road
☎ (01656) 654884
11.30–3, 5 (5.30 Sat)–11
Bass Worthington BB,
Draught Bass; Hancock's HB;
guest beer Ⓗ
Smart, old converted
farmhouse with a stone
fireplace, beams and a
restaurant.
⌂ Q ✿ ◑ ♪ ⌺ ♣ P

Coychurch

Prince of Wales
Main Road ☎ (01656) 860600
12–11
Banks's Mild, Bitter;
Marston's Pedigree Ⓗ
Pleasant village local with
exposed stone walls and
flagstone floors. A rare Banks's
outlet for the area. Q ◑ ⌺ P

White Horse
Main Road ☎ (01656) 652583
11.30–4, 5.30–11; 11.30–11 Sat
Brains Dark, Bitter, SA Ⓗ
Plush, restaurant-style lounge
(emphasis on food) and a
comfortable public bar.
✿ ◑ ♪ ⌺ ♣ P

Efail Isaf

Carpenter's Arms
Heol Ffrwd Phillip
☎ (01443) 202426
12–11
Brains Bitter; Hancock's HB Ⓗ
Popular village local with a
comfortable lounge and a
more basic bar with a TV.
✿ ⌺ ♣ P

Gilfach Fargoed

Capel
Park Place ☎ (01443) 830272
12–4, 7–11; 12–11 Fri & Sat
Brains SA; Courage Best
Bitter; John Smith's Bitter;
guest beer Ⓗ
Large, traditional Valleys pub
with lots of interesting
features.
Q ✿ ⍟ ◑ ⌺ ≠ ♣ P

Gilfach Goch

Griffin
Hendreforgan (600 yds S of
A4093) OS988875
7 (12 Sat)–11
Brains SA Ⓗ
Exceptional, traditional local,
remotely situated in a small
valley bottom. Interesting old
furniture and bric-a-brac;
convivial atmosphere. Easy to
miss at the end of a rough
lane, and not signed, but
worth the effort. Q ✿ P

Glan-y-Llyn

Fagin's Ale & Chop House
Cardiff Road ☎ (01222) 811800
12–11
Brains Bitter; Felinfoel
Double Dragon; Wadworth
6X; Whitbread Boddingtons
Bitter Ⓗ; guest beers Ⓖ
Pub and restaurant converted
from an old terraced cottage,
offering a terrific range of ales
from independents (up to
eight guests). Fagin's own
brew from Crown Buckley.
Regional CAMRA *Pub of the
Year* 1994. Occasional cider.
✿ ◑ ♪ ≠ (Taff's Well) ⌂

Groeswen

White Cross Inn
On hillside, 1 mile N of A468
OS128870 ☎ (01222) 851332
12–3.30, 6–11; 11–11 Sat (supper
licence)
Bass Worthington Dark, BB,
Draught Bass; Hancock's HB;
S&N Theakston Best Bitter Ⓗ
Pub with a small bar and
two additional rooms, the
larger allowing for live
entertainment. The patio has a
view of Caerphilly Castle.
Children welcome.
⌂ Q ✿ ⌂ ◑ ♪ ⅙ ⚶ ♣ P

Hengoed

Junction Inn
9 King's Hill (by station)
☎ (01443) 812192
12–4 (4.30 Fri & Sat), 7–11
Bass Worthington BB;
Hancock's HB Ⓗ
Immaculately appointed local,
featuring railway memorabilia.
On the western bank of a
viaduct. ◑ ♪ ⌺ ≠ ♣

Hopkinstown

Hollybush
Tŷ Mawr Road (main road to
Rhondda) ☎ (01443) 402325
11.30–5, 6.15–11
Bass Worthington BB;
Hancock's HB; guest beer Ⓗ
Small bar, dedicated to sports,
both physical and mental. A
comfortable lounge doubles as
an eating area. ◑ ♪ ⌺ ⅙ ♣ P

Llanharan

High Corner House
The Square ☎ (01443) 238056
11–11
Brains Bitter; Wadworth 6X;
Whitbread Boddingtons
Bitter, Flowers Original Ⓗ
Typical Brewer's Fayre pub
with families well catered for
(baby changing cubicle).
⛄ ✿ ◑ ♪ P ⊁

Llantrisant

Cross Keys
High Street ☎ (01443) 222155
12–3 (not Mon), 7–11; 11–11 Fri & Sat
Brains Bitter; Whitbread
Boddingtons Bitter, Flowers
IPA Ⓗ
Open-plan, central, village pub
popular with the younger set
eves. Folk club Wed. ✿ ◑ ♣

Llantwit Fardre

Bush Inn
Main Road ☎ (01443) 203958
2.30 (12 Sat)–11
Bass Worthington BB,
Draught Bass; Brains Dark;
Hancock's HB Ⓗ
Single-room village local with
a small car park. Q ◑ ♪ ♣ P

Machen

White Hart Inn
Nant y Ceisiad (100 yds N of
A468, under railway bridge)
☎ (01633) 441005
12–2 (may vary), 6.30–11
Felinfoel Dark, Double
Dragon; guest beers Ⓗ
Mid Glam. CAMRA *Pub of the
Year* 1991/92: a rambling pub
with extensive wood
panelling. Excellent range of
guest beers from
independents. Three mini-beer
festivals per year. Small
restaurant (no lunches Sat).
⌂ Q ✿ ◑ ♪ P

Maesycwmmer

Maesycwmmer Inn
Main Road ☎ (01443) 814385
12–4, 7–11
Brains SA Ⓗ
Small bar and a comfortable
lounge in a pub by the eastern
side of the Hengoed Viaduct.
No lunches Sat. Q ✿ ◑ ⌺ ≠
(Hengoed) ♣ P

Merthyr Tydfil

Lanterns
Bethesda Street, Georgetown
☎ (01685) 383683
12–5, 7–11
Crown Buckley Best Bitter,
Rev. James Ⓗ
200-year-old pub: a single
horseshoe-shaped bar with a
raised dining area. House beer
from Crown Buckley.
✿ ◑ ♪ ≠

Wellington
Bethesda Street, Georgetown
☎ (01685) 370665
12–3 (may extend Fri & Sat), 7–11
Bass Worthington BB;
Hancock's HB; guest beer Ⓗ
Comfortable and friendly pub
with an Italian restaurant

Mid Glamorgan

upstairs. Lunches served Sun only, eve meals Tue–Sat. ◗

Nelson

Dynevor Arms
Commercial Street (near bus station) ☎ (01443) 450295
11–11; 11.30–4.30, 6–11 Tue & Thu
Bass Worthington BB; Brains Bitter; Hancock's HB Ⓗ
Former brew pub (and mortuary), over 200 years old, used by farmers after market. Busy public bar. ⊞ & ♣ P

Tyler's Arms
Feol Fawr (main street) ☎ (01443) 450430
11.30–4, 6.30–11; 11–11 Thu–Sat
Bass Worthington BB; Hancock's HB; John Smith's Bitter Ⓗ
Small, comfortably-appointed lounge and a busy public bar. Good food (book Sun lunch). This recently became an Ushers pub and the beers may change. Q ◖ ◗ ⊞ ♣ P

Ogmore

Pelican
Ewenny Road (B4524, opp. castle) ☎ (01656) 880049
11.30–3, 5 (6.30 Tue, Thu & Fri)–11; 11–11 Sat
Brains SA; Courage Best Bitter; John Smith's Bitter; Wadworth 6X; guest beer Ⓗ
Smart, comfortable country pub and restaurant serving an excellent range of fare.
❀ ◖ ◗ ▲ ♣ P

Pen-y-Cae

Tŷ'r Isha
Off A4061/A4063, Bridgend side of M4 services ☎ (01656) 725287
11–4, 6–11; 11–11 Sat
Bass Worthington BB, Draught Bass; Hancock's HB Ⓗ
Popular, converted 15th-century farmhouse, also once a courthouse. ⌂ ❀ ◖ ◗ & ⇌ (Sarn) P

Pontypridd

Bunch of Grapes
Ynysangharad Road (off A470 at Ynysybwl jct) ☎ (01443) 402934
11–11
Bass Worthington BB; Brains Bitter, SA; Hancock's HB; guest beer Ⓗ
Large, comfortable pub and restaurant. ❀ ◖ ◗ ♣ P

Llanover Arms
Bridge Street (off A470 at Ynysybwl jct) ☎ (01443) 403215
11–11

Bass Worthington BB; Brains Dark, Bitter, SA; guest beer Ⓗ
Bustling town pub with three drinking areas. ❀ ⊞ ♣ P

Market Tavern
Market Square ☎ (01443) 485331
11–11
Bass Worthington BB; Courage Best Bitter; Hancock's HB; John Smith's Bitter; Wadworth 6X Ⓗ
Busy town tavern with a restaurant/function room. The cellar bar stages live music weekends. Q ⌂ ◖ ◗ ⇌

Quakers Yard

Glantaff Inn
On A4054 ☎ (01443) 410822
12–4, 7–11
Brains Bitter; Courage Best Bitter, Directors; Ruddles Best Bitter; John Smith's Bitter; guest beer Ⓗ
Comfortable inn with a warm atmosphere, and a collection of water jugs. No eve meals Sun. Upstairs restaurant. Q ❀ ◖ ◗ & ⇌ (Abercynon) P

St Bride's Major

Farmer's Arms
Wick Road ☎ (01656) 880224
12–3, 6–11
Courage Best Bitter; John Smith's Bitter; Ushers Best Bitter, Founders; guest beer Ⓗ
Cosy, roadside inn by the village pond. Safe play area for children. ⌂ Q ❀ ◖ ◗ P

Fox & Hounds
Wick Road ☎ (01656) 880285
12–3, 5.30–11; 12–11 Fri, Sat & sometimes Mon–Fri in summer
Brains Bitter; John Smith's Bitter; Wadworth 6X; guest beer (weekends) Ⓗ
Friendly, 16th-century village pub with a busy bar. Food is served in a raised area. Great atmosphere. ❀ ◖ ◗ ⊞ P

Tondu

Llynfi Arms
Maesteg Road ☎ (01656) 720010
1 (12 Fri & Sat)–4, 6.30–11
Bass Worthington BB; Hancock's HB; guest beer Ⓗ
Roadside pub with a lively bar and a comfy lounge. Lunches served Sat; eve meals Thu–Sat. ◗ ⊞ ⇌

Treforest

Otley Arms
Forest Road ☎ (01443) 402033
11–11
Bass Worthington BB; Brains SA; Crown Buckley SBB, Rev. James; guest beer Ⓗ

Deceptively large pub, used by students. ❀ ◖ ◗ ⊞ ⇌ ♣ P

Tyle Garw

Boar's Head
Coed Cae Lane (½ mile off A473) ☎ (01443) 225400
12–4, 7–11
Beer range varies Ⓗ
Small, simply furnished, friendly, unspoilt local. Forest walks opposite. Two guest beers. Q ❀ ♣

Upper Church Village

Farmer's Arms
St Illtyd's Road ☎ (01443) 205766
11–11
Bass Worthington BB, Draught Bass; Hancock's HB; guest beer Ⓗ
Busy village pub where the open-plan bar is still cosy. The menu is mainly home-made and includes Sat breakfast. No meals Sun; eve meals on request. ❀ ◖ ◗ P

Wick

Lamb & Flag
St Bride's Road ☎ (01656) 890278
11.30–5, 6–11; 11–11 Fri & Sat
Bass Worthington BB, Draught Bass; Hancock's HB Ⓗ
Warm welcome in a village pub where much bric-a-brac adorns the lounge bar and adjoining rooms. Comfortable furnishings include small settles. ⌂ Q ◖ ◗ ⊞ ♣ P

Ynyswen

Crown Hotel
Ynyswen Road ☎ (01443) 772805
11–11 (may vary)
Courage Best Bitter, Directors; Ushers Founders Ⓗ; **guest beers** Ⓗ / Ⓖ
Popular, welcoming main road pub. The public bar features a red phone box. Separate lounge. ⌂ ⊞ ⇌ ♣

Ystrad Mynach

Royal Oak
Commercial Street (A469) ☎ (01443) 814196
12–3, 5.30–11; 12–11 Sat
Bass Worthington BB, Draught Bass; Hancock's HB Ⓗ
Unmistakable brewer's Tudor pub with a busy public bar. Good food. Q ❀ ◖ ◗ ⊞ & ⇌ (Pengam Halt) P

South Glamorgan

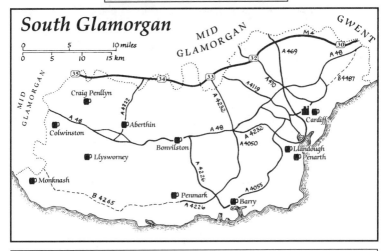

 Brains, Bullmastiff, *Cardiff*

Aberthin

Hare & Hounds
On A4222 ☎ (01446) 774892
11.30–11
**Bass Worthington BB,
Draught Bass** Ⓖ; **Hancock's
HB** Ⓗ
Small community pub
unchanged for many years.
Mature males in the bar;
family room and garden play
area. Meals in summer (only).
Limited parking.
🛏 Q ☘ ❀ ◖ ♣ P

Barry

Castle Hotel
Jewel Street ☎ (01446) 701035
12–11
Brains Dark, Bitter, SA Ⓗ
Large, back-street local with
four rooms downstairs and an
upstairs function room. The
lounge is adorned with prints
of old Barry.
Q ⊟ ≢ (Dock) ♣

Bonvilston

Red Lion
☎ (01446) 781208
11.30–3, 5–11 (11.30–11 summer);
11–11 Sat
Brains Dark, Bitter, SA Ⓗ
Roadside pub with a separate
area for eating and a darts
room. Good mix of visitors
and local characters. No eve
meals Sun/Mon. ❀ ◖ ▶ ♣ P

Cardiff

Baroness Windsor
Penarth Road
☎ (01222) 231380
11–11

Brains Dark, Bitter Ⓗ
Basic Brains pub on a busy
main road. Public bar at the
front; lounge at the rear;
serving area in-between.
Q ⊟ ≢ (Grangetown)

Black Lion
High Street, Llandaff
11–11
Brains Dark, Bitter, SA Ⓗ
Traditional Brains house on a
busy road near Llandaff
Cathedral. Spacious lounge. A
Brains cellarmanship award-
winner.
Q ◖ ▶ ⊟ ≢ (Fairwater)

Butcher's Arms
Llandaff Road, Canton
11–11
Brains Dark, Bitter, SA Ⓗ
Welcoming corner local near
the Chapter arts centre.
Refreshingly untrendy and
comfortable. ⊟ ♣

City Arms
10–12 Quay Street
☎ (01222) 225258
11–11
Brains Dark, Bitter, SA; guest
beer Ⓗ
Simple, two-bar pub
contrasting with other city-
centre leisure experiences.
Deservedly popular with all
ages. Close to the Arms Park.
Q ◖ ⊟ ≢ (Central) ♣

Conway
Conway Road, Canton (100
yds off A4119)
☎ (01222) 232797
12–11
**Whitbread Boddingtons
Bitter, Flowers IPA, Original;**
guest beers Ⓗ

Lively, back-street local in the
Bohemian quarter: a small bar
and comfy lounge with a
'book exchange' facility.
Quizzes Tue/Sun. No meals
Sun. Q ❀ ◖ ⊟ ♣

Discovery Inn
Celyn Avenue, Lakeside
☎ (01222) 755015
11–3, 5.30–11; 11–11 Fri & Sat
**Courage Best Bitter,
Directors; Marston's Pedigree;
Ruddles County; John
Smith's Bitter** Ⓗ
Comfortable, two-lounge,
1960s pub in a pleasant North
Cardiff location, near a lake.
The younger element takes
over one bar. Tidy dress
preferred. Good, home-made
lunches. Q ❀ ◖ ♿ P

Goat Major
High Street
11–11
Brains Dark, Bitter, SA Ⓗ
Smart, city-centre lounge bar
decorated with military
memorabilia and old local
photographs. Eve meals till
7pm. Q ◖ ▶ ≢ (Central)

Maltster's Arms
75 Merthyr Road, Whitchurch
☎ (01222) 624326
12–4, 5.30–11; 11–11 Wed–Sat
Brains Dark, Bitter Ⓗ
Small, real local offering a
piano sing-song Sat night and
skittles and darts matches
Mon-Fri. Many charity
activities. Q ❀ ◖ ▶ ⊟ ♣

Newt & Cucumber
4 Wharton Street
☎ (01222) 222114
12–11; closed Sun
Bass Worthington BB; Greene

South Glamorgan

King Abbot; S&N Theakston Best Bitter, XB *or* Old Peculier; guest beers H
Pub converted from a failed café-bar by Unicorn Inns, with enthusiastic management and staff. No-smoking area during dining hours (food served until 8pm, except Sun). Very busy with young people Fri and Sat nights. Dress restrictions apply.
◖ ▶ ⇌ (Central) ⊭

Royal Oak
Merthyr Road, Whitchurch
☎ (01222) 522050
11–3, 5–11; 11–11 Thu–Sat
Draught Bass; Hancock's HB H
Cosy, terraced pub in a shopping street: a friendly local organizing many charity activities. A tiny public bar hides a larger lounge at the rear. A guest beer from the Bass Caskmaster range often substitutes Bass.
Q ❀ ⊞

Three Horseshoes
Merthyr Road, Gabalfa
(400 yds N of Gabalfa interchange, A48/A470 jct)
☎ (01222) 625703
11–11
Brains Dark, Bitter, SA H
Pub of unremarkable appearance but with a friendly welcome and good food (Mon–Fri only). Built in 1968 to replace the previous Three Horseshoes, demolished to make way for the A470.
Q ❀ ◖ ⊞ ♣ P

Tut 'n' Shive
City Road
☎ (01222) 493526
11–11
Greene King Abbot; Wadworth 6X; Whitbread Boddingtons Bitter, Flowers Original H
Loud, bustling ale house, popular with students and followers of live music. Beers occasionally vary. Gravity dispense is no longer in use. No meals Sun. ◖

Vulcan
10 Adam Street
☎ (01222) 461580
11–11 (may close earlier in winter)
Brains Dark, Bitter H
Smallish, two-bar pub (though

one bar is open). This ex-Irish boarding house was used during the construction of the docks and is probably the oldest pub in Cardiff that has continuously sold beer. Eve meals on request.
Q ◖ ▶ ⊞ ⇌ (Queen St) ♣

White Hart
6 James Street
☎ (01222) 472561
11–11
Brains Dark, Bitter H
Single-bar, refurbished pub in the docks area. Walls are adorned with shipping and old Cardiff photographs. Brains *Best Cellar of the Year* 1994 in the tenanted trade. Meals on request.
Q ◖ ▶ ⇌ (Bay)

Colwinston

Sycamore Tree
Off A48 ☎ (01656) 652827
12–4 (not Mon/Tue in winter), 6–11
Draught Bass; Hancock's HB; guest beer H
Welcoming pub in a relatively unspoiled part of the Vale. Food is good quality; home made fare sometimes includes rabbit pie. Extensive pizza and pasta menu. Summer barbecues; the garden catches the eve sun.
🏚 Q ❀ ◖ ▶ ⊞ ♿ ▲ ♣ P

Craig Penllyn

Barley Mow
1½ miles N of A48 OS978773
☎ (01446) 772558
12–3 (not Mon), 6–11
Bass Worthington BB; Hancock's HB; guest beers H
Popular, three-roomed village pub, serving changing guest beers from an interesting range. Good food (no meals Sun eve) in the bar and quieter dining area.
🏚 ❀ ◖ ▶ ⊞ ▲ ♣ P

Llandough

Merrie Harrier
Penlan Road
☎ (01222) 707706
12–11; 12–2, 7–10.30 Sun
Brains Dark, Bitter, SA H
Popular pub near Llandough Hospital. No food Sun.
Q ❀ ◖ ⊞ ⇌ (Cogan) ♣ P

Llysworney

Carne Arms
On B4268 ☎ (01446) 773553
12–3, 6–11
Courage Best Bitter; Ruddles County; Wadworth 6X H
Friendly village local, originally a rectory for the area's first non-conformist minister. Excellent range of whiskies; good value food, mostly home made. Children welcome; large play area behind the pub. The beer range may vary.
🏚 Q ◖ ▶ ⊞ ▲ ♣ P ⊟

Monknash

Plough & Harrow
Off B4265 between Llantwit Major and Wick
☎ (01656) 890209
12 (6 Mon)–11
Bass Worthington BB, Draught Bass; Hancock's HB H; guest beers G
Lively local on the site of an 11th-century monastic grange, just off the Heritage Coast Path and frequented by trippers of all kinds. Live folk music Sun; quizzes; poetry; cider in summer. The house beer is brewed at Castle Eden. Meals in winter: weekends only.
🏚 Q ❀ ◖ ♣ ⮌ P

Penarth

Golden Lion
Glebe Street (off A4160)
☎ (01222) 701574
12–11
Cains Bitter; Hancock's HB H
Traditional local popular with all ages.
Q ⊞ ⇌ (Penarth/Dingle Rd)

Penmark

Six Bells
☎ (01446) 710229
12–11
Hancock's HB H
Village local where recent extension/refurbishment represents substantial investment by the licensee. Separate lounge/restaurant with an extensive menu. Close to Cardiff airport.
Q ❀ ▶ ⊞ P

UPDATES

Updates to *Good Beer Guide* entries and information about new breweries are provided by *What's Brewing*, CAMRA's monthly newspaper. Make sure of your copy by joining CAMRA today.

West Glamorgan

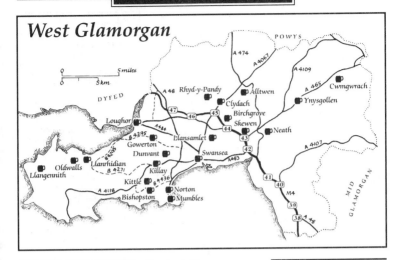

Occasional cider.
🏠 ⊛ ◖ ▶ ⌂ P

Clydach

New Inn

The Lone (1 mile NW of
Clydach, off B4603)
☎ (01792) 842839
11–4, 6–11; 11–11 Fri & Sat
**Bass Worthington BB; Greene
King Abbot; Morland Old
Speckled Hen; Whitbread
Flowers Original; guest
beers** Ⓗ
Three-roomed pub set in a
very scenic area of the
Swansea Valley. Beer is in the
'Real Ale Bar'.
🏠 Q ⊛ ◖ ▶ 🍴 & P

Cwmgwrach

Star

17 Glannant Place (off A465)
☎ (01639) 720365
12–2, 7–11; 11–11 Fri & Sat
**Bass Worthington BB; Crown
Buckley Best Bitter** Ⓗ
Two bars, a bar-lounge and a
small outside children's area at
a typical Neath Valley house
built over 100 years ago and
refurbished by the current
landlord. The owner also runs
mini coaches and taxis. No
meals Sun eve. ⊛ ▶ 🍴 P

Dunvant

Found Out Inn

8 Killan Road
☎ (01792) 203596
11–11
**Marston's Pedigree;
Whitbread Flowers Original;
guest beer** Ⓗ
Friendly local with a bar and a
lounge offering pool, darts,
regular quiz nights and good
quality lunches.
⊛ ◖ 🍴 ♣ P

Alltwen

Butcher's Arms

Alltwen Hill ☎ (01792) 863100
12–3, 6.30–11
**Courage Directors; Everards
Old Original; John Smith's
Bitter; Wadworth 6X; guest
beers** Ⓗ
Well-established traditional
village inn and restaurant,
offering a widely varied bar
menu of good quality meals
(no meals Sun eve). Families
are welcome. Outside bench
and table, but no garden.
🏠 Q ⊛ ◖ ▶ & P

Birchgrove

Bridgend Inn

265 Birchgrove Road (off M4
jct 44) ☎ (01792) 321878
12–2, 6–11; 12–11 Fri & Sat
**Brains Dark; Marston's
Pedigree; John Smith's Bitter;
Wadworth 6X; guest beer** Ⓗ
Local pub with a bar, a pool
room and a comfortable
lounge. Families are welcome.
Eve meals are cooked to order.
Weekly guest ale.
Q ⊛ ◖ & ♣ P

Bishopston

Joiner's Arms

50 Bishopston Road
☎ (01792) 232658
12–11
**Brains Dark; Courage Best
Bitter, Directors; John Smith's
Bitter; guest beers** Ⓗ
Superb free house, popular
with Gower visitors and locals.
A varied menu offers good
value food. There are always
at least two guest ales, and
occasional 'beer months'
feature a wide range.

Gowerton

Welcome to Gower

2 Mount Street
☎ (01792) 872611
11.30–3, 7–11
**Crown Buckley Dark, Best
Bitter, Rev. James** Ⓗ
Very popular lounge bar and
restaurant with a relaxing,
friendly environment. Families
welcome. Ample parking.
Q ⊛ ◖ ▶ ⇌ P

Killay

Railway Inn

553 Gower Road
☎ (01792) 203946
12–11
**Crown Buckley Dark, Best
Bitter, Rev. James** Ⓗ
Old-fashioned pub, which
used to be a railway station,
and now has three small bars
with a very cosy atmosphere.
Set in the Clyne Valley.
Q ⊛ ◖ 🍴 ▲ ⌂ P

Try also: Village Inn, Gower
Rd (Bass)

Kittle

Beaufort Arms

18 Pennard Road
☎ (01792) 234521
12–11
**Crown Buckley Best Bitter,
Rev. James** Ⓗ
Fine pub and restaurant (Mrs
B's) featuring pictures of old
Swansea and its surrounding
district. Children's play area
outside. Good value food.
⊛ ◖ ▶ P

Llangennith

King's Head

☎ (01792) 386212

11–11
Crown Buckley Best Bitter, Rev. James Ⓗ
There's a great view of Rhossili Bay from this cosy, stone-walled pub with an adjoining eating area. Separate bar for games. Popular in summer. ❀ ◖ ◗ ▲ ♣ P ⊟

Llanrhidian

Welcome to Town
Off B4295 ☎ (01792) 390015
12–3, 7–11 (may vary)
Wadworth 6X; guest beer (occasional) Ⓗ
Pleasant pub overlooking Loughor Estuary. The village green opposite is pleasant on sunny afternoons. Q ❀ ◖ ◗ P

Llansamlet

Birchgrove Inn
396 Heol Las Close, Heol Las
☎ (01792) 771181
2.30 (12 Fri & Sat)–11
Bass Worthington BB; Crown Buckley Dark, Best Bitter Ⓗ
Three-storey, 19th-century village inn, popular with the locals. It features a wood fire plus a pool room at the rear.
♨ Q P

Loughor

Reverend James
180 Borough Road
☎ (01792) 892943
12–11
Crown Buckley Dark, Best Bitter, SBB, Rev. James Ⓗ
Welcoming local with a comfortable lounge and an adjoining restaurant. Note the history of Buckley's brewery on the wall. ♨ ◖ ◗ ⊞ P

Mumbles

Park Inn
23 Park Street
☎ (01792) 366738
12–2.30, 5.30–11
Bass Worthington BB; Marston's Pedigree; Ruddles County; guest beers Ⓗ
Old-fashioned local: a popular, bright, but cosy free house offering a variety of ales and a wide range of home-cooked food. The welcome is warm and genuine in its single lounge/bar. Q ◖ ♿

Victoria Inn
21 Westbourne Place (turn at church in Oystermouth then 2nd left) ☎ (01792) 368546
11.30–11
Bass Worthington Dark, BB, Draught Bass Ⓗ
Recently refurbished old local featuring lots of wood and an interesting well. Popular for darts in winter. ♣

Vincent's
580 Mumbles Road
☎ (01792) 368308
11–11
Bass Worthington BB, Draught Bass; guest beer Ⓗ
Seafront pub with a Spanish theme, offering an extensive Tapas menu until 8pm. Regularly changed guest ale.
◖

Neath

Dyffryn Arms
Bryncoch (3 miles from town on A474, Pontardawe road)
☎ (01639) 636184
12–3, 7–11; 12–3, 7 (8 winter)–10.30 Sun
Fuller's London Pride; Whitbread Boddingtons Bitter; guest beer Ⓗ
Very popular rural pub serving good quality meals (late supper licence in the restaurant). No meals Sun eve (quiz night). Families welcome. Large outdoor children's play area. ❀ ◗ P ⊟

Highlander
2 Lewis Road, Melyn
☎ (01639) 633586
12–3, 6–11
Bass Worthington BB; guest beer Ⓗ
Welcoming, pleasantly furbished free house serving good value quality meals; cod is a house speciality. Late supper licence in the restaurant. No meals Sun eve. Live music Tue, Wed and Thu in the bar, plus monthly cabaret in the restaurant. Two guest beers. ◖ ◗ ⇌

Star
Pen-y-Dre ☎ (01639) 637745
12–4.30, 6–11; 12–11 Sat
Bass Worthington Dark, Draught Bass; Hancock's HB Ⓗ
Traditional, friendly local with two rooms, of which one is a snug. Mature clientele; impromptu sing-alongs. Lunchtime bar snacks. Q P

Norton

Beaufort Arms
1 Castle Road (turn by Norton House Hotel off Mumbles Road) ☎ (01792) 406420
11.30–3, 5.30–11; 11–11 Fri & Sat
Bass Worthington Dark, BB, Draught Bass Ⓗ
Old-fashioned country pub, popular with locals and tourists alike: a cosy lounge and a separate bar with traditional games.
♨ Q ❀ ◖ ⊞ ♿ ♣

Oldwalls

Greyhound
☎ (01792) 390146
12–11
Beer range varies Ⓗ
Popular Gower pub with a warm atmosphere in the locals' bar and plenty of room outside to enjoy the Gower countryside. The excellent menu features fresh fish dishes. At least four ales from the Whitbread Cask Collection.
♨ Q ⚘ ❀ ◖ ◗ ⊞ P

Rhyd-y-Pandy

Masons Arms
Rhyd-y-Pandy Road, Morriston (2 miles N of M4 jct 46) ☎ (01792) 842535
11–11
Bass Worthington BB; Courage Best Bitter; Marston's Pedigree Ⓗ
Pub dating back to the 17th century. Live folk/blues bands Fri nights. A bit difficult to find but worth the effort.
♨ Q ❀ ◖ ◗ ⊞ ♿ P

Skewen

Crown Hotel
216 New Road
☎ (01792) 813309
12–11
Brains Dark, MA, SA Ⓗ
Friendly bar and a comfortable lounge in what is still the only pub to offer MA on a regular basis (a brewery mix of Bitter and Dark). ⊞ ⇌ ♣

Swansea

Builder's Arms
36 Oxford Street
☎ (01792) 476189
11–11; closed Sun except for parties
Crown Buckley Dark, Best Bitter, Rev. James Ⓗ
Comfortable, split-level lounge bar near the Grand Theatre. Parties are catered for either in the dining area or on the upstairs balcony. Eve meals by reservation only. Q ◖ ♿

Cockett Inn
Waunarlwydd Road
☎ (01792) 582083
11–11
Crown Buckley Dark, Best Bitter Ⓗ
Pub with a large bar with a pool table, drawing mainly local trade, plus a comfortable lounge. ❀ ◖ ⊞ ♣ P

Commercial Inn
311 Neath Road, Plasmarl
☎ (01792) 771120
2 (12 Sat)–11

Courage Best Bitter; John Smith's Bitter; Webster's Dark; guest beers (occasional) H
Small local, a centre for various clubs and societies (sea shanty practice Fri). Watch out for the sharks in the aquarium in the lounge. Families welcome in the upstairs function room.
🏮 ⌬ ♣

Cross Keys
12 St Mary's Street
☎ (01792) 473417
11–11
Bass Worthington BB; Hancock's HB; Wadworth 6X H
Well-appointed, city-centre pub and restaurant catering for a variety of tastes.
🏮 ◖ ▶ ⇌

Hanbury
The Kingsway
☎ (01792) 641824
11–11
Courage Directors; S&N Theakston Best Bitter; John Smith's Bitter H
Typical post-war, city-centre pub, now one large bar with its entrance between two shops. A good pre-night club and after-cinema house. Inexpensive carvery. ◖ ⇌ P

JC's
Swansea University, Singleton Park
12–11 (term time only)
Beer range varies H

Comfortable campus bar serving students and visitors. Snacks and coffee are always available. Typically, the range of beers (from the Whitbread Cask Collection) is changed at the beginning of each term.
Q ♣ ⌒

Queen's Hotel
Gloucester Place
☎ (01792) 643460
11–11
Crown Buckley Best Bitter; S&N Theakston Mild, Best Bitter, Old Peculier; guest beer H
One-roomed lounge bar on the edge of the marina. Numerous pictures show the maritime history of the area. Excellent Sun lunches. Outside seating at pavement tables.
Q 🏮 ◖ & 🏮

St George
30 Walter Road
☎ (01792) 469317
11.30–11
Bass Worthington BB; Felinfoel Double Dragon; Hancock's HB H
Lounge bar on the edge of the city centre – the only regular outlet for Felinfoel in the city. Regular events include live music (Sun) and a quiz (Tue). Q ◖ &

Star Inn
1070 Carmarthen Road, Fforestfach ☎ (01792) 586910
11–11
Crown Buckley Dark, Best Bitter H

Friendly local on the edge of an industrial estate. Bar snacks lunchtime. Q ⌬ ♣ P

Vivian Arms
Vivian Road, Sketty
☎ (01792) 203015
12–11
Brains Dark, Bitter, SA H
Pub with a wood-panelled bar, featuring pictures of old Swansea, and a well-appointed lounge, popular at lunchtime. Quiz Sun eve. Good value food (no meals Sun). 🏮 ◖ ⌬ ♣

Westbourne Hotel
1 Brynymor Road
☎ (01792) 459054
12–11
Bass Worthington Dark, Draught Bass; Hancock's HB; guest beers H
Striking street-corner pub, close to the Guildhall. The imposing slate plaque in the bar is of uncertain age.
🏮 ◖ ⌬

Ynysgollen

Rock & Fountain
On A465 ☎ (01639) 642681
11.30–3, 6.30–11
Bass Worthington BB; Felinfoel Double Dragon; Wadworth 6X H
Comfortable, well-appointed pub. The adjoining restaurant offers a wide choice of meals; children welcome.
Q 🏮 ◖ ▶ P

OUT OF HOURS

The opening times of the British pub are a source of much amusement and confusion for overseas visitors. Travellers from the Continent, used to enjoying a relaxing, civilised drink in the small hours, never fail to remark on the arcane UK licensing system that calls for all drinks to be ordered and paid for by 11pm and consumed within 20 minutes. They rightly recognise the folly of setting such an early 'deadline' for knocking back alcohol and wince at the sight of hundreds of tanked up boozers being turned out on the streets at the same time, with all its social consequences.

Reform seems to be on the way. A few years ago, publicans in England and Wales were given the right to join Northern Ireland in opening all day (sic), from 11am to 11pm, Monday to Saturday, if they so desired. At the same time, Sunday hours were marginally extended to 12–3, 7–10.30, and now all day Sunday opening (12–10.30) has finally arrived. Considering that pubs serving meals and other restaurants were already able to stay open and serve alcohol all day on Sunday, this has been more than overdue.

Scottish drinkers have long been treated with more respect. Extended hours are common North of the Border and have proved to be a great success.

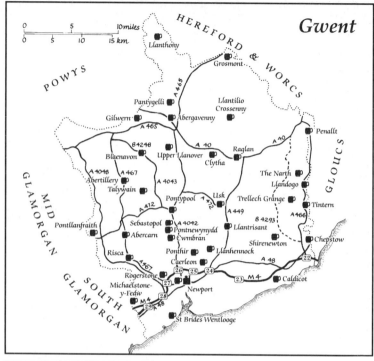

 Newport Brewhouse, Newport

Abercarn

Old Swan
58 Commercial Road
☎ (01495) 243161
12–11
Courage Best Bitter; Ushers Best Bitter, Founders Ⓗ
Friendly Valleys local where photographs commemorate the area's mining heritage. A comfortable lounge leads off the bar; pool room. Good value food. Bulmer's cider in summer; snuff available. Camp at the Cwmcarn Forest Drive. 🏕 ❀ ◖ ⊟ ▲ ♣ ◌

Abergavenny

Coach & Horses
Cross Street
10.30–11
Draught Bass; Brains SA; Wadworth 6X; Whitbread Flowers IPA Ⓗ
With a carefully chosen beer range this single-bar pub, now free of tie, is going from strength to strength – a tribute to the landlord and his family. Near the bus station and ten mins' walk from the BR station. ❀ ♣

Hen & Chickens
5 Flannel Street
☎ (01873) 853613
10.30 (10 Tue)–11; 10.30–4, 7–11 Mon
Draught Bass; Hancock's HB, guest beer Ⓗ
Old and venerable South Wales drinkers' institution, making few concessions to modernity, but selling huge amounts of draught beer. Always popular. No food Sun. Q ⊠ ◖ ♣

Somerset Arms
Victoria Street (Merthyr Rd jct)
☎ (01873) 852158
7–11; 12–2, 7–11 Sat
Draught Bass; Felinfoel Bitter; guest beers Ⓗ
Two fairly small, cosy rooms, including an excellent bar with an open fire, set the tone for this popular family-run pub. First class food and accommodation. No meals Sun eve. 🏕 Q ❀ ◖ ⟊ ◖ ⊟ ♣

Station
37 Brecon Road
☎ (01873) 854759
12–3 (not Mon–Thu), 5–11; 12–11 Sat
Draught Bass; Freeminer Bitter; Tetley Bitter; guest beer Ⓗ
Basic two roomer, providing a rare outlet for Freeminer ale in the area. The charm of the place is partly due to the wide cross-section of customers. 🏕 ⊟ ♣ P

Abertillery

Clynmawr Hotel
Tŷ Bryn Road (off A467)
☎ (01495) 212323
2 (1 Sat)–11
Crown Buckley Best Bitter Ⓗ
Traditional pub, a useful watering hole for the local RFC. The public bar is adjoined by a challenging skittle alley. Family room upstairs. ⊠ ❀ ⊟ ♣

Blaenavon

Cambrian Inn
Cambrian Row
☎ (01495) 790327
6 (1 Fri, 12 Sat)–11
Draught Bass; Brains Dark, Bitter, SA; guest beer Ⓗ
Pleasant, street-corner local with a cosy lounge, a public bar adorned with local photos, and a pool room. Interesting guest beers enhance the choice of cask ales in the area. Near Big Pit Mining Museum. Q ⊟ ♣

Caerleon

Angel

Goldcroft Common
☎ (01633) 420264
12–11
**Bass Worthington BB,
Draught Bass; Hancock's HB;
guest beer** H
Very popular pub especially
with locals; a nice change from
the student haunts, it is
frequented by local sports
teams. Handy for all the
Caerleon Roman attractions.
No gimmicks – just a good
honest pub offering good
value meals and
accommodation. No food Sun
eve. 🏨 ❀ 🛏 ◑ ▶ ⅘ ♣ P

Tabard Brasserie

9 High Street
☎ (01633) 422822
6.30–11 (may open summer lunch)
**Hardington Bitter,
Moonshine; guest beers** H
Popular pub and restaurant
serving five beers including
unusual guests, all from
independent breweries. A la
carte and bar meals are
available in comfortable
surroundings; very busy at
weekends. Occasional ciders.
Worth a visit. ❀ ◑ ▶ P

Caldicot

Cross Inn

Newport Road
☎ (01291) 420692
11–4, 7–11; 11–11 Sat
**Brains Dark; Courage Best
Bitter; Ruddles County; John
Smith's Bitter; Wadworth 6X;
guest beer** H
Handily placed by bus stops,
this popular pub offers the
best range of cask ales in town
in a lively public bar and a
spacious lounge, where a
central fireplace divides the
room. ❀ 🍺 ♣ P

Chepstow

Coach & Horses Inn

Welsh Street (near Town Arch)
☎ (01291) 622626
11–3, 6–11
**Brains SA; Crown Buckley
Best Bitter, Rev. James; Taylor
Landlord; guest beer** H
Long-time favourite haunt of
cask ale fans and venue of a
highly successful beer festival
in July. A big TV screen is
used for major sporting
events. Close to the bus and
rail stations and 1 mile from
the racecourse. Lunches
Mon–Fri. ❀ 🛏 ◑ ⅘

Five Alls

Hocker Hill Street
☎ (01291) 622528

11–5, 7–11
**John Smith's Bitter; Ushers
Best Bitter, Founders; guest
beer** H
L-shaped bar with a games
area at the rear. Old local
photos and sporting souvenirs
add to the character. Ushers
seasonal ales are also sold. Ten
mins' from the BR station.
◑ ⅘

Clytha

Clytha Arms

On old Abergavenny–Raglan
road, off B4598
☎ (01873) 840206
11.30–3.30 (not Mon), 6–11; 11–11 Sun
**Draught Bass; Hook Norton
Best Bitter; S&N Theakston
XB; guest beers** H
CAMRA South and Mid Wales
Pub of the Year 1994; a
converted dower house
which acquired its licence
from the Swan after it fell
into the River Usk in 1942!
Excellent food (book the
restaurant). Eve meals
Tue–Sat.
🏨 Q ❀ 🛏 ◑ ▶ ♣ 🜪 P 🍴

Cwmbran

Bush Inn

Graig Road, Upper Cwmbran
☎ (01633) 483764
11–3, 7 (6 Fri & Sat)–11
**Courage Best Bitter; guest
beer** H
Two-roomed pub, very busy at
weekends (karaoke and a
disco). One room is mainly for
diners, the other is an
extremely comfortable bar.
Book Sun lunch and eve
meals. Limited parking.
❀ ◑ ▶ ♣ P

Commodore Hotel

Mill Lane, Llanyrafon
☎ (01633) 484091
11–5, 7–11
**Crown Buckley Rev. James;
guest beers** H
Comfortable and welcoming
modern hotel. Cask ales are
served in the Pilliner's lounge
at upmarket prices. R&B
bands occasionally perform in
the adjacent ballroom. Tasty
bar meals plus a restaurant.
❀ 🛏 ◑ ▶ P

Mount Pleasant Inn

Wesley Street
☎ (01633) 484289
12–3, 7 (6.30 Fri & Sat)–11
**Ushers Best Bitter,
Founders** H
Homely pub, comfortably
furnished throughout its bar
and lounge areas. Ideal for
a quiet drink. No meals
Sun lunchtime.
❀ ◑ ▶ 🍺 ♣ P 🍴

Gilwern

Corn Exchange Inn

Crickhowell Road
☎ (01873) 830337
12–3, 6 (5 Fri)–11; 12–11 Sat
**Bass Worthington BB,
Draught Bass; Hancock's HB;
guest beer** H
Good refreshment stop for
those exploring this scenic
locality and its historic
industrial past. Real ale is in
the pleasant public bar, while
a comfortable lounge and
dining room are at the rear
(book Sun lunch).
❀ ◑ ▶ 🍺 ▲ ♣ P

Grosmont

Angel

Main Street ☎ (01981) 240646
12–3, 7–11
**Crown Buckley Best Bitter,
Rev. James** H
Single-bar, ancient pub at the
centre of village life,
charmingly set amidst a castle,
large church and a tiny town
hall, all reflecting a former
importance. A good stop on
the 18-mile way marked *Three
Castles Walk*. 🏨 ❀ 🛏 ◑ ▶ ♣

Llandogo

Sloop Inn

On A466 ☎ (01594) 530291
11–3, 6–11; 11–11 Sat
**Draught Bass; Brains SA;
Wye Valley Bitter** H
With its high standard of
accommodation, this pub
makes a splendid base from
which to explore the scenic
locality. The rear lounge
provides a fine view of the
Wye Valley, whilst the public
bar features a welcoming log
fire. 🏨 ❀ 🛏 ◑ ▶ 🍺 ♣ P

Llanhennock

Wheatsheaf Inn

1 mile off the Caerleon–Usk
road OS353929
☎ (01633) 420468
11–3.30, 5.30–11; 11–11 Sat &
summer
**Bass Worthington BB,
Draught Bass; guest beer** H
Unchanged for many years
and full of character, this pub
is very popular in summer due
to the pleasant surroundings.
Boules is a favourite game.
Good value lunches; the
doorstep sandwiches are as
popular as ever. No food Sun.
🏨 Q ❀ ◑ 🍺 ♣ P

Llanthony

Half Moon

200 yds N of the Priory
OS288279 ☎ (01873) 890611

Gwent

11–3, 6–11; 11–3 (Sat only), 6–11 (Fri
& Sat only) Jan & Feb
**Bullmastiff Son of a Bitch;
Hook Norton Best Bitter;
guest beer** (summer) H
Set in good hiking and horse
riding country, near monastic
ruins, this basic, one-bar pub is
a regular refuelling stop for
many walkers. A rare regular
outlet for Bullmastiff beer.
Check opening times before
visiting.
🏨 Q 🏵 ◖ ▷ ▲ ♣ ⌂ P

Try also: Abbey Hotel (Free)

Llantilio Crossenny

Hostry Inn
On B4233, Monmouth–
Abergavenny Road
☎ (01600) 780278
12–3, 6–11
Wye Valley Bitter; guest beer
(summer) H
Welcoming, 15th-century
village pub with friendly
licensees. Good selection of
meals; Sun lunch is very
popular.
🏵 🚪 ◖ ▷ ▲ ♣ P ✕

Llantrisant

Greyhound Inn
3 miles S of Usk, by A449
☎ (01291) 672505
11–3, 6–11
**Marston's Pedigree;
Wadworth 6X; Whitbread
Boddingtons Bitter, Flowers
Original; guest beers** H
Originally a 17th-century
farmhouse, this large pub
includes a stone stable block
that has recently been
converted to accommodation,
including a room for disabled
guests. Splendidly traditional
bar. No access from A449.
🏨 Q ⛲ 🏵 🚪 ◖ ▷ 🍴

Michaelstone-y-Fedw

Cefn Mably Arms
Off A48 at Castleton (follow
signs) ☎ (01633) 680347
12–3 (not Mon), 6.30–11
**Hancock's HB; Marston's
Pedigree; Tetley Bitter** H
Popular, traditional pub in a
charming, rural location. The
large car park is dominated by
an oak tree. Friendly hosts
provide a warm welcome
within a decor of timber, stone
and copper. Hard to resist
food (no meals Sun eve or
Mon). 🏵 ◖ ▷ P

The Narth

Trekkers
OS525064 ☎ (01600) 860367

11–3, 6–11
**Draught Bass; Felinfoel
Bitter; Freeminer Bitter; guest
beer** H
Unusual pub of log cabin
design, with its own post
office. The very large garden
has children's swings.
Excellent variety of meals.
Skittle alley.
🏨 Q 🏵 ◖ ▷ ⛴ ♣ P

Newport

Lyceum Tavern
110 Malpas Road (near M4 jct
26) ☎ (01633) 858636
11.30–11
**Courage Best Bitter; John
Smith's Bitter; Wadworth
6X** H
This thriving town pub, a
venue for frequent live music,
features a central bar area plus
a popular games room. Book
Sun lunch. 🏵 ◖ ▷ ♣

St Julian Inn
Caerleon Road
☎ (01633) 258663
11.30–11
**Courage Best Bitter; Ruddles
Best Bitter; John Smith's
Bitter; guest beers** H
Deservedly popular pub on
the banks of the River Usk.
Well-established, it caters for
all ages with a good range of
changing guest beers and good
value food (no meals Sun).
Beautiful views in summer.
Gwent CAMRA *Pub of the Year*
1994. Worth finding.
🏵 ◖ ▷ ♣ P

Windsor Castle
19 Upper Dock Street (opp.
Passport Office)
☎ (01633) 266819
11–3, 5–11; 11–11 Fri & Sat
**Draught Bass; Hancock's
HB** H
Almost next to the bus station,
one of the very few traditional
pubs left in the town centre. It
attracts a good mix of
shoppers, office workers and
serious drinkers; packed Fri
and Sat. Reasonably priced
meals. Wheelchair access is via
the side door. ◖ ♿ ⇌

Try also: Ale House, John
Frost Sq (Carlsberg-Tetley);
Newport Brewhouse, Market
St (Ross)

Pantygelli

Crown Inn
Old Hereford Road (2 miles off
A465, near Abergavenny)
☎ (01873) 853314
11.30–2.30, 7–11
**Draught Bass; Felinfoel
Double Dragon** H
Pub popular for beer and food
(families welcome), at the

gateway to the Black
Mountains. The fine views
from the flower-bedecked
patio might tempt you to
explore the surrounding hills.
🏨 🏵 🚪 ◖ ▷ P

Penallt

Boat Inn
Lone Lane (off A466; access by
footbridge from Redbrook)
OS536098 ☎ (01600) 712615
11–3, 6–11
**Adnams Broadside; Fuller's
London Pride; S&N
Theakston Best Bitter, Old
Peculier; Wadworth 6X; guest
beers** G
Very popular riverside pub
with a small bar and another
adjoining room, in a scenic
setting. The freshly prepared
food is highly recommended.
Live music Tue and Thu.
Cider in summer.
🏨 ⛺ 🏵 ◖ ▷ ⌂ P

Ponthir

Ponthir House Inn
Candwr Road (B4236)
☎ (01633) 420479
11.30–11
**Bass Worthington BB,
Draught Bass; Hancock's HB;
guest beer** H
Attractive village pub with
several linked areas, including
one set aside for diners.
🏵 ◖ ▷ ♣ P

Pontllanfraith

Crown
The Bryn (near A472/A4049
jct) ☎ (01495) 223404
12–3, 6–11; 12–11 Fri & Sat
**Courage Best Bitter; Felinfoel
Double Dragon; John Smith's
Bitter; guest beer**
(occasional) H
Once surrounded by a road
system, this friendly pub is
well placed to attract passing
trade. The lounge
accommodates lunchtime
diners and has a no-smoking
section. Good outdoor play
facilities. 🏵 ◖ 🍴 ♣ P ✕

Pontnewynydd

Horseshoe Inn
Hill Street ☎ (01495) 762188
12–11
**John Smith's Bitter; Ushers
Best Bitter, Founders; guest
beer** H
Georgian coaching inn with
lounge and public bars, a pool
room, a children's room, and a
restaurant. The small, fully
enclosed garden has a play
area. Book Sun lunch. Ushers
seasonal beers also sold. Note:
a cask breather is sometimes

used on guest beers.
♿ ❀ ◐ ▷ ⊟ ♿ ♣

Pontypool

George
Commercial Street
☎ (01495) 764734
11.30–11
**John Smith's Bitter; guest
beer** (occasional) Ⓗ
Popular town-centre bar with
an upstairs restaurant. The
Georgian-style interior
features pictures with a
'George' theme. Handy for
Pontypool Park. Book Sun
lunch. ◐

Raglan

Ship Inn
High Street ☎ (01291) 690635
11.30 (12 Mon)–11
Draught Bass; guest beers Ⓗ
Coaching inn dating from the
16th-century, with a cobbled
forecourt. At least two guest
ales are available, plus award-
winning local cider in
summer.
🏠 Q ❀ ◐ ▷ ⊟ ♣ ○

Risca

Exchange Inn
52 St Mary Street
☎ (01633) 612716
11–11
**Crown Buckley Best Bitter,
SBB, Rev. James; guest beer** Ⓗ
Smart, colourful free house on
the main road. The large
public bar boasts trophy
cabinets and Hancock's prints.
Smaller, but more comfortable,
lounge. The house beer (4.1%
ABV) is brewed by Crown
Buckley. ❀ ◐ ⊟ ♣ P

Rogerstone

Old Globe
1 St John's Crescent
☎ (01633) 897154
12–3, 5.30 (6 Sat)–11; 12–2.30, 7–10.30
Sun
Hancock's HB; guest beers Ⓗ
Relaxed and comfortable local
where two small rooms have
been converted into a single
open lounge with a pool table.
❀ ♣ P

St Brides
Wentlooge

Church House
Church Road (B4239)
☎ (01633) 681289
11–4, 7–11 (11–11 May–Sept)
Brains Dark, Bitter, SA Ⓗ
Traditional, two-bar Brains
pub: very much a local in
winter and popular with
families in summer, due to its
large garden. A bistro

restaurant is open eves. No
food Sun eve. A good location
to start coastal walks.
🏠 ❀ ◐ ▷ ⊟ ♣ P

Sebastopol

Open Hearth
Wern Road (off South St)
☎ (01495) 763752
11–3, 6–11
**Archers Golden; Draught
Bass; Brains Dark, SA;
Whitbread Boddingtons
Bitter; guest beers** Ⓗ
Canalside favourite offering a
wide range of ales which may
vary from those listed. Well
balanced menu of tasty dishes,
plus blackboard specials.
Q ❀ ◐ ▷ ⊟ P

Shirenewton

Carpenter's Arms
Usk Road (B4235)
☎ (01291) 641231
11–2.30, 6–11
**Fuller's London Pride;
Marston's Pedigree, Owd
Rodger; Wadworth 6X;
Whitbread Boddingtons
Bitter, Flowers IPA** Ⓗ
Charming country pub where
the bar services many linked
rooms, each with its own style
of decor, old pictures and
interesting artefacts. Locally
produced dishes; no Sun eve
meals in winter.
🏠 Q ❀ ◐ ▷ P

Talywain

Globe Inn
Commercial Road (B4246)
☎ (01495) 772053
6.30 (11 Sat)–11
**Brains Bitter; Hancock's HB;
guest beer** Ⓗ
Friendly local with a
traditional public bar, a
comfortable, narrow lounge,
and a pool room. The
landlord's enthusiasm for new
guest ales has stimulated local
interest. Cider in summer.
🏠 ⊟ ♣ ○

Tintern

Cherry Tree
Devauden Road (off A466)
☎ (01291) 689292
11–2.30 (not winter Mon), 6–11
Hancock's HB Ⓖ
One-roomed, village pub; a
fine example of a 'pub that
time forgot'. Friendly locals
and a welcoming fire. Limited
parking. 🏠 Q ❀ ♣ ○ P

Trellech Grange

Fountain Inn
Off B4293 OS503011
☎ (01291) 689303

12–3, 6–11
Wadworth 6X; guest beer Ⓗ
Situated in the Wye Valley,
this popular 17th-century pub
is the centre of the local
community. Good value
meals; Fri night fish and chip
suppers are a speciality.
🏠 ❀ 🏠 ◐ ▷ ▲ ♣ P

Upper Llanover

Goose & Cuckoo
Off A4042 OS292073
☎ (01873) 880277
11.30–3, 7–11
**Bullmastiff Best Bitter; guest
beer** Ⓗ
Situated two miles up a long,
winding, narrow lane, this pub
offers home-made vegetarian
food, a good range of
whiskies, beautiful views and
excellent walks. A very
friendly, genuine, unspoilt,
old country pub well
worth finding. No meals
Thu eve.
🏠 Q ❀ ◐ ▷ ♣ P

Usk

Greyhound Inn
1 Old Chepstow Road
☎ (01291) 672074
11.30–3, 6–11
**Draught Bass; Hancock's HB;
guest beer** Ⓗ
Comfortable, unassuming pub
in a quiet backwater near the
town square. An open-plan
lounge bar caters for diners
and drinkers. Interesting guest
ales. Q ❀ ◐ ▷

King's Head Hotel
18 Old Market Street
☎ (01291) 672963
11–11
**Fuller's London Pride; Hall &
Woodhouse Tanglefoot;
Marston's Pedigree;
Whitbread Flowers
Original** Ⓗ
Pub where the comfortable
lounge features an impressive
fireplace as a centrepiece. The
landlord's angling triumphs
are displayed.
🏠 Q 🏠 ◐ ▷ ⊟ ♣ P

New Court Hotel
56 Maryport Street
☎ (01291) 673364
11–11
**Draught Bass; Marston's
Pedigree; Tetley Bitter; guest
beer** Ⓗ
Inviting pub which takes its
name from the original court
(and prison) opposite. It has a
dining area, a large garden
and a tie collection!
❀ 🏠 ◐ ▷ ⊟

Try also: Cardiff Arms, Bridge
St (Free)

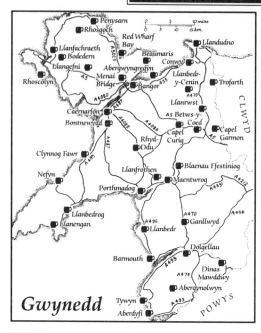

Gwynedd

Aberdyfi

Penhelig Arms
☎ (01654) 767215
11–3, 6–11
Ansells Mild; Ind Coope Burton Ale; Tetley Walker Bitter; guest beer Ⓗ
Bar overlooking the estuary, popular with the yachting fraternity. Good food.
🏚 Q 🚪 ◑ ▶ ▲ 🚲 P

Abergwyngregyn

Aber Hotel
Station Road
☎ (01248) 681770
12–11
Marston's Bitter, Pedigree Ⓗ
Quiet, multi-room pub off the A55, near the railway line, with a restaurant and a small and friendly public bar.
🏚 Q 🚲 🚪 ◑ ▶ 🍺 🌺 P

Abergynolwyn

Railway Inn
On B4405
☎ (01654) 782279
12–2.30, 7–11; 12–11 Sat & summer
Ansells Mild; Tetley Walker Bitter; guest beer Ⓗ
Three-roomed pub in a picturesque valley village, at the end of the Tal-y-Llyn railway. A brewery is planned for early 1996. Beware the fake handpump for keg cider.
🏚 Q 🌺 ◑ 🍺 ▲ P

Bangor

Belle Vue Hotel
Holyhead Road
☎ (01248) 364439
11–11
Marston's Pedigree; Whitbread Boddingtons Bitter, Flowers IPA; guest beers Ⓗ
Popular pub in the student area. The public bar, popular for Sky sports, and the lounge, popular for Sun lunches, are separated by a central bar. Pool room. Q 🌺 ◑ 🍺 🚆

Bulkeley Arms
60 Caernarfon Road
☎ (01248) 361478
11–11
Marston's Bitter, Pedigree Ⓗ
Small local where the U-shaped bar has pool at one end. The cheapest Marston's house in Bangor, but it can be quite smoky. 🏚 🚆

Fat Cat Café Bar
159–161 High Street
☎ (01248) 370455
11–11
S&N Theakston Best Bitter, XB; Whitbread Boddingtons Bitter; guest beers Ⓗ
Café bar close to the cathedral, popular with students, locals and tourists. Recently expanded into an old fabric shop, it features wooden floors, bench seating and bookshelves. Good range of food from 10am. ◑ ▶ 🚆

Union Hotel
Garth Road ☎ (01248) 362462
11–11
Burtonwood Bitter, Top Hat Ⓗ
A nautical theme pervades this pub with lots of rooms off a single bar. Very friendly. No eve meals Tue.
Q 🌺 🚪 ◑ ▶ P

Barmouth

Tal y Don
High Street ☎ (01341) 280508
11–3.30, 6–11; 11–11 Sat & summer
Burtonwood Mild, Bitter Ⓗ
Town pub with two separate drinking areas, which development plans by the brewery may spoil.
🏚 🌺 🚪 🍺 ▲ 🌺

Beaumaris

Olde Bull's Head
Castle Street ☎ (01248) 810329
11–11
Bass Worthington BB; Draught Bass; guest beers Ⓗ
This is the Anglesey 'not to be missed' pub, an historic Grade II-listed building whose past guests include Dr Johnson. The two bars are full of antique weaponry and china. Sun lunch in the restaurant, but not in the bars.
🏚 Q 🚪 ◑ P

Betws-y-Coed

Glan Aber Hotel
Holyhead Road
☎ (01690) 710325
11–11
Marston's Pedigree; Tetley Walker Dark Mild, Bitter Ⓗ
Popular hotel in the centre of town with three separate rooms for non-residents. Good welcome: all tastes catered for. Food is highly recommended.
Q 🚲 🌺 🚪 ◑ ▶ ▲ 🚆 🌺 P

Blaenau Ffestiniog

Manod
Manod Road ☎ (01766) 830346
11–11
S&N Theakston Mild, Best Bitter, XB Ⓗ
Traditional town pub with a sympathetic new lounge extension. Don't miss the smoke room. 🏚 🍺 🚆 🌺 P

Bodedern

Crown Hotel
☎ (01407) 740734
12–3.30, 6–11; 11–11 Sat & bank hols
Burtonwood Bitter Ⓗ
Friendly little village pub, always popular with visitors,

offering good food and pleasant accommodation. It features a lounge, a bar, and a pool room which doubles as a children's room. A community pub. 🏰 ❀ 🛏 ◖ ▶ 🍴 ♣ P

Bontnewydd

Newborough Arms

Main Road ☎ (01286) 673126
11-3, 6-11; 11-11 Sat
Draught Bass; Everards Tiger; Ind Coope Burton Ale; Tetley Walker Dark Mild, Bitter Ⓗ
Busy, often crowded village pub, recently extended. Very popular for food. Friendly staff. Families welcome.
❀ ◖ & P

Caernarfon

Black Boy Inn

Northgate Street
☎ (01286) 673604
11-11
Draught Bass; guest beer Ⓗ
Pub within the old town walls featuring a public bar, a small lounge and a separate restaurant. Open fires in both bars. The guest beer changes weekly. 🏰 Q ❀ 🛏 ◖ ▶ 🍴

Y Goron Fach

Hole in the Wall Street
☎ (01286) 673338
11-11
Draught Bass; Cains Bitter; Tetley Walker Bitter; guest beer Ⓗ
Long, narrow pub with a bar in the lounge. Part-stone walls and bench seating feature in the bar; the lounge is slightly quieter and more comfortable. Sun lunch and eve meals in the tourist season only.
❀ ◖ ▶ 🍴 ♣

Capel Curig

Cobden's Hotel

☎ (01690) 720243
11-3, 6-11; 11-11 Sat
Greenalls Original; Ind Coope ABC Best Bitter; Tetley Walker Bitter Ⓗ
Informal, family-run hotel in the heart of Snowdonia, offering a lounge, a restaurant and a climbers' bar, making a feature out of a natural rock face. Freshly prepared food, with local influence. Warm welcome. Q 🛏 ❀ 🏰 ◖ ▶ 🍴 & A ♣ P

Capel Garmon

White Horse Inn

☎ (01690) 710271
12-3, 6-11
Bass Worthington BB, Draught Bass Ⓗ
Cosy, two-bar pub with

character in a small village. Interesting collection of teapots and jugs. Popular with tourists. Good food.
🏰 Q 🛏 ❀ 🛏 ◖ ▶ 🍴 ♣ ✗

Clynnog Fawr

Coach Inn

On A499 ☎ (01286) 660212
12-11; closed Sun
Banks's Mild; Marston's Bitter, Pedigree; guest beers Ⓗ
Grade I-listed building (c1600), full of character and overlooking the sea.
🏰 Q 🛏 ❀ 🛏 ◖ ▶ A ♣ P 🖃

Conwy

Groes

Tyn-y-Groes (B5106 1 mile from centre) ☎ (01492) 650545
12-3, 7-11 (12-11 summer); closed Sun
Ind Coope Burton Ale; Tetley Walker Bitter Ⓗ
The first licensed house in Wales, dating from 1573. It was extended during the high period of coach travel. A pub of great character. Excellent meals. 🏰 Q ❀ ◖ ▶

Dinas Mawddwy

Red Lion

Off A470 ☎ (01650) 531247
11-3, 6-11; 11-11 Sat & summer
Bass Worthington Dark, BB, Draught Bass; guest beers Ⓗ
Friendly local with a large lounge; a popular meeting place for hillwalkers. Don't miss the brasses bar. 🏰 Q 🛏 ❀ 🛏 ◖ ▶ 🍴 & A ♣ P

Dolgellau

Cross Keys

Mill Street ☎ (01341) 423342
11-11
Bass Worthington BB, Draught Bass Ⓗ
Unspoilt town local: a good, old-fashioned, back-street tavern. 🏰 A ♣

Ganllwyd

Tyn y Groes

On A470 ☎ (01341) 402775
12-3, 7-10.30 (11 Fri & Sat) (11.30-4, 6-11 summer)
John Smith's Bitter; Whitbread Flowers IPA; guest beers (summer) Ⓗ
Roadside inn situated in mountainside forest. The emphasis is on food. Separate locals' bar.
🏰 Q ❀ 🛏 ◖ ▶ A P

Llanbedr

Victoria Hotel

Main Road ☎ (01341) 241213

11-11
Robinson's Best Bitter Ⓔ, **Frederic's** Ⓗ
Pleasant hotel with three separate drinking areas, built with locally quarried stone.
🛏 🛏 ◖ ▶ 🍴 A ⇄ ♣ P

Llanbedrog

Ship Inn

☎ (01758) 740270
11-3.30, 5.30-11 (11-11 summer); closed Sun
Burtonwood Mild, Bitter Ⓗ
Cosy, friendly pub with a seafood restaurant and an unusually-shaped, no-smoking family room.
🏰 Q 🛏 ◖ ▶ & ♣ P ✗ 🖃

Llanbedr-y-Cenin

Bull

☎ (01492) 660508
12-3, 7-11
Lees GB Mild, Bitter Ⓗ
Small pub on the side of a hill, with splendid views over the Conwy Valley. Good food.
🏰 Q ❀ ◖ ▶ P

Llandudno

Cross Keys

28 Madoc Street
☎ (01492) 876132
11-11
Whitbread Boddingtons Bitter; guest beers Ⓗ
Friendly, family-run pub in the heart of town; renovated in a mismatch of styles. It can get very busy on weekends and bank holidays. Guests come from the Whitbread list.
🏰 ❀ ◖ & ♣

London Hotel

131 Mostyn Street
11.30-4 (5 Sat), 7-11
Burtonwood Bitter, Forshaw's, Top Hat Ⓗ
Large, friendly town pub, with a collection of jugs and an original red telephone box. Family room lunchtime only. Ten minutes' walk from the station. 🛏 🛏 ◖ ♣

Snowdon Hotel

11 Tudno Street (off Upper Mostyn St) ☎ (01492) 875515
11-11
Tetley Walker Bitter; guest beers Ⓗ
Popular and friendly, comfortable, back-street local. Large lounge area; darts in the small bar. Two-pint 'steins' sold at a 30p discount. Eve meals in summer only (till 8.30). ❀ 🛏 ◖ ▶ ♣

Llanengan

Sun

☎ (01758) 712660

Gwynedd

11–3, 5.30–11; closed Sun
Ind Coope Burton Ale; Tetley Walker Bitter; guest beers Ⓗ
Popular pub near Hell's Mouth beach. Excellent food and safe gardens.
🏚 ❀ ◑ ♪ ▲ ♣ P

Llanfachraeth

Holland Hotel
On A5025 ☎ (01407) 740252
11–3.30, 7–11 (11–11 summer)
Lees GB Mild, Bitter Ⓗ
Pleasant little village pub with separate rooms and a passage, all served from a central bar. An ideal spot to stay if driving round the island or walking the Anglesey coastal path.
Q ❀ 🛏 ◑ ♪ ♣ P

Llanfrothen

Brondanw Arms
On A4085 ☎ (01766) 770555
12–3, 6–11 (12–11 summer)
Robinson's Hartleys XB, Best Bitter Ⓗ
Hard to find local worth seeking out. Uninspiring from the outside, but the large lounge is popular with both locals and hillwalkers.
🏚 Q 🛏 ◑ ♪ ♣ P

Llangefni

Railway Inn
High Street ☎ (01248) 722166
12–2, 7–11; 11–3.30, 6.30–11 Fri & Sat
Lees GB Mild, Bitter Ⓗ
Friendly pub, just away from the bustle of this busy market town. Close to the now defunct station, it retains a railway theme in its different rooms. ♣

Llanrwst

New Inn
1 Denbigh Street
☎ (01492) 640476
11–11
Bateman Mild; Marston's Bitter, Pedigree; guest beer Ⓗ
One-roomed, town-centre pub, popular with young people.
🏚 Q ❀ 🛏 ⇥

Maentwrog

Grapes Hotel
☎ (01766) 85208
11–11
Bass Worthington BB, Draught Bass; Dyffryn Clwyd Four Thumbs; guest beers Ⓗ
Very busy, 13th-century, family-run hotel, overlooking the Vale of Ffestiniog. The basement restaurant enjoys a good reputation.
🏚 🛏 ❀ 🛏 ◑ ♪ ▲ ♣ P

Menai Bridge

Victoria Hotel
Telford Road (¼ mile from bridge towards Beaumaris)
☎ (01248) 712309
11–11
Draught Bass; guest beer Ⓗ
Popular and comfortable hotel bar near the Menai suspension bridge. Excellent views from the garden. The guest beer comes from Marston's.
🏚 🛏 ❀ 🛏 ◑ ♪ ⊟ ♿ P

Nefyn

Sportsman
Stryd Fawr (main street)
☎ (01758) 720205
12 (11 summer)–11; closed Sun
Bass Worthington BB, Draught Bass Ⓗ
Friendly pub, popular with locals and tourists; tastefully renovated. 🏚 Q ◑ ♪ ♿ ▲

Penysarn

Bedol
Off A5025 ☎ (01407) 832590
12–11
Marston's Bitter, Pedigree; guest beers Ⓗ
Welcoming, family-run village pub which has a lounge and a separate pool/games room. Mainly local trade is supplemented by visitors in summer. Guest beers are from the Marston's list. Meals in summer only.
🏚 Q ❀ ◑ ♪ ⊟ ▲ ♣ P

Porthmadog

Ship
Lombard Street
☎ (01766) 512990
11.30–11
Ind Coope Burton Ale; Tetley Walker Dark Mild, Bitter; guest beers Ⓗ
Good local, popular with all ages; one to visit when in the area. Welcoming licensee. Cantonese restaurant upstairs.
🏚 🛏 ❀ ◑ ♪ ⊟ ▲ ⇥

Red Wharf Bay

Ship Inn
☎ (01248) 852568
11–3.30, 7–11 (11–11 summer)
Ind Coope Friary Meux BB; Tetley Walker Bitter; guest beers (summer) Ⓗ
The best pub site on Anglesey, with views across the bay to the surrounding hills. Full of character, it features stone walls, wooden beams and huge fireplaces. An award-winning food pub.
🏚 Q 🛏 ❀ ◑ ▲ ♣ P ✕

Rhoscolyn

White Eagle Inn
Signed from Trearddur Bay/Rhoscolyn
☎ (01407) 860267
12–3, 7–11 (11–11 summer)
Ind Coope Burton Ale; Marston's Bitter, Pedigree; guest beer Ⓗ
Slightly out of the way, but worth the detour: a large, multi-roomed pub with an extensive garden and views over the bay towards Snowdonia.
🏚 Q ❀ ◑ ♪ ♿ P

Rhosgoch

Rhosgoch Hotel (Ring)
Off B5111 ☎ (01407) 830720
5.30 (12 Fri & Sat)–11
Bass Worthington BB, Draught Bass; Stones Best Bitter Ⓗ
Off the beaten track, a pub where a central bar serves several drinking areas, including a pool room. Good outside area for children. A Caravan Club site adjoins the pub.
🏚 Q ❀ ◑ ♪ ▲ ♣ P

Rhyd-Ddu

Cwellyn Arms
On A4085 ☎ (01766) 890321
11–11
Bass Worthington BB, Draught Bass; guest beers Ⓗ
Isolated but busy pub, popular with locals and tourists alike. An ideal place to end a day's walking. 🏚 Q ❀ ◑ ♪

Trofarth

Holland Arms
On B5113 ☎ (01492) 650777
12–2.30, 7–11
Ansells Mild; Tetley Walker Bitter Ⓗ
Friendly 18th-century coaching house set in country landscapes, within sight of Snowdonia, and featuring bar, lounge, and restaurant areas. Families welcome up to 9pm. Good meals. Q ❀ ◑ ♪ ♣ P

Tywyn

Corbett Arms Hotel
High Street
☎ (01654) 710264
11–11
Bass Worthington BB, Draught Bass; Hancock's HB Ⓗ
Plush, pleasant hotel lounge whose dress code encourages the over-25s. Very good winter break offers. 🛏 ◑ ♪ ▲ ⇥ P

Powys

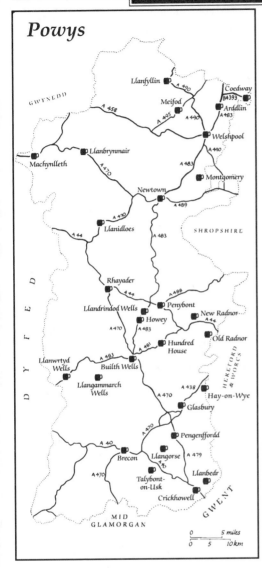

GWYNEDD

Llanfyllin

Coedway
B4393

Meifod

Arddlîn

A 458

A 495

A 490

A 483

Welshpool

Llanbrynmair

A 490

Machynlleth

A 470

A 483

Newtown

Montgomery

SHROPSHIRE

A 470

A 489

Llanidloes

A 44

A 483

Rhayader

A 44

A 488

Llandrindod Wells

Penybont

New Radnor

Howey

A 44

A 470

A 483

Hundred
House

Old Radnor

Llanwrtyd
Wells

A 481

HEREFORD & WORCS

Builth Wells

Llangammarch
Wells

A 438

Hay-on-Wye

A 470

Glasbury

A 470

Pengenffordd

A 40

Brecon

Llangorse

A 479

Llanbedr

Talybont-
on-Usk

Crickhowell

GWENT

MID
GLAMORGAN

0 — 5 miles
0 — 5 — 10km

Arddlîn

Horseshoe

On A483/B4392
☎ (01938) 590318
12–3, 5.30–11
**Bass Worthington BB;
Marston's Pedigree** Ⓗ
Welcoming village pub: a
traditional public bar with a
comfortable lounge/
restaurant. Wide range of
reasonably priced food.
Children's play area in the
garden. Weston's ciders
available.
🏨 ✿ ◑ ▶ ⊞ ♣ ⌂ P

Brecon

George Hotel

George Street (off The Struet,
by car park)
☎ (01874) 623421
10–11
**Tetley Bitter; Wadworth 6X;
guest beers** Ⓗ
Historic, 17th-century inn with
comfortable bars, much
frequented by the local
business community.
Interesting guest beers;
excellent range of bar meals
(all day).
🏨 ◑ ▶ P

Old Boar's Head

14 Ship Street
☎ (01874) 622856
11–3, 5.30–11; 11–11 Fri & Sat (& Tue
in summer)
**Fuller's London Pride, ESB;
Hook Norton Best Bitter;
Tetley Bitter; guest beers** Ⓗ
Old pub overlooking the River
Usk, adjacent to the bridge.
The comfortable public bar has
recently been modernised; the
spacious rear bar has a pool
table and is frequented by the
younger element. Snacks
always available, but meals in
summer only. Limited
parking. ✿ ◑ ⊞ ♣ P

Builth Wells

Greyhound Hotel

3 Garth Road
☎ (01982) 553255
12–3, 6.30–11
**Bass Worthington BB,
Draught Bass** Ⓗ
Attractively decorated hotel
comprising a lounge bar, for
quiet eating and drinking, and
a public bar with pool table.
Q 🏨 ◑ ▶ ⊞ & P

Coedway

Old Hand & Diamond

On B4393 ☎ (01743) 884379
11–11
**Bass Worthington BB,
Draught Bass; M&B Mild;
guest beer** Ⓗ
A plain exterior hides this
immaculate, comfortable pub
of character. Four rooms
include a restaurant with a
good reputation.
🏨 ✿ ◑ ▶ ⊞ ♣ P

Crickhowell

Bear Hotel

On A40 ☎ (01873) 810408
11–3, 6–11
**Draught Bass; Ruddles Best
Bitter, County; John Smith's
Bitter; guest beers**
(occasional) Ⓗ
Delightful, historic coaching
inn from the 15th century,
winner of many awards for its
bar and cuisine. Very popular
with locals and can get busy.
🏨 Q ☎ ✿ 🏨 ◑ ▶ P

White Hart Inn

Brecon Road (A40, W of
centre) ☎ (01873) 810473
12–3, 6–11; 12–11 Sat
**Brains Bitter, SA; Hancock's
HB; S&N Theakston XB;
guest beer** Ⓗ
Small, friendly old inn,
formerly a toll-house (the tolls
are still displayed outside),
with a growing reputation.
The landlord has the knack of
making the most casual visitor

feel at home. Good range of food at reasonable prices.
◑ ▶ P

Glasbury

Harp Inn

On B4350, near A438 jct
☎ (01497) 847373
11–3, 6 (6.30 winter)–11
Robinson's Best Bitter; Thwaites Bitter; Whitbread Boddingtons Bitter, Flowers Original ⊞
Warm, welcoming inn bordering the River Wye and popular with locals. Formerly a 17th-century cider house, it is a good base for sampling the many activity-based attractions of the area. Good bar meals at reasonable prices.
▨ Q ❀ ⨌ ◑ ▶ ⊟ ♣ P

Hay-on-Wye

Blue Boar

Castle Street ☎ (01497) 820884
11–3, 6–11 (11–11 summer)
Draught Bass; Fuller's London Pride; Morland Old Speckled Hen; Wadworth 6X; Whitbread Flowers IPA, Original ⊞
Characterful old pub close to the car park and castle, popular with locals and visitors but bar prices reflect the town's status as a tourist centre and Mecca for second-hand book-buyers. Live music eves. No eve meals in winter.
▨ Q ◑ ⊟

Try also: **Swan Hotel**, Church St (Free)

Howey

Drover's Arms

Off A483, 1½ miles S of Llandrindod Wells
☎ (01597) 822508
12–2.30 (not Tue), 7–11
Fuller's London Pride; Wood Special; guest beers ⊞
Picturesque, two-bar, village inn on the original drovers' route, with a 13th-century cellar. Outside seating at the front; attractive patio garden overlooking a brook. The interesting and varied, home-cooked food uses only local produce.
▨ Q ❀ ⨌ ◑ ▶ ⊟ ▲ ♣ P

Hundred House

Hundred House Inn

On A481 ☎ (01982) 570231
11–3.30, 6.30–11
Bass Worthington BB; Hancock's HB; guest beers (summer) ⊞
Former drovers' pub set among fine upland scenery.

No fewer than five rooms: a pool room, a farmers' bar, a lounge, a dining room and a garden bar. Families welcome.
▨ Q ❀ ⨌ ◑ ▶ ⊟ ▲ ♣ P

Llanbedr

Red Lion

☎ (01873) 810754
12–2.30 (not Mon or Tue in winter), 7–11; 12–11 Sat
Beer range varies ⊞
Friendly old country pub in a small village at the foot of the Black Mountains. The house beer is brewed by Wye Valley. Good pub food (mostly home cooked). ▨ ዼ ᕤ ❀ ◑ ▶ P ⊁

Llanbrynmair

Wynnstay Arms Hotel

On A470
☎ (01650) 521431
11–2.30, 6–11
Whitbread Boddingtons Bitter, Flowers IPA; guest beer ⊞
Well-kept, comfortable village local with a pool room.
▨ ❀ ⨌ ◑ ▶ ⊟ ♣ P

Llandrindod Wells

Llanerch Inn

Waterloo Road (across station footbridge, 100 yds)
☎ (01597) 822086
11.30–2.30 (3 Sat), 6–11
Bass Worthington BB; Hancock's HB; guest beer ⊞
16th-century coaching inn with a beamed ceiling and a large stone hearth. Annual beer tasting (end of Aug).
Q ❀ ⨌ ◑ ▶ ⨝ P

Royal British Legion Club

Tremont Road (by fire station)
☎ (01597) 822558
7.30–11; 12–3, 7–11 Fri; 11–11 Sat
Hancock's HB; M&B Brew XI; guest beer ⊞
Non-members must be signed in to this British Legion Club.
ዼ ⨝ ♣ P

Llanfyllin

Cain Valley Hotel

On A490
☎ (01691) 648366
11–11
Ansells Bitter; Draught Bass; Tetley Bitter ⊞
Excellent, 17th-century coaching inn: a plush lounge with two basic bars, one serving as a games room. Imposing stone fireplace.
❀ ⨌ ◑ ▶ ⊟ ♣ P

Llangammarch Wells

Aberceiros Inn

☎ (01591) 620227
6.30 (11 Sat)–11
Draught Bass; Hancock's HB; guest beer ⊞
A little way out (SW) of the village centre, this pub is worth finding. It has been in the licensee's family for 150 years and has been tastefully modernised retaining much of its character.
▨ Q ❀ ◑ ▶ ▲ ⨝ ♣ P ⊟

Llangorse

Castle Inn

☎ (01874) 658225
12–2.30 (extends in summer), 6–11
Whitbread Wethered Bitter, Castle Eden Ale; guest beer (summer) ⊞
Friendly old village inn in the heart of Brecon Beacons National Park. Being close to Llangorse Lake, a popular centre for boating activities, it can get very busy in summer. Good food. Limited parking.
▨ Q ❀ ◑ ▶ ⊟ ▲ ♣ P

Llanidloes

Mount Inn

China Street (off A470)
☎ (01686) 412247
11–2.30, 5.30–11; 11–11 Sat
Bass Worthington Dark, BB ⊞
Many-roomed, 17th-century pub with a cast iron stove and a listed floor.
▨ Q ⨌ ◑ ▶ ⊟ ♣ P

Unicorn

Longbridge Street
☎ (01686) 413167
12–2.30, 6–11
Draught Bass; Tetley Mild, Bitter ⊞
A rare outpost for Tetley Mild in a town where all the pubs sell real ale. ◑ ▶

Try also: **Crown & Anchor**, Longbridge St (Free)

Llanwrtyd Wells

Neuadd Arms Hotel

The Square (A483)
☎ (01591) 610236
11.30–11 (may close afternoons)
Bass Worthington Dark, Draught Bass; Felinfoel Double Dragon; Hancock's HB; guest beer ⊞
Georgian hotel, enlarged in the 1860s. An excellent centre for outdoor activities in the surrounding mountains and forests. Cycle hire available. Real ale rambles held. The

venue for the Mid-Wales beer festival (Nov) and a winter ale festival (Jan).
🏠 Q ❀ 🍴 ◖ ▶ ⊟ 𝗔
🚆 (not winter Sun)

Stonecroft Inn

Dolecoed Road (100 yds W of town square)
☎ (01591) 610332
5–11; 12–3, 5–11 Thu & Fri; 11–11 Sat
Brains SA; S&N Theakston XB; Younger Scotch Ⓗ
Friendly Victorian pub in Britain's smallest town, amid beautiful scenery, on the spectacular Heart of Wales BR line. Large riverside garden with barbecue patio; regular special events. Children welcome. Meals at all times when open. 🏠 Q ❀ 🍴 ◖ ▶ ⬤ 𝗔 🚆 (not winter Sun)
➕ P

Machynlleth

White Horse

Maengwyn Street
☎ (01654) 702247
11–3, 6–11; 11–11 Wed, Fri & Sat
Hancock's HB Ⓗ
Popular public and lounge bars in an old coaching inn.
❀ ◖ ▶ ⊟ 🚆 ➕

Try also: **Wynnstay Arms Hotel**, Maengwyn St (Free)

Meifod

King's Head

On A495 ☎ (01938) 500256
12 (11 summer)–3, 7 (6 summer)–11
Bass Worthington BB Ⓗ
Impressive, ivy-clad, stone-built inn at the centre of the village: a basic bar and a plush lounge with a restaurant.
❀ 🍴 ◖ ▶ ⊟ ➕ P

Montgomery

Dragon Hotel

Off B4385 ☎ (01686) 668359
11–11
Felinfoel Double Dragon; Wood Old Sam; guest beer Ⓗ
Excellent, comfortable bar in an hotel which was formerly a coaching inn from the 1600s. The stone and timber behind the bar are reputed to have come from the local castle. The hotel has an indoor swimming pool. Q ❀ 🍴 ◖ ▶ ➕

New Radnor

Eagle Hotel

Broad Street ☎ (01544) 350208
11–3, 7–11 (may extend; 1.30am Fri); 11–11 Sat
Draught Bass; Hook Norton Best Bitter; guest beers Ⓗ
Old coaching inn with comfortable, beamed bars. Vegetarian and vegan

specialities on the menu. Local outdoor activities. 🏠 Q ❀ 🍴 ◖ ▶ ⊟ ⬤ 𝗔 ➕ ⬤ P ⊁

Try also: **Red Lion**, Llanfihangel-nant-Melan (Hook Norton)

Newtown

Railway Tavern

Old Kerry Road (off A483)
☎ (01686) 626151
11–3.30 (4.30 Tue, Fri & Sat), 6.30–11
Bass Worthington BB; guest beer Ⓗ
Friendly, small, one-roomed local. 🚆 ➕

Sportsman

Severn Street (off A483)
☎ (01686) 625885
11–2.30, 5.30–11; 11–11 Fri & Sat
Ind Coope Burton Ale; Tetley Bitter; guest beer Ⓗ
Friendly, town-centre local, popular with a wide range of customers. Traditional music jam sessions every Tue.
Q ❀ ◖ ▶ 🚆 ➕

Try also: **Pheasant**, Market St (Burtonwood)

Old Radnor

Harp

1 Mile W of A44/B4362 jct
☎ (01544) 21655
11.30–11
Wood Special; Wye Valley HPA; guest beer (Christmas/summer) Ⓗ
15th-century inn beautifully restored by the Landmark Trust, with a flagged floor, stone walls, beamed ceiling, antique furniture and bric-a-brac. Memorable view of Radnor Forest.
🏠 Q ❀ 🍴 ◖ ▶ 𝗔 ➕ P

Pengenffordd

Castle Inn

On A479 ☎ (01874) 711353
11–3, 7–11 (11–11 Sat in summer & bank hols)
Greene King Abbot; Wadworth 6X; guest beer (summer) Ⓗ
Friendly country pub popular with pony-trekkers and hillwalkers, situated at the summit of the A479, between Talgarth and Crickhowell. Castell Dinas, the highest hillfort in England and Wales, forms the backdrop.
🏠 ❀ 🍴 ◖ ▶ ⊟ 𝗔 ➕ P

Penybont

Severn Arms Hotel

At A44/A488 jct
11–2.30, 6–11
Bass Worthington BB, Draught Bass; Tetley Bitter Ⓗ

Roadside inn with extensive gardens sloping down to the River Ithon (fishing rights): a large public bar with an open fire, a games room, a lounge bar and a restaurant.
🏠 Q ❀ 🍴 ◖ ▶ ⊟ ⬤ 𝗔 ➕ P

Rhayader

Cornhill Inn

West Street ☎ (01597) 810869
7–11; 11–3, 7–11 Sat & summer
Marston's Pedigree; Wye Valley Bitter; guest beers (summer) Ⓗ
Friendly, low-beamed, 400-year-old pub, reputedly haunted: a single L-shaped bar with items to interest the motorcyclist.
🏠 Q ❀ 🍴 ◖ 𝗔 ➕

Triangle Inn

Cwmdauddwr (off Bridge St, B4518) ☎ (01597) 810537
12–3, 6.30–11; 11–11 Fri & Sat
Draught Bass; Hancock's HB Ⓗ
Beautiful, little weatherboarded gem overlooking the River Wye. The ceilings are so low that customers have to stand in a hole in the floor to play darts.
❀ ◖ ▶ ➕

Talybont-on-Usk

Star Inn

On B4558 ☎ (01874) 87635
11–3, 6–11; 11–11 Sat
Beer range varies Ⓗ
Canalside pub recently renovated after a disastrous flood in 1994. The pub's character has been retained and improvements carried out. Not to be missed if you are in the area; 12 beers on sale. Good pub food. Live music Wed. 🏠 ❀ ❀ ◖ ▶ 𝗔 ⬤

Welshpool

Pheasant

High Street ☎ (01938) 553104
11–11
Bass Worthington BB, Draught Bass Ⓗ
Long, narrow bar with a garden at the rear. ❀ ◖ ➕ ➕

Royal Oak Hotel

Severn Street (off A483)
☎ (01938) 552217
11–3, 5.30–11; 11–11 Mon
Bass Worthington BB; Whitbread Boddingtons Bitter; guest beers Ⓗ
Plush, 350-year-old coaching inn; formerly the manor house of the Earls of Powis, now an hotel which has been in the same family for 60 years. Two or more guest beers. Separate restaurant.
🏠 Q 🍴 ◖ ▶ 🚆 P

Borders

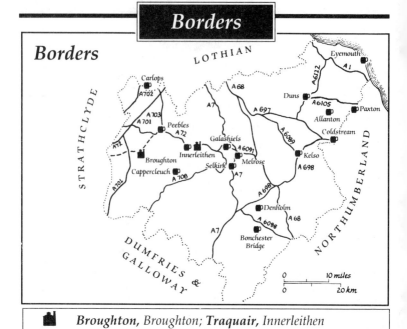

Borders

🏰 **Broughton**, Broughton; **Traquair**, Innerleithen

Allanton

Allanton Inn
On B6437 ☎ (01890) 818260
12–2.30, 6–11 (midnight Fri); 12–11.45
Sat; 12.30–11 Sun
**Belhaven 80/-, St Andrew's
Ale; guest beer** ⊞
Old coaching house with a
restaurant. The unchanged
exterior still boasts iron
hitching rings for horses. Stone
flags surround the bar in a
comfortable, functional
interior.
🏨 Q ❀ 🚪 ◁ ▶ & ♣ P

Bonchester Bridge

Horse & Hound
Country Inn
On A6088 ☎ (01450) 86645
11–2.30, 6–11 (midnight Sat); 11–3,
5.30–midnight Sun; closed Tue
**Alloa Arrol's 80/-; Orkney
Dark Island; guest beers** ⊞
18th-century coaching inn
with a cosy bar, lounge and a
restaurant; ideally placed for
hill-walking, fishing or golfing.
Meals include a massive 72-oz
steak – free if eaten within the
hour! 🏨 Q ❀ 🚪 ◁ ▶ 🍴 ▲
♣ P ½ 🎄

Cappercleuch

Tibbie Shiels Inn
St Mary's Loch (on A708)
☎ (01750) 42231
11 (12.30 Sun)–11 (midnight Fri & Sat)
(closed Mon Nov–Easter)

**Belhaven 80/-; Broughton
Greenmantle Ale** ⊞
Isolated rural retreat, nestling
by the loch and surrounded by
rolling hills. A low ceiling and
thick walls impart an intimate
feel. The outside gents' can
pose a dilemma in inclement
weather.
🏨 Q 🚪 ◁ ▶ & ▲ ♣ P

Carlops

Allan Ramsay Hotel
On A702
☎ (01968) 660258
11–midnight
**Belhaven Sandy Hunter's Ale,
80/-** ⊞
Old coaching inn in a village
high on a shoulder of the
Pentland Hills. Despite the bar
being knocked into a single
eating/drinking area, the
atmosphere is retained by dark
panelling and log fires.
Children welcome.
🏨 Q ❀ 🚪 ◁ ▶ & P

Coldstream

Crown Hotel
Market Square (off A697)
☎ (01890) 882558
11–midnight (11.30 Sat); 12.30–11.30
Sun
Caledonian 80/- ⊞
Pub on a quiet residential
square. A labyrinthine
passageway leads into a snug
bar with an angling theme and
an impressive collection of
whisky miniatures. Children's
certificate.
❀ 🚪 ◁ ▶ 🍴 ♣

Denholm

Auld Cross Keys Inn
On A698 ☎ (01450) 87305
11–2.30, 5–11 (midnight Thu, 1am Fri);
11–midnight Sat; 12.30–11 Sun
**Broughton Greenmantle Ale;
guest beer** ⊞
Picturesque, 17th-century inn
overlooking the village green.
A low ceiling lends to the
conviviality. The cheesy eggs
at the bar and high teas in the
restaurant are both famous.
Children's certificate.
🏨 Q ◁ ▶ 🍴 & ▲ ♣ P

Duns

Whip & Saddle
Market Square (A6105)
☎ (01361) 883215
11–11 (midnight Fri, 11.30 Sat);
12.30–11 Sun
**Caledonian Deuchars IPA;
S&N Theakston XB; guest
beer** ⊞
Town-centre bar with a
modern interior, wood floors
and views over the town
square. The family room is
upstairs. Q ☎ ◁ 🍴 ♣

Eyemouth

Ship Hotel
Harbour Road
☎ (01890) 750224
11–midnight
**Caledonian 70/-; Tetley Bitter
(summer); guest beer** Ⓐ
Family-run hotel, right on the
harbour front. The public bar

---

is warmed by a coal fire and there is a vast selection of rums, as befits a fisherman's haunt. Limited parking.
🛏 ❀ 🛌 ◖ ▶ 🛗 ⚹ ♣ P

Galashiels

Auld Mill Inn
57–58 Bank Street (A7, town centre) ☎ (01896) 758655
11–11 (midnight Thu–Sat); 12.30–midnight Sun
Caledonian Deuchars IPA; guest beer 🅷
Single-roomed locals' bar with a welcoming atmosphere and half-panelled walls. The Addlestones cider is *not* kept under CO_2. 🍺 ♣ ♨

Ladhope Inn
33 High Buckholmside (A7, ½ mile N of centre)
☎ (01896) 752446
11 (12.30 Sun)–11 (midnight Thu–Sat)
Caledonian 80/-; guest beer 🅷
Neat, local bar built into the hillside, dating from 1792, though much altered. Vibrant atmosphere. Note: the Tetley Bitter is kept under a cask breather. ♣

Innerleithen

Traquair Arms Hotel
Traquair Road (B709, off A72)
☎ (01896) 830229
11 (12 Sun)–11 (midnight Sat)
Broughton Greenmantle Ale; Traquair Bear Ale 🅷
Family-run, 18th-century hotel with a plush lounge, warmed by a log fire. Good, home-cooked food from local produce. Beware the Theakston Best Bitter and

Addlestones cider, both kept under CO_2.
🛏 Q ❀ 🛌 ◖ ▶ 🛗 P

Kelso

Red Lion
Crawford Street (off town square) ☎ (01573) 224817
11–midnight (1am Fri); 12.30–11 Sun
Belhaven 80/-; Courage Directors; Tetley Bitter; guest beer 🅷
Pub where the interior features a fine wood and plaster vaulted ceiling and wood panelling. Old spirit barrels decorate the rear of the bar, on top of a painted gantry with original mirrors. 🛏 🍺 ♣

Melrose

King's Arms Hotel
High Street ☎ (01896) 822143
11–2.30, 5–11 (midnight Fri); 11–midnight Sat; 11–11 Sun
Ind Coope Burton Ale; Tetley Bitter; guest beer 🅷
Small, lively local, sporting wood floors and church pew seating. The main theme of the decor is rugby, which is the local religion.
🛏 Q 🛌 ◖ ▶ 🛗 ⚹ 🛗 ♣ P

Paxton

Hoolit's Nest
On B6460 ☎ (01289) 386267
11–2.30, 6.30–11
Alloa Arrol's 80/-; guest beer 🅷
Village pub with more hoolits (owls) than you can shake a stick at – of every shape and description, they survey the

clientele from every nook and cranny. A stately home, Paxton House, is nearby.
◖ ▶ 🛗 ⚹ ♣ P

Peebles

Cross Keys Hotel
Northgate (off A72)
☎ (01721) 724222
11–midnight
Beer range varies 🅷
Located just off the main street, this rambling historic building includes a smart bar, a restaurant and enough spare room for festivals featuring beer from the wood. Barbecues held in the garden. The Addlestones cider is *not* kept under CO_2.
🛏 ❀ 🛌 ◖ ▶ 🛗 ⚹ 🛗 ♣ ♨

Green Tree Hotel
41 Eastgate (E end of High Street, A72) ☎ (01721) 720582
11 (12 Sun)–midnight
Caledonian 80/-; guest beer 🅷
Bustling hotel bar with interesting leaded windows. Very much a local in the front; the back room is more relaxed (children welcome). 🛏 Q ❀ 🛌 ◖ ▶ 🛗 ⚹ 🛗 P ⚹

Selkirk

Cross Keys Inn
Market Place (A7)
☎ (01750) 21283
11 (12.30 Sun)–11 (midnight Thu–Sat)
Caledonian 80/-; guest beer 🅷
Vibrant, wee, wood-panelled public bar with steps leading up to a comfortable lounge. Often packed. Excellent meals (not served Sat eve). ◖ ▶ 🛗

WHAT'S BREWING

Members of the Campaign for Real Ale receive numerous benefits from their annual subscription. These include discounts on products and books like the *Good Beer Guide* and reduced price admission to CAMRA beer festivals. They also receive the acclaimed *What's Brewing* newspaper each month, free of charge.

What's Brewing is the leading national newspaper on beer and pub matters. Edited by award-winning beer writer Roger Protz, it offers up to the minute news of events in the beer and pub world, as well as entertaining features by world-renowned beer hunter Michael Jackson, pub food articles by Susan Nowak and cartoons by Bill Tidy.

Campaign news, interviews, guest writers, beer festival information and profiles of breweries big and small also figure prominently in the tabloid, with many pages in full colour. In addition, the paper carries *Good Beer Guide* updates and details of all the latest brewing ventures.

Keep in touch with events in the fast-changing world of beer. Join CAMRA and make sure of your copy of *What's Brewing* every month.

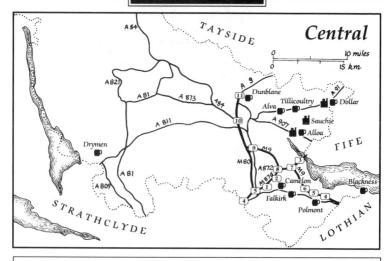

Central

 Harviestoun, Dollar; **Maclay,** Alloa; **Mansfield Arms,** Sauchie

Alloa

Crams Bar
8 Candleriggs
11–11
Maclay 80/- Ⓐ
Traditional workingmen's bar in the town centre.
Q & ♣

Alva

Cross Keys
120 Stirling Street
(main street)
☎ (01259) 760409
11–11 (midnight Thu, 1am Fri & Sat);
12.30–11 Sun
Maclay 80/-, Kane's Amber Ale; guest beers Ⓗ
Comfortable two-bar local with a spacious lounge.
🏰 🕪 ▶ 🕀 &

Blackness

Blackness Inn
The Square (B903)
☎ (01506) 834252
11–2.30, 6–11 (midnight Fri & Sat);
12.30–11 Sun
Ind Coope Burton Ale; Whitbread Boddingtons Bitter; guest beers Ⓔ
Typical country inn, nicely situated on the edge of the River Forth, near Blackness Castle. A warm welcome is assured, with real fires in both bars and award-winning, home-cooked food (fish a speciality).
🏰 ❀ 🚗 🕪 ▶ 🕀 ♣

Camelon

Rosebank
Main Street ☎ (01324) 611842
11–11 (midnight Fri & Sat); 12.30–
11.30 Sun
Whitbread Boddingtons Bitter; guest beers Ⓗ
Beefeater renovation of the former Rosebank Distillery bonded warehouse, on the Forth & Clyde Canal. Its unusual architecture and bulk dominates the crossroads on which it stands.
🕪 ▶ & ⇌ P

Dollar

King's Seat
19 Bridge Street
☎ (01259) 742515
11–2.30, 5–11 (midnight Thu–Sat)
Harviestoun 80/-; guest beers Ⓗ
Comfortable pub on the main street, offering a regularly changing selection of seven beers. A wide range of food is served in both lounge areas. Families welcome.
🕪 ▶ & 🅰

Lorne Tavern
17 Argyll Street
☎ (01259) 743423
11–2.30, 5–11 Mon; 5–11 Tue; 3–11
Wed; 3–midnight Thu; 11–1am Fri &
Sat; 12.30–11 Sun
Greene King IPA Ⓐ;
Harviestoun 70/-, 80/- Ⓗ; **guest beer** Ⓐ
Pub holding the oldest licence in Dollar (1850); ideal for a stop after a walk up Dollar Glen. Lunches Sat and Sun;

eve meals Thu–Sun. Children's certificate. 🕪 ▶ 🕀 🅰 ♣ P

Drymen

Winnock Hotel
The Square ☎ (01360) 660245
11 (12 Sun)–midnight (1am Fri & Sat)
Draught Bass Ⓗ; **Broughton Greenmantle Ale; Courage Directors; Ruddles Best Bitter; Webster's Yorkshire Bitter** Ⓗ
Well-appointed, 18th-century hotel in the centre of the village, within easy driving distance of Loch Lomond.
🏰 🛏 ❀ 🚗 🕪 ▶ P

Dunblane

Tappit Hen
Kirk Street
☎ (01786) 825226
11 (12.30 Sun)–11.30 (12.30am Fri &
Sat)
Harviestoun Original 80/-; Maclay Kane's Amber Ale, Wallace; guest beers Ⓗ
Traditional local opposite the cathedral. Seven handpumps serve an extensive range of guest beers. Good choice of malt whiskies, too. Local CAMRA *Pub of the Year* 1995.
⇌ ♣

Falkirk

Eglesbrech Ale House (Behind The Wall)
14 Melville Street
☎ (01324) 633338
12–11.30; 11.30–12.45am Fri & Sat;
12.30–midnight Sun

S&N Theakston XB, Newcastle Exhibition; Whitbread Flowers Original; guest beers Ⓗ
The ale house is on the upper floor of this former Playtex bra factory. German and Belgian bottled beers are also available. A good variety of food is served in all areas, as well as in the downstairs bistro. Live folk music Thu eve. ❀ ◖ ▮ ➡ (Grahamston)

Polmont

Black Bull
Main Street
☎ (01324) 714424

11–11 (midnight Fri–Sun)
Maclay 80/-; guest beers Ⓗ
Popular village local with a comfortable lounge.
Q ◖ ▮ ➡ ♣ P

Whyteside
Gilston Crescent
☎ (01324) 712394
11–11 (including Sun)
Whitbread Boddingtons Bitter, Flowers Original; guest beers Ⓗ
Imposing building in a modern housing estate. Legend has it that Burke and Hare (the infamous grave robbers) stayed nearby when they worked as labourers

on the Union Canal. Refurbished in 1990 as a Brewer's Fayre outlet.
◖ ▮ & ➡ P

Tillicoultry

Woolpack Inn
1 Glassford Square
☎ (01259) 750332
11–midnight (1am Fri & Sat); 11–midnight Sun
Beer range varies Ⓗ
Traditional, old drovers' inn dating back to 1743. Very strong local trade, but it also caters for hill-walking enthusiasts. Meals Fri–Sun.
⇞ Q ⛬ ◖ ▮ ▲ ♣

WHO OWNS WHOM?

Space restrictions in the pub entries prohibit full and clear explanations of just who owns the major beer brands in the UK.

Full details are, of course, given in the breweries section and the Beers Index, but here, as a quick guide, are the main ownership details of well-known cask ale brands.

Bass

Aitken's
Hancock's
M&B
Stones
Worthington

Carlsberg-Tetley

ABC (Aylesbury)
Ansells
Arrol's
Benskins
Dartmoor
Firkin
Friary Meux
HP&D (Holt, Plant & Deakin)
Ind Coope
Nicholson's
Tetley
Tetley Walker
Peter Walker

Courage

John Smith's
Webster's
Wilson's

Greenalls (pub group)

Cornish
Davenports
Devenish
Shipstone's

Scottish & Newcastle

Home
Matthew Brown
McEwan
Theakston
Younger

Whitbread

Bentley's
Boddingtons
Castle Eden
Chester's
Flowers
Fremlins
Higsons
Oldham
Strong
Wethered

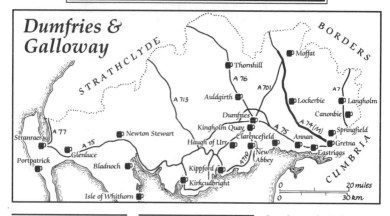

Dumfries & Galloway

STRATHCLYDE · BORDERS · CUMBRIA

Moffat · Thornhill · A 76 · A 701 · Auldgirth · Lockerbie · Langholm · Canonbie · Dumfries · Kingholm Quay · A 74(M) · Springfield · Newton Stewart · A 77 · A 75 · Haugh of Urr · Clarencefield · Annan · Gretna · Stranraer · Glenluce · New Abbey · Eastriggs · Portpatrick · Bladnoch · Kippford · Kirkcudbright · Isle of Whithorn

0 · 20 miles · 0 · 30 km

Annan

Blue Bell Inn
High Street ☎ (01461) 202385
11 (12.30 Sun)–11 (midnight Thu–Sat)
**S&N Theakston Best Bitter;
guest beers** Ⓗ
Excellent, traditional boozer
with impressive wood
panelling; friendly and very
popular. Local CAMRA *Pub of
the Year 1994.* Q ❀ ▲ ⇌ ♣

Auldgirth

Auldgirth Inn
Off A76 ☎ (01387) 740250
11–2.30, 5–11 (midnight Thu & Fri);
11–midnight Sat; 12.30–11 Sun
**Draught Bass; Caledonian
80/-** Ⓗ
Quaint country inn, bypassed
by a road diversion. The
comfortable lounge bar is
decorated in olde-worlde style.
Children's certificate.
🏨 Q ❀ 🛏 ◖▶ ⌂ P

Bladnoch

Bladnoch Inn
On A714 ☎ (01988) 402200
11 (12 Sun)–11 (midnight Fri & Sat)
**Fuller's London Pride; guest
beers** Ⓗ
Friendly village local, popular
with farmers, anglers and
wildfowlers, opposite
Bladnoch distillery (sadly out
of production but maintaining
a visitor centre). Children's
certificate. 🏨 🛏 ❀ 🛏 ◖▶ P

Canonbie

Riverside Inn
☎ (0138 73) 71512
12–3, 6.30–11; 12–3 (not winter),
7–10.30 Sun
Yates Bitter; guest beer Ⓗ
Charming, comfortable,
country inn on the River Esk.
Good quality food.
🏨 Q ❀ 🛏 ◖▶ ⌂ P ⊟

Clarencefield

Farmers Inn
Main Street ☎ (01387) 87675
11–2.30, 6–11 (midnight Fri);
11–midnight Sat; 12.30–11 Sun
**Caledonian 70/-, 80/-; guest
beer** Ⓗ
Welcoming, 18th-century inn,
once a temperance hotel.
🏨 🛏 ❀ 🛏 ◖▶ ⌂ ▲ ♣ P

Dumfries

Douglas Arms
Friars Vennel ☎ (01387) 56002
11 (12.30 Sun)–11 (midnight Thu–Sat)
**Broughton Greenmantle Ale,
Oatmeal Stout, Old Jock;
Jennings Cumberland Ale;
guest beers** Ⓗ
Town-centre pub with a cosy
snug bar. 🏨 Q 🛏 ♣

Moreig Hotel
67 Annan Road
☎ (01387) 55524
11 (12 Sun)–11 (midnight Thu–Sat)
**S&N Theakston Best Bitter;
John Smith's Bitter** Ⓗ
Friendly, comfortable hotel,
serving an excellent choice of
meals. Weekend restaurant.
🏨 Q 🛏 ❀ 🛏 ◖▶ ⌂ ♣ P

New Bazaar
38 Whitesands
☎ (01387) 68776
12–midnight; 12.30–11 Sun
**Broughton Greenmantle Ale;
Maclay Wallace; McEwan
80/-; guest beers** Ⓗ
Excellent traditional bar with
Victorian fittings. Handy for
shoppers. Varied guest beers.
🏨 Q 🛏 ⌂ ♣

Ship Inn
97 St Michael Street
☎ (01387) 55189
11–2.30, 5–11
**Caledonian Double Amber
Ale; McEwan 70/-, 80/-;
Marston's Pedigree; S&N
Theakston XB; guest beers** Ⓗ

Superb, award-winning,
traditional pub – a gem not to
be missed. Q ▲ ⇌ ♣

Troqueer Arms
Troqueer Road
☎ (01387) 54518
11–11 (midnight Thu, 1am Fri & Sat);
12.30–midnight Sun
Maclay 60/- Ⓗ
Traditional inn, nicely fitted
out, handy for the Camera
Obscura and Burns Trail
Museums. The fine, long bar
boasts views across the town.
Q 🛏 ❀ ♣ P

Eastriggs

Graham Arms
The Rand (main road from
Annan) ☎ (01461) 40244
11 (12.30 Sun)–11 (midnight Thu–Sat);
(varies in winter)
**Bass Worthington BB; Stones
Best Bitter; guest beers** Ⓗ
Traditional pub with lounge
and public bars. The bowling
green is popular in season.
Pleasant staff; excellent food.
🏨 ❀ ◖▶ ⌂ ♣ P

Glenluce

Kelvin House Hotel
53 Main Street (off A75)
☎ (01581) 300303
11–11 (midnight Sat & Sun)
**Alloa Arrol's 80/-; guest
beer** Ⓗ
Small hotel at the head of Luce
Bay, in a village now
bypassed. Children's
certificate.
Q ❀ 🛏 ◖▶ ⌂ ▲ ♣

Gretna

Solway Lodge
Annan Road (main road S
from Gretna) ☎ (01461) 338266
12–11 (midnight Sat)–midnight
Fri; 12–11 Sun (12–3 winter Sun)
**Broughton Special; Tetley
Mild, Bitter** Ⓗ

Excellent restaurant/hotel in its own grounds with good food at reasonable prices.
🏚 ⛵ ◁ ▷ ⅃ P

Haugh of Urr

Laurie Arms Hotel
1 mile S of A75
☎ (01556) 660246
11.45–2.30, 5 (5.30 winter)–midnight
Beer range varies H
Comfortable and friendly country inn just off the beaten track. Up to three guest beers. Children's certificate. Beware the keg cider from a fake handpump.
🏚 Q ☀ 🛏 ◁ ▷ P

Isle of Whithorn

Steam Packet Hotel
Harbour Row (A750)
☎ (01988) 500334
11 (12 Sun)–11
S&N Theakston XB; Whitbread Boddingtons Bitter (summer) H
Very attractive harbourside inn, in a picturesque village. The bar walls are stone-clad. The hotel has its own sailing and fishing boats.
🏚 Q ☀ 🛏 ◁ ▷ 🍴 ⅃ ♣

Kingholm Quay

Swan Hotel
On B726, 1½ miles S of Dumfries ☎ (01387) 253756
11.30–2.30, 5–11 (midnight Thu–Sun; 11.30–midnight Sun April–Oct)
McEwan 80/-; S&N Theakston Best Bitter H
Attractive and friendly hotel overlooking the River Nith. Excellent bar meals.
🏚 Q ⛵ ☀ ◁ ▷ 🍴 🛏 ♣ P ✗

Kippford

Anchor Hotel
☎ (01556) 620205
11–midnight; 12.30–11 Sun
S&N Theakston Best Bitter; guest beers H
Traditional village inn set opposite a busy yachting haven. The chef/proprietor takes pride in his food. The traditional bar has great atmosphere and original fixtures. Children's certificate.
🏚 ⛵ 🛏 ◁ ▷ ⅃ ♣ P ✗ ⛴

Mariner Hotel
Main Street ☎ (01556) 620206
12–2.30, 6–11 (12–11 Sat & Sun in summer)
Morland Old Speckled Hen; Whitbread Boddingtons Bitter; guest beers (summer) H
Hotel with a comfortable lounge bar affording beautiful views over the estuary to the hills. Split-level bar; children's play area and children's

certificate. Three guest beers.
🏚 🛏 ◁ ▷ ⅃ P ⛴

Kirkcudbright

Masonic Arms
19 Castle Street (opp. castle, near harbour)
☎ (01557) 330517
11 (12.30 Sun)–midnight
Draught Bass; guest beers H
Interesting pub making use of barrels for the bar front, stools and tables, and displaying a selection of old bar mirrors. A friendly local in a town famous for its artists. 🏚 ☀ 🍴

Langholm

Crown Hotel
High Street ☎ (013873) 80247
11 (12 Sun)–11 (midnight Thu–Sat)
Beer range varies H
Comfortable, 18th-century inn offering high teas. Children's certificate.
🏚 ⛵ 🛏 ◁ ▷ 🍴 🛏 ⅃ ♣

Lockerbie

Somerton House Hotel
35 Carlisle Road
☎ (01576) 202583
11–11 (midnight Thu–Sat)
Broughton Greenmantle Ale; guest beer H
Deservedly popular, well-appointed hotel with friendly service. Excellent meals.
🏚 Q ⛵ ☀ 🛏 ◁ ▷ 🍴 P

Moffat

Black Bull Hotel
Church Gate ☎ (01683) 20206
11 (12 Sun)–11 (midnight Thu–Sat)
McEwan 80/-; S&N Theakston Best Bitter; guest beers H
Historic, 16th-century hotel with a comfortable lounge and a traditional bar.
🏚 ⛵ ☀ 🛏 ◁ ▷ 🍴 ⅃ ♣

Star Hotel
High Street ☎ (01683) 20156
11 (12 Sun)–11 (midnight Thu–Sat)
S&N Theakston Best Bitter; guest beer (summer) H
Welcoming, family-run hotel; the narrowest detached hotel in Britain. High teas served.
🛏 ◁ ▷ 🍴

New Abbey

Criffel Inn
The Square ☎ (01387) 850305
12 (12.30 Sun)–2.30, 5.30 (6.30 Sun)–11
Broughton Special A
Traditional bar in a small hotel in a picturesque village near the ruins of Sweetheart Abbey. Old photos and timetables of

local interest are displayed. Children's certificate.
🏚 Q ⛵ ☀ 🛏 ◁ ▷ 🍴 ♣ P

Newton Stewart

Creebridge House Hotel
On old main road, E of river
☎ (01671) 402121
12–2.30, 6–midnight; 12.30–3, 7–11 Sun
Beer range varies H
Country house hotel set in spacious grounds on the outskirts of Minnigaff. It has been reorganised internally, to form a larger lounge. Children's certificate. Up to three guest beers.
Q ⛵ ☀ 🛏 ◁ ▷ ⅃ ♣ P

Portpatrick

Harbour House Hotel
53 Main Street (harbour)
☎ (01776) 810456
11 (12 Sun)–11.15 (11.45 Fri & Sat if there is entertainment)
Beer range varies H
Open-plan lounge bar in a hotel looking on to a picturesque fishing port. Children's certificate. Two guest beers. 🏚 🛏 ◁ ▷ ⅃ P

Springfield

Queen's Head
Main Street
☎ (01461) 37173
12–2.30, 7–11 (midnight Thu–Sat)
McEwan 70/-, 80/-; S&N Theakston Mild, Best Bitter H
Welcoming, single-room local. Snacks available. ♣ P

Stranraer

Rudicott Hotel
London Road
(A75, 400 yds E of centre)
☎ (01776) 702684
12–2.30, 5–11
Beer range varies H
Small, family-run hotel, handy for ferry terminals and football and rugby grounds. Two guest beers. Q ☀ 🛏 ◁ ⅃ P

Thornhill

Buccleugh & Queensbury Hotel
112 Drumlanrig Street (A76)
☎ (01848) 330215
11–1am (midnight Thu)
Beer range varies H
Hotel with a comfortable lounge where meals are served all day (breakfast from 7.30 in the fishing season, late Feb–Nov). One guest beer all year; one more in the public bar in summer. 🏚 Q ⛵ 🛏 ◁ ▷ 🛏 🍴 ♣ P

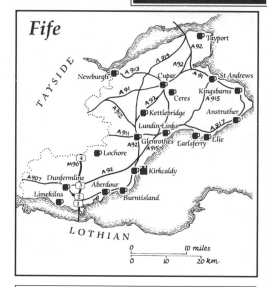

Fife

Fife

Fyfe, Kirkcaldy

Aberdour

Aberdour Hotel
High Street (A921)
☎ (01383) 860325
4 (11 Fri & Sat, 12.30 Sun)–11 (midnight Thu–Sat)
Alloa Arrol's 80/-; Draught Bass; Ind Coope Burton Ale Ⓗ
Old coaching inn with stables in a cobbled yard. The public bar has a rare Deuchars mirror. Golf courses, tennis courts and lovely beaches are nearby. Tiny car park. Lunches weekends only in winter.
🚪 ❀ 🛏 ◖ ▶ ≑ ♣ P

Anstruther

Dreel Tavern
High Street ☎ (01333) 310727
11–midnight
Beer range varies Ⓗ
On the bank of the Dreel burn, next to the old ford, this popular stone pub provides good quality food.
🚪 Q ❀ ◖ ▶ ♣

Burntisland

Crown Tavern
19 Links Place (off High St)
☎ (01592) 873697
4 (12 Fri & Sat); 12.30–midnight Sun
Belhaven Sandy Hunter's Ale; Broughton Greenmantle Ale Ⓗ
Well-appointed lounge bar opposite the town's links, where a fair is situated all summer. Near the beach. ≑

Ceres

Brands Inn
High Street (behind Folk Museum)
☎ (01334) 828325
11.30–3, 5.30–midnight (1am Fri); 11–midnight Sat; 12.30–11.30 Sun
Caledonian 80/-; guest beer Ⓗ
Friendly local where the old stone walls and wooden beams have now been restored, and a large, open fireplace is a focal point. The rare Ballingall's Brewery mirror is again on display. Children welcome in the games room. 🚪 Q ◖ 🎱

Ceres Inn
The Cross
☎ (01334) 828305
11–2.30, 5 (6 Tue)–11 (1am Thu & Fri, midnight Sat)
Beer range varies Ⓗ
Long, single bar with a collection of brasses, a pool table in an alcove and snug tables. Restaurant downstairs (eve meals Thu–Sat, plus Mon–Wed in summer). Two real ales. ❀ ◖ ▶ ♣ P

Cupar

Drookit Dug
43 Bonnygate
☎ (01334) 655862
11–1am; 12.30–11 Sun
Beer range varies Ⓗ
Town-centre pub, popular with the young, offering regular cut-price bargains in real ales. Occasional festivals.
🚪 ◖ ≑

Dunfermline

City Hotel (Cask & Barrel Bar)
18 Bridge Street
☎ (01383) 722538
11 (12.30 Sun)–11 (midnight Fri & Sat)
Maclay 70/-, 80/-; guest beers Ⓗ
Originally a coaching inn, from around 1775, this is now a prestigious town-centre hotel. Cask beers are in the ground floor bar, which is comfortable if a little lacking in atmosphere. Near the famous abbey and Pittencrieff Park. 🚪 ◖ 🍴 🍺 P

Coady's
16 Pilmuir Street (near bus station) ☎ (01383) 723865
11–11.30 (11.45 Fri & Sat); 12.30–11 Sun
S&N Theakston Best Bitter Ⓗ
Busy, street-corner local with bare wooden floorboards and a back sitting room, plus a pool room upstairs. Named after an Irish painter whose works adorn the walls. Occasional live music. Car park opposite. ♣

Earlsferry

Golf Tavern, 19th Hole
Links Road ☎ (01333) 330610
11–midnight (1am Fri); 12.30–11 Sun (11–2.30, 5–midnight Oct–April)
Caledonian Deuchars IPA; Maclay 80/-; guest beers Ⓗ
Excellent public bar and lounge with a lovely outlook over a golf links and a strong golf theme throughout. Children welcome until 8pm.
🚪 Q ❀ 🛏 ◖ ▶ ▲ ♣

Elie

Ship Inn
The Toft ☎ (01333) 330246
11–midnight; 12.30–11 Sun
Belhaven 80/-; Courage Directors; guest beers Ⓗ
Excellent, renovated pub overlooking Elie Bay and the harbour. Its restaurants and an outdoor barbecue area attract locals and visitors to this ale house opened in 1838.
🚪 Q ❀ ◖ ▶ ▲

Glenrothes

Glenrothes Snooker Club
Plot 7, Caskieberran Road (off A92) ☎ (01592) 758916
11–11 (including Sun); 11–midnight Thu–Sat
Alloa Arrol's 80/-; Ind Coope Burton Ale; guest beer Ⓗ
Plush lounge bar, more like a pub than a club. The central

bar area has couches and is surrounded by private rooms with snooker tables. & ♣ P

Kettlebridge

Kettlebridge Inn
9 Cupar Road (A92, Markinch road) ☎ (01337) 830232
11.30–2.30, 5–11 (4.30–midnight Fri); 12–midnight Sat; 12.30–11 Sun
Belhaven 80/-, Sandy Hunter's Ale, St Andrew's Ale; guest beers Ⓗ
Local CAMRA *Pub of the Year* 1994; a small, friendly bar and restaurant, well worth seeking out. Eve meals finish at 8.30 (not served Mon). Q ❀ ◑ ◐

Kingsbarns

Cambo Arms
5 Main Street
☎ (01334) 880226
11–11 (midnight Fri & Sat); 12.30–11 Sun
Belhaven 80/-, St Andrew's Ale; guest beer Ⓗ
Small, friendly bar with books and board games. The dining room serves good home cooking using local produce (eve meals in summer only).
🏚 Q ⛴ ❀ ◑ ◐ ♣ P

Kirkcaldy

Betty Nicol's
297 High Street
☎ (01592) 642083
11 (6 Sun)–11 (midnight Wed–Sat)
Alloa Arrol's 80/-; Caledonian Deuchars IPA; Ind Coope Burton Ale; Tetley Bitter; guest beer Ⓗ
Town-centre ale house with some remaining vestiges of its former glory, sympathetically restored by the present management. The marvellous back room has a coal fire and can be used for families. No food Sun. 🏚 ◑ & ♣

Harbour Bar
471–473 High Street (opp. harbour) ☎ (01592) 274270
11–2.30, 5–midnight; 11–midnight Fri & Sat; 12.30–midnight Sun
Belhaven St Andrew's Ale; Fyfe Auld Alliance; guest beers Ⓗ
Marvellous, unspoilt town

boozer with lovely etched windows and a rare jug bar. Both lounge and public bars are wood-panelled. Four guest beers complement the home-brewed ale. Try the home-made pies. Q ⊞

Limekilns

Ship Inn
Halkett's Hall (off A985)
☎ (01383) 872247
11 (12.30 Sun)–11 (midnight Thu–Sun)
Belhaven 80/-, St Andrew's Ale; Courage Directors Ⓗ
Small, but nonetheless friendly and comfortable, one-room lounge bar with nautical bric-a-brac and fine views over the Firth of Forth. Children catered for. ◑ & ♣

Lochore

Miners' Welfare Society Social Club
1 Lochleven Road (B920)
☎ (01592) 860358
12 (12.30 Sun)–3.30, 6.30–11.30
Maclay 70/- Ⓗ
Large club, with a public bar, lounge, two dance halls and an upstairs games room, in what was once part of Fife's thriving coalfield. Non-members must be signed in but are made most welcome. Close to Lochore Meadows Country Park, reclaimed from pit wasteland. Bowling green.
⊞ & ♣

Lundin Links

Coachman's (Old Manor Hotel)
Leven Road ☎ (01333) 320368
11–3, 5–11
Beer range varies Ⓗ
Converted coach house where the restaurant provides good food to accompany the ever changing ales. Children's certificate. Q ⛴ 🏚 ◑ ◐ P

Newburgh

Abbey Inn
East Port, Cupar Road (E end of town) ☎ (01337) 840761

11 (12.30 Sun)–11 (midnight Wed, Thu & Sat; 1am Fri)
Beer range varies Ⓗ
Small, L-shaped bar with a games room extension; also a cosy lounge. This lively social centre is patronised by local sports teams. Good pub food served till 8pm (not Tue). Four real ales. Q ❀ 🏚 ◑ ◐ ⊞ ♣

St Andrews

Bert's Bar
99 South Street (opp. St Mary's College) ☎ (01334) 474543
11 (12 Sun)–midnight (11.45 Sat)
Alloa Arrol's 80/-; Ind Coope Burton Ale; Taylor Landlord; Tetley Bitter; guest beer Ⓗ
Comfortable, single-bar town pub, popular with students. Note the marble-topped bar. A successful survivor of Alloa's chain of Bert's Bars. ◑ & ♣

Cellar Bar (Aikman's)
32 Bell Street ☎ (01334) 477425
11–3, 5–midnight; 11–11.45 Sat; 6.30–11 Sun
Belhaven 80/-; guest beers Ⓗ
The busy basement of Aikman's bar/restaurant. Food may be ordered from the ground floor restaurant. Occasional beer festivals. ◑ ◐

Whey Pat Tavern
1 Bridge Street (opp. West port) ☎ (01334) 477740
11–midnight (including Sun)
S&N Newcastle Exhibition, Theakston XB; guest beer Ⓗ
Pleasant lounge, popular with students, with a new extension to the rear; noted for the quality of its bar service. The name derives from a pot used to heat whey. ◑ & ♣

Tayport

Bell Rock
4–6 Dalgleish Street (opp. harbour) ☎ (01382) 552388
11 (12.30 Sun)–midnight (1am Thu & Fri)
Beer range varies Ⓗ
Split-level bar reflecting a close association with the sea. The walls are festooned with pictures of local rail, sea and air history. Children's certificate. Price reductions for pensioners. Q ❀ ◑ ▲ ♣

Every effort is made to ensure that information given in the *Good Beer Guide* is accurate. However, as the pub trade is in a state of flux, with landlords changing, new beers being introduced and facilities being up- (or down-) graded, we suggest that readers check important facts before visiting. With the arrival, in August 1995, of all day opening on Sunday, readers should also check pubs' new Sunday hours.

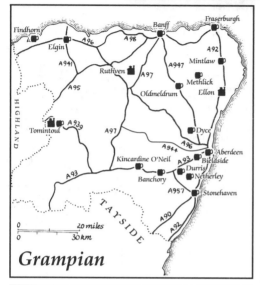

Grampian

 Aberdeenshire, Ellon; **Borve**, Ruthven; **Tomintoul**, Tomintoul

Aberdeen

Adam Lounge
145 Holburn Street
☎ (01224) 587932
11–midnight; 12.30–11 Sun
Beer range varies Ⓗ
Popular meeting place for all ages. A model train runs overhead round both the lounge and public bar. Real ale is served in the lounge only.
Ⓔ

Betty Burke's
10 Bon Accord Square
☎ (01224) 210359
11–midnight; 12.30–11 Sun
Caledonian 80/-; Ind Coope Burton Ale; Tetley Bitter; guest beers Ⓗ
Popular, city-centre bar, noted for its good food and a large selection of bottled beers from all over the world. Very busy at weekends. Coffee served from 10am.
◐ ▶ ⇌

Blue Lamp
121–123 Gallowgate
☎ (01224) 647472
11–midnight
Caledonian Deuchars IPA, 80/-; S&N Theakston Best Bitter Ⓗ**; Younger No. 3** Ⓐ**; guest beers**
Excellent pub set in an old granite building. The large, sympathetic, modern lounge (note the slate floor) is popular with students, hosting live bands at weekends. The smaller, old-fashioned public bar is popular with locals. Free jukebox. The lounge (closed Sun eve) gives access to a wheelchair WC.
Ⓔ & ⌂

Carriages
101 Crown Street
☎ (01224) 595440
11–2.30, 5–midnight; 6–11.30 Sun, closed Sun lunch
Caledonian Deuchars IPA; S&N Theakston Best Bitter; Whitbread Boddingtons Bitter, Castle Eden Ale, Flowers Original; guest beers Ⓗ
Relaxed and friendly, but busy, city-centre bar; quieter at weekends. Excellent selection of real ales, plus good food in the bar and restaurant.
Q ⇔ ◐ ▶ ⇌ ⌂ P

Cocky Hunter's
504 Union Street
☎ (01224) 626720
11–midnight; 12.30–11 Sun
Caledonian 80/-; Whitbread Boddingtons Bitter, Flowers Original; guest beers Ⓗ
Very popular, city-centre pub decorated throughout with bric-a-brac. Live music or entertainment is staged every night. There is seating in wooden alcoves if a quieter time is required. ◐ &

Donview
2 Ellon Road, Bridge of Don (A92, at River Don bridge, 2½ miles N of Aberdeen centre) ☎ (01224) 703239
11–midnight; 12.30–11 Sun
Ind Coope Burton Ale; Tetley Bitter; guest beer Ⓗ
Local pub on the main route north from the city centre; handy for beach and riverside walks and bird and seal watching. Food is served in the lounge everyday; entertainment Fri eve.
◐ ▶ Ⓔ ♣ P

Ferryhill House Hotel
169 Bonaccord Street
☎ (01224) 590867
11–11; 11.30–midnight Fri & Sat
Caledonian 80/-; S&N Theakston Best Bitter; Taylor Landlord; guest beer Ⓗ
One of the few hotels with a garden drinking area. The wood-panelled bar features a subdued tartan theme and an open fire. Children welcome; something for everyone. ⇔ Q ✿ ⇔ ◐ ▶ P

Globe
13 North Silver Street
☎ (01224) 624528
11–midnight (11 Sun)
Draught Bass; Caledonian 80/-; S&N Theakston Best Bitter; guest beer Ⓗ
Pleasant, one-room pub, popular with office workers and theatre-goers. Excellent bar food (booking advised).
◐ ▶

Grill
213 Union Street
11–11
Draught Bass Ⓗ**; McEwan 80/-** Ⓐ**; Whitbread Boddingtons Bitter; guest beers** Ⓗ
Superb, traditional, high-ceilinged pub. No female toilets, but a wide-ranging clientele. Try the stovies.
Q ◐ ⇌

Mains of Scotstown
1 Jesmond Square East, Bridge of Don
☎ (01224) 825222
11–11 (midnight Thu–Sat)
Draught Bass; Caledonian 80/- Ⓗ
Popular local, comprising a bar, lounge and a restaurant with a good reputation. Food is also served all day in the lounge. Regular and varied events are staged.
✿ ◐ ▶ ♣ P

Mill of Mundurno
Bridge of Don (B999/A92 jct, 4½ miles N of Aberdeen centre)
☎ (01224) 821217
11 (12 Sun)–11

Whitbread Boddingtons Bitter, Castle Eden Ale, Flowers Original ℍ
Converted mill restored in a traditional manner with a waterwheel attached. Travel lodges are available. Popular with passing trade, especially business travellers.
☎ ❀ ⇦ ⇦ ▶ ✕

Moorings

2 Trinity Quay (harbour front)
☎ (01224) 587062
11–midnight; 12.30–11 Sun
Beer range varies ℍ
Pub for lovers of heavy rock who like a decent pint and appreciate the excellent jukebox selection. Not for devotees of a quiet life, but worth checking out. Five guest beers. ⇦ ≋

Old Blackfriars

52 Castle Street
☎ (01224) 581992
11–midnight; 12–11 Sun
Caledonian Deuchars IPA, 80/-; Ind Coope Burton Ale; Tetley Bitter; guest beers ℍ
Characterful Scottish tavern on split levels, recently restored: brick and stone walls, wood panelling, stunning stained-glass panels behind the bar. Plenty of nooks and corners. Generously portioned food is served all day; children welcome. Coffee served from 10am. ⇦ ▶ & ≋

Prince of Wales

5 St Nicholas Lane
☎ (01224) 640597
11–11.45; 12.30–10.45 Sun
Draught Bass; Caledonian 80/-; Orkney Dark Island; S&N Theakston Old Peculier; Younger No. 3; guest beers ℍ
Friendly, welcoming city-centre pub. The long, traditional bar boasts two fine gantries and other features. Live music Sun afternoons. Full of atmosphere. Good, wholesome food. Q ⇦ ≋ ✦

Tilted Wig

55 Castle Street (opp. Court House) ☎ (01224) 583248
12–midnight; 7–11 Sun
Alloa Arrol's 80/-; Caledonian Deuchars IPA, 80/-; Ind Coope Burton Ale; Marston's Pedigree; Tetley Bitter; guest beers ℍ
Brimming and bouncing with friendly folk, a pub where legal eagles and their clients mix. Recently renovated.
⇦ ▶ & ≋

Banchory

Ravenswood Club, Royal British Legion

Ramsay Road
☎ (01330) 822347

11–2.30, 5–midnight; 11–midnight Sat; 12–midnight Sun
Draught Bass; Shepherd Neame Spitfire ℍ
Old house with added function rooms. The bar is like an ordinary pub, with a very friendly atmosphere and prices considerably lower than normal for the area. Large snooker room with two full-size tables and a pool table. ❀ ⇦ ⇦ & ♣ ▲ ▶ P

Scott Skinner's Lounge

North Deeside Road (E side of town) ☎ (01330) 824393
11–3, 5–11.30 (midnight Thu & Fri); 11–midnight Sun
Draught Bass; guest beers ℍ
Pleasant, friendly pub serving lunches and dinners everyday in summer and Wed–Sun in winter. Three guest beers.
⚌ ❀ ⇦ ▲ P

Tor Na Coille Hotel

Inchmarlo Road (W side of town) ☎ (01330) 822242
12–midnight
Whitbread Boddingtons Bitter ℍ
Imposing, old country residence, now an hotel. Excellent accommodation and restaurant; also bar meals.
⚌ Q ☎ ⇦ ⇦ ▲ P

Banff

Ship Inn

7–8 Deveronside (by harbour)
☎ (01261) 812620
11–midnight
Marston's Pedigree; guest beer ℍ
Cosy harbourfront bar, with a larger lounge. Friendly welcome. ⚌ Q ⇦ ✦

Bieldside

Bieldside Inn

37 North Deeside Road
☎ (01224) 867891
11 (12.30 Sun)–midnight
Whitbread Boddingtons Bitter ℍ
Large village pub with two bars; cask beer is only served in the lounge. ⇦ ⇦ ▶ ⇦ P

Durris

Crofters Inn

Lochton of Durris (A957, Stonehaven–Crathes road)
☎ (01330) 844543
12–3, 6–10 (midnight Fri & Sat); 12.30–3, 5.30–11 Sun (closed winter Tue)
Ind Coope Burton Ale ℍ
Cosy country inn with a friendly atmosphere; set in a remote location. Choose between the homely-furnished lounge and the small, basic

---

bar. It is advisable to book for meals. Q ☎ ⇦ ⇦ & ✦ P

Dyce

Tap & Spile

Aberdeen Airport (off A96, 6 miles from Aberdeen centre)
☎ (01224) 722331
9–10 (7 winter Sat); 12.30–10 Sun
Marston's Pedigree; S&N Theakston XB; Tetley Bitter; guest beers ℍ
Smart, open lounge bar, popular with city and oil workers waiting for their flights. Snacks available. Five guest beers. & ✦ P ✕

Elgin

Sunninghill Hotel

Hay Street (near station)
☎ (01343) 547799
11–2.30, 5–11
Ind Coope Burton Ale; guest beers ℍ
Pleasant and relaxing hotel lounge; friendly and family run. Q ⇦ ⇦ ▶ ≋ P

Thunderton House

Thunderton Place (off High St)
☎ (01343) 546871
11–11.30 (11.45 Fri & Sat)
Beer range varies ℍ
Contained in a beautiful old building, this town-centre conversion comprises one split-level room, popular with all. Q ⇦ ▶

Findhorn

Crown & Anchor Inn

Off A96, 3 miles from Forres
☎ (01309) 690243
11–11 (11.45 Thu, 12.30am Fri & Sat); 12–11.45pm Sun
Draught Bass; Whitbread Boddingtons Bitter; guest beers ℍ
Situated on picturesque Findhorn Bay, a haven for watersports and wildlife enthusiasts, this is a busy, lively pub with RAF connections (near Kinloss airbase). The real ale visitors' book makes interesting reading.
⚌ ☎ ❀ ⇦ ⇦ ▶ ⇦ & ▲ ✦ P

Fraserburgh

Crown Bar

125 Shore Street (alley between Broad St and Shore St)
☎ (01346) 518452
11–11.30; 12.30–11 Sun
Beer choice varies ℍ
Unspoilt, but cosy, old-fashioned bar overlooking the harbour. A real gem in a real ale desert, serving a single, varying cask beer. ⇦ ✦

Grampian

Kincardine O'Neil

Gordon Arms Hotel
Main Street (A93)
☎ (0133 98) 84236
11–midnight
S&N Theakston Best Bitter; guest beers Ⓗ
Pleasant, friendly inn providing accommodation and serving excellent food. Close to the River Dee, it caters for salmon fishers (fishing can be arranged by the inn during the season). ♨ Q ☎ ⋈ ◖ ▶ P

Methlick

Gight House Hotel
Sunnybrae (over bridge at top of hill) ☎ (01651) 806389
12–2.30, 5–midnight; 12–11.45 Sat;
12–11 Sun
Draught Bass; guest beers Ⓗ
Attractive lounge bar in a former church manse, popular with the local farming community. Excellent, home-cooked meals incorporate local produce. Families welcome.
Q ☎ ❀ ⋈ ◖ ▶ & ♣ P

Mintlaw

Country Park Inn
Station Road (A950, ½ mile W of Mintlaw) ☎ (01771) 622622
11–11.30

Beer range varies Ⓗ
Friendly country inn which welcomes families. It offers a good, varied food selection and a beer range (two) which changes regularly. Nightclub.
♨ ☎ ⋈ ◖ ▶ & P

Netherley

Lairhillock Inn
On B979 ☎ (01596) 30001
11–midnight; 12.30–3.30, 6.30–11 Sun
Courage Directors; McEwan 80/-; Thwaites Craftsman Ⓐ;
Whitbread Flowers Original; guest beers Ⓗ
Pub set in lovely countryside: look out for 'Inn' on the roof. The large lounge boasts a central fire; families are welcome in the conservatory. The public bar has two fires and a friendly atmosphere. Excellent food.
♨ Q ☎ ❀ ◖ ▶ P

Oldmeldrum

Redgarth
Kirk Brae (off A947, look for the golf course sign) OS812273
☎ (01651) 872353
11–2.30, 5–11 (11.45 Fri & Sat);
12.30–2.30, 5.30–11 Sun
Caledonian 80/- Ⓗ; **guest beers** Ⓗ/Ⓖ
Very popular bar enjoying magnificent panoramic views.

Good value, fresh, home-cooked food includes a vegetarian choice. The attentive host is a previous national CAMRA *Pub of the Year* winner. Children welcome. ❀ ⋈ ◖ ▶ P

Stonehaven

Marine Hotel
Shorehead (harbour front)
☎ (01569) 762155
11–midnight; 12–11 Sun
Draught Bass; McEwan 80/-; S&N Theakston Best Bitter; Taylor Landlord; guest beers Ⓗ
Popular village hotel on a small, picturesque harbour. Very crowded in summer, but sit on the wall and soak up the sun and sights. The family room is upstairs.
♨ ☎ ❀ ⋈ ◖ ▶ ▲ ♣ P

Tomintoul

Glen Avon Hotel
1 The Square ☎ (01807) 580218
11.30–11.30
Tomintoul Caillie *or* **Stag; guest beer** Ⓗ
Warm and welcoming village pub, set on the edge of the Cairngorms, and used by walkers and skiers. Look out for odes to locals.
♨ Q ⋈ ◖ ▶ & ▲ ♣

DOES YOUR PINT MEASURE UP?

It's now official. You don't have to be given a pint when you pay for one. Four years ago, there was much excitement when Trade and Industry minister Edward Leigh declared that Section 43 of the 1985 Weights and Measures Act was going to be implemented.

In layman's terms, this meant that the Government was going to enforce the law which stated that a pint of beer should be a pint of beer, with any froth or head counted as extra. The brewers, of course, were up in arms. Implementing the act would cost brewers and publicans millions, they declared. Brim-measure glasses would have to be replaced with oversized glasses and handpumps would have to be ripped out of every bar in the land to make way for metered dispense.

Over the following months, the brewers' estimates of the cost of the change dipped sharply, as each figure they produced was challenged. Nevertheless, they got their way and persuaded the Government to scrap its plans. Consequently, drinkers are today entitled to 95% liquid plus a head, if the beer is handpumped. Electric metered dispense pints may be six millilitres above or below measure. However, if you think you are being short-measured on hand-pumped pints, you can ask for a top-up, which should be given with good grace and not unreasonably refused.

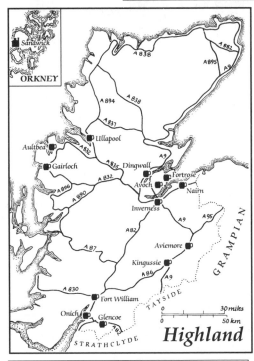

Orkney, *Sandwick, Orkney*

Aultbea

Drumchork Lodge Hotel
Off A832 at southern
edge of village
☎ (01445) 731242
11–11 (1am Fri, 11.30 Sat); 12.30–11
Sun
Bateman XXXB; guest beers Ⓗ
Popular holiday hotel with
splendid views of Loch Ewe
and west coast sunsets. An old
shooting lodge in a lovely
walking area, managed/
owned by an ex-Lincolnshire
publican. Very peaceful. One
or two guest beers.
🏨 🛏 🕜 🍽 ♣ P

Aviemore

Winking Owl
Grampian Road (main street)
☎ (01479) 810646
11–midnight; 12.30–11 Sun
**Alloa Arrol's 80/-; Ind Coope
Burton Ale; Tetley Bitter;
guest beers** Ⓗ
Conversion from a farm
building many years ago,
well-patronised by skiers,
hill-walkers and locals alike.
One of the three guest beers
comes from Tomintoul.
🌸 🕜 🅰 🥾 P

Avoch

Station Hotel
Bridge Street ☎ (01381) 620246
11–2.30, 5–11 (midnight Fri); 11–11.30
Sat & Sun
Beer choice varies Ⓗ
Busy local in a pleasant Black
Isle fishing village with good
walking, golfing and sailing
nearby. Popular for its good
value food (served all day Sat
and Sun). Children's play area
in the garden. 🌸 🕜 🍽 ♣ P

Dingwall

National Hotel
High Street ☎ (01349) 862166
11–midnight (1am Fri, 11 Sun)
**Alloa Arrol's 80/-; Caledonian
80/-; Ind Coope Burton Ale;
Orkney Raven Ale, Dark
Island; Tetley Bitter; guest
beers** Ⓗ
Friendly, comfortable but
utilitarian bar in a modern
extension to a 1930s-style hotel
in the town centre. Occasional
mini-beer festivals with up to
20 guest ales. 🌸 🏨 🕜 🍽 🥾 P

Fortrose

Royal Hotel
High Street ☎ (01381) 620236
11–2.30, 5–midnight; 11–11.30 Sat;
12.30–11 Sun
Beer choice varies Ⓗ
Traditional Scottish village
hotel with a warm and
friendly atmosphere in the
locals' bar. The lounge bar
caters for family groups. Hotel
guests include golfers, sailors
and walkers. One guest ale.
🏨 🕜 🍽 🅰 ♣

Fort William

Alexandra Hotel
The Parade (northern end of
town) ☎ (01397) 702241
11 (12.30 Sun)–11
**Draught Bass; Caledonian
Deuchars IPA, 80/-** Ⓗ
Bright, friendly lounge bar in
the town's main hotel (AA
three-star), modern-looking
and tastefully decorated
though built in the last
century. Popular with coach
parties, with live music most
nights. Good value food in the
restaurant next to the bar,
much frequented by hill-
walkers. 🍼 🌸 🏨 🚻 🅰 P

Gairloch

Old Inn
The Harbour (southern edge
of village) ☎ (01445) 712006
11 (11.30 Sat)–midnight; 12.30–11 Sun
Beer range varies Ⓗ
Small Highland hotel in a
delightful setting by a burn
and an old bridge, featuring a
busy public bar and a quiet
lounge. Busy in the holiday
season, but popular all year
round with sailing, climbing
and walking clients. Very safe
garden for children.
Q 🌸 🏨 🕜 🍽 🅰 ♣ P

Glencoe

Clachaig Inn
On old riverside road, at rear
of NT centre ☎ (01855) 811252
11 (12.30 Sun)–11 (midnight Fri, 11.30
Sat)
**Alloa Arrol's 80/-; Caledonian
80/-** Ⓗ
Vibrant public bar, usually full
of climbers, walkers and
tourists from all over Britain
and beyond. Live folk music.
CAMRA's Scottish *Pub of the
Year* 1994. Beer festivals held.
🏨 🌸 🏨 🕜 🅰 P

Inverness

Blackfriars
93–95 Academy Street
☎ (01463) 233881
11–11 (1am Thu & Fri, 11.45 Sat);
11–11 Sun
**McEwan 80/-; Marston's
Pedigree; S&N Theakston
Best Bitter, Old Peculier;
guest beers** Ⓗ

Pub recently refurbished by S&N in the guise of its T&J Bernard's chain: a very well managed beer drinkers' pub with a good selection of German, Belgian and other foreign brews. Just the one large bar, but with snug alcoves. Speciality pies available most of the day. Live music some midweek eves.
◑ ▮ ≢ ○

Clachnaharry Inn
17–19 High Street, Clachnaharry (Beauly Road, N of town) ☎ (01463) 239806
11–11 (midnight Thu & Fri, 11.45 Sat); 12.30–11 Sun
McEwan 80/-; S&N Theakston XB; guest beers Ⓗ
300-year-old coaching inn looking onto the railway, the Beauly Firth and the sea lock of the Caledonian Canal. The beer garden was once the platform of the old Clachnaharry station.
❧ ❀ ◑ ▮ ◱ ♣ P

Phoenix
108 Academy Street
☎ (01463) 233685
11 (12.30)–11 (12.30am Thu & Fri, 11.30 Sat)
Bass Worthington BB, Draught Bass; guest beers Ⓗ
Traditional pub, 100 years old in 1994, featuring a rare example of an island bar. A busy pub with a mixed clientele and white-aproned staff. Sawdust on the floor. Regular live entertainment in the lounge bar.
❧ ◑ ▮ ◱ ⅋ Å ≢ ⅍

Kingussie

Royal Hotel
High Street
☎ (01540) 661898
11 (12.30 Sun)–midnight (1am Thu–Sat)
Alloa Arrol's 80/-; Ind Coope Burton Ale; Orkney Dark Island; Robinson's Best Bitter; Tetley Bitter; guest beers Ⓗ
Large, extended hotel, a coaching house in its earlier days, and still popular with coach parties. The large lounge bar serves good value food and offers music at weekends. Special beer prices and bargain accommodation Nov–Dec. Many guest ales.
❧ ❀ ⛵ ◑ ▮ ⅋ Å ≢ ♣ P ⅍

Nairn

Claymore House Hotel
Seabank Road
☎ (01667) 453731
12–3, 5–11.30 (12.30am Thu & Fri); 12–3, 5–11.30 Sun
Whitbread Boddingtons Bitter; guest beer (summer) Ⓗ
Nicely decorated bar in a hotel in Nairn's west end, conveniently on the way to Nairn Golf Club and not far from the seafront. Friendly atmosphere; a popular venue for bar suppers. Children's licence till 9. Occasional live music.
🏚 Q ❀ ⛵ ◑ ▮ P

Invernairne Hotel
Thurlow Road
☎ (01667) 452039
11–11.30 (12.30am Fri)
Beer range varies Ⓗ
Nice, friendly bar in a Victorian seaside hotel, with lovely wooden-panelling, a superb fireplace and a panoramic view of the Moray Firth. A path leads from the garden to the promenade and beach. Children's certificate till 8. High teas are popular in summer.
🏚 Q ⛵ ❀ ⛵ ◑ ▮ P

Onich

Nether Lochaber
Off A82, by terminal of Corran Ferry ☎ (01855) 821235
11–2.30, 5–11; 12.30–2.30, 6.30–11 Sun
Draught Bass Ⓗ
Smashing wee public bar tucked behind an hotel on the slipway to the ferry. Owned by the same family for 70 years. Q ❀ ⛵ ◑ ▮ Å ♣ P

Ullapool

Ferryboat Inn
Shore Street (southern end of village)
☎ (01854) 612366
11 (12.30 Sun)–11
Beer range varies Ⓗ
Small, comfortable lounge bar on the village waterfront, with open views inland over Loch Broom. Busy throughout the tourist season.
🏚 Q ❧ ⛵ ◑ ▮ Å

LINED GLASSES

A new symbol makes its debut in the 1996 *Good Beer Guide*. The oversized, lined glasses icon has now been awarded to pubs which use lined pint glasses to serve some or all of their beers.

CAMRA has long campaigned for full measures and has introduced lined glasses into all its beer festivals as a means of ensuring that drinkers get a pint when they pay for a pint. The glasses are larger than normal pint glasses, allowing any froth to sit above a line which indicates a full measure.

Many exemplary publicans have carefully and properly used normal brim-measure glasses and have always given value for money. Sadly, with the development of the swan neck and sparkler system, designed to whip up deep, creamy heads on beer, too many landlords and brewers have seized their chance to short-measure customers by serving excessively frothy beer in standard pint pots.

The oversized, lined glass is your best guarantee of getting a full pint in such circumstances, so we are happy to recognise pubs using these glasses by awarding the new symbol.

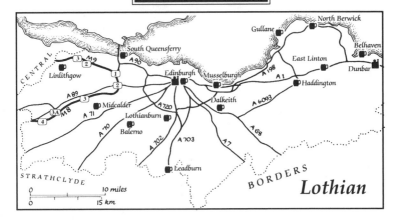

Lothian

 Belhaven, Dunbar; *Caledonian*, Edinburgh

Balerno

Johnsburn House
64 Johnsburn Road (off A70)
☎ (0131) 449 3847
12–2.30, 6.30–11 (midnight Fri);
12–midnight Sat; 12.30–10.45 Sun;
closed Mon
**Hambleton Bitter; S&N
Theakston Best Bitter; guest
beers** Ⓗ
Baronial mansion dating from
1760 and now Grade B listed.
Well-deserved reputation for
meals. The cosy bar has a
convivial atmosphere. Four
guest beers; cider in summer.
🏨 Q ✿ ◖ ▶ & ♣ ⌂ P

Belhaven

Mason's Arms
8 High Street (A1087, ½ mile W
of Dunbar) ☎ (01368) 863700
11–2.30 (4 Fri; not Wed), 5–11 (1am
Thu & Fri); 11–midnight Sat; 12.30–5
Sun
Beer choice varies Ⓗ
Friendly locals' bar close to the
brewery, affording fine views
to the Lammermuir Hills.
Aviary in the back yard. Eve
meals Thu–Sat. Q ▶ ⊞ ▲ ♣

Dalkeith

Black Bull
1 Lothian Street (off A68, S of
shopping precinct)
☎ (0131) 663 2095
11–11.30 (midnight Thu–Sat);
12.30–midnight Sun
**Caledonian Deuchars IPA,
80/-; Orkney Dark Island;
guest beer** Ⓗ
A good example of a
'Gothenburg': a busy,
traditional bar with fine
arched windows, cornice work
and a well-crafted gantry.

Large TV for sport. The quieter
lounge is contrastingly
modern. ✿ ◖ ⊞ & ♣

East Linton

Crown Hotel
27 Bridge Street (B1377)
☎ (01620) 860335
11–2.30, 5–11 (midnight Thu); 11–1am
Fri & Sat; 12.30–midnight Sun
Belhaven 80/-; guest beer Ⓗ
Cosy, wood-panelled locals'
bar with a pair of rare
Dudgeon (predecessor of
Belhaven) windows. Note the
cabinet of sporting trophies.
Large lounge to the rear.
🏨 Q ⊨ ◖ ⊞ ▲ ♣

Drover's Inn
5 Bridge Street (B1377)
☎ (01620) 860298
12–2, 5–11; 12–11 Sun & summer
Beer range varies Ⓗ
Characterful bar with a dark,
intimate feel. An interesting
range of five beers is served
across the marble top bar. The
restaurant upstairs offers
excellent meals. Be prepared to
pay for the quality.
🏨 Q ◖ ▶ ▲

Edinburgh

Baron Bailie
2–4 Lauriston Street (West Port
off the Grassmarket)
☎ (0131) 229 3201
12 (12.30 Sun)–1am
**Caledonian Deuchars IPA,
80/-; Ind Coope Burton Ale;
guest beer** Ⓗ
Alehouse on the fringe of the
Old Town, attracting students.
The fine selection on the
jukebox is unashamedly
played loud. Well used pinball
machine. ♣ ⌂

Bow Bar
80 West Bow (between Royal
Mile and Grassmarket)
☎ (0131) 226 7667
11–11.15; 7–11 Sun
**Draught Bass; Caledonian
70/-, Deuchars IPA, 80/-, ERA;
Taylor Landlord; guest
beers** Ⓐ
Traditional one-room,
stand-up bar with efficient,
friendly service. Several
extinct brewery mirrors and
old cigarette ephemera cover
the walls. Large selection of
malts and 11 beers. Q

Cask & Barrel
115 Broughton Street (between
Leith Walk and Canonmills)
☎ (0131) 556 3132
11–midnight; 12.30–11 Sun
**Draught Bass; Caledonian
Deuchars IPA, 80/-; guest
beers** Ⓗ
Spacious and extremely busy,
suburban alehouse with an
imposing horseshoe bar,
wooden floorboards and a
splendid cornice. Collection of
brewery mirrors; ten
handpumps. ◖ &

Cumberland Bar
1–3 Cumberland Street (off
Dundas St in New Town)
☎ (0131) 556 9409
12–11.30; closed Sun
**Caledonian Murrays Summer
Ale, Deuchars IPA, 80/-; guest
beers** Ⓐ
Completely rebuilt New Town
bar, turned into a superb
public bar with some
peripheral seating and a cosy
sitting room. Half-wood
panelling and rare old
brewery mirrors feature. Often
extremely busy, but the service
is fast.
🏨 Q ✿ ⊞

Lothian

Drew Nicol's (Coppers)

19 Cockburn Street (between Royal Mile and Waverley Bridge) ☎ (0131) 225 1441
11–11.30; 12.30–11 Sun
Alloa Arrol's 80/-; Caledonian Deuchars IPA; guest beers H
One-roomed pub for lovers of the turf. Three guest beers; the Arrol's 80/- is sold as Drew Nicol's 80/-. It can get extremely smoky when busy.
Q ⒟ ⇄ (Waverley)

Golden Rule

30 Yeaman Place (off Dundee St, near the S&N factory)
☎ (0131) 229 3413
11 (12.30 Sun)–11.30 (11 Mon, Tue & Sun)
Draught Bass; Belhaven 80/-; Caledonian Deuchars IPA, 80/-; Harviestoun 80/-; Maclay Kane's Amber Ale H
Busy, split-level lounge bar in a Victorian tenement building which can be smoky and hot. Two guest beers. Snacks served. ⒟

Guildford Arms

1 West Register Street (behind Burger King, E end of Princes St) ☎ (0131) 556 4312
11–11 (midnight Thu–Sat); 12.30–11 Sun
Draught Bass; Belhaven 60/-; Caledonian 80/-; Harviestoun 70/-, 80/-; Orkney Dark Island H
Pub laid out with ornate plasterwork and ceilings, spectacular cornices and friezes, window arches and screens and an unusual, wood-panelled gallery bar overlooking the busy main bar. Four guest beers.
Q ⒟ ⒬ ⇄ (Waverley)

Halfway House

24 Fleshmarket Close (between Cockburn St and Waverley station rear entrance)
☎ (0131) 225 7101
11 (10 Sat)–11.30 (midnight Wed, 1am Thu–Sat); 12.30–11 Sun (7–11 winter Sun)
Belhaven 80/-, St Andrew's Ale; guest beer H
Cosy, friendly, wee L-shaped howff down an Old Town close; often crowded and smoky. Railway memorabilia features. ⇄ (Waverley)

Home's Bar

102 Constitution Street (between foot of Leith Walk and The Shore)
☎ (0131) 553 7710
12–11 (12.30am Fri & Sat); 12–11 Sun
Belhaven St Andrew's Ale; guest beers H
Fine traditional bar with no frills. Interesting decor

includes enamelled railway signs and displays of antique tin boxes. Live folk music Fri and Sat. ⒟

Jamie's Lounge Bar

1 Grange Road (Newington end) ☎ (0131) 667 2335
11 (12.30 Sun)–midnight
Caledonian Deuchars IPA; Orkney Dark Island; guest beers H
Comfortable corner bar, full of couthy locals. Three guest ales.
⒟

Kay's Bar

39 Jamaica Street (mews between India and Howe Sts in New Town)
☎ (0131) 225 1858
11–11.45; 12.30–11 Sun
Belhaven 80/-; S&N Theakston Best Bitter, XB; guest beers H
Cosy, convivial, comfortable and consistent New Town bar featuring clever and interesting furniture. Good, varied lunches. Fifty single malts. ♨ Q ⒟

K Jackson's

40–44 Lady Lawson Street (West Port off the Grassmarket)
☎ (0131) 228 4284
11–midnight (1am Thu–Sat); 12.30–11 Sun
Draught Bass; Broughton Merlin's Ale; Caledonian Deuchars IPA; guest beers H
Small, busy locals' bar. It can be quite smoky. Five guest beers. ⌣

Leslie's Bar

45 Ratcliffe Terrace (between Newington and the Grange)
☎ (0131) 667 7205
11 (12.30 Sun)–11 (12.30am Fri, 11.45 Sat)
Draught Bass; Belhaven 80/-; Caledonian 70/-, Deuchars IPA, 80/-; guest beer H
Superb, busy Victorian pub with one of the finest interiors in the city. A snob screen separates the saloon and snug from the public bar.
♨ Q ⒬ ♣

Malt & Hops

45 The Shore (on the waterfront) ☎ (0131) 555 0083
12 (12.30 Sun)–11 (midnight Thu, Fri & Sat)
Alloa Arrol's 80/-; Ind Coope Burton Ale; Marston's Pedigree; guest beers H
One-room public bar dating from 1749 and facing onto the Water of Leith. It is said to be haunted by the ghost of a previous licensee. Large collection of pump clips. No food Sun. ♨ Q ⒟ ♣ ⌣

Olde Inn

25 Main Street, Davidsons Mains (off A90, 3 miles W of centre) ☎ (0131) 336 2437
11 (12.30 Sun)–11
Caledonian 80/-; Ind Coope Burton Ale; guest beer H
Thriving, large village local with a conservatory (no-smoking lunchtime) and a garden drinking area. Petanque played.
Q ✿ ⒟ ♪ ⒬ ♣ ⒴

Oxford Bar

8 Young Street (near Charlotte Sq) ☎ (0131) 225 4262
11 (12.30 Sun)–1am
Belhaven 80/- Ⓐ, St Andrew's Ale; Caledonian Deuchars IPA H
Tiny yet vibrant New Town drinking shop, retaining signs of its original, early 19th-century parlour arrangement.
Q ⒬

Royal Ettrick Hotel

13 Ettrick Road (behind Merchiston Bowling & Tennis Club) ☎ (0131) 228 6413
11 (12.30 Sun)–midnight
Draught Bass; Caledonian Deuchars IPA, 80/-; Maclay Kane's Amber Ale; guest beers H
Built as a town house in 1875 and now a splendid, family-run hotel, set in leafy suburbs. The lounge bar is comfortably appointed and the restaurant is bright and airy. Excellent meals. Q ✿ ⌂ ⒟ ▶ P

Southsider

3–7 West Richmond Street (near Surgeons' Hall)
☎ (0131) 667 2003
11.30 (11 Sat)–midnight (1am Fri); 12.30–11 Sun
Maclay 60/-, 70/-, 80/-, Kane's Amber Ale; guest beers H
Busy Southside lounge bar, popular with discerning locals and students. The public bar is a handy refuge if the lounge gets too smoky. ⌘ ⒟ ⒬ ⌣

Stable Bar

Mortonhall Park, 30 Frogston Road East (off B701, E of A702; road by garden centre)
☎ (0131) 664 0773
11–midnight; 12.30–11 Sun
Caledonian 80/- H
Friendly bar approached through an arch and a cobbled courtyard. Food all day. Adjacent to a camping/caravan park in rural surroundings on the southern edge of the city. Children welcome. No-smoking skittle alley.
♨ Q ✿ ⒟ ▶ ♿ ♣ ♣ P ⒴

Starbank Inn
64 Laverockbank Road (between Leith and Granton)
☎ (0131) 552 4141
11 (12.30 Sun)–11 (midnight Thu–Sat)
Belhaven Sandy Hunter's Ale, 80/-, St Andrew's Ale; Taylor Landlord; guest beers Ⓗ
Pub transformed into a bright and airy bare-floorboarded house without loss of atmosphere. Three separate areas. Fine views across the Forth. Q ❀ ◐ ◑

Winston's
20 Kirk Loan (off St John's Road, A8) ☎ (0131) 539 7077
11–11.30 (midnight Fri & Sat); 12.30–3.30, 5–11 Sun
Alloa Arrol's 80/-; Caledonian 70/-, Deuchars IPA; Ind Coope Burton Ale; guest beer Ⓗ
Busy locals' lounge bar housed in an ex-launderette, in a western suburb. A modern one-roomed pub with a golfing and rugby theme. Q ◐

World's End
4 High Street (Royal Mile)
☎ (0131) 556 3628
11–midnight (1am Fri & Sat); 12.30–11 Sun
Belhaven Sandy Hunter's Ale, 80/-, St. Andrew's Ale Ⓗ
Bustling, friendly pub in the heart of the Old Town.
◐ ⇌ (Waverley)

Gullane

Bisset's Hotel
Main Street ☎ (01620) 843320
11–11 (1am Fri & Sat, midnight Sun)
Ind Coope Burton Ale; guest beers Ⓐ
Functional bar, with a pool table and dartboard, decorated by modern pub mirrors. Steps lead down to a small comfortable lounge. Children's certificate.
🛏 ◐ ◑ ⊞ ♿ ⛺ ♣ P

Haddington

Pheasant
72 Market Street
☎ (01620) 824428
11–11 (midnight Thu–Sat)
Alloa Arrol's 80/-; Ind Coope Burton Ale; Tetley Bitter; guest beers Ⓗ
Vibrant and sometimes noisy pub attracting younger folk. A long thin bar leads to a games area where Basil (surely a Norwegian Blue) overlooks the pool table. ♣

Leadburn

Leadburn Inn
At A703/A701/A6094 jct
☎ (01968) 672952
11–midnight (including Sun)
Beer range varies Ⓗ
Large, food-oriented hostelry where a converted railway coach serves as a restaurant. The public bar has two pot-bellied stoves and a picture window with views to the Pentland Hills. A conservatory links the bar to a plush lounge. Excellent menu.
♨ Q ❀ 🛏 ◐ ◑ ⊞ ♿ ♣ ⛀
P ⅟

Linlithgow

Four Marys
High Street ☎ (01506) 842171
12–2.30, 5–11; 5–midnight Fri; 12–midnight Sat; 12.30–2.30, 7–11 Sun
Belhaven 60/-, 70/-, 80/-, St Andrew's Ale; Caledonian Deuchars IPA; Harviestoun Ptarmigan; guest beers Ⓗ
Attractive lounge with antique furniture and items reflecting the town's history. Nine handpumps serve constantly changing guest beers; large range of whiskies. CAMRA Scotland *Pub of the Year* 1995. No food Sun eve. ◐ ◑ ⇌

Lothianburn

Steading
118 Biggar Road (A702, near dry ski slope)
☎ (0131) 445 1128
11–11.30; 12.30–11 Sun
Caledonian Deuchars IPA, 80/-; Ind Coope Burton Ale; Orkney Dark Island; Taylor Landlord; guest beers Ⓗ
Stone cottages converted into an attractive bar and restaurant with a conservatory extension. A popular eating establishment but there's still a drinking area where only snacks are served.
♨ Q ❀ ◐ ◑ ♿ P

Midcalder

Torphichen Arms
36 Bank Street
☎ (01506) 880020
11–midnight (including Sun)
Caledonian Deuchars IPA, 80/-; Greenalls Shipstone's Bitter; Orkney Dark Island; guest beers Ⓗ
Village local, originally several rooms, now one L-shaped bar with public and lounge areas. Live music at weekends. Occasional beer festivals.
❀ ◐ ♣ P

Musselburgh

Volunteer Arms (Stagg's)
78–81 North High Street (behind Brunton Hall)
☎ (0131) 665 9654
11–2.30, 5–11; 11–11.30 Thu; 11–midnight Fri & Sat; closed Sun
Draught Bass; Caledonian Deuchars IPA, 80/-; guest beers Ⓗ
Established in 1858: a busy family-run pub with an olde-worlde bar with dark wood panelling, brewery mirrors and a superb gantry. A comfortable lounge to the rear has no real ale.
❀ ⊞ ♿ ♣ P

North Berwick

Nether Abbey Hotel (Fly Half Bar)
20 Dirleton Avenue (A198 W of centre)
☎ (01620) 892802
11 (12.30 Sun)–2.30, 5–11 (11.45 Thu & Fri); 11–12.45am Sat
Beer range varies Ⓐ
Extended bar in a well-appointed, family-run Victorian hotel: an ideal base for exploring the E Lothian coast. Four ales sold. Beer festival Feb.
❀ 🛏 ◐ ◑ ⛺ ⇌ P

South Queensferry

Ferry Tap
High Street
☎ (0131) 331 2000
11–11.30 (12.30am Thu–Sat); 12.30–11.30 Sun
Caledonian Deuchars IPA, 80/-; Orkney Dark Island; guest beers Ⓗ
Well-appointed, friendly one roomer with an unusual barrel-vaulted ceiling. No food Sun. Q ◐

For further information about the beers listed in the above entries, check the breweries section at the rear of the book.

Strathclyde

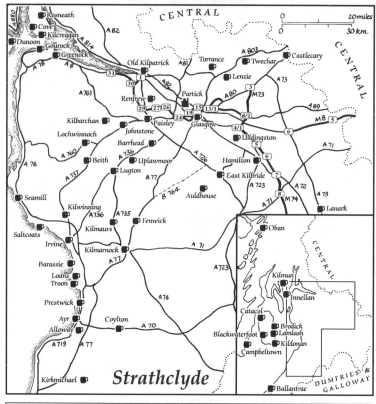

 Glaschu, Heather, Glasgow

Note: Licensing laws permit no entry after 11pm to pubs in the following locations: Barrhead, Gourock, Greenock, Houston, Johnstone, Kilbarchan, Lochwinnoch, Paisley, Renfrew and Uplawmoor.

Alloway

Balgarth
Dunure Road (A719, at Doonfoot, S of Ayr)
☎ (01292) 442441
11 (12.30 Sun)–11 (midnight Fri & Sat)
Whitbread Boddingtons Bitter, Flowers Original; guest beer Ⓗ
Former country hotel opposite a popular garden centre, well refurbished into a Brewer's Fayre pub/restaurant. The main bar features prints of sporting activities. Children's certificate – families welcome. Food available all day.
⚅ Q ☎ ✿ ◑ ▶ & P ⊁

Auldhouse

Auldhouse Arms
6 Langlands Road (from E Kilbride, right from Strathaven road, follow signs) OS624502

☎ (0135 52) 63242
11–2.30, 5–11; 11–midnight Fri & Sat; 12.30–11 Sun
Belhaven 80/–; guest beer Ⓐ
Traditional village pub with side rooms warmed by well-fed fires. The handpump on the bar activates an air pressure pump. The recently-opened modern lounge houses the guest beer. ⚅ ✿ ◑ ▶ P

Ayr

Burrowfields
13 Beresford Terrace
☎ (01292) 269152
11–midnight (12.30am Fri & Sat)
Ind Coope Burton Ale; Tetley Bitter; guest beer Ⓗ
Pleasant, wood-panelled café-bar in a corner location in the town centre. Formerly an insurance office, it has been converted tastefully in Art Deco style. Very handy for the station. ◑ & ⇌

Chestnuts Hotel
52 Racecourse Road (A719, S of centre) ☎ (01292) 264393
11 (12 Sun)–midnight
Draught Bass; Broughton Special; guest beers Ⓗ
Comfortable lounge bar with a vaulted ceiling and a collection of over 300 water jugs. Excellent bar meals. Children's certificate.
⚅ Q ✿ ⊨ ◑ ▶ P ⊁

Geordie's Byre
103 Main Street (over river towards Prestwick)
☎ (01292) 264925
11 (12.30 Sun)–11 (midnight Thu–Sat)
Caledonian Deuchars IPA, 80/–; guest beers Ⓐ
Excellent, friendly, traditional pub. The back lounge (open weekends) features a collection of Victoriana and bric-a-brac. The three guest beers come from anywhere between Orkney and

394

Cornwall. A monthly venue for 'Poems and Pints' nights. 🍺 ⚅ ♣

Tam O'Shanter

230 High Street
☎ (01292) 611684
11 (12.30 Sun)–midnight
Beer range varies Ⓗ
Small, traditional town-centre bar which has returned to its original use after years as a Burns Museum. Note the flagstoned floor and thatched roof. Two guest beers are rotated on a regular basis. The music can be loud on occasions. ⚅ ⚅ ⇌

Wellington's

17 Wellington Square (behind seafront) ☎ (01292) 262794
11–12.30am; 12–midnight Sun
Draught Bass Ⓗ
Basement lounge bar in a Georgian square near the beach. Regular Sun eve folk sessions are held. ⚅ ▶ ♣

Ballantrae

King's Arms Hotel

40 Main Street (A77, coast road) ☎ (01465) 831202
11–12.30am; 12–midnight Sun
Beer range varies Ⓗ
Comfortable village hotel on the main route between Central Scotland and Northern Ireland, close to the seafront. Up to three guest beers are stocked. Children's certificate. 🛏 ❀ ⇦ ⚅ ▶ 🍺 P

Barassie

Tower Hotel

23 Beach Road (B748, seafront N of Troon) ☎ (01292) 311142
11 (12.30 Sun)–12.30am
Draught Bass, M&B Highgate Dark; guest beers Ⓗ
Attractive hotel with two bars and a restaurant, but no accommodation. Fine views over the Firth of Clyde to Arran. Real ale is available in both bars, but the beer range may be reduced in winter. Children's certificate.
Q ❀ ⚅ ▶ 🍺 ⇌ ♣ P

Barrhead

Cross Stobs Inn

4 Grahamston Road
☎ (0141) 881 1581
11–midnight (11.45 Sat, 11 Sun)
Courage Directors; guest beer Ⓗ
Roadside pub in the form of a coaching inn. Glass panelling provides a separate lounge bar. Friendly and efficient staff. ❀ 🍺 P

Beith

Anderson Hotel

17 Eglinton Street (B7049, S of centre) ☎ (01505) 502034
11–midnight (1am Thu–Sat)
John Smith's Magnet Ⓗ
Small hotel in the town centre, which prides itself on its home-cooked food. A second real ale is planned for the public bar. A rare John Smith's outlet in Ayrshire.
🛏 Q ⇦ ⚅ ▶ ♣ 🍴

Blackwaterfoot

Kinloch Hotel

☎ (01770) 860444
11.30 (12 Sun)–midnight (1am Thu–Sat);
Courage Directors; Whitbread Boddingtons Bitter; guest beer Ⓐ
Prominent hotel on the seafront with good views of the Kintyre peninsula. Recently modernised, it has a swimming pool, squash court and other leisure facilities, all open to the public.
⇦ ⚅ ▶ 🍺 ⚅ ▲ P

Brodick

Brodick Bar

Alma Road (behind post office) ☎ (01770) 302169
11–midnight; closed Sun
Beer range varies Ⓗ
Modernised public and lounge bars in a single-storey building close to the seafront.
⚅ ▶ 🍺 ⚅ ▲ P

Campbeltown

Ardshiel Hotel

Kilkerran Road
☎ (01586) 552133
11–2.30, 5–midnight
S&N Theakston XB *or* **guest beer** Ⓗ
Family-run hotel on the beautiful South Kintyre peninsula. Children welcome. Q ⚡ ❀ ⇦ ⚅ ▶ P

Commercial Inn

Cross Street ☎ (01586) 553703
11 (12.30 Sun)–1am
Caledonian Deuchars IPA; guest beers Ⓗ
Superb, friendly, family-run pub, very popular with locals and most welcoming to visitors. It has an increasing commitment to cask beers with a good guest beer range. 🍺

Castlecary

Castlecary House Hotel

Main Street (off A80)
☎ (01324) 840233

11 (12.30 Sun)–11 (11.30 Thu–Sat)
Draught Bass; Belhaven 80/-; Caledonian Deuchars IPA; guest beers Ⓗ
Small private hotel with three drinking areas. The village is on the site of one of the major Roman forts along the Antonine Wall. The Castlecary Arches – a large viaduct carrying the main Glasgow–Edinburgh railway line – are nearby. Q ⇦ ⚅ ▶ 🍺 P

Catacol

Catacol Bay Hotel

☎ (01770) 830231
11–midnight (1am Thu–Sat)
Ruddles Best Bitter; John Smith's Magnet; guest beer Ⓗ
Seafront hotel with superb views to Kintyre. Originally a manse when built in the 19th century, next to the Twelve Apostles, an unusual listed terrace of houses. Wheelchair access is via the garden.
🛏 ❀ ⚅ ▶ ⚅ P

Cove

Knockderry Hotel

204 Shore Road (B833)
☎ (01436) 842283
11–midnight; 12–11 Sun
S&N Theakston Best Bitter, XB; guest beer Ⓗ
Fine example of Victorian architecture, situated on the picturesque Rosneath peninsula. The wood-panelled lounge bar offers superb views over Loch Long. Local CAMRA 1994 *Pub of the Year*.
🛏 ❀ ⇦ ⚅ ▶ ♣ P

Coylton

Finlayson Arms Hotel

Hillhead (A70, 4 miles E of Ayr) ☎ (01292) 570298
11–2.30, 5–midnight (12.30am Fri);
11–12.30am Sat; 12.30–midnight Sun
Belhaven Sandy Hunter's Ale; Broughton Special; guest beer (summer) Ⓗ
Village inn, ideally positioned for the Burns Heritage Trail. The comfortable lounge has a log fire. Children's certificate. 🛏 Q ❀ ⇦ ⚅ ▶ 🍺 P

Dunoon

Lorne Bar

249 Argyll Street (A815)
☎ (01369) 705064
11 (12.30 Sun)–midnight (1am Fri & Sat)
Draught Bass; guest beers Ⓗ
Small, traditional public bar, and a modern comfortable lounge. Special high tea is served every day. Live music Fri and Sat eve. Dunoon's only real ale pub. 🛏 ⚅ ▶ ⚅ ♣

Strathclyde

East Kilbride

East Kilbride Sports Club
Torrance Avenue. Strathaven road (follow signs for country park) ☎ (0135 52) 36001
11 (12.30 Sun)–11 (midnight Fri & Sat)
Caledonian Deuchars IPA; guest beers Ⓗ
Private club offering a wide variety of sporting activities within the exquisite setting of Calderglen Country Park. Show the *Guide* or a CAMRA membership card to get signed in. The club president runs a beer agency. Beer festivals sometimes held. Weekend lunches served. ⑤ ❀ ⓓ P

Fenwick

King's Arms
89 Main Road (B7061, just off A77) ☎ (01560) 600276
12.45–3, 5–midnight; 11–midnight Fri & Sat; 12.30–midnight Sun
Beer range varies Ⓐ
Fine village inn on the edge of moorland. A listed building with an unusual exterior, it has been recently renovated, retaining original features. The new lounge is now a meals area. The bar features artwork by a well-known local cartoonist. A bus service passes. Children's certificate. ⓓ ▮ ⊟ ዼ ♣ P

Glasgow

Aragon
131 Byres Road ☎ (0141) 339 3252
11 (12.30 Sun)–11 (11.45 Fri & Sat)
Beer range varies Ⓗ
Small T&J Bernard's chain pub in the heart of the West End, drawing a mixed clientele. ⊖ (Kelvinhall) ⓒ

Athena Taverna
780 Pollokshaws Road ☎ (0141) 424 0858
11–2.30, 5–11; closed Sun
Belhaven 80/-; guest beers Ⓐ
Modern-style, single-bar café attached to a Greek restaurant, selling an excellent range of five guest ales, plus a good choice of Belgian and German bottled beers. The bar has an unusual goldfish bowl effect and can be extremely busy weekend eves. ⓓ ▮ ⇌ (Queen's Pk)

Babbity Bowster
16–18 Blackfriars Street ☎ (0141) 552 5055
11 (12.30 Sun)–midnight
Maclay 70/-, 80/-, Kane's Amber Ale; guest beers Ⓐ
Distinctive bar where café-style furniture and tall windows provide an airy feel; a definitely Scottish pub though, whose regulars include folk musicians. Open for food from 8am.
⌸ Q ❀ ⨝ ⓓ ▮ ⇌ (High St) ⓒ P

Blackfriars
36 Bell Street ☎ (0141) 552 5924
11 (12.30 Sun)–midnight
Alloa Arrol's 80/-; Caledonian Deuchars IPA; Ind Coope Burton Ale; Tetley Bitter; guest beers Ⓗ
Lively bar with a mostly youthful clientele. The walls are covered with posters advertising local events. Live bands three nights a week, with club nights in the downstairs bar. Draught and bottled Belgian beer.
ⓓ ▮ ⇌ (High St/Argyle St) ⓒ

Bon Accord
153 North Street ☎ (0141) 248 4427
11–11.45; 12.30–11 Sun
Beer range varies Ⓗ
One of the Victorian-style T&J Bernard's alehouses, selling six guest beers with independent breweries well-represented. Beer festivals. No food weekends, except Sat eve. ⓓ ዼ ⇌ (Charing Cross) ⓒ

Brewery Tap
1055 Sauchiehall Street ☎ (0141) 339 8866
12 (12.30 Sun)–11 (midnight Fri & Sat)
Alloa Arrol's 80/-; Belhaven 60/- Ⓐ; **Ind Coope Burton Ale** Ⓗ; **Tetley Bitter** Ⓐ; **guest beers** Ⓐ / Ⓗ
Lively two-roomed pub across from Kelvingrove Park; very busy eves. Live music at weekends. A small selection of Belgian and German traditional beers is stocked, plus three guest ales. Friendly and efficient staff.
❀ ⓓ ⊖ (Kelvinhall) ⓒ

Dr Thirsty's Alehouse
65 Old Dumbarton Road ☎ (0141) 334 4197
11 (12.30 Sun)–11 (midnight Fri & Sat)
Draught Bass; Maclay 80/-; Taylor Landlord; guest beer Ⓗ
Tastefully renovated tenement corner local in the West End conservation area, behind Kelvin Hall sports arena. The name is a parody on the proximity of the nearby children's and maternity hospitals. ⓓ ⊖ (Kelvinhall)

Mitre
12 Brunswick Street (off Trongate) ☎ (0141) 552 3764
11–midnight (11 Tue & Wed); 12.30–8 Sun

Belhaven 60/-, 80/-, St Andrew's Ale; guest beer Ⓗ
Small, basic and friendly pub just off the busy Trongate. Unspoilt, original (1866) decor includes a mini-horseshoe bar and dividing screens. Selection of bottled Belgian beers; reasonably priced food (eve meals finish at 6).
ⓓ ▮ ⊟ ⇌ (Argyle St) ⊖ (St Enoch)

Ritz
241 North Street ☎ (0141) 226 4419
11–midnight; 6.30–11 Sun
McEwan 80/-; Marston's Pedigree; S&N Theakston Best Bitter, Old Peculier; Younger No. 3; guest beers Ⓗ
Busy city-centre bar, popular with office workers in the afternoon, and virtually unchanged since becoming a T&J Bernard's pub group member. Well worth a visit to see the original woodwork and interior. Three guest ales. ⓓ ⇌ (Charing Cross) ⊖ (St George's Cross) ⓒ

State Bar
148 Holland Street ☎ (0141) 332 2159
11 (12.30 Sun)–midnight
McEwan 80/-; S&N Theakston Best Bitter, Newcastle Exhibition; Younger No. 3; guest beers Ⓗ
Modern city-centre bar hosting live folk music twice a week, plus beer festivals. Good quality food – try the legendary hot dogs. Much frequented by the local business clientele, and trendy students at weekends. ⓓ ⇌ (Charing Cross) ⊖ (Cowcaddens/Buchanan St)

Station Bar
55 Port Dundas Road, Cowcaddens ☎ (0141) 332 3117
11–midnight; 12.30–11 Sun
Caledonian Deuchars IPA; guest beers Ⓗ
Friendly, street-corner local, popular with office workers at lunchtime. Friendly staff. A real gem; not to be missed. ⇌ (Queen St) ⊖ (Cowcaddens)

Three Judges
141 Dumbarton Road ☎ (0141) 337 3055
11 (12.30 Sun)–11 (midnight Fri & Sat)
Maclay 80/-, Wallace IPA; guest beers Ⓗ
Busy, lively West End saloon bar, serving over 700 guest ales (six at a time) in three years. Current holder and frequent past winner of the local CAMRA *Landlord* and *Pub of the Year* awards. Fast and friendly service. An

absolute must. & ≠ (Partick)
⊖ (Kelvinhall) ☼

Ubiquitous Chip

12 Ashton Lane, Hillhead
(behind underground station)
☎ (0141) 334 5007
11 (12.30 Sun)–11 (midnight Fri & Sat)
**Caledonian Deuchars IPA,
80/-** Ⓐ
Often busy bar above a
famous restaurant. Open
rafters and wooden furniture
help provide a different
atmosphere to the more
frenetic bar nearby. Good
selection of wines.
♨ Q ◖ ▶ ⊖ (Hillhead) ☼

Victoria Bar

157 Bridgegate
☎ (0141) 552 6040
11 (12.30 Sun)–midnight
**Maclay 70/-, 80/-, Kane's
Amber Ale, Wallace IPA;
Whitbread Boddingtons
Bitter; guest beer** Ⓐ
Legendary, old, wood-
panelled bar, situated in the
oldest part of Glasgow; full of
character. Live folk music five
times a week. Q ≠ (Argyle
St) ⊖ (St Enoch)

Gourock

Spinnaker Hotel

121 Albert Road
☎ (01475) 633107
11–11.30; 12.30–11 Sun
Belhaven 80/-; guest beer Ⓐ
Small hotel on the Clyde coast,
affording excellent sea views.
The alcove bar in the airy front
room is a welcome retreat for
many locals. Full restaurant;
bar snacks and coffee available
all day. ⋈ ◖ ▶

Greenock

Argyle & Sutherland

1 Bruce Street
☎ (01475) 723582
11–midnight (1am Fri & Sat); 12.30–11
Sun
**Belhaven 80/-; S&N
Theakston Old Peculier** Ⓗ
Victorian workingman's pub
(1831) unspoilt by
refurbishment and
complemented by a recent
(1993) modern bar and beer
garden, creating a 'Tardis'
effect. Well worth a visit!
❀ ◖ ⊞ & ≠ (West) P

Hamilton

George

18 Campbell Street (off
Cadzow St, 100 yds from
Bottom Cross)
☎ (01698) 424225
11–11.45; 6.30–11 Sun
**Maclay 80/-, Oat Malt Stout;
guest beer** Ⓗ

Small family-run pub with a
friendly atmosphere. CAMRA
Lanarkshire *Pub of the Year* for
the past two years. Somewhat
difficult to find, but well worth
the effort. ◖ ≠ (Central) ⅃

Houston

Fox & Hounds

1 South Street
11 (12.30 Sun)–midnight (11.45 Sat)
**Broughton Greenmantle Ale;
Caledonian Deuchars IPA;
Whitbread Boddingtons
Bitter** Ⓗ
Lively country pub in a rural
village now easily accessible
from the M8 motorway.
Excellent restaurant with full à
la carte menu, plus bar food,
regular summer beer festivals
(in a marquee) and barbecues.
A Maclay beer is also sold.
❀ ◖ ▶ ⊞ & P

Innellan

Braemar Hotel

Shore Road (A815, 4 miles S of
Dunoon) ☎ (01369) 830792
12 (12.30 Sun)–midnight
**Whitbread Flowers
Original** Ⓗ
Built in the 19th century as the
superb seaside home of textile
magnate JP Coates, this hotel
boasts a splendid view over
the Firth of Clyde from its
large outdoor seating area. A
children's play area and
practice cricket nets are
available.
⛱ ❀ ⋈ ◖ ▶ & ♣ P

Irvine

Ship Inn

120–122 Harbour Street (next
to Magnum Leisure Centre)
☎ (01294) 279722
11–2.30, 5–midnight (1am Fri);
11–1am Sat; 12.30–11 Sun
S&N Theakston Best Bitter Ⓗ
Harbourside pub, the oldest
licensed premises in town,
renowned for its well-cooked
and good value meals. Quiet
lunchtime and early eve, it
gets rather lively later on. See
the local scenes drawn on the
ceiling. Children's certificate.
Q ⛱ ❀ ◖ ▶ & ≠

Turf Hotel

32–34 Eglinton Street
☎ (01294) 275836
11–midnight (1am Fri & Sat); 12.30–11
Sun
**S&N Theakston Best Bitter;
guest beer** (occasional) Ⓗ
Totally unspoilt, traditional
Scottish bar, with a lounge to
the rear which has its own
character. Quite cosmopolitan
at lunchtime, when quality
lunches of amazing value are
served, it is more of a local at
night. ♨ ◖ ⊞ ♣

Johnstone

Coanes

26 High Street
☎ (01505) 322925
11–11.30 (1am Fri, 11.45 Sat); 6.30–11
Sun
**Draught Bass; Caledonian
Deuchars IPA; Orkney Dark
Island; Whitbread
Boddingtons Bitter; guest
beers** Ⓗ
Comfortable town-centre pub
with a relaxing atmosphere.
The bar is wood-panelled and
the lounge is open-plan. Both
drinking areas are decorated
with period pictures and
memorabilia. Nine ales on tap.
No food Sun. ◖ ⊞ ≠ ♣ *

Kilbarchan

Trust Inn

8 Low Barholm
☎ (01505) 72401
11–midnight (11.45 Sat, 11 Sun)
Beer range varies Ⓗ
Traditional pub in a former
weaving village; a comfortable
lounge with cosy nooks,
beamed ceiling and decorative
brasses: a popular local. The
beers are from the Alloa range.
◖ ▶ ≠ (Milliken Pk)

Kilcreggan

Kilcreggan Hotel

Argyll Road (600 yds from
B833) ☎ (01436) 842243
11–midnight (1am Fri & Sat)
**Orkney Dark Island; S&N
Theakston Best Bitter;
Younger No. 3; guest beer** Ⓗ
Friendly, well-run, family
hotel offering good views over
the Firth of Clyde; only five
mins' walk from the Gourock
Ferry. Live entertainment is
staged in the lounge Sat eve.
Children's certificate (toys
available). Eve meals finish at
8.45. Real ale is served in the
lounge but can be brought
through to the bar. ♨ Q ⛱
❀ ⋈ ◖ ▶ ⊞ ♣ ♣ P

Kildonan

Breadalbane Hotel

On village loop road
☎ (01770) 820284
11–midnight (1am Thu–Sat)
Draught Bass Ⓗ
Friendly seaside hotel in a
quiet village off the beaten
track, with superb scenic
views.
♨ ⛱ ❀ ⋈ ◖ ▶ & ♣ P

Kilmarnock

Hunting Lodge

14–16 Glencairn Square (opp.
Safeway) ☎ (01563) 522920

11–3, 5–midnight; 11–12.30am Fri & Sat; 12.30–midnight Sun
Draught Bass; Broughton Greenmantle Ale; Caledonian 80/-; guest beers Ⓗ
The biggest selection of real ales in the area is served in this pub's attractive Malty Hop lounge. An additional ten handpumps are used for mini-festivals. The venue for the local folk club (Thu), quizzes (Mon) and occasional ceilidhs. Children's certificate.
◐ ◑ ⊟ ⅟

Kilmaurs

Weston Tavern
27 Main Street (A735)
☎ (01563) 538805
11 (12.30 Sun)–midnight
Beer range varies Ⓗ
In an historic conservation area next to the 'Jougs', this pub dates back to 1500 or earlier. The partly tiled floor is a listed feature. A low-beamed panelled games area and a craggy stoneworked bar add to its charm. The rear lounge is for families and meetings. Book eve meals.
Q ꝏ ◐ ◑ ⊟ ♿ ⇌ ♣ P ⊞

Kilmun

Coylet Inn
Loch Eck (A815, 9 miles N of Dunoon) ☎ (01369) 840426
11 (12.30 Sun)–2.30, 6.30–11 (5–midnight Fri & Sat)
Caledonian Deuchars IPA; McEwan 80/-; Younger No. 3 Ⓔ
Attractive and inviting lochside bar where you can relax around the open fire after a day's fishing, touring or walking in the hills. The setting for the film *The Blue Boy*. Good bar food.
🔥 ❀ 🛏 ◐ ◑ ▲ P

Kilwinning

Claremont Hotel
67 Byres Road (A738)
☎ (01294) 558445
12–2.30, 5–midnight (1am Fri); 12–1am Sat; 12–midnight Sun
Beer range varies Ⓗ
Attractive, comfortable lounge in a small hotel right next to the station. Three guest beers, two from the Scottish Brewers list and one free of tie. The traditional Scottish bar has longer opening hours, but no real ale. Children's certificate.
🛏 ◐ ◑ ⊟ ♿ ⇌ P

Kirkmichael

Kirkmichael Arms
3 Straiton Road
☎ (01655) 750375
11–2.30, 5–11; 11–11 Fri, Sat & summer; 12.30–11 Sun
Beer range varies Ⓗ
Rural gem with low ceilings, set in a conservation village. The comfortable lounge and small bar are made cosy by a real fire. Children's certificate. Excellent value home-cooked meals. 🔥 ◐ ◑ ⊟

Lamlash

Pier Head Tavern
☎ (01770) 600380
9am (12.30 Sun)–midnight (1am Thu–Sat)
Draught Bass; guest beer Ⓗ
Seafront pub known locally as the PHT. Generous opening hours make it a popular starting place for local boaters and yachtsmen. Handy for Arran Rugby Club. 🔥 ◐ ◑ P

Lanark

Horse & Jockey
56 High Street
☎ (01555) 664825
11–1am (midnight Sat); 12.30–11 Sun
Beer choice varies Ⓗ
Friendly, unpretentious town-centre local, whose name commemorates Lanark's former association with horse racing. Real ale in the public bar only. ◐ ⊟ ⇌

Lenzie

Carriages
Millersneuk Shopping Centre, Millersneuk Avenue
☎ (0141) 777 7611
11 (12.30 Sun)–midnight (1am Fri)
Broughton Greenmantle Ale; guest beer Ⓗ
Comfortable lounge bar in a modern shopping centre, a local oasis run by the nephews of a former owner of Glasgow's legendary Bon Accord. ◐ ⇌ P

Loans

Bruce Inn
31–33 Main Street (A759)
☎ (01292) 315976
11 (12.30 Sun)–midnight (12.30am Fri)
Draught Bass Ⓗ; guest beer Ⓔ
Smart village bar and restaurant in the centre of Loans. Real ale is available in both; constantly changing guest beer. Q ꝏ ◐ ◑ ♿ ♣ P

Lochwinnoch

Brown Bull
33 Main Street
☎ (01505) 843250
11 (12.30 Sun)–11 (midnight Fri, 11.45 Sat)
Belhaven Sandy Hunter's Ale; Orkney Dark Island; guest beers Ⓗ
Excellent country pub with real hop flowers lavishly adorning the bar gantry. Note the 1930s telephone (sadly not working). The pub was used in filming the TV series *Dr Finlay*. Well worth a visit. Step through the door and backwards in time. 🔥 ❀ ♿

Mossend

Largs Road ☎ (01505) 842672
11–11
Whitbread Boddingtons Bitter, Flowers Original; guest beers Ⓗ
Brewer's Fayre stereotype, ideal for families, with a children's play area. Occasional mini-beer festivals with an outdoor marquee and barbecue. Bouncy castle in summer when more guest beers are available. A bird sanctuary and a water sports centre are nearby.
❀ ◐ ◑ ♿ ⇌ P

Lugton

Paraffin Lamp
1 Beith Road (A736/B777 jct)
☎ (01505) 850510
11 (12.30 Sun)–11
Marston's Pedigree; Whitbread Boddingtons Bitter, Castle Eden Ale, Flowers Original; guest beer Ⓗ
Whitbread Brewer's Fayre country eatery with a separate bar. Food is available all day. The real ale choice has increased recently; the guest beer is from the Whitbread range. Popular with families as children are well catered for (certificate). Q ❀ ◐ ◑ ♿ ♣ P

Oban

Caledonian Hotel
Queens Park Place
☎ (01631) 563133
11–11
Caledonian 80/- Ⓗ
Grand Victorian seafront hotel next to the station and the islands ferry terminal, with a large, plush, open-plan lounge. ❀ 🛏 ◐ ◑ ♿ ⇌

Lorne Hotel
Stevenson Street
☎ (01631) 566766
11–1am
S&N Theakston Best Bitter; guest beers Ⓗ
Hotel boasting a lively, busy locals' bar and a pleasant, modern lounge with a snug. A marble-topped island bar and a gleaming Italian coffee machine are features. Occasional live rock bands.
🛏 ◐ ◑ ♿ ⇌

Old Kilpatrick

Ettrick
159 Dumbarton Road (A814)
☎ (01389) 72821
11 (12.30 Sun)–11.30 (midnight Thu–Sat)
S&N Theakston Best Bitter; Younger No. 3; guest beer Ⓗ
Traditional village local (estd. 1893) with a horseshoe-shaped public bar, named after the Ettrick shepherd, James Hogg, a friend of Sir Walter Scott and a famed poet in his own right. The pub is close to Erskine Bridge. No smoking in the lounge during the day. ⚘ Ɑ ⬥ ⟰ (Kilpatrick) ♦ ⚲

Paisley

Abbey Bar
8 Lawn Street
☎ (0141) 839 8451
11–midnight (1am Fri, 11.45 Sat, 11 Sun)
McEwan 80/- Ⓗ
Small town tavern, situated across from the magnificent Paisley Abbey, with a cosy, homely atmosphere. Live music Fri and Sat; wide range of social events. No food Sun. Ɑ ⟰ (Gilmour St)

Bar Point
42 Wellmeadow Street
☎ (0141) 889 5188
11 (12.30 Sun)–11 (midnight Thu, 1am Fri, 11.45 Sat)
Beer range varies Ⓗ
Fine modern pub which has matured through its 18 years. Good food, exotic entertainment and a club atmosphere are features, thanks to its illustrious owner. The beer range (from Belhaven) is restricted due to cellar size. ⚘ Ɑ ▶ ⬥

Gabriel's
33 Gauze Street (Silk St jct)
☎ (0141) 887 8204
11–midnight (1am Fri, 11.45 Sat, 11 Sun)
Caledonian Deuchars IPA; Orkney Dark Island; guest beers Ⓗ
Pub with a large, oval-shaped central bar. Period advertising on the walls serves as a reminder of Britain's manufacturing heyday. Regular beer festivals. Friendly and efficient staff. Children's certificate. Ɑ ▶

Lord Lounsdale
Lounsdale Road
☎ (0141) 889 6263
11–midnight (11.45 Sat, 11 Sun)
Draught Bass Ⓗ**; Broughton Greenmantle Ale** Ⓐ
Mock hunting lodge with fake oak beams. It can get very busy. Excellent food.
⚘ Ɑ ▶ ⬚ ⬥ P

RH Finlay's
33 Causeyside Street
☎ (0141) 889 9036
11–midnight (1am Fri, 11.45 Sat); 12–11 Sun
Draught Bass; guest beer Ⓗ
Two friendly lounge bars furnished to a high standard and serving quality bar lunches. Located in the town centre; an ideal meeting place. Ɑ ⟰ (Gilmour St/Canal St)

Tannahills
100 Neilston Road (opp. South Primary School)
☎ (0141) 889 2491
11–11 (midnight Thu & Fri, 11.45 Sat)
Caledonian Deuchars IPA Ⓐ
Pub where the bar is in the form of a house, complete with roof tiles. Pictures of old Paisley and the poet Robert Tannahill adorn the walls. Friendly atmosphere. Ɑ

Wee Howff
53 High Street
☎ (0141) 889 2095
11–11 (11.30 Fri & Sat); closed Sun
Ind Coope Burton Ale; Tetley Bitter; guest beers Ⓗ
Long, narrow bar with a mock Tudor interior, popular with students from the university. The publican was the first Burton *Master Cellarman* in Scotland. Friendly and efficient bar staff. Its 12th appearance in the *Guide*.
⟰ (Gilmour St) ♦

Prestwick

Parkstone Hotel
6–8 Ardayre Road
☎ (01292) 477286
11 (12.30 Sun)–12.30am (midnight Sun)
Belhaven 80/- Ⓗ
Comfortable lounge bar in a seafront hotel with views over to Arran; a long-established outlet for Belhaven, and definitely the best bet in Prestwick. Children's certificate. ⚌ Q ⚘ ⬚ Ɑ ▶
⟰ (Town) P

Renfrew

Ferry Inn
1 Clyde Street
☎ (0141) 886 2104
11 (12.30 Sun)–11 (1am Fri, 11.45 Sat)
Beer range varies Ⓗ
Riverside local for cyclists, dogs and ex-radio presenters. Photographs of past and present Clyde shipping adorn the walls. ⚌

Tap & Spile
Terminal Building, Glasgow Airport ☎ (0141) 848 4869
8am (12.30 Sun)–11 (1am Fri, 11.45 Sat)

Beer range varies Ⓗ
Stained-glass adds a traditional touch to this busy lounge at Glasgow's international airport. One-third pints are available. The beer range doubles to eight ales in summer. ⬥ ⚲

Rosneath

Rosneath Bistro
Rosneath Castle Holiday Park, near Helensburgh (1 mile from B833) ☎ (01436) 831333
11.30–2.30, 5.30–11 (11–11 summer); 11–midnight Fri & Sat; 12.30–11 Sun
Beer range varies Ⓗ
Newly-refurbished bistro bar on the picturesque Rosneath peninsula, providing a superb holiday base for campers and caravanners. A merry-go-round of Harviestoun beers is available. Children's certificate. Eve meals finish at 8.45. Q ⚘ Ɑ ▶ ⬥ ⚷ ♦ P

Saltcoats

Hip Flask
13 Winton Street (near seafront) ☎ (01294) 465222
11–midnight (1am Thu–Sat)
Belhaven St Andrew's Ale; guest beer Ⓗ
Small café-bar, well-placed for both the town centre and the beach, with a friendly atmosphere. The raised seating area can double as a small stage. Live music and quizzes some eves. Good value food. Newspapers and magazines supplied. Children's certificate. ⚘ Ɑ ▶

Seamill

Waterside Inn
Ardrossan Road (A78)
☎ (01294) 823238
11–midnight (1am Fri & Sat); 12.30–11 Sun
Marston's Pedigree; Whitbread Boddingtons Bitter; guest beers Ⓗ
Former run-down seaside hotel transformed into a Brewer's Fayre pub/restaurant, right on the beach with wonderful sea views. A summer beer festival is held in a marquee. Food available all day. Children's certificate. ⚘ Ɑ ▶ ♦ P

Torrance

Wheatsheaf Inn
77 Main Street
☎ (01360) 620374
11 (12.30 Sun)–midnight
Belhaven 70/-; guest beer Ⓗ
Busy village local with a fine display of old brewery mirrors and windows. Children welcome until 8.
⚌ ⚷ ⚘ Ɑ ▶ ⬚ P

Strathclyde

Troon

Harbour Bar
169 Templehill (B749, to harbour) ☎ (01292) 312668
11–12.30am; 12.30–midnight Sun
Broughton Greenmantle Ale; Greene King Abbot; guest beers Ⓗ
Friendly local with a lounge area and a games room served from the same bar; near the marina with views over the Firth of Clyde. Nautical prints are a feature. ⊁ ⊞ ⅋ ♣ P

McKay's
69 Portland Street (A759)
☎ (01292) 311079
11–12.30am; 12.30–midnight Sun
Maclay 80/- ; Ⓔ; Whitbread Boddingtons Bitter Ⓗ; **guest beers** Ⓔ
Popular, town-centre lounge bar which can get very busy Sat night. A constant rotation of guest beers includes four ales dispensed by electric handpump. ⊛ ⅅ ⇌

Piersland House Hotel
15 Craigend Road (B749)
☎ (01292) 314747
11–midnight
Broughton Greenmantle Ale; Courage Directors; Ruddles County; guest beer Ⓗ
Fine three-star hotel overlooking Royal Troon Golf Course. Good reputation for food. Beer prices tend to reflect the quality of the hotel. Croquet played.
⋈ Q ⊛ ⊞ ⅅ ▶ ⅍ ♣ P ⊟

Twechar

Quarry Inn
Main Street ☎ (01236) 821496
11–11.30 (1am Fri); 12.30–11 Sun
Maclay 70/-; Wallace IPA; guest beers Ⓗ
Extremely popular village local with an unchanged, friendly atmosphere, in a former mining community. An annual beer festival in Oct offers some 25 beers. Note the brewery mirrors. A real basic gem of a boozer! Other Maclay and guest beers sold.
⋈ ⊞ ♣ P

Uddingston

Rowan Tree
60 Old Mill Road
☎ (01698) 812678
11–11.45; 12.30–11 Sun
Maclay 80/-; guest beers Ⓗ
Pub featuring an unspoilt wooden interior with a fireplace at both ends of the bar, an abundance of brewery mirrors, and a stained-glass phone booth. It's reputed to be haunted by a stable lad who was kicked by a horse here when it was a coaching inn. Children welcome lunchtime. Maclay seasonal ales stocked.
⋈ ⊁ ⅅ ⇌ P

Uplawmoor

Uplawmoor Hotel
66 Neilston Road (off A736, Barrhead–Irvine road)
☎ (01505) 850565
12–2.30, 5–11 (midnight Fri);
12–midnight Sat; 12.30–11 Sun
Draught Bass; S&N Theakston Best Bitter Ⓗ
Village hotel: a comfortable lounge and a large, airy cocktail bar/restaurant with a central feature fireplace. Not easily accessible, but well worth the effort.
⋈ ⊁ ⊛ ⅅ ▶ ⅍ P

PRICE INSENSITIVE

It is the law that all licensed premises must prominently display a representative sample of their drink prices. Not that you'd know that by visiting some pubs. As CAMRA annual prices surveys repeatedly reveal, hundreds of pubs around the country openly flout the law by not placing a price list on show.

Others try to bend the rules by tucking the price list away around a corner of the bar, or by printing it small and only pinning it to the back of the bar where not even eagle-eyed drinkers can easily read the information. At a time when beer prices are continuing to soar ahead, this, clearly, is not good enough.

An even worse evil seems to have reared its ugly head in recent months. New electronic point of sale equipment in some houses enables bar staff to adjust prices at the flick of a switch. This technology has proved to be a useful asset where 'happy hours' have been introduced, saving time and complication in resetting tills. However, in some outlets, this gadgetry has been employed to *raise* prices on weekend evenings or at other peak times, allowing the pub to charge up to 30p or more extra per pint, without always informing the customer first. This sleight of hand is clearly designed to take advantage of young 'circuit' followers who drink in rounds in noisy, busy pubs and who are less inclined to check their change.

CAMRA would remind publicans engaged in this sort of practice that unless price lists on display are amended at the same time as the tills are reprogrammed, they are falling foul of the law. Trading standards officers will no doubt take an interest in such cases.

Tayside

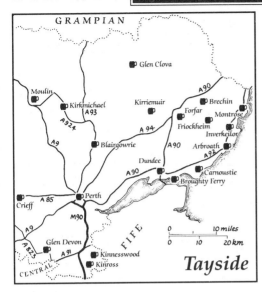

Best Bitter, XB; guest beers Ⓐ
Modernised, sensibly
partitioned, one-room bar.
Extremely busy late eve and at
weekends. Occasional beer
festivals. Eve meals in
summer. No-smoking area
mealtimes. Family room
lunchtime. ⍭ ◖ ▶ ⅋
⇌ (limited service) ♣ ⚇

Carnoustie

Morven Hotel
West Path ☎ (01241) 852385
11–2.30, 4.30–11 (midnight Fri);
11–midnight Sat; 12.30–11 Sun
Beer range varies Ⓗ
After some changes, this
popular small hotel is now
back on form. Four ales.
Q ⍭ ⇴ ▲ ⇌ (Golf St) P ⎅

Crieff

Oakbank Inn
Turret Bridge (by Lady Mary's
Walk) ☎ (01764) 652420
6–11 Mon–Wed; 12–3, 6–11 Thu; 12–3,
6–11.45 Fri; 12–11.45 Sat; 12.30–11
Sun (12–11 (11.45 Sat) summer)
Belhaven 80/- Ⓗ
Popular bar with families and
locals alike. A 500-year-old
tree in the grounds provides
the name. Close to Glenturret
Distillery. ⚇ ◖ ▶ ▲ ♣ P

Dundee

Frew's Bar
117 Strathmartine Road (opp.
Coldside library)
☎ (01382) 810975
11–11.45; 12.30–11 Sun
Draught Bass Ⓗ
Friendly corner bar retaining
traditional features; close to
both football grounds.
⊞ ⅊

Galleon Bar
2 Whitehall Crescent (near
City Sq) ☎ (01382) 224376
10–midnight; 12–11 Sun
Caledonian 80/-; Ind Coope
Burton Ale; Orkney Dark
Island; guest beers Ⓗ
Large pub with a sitting area
upstairs and a function suite.
Curios from around the world
provide decor. Beer festivals
held. ◖ ▶ ⇌

Mickey Coyle's
21–23 Old Hawkhill
☎ (01382) 225871
11–11.30; 7–11 Sun
Draught Bass Ⓗ; Broughton
Greenmantle Ale; S&N
Newcastle Exhibition Ⓐ;
Whitbread Boddingtons
Bitter Ⓗ; Younger No.3 Ⓐ;
guest beers
Very popular, L-shaped bar
close to the university.
Frequented by students and
locals alike. ◖ ▶ ⅊ ⇌

Arbroath

Lochland
14–16 Lochlands Street (100
yds W of station)
☎ (01241) 873286
11–11 (including Sun)
Draught Bass; Ruddles
County Ⓗ
Welcoming town bar with an
active social life; noisy and
smoky when in full swing. The
beers may change. ◖ ⊞ ⇌ ♣

Victoria
12 Catherine Street (between
rail and bus stations)
☎ (01241) 874589
11–2.30, 5–11; 11–midnight Fri & Sat;
12.30–6 Sun
S&N Theakston Best Bitter;
guest beers Ⓗ
Pub offering two ales in the
spartan, but welcoming, bar,
and one in the lounge (orders
brought through).
⊞ ▲ ⇌ ♣

Blairgowrie

Kintrae House Hotel
Balmoral Road, Rattray (A93,
N side of town)
☎ (01250) 872106
11–2.30, 5.30–11 (11.45 Fri & Sat);
12–3, 6.30–11 Sun
Beer range varies Ⓗ
Lounge bar in a small hotel.
The hours may be extended at
weekends May–Aug and the
pub sometimes closes lunchtime out of season (check).
Two ales. ⚔ Q ⇴ ◖ ▶ P

Stormont Arms
101 Perth Street
☎ (01250) 873142

11–3, 5–11; 11–11 Fri & Sat; 12.30–3,
6.30–11 Sun
Belhaven St Andrew's Ale;
Caledonian Golden Promise;
guest beer Ⓗ
Traditional, busy local with a
modern lounge. Large whisky
mirrors in the bar. ⊞ ♣

Brechin

Dalhousie
1 Market Street (top of High
St) ☎ (01356) 622096
11 (12.30 Sun)–11
Beer range varies Ⓗ
High-ceilinged bar with
assorted memorabilia and an
unusual, near-circular, bar
counter. Two ales. ⊞ ♣

Broughty Ferry

Fisherman's Tavern
10 Fort Street (by lifeboat
station) ☎ (01382) 775941
11–midnight; 12.30–11 Sun
Belhaven 60/-, 80/-, St
Andrew's Ale; Maclay 80/-;
Whitbread Boddingtons
Bitter; guest beers Ⓗ
In every Good Beer Guide since
Scotland was first included in
1975: national CAMRA Urban
Pub of the Year 1993. A new
lounge and a range of Belgian
beers are proving popular, but
sadly the jug and bottle is no
more. Q ⍭ ⇴ ◖ ⊞
⇌ (limited service) ♣

Old Anchor
48 Gray Street (S of station)
☎ (01382) 737899
11–11.30; 11–midnight Fri & Sat);
12.30–11 Sun
McEwan 80/-; Marston's
Pedigree; S&N Theakston

401

Tayside

Phoenix

103–105 Nethergate
☎ (01382) 200014
11–midnight; 12.30–11 Sun
Beer range varies H
Justly popular, Victorian-style
pub frequented by students
and locals: a former local
CAMRA *Pub of the Year*. Busy
Fri/Sat nights. Food all day till
7pm. Five ales. ◖ ➤ ≢ ♠

Planet Bar

161 South Road, Lochee
☎ (01382) 623258
11–11.30 (midnight Fri & Sat);
12.30–11 Sun
**Orkney Dark Island; guest
beers** H
A modern-style exterior belies
this traditional, friendly public
bar and large refurbished
lounge. A hub of sporting and
social activity. ⊞ ⚹ P

Tavern

168–172 Perth Road
☎ (01382) 227135
11–2.30, 5–11.30; 11–11.30 Wed &
Thu; 11–midnight Fri & Sat; 7–11 Sun
**Caledonian 80/-; guest
beers** H
Popular pub with both locals
and students, busy in term
time while showing live
football (Sun opening may be
brought forward for matches).
Eve meals 5–7. ◖ ▶ ⚹

Forfar

O'Hara's

41 West High Street
☎ (01307) 464350
11–2.30, 5.30–11 (midnight Fri & Sat)
Beer choice varies H
Enterprising bistro above a
small restaurant. Excellent
food. One beer. ⚏ ◖ ▶

Friockheim

Star Inn

13 Gardyne Street
☎ (01241) 828980
11–2.30, 5–11; 11–11 Fri & Sat;
12.30–11 Sun
**McEwan 80/-; S&N Theakston
Best Bitter; guest beer** H
Delightful country pub, once a
coaching inn; an oasis in rural
Angus. The village name is
pronounced 'freak'em'. ⚏ ⚹
🏠 ◖ ⊞ ≢ (Montrose) ♠

Glen Clova

Clova Hotel

On B955, 15 miles N of
Kirriemuir ☎ (01575) 550222
11–midnight; 12.30–11 Sun
**Orkney Dark Island; guest
beers** H
Real ale haven for climbers
and tourists. Easter beer
festival.
⚏ ⚏ 🏠 ◖ ▶ ⊞ ▲ P

Glen Devon

Tormaukin Hotel

☎ (01259) 781252
11–2.30, 5–11; 11–11 Fri & Sat; 12–11
Sun
**Harviestoun 80/-,
Schiehallion; Ind Coope
Burton Ale** H
Comfortable, friendly hotel
with a cosy lounge and a
restaurant. Formerly a
drovers' inn dating from 1720,
its name means 'hill of the
mountain hare'. Food all day
Sun. ⚏ Q ⚏ 🏠 ◖ ▶ ⚹ ▲ P

Inverkeilor

Chance Inn

Main Street ☎ (01241) 830308
12–2.30, 5–11; 12.30–11 Sat, Sun &
summer
Beer range varies H
Renovated public bar with a
pleasant lounge behind. Large
garden. Family room till 8pm.
⚏ ⚹ 🏠 ◖ ▶ ⊞ ⚹ ♠ P

Kinnesswood

Lomond Country Inn

Main Street ☎ (01592) 840253
11–11 (midnight Fri & Sat)
**Draught Bass; Caledonian
Deuchars IPA; Jennings
Bitter** H
Popular inn with an open-plan
restaurant and bar, and fine
views over Loch Leven.
⚏ Q ⚹ ⚹ 🏠 ◖ ▶ ⚹ ▲ P ⚹

Kinross

Kirklands Hotel

High Street ☎ (01577) 863313
11.30–2.30, 5–11 (11.30 Fri & Sat);
12.30–11 Sun
**Maclay 80/-; Whitbread
Flowers Original; guest
beer** H
Small, comfortable hotel. The
public bar is popular with
locals. Q 🏠 ◖ ▶ ⊞ ⚹ P ⚹

Muirs Inn

49 The Muirs (N of town on
Milnathort road)
☎ (01577) 862270
11–2.30, 5–11 (11.45 Fri); 11–11.45 Sat;
12.30–11 Sun
**Belhaven 80/-; Orkney Dark
Island; guest beers** H
Small, panelled bar with rare
brewery mirrors hidden
behind the gantry. Snacks
available (meals in the
attached restaurant). Six guest
beers: Scottish ales are
featured. Q ⚹ 🏠 ⊞ ⚹ ▲ P

Kirkmichael

Aldchlappie Hotel

By A924/B950
☎ (01250) 881224
11–3 (not Mon), 5.30–11.45; 12.30–3,
6.30–11 Sun

Glen Devon *(cont.)*

Beer range varies H
Comfortable lounge in a small
hotel, popular with walkers
and skiers. Eve meals end at
8.45. Beware the keg cider on a
fake handpump.
⚏ ⚏ 🏠 ◖ ▶ ⚹ ▲ P

Kirriemuir

Roods Bar

10 Roods (lane near car park)
☎ (01575) 572945
11–1am; 12.30–11 Sun
Beer choice varies H
Friendly, basic local with a
Robert Younger window and
an Aitken mirror. One beer. ♠

Thrums Hotel

Bank Street ☎ (01575) 572758
11 (12 Sun)–midnight
Beer range varies H
Large, open-plan lounge
taking its name from one of
Barrie's novels. Two beers;
meals all day. 🏠 ◖ ▶ ♠

Montrose

George Hotel

22 George Street (by police
station) ☎ (01674) 675050
11 (12 Sun)–11
Beer range varies H
Long, brightly-lit lounge
which doubles as a restaurant.
Four ales. ⚹ 🏠 ◖ ▶ ⚹ P ⚹

Moulin

Moulin Inn

11–13 Kirkmichael Road
(⅔ mile NE of Pitlochry on
Braemar road)
☎ (01796) 472196
11 (12 Sun)–11 (11.45 Fri & Sat)
**Whitbread Boddingtons
Bitter; guest beers** H
Century-old inn with four real
ales in the public bar, which
has been extended into a
family and games area.
⚏ ⚹ 🏠 ◖ ▶ ⚹ ▲ P

Perth

Greyfriars

15 South Street
☎ (01738) 633036
11–10.30 (11 Tue–Thu, 11.45 Fri &
Sat); 12.30–11 Sun
**Ind Coope Burton Ale;
Orkney Raven Ale; guest
beers** H
Small, friendly pub near the
River Tay. Restaurant upstairs.
Four guest beers. ◖ ⚹

Old Ship Inn

Skinnergate ☎ (01738) 624929
11–2.30, 5–11; 11–11 Fri & Sat; closed
Sun
**Alloa Arrol's 80/-; Caledonian
Deuchars IPA; Ind Coope
Burton Ale; guest beer** H
Quiet pub – Perth's oldest
(1665). Dominoes night held.
Eve meals Sat. Q ◖ ⊞ ♠

Northern Ireland

0 — 10 miles
0 — 20 km

Limavady

Crosskeys

A37
A2
A2
A26
A44
A42
A26
B52
A6
M22
M2
A8
Ballyeaston
Glengormley
Bangor
Belfast
Holywood
A2
M1
A26
Lisburn
Saintfield
Hillsborough
A24
A1
A3
A4

🏰 *Hilden, Lisburn*

Ballyeaston

Carmichael's (Staffies)
16 Ballyeaston Village
Eve only (times vary); closed Sun
Worthington White Shield
Very quiet, rural house, one of
the few remaining pubs in
Ireland selling bottled beer
only. A peaceful country
haven. The gents' has been
described as 'quaint'.
🏚 Q P

Bangor

Jenny Watts
41 High Street (200 yds from
seafront, close to shops and
marina) ☎ (01247) 270401
11.30–11; 12.30–2.30, 7–10 Sun
S&N Theakston Best Bitter Ⓗ
Dating back to 1740, a
tastefully modernised, open-
plan bar with a stone floor and
old memorabilia on the walls.
Popular with all ages. Folk
music Tue and Sun eve; jazz
Sun lunchtime. Excellent food.
🏚 ☀ Ⓓ ▶ Ꮙ

Belfast

Beaten Docket
48 Great Victoria Street
☎ (01232) 242986
11.30–11 (1am Thu–Sat); 12.30–2.30,
7–10 Sun
S&N Theakston Best Bitter Ⓗ
Often busy, modern, tiled-
floor pub with a horse racing
theme (next door to a
bookie's). The upstairs lounge
features music. Good food.
Ⓓ 🍺 Ꮙᚯ (Botanic, NIR)

Bittles
103 Victoria Street (corner of
Victoria Sq) ☎ (01232) 311088
11.30–11.30; 12–3 Sun, closed Sun
eve
Worthington White Shield
Interesting backwater pub, on
an unusual junction of two
streets. Its triangular, bijou
lounge bar has a tiled floor
and a high, wood-panelled
ceiling. Paintings of local
landmarks and characters
provide decor.
Ⓓ Ꮙᚯ (Central, NIR)

Brown's
30 Chichester Street
☎ (01232) 232920
12–11; 12–6 Sun
Worthington White Shield
Small bar and comfortable
restaurant with a long, narrow
entrance. Good atmosphere
and friendly staff. There's also
an upstairs bar and a circular,
verandah-style lounge/eating
area. Good food.
Q Ⓓ ▶ Ꮙᚯ (Central, NIR)

Crown Liquor Saloon
42–44 Great Victoria Street
☎ (01232) 231478
11.30–11; 12.30–2.30, 7–10 Sun
Draught Bass Ⓗ
Famous, gas-lit Victorian gin
palace: a National Trust gem,
with ornate tiling, pillars,
booths and other trappings of
a bygone drinking age. Good
food includes local oysters.
Beloved of locals and tourists
alike. Ⓓ Ꮙᚯ (Botanic, NIR)

Crow's Nest
22–28 Skipper Street
☎ (01232) 325491

11–11 (extends weekends); 7–10 Sun,
closed Sun lunch
Worthington White Shield
Typical, large, single-room
(mind the step) city pub. Good
lunchtime trade. The quiet
upstairs lounge offers karaoke
some nights; weekend music
downstairs. Ⓓ

Elms
36 University Road
☎ (01232) 322106
11.30–1am; 7–10.30 Sun, closed Sun
lunch
Worthington White Shield
Bustling and lively university
pub, featuring often noisy live
music nightly. The long bar,
with lots of space and friendly
staff, attracts all types. Sports
events are covered on a large
screen. Ⓓ Ꮙᚯ (Botanic, NIR)

Kitchen Bar & Parlour Bar
16 Victoria Square (corner of
Telfair St) ☎ (01232) 324901
11.30–11 (may extend weekends);
usually closed Sun
**S&N Theakston Best Bitter;
guest beers** Ⓗ
Family-run, long, narrow bars,
famous for superb food, ales
and beer festivals. Winner of
several local CAMRA awards.
Packed and lively; occasional
folk music sessions.
🏚 Q Ⓓ 🍺 Ꮙᚯ (Central, NIR)

Nick's Warehouse
35–43 Hill Street
☎ (01232) 439690
11.30–11; closed Sun
A popular wine bar
downstairs and a good
restaurant upstairs, in the
oldest quarter of Belfast;
formerly a bonded warehouse
for Bushmills, dating back to
1830. No food Sun. No
draught ales but an ever-
changing selection of bottle-
conditioned and foreign beers.
Ⓓ ▶ ᚯ

Roost
46 Church Lane
☎ (01232) 233282
11.30–11 (may close earlier); closed
Sun
Worthington White Shield
Tastefully refurbished pub with
a wooden floor, a balcony bar
upstairs and lots of mixed
memorabilia. Cosy atmosphere;
good lunch trade. Ⓓ

Thompson's Garage
3 Patterson Place, Donegall
Square East (down lane beside
taxi rank, E side of City Hall)
☎ (01232) 323762
11.30–11 (may close earlier); closed
Sun
Worthington White Shield
High-roofed, ex-garage with
motoring memorabilia on bare
brick walls. Good food (special
menus). Occasional live music.
Ⓓ ᚯ

Northern Ireland

Crosskeys

Crosskeys
39 Grange Road, Toomebridge
(left off B52 7 miles N of
Randalstown) ☎ (01648) 50694
11 (6.30 winter)–11; 7–10 Sun, closed
Sun lunch (ring to confirm)
Worthington White Shield
Picturesque, listed, rural pub
seen on postcards and
calendars: a timeless slice of
history with its whitewashed
stone walls and thatched roof.
A beautiful aroma comes from
the turf fire. Occasional
traditional folk bands. With its
very friendly owner, this
should be No 1 on your list.
🍴 Q ❀ ⊕ P

Glengormley

Crown & Shamrock
540 Antrim Road (A6, 1½ miles
W of Glengormley)
☎ (01232) 832889
11.30–11.30; 7–10.30 Sun, closed Sun
lunch
Worthington White Shield
Traditional, family-run, Irish
one-bar pub with a high
counter and a warm welcome.
Small, cosy lounge. Occasional
folk music and draught guest
beers. 🍴 Q ❀ P

Whittley's
401 Ballyclare Road (B56, 2½
miles NW of Glengormley)
☎ (01232) 832438
11.30–11; 5.30–10.30 Sun, closed Sun
lunch
Worthington White Shield
Welcoming pub with a quiet,
homely public bar featuring
real fires and a wood and
stone floor. There's also a
games room, a large lounge

and a railway-themed
restaurant. Occasional passing
steam locomotives. Children
welcome till 7pm.
🍴 Q ❀ ⊕ ▶ P

Hillsborough

Hillside Inn
Main Street ☎ (01846) 682765
11.30–11; 12.30–3, 7–10 Sun
**Hilden Ale; S&N Theakston
Old Peculier; guest beers** Ⓗ
Appropriately named village
bar with three different
drinking areas. The upper
floor contains a highly
recommended restaurant. No
bar food Sun eve. Special
events often held.
🍴 Q ❀ ⊕ ▶

Plough Inn
The Square (top of the hill)
☎ (01846) 682985
11.30–11; 12.30–2, 7–10 Sun
S&N Theakston Best Bitter
Well-decorated, multi-level
bar with much wooden
furniture and 'equine'
memorabilia. There is a wine
bar upstairs, plus a separate
restaurant (good food) with its
own bar. Local CAMRA *Pub of
the Year* 1994.
🍴 Q ❀ ⊕ ▶ ⊕ P

Holywood

Bear Tavern
62 High Street
☎ (01232) 426837
11.30–11 (1am Wed–Sat); 12.30–2.30,
7–10.30 Sun
**McEwan 80/- or S&N
Theakston Best Bitter** Ⓗ
Lively, long, narrow bar with
mahogany fittings, mirrors
and glass: cosy inglenooks and

a sloping stone floor beneath a
Paris docks-style first floor
lounge. A roof patio is open
during summer months.
🍴 Q ❀ ⊕ ⊕ ⊕ ⅙ ≠ (NIR)

Seaside Tavern
19 Stewarts Place
☎ (01232) 423152
11.30–11 (1am Thu–Sat); 12.30–2.30,
7–10 Sun
S&N Theakston Best Bitter Ⓗ
Popular bar with wooden and
stone flooring. The upstairs
lounge is tastefully decorated.
Eve meals end at 8.30pm; no
eve meals Sun.
Q ❀ ⊕ ▶ ⊕ ⅙ ≠ (NIR)

Limavady

Owens Bar
50 Main Street
☎ (0150 47) 22328
11–11; closed Sun
Worthington White Shield
Old, traditional, family-run
pub with a wide-ranging
clientele. Barbecues in
summer. Ask for
'Worthington's' when
requesting White Shield.
🍴 Q

Saintfield

White Horse Inn
49 Main Street
☎ (01238) 510417
11–11; closed Sun
**S&N Theakston Best Bitter;
guest beers** Ⓗ
Family-run pub and basement
restaurant with friendly staff
and locals and a comfortable
atmosphere. Noted for its
ostrich steaks. The adjoining
off-licence sells ale from the
handpump. 🍴 Q ⊕ ▶

BLANKET COVERAGE FOR WORTHINGTON

Real ale campaigners in Northern Ireland are at last beginning to
see the fruits of their efforts. Until recently, apart from limited
sales of Hilden Brewery products, the only real ale available in the
province was bottle-conditioned Worthington White Shield. Now
S&N has introduced Theakston Best Bitter into some bars and Bass,
too, has entered the cask ale fray with Worthington Best Bitter.
Unfortunately, the company has decided that this beer must be kept
under a blanket of gas in all outlets, in order to prolong its shelf life.
CAMRA does not accept the application of gas to cask ales as such a
procedure inevitably prevents the beer from developing its full
flavour. Furthermore, a few outlets which had bravely offered
genuine, cask-conditioned Draught Bass have now taken the
neutered Worthington instead. However, at least pub users in the six
counties are growing used to the sight of handpumps on the bar and
if Bass can be persuaded to abandon its early caution, lift the gas
blanket and allow Worthington Best Bitter to become 'real', things
really will be looking up in Northern Ireland.

Channel Islands

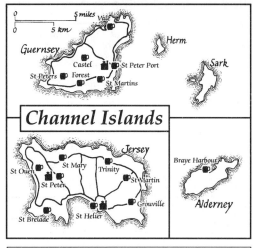

 Guernsey, St Peter Port; **Jersey,** St Helier; **Randalls,** St Peter Port; **Tipsy Toad,** St Peter/St Helier

Alderney

Braye Harbour

Moorings Hotel
Braye Street ☎ (01481) 823558
11–midnight (1am summer)
Guernsey Moorings Ale Ⓗ
Conservatory bar overlooking Braye Bay, stocking a large selection of bottled beers from around the world. Occasional 'guest' beer from the Guernsey Brewery stable, in addition to the house beer shown above.
❀ 🛏 ◖ ▶ ⇌ (Braye Rd)

Try also: **Georgian House Hotel**, Victoria St (Free)

Guernsey

Castel

Fleur du Jardin
King's Mills ☎ (01481) 57996
11–3, 5.30–11.45; 12–3.30, 6–11 Sun
Guernsey Sunbeam Ⓗ
Comfortable hotel in an attractive setting, renovated in keeping with its farmhouse origins. The garden has a play area. The public bar does not open winter lunchtimes.
Q ❀ 🛏 ◖ ▶ ⊞ ♠ P

Forest

Deerhound Inn
Le Bourg ☎ (01481) 38585
10.30–11.45; 12–3.30, 7–11 Sun
Guernsey Sunbeam Ⓗ
Welcoming roadside tavern, handy for the airport. Excellent bar meals (till 7pm); separate restaurant (last food orders 9.30). ❀ 🛏 ◖ ▶ P

Venture Inn
Rue de la Villiaze (New Road)
☎ (01481) 63211
10–11.45; 12–1.45pm Sun
Randalls Best Bitter Ⓗ
Well-run hostelry not far from the airport. The functional bar contrasts with a cosy lounge. No eve meals Mon; no lunches Mon in winter.
🏭 Q ❀ 🛏 ◖ ▶ ⊞ ♠ P

St Martins

Captain's Hotel
La Fosse ☎ (01481) 38990
10.30–11.45; closed Sun
Guernsey Sunbeam Ⓗ
Attractive and cosy lounge bar boasting an impressive handpump. Moulin Huet Bay and Pottery are nearby. Separate bistro-type restaurant. ❀ 🛏 ◖ ▶ P

St Peter Port

Britannia Inn
Trinity Square
☎ (01481) 721082
10–11.45; closed Sun
Guernsey Braye, Britannia, Sunbeam Ⓗ
Single-roomed lounge bar in the old quarter of town. An occasional 'guest' beer from the Guernsey Brewery is also sold. Note: Braye is kept under a cask breather in winter. ♣

Drunken Duck
La Charroterie
☎ (01481) 725045
11.30–2.30, 4–11.45; 11.30–11.45 Fri & Sat; closed Sun
Ringwood Best Bitter, XXXX Porter, Fortyniner, Old Thumper; guest beers Ⓗ
Cosy, two-roomed pub well worth the climb up from town. Impromptu folk nights Tue; live band Thu; regular quiz nights. Beware the keg Scrumpy Jack cider on a fake handpump.
♣ ᗒ

Prince of Wales
Manor Place (Smith Street)
☎ (01481) 721066
10.30–11.45; closed Sun
Randalls Best Bitter Ⓔ
A welcome return to the *Guide* for this busy town pub boasting many original Victorian features. The only outlet for cask Randalls in town. ◖ ⊞

Ship & Crown
North Pier Steps
☎ (01481) 721368
12–3.30, 6–11
Guernsey Sunbeam Ⓗ
Busy, single-bar town pub, opposite the marina for visiting yachts. Walls are covered with pictures of ships and local shipwrecks. Popular with yachtsmen and bankers at lunchtime. One other Guernsey beer is also sold. ◖

Try also: **Thomas de la Rue**, The Pollet (Guernsey)

St Peters

Longfrie Inn
Rue de Longfrie
☎ (01481) 63107
11–3, 5.30–11.45; 12–3.30, 6–11 Sun
Guernsey Sunbeam Ⓗ
Family-orientated hostelry with a heavy emphasis on food. One other Guernsey beer is stocked.
🏭 Q ❀ 🛏 ◖ ▶ P

Vale

Houmet Tavern
Grande Havre
☎ (01481) 43037
10.30–11.45; closed Sun
Guernsey Braye Ⓗ
Busy pub with a lively bar and a cosy lounge overlooking Grande Havre Bay. No eve meals Sun, Mon or Thu. Bar billiards played.
Q ❀ ◖ ▶ ⊞ ♠ ♣ P

Try also: **Pony Inn** (Guernsey)

405

Channel Islands

Grouville

Pembroke
Coast Road
☎ (01534) 855756
9–11; 11–1, 4.30–11 Sun
**Draught Bass; Whitbread
Boddingtons Bitter; guest
beers** Ⓗ
Recently refurbished, large
family pub next to a golf
course. Range of games in the
public bar. Good food.
🏾 Q 🍽 ❀ ◑ ▶ ⊟ ♣ P

Seymour Inn
La Rocque
☎ (01534) 854558
9–11; 11–1, 4.30–11 Sun
**Guernsey Sunbeam; Jersey
Old Jersey Ale, Ann's Treat,
Winter Ale** Ⓗ
Friendly coastal pub with a
separate real ale bar. Ask for
real ale if this bar is shut.
Good food (no meals Sun). Bar
billiards played.
🏾 🍽 ❀ ◑ ▶ ⊟ ♣ P

St Brelade

Old Smugglers Inn
Ouaisne Bay
☎ (01534) 41510
11–11; 11–1, 4.30–11 Sun
**Draught Bass; Ringwood
XXXX Porter; S&N
Theakston Old Peculier; guest
beers** Ⓗ
Converted 17th-century
fisherman's cottage close to
the beach. Beware the purple
carpet with the smuggler's
head. It is worth checking
which beers are on before
visiting. Live folk and blues
some nights (usually Sun).
Good food.
🏾 🍽 ◑ ▲

Try also: Old Portelet Inn
(Whitbread Boddingtons)

St Helier

Lamplighter
Mulcaster Street (50 yds from
bus station)
☎ (01534) 23119
9.30–11; 11–1, 4.30–11 Sun
**Draught Bass; Marston's
Pedigree; S&N Theakston
Old Peculier; Whitbread
Boddingtons Bitter; guest
beers** Ⓗ
Gas-lit town pub with a varied
clientele and a good
atmosphere in its single bar;
no TV, music or electronic
games. Good range of guest
beers; Bulmers Traditional
Cider served. No food Sun;
no lunches Sat.
Q ◑ ♻ ⊟

Town House
New Street
☎ (01534) 615000
9.30–11; 11–1, 4.30–11 Sun
**Tipsy Toad Cyril's Bitter,
Jimmy's Bitter, Black Tadger,
Horny Toad, Star Drooper** Ⓗ;
guest beers Ⓗ/Ⓖ
Possibly the largest brew pub
in Britain, this has a massive
bar with upstairs rooms for
live music and functions.
Good food in the bar and
restaurant. Bulmers
Traditional cider served. Local
CAMRA *Pub of the Year* 1994.
🍽 ◑ ▶ ♻ ⊟

St Martin

Anne Port Bay Hotel
Anne Port
☎ (01534) 852058
11–2.30, 5–11; 11–11 Sat; 11–1,
4.30–11 Sun
**Draught Bass; Marston's
Pedigree; guest beers** Ⓖ
Small, homely hotel bar near
the beach. Popular with locals.
Q ❀ 🛏 ◑ ▲

Royal Hotel
La Grande Route de St Martin
☎ (01534) 856289
11–11; 11–1, 4.30–11 Sun
**Marston's Pedigree;
Whitbread Boddingtons
Bitter** Ⓗ
Traditional granite bar which
has been extended by the
addition of a conservatory for
meals. Large terrace with
barbecues in summer and a
play area for children.
Separate restaurant upstairs.
Bar billiard table.
🏾 🍽 ❀ ◑ ▶ ⊟ ♣ ♣ P

Rozel Bay Hotel
Rozel Bay
☎ (01534) 863438
10–11.30
Draught Bass Ⓗ
Characteristic, two-bar village
pub at picturesque Rozel
Harbour. Enjoy the log fire in
winter and the garden in
summer. Eve meals in summer
only, 6–8.
🏾 Q ❀ ◑ ▶ ⊟ ♣ P

St Mary

St Mary's Country Hotel
Rue des Buttes (opp. church)
☎ (01534) 481561
9.30–11; 11–1, 4.30–11 Sun
**Bass Worthington BB,
Draught Bass** Ⓗ
Large, friendly and
comfortable country pub with
a conservatory and outdoor
drinking areas. Log fires in the
bar and lounge. Good food
from a varied menu with daily
specials. No food Sun. Eve
meals 6–8 in summer (plus Fri
and Sat in winter).
🏾 Q 🍽 ❀ ◑ ▶ ⊟ P ⊬

St Ouen

Moulin de Lecq
Greve de Lecq Bay (200 yds
from beach) ☎ (01534) 482818
11–11; 11–1, 4.30–11 Sun
**Guernsey Sunbeam; Jersey
Old Jersey Ale, Ann's Treat,
Winter Ale** Ⓗ
Picturesque, converted 12th-
century watermill featuring a
working drivewheel behind
the bar. Large outdoor play
area (barbecues in summer).
No food Sun eve.
🏾 Q 🍽 ❀ ◑ ▶ P

St Peter

Star & Tipsy Toad Brewery
La Grande Route de St Pierre
☎ (01534) 485556
10–11; 11–1, 4.30–11 Sun
**Tipsy Toad Jimmy's Bitter,
Horny Toad, Star Drooper;
guest beers** Ⓗ
One of two Tipsy Toad brew
pubs in Jersey. Spacious
rooms; regular live music;
good food and an outdoor
play area for children. Bulmers
cider.
🏾 🍽 ❀ ◑ ▶ ♣ ♣ ▲ ♻ P

Trinity

Trinity Arms
On B31, close to Trinity
Church, near zoo
☎ (01534) 864691
10.30–11; 11–1, 4.30–11 Sun
Guernsey Sunbeam Ⓗ
Modern granite country pub
which may also sell one more
real ale. Lunches Mon–Sat; eve
meals in summer.
🏾 ❀ ◑ ▶ ⊟ ♣ P

**Do you care about your pub and your pint?
Join CAMRA and help us protect your pleasure.**

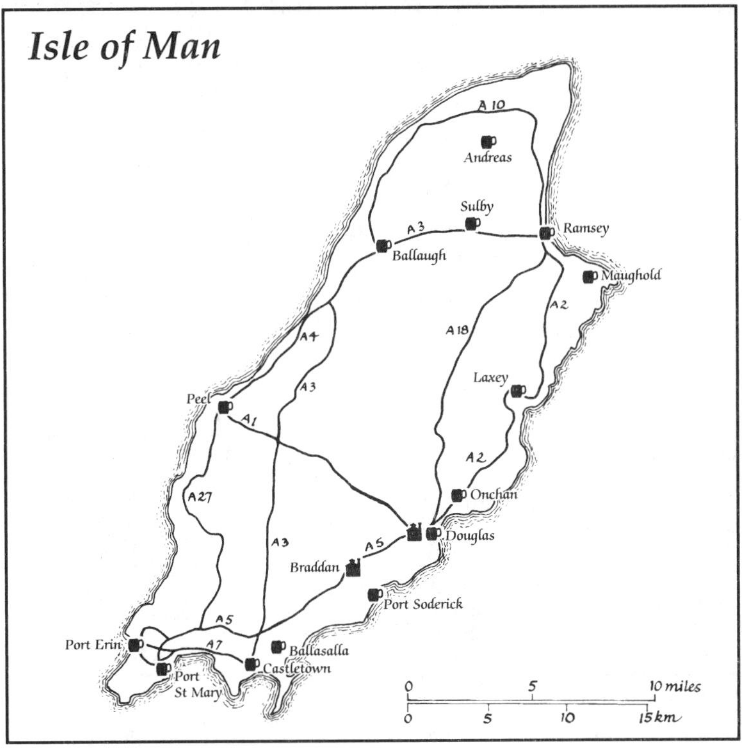

Bushy's, *Braddan*; **Isle of Man**, *Douglas*

Sunday hours on the Isle of Man are 12–1.30, 8–10

Andreas

Grosvenor

☎ (01624) 880227
12–10.45
Cains Bitter; Okells Bitter H
Large country pub with separate bars and restaurant areas. Good home cooking. Occasional eve meals in summer.
Q ❀ ◐ ⊞ ♿ ♣ P

Ballasalla

Whitestone Inn

☎ (01624) 822334
12–10.45
Okells Bitter H
Pub where the lounge serves almost as a dining room at lunchtime with strong local support for good value meals. However, the comfortable public bar remains for those who just want a drink and who want to avoid food.
◐ ⊞ ♿ ⇌ (IMR) ♣ P

Ballaugh

Raven

☎ (01624) 897272
12–10.45
Bushy's Best Bitter; Marston's Pedigree; Okells Bitter; Whitbread Boddingtons Mild; guest beer H
Country pub on the famous TT course. First class service; good quality food. Occasional eve meals in summer.
❀ ◐ ▲ ♣ P

Castletown

Castle Arms (Gluepot)

Quayside
☎ (01624) 824673
11–10.45
Cains Mild, Bitter; Tetley Bitter H
One of the oldest pubs on the island, on the harbour opposite Castle Rushen. Its comfortable interior has a strong nautical flavour. Good food trade (no meals Sun).
⌂ Q ❀ ◐ ◗ ♿ ▲
⇌ (IMR) ♣

Viking

Victoria Road
11–10.45
Cains Bitter; Tetley Bitter; Whitbread Boddingtons Bitter; guest beers H
Very popular family-run pub serving good food. Barbecues in the garden.
Q ♘ ❀ ◐ ◗ ⊞ ♿ ▲
⇌ (IMR) ♣ P

Try also: Union (Okells)

Douglas

Albert

Church Row (between bus station and market hall)
☎ (01624) 673632
12–10.45
Okells Mild, Bitter H
Very busy and popular, town-centre, straight-forward drinkers' pub. Well worth a visit. ⊞ ⇌ (IMR) ⊖ ♣

Bushy's

Victoria Street (near sea terminal) ☎ (01624) 675139
12–10.45

Isle of Man

Bushy's Mild, Best Bitter, Old Bushy Tail H
Pub which is very popular with younger drinkers, although it caters for all tastes and ages. The separate music room also has real ale. TT motor cycle history displayed. Families can use the lounge.
🏠 🕭 🕯 ⇌ (IMR)

Foresters Arms
St George's Street (50 yds from circular road)
☎ (01624) 676509
12–10.45
Okells Mild, Bitter H
Traditional Manx local with a good social side; popular with business people. Baps and toasties available all day.
🏠 🕭 ⇌ (IMR) ♣

Old Market Inn
Church Row (near bus station and market hall)
☎ (01624) 675202
12–10.45
Bushy's Best Bitter; Okells Bitter H
Genuine Manx pub close to the shops and harbour. Well worth a visit; very good atmosphere.
🏠 🍺 ⇌ (IMR) ⊖ ♣

Rovers Return
Church Road (rear of town hall) ☎ (01624) 676459
12–10.45
Bushy's Mild, Best Bitter, Old Bushy Tail H
Centrally located pub in the business district, popular with locals. Note the pictures of old fire engines (the pub used to be known as the Firemans). Other pictures show old pubs and Blackburn Rovers teams. Good meals.
🏠 🕭 🕯 ⇌ (IMR) ⊖ ♣

Samuel Webb
Marina Road ☎ (01624) 625595
11–10.45
Courage Directors; Marston's Pedigree; Ruddles County; John Smith's Bitter; Tetley Bitter; guest beers H
Town-centre pub, very popular with all age groups. Good food served.
Q 🕭 🕯 ♦ ⊖ ♣

Terminus Tavern
Strathalan Crescent
☎ (01624) 624312
12–10.45
Okells Mild, Bitter H
Pub at the end of the promenade, by the electric tram terminus. Very good selection of home-cooked food.
🏠 Q ⛄ 🕭 🕯
⇌ (MER) ♣ P

Tramshunter's Arms
Harris Promenade
☎ (01624) 626011
11–10.45

Draught Bass; Okells Mild, Bitter; Whitbread Flowers Original; guest beers H
Very popular, town-centre pub, local CAMRA *Pub of the Year* 1993. Choose from 13 real ales. Beef baps a speciality.
🏠 🍺 🕯 ⊖ ♣ P

Laxey

Mines Tavern
Captains Hill (by station)
☎ (01624) 861484
12–10.45
Bushy's Best Bitter; Cains Bitter; Tetley Bitter H
Old-world-style bar in the shape of a tramcar, featuring brass and dark wood.
🕭 🕯 ♦ 🍺 ⇌ (MER) ♣ P

New Inn
New Road ☎ (01624) 861077
12–10.45
Okells Bitter; Whitbread Castle Eden Ale; guest beers (summer) H
Popular local with a welcoming landlord. Accommodation and meals in TT week only.
Q 🕭 🏠 ♦ ⇌ (MER) ♣

Queens Hotel
New Road ☎ (01624) 861195
12–11
Bushy's Best Bitter; Whitbread Boddingtons Bitter; Flowers Original; guest beers H
One-bar village pub popular with motor and motorcycle clubs. Large garden. Summer barbecues. Limited accommodation.
🕭 🏠 ▲ ⇌ (MER) ♣ P

Maughold

Glen Mona
☎ (01624) 861263
12–3, 6–11
Okells Bitter; Tetley Bitter (summer); **guest beer** (summer) H
Country pub in unspoilt and dramatic scenery, between Laxey and Ramsey, 100 yds from the Manx Electric Railway station. No meals Sun eve. Families welcome till 9pm. 🏠 🕭 🕯 ▲
⇌ (Glen Mona, MER) ♣ P

Onchan

Liverpool Arms
Main Road, Baldrine (Laxey road) ☎ (01624) 674787
12–10.45
Okells Mild, Bitter H
Former Castletown Brewery pub with appropriate livery still on the building: an old halfway house with popular

---

licensees. Good lunches; convivial atmosphere.
🏠 Q 🕭 🕯 🍺
⇌ (MER, request stop) ♣ P

Manx Arms
Main Road ☎ (01624) 675484
12–10.45
Okells Mild, Bitter H
Large, busy pub in the centre of the village, on the corner of the former car racing course with old photos to prove it. Family room lunchtime.
Q ⛄ 🕭 🍺 ♣ P

Peel

White House
2 Tynwald Road (100 yds from bus station along Atholl St)
☎ (01624) 842252
11–10.45
Draught Bass; Bushy's Best Bitter; Okells Mild, Bitter; Whitbread Flowers Original; guest beers H
Comfortable, friendly pub with a cosy snug (Captain's Cabin) and games and music rooms. Manx music Sat. CAMRA local *Pub of the Year* 1992 and 1994. Always three guest beers.
🏠 Q 🕭 ▲ ♣ P

Port Erin

Falcon's Nest Hotel
Station Road
☎ (01624) 834077
11–10.45
Okells Bitter; Tetley Bitter; Whitbread Boddingtons Bitter, Castle Eden Ale, Flowers Original; guest beers H
Traditional hotel overlooking the beach, with original features and comfortable bars. Friendly and helpful service.
🏠 🏠 🕯 ♦ 🍺 ⇌ (IMR) P

Port St Mary

Albert
Athol Street (near harbour)
☎ (01624) 832118
12–10.45
Bushy's Best Bitter; Cains Mild; Okells Bitter; S&N Theakston Best Bitter; Whitbread Flowers Original H
The Albert has been renovated without significant structural alterations, leaving it still totally recognisable as the much-appreciated fishermen's and yachtsmen's pub of old. Wide range of real ales.
🏠 🕯 🍺 ♣

Bay View Hotel
Bay View Road
☎ (01624) 832234
12–10.45
Okells Mild, Bitter H

Pub offering live entertainment in its new lounge bar, particularly at weekends. The public bar remains little altered and offers a lively and sociable atmosphere. Regular locals are joined by summer visitors. Mild is not always available.
🛏 ⊛ 🍴 ◖ 🍺 ♣ P

Station
☎ (01624) 832249
12–10.45
Okells Mild, Bitter Ⓗ
Comfortable premises with a separate dining room. However, if you are 'only here for the beer' you can alight from the steam train almost straight into the public bar.
◖ ▶ 🍺 🚅 (IMR) ♣ P

Port Soderick

Anchor
☎ (01624) 620500
12–midnight (11 winter)
Cains Bitter; Okells Bitter Ⓗ

Clean, well-managed pub on the seafront of this scenic port. Live bands at weekends in summer.
⊛ ◖ ▶ P

Ramsey

Britannia
Waterloo Road
☎ (01624) 816547
12–10.45
Okells Mild, Bitter Ⓗ
Pub opposite the Electric Railway terminus: a good locals' bar and a cosy lounge.
Q 🛏 ⊛ ◖ 🍺 🚅 (MER) ♣

Swan
Parliament Square
☎ (01624) 814236
12–10.45
Okells Mild, Bitter Ⓗ
Recent purpose-built, town-centre pub situated on the TT course – customers can watch the races. Popular with locals and visitors. Large lounge and bar areas, plus a garden at the rear.
⊛ ◖ 🍺 ♿ 🚅 (MER) ♣

Trafalgar
West Quay
☎ (01624) 814601
12–10.45
Bushy's Best Bitter; Cains Mild, Bitter; guest beers Ⓗ
Harbourside pub which re-opened two years ago and is popular with harbour workers. The upstairs dining room serves food lunchtimes; the small, cosy downstairs room has a bar at one end. Accessible from one of the many lanes off the shopping street or from the harbour itself. ◖ 🚅 (MER)

Sulby

Sulby Glen Hotel
☎ (01624) 897240
12–10.45
Bushy's Best Bitter; Cains Mild; Okells Mild, Bitter Ⓗ
Typical, friendly Manx country pub on the famous TT course (the Sulby Straight). Local history and TT memorabilia displayed.
🛏 ⊛ 🍴 ◖ ▶ 🍺 🛏 ♣ P

THE BREWERIES

W hen CAMRA took to the streets for the first time there were under 100 surviving real ale breweries in the UK. Today, we can enjoy the beers of well over 300 breweries and new producers are setting up shop all the time. This year's *Good Beer Guide* lists more than 50 new micros to add to the 85 it has listed in the last three years. Unfortunately, the market place is becoming increasingly congested and some brewers have had difficulty in finding bar room. When the national breweries control sales in over 80% of pubs, this is hardly surprising. Consequently, a handful of concerns have packed up their coppers and called it a day, for the moment at least. These include Cook's in Dorset, West Coast in Manchester and West Highland in Scotland.

The market is set to become even tighter now that Scottish & Newcastle's take-over plans for Courage have been approved by the Government. Ironically, seven years ago Courage's parent company, Foster's of Australia, attempted to purchase S&N. S&N put up a staunch defence which effectively conveyed to the Monopolies and Mergers Commission that such a merger would not be in the public interest and would cost jobs. It cited loss of competition with its effect on consumer choice, and it declared that further concentration of control in so few hands would be detrimental to the trade. The MMC agreed and the bid was foiled. With the boot on the other foot, S&N has now refuted its former findings and the Government has been happy to nod the deal through with only a couple of small conditions – that S&N cuts its tied estate by 115 pubs within a year and also releases 1,000 Inntrepreneur pubs (see Pub Groups) from their Courage supply agreement.

NEW MERGER MANIA?

S&N, with Courage's breweries on board, will now control over a quarter of UK brewing production, making it comfortably Britain's biggest brewer. Bass, until now holders of that title, will be unlikely to sit back and allow its position and influence to be so eroded. One or two regional brewers are rumoured to be already in the company's sights, evidence that further mergers and acquisitions will almost certainly follow the S&N/Courage deal. It is time the Government began to act on behalf of the pub user. It has no qualms about taking billions of pounds of tax from the beer drinker, but gives little back in return. Plans to regulate on full measures were scrapped after intense lobbying by the big brewers, and the best response it could give to the call for lowering beer duty, to cut cheap foreign imports, was to raise it by one penny. The net result is a wider grin on the faces of the organised gangs who now control the illegal cross-Channel trade, and further

despair for publicans and smaller breweries whose profits are being squeezed by the millions of gallons of Eurofizz which keep people at home instead of in their local.

THE BREWERIES SECTION

The breweries information is divided into three sections: Independents, Nationals and Pub Groups. The Independents are those breweries and brew pubs (pubs brewing beer on the premises) which are not controlled by the big national breweries. Brew pubs are easily identified by the pub sign symbol at the start of their address, but brew pubs which are owned and run by Nationals (such as the Firkin chain) are included this year with their parent companies, rather than as Independents. A brief history and description of each brewery is given, including, for the first time this year, details of brewery shops and the availability of tours. Each brewery's real ales are also listed, in increasing order of original gravity (OG). The OG was for many years the standard method of gauging the approximate strength of a brew and was used as the basis for evaluating the duty payable to the Government. It is a reading taken before fermentation begins and indicates how much fermentable material (sugars) are in the brew. Usually, the more sugars, the greater the ultimate strength. A beer with an OG of 1040 is likely to brew out to around 4% alcohol by volume (ABV), although brewers will terminate the fermentation early, or allow it to continue longer, to provide sweeter or dryer beers and this will obviously affect the ABV. Beer duty is now assessed from each brew's actual strength when brewing has finished and therefore many breweries now only declare ABV figures, making OG details harder to come by. All the same, where we have been able to obtain these figures, they have been included.

Most beers are furnished with tasting notes. These notes have been supplied by CAMRA tasting panels, organised groups of trained activists. Because of the hundreds of new beers which arrive each year, it has proved impossible to 'taste' every real ale now available. Some basic descriptions, which will provide a little guidance, have been obtained from limited samplings and the beers with these 'unofficial' tasting notes are marked with an asterisk. Tasting notes are not supplied for brew pub beers which can only be discovered in one or two outlets, nor for other breweries' beers which are available only for very limited periods each year. These 'occasional beers' are listed in the main body of brewery information, next to details of bottle-conditioned beers, where available.

Beers marked with a tankard are *Good Beer Guide Beers of the Year* (see full list on page 273). These beers were finalists in the *Champion Beer of Britain* contest held at the Great British Beer Festival in August 1995.

The Pub Groups section looks at the non-brewing companies which own many of our pubs these days. Because of space restrictions only those running about 30 or more pubs have been featured.

The Independents

ABC See Nationals, Carlsberg-Tetley.

ABERDEEN-SHIRE **Aberdeenshire Ales Ltd., Mains of Inverebrie, Ellon, Grampian AB41 8PX. Tel./Fax. (01358) 761457**

Brewery founded in May 1995 by Simon and Valerie Lister who commissioned a hand-made real copper kettle for the venture.

Buchan Gold* (ABV 4%)

ABERYSTWYTH **Aberystwyth Ales, Tregynnan Brewery, Llanrhystyd, Dyfed SY23 5DW. Tel./Fax. (01974) 202388**

Set up in a farm cowshed, using its own well water, this brewery went into production in March 1994. The business has grown rapidly and now around 40 free trade outlets are supplied. Expansion is planned and more tied houses are being sought (one at present). Tours by arrangement.

Dinas Dark Mild* (OG 1036, ABV 3.6%)

Dinas Draught* (OG 1038, ABV 3.6%)

Premium* (OG 1046, ABV 4.4%)

ABINGTON PARK See Nationals, Scottish & Newcastle.

ADNAMS **Adnams and Company PLC, Sole Bay Brewery, Southwold, Suffolk IP18 6JW. Tel. (01502) 722424 Fax. (01502) 722740**

East Anglia's seaside brewery, established in 1890, whose local deliveries are still made by horse drays. Real ale is available in all its 101 pubs, and it also supplies some 650 other outlets direct, with the beers available nationwide via agents. A gradual expansion is planned for the tied estate, 32 ex-Lacon pubs having been acquired from Whitbread in April 1995. Brewery shop open Mon–Fri. Tours by arrangement. Occasional beers: Mayday (OG 1050, ABV 5%, May), Barley Mow (OG 1050, ABV 5%, August), Tally Ho (OG 1075, ABV 6.4%, Christmas).

Mild (OG 1034, ABV 3.2%) A fine black/red mild. The aroma is a subtle balance of fruit and malt with some roast malt, followed by a taste which blends roast malt, grain, hops and fruit on a bittersweet base. Dry finish with faint malt.

Bitter (OG 1036, ABV 3.6%) A fine session bitter with the characteristic Adnams nose of hops, citrus fruits and some sulphur. Dry and hoppy on the palate with some fruit, and a long, dry, hoppy finish. Also known as Southwold Bitter.

Old Ale (OG 1042, ABV 4.1%) A rich, dark brown winter ale with red highlights: a well-balanced blend of fruit, malt and roast grain on a bittersweet base, with an aroma of rich fruit and malt. Dry aftertaste with faint malt and fruit.

Extra (OG 1043, ABV 4.3%) A pungent hop and citrus fruit aroma leads into hops and bitter orange fruit on the palate. Very dry finish with some hops and fruit. *Champion Beer of Britain 1993.*

Broadside (OG 1049, ABV 4.7%) Mid-brown beer with a rich flavour of raisins, plus malt, hops and some dryness. The aroma is dominated by fruit and malt. Long, dry finish with some fruit.

AITKEN'S See Nationals, Bass.

ALFORD ARMS See Nationals, Whitbread.

The pub sign indicates breweries which are also brew pubs, i.e. produce beer in part of a pub or in its grounds.

412

The Independents

ALL NATIONS

All Nations, Coalport Road, Madeley, Telford, Shropshire TF7 5DP. Tel. (01952) 585747

One of few brew pubs left before the new wave arrived, which has, in fact, been brewing for 200 years. Still known as Mrs Lewis's, the inn has been in the same family since 1934. Beer: Pale Ale (OG 1032, ABV 3%).

ALLIED BREWERIES

See Nationals, Carlsberg-Tetley.

ALLOA

See Nationals, Carlsberg-Tetley.

ANCIENT DRUIDS

Ancient Druids, Napier Street, Cambridge CB1 1HR. Tel. (01223) 576324

Brew pub set up in 1984 by Charles Wells, brewing with malt extract. Tours by arrangement. Beer: Ellies SB (ABV 6%, but varies).

ANN STREET

See Jersey.

ANSELLS

See Nationals, Carlsberg-Tetley.

ARCHERS

Archers Ales Ltd., Station Industrial Estate, London Street, Swindon, Wiltshire SN1 5DY. Tel. (01793) 496789 Fax. (01793) 421598

Small brewery, set up in 1979 in the old Great Western Railway works, which has grown very successfully and now supplies 180 free trade outlets from Oxford to Bath (via wholesalers), plus three tied houses. Plans to move to larger premises are well advanced. Tours by arrangement for customers and CAMRA groups.

Village Bitter

(OG 1035, ABV 3.5%) A dry, well-balanced beer, with a full body for its gravity. Malty and fruity in the nose, then a fresh, hoppy flavour with balancing malt, and a hoppy, fruity finish.

Best Bitter

(OG 1040, ABV 4%) Slightly sweeter and rounder than Village, with a malty, fruity aroma and a pronounced bitter finish.

Black Jack Porter

(OG 1046, ABV 4.6%) A winter brew: a black beer with intense roast malt dominant on the tongue. The aroma is fruity and there is some sweetness on the palate, but the finish is pure roast grain.

Golden Bitter

(OG 1046, ABV 4.7%) A full-bodied, hoppy, straw-coloured brew with an underlying fruity sweetness. Very little aroma, but a strong bitter finish.

Old Cobleigh's

(OG 1065, ABV 6.3%) Formerly Headbanger. Almost a barley wine in style, enjoying a full flavour. Sweet and powerful, with a pleasant, dry finish.

ARKELL'S

Arkell's Brewery Ltd., Kingsdown, Swindon, Wiltshire SN2 6RU. Tel. (01793) 823026 Fax. (01793) 828864

Established in 1843 and now one of the few remaining breweries whose shares are all held by one family, with its managing director, James Arkell, a great-great-grandson of founder John Arkell. A gradual expansion is taking place in the tied estate, mainly along the M4 corridor, with four new pubs acquired in the last 12 months. All 82 tied pubs serve real ale, which is also supplied direct to 220 free trade accounts. Tours by arrangement. Occasional beers: Mash Tun Mild (OG 1036, ABV 3.5%), Summer Ale (OG 1038, ABV 3.8%), Yeomanry Bicentenary Ale (OG 1045, ABV 4.5%), Peter's Porter (OG 1049, ABV 4.8%), Noel Ale (OG 1055, ABV 5.5%, Christmas). These may not be available in all Arkell's pubs and may need seeking out.

2B

(OG 1032, ABV 3.2%) Hoppy, pale beer with a hint of fruit and honey. A most refreshing lunchtime or session ale, with a good body for its OG.

The Independents

3B

(OG 1040, ABV 4%) An unusual and distinctive bitter. The crystal malt gives a nutty taste which persists throughout and combines with bitterness in the aftertaste.

Kingsdown Ale

(OG 1052, ABV 5%) 3B's big brother with which it is parti-gyled (uses the same mash). A powerful roast malt/fruit flavour is followed by a lingering, dry aftertaste.

ARUNDEL

Arundel Brewery, Ford Airfield Estate, Ford, Arundel, W. Sussex BN18 0BE. Tel. (01903) 733111 Fax. (01903) 733381

Set up in 1992, Arundel produces beers from authentic Sussex recipes, without the use of additives. Demand has steadily increased and the brewery now serves over 60 outlets, plus its single tied house, the Swan in Arundel. Old Knucker was named after a legendary dragon, Knucker, who allegedly terrorised townsfolk before being slain by a local hero. Tours by arrangement. Occasional beers: Old Conspirator (OG 1050, ABV 5%, October–November), Romeo's Rouser (OG 1053, ABV 5.3%, February), Old Scrooge (OG 1060, ABV 6%, Christmas).

Best Bitter

(OG 1040, ABV 4%) Pale tawny brew with a good hop and fruit aroma with underlying malt. Its dry, hoppy flavour is balanced by malt and fruit and leads through to a fruity, dry aftertaste.

Gold

(OG 1042, ABV 4.2%) A light golden 'summer'-style ale which could benefit from a higher hop content to balance the predominant maltiness.

Stronghold

(OG 1050, ABV 5%) Rich malt predominates in this brew, with a good balance of roast malt, fruit and hops on a bittersweet base.

Old Knucker

(OG 1055, ABV 5.5%) A dark, full-bodied beer. The flavour is a complex blend of sweet fruit and caramel maltiness, which balances dry roast bitterness. This is mirrored in the aftertaste. Roast malt, fruit, caramel and malt feature in the aroma, with some hops. Brewed September–April.

ASH VINE

Ash Vine Brewery (South West) Ltd., The White Hart, Trudoxhill, Frome, Somerset BA11 5DP. Tel./Fax. (01373) 836344

Brewery set up in 1987 near Taunton, but moved to the White Hart pub in January 1989. Ash Vine acquired its third pub in 1995 and some 50 free trade outlets are now supplied locally, following a 50% increase in brewing capacity. Other recent changes have included reducing the beer range, lowering the ABVs of the bitter and Hop & Glory, and the launch of the latter as a bottle-conditioned beer. A different beer is offered each month, always to a new recipe. Tours by arrangement. Bottle-conditioned beer: Hop & Glory (OG 1052, ABV 5%).

Bitter

(OG 1036, ABV 3.5%) A light gold bitter with a floral hop aroma. A powerful, bitter hoppiness dominates the taste and leads to a dry, and occasionally astringent, finish. An unusual and distinctive brew.

Challenger

(OG 1042, ABV 4.1%) A mid-brown beer with a solid malt flavour balanced by a good hoppy bitterness and subtle citrus fruits. It can be sulphurous and slightly metallic.

Black Bess Porter

(OG 1043, ABV 4.2%) A dark copper-brown, bitter porter with roast malt, hops and a sweet fruitiness. Roast malt and hop nose; dry, bitter finish.

Hop & Glory

(OG 1052, ABV 5%) A copper-coloured beer with a malt, fruit and hop aroma. The taste is bittersweet, with hops in abundance and some citrus fruits. Similar finish. A complex, rich and warming winter ale.

ASTON MANOR

Aston Manor Brewery Company Ltd., 173 Thimblemill Lane, Aston, Birmingham, W. Midlands B7 5HS. Tel. (0121) 328 4336 Fax. (0121) 328 0139

Aston Manor ceased brewing cask-conditioned beer in 1994, due to lack of free trade outlets in Birmingham. It now concentrates on canned and bottled beers.

AYLESBURY (ABC)

See Nationals, Carlsberg-Tetley.

B&T

B&T Brewery Ltd., The Brewery, Shefford, Bedfordshire SG17 5DZ. Tel. (01462) 815080 Fax. (01462) 850841

Founded in 1981 in a small industrial unit as Banks & Taylor, the company sadly fell into receivership in April 1994. The next month, Lewis Shepherd acquired all the trading rights and his new company retained Banks & Taylor men Martin Ayres and Mike Desquesnes, together with brewer John Waters, to produce the same extensive range of beers, including the monthly special brews. B&T now supplies 60 outlets direct. Brewery tours by arrangement. Occasional beers: Midsummer Ale (OG 1035, ABV 3.5%), Bedfordshire Clanger (OG 1038, ABV 4%, March), Santa Slayer (OG 1040, ABV 4%), Madhatter (OG 1042, ABV 4.2%, May), Maiden's Rescue (OG 1042, ABV 4.2%, April), Bodysnatcher (OG 1044, ABV 4.4%, October), Guy Fawkes Bitter (OG 1045, ABV 4.5%, November), Romeo's Ruin (OG 1045, ABV 4.5%, February), Emerald Ale (OG 1050, ABV 5%, March), Juliet's Revenge (OG 1050, ABV 5%, February), Shefford Wheat Beer (OG 1050, ABV 5%, July–August), Frostbite (OG 1055, ABV 5.5%, December–January), Bat out of Hell (OG 1060, ABV 6%, November), Skeleton Special (OG 1060, ABV 6%).

Shefford Bitter

(OG 1038, ABV 3.8%) Pleasant, well-balanced session beer with a distinct bitter aftertaste.

Shefford Mild

(OG 1038, ABV 3.8%) A dark beer with a well-balanced taste. Sweetish, roast malt aftertaste.

Dragonslayer

(OG 1045, ABV 4.5%) A straw-coloured beer, dry, malty and lightly hopped.

Edwin Taylor's Extra Stout

(OG 1045, ABV 4.5%) A pleasant, bitter beer with a strong roast malt flavour.

Shefford Pale Ale (SPA)

(OG 1045, ABV 4.5%) A well-balanced beer, with hops, fruit and malt flavours. Dry, bitter aftertaste.

Shefford Old Dark (SOD)

(OG 1050, ABV 5%) SOS with caramel added for colour. Often sold under house names.

Shefford Old Strong (SOS)

(OG 1050, ABV 5%) A malty, fruity beer with a bitter aftertaste.

Black Bat

(OG 1060, ABV 6%) A powerful, sweet, fruity and malty beer for winter. Fruity, nutty aroma; strong roast malt aftertaste.

2XS

(OG 1060, ABV 6%) A reddish beer with a strong, fruity, hoppy aroma. The taste is full-flavoured and the finish strong and sweetish.

Old Bat

(OG 1070, ABV 7%) Powerful-tasting, sweet winter beer, with bitterness coming through in the aftertaste. Fruit is present in both aroma and taste.

BALLARD'S

Ballard's Brewery Ltd., Unit C, The Old Sawmill, Nyewood, Petersfield, Hampshire GU31 5HA. Tel. (01730) 821301 Fax. (01730) 821742

Founded in 1980 at Cumbers Farm, Trotton, Ballard's has been trading at Nyewood (in West Sussex, despite the postal address) since 1988 and now supplies around 50 free trade outlets. Shop open 8–4.30 Mon–Fri. Tours by arrangement. Ballard's brews a Christmas ale with a gravity to match the number of the year.

The Independents

Bottle-conditioned beers: Wassail (OG 1060, ABV 6%), Off the Wall (OG 1094, ABV 9.6%).

Midhurst Mild*   (OG 1034, ABV 3.5%) A rarely seen, basic mild.

Trotton Bitter   (OG 1035, ABV 3.6%) Complex for its gravity, this well-balanced beer has an initial maltiness which fades to a hoppy finish.

Best Bitter   (OG 1042, ABV 4.2%) Copper-red, with a malty aroma. Indeed, a notably malty beer altogether, but well-hopped and with a satisfying finish.

Golden Bine*   (OG 1042, ABV 4.2%)

Wild*   (OG 1047, ABV 4.7%)

Wassail   (OG 1060, ABV 6%) A strong, full-bodied, fruity beer with a predominance of malt throughout, but also an underlying hoppiness. Tawny/red in colour.

BANKS & TAYLOR   See B&T.

BANKS'S

Unspoilt by Progress

The Wolverhampton & Dudley Breweries PLC, PO Box 26, Park Brewery, Bath Road, Wolverhampton, W. Midlands WV1 4NY. Tel. (01902) 711811 Fax. (01902) 29136

Wolverhampton & Dudley Breweries was formed in 1890 by the amalgamation of three local companies. Hanson's was acquired in 1943, but its Dudley brewery was closed in 1991 and Hanson's Mild is now brewed at Wolverhampton. The 150 Hanson's pubs keep their own livery. In 1992, W&D bought Camerons Brewery and 51 pubs from Brent Walker, bringing the total estate for the whole group up to 950 houses, virtually all serving traditional ales, mostly through electric, metered dispense. Extensive free trade throughout the country, in pubs and clubs. Tours by arrangement.

Hanson's Mild   (OG 1030, ABV 3.2%) A mid- to dark brown mild with a malty roast flavour and aftertaste.

Mild   (OG 1036, ABV 3.4%) A top-selling, amber-coloured, malty mild, with hints of bitterness, roast malt and caramel. It is now being marketed simply as 'Banks's'.

Bitter   (OG 1039, ABV 3.6%) A malty, pale brown, bittersweet beer, with more hops in the bitter aftertaste.

BARLEY   See Fox & Hounds.

BASS   See Nationals.

BATEMAN

George Bateman & Son Ltd., Salem Bridge Brewery, Mill Lane, Wainfleet, Skegness, Lincolnshire PE24 4JE. Tel. (01754) 880317 Fax. (01754) 880939

A family-owned and -run brewery, established in 1874 by the present chairman's grandfather, then a bankrupt farmer, to serve local landworkers. In the mid-1980s a family dispute threatened the brewery's future, but, after a three-year battle, Chairman George Bateman secured the brewery's independence and is now steadily expanding its sales area to cover nearly the whole of the UK. All its 57 tied houses serve real ale. Shop open 8.45–5 Mon–Fri. Tours by arrangement.

Dark Mild ⊟   (OG 1033, ABV 3%) Ruby black, topped by a cream head, this is the epitome of a mild. Roast malt leads the way with hops and bitterness appearing in the taste and finish.

XB   (OG 1037, ABV 3.8%) Prominent hops are backed up with malt and some slight fruitiness in this light brown, satisfying, bitter beer.

Valiant   (OG 1043, ABV 4.3%) Golden brown and hoppy: a fine beer with fruit present throughout. Malt comes strongly through in the aftertaste. Sometimes difficult to find in the tied trade.

Salem Porter   (OG 1049, ABV 5%) A black beer with a ruby hue. Malty and fruity, it matures well, tempering some of the initial liquorice taste and developing other fruit flavours in its dry aftertaste.

XXXB (OG 1049, ABV 5%) Malty, yet hoppy and bitter, beer with faint fruit detectable in the taste and aftertaste. Still an outstanding beer of its class.

Victory Ale (OG 1059, ABV 6%) A fruity, powerful, strong beer. Malty and sweet to the taste, developing into a lighter, fruity, hoppy and bitter finish, that makes it dangerously drinkable for its strength.

BATHAM **Bathams (Delph) Ltd., Delph Brewery, Delph Road, Brierley Hill, W. Midlands DY5 2TN. Tel. (01384) 77229 Fax. (01384) 482292**

Small brewery hidden behind one of the Black Country's most famous pubs, the Vine (or the 'Bull & Bladder', as it is commonly known). Established in 1877 and now in its fifth generation of family ownership, Batham currently supplies over 20 free trade outlets. A programme of upgrading and refurbishment is underway in its tied estate (nine houses) and there are plans to acquire more pubs. Tours on Saturdays by arrangement (max. ten people).

Mild Ale (OG 1037, ABV 3.5%) Fruity, dark brown mild with a malty sweetness and a roast malt finish.

Best Bitter (OG 1044, ABV 4.3%) A pale yellow, very fruity and lightly refreshing bitter. The initial sweetness progresses to a complex, dry, hoppy taste.

XXX* (OG 1064, ABV 6.3%) A winter ale.

BEARTOWN **Beartown Brewery, Unit 9, Varey Road, Eaton Bank Trading Estate, Congleton, Cheshire CW12 1UW. Tel. (01260) 299964**

Congleton's links with brewing can be traced back to 1272, when the town received charter status. Two of its most senior officers at the time were Ale Taster and Bear Warden, hence the name of this new brewery, set up in November 1994 on land which once housed Samuel Bull's silk mill (giving rise to the name of SB Bitter).

SB Bitter* (OG 1043, ABV 4.2%)

Th'underback* (OG 1055, ABV 5.3%) A winter brew.

BEER ENGINE **The Beer Engine, Sweetham, Newton St Cyres, Exeter, Devon EX5 5AX. Tel. (01392) 851282**

Brew pub set up in 1983, next to the Barnstaple branch railway line (hence the beer names), and expanded in 1989 with the acquisition of a second pub, the Sleeper in Seaton. This was sold in 1994, but two other free trade outlets are currently supplied and the beers are also distributed via agencies. Tours by arrangement. Occasional beers: Porter (OG 1042, ABV 4.3%), Whistlemas (OG 1070, ABV 7.2% but varies, Christmas).

Rail Ale (OG 1036, ABV 3.8%) Amber-coloured beer with a malty aroma and a fruity, sweet taste.

Piston Bitter (OG 1042, ABV 4.3%) Mid-brown, sweet-tasting beer with a pleasant bittersweet aftertaste.

Sleeper Heavy (OG 1052, ABV 5.4%) Red-coloured beer with a fruity, sweet taste and a bitter finish.

BELCHERS See Hedgehog & Hogshead.

BELHAVEN **Belhaven Brewery Co. Ltd., Spott Road, Dunbar, Lothian EH42 1RS. Tel. (01368) 862734 Fax. (01368) 864550**

With a tradition of brewing going back almost 800 years, Scotland's oldest brewery has had a chequered recent history. It was

bought in 1989 by the London-based Control Securities PLC, but in 1993 its employees successfully engineered a management buy-out of the brewery. Despite all its ups and downs, it continues to produce award-winning beers, supplying 56 of its 65 houses, and a further 400 outlets, with cask beer. Shop open 9–5 Mon–Fri. Tours by arrangement. Occasional beer: 90/- (OG 1071, ABV 8%).

60/- Ale*	(OG 1030, ABV 2.9%)
70/- Ale*	(OG 1035, ABV 3.5%)
Sandy Hunter's Traditional Ale	(OG 1038, ABV 3.6%) A distinctive, medium-bodied beer named after Belhaven's recent chairman and head brewer. An aroma of malt, hops and characteristic sulphur greets the nose; caramel and a hint of roast malt combine with the malt and hops to give a bittersweet taste and finish.
Festival Gold*	(OG 1039, ABV 3.8%)
80/- Ale	(OG 1041, ABV 4.2%) Incredibly robust, malty beer with a sulphury aroma. This classic ale has a burst of complex flavours in the taste and a rich, bittersweet finish.
St Andrew's Ale*	(OG 1046, ABV 4.9%)

BELVOIR — **Belvoir Brewery, Woodhill, Nottingham Lane, Old Dalby, Leicestershire LE14 3LX. Tel. (01664) 823455**

Belvoir Brewery

Brewery founded by former Theakston and Shipstone's brewer Colin Brown in summer 1995 to supply local free trade outlets.

Beaver Bitter* — (OG 1044, ABV 4.3%)

BENSKINS — See Nationals, Carlsberg-Tetley.

BENTLEY — See Nationals, Whitbread.

BERKELEY — **Berkeley Brewing Co., The Brewery, Bucketts Hill Farm, Berkeley, Gloucestershire GL13 9NQ. Tel. (01453) 811895**

This small operation was set up in an old farm cider cellar early in 1994, and brewing began in September that year. It now brews 'on demand' and supplies six local pubs.

Old Friend — (OG 1039, ABV 3.8%) A hoppy aroma leads into this fruity, hoppy beer which has a moderately hoppy, bitter finish.

Berkeley Vale Ale* — (ABV 4.5%)

BERROW — **Berrow Brewery, Coast Road, Berrow, Burnham-on-Sea, Somerset TA8 2QU. Tel. (01278) 751345**

Brewery founded in June 1982 to supply pubs and clubs locally (about ten free trade outlets). Tours by arrangement.

Best Bitter (BBBB or 4Bs) — (OG 1038, ABV 3.9%) A pleasant, pale brown session beer, with a fruity aroma, a malty, fruity flavour and bitterness in the palate and finish.

Porter* — (OG 1044, ABV 4.4%)

Topsy Turvy (TT) — (OG 1055, ABV 6%) A straw-coloured beer with an aroma of malt and hops, which are also evident in the taste, together with sweetness. The aftertaste is malty. Very easy to drink. Beware!

BIG END — See Daleside.

BIG LAMP — **Big Lamp Brewers, 1 Summerhill Street, Newcastle upon Tyne, Tyne & Wear NE4 6EJ. Tel. (0191) 261 4227**

Big Lamp was set up in 1982 and changed hands at the end of 1990. The plant was expanded in February 1995, to double the capacity, and Big Lamp currently supplies one tied house and a growing free trade (about 55 outlets). Occasional beers: Old Genie (OG 1070, ABV 7.4%), Blackout (OG 1100, ABV 11%).

Bitter	(OG 1038, ABV 3.9%) A bitter, hoppy beer with a strong hop aroma and taste. There is some fruit in the background, but the finish is lightly dry.
Prince Bishop Ale	(OG 1044, ABV 4.8%) A deceptively light-coloured beer for its gravity. The aroma and taste feature well-balanced hops and malt, with a background spikiness. A beer full of flavours.
Summerhill Stout	(OG 1048, ABV 4.8%) Another beer with many features, including a rich roast aroma and a malty mouthfeel. Look for a light bitterness and some sweetness.
Premium	(OG 1046, ABV 5%) Formerly ESB, a complex beer with a red hue. Hops balance malt against a background fruitiness and a lingering bitterness. A distinctive and special bitter.
Winter Warmer	(OG 1048, ABV 5.2%) A strong bitter, fortified with roast malt character and rich maltiness. Try it for its mouthfeel and lasting bitterness.

BIRD IN HAND

 Wheal Ale Brewery Ltd., Paradise Park, Hayle, Cornwall TR27 4HY. Tel. (01736) 753974

Unusual brewery in a bird park, founded in 1980 as Paradise Brewery. Three other pubs are supplied, plus more in summer. Beers: Paradise Bitter (OG 1040, ABV 3.8%), Miller's Ale (OG 1045, ABV 4.3%), Artists Ale (OG 1055, ABV 5.1%), Old Speckled Parrot (ABV 6.3%).

BISHOPS

Bishops Brewery, 2 Park Street, Borough Market, London SE1 9AB. Tel./Fax. (0171) 357 8343

Small brewery established in December 1993 by the former brewer at the Market Porter brew pub. Malt extract is added to the mashes.

Traditional Ale*	(OG 1035, ABV 3.5%)
Cathedral Bitter*	(OG 1037, ABV 3.7%)
Cardinal Ale*	(OG 1047, ABV 4.7%)

BLACKAWTON

Blackawton Brewery, Washbourne, Totnes, Devon TQ9 7UF. Tel. (01803) 732339 Fax. (01803) 732151

Situated just outside the village of Washbourne, this small family brewery was founded in 1977 and is now the oldest in Devon. It originated in the village of Blackawton, but moved to its present site in 1981 and, although it changed ownership in 1988, it retains a loyal local following, serving around 50 free trade outlets, but having no pubs of its own. Occasional beers: Winter Fuel (ABV 4.1%, Christmas–January), Shepherd's Delight (OG 1044, ABV 4.6%, April).

Bitter	(OG 1038, ABV 3.8%) Tawny in colour, with a bitter/fruity taste and a bitter aftertaste.
Devon Gold*	(OG 1041, ABV 4.1%) A summer brew, available April–October. A very pleasant, straw-coloured beer.
44 Special	(OG 1045, ABV 4.5%) Tawny, fruity-flavoured bitter with a slightly sweet taste and finish.
Headstrong	(OG 1052, ABV 5.2%) Mid-brown, strong beer, with a pleasant, fruity, sweet taste and finish.

BLACKBEARD See Fox & Hounds, Freeminer and Hanby.

BLACK BULL

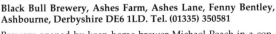

Black Bull Brewery, Ashes Farm, Ashes Lane, Fenny Bentley, Ashbourne, Derbyshire DE6 1LD. Tel. (01335) 350581

Brewery opened by keen home brewer Michael Peach in a converted building on his own farm in April 1994. Twenty-five outlets currently take the beer and plans for bottle-conditioned beers are in hand. Tours by arrangement.

Dovedale Bitter*	(OG 1036, ABV 3.6%)
Best Bitter*	(OG 1040, ABV 4%) A dark ruby bitter.
Raging Bull*	(OG 1049, ABV 4.9%)
Owd Shrovetider*	(OG 1060, ABV 5.9%) A winter warmer, available November–February.

BLACK HORSE & RAINBOW

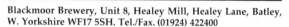

The Liverpool Brewing Company Ltd., The Black Horse & Rainbow, 21–23 Berry Street, Liverpool, Merseyside L1 9DF. Tel. (0151) 709 5055 Fax. (0151) 709 9405

Brewery with a five-barrel plant, set up in July 1990 to brew solely for the Black Horse & Rainbow pub, although a second pub is now being considered to take the brewery's excess capacity. The beer is stored in cellar tanks and the brewery can be viewed both from inside the pub and from the street. Beers: Black Horse Bitter (OG 1045, ABV 4.3%), Winter Ale (OG 1045, ABV 4.3%), Celebration Bitter (OG 1050, ABV 4.8%).

BLACKMOOR

Blackmoor Brewery, Unit 8, Healey Mill, Healey Lane, Batley, W. Yorkshire WF17 5SH. Tel./Fax. (01924) 422400

Brewery founded in December 1994 and now supplying around ten outlets. There are plans for a brew pub and also a shop.

Batley Bitter*	(OG 1036, ABV 3.6%)
Bog Standard Bitter	(OG 1042, ABV 4.2%) An initially very bitter and hoppy beer, with sweet, malty flavours lingering in the finish. Copper coloured.
Nectar Soup*	(OG 1042, ABV 4.2%)
Batley Shampayne*	(OG 1048, ABV 4.8%)
DOA*	(OG 1050, ABV 5%)

BLACK SHEEP

The Black Sheep Brewery PLC, Wellgarth, Masham, Ripon, N. Yorkshire HG4 4EN. Tel. (01765) 689227 Fax. (01765) 689746

Set up in 1992 by Paul Theakston, a member of Masham's famous brewing family, in the former Wellgarth Maltings, Black Sheep is currently brewing 300 barrels a week, with all beer fermented exclusively in Yorkshire slate squares. Expansion is imminent, to cater for an expanding free trade, which now extends to some 300 outlets. Brewery shop, open 9–5 Mon–Fri all year; 10.30–5 Sat, 11–4.30 Sun, Easter–end September. Tours by arrangement.

Best Bitter	(OG 1039, ABV 3.8%) A beer offering a subtle aroma of malt, with traces of fruit and hops. The flavour is malty with underlying faint fruit and hop bitterness. Dry finish but little depth of flavour.
Special Strong Bitter	(OG 1046, ABV 4.4%) A well-hopped, initially smooth beer becoming dry and astringent and giving a strong, bitter aftertaste, with some hop and fruit.

BLEWITTS

Blewitts Brewery, South Hams Business Park, First Farm, Churchstow, Devon TQ7 3QR. Tel. (01548) 856351

Originally set up as a brew pub at the Ship & Plough in Kingsbridge, this brewery was moved in February 1995 to new premises. There are plans to reinstate the brew pub to produce three or four of the beers listed below for its own customers. The new brewery currently supplies six other outlets. Tours by arrangement.

Best*	(OG 1040, ABV 3.8%)
Wages*	(OG 1044, ABV 4.2%)

The tankard symbol indicates the *Good Beer Guide Beers of the Year*, finalists in the *Champion Beer of Britain* contest held at the *Great British Beer Festival* at Olympia in August 1995.

Nose*	(OG 1048, ABV 4.6%)
Head Off*	(OG 1050, ABV 4.8%)
Top*	(OG 1055, ABV 5.2%)

BLUE ANCHOR  Blue Anchor, 50 Coinagehall Street, Helston, Cornwall TR13 8EL. Tel. (01326) 562821

Historic thatched brew pub, possibly the oldest in the UK, originating as a monks' resting place in the 15th century. It produces powerful ales known locally as 'Spingo' beers. Beers: Middle (OG 1050, ABV 4.9%), Best (OG 1053, ABV 4.9%), Special (OG 1066, ABV 6.3%, summer), Extra Special (OG 1076, ABV 7.3%, winter).

BODDINGTONS See Nationals, Whitbread and Pub Groups.

BODICOTE See Plough Inn.

BORDER Border Brewery Company, The Old Kiln, Brewery Lane, Tweedmouth, Berwick-upon-Tweed, Northumberland TD15 2AH. Tel. (01289) 303303 Fax. (01289) 306115

Do not confuse with the Wrexham brewery taken over and closed by Marston's. This operation opened in 1992 in an old kiln on the site of Berwick's original Border Brewery, which was established in the 17th century, but which lay idle for 50 years. A change of ownership took place in June 1994, with the company becoming a partnership. The output is slowly increasing, and the brewery regularly supplies 15 outlets. Tours by arrangement. Occasional beer: Rudolph's Ruin (OG 1068, ABV 7.1%, Christmas).

Old Kiln Bitter	(OG 1037, ABV 3.8%) A richly hoppy bitter, with strong mouthfeel and lasting maltiness.
Special Bitter*	(OG 1037, ABV 3.8%)
Old Kiln Ale	(OG 1039, ABV 4%) A light-tasting bitter with a hoppy and fruity character and lasting sweetness.
Noggins Nog	(OG 1041, ABV 4.2%) An unusual mix of malt and roast malt leaves an impressive chocolate character in the aftertaste of this solidly made beer.
SOB*	(OG 1048, ABV 5%)

BORVE Borve Brew House, Ruthven, Huntly, Grampian AB54 4SR. Tel. (01466) 760343

Borve moved from its original site on the Isle of Lewis in 1988, taking up residence in a former school on the mainland. The school is now a pub, with the brewhouse adjacent. A few free trade outlets are also supplied. Tours by arrangement. Beers: Borve Ale (OG 1040, ABV 3.9%), Tall Ships IPA (OG 1050, ABV 4.9%), Union Street 200 (OG 1050, ABV 4.8%). Bottle-conditioned beers: as cask, plus Extra Strong (OG 1085, ABV 9.8%).

BRAINS SA Brain & Co. Ltd., The Old Brewery, 49 St Mary Street, Cardiff, S. Glamorgan CF1 1SP. Tel. (01222) 399022 Fax. (01222) 383127

A traditional brewery which has been in the Brain family since Samuel Brain and his Uncle Joseph bought the Old Brewery in 1882. It supplies cask-conditioned beer to all its 114 pubs and over 500 free trade outlets, including many clubs. Several Brains houses have joined in a series of 'Guest beer of the month' promotions, some of which feature occasional brews by Brains itself. Others come from other independent brewers. Brains beers also appear as guests in many big brewers' outlets in South Wales and beyond, and the company still has interests in hotel and leisure projects in Wales and the West Country. MA (OG 1035, ABV 3.6%, a mix of Dark and Bitter) is usually only available at the Crown Hotel,

Skewen, West Glamorgan. Brewery shop open 9–5.40 Mon–Sat. Tours by arrangement.

Dark

(OG 1035, ABV 3.5%) A full-bodied, dark brown mild with traces of chocolate followed by a rounded, bittersweet finish.

Bitter

(OG 1035, ABV 3.7%) A distinctively bitter beer, pale and somewhat hoppy, with faint malt and a dry finish. Commonly known as 'Light'.

SA Best Bitter

(OG 1042, ABV 4.2%) A full-bodied, malty, hoppy, premium bitter; well-balanced, with a smooth, dry finish.

BRAKSPEAR

WH Brakspear & Sons PLC, The Brewery, New Street, Henley-on-Thames, Oxfordshire RG9 2BU. Tel. (01491) 573636 Fax. (01491) 410254

Brewing took place before 1700 on this Henley site, but the Brakspear family involvement only began in 1799, when Robert Brakspear formed a partnership with Richard Hayward. It was Robert's son, William Henry, who greatly expanded the brewery and its trade. Brakspear today boasts many excellent, unspoilt pubs (though the estate is being rationalised) and all its 106 houses serve traditional ales. Around 350 free trade outlets are supplied direct and trading arrangements with Whitbread and others mean that Brakspear's ales are available throughout southern England. Improvements to the brewery site are likely to include a new bottling line with scope for producing a bottle-conditioned ale. Shop at 38 Hart Street open 9–6 Mon–Wed and Sat, 9–7 Thu and Fri.

Mild

(OG 1030, ABV 3%) A thin beer with a red/brown colour and a sweet, malty, fruity aroma. The well-balanced taste of malt, hops and caramel has a faint bitterness, complemented by a sweet, fruity flavour. The main characteristics extend through to the bittersweet finish.

Bitter

(OG 1035, ABV 3.4%) Amber in colour, with a good fruit, hop and malt nose. The initial taste of malt and the dry, well-hopped bitterness quickly dissolves into a predominantly bitter, sweet and fruity aftertaste.

Old Ale

(OG 1043, ABV 4.3%) Red/brown with good body. The strong, fruity aroma is well complemented by malt, hops and roast caramel. Its pronounced taste of malt, with discernible sweet, roast malt and caramel flavours, gives way to fruitiness. The aftertaste is of bittersweet chocolate, even though chocolate malt is not present.

Special

(OG 1043, ABV 4.3%) Tawny/amber in colour; its good, well-balanced aroma has a hint of sweetness. The initial taste is moderately sweet and malty, but is quickly overpowered by the dry bitterness of the hops, before a slightly sweet fruitiness. A distinct, dry, malty finish.

OBJ*

(OG 1050, ABV 5%)

BRANSCOMBE VALE

The Branscombe Vale Brewery, Great Seaside Farm, Branscombe, Seaton, Devon EX12 3DP. Tel. (01297) 680511

Brewery set up in July 1992 in two cowsheds owned by the National Trust, by former dairy workers Paul Dimond and Graham Luxton, who converted the sheds and dug their own well. It currently supplies 30 outlets regularly and there are plans to double capacity by summer 1996. An own label house beer (OG 1044, ABV 4.6%) is produced for several local pubs in East Devon and one beer is brewed for the Lock, Stock and Barrel wholesalers – tel. (01364) 644124. Tours by arrangement. Occasional beer: Anniversary Ale (OG 1044, ABV 4.6%, December).

Branoc

(OG 1040, ABV 3.8%) A well-balanced bitter with a hoppy, bitter taste and aftertaste.

Olde Stoker

(OG 1054, ABV 5.6%) A dark brown beer with a distinct aroma and taste of roast and fruit, and a bitter aftertaste.

For Lock, Stock and Barrel:

Pistol Knight* (OG 1041, ABV 4.3%)

BREWERY ON SEA

The Brewery on Sea Ltd., Unit 24, Winston Business Centre, Chartwell Road, Lancing, W. Sussex BN15 8TU. Tel. (01903) 851482

Brewery established in 1993. The capacity was increased early in 1995 to around 55 barrels a week, the majority of which is taken by wholesalers, although some is sold in the immediate vicinity of the brewery. Beers are also brewed for East-West Ales – tel. (01892) 834040 – some of which are sold exclusively in JD Wetherspoon houses, and the London Beer Company – tel. (0171) 739 3701. Occasional beers: Spinnaker Porter (OG 1047, ABV 5%), Tidal Wave (OG 1065, ABV 7%).

Spinnaker Bitter* (OG 1036, ABV 3.5%) Hoppy tasting, smooth, basic ale.

Spinnaker Mild or Lancing Special Dark* (OG 1036, ABV 3.5%) A traditional style mild.

Spinnaker Classic* (OG 1040, ABV 4%)

Spinnaker Buzz (OG 1044, ABV 4.5%) An amber-coloured, interesting beer, primed with honey. Honey predominates in the aroma, while an initial sweetness gives way to an intriguing flavour, blending malt, honey and hops. Hoppy aftertaste.

Black Rock* (OG 1050, ABV 5.5%)

Special Crew* (OG 1050, ABV 5.5%)

Spinnaker Ginger* (OG 1050, ABV 5.5%)

Riptide* (OG 1060, ABV 6.5%)

For East-West Ales:

Winter Widget* (OG 1043, ABV 4.5%)

Wicked Widget* (OG 1045, ABV 4.7%)

For London Beer Company:

Pitfield Bitter* (OG 1036, ABV 3.5%)

Hoxton* (OG 1048, ABV 5.5%)

BRIDGWATER

Bridgwater Brewing Company, Unit 1, Lovedere Farm, Goathurst, Bridgwater, Somerset TA5 2DD. Tel. (01278) 663996

Brewery established in spring 1993. Within the first 12 months, the equipment had been upgraded from a four- to a 15-barrel plant and over 40 free trade outlets are now supplied. Tours by arrangement. Occasional beers: Carnival Special Brew (OG 1035, ABV 3.5%, October–November), Krimbleale (OG 1050, ABV 4.8%, Christmas).

Blake's Bitter* (OG 1035, ABV 3.4%)

Amber Ale* (OG 1040, ABV 3.8%)

Bosun's Tickle* (OG 1042, ABV 4.1%)

Coppernob* (OG 1045, ABV 4.4%)

Sunbeam* (OG 1052, ABV 5.4%)

Bluto's Revenge* (OG 1060, ABV 6%).

BRISTOL BREWHOUSE See Ross.

The Independents

BRITANNIA

The Britannia Ales Brewery, Britannia Inn, Kent Street, Upper Gornall, W. Midlands DY3 1UX. Tel. (01902) 883253

Historic brew pub which ceased production in 1959 but began brewing again in May 1995. The two full mash beers are available in the pub itself and occasionally at local beer festivals. A third brew, Yule Britannia, is planned for Christmas. Beers: Sally Perry Mild (ABV 3.5%), Wally Williams Bitter (ABV 4.5%).

BRITISH OAK

British Oak Brewery, Salop Street, Eve Hill, Dudley, W. Midlands DY1 3AX. Tel. (01384) 236297

British Oak began life as a family-run brew pub in May 1988, and now usually only supplies this and a second pub of its own. Tours by arrangement. Beers: Mild (OG 1038, ABV 3.7%), Eve'ill Bitter (OG 1042, ABV 4%), Colonel Pickering's Porter (OG 1046, ABV 4.6%, occasional), Dungeon Draught (OG 1050, ABV 4.8%, occasional), Old Jones (OG 1062, ABV 6.2%, September–April).

BROUGHTON

Broughton Brewery Ltd., Broughton, Biggar, Borders ML12 6HQ. Tel. (01889) 830345 Fax. (01889) 830474

Go-ahead brewery, founded in 1980 by former S&N executive David Younger to brew and distribute real ale in central and southern Scotland. It currently supplies 250 outlets, plus two tied houses in Dumfries. While this remains the priority, a strong bottled beer trade (not bottle-conditioned) has developed nationwide. Shop open 10–4. Tours by arrangement.

Scottish Oatmeal Stout*	(OG 1038, ABV 3.8%) Also sold by Jennings.
Greenmantle Ale*	(OG 1039, ABV 3.9%) A beer lacking aroma, but bittersweet in taste, with a hint of fruit, and a very dry finish.
Special Bitter*	(OG 1039, ABV 3.9%) A dry-hopped version of Greenmantle.
80/- Ale*	(OG 1042, ABV 4.2%)
Merlin's Ale*	(OG 1042, ABV 4.2%)
Old Jock*	(OG 1070, ABV 6.7%) Strong, sweetish and fruity in the finish.

MATTHEW BROWN See Nationals, Scottish & Newcastle.

ABEL BROWN'S See Stag.

TOM BROWN'S See Goldfinch.

BRUNSWICK

The Brunswick Inn Ltd. Brewing Co., 1 Railway Terrace, Derby DE1 2RU. Tel. (01332) 290677 Fax. (01332) 370226

Purpose-built tower brewery attached to the Brunswick Inn, a famous railway hotel partly restored by the Derbyshire Historic Building Trust and bought by the present owners in 1987. Brewing began in 1991 and a viewing area allows pub-users to watch production. The beers are currently only sold at the pub. Tours by arrangement. Beers: The Recession Ale (OG 1033, ABV 3.3%), First Brew (OG 1036, ABV 3.6%), Recession Extra (OG 1038, ABV 3.8%), Second Brew (OG 1042, ABV 4.2%), Railway Porter (OG 1045, ABV 4.3%), Festival Ale (OG 1046, ABV 4.6%), Old Accidental (OG 1050, ABV 4.9%), Owd Abusive (OG 1066, ABV 6%). Bottle-conditioned beer: Old Vicarage Ale (OG 1074, ABV 7%).

BUCKLEY See Crown Buckley.

424

The Independents

BUFFY'S

Buffy's Brewery, Mardle Hall, Rectory Road, Tivetshall St Mary, Norwich, Norfolk NR15 2DD. Tel. (01379) 676523

Situated alongside a 15th-century house, Buffy's started life as Mardle Hall Brewery in November 1993, but was forced to change its name after a complaint from another brewery. Twenty local free houses are supplied with the beer which is now available more widely via wholesalers. Tours by arrangement.

Bitter
(OG 1038, ABV 4%) Very well-balanced throughout, this is a flavoursome session beer, not at all bland or cloying, with more complexity than its gravity may suggest.

Polly's Folly ⊟
(OG 1041, ABV 4.3%) A well-balanced amber beer with a flowery hop character in its aroma. The palate is clean and bitter, with malt and some citrus notes which die away in the aftertaste to let the hops and bitterness come through.

Best Bitter
(OG 1046, ABV 4.9%) Much like the bitter, only stronger and fuller-bodied. It is just as well-balanced, but with a rounder, fruitier palate. It is also moreish, with a clean, bitter finish.

Ale
(OG 1052, ABV 5.5%) A pale brown beer which is a smooth and malty, strong bitter throughout. Slightly warming and easy to drink.

Strong Ale
(OG 1062, ABV 6.5%) A rich, hearty and complex, darkish brown beer which is full of malt and fruit, with some hoppiness. Very drinkable for its strength.

BULLMASTIFF

Bullmastiff Brewery, 14 Bessemer Close, Leckwith, Cardiff, S. Glamorgan CF1 8DL. Tel. (01222) 665292

Small brewery set up in the Penarth docklands in 1987 and moved to larger premises in Cardiff in 1992. Bullmastiff now supplies about 30 outlets locally, but not on a regular basis, so the beers may be rather hard to find on the brewery's home patch. Much of the production is sold in other parts of the country through wholesalers. Occasional beer: Ebony Dark (OG 1040, ABV 3.8%)

Bitter
(OG 1036, ABV 3.5%) A pale brown, bitter beer, slightly malty with a dry finish. A popular session beer.

Best Bitter
(OG 1042, ABV 4%) A well-balanced, malty, bitter beer with a balanced, hoppy, fruity finish. Very drinkable.

Brindle*
(OG 1050, ABV 5%)

Son of a Bitch ⊟
(OG 1064, ABV 6%) A full-bodied, notably hoppy and malty, bitter beer. This premium bitter has a distinctive aroma and aftertaste.

BULL'S HEAD

Bull's Head Brewery, The Three Tuns, 34 High Street, Alcester, Warwickshire B49 5AC. Tel. (01789) 766550

Brewery founded on a farm at Inkberrow, Hereford & Worcester in December 1994, which moved to the rear of the Three Tuns in Alcester, Warwickshire in 1995. It now brews mostly for the pub itself, where beer is kept in cellar tanks (without a blanket of gas). Beer: Light (OG 1046, ABV 4.5%).

BUNCES

Bunces Brewery, The Old Mill, Netheravon, Wiltshire SP4 9QB. Tel./Fax. (01980) 670631

Tower brewery housed in a listed building on the Wiltshire Avon, established in 1984 and sold to Danish proprietors in summer 1993. Its cask-conditioned beers are delivered to around 30 free trade outlets within a radius of 50 miles, and a number of wholesalers are also supplied. Shop open 8.30–5.30 Mon–Fri; 10–1 Sat. Tours by arrangement. Occasional beer: Rudolph (OG 1050, ABV 5%, Christmas).

Vice Beer*
(OG 1033, ABV 3.2%) A wheat beer for summer.

Benchmark
(OG 1035, ABV 3.5%) A pleasant, bitter ale of remarkable character, which maintains one's interest for a long time. The taste is malty, the aroma subtle and the very long finish is quite dry on the palate.

The Independents

Pigswill*	(OG 1040, ABV 4%)
Best Bitter	(OG 1042, ABV 4.2%) A first-rate beer. The piquant aroma introduces a complex, malty and bitter taste with a hint of fruit. Long, fresh, bitter aftertaste.
Old Smokey	(OG 1050, ABV 5%) A delightful, warming, dark bitter ale, with a roasted malt taste and a hint of liquorice surrounding a developing bitter flavour. Very appealing to the eye.

BURTON BRIDGE

Burton Bridge Brewery, 24 Bridge Street, Burton upon Trent, Staffordshire DE14 1SY. Tel. (01283) 510573

Established in 1982, with one tied outlet at the front of the brewery. Conversion of the adjoining premises into a new brewhouse has begun and the pub will eventually be extended into the old brewery buildings. Guest beers are supplied to around 250 outlets virtually nationwide, and Burton Bridge specialises in commemorative bottled beers to order. The brewery also brews for the Heritage Brewery Museum in Burton – tel. (01283) 510246. Occasional beers: Spring Ale (OG 1047, ABV 4.7% March–April), Battle Brew (OG 1050, ABV 5%, July–August), Hearty Ale (OG 1050, ABV 5%, Christmas). Bottle-conditioned beer: Burton Porter ⊲ (OG 1045, ABV 4.5%).

Summer Ale*	(OG 1038, ABV 3.8%) Only available during British Summer Time.
XL Bitter	(OG 1040, ABV 4%) A golden, malty drinking bitter, with a faint, hoppy and fruity aroma. An excellent mix of flavours follows, with fruitiness dominating.
Bridge Bitter	(OG 1042, ABV 4.2%) An amber-coloured, robust and malty beer. The taste is bittersweet with fruit and gives way to a dominating hoppy finish.
Burton Porter	(OG 1045, ABV 4.5%) A ruby-red, sweetish porter. Roast malt and fruit flavours emerge and fruit lingers, before giving way to a subtly bitter finish.
Knot Brown Ale*	(OG 1048, ABV 4.8%) An autumn beer.
Top Dog Stout	(OG 1050, ABV 5%) A winter brew with a strong roast malt and fruit mix, developing into a potent malt and roast malt aftertaste.
Burton Festival Ale	(OG 1055, ABV 5.5%) A full-bodied, copper-coloured, strong but sweet beer. The aroma is hoppy, malty and slightly fruity. Malt and hops in the flavour give way to a fruity finish. Tremendous mouthfeel.
Old Expensive*	(OG 1065, ABV 6.7%) A winter warmer, virtually a barley wine. Its wonderful mix of sweetness and fruit certainly hits the throat.
	For Heritage:
Thomas Sykes Old Ale*	(OG 1100, ABV 10%) Available in winter and spring. Also bottled-conditioned and sometimes sold as Christmas Ale.

BURTONWOOD

Burtonwood Brewery PLC, Bold Lane, Burtonwood, Warrington, Cheshire WA5 4PJ. Tel. (01925) 225131 Fax. (01925) 224562

A family-run public company established in 1867 by James Forshaw, who had learned his trade at Bath Springs Brewery in Ormskirk. In the 1980s, Burtonwood embarked on a £6 million extension plan and a new brewhouse was completed in 1990. Real ale is supplied to over 400 of its 500 tied houses (138 of which are on long lease from Allied), and to 135 pubs in the free trade. Burtonwood also has a stake in the Paramount pub chain (see Pub Groups). Evening tours by arrangement.

Mild	(OG 1032, ABV 3%) A smooth, dark brown, malty mild with a good roast flavour, some caramel and a hint of bitterness. Slightly dry finish.
Bitter	(OG 1037, ABV 3.7%) A well-balanced, refreshing, malty bitter, with good hoppiness. Fairly dry aftertaste.

James Forshaw's Bitter   (OG 1038, ABV 4%) A malty and hoppy, well-balanced bitter. More hoppy and characterful than the ordinary bitter.

Top Hat   (OG 1046, ABV 4.8%) Soft, nutty, malty and a little sweet. Fairly thin for its gravity.

Buccaneer*   (OG 1052, ABV 5.2%)

For Whitbread:

Chester's Best Bitter*   (OG 1033, ABV 3.6%)

OB Bitter   (OG 1037.5, ABV 3.8%) Copper-coloured beer with an aroma of malt and fruit. The flavour is malty and bitter, with a bittersweet tinge and a dry, malty finish. A relic of the Oldham Brewery closed by Boddingtons.

BURTS

Mr Burt

Burts Brewery (Newport) Ltd., Dodnor Industrial Estate, Newport, Isle of Wight PO30 5FA. Tel./Fax. (01983) 528098

Brewery originally founded in 1840, but which went into receivership in 1992. The name and brands were bought by Hampshire soft drinks firm Hartridges, owners of Island Brewery, who now use the Burts name for all their brewing operations, supplying pubs both on the island and the mainland. The first tied house was acquired in March 1995. Brewery tours by arrangement.

Nipper Bitter*   (OG 1038, ABV 3.8%)

Parkhurst Porter*   (OG 1039, ABV 3.8%)

Ventnor Premium Ale or VPA*   (OG 1041, ABV 4.2%)

Newport Nobbler*   (OG 1043, ABV 4.4%)

Tanner Bitter*   (OG 1048, ABV 4.8%)

Old Vectis Venom*   (OG 1049, ABV 5%)

BUSHY'S

The Mount Murray Brewing Co. Ltd., Mount Murray, Castletown Road, Braddan, Isle of Man IM4 1JE. Tel. (01624) 661244 Fax. (01624) 611101

Set up in 1986 as a brew pub, Bushy's moved to its present site in 1990, when demand outgrew capacity. The beers, all brewed to the stipulations of the Manx Brewers' Act of 1874, are supplied to four tied houses and 25 other outlets. Tours by arrangement. Occasional beers: Piston Brew (OG 1045, ABV 4.5%, for the TT races in May–June), Lovely Jubbely Christmas Ale (OG 1055, ABV 5.2%).

Dark Mild   (OG 1035, ABV 3.4%) With a hoppy aroma, and notes of chocolate and coffee to the malty flavour, this rich, creamy, fruity, very dark brew is reminiscent of a porter.

Best Bitter   (OG 1038, ABV 3.8%) An aroma full of pale malt and hops introduces you to a beautifully hoppy, bitter beer. Despite the predominant hop character, malt is also evident. Fresh and clean-tasting.

Old Bushy Tail   (OG 1045, ABV 4.5%) An appealing reddish-brown beer with a pronounced hop and malt aroma, the malt tending towards treacle. Slightly sweet and malty on the palate, with distinct orangey tones. The full finish is malty and hoppy, with hints of toffee.

BUTCOMBE

Butcombe Brewery Ltd., Butcombe, Bristol, Avon BS18 6XQ. Tel. (01275) 472240

One of the most successful of the new wave of breweries, set up in 1978 by a former Courage Western MD, Simon Whitmore. During 1992–93, the brewery virtually doubled in size (for the third time), allowing for an 80-barrel brew. A fourth tied house has now been acquired. Real ale is supplied to over 300 outlets, mostly within a

The Independents

50-mile radius of the brewery, as well as further afield via wholesalers. Tours by arrangement.

Bitter (OG 1039, ABV 4%) An amber, malty bitter with subtle citrus fruit qualities. It has a hoppy, malty aroma and a dry, bitter finish. A well-regarded, refreshing bitter.

BUTTERKNOWLE

Butterknowle Brewery, The Old School House, Lynesack, Butterknowle, Bishop Auckland, Co. Durham DL13 5QF. Tel. (01388) 710109 Fax. (01388) 710373

Since its launch in August 1990, Butterknowle has continued to prosper and grow by producing award-winning ales. It now supplies almost 100 outlets nationwide on a regular basis. A new bottling room should soon be producing a full range of bottle-conditioned beers. The brewery is situated in Victorian buildings once home to the Lynesack National School. Occasional beer: West Auckland Mild (OG 1034, ABV 3.3%). Bottle-conditioned beer: Conciliation Ale (OG 1042, ABV 4.3%).

Bitter (OG 1036, ABV 3.6%) A good, hoppy bitter. Very drinkable, with a light bitterness and a malty aftertaste.

Banner Bitter* (OG 1040, ABV 4%)

Conciliation Ale (OG 1042, ABV 4.2%) Butterknowle's flagship brand. Fruit and hop compete for prominence in this classic bitter. Light mouthfeel, with rich, citrus bitterness leaving a crisp, dry aftertaste.

Black Diamond (OG 1050, ABV 4.8%) Actually red-brown in colour. A richly pungent ale with a good body and a sweet taste. Hop and bitter flavours are mild, leaving a grainy finish.

High Force (OG 1060, ABV 6.2%) A smooth strong ale, well-hopped with some fruity sweetness. A good depth of flavour develops in the aftertaste: a multi-dimensional beer.

Old Ebenezer (OG 1080, ABV 8%) A splendid, rich and fruity, seasonal barley wine: liquid Christmas cake with a potent punch. Surprisingly moreish, if only in sips!

BUTTS

Butts Brewery Ltd., Northfield Farm, Great Shefford, Newbury, Berkshire RG16 7DQ. Tel. (01488) 648133 Fax. (01734) 345860

This new brewery was set up in autumn 1994 with plant acquired from Butcombe. It is looking to build on its present clientele of 25 outlets in Berkshire and the surrounding counties of Hampshire, Oxfordshire and Wiltshire. Brewery tours by arrangement.

Bitter* (OG 1040, ABV 4%)

CAINS

Robert Cain & Co. Ltd., The Robert Cain Brewery, Stanhope Street, Liverpool, Merseyside L8 5XJ. Tel. (0151) 709 8734 Fax. (0151) 708 8395

Robert Cain's brewery was first established on this site in 1850, but was bought out by Higsons in the 1920s, then by Boddingtons in 1985. Whitbread took control of the Boddingtons breweries in 1990 and closed the site, switching the brewing of Higsons to Sheffield. The site was then bought by GB Breweries to brew canned beers, but with enthusiastic staff and CAMRA support, it soon moved on to cask ales. The company is now a division of the brewery group Denmark A/S. It won CAMRA's 1994 *Best Refurbishment* award for its single tied house. Over 300 free trade outlets are supplied in Merseyside and the North-West. Tours by arrangement. Occasional beer: Superior Stout (OG 1045, ABV 4.8%).

Dark Mild (OG 1033, ABV 3.2%) A smooth, dry and roasty dark mild, with some chocolate and coffee flavour. Tasty and satisfying.

Traditional Bitter (OG 1039, ABV 4%) A darkish, full-bodied bitter, with a good, hoppy nose and a dry aftertaste that marks a return to form.

Formidable Ale (FA) (OG 1048, ABV 5%) A bitter and hoppy beer with a good, dry aftertaste. Sharp, clean and dry.

The Independents

CALEDONIAN

The Caledonian Brewing Company Ltd., 42 Slateford Road, Edinburgh, Lothian EH11 1PH. Tel. (0131) 337 1286 Fax. (0131) 313 2370

Described by Michael Jackson as a 'living, working museum of beer making', Caledonian operates from a Victorian brewhouse, using the last three direct-fired open coppers in Britain, one of which dates back to 1869, when the brewery was started by George Lorimer and Robert Clark. The site was taken over by Vaux of Sunderland in 1919, who continued to brew there until 1987, when, under threat of closure, it was acquired by a management buy-out team. It has no tied estate, but around 350 free trade outlets are supplied, and the beers are increasingly available South of the Border. Tours by arrangement.

60/- Ale*	(OG 1032, ABV 3.2%)
70/- Ale*	(OG 1036, ABV 3.5%)
Murrays Summer Ale*	(OG 1036, ABV 3.6%)
Deuchars IPA ⊟	(OG 1038, ABV 3.8%) A refreshing, amber-coloured beer, with malt, hops and hints of fruit evident throughout, leading to a hoppy bitter finish. Surprisingly bitter for a Scottish beer.
Edinburgh Real Ale or ERA*	(OG 1042, ABV 4.1%)
80/- Ale	(OG 1042, ABV 4.1%) A predominantly malty bitter, well balanced by hop and fruit, with the characteristics of a Scottish heavy. A complex-tasting, copper-coloured beer.
Porter*	(OG 1042, ABV 4.1%)
Murrays Heavy*	(OG 1044, ABV 4.3%)
Campbell, Hope & King's Double Amber Ale*	(OG 1045, ABV 4.6%)
125*	(OG 1046, ABV 4.5%) Originally brewed to celebrate the brewery's 125th anniversary in 1994.
Phoenix*	(OG 1046, ABV 4.6%) Brewed to celebrate the brewery's recovery from a fire in 1994.
Golden Promise*	(OG 1049, ABV 5%) An organic beer.
Merman XXX*	(OG 1049, ABV 4.8%) Based on a Victorian recipe.
Edinburgh Strong Ale or ESA*	(OG 1063, ABV 6.4%)

CAMERONS

The Camerons Brewery Company, Lion Brewery, Hartlepool, Cleveland TS24 7QS. Tel. (01429) 266666 Fax. (01429) 868195

This major brewer of real ale, established in 1865, went through a difficult period during the late 1980s when it was acquired by the ill-fated Brent Walker group. However, since being bought by Wolverhampton & Dudley Breweries in 1992, the future has looked much rosier. W&D has invested heavily in the brewery and pub refurbishments, and successfully relaunched the beers, the latest being Crown Special in 1995, originally brewed for the Queen's Silver Jubilee. Real ale is supplied to all 100 local W&D tied houses and around 350 other outlets. Tours by arrangement.

Bitter	(OG 1036, ABV 3.6%) A light bitter, but well-balanced, with hops and malt.

OG stands for Original Gravity, the reading taken before fermentation of the amount of fermentable material in the brew. It is a rough indicator of strength. More reliable is the ABV (Alcohol by Volume) rating, which gives the percentage of alcohol in the finished beer.

Crown Special*	(OG 1041, ABV 4%)
Strongarm	(OG 1041, ABV 4%) Now substantially improved, and with consistent character. A rich, ruby red bitter with a full body and robust bitterness. Hop aroma is spicy and balances a lasting fruitiness.

CANNON

Parker & Son Brewers Ltd., The Cannon, Cannon Street, Wellingborough, Northamptonshire NN8 4DJ. Tel. (01933) 279629

Brewery founded in January 1993, in the old bottle store of the Cannon pub. A family-run business, it supplies the pub and ten other free trade outlets.

Light Brigade*	(OG 1036, ABV 3.6%)
Pride*	(OG 1042, ABV 4.2%)
Florrie Night-in-Ale*	(OG 1048, ABV 4.8%)
Fodder*	(OG 1055, ABV 5.5%)

CANNON ROYALL

Cannon Royall Brewery, The Fruiterer's Arms, Uphampton, Ombersley, Hereford & Worcester WR9 0JW. Tel. (01905) 621161

This five-barrel plant was set up in 1993, in a converted cider house behind the Fruiterer's Arms pub, by the former brewer at the Fox & Hounds in Stottesdon. It now brews 12 barrels a week, with plans for expansion. Free trade sales have increased to 20 outlets. Tours by arrangement.

KPA*	(OG 1034, ABV 3.4%) A new summer beer.
Mild*	(OG 1037, ABV 3.7%) A new brew to replace Millward's Musket Mild.
Arrowhead*	(OG 1039, ABV 3.9%) A beer in which hoppiness gradually increases leaving a strongly hoppy finish.
Buckshot*	(OG 1045, ABV 4.5%) Initially rich and malty beer, leaving a rounded, hoppy taste in the mouth.
Heart of Oak*	(OG 1054, ABV 5.4%)
Olde Merrie*	(OG 1060, ABV 6%) A strong, malty winter brew, almost a barley wine.

CARTMEL

Cartmel Brewery, Unit 7, Fell View Trading Park, Shap Road, Kendal, Cumbria LA9 6NZ. Tel. (01539) 724085

Set up by Nick Murray, in a disused barn at the Cavendish Arms, Cartmel in September 1994, this new brewery took off so successfully that larger premises were soon required and the plant was moved to nearby Kendal. Around 40 outlets are supplied, mostly in Cumbria and Lancashire, with a few in Scotland. Tours by arrangement.

Buttermere Bitter*	(OG 1035, ABV 3.6%)
Lakeland Gold*	(OG 1038, ABV 4%)
Thoroughbred*	(OG 1044, ABV 4.5%)
Winter Warmer*	(OG 1052, ABV 5.2%)

CASTLE EDEN	See Nationals, Whitbread.
CASTLETOWN	See Isle of Man Breweries.

CHALK HILL

Chalk Hill Brewery, Rosary Road, Thorpe Hamlet, Norwich, Norfolk NR1 4DA. Tel./Fax. (01603) 620703

Run by former Reindeer brew pub owner Bill Thomas and his partners, Chalk Hill began production with a 15-barrel plant in December 1993, supplying local free trade. It now has some 50 outlets and the beers are available nationwide via beer agencies. Further expansion of the brewery is underway.

Tap Bitter	(OG 1036, ABV 3.6%) A simple and unpretentious session beer, hoppy and quite well-balanced, but not strongly flavoured. A gentle, hoppy bitterness lingers in the aftertaste.
CHB	(OG 1042, ABV 4.2%) A fairly well-balanced, mid-brown beer, not very strongly flavoured.
Dreadnought	(OG 1049, ABV 4.9%) A strong brown bitter which, despite having little aroma, is full-flavoured, well-balanced, rounded and fruity. The aftertaste is similar but short. A beer which is easier to drink than its strength may suggest.
Old Tackle	(OG 1056, ABV 5.6%) A reddish brown beer with little aroma but a fairly full body and a full palate. The taste is complex, with mainly fruit but even hints of liquorice.

CHARRINGTON   See Shepherd Neame and Nationals, Bass.

CHERITON

The Cheriton Brewhouse, Cheriton, Alresford, Hampshire SO24 0QQ. Tel. (01962) 771166

A purpose-built brewery, opened at Easter 1993 by the licensees of the Flower Pots Inn next door, and two partners. With a ten-barrel plant, it now supplies around 40 free trade outlets, as well as a second pub, the Tally Ho! at Broughton, and the Watercress Line steam railway. Cheriton also produces occasional special brews.

Pots Ale	(OG 1037, ABV 3.8%) Golden in colour with a hoppy nose, a well-balanced bitter taste and a bitter aftertaste.
Best Bitter*	(OG 1041, ABV 4.2%)
Diggers Gold*	(OG 1046, ABV 4.6%)

CHESTER'S   See Nationals, Whitbread.

CHILTERN

The Chiltern Brewery, Nash Lee Road, Terrick, Aylesbury, Buckinghamshire HP17 0TQ. Tel. (01296) 613647 Fax. (01296) 612419

Set up in 1980 on a small farm, Chiltern specialises in an unusual range of beer-related products, like beer mustards, Old Ale chutneys, cheeses and malt marmalade. These products are available from the brewery shop (open 9–5 Mon–Sat) and also from a dozen other retail outlets. The beer itself is regularly supplied to up to 20 free trade outlets (no tied houses). There is a small museum (due to be expanded) and brewery tours are at noon Saturday, or by arrangement. Bottle-conditioned beer: Bodgers Barley Wine (OG 1080, ABV 8%).

Ale*	(OG 1038, ABV 3.7%) A distinctive, tangy light bitter.
Beechwood Bitter*	(OG 1043, ABV 4.3%) Full-bodied and nutty.
Three Hundreds Old Ale*	(OG 1050, ABV 4.9%) A strong, rich, deep chestnut-coloured beer.

CHURCH END

Church End Brewery Ltd., The Griffin Inn, Church Road, Shustoke, Warwickshire B46 2LP. Tel. (01675) 481567

Brewery founded in autumn 1994 in an old stable and coffin workshop behind the Griffin Inn. Brewing about six barrels a week, it produces guest and special brews for its free trade outlets (between 20 and 50). Tours by arrangement. Occasional beer: R-I-P (OG 1070, ABV 7%, Christmas).

The Independents

Gravediggers*	(OG 1038, ABV 3.8%) Spring/summer.
What the Fox's Hat*	(OG 1045, ABV 4.2%)
Pews Porter*	(OG 1045, ABV 4.5%) Autumn/winter.
M-Reg GTi*	(OG 1046, ABV 4.4%)
Old Pal*	(OG 1055, ABV 5.5%)

WILLIAM CLARK — **William Clark Brewing Company, c/o The Highlander, 15–16 Esplanade, South Cliff, Scarborough, N. Yorkshire YO11 2AF. Tel. (01723) 365627**

Brewery which has also been known as North & East Riding Brewers and which now supplies only its parent outlet, the Highlander on Scarborough's Esplanade. Beers: Thistle Mild (OG 1040, ABV 4%), EXB (OG 1040, ABV 4.1%, occasional), Thistle Bitter (OG 1040, ABV 4.1%), Two Bays Best Bitter (OG 1040, ABV 4.1%), No. 68 (OG 1050, ABV 5.1%), XXXPS (OG 1051, ABV 5.1%, occasional).

CLARK'S

HB Clark & Co. (Successors) Ltd., Westgate Brewery, Westgate, Wakefield, W. Yorkshire WF2 9SW. Tel. (01924) 373328 Fax. (01924) 372306

Founded in 1905, Clark's ceased brewing during the keg revolution of the 1960s and 1970s, although it continued to operate as a drinks wholesaler. It resumed cask ale production in 1982 and, within two months, Clark's Traditional Bitter was voted *Best Bitter* at the *Great British Beer Festival* in Leeds. It now has three tied houses and Clark's beers are widely available (including in Scotland and London) either supplied directly from the brewery or via beer agencies. Old Drovers Heavy, a house beer, is brewed for the Drovers Inn near Dunbar. Brewery shop open 8–5 Mon–Fri, 9–12 Sat and Sun. Tours by arrangement.

Traditional Bitter — (OG 1038, ABV 3.8%) Initial maltiness combines with lingering hops to provide a well-balanced bitter beer, thinner than in previous years.

Festival Ale — (OG 1042, ABV 4.2%) A light, fruity, premium bitter, pleasantly hopped. Peaches feature in the taste and linger for a while in the finish with hop bitterness.

Burglar Bill — (OG 1044, ABV 4.4%) A good, hoppy aroma precedes an excellent, strong hop flavour, combined with rich malt and fruit. A long finish of hops and malt completes this full-bodied, strong bitter.

Rams Revenge — (OG 1046, ABV 4.8%) Rounded, dark brown ale with malt and caramel predominant in the flavour, with some balancing fruit and hops declining rapidly in the finish.

Hammerhead — (OG 1055, ABV 5.5%) Rich malt in the mouth, but with hop flavour and bitterness to balance. The malty, hoppy aroma is faint, but the finish is long, malty and dry. A robust, strong bitter.

Winter Warmer — (OG 1060, ABV 6.4%) A dark brown, powerful strong ale. A strong mouth-filling blend of roast malt, hop flavour, sweetness and fruit notes concludes with a satisfying finish of bittersweet roast malt.

Tow'd Dreadnought* — (OG 1080, ABV 9%)

COACH HOUSE

The Coach House Brewing Company Ltd., Wharf Street, Howley, Warrington, Cheshire WA1 2DQ. Tel. (01925) 232800 Fax. (01925) 232700

Founded in 1991 and run mainly by ex-Greenall Whitley employees, Coach House quickly became established and in March 1995 increased its brewing capacity to cope with growing demand (currently 500 outlets, including some in northern Scotland and southern England via the Tap & Spile chain). The brewery also produces specially commissioned beers and brews two

beers for John Joule of Stone (a brewery closed by Bass in 1972 and about to be resurrected as an independent – tel. (01785) 814909). Tours by arrangement. Occasional beers: Wizards Wonder (OG 1042, ABV 4.2%, October), Cracker Barrel (OG 1044, ABV 4.4%, November), Dewi Sant (OG 1044, ABV 4.4%, April), Regal Ale (OG 1044, ABV 4.4%, April), St George's Ale (OG 1044, ABV 4.8% March), Bootleg Valentines Ale (OG 1050, ABV 5%, February), Burns Auld Sleekit (OG 1055, ABV 5.5%, January), Three Kings Christmas Ale (OG 1055, ABV 5.5%), Anniversary Ale (OG 1060, ABV 6%, January).

Coachman's Best Bitter
(OG 1037, ABV 3.7%) A well-hopped, malty bitter, moderately fruity with a hint of sweetness and a peppery, hop nose. A refreshing beer.

Gunpowder Strong Mild
(OG 1037, ABV 3.8%) Full-bodied and roasty dark mild with hints of pepper, fruit and liquorice, plus chocolate overtones. Malty aroma and full finish.

Ostlers Summer Pale Ale
(OG 1038, ABV 3.9%) Light, refreshing and very bitter, with a hint of pepper and a very dry finish.

Squires Gold Spring Ale
(OG 1042, ABV 4.2%) A golden spring beer. New Zealand hops give intense bitterness which is followed by a strong chocolate flavour from amber malt. Uncompromising and characterful.

Innkeeper's Special Reserve
(OG 1045, ABV 4.7%) A darkish, full-flavoured bitter. Quite fruity, with a strong, bitter aftertaste.

Posthorn Premium Ale
(OG 1050, ABV 5%) Well-hopped and very fruity, with bitterness and malt also prominent. Hoppy aroma; fruity aftertaste.

Taverners Autumn Ale
(OG 1050, ABV 5%) Fruity, bitter, golden ale with a slightly dry aftertaste. A warming, autumnal ale.

Blunderbus Old Porter
(OG 1055, ABV 5.5%) A super winter beer. The intense roast flavour is backed up by coffee, chocolate and liquorice, and hints of spice and smoke. Very well-hopped with massive mouthfeel. An intense, chewy pint which is surprisingly refreshing and moreish.

For Joule:

Old Priory
(OG 1047, ABV 4.7%)

Victory Brew
(OG 1052, ABV 5.2%)

COMBE
Combe Brewery, Mullacott Industrial Estate, Ilfracombe, Devon EX34 8PL. Tel. (01271) 864020

One man, part-time brewery founded in October 1994 to serve local outlets. Occasional beer: Gold (OG 1040, ABV 4%).

Shipwrecker's Ale*
(OG 1042, ABV 4.4%)

Wallop*
(OG 1047, ABV 5%)

COMMERCIAL

Commercial Brewing Co. Ltd., Worth Brewery, Worth Way, Keighley, W. Yorkshire BD21 5LP. Tel. (01535) 611914 Fax. (01535) 691883

Set up in a former garage, this brewery's first beer was produced in February 1992. Its direct free trade now extends to over 50 outlets throughout the North and Midlands. Shop open 11–2 Mon–Fri, 10–11am Sat. Tours by arrangement. Occasional beers: Hi Summer (OG 1034, ABV 3.2%, June–July), Beckside (OG 1034, ABV 3.4%, May), Harvest Festival (OG 1045, ABV 4.5%, August–Sept), Rampant Spring (OG 1048, ABV 4.8%, March–April), Winter Blues (OG 1048, ABV 5.2%, January–February), Knöbwilter (OG 1050, ABV 5.2%, wheat beer, summer), Ruggie's Russet Nectar (OG 1070, ABV 7.5%, October–November), Santa's Toss (OG 1080, ABV 8%,

The Independents

December). Bottle-conditioned beers: Alesman (OG 1036, ABV 3.7%), Neary's Stout (OG 1042, ABV 4.1%), Worth Best Bitter (OG 1045, ABV 4.5%), Worth Porter (OG 1045, ABV 4.5%), Old Toss (OG 1065, ABV 6.5%), Santa's Toss (OG 1080, ABV 8%).

Worth Wayfarer*	(OG 1034, ABV 3.4%)
Alesman or Keighlian Bitter	(OG 1036, ABV 3.7%) A clean, fruity beer with a pungent hop/citrus fruit character on the nose. Bitter fruit aftertaste.
Wild Boar*	(OG 1041, ABV 4%)
Neary's Stout*	(OG 1042, ABV 4.1%)
Worth Best Bitter*	(OG 1045, ABV 4.5%)
Worth Porter*	(OG 1045, ABV 4.5%)
Old Toss*	(OG 1065, ABV 6.5%)

CONCERTINA

The Concertina Brewery, The Mexborough Concertina Band Club, 9a Dolcliffe Road, Mexborough, S. Yorkshire S64 9AZ. Tel. (01709) 580841

Brewery in the cellar of a club, which began production in 1993, brewing eight barrels a week and supplying about 25 occasional outlets. The partners are still planning to acquire a pub.

Best Bitter	(OG 1038, ABV 4%) A mid-brown bitter with lots of hops on the nose, a subtle, hoppy taste and a dry finish. A gentle fruitiness throughout.
Old Dark Attic*	(OG 1038, ABV 4%)
Hackett VC	(OG 1040, ABV 4.2%) A well-balanced, malty ale with a hop underlay and even coffee tastes, though the finish has a bitter edge. Mid-brown to amber in colour.
Shot Firers Porter*	(OG 1040, ABV 4.5%)
KW Special Pride	(OG 1042, ABV 4.5%) A smooth, medium-bodied premium bitter with a fine mixture of grain, fruit and hop in the mouth, followed by a balanced, mellow aftertaste. Easy drinking for its strength.
Fitzpatricks Stout*	(OG 1043, ABV 4.5%)
Bengal Tiger*	(OG 1043, ABV 4.5%)
Bandsman Strong Ale*	(OG 1048, ABV 5.2%)

COOK'S

The Cook Brewery Company, Bockhampton, Dorset.

Brewery closed.

CORNISH

See Nationals, Whitbread, and Pub Groups, Greenalls.

COTLEIGH

Cotleigh Brewery, Ford Road, Wiveliscombe, Somerset TA4 2RE. Tel. (01984) 624086 Fax. (01984) 624365

Continued growth has taken this brewery a long way from its first home, a stable block at Cotleigh Farmhouse in 1979. It is now housed in specially converted premises in Wiveliscombe where recently installed plant has increased the capacity to 140 barrels a week. Cotleigh now serves some 120 outlets, mostly in Devon and Somerset, although the beers are also available across the country via wholesalers. Two beers are produced exclusively for the Kent wholesalers, East-West Ales Ltd. – tel. (01892) 834040. Occasional beers (made available to customers on a monthly rota): Swift (OG 1030, ABV 3.2%), Nutcracker Mild (OG 1036, ABV 3.6%), Hobby Ale (OG 1042, ABV 4.2%), Peregrine Porter (OG 1045, ABV 4.4%), Golden Eagle (OG 1045, ABV 4.5%), Old Buzzard ⊞ (OG 1048, ABV 4.8%), Powderkeg (OG 1050, ABV 5%), Snowy Ale (OG 1050, ABV 5%), Red Nose Reinbeer (OG 1060, ABV 5.6%, Christmas).

Harrier SPA   (OG 1035, ABV 3.6%) A straw-coloured beer with a very hoppy aroma and flavour, and a hoppy, bitter finish. Plenty of flavour for a light, low gravity beer.

Tawny Bitter 🍺   (OG 1038, ABV 3.8%) A mid-brown-coloured, very consistent beer. A hoppy aroma, a hoppy but quite well-balanced flavour, and a hoppy, bitter finish.

Barn Owl Bitter*   (OG 1045, ABV 4.5%) Brewed for the Hawk & Owl Trust charity.

For East-West Ales:

Aldercote Ale*   (OG 1042, ABV 4.2%)

Aldercote Extra*   (OG 1046, ABV 4.7%)

COTTAGE   **Cottage Brewing Company, High Street, West Lydford, Somerset TA11 7DQ. Tel. (01963) 240551 Fax. (01963) 240383**

Brewery founded in 1992 and upgraded to a ten-barrel plant in 1994. The beers are served in over 100 outlets locally, with deliveries made by the company's steam lorry and horse-drawn dray. The names mostly follow a railway theme. Tours by arrangement. Occasional beers: Bitter (OG 1031, ABV 3.7%), Christmas Cottage (OG 1058, ABV 6%).

Southern Bitter*   (OG 1039, ABV 3.7%)

Wheeltappers Ale*   (OG 1041, ABV 4%)

Somerset & Dorset Ale (S&D)*   (OG 1043, ABV 4.4%) Named after the Somerset & Dorset Railway: a well-hopped, malty brew, with a deep red colour.

Great Western Real Ale (GWR)*   (OG 1052, ABV 5.4%) Similar to S&D but stronger and darker, with a full-bodied maltiness.

Norman's Conquest 🍺   (OG 1066, ABV 7%) A dark strong ale, with plenty of fruit flavour and a touch of bitterness.

COURAGE   See Nationals.

CROPTON   **Cropton Brewery Co., The New Inn, Cropton, Pickering, N. Yorkshire YO18 8HH. Tel./Fax. (01751) 417310**

Brewery set up in 1984 in the cellar of the New Inn just to supply the pub. The plant was expanded in 1988, but by 1994 it had outgrown the cellar and a new purpose-built brewery was installed behind the pub. It currently brews 40 barrels of its additive-free beers per week to supply some 45 outlets locally, plus wholesalers. Tours by arrangement.

King Billy Bitter   (OG 1037, ABV 3.6%) Initially brewed for the King William pub in Hull: a gold-coloured, beautifully clean, hoppy bitter, light on the palate but with strong hop flavour and bitterness. Long, hoppy and bitter finish, but only a slight aroma.

Two Pints Best Bitter   (OG 1042, ABV 4%) A hop aroma precedes a powerful, flowery hop character in the taste with some malt and bitterness. Long, smooth, hoppy and sweet finish. A fine, distinctive bitter.

Scoresby Stout 🍺   (OG 1043, ABV 4.2%) A rich assault of roast malt and bitterness leads to a long, bitter finish of roast malt and chocolate. Jet black, and a stout in every sense.

Special Strong Bitter*   (OG 1060, ABV 6%) A powerful ale, produced all year but popular at Christmas.

CROUCH VALE   **Crouch Vale Brewery Ltd., 12 Redhills Road, South Woodham Ferrers, Chelmsford, Essex CM3 5UP. Tel. (01245) 322744 Fax. (01245) 329082**

Founded in 1981, Crouch Vale has expanded slowly but surely. Recent growth in the guest beer and wholesale markets has resulted in the building of new offices and the installation of new brewing plant. The brewery's single tied house, the Cap & Feathers at Tillingham, was the CAMRA national *Pub of the Year* in

1989. Crouch Vale currently delivers its wares by liveried dray to over 250 free trade outlets in Suffolk, Essex and Greater London. Tours by arrangement. Occasional beers: Best Dark Ale (OG 1035, ABV 3.6%).

Woodham IPA (OG 1036, ABV 3.6%) An amber beer with a fresh, hoppy nose with slight fruitiness. A good session bitter with a well-balanced taste leading to a fruit and hop finish.

Best Bitter (OG 1040, ABV 4%) The fruity aroma of this red/brown brew invites drinkers into a splendid taste of malt and fruit, with some hops, leading to a bitter finish.

Millennium Gold (OG 1042, ABV 4.2%) A golden beer featuring a strong, hoppy nose with maltiness. A powerful mixture of hops and fruit combines with pale malt to give a final sharp, bitter flavour with malty undertones.

Kursaal Flyer* (OG 1045, ABV 4.6%) A new beer, probably seasonal only.

Strong Anglian Special or SAS (OG 1050, ABV 5%) A tawny-coloured beer with a fruity nose. Well-balanced, full-bodied and sharply bitter, with a dry aftertaste.

Essex Porter (OG 1050, ABV 5%) A dark brew with a complex aroma followed by a flavour that is fruity and slightly nutty on a sweet base. Balanced sweet finish. This beer can be difficult to find.

Santa's Revenge (OG 1057, ABV 5.7%) A Christmas ale, also sold throughout the year under house names. Despite its strength, it is dry and winey, not sweet.

Willie Warmer (OG 1060, ABV 6.4%) A meal in a mug! This very dark red ale brims with malt and fruit aromas. Sweet fruitiness fills the taste, offset by roast malt and hops.

CROWN BUCKLEY

Crown Buckley Ltd, Gilbert Street, Llanelli, Dyfed SA15 3PP. Tel. (01554) 777004 Fax. (01554) 777017

Following several take-overs, Buckley, the oldest brewery in Wales (est. 1767) merged with Crown Brewery (the former United Clubs Brewery) in 1989, with Harp financial backing. This ultimately meant that the new company was owned by Guinness but represented a genuine lifeline. Crown Buckley subsequently underwent heavy rationalisation and restructuring, before a management buy-out in June 1993 ensured its true independence once more. Today, all beer production is carried out at the Llanelli (Buckley) site, with kegging and bottling taking place at Pontyclun (the old Crown brewery). A tied estate (mostly Harp houses) of 76 pubs, and a free trade of around 400 outlets, are supplied direct from the brewery. The clubs trade is still important, too. Special beers (OG 1041, ABV 4.1%) are occasionally brewed for festivals.

Crown Pale Ale* (OG 1033, ABV 3.4%)

Buckley's Dark Mild ⊕ (OG 1034, ABV 3.4%) A very dark, malty mild, fairly sweet with traces of chocolate, followed by a nutty, bitter finish. Very drinkable.

Buckley's Best Bitter (OG 1036, ABV 3.7%) A well-balanced, medium gravity bitter which has a rather sweet, malty flavour and a pleasant, bitter finish.

Special Best Bitter (SBB) (OG 1036, ABV 3.7%) Distinctively malty and clean-tasting, with a pronounced bitter flavour and a rather dry aftertaste.

James Buckley Ale* (OG 1038, ABV 3.9%)

Reverend James Original Ale (OG 1045, ABV 4.5%) A malty, full-bodied bitter with hoppy and fruity overtones, followed by a bittersweet aftertaste.

CROWN HOTEL	See Scott's.

CROWN INN

The Crown
at Munslow

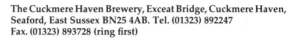 **Munslow Brewhouse, The Crown Inn, Munslow, Shropshire SY7 9ET. Tel (01584) 841205**

Pub brewery established in September 1994 and generally only supplying the pub itself. A Christmas ale has also been produced. Beers: Munslow Boy's Pale Ale (OG 1038, ABV 3.6%), Munslow Ale (OG 1042, ABV 4%).

CUCKMERE HAVEN

The Cuckmere Haven Brewery, Exceat Bridge, Cuckmere Haven, Seaford, East Sussex BN25 4AB. Tel. (01323) 892247 Fax. (01323) 893728 (ring first)

This tiny brewhouse went into production in June 1994 to serve the Golden Galleon pub (the brewery's owner), plus five other outlets on an occasional basis. Deliveries are made in the brewery's much publicised, 1957 Ford 10 pickup truck. Plans are in hand to expand both the pub and the brewery. Tours by arrangement. Occasional beers: Summer Pale Ale (OG 1034, ABV 3.4%), Seven Sisters Sussex Special (OG 1044, ABV 4.3%), Velvet Dark Mild (OG 1049, ABV 4.7%, summer), Fuggl'olmullable (OG 1063, ABV 6.2%, winter).

Best Bitter	(OG 1041, ABV 4.1%) Malty overtones in the aroma are joined by a hoppy bitterness in the flavour. Hop character increases in the aftertaste.
Saxon King Stout*	(OG 1042, ABV 4.2%)
Gentlemen's (Smuggler's) Gold*	(OG 1046, ABV 4.5%)
Guv'ner	(OG 1047, ABV 4.7%) Pleasant bitter in which malt and roast malt in the aroma give way to a hoppy bitterness in the taste and aftertaste.

CYDER HOUSE INN

SHACKLEFORD BREWERY CO.

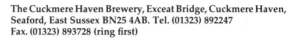 **The Shackleford Brewery Co., The Cyder House Inn, Peperharow Lane, Shackleford, Godalming, Surrey GU8 6AN. Tel. (01483) 810360 Fax. (01483) 811940**

Full mash brewery set up in 1992, which also supplies beer to its second pub, the Thurlow Arms at Cranleigh, acquired in 1993. Brewing was suspended for a while in 1994, owing to mechanical problems, and the equipment is now being relocated to a new, bigger building. Tours by arrangement. Beers: Piston Broke (OG 1041, ABV 4%), Norfolk n' Chance (OG 1045, ABV 4.6%), Old Shackle (OG 1047, ABV 4.8%, occasional), Overdraught (OG 1048, ABV 4.8%, Christmas).

DALESIDE

Daleside Brewery, Camwal Road, Starbeck, Harrogate, N. Yorkshire HG1 4PT. Tel. (01423) 880041

Formerly Big End brewery, founded in 1988 by Bill Witty and now run with his son, Craig. The company moved to new premises and changed its name in 1992. It supplies 200 outlets, mainly on the A1 corridor between North London and Northumberland, plus other outlets nationwide via wholesalers. It began bottling in 1995.

Bitter	(OG 1038, ABV 3.7%) A pale brown bitter with a strong, fruity aroma. The clean, fruity taste with balancing malt and bitterness, is finished with a long bitter, fruit aftertaste. It may be sold under house names.
Country Stile*	(OG 1042, ABV 4.1%) Also sold as Old Legover.
Dalesman Old Ale	(OG 1042, ABV 4.1%) Satisfying, dark brown, strong bitter, with rich malt and roast in the mouth, complemented by fruit and hop flavour. Light hop and roast malt finish. It can also have house names.

437

The Independents

Monkey Wrench (OG 1056, ABV 5.3%) A powerful strong ale, dark ruby/brown in hue. A strong aroma of fruit leads to a rich assault of malt and roast malt, plus a strong fruit flavour with balancing bitterness. Long, fruity, malty and bitter finish; some sweetness throughout. It can be difficult to find, however.

DARK HORSE

🍺 **Dark Horse Brewing Co. (Hertford) Ltd., 33–35 Castle Street, Hertford SG14 1HH. Tel. (01992) 501950**

Brewery in the cellar of the White Horse free house which launched its first beers in November 1994. The White Horse is still the main outlet. In addition to the following, some occasional beers are also produced. Beers: Dark Horse Ale (OG 1036, ABV 3.6%), Fallen Angel (OG 1037, ABV 3.5%, a ginger beer), Sun Runner (OG 1040, ABV 4.1%), Black Widow (OG 1048, ABV 4.6%, a stout), Death Quest (OG 1053, ABV 5.3%).

DARK STAR See Skinner's.

DARLEY See Wards.

DARTMOOR See Nationals, Carlsberg-Tetley.

DARWIN

Darwin Brewery, Brewlab, University of Sunderland, Chester Road, Sunderland SR1 3SD. Tel. (0191) 515 2535 Fax. (0191) 515 2531

Brewery founded in late 1994 as a research facility for the staff and students at the University of Sunderland. Three or four local pubs now take the regular beers, as do beer festivals, but numerous experimental beers are also produced.

Evolution Ale* (OG 1040, ABV 4%) Dark amber, full-bodied bitter with a malty flavour and a clean, bitter aftertaste.

Sinner Strong Ale* (OG 1053, ABV 5%) A rich, smooth-tasting, ruby red ale with a fruity aroma and hop character in the taste.

Killer Bee* (OG 1060, ABV 6%) A strong beer made with honey.

DAVENPORTS See Nationals, Carlsberg-Tetley, and Pub Groups, Greenalls.

DAVENPORTS ARMS

🍺 **Worfield Brewery, Davenports Arms, Main Street, Worfield, Shropshire WV15 5LF. Tel. (01746) 716320**

Pub brewery established in March 1994 and currently supplying just the pub itself. In addition to the beer listed below, WB Stout (OG 1040, ABV 4%) is produced. However, this is served under mixed gas dispense. A barley wine at 9.1% ABV has also been brewed. Beer: JLK Pale Ale (OG 1040, ABV 4%).

DENT

Dent Brewery, Hollins, Cowgill, Dent, Cumbria LA10 5TQ. Tel./Fax. (01539) 625326

Brewery set up in a converted barn in the Yorkshire Dales in March 1990, originally to supply just three local pubs. It now has two tied houses and supplies 12 free trade outlets directly. Its own distribution company, Flying Firkin Distribution, delivers all over northern England and is making some inroads into the South, too. All Dent's beers are brewed using the brewery's own spring water. Tours by arrangement (minimum six people).

Bitter* (OG 1036, ABV 3.7%)

Ramsbottom Strong Ale* (OG 1044, ABV 4.5%)

T'Owd Tup* (OG 1058, ABV 6%)

For Flying Firkin Distribution:

Kamikaze* (OG 1048, ABV 5%)

The Independents

DEVENISH   See Pub Groups, Greenalls, and Nationals, Whitbread.

DONNINGTON   **Donnington Brewery, Stow-on-the-Wold, Gloucestershire GL54 1EP. Tel. (01451) 830603**

Possibly the most attractive brewery in the country, set in a 13th-century watermill in idyllic surroundings. Bought by Thomas Arkell in 1827, it became a brewery in 1865, and is still owned and run by the family. Donnington currently supplies 15 tied houses, and 12 free trade outlets, though XXX is only available in a few pubs.

BB   (OG 1036, ABV 3.5%) Little aroma, but a pleasing, bitter beer, with a good malt/hop balance. Not as distinctive as it used to be.

XXX   (OG 1036, ABV 3.5%) Again, thin in aroma, but flavoursome. More subtle than others in its class, with some fruit and traces of chocolate and liquorice in the taste, and a notably malty finish.

SBA   (OG 1046, ABV 4%) Malt dominates over bitterness in the flavour of this subtle premium bitter, with just a hint of fruit and a dry, malty finish. Faintly malty aroma.

DRINKLINK   See Eldridge Pope.

DURHAM   **The Durham Brewery, Units 6D/E, Bowburn North Industrial Estate, Bowburn, Co. Durham DH6 5AD. Tel./Fax. (0191) 377 1991**

When this new brewery launched its first beers at the 1994 Durham Beer Festival, Celtic was voted *Best Beer*. It now supplies around 70 outlets and there are plans to acquire a pub. Off-sales are available from the brewery (ring first).

Magus*   (OG 1039, ABV 3.8%)

Celtic*   (OG 1042, ABV 4.2%)

Pagan*   (OG 1047, ABV 4.8%)

Sanctuary*   (OG 1058, ABV 6%) An old ale for winter.

DYFFRYN CLWYD   **Bragdy Dyffryn Clwyd Brewery, Chapel Place, Denbigh, Clwyd LL16 3TJ. Tel. (01745) 815007**

Brewery founded by local pub landlord Ioan Evans in 1993. The beers have bilingual pump clips and are sold in free houses in Clwyd and Gwynedd, but are more widely available in England than Wales via wholesalers. Tours by arrangement. Occasional beer: De Laceys ⊞ (OG 1062, ABV 6.2%, Christmas). Bottle-conditioned beer: Pedwar Bawd or Four Thumbs (OG 1045, ABV 4.8%).

Cysur or Comfort Bitter   (OG 1036, ABV 3.6%) A sharp, clean bitter with good hop character. Fairly dry finish; refreshing.

Druid   (OG 1039, ABV 3.9%) A dry, darkish bitter with hints of coffee and roast malt. A blend of Cysur and Castell.

Cwrw Castell or Castle Bitter ⊞   (OG 1042, ABV 4.2%) A darkish, smooth bitter, with good hop character. Fairly fruity, with some roast malt flavour. A complex bitter.

Jolly Jack Tar Porter   (OG 1045, ABV 4.5%) A smooth, dry porter with good roast malt and chocolate flavours; reasonably well-hopped.

Pedwar Bawd or Four Thumbs* ⊞   (OG 1045, ABV 4.8%) A well-balanced, hoppy pale bitter with hints of sweetness, plus citrus overtones.

439

The Independents

EARL SOHAM **Earl Soham Brewery, The Victoria, Earl Soham, Wood-bridge, Suffolk IP13 7RL. Tel. (01728) 685758**

Brewery established in April 1985 to supply its own pub, the Victoria, and a few years' later acquiring a second pub, the Tram Depot in Cambridge, which has since been sold to Everards. A few other free trade outlets take the beer. Beers: Gannet Mild (OG 1032, ABV 3%), Victoria (OG 1036, ABV 3.5%), Albert Ale (OG 1044, ABV 4.3%), Jolabrugg (OG 1060, ABV 5.4%).

EAST-WEST ALES   See Brewery on Sea, Cotleigh and Foxley.

EASTWOOD'S   Eastwood's Brewery, Huddersfield, W. Yorkshire.

Brewery closed and planning to relocate in Walkleys Clog Factory (a tourist attraction) at Hebden Bridge.

ECCLESHALL **Eccleshall Brewery, George Hotel, Castle Street, Eccleshall, Stafford ST21 6DF. Tel. (01785) 850300
Fax. (01785) 851452**

Brewery opened in outbuildings behind the George Hotel in March 1995, producing 'Slaters Ales'. Some other local pubs and wholesalers are also supplied with the beers. Beers: Slaters Bitter (OG 1036, ABV 3.8%), Slaters Original (OG 1040, ABV 4%), Slaters Premium (OG 1044, ABV 4.4%).

EDGCOTE   **Merivales Ales, Edgcote Brewery, 3 Snobs Row, Edgcote, Banbury, Oxfordshire OX17 1AG. Tel. (01295) 660335**

This very small operation (single-barrel brew plant) was set up in June 1994, but there are plans to expand into nearby premises. Eight outlets are supplied. Beers: Ordinary Bitter (OG 1040, ABV 3.9%), Best Bitter (OG 1044, ABV 4.8%).

ELDRIDGE POPE   **Eldridge, Pope & Co. PLC, Weymouth Avenue, Dorchester, Dorset DT1 1QT. Tel. (01305) 251251 Fax. (01305) 258300**

Charles and Sarah Eldridge started the Green Dragon Brewery in Dorchester in 1837. By 1880, Edwin and Alfred Pope had bought into the company and it had moved to its present site. The brewery is still run by the Pope family, owning some 200 pubs and producing award-winning ales, with Thomas Hardy's Ale long notable as the strongest naturally-conditioned bottled beer available in the UK. Free trade extends as far as London, Bristol and Exeter, and the brewery also produces occasional beers and brews under contract for Ross (qv), the Liquid Assets wholesaler – tel. (0161) 864 5000 – and the Drinklink wholesaler – tel. (01271) 862016. Tours by arrangement. Bottle-conditioned beers: Thomas Hardy Country Bitter (OG 1040, ABV 4.2%), Thomas Hardy's Ale ⊞ (OG 1125, ABV 12%).

Dorchester Bitter   (OG 1032, ABV 3.3%) A light session beer which is hoppy and bitter throughout, with some balancing malt.

Best Bitter   (OG 1036, ABV 3.8%) A mixture of malt and hop, with a hint of fruit. Difficult to find in cask-conditioned form.

Blackdown Porter   (OG 1040, ABV 4%) A dark, winter beer with an intense roast malt aroma. There are traces of coffee, chocolate and blackcurrant in the taste, leading into a dry, bitter finish.

Thomas Hardy Country Bitter   (OG 1040, ABV 4.2%) A dry, hoppy beer, with faint undertones of malt and fruit. The taste is smooth despite a bitter edge which continues into the aftertaste.

Beers marked with an asterisk have not been tasted by official CAMRA tasting panels. However, some of these beers do carry brief descriptions derived from limited samplings or other sources which can be used for rough guidance.

The Independents

Royal Oak	(OG 1048, ABV 5%) A full-bodied beer with a distinctive banana aroma and a mainly sweet, fruity taste. This is balanced by malt and some hop, and there is a fruity finish to this smooth, well-rounded brew.

For Liquid Assets:
Potter's Pride* (ABV 3.8%)

For Drinklink:
Parson's Nose* (OG 1039, ABV 3.7%) The recipe may change in the coming year.

For Ross:
Bottle-conditioned beer: Saxon Strong Ale (OG 1050, ABV 5%)

ELGOOD'S — Elgood & Sons Ltd., North Brink Brewery, Wisbech, Cambridgeshire PE13 1LN. Tel. (01945) 583160 Fax. (01945) 587711

From its classical Georgian, riverside premises (converted in the 1790s from a mill and granary and acquired by Elgood's in 1878), this brewery supplies real ale to all but two of its 47 tied houses, and to a free trade of around 100 outlets. In addition, a mini-brewery produces a variety of beers in small volumes for sale as guests. A visitors' centre and brewery museum were opened in 1995. Tours by arrangement.

Black Dog Mild* (OG 1035, ABV 3.6%) Malt dominates the aroma of this black/red seasonal (spring) mild. Malt and roast grain on the palate are blended with hops and fruit. Dry, roast grain finish.

Cambridge Bitter (OG 1037, ABV 3.8%) An amber beer whose malty aroma is accompanied by some hops and fruit. The flavour is a good balance of malt and hops, with a pungent, slightly fruity bitterness. Long, dry finish with some malt and hops.

Bicentenary Pageant Ale* (OG 1040, ABV 4.3%)

Barleymead* (OG 1046, ABV 4.8%) A seasonal, autumn brew.

Greyhound Strong Bitter or GSB (OG 1046, ABV 5.2%) Much improved in recent years; a balanced aroma of malt and fruit is followed by a robust flavour of malt, hops and fruit on a bitter base. Very dry finish with some malt, hops and fruit.

North Brink Porter (OG 1048, ABV 5%) A winter beer of some character. The flavour is a complex blend of roast malt and rich fruits on a dry base with liquorice notes. The complex aroma of roast grain, malt and fruit often has some sulphur. Long, dry finish of roast grain and fruit.

Wenceslas Winter Warmer (OG 1065, ABV 7.5%) A robust winter ale with a rich fruit and roast grain aroma. On the palate, it is wine-like and warming, with rich, ripe fruits on a bittersweet base. Dry, faint fruit finish.

ENVILLE — Enville Ales, Enville Brewery, Cox Green, Enville, Stourbridge, W. Midlands DY7 5LB. Tel./Fax. (01384) 873770

Brewery on a picturesque Victorian farm complex. Using the same water source as the original village brewery (closed in 1919), the beers also incorporate over three tons of honey annually, produced by the beekeeper owner, using recipes passed down from his great-great aunt. Enville (in Staffordshire, despite the postal address) also runs the Victoria Pub Co. Tours by arrangement. Bottle-conditioned beers: Gothic (OG 1051, ABV 5.2%, occasional).

Enville Bitter (OG 1037, ABV 3.8%) A straw-coloured, hoppy and bitter beer which leaves a malty, moreish aftertaste.

Simpkiss Bitter (OG 1038, ABV 3.9%) Medium-bodied, golden bitter. The refreshing, hoppy taste lingers.

White (OG 1041, ABV 4.2%) A clean, refreshing beer, with no dominant flavours, but appealing nevertheless.

Ale (OG 1045, ABV 4.5%) A pale gold, medium-bodied bitter. Light hops and sweet fruitiness are present in the taste, with a tang of honey in the aftertaste.

The Independents

Gothic Ale	(OG 1051, ABV 5.2%) Malt, hops and caramel combine with a strong roast malt taste in this dark, stout-like beer. Well-balanced, with lurking hints of honey.

EVENING STAR	See Skinner's.

EVERARDS	**Everards Brewery Ltd., Castle Acres, Narborough, Leicester LE9 5BY. Tel. (0116) 2814100 Fax. (0116) 2814199**

Small, family-owned brewery, founded in 1849 with the acquisition of an existing Leicester brewery, by the great-great-grandfather of the current chairman, Richard Everard. Over the years its beers were brewed in both Leicester and Burton upon Trent, until all production was transferred to Castle Acres in 1991. Ninety per cent of its 150 tied houses sell real ale, but some use cask breathers. Everards also services some 500 free trade accounts. The Wine Warehouse next to the brewery sells some Everards products (open 9–6 Mon–Fri). Brewery tours by arrangement.

Mild	(OG 1036, ABV 3.3%) A smooth, well-balanced, dark red beer, malty throughout. The sweet fruitiness in the taste leads to a satisfying dry aftertaste. Beware: often on a cask breather.
Beacon Bitter ⊞	(OG 1036, ABV 3.8%) A copper-coloured session beer with a bitter hoppiness as its main characteristic. It can also have an intense sulphurous character, particularly in fresh casks, but is always very drinkable.
Tiger Best Bitter	(OG 1041, ABV 4.2%) A gentle aroma of malt, hops and fruit, with more than a dash of sulphur, leads to a soft, malty palate. Well-balanced, with a finish that is bitter and hoppy. A pleasant, medium-bodied bitter.
Old Original	(OG 1050, ABV 5.2%) A mid-brown beer with a sulphurous, hoppy aroma and a complex, malty, bittersweet palate. The finish is intensely bitter, but equally complex.
Daredevil Winter Warmer	(OG 1068, ABV 7.1%) Brewed December–January, a full-flavoured, fruity beer, with an aroma of malt and fruit, preceding a sweetish, powerful blend of hops, malt and fruit in the taste. Hops and liquorice linger on the palate.
	For Whitbread:
Chester's Best Mild*	(OG 1032, ABV 3.5%)

EVESHAM	**Evesham Brewery, Oat Street, Evesham, Hereford & Worcester WR11 4PJ. Tel./Fax. (01386) 443462**

Brewery based in the old bottle store at the Green Dragon Inn in Evesham. The owner and licensee, Steve Murphy, who also owns another pub, currently supplies some 20 outlets direct and others around the country via agents. The brewery has become a local tourist attraction; tours by arrangement. 'Asum' is the local pronunciation of Evesham.

Asum Ale*	(OG 1038, ABV 3.8%) Distinctive and malty session ale.
Asum Gold*	(OG 1050, ABV 5.2%) Fruity, malty and sweet strong ale.

EXE VALLEY	**Exe Valley Brewery, Land Farm, Silverton, Exeter, Devon EX5 4HF. Tel. (01392) 860406**

Founded as Barron Brewery in 1984, by Richard Barron, this company's name changed in 1991 when Richard was joined as partner by Guy Sheppard. It operates from an old barn (using the farm's own spring water), and new plant was installed in 1993, to treble capacity. More seasonal beers may be produced after the success of the new spring beer. The brewery is aiming to consolidate its local trade (over 50 outlets) and looking for wider distribution of the beers via wholesalers. Tours for groups by arrangement.

Bitter	(OG 1038, ABV 3.7%) A pale brown-coloured beer, with a fruity aroma and taste. The aftertaste is a mix of malt and fruit, and slightly sweet.
Dob's Best Bitter	(OG 1040, ABV 4.1%) Malt and fruit dominate the aroma and taste, whilst the finish is hoppy, malty and dry.
Spring Beer	(OG 1043, ABV 4.3%) A straw-coloured, fruity tasting beer with a bittersweet finish.
Devon Glory	(OG 1047, ABV 4.7%) A tawny-coloured beer, with malt and fruit running through from the aroma to the finish.
Exeter Old Bitter	(OG 1047, ABV 4.8%) A mid-brown beer with a fruity aroma and taste. Bitter, fruity aftertaste.

EXMOOR

Exmoor Ales Ltd., Golden Hill Brewery, Wiveliscombe, Somerset TA4 2NY. Tel. (01984) 623798 Fax. (01984) 624572

Somerset's largest brewery was founded in 1980 in the old Hancock's brewery, which had been closed since 1959. It quickly won national acclaim, as its Exmoor Ale took the *Best Bitter* award at CAMRA's *Great British Beer Festival*, the first of over 30 prizes. Brewing capacity is being increased all the time to meet demand from over 200 pubs in the South-West that are supplied directly, and wholesalers and pub chains nationwide. Tours by arrangement. Occasional beers: Dark (OG 1042, ABV 4.1%), Stoat (OG 1044, ABV 4.2%), Exmas (OG 1058, ABV 6%, Christmas).

Exmoor Ale	(OG 1039, ABV 3.8%) A pale brown beer with a malty aroma, a malty, dry taste and a bitter and malty finish. Very drinkable.
Exmoor Gold	(OG 1045, ABV 4.5%) Yellow/golden in colour, with a malty aroma and flavour, and a slight sweetness and hoppiness. Sweet, malty finish.
Exmoor Stag	(OG 1050, ABV 5.2%) A pale brown beer, with a malty taste and aroma, and a bitter finish. Slightly sweet. Very similar to Exmoor Ale and drinks as easily.
Exmoor Beast*	(OG 1066, ABV 6.6%) A winter brew, available October–March.

FARMERS ARMS

Mayhem's Brewery, Lower Apperley, Gloucestershire GL19 4DR. Tel. (01452) 780172 Fax. (01452) 780307

Brewery opened in 1992 in the grounds of the Farmers Arms, which also produces its own cider. The beers are stored in cellar tanks and are only available at the pub. Beers: Odda's Light (OG 1038, ABV 3.8%), Sundowner (OG 1044, ABV 4.5%).

FEATHERSTONE

Featherstone Brewery, Unit 3, King Street Buildings, King Street, Enderby, Leicester LE9 5NT. Tel./Fax. (0116) 2750952

Small brewery which has moved site several times. It specialises in supplying custom beers to pubs for sale under house names and turnover has grown considerably since it started in 1989. Four local outlets take the beers regularly. Occasional beer: Stout (OG 1037, ABV 3.8%).

Hows Howler*	(OG 1036, ABV 3.6%)
Best Bitter*	(OG 1042, ABV 4.2%)
Stage Ale*	(OG 1045, ABV 4.8%)
Vulcan Bitter*	(OG 1049, ABV 5.1%)
Kingstone Strong*	(OG 1058, ABV 6.4%)

FEDERATION

Federation Brewery Ltd., Lancaster Road, Dunston, Tyne & Wear NE11 9JR. Tel. (0191) 460 9023 Fax. (0191) 460 1297

A co-operative, founded by local clubs in 1919 to overcome the post-war beer shortage. It moved to John Buchanan's Brewery in 1930, but was forced to expand again in 1980 to a green field site at Dunston. The brewery is still owned by local clubs, and their business accounts for the majority of the brewery's trade. Cask

beers were reinstated in 1986, but only since the introduction of the Buchanan range in 1991 have sales taken off. However, real ales still only amount to a small percentage of the brewery's output. Tours by arrangement.

Buchanan's Best Bitter	(OG 1034, ABV 3.6%) Very difficult to find, especially on top form, when it has a pleasant aroma, a bitter flavour and a well-balanced aftertaste, with a hint of fruit throughout. Really an ordinary bitter, not a best.
Buchanan's Special	(OG 1040, ABV 4%) A clean, hoppy and bitter ale, finishing dry, with fruit and hop lingering.
Buchanan's Original	(OG 1042, ABV 4.4%) A rich, ruby red bitter with a smooth, creamy taste and lingering mouthfeel. A robust malt character makes this a better than average drinking bitter.

FELINFOEL

Felinfoel Brewery Co. Ltd., Farmers Row, Felinfoel, Llanelli, Dyfed SA14 8LB. Tel. (01554) 773357 Fax. (01554) 752452

This renowned Welsh brewery was built in 1878, when the village brew pub could no longer keep up with demand. Despite recent predators, it is still managing to hang on to its independence. The first brewery in Europe to can beer (in the 1930s), Felinfoel now supplies cask ale to most of its 85 houses (though some use top pressure) and serves roughly 160 free trade outlets. Shop open Mon–Fri 9–4.30. Occasional beer: Festive (OG 1061, ABV 6%, Christmas).

Bitter	(OG 1032, ABV 3.2%) A light brown, slightly malty, bitter beer with a distinct hop flavour and a bitter finish. Very drinkable.
Dark	(OG 1032, ABV 3.2%) A dark brown/red mild, rather thin, with a slightly bitter flavour and aftertaste.
Double Dragon	(OG 1042, ABV 4.2%) A fine, well-balanced, rich bitter with a nutty malt flavour, a fruity nose and a rounded, bittersweet finish. It is now back at its lower strength after a time at 5%.

FELLOWS, MORTON & CLAYTON

Fellows, Morton & Clayton Brewhouse Company, 54 Canal Street, Nottingham NG1 7EH. Tel. (0115) 9506795 Fax. (0115) 9551412

This pub, leased from Whitbread, began brewing in 1980 and still uses malt extract. Tours by arrangement. Beers: Samuel Fellows Bitter (OG 1040, ABV 3.7%), Matthew Clayton's Original Strong Ale (OG 1050, ABV 4.3%).

FILO   See First In, Last Out.

FIRKIN   See Nationals, Carlsberg-Tetley.

FIRST IN, LAST OUT

FILO Brewery, 14–15 High Street, Old Town, Hastings, E. Sussex TN34 3EY. Tel. (01424) 425030 Fax. (01424) 420802

The First In, Last Out began brewing in 1985, but the establishment changed hands three years later. Brewing currently takes place once a week just to serve the pub, but planned expansion will allow some free trade to be supplied. Tours by arrangement. Beers: Crofters (OG 1040, ABV 4%), Cardinal (OG 1044, ABV 4.2%).

FLAGSHIP

The Flagship Brewery, Unit 2, Building 64, The Historic Dockyard, Chatham, Kent ME4 4TE. Tel. (01634) 832828

Brewery set up in February 1995 in Chatham's preserved Georgian dockyard, now a major tourist site. Plans include a visitors' area. Some 20 outlets are supplied direct.

Capstan Ale* (OG 1040, ABV 3.8%)

The Independents

Ensign Ale*	(OG 1044, ABV 4.2%)
Crow's Nest Ale*	(OG 1050, ABV 4.8%)
Futtock Ale*	(OG 1053, ABV 5.2%)
Gangplank Ale*	(OG 1060, ABV 5.8%) A winter brew.

FLAMINGO **The Kingston Brewery, 88 London Road, Kingston upon Thames, Gtr London KT2 6PX. Tel. (0181) 541 3717**

Previously part of the Firkin chain, but now owned by Saxon Inns, this five-barrel brewhouse is situated behind the Flamingo pub. Some of the beer is stored under mixed gas in cellar tanks. A couple of other pubs are supplied with cask beer. Beers: Fairfield Bitter (OG 1037, ABV 3.5%), Royal Charter (OG 1044, ABV 4.2%), Coronation (OG 1059, ABV 5.7%), Crucifixion Ale (ABV 6.3%, Easter), Rudolph's Revenge (OG 1070, ABV 7.2%, Christmas).

FLOWER POTS INN See Cheriton.

FLOWERS See Nationals, Whitbread.

FLYING FIRKIN See Dent.

FOX & HOUNDS **Barley Brewery, Fox & Hounds, Barley, Hertfordshire SG8 8HU. Tel. (01763) 848459**

An early member of the pub brewing revival, using a 19th-century brewhouse at what used to be the Waggon & Horses before changing its name. Beers: Nathaniel's Special (OG 1037, ABV 3.3%), Flame Thrower (OG 1048, ABV 4.2%), Old Dragon (OG 1052, ABV 5.3%).

FOX & HOUNDS **Woody Woodward's Brewery, The Fox & Hounds, High Street, Stottesdon, Kidderminster, Hereford & Worcester DY14 8TZ. Tel. (01746) 718222**

Shropshire pub (despite the postal address) which started brewing in 1979 and which had two owners before the present landlord. It is still looking to increase its outside trade from the two outlets currently supplied. 'Wust' and 'Bostin' are Black Country expressions meaning worst and best. The pub also brews under contract for the Blackbeard Trading Company – tel. (01584) 872908. Beers: Wust Bitter (OG 1037, ABV 3.7%), Bostin Bitter (OG 1043, ABV 4.2%), Wild Mild (OG 1043, ABV 4.2%), Gobstopper (OG 1065, ABV 6.5%, winter).

For Blackbeard Trading:

Brew 37*	(OG 1052, ABV 5.1%).

FOX & NEWT See Nationals, Whitbread.

FOXLEY **Foxley Brewing Company Ltd., Unit 3, Home Farm Workshops, Mildenhall, Marlborough, Wiltshire SN8 2LR. Tel. (01672) 515000**

Rob Owen and Neil Collings, both keen home brewers, started this, their first commercial venture, in June 1992. Production increased steadily and the range was quickly extended to four beers. Foxley now directly supplies around 80 free trade outlets within a 50-mile radius, and pubs further afield via wholesalers. One beer is brewed occasionally for wholesalers East-West Ales Ltd. – tel. (01892) 834040.

Best Bitter*	(OG 1038, ABV 3.8%)
Barking Mad*	(OG 1043, ABV 4.3%)

445

The Independents

Dog Booter*	(OG 1046, ABV 4.6%)
Howling Wolf or Strong Bitter*	(OG 1048, ABV 4.8%)
	For East-West Ales:
Roadhog*	(OG 1042, ABV 4.2%)

FRANKLIN'S

Franklin's Brewery, Bilton Lane, Bilton, Harrogate, N. Yorkshire HG1 4DH. Tel. (01423) 322345

Brewery set up in 1980 by Sean Franklin, who devised a beer to copy the bouquet of the wines in which he specialised. It is now run by Leeds CAMRA founder-member Tommy Thomas and around ten free trade outlets, plus beer festivals, are supplied.

Bitter	(OG 1038, ABV 3.9%) A tremendous hop aroma precedes a flowery hop flavour, combined with malt. Long, hoppy, bitter finish. A fine, unusual amber bitter.
DTs*	(OG 1055, ABV 4.7%)
Summer Blotto*	(OG 1055, ABV 4.7%) Seasonal.
Winter Blotto*	(OG 1055, ABV 4.7%) Seasonal.

FREEDOM

The Freedom Brewing Company Ltd., The Coachworks, 80 Parsons Green Lane, Fulham, London SW6 4HU. Tel. (0171) 731 7372 Fax. (0171) 731 1218

Brewery opened in April 1995 to produce one ale and one premium lager. The lager (ABV 5.4%) is brewed to the German beer purity law standard and is unpasteurised. It is also available unpasteurised in bottled form.

Fulham Ale*	(OG 1043, ABV 4.3%)

FREEMINER

Freeminer Brewery Ltd, The Laurels, Sling, Coleford, Gloucestershire GL16 8JJ. Tel./Fax. (01594) 810408

Established at the edge of the Forest of Dean in November 1992, Freeminer is now brewing to full capacity. It has one tied house (the Miners Arms in Sling) and supplies over 50 free trade outlets directly, including several in Manchester, plus others nationwide via wholesalers. It also produces cider and perry and has extended its range of bottle-conditioned beers. Beers are also brewed under contract for the Blackbeard Trading Company – tel. (01584) 872908. Evening tours by arrangement. Occasional beers: Iron Brew (OG 1042, ABV 4.4%), Trafalgar IPA (OG 1060, ABV 6%). Bottle-conditioned beers: Shakemantle Ginger Ale (OG 1050, ABV 5%), Slaughter Porter (OG 1055, ABV 5.2%), Deep Shaft Stout (OG 1060, ABV 6%), Trafalgar IPA (OG 1060, ABV 6%).

Bitter	(OG 1038, ABV 4%) A light, hoppy bitter with a wonderful hop aroma and very dry, hoppy finish. Very moreish.
Speculation Ale	(OG 1047, ABV 4.8%) A smooth, well-balanced mix of malt and hop, with a predominantly hoppy finish.
Shakemantle Ginger Ale*	(OG 1050, ABV 5%) A summer brew.
Slaughter Porter*	(OG 1055, ABV 5%) Brewed in spring and autumn.
Deep Shaft Stout	(OG 1060, ABV 6.2%) A winter beer: a jet black stout. Roast and malt hit you immediately, then a very dry, biscuity, hoppy finish follows.
	For Blackbeard Trading:
Dead Ringer*	(OG 1048, ABV 4.8%)
Stairway to Heaven*	(OG 1050, ABV 5%)
Old Sally MacLennon*	(OG 1055, ABV 5.5%)

446

Low Rider*	(OG 1060, ABV 6%)
FREETRADERS	See King & Barnes.
FREMLINS	See Nationals, Whitbread.
FRIARY MEUX	See Nationals, Carlsberg-Tetley.
FROG & PARROT	See Nationals, Whitbread.

FROG ISLAND

Frog Island Brewery, The Maltings, Westbridge Street, James Road, Northampton NN5 5HS. Tel. (01604) 587772

Based in an old malthouse, once owned by the defunct Thomas Manning brewery, this new company has been in operation since September 1994. Frog Island is a local name for an area once prone to flooding. Future plans include a winter ale and occasional brews. Forty free trade outlets are currently supplied. Tours by arrangement.

Best Bitter*	(OG 1039, ABV 3.8%)
Natterjack*	(OG 1048, ABV 4.8%)

FROMES HILL

Fromes Hill Brewery, Wheatsheaf Inn, Fromes Hill, Ledbury, Hereford & Worcester HR8 1HT. Tel. (01531) 640888

Brewery founded in April 1993, owning two pubs and supplying over a dozen other local outlets. Local hops are used. Tours by arrangement.

Buckswood Dingle*	(OG 1036, ABV 3.6%)
Overture*	(OG 1040, ABV 4.2%)
IDK*	(OG 1048, ABV 4.8%).

FRUITERER'S ARMS	See Cannon Royall.

FULLER'S

Fuller, Smith and Turner PLC, Griffin Brewery, Chiswick Lane South, Chiswick, London W4 2QB. Tel. (0181) 996 2000 Fax. (0181) 995 0230

Beer has been brewed on the Fuller's site for over 325 years, John Fuller being joined by Henry Smith and John Turner in 1845. Descendants of the original partners are still on the board today. The brewery recently completed a £1.6 million brewhouse redevelopment to cope with growing demand, and the installation of new mash tuns in 1993 led to an increase in capacity of 50%. It owns 200 pubs and all but two serve real ale. Fuller's also supplies an extensive free trade, both directly and through its subsidiary real ale distributor, Classic Ales. Shop open 8–4 Mon–Thu, 8–3 Fri. Tours by arrangement. Occasional beer: Golden Pride (OG 1089, ABV 9.2%, a barley wine for Christmas). Bottle-conditioned beer: 1845 Ale (OG 1062, ABV 6.3%).

Hock	(OG 1033, ABV 3.2%) A reddish brown, malty mild with a pleasant, dry finish. Available in spring only.
Chiswick Bitter	(OG 1034, ABV 3.5%) A distinctively hoppy, refreshing beer, with moderate maltiness and a lasting bitter finish. *Champion Beer of Britain* 1989.
Summer Ale*	(OG 1037, ABV 3.9%) A crisp, golden seasonal brew, available June–September.
London Pride ⊟	(OG 1040, ABV 4.1%) An award-winning beer with a strong, malty base and a rich balance of well-developed hop flavours.

The Independents

India Pale Ale*	(OG 1047, ABV 4.8%) A new, hoppy and full-bodied beer for February–May.
Mr Harry*	(OG 1048, ABV 4.8%) Available November–February.
ESB ⌺	(OG 1053, ABV 5.5%) A strong and aromatic beer of great character. The immediate full-bodied maltiness gives way to a rich hoppiness in the finish.

FURGUSONS	See Nationals, Carlsberg-Tetley.

FYFE

Fyfe Brewery Company, 496 High Street, Kirkcaldy, Fife KY1 2SN. Tel. (01592) 646211

Established in May 1995 behind the Harbour Bar, this is Fife's first brew pub this century, producing the Kingdom's first beer since the 1920s. The brewing capacity is two and a half barrels, most of which is supplied to the pub, the remainder being available to the free trade.

Auld Alliance*	(OG 1040, ABV 4%) A fruity, bitter beer with a long, dry aftertaste.

GALE'S

George Gale & Co. Ltd., The Hampshire Brewery, Horndean, Hampshire PO8 0DA. Tel. (01705) 571212 Fax. (01705) 598641

Hampshire's major brewery, Gale's was founded in 1847. The original building was largely destroyed by fire and a new, enlarged brewery was built on the site in 1869. Still family owned, it has grown slowly and steadily and all 131 tied houses (which include some very attractive old inns) serve real ale. Gale's also supplies around 300 free trade outlets directly, and other pubs via the big breweries. Licensees who join the Gale's Beer Club can take a series of special one-off brews. However, the mild, XXXD, is no longer produced. Bottle-conditioned beer: Prize Old Ale ⌺ (OG 1094, ABV 9%).

BBB or Butser Brew Bitter	(OG 1035, ABV 3.4%) Golden brown in colour, with little aroma. Fairly sweet-tasting, with the sweetness not appearing to come entirely from malt. Some grain and maltiness are also present, with some bitterness and hop flavour to finish.
Best Bitter	(OG 1040, ABV 3.8%) Probably the best-balanced beer of the Gale's range: sweet and malty, with some fruit leading to a malty finish with some hop character. A reddish brown brew.
Gold*	(OG 1040, ABV 4%) A straw-coloured beer, served a few degrees cooler than most ales.
5X	(OG 1044, ABV 4.2%) Available October–March. A very fruity beer, occasionally with liquorice and aniseed flavours, too. There is a winey fruitiness to the nose and some bitterness in the finish.
HSB	(OG 1050, ABV 4.8%) Too sugary-sweet for some palates: a deep-brown beer with little aroma but a flavour of malt grain and mixed fruit (apples, bananas and damson), leading to a dry, hoppy finish.
Festival Mild*	(OG 1051, ABV 4.8%) A dark, strong mild.
	For Whitbread:
Pompey Royal	(OG 1043, ABV 4.5%) A brown beer with a hint of red. Low in aroma, with the flavour dominated by sweetness and pear fruit. The finish can be a little cloying.

GIBBS MEW

Gibbs Mew PLC, Anchor Brewery, Gigant Street, Salisbury, Wiltshire SP1 2AR. Tel. (01722) 411911 Fax. (01722) 410013

Gibbs Mew was established in 1898 by the amalgamation of Salisbury brewers Bridger Gibbs & Sons and Herbert Mew & Co. Charrington bought a stake in the company in the 1960s, which the Gibbs family bought back in 1972, and, in 1992, with CAMRA support, it saw off new predators Brierly Investments. The tied

estate is still growing: in 1994 it bought the Centric Pub Company (197 pubs) and in 1995 it exchanged the Castle Leisure Complex in Cardiff for the six pubs formerly owned by Harmony Leisure Group. Real ale is now supplied to most of its 305 pubs (280 of which are tied), and to 100 free trade outlets. Tours by arrangement. Occasional beer: Premium (OG 1042, ABV 4%)

Wiltshire Traditional Bitter
(OG 1036, ABV 3.6%) A beer with a pleasant enough flavour of malt and hops, and a dry finish.

Overlord*
(OG 1036, ABV 3.6%) Produced to commemorate the 50th anniversary of D-Day and continued as a regular brew.

Salisbury Best Bitter
(OG 1042, ABV 4%) A rather chewy, sweet ale, decidedly lacking in bitterness. All the same, a pleasant beer.

Deacon
(OG 1050, ABV 5%) A pale, golden beer with a faint orange aroma, an initial bitter taste, and a lingering, dry aftertaste.

Wake Ale*
(OG 1050, ABV 5%) Available October–March.

The Bishop's Tipple
(OG 1066, ABV 6.5%) Weaker than the average barley wine, but not lacking in flavour. The full-bodied taste is marvellously malty with a kick that leaves the brain rather less clear than the beer.

GLASCHU

The Glaschu Brewery, 250 Woodlands Road, Glasgow, Strathclyde G3 6ND. Tel. (0141) 332 2862

Brewery opened in August 1994, serving four or five local outlets. It also owns one tied house and two hotels. Shop open Tue–Sat 12–8. Tours by arrangement.

Best Bracken*
(OG 1044, ABV 4%)

Pride of the Clyde*
(OG 1054, ABV 5%)

Double Whammy*
(OG 1063, ABV 6%)

GOACHER'S

P&DJ Goacher, Unit 8, Tovil Green Business Park, Tovil, Maidstone, Kent ME15 6TA. Tel. (01622) 682112

Kent's most successful small independent brewer, set up in 1983 by Phil and Debbie Goacher, producing all-malt ales with Kentish hops for its single free house and around 30 free trade outlets in the Maidstone area. Special, a 75%/25% mix of Light and Dark, is also available to pubs for sale under house names. Tours for local pub and club groups by arrangement.

Real Mild Ale*
(OG 1033, ABV 3.4%) A full-flavoured malty ale with a background bitterness.

Fine Light Ale*
(OG 1036, ABV 3.7%) A pale, golden brown bitter ale with a strong, hoppy aroma and aftertaste. A very hoppy and moderately malty session beer.

Best Dark Ale
(OG 1040, ABV 4.1%) An intensely bitter beer, balanced by a moderate maltiness, with a complex aftertaste. Lighter in colour than it once was, but still darker than most bitters.

Gold Star*
(OG 1050, ABV 5.1%) A summer pale ale.

Maidstone Porter*
(OG 1050, ABV 5.1%) A dark ruby winter beer with a roast malt flavour.

Old 1066 Ale*
(OG 1066, ABV 6.7%) Black, potent old ale, produced in winter.

GODDARD'S

Goddard's Brewery, Barnsley Farm, Bullen Road, Ryde, Isle of Wight PO33 1QF. Tel. (01983) 295024 Fax. (01983) 293898

Farm-based brewing company, formed in 1993. A bottled (not bottle-conditioned) version of Fuggle-Dee-Dum has been produced using the equipment at Bateman's brewery.

Special Bitter*
(OG 1039, ABV 4%)

Fuggle-Dee-Dum 🍺
(ABV 4.8%) A golden, full-bodied ale with a hoppy aroma, a malty bitter taste with a little sweetness and a hoppy, bitter finish.

The Independents

GOFF'S

Goff's Brewery Ltd., 9 Isbourne Way, Winchcombe, Gloucestershire GL54 5NS. Tel. (01242) 603383 Fax. (01242) 603959

A family concern which started brewing in September 1994, using plant purchased from Nethergate brewery. It supplies 15 outlets in the Cotswolds, but the beer is more widely available via wholesalers. A second beer is planned. Tours by arrangement.

Jouster Ale

(OG 1040, ABV 4%) A very drinkable, tawny-coloured ale. Malt and fruit predominate in the aroma and in the mouth. Some hoppiness in the taste sometimes persists into the aftertaste.

GOLDFINCH

Goldfinch Brewery, 47 High East Street, Dorchester, Dorset DT1 1HU. Tel. (01305) 264020

Brewery established in 1987 at Tom Brown's Public House, whose theme is broadly based on *Tom Brown's Schooldays*. It has expanded from a one-barrel to a four-barrel plant and supplies Tom Brown's (which is run as a free house), six other free trade outlets direct, plus others via wholesalers. Tours by arrangement.

Tom Brown's Best Bitter

(OG 1039, ABV 4%) A pale-coloured bitter which is fruity in both aroma and taste, with hop and some malt. The bittersweet taste gives way to a predominantly bitter finish.

Flashman's Clout Strong Ale

(OG 1043, ABV 4.5%) A tawny/mid-brown beer with an attractive, honeyed aroma, and, again, a bittersweet taste with malt and some hop. Hoppiness continues through to give a bitter edge to the aftertaste.

Midnight Blinder

(OG 1050, ABV 5%) A ruby red-coloured beer with an intense fruit aroma. Malt, hop and fruit combine to give the familiar bittersweet taste of Goldfinch beers, leading into a hoppy, bitter finish.

DOROTHY GOODBODY

See Wye Valley.

GOOSE EYE

Goose Eye Brewery, Ingrow Bridge, South Street, Keighley, W. Yorkshire BD21 5AX. Tel. (01535) 605807

After an absence of four years from the brewing scene, Goose Eye was re-opened in 1991 in a converted carpet warehouse by Bryan Eastell, with a new partner, Jack Atkinson, who went on to become the sole proprietor in 1993. The brewery supplies around 50 free trade outlets, and is still expanding, with a new summer bitter (4% ABV) in the offing. Tours by arrangement. Occasional beer: Black Goose Mild (OG 1036, ABV 3.5%).

Bitter*

(OG 1038, ABV 3.8%)

Bronte*

(OG 1040, ABV 4%)

Wharfedale*

(OG 1045, ABV 4.5%)

Pommie's Revenge*

(OG 1052, ABV 5.2%)

GRAND METROPOLITAN

See Nationals, Courage, and Pub Groups, Inntrepreneur.

GREENALLS

See Pub Groups and Nationals, Carlsberg-Tetley.

GREEN DRAGON

Green Dragon, 29 Broad Street, Bungay, Suffolk, NR35 1EE. Tel (01986) 892681

The Green Dragon was purchased from Brent Walker in 1991 and the buildings at the rear converted to a brewery. In December 1994, the plant was expanded and moved into a converted barn. Seasonal ales are occasionally brewed, but the beers are at present only available at the pub. Tours by arrangement. Beers: Mild (OG 1034, ABV 3.4%), Chaucer Ale (OG 1037, ABV 3.7%), Bridge Street Bitter (OG 1046, ABV 4.5%), Dragon (OG 1055, ABV 5.5%).

GREEN DRAGON   See Evesham.

GREEN JACK   **Green Jack Brewing Co. Ltd., Oulton Broad Brewery, Harbour Road Industrial Estate, Oulton Broad, Suffolk NR32 3LZ. Tel. (01502) 587905**

Green Jack opened in November 1993, on the site of the Forbes Brewery (which closed in February the same year), with new owners in charge. The attached Brewery Bar has just been refurbished, and this and a second tied house take most of the output; five other local outlets are also supplied. Tours by arrangement. Occasional beer: Ripper (OG 1077, ABV 8%).

Moild   (OG 1031, ABV 3%) A flavoursome dark mild with malt, roast malt and pleasant hoppiness prominent. Big mouthfeel for a mild of this type.

Bitter   (OG 1034, ABV 3.5%) A malty, light bitter with a fresh floral hoppiness.

Best Bitter   (OG 1044, ABV 4.5%) A hoppy bitter with a slightly astringent finish. Noticeably sweeter when young.

Golden Sickle   (OG 1048, ABV 4.9%) An uncomplicated light bitter, stronger than it tastes.

Norfolk Wolf Porter   (OG 1051, ABV 5.2%) An excellent, dry, roasty porter.

Lurcher Strong Ale   (OG 1057, ABV 6%) A sharp-tasting, fruity, strong bitter.

GREENE KING   **Greene King PLC, Westgate Brewery, Westgate Street, Bury St Edmunds, Suffolk IP33 1QT. Tel. (01284) 763222 Fax. (01284) 706502**

East Anglia's largest regional brewery (established 1799), producing cask-conditioned beers at Bury (its Biggleswade brewery is entirely given over to lager production). Having recently acquired 85 new pubs from Bass, its tied estate now amounts to 900 pubs (90% of which take cask ale), stretching from East Anglia down into London, Kent, Surrey and Sussex. The majority of pubs have a cask breather device fitted in the cellar, but, thankfully, some licensees choose not to use it. Extensive free trade. Greene King's new seasonal beers are sold under the 'King's Court' banner.

XX Dark Mild   (OG 1032, ABV 3%) Fuller in body and sweeter than before its 1994 OG increase. Smooth and sweetish, with a bitter, slightly astringent aftertaste. It is still under threat due to low volumes.

IPA   (OG 1036, ABV 3.6%) A blandish session bitter. Not unpleasant, it is hoppy on the nose, with hop and bitterness in the taste, ending in an astringent, bitter finish. Hop oils can be noticeable.

King's Champion*   (OG 1040, ABV 3.8%) A summer beer, available June–September.

Rayments Special Bitter   (OG 1040, ABV 4%) Very different to the other Greene King beers: predominantly malty and sweet, with a complex bitterness and hops lingering in the aftertaste.

Black Baron   (OG 1044, ABV 4.3%) A new winter beer. A plum red, strong mild, robust and flavoursome, with a complex fruity and sweet taste, and developing bitterness in the finish.

Sorcerer   (OG 1048, ABV 4.5%) A spring beer, available March–May. Early samples were well received. Its aroma gives little indication of the crisp, citrus, hoppy flavour which follows.

Abbot Ale   (OG 1049, ABV 5%) A complex, strong ale, with a good balance of malt, fruit and hops. However, some still find the hop oils intrusive.

Winter Ale   (OG 1060, ABV 6%) Available November–January. A dark red/brown, warming old ale of substance, like a good wine in many ways. A predominantly fruity nose with some chocolate

leads through to a rich blend of fruit, roast malt and some sweetness in the taste. Surprisingly dry aftertaste.

GREENWOOD'S

Greenwood's Brewery, Bell Farm, Bell Foundry Lane, Wokingham, Berkshire RG11 5QF. Tel. (01734) 793516 Fax. (01276) 675049

It was the fondness for teddy bears of Andrew Greenwood's partner, Helen Glennon, that inspired the logo for this new brewery, which was set up in converted farm buildings in November 1994. The beer is supplied direct (but intermittently) to around 50 pubs and also to wholesalers. Special beers are brewed to order and some occasional beers are produced.

Hop Pocket Bitter*	(OG 1038, ABV 3.8%)
Gold Prospector*	(OG 1046, ABV 4.6%) A summer brew.
Prohibition*	(OG 1048, ABV 4.8%)
Amber Gambler*	(OG 1055, ABV 5.5%)
Draught Excluder*	(OG 1060, ABV 6%) A winter brew.

GREYHOUND   See Nationals, Scottish & Newcastle.

GRIBBLE

The Gribble Inn, Oving, Chichester, W. Sussex PO20 6BP. Tel. (01243) 786893

Brew pub owned by Hall & Woodhouse and sometimes supplying other Hall & Woodhouse pubs. Black Adder II is not to be confused with the 1991 *Champion Beer of Britain* from Mauldons, nor Pig's Ear with the brew from Uley. Tours by arrangement. Beers: Harvest Pale (OG 1030, ABV 2.7%, summer), Gribble Ale (OG 1043, ABV 4.1%), Reg's Tipple (OG 1055, ABV 5%), Plucking Pheasant (OG 1055, ABV 5.2%), Black Adder II (OG 1060, ABV 5.8%), Pig's Ear Old Ale (OG 1060, ABV 6%), Wobbler (OG 1080, ABV 7.2%, Christmas).

GRIFFIN INN   See Church End.

GUERNSEY

The Guernsey Brewery Co. (1920) Ltd., South Esplanade, St Peter Port, Guernsey GY1 1BJ. Tel. (01481) 720143 Fax. (01481) 710658

One of two breweries on this Channel Isle, serving its stronger than average real ales in 13 of its 34 tied houses. Originally opened as the London Brewery in 1856, it became a Guernsey registered company in 1920 upon the introduction of income tax on the mainland. It was taken over by Ann Street (now Jersey) Brewery in 1988 and Guernsey real ale is still available in selected Jersey Brewery houses. A new microbrewery on the same premises produces an ever-changing range of real ales and stouts, and has also helped secure the future of Braye Ale. Sadly, more beer is now being sold as keg, dispensed with mixed gas. Eight free trade outlets in the Channel Isles are supplied with the real thing, with Britannia Bitter often sold under house names. Tours occasionally by arrangement.

Braye Ale	(OG 1038, ABV 3.8%) Copper-red in colour, with a complex aroma of malt, hops, fruit and toffee. The rich, mellow flavour combines malt, fruit, hops and butterscotch, whilst the finish has malt and hops. Full-flavoured, surprisingly dry and hoppier than before.
Britannia Bitter	(OG 1042, ABV 4%) A blend of Sunbeam and Braye; amber/tawny in colour, with an aroma of malt, fruit and toffee. Very malty on the palate and again in the finish. Full-bodied and satisfying.
Sunbeam Bitter	(OG 1045, ABV 4.2%) Golden in colour, with a fine malt aroma. Malt and fruit are strong on the palate and the beer is quite dry for its strength. Excellent, dry malt and hop finish.

GUINNESS	See Nationals.
HP&D	See Nationals, Carlsberg-Tetley.

HADRIAN

Hadrian Brewery Ltd., Unit 10, Hawick Crescent Industrial Estate, Newcastle upon Tyne, Tyne & Wear NE6 1AS. Tel. **(0191) 276 5302**

Brewery started with a five-barrel plant in 1987. It grew steadily, and moved to new premises in 1991 in order to expand. Financial problems followed, but the brewery was saved from receivership and now supplies 60 free trade outlets with its additive-free beers. It also brews for the Tap & Spile pub chain and Village Brewer, a wholesale operation based near Richmond, N. Yorkshire – tel. (01325) 374887. Tours by arrangement. Occasional beer: Yule Fuel (OG 1060, ABV 6.2%, Christmas).

Gladiator Bitter

(OG 1038, ABV 3.8%) Renowned as a fresh-tasting, full-flavoured premium bitter. Hoppiness dominates, to accompany a lasting bitterness and a dry finish.

Legion Ale*

(OG 1042, ABV 4.2%)

Centurion Best Bitter

(OG 1045, ABV 4.5%) Excellently-balanced beer with a prolonged malt and bitter character, balancing a lingering hoppiness.

Emperor Ale

(OG 1050, ABV 5%) A beautiful old ale, well-crafted to give lasting flavours. Highly-hopped, with a good balance of fruit and bitterness, finishing rich but dry.

For Tap & Spile:

Tap & Spile Bitter*

(OG 1036.5, ABV 3.8%)

For Village Brewer:

Zetland Best Bitter*

(OG 1042, ABV 4.2%)

HALL & WOODHOUSE

Hall & Woodhouse Ltd., The Brewery, Blandford St Mary, Blandford Forum, Dorset DT11 9LS. Tel. (01258) 452141 Fax. (01258) 454700

Founded as the Ansty Brewery in 1777 by Charles Hall, whose son, Robert, took Mr GEI Woodhouse into partnership in 1847. More usually known as 'Badger's', the brewery serves cask beer in all of its 160 houses (although an increasing number now use cask breathers), as well as supplying around 300 free trade outlets in southern England. Brewery tours by arrangement. Hall & Woodhouse also owns the Gribble Inn brew pub in Oving, W. Sussex (see Gribble).

Badger Best Bitter

(OG 1041, ABV 4%) A fine best bitter whose taste is strong in hop and bitterness, with underlying malt and fruit. A hoppy finish with a bitter edge.

Hard Tackle

(OG 1045, ABV 4.6%) A well-balanced, tawny-coloured beer. The nose is fruity and hoppy with some malt, and the palate has similar characteristics. A mainly bitter aftertaste.

Tanglefoot

(OG 1048, ABV 5.1%) A pale-coloured beer with a full fruit character throughout. Some malt and hop are also present in the palate, whilst the finish is bittersweet. Dangerously drinkable.

HALLCROSS	See Stocks.

HAMBLETON

Hambleton Ales, Holme-on-Swale, Thirsk, N. Yorkshire YO7 4JE. Tel. (01845) 567460 Fax. (01845) 567741

Brewery set up in March 1991 in a Victorian barn on the banks of the River Swale. Production, now averaging 50 barrels a week, has outgrown the original site, and a new brewery should soon be completed, 300 yards away in a former sheep nursery. Hambleton

now supplies over 100 free trade outlets and brews three beers under contract for the Village Brewer wholesale company – tel. (01325) 374887.

Bitter (OG 1036, ABV 3.6%) A crisp, satisfying bitter, with early malt character and final dryness. Strong hop aroma; smooth mouthfeel.

Goldfield (OG 1040, ABV 4.2%) A light amber bitter with good hop character and increasing dryness. A fine blend of malts gives a smooth overall impression.

Stallion (OG 1040, ABV 4.2%) A premium bitter with strong fruit flavours. Excellently hoppy and richly balanced with bitterness. Lasting, dry mouthfeel; fruity finish.

Nightmare (OG 1048, ABV 5%) Roast malt rears out of this complex mixture to balance a rich creamy sweetness and a lingering dry aftertaste. Available in winter.

Thoroughbred* (OG 1048, ABV 5%) Available in summer.

For Village Brewer:

White Boar (OG 1036, ABV 3.8%) Light, dry bitter, with a sharp aftertaste, leaving a dry mouthfeel.

Bull* (OG 1039, ABV 4%)

Old Raby (OG 1048, ABV 4.8%) A full-bodied beer with a pleasing, fruity aroma and a powerful maltiness. Excellently-balanced.

HAMPSHIRE

HAMPSHIRE ~BREWERY~

Hampshire Brewery, 5 Anton Trading Estate, Andover, Hampshire SP10 2NJ. Tel. (01264) 336699 Fax. (01264) 332338

Brewery set up in 1992 with a purpose-built, 25-barrel plant. The first brew was named after Alfred the Great, whose parliament resided in Andover. Sales have doubled in the last couple of years (to 200 outlets) and the brewery is approaching full capacity. There are plans to move to a larger site at the end of 1996. Brewery shop open 9–5.

King Alfred's (OG 1038, ABV 3.8%) A session beer. The well-hopped, fruity, slightly perfumed flavour is followed by a lingering bitter finish.

Lionheart* (OG 1042, ABV 4.2%)

Pendragon* (OG 1048, ABV 4.8%)

1066* (OG 1066, ABV 6%)

HANBY

Hanby Ales Ltd., New Brewery, Aston Park, Soulton Road, Wem, Shropshire SY4 5SD. Tel./Fax. (01939) 232432

Following the closure of Wem Brewery by Greenalls in 1988, the former head brewer, Jack Hanby, set up his own business. Brewing commenced the following spring and by February 1990 he had moved into a new, larger brewhouse (which was improved in 1991), supplying pubs directly and via wholesalers. Hanby acquired its first tied house in 1994 and started brewing monthly 'specials' that summer. It also brews for Blackbeard Trading – tel. (01584) 872908.

Black Magic Mild (OG 1033, ABV 3.3%) A dark, reddish brown mild, which is dry and bitter with a roast malt taste.

Drawwell Bitter (OG 1039, ABV 3.9%) A hoppy beer with excellent bitterness, both in taste and aftertaste. Beautiful amber colour.

Shropshire Stout (OG 1044, ABV 4.4%) Full-bodied, rich ruby stout, with a very distinctive, chocolate malt, dry flavour.

Scorpio* (OG 1045, ABV 4.5%)

Treacleminer Bitter (OG 1046, ABV 4.6%) A pale brown beer which is sweeter and fruitier than the beers above. Slight malt and hop taste.

Nutcracker Bitter (OG 1060, ABV 6%) A warming, smooth, mid-brown beer, with malt and hops coming through. Definitely more bitter than sweet.

	For Blackbeard Trading:
Happy Jack*	(OG 1030, ABV 3%)
Black Betty*	(OG 1045, ABV 4.4%)
Cherry Bomb*	(OG 1060, ABV 5.9%)
Joy Bringer*	(OG 1060, ABV 5.9%)
Queen Ann's Revenge*	(OG 1080, ABV 7.6%)

HANCOCK'S — See Nationals, Bass.

HAND IN HAND — See Kemptown.

HANSEATIC — See McMullen.

HANSON'S — See Banks's.

HARDINGTON

Hardington Brewery, Albany Buildings, Dean Lane, Bedminster, Bristol, Avon BS3 1BT. Tel. (0117) 9636194

Set up in April 1991, Hardington, however, has no connection with the old Somerset brewery of the same name. Demand for its beers continues to grow and it now serves 200 outlets. A second tied house was acquired in 1994. Tours by arrangement. Occasional beer: Rocket Best Bitter (OG 1040, ABV 4%).

Special Pale — (OG 1035, ABV 3.5%) A refreshing, golden pale ale. Malt, with a touch of hops and citrus fruit, is evident in the aroma, and a delicate, creamy body with similar characteristics and a dry bitterness lasts through to the finish.

Traditional Bitter — (OG 1036, ABV 3.6%) An amber-coloured, clean, refreshing bitter with a floral hop and citrus fruit aroma. The taste is similar, with balancing malt and a little sweetness. Long, dry, bitter hop finish.

Best Bitter — (OG 1041, ABV 4.1%) A crisp, refreshing pale brown best bitter with malt complexity and slight sweetness, becoming bitter and finishing dry. Floral hop and citrus fruit aroma. Moreish.

Jubilee — (OG 1050, ABV 5%) A mid-brown, strong bitter, rich in fruit and malt. Beautifully balanced with a contrasting dry, bitter finish.

Moonshine — (OG 1050, ABV 5%) A yellow/gold beer, with a wheaty malt and slight citrus fruit aroma. The smooth, sweetish taste of pale malt has hints of fruit and spice; dry, bitter finish.

Old Lucifer — (OG 1055, ABV 5.5%) A pale brown, smooth and powerful, distinctive strong bitter, sweet, hoppy, fruity and warming, with a complex biscuit and chocolate malt balance and a dry, bitter finish. Full-bodied.

Old Ale — (OG 1060, ABV 6%) A rich, copper-red, full-bodied, warming ale. The fruity, hoppy, roast malt aroma is well balanced; similar bittersweet, vinous taste with fruit notes and spices. Complex finish. A powerful, well-crafted old ale.

HARDYS & HANSONS

Hardys & Hansons PLC, Kimberley Brewery, Nottingham NG16 2NS. Tel. (0115) 9383611 Fax. (0115) 9459055

Established in 1832 and 1847 respectively, Hardys and Hansons were two competitive breweries until a merger in 1930 produced the present company. Nottingham's last independent brewery is today controlled by descendants of the original Hardy and Hanson families, who are committed to keeping it that way. It acquired almost 50 new pubs at the beginning of this decade, and now roughly 200 of its 250 tied houses take its real ales, although there is still a tendency to spoil them with top pressure (though never used on the strong Kimberley Classic). The brewery supplies around 60 other free trade outlets. Tours by arrangement.

The Independents

Kimberley Best Mild — (OG 1035, ABV 3.1%) A deep ruby, sweetish mild with malt and roast malt flavours and fruit and some hop coming through in the aftertaste.

Kimberley Best Bitter — (OG 1039, ABV 3.9%) Well-balanced, light amber brew which seems to have become more bitter in recent years. However, malt is still present in the taste and aftertaste.

Kimberley Classic — (OG 1047, ABV 4.8%) Malt and hops on the nose and in the taste, with some fruit throughout, but bitterness predominates. Undeservedly becoming more difficult to find.

HARPENDEN

Harpenden Brewery, The Red Cow, 171 Westfield Road, Harpenden, Hertfordshire AL5 4ND. Tel. (01582) 460156

Brew pub which started production in August 1994, but which is restricted to selling only one beer outside the list approved by Inntrepreneur, which owns the pub lease. Tours by arrangement. Beer: Harpenden Special Ale (OG 1038, ABV 3.8%).

HART

Hart Brewery, Cartford Hotel, Cartford Lane, Little Eccleston, Lancashire PR3 0YP. Tel. (01995) 670166

Brewery founded in 1994 in a small private garage, which moved to premises at the rear of the Cartford Hotel in summer 1995. Some local free houses are supplied as well as the hotel. Beers: Sun Rays (OG 1032, ABV 3.5%), Liberator (ABV 3.8%), Mayson Premier (OG 1040, ABV 4%), Criminale Porter (OG 1040, ABV 4%), Nemesis (ABV 4.5%), Old Ram (OG 1050, ABV 5%), Amadeus (ABV 5.5%), Nemesis Special (ABV 5.5%).

HARTLEYS — See Robinson's.

HARVEYS

Harvey & Son (Lewes) Ltd., The Bridge Wharf Brewery, 6 Cliffe High Street, Lewes, E. Sussex BN7 2AH. Tel. (01273) 480209 Fax. (01273) 483706

Established in the late 18th century by John Harvey, on the banks of the River Ouse, this Georgian brewery was partly rebuilt in 1880. The Victorian Gothic tower and brewhouse remain a very attractive feature in Lewes town centre. Still a family-run company, Harveys is slowly building up its tied estate, supplying real ale to all its 37 pubs and about 600 free trade outlets in Sussex and Kent. One of the first breweries to introduce seasonal ales, it also frequently produces commemorative beers, which are sometimes available on draught. Tours by arrangement. Shop open 9.30–1, 2–4.45 Mon–Wed, 9.30–4.45 Thu–Sat. Occasional beers: Knots of May Mild (OG 1030, ABV 3%, May), 1859 Porter ⊞ (OG 1053, ABV 4.8%, March), Tom Paine (OG 1055, ABV 5.5%, July), Christmas Ale (OG 1090, ABV 8.1%, December). Bottle-conditioned beer: 1859 Porter (OG 1053, ABV 4.8%).

XX Mild Ale — (OG 1030, ABV 3%) A dark, malty brew with some roast malt in the aroma. The flavour also enjoys some fruity sweetness. Roast malt finish.

Sussex Pale Ale — (OG 1033, ABV 3.5%) An agreeable light bitter, well-flavoured for its strength. Malt and hops predominate in the aroma, whilst a hoppy bitterness develops in the flavour to dominate the aftertaste.

Sussex Best Bitter (BB) — (OG 1040, ABV 4%) Medium strength bitter with a good balance of malt and hops in the flavour, which develops into a bitter, hoppy aftertaste.

XXXX or Old Ale — (OG 1043, ABV 4.3%) Brewed October–May: a rich, dark beer with a good malty nose, with some undertones of roast malt, hops and fruit. The flavour is a complex blend of roast malt, grain, fruit and hops with some caramel. Malty caramel finish with roast malt.

Armada Ale — (OG 1045, ABV 4.5%) Full-bodied beer in which hops are dominant throughout.

The Independents

HARVIESTOUN

Harviestoun Brewery Ltd., Devon Road, Dollar, Clackmannanshire, Central FK14 7LX. Tel./Fax. (01259) 742141

Hand-built in a 200-year-old stone byre by two home-brew enthusiasts in 1985, this small brewery operates from a former dairy at the foot of the Ochil Hills, near Stirling. To cope with demand a new custom-built brew plant was installed in 1991 and now serves 70 outlets in central Scotland as well as wholesale customers throughout Britain. Tours by arrangement. Occasional brew: Nouveau (OG 1095, ABV 9.5%, a barley wine brewed for Christmas and the New Year, with the OG increasing with the year).

Waverley 70/-*
(OG 1037, ABV 3.7%) A light session beer with hints of roast malt in the aftertaste.

Original 80/-*
(OG 1041, ABV 4.1%)

Montrose*
(OG 1042, ABV 4.2%)

Ptarmigan 85/-*
(OG 1045, ABV 4.5%) The first known 85/- ale, brewed with Bavarian hops and Scottish malt.

Schiehallion*
(OG 1048, ABV 4.8%) A cask-conditioned lager, served at cellar temperature by handpump.

Old Manor*
(OG 1050, ABV 5%)

HEATHER

Heather Ale Ltd., 736 Dumbarton Road, Glasgow, Strathclyde G11 6RD. Tel. (0141) 339 3479 Fax. (0141) 337 6298

Bruce Williams started brewing Fraoch (Gaelic for heather) in 1992 at the West Highland Brewery in Argyll, then moved his production to Maclay's Thistle brewery in 1993 from where he supplies almost 50 outlets (Bruce brews the beer himself, using Maclay's equipment). Fraoch is made with flowering heather, hence its seasonal nature.

Fraoch Heather Ale*
(OG 1041, ABV 4.1%) Available June–December.

Fraoch Pictish Ale*
(OG 1052, ABV 5.3%) Available December–March.

HEDGEHOG & HOGSHEAD

Belchers Brewery, 100 Goldstone Villas, Hove, E. Sussex BN3 3RX. Tel. (01273) 324660; 163 University Road, Highfield, Southampton, Hampshire SO17 1TS. Tel. (01703) 581124

Two brew pubs set up in 1990 by David Bruce (of Firkins fame), then sold in March 1994 to Grosvenor Inns for shares, with Bruce taking a seat on the Grosvenor board (see Pub Groups). The beers are stored in cellar tanks and a cask breather is used on slower sellers. There are also two Hedgehog & Hogsheads in London, but these do not brew. The beers are also supplied to some other outlets. Tours by arrangement. Beers: Belchers Original (OG 1034, ABV 3.4%), Belchers Best Bitter (OG 1042, ABV 4.2%), Old Slug Porter (OG 1042, ABV 4.2%), Bootleg Bitter (OG 1052, ABV 5.2%), New Barbarian (OG 1052, ABV 5.2%, occasional), Hogbolter (OG 1058, ABV 5.8%).

HENSTRIDGE

Henstridge Brewery, Bow Bridge Works, Henstridge Trading Estate, Henstridge, Somerset BA8 0TH. Tel. (01963) 363150 Fax. (01963) 363864

Brewery founded in 1994 and supplying one beer to outlets locally, and further afield via an agent.

Vickery's Brew*
(ABV 4.1%)

HERITAGE
See Burton Bridge and Lloyds.

The Independents

HESKET NEWMARKET

 Hesket Newmarket Brewery, Old Crown Barn, Hesket Newmarket, Cumbria CA7 8JG. Tel. (0169 74) 78288

Brewery set up in a barn behind the owners' pub in an attractive North Lakes village. Most of the beers are named after local fells and around 22 outlets are supplied. Tours by arrangement. Occasional beers: Show Ale (OG 1040, ABV 3.9%, September), Westmorland Ale (OG 1045, ABV 4.3%), Ayala's Angel (OG 1080, ABV 7%, Christmas).

Great Cockup Porter*	(OG 1035, ABV 2.8%) A refreshing, chocolate-tasting beer.
Blencathra Bitter*	(OG 1035, ABV 3.1%)
Skiddaw Special Bitter*	(OG 1035, ABV 3.7%) A golden session beer, despite its name.
Doris's 90th Birthday Ale*	(OG 1045, ABV 4.3%) A fruity premium ale.
Catbells Pale Ale*	(OG 1052, ABV 5.1%)
Old Carrock Strong Ale*	(OG 1060, ABV 5.6%) A dark red, powerful ale.

HEXHAMSHIRE

Hexhamshire Brewery, Leafields, Ordley, Hexham, Northumberland NE46 1SX. Tel. (01434) 673031

Brewery set up in a redundant farm building in November 1992 by the owner of the Dipton Mill Inn with two partners. No adjuncts are used in the beers, which are produced for the inn and other local outlets. Occasional beers: Blackhall Stout (OG 1043, ABV 4.3%), Old Humbug (OG 1055, ABV 5.5%).

Low Quarter Ale	(OG 1035, ABV 3.5%) Full-bodied, hoppy ale, with low bitterness and a golden hue.
Shire Bitter	(OG 1037, ABV 3.8%) Thicker than expected: a more bitter beer than Low Quarter, but with a malty overtone.
Devil's Water	(OG 1041, ABV 4.1%) A beer of mixed character and an unexpected range of flavours. Malt dominates and bitterness gradually declines, giving a strong, sweet finish.
Whapweasel or Strong	(OG 1048, ABV 4.8%) This malty bitter has a lasting hoppiness and a smooth mouthfeel.

HIGHGATE   See Nationals, Bass.

HIGH PEAK   See Lloyds.

HIGHWOOD

Highwood Brewery Ltd., Melton Highwood, Barnetby, Humberside DN38 6AA. Tel. (01652) 680020 Fax. (01652) 680729

Located in a converted granary on the edge of the Lincolnshire Wolds, this brewery went into production in March 1995. Tours by arrangement. Some 40 pubs take the beer locally and deliveries are also made to the West Midlands. Seasonal beers are planned, including a German-style smoked beer.

Tom Wood Best Bitter*	(OG 1036, ABV 3.5%)
Old Timber*	(OG 1042, ABV 4.5%)

HIGSONS   See Cains and Nationals, Whitbread.

HILDEN

Hilden Brewery, Hilden House, Lisburn, Co. Antrim BT27 4TY. Tel. (01846) 663863

Mini-brewery beside a Georgian country house, set up in 1981 to counter the local Guinness/Bass duopoly. It is presently the only real ale brewery in Northern Ireland, supplying Hilden Ale to just a single pub there, and the full range to some pubs in England.

Hilden Ale   (OG 1038, ABV 4%) An amber-coloured beer with an aroma of

malt, hops and fruit. The balanced taste is slightly slanted towards hops, and hops are also prominent in the full, malty finish. Bitter and refreshing.

Great Northern Porter (OG 1039, ABV 4%) A beer with a rich, tawny colour and a pronounced malty aroma. Crystal malt is dominant in both the flavour and aftertaste.

Special Reserve (OG 1040, ABV 4%) Dark red/brown in colour and superbly aromatic – full of dark malts, producing an aroma of liquorice and toffee. Malt, fruit and toffee on the palate, with a sweet, malty finish. Mellow and satisfying, but not always available.

HOBSONS

Hobsons Brewery & Co., The Brewery, Cleobury Industrial Estate, Cleobury Mortimer, Kidderminster, Hereford & Worcester DY14 8DP. Tel. (01299) 270837

Opened at Easter 1993 in a former sawmill, Hobsons is run by Nick Davies and his parents, supplying their own pub and 80 other pubs and clubs within an hour's drive. The brewery is actually in Shropshire, despite the postal address. Tours by arrangement. Bottle-conditioned beer: Town Crier (OG 1043, ABV 4.5%, occasional).

Best Bitter (OG 1038, ABV 3.8%) A pale brown to amber, medium-bodied beer with strong hop character throughout. It is consequently bitter, but with malt discernible in the taste.

Town Crier* (OG 1043, ABV 4.5%) A straw-coloured bitter.

Old Henry* (OG 1050, ABV 5.2%) A winter brew.

HODGES

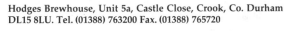

Hodges Brewhouse, Unit 5a, Castle Close, Crook, Co. Durham DL15 8LU. Tel. (01388) 763200 Fax. (01388) 765720

Hodges has raced to a flying start after its official opening in October 1994 by Dr David Bellamy. Sixteen local outlets are now supplied.

Original* (OG 1040, ABV 4.1%)

Best* (OG 1045, ABV 4.5%)

HOGS BACK

Hogs Back Brewery, Manor Farm, The Street, Tongham, Surrey GU10 1DE. Tel. (01252) 783000 Fax. (01252) 782328

This purpose-built brewery was set up in a restored farm building (circa 1768) in August 1992. It supplies over 200 outlets and has a well-stocked shop/off-licence on site, offering a wide range of English and foreign (particularly Belgian) bottled beers; open 9–6 Mon–Sat (9–8.30 Wed). Tours by arrangement. Occasional beers: Santa's Wobble (OG 1077, ABV 7.5%, Christmas), Brewster's Bundle (OG 1076, ABV 7.5%), Still Wobbling (OG 1077, ABV 7.5%, summer), A over T or Aromas over Tongham (OG 1091, ABV 9%).

Dark Mild (OG 1036, ABV 3.4%) A reddish brown, malty mild with an underlying fruitiness and a bitter finish.

APB or A Pinta Bitter (OG 1037, ABV 3.5%) A thin bitter with a malty aroma, balanced in flavour by an underlying fruitiness.

TEA or Traditional English Ale 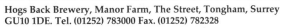 (OG 1044, ABV 4.2%) Orange/brown, malty bitter with a developing hop balance. Slightly fruity.

Blackwater Porter* (OG 1046, ABV 4.4%)

Hop Garden Gold (OG 1048, ABV 4.6%) Malty, golden beer with a hoppy finish.

Rip Snorter (OG 1052, ABV 5%) Strong, malty and fruity, reddish brown bitter with a slight hop flavour.

OTT or Olde Tongham Tasty (OG 1066, ABV 6%) Black winter ale, with a pleasant fruity, roast malt aroma and flavour. Hops are also present in the finish with lingering roast malt and bitterness.

The Independents

HOLDEN'S

Holden's Brewery Co. Ltd., Hopden Brewery, George Street, Woodsetton, Dudley, W. Midlands DY1 4LN. Tel. (01902) 880051 Fax. (01902) 665473

A fourth generation of the Holden family has recently joined this long-established Black Country brewery, which started as a brew pub at the Park Inn (now the brewery tap) in 1916. It produces a good range of real ales for its 21 pubs and around 60 free trade customers, and also bottles its own beers and others under contract at the only remaining bottling hall in the Black Country. Shop open daily 10.30–2, 4 (6 Sat and Sun)–10. Tours by arrangement. Occasional beers: Stout (OG 1035, ABV 3.6%), Old Ale (OG 1072, ABV 6.9%, Christmas).

Mild
(OG 1037, ABV 3.7%) Medium-bodied, dark red/brown mild, typical of the area. A blend of roast malt, hops and fruit, but dominated by maltiness throughout.

Bitter
(OG 1039, ABV 3.9%) Medium-bodied, golden ale. A light, clean bitter with malt and hops pleasantly balanced and a dry, hoppy, bitter finish.

XB or Lucy B
(OG 1042 ABV 4.1%) Named after Lucy Blanche Holden, this is a sweeter, slightly fuller version of the bitter.

Special Bitter
(OG 1052, ABV 5.1%) A sweet and malty, full-bodied amber ale, with a pleasant, bittersweet aftertaste.

HOLT

EST. 1849

Joseph Holt PLC, Derby Brewery, Empire Street, Cheetham, Manchester M3 1JD. Tel. (0161) 834 3285 Fax. (0161) 834 6458

Successful family brewery, founded in 1849 (not to be confused with Carlsberg-Tetley's Midlands company Holt, Plant & Deakin). All 110 tied houses serve real ale, most of them taking hogsheads (54-gallon casks), because their low prices result in a high turnover. The beers are popular as guests and, with a free trade of around 80 outlets (plus another 40 or so via an agent), the brewery was extended in 1992 to cope with growing demand. Occasional beer: Sixex (OG 1060, ABV 6%, Christmas).

Mild
(OG 1032, ABV 3.2%) Very dark beer with a complex aroma and taste. Roast malt is prominent, but so are hops and fruit. Strong in bitterness for a mild, with a long-lasting, satisfying aftertaste.

Bitter
(OG 1039, ABV 4%) Tawny beer with a good hop aroma. Although balanced by malt and fruit, the uncompromising bitterness can be a shock to the unwary. It has gained a little sweetness in recent years.

HOLTS
See Nationals, Carlsberg-Tetley.

HOME
See Nationals, Scottish & Newcastle.

HOOK NORTON

The Hook Norton Brewery Co. Ltd., Hook Norton, Banbury, Oxfordshire OX15 5NY. Tel. (01608) 737210 Fax. (01608) 730294

Built by John Harris on the family farm in 1850, Hook Norton remains one of the most delightful traditional Victorian tower breweries in Britain. It retains much of its original plant and machinery, the showpiece being a 25-horsepower stationary steam engine which still pumps the Cotswold well water used for brewing. The brewery boasts some fine old country pubs, with all 34 of its tied houses serving real ale, and some 400 free trade outlets also supplied. Occasional beers: Haymaker (ABV 4.9%, July), Twelve Days (OG 1058, ABV 5.5%, Christmas).

Beers marked with an asterisk have not been tasted by official CAMRA tasting panels. However, some of these beers do carry brief descriptions derived from limited samplings or other sources which can be used for rough guidance.

PAB Mild (OG 1032, ABV 2.9%) A dark, red/brown mild with a malty aroma and a malty, sweetish taste, tinged with a faint hoppy balance. Malty in the aftertaste. Highly drinkable.

Best Bitter (OG 1036, ABV 3.4%) An excellently-balanced, golden bitter. Malty and hoppy on the nose and in the mouth, with a hint of fruitiness. Dry, but with some balancing sweetness. A hoppy bitterness dominates the finish.

Old Hooky (OG 1049, ABV 4.5%) An unusual, tawny beer with a strong fruity and grainy aroma and palate, balanced by a hint of hops. Full-bodied, with a bitter, fruity and malty aftertaste.

HOP BACK

Hop Back Brewery PLC, Unit 21–23 Batten Road Industrial Estate, Downton, Salisbury, Wiltshire SP5 3HU. Tel. (01725) 510986 Fax. (01725) 513116

Originally a brew pub, the Wyndham Arms, set up in 1987 with a five-barrel plant, Hop Back switched most of its production to a new brewery at Downton in 1992. New plant was added in 1995 to cope with increased demand, and in the same year a fourth tied house, the Hop Leaf in Reading, was opened (see Hop Leaf). Hop Back also sells directly to 85 free trade outlets and produces special brews for the Westbury Ales wholesaler – tel. (01749) 870719. Tours by arrangement.

Mild (OG 1032, ABV 3.2%) A dark, well-balanced, very tasty mild, with bags of chocolate malt. Dry, clean-tasting and well-hopped. A very quaffable session ale.

GFB (OG 1035, ABV 3.5%) Golden, with the sort of light, clean, tasty quality which makes an ideal session ale. A hoppy aroma and taste lead to a good, dry finish. Refreshing.

Special (OG 1041, ABV 4%) A medium bitter. Slightly sweet, but with a good balance of malt and hops and a long finish.

Wilt Alternative (OG 1041, ABV 4%) A light, straw-coloured, crisp, clean-tasting best bitter, with a fine aroma and a taste of honey. Well-hopped for bitterness, which lasts.

Entire Stout (OG 1043, ABV 4.5%) A rich dark stout with a strong roasted malt flavour and a long, sweet and malty aftertaste. A vegan beer.

Wheat Beer (OG 1048, ABV 5%) Very pale in colour. A full-bodied beer, with a rich, fruity taste and a dry, clean apricot finish. Very moreish.

Powerhouse* (OG 1049, ABV 5%) A new winter brew.

Summer Lightning (OG 1049, ABV 5%) A very pleasurable pale bitter with a good, fresh, hoppy aroma and a malty, hoppy flavour. Finely balanced, it has an intense bitterness leading to a long, dry finish. Though strong, it tastes like a session ale.

HOP LEAF

The Hop Leaf, 163–165 Southampton Street, Reading, Berkshire RG1 2QZ. Tel. (01734) 314700

Inntrepreneur pub taken over by Hop Back; Reading's first real ale brewery since Courage closed the old Simonds site in the late 1970s. Its five-barrel plant came from the Wyndham Arms in Salisbury. Occasional beers are brewed for other Hop Back pubs and the free trade. Beer: Bitter (OG 1035, ABV 3.5%).

HOPE & ANCHOR

The Lucifer Live Beer Brewing Company, Hope & Anchor, 38 Jacob's Wells Road, Clifton, Bristol, Avon BS8 1DR. Tel./Fax. (0117) 9292987

Brewery currently inoperative, but with plans to resume production.

HORSEBRIDGE See Royal Inn.

The Independents

HOSKINS

Tom Hoskins Brewery PLC, Beaumanor Brewery, 133 Beaumanor Road, Leicester LE4 5QE. Tel. (0116) 2661122 Fax. (0116) 2610150

Established in 1877, this traditional tower brewery was family-owned until 1983, when it was acquired and expanded by TRD Estates Ltd. Following the sale of eight pubs to Wolverhampton & Dudley in 1992, the brewery was taken over by Halkin Holdings in 1993 and in 1995 was subject to a management buyout – look out for changes to the beer range. It has five tied houses (all serving real ale), and supplies 12 free trade outlets, as well wholesalers. Tours by arrangement.

Beaumanor Bitter

(OG 1039, ABV 3.7%) This pale brown/tawny brew is dominated by a bitterness that becomes astringent in the aftertaste. Unbalanced and unsophisticated; yeast can also be detected. Early promise is not sustained.

Penn's Bitter

(OG 1045, ABV 4.6%) An overwhelming bitterness is this beer's most obvious characteristic. A reddish-brown brew that has an astringent, soapy finish.

Premium

(OG 1050, ABV 4.9%) Very grainy, with a sweet, hoppy taste, leading to an intensely bitter, astringent aftertaste.

Churchill's Pride*

(OG 1050, ABV 4.9%)

Old Nigel Winter Warmer

(OG 1060, ABV 5.8%) A full-bodied, smooth beer with many flavours, but totally dominated by a sweet, cloying taste and finish, somewhat tempered by its fruitiness. Overly yeasty.

HOSKINS & OLDFIELD

Hoskins & Oldfield Brewery Ltd., North Mills, Frog Island, Leicester LE3 5DH. Tel. (0116) 2510532

Brewery set up by two members of Leicester's famous brewing family, Philip and Stephen Hoskins, in 1984, after the sale of the old Hoskins Brewery. The number of outlets supplied direct from the brewery has increased considerably in the last 12 months, and the wholesale trade has remained steady. Plans are in hand to resume production of bottle-conditioned beers. Occasional beers: Tom Kelly's Christmas Pudding Porter (OG 1052, ABV 5%, Christmas), Reckless Raspberry (ABV 5.5%, a stronger version of the wheat beer with added raspberries).

HOB Best Mild ⊟

(OG 1036, ABV 3.5%) Toffee notes dominate this almost black-coloured beer, but malt and hops are both present in the taste, which leads to a long, bitter finish with fruity overtones.

Brigadier Bitter

(OG 1036, ABV 3.6%) A pleasant ordinary bitter. Fruity, but somewhat lacking in balancing bitterness.

HOB Bitter

(OG 1041, ABV 4%) A tawny-coloured, well-balanced best bitter with a hoppy nose, a sweetish, malty flavour and an astringent, hoppy aftertaste that leads to a late, lingering bitter finish with hints of sweetness.

Little Matty

(OG 1041, ABV 4%) Very complex brown/red beer. Hops and fruit blend with malt and caramel for an almost 'nuts and raisins' aroma. Malt sweetness and fruit combine to give a dry, nutty taste, with hops appearing in the finish.

White Dolphin

(OG 1041, ABV 4%) Citrus fruit predominates, with sweetness tempering the lactic sharpness of this wheat beer.

Tom Kelly's Stout

(OG 1043, ABV 4.2%) A satisfying stout, dark in colour, with an attractive, golden, creamy head and an aroma of malt and fruit. The flavour is exceedingly bitter but malty, and the finish is dry and chocolatey.

Supreme*

(OG 1045, ABV 4.4%) A very light gold best bitter.

Tom Hoskins Porter*

(OG 1050, ABV 4.8%) Brewed using honey and oats.

EXS Bitter*

(OG 1051, ABV 5%) A tawny-coloured premium bitter.

Ginger Tom*	(OG 1053, ABV 5.2%) A ginger beer.
Old Navigation Ale ⊕	(OG 1071, ABV 7%) Ruby/black beer, with an aroma reminiscent of sherry. Plenty of mouthfeel, with liquorice and raisins in a sweet, fruity stout-like malt flavour. May sometimes have too strong a caramel taste for some palates.
Christmas Noggin	(OG 1100, ABV 10%) Russet-coloured beer with a spicy, fruity aroma. The taste is of malt and fruit, and the finish balances malt and hops. Sweet but not cloying. Available throughout the year.

HP&D	See Nationals, Carlsberg-Tetley.

SARAH HUGHES

Sarah Hughes Brewery, Beacon Hotel, 129 Bilston Street, Sedgley, Dudley, W. Midlands DY3 1JE. Tel. (01902) 883380

Brewery re-opened in 1988 after lying idle for 30 years, to serve the village pub and a few other outlets, but which now also produces beers for the free trade. A Victorian-style conservatory acts as a reception area for brewery visits. Bottle-conditioned beer: Original Dark Ruby Mild (OG 1058, ABV 6%).

Sedgley Surprise	(OG 1048, ABV 5%) A bittersweet, medium-bodied, hoppy ale with some malt.
Original Dark Ruby Mild ⊕	(OG 1058, ABV 6%) A near-black, strong ale with a good balance of fruit and hops, leading to a pleasant, lingering hops and malt finish.

HULL

The Hull Brewery Co. Ltd., 144–148 English Street, Hull, Humberside HU3 2BT. Tel. (01482) 586364 Fax. (01482) 586365

Hull Brewery was resurrected in 1989 after a 15-year absence, and was taken over by a new owner in March 1994. Improvements have since been made to the brewery to ensure consistency. Tours by arrangement. Around 100 free trade outlets throughout northern England are currently supplied. Occasional beers: Electric Light Ale (OG 1038, ABV 3.7%, summer), John Barleycorn (OG 1042, ABV 4.2%, June–July), Nuclear Brown Ale (OG 1046, ABV 4.6%, autumn), Coal Porter (OG 1048, ABV 4.8%, October–November), Old Acquaintance (OG 1048, ABV 4.8%, Christmas), Belly Rumbler (OG 1050, ABV 5%, spring).

Mild*	(OG 1034, ABV 3.3%)
Elwood's Best Bitter*	(OG 1038, ABV 3.8%)
Bitter*	(OG 1039, ABV 3.8%)
Amber Ale*	(OG 1040, ABV 4%)
Governor Strong Ale*	(OG 1046, ABV 4.4%)

HYDES' ANVIL

Hydes' Anvil Brewery Ltd., 46 Moss Lane West, Manchester M15 5PH. Tel. (0161) 226 1317 Fax. (0161) 227 9593

Family-controlled traditional brewery, first established at the Crown Brewery, Audenshaw, Manchester in 1863 and on its present site, a former vinegar brewery, since the turn of the century. The smallest of the established Manchester breweries, it supplies cask ale to all its 62 tied houses and around 35 free trade outlets. A new 4.5% ABV beer is planned. Tours by arrangement.

Dark Mild	(OG 1032, ABV 3.5%) A mild with a caramel and fruit aroma: quite sweet and fruity, with a pleasant aftertaste. Sold mainly in the company's Welsh pubs, but rare in the Manchester area.
Mild	(OG 1032, ABV 3.5%) A light, refreshing and quite fruity drink, with a short, dry aftertaste. This mid-brown beer has a fruity and malty aroma.

The Independents

Light	(OG 1034, ABV 3.7%) A lightly-hopped session beer, with malt and a refreshing fruitiness dominating before a brief but dry finish.
Bitter	(OG 1036, ABV 3.8%) A good-flavoured bitter, with a malty and hoppy nose, fruity background and malt and hops in the finish. A hint of bitterness and astringency throughout.

ICENI

The Iceni Brewery, 3 Foulden Road, Ickburgh, Mundford, Norfolk IP26 5BJ. Tel./Fax. (01842) 878922

Owner Brendan Moore had a dream one night of opening a brewery. A year later, without any prior experience, but armed with redundancy money and a grant from the Rural Development Commission, he went ahead and his first brew rolled out in January 1995. Some 20 local outlets are now supplied with beers which are all named after Celtic queens. Tours by arrangement.

Boadicea Chariot Ale*	(OG 1038, ABV 3.8%)
Deirdre of Sorrows*	(OG 1044, ABV 4.4%)
Queen Maev Stout*	(OG 1055, ABV 4.9%)

IND COOPE	See Nationals, Carlsberg-Tetley.

ISLAND	See Burts.

ISLE OF MAN

Isle Of Man Breweries Ltd., Kewaigue, Douglas, Isle of Man IM2 1QG. Tel. (01624) 661120 Fax. (01624) 661160

The main brewery on the island, having taken over and closed the rival Castletown brewery in 1986. Production of Castletown beers ceased completely in 1992 after a period at the Victorian Falcon Brewery, which itself was closed in 1994, when production moved to a new, purpose-built brewery at Kewaigue. All beers are produced under the unique Manx Brewers' Act 1874 (permitted ingredients: water, malt, sugar and hops only). All the company's 42 tied houses sell real ale and 12 free trade outlets are also supplied. Tours by arrangement. Occasional beers: Olde Skipper (OG 1045, ABV 4.5%, May), St Nick (OG 1050, ABV 5%, Christmas).

Okells Mild	(OG 1034, ABV 3.4%) A genuine, well-brewed mild ale, with a fine aroma of hops and crystal malt. Reddish-brown in colour, this beer has a full malt flavour with surprising bitter hop notes and a hint of blackcurrants and oranges. Full, malty finish.
Okells Bitter	(OG 1035, ABV 3.7%) Golden, malty and superbly hoppy in aroma, with a hint of honey. Rich and malty on the tongue, with a wonderful, dry malt and hop finish. A complex but rewarding beer.
Doolish*	(OG 1045, ABV 4.1%) A new cask-conditioned stout.

JENNINGS

ESTᴰ. 1828

Jennings Bros PLC, Castle Brewery, Cockermouth, Cumbria CA13 9NE. Tel. (01900) 823214 Fax. (01900) 827462

Founded in 1828, and moved to its present site in 1874, Jennings has gradually expanded over the years (particularly during the 1920s). Although there is no longer any family involvement, many of the company's shares are owned by local people. Over 450 free trade outlets are now supplied from its own Leyland and Newcastle depots, and many more via wholesalers throughout the UK. Real ale is also available at 92 of the 107 tied houses. Oatmeal Stout (OG 1042, ABV 3.8%) is brewed for Jennings by Broughton. Shop open 9–4.45 Mon–Fri. Tours by arrangement.

Dark Mild*	(OG 1031, ABV 3.1%) A dark, mellow mild.
Bitter	(OG 1035, ABV 3.5%) A distinctive, red/brown brew with a

hoppy, malty aroma. A good, strong balance of grain and hops in the taste, with a moderate bitterness, develops into a lingering, dry, malty finish.

Cumberland Ale (OG 1040, ABV 4%) A light, but hoppy, bitter, with a creamy taste and smooth mouthfeel. The aroma can be sulphury, but the taste ends crisp and dry with a spicy bitterness.

Cocker Hoop* (OG 1047, ABV 4.8%)

Sneck Lifter* (OG 1055, ABV 5.1%) A dark, strong warmer.

JERSEY

The Jersey Brewery, Ann Street Brewery Co. Ltd., 57 Ann Street, St Helier, Jersey JE1 1BZ. Tel. (01534) 31561 Fax. (01534) 67033

Brewery under a new name. Jersey (formerly known by its parent company's title of Ann Street) began brewing cask beer again in 1990 after a break of 30 years. It has 50 tied houses, of which 12 take real ale. Tours by arrangement.

Old Jersey Ale (OG 1036, ABV 3.5%) An attractive tawny/copper colour, this bitter ale packs an immense depth of malt flavours, the crystal malt giving hints of barley sugar. The malty bitterness is quite intense in the aftertaste.

Ann's Treat (OG 1049, ABV 5.1%) An amber-coloured beer with a fruity aroma. Sweetish and full-bodied, it has a good balance of malt and hop, but with fruit flavours to the fore, plus hints of dates and ginger. The finish is malty and less sweet.

Winter Ale (OG 1070, ABV 7.5%) Very dark brown, with hues of copper, this is a complex beer, full of roast barley and malt flavours, giving glimpses of chocolate, coffee and butterscotch. Quite bitter for its strength and very rewarding.

JOHN THOMPSON INN

 John Thompson Brewery, Ingleby, Derbyshire DE73 1HW. Tel. (01332) 862469

This 15th-century farmhouse was converted to a pub in 1969. It has brewed since 1977, with most of the production supplied to the free trade through Lloyds Country Beers (see Lloyds), a separate enterprise. Beers (on sale here): Summer Gold (OG 1040, ABV 4%), JTS XXX (OG 1042, ABV 4.1%, sold elsewhere as Lloyds Derby Bitter), JTS Rich Porter (OG 1045, ABV 4.3%, winter).

JOLLYBOAT

The Jollyboat Brewery Ltd., 4 Buttgarden Street, Bideford, Devon EX39 2AU. Tel. (01237) 424343

Brewery established in April 1995 and currently supplying around 30 local outlets, plus wholesalers.

Buccaneer* (OG 1038, ABV 3.8%)

Mainbrace Bitter* (OG 1041, ABV 4.2%)

Plunder* (OG 1049, ABV 5%)

JOLLY ROGER

 Jolly Roger Brewery, 31–33 Friar Street, Worcester, Hereford & Worcester WR1 2NA. Tel. (01905) 22222 Fax. (01905) 20977

Founded as a brew pub in Upton upon Severn in 1982, Jolly Roger made its new home in Worcester in 1985 and expanded quickly thereafter. Setbacks in 1993 led to changes in control and a scaling down of operations, but there are plans to expand again, with the acquisition of two new pubs (to make a total of six) and a move to larger office premises. Additions to the beer range are also planned. Five local free trade outlets are supplied. Two brews are produced exclusively for the Brewery Tap in Lowesmoor, Worcester, a former brew pub: Quaff (OG 1039, ABV 3.9%), Old Lowesmoor (OG 1056, ABV 5.6%). Bottle-conditioned beer: Winter Wobbler (OG 1095, ABV 9%, the OG increasing with each year).

The Independents

Ale*	(OG 1038, ABV 3.8%)
Broadsword*	(OG 1039, ABV 3.9%)
Shipwrecked*	(OG 1040, ABV 4%)
Goodness Stout*	(OG 1042, ABV 4.2%)
Flagship*	(OG 1052, ABV 5.2%) A sweet, dark and smooth beer that does not disguise its strength.
Winter Wobbler*	(OG 1094, ABV 9.6%) A winter ale, like liquid liquorice; very strong.

JOULE — See Coach House and Nationals, Bass.

JUDGES — **Judges Brewery, Unit 15a, Boughton Road, Rugby, Warwickshire CV23 9HD. Tel. (01788) 535356**

Brewery set up by Graham and Anne Judge in May 1992 in a sleepy Warwickshire village, but since moved to a larger site in Rugby. It is now at the forefront of a brewing revival in the county and supplies around 20 local outlets. Tours by arrangement. Occasional beer: Santa's Surprise (OG 1052, ABV 5%, a Christmas porter).

Barristers Bitter	(OG 1038, ABV 3.5%) A well-balanced, pale-coloured session beer; light and easily drinkable.
Coombe Ale*	(OG 1042, ABV 4.2%) A new beer, primed with local honey.
Old Gavel Bender	(OG 1050, ABV 5%) Full-bodied, with a caramel aroma and taste. Good, dry, sharp aftertaste.
Solicitor's Ruin	(OG 1056, ABV 5.6%) A full-flavoured, smooth and sweet beer with malt and fruit abounding. Fruity, dry aftertaste.

JUWARDS — **Juwards Brewery, c/o Fox Brothers & Co. Ltd., Wellington, Somerset TA21 0AW. Tel. (01823) 667909**

Juwards, the latest venture of Ted Bishop, former brewer at Cotleigh and Ash Vine, went into production in June 1994, based in an old wool mill. It supplies around 30 outlets direct in the West Country, plus others in the Midlands and North of England via agents.

Bitter*	(OG 1040, ABV 3.9%)
Premium*	(OG 1048, ABV 4.9%)

KELHAM ISLAND — **Kelham Island Brewery, 23 Alma Street, Sheffield, S. Yorkshire S3 8SA. Tel. (0114) 2781867 Fax. (0114) 2786850**

Brewery opened in 1990 at the Fat Cat pub, using equipment purchased from the former Oxford Brewery and Bakehouse, serving around 100 outlets in Derbyshire, Nottinghamshire and South Yorkshire.

Fat Cat Pale Ale*	(OG 1036, ABV 3.6%)
Bitter	(OG 1038, ABV 3.8%) A strong assault of hops on the nose is followed by hoppiness throughout this pale brown, clean and refreshingly crisp beer, with a dry aftertaste.
Golden Eagle*	(OG 1042, ABV 4.2%)
Wheat Beer*	(OG 1050, ABV 5%)
Pale Rider	(OG 1052, ABV 5.2%) A fruity, sweet, straw-coloured ale with a dry hoppiness in the taste and lingering finish.
Bête Noire	(OG 1055, ABV 5.5%) A beer with a thin aroma with hints of coffee. Malt and caramel chocolate are prominent in the mouth, developing into plum notes and a sweet, yet dry, aftertaste.

The pub sign indicates breweries which are also brew pubs, i.e. produce beer in part of a pub or in its grounds.

The Independents

KEMPTOWN

The Kemptown Brewery Co. Ltd., 33 Upper St James's Street, Kemptown, Brighton, E. Sussex BN2 1JN. Tel. (01273) 699595

Brewery established in 1989, built in the 'tower' tradition behind the Hand in Hand, which is possibly the smallest pub in England with its own brewery. It takes its name and logo from the former Charrington's Kemptown Brewery 500 yards away, which closed in 1964. Fifteen free trade outlets are supplied. Tours by arrangement.

Budget Bitter*	(OG 1036, ABV 3.5%)
Bitter*	(OG 1040, ABV 4%)
Crewsaver*	(OG 1045, ABV 4.5%) Brewed to benefit the Brighton Marina Lifeboat.
Tipper's Tipple	(OG 1045, ABV 4.5%)
Celebrated Staggering Ale*	(OG 1050, ABV 5%)
Staggering in the Dark (SID)*	(OG 1050, ABV 5.2%)
Old Grumpy*	(OG 1060, ABV 6%) Available November–February.

KING & BARNES

King & Barnes Ltd., The Horsham Brewery, 18 Bishopric, Horsham, W. Sussex RH12 1QP. Tel. (01403) 270470 Fax. (01403) 270570

Long-established brewery, dating back almost 200 years and in the present premises since 1850. It is run by the King family, which united with the Barnes family brewery in 1906. Its 'Fine Sussex Ales' are served in all 57 country houses and to around 150 free trade outlets, mostly within a radius of 40 miles. Twelve Bore Bitter is produced for the Freetraders Group wholesalers – tel. (0181) 965 0222. Tours by arrangement. Brewery shop open 9–5. Occasional beers: Harvest Ale (OG 1045, ABV 4.5%), Easter Ale (OG 1048, ABV 4.5%), Christmas Ale (OG 1075, ABV 8%). Bottle-conditioned beer: Festive (OG 1050, ABV 5.3%), Old Porter (OG 1055, ABV 5.5%).

Mild Ale	(OG 1034, ABV 3.5%) A smooth, malty, very dark mild, with a fruity, malty aroma. The bittersweet finish soon disappears, leaving you wanting more. Becoming more difficult to find.
Sussex	(OG 1034, ABV 3.5%) Whilst hops still dominate this pale brown bitter, they are not as evident as they used to be, more's the pity.
Wealdman*	(OG 1037, ABV 3.8%)
Broadwood	(OG 1040, ABV 4.2%) A tawny-coloured, well-balanced beer from aroma to finish, with hops winning through in the end.
Old Ale	(OG 1045, ABV 4.5%) A classic, black old ale. A fruity, roast malt flavour, with some hops, leads to a bittersweet, malty finish. Lovely roast malt aroma. Available October–March.
Festive	(OG 1050, ABV 5%) A red-brown beer, with a fruity aroma. The flavour is also fruity and malty, but with a noticeable hop presence. Malt and fruit dominate the aftertaste.

For Freetraders:

Twelve Bore Bitter	(OG 1035, ABV 3.7%) A thin, mid-brown bitter, with a clean finish. Good balance of malt and hops throughout.

KING'S HEAD

Ale House & Brewery

King's Head Ale House and Brewery, 21 Bretonside, Plymouth, Devon PL4 0BB. Tel. (01752) 665619

Plymouth's first brew pub, founded in January 1994 in the oldest pub in the town. The business has quickly taken off and it now supplies two other tied houses and around 20 other outlets. Plans are in hand to enlarge the brewery. Tours by arrangement. Occasional beer: Santa's Blotto (OG 1060, ABV 6%, Christmas).

The Independents

King's Ransom*	(OG 1040, ABV 4%)
Bretonside's Best (BSB)*	(OG 1042, ABV 4.2%)
Gez's Ale*	(OG 1050, ABV 5%)
Golden Goose	(OG 1050, ABV 5%) A straw-coloured beer with a hoppy, fruity aroma, taste and finish.
Ma Husson's Strong Olde Ale*	(OG 1056, ABV 5.6%)
Old Hoppy*	(OG 1056, ABV 5.6%)

KINGSTON — See Flamingo.

LAKELAND — See Masons Arms.

LARKINS

Larkins Brewery Ltd., Chiddingstone, Edenbridge, Kent TN8 7BB. Tel. (01892) 870328

Larkins brewery was founded in 1986 by the Dockerty family (who are farmers and hop-growers), with the purchase of the Royal Tunbridge Wells Brewery. Brewing was transferred to a converted barn at the family farm in 1990 and an additional copper and fermenter were acquired in 1991 to keep up with the growing local free trade. The additive-free beers can now be found in around 85 pubs and tourist venues in the South-East. Only Kent hops are used, some from the farm itself. Tours by arrangement for groups of 15 or more people on Saturday mornings.

Traditional Bitter*	(OG 1035, ABV 3.4%) A tawny-coloured beer.
Sovereign	(OG 1040, ABV 4%) A malty and slightly fruity, bitter ale, with a very malty finish. Copper-red in colour.
Best Bitter	(OG 1045, ABV 4.4%) Full-bodied, slightly fruity and unusually bitter for its gravity. Dangerously drinkable!
Porter	(OG 1053, ABV 5.2%) Each taste and smell of this potent black winter beer reveals another facet of its character. An explosion of roasted malt, bitter and fruity flavours leaves a bittersweet aftertaste.

LASS O'GOWRIE — See Nationals, Whitbread.

LASTINGHAM

Lastingham Brewery Co. Ltd., Unit 5, Westgate Carr Road, Pickering, N. Yorkshire YO18 8LX. Tel. (01751) 477628

Though only set up in May 1993, this brewery quickly outgrew its original premises and moved in October of the same year. It has won a number of local and national business awards and, at one London function, the Prince of Wales sampled the ale. The brewery then began brewing Royal Oui to commemorate the fact. It has one tied house, but is looking to buy more and currently supplies 70 other outlets. Tours by arrangement.

Church Bitter*	(OG 1038, ABV 3.7%)
Curate's Downfall*	(OG 1043, ABV 4.3%)
Royal Oui*	(OG 1044, ABV 4.5%)
Amen*	(OG 1052, ABV 5.4%)

LEAKING BOOT

Leaking Boot Brewery, Unit 3, 400 Cromwell Road, Grimsby, Humberside DN31 2BN. Tel. (01472) 242303

Brewery launched in April 1995 by a former Shipstone's brewer. The curious name comes from a famous statue of a boy with a leaking boot in Cleethorpes. Two pubs are supplied on a regular basis and others take the beer sporadically.

Bitter*	(OG 1038.5, ABV 3.9%).

LEATHER-BRITCHES

Leatherbritches Brewery, Bently Brook, Brewery Yard, Fenny Bentley, Ashbourne, Derbyshire DE6 1LF. Tel. (01335) 350278 Fax. (01335) 350422

Beer sausages are an unusual sideline at this new brewery which keeps its own pigs. Leatherbritches has already outgrown an initial capacity of five barrels a week, and new plant has been installed. It serves a single tied house and 30 other local outlets, as well as wholesalers, and the purchase of a second pub is likely. Bottle-conditioned beer: Ashbourne Ale (ABV 4.5%).

Light Summer*	(ABV 3.3%)
Belter*	(ABV 4%)
Ashbourne Ale*	(ABV 4.5%)
Belt 'n' Braces*	(ABV 4.8%)
Bespoke*	(ABV 5%)
Tarebrain*	(ABV 6.5%)

LEES

JW Lees & Co. (Brewers) Ltd., Greengate Brewery, PO Box 2, Middleton Junction, Manchester M24 2AX. Tel. (0161) 643 2487 Fax. (0161) 655 3731

Family-owned brewery, founded in 1828 by John Willie Lees, a retired cotton manufacturer, and recently joined by sixth-generation family members. The existing brewhouse dates from 1876 but has been expanded and refitted recently, doubling the capacity. All the brewery's 175 pubs (most in northern Manchester) serve real ale. Free trade in the North-West is approaching 100 regular outlets (and still growing), of which about 85 take real ale. Tours by arrangement.

GB Mild	(OG 1032, ABV 3.5%) Malty and fruity in aroma. The same flavours are found in the taste, but do not dominate in a beer with a rounded and smooth character. Dry, malty aftertaste.
Bitter	(OG 1037, ABV 4%) A pale beer with a malty, fruity aroma and a distinctive, malty, dry and slightly metallic taste. Clean, dry Lees finish.
Moonraker	(OG 1073, ABV 7.5%) Reddish-brown beer with a strong, malty, fruity aroma. The flavour is rich and sweet, with roast malt, and the finish is fruity yet dry. Only available in a handful of outlets.

LICHFIELD

Lichfield Brewery, 3 Europa Way, Boley Park, Lichfield, Staffordshire WS14 9TZ. Tel. (01543) 419919

Two CAMRA members began brewing at Lichfield in 1992, bringing production back to the city after 60 years. Its capacity has since doubled and a dozen local outlets regularly take the beers, which are also becoming popular as guest ales around the Midlands. Look out for the special beer to commemorate Lichfield Cathedral's 800th anniversary. Occasional beer: Mincespired (OG 1060, ABV 5.8%, Christmas).

Steeplechase*	(OG 1037, ABV 3.7%) A summer beer.
Inspired	(OG 1040, ABV 4%) Dark and malty, with a proper bitter aftertaste.
Sheriff's Ride*	(OG 1042, ABV 4.2%)
Steeplejack	(OG 1045, ABV 4.5%) Refreshing, pale brown, hoppy beer, with a bitter finish.
Xpired	(OG 1050, ABV 4.8%) A dark bitter, with malt and chocolate flavours.

The Independents

LINFIT

Linfit Brewery

Linfit Brewery, Sair Inn, Lane Top, Linthwaite, Huddersfield, W. Yorkshire HD7 5SG. Tel. (01484) 842370

Nineteenth-century brew pub which recommenced brewing in 1982, producing an impressive range of ales for sale at the Sair Inn and in the free trade as far away as Manchester (seven regular outlets). New plant installed in 1994 has almost doubled its capacity. Linfit also brews West Riding Bitter for the West Riding Licensed Refreshment Rooms in Dewsbury, as well as special occasional beers. Tours by arrangement. Occasional beers: Xmas Ale (OG 1080, ABV 8.6%). Bottle-conditioned beer: English Guineas Stout (OG 1050, ABV 5.5%).

Summer Ale* — (OG 1030, ABV 3.1%)

Dark Mild — (OG 1032, ABV 3%) Roast malt dominates in this straightforward dark mild. Some hop aroma; slightly dry flavour. Malty finish.

Bitter — (OG 1035, ABV 3.7%) A session beer. A dry-hopped aroma leads to a clean-tasting, hoppy bitterness, balanced with some maltiness. The finish is well-balanced, too, but sometimes has an intense bitterness.

Special — (OG 1041, ABV 4.3%) Dry-hopping provides the aroma for this rich and mellow bitter, which has a very soft profile and character: it fills the mouth with texture rather than taste. Clean, rounded finish.

Janet Street Porter* — (OG 1043, ABV 4.5%)

Autumn Gold* — (OG 1045, ABV 4.7%) The latest addition to the range.

English Guineas Stout — (OG 1050, ABV 5.3%) A fruity, roasted aroma preludes a smooth, roasted malt, chocolatey flavour which is bitter but not too dry. Excellent appearance; good, bitter finish.

Old Eli — (OG 1050, ABV 5.3%) A well-balanced premium bitter with a dry-hopped aroma and a fruity, bitter finish.

Springbok Bier* — (OG 1053, ABV 5.7%)

Leadboiler — (OG 1063, ABV 6.6%) Flowery and hoppy in aroma, with a very moreish, strong bitter flavour which is well-balanced by a prominent maltiness. Soft mouthfeel; rounded, bitter finish.

Enoch's Hammer — (OG 1080, ABV 8.6%) A straw-coloured, vinous bitter with no pretensions about its strength or pedigree. A full, fruity aroma leads on to a smooth, alcoholic-tasting, hoppy, bitter flavour, with an unexpectedly bitter finish.

LIQUID ASSETS

See Eldridge Pope.

LITTLE AVENHAM

The Little Avenham Brewery, Arkwright Mill, Hawkins Street, Preston, Lancashire PR1 7HS. Tel. (01772) 555305 Fax. (01772) 556900

Previously based at the CAMRA award-winning Gaston's Real Ale and Fine Wine Pub, this brewery quickly outgrew its original premises and moved in April 1995 to a new brewhouse, from where it now serves 70 free trade customers. Tours by arrangement. Occasional beers: Hedge Row Bitter (ABV 1038, ABV 3.8%, September, using wild hops and nettles), Stocking Filler (OG 1060, ABV 6%, a Christmas porter).

Arkwright Mild — (OG 1035, ABV 3.5%) A dark mild with intense fruit flavours and a dry aftertaste.

Arkwright Ale — (OG 1036, ABV 3.6%) A mid-brown session beer with a gentle aroma but strong fruit and hop flavours which continue through to the aftertaste. A sourness and wine-like tartness are not unpleasant.

Clog Dancer — (OG 1038, ABV 4%) A golden yellow, distinctive bitter. Though well-balanced, complex fruit and hop flavours make it rich and moreish.

Porter	(OG 1040, ABV 4%) An excellent dark beer with hints of ruby red. Thinner than you would expect from its colour, but very satisfying. Chocolate and roast malt flavours are prominent, with a slight hoppiness and a dry aftertaste.
Pickled Priest	(OG 1043, ABV 4.3%) A pale, thin and tart bitter in which fruit flavours give way to a lasting dryness in the finish.
Torchlight	(OG 1050, ABV 5%) A dark to mid-brown premium ale. Malt and fruit are prominent in the aroma and flavour. Enjoyable and distinctive, it is mild and complex in the mouth, with some sweetness.
Pierrepoints Last Drop	(OG 1063, ABV 7%) A pale, strong ale with prominent fruit flavours and a dry aftertaste.

LIVERPOOL See Black Horse & Rainbow.

LLOYDS **Lloyds Country Beers Ltd., John Thompson Brewery, Ingleby, Derbyshire DE7 1HW. Tel. (01332) 863426**

Lloyds is the separate business set up to supply the beers brewed at the John Thompson Inn (qv) to the free trade. It currently has around 100 outlets, mainly in the Midlands, and the company hopes to acquire a pub of its own. Lloyds also provides beer for the Heritage Brewery Museum in Burton – tel. (01283) 510246 – and the High Peak brewery in Chinley, Derbyshire, which is yet to go into production, is still using the premises for its own brews. These have included Bagman's Bitter (OG 1045, ABV 4.3%) and Cracken (OG 1049, ABV 4.9%, Christmas), as well as a 3.8% bitter. Lloyds also produces one-off brews (generally ABV 4–5%) for special events. Occasional beer: Overdraft (OG 1060, ABV 6%, Christmas).

Country Gold*	(OG 1040, ABV 4%) Brewed in summer.
Derby Bitter or JTS XXX*	(OG 1042, ABV 4.1%) Full and fruity.
Vixen Velvet*	(OG 1045, ABV 4.5%) A winter porter.
VIP (Very Important Pint)*	(OG 1048, ABV 4.8%) A heavier, darker version of the bitter.
	For Heritage:
Dark Amber*	(OG 1045, ABV 4.2%)

LONDON BEER COMPANY See Brewery on Sea and Skinner's.

LONGSTONE **Longstone Brewery, Station Road, Belford, Northumberland NE70 7DT. Tel./Fax. (01668) 213031**

Brewery operational since 1991, the first in Northumberland for many years. Following an injection of cash in 1994, Longstone invested in extra equipment and increased its brewing capacity, adding two new beers. It now supplies 60 outlets regularly in the North and Scotland, and others further afield via beer agencies. Tours by arrangement.

Hotspur Bitter*	(OG 1037, ABV 3.7%)
Bitter	(OG 1039, ABV 4%) An imaginative beer with pungent and sometimes undefinable flavours. Hop character dominates but there is also underlying fruit, a solid body and lasting sweetness.
Old Grace Bitter*	(OG 1042, ABV 4.2%)

LUCIFER See Hope & Anchor.

LUNDY **Lundy Company, Marisco Tavern Brewery, Lundy Island, Bristol Channel EX39 2LY. Tel. (01237) 431831 Fax. (01237) 431832**

Brewery opened in 1984 but closed and relocated in 1992. It recommenced brewing in March 1995, producing beer from malt extract and spring water for visitors to the island's pub. Tours by arrangement. Beer: Old Light Bitter (OG 1055, usually only in summer).

471

The Independents

McEWAN	See Nationals, Scottish & Newcastle.

THOMAS McGUINNESS

 Thomas McGuinness Brewing Company, Cask & Feather, 1 Oldham Road, Rochdale, Lancashire OL16 1UA. Tel. (01706) 711476

Small brewery established in 1991 behind the Cask & Feather pub, by the late Thomas McGuinness and brewer Eric Hoare. Plans are in hand to expand the brewery in 1996. It currently supplies real ale to two tied houses and 70 other outlets. Tours by arrangement.

Feather Plucker Mild* (OG 1034, ABV 3.4%) Dark brown beer, with roast malt dominant in the aroma and taste. There's a touch of bitterness, too.

Best Bitter (OG 1038, ABV 3.8%) Gold in colour with a hoppy aroma: a clean, refreshing beer with hop and fruit tastes and a hint of sweetness. Bitter aftertaste.

Special Reserve Bitter (OG 1040, ABV 4%) A tawny beer, sweet and malty, with underlying fruit and bitterness, and a bittersweet aftertaste.

Stout* (OG 1040, ABV 4%)

Junction Bitter (OG 1042, ABV 4.2%) Mid-brown in colour, with a malty aroma. Maltiness is predominant throughout, with some hops and fruit in the taste and bitterness coming through in the finish.

Tommy Todd Porter (OG 1050, ABV 5%) A winter warmer, with a fruit and roast aroma, leading to a balance of malt and roast malt flavours, with a touch of chocolate. Not too sweet for its gravity.

MACLAY

Maclay & Co. Ltd., Thistle Brewery, East Vennel, Alloa, Clackmannanshire, Central FK10 1ED. Tel. (01259) 723387 Fax. (01259) 216511

Founded in 1830 and moved to the present Victorian tower brewery in 1869, Maclay still uses traditional brewing methods and direct-fired coppers, with the beers produced using only bore-hole water (the only Scottish brewery to do so) without any adjuncts. Until 1992, the company had been run by descendants of the founder, James Maclay, but is now owned by the family of the present chairman, Evelyn Matthews. Plant improvements are underway, to increase volume and sales. All 30 tied houses offer real ale, which is also supplied to over 200 other outlets.

Jacobite* (ABV 3.2%)

60/- Ale* (OG 1034, ABV 3.4%)

70/- Ale (OG 1036, ABV 3.6%) A well-rounded, malty, fruity, clean-tasting beer. There is malt in the nose and a characteristically dry finish.

Broadsword* (OG 1038, ABV 3.8%)

80/- Export (OG 1040, ABV 4%) A rich, creamy bittersweet beer, well worth seeking out. It has plenty of malt, balanced with bitterness, some hops and a little fruit.

Porter* (OG 1040, ABV 4%)

Oat Malt Stout* (OG 1045, ABV 4.5%)

Wallace IPA (OG 1045, ABV 4.5%) A recent addition. Hops and fruit are to the fore in the aroma and remain in the taste, with a surprisingly bitter finish.

Scotch Ale* (OG 1050, ABV 5%)

McMULLEN

McMullen & Sons Ltd., The Hertford Brewery, 26 Old Cross, Hertford SG14 1RD. Tel. (01992) 584911 Fax. (01992) 500729

Hertfordshire's oldest independent brewery, founded in 1827 by Peter McMullen. The Victorian tower brewery, which houses the original oak and copper-lined fermenters still in use today, was built on the site of three wells. Real ale is served in all McMullen's

472

145 pubs in Hertfordshire, Essex and London, and also supplied to around 200 free trade outlets. Seasonal beers are brewed for a limited period under the banner of McMullen Special Reserve. The company also brews bottle-conditioned beers for Hanseatic Trading Company – tel. (01778) 560662 – for sale largely through Oddbins off-licences. In April 1995, head brewer Tony Skipper was voted *Brewer of the Year* by the Parliamentary Beer Club. Tours by arrangement.

Original AK (OG 1034, ABV 3.7%) A bitter-tasting beer, with a pleasant mix of hops and malt. Distinctive, dry aftertaste.

Country Best Bitter (OG 1042, ABV 4.3%) A full-bodied beer with a well-balanced mix of malt, hops and fruit flavours and a strong, dry aftertaste.

Gladstone* (ABV 4.3%) A new beer, launched in May 1995.

Stronghart (OG 1070, ABV 7%) A sweetish, rich, dark beer, full of fruit and hop aromas and flavours.

For Whitbread:

Wethered Bitter* (OG 1035, ABV 3.6%)

For Hanseatic:

Bottle-conditioned beers: BCA (OG 1045, ABV 4.5%), IPA (OG 1045, ABV 4.5%), Vassilenski's Black Russian (OG 1048, ABV 4.8%)

MALTON

Malton Brewery Company Ltd., Crown Hotel, Wheelgate, Malton, N. Yorkshire YO17 0HP. Tel. (01653) 697580

Malton began brewing in 1985 in a stable block at the rear of the Crown Hotel, where the former Grand National winner Double Chance was once stabled, hence the name of the bitter. The additive-free beers are supplied to around ten free trade outlets directly and pubs further afield via wholesalers. Tours by arrangement.

Pale Ale (OG 1034, ABV 3.2%) With a light aroma, but immediately hoppy in the mouth, this is a thin, light, golden yellow brew, with a balanced smoothness ending in a delicate, dry finish.

Double Chance Bitter (OG 1038, ABV 3.8%) The aroma is more subtle and the taste more malty than last year, but this beer still offers hops on the nose and tongue. However, the dry and lightly bitter aftertaste has lost its sweet edge and its bite.

Pickwick's Porter (OG 1040, ABV 4%) Heavy malt and roast malt in both the nose and the mouth lead to a dry mixture of tart fruit and dark chocolate. The dry and nutty, yet sticky, finish persists, but the brew is more full-bodied and rounded this year.

Nutbrown (ABV 4.1%) A new brew that is yet to find itself. It has a full hop nose and a chocolate tone upfront, but fades into a dry and malty taste with bitter interludes. Little body and no great depth.

Owd Bob (OG 1055, ABV 5.9%) A rich and warming combination of hops and roast malt leads to floral, fruit and chocolate tastes. The roast malt lingers through to the slightly sweet, yet still bitter, finish. Red hints to the dark brown body.

M&B See Nationals, Bass.

MANSFIELD

Mansfield Brewery PLC, Littleworth, Mansfield, Nottinghamshire NG18 1AB. Tel. (01623) 25691 Fax. (01623) 658620

Founded in 1855, and now one of the country's leading regional brewers, Mansfield resumed brewing cask beer in 1982 after a break of ten years. Its award-winning ales are all fermented in traditional Yorkshire squares and have enjoyed steadily rising sales, aided in 1991 by the acquisition of a substantial number of pubs from Courage and another dozen from S&N in 1993. Over 80% of its 468 pubs serve cask beer. An extensive free trade

The Independents

(particularly in East Midlands clubs) is also supplied and Mansfield enjoys a reciprocal trading arrangement with Charles Wells. The growing range of Deakin's seasonal beers has been well received. Shop open 8.30–4, Mon–Fri. Tours by arrangement. Occasional 'Deakin's' beers: White Rabbit (OG 1041, ABV 4.3%, Easter), 1855 (OG 1042, ABV 4.3%), Red Admiral (OG 1042, ABV 4.4%, summer), Red Squirrel (OG 1042, ABV 4.4%), Royal Stag (OG 1042, ABV 4.5%, autumn), Wild Boar (OG 1053, ABV 5.5%, winter), Yule Brew (OG 1053, ABV 5.5%, Christmas).

Riding Mild (OG 1035, ABV 3.5%) A dark ruby mild, with a roast malt nose. An initial sweetness develops into a complex fruitiness and nuttiness, leading to a dry, malty finish.

Riding Bitter (OG 1035, ABV 3.6%) A wonderfully hoppy aroma dominates this beer, although malt is always there. This pale brown brew stays faithful to hops and malt in the taste, with the malt coming through towards the finish.

Bitter (OG 1038, ABV 3.9%) Now firmly established in cask form, this well-balanced, medium brown bitter has an initial malt sweetness, soon joined by hops and bitterness. The malt remains present throughout.

Old Baily (OG 1045, ABV 4.8%) A fine, complex beer, coppery in colour. Malt and fruit mingle in the aroma, with hops joining in the taste. There are also bitterness and sweetness, with bitterness lasting longer.

For Scottish & Newcastle:

Home Mild* (OG 1036, ABV 3.6%)

MANSFIELD ARMS

 Mansfield Arms, 7 Main Street, Sauchie, Alloa, Central FK10 3JR. Tel. (01259) 722020 Fax. (01259) 218409

Brewing at CAMRA's 1993 *Scottish Pub of the Year* started in spring 1994. Plans are afoot to expand the brewery, just to keep up with demand from this and the owners' other pub. Beers: Devon Original (OG 1037, ABV 3.8%), Devon Thick Black (OG 1040, ABV 4.1%), Devon Pride (OG 1046, ABV 4.6%).

MARCHES

ᛗᚪᚱᚳᚻᛖᛋ ᚪᛚᛖᛋ

Marches Ales, Unit 6, Western Close, Southern Avenue Industrial Estate, Leominster, Hereford & Worcester HR6 0QD. Tel. (01568) 611084

The Solstice brewery of Kington was taken over by Paul Harris in 1995 and moved to this new purpose-built brewery, which takes its name from its location at the edge of the Marches. It currently supplies six outlets. Tours by arrangement Fri and Sat evenings. Three beers are produced for the Black Horse pub in Leominster: Black Horse Bitter (ABV 3.8%), Flakey Dove (ABV 4.8%), Woody's Crown (ABV 5.2%).

Best Bitter* (OG 1036, ABV 3.8%)

Priory Ale* (OG 1048, ABV 4.8%)

Jenny Pipes Summer Ale* (OG 1050, ABV 5.2%)

Earl Leofric Winter Ale* (OG 1070, ABV 7.2%)

MARISCO TAVERN See Lundy.

Beers marked with an asterisk have not been tasted by official CAMRA tasting panels. However, some of these beers do carry brief descriptions derived from limited samplings or other sources which can be used for rough guidance.

The Independents

| **MARSTON MOOR** | **Marston Moor Brewery, Crown House, Kirk Hammerton, York, N. Yorkshire YO5 8DD. Tel. (01423) 330341** |

Small, but expanding brewery, set up in 1983 and moved to the rear of its first tied house, the Crown, in 1988. This pub was closed in December 1993 after the acquisition of the Beer Exchange at Woodhouse in Leeds, but more pubs are being sought. The company currently produces 1,000 barrels a year and supplies around 60 free trade outlets. Tours by arrangement.

Cromwell Bitter*	(OG 1036, ABV 3.6%) A distinctive, bitter beer.
Brewers Pride*	(OG 1042, ABV 4.2%) An amber-coloured, premium beer.
Porter*	(OG 1042, ABV 4.2%) A seasonal brew (October–May), ruby-coloured and stout-like.
Black Tom Stout*	(OG 1045, ABV 4.5%) Also brewed for October–May.
Merrie Maker*	(OG 1045, ABV 4.5%)
Brewers Droop*	(OG 1050, ABV 5.1%) A potent, straw-coloured ale.
ESB*	(OG 1050, ABV 5.1%)
Trooper*	(OG 1050, ABV 5.1%)

| **MARSTON'S** | **Marston, Thompson & Evershed PLC, Shobnall Road, Burton upon Trent, Staffordshire DE14 2BW. Tel. (01283) 531131 Fax. (01283) 510378** |

The only brewery still using the Burton Union system of fermentation (for its stronger ales), Marston's reinforced its commitment to this method in 1992 with a £1 million investment in a new Union room. Real ale is available in 830 of the company's 885 pubs, which stretch from Yorkshire to Hampshire. Marston's also enjoys an enormous free trade, thanks to trading agreements with Wolverhampton & Dudley and the fact that many national brewers' houses stock Pedigree Bitter. Although there are now only three standard beers, the Head Brewer's Choice scheme offers a range of new brews to selected outlets for two weeks at a time. Shop open 10.30–2.30 Mon–Fri; 9.30–12 Sat. Tours by arrangement. Bottle-conditioned beer: Oyster Stout (OG 1045, ABV 4.5%).

Bitter	(OG 1038, ABV 3.8%) An amber/tawny session beer which can often be markedly sulphury in aroma and taste. At its best, a splendid, subtle balance of malt, hops and fruit follows a faintly hoppy aroma and develops into a balanced, dry aftertaste.
Pedigree	(OG 1043, ABV 4.5%) Variable; it can be excellent, but is often spoilt by swan-necked dispense which removes the unique sulphury aroma and hoppy taste. When on form, its perfect balance of hop and malt lingers through the taste to leave an astringent, hoppy and malty finish.
Owd Rodger	(OG 1078, ABV 7.6%) A dark, ruby-red barley wine, with an intense fruity nose before a deep, winey, heavy fruit flavour, with malt and faint hops. The finish is dry and fruity (strawberries). Misunderstood, moreish and strong.

| **MASONS ARMS** | **Lakeland Brewing Co., Strawberry Bank, Cartmel Fell, Cumbria LA11 6NW. Tel. (0153 95) 68686 Fax. (0153 95) 68780** |

Famous pub, known for its large selection of bottled beers, which began brewing in May 1990. Beer names are based on books by local author Arthur Ransome. Some unusual fruit beers are planned. Tours by arrangement. The pub was placed on the market in spring 1995. Beers: Amazon Bitter (OG 1038, ABV 4%), Captain Flint (OG 1040, ABV 4%), Great Northern (OG 1045, ABV 4.5%), Big Six (OG 1060, ABV 6%), Damson Beer (OG 1070, ABV 7%). Occasional bottle-conditioned beers: Amazon Bitter (OG 1038, ABV 4%), Great Northern (OG 1045, ABV 4.5%), Big Six (OG 1060, ABV 6%), Damson Beer (OG 1070, ABV 9%).

The Independents

MAULDONS

Mauldons Brewery, 7 Addison Road, Chilton Industrial Estate, Sudbury, Suffolk CO10 6YW. Tel./Fax. (01787) 311055

Company set up in 1982 by former Watney's brewer Peter Mauldon, whose family had its own local brewery in the late 18th century. Its extensive beer list changes frequently and is supplied to 150 free trade outlets in East Anglia, as well as pubs further afield via wholesalers. Occasional beers: Broomstick Bitter (OG 1040, ABV 4%, Hallowe'en), Mother's Ruin (OG 1040, ABV 4%, Mothering Sunday), George's Best (OG 1045, ABV 4.4%, St George's Day), Love Potion No. 9 (OG 1045, ABV 4.5%, Valentine's Day), Gunpowder Blast (OG 1063, ABV 6%, Guy Fawkes Day), Christmas Reserve (OG 1066, ABV 6.6%).

Best Bitter
(OG 1037, ABV 3.8%) A well-balanced session beer with a crisp, hoppy bitterness balancing sweet malt.

Midsummer Gold*
(OG 1040, ABV 4%) A light-coloured summer beer.

Eatanswill Old XXXX
(OG 1042, ABV 4%) Formerly Old XXXX, renamed in 1994, after the name used for Sudbury by Dickens in *Pickwick Papers*. A winter ale of deep red and brown hue, with well-balanced fruit and malt plus a slight sweetness on the palate, ending in a pleasant roast bitterness.

Original Porter
(OG 1042, ABV 3.8%) A black beer with malt and roast malt flavours dominating. Some hop in the finish.

Special Bitter
(OG 1044, ABV 4.2%) By far the hoppiest of the Mauldons beers, with a good, bitter finish and some balancing malt.

Squires Bitter
(OG 1044, ABV 4.2%) A best bitter with a good, malty aroma and a reasonably balanced flavour, which leans towards malt. Hops come through late and crisply into the aftertaste.

Suffolk Punch
(OG 1050, ABV 4.8%) A full-bodied, strong bitter. The malt and fruit in the aroma are reflected in the taste and there is some hop character in the finish. Deep tawny/red in colour.

Black Adder
(OG 1053, ABV 5.3%) A dark stout. Roast malt is very strong in the aroma and taste, but malt, hop and bitterness provide an excellent balance and a lingering finish. *Champion Beer of Britain* 1991.

White Adder
(OG 1053, ABV 5.3%) A pale brown, almost golden strong ale. A warming, fruity flavour dominates and lingers into a dry, hoppy finish.

Suffolk Comfort
(OG 1065, ABV 6.6%) A clean, hoppy nose leads to a predominantly malty flavour in this full-bodied beer. Dry, hoppy aftertaste.

MAYHEM'S
See Farmers Arms.

MAYPOLE
Maypole Brewery, North Laithes Farm, Wellow Road, Eakring, Nottinghamshire NG22 0AN. Tel. (01623) 871690

Brewery established in 1995 with equipment purchased from Springhead Brewery. It currently supplies around ten pubs a week.

Celebration*
(OG 1040, ABV 4%)

Mayday*
(OG 1046, ABV 4.6%)

MERIVALES ALES
See Edgcote.

MERRIMANS
Merrimans Brewery, Old Fart Ltd, Marpak House, Westland Square, Leeds, W. Yorkshire LS11 5SS. Tel. (0113) 2704542 Fax. (0113) 2700778

After the demise of Robinwood Brewery, Tim Fritchley set up this new operation in June 1994 with the intention of rejuvenating the 'Old Fart' name. It has concentrated on bottling, with an eye to the export market, but also supplies 40 local outlets with the cask-conditioned version.

Old Fart*
(OG 1050, ABV 5%)

476

MILDMAY

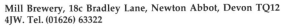 The Mildmay Brewery, Holbeton, Plymouth, Devon PL8 1NA. Tel. (01752) 830320 Fax. (01752) 830540

Mildmay started brewing in October 1993, for its tied house, the Mildmay Colours Inn. In the winter of 1994, the brewery was expanded to triple its capacity to around 50 barrels per week and the beers are now much in demand. Brewery shop open most days. Tours by arrangement.

Colours Best

(OG 1040, ABV 3.8%) A pale brown beer with a good hop aroma. The initial taste is bitter and hoppy, but sweetness develops later. Bitter finish.

SP or Starting Price Ale

(OG 1045, ABV 4.5%) A mid-brown bitter with a malty, fruity aroma and taste, and a sharp, bitter aftertaste.

50/1*

(OG 1050, ABV 5.1%)

Old Horse Whip*

(ABV 5.7%)

MILL

MILL BREWERY

Mill Brewery, 18c Bradley Lane, Newton Abbot, Devon TQ12 4JW. Tel. (01626) 63322

Brewery founded in 1983 on the site of an old watermill and run on a part-time basis until changing hands in March 1994. The new owners, brewing full-time, have dropped the original 'Janners' name from all but one of the beers and now brew a different guest beer each month. Over 20 outlets take the beers regularly. Tours by arrangement.

Janner's Ale

(OG 1038, ABV 3.8%) A pale brown beer, with a fruity aroma and a bitter taste and aftertaste.

Ruby Ale*

(OG 1044, ABV 4.5%) Ruby-red beer with a strong malty, bitter taste.

Old Original*

(OG 1048, ABV 5%) A golden beer with plenty of fruit and hops in both aroma and flavour.

Black Bushel*

(ABV 6%) A winter beer.

MILLGATE

 The Millgate Brewery, The Millgate, Ashton Road West, Failsworth, Manchester M35 0ES. Tel./Fax. (0161) 688 4910

After a few teething problems with the trial brews, this new brewery eventually took off in February 1995 and now supplies two tied houses. Beers: Bitter (OG 1039, ABV 3.8%), Willy Booth's Best Bitter (OG 1039, ABV 3.8%).

MINERVA

See Nationals, Carlsberg-Tetley.

MIN PIN INN

North Cornwall Brewers, Tintagel, Cornwall.

Brewery closed.

MITCHELL'S

Mitchell's of Lancaster (Brewers) Ltd., 11 Moor Lane, Lancaster, Lancashire LA1 1QB. Tel. (01524) 63773 Fax. (01524) 846071

The only surviving independent brewery in Lancaster (est. 1880), wholly owned and run by direct descendants of founder William Mitchell. The company is very traditional: many of the casks are still wooden and its award-winning beers are brewed with natural spring well water. There have been considerable changes to the beer range in the last 12 months and seasonal beers (a new one every month) are also now being brewed. Real ale is sold in all but one of its 53 pubs and is available virtually countrywide in the free trade. Occasional beers: Brewers Pride (OG 1040, ABV 4%), Stout (OG 1041, ABV 4.1%), Resolution Ale (OG 1052, ABV 5%), Christmas Cracker (OG 1057, ABV 5.5%), Guy Fawkes Bitter (OG 1058, ABV 5.7%).

William Mitchell's Original Bitter*

(OG 1038, ABV 3.8%) A replacement for the old Best Bitter.

The Independents

Lancaster Bomber*   (OG 1044, ABV 4.4%)

Single Malt   (OG 1064, ABV 7.2%) A winter brew (November–January), mid-brown in colour and suggestive of malt whisky in aroma and flavour. Strongly malty throughout, with a subtle, bittersweet, hoppy balance in the taste.

MITCHELLS & BUTLERS (M&B)   See Nationals, Bass.

MOLE'S   Mole's Brewery (Cascade Drinks Ltd.), 5 Merlin Way, Bowerhill, Melksham, Wiltshire SN12 6TJ. Tel. (01225) 704734 Fax. (01225) 790770

Brewery established in 1982 and run on very traditional lines by former Ushers brewer Roger Catté (the brewery name came from his nickname). With 100 free trade outlets now supplied, plans are in hand to expand the brewery and add to the tied estate (currently 15 pubs). Mole's also acts as a distributor for other members of the Small Independent Brewers Association (SIBA). Shop open 9–5 Mon–Fri; 9–12 Sat. Tours by arrangement. Bottle-conditioned beer: Brew 97 (OG 1050, ABV 5%).

Tap Bitter   (OG 1035, ABV 3.5%) A pale brown beer with a trace of malt in the aroma. A gentle, malty, dry flavour with apple and pear fruits follows, then a bitter finish.

Best Bitter   (OG 1040, ABV 4%) A pale brown/golden-coloured beer with a light malt aroma. The taste is clean, dry and malty, with some bitterness and delicate floral hop. A well-balanced, light and subtle ale.

Landlords Choice*   (OG 1045, ABV 4.5%) A dark bitter, not widely available.

Brew 97   (OG 1050, ABV 5%) A mid-brown, full-bodied beer with a gentle malt and hop aroma. The rich flavour is malty, with fruit, hop and traces of vanilla. A wonderfully warming, malty ale.

XB*   (OG 1060, ABV 6%) A winter brew.

MOORHOUSE'S   Moorhouse's Brewery (Burnley) Ltd., 4 Moorhouse Street, Burnley, Lancashire BB11 5EN. Tel. (01282) 422864 Fax. (01282) 838493

Long-established (1865) producer of hop bitters, which in 1978 began brewing cask beer. A succession of owners failed to develop the company until it was taken over in 1985 by Bill Parkinson, since when it has grown considerably. A modern brewhouse was installed in 1988 and further expansion is being undertaken. Plans include a brewery shop. The brewery supplies real ale to its own six pubs and 150 free trade outlets. Tours by arrangement.

Black Cat Mild*   (OG 1034, ABV 3.4%)

Premier Bitter   (OG 1036, ABV 3.7%) Pale brown in colour but not in character, this brew has a superb hop flower aroma, with some fruit and malt. On the palate, citrus flavours are balanced by malt and hoppy bitterness. Dry, hoppy finish.

Pendle Witches Brew   (OG 1050, ABV 5.1%) A good hoppy aroma leads through to a full-bodied, malty sweetness, with a trace of hop bitterness. Bittersweet aftertaste.

Owd Ale*   (OG 1064, ABV 6%) A winter brew, available November–February.

OG stands for Original Gravity, the reading taken before fermentation of the amount of fermentable material in the brew. It is a rough indicator of strength. More reliable is the ABV (Alcohol by Volume) rating, which gives the percentage of alcohol in the finished beer.

The Independents

MORDUE

Mordue Brewery, Unit 22c Middle Engine Lane, West Chirton North Industrial Estate, North Shields, Tyne & Wear NE29 8SF. Tel. (0191) 296 1879

The new Mordue brewery takes its name from an original family brewery which operated in Wallsend in the 19th century. Future plans include the acquisition of a pub and expansion of the five-barrel plant. Occasional beers are planned. Tours by arrangement.

Five Bridges* (OG 1039, ABV 3.8%)

Workie Ticket* (OG 1045, ABV 4.5%)

MORLAND

Morland & Co. PLC, PO Box 5, Ock Street, Abingdon, Oxfordshire OX14 5DD. Tel. (01235) 553377 Fax. (01235) 529484

Established in 1711, Morland is the second oldest independent brewer in the UK and has been on its present site since 1861. In 1992 it survived a take-over bid by Greene King. The East Anglian giant, after buying Whitbread Investment Company's 43.4% stake, tried (but failed) to pick up a further 6.7% to take overall control and close the Abingdon brewery. Nearly all Morland's 350-plus pubs serve cask ale, but in some cases the licensee uses cask-breathers. The company also supplies around 500 free trade outlets around the Thames Valley and Surrey (with Old Speckled Hen particularly prominent). A recent £5 million investment in the brewery has improved and expanded production facilities. Morland also brews under contract for Courage. Tours by arrangement.

Original Bitter (OG 1035, ABV 4%) A light amber beer with malty, hoppy nose with a hint of fruitiness. The distinct, but lightish malt and hops carry over to the flavour and leave a sweet but dry, hoppy aftertaste.

Independent IPA* (OG 1037, ABV 3.4%)

Old Masters (OG 1040, ABV 4.6%) A well-balanced tawny/amber beer with not outstandingly strong flavours. The initial aroma of malt and hops leads to a moderately malty, but dry and hoppy flavour, with a hint of fruit which can be faintly sulphurous. Dry, bitter finish.

The Tanner's Jack* (OG 1042, ABV 4.4%) The latest addition to the range.

Old Speckled Hen (OG 1050, ABV 5.2%) Morland's most distinctive beer, deep tawny/amber in colour. A well-balanced aroma of roasted malt and hops is complemented by a good hint of caramel. An initial sweet, malty, fruity, roast caramel taste soon allows the dry hop flavour through, leaving a well-balanced aftertaste.

For Courage:

Wilson's Original Mild* (OG 1032, ABV 3%)

MORRELLS

MORRELLS BREWERY
Oxford

Morrells Brewery Ltd., The Lion Brewery, St Thomas' Street, Oxford OX1 1LA. Tel. (01865) 792013 Fax. (01865) 791868

The oldest brewery in Oxford is run by the Morrell family, as it has been since 1782. Of its 144 pubs, over 50 are within the city limits and all but one of the outlets serve cask ale, though some employ blanket pressure. Some 130 other outlets stock Morrells beers. Shop open during office hours. Tours by arrangement. Occasional beer: College Ale (OG 1073, ABV 7.4%, winter).

Oxford Bitter (OG 1036, ABV 3.7%) Golden in colour and light in body, but not in flavour, with a good aroma of hops complemented by malt and fruitiness. An initial dry hop bitterness is well balanced by malt, which gives way to a refreshing, slightly sweet fruitiness, with a hint of roast caramel. A bittersweet, hoppy finish.

Oxford Mild* (OG 1037, ABV 3.7%) A full-bodied dark mild.

Varsity (OG 1041, ABV 4.3%) A tawny/amber beer. Malt, hops and fruit are the main features in both aroma and taste, but are well-balanced. The slightly sweet, malty, fruity start fades away to a distinctive, bittersweet finish.

Graduate (OG 1048, ABV 5.2%) An intense malt and roast malt aroma is complemented by a moderate hoppiness in the taste. Pleasant, bitter finish.

The Independents

Strong Country Bitter*	For Whitbread: (OG 1037, ABV 3.9%)

MUNSLOW — See Crown Inn.

NENE VALLEY — **Nene Valley Brewery, Unit 1, Midland Business Centre, Midland Road, Higham Ferrers, Northamptonshire NN9 8PN. Tel. (01933) 412411**

Brewery which opened with a single-barrel outfit in April 1992 before moving to its present site in October that year with a five-barrel plant. It now has one tied house and also supplies over 20 free trade outlets. Occasional beer: Santa's Tipple (OG 1130, ABV 12.8%, Christmas).

Union Bitter* — (OG 1036, ABV 3.6%)

Trojan Bitter — (OG 1038, ABV 3.8%) A well-presented beer, but with little depth of flavour. Clean and dry, with a dried grass hop character and a palate-cleansing dry finish.

Griffin — (ABV 4.2%) A pale brown beer with a faint, fruity aroma. The flavour is a subtle blend of fruit, hops and malt on a bitter base. Dry finish.

Shopmates Ale* — (OG 1044, ABV 4.4%)

Old Black Bob — (OG 1047, ABV 4.7%) This dark brown/red beer has a pungent, smoky, roast malt aroma with underlying fruit. The roast malt follows through into the flavour and aftertaste, leading to a persistent bitterness. Faint malt and hops.

Rawhide* — (OG 1050, ABV 5.1%)

Midas — (ABV 5.2%) A pale brew with good hop aroma, backed up by malt and fruit. The flavour is a balance of hops and fruit with some malt on a bitter base. Very dry finish.

Medusa Ale* — (OG 1080, ABV 7.8%)

NETHERGATE — **Nethergate Brewery Co. Ltd., 11–13 High Street, Clare, Suffolk CO10 8NY. Tel. (01787) 277244 Fax. (01787) 277123**

Small brewer of award-winning beers, set up in 1986, which continues to use traditional methods and no additives. The Umbel beers (introduced in 1994 but now renamed) are infused with coriander seeds, reflecting an ancient brewing style. A new beer at OG 1045 is planned. Some 160 free trade outlets are now supplied, most in East Anglia. Brewery tours by arrangement.

IPA — (OG 1036, ABV 3.6%) An apple crisp, refreshing session beer, hoppy throughout, without fully masking the malt. Lingering, bitter aftertaste.

Umbel Ale — (OG 1038.5, ABV 3.8%) Wort is percolated through coriander seeds to give a wonderful, warming, spicy fruit tang to both the taste and aroma. The hops are strong enough to make themselves known and a strong, bitter malt finish hits late.

Bitter — (OG 1039, ABV 4%) A dark bitter in which delightful malt and hop aromas give way to a well-balanced palate. Rich malts and powerful bitterness dominate the flavour; strong, bitter finish.

Old Growler ⏛ — (OG 1055, ABV 5.5%) A complex and satisfying porter, smooth and distinctive. Sweetness, roast malt and fruit feature in the palate, with bitter chocolate lingering. The finish is powerfully hoppy.

Umbel Magna — (OG 1055, ABV 5.5%) The addition of coriander to the Old Growler wort completes the original 1750s recipe for this very distinctive dark porter. The powerful spiciness only adds to the appeal.

480

NEWALE

Newale Brewing Company Ltd., 6 Viscount Court, Southway, Walworth Industrial Estate, Andover, Hampshire SP10 5NW. Tel. (01264) 336336 Fax. (01264) 333310

Set up in September 1993 by Phil Newton, owner of an air-conditioning company, this brewery has been voted the *Most Environmentally Friendly Company* in Andover. Around 25 outlets take the beers. Brewery shop open 9–5 Mon–Fri; 10–1 Sat. Tours by arrangement.

New Tun Mild* (OG 1035, ABV 3.5%)

Anna Valley Ale* (OG 1038, ABV 4%)

Balksbury Bitter* (OG 1044, ABV 4.5%)

Clatford Clout* (OG 1048, ABV 5%)

Old Hatch Ale* (OG 1057, ABV 6%)

NEWPORT

Newport Brewhouse, 4–5 Market Street, Newport, Gwent NP9 1FU. Tel. (01633) 212188

A brew pub offshoot of the Bristol-based Ross brewery, set up in September 1994. Beers: Casnewydd Cask (OG 1035, ABV 3.5%), Black & Amber Bitter (OG 1045, ABV 4.5%), Castle Ruin Ale (OG 1050, ABV 5%), Uncle Igor's (ABV 21%, brewed only in very small quantities).

NICHOLSON'S See Nationals, Carlsberg-Tetley.

NIX WINCOTT

Nix Wincott Brewery, Three Fyshes Inn, Bridge Street, Turvey, Bedfordshire MK43 8ER. Tel./Fax. (01234) 881264

Brew pub founded in 1987 which quickly doubled its capacity to meet demand from the local free trade and wholesalers, then doubled again in 1993, with the addition of a new fermenting room. It now supplies 16 free trade outlets locally, as well as the Three Fyshes. Tours by arrangement.

Old Cock Up Mild (OG 1032, ABV 3.4%) A subtly-flavoured black/red beer. A faint fruit aroma leads through into a blend of roast malt and fruit, then a dry finish.

Turvey Bitter (OG 1034, ABV 3.4%) A faint, fruity aroma precedes a subtle blend of hops and fruit in the taste, on a bittersweet base. Faint, dry finish with a little fruit.

Two Henrys Bitter (OG 1038, ABV 3.9%) A fairly well-balanced blend of malt and hops with an aroma of hops and fruit, and a slightly dry finish.

THAT (OG 1048, ABV 4.8%) Fruit dominates the aroma of this pale brown beer and also the flavour, against a background of hops and toffee/malt. Dry finish with a little fruit. 'THAT' stands for Two Henrys Alternative Tipple.

Old Nix (OG 1059, ABV 6%) A robust beer with an aroma of fruit and malt. A blend of fruit, malt and caramel gives a raisin-fudge character to the flavour. Faint, dry finish with a little fruit.

Winky's Winter Warmer* (OG 1059, ABV 6.1%) Available October–Easter.

Winky Wobbler (OG 1072, ABV 7.5%) A potent winter brew that has an aroma of fruit and wine. The flavour is a powerful combination of bittersweet malt, fruit, roast malt and some hops. Dry, fruity aftertaste.

NORTH YORKSHIRE

North Yorkshire Brewing Co., 84 North Ormesby Road, Middlesbrough, Cleveland TS4 2AG. Tel. (01642) 226224 Fax. (01642) 226225

Company started in March 1990 with a purpose-built brewery. The traditionally brewed beers are in much demand, and an extra beer is brewed every month to a new recipe. A real cider, Scatterbrain Scrumpy (ABV 6%), is also produced. Two tied houses and over 100 free trade outlets are currently supplied.

The Independents

Best Bitter
(OG 1036, ABV 3.6%) Light and very refreshing. Surprisingly full-flavoured for a pale, low gravity beer, with a complex, bitter-sweet mixture of malt, hops and fruit carrying through into the aftertaste.

Yorkshire Brown
(OG 1038, ABV 3.8%) A ruby-red beer with a soft, malty taste and a hoppy aftertaste. Dry finish.

Erimus Dark
(OG 1040, ABV 3.7%) A dark, full-bodied, sweet brew with lots of roast malt and caramel flavour, and an underlying hoppiness. At its best it is very smooth indeed, with a tight, creamy head and a sweet, malty finish.

Yorkshire Porter
(OG 1040, ABV 3.7%) A very dark brew with good burnt malt and liquorice flavours and a burnt, dry finish.

Fools Gold
(OG 1046, ABV 4.6%) A well-hopped, lightly malted, golden premium bitter, using Styrian and Goldings hops.

Flying Herbert
(OG 1048, ABV 4.7%) A refreshing, red/brown beer with a hoppy aroma. The flavour is a pleasant balance of roast malt and sweetness which predominates over the hops. The malty, bitter finish develops slowly.

Dizzy Dick
(OG 1080, ABV 7%) A smooth, strong, dark, aromatic ale with an obvious bite, although too sweet for some. The very full, roast malt and caramel flavour has hints of fruit and toffee. The malty sweetness persists in the aftertaste.

OAK

Oak Brewing Company Ltd., Phoenix Brewery, Green Lane, Heywood, Gtr. Manchester OL10 2EP. Tel. (01706) 627009

Brewery established in 1982 in Ellesmere Port which moved in 1991 to Heywood and now supplies over 100 free trade outlets, from West Cheshire to West Yorkshire. Its special 'one-off' brews have been so successful that three of them are now regulars. Occasional beer: March Hare (OG 1042, ABV 4.2%, March).

Hopwood Bitter*
(OG 1035, ABV 3.5%)

Bantam Bitter*
(ABV 3.5%)

Best Bitter
(OG 1038, ABV 3.9%) A tawny, hoppy session beer with some balancing malt in the aroma and taste. Strong, dry and hoppy finish.

Tyke Bitter*
(OG 1042, ABV 4.3%)

Midsummer Madness*
(OG 1044, ABV 4.4%) Available June–August.

Old Oak Ale
(OG 1044, ABV 4.5%) A well-balanced, brown beer with a multitude of mellow fruit flavours. Malt and hops balance the strong fruitiness in the aroma and taste, and the finish is malty, fruity and dry.

Thirsty Moon*
(ABV 4.6%)

Bonneville*
(ABV 4.8%)

Double Dagger
(OG 1050, ABV 5%) A pale brown, malty brew, more pleasantly dry and light than its gravity would suggest. Moderately fruity throughout; a hoppy bitterness in the mouth balances the strong graininess.

Porter
(OG 1050, ABV 5%) The roast malt promised by the aroma is joined in the taste by malt, caramel and hops. Long and pleasant aftertaste. Brewed October–January.

Wobbly Bob
(OG 1060, ABV 6%) A red/brown beer with a malty, fruity aroma. Strongly malty and fruity in flavour and quite hoppy, with the sweetness yielding to a dryness in the aftertaste.

Humbug*
(OG 1064, ABV 7%) Available November–January.

The Independents

OAKHAM

Oakham Ales, 12–13 Midland Court, Station Approach, Oakham, Rutland, Leicestershire LE15 6QW. Tel. (01572) 755333

One-man brewery, established in October 1993 in industrial units on a trading estate, with a custom-built, ten-barrel plant. It has slowly built up a wholesale trade, whilst its direct business has increased to 50 free trade outlets, within a 50-mile radius.

Jeffrey Hudson Bitter or JHB (OG 1038, ABV 3.8%) A golden beer whose aroma is dominated by hops that give characteristic citrus notes. Hops and fruit on the palate are balanced by malt and a bitter base. Dry, hoppy finish with soft fruit flavours.

Hunky Dory (OG 1044, ABV 4.5%) A robust, well-balanced beer. The blend of malt and hops on a bitter fruit base is preceded by a subtle aroma of hops, fruit and malt. Dry finish with hops and fruit.

Old Tosspot* (OG 1052, ABV 5.2%) A full-flavoured, fruity brew.

OAKHILL

Oakhill Brewery, High Street, Oakhill, Bath, Avon BA3 5AS. Tel. (01749) 840134 Fax. (01749) 840531

Situated high in the Mendip Hills in Somerset (despite the Avon address), this brewery was set up by a farmer in 1984 in an old fermentation room of the original Oakhill Brewery (est. 1767, but burnt down in 1924). However, growing trade has necessitated larger premises and a move is underway to the old Maltings building in Oakhill. A third tied house has now been acquired and some 100 other outlets are also supplied. Shop open 8–5 Mon–Fri; 9–12 Sat. Tours by arrangement.

Somer Ale (OG 1035, ABV 3.5%) An amber, light and refreshing, fruity pale ale, with a pleasant, dry, bitter finish. A summer brew.

Best Bitter (OG 1039, ABV 4%) A clean-tasting, tangy bitter, with good hop content and citrus fruit and malt balance. Dry finish; light hop aroma. Very quenching.

Black Magic (OG 1044, ABV 4.5%) A black/brown bitter stout with roast malt and a touch of fruit in the nose. Smooth roast malt and bitterness in the taste, with mellow coffee and chocolate.

Yeoman Strong Ale (OG 1049, ABV 5%) A strong, pale brown, full-bodied bitter, with a floral hop palate and notable fruitiness. Dry, bitter, lasting finish.

Mendip Tickler* (ABV 6.3%)

OKELLS See Isle of Man Breweries.

OLD BEAR

Old Bear Brewery, 6 Keighley Road, Cross Hills, Keighley, N. Yorkshire BD20 7RN. Tel. (01535) 632115

Brewery founded in June 1993 by former Goose Eye Brewery owner Bryan Eastell, next to his Whitbread tied house. His aim is to produce 'natural' beers, brewed with local spring water. Four free trade outlets are also supplied and some occasional beers are produced. Tours by arrangement.

Bitter* (OG 1038, ABV 3.9%)

Barnsey Bitter* (OG 1038, ABV 3.9%)

OLD CHIMNEYS

Old Chimneys Brewery, The Street, Market Weston, Diss, Norfolk IP22 2NZ. Tel. (01359) 221411

Tiny craft brewery opened in 1995 by former Greene King/Broughton brewer Alan Thomson. The beers are brewed with wild hops gathered from local hedgerows and are named after local endangered species. Despite the postal address, the brewery is in Suffolk.

Swallowtail IPA* (OG 1036, ABV 3.6%) A crisp, clean-tasting bitter.

Great Raft Bitter* (OG 1043, ABV 4.2%) A malty best bitter with distinctive hop character.

The Independents

Natterjack Premium Ale*	(OG 1050, ABV 5%) A rich, full-bodied, fruity ale.

OLD COURT

🏮 **The Old Court Brewhouse, Queen Street, Huddersfield, W. Yorkshire HD1 2SL. Tel. (01484) 454035**

New brew pub opened in 1994 in Huddersfield's former County Court. The building's character has been retained and the brewing copper protruding from the lower ground floor into the ground floor public bar provides an unusual talking point. Beers: M'Lud (OG 1035, ABV 3.5%), 1825 (OG 1045, ABV 4.5%), Maximum Sentence (OG 1055, ABV 5.5%).

OLDHAM

See Burtonwood, Nationals, Whitbread, and Pub Groups, Boddingtons.

OLD FORGE

Pett Brewing Company, The Old Forge Brewery, c/o The Two Sawyers, Pett, Hastings, E. Sussex TN35 4HB. Tel. (01424) 813030

Brewery established in early 1995 in a restored old village forge. Around a dozen local outlets now take the beer and the brewery is currently operating to full capacity.

Brothers Best*	(OG 1037, ABV 3.9%)
Pett Progress	(OG 1043, ABV 4.6%) A mid-brown beer marked by its maltiness which dominates the aroma and taste. Caramel comes through in the aftertaste.
Old Farnes*	(OG 1052, ABV 5.3%)

OLD LUXTERS

Old Luxters Farm Brewery, Hambleden, Henley-on-Thames, Oxfordshire RG9 6JW. Tel. (01491) 638330 Fax. (01491) 638645

Brewery set up in May 1990 in a 17th-century barn by David Ealand, owner of Chiltern Valley Wines. Apart from the brewery and vineyard, the site also houses a fine art gallery and a cellar shop. The brewery supplies 12 local free trade outlets and pubs further afield via wholesalers. Note: Hambleden is in Buckinghamshire, despite the postal address. Brewery shop open daily 9–6. Tours by arrangement. Bottle-conditioned beer: Barn Ale (OG 1052, ABV 5.4%).

Barn Ale	(OG 1042, ABV 4.5%) Predominantly malty, fruity and hoppy in taste and nose, and tawny/amber in colour. Fairly strong in flavour: the initial, sharp, malty and fruity taste leaves a dry, bittersweet, fruity aftertaste, with hints of black cherry. It can be slightly sulphurous.

OLD MILL

Old Mill Brewery Ltd., Mill Street, Snaith, Goole, Humberside DN14 9HS. Tel. (01405) 861813 Fax. (01405) 862789

Small brewery opened in 1983 in a 200-year-old former malt kiln that had been used to manufacture clog soles until 1946. The purpose-built brewing plant was expanded in 1992, increasing capacity by 50%. Since then new offices and a warehouse have also been added, and most recently, additional fermenters for seasonal and special brews have been introduced. The tied estate now stands at 12 houses. Some 150 free trade outlets are also supplied. Occasional beer: Porter (ABV 5%)

Traditional Mild	(OG 1034, ABV 3.5%) A thin, but easy drinking dark brown/red brew. The malty aroma has hints of burnt chocolate and the same elements are found on the palate. The dry and nutty finish fades away.
Traditional Bitter	(OG 1037, ABV 3.9%) This year has witnessed the return of the Old Mill character to this beer, though bitterness remains at a premium. It has a malty nose and initial flavour, with hops hiding until the lingering finish. Improving.

Bullion   (OG 1044, ABV 4.7%) The malty and hoppy aroma is followed by a neat mix of hop and fruit tastes within an enveloping brewery maltiness that one remembers from a couple of years ago. Generally dark brown, but an amber colour is more discernible.

ORANGE   See Nationals, Scottish & Newcastle.

ORKNEY   **The Orkney Brewery, Quoyloo, Orkney KW16 3LT. Tel. (01856) 841802 Fax. (01856) 841754**

The Orkney's first brewery in living memory, set up in 1988 by former licensee Roger White. Initially only brewing keg beer for local outlets, Roger's personal commitment to real ale has resulted in cask ales now representing 90% of sales (mostly to central Scotland, but also to one pub on Orkney). The brewery now employs six people. Tours by arrangement.

Raven Ale*   (OG 1038, ABV 3.8%) Still mainly keg on the island, but worth seeking out when in 'real' form. Smooth, mellow and malty, with a distinctive aroma and finish.

Dragonhead Stout*   (OG 1040, ABV 4%)

Dark Island ⊞   (OG 1045, ABV 4.6%) Dark, beautifully balanced and full of roast malt and fruit. A bittersweet taste leads to a long-lasting, roasted, slightly bitter finish. Full-bodied and deceptive.

Skullsplitter*   (OG 1080, ABV 8.5%)

OTTER   **Otter Brewery, Mathayes Farm, Luppitt, Honiton, Devon EX14 0SA. Tel. (01404) 891285**

Otter began brewing in November 1990 and has grown steadily, with a major expansion in May 1994 leading to improved sales and the production of two seasonal beers. Sixty pubs now take the beers, which are produced using local malt and the brewery's own spring water. Tours by arrangement.

Bitter   (OG 1036, ABV 3.6%) A pale brown beer: a true bitter from the hoppy, fruity aroma, through the hop/bitter taste to the dry, bitter finish.

Bright*   (OG 1039, ABV 4.3%) A summer beer.

Ale ⊞   (OG 1043, ABV 4.5%) Mid brown-coloured, well-balanced beer with a malty aroma and a hoppy, bitter taste and aftertaste.

Dark   (OG 1046, ABV 4.8%) Dark brown with a definite chocolate malt aroma and taste, and a bitter finish.

Head   (OG 1054, ABV 5.8%) A mid-brown beer with a strong malt aroma and taste. Pleasant, bitter, malty finish.

PALMERS   **JC & RH Palmer Ltd., The Old Brewery, West Bay Road, Bridport, Dorset DT6 4JA. Tel. (01308) 422396 Fax. (01308) 421149**

Britain's only thatched brewery, founded in 1794, is situated by the sea in former mill buildings. The company is managed by the great-grandsons of brothers John Cleeves and Robert Henry Palmer, who acquired the brewery in the late 19th century. It is still slowly developing its tied estate (presently 64 houses) with very selective acquisitions. All its pubs serve real ale, although top pressure and cask breathers are widely in use. A hundred free trade outlets are serviced directly, but Palmers' beers are reaching a wider audience throughout the South via wholesalers. Shop open 9.30–6 Mon–Thu; 9.30–8 Fri and Sat. Tours by arrangement.

Bridport Bitter or BB   (OG 1030, ABV 3.2%) A light beer with a hoppy aroma, a bitter, hoppy taste with some malt, and a bitter aftertaste.

Best Bitter or IPA   (OG 1040, ABV 4.2%) A beer that is hoppy and bitter throughout. Fruit and malt undertones give some balance to the aroma and

485

	taste, and there is a lingering bitter aftertaste.
Tally Ho!	(OG 1046, ABV 4.7%) A dark and complex brew with a mainly malty aroma. The nutty taste is dominated by roast malt and the aftertaste is malty and bitter. Limited availability, especially in winter.
200*	(OG 1052, ABV 5%) The anniversary ale, now a permanent feature.

PARADISE   See Bird in Hand.

PARISH   **Parish Brewery, The Old Brewery Inn Courtyard, Somerby, Leicestershire LE14 2PZ. Tel. (01664) 454781**

The Old Brewery Inn — Home of The Parish Brewery

The first brewery to be established in Somerby since the 16th century, Parish started life at the Stag & Hounds, Burrough on the Hill, in 1983. It moved in 1991, acquiring a new 20-barrel plant to keep up with demand for the beers, which are now supplied to around 20 free trade outlets, as well as the Old Brewery Inn (which is a free house). Tours by arrangement. Occasional beer: Baz's Super Brew (OG 1150, ABV 23%, Christmas).

Mild	(OG 1035, ABV 3.5%) A thin, smooth, dark brew with caramel dominant throughout. The palate and aftertaste also feature a dry maltiness, but can be too yeasty.
Special Bitter or PSB	(OG 1038, ABV 3.8%) A thin-bodied beer, dominated by hops, but with a tangy fruitiness. Refreshing bitter aftertaste.
Farm Gold*	(OG 1039, ABV 4%)
Somerby Premium	(OG 1040, ABV 3.9%) A tawny, medium-bodied beer with a malty, hoppy fragrance and a bitter, fruity taste. There are hints of ginger in the aftertaste.
Porter*	(OG 1048, ABV 4.8%) A winter beer.
Poachers Ale	(OG 1060, ABV 6%) A complex, full-flavoured ale, ruby-coloured, with plenty of hops and malt throughout. Caramel is present, but is overtaken by an Olde English marmalade taste. Long, yeasty finish.
Baz's Bonce Blower or BBB	(OG 1105, ABV 11%) A robust and vigorous Christmas pudding of a beer, almost black in colour, with caramel again dominant. It has a rich palate and an exceedingly long finish.

PARKER   See Cannon.

PASSAGEWAY   **Passageway Brewing Company, Unit G8, Mariners House, Norfolk Street, Liverpool, Merseyside L1 0BG. Tel. (0151) 708 0730 Fax. (0151) 709 0925**

THE **PASSAGEWAY** BREWING Cᵒ

Brewery established in May 1994. Its two founders, Steve Dugmore and Phil Burke, painstakingly researched the history of St Arnold, the Belgian patron saint of brewing, before beginning production. They use yeast from a Belgian monastic brewery, and half a pint of water from St Arnold's well in Belgium is added to the copper before each mash. Passageway now supplies 20 free trade outlets. Tours by arrangement.

Docker's Hook*	(OG 1036, ABV 3.8%)
Redemption*	(OG 1038, ABV 4%) A rye beer.
St Arnold	(OG 1048, ABV 5%) Deep ruby in colour, this is a very fruity and bitter beer, yet not sweet. Hop, roast malt, chocolate and liquorice flavours also fight for attention in the taste and dry aftertaste. A complex, heavy beer, reminiscent of a Belgian brown ale. Highly drinkable.

The Independents

PEMBROKE

Pembroke Brewery Co., Eaton House, 108 Main Street, Pembroke, Dyfed SA71 4HN. Tel. (01646) 682517 Fax. (01646) 682008

Brewery founded in May 1994 in historic former stables behind the proprietors' house. A redundant building at Pembroke Dock railway station has since been converted into a tied house. Seasonal ales, plus a cask-conditioned lager, are planned and over 20 free trade outlets are currently supplied.

The Darklin*	(OG 1035, ABV 3.5%)
Main Street Bitter*	(OG 1039, ABV 4.1%)
Golden Hill Ale*	(OG 1043, ABV 4.5%)

PENNINE

Pennine Brewing Company, Keighley, W. Yorkshire.
Brewery closed.

PETT

See Old Forge.

PILGRIM

Pilgrim Ales, The Old Brewery, West Street, Reigate, Surrey RH2 9BL. Tel. (01737) 222651 Fax. (01737) 225785

Set up in 1982, and moved to Reigate in 1985, Pilgrim has gradually increased its capacity and its beers have won both local and national awards, although sales are mostly concentrated in the Surrey area. Tours are available by arrangement on the last Friday of the month in summer. Occasional beers: Autumnal (ABV 4.5%, mid-September–mid-October), The Great Crusader (ABV 6.5%, June–July), Conqueror (OG 1070, ABV 6.5%), Pudding (ABV 7.3%, November–December).

Surrey	(OG 1037, ABV 3.7%) A well-balanced session bitter with an underlying fruitiness. Hop flavour comes through in the finish.
Porter	(OG 1042, ABV 4%) A black beer with a pleasant roast malt flavour, balanced by a faint hoppiness which is also there at the finish. Noticeable roast malt aroma.
Progress	(OG 1042, ABV 4%) Reddish-brown in colour, with a predominantly malty flavour and aroma, although hops are also evident in the taste.
Saracen	(OG 1047, ABV 4.5%) Roast malt dominates the aroma of this black stout, but hops balance the roast malt flavour, leading to a bitter finish. Tasty.
Crusader	(OG 1048, ABV 4.9%) A summer brew; a light, golden beer with a good marriage of malt and hops from aroma through to finish. Very drinkable.
Talisman	(OG 1049, ABV 5%) A strong ale with a mid-brown colour, a fruity, malt flavour and a faint hoppiness.
Spring Bock*	(ABV 5%) A new wheat beer for spring.

PIONEER

See Rooster's.

PITFIELD

See Brewery on Sea.

PLASSEY

Plassey Brewery, The Plassey, Eyton, Wrexham, Clwyd LL13 0SP. Tel. (01978) 780922 Fax. (01978) 780019

Brewery founded in 1985 on the 250-acre Plassey Estate, which also incorporates a touring caravan park, craft centres, a golf course and three licensed outlets for Plassey's ales. Twenty free trade outlets also take the beers. Work has started on a new brewery, with plans for the old one to be turned into a brewery shop. Tours by arrangement.

Bitter	(OG 1039, ABV 4%) A well-hopped, straw-coloured beer, with blackcurrant fruitiness.
Stout*	(OG 1045, ABV 5%) A new stout.
Glyndwr's Revenge*	(OG 1046, ABV 4.8%) A new dark beer.
Cwrw Tudno	(OG 1048, ABV 5%) More malty and sweet and less bitter than the bitter, but with a fairly dry aftertaste.

The Independents

Dragon's Breath (OG 1060, ABV 6%) A fruity, strong bitter, smooth and quite sweet, though not cloying, with an intense, fruity aroma. A dangerously drinkable winter warmer.

PLOUGH INN   **Bodicote Brewery, Plough Inn, Bodicote, Banbury, Oxfordshire OX15 4BZ. Tel. (01295) 262327**

Brewery founded in 1982 at the Plough, No. 9 High Street (hence the beer name), which has been in the same hands since 1957. Three other outlets are also supplied with its full mash beers. Tours by arrangement. Beers: Bitter (OG 1035, ABV 3.2%), No. 9 (OG 1045, ABV 4.4%), Old English Porter (OG 1045, ABV 4.5%, winter), Triple X (OG 1055, ABV 5%, winter).

POOLE   **The Brewhouse Brewery, 68 High Street, Poole, Dorset BH15 1DA. Tel. (01202) 682345**

Brewery established in 1980, three years before the Brewhouse pub was opened. Brewing was transferred to the Brewhouse in 1987. The brewery was extended in 1990 and an additional fermenting vessel was put into operation in 1995 to meet growing demand for the beers which are sold to around 35 outlets. The beers are kept at the Brewhouse pub in cellar tanks and casks, but blanket pressure is no longer applied. Occasional tours by arrangement.

Best Bitter or Dolphin* (OG 1038, ABV 3.8%) An amber-coloured, balanced bitter.

Bosun Bitter* (OG 1047, ABV 4.6%) Amber and rich.

PORTER   **Porter Brewing Co. Ltd., Rossendale Brewery, The Griffin Inn, Haslingden, Lancashire BB4 5AF. Tel./Fax. (01706) 214021**

The Griffin Inn was refurbished and re-opened, complete with microbrewery, by new owner David Porter in March 1994. A second tied house was acquired in June 1995 and other local outlets also take the beer.

Dark Mild* (OG 1033, ABV 3.3%)

Bitter* (OG 1038, ABV 3.8%)

Porter* (OG 1049, ABV 5%)

Sunshine* (OG 1051, ABV 5.3%)

Stout* (ABV 5.5%)

POWELL See Wood.

PRINCETOWN Princetown Breweries Ltd., The Brewery, Tavistock Road, Princetown, Devon PL20 6QF. Tel. (01822) 890789 Fax. (01822) 890719

Brewery established in late 1994 by a former Gibbs Mew and Hop Back brewer. It serves five tied pubs with any surplus beer sold to local free trade outlets.

Dartmoor IPA or Best Bitter* (OG 1041, ABV 4%) This beer is sold under both names.

Jail Ale (OG 1049.5, ABV 4.8%) Hop and fruit predominate in the flavour of this mid-brown beer which has a slightly sweet aftertaste.

RAINBOW   **The Rainbow Inn, 73 Birmingham Road, Allesley, Coventry, W. Midlands CV5 9GT. Tel. (01203) 402888**

Pub which began brewing in October 1994, just to serve its own customers. Beers: Piddlebrook (OG 1038, ABV 3.8%), Belcher's Wood (OG 1042, ABV 4.2%), Fire Cracker (OG 1048, ABV 4.8%), Sley Alle (OG 1054, ABV 5.2%, occasional).

The Independents

RANDALLS

RW Randall Ltd., Vauxlaurens Brewery, St Julian's Avenue, St Peter Port, Guernsey GY1 3JG. Tel. (01481) 720134 Fax. (01481) 713233

The smaller of Guernsey's two breweries, which was purchased by RW Randall from Joseph Gullick in 1868. Successive generations have continued to run the business, except during the period of the German occupation, when brewing ceased until after the war. It currently owns 18 houses, but only two serve real ale. Do not confuse with Randalls Vautier of Jersey, which no longer brews but which still runs 29 pubs on that island. Shop open 10–5.15 Mon–Sat. Tours at 2.30 on Thursdays, May–September. Bottle-conditioned beer: Stout (OG 1050, ABV 5.5%).

Bitter

(OG 1046, ABV 5%) Amber in colour, with a hoppy aroma. Bitter and hoppy both in the palate and finish.

RAT & RATCHET

 The Rat & Ratchet Brewery, 40 Chapel Hill, Huddersfield, W. Yorkshire HD1 3EB. Tel. (01484) 516734

Well-known ale house which began brewing in December 1994. No regular beers have been confirmed to date. One or two outside outlets have taken some of the ales.

RAYMENTS

See Greene King.

RCH

RCH Brewery, West Hewish, Weston-super-Mare, Avon BS24 6RR. Tel. (01934) 834447 Fax. (01934) 834167

Brewery originally installed in the early 1980s behind the Royal Clarence Hotel at Burnham-on-Sea, but moved in October 1993 to a new site to begin brewing on a commercial basis, with a new beer range. It now supplies around 50 free trade outlets through its own beer agency, and other pubs nationwide via wholesalers. Tours by arrangement. Occasional beer: Santa Fé (OG 1071, ABV 7.3%, Christmas).

PG Steam*

(OG 1039, ABV 3.9%)

Pitchfork*

(OG 1043, ABV 4.3%)

Old Slug Porter ⊞

(OG 1045, ABV 4.5%) A traditional-style porter with a nutty, woody flavour and a toffee and honey aroma.

East Street Cream*

(OG 1050, ABV 5%)

Firebox*

(OG 1060, ABV 6%)

REBELLION

REBELLION BEER CO.

Rebellion Beer Company, Unit J, Rose Industrial Estate, Marlow Bottom Road, Marlow, Buckinghamshire SL7 3ND. Tel. (01628) 476594 Fax. (01628) 482354

Opened in 1993, Rebellion helps to fill the gap left in Marlow by Wethered's brewery, closed by Whitbread in 1988. The brewery water is 'Marlowised', i.e. treated to recreate the mineral composition of the water used by the old brewery. Some 50 pubs regularly take the beers and others are supplied via wholesalers. Shop open 8–6 Mon–Fri; 10–4 Sat.

IPA*

(OG 1037, ABV 3.9%)

Mutiny*

(OG 1046, ABV 4.5%) Formerly ESB.

24 Carat*

(OG 1048, ABV 5%)

RECKLESS ERIC'S

Reckless Brewing & Supply Co. Ltd., Unit 4, Albion Industrial Estate, Cilfynydd, Pontypridd, Mid Glamorgan CF37 4NX. Tel. (01443) 409229

Small brewery, opened in late 1993 and supplying over 50 free trade outlets some distance from its South Wales base. Other beers beginning with 'R' are brewed from time to time.

Retribution*

(ABV 3.4%)

The Independents

Renown*	(OG 1040, ABV 4%)
Restoration*	(ABV 4.3%)
'Recked 'Em*	(OG 1052, ABV 5.2%)
Rejoice*	(OG 1060, ABV 6%) A stout.

RED CROSS

Red Cross Brewery, Perryfields Road, Bromsgrove, Hereford & Worcester B61 8QW. Tel. (01527) 871409

After battling for two years with planning problems, this brewery opened in October 1993 in the old bull pen of Red Cross Farm, a 17th-century yeoman farmhouse. Initially just brewing for the Hop Pole Inn in Bromsgrove (an M&B tied house), it still plans to expand into the free trade. Beer: Nailers OBJ (OG 1046, ABV 4.5%).

REDRUTH

Redruth Brewery (1792) Ltd., The Brewery, Redruth, Cornwall TR15 1AT. Tel. (01209) 212244

The old Cornish Brewery, originally founded in 1792, is now owned by the Dransfield Group PLC of Hong Kong. With no tied estate and most local pubs being tied to other breweries, Redruth has few outlets for beers of its own and therefore concentrates on contract packaging and brewing.

REEPHAM

Reepham Brewery, Unit 1, Collers Way, Reepham, Norfolk NR10 4SW. Tel. (01603) 871091

Family brewery, founded in 1983 by a former Watney's research engineer with a purpose-built plant in a small industrial unit. The company was launched on a single beer, Granary Bitter, but now produces quite a range, which varies from year to year and includes some award-winners. Reepham now has a brewery tap (the Crown – by agreement with the owners) and 20 other local outlets are supplied directly.

Granary Bitter	(OG 1038, ABV 3.8%) An amber beer which is well-balanced and makes easy drinking. The malt and hops are complemented by a pleasing amount of bitterness and hints of fruit.
Dark*	(OG 1039, ABV 3.9%) A strong mild.
Rapier Pale Ale	(OG 1042, ABV 4.2%) A beer which appears to be slightly more attenuated than before. It still possesses a flowery hop aroma and maltiness in the taste on a fruit and hop background, but it has lost some of its clean edge and a little body.
Summer Velvet*	(OG 1042, ABV 4.2%)
Velvet Stout	(OG 1043, ABV 4.2%) The fruity, malt aroma of this darkish brown beer gives way to a sweet, mellow taste explosion of malt, roast malt, fruit and hops. This subsides to a pleasant aftertaste with hints of liquorice.
Old Bircham Ale	(OG 1046, ABV 4.6%) An amber/tawny beer with good body for its gravity. The fruity aroma precedes a complex, malty, hoppy palate, which also has a sweetness that dies away in the malty, dry finish. A winter brew.
Brewhouse*	(OG 1055, ABV 5%) A strong winter ale.
Anniversary Ale*	(OG 1076, ABV 7.3%)

REINDEER   See Nationals, Carlsberg-Tetley.

RIDLEYS

TD Ridley & Sons Ltd., Hartford End Brewery, Felsted, Chelmsford, Essex CM3 1JZ. Tel. (01371) 820316 Fax. (01371) 821216

Ridleys was established by a miller, Thomas Dixon Ridley, on the banks of the picturesque River Chelmer in 1842. A programme of improvement is still underway in the tied estate and all 62 pubs sell real ale. Around 150 other outlets are also supplied. Tours by arrangement. Occasional beer: Winter Ale (OG 1050, ABV 5%, Christmas). Bottle-conditioned beer: Chelmer Gold (OG 1051, ABV 5%).

490

IPA Bitter (OG 1034, ABV 3.5%) A refreshing, hoppy bitter, well-balanced by malt in the flavour and delicate fruit in the finish, with lingering bitterness.

Mild ⏚ (OG 1034, ABV 3.5%) A very dark mild with a light aroma of roast malt and caramel. Quite bitter for a mild, with roast malt flavours. The finish has hops, roast malt and caramel, with none dominant.

ESX Best Bitter (OG 1043, ABV 4.3%) Harmonious malt and hops dominate the taste of this best bitter, with a hint of fruit. Hops just gain over malt in the finish.

Witchfinder Porter (OG 1045, ABV 4.3%) A very dark red, sweet brew, not too heavy. Malt is much in evidence in the aroma, taste and finish, with a careful hoppiness. Winter only.

Spectacular Ale* (OG 1048, ABV 4.6%) A summer beer, available May–October.

RINGWOOD **Ringwood Brewery Ltd., 138 Christchurch Road, Ringwood, Hampshire BH24 3AP. Tel. (01425) 471177 Fax. (01425) 480273**

Hampshire's first new brewery in the real ale revival, founded in 1978 and housed in attractive 18th-century buildings, formerly part of the old Tunks brewery. A new brewhouse was commissioned just before Christmas 1994. Famous for its award-winning Old Thumper, it has two tied houses and around 350 free trade accounts, from Weymouth to Chichester and across to the Channel Isles. Shop open 10–5 Mon–Fri; 9.30–noon Sat. Tours by arrangement.

Best Bitter (OG 1038, ABV 3.8%) A golden brown, moreish beer, with flavours for all. The aroma has a hint of hops and leads to a malty sweetness, which becomes dry, with a hint of orange. Malt and bitterness in the finish.

XXXX Porter (OG 1048, ABV 4.7%) Sadly only available October–March: a rich, dark brew with a strong aroma of roasted malt, hops and fruit. Rich in flavour, with coffee, vanilla, damsons, apples and molasses evident. The overall roast maltiness continues into the drying, hoppy, bitter finish.

Fortyniner (OG 1048, ABV 4.8%) A good premium beer, with malt and hops in good balance. The flavours slowly increase to a fruity finish.

Old Thumper (OG 1058, ABV 5.8%) A golden beer with a surprisingly bitter aftertaste, which follows a middle period tasting of various fruits. It may be a little sweet for some.

RISING SUN **The Rising Sun Inn, Knowle Bank Road, Shraley Brook, Audley, Stoke-on-Trent, Staffordshire ST7 8DS. Tel. (01782) 720600 Fax. (01782) 721288**

Brewing began in June 1989 at the Rising Sun and the brewery now supplies the busy pub and a thriving free trade (ten outlets). Tours by arrangement. Occasional beer: Mild (OG 1034, ABV 3.3%).

Sunlight* (OG 1036, ABV 3.5%) Summer only.

Rising (OG 1040, ABV 3.8%) A lightly-flavoured, easy-drinking amber beer, tasting fruity and hoppy with a little malt. Bittersweet aftertaste; slight aroma of hops.

Setting (OG 1045, ABV 4.4%) The faint aroma implies fruit and hops, and this bittersweet, dark brown, medium-flavoured ale does have fruit and hops, but largely malt characteristics.

Sunstroke (OG 1056, ABV 5.6%) A dark, red/brown, medium-bodied ale. The aroma has roast malt and some hops, whilst the taste is bittersweet with a dominating maltiness. The aftertaste sees malt, roast malt and hops coming through.

The Independents

| Total Eclipse* | (OG 1072, ABV 6.8%) |
| Solar Flare* | (OG 1100, ABV 11%) Winter only. |

ROBINSON'S

Frederic Robinson Ltd., Unicorn Brewery, Lower Hillgate, Stockport, Cheshire SK1 1JJ. Tel. (0161) 480 6571 Fax. (0161) 476 6011

Major Greater Manchester family brewery, founded in 1838. Robinson's took over Hartleys of Ulverston in 1982, but closed that brewery in October 1991. Only Hartleys XB is still brewed (at Stockport). The brewery supplies real ale to most of its 412 tied houses (70 from the Hartleys Cumbrian estate, but most in southern Manchester and Cheshire). Shop open 9–5.30 Mon–Sat. Tours by arrangement.

Dark Best Mild
(OG 1033, ABV 3.3%) Toffee/malt-tasting, with a slight bitterness. A very quaffable beer with a fruity malt aroma and a dry finish. A very rare find.

Hatters Mild
(OG 1033, ABV 3.3%) A light mild with an unpronounced malty aroma and a refreshing, dry, malty flavour. Short bitter/malty aftertaste.

Old Stockport Bitter
(OG 1035, ABV 3.5%) A beer with a refreshing, malty and fruity taste, a characteristic fruity aroma, with a touch of sulphur, and a short, dry finish. The number of outlets has trebled since it was renamed from Robinson's Bitter last year.

Hartleys XB
(OG 1040, ABV 4%) Little aroma, but malty with some hop bitterness in the taste; dry finish.

Best Bitter
(OG 1041, ABV 4.2%) A pale brown beer with a malty, hoppy nose. There are malt, hops and bitterness in the flavour and the aftertaste is short and bitter.

Frederic's*
(OG 1050, ABV 5%)

Old Tom ⌸
(OG 1079, ABV 8.5%) A full-bodied, dark, fruity beer. The aroma is fruity and mouth-watering; the aftertaste is bittersweet, with an alcoholic kick. A beer to be sipped respectfully by a winter fire.

ROBINWOOD
See Merrimans.

ROOSTER'S

Rooster's Brewery, Unit 20, Claro Court, Claro Business Centre, Claro Road, Harrogate, N. Yorkshire HG1 4BA. Tel. (01423) 561861 Fax. (01423) 520996

Brewery set up in 1992 by Sean Franklin, formerly of Franklin's Brewery. Rooster's is now successfully building up its business and expanded the plant in 1994 to cope with increased demand. A subsidiary label, Pioneer, produces a different, experimental beer each month for the guest beer market. These beers have included Mayflower II (OG 1037, ABV 3.7%) and Zulu (OG 1049, ABV 4.7%, a porter). Rooster's occasional beers: Hop Along (ABV 4.7%, Easter), Nector (OG 1058, ABV 5.8%, Christmas).

Jak's*
(OG 1039, ABV 3.9%)

Special*
(OG 1039, ABV 3.9%)

Yankee
(OG 1043, ABV 4.3%) A straw-coloured beer with a delicate aroma. The flavour is an interesting mix of malt and hops, with a gentle sweetness and a bite of orange peel, leading to a short, pleasant finish.

Cream*
(OG 1047, ABV 4.7%)

Rooster's
(OG 1047, ABV 4.7%) A light amber beer with a subtle, sweet, slightly hoppy nose. Intense malt flavours, reminiscent of treacle toffee with chocolate and orange undertones, precede an unexpected hoppy finish.

ROSE STREET
See Nationals, Carlsberg-Tetley.

ROSS

Ross Brewing Company, The Bristol Brewhouse, 117–119 Stokes Croft, Bristol, Avon BS1 3RW. Tel. (0117) 9420306 Fax. (0117) 9428746

Set up in Hartcliffe in 1989, Ross was the first brewery to brew with organic Soil Association barley, initially producing bottle-conditioned beers only. The brewery later moved to the Bristol Brewhouse pub and the one remaining bottled beer, Saxon Strong Ale, is now brewed under contract by Eldridge Pope (qv). In September 1994 Ross set up the Newport Brewhouse in Gwent (see Newport), and now brews cask beers for consumption in its two pubs and for a very limited free trade. Beers: Pictons Pleasure (OG 1042, ABV 4.2%), Hartcliffe Bitter (OG 1045, ABV 4.5%), Porter (OG 1053, ABV 5%), SPA (OG 1055, ABV 5.5%), Numbskull (OG 1063, ABV 6%, winter).

ROSSENDALE   See Porter.

ROTHER VALLEY   **Rother Valley Brewing Company, Gate Court, Northiam, Rye, E. Sussex TN31 6QT. Tel. (01797) 252444 Fax. (01797) 252757**

Brewery founded jointly by a hop farmer and a publican, as a part-time venture in August 1993. The publican left the retail trade in April 1994 to brew full-time. Using their own yeast strain and local hops, the partners currently supply 30 free trade outlets, from Maidstone to the south coast.

Level Best   (OG 1040, ABV 4%) Light in aroma, this beer has a good, bitter taste, but is somewhat thin for its gravity.

ROYAL CLARENCE   See RCH.

ROYAL INN

Royal Inn & Horsebridge Brewery, Horsebridge, Tavistock, Devon PL19 8PJ. Tel. (01822) 870214

Fifteenth-century country pub, once a nunnery, which began brewing in 1981. After a change of hands, and a period of inactivity, the single-barrel plant recommenced production in 1984. The beers are only available at the pub. Beers: Tamar (OG 1039, ABV 3.9%), Horsebridge Best (OG 1045, ABV 4.5%), Right Royal (OG 1050, ABV 5%), Heller (OG 1060, ABV 6%).

RUDDLES

Ruddles Brewery Ltd., Langham, Oakham, Leicestershire LE15 7JD. Tel. (01572) 756911 Fax. (01572) 756116

Famous real ale brewery, founded in 1858, which lost its independence when it was taken over by Grand Metropolitan in 1986. Ruddles beers subsequently became national brands. The brewery is now in the hands of Dutch lager giants Grolsch, who purchased the business from Courage in 1992. Tours by arrangement.

Best Bitter   (OG 1037, ABV 3.7%) A medium-bodied bitter, mid-brown in colour with an aroma of sulphur, malt and hops, leading to a bitter, hoppy flavour and dry, bitter finish.

County   (OG 1050, ABV 4.9%) Hoppy bitterness, softened by malt, characterises this mid-brown, good-bodied, notably sulphurous bitter. Although it has improved of late, it is still nothing like the County of old.

RUDGATE

Rudgate Brewery Ltd., 2 Centre Park, Marston Business Park, Rudgate, Tockwith, York, N. Yorkshire YO5 8QF. Tel. (01423) 358382

Brewery founded in April 1992, which was bought by two former Bass executives in November that year. It operates from an old armoury building on Tockwith's disused airfield and now supplies 100 outlets, from Tyneside to Nottingham. Open square fermenters are used and a third vessel has recently been added to produce seasonal and special beers. Rudgate itself lies on an old

Viking road, hence the beer names. Tours by arrangement. Occasional beers: Maypole (OG 1045, ABV 4.5%), Easter Special (OG 1052, ABV 5%), Thor's Hammer (OG 1055, ABV 5.5%), Rudolf's Ruin (OG 1060, ABV 6%, Christmas).

Viking*	(OG 1039, ABV 3.8%)
Pillage Porter*	(OG 1042, ABV 4%)
Battleaxe*	(OG 1044, ABV 4.2%)

RYBURN

Ryburn Brewery, Owenshaw Mill, Old Cawsey, Sowerby Bridge, Halifax, W. Yorkshire HX6 2AJ. Tel./Fax. (01422) 835413

Brewery founded with a tiny, two-barrel plant in a former dye works in 1990. The growing popularity of the beers called for new plant early in 1993 and a move to larger premises in October 1994. Ryburn supplies a single tied house and 15 other outlets with the beers below. It also produces occasional special brews and a number of pub house beers. Tours by arrangement. Occasional beer: Porter (OG 1044, ABV 4.2%, Christmas).

Best Mild (OG 1033, ABV 3.3%) Stout-like in taste and colour, with a rich, roast malt flavour and balancing bitterness, which is reflected in the finish and aroma.

Best Bitter* (OG 1038, ABV 3.8%)

Rydale Bitter (OG 1044, ABV 4.2%) Mid-brown in colour with little aroma. A smooth, malty bitter with hop character and bitterness, plus some fruit notes. Long, malty and bitter finish.

Old Stone Troff Bitter* (OG 1047, ABV 4.7%)

Luddite* (OG 1048, ABV 5%) A dark beer.

Stabbers Bitter (OG 1052, ABV 5.2%) A malty aroma leads to a rich maltiness in the mouth, with bittersweet, fruity elements. Malty and bitter finish. A mid-brown, powerful strong ale.

Coiners* (OG 1060, ABV 6%)

ST AUSTELL

St Austell Brewery Co. Ltd., 63 Trevarthian Road, St Austell, Cornwall PL25 4BY. Tel. (01726) 74444 Fax. (01726) 68965

Brewing company set up in 1851 by maltster and wine merchant Walter Hicks. It moved to the present site in 1893 and remains a family business, with many of Hicks's descendants employed in the company. It owns 140 pubs, spread right across Cornwall. Most of these serve traditional ale, and some 1,500 other outlets are also supplied. Shop open 9–5. There is also a visitors' centre (tours by arrangement).

Bosun's Bitter (OG 1034, ABV 3.4%) A refreshing session beer, sweetish in aroma and bittersweet in flavour. Lingering, hoppy finish.

XXXX Mild (OG 1037, ABV 3.6%) Little aroma, but a strong, malty character. A caramel-sweetish flavour is followed by a good, lingering aftertaste which is sweet, but with a fruity dryness. Very drinkable.

Tinners Ale (OG 1038, ABV 3.7%) A deservedly popular, golden beer with an appetising malt aroma and a good balance of malt and hops in the flavour. Lasting finish.

Hicks Special Draught or HSD (OG 1050, ABV 5%) An aromatic, fruity, hoppy bitter which is initially sweet and has an aftertaste of pronounced bitterness, but whose flavour is fully-rounded. A good premium beer.

Winter Warmer (OG 1060, ABV 6%) A red/brown winter beer, available November–February: full-bodied with a pronounced malty aroma which leads into a palate featuring strong malt and hop flavours. Worth seeking out.

SCOTT'S

 Scott's Brewing Company, Crown Street East, Lowestoft, Suffolk NH32 1SH. Tel. (01502) 537237

Brewery founded in 1988, in the former stables at the rear of the Crown Hotel, the site of a brewery owned by William French 400 years ago. It supplies real ales to five pubs owned by its parent company (Scott's Inns) and a further tied house, plus 70 local free trade outlets. Centenary Ale (ABV 4.2%) is brewed for the Eaton Cottage pub in Norwich. Tours by arrangement. Occasional beers: Festival Staggers (ABV 7%), Santa's Quaff (ABV 7%).

Golden Best Bitter (OG 1033, ABV 3.4%) A golden beer which is not at all strong tasting. The flavour is a reasonable balance of malt and (pungent) hop and the latter dominates the aftertaste.

Blues and Bloater (OG 1036, ABV 3.7%) This pleasant, malty, fruity beer has some bitterness in the aftertaste. More of a light mild than a bitter.

Mild* (OG 1044, ABV 4.4%) A dark, full-bodied mild/porter.

William French (OG 1052, ABV 5%) A full and beautifully-balanced beer. A faint, malty aroma leads into strong malt and hop flavours, with considerable fruitiness. Full and balanced aftertaste, too.

Dark Oast (OG 1054, ABV 5%) Red/brown in colour, with less body than its gravity would suggest. The taste has roast malt as its main characteristic, with hoppiness prominent in the aftertaste.

SCOTTISH & See Nationals.
NEWCASTLE

SELBY **Selby (Middlebrough) Brewery Ltd., 131 Millgate, Selby, N. Yorkshire YO8 0LL. Tel. (01757) 702826**

Old family brewery which resumed brewing in 1972 after a gap of 18 years and is now mostly involved in wholesaling. Its single real ale is brewed once a year in November and is available, while stocks last, primarily through its Brewery Tap off-licence in Selby (open 10–2, 6–10, Mon–Sat), and not at the company's single pub. Beer: Old Tom (OG 1065, ABV 6.5%).

SHACKLEFORD See Cyder House Inn.

SHARDLOW **Shardlow Brewery Ltd., British Waterways Yard, Cavendish Bridge, Leicestershire DE72 2HL. Tel. (01332) 799188**

shardlow

This new brewery opened in October 1993 in the old kiln house of the original Cavendish Bridge Brewery, which closed in the 1920s. It stands on the River Trent, opposite Shardlow Marina, and currently supplies 50 free trade outlets. Wide-Eyed and Crownless (OG 1044, ABV 4.4%) is brewed exclusively for the Old Crown at Cavendish Bridge.

Session* (OG 1036, ABV 3.6%) A summer brew.

Bitter* (OG 1042, ABV 4.2%)

Cavendish 47 (OG 1047, ABV 4.7%)
Bridge*

Sleighed* (OG 1057, ABV 5.7%) A winter brew, available October–March.

SHARP'S **Sharp's Brewery, Pityme Industrial Estate, Rock, Wadebridge, Cornwall PL27 6NU. Tel. (01208) 862121 Fax. (01208) 863727**

Brewery established in an industrial unit in summer 1994 by silversmith Bill Sharp. It is now working to full capacity, supplying free houses throughout Cornwall and hoping for sales further afield via agents. Tours by arrangement.

Cornish Coaster* (OG 1037, ABV 3.6%)

Doom Bar Bitter* (OG 1042, ABV 4%)

The Independents

Own*	(OG 1044, ABV 4.4%)

SHEPHERD NEAME

Shepherd Neame Ltd., 17 Court Street, Faversham, Kent ME13 7AX. Tel. (01795) 532206 Fax. (01795) 538907

Shepherd Neame is believed to be the oldest continuous brewer in the land (since 1698), but records show brewing commenced as far back as the 12th century, and the same water source is still used. Steam engines have been brought back into use and the mash is produced in two teak tuns which date from 1910. A visitors' reception centre is housed in a restored medieval hall (tours by arrangement). Its tied estate of some 370-plus pubs are mostly in Kent, with a few in Surrey, Sussex, Essex and London. All sell cask ale, but tenants are encouraged to keep beers under blanket pressure if the cask is likely to be on sale for more than three days. Over 1,000 other outlets are supplied directly by the brewery, while Spitfire and Bishops Finger are available nationwide via wholesalers. Charrington IPA is brewed for Bass. Shop open 8.30–4. Bottle-conditioned beer: Spitfire ⊕ (OG 1043, ABV 4.7%).

Master Brew Bitter — (OG 1034, ABV 3.7%) A very distinctive bitter, mid-brown in colour, with a very hoppy aroma. Well-balanced with a nicely aggressive bitter taste from its hops, leaving a hoppy/bitter finish, tinged with sweetness.

Best Bitter — (OG 1038, ABV 4.1%) Mid-brown, with less marked characteristics than the bitter. However, the nose is very well-balanced and the taste enjoys a malty, bitter smokiness. A malty, well-rounded finish.

Spitfire Ale* — (OG 1043, ABV 4.7%) A commemorative brew (Battle of Britain) for the RAF Benevolent Fund's appeal, now a permanent feature.

Bishops Finger* — (OG 1049, ABV 5.2%) A well-known bottled beer, introduced in cask-conditioned form in 1989.

Original Porter — (OG 1049, ABV 5.2%) Rich, black, full-bodied, winter brew. The good malt and roast malt aroma also has a fine fruit edge. The complex blend of flavours is dominated by roast malt, which is also present in a very dry aftertaste.

For Bass:

Charrington IPA — (OG 1036, ABV 3.4%) Well-balanced pale brown bitter with a hoppy bitterness in the finish. Improved by its move to Faversham.

SHIP & PLOUGH — See Blewitts.

SHIPSTONE'S — See Nationals, Carlsberg-Tetley, and Pub Groups, Greenalls.

SKINNER'S

SKINNER'S OF BRIGHTON

Skinner's Ales, The Evening Star, 55–56 Surrey Street, Brighton, E. Sussex BN1 3PB. Tel. (01273) 328931

Brewing started in December 1994 in the cellar of the Evening Star with a tiny plant designed by Rob Jones, formerly of Pitfield Brewery. The beers are supplied to Peter Skinner's two pubs (the other being the Gardener's Arms in Lewes) which also take most of Rob's own Dark Star beers, also brewed at the Evening Star. Beers: Ale Trail Roast Mild (OG 1035, ABV 3.5%, mostly brewed in spring), Pale Ale (OG 1037, ABV 3.7%), 42 (OG 1042, ABV 4.2%), Old Ale (OG 1042, ABV 4.2%, winter), Penguin Stout (OG 1042, ABV 4.2%), Old Familiar (OG 1050, ABV 5%), Summer Haze (OG 1050, ABV 5%, a summer wheat beer), Cliffe Hanger Porter (OG 1055, ABV 5.5%), Pavilion Beast (OG 1060, ABV 6%).

For Dark Star:

Dark Star* — (OG 1050, ABV 5%) Also supplied to the London Beer Company – tel. (0171) 739 3701.

Meltdown* (OG 1060, ABV 6%) An occasional ginger beer.

SLATERS See Eccleshall.

SMILES **Smiles Brewing Co. Ltd., Colston Yard, Colston Street, Bristol, Avon BS1 5BD. Tel. (0117) 9297350 Fax. (0117) 9258235**

Brewery established in 1977 to supply a local restaurant, which began full-scale brewing early in 1978. In 1991 it came under the ownership of Ian Williams, via a management buyout, and he has since increased the tied estate to 14 houses, all selling real ale. Noted for its quality ales and good pubs (winners of CAMRA's *Pub Design* awards), the brewery also supplies over 200 other outlets. Tours by arrangement.

Bitter (OG 1036, ABV 3.7%) A golden/amber, lightly malted beer. Its slightly sweet, fruit palate is followed by a pleasant, bitter, dry finish. Light, fruity nose.

Best Bitter (OG 1040, ABV 4.1%) A mid-brown, fruity beer with some malt and hops in both nose and taste, plus a slight blackcurrant sweetness. A well-rounded bitter, with a brief, but dry finish.

Bristol Stout (OG 1046, ABV 4.7%) A dark, red/brown stout with a roast malt and coffee aroma. The predominantly rich roast malt taste features some hops and fruit. Roast, bitter, dry finish. Available September – March.

Exhibition Bitter (OG 1051, ABV 5.2%) A dark copper-brown ale with a pronounced malt, hop and fruit taste, turning to a dry, roast malt and bitter finish.

JOHN SMITH'S See Nationals, Courage.

SAMUEL SMITH **Samuel Smith Old Brewery (Tadcaster), High Street, Tadcaster, N. Yorkshire LS24 9SB. Tel. (01937) 832225 Fax. (01937) 834673**

Small company operating from the oldest brewery in Yorkshire, dating from 1758 and once owned by John Smith. Although John Smith's is now Courage-owned, 'Sam's' remains family-owned and firmly independent. Beers are brewed from well water without the use of any adjuncts and all cask beer is fermented in Yorkshire stone squares and racked into wooden casks provided by the brewery's own cooperage. Real ale is served in the majority of its 200-plus tied houses, although some of the 27 London pubs no longer sell cask beer, switching instead to nitrokeg Sovereign Bitter. Tours by arrangement.

Old Brewery Bitter (OBB) (OG 1040, ABV 4%) Malt dominates the nose, the taste and aftertaste, although this is underscored at all stages by a gentle hoppiness. A 'big' beer with loads of flavour, complemented by an attractive amber colour.

Museum Ale (OG 1049, ABV 5%) Even though this rich, sweet beer may be mentioned in some pub entries, it was sadly phased out by the brewery from August 1995.

SNOWDONIA **Snowdonia Brewing Co. Ltd., Gellilydan, Gwynedd.**

Brewery closed.

SOLSTICE See Marches.

The pub sign indicates breweries which are also brew pubs, i.e. produce beer in part of a pub or in its grounds.

The Independents

SOLVA	The Solva Brewing Co. Ltd., Panteg, Solva, Haverfordwest, Dyfed SA62 6TL. Tel. (01437) 720350

Brewery in operation since late 1993. The beers are available in about a dozen other outlets, mainly in summer, as well as in The Ship, home of the brewery. Beers: Ramsay Bitter (OG 1041, ABV 4.1%), Bishops & Clerks (OG 1050, ABV 5%).

SOUTH YORKSHIRE

South Yorkshire Brewing Co., Elsecar Brewery, Wath Road, Elsecar, Barnsley, S. Yorkshire S74 8HJ. Tel. (01226) 741010

Commissioned in March 1994, this brewery uses the old yeast culture from the long-closed Oakwell Brewery in Barnsley. New fermenting and conditioning vessels have increased capacity to 100 barrels a week and free trade has grown to more than 100 outlets. Tours by arrangement.

Barnsley Bitter (OG 1037, ABV 3.8%) A well-rounded, smooth, ruby/mid-brown-coloured beer. There is little aroma, but an even-balanced taste of malt and hops compensates, followed by a distinctive bitter aftertaste. Rapidly gaining recognition.

Black Heart Stout* (ABV 4.6%) Launched on St Patrick's Day 1995.

SPIKES

Spikes Brewery, The Wine Vaults, 43–47 Albert Road, Southsea, Portsmouth, Hampshire PO5 2SF. Tel. (01705) 864712

Brewery installed above the Wine Vault pub in November 1994. There are plans to move to a different site in order to supply a wider market beyond this one pub. Tours by arrangement. Beers: Impaled Ale (ABV 3.6%), Porter (ABV 4%), Stinger (ABV 4.5%).

SPRINGHEAD

Springhead Brewery, Unit 3, Sutton Workshops, Old Great North Road, Sutton on Trent, Nottinghamshire NG23 6QS. Tel./Fax. (01636) 821000

Springhead started in 1990 as the smallest brewery in the country, but was forced to move to larger premises in 1994 to expand the plant. Some 100 outlets are now supplied. Brewery visits are very popular (by arrangement).

Bitter (OG 1040, ABV 4%) Clean, pale brown bitter. Hop predominates in the nose and taste, giving the beer a bitterness which is tempered by malt coming through in the taste and aftertaste.

The Leveller (OG 1048, ABV 4.8%) Darkish brown; a very complex beer. Roast malt and malt combine to produce an almost coffee-like aroma and taste. However, hops appear to give a bitter finish to the beer.

Roaring Meg (OG 1052, ABV 5.5%) Almost Belgian in style; a splendid bottom-fermented blonde beer. An intense hop and citrus (mainly orange) nose gives an indication of tastes to come. Lingering dry finish. Very drinkable.

Cromwell's Hat* (OG 1058, ABV 6%) A new beer using juniper berries in the recipe.

STAG

Abel Brown's Brewery, The Stag, 35 Brook Street, Stotfold, Bedfordshire SG5 4LA Tel. (01462) 730261

Pub which began brewing in spring 1995, using the name of its first publican, Abel Brown, on its pump clips. The beers are named after the village's famous traction engines. Beers: Jack of Hearts (OG 1040 ABV 4%), Lord Douglas Dark Mild (OG 1040, ABV 4%).

STANWAY

Stanway Brewery, Stanway, Cheltenham, Gloucestershire GL54 5PQ. Tel. (01386) 584320

Small brewery founded in March 1993 with a five-barrel plant, which confines its sales to the Cotswolds area (25 outlets). Occasional beer: Old Eccentric (OG 1052, ABV 5.5%).

Stanney Bitter (OG 1042, ABV 4.5%) Light, refreshing, amber-coloured beer, dominated by hops in the aroma, with a bitter taste and a hoppy, bitter finish.

STAR & TIPSY TOAD	See Tipsy Toad.

STEAM PACKET

 The Steam Packet Brewery, The Bendles, Racca Green, Knottingley, W. Yorkshire WF11 8AT.
Tel./Fax. (01977) 674176

Brewery which began producing beers for the Steam Packet pub in November 1990, but which has expanded to supply 50 outlets regularly (and more on an occasional basis), mainly in the North-West. New brews are regularly added.

Summer Lite* (OG 1030, ABV 3.5%) Summer only.

Mellor's Gamekeeper Bitter (OG 1036, ABV 3.6%) A malty brew, with a dry, malty initial taste, but sometimes a very weak aftertaste. Light brown in colour.

Chatterley (OG 1038, ABV 3.7%) A wheat malt brew, with a light golden colour and a quite fruity, hoppy taste. A session beer with a lemon aftertaste.

Foxy (OG 1039, ABV 3.9%) A new, russet-coloured beer brewed with a small amount of wheat malt. The very well-balanced malt and hop flavour is also fruity, with a slight lemon flavour in the aftertaste.

Bit o Black (OG 1040, ABV 4%) A dark, malty brew with a well-balanced taste and a lightly vinous nose and aftertaste. Like a good, dark strong mild.

Brown Ale* (OG 1045, ABV 4.5%)

Packet Porter* (OG 1045, ABV 4.5%)

Bargee (OG 1048, ABV 4.8%) A splendid Belgian-style beer of a slightly darker colour than Foxy. A very malty initial flavour bursts into a fruity aftertaste.

Poacher's Swag (OG 1050, ABV 5%) A mid-brown beer with a full, sweetish, malty mouthfeel. However, it is let down by the aroma and a dominant, lingering astringency.

Giddy Ass (OG 1080, ABV 8%) A beer with a winey taste and no hint of sweetness. Dangerously drinkable.

STOCKS

Stocks Brewery, Cooplands (Doncaster) Ltd., The Hall-cross, 33–34 Hallgate, Doncaster, S. Yorkshire DN1 3NL.
Tel. (01302) 328213 Fax. (01302) 329776

Brewery founded in December 1981 in a former baker's shop behind the Hallcross pub, which was its sole outlet. The company has slowly grown and now has two further tied houses and a free trade of some 20 outlets, including some Tap & Spile pubs. Off-sales are available from the Hallcross (during pub hours). Tours by arrangement.

Best Bitter (OG 1037, ABV 3.9%) A thin session beer, with malty overtones and little else. Dry, but weak in the aftertaste.

Select (OG 1044, ABV 4.7%) A tawny-coloured drink with little aroma. Malt dominates, with a short, bittersweet finish.

Golden Wheat* (OG 1044, ABV 4.7%) A new wheat beer available in summer.

St Leger Porter (OG 1050, ABV 5.1%) Black with ruby hues, this beer is thin for its gravity. A nutty and malty aroma develops into a malty taste and then a weak roast malt finish. Winter only.

Old Horizontal (OG 1054, ABV 5.4%) This used to be the pride of the pack, but even this is now a thin, bland-tasting beer. However, roasted malt can be detected in the aroma and taste of this dark brown ale, which has a dry, malty aftertaste.

STONES	See Nationals, Bass.

STRONG	See Morrells and Nationals, Whitbread.

The Independents

SUMMERSKILLS

Summerskills Brewery, Unit 15, Pomphlett Farm Industrial Estate, Broxton Drive, Billacombe, Plymouth, Devon PL9 7BG. Tel. (01752) 481283

Summerskills was initially set up in 1983 in a vineyard, but was only operational for two years. It was relaunched by new owners in 1990, with plant from the old Penrhos brewery, and production has grown at a steady rate. It currently supplies its award-winning beers to around 35 free trade outlets directly, and others nationally via wholesalers. The brewery logo comes from the ship's crest of *HMS Bigbury Bay*. Tours by arrangement.

Best Bitter
(OG 1042, ABV 4.3%) A mid-brown beer, with plenty of malt and hops through the aroma, taste and finish. A good session beer.

Whistle Belly Vengeance
(OG 1046, ABV 4.7%) Red/brown beer with a beautiful malt and fruit taste and a pleasant, malty aftertaste.

Ninjabeer
(OG 1049, ABV 5%) A dark gold beer, with a strong, fruity aroma and a predominantly fruity taste and aftertaste. Very drinkable. Brewed October–April.

Indiana's Bones
(OG 1056, ABV 5.6%) Mid-brown beer with a good balance of fruit and malt in the aroma and taste, and a sweet, malty finish.

SUTTON

Sutton Brewing Company, 31 Commercial Road, Coxside, Plymouth, Devon PL4 0LE. Tel. (01752) 255335 Fax. (01752) 672235

This brewery was built alongside the Thistle Park Tavern, near Plymouth's Sutton Harbour, in 1993. It went into production the following year to supply that pub and the free trade. Such was the demand (currently 30 outlets) that additional fermenters and a redesign of the plant were quickly needed. Occasional celebration ales are produced. Tours by arrangement.

Plymouth Pride
(OG 1039, ABV 3.8%) A pale brown beer, with a malty, hoppy aroma and taste and a bitter finish.

XSB
(OG 1042, ABV 4.2%) A pale brown beer with a hoppy, fruity taste and a bitter finish.

Gold*
(ABV 4.4%)

Old Pedantic*
(ABV 4.9%) An old ale.

Weetablitz*
(ABV 5%) A new wheat beer.

Eddystone Light*
(OG 1052, ABV 5%)

Knickadroppa Glory*
(ABV 5.4%)

Plymouth Porter
(OG 1055, ABV 5.5%) A winter brew, dark brown in colour with a distinct roast malt aroma, taste and finish.

TALLY HO

Tally Ho Country Inn and Brewery, 14 Market Street, Hatherleigh, Devon EX20 3JN. Tel. (01837) 810306

The Tally Ho recommenced brewing at Easter 1990, reviving the tradition of the former New Inn brewery on the same site. New owners took over in December 1994. Its beers are produced from a full mash, with no additives, and, although no other pubs are supplied direct, the beer is available through an agency. Tours by arrangement. Beers: Potboiler's Brew (OG 1036, ABV 3.5%), Master Jack's Mild (OG 1040, ABV 3.5%, summer), Tarka's Tipple (OG 1042, ABV 4%), Nutters Ale (OG 1048, ABV 4.6%), Thurgia (OG 1056, ABV 5.7%), Janni Jollop (OG 1066, ABV 6.6%, winter). Bottle-conditioned beers: Tarka's Tipple (OG 1048, ABV 4.6%), Thurgia (OG 1056, ABV 5.7%), Creber (ABV 6%).

TAYLOR

Timothy Taylor & Co. Ltd., Knowle Spring Brewery, Keighley, W. Yorkshire BD21 1AW. Tel. (01535) 603139 Fax. (01535) 691167

Timothy Taylor began brewing in Keighley in 1858 and moved to the site of the Knowle Spring in 1863. The business was continued by his sons and remains an independent family-owned company to this day. Its prize-winning ales are served in all 29 of the brewery's pubs as well as a wide free trade.

Golden Best	(OG 1033, ABV 3.5%) A soft and smooth, slightly sweet, malty taste follows a light malt and hop aroma. There is a hint of bitterness in the delicate and short finish. Golden colour, tinged with amber.
Dark Mild	(OG 1034, ABV 3.5%) A dark brown beer with red hints. Caramel conceals the Golden Best it is based on until the finish, which sometimes has a resinous or dry edge.
Best Bitter	(OG 1037, ABV 4%) A fine bitter which has not yet regained its form of a few years ago but which remains a good drink. The nose combines flowers, fruit and malt but the big taste is one of dry bitterness. The finish is usually short.
Porter	(OG 1041, ABV 3.8%) Roast malt and caramel dominate the whole drink until the aftertaste, when sweetness wins through. In an age of new, true porters, this brew looks lost. Perhaps that is why it is increasingly difficult to find.
Landlord	(OG 1042, ABV 4.3%) The nose dominates this drink, with lots of hops and a hint of malt. The taste is weak in comparison, having lost the complex multi-layering of previous years which has been replaced by malt tinged with a hoppy bitterness. *Champion Beer of Britain* 1994.
Ram Tam (XXXX)	(OG 1043, ABV 4.3%) Rather than smothering other characteristics, the caramel in this brew now adds to both the body and depth, and allows the dry hop bitterness and fruity aftertaste to emerge from under a relatively gentle sweetness.

TAYLOR WALKER	See Nationals, Carlsberg-Tetley.

TEIGNWORTHY	**Teignworthy Brewery, The Maltings, Teign Road, Newton Abbot, Devon TQ12 4AA. Tel. (01626) 332066**

Brewery founded in June 1994 with a 15-barrel plant by former Oakhill and Ringwood brewer John Lawton, using part of the historic Victorian malthouse of Edward Tucker & Sons. About 50 other outlets take the beer. Bottle-conditioned beer: Reel Ale (OG 1039, ABV 4%).

Reel Ale*	(OG 1039, ABV 4%)
Spring Tide*	(OG 1043, ABV 4.3%)
Beachcomber*	(OG 1045, ABV 4.5%)

TENNENT CALEDONIAN	See Nationals, Bass.

JOSHUA TETLEY	See Nationals, Carlsberg-Tetley.

THEAKSTON	See Nationals, Scottish & Newcastle.

THOMPSON'S	**Thompson's Brewery, 11 West Street, Ashburton, Devon TQ13 7BD. Tel. (01392) 467797 Fax. (01392) 464760**

Brewery which began operation in 1981 by brewing for its own pub, the London Inn in Ashburton. Around 50 other outlets also take the beer. Tours by arrangement.

Lunchtime Bitter*	(OG 1035, ABV 3.4%)
Best Bitter	(OG 1040, ABV 4.1%) A pale brown beer with a hoppy aroma and taste. Bitter finish.
Black Velvet Stout*	(OG 1040, ABV 4.2%)
IPA	(OG 1044, ABV 4.4%) A mid-brown-coloured ale with a distinct hoppy aroma and a bitter taste and finish.
Figurehead	(OG 1050, ABV 5.1%) A dark brown, full-bodied winter beer with a malty nose and a roasty, bitter taste and finish.

The Independents

Man 'O' War	(OG 1050, ABV 5.1%) A golden, summer beer with a fruity sweet taste and aftertaste.
Celebration Porter*	(OG 1059, ABV 6%)

THREE FYSHES INN   See Nix Wincott.

THREE TUNS **The Three Tuns Brewery, Salop Street, Bishop's Castle, Shropshire SY9 5BW. Tel. (01588) 638797**

Historic brew pub which first obtained a brewing licence in 1642. The tower brewery was built in 1888 and is still in use, serving some other outlets in addition to the pub. Beers: Mild (OG 1035, ABV 3.5%), XXX Bitter (OG 1042, ABV 4.3%), XXX Stout (ABV 4.3%), Jim Wood's Porter (OG 1058, ABV 5.8%), Old Scrooge (ABV 5.5%, Christmas).

THWAITES **Daniel Thwaites PLC, PO Box 50, Star Brewery, Blackburn, Lancashire BB1 5BU. Tel. (01254) 54431 Fax. (01254) 681439**

Lancashire brewery, founded by excise officer Daniel Thwaites in 1807 and now run by his great-great grandson. It still uses shire horse drays and nearly all its 424 pubs serve real ale. A substantial free trade is also supplied. Tours by arrangement. A new range of monthly beers, known as the Connoisseur Cask Ale Collection, has been introduced in the last year: White Oak Bitter (OG 1038, ABV 3.8%), Snigbrook Ale (OG 1040, ABV 4%), Scallywag (OG 1043, ABV 4.5%), Thunderbolt (OG 1043, ABV 4.5%), Town Crier (OG 1045, ABV 4.5%), Fawkes Folly Porter (OG 1046, ABV 4.8%), Daniel's Hammer (OG 1048, ABV 5.2%), Big Ben (OG 1050, ABV 5%), Old Dan (OG 1065, ABV 6.5%).

Best Mild	(OG 1034, ABV 3.3%) A rich, dark mild presenting a smooth, malty flavour and a pleasant, slightly bitter finish.
Bitter	(OG 1036, ABV 3.6%) A gently-flavoured, clean-tasting bitter. Malt and hops lead into a full, lingering, bitter finish.
Craftsman*	(OG 1042, ABV 4.5%) A hoppy, golden premium ale.

TIPSY TOAD **The Tipsy Toad Brewery, St Peter, Jersey JE3 7AA. Tel. (01534) 485556 Fax. (01534) 485559; The Tipsy Toad Townhouse and Brewery, 57–59 New Street, St Helier, Jersey JE2 3RB. Tel. (01534) 615002 Fax. (01534) 615003**

Following refurbishment of the Star pub, brewing began on the St Peter premises in spring 1992. Two other outlets are now supplied on a regular basis with the full mash brews. Tours by arrangement. Beers: Cyril's Bitter (OG 1036, ABV 3.7%), Jimmy's Bitter (OG 1040, ABV 4%), Black Tadger (OG 1045, ABV 4.4%, a porter), Horny Toad (OG 1050, ABV 5%), Star Drooper (OG 1060, ABV 6%, winter). The brewery opened a second brew pub-cum-real ale shop, The Tipsy Toad Townhouse and Brewery, in St Helier in 1994 and this brews Cyril's Bitter (OG 1036, ABV 3.7%).

TISBURY **Tisbury Brewery Ltd., Church Street, Tisbury, Wiltshire SP3 6NH. Tel. (01747) 870986 Fax. (01747) 871540**

Housed in the old Wiltshire Brewery buildings, Tisbury began production in April 1995, providing beer for free trade outlets within a 50-mile radius as well as wholesalers.

Best Bitter*	(OG 1040, ABV 3.8%)
Archibald Beckett*	(OG 1046, ABV 4.3%)
Old Wardour*	(OG 1048, ABV 4.8%)

TITANIC

Titanic Brewery, Unit G, Harvey Works, Lingard Street, Burslem, Stoke-on-Trent, Staffordshire ST6 1ED. Tel. (01782) 823447 Fax. (01782) 812349

This brewery, named in honour of the Titanic's Captain Smith, who hailed from Stoke, was founded in 1985 but fell into difficulties until rescued by the present owners. A move to larger premises took place in 1992, and the brewery now supplies over 100 free trade outlets, as well as two pubs of its own (which also sell other Independents' guest beers). New brewing plant is being installed. Tours by arrangement. Occasional beer: Anniversary Ale (OG 1050, ABV 4.8%, April). Bottle-conditioned beers: Stout (OG 1046, ABV 4.5%), Christmas Ale (OG 1080, ABV 7.8%).

Best Bitter

(OG 1036, ABV 3.5%) A refreshing, clean-drinking bitter with balanced fruit, malt and hops.

Lifeboat Ale

(OG 1040, ABV 3.9%) A fruity and malty, dark red/brown beer, with a dry and fruity finish.

Premium Bitter

(OG 1042, ABV 4.1%) An impressive, well-balanced pale brown bitter with a fruity and hoppy taste. The flavour has been more consistent since a change of hops.

Stout

(OG 1046, ABV 4.5%) A dark combination of malt and roast with some hops. Strongly flavoured and well-balanced.

Captain Smith's Strong Ale

(OG 1050, ABV 4.8%) A red/brown, full-bodied beer, hoppy and bitter with a malty sweetness and roast malt flavour, and a good finish.

Wreckage

(OG 1080, ABV 7.8%) A dark winter brew, full-flavoured with a rich bittersweet finish.

TOLLY COBBOLD

Tollemache & Cobbold Brewery Ltd., Cliff Road, Ipswich, Suffolk IP3 0AZ. Tel. (01473) 231723 Fax. (01473) 280045

One of the oldest breweries in the country, founded by Thomas Cobbold in 1723 at Harwich. Tolly moved to Ipswich in 1746 and celebrates 250 years in the town in 1996. In 1989, Brent Walker took over the company, closed the Cliff Brewery and transferred production to Camerons in Hartlepool. However, a management buy-out saved the day and Tolly Cobbold Ipswich-brewed ales were back on sale in September 1990. The new company acquired no pubs from Brent Walker, but secured a long-term trading agreement with Pubmaster (the company which runs former Brent Walker pubs), supplying a total of 550 outlets. It opened a brewery tap, the only tied house, in 1992. Tours (daily) by arrangement. Brewery shop open lunchtimes in the tourist season.

Mild

(OG 1032, ABV 3.2%) A tasty mild with fruit, malt and roast malt characters. Pleasing aftertaste. It tends to lose complexity when forced through a sparkler.

Bitter

(OG 1035, ABV 3.5%) A light, mid-brown-coloured malty beer lacking bitterness.

Original Best Bitter

(OG 1038, ABV 3.8%) A slightly stronger bitter with assertive hop character throughout. The finish is bitter, but with a good balancing maltiness. Disappointingly hard to find.

IPA*

(OG 1045, ABV 4.2%) A best bitter, full of citrus fruit flavours and flowery hoppiness.

Old Strong Winter Ale

(OG 1048, ABV 5%) Available November–February. A dark winter ale with plenty of roast character throughout. Lingering and complex aftertaste.

Tollyshooter

(OG 1052, ABV 5%) A reddish premium bitter with a full, fruity flavour and a long, bittersweet aftertaste. Good hop character, too. Named after the Sir John Harvey-Jones TV series, *Troubleshooter*, in which Tolly featured.

The Independents

TOMINTOUL	**Tomintoul Brewery Co. Ltd., Mill of Auchriachan, Tomintoul, Ballindalloch, Grampian AB37 9EQ. Tel. (01807) 580333 Fax. (01807) 580358**

Brewery opened in November 1993 in an old watermill, in an area better known for malt whisky and snow-blocked roads. Around a dozen outlets are currently supplied. Tours by arrangement. Occasional beers: 80/- (ABV 4.2%), Ginger Tom (OG 1044, ABV 4.5%).

Caillie*	(OG 1036, ABV 3.6%)
Stag*	(OG 1039.5, ABV 4.1%)
Wildcat*	(OG 1049.5, ABV 5.1%)

TOMLINSON'S

Tomlinson's Old Castle Brewery, Unit 5, Britannia Works, Skinner Lane, Pontefract, W. Yorkshire WF8 1HU. Tel. (01977) 780866

Marking a return to brewing in Pontefract after over 60 years, Tomlinson's was built in 1993 and is run by a former pipe fitter and fabricator. The award-winning brews take their names from various local historical connections. Some 40 outlets are now supplied. Tours by arrangement. Occasional beers: Hermitage Mild (OG 1036, ABV 3.7%), Down With It! (OG 1042, ABV 4.3%), Femme Fatale (OG 1043, ABV 4.5%), Fractus XB (OG 1045, ABV 4.5%).

Sessions	(OG 1038, ABV 4%) A dry, well-hopped bitter with a faint, smoky aroma and a little fruitiness in the taste and aftertaste.
De Lacy	(OG 1044, ABV 4.6%) A pleasant, amber, very dry beer with a well-hopped taste and a slight fruitiness. Hops persist from the aroma through to the finish. Coffee also comes through in the taste and finish.
Deceitful Rose	(OG 1048, ABV 5%) Superbly dry, straw-coloured beer with a long, bitter aftertaste and some lingering hop character. Very reminiscent of an old-style IPA.
Richard's Defeat	(OG 1050, ABV 5%) A black, full-bodied, smooth and sweetish porter for winter, with strong roast malt character and a bitter finish.
Three Sieges*	(OG 1058, ABV 6%) A liquorice beer, brewed in winter.

TOWNES

Townes Brewery, Bay 9, Suon Buildings, Lockoford Lane, Chesterfield, Derbyshire S41 7JJ. Tel. (01246) 277994

Brewery established in an old bakery in May 1994 by photographer Alan Wood, bringing brewing back to Chesterfield after nearly 40 years. Now some 40 outlets are supplied and there are plans to increase brewing capacity. A series of six, monthly 'Spirite' beers (all at 5% ABV) has also been produced.

Muffin Ale*	(OG 1035, ABV 3.5%) Full-bodied, red/brown ale with a smooth, chocolatey flavour which belies its relatively low alcohol content. Easy to drink.
Sunshine*	(OG 1036, ABV 3.6%) A very pale, spicy summer beer, with a full finish.
Best Lockoford Bitter*	(OG 1040, ABV 4%) A golden, satisfying session bitter, with plenty of hop character throughout.
IPA*	(OG 1045, ABV 4.5%) A refreshing, medium-bodied pale ale with a prominent hop character and a fruity aroma.
Pynot Porter*	(OG 1045, ABV 4.5%) A very dark, rich and mellow winter brew, with hints of roast malt, chocolate and fruit. The finish is dry and satisfying.
Double Bagger*	(OG 1050, ABV 5%) A full-bodied beer with an aroma of fruit and malt, leading to a well-balanced taste and finish.

The Independents

TRAQUAIR

Traquair House Brewery, Innerleithen, Peeblesshire, Borders EH44 6PW. Tel. (01896) 830323 Fax. (01896) 830639

This 18th-century brewhouse is situated in one of the wings of Traquair House (over 1,000 years old) and was rediscovered by the 20th Laird, Peter Maxwell Stuart, in 1965. He began brewing again using all the original equipment (which remained intact, despite having lain idle for over 100 years). The brewery passed to Catherine Maxwell Stuart in 1990. All the beers are oak-fermented and 60% of production is exported (mostly bottled Traquair House Ale). Tours by arrangement, April–September. Shop open daily Easter–end of September.

Bear Ale*	(OG 1050, ABV 5%)
Fair Ale*	(OG 1055, ABV 6%)
Traquair House Ale*	(OG 1070, ABV 7.2%)
Jacobite Ale*	(OG 1080, ABV 8%)

TRING

Tring Brewery Company Ltd., 81–82 Akeman Street, Tring, Hertfordshire HP23 6AF. Tel. (01442) 890721 Fax. (01442) 890740

Established in December 1992, bringing brewing back to this Hertfordshire town after almost 60 years, Tring now supplies around 100 outlets. Tours by arrangement. Occasional beer: Death or Glory Ale (OG 1070, ABV 7.2%, brewed October 25 to commemorate the Charge of the Light Brigade in 1854 and sold in December). Bottle-conditioned beer: Death or Glory Ale (OG 1070, ABV 7.2%).

Finest Summer Ale*	(OG 1037, ABV 3.7%) Available June–September.
The Ridgeway Bitter	(OG 1039, ABV 4%) A beer with a pleasant mix of hop and malt flavours in the aroma and taste, leading to a dry, often flowery hop, aftertaste.
Old Cantankerous*	(OG 1048.5, ABV 4.8%) A winter porter.
Old Icknield Ale	(OG 1049, ABV 5%) A beer with a distinct, hoppy flavour and a dry, bitter aftertaste.

ULEY

Uley Brewery Ltd., The Old Brewery, Uley, Dursley, Gloucestershire GL11 5TB. Tel. (01453) 860120

Brewing at Uley began in 1833, but Price's Brewery, as it was then, remained inactive for most of this century. Work commenced on restoring the premises in 1984 and Uley's brewery was reborn in 1985. The brewery has no pubs of its own but now serves 50 free trade outlets in the Cotswolds area.

Bitter or Hogshead or UB40	(OG 1040, ABV 3.8%) Copper- coloured beer with malt, hops and fruit in the aroma and a malty, fruity taste, underscored by a hoppy bitterness. The finish is dry, with a balance of hops and malt.
Old Ric*	(ABV 4.5%)
Old Spot Prize Ale	(OG 1050, ABV 4.8%) A fairly full-bodied, red/brown ale with a fruity aroma, a malty, fruity taste (with a hoppy bitterness), and a strong, balanced aftertaste.
Pig's Ear Strong Beer	(OG 1050, ABV 4.8%) A pale-coloured, light beer, deceptively strong. Notably bitter in flavour, with a hoppy, fruity aroma and a bitter finish.
Pigor Mortis	(OG 1060, ABV 6%) A winter brew, another beer which belies its strength. No distinct aroma, but a sweet, smooth flavour, with hints of fruit and hops. Dry finish.

UNITED BREWERIES

See Pub Groups, Inn Business.

The Independents

USHERS

Ushers of Trowbridge PLC, Directors House, 68 Fore Street, Trowbridge, Wiltshire BA14 8JF. Tel. (01225) 763171 Fax. (01225) 753661

This famous West Country brewery was founded in 1824, but lost its identity after being swallowed up by Watney (later Grand Met) in 1960. A successful management buy-out from Courage in 1991 gave Ushers back its independence. It has since invested in pubs and plant, with over £2 million spent on the brewery. Ushers supplies real ale to nearly all its 520 houses (most tenanted and all in the South, South-West and South Wales) and also to Courage/Grand Met Inntrepreneur pubs. Keg and bottled products are brewed for Courage and one cask beer is produced for the Tap & Spile chain. Occasional beers: Summer Madness (OG 1037, ABV 3.6%), Spring Fever (OG 1040, ABV 4%), Autumn Frenzy (OG 1041, ABV 4%), 1824 Particular (OG 1063, ABV 6%, winter).

Best Bitter

(OG 1038, ABV 3.8%) An amber/pale brown, clean bitter with good malt character and tangy hops in the flavour. Refreshing, dry, bitter finish. Continually improving.

Founders Ale

(OG 1046, ABV 4.5%) A pale brown beer with a bitter hop taste, balanced by sweet maltiness and faint citrus fruit. Predominantly bitter finish.

For Tap & Spile:

Tap & Spile Premium*

(ABV 4.3%)

VALE

Vale Brewery Co., Thame Road, Haddenham, Buckinghamshire HP17 8BY. Tel. (01844) 290008 Fax. (01844) 292505

After many years working for large regional breweries and allied industries, brothers Mark and Phil Stevens combined their experience and opened a small, purpose-built brewery in Haddenham. This revived brewing in a village where the last brewery closed at the end of World War II. Around 50 local outlets now take the beers, which are brewed from premium barley and whole hops.

Wychert Ale*

(OG 1040, ABV 3.9%)

Grumpling Old Ale*

(OG 1046.5, ABV 4.6%)

VAUX

Vaux Breweries Ltd., The Brewery, Sunderland, Tyne & Wear SR1 3AN. Tel. (0191) 567 6277 Fax. (0191) 514 0422

First established in 1837 and now one of the country's largest regional brewers, Vaux remains firmly independent. It owns Wards of Sheffield, but sold off Lorimer & Clark in Edinburgh to Caledonian in 1987. Real ale is sold in over 300 of its 700 houses (which include those run by Wards and Vaux Inns Ltd.) and is also provided to 10% of its 700 free trade customers. Tours by arrangement. Vaux Extra Special (OG 1049, ABV 5%) and Waggle Dance (OG 1047, ABV 5%) are produced at Wards (qv). Vaux Mild is Wards Mild rebadged.

Lorimer's Best Scotch

(OG 1036, ABV 3.6%) A replica of the original Scottish Scotch. Aroma is often lacking, but, when fresh, there can be a subtle hop character to balance a sweet and malty taste.

Bitter

(OG 1038, ABV 3.9%) A light and drinkable bitter with low bitterness and some fruit evident. Aroma is easily lost, but can be hoppy.

Samson

(OG 1041, ABV 4.2%) A very light bitter with a grainy aftertaste, and a sulphury aroma when fresh. Bitterness is moderate and sweetness may persist in the taste.

Double Maxim

(ABV 4.7%) A smooth brown ale, rich and well-balanced, with lasting fruit and good body. The strength was increased in 1995.

VILLAGE BREWER

See Hadrian and Hambleton.

506

WADWORTH

Wadworth & Co. Ltd., Northgate Brewery, Devizes, Wiltshire SN10 1JW. Tel. (01380) 723361 Fax. (01380) 724342

Delightful market town tower brewery set up in 1885 by Henry Wadworth. Though solidly traditional (with its own dray horses), it continues to invest in the future and to expand, producing up to 2,000 barrels a week to supply a wide-ranging free trade in the South of England, as well as its own 200 tied houses. All the pubs serve real ale and 6X remains one of the South's most famous beers. Shop (reception) open in office hours. Some tours by arrangement. Occasional beers: Valentine's Ale (OG 1044, ABV 4.5% February), Easter Ale (OG 1044, ABV 4.5%), Malt & Hops (OG 1044, ABV 4.5%, September), Summersault (OG 1044, ABV 4.5%, June–July).

Henry's Original IPA

(OG 1034, ABV 3.8%) A golden brown-coloured beer with a gentle, malty and slightly hoppy aroma, a good balance of flavours, with maltiness gradually dominating, and then a long-lasting aftertaste to match, eventually becoming biscuity. A good session beer.

6X

(OG 1040, ABV 4.3%) Mid-brown in colour, with a malty and fruity nose and some balancing hop character. The flavour is similar, with some bitterness and a lingering malty, but bitter finish. Full-bodied and distinctive.

Farmer's Glory

(OG 1046, ABV 4.5%) This dark beer can be delightfully hoppy and fruity, but varies in flavour and conditioning. The aroma is of malt and it should have a dryish, hoppy aftertaste.

Old Timer

(OG 1055, ABV 5.8%) Available from October to March only: a rich, copper-brown beer with a strong, fruity, malty aroma. The flavour is full-bodied and complete, with hints of butterscotch and peaches, beautifully balanced by a lasting, malty, dry finish.

PETER WALKER

See Nationals, Carlsberg-Tetley.

WARDS

Wards Brewery, Ecclesall Road, Sheffield, S. Yorkshire S11 8HZ. Tel. (0114) 2755155 Fax. (0114) 2751816

Established in 1840 by Josiah Kirby, Wards has been a subsidiary of Vaux of Sunderland since 1972. Since the closure of the neighbouring Thorne brewery in 1986, it has also produced Darley's beers. Real ale is available in about two-thirds of the brewery's 293 tied houses and around 200 free trade outlets are supplied directly. Tours for organisations by arrangement.

Mild or Darley's Dark Mild

(OG 1034, ABV 3.4%) Also sold as Vaux Mild. This beer's rich dark brown and red hue promises more than is delivered. A strong malt nose precedes a roast malt taste, with hints of chocolate. The dry finish can be tinged with sweetness, if it lasts long enough.

Thorne Best Bitter

(OG 1037, ABV 3.8%) Although thin in character, this malty-nosed, mid-brown beer can be tasty, with some hoppiness. The finish is malty and dry.

Best Bitter

(OG 1038, ABV 4%) An unmistakable, rich malty aroma opens into a full malty taste. The body can be variable, but it has a pleasant, bittersweet, dry finish.

For Vaux:

Waggle Dance

(OG 1047, ABV 5%) A new beer brewed with honey. Gold in colour and typically malty throughout, it can also be very sweet, with a little hop bitterness and a dry aftertaste.

Extra Special Bitter*

(OG 1049, ABV 5%)

WATNEY

See Nationals, Courage.

WEBSTER'S

See Nationals, Courage.

The Independents

WEETWOOD
WEETWOOD ALES

Best Bitter

Old Dog Bitter

Weetwood Ales Ltd., Weetwood Grange, Weetwood, Tarporley, Cheshire CW6 0NQ. Tel. (01829) 752377

Brewery set up at an equestrian centre in 1993, with the first brew on sale in March of that year. Over 30 regular customers are now supplied.

(OG 1040.5, ABV 3.8%) A clean, dry and fruity bitter. Less distinctive than before.

(OG 1046.5, ABV 4.5%) A fuller-bodied version of the bitter: fruitier, with a dry, lingering aftertaste and a sulphurous nose.

WELLS

CHARLES WELLS

Eagle IPA

Bombardier Premium Bitter

Fargo Strong Ale

Charles Wells Ltd., The Eagle Brewery, Havelock Street, Bedford MK40 4LU. Tel. (01234) 272766 Fax. (01234) 279000

Successful, family-owned brewery, established in 1876 and still run by descendants of the founder. The brewery has been on this site since 1976 and now all 325 tied pubs serve cask ale, though about 50% apply cask breathers. Wells also supplies around 350 other outlets direct and owns the Ancient Druids brew pub in Cambridge (see Ancient Druids).

(OG 1035, ABV 3.6%) A good session beer that is often served too fresh. The aroma is of hops and some sulphur. Dry and hoppy on the palate, with faint fruit and malt. The long, dry finish can be faintly astringent.

(OG 1042, ABV 4.3%) A beer with a well-balanced flavour of hops, fruit and some faint malt, on a bittersweet base. The aroma is hoppy and faintly fruity; good, dry finish with some fruit.

(ABV 5%) A new beer with an old name. The good, hoppy aroma has some citrus fruit notes, the flavour is a well-balanced blend of hops, fruit and malt on a bittersweet base, and the finish is dry and faintly fruity.

WELSH BREWERS

See Nationals, Bass.

WESTBURY ALES

See Hop Back.

WEST COAST

West Coast Brewing Co. Ltd., Chorlton-on-Medlock, Gtr Manchester.
Brewery closed.

WEST HIGHLAND

West Highland Brewers, Taynuilt, Strathclyde.
Brewery closed.

WETHERED

See McMullen and Nationals, Whitbread.

WHEATSHEAF INN

See Fromes Hill.

WHEAL ALE

See Bird in Hand.

WHIM

BREWED AT HARTINGTON IN
The Derbyshire Dales

Hartington Bitter*

Magic Mushroom Mild*

Whim Ales, Whim Farm, Hartington, Buxton, Derbyshire SK17 0AX. Tel. (01298) 84702

Brewery opened in December 1993 in redundant outbuildings at Whim Farm. Around 30 outlets are currently supplied. Old Izaak is named after Dovedale's Father of Fishing, Izaak Walton. A wheat beer is sometimes brewed in summer. Occasional beer: Black Christmas (OG 1062, ABV 6.5%, a more attenuated version of Black Bear Stout). Bottle-conditioned beer: Black Bear Stout (OG 1062, ABV 6.2%).

(OG 1038, ABV 4%) Light, golden, hoppy bitter with a dry finish.

(OG 1042, ABV 3.8%) A well-balanced mild with a complex mix of flavours. Black/ruby in colour.

Special*	(OG 1045, ABV 4.7%) Full-bodied bitter. Good balance of fruit and hops; dry, crisp finish.
Old Izaak*	(OG 1052, ABV 5.2%) A dry, dark brown beer with good flavour balance. Dry, bitter finish.
Black Bear Stout*	(OG 1062, ABV 6.2%)

WHITBREAD   See Nationals.

WHITBY'S

Whitby's Own Brewery Ltd., St Hilda's, The Ropery, Whitby, N. Yorkshire YO22 4ET. Tel. (01947) 605914

Brewery opened in a former workhouse in 1988 and moved 50 yards in 1992 into newer, larger premises. Free trade (mostly as guest beers) extends from Newcastle upon Tyne to Huddersfield and takes in roughly 40 outlets, but the brewery is still looking for a first pub of its own.

Golden Pale Bitter*	(OG 1033, ABV 3.3%)
Merryman's Mild*	(OG 1036, ABV 3.5%) A dark mild.
Wallop	(OG 1038, ABV 3.6%) Formerly known as Ammonite Bitter. A light, refreshing beer, pleasant and fruity, with a hoppy aftertaste. Difficult to track down, but well worth the effort.
Nut Brown Ale*	(OG 1045, ABV 4.5%)
Wobble	(OG 1045, ABV 4.5%) A copper-red, full-bodied, malty bitter, with a burnt roast flavour and a dry, hoppy finish.
Force Nine	(OG 1055, ABV 5.5%) Strong and dark, with a well-balanced blend of contrasting flavours: sweet and fruity, dry and malty, with a strong, bitter finish. A beer of the winter ale type, excellent in its class.

WHITE

White Brewing Company, The 1066 Country Brewery, Pebsham Farm Industrial Estate, Pebsham Lane, Bexhill, E. Sussex TN40 2RZ. Tel. (01424) 731066

Brewery founded in May 1995 by husband and wife David and Lesley White to serve local free trade outlets and a wholesaler. Visits by appointment only.

1066 Country Bitter*	(OG 1040, ABV 4%)

WHITWORTH HALL

Whitworth Hall Brewery, Whitworth Lane, Spennymoor, Co. Durham DL16 7QX. Tel. (01388) 817419

A small brewery set up mainly to supply the Whitworth Hall tearoom, catering for visitors to the house and grounds. Outside sales have been limited by the brewery's lack of small casks. Occasional beer: Plum Beer (ABV 8%, Bobby Shafto further fermented with plum juice). Bottle-conditioned beer: Bobby Shafto Wheat Beer (ABV 5%).

Bonnie Bobby Shafto	(OG 1062, ABV 6%) A Belgian-styled brown ale with an unusual spicy character and strong hoppiness.

WICKWAR

The Wickwar Brewing Co., The Old Cider Mill, Station Road, Wickwar, Avon GL12 8NB. Tel. (01454) 294168

Brewery launched on the 'Glorious First of May 1990' (guest beer law day) by two Courage tenants, Brian Rides and Ray Penny, with the aim of providing guest ales for their three tenancies. The business proved so successful that they dropped the pubs to concentrate on supplying their other regular outlets (now totalling over 100). The brewery operates from an old cider mill, originally the site of the Arnold, Perrett & Co. Ltd. brewery. Tours by arrangement.

The Independents

Coopers WPA	(OG 1036, ABV 3.5%) A yellow/gold, well-balanced, light, refreshing brew with hops, citrus fruit, peardrop flavour and notable malt character. Bitter, dry finish.
Brand Oak Bitter	(OG 1040, ABV 4%) A distinctive blend of hops, malt and citrus fruits. The slightly sweet taste turns into a fine, dry bitterness with a similar lasting finish. Moreish and known locally as 'Bob'.
Olde Merryford Ale	(OG 1050, ABV 5.1%) A pale brown, full-flavoured, well-balanced beer, with malt, hops and fruit elements throughout. Slightly sweet, with a long lasting, malty, dry finish.
Station Porter	(OG 1061, ABV 6.1%) A smooth, warming, dark brown ale with an aroma of roast malt, coffee and rich fruit. It has a similar, complex and spicy, rich, bittersweet taste and a long, smooth, roast finish. Brewed in winter.

WILD'S

Wild's Brewery, Unit 3E, Spa Field Industrial Estate, Slaithwaite, Huddersfield, W. Yorkshire HD7 5BB. Tel. (01484) 648387

Brewery founded in March 1994 by accountant Pete Wild, beginning serious production in August that year after five months of experimentation. There are plans to double capacity and, at present, around 12 outlets are supplied.

Bitter*	(OG 1038, ABV 3.8%)
Wild Oats*	(OG 1041, ABV 4.1%)
Wild Blonde*	(OG 1045, ABV 4.5%)
Wild Redhead*	(OG 1045, ABV 4.5%)
Wild Thing*	(OG 1050, ABV 5%)

WILLY'S

Willy's Pub and Brewery, 17 High Cliff Road, Cleethorpes, Humberside DN35 8RQ. Tel. (01472) 602145 Fax. (01472) 603578

Brewery opened in May 1989 to supply a seafront pub and some free trade. Some 60% of production is now sold outside the pub and Old Groyne is particularly popular as a guest beer through wholesalers. Another outlet, SWIGS (Second Willy's In Grimsby), was bought in December 1989. Some occasional beers. Tours by arrangement.

Original Bitter	(OG 1038, ABV 3.7%) Very quaffable, mid-brown beer with an intense hop aroma and taste, complemented by fruit and malt. Good bitter finish.
Burcom Bitter*	(OG 1044, ABV 4.2%) A dark bitter.
Coxswains Special Bitter*	(OG 1049, ABV 4.9%)
Old Groyne*	(OG 1060, ABV 6.2%) Fruit and malt in the nose lead to fruit and malt in the taste, but with hop character present throughout. Bittersweet finish.

WILSON'S	See Morland, and Nationals, Courage.

WOLVERHAMPTON & DUDLEY	See Banks's and Camerons.

WOOD

The Wood Brewery Ltd., Wistanstow, Craven Arms, Shropshire SY7 8DG. Tel. (01588) 672523 Fax. (01588) 673939

A village brewery, founded by the Wood family in 1980, in buildings adjacent to the Plough Inn. The brewery has enjoyed steady growth in recent years and now supplies around 200 other outlets. Sam Powell beers have been brewed here since the Powell brewery in Newtown went into receivership in 1991. One pub is owned at present, but more may be acquired. Tours by arrangement. Oc-

casional beers: Anniversary Ale (OG 1050, ABV 5%, April), Christmas Cracker (OG 1060, ABV 6%).

Wallop* (OG 1035, ABV 3.4%)

Sam Powell Original Bitter* (OG 1038, ABV 3.7%)

Parish Bitter (OG 1040, ABV 4%) A blend of malt and hops with a bitter aftertaste. Pale brown in colour.

Special Bitter (OG 1042, ABV 4.2%) A tawny brown bitter with malt, hops and some fruitiness.

Woodcutter* (OG 1042, ABV 4.2%) An autumn brew.

Shropshire Lad* (OG 1046, ABV 4.5%) A spring brew.

Sam Powell Old Sam* (OG 1047, ABV 4.6%)

Wonderful (OG 1048, ABV 4.8%) A mid-brown, fruity beer, with a roast and malt taste.

WOODFORDE'S

WOODFORDE'S
Norfolk Ales

Woodforde's Norfolk Ales (Woodforde's Ltd.), Broadland Brewery, Woodbastwick, Norwich, Norfolk NR13 6SW. Tel. (01603) 720353 Fax. (01603) 721806

Founded in late 1980 in Norwich, to bring much-needed choice to a long Watney-dominated region, Woodforde's moved to a converted farm complex, with greatly increased production capacity, in the picturesque Broadland village of Woodbastwick in 1989. It brews an extensive range of beers and runs two tied houses, with some 200 other outlets supplied on a regular basis. Tours by arrangement. Shop open 11–5.30 weekdays in winter and 11–7 Tue–Sun in summer. Occasional beers: Mother-in-Law's Tongue (OG 1041, ABV 4.1%, for Mother's Day), Norfolk Porter (OG 1043, ABV 4.1%), John Browne's Ale (OG 1043, ABV 4.3%). Bottle-conditioned beer: Norfolk Nips (OG 1085, ABV 8.6%, sometimes also on draught).

Broadsman Bitter (OG 1035, ABV 3.5%) A session beer which is a straightforward combination of malt and hops, with hints of sweetness and fruit. Hops and bitterness dominate the aftertaste.

Mardler's Mild (OG 1035, ABV 3.5%) A red/brown mild which is fairly dry (for a mild), smooth and malty. Well-balanced, with some subtle fruitiness. The aftertaste is pleasant but short.

Wherry Best Bitter (OG 1039, ABV 3.8%) This award-winning, amber beer has a distinctly hoppy nose and a well-balanced palate with pronounced bitterness and, usually, a flowery hop character. A long-lasting, satisfying, bitter aftertaste.

Emerald Ale (OG 1042, ABV 4.2%) Very black and very dry, with lots of roast malt throughout, this is a full-bodied and full-flavoured stout.

Old Bram (OG 1043, ABV 4.1%) A distinctly fruity old ale, full-bodied and flavoursome. Roast malt and hints of chocolate feature.

Great Eastern Ale* (OG 1043, ABV 4.3%)

Nelson's Revenge (OG 1045, ABV 4.5%) This premium bitter has quite a strong, pleasant, malty, fruity, hoppy aroma which the rounded and complex, malty palate doesn't quite live up to. The hoppiness and bitterness come through more distinctly at the end to give a good, lasting aftertaste.

Phoenix XXX* (OG 1047, ABV 4.8%)

Norfolk Nog (OG 1049, ABV 4.6%) A full-bodied red/brown beer with plenty of flavour and aroma. Roast malt balances the sweeter components of the palate. A very good, dark winter brew. *Champion Beer of Britain 1992.*

Baldric (OG 1052, ABV 5.6%) Much changed. Now an amber/golden, light

beer, with almost delicate hopping. A pleasing combination of malt, hops and fruit, with some sweetness in the palate and bitterness in the finish.

Headcracker (OG 1069, ABV 7%) This fairly pale brown barley wine is full-bodied and fruity throughout. The sweetness in the palate is balanced by the hoppiness and bitterness, and the aftertaste is warming.

WOODY WOODWARD'S   See Fox & Hounds.

WORLDHAM

Worldham Brewery, Smith's Farm, East Worldham, Alton, Hampshire GU34 3AT. Tel. (01420) 83383 Fax. (01420) 83600

It took 18 months for experienced brewer Hugo Sharpe to convert a hop kiln into a ten-barrel brewery, using plant acquired from a number of different breweries. Worldham eventually launched its first beer at the 1991 CAMRA Farnham Beerex and now serves around 50 free trade outlets.

Session Bitter*   (OG 1036, ABV 3.6%) Quaffable bitter with a clean, hoppy finish.

Old Dray Bitter   (OG 1043, ABV 4.4%) Mid- to deep brown beer, low in aroma and with a dry flavour with some grain. Strong on hops in the slightly cloying finish.

Barbarian Bitter*   (OG 1053, ABV 5.2%) A well-hopped premium bitter.

WORTH   See Commercial.

WORTHINGTON   See Nationals, Bass.

WORTLEY

Wortley Arms Brewery, Wortley Arms Hotel, Halifax Road, Wortley, Sheffield, S. Yorkshire S30 7DB. Tel. (0114) 2882245

Brewery opened in December 1991 in the cellar of the Wortley Arms Hotel. This and some other regular outlets are supplied. Tours by arrangement. Beers: Best Bitter (OG 1038, ABV 3.6%), Earls Ale (OG 1044, ABV 4.2%), Countess Ale (OG 1058, ABV 5.8%, Christmas).

WYCHWOOD

Wychwood Brewery Ltd., Eagle Maltings, The Crofts, Witney, Oxfordshire OX8 7AZ Tel. (01993) 702574 Fax. (01993) 772553

Formerly Glenny Brewery, set up in 1983 in the old maltings of the extinct Clinch's brewery. It moved to a new site in 1987 and was radically revamped during 1992, when nine pubs were acquired (leased from Allied or Inntrepreneur) by its sister company Hobgoblinns Ltd. Since then 23 more pubs have been taken on, in various towns across the South and South-West, all restyled in the bare boards and breweriana idiom, most renamed Hobgoblin and all taking real ale, which is also supplied to 100 other outlets. As a consequence of the extra demand, the brewery moved back to the old Clinch's site in 1994. Tours by arrangement. Shop open 9–5 weekdays and 10–11.30 Saturday.

Shires Bitter   (OG 1034, ABV 3.4%) A pleasantly hoppy and malty, light brown session beer, with a roast malt and fruit aroma.

Fiddlers Elbow*   (OG 1040, ABV 4%) Brewed May–September, a straw-coloured beer containing barley and wheat malts.

Best   (OG 1042, ABV 4.2%) Mid-brown, full-flavoured premium bitter. Moderately strong in hop and malt flavours, with pleasing, fruity overtones which last through to the aftertaste.

Dr Thirsty's Draught*   (OG 1052, ABV 5.2%) A robust bitter with a full malt flavour, balanced with hops.

Black Wych Stout*   (OG 1050, ABV 5%) A rich black stout, available October–April.

The Independents

Hobgoblin	(OG 1059, ABV 6%) Powerful, full-bodied, copper-red, well-balanced brew. Strong in roasted malt, with a moderate, hoppy bitterness and a slight fruity character.
The Dog's Bollocks*	(OG 1064, ABV 6.5%) A full-bodied, hoppy, golden brew, incorporating Styrian hops and wheat.

WYE VALLEY

 Wye Valley Brewery, 69 St Owen Street, Hereford, Hereford & Worcester HR1 2JQ. Tel./Fax. (01432) 342546

Brewery which started production in 1985 and moved to its present address in 1986. New plant was installed in 1992 to increase capacity and cater for a rapidly growing free trade (currently 75 outlets). Tours by arrangement. The company now also has two pubs of its own and has produced the following seasonal beers under the Dorothy Goodbody name. These account for 40% of sales: Springtime Bitter (OG 1040, ABV 4%, April–June), Golden Summertime Ale (OG 1042, ABV 4.2%, July–Sept), Glowing Autumn Ale (OG 1044, ABV 4.5%), Wholesome Stout (OG 1046, ABV 4.5%, January–March), Warming Wintertime Ale (OG 1055, ABV 5.6%, October–November), Father Xmas Ale (OG 1078, ABV 8.5%, December).

Bitter	(OG 1036, ABV 3.5%) Very little nose, but a crisp, dry and truly bitter taste, with a balancing malt flavour. The initial bitter aftertaste mellows to a pleasant, lingering malt.
Hereford Pale Ale or HPA	(OG 1040, ABV 4%) Beer with a distinctive colour of old pine and a malty nose. On the tongue, it is malty, with some balancing bitterness and a hint of sweetness. Good, dry finish.
Supreme	(OG 1045, ABV 4.4%) This rich, copper-red beer has a good malty, fruity aroma. In the complex flavour, the malt, fruit and bitterness are distinctive. The finish has bitterness but can be malty.
Brew 69	(OG 1055, ABV 5.6%) A pale beer which disguises its strength. It has a well-balanced flavour and finish, without the sweetness which normally characterises beer of this strength.

WYRE PIDDLE

Wyre Piddle Brewery, Unit 21, Craycombe Farm, Fladbury, Evesham, Hereford & Worcester WR10 2QS. Tel. (01386) 860473

Brewery established by a former publican and master builder in autumn 1994. Over 20 outlets now take the beer in locations throughout the southern Midlands.

Piddle in the Hole*	(OG 1038, ABV 3.9%) A malty session ale.
Piddle in the Snow*	(ABV 5.2%) A thick, rich, hoppy brew for December and January.

YATES

Yates Brewery, Ghyll Farm, Westnewton, Aspatria, Cumbria CA5 3NX. Tel. (0169 73) 21081

Small, traditional brewery set up in 1986 by Peter and Carol Yates in an old farm building on their smallholding, where a herd of pedigree goats makes good use of the brewery's by-products. Brewing award-winning beers to their capacity of 34 barrels a week during summer and other peak times, they serve over 20 free trade outlets and own one pub.

Bitter	(OG 1035, ABV 3.7%) A fruity, bitter, straw-coloured ale with malt and hops in the aroma and a long, bitter aftertaste.
Premium	(OG 1048, ABV 5.5%) Available at Christmas and a few other times of the year. Straw-coloured, with a strong aroma of malt and hops, and full-flavoured, with a slight toffee taste. The malty aftertaste becomes strongly bitter.
Best Cellar	(OG 1052, ABV 6%) Brewed only in winter and the strength changes from year to year. An excellent, red/brown beer with a

fruity aroma and a sweet, malty flavour, contrasted by a hoppy bitterness. The finish is a bittersweet balance, with grain and hops.

YORKSHIRE GREY　　See Nationals, Scottish & Newcastle.

YOUNGER　　See Nationals, Scottish & Newcastle.

YOUNG'S

Young & Co.'s Brewery PLC, The Ram Brewery, High Street, Wandsworth, London SW18 4JD. Tel. (0181) 870 0141 Fax. (0181) 870 9444

Brewery founded in 1675 by the Draper family, and bought by Charles Young and Anthony Bainbridge in 1831. Their partnership was dissolved in 1884 and the business was continued by the Young family. Though a public company since 1898, Young's is still very much a family affair and was the only London brewer not to join the keg revolution in the 1970s. It still brews award-winning beers in the traditional manner, with some of its pub deliveries made by horse-drawn drays. Around 400 free trade outlets are supplied, mostly within the M25 ring, though the brewery's presence is extending westward, and the brewery's tied estate has now increased to 188 houses. The Bill Bentley's wine bar chain is also now part of the business. Tours by arrangement.

Bitter　　(OG 1036, ABV 3.7%) A light gold, distinctive beer with well-balanced malt and hop characters. A strong, hoppy bitterness is followed by a delightfully astringent and hoppy, bitter aftertaste.

Special　　(OG 1046, ABV 4.6%) A strong, full-flavoured, bitter beer with a powerful hoppiness and a balancing malt flavour. Hops persist in the aftertaste.

Winter Warmer　　(OG 1055, ABV 5%) A dark reddish-brown ale with a malty, fruity aroma, a flavour of roast malt, and a bittersweet finish, including some lingering malt.

NEW BREWERIES

Use this space to record details of new breweries and beers.

BASS

Bass Brewers Ltd., 137 High Street, Burton upon Trent, Staffordshire DE14 1JZ Tel. (01283) 511000 Fax. (01283) 513256

Founded by William Bass in 1777, Bass today commands some 23% of all beer production in the UK, with two of the company's ale brands (Stones Best Bitter and Worthington Best Bitter) featuring amongst the top five sellers, and Draught Bass the biggest-selling premium cask ale. Following the closures of the breweries in Edinburgh (Heriot), Sheffield (Hope) and Wolverhampton (Springfield), Bass now brews at just nine sites, with those at Alton, Belfast and Tadcaster producing only keg beer.

The Belfast site is now being extended, to cater for demand for Caffrey's Ale, the company's major innovation of recent years. Launched on St Patrick's Day 1994, Caffrey's is one of the new breed of nitrokeg beers – brewery-conditioned, pasteurised beers which are served under mixture of CO_2 and nitrogen (in effect a smoother keg beer than established keg brands). Despite the fact that Bass did not initially advertise this product, sales roared ahead and brought with them new fears for the survival of some of the company's lesser-known cask brands.

On the pub side, the company controls around 4,100 houses (74% cask) of which about 2,600 are managed and the balance tenanted or leased. Many pubs still bear the liveries of former Bass trading divisions like Charrington, Tennents, M&B and Welsh Brewers. In recent years, Bass has sold about 2,730 pubs to comply with the DTI Orders restricting the number of tied houses run by national brewers, although many of these have been to new pub chain companies which have also agreed to take their beer from Bass. Free trade represents about half of sales, the tied estate accounts for a third, and the balance comes from the take-home trade.

BIRMINGHAM	**Cape Hill Brewery, PO Box 27, Smethwick, Birmingham, W. Midlands B16 0PQ. Tel. (0121) 558 1481**

One of the largest cask beer production centres in the country, subject of a £60 million investment programme in recent years. One-off brews are produced for Bass's Caskmaster 'guest' beer range. Bottle-conditioned beer: Worthington White Shield ⚑ (OG 1050.5, ABV 5.6%)

M&B Mild
(OG 1034.5, ABV 3.2%) A dark brown quaffing mild with roast and malt flavours. Dry, slightly bitter finish.

Joule's Crown Ale*
(OG 1039.5, ABV 3.9%) A revival of the old Joule name from a brewery closed by Bass in 1972. Do not confuse with the new John Joule & Son whose beers are produced by Coach House.

M&B Brew XI
(OG 1039.5, ABV 3.9%) A sweet, malty beer with a hoppy, bitter aftertaste.

BURTON	**Burton Brewery, Station Street, Burton upon Trent, Staffordshire DE14 1JZ. Tel. (01283) 513578**

The original home of Bass, producing one of Britain's most famous ales, available throughout its estate and the free trade.

Draught Bass
(OG 1043, ABV 4.4%) Can be a classic, but swan neck and sparkler dispense reduces aroma, taste and aftertaste to minimal levels. At its best, it is malty with underlying hops and a dry finish.

CARDIFF	**The Brewery, Crawshay Street, Cardiff, S. Glamorgan CF1 1TR. Tel. (01222) 233071 Fax. (01222) 372668**

The Hancock's brewery (founded in 1884) which was taken over by Bass Charrington in 1968. Tours by arrangement.

Worthington Dark
(OG 1034, ABV 3%) A dark brown, creamy mild with a somewhat malty flavour, followed by a sweet finish. Very popular in the Swansea area.

Hancock's HB	(OG 1038, ABV 3.6%) A slightly malty beer, with a bittersweet aftertaste. The brewery's quality control is of a high standard.
Worthington Best Bitter	(OG 1038, ABV 3.6%) A fairly malty, light brown beer, with a rather bitter finish. A very consistent national brand.

GLASGOW — **Wellpark Brewery, 161 Duke Street, Glasgow, Strathclyde G31 1JD. Tel. (0141) 552 6552 Fax. (0141) 552 2885**

The home of J&R Tennent Ltd., founded in 1745 and taken over by Charrington in 1963. In recent years it has predominantly brewed lagers. The cask beer below (named after one of the breweries subsumed by the company) was introduced in 1995.

Aitken's 80/-* (ABV 4.2%)

SHEFFIELD — **Cannon Brewery, 43 Rutland Road, Sheffield, S. Yorkshire S3 8BE. Tel. (0114) 2720323**

The original home of William Stones Ltd., dating from at least 1860. It was taken over by Bass in 1968.

Mild (OG 1032, ABV 3.1%) Formerly XXXX Mild. A pleasant, smooth, dark mild with a faint aroma of caramel, which leads to a caramel and roast rich taste, with complementing sweetness and bitterness. A good, long, satisfying, roast malt and caramel-sweet finish.

Light (OG 1032, ABV 3.2%) An amber-coloured mild: a lightly-flavoured blend of malt, sweetness and bitterness. At its best, it has a delicate, pleasing, flowery taste, but can too often be bland. A disappointing, short, sweetish finish and little aroma. Also known as Toby Light.

William Butler's Black Country Ale* (OG 1032, ABV 3.5%)

Special Bitter (OG 1034, ABV 3.4%) Certainly not special. Pale brown in hue, with little aroma. The generally bland taste has sweetness, malt and a slight bitterness. The poor, sweet and dryish finish can be cloying. Unexciting.

Worthington Best Bitter* (OG 1038, ABV 3.6%) This supplements supplies from the Cardiff brewery.

Stones Best Bitter (OG 1039, ABV 3.9%) Although generally more hoppy than recently, this golden straw-coloured brew retains a careful balance of malt, hop and fruit on the nose, mellow tastes in the mouth and a clean and bitter finish.

WALSALL — **Highgate Brewery, Sandymount Road, Walsall, W. Midlands WS1 3AP. Tel. (01922) 23168**

Built in 1895 and now a listed building, the Highgate Brewery is the smallest in the Bass group and has remained unchanged for many years.

M&B Highgate Dark Ale (OG 1034.5, ABV 3.2%) A classic Black Country dark mild, increasingly being shared with the rest of the country. Smooth, dry and nutty, with well-balanced hints of fruit, roast and bittersweet maltiness.

M&B Highgate Old Ale (OG 1053.5, ABV 5.1%) November–January only: a dark brown/ruby-coloured old ale. A full-flavoured, fruity, malty ale with a complex aftertaste, with touches of malt, roast, hops and fruit.

CARLSBERG-TETLEY

Carlsberg-Tetley Brewing Ltd., 107 Station Street, Burton upon Trent, Staffordshire DE14 1BZ. Tel. (01283) 531111 Fax. (01283) 502053

The company formed by the merger of the Allied Lyons breweries with Danish giant Carlsberg. Allied was established in 1961 with

the amalgamation of Ansells, Tetley Walker and Ind Coope. Carlsberg has long been a world-famous brewer, with quality lagers in its own country but lacklustre copies in Britain. It has owned no pubs, but, with its modern Northampton brewery now added to Allied's under-capacity sites, worries about brewery closures remain. The Allied lager plant at Wrexham still looks vulnerable. The company's biggest ale brand is Tetley Bitter.

On the pub front, Allied Domecq (as the company is now known) is keen to keep its local brewery image. Though the Tetley Pub Company now manages the former Joshua Tetley and Tetley Walker pubs, the traditional brewery liveries still decorate the pubs, as they do in the South-East, where Ind Coope Retail runs the former pubs of Friary Meux, Benskins, ABC and Halls. In London, Taylor Walker is complemented by the small Nicholson's chain of upmarket pubs, and the Ansells trademark is very prominent in the Midlands and South Wales. However, many former Allied pubs have been sold or leased to regional breweries and pub chains, some with the Carlsberg-Tetley beer tie still in place. The current stock stands at around 4,100 pubs.

ALLOA	**Carlsberg-Tetley Alloa Ltd., Alloa Brewery, Whins Road, Alloa, Clackmannanshire, Central FK10 3RB. Tel. (01259) 723539**

The company's Scottish arm, established in 1810, which was taken over by Archibald Arrol in 1866. It fell to Ind Coope & Allsopp's in 1951, becoming part of Allied in the 1961 merger. Less than half of Alloa's 310 pubs sell real ale. Tours by arrangement.

Archibald Arrol's 80/- (OG 1041, ABV 4.4%) A fruity Scottish heavy, dominated by malt, fruit and hops, with increasing bitterness in the aftertaste. Well worth seeking out when in top form.

HP&D	**Holt, Plant & Deakin Ltd., Dudley Road, Wolverhampton, W. Midlands WV2 3AF. Tel. (01902) 450504**

Trades under the name of Holts, but do not confuse it with Manchester's Joseph Holt brewery. This is a Black Country company set up in 1984 and now running 23 traditional pubs, all serving real ale. Holts Mild and Bitter are brewed by Tetley Walker in Warrington.

Entire (OG 1043, ABV 4.4%) A tawny beer with a complex fruit and hops flavour and a strongly bitter aftertaste.

Deakin's Downfall (OG 1060, ABV 6.1%) A full-bodied, strong winter ale. Malt dominates the flavour, with hops in the aftertaste.

IND COOPE	**Ind Coope Burton Brewery Ltd., 107 Station Street, Burton upon Trent, Staffordshire DE14 1BZ. Tel. (01283) 531111**

The major brewery in the group which resulted from the merger of the adjoining Allsopp's and Ind Coope breweries in 1934. It currently has a capacity of two and a half million barrels a year and brews eight real ales for the South and the Midlands, providing beer for the Ansells, Ind Coope Retail and Nicholson's trading divisions. These 'local' beers are derived from two mashes: ABC and Friary from one, Benskins and Nicholson's from the other. Taylor Walker Best Bitter is no longer brewed. Lumphammer (OG 1039) is brewed for the Worcestershire-based Little Pub Co. chain. Tours by arrangement.

For Ind Coope Retail:

ABC Best Bitter* (OG 1035, ABV 3.7%) A light, refreshing bitter, owing much of its character to dry hopping.

Benskins Best Bitter (OG 1035, ABV 3.7%) A predominantly hoppy session beer, which can be a very suppable pint but sometimes suffers from an astringent aftertaste.

The Nationals

Friary Meux Best Bitter (OG 1035, ABV 3.7%) Malt just dominates over hops in the aroma and flavour of this beer, and a strange, fruity taste lurks in the background.

Ind Coope Burton Ale (OG 1047, ABV 4.8%) At its best, this is still a full-bodied beer, rich with the aroma and taste of malt, hops and fruit (fruit dominating the hops), offering a reminder of why it was judged *Champion Beer of Britain* in 1990. Lingering aftertaste, bitter and astringent.

For Ansells:

Ansells Mild (OG 1033, ABV 3.4%) A red-brown, malty beer, striking in its smooth mouthfeel. Caramel dominates the fruit and hop background and leaves a smooth, but slightly grainy, roast caramel aftertaste.

Ansells Bitter (OG 1035, ABV 3.7%) A pale brown bitter with a mellow aroma and no dominant flavours. The strong, bitter aftertaste is slightly astringent and refreshing.

For Nicholson's:

Nicholson's Best Bitter* (OG 1035, ABV 3.7%)

PLYMPTON **Carlsberg-Tetley Brewing Ltd., Plympton Brewery, Valley Road, Plympton, Plymouth, Devon PL7 3LQ. Tel. (01752) 330171 Fax. (01752) 342385**

Set up in the Halls Plympton depot in 1984, this brewery's business expanded rapidly from 1987 under the trading name of Furgusons. The name has now been dropped, following the Carlsberg-Tetley merger but the brewery still offers three ales of its own for sale to Allied pubs in the area and to free trade in the South-West. Tours by arrangement.

Dartmoor Best Bitter (OG 1038, ABV 3.9%) Award-winning, mid-brown-coloured beer with malt and fruit in both the aroma and taste. Bitter aftertaste.

Dartmoor Legend (OG 1045, ABV 4.6%) Formerly Dartmoor Strong. A pale brown, fruity and sweet-tasting beer with a fruity aroma.

Dartmoor Cockleroaster (OG 1059, ABV 6%) Around Christmas only. An amber-coloured, full-bodied beer. Smooth and well balanced, yet slightly sweet-tasting, with a strong, multi-flavoured finish.

JOSHUA TETLEY **Carlsberg-Tetley Brewing Ltd., Joshua Tetley & Son, PO Box 142, The Brewery, Leeds, W. Yorkshire LS1 1QG. Tel. (0113) 2594594**

Yorkshire's best-known brewery, founded in 1822 by maltster Joshua Tetley. The brewery site covers 20 acres and includes a brewhouse opened in May 1989 to handle the increased demand for Tetley Bitter, though versions of both Tetley Bitter and Mild are also brewed at the Tetley Walker plant in Warrington, with no point of origin declared on the pump clips. A £6 million visitor centre and museum, Tetley's Brewery Wharf, opened in 1994.

Mild (OG 1032, ABV 3.2%) Red/brown in colour, with a light hint of malt and caramel in the aroma. A rounded taste of malt and caramel follows, with balancing bitterness, then a generally dry finish. A smooth, satisfying mild.

Bitter (OG 1035.5, ABV 3.7%) A beer with a faint, hoppy aroma, which is reflected in the taste and finish. The body is malty, with moderate bitterness coming through in the aftertaste, together with some sweetness.

Imperial* (OG 1042, ABV 4.3%)

TETLEY WALKER Tetley Walker Ltd., Dallam Lane, Warrington, Cheshire WA2 7NU. Tel. (01925) 631231

Brewery founded by the Walker family in 1852 which merged with Joshua Tetley in 1960 and currently brews Tetley Walker, Peter Walker, HP&D and Greenalls brands. The Tetley Mild and Bitter brewed here are versions of the beers from Tetley's Leeds brewery but are sold with identical pump clips. In the *Good Beer Guide* pub section we state Tetley Walker instead of Tetley when we are aware that the beer comes from Warrington and not Leeds.

Tetley Dark Mild (OG 1032, ABV 2.9%) A smooth, dark, malty mild with balanced roast and caramel flavours, and a hint of fruit and liquorice. Some dryness.

Walker Mild (OG 1032, ABV 2.9%) A smooth, dark mild with fruit and hints of caramel, roast and bitterness. The malty aftertaste quickly gives way to a faint dryness.

Tetley Mild (OG 1032, ABV 3.2%) A smooth, malty mild with some fruitiness and bitter notes. The aftertaste is malty, with a little dryness. A refreshing, darkish mild.

Walker Bitter (OG 1033, ABV 3.6%) A light, refreshing, well-balanced bitter with some hop and a little fruit.

Tetley Bitter (OG 1036, ABV 3.7%) A fruity session beer with a dry finish. Bitterness tends to dominate malt and hop flavours. Sharp, clean-tasting and popular.

Walker Best Bitter (OG 1036, ABV 3.7%) A bitter, fruity beer with a dry finish. Reasonably hoppy, but less fruity than last year.

Wild Rover (OG 1055, ABV 5.6%) A fruity, full-bodied bitter in which strong bitterness subsumes the hops. A fairly clean palate and a dry aftertaste.

Walker Winter Warmer (OG 1060, ABV 6.2%) Brewed November–February. A smooth, dark and sweet winter ale, with a strong, fruity flavour, balanced to some degree by a bitter taste and a dry finish.

For HP&D:

HP&D Bitter (OG 1036, ABV 3.7%) Brewed not to give offence: pale, sweet, malty and brown.

HP&D Mild (OG 1036, ABV 3.7%) An innocuous mild that doesn't trouble the tastebuds. Dark brown, sweet and malty.

For Greenalls:

Greenalls Mild (OG 1032, ABV 3.3%) A dark, malty mild with a faint fruit aroma. Some fruit and roast flavours follow, with a hint of caramel and bitterness.

Shipstone's Mild* (OG 1034, ABV 3.4%)

Greenalls Bitter (OG 1036, ABV 3.8%) A well-balanced beer which is quite fruity and well-hopped, with a good, dry finish.

Davenports Traditional Bitter* (OG 1037, ABV 3.9%)

Shipstone's Bitter* (OG 1037, ABV 3.9%)

Thomas Greenall's Original Bitter (OG 1045, ABV 4.6%) A smooth, malty and well-hopped premium bitter, fairly fruity with a dry aftertaste.

Carlsberg-Tetley Brew Pubs:

MINERVA Minerva Hotel, Nelson Street, Hull, Humberside HU1 1XE. Tel. (01482) 26909

Full mash operation, set up in 1983 and storing its beer under blanket pressure in cellar tanks. It was closed for a short period for

refurbishment during 1995, but generally produces special brews for events all year round. Beers: Pilots Pride (OG 1039, ABV 4.2%), Antlers Pride (OG 1039, ABV 4.2%, Christmas).

REINDEER

 Reindeer Trading Company Ltd., 10 Dereham Road, Norwich, Norfolk NR2 4AY. Tel. (01603) 666821 Fax. (01603) 666872

Brew pub which opened in 1987 and has progressed rapidly. It was taken over by Ind Coope Retail as part of the Firkin group in June 1995, but both the identity and the operation of the brewery have been unaltered. The pub is still the brewery's biggest customer, taking at least a third of its 60-barrel weekly output. The rest goes to 27 local free houses and to East-West Ales wholesalers for nationwide distribution. At the pub, most of the beers are now kept in casks, but Reindeer and Bevy are still kept under blanket pressure at weekends. Occasional beers: Porter (OG 1045, ABV 4.5%), Sanity Clause (OG 1065, ABV 7%), Sledgehammer (OG 1066, ABV 7.5%), the last two both Christmas.

Moild

(OG 1034, ABV 3.5%) Full-bodied (for a mild) and definitely full-flavoured. The palate has a malt and roast malt base with hops, sweetness and some bitterness. Usually dry, but it can be quite fruity initially.

Pale Ale or RPA

(OG 1034, ABV 3.5%) An amber-coloured, simple and unpretentious session beer, with malt and hops well balanced throughout and variable degrees of sweetness and bitterness.

Bevy

(OG 1037, ABV 3.9%) A stronger session beer than the RPA, with a bias towards hoppiness in the nose and palate, and a little less sweetness.

Stout

(OG 1039) A red-brown, dry stout which, although not strong, does not lack flavour or body. Plenty of roast malt and a moderate amount of bitterness.

Gnu Bru

(OG 1042, ABV 4.5%) A fairly full-bodied beer for its strength, well-balanced throughout. Hops and malt feature in the taste, with some fruit.

Reindeer

(OG 1047, ABV 5%) A full-bodied beer which is complex and flavoursome: fruity, hoppy and malty throughout, with some lingering hop bitterness.

Red Nose

(OG 1057, ABV 6%) A dark red/brown, very full-bodied beer. Mainly fruity and malty, it is a rich, complex brew, good for cold evenings, although some may find it a touch cloying.

ROSE STREET

 Rose Street Brewery, 55 Rose Street, Edinburgh, Lothian EH2 2NH. Tel. (0131) 220 1227

Founded in 1983 and run by Alloa Brewery, supplying six other Alloa outlets with beers produced from malt extract. Beers: Auld Reekie 80/- (OG 1043, ABV 4.1%), Auld Reekie 90/- (OG 1055, ABV 5.2%).

FIRKIN

 The Firkin Brewery, 77 Muswell Hill, London N10 3PH. Tel. (0181) 365 2823 Fax. (0181) 442 2000

This famous pub brewery chain was founded by David Bruce in 1979, relaunching the brew pub concept in what used to be run-down national brewers' houses. The pubs were refurbished in a back-to-basics fashion and were given in-house breweries, tucked away behind viewing windows. The Bruce's Brewery chain rapidly grew in number until 1988, when he sold all the pubs to Midsummer Leisure (later European Leisure), which, in turn, sold them to Stakis Leisure in 1990. Since 1991, the chain has been owned by Allied-Domecq, through its subsidiaries Taylor Walker, Ind Coope Retail, Ansells Retail and Tetley Pub Co. Much expansion has taken place, with new sites opened in university towns. The destruction of some classic Midlands pubs to create new Firkins has caused much resentment amongst local drinkers. The estate currently runs to over 60 pubs, but only 21of them brew. The

remainder are supplied by the brew pubs (mainly the Falcon & Firkin in London), so only the actual brew pubs are listed here. Four basic brews are available, usually sold under house names, a 1034 OG/3.4% ABV mild, a 1036 OG/3.5% ABV bitter, a stronger bitter at 1043/4.3%, and Dogbolter (OG 1057, ABV 5.6%). Some pubs offer extra one-off brews, including summer and winter ales, and also seen are Stout (OG 1047, ABV 4.6%) and Golden Glory (OG 1051, ABV 5%). All the brews are full mash and most pubs now offer some cask-conditioned beer with no additional gas applied. However, cellar tanks with mixed gas breathers are still used in some outlets. The Flamingo & Firkin in Kingston now belongs to Saxon Inns (see Independents, Flamingo).

Current brew pubs:

Faculty & Firkin, Holt Street, Aston University Campus, Gosta Green, Birmingham, W. Midlands B7 4BD. Tel. (0121) 359 4520

Falcon & Firkin, 360 Victoria Park Road, Hackney, London E9 7BT. Tel. (0181) 985 0693

Feast & Firkin, 229 Woodhouse Lane, Leeds, W. Yorkshire LS2 3AP. Tel. (0113) 2453669

Ferret & Firkin, 114 Lots Road, Chelsea, London SW10 0RJ. Tel. (0171) 352 6645

Fiddler & Firkin, 14 South End, Croydon, London CR0 1DL. Tel. (0181) 680 9728

Fieldmouse & Firkin at the Fighting Cocks, St Mary's Row, Moseley, Birmingham, W. Midlands B13 0HN. Tel. (0121) 449 0811

Finch & Firkin, 487 Smithdown Road, Liverpool, Merseyside L15 5AE. Tel. (0151) 733 2403

Fizgig & Firkin, St Anne's Well, Lower North Street, Exeter, Devon EX4 3ET. Tel. (01392) 437667

Flamingo & Firkin, 1-7 Becket Street, Derby DE1 1HT. Tel. (01332) 45948

Flea & Firkin, 137 Grosvenor Street, Manchester M1 7BZ. Tel. (0161) 274 3682

Flounder & Firkin, 54 Holloway Road, Holloway, London N7 8JP. Tel. (0171) 609 9574

Fly & Firkin, 18 Southfield Road, Middlesbrough, Cleveland, TS1 3BZ. Tel. (01642) 244792

Forrester & Firkin, 3 Eastgate Street, Stafford ST16 2NQ. Tel. (01785) 223742

Fowl & Firkin, 1–2 The Butts, Coventry, W. Midlands CV1 3GR. Tel. (01203) 221622

Fox & Firkin, 316 Lewisham High Street, Lewisham, London SE13 3HL. Tel. (0181) 690 8925

Friar & Firkin, 120 Euston Road, Euston, London NW1 2AL. Tel. (0171) 387 2419

Friesian & Firkin, 87 Rectory Grove, Clapham, London SW4 0DR. Tel. (0171) 622 4666

Phantom & Firkin, Leicester Road, Loughborough, Leics. LE11 2AG. Tel. (01509) 263226

Philanthropist & Firkin, Victoria Street, St Albans, Herts. Tel. (01727) 847021

Phoenix & Firkin, 5 Windsor Walk, Camberwell, London SE5 3BB. Tel. (0171) 701 8282

Physician & Firkin, 58 Dalkeith Road, Edinburgh, Lothian EH16 5AD. Tel. (0131) 667 1816

The Nationals

COURAGE

Courage Ltd., Ashby House, 1 Bridge Street, Staines, Surrey TW18 4TP. Tel. (01784) 466199 Fax. (01784) 468131

After months of speculation, the sale of Courage by its Australian owner, Foster's, to Scottish & Newcastle was agreed in May 1995 and nodded through by the Government in July. Courage had been a brewer with no pubs since 1991, following the sale of its pub empire to Inntrepreneur Estates, a company Foster's jointly owns with Grand Metropolitan. This ruse to avoid the full implications of the Government's Beer Orders, which sought to restrict the number of tied houses owned by the national brewers, left Courage in a very exposed position. As part of the Grand Metropolitan deal, Courage took over all Grand Met.'s breweries (the former Watney's plants). Some of these must now be under threat. The old Webster's site at Halifax would seem ripe for closure and its brands, including the much vaunted Yorkshire Bitter, could well disappear altogether. Even Courage's southern real ale base, the Bristol brewery, may not survive in the long term.

Prior to the S&N take-over, in addition to the cask ale plants listed below, Courage operated keg beer factories in Mortlake (now a joint venture with Anheuser-Busch known as The Stag Brewing Company and largely responsible for Budweiser production) and on the outskirts of Reading. Foster's also owns the Beamish & Crawford brewery in Cork, Ireland.

BRISTOL

Bristol Brewery, Counterslip, Victoria Street, Bristol, Avon BS1 6EX. Tel. (0117) 9297222

The former Georges brewery (established 1788), and now Courage's only real ale brewery in the South. Growing demand for cask beer has resulted in expansion at this plant in recent years, with Best and Directors very well promoted nationally but Bitter Ale (now renamed Georges Bitter Ale) sales confined mostly to the West Country and South-East Wales. However, the three beers are all diluted versions of the same original high-gravity brew.

Georges Bitter Ale

(OG 1031, ABV 3.3%) A pale, light-bodied session bitter, with a slightly grainy taste, a hoppy aroma and a dry, bitter finish. There are occasional subtle fruit flavours, too.

Best Bitter

(OG 1039, ABV 4%) A pale brown bitter with a grainy malt taste. The aroma is hoppy; the finish is bitter and dry with some hops.

Directors

(OG 1048, ABV 4.8%) A well-balanced, full-bodied, mid-brown malty ale, with hops and fruit in the nose. The grainy malt taste has some fruit and develops into a powerful, bitter, dry finish.

FOUNTAIN HEAD

Fountain Head Brewery, Ovenden Wood, Halifax, W. Yorkshire HX2 0TL. Tel. (01422) 357188

The original Samuel Webster brewery, merged by Watney in 1985 with Wilson's of Manchester, a move which saw the closure of Wilson's own brewery. Wilson's Mild has since been contracted out to Morland (see Independents). Webster's Dark (OG 1031, ABV 3%) and Truman IPA (ABV 3.5%) have been trialled here in the last year.

Webster's Green Label Best

(OG 1034, ABV 3.2%) A faint, hoppy aroma, with a little fruitiness at times. Some sweetness in the malty taste, and a bitter finish.

Webster's Yorkshire Bitter

(OG 1036, ABV 3.5%) A disappointing beer with a faintly malty and fruity aroma (sometimes metallic). Often very bland in taste to offend no-one. If you are lucky it can have a good, fresh, hoppy-bitter flavour and finish (but very rare!).

Wilson's Original Bitter	(OG 1037, ABV 3.5%) A fairly thin, golden beer with a malty and fruity aroma and a flowery hop flavour, which can be very bitter at times. Malty overtones in the taste and finish.

JOHN SMITH'S	John Smith's Brewery, Tadcaster, N. Yorkshire LS24 9SA. Tel. (01937) 832091

A business founded at the Old Brewery in 1758 and taken over by John Smith (brother of Samuel Smith – see Independents) in 1847. The present brewery was built in 1884 and became part of the Courage empire in 1970. John Smith's Bitter is Courage's best known ale, thanks to extensive television advertising. Bottle-conditioned beer: Imperial Russian Stout ⊟ (OG 1098, ABV 10%), a famous export beer which is now only occasionally brewed.

Bitter	(OG 1036, ABV 3.8%) Copper-coloured beer with a pleasant mix of hops and malt in the nose. Malt dominates the taste but hops take over in the finish. The brewery's quality control for this beer is excellent. Widely available nationally.
Magnet	(OG 1040, ABV 4%) A well-crafted beer, almost ruby coloured. Hops, malt and citrus fruit can be identified in the nose and there are complex flavours of nuts, hops and fruit. Long, malty finish.

GUINNESS

Guinness Brewing (GB), Park Royal Brewery, London NW10 7RR. Tel. (0181) 965 7700 Fax. (0181) 963 0801

One of the world's most famous brewing names, Guinness has swum against the tide somewhat in recent years. In 1993, at a time when interest in bottle-conditioned beers was reviving, and with stout making an overdue comeback in many breweries, the company decided to axe its naturally-conditioned, bottled stout, Guinness Original. Guinness Original is still on sale, but only in a brewery-conditioned, pasteurised version, which lacks the complexity and freshness of the bottle-conditioned beer. On the plus side, the stronger bottled Foreign Extra Stout (not bottle-conditioned), a beer sold all over the world, has been reintroduced to British pubs.

Guinness has put more effort into promoting 'Draught' Guinness in a can and has also produced a Draught Bitter in a can, even though the company brews no genuine draught bitter. All Draught Guinness sold in the UK is keg, despite the clumsy attempt to suggest otherwise to drinkers, by introducing a small handpump-style fount. In Ireland, Draught Guinness (OG 1038, brewed at Arthur Guinness, St James's Gate, Dublin 8) is not pasteurised but is served with gas pressure.

SCOTTISH & NEWCASTLE

Scottish & Newcastle Beer Production Ltd., Scottish & Newcastle PLC, Abbey Brewery, 111 Holyrood Road, Edinburgh, Lothian EH8 8YS. Tel. (0131) 556 2591 Fax. (0131) 556 4571

Scottish & Newcastle was formed in 1960, as a merger between Scottish Brewers Ltd. (the former Younger and McEwan breweries) and Newcastle Breweries Ltd. The company runs approximately 2,750 pubs, including some former Chef & Brewer houses it purchased in 1994 from Grand Metropolitan, which gave S&N a foothold in southern England. S&N also continues to have a massive presence in the free trade (particularly through McEwan

and Theakston brands and the infamous Newcastle Brown Ale), and the company also dominates many free houses through the loan-tie system of offering financial loans in return for beer sales.

In May 1995, it was announced that S&N had agreed to purchase Courage from its Australian owner, Foster's. This means that S&N will now become Britain's biggest brewer, cornering over one quarter of the country's beer production. The consequences for the UK industry will be severe. It will inevitably lead to reduced competition, higher prices and less choice. Brewery rationalisation will be another reality. The Home Brewery in Nottingham could be top of the closures list, a move that would be fiercely resisted by Midlands drinkers keen not to see their local brewery disposed of by S&N in the same contemptuous way as Matthew Brown in Blackburn was closed in 1991, despite assurances that it was 'sacrosanct'.

Excluding the Courage sites, S&N operates five breweries, including a keg beer plant in Manchester. Theakston beers are produced at the Tyne Brewery in Newcastle, as well as in Theakston's own brewery in Masham.

FOUNTAIN	**Fountain Brewery, 159 Fountainbridge, Edinburgh, Lothian EH3 9YY. Tel. (0131) 229 9377 Fax. (0131) 229 1282**

The Scottish production centre, formerly the home of William McEwan & Co. Ltd, founded in 1856. Its beers are sold under two separate names – McEwan and Younger, depending on the trading area. New this year is Younger Best Bitter (brewed at Home, see below). Occasional beer: McEwan 90/- (OG 1052, ABV 5.5%).

McEwan 70/- or Younger Scotch Bitter* (OG 1036, ABV 3.7%) A well-balanced, sweetish brew, becoming more and more rare. Often competitively priced in Wetherspoon pubs.

McEwan 80/- or Younger IPA (OG 1042, ABV 4.5%) Thin-bodied beer with a cloying metallic aftertaste. Once a classic, now bland and sweet with some maltiness.

Younger No. 3* (OG 1042, ABV 4.5%) This beer's recipe was reformulated in summer 1995 and the brand was relaunched.

McEwan Export* (OG 1043, ABV 4.5%) A new beer for the guest ale market.

HOME	**Home Brewery, Mansfield Road, Daybrook, Nottingham NG5 6BU. Tel. (0115) 9675030 Fax. (0115) 9670122**

Founded in 1875 and acquired by S&N in 1986, Home's tied estate offers real ale in 180 of its 400 pubs and the brewery enjoys extensive free trade in the Midlands and the North. It now also brews the beers from the closed Matthew Brown brewery in Blackburn and these are still sold in 184 of the 403 Matthew Brown pubs in the North-West. Home Mild (OG 1036, ABV 3.6%), however, is now contract-brewed at Mansfield (see Independents).

Matthew Brown Lion Mild* (OG 1030, ABV 3.1%)

Matthew Brown Lion Bitter* (OG 1034, ABV 3.5%)

Younger Best Bitter* (OG 1035, ABV 3.7%)

Home Bitter (OG 1038, ABV 3.8%) A beer with little aroma. The flavour balances malt and hops well, with a smooth, initial taste and a lingering, dry, bitter finish. Golden/copper in colour.

THEAKSTON	**T&R Theakston Ltd., Wellgarth, Masham, Ripon, N. Yorkshire HG4 4DX. Tel. (01765) 689544 Fax. (01765) 689769**

Company formed in 1827 and based at this brewery since 1875. Theakston became part of S&N when its parent company,

Matthew Brown, was swallowed up. More than £1 million has been spent on this brewery in the last few years, reflecting the 'national' status its brews have been given by S&N. Although Theakston itself runs just ten tied houses, the free trade is enormous and, consequently, most of Theakston's production now takes place in Newcastle. The same pump clips are used for Masham and Newcastle beers, so the consumer is still not told whether the beer actually comes from Theakston's brewery. Tours by arrangement. Occasional beers: Hogshead Bitter (OG 1041, ABV 4.1%), Masham Ale (OG 1065, ABV 6.6%).

Mild Ale ⊕ (OG 1035, ABV 3.5%) A rich and smooth mild ale with a creamy body and a rounded liquorice taste. Dark ruby/amber in colour, with a mix of malt and fruit in the nose and a dry, hoppy aftertaste.

Black Bull Bitter* (OG 1037, ABV 3.9%) An occasional beer made part of the regular range in summer 1995.

Best Bitter (OG 1039, ABV 3.8%) A light drinking bitter with little body or aftertaste. Hoppiness rapidly declines, leaving a low bitterness and little to remember.

XB (OG 1045, ABV 4.6%) Although often lacking character, this can be a good drinking bitter, with hop and fruit character, and a smooth, slightly creamy aftertaste.

Old Peculier ⊕ (OG 1057, ABV 5.7%) A deservedly acclaimed old ale, complex and unforgettable. It is smooth and rich, with a solid body of malts giving lasting roast and liquorice tastes and an underlying fruitiness.

TYNE **Tyne Brewery, Gallowgate, Newcastle upon Tyne, Tyne & Wear NE99 1RA. Tel. (0191) 232 5091 Fax. (0191) 261 6297**

The home of Newcastle Breweries Ltd., formed in 1890 as an amalgamation of five local breweries. It brewed no real ale until most of Theakston's production was transferred here a few years ago. No indication is given at the point of sale or in advertising that Theakston beers are brewed in Newcastle (for tasting notes, see Theakston).

Theakston Mild Ale (OG 1035, ABV 3.5%)

Theakston Best Bitter (OG 1039, ABV 3.8%)

Newcastle Exhibition* (OG 1040, ABV 4.4%)

Theakston XB (OG 1045, ABV 4.6%)

Theakston Old Peculier (OG 1057, ABV 5.7%)

S&N Brew Pubs:

ABINGTON PARK 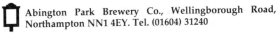 **Abington Park Brewery Co., Wellingborough Road, Northampton NN1 4EY. Tel. (01604) 31240**

A Victorian-styled brew pub, opened in 1984 by Chef & Brewer and now owned by S&N Retail (Trent Inns Ltd.). Equipped with a five-barrel plant, the pub stores its beer in cellar tanks under CO_2 at atmospheric pressure. Beers: Cobblers Ale (OG 1037, ABV 3.3%), Becket (brewed with malt, wheat and maize, OG 1042, ABV 3.6%), Dark (OG 1044, ABV 3.6%, occasional), Extra (OG 1047, ABV 4.3%), Special (OG 1062, ABV 5%, occasional).

Beers marked with an asterisk have not been tasted by official CAMRA tasting panels. However, some of these beers do carry brief descriptions derived from limited samplings or other sources which can be used for rough guidance.

The Nationals

GREYHOUND

 Greyhound Brewery Company Ltd., 151 Greyhound Lane, Streatham Common, London SW16 5NJ. Tel. (0181) 677 9962

Set up in 1984, the Greyhound brew pub was acquired by Scottish & Newcastle in November 1993. Improvements to the plant began in 1994. Cellar tanks, with a blanket of CO_2, are used at the pub. Beers: Special (OG 1038, ABV 3.6%), Streatham Strong (OG 1048, ABV 4.3%), Dynamite (OG 1055, ABV 5%).

ORANGE

 Orange Brewery, 37–39 Pimlico Road, Pimlico, London SW1W 8NE. Tel. (0171) 730 5984

Brewery opened in 1983, which, after refurbishment, opened again in April 1995. The full mash brews are stored in cellar tanks and are kept under blanket pressure. Tours by arrangement. Beers: SW1 (OG 1040, ABV 3.8%), Pimlico Porter (OG 1046, ABV 4.5%), SW2 (OG 1050, ABV 4.8%).

YORKSHIRE GREY

 Yorkshire Grey, 26 Theobalds Road, Holborn, London WC1X 8PN. Tel. (0171) 405 2519

Brew pub on the corner of Gray's Inn Road. Malt extract is used but there are plans to develop the brewery into a full mash outfit. A CO_2 blanket is applied to the cellar tanks. Beers: Headline Bitter (OG 1040, ABV 3.8%), Holborn Best Bitter (OG 1047, ABV 4.8%).

WHITBREAD

The Whitbread Beer Company, Whitbread PLC, Porter Tun House, Capability Green, Luton, Bedfordshire LU1 3LS. Tel. (01582) 391166 Fax. (01582) 397397

The name of Whitbread conjures up just one image for many beer drinkers, that of brewery closures. By destroying the likes of Strong's of Romsey, Wethered of Marlow, Fremlins of Faversham, Chester's of Salford and Higsons of Liverpool in the 1970s and 1980s, Whitbread effectively raised two fingers to local preference and killed off an important part of many beer drinkers' lives. The most recent closure was the Exchange Brewery in Sheffield in 1993. Since then Whitbread seems to have rediscovered cask-conditioned beer and has been investing heavily in its cask ale portfolio. The retail side of the company has turned a number of pubs into 'alehouses' to support this initiative and there have also been some noteworthy special brew promotions, involving limited edition beers brewed in Cheltenham and Castle Eden which have rolled out under 'The Beer Thinkers' banner. In addition to the cask ale breweries, the company operates keg beer factories in Magor in Gwent and Samlesbury in Lancashire.

Whitbread's 4,700 pubs are more or less equally controlled by two divisions: Whitbread Inns (managed houses) and Whitbread Pub Partnerships (pubs leased out, usually on 20-year terms).

BODDINGTONS

Strangeways Brewery, PO Box 23, Strangeways, Manchester M60 3WB. Tel. (0161) 828 2000 Fax. (0161) 828 2213

Brewery established in 1778 and acquired by Whitbread in 1989, when the Boddingtons company, which had already taken-over and closed Oldham Brewery, retreated to pub owning. Now Whitbread is pushing Boddingtons Bitter nationwide and the beer takes up 90% of the brewery's already expanded production capacity. Oldham Best (OB) Bitter (OG 1037.5, ABV 3.8%) has been transferred to Burtonwood Brewery (see Independents).

The pub sign indicates breweries which are also brew pubs, i.e. produce beer in part of a pub or in its grounds.

Boddingtons Mild (OG 1032, ABV 3%) A thin, dark mild with a sweet caramel and malt flavour, and a short aftertaste. It has now disappeared from many tied houses.

OB Mild (OG 1032, ABV 3%) Reddish brown beer with a malty aroma. A smooth roast malt and fruit flavour follows, then a malty and surprisingly bitter aftertaste.

Boddingtons Bitter (OG 1034.5, ABV 3.8%) A pale beer in which the grainy malt, hop and bitter character can be spoiled by a rather cloying sweetness.

CASTLE EDEN **Castle Eden Brewery, PO Box 13, Castle Eden, Hartlepool, Cleveland TS27 4SX. Tel. (01429) 836007**

Originally attached to a 17th-century coaching inn, the old Nimmo's brewery (established in 1826) was purchased by Whitbread in 1963. It actually stands in County Durham, despite the Cleveland postal address, and now produces some of Whitbread's better quality beers. Winter Royal, once brewed by Wethered of Marlow, has arrived here after a time at Gale's in Horndean, as have the Higsons beers from Sheffield – all helping to secure the future of this small brewery. Castle Eden is also responsible for many of the Whitbread special, limited-edition brews.

Higsons Mild (OG 1032, ABV 3.4%) A fruity, dark mild with some roast malt and caramel. Fairly bitter and dry.

Eden Bitter* (OG 1037, ABV 3.6%)

Higsons Bitter (OG 1037, ABV 3.7%) A hoppy and fruity beer with some sweetness and vanilla notes. Thin, inoffensive and bland.

Castle Eden Ale (OG 1040, ABV 4.2%) A fruity bitter with well-developed hop character, solid body and a creamy taste. The aroma may be spicy and sulphur may dominate when fresh.

Old Dambuster* (OG 1043, ABV 4.6%)

Whitbread Porter (OG 1052, ABV 4.6%) A deservedly proud beer, rich in coffee and liquorice flavours. Very smooth and well-balanced, with an impressively rich, dry aftertaste. Now only available February–May.

Fuggles Imperial IPA* (OG 1053, ABV 5.5%)

Winter Royal (OG 1055, ABV 5.5%) The former Wethered winter ale. A rich, fruity and full-flavoured beer with a malty palate, tasting even stronger than its gravity suggests.

FLOWERS **The Flowers Brewery, Monson Avenue, Cheltenham, Gloucestershire GL50 4EL. Tel. (01242) 261166 Fax. (01242) 265404**

Brewery established in 1760 by banker John Gardner, which became the Cheltenham Original Brewery when rebuilt in 1898. It merged in 1958 with Stroud Brewery to form West Country Breweries Ltd. and was acquired by Whitbread in 1963. The Flowers brewing operation and title were transferred from Stratford-upon-Avon in 1968. In recent years it has become the centre for Whitbread cask ale in the South, absorbing the Wethered, Strong and Fremlins production as these breweries were closed. Wethered Bitter (see McMullen), Pompey Royal (see Gale's) and Strong Country Bitter (see Morrells) have since been contracted out to other breweries, while Fremlins Bitter has been joined at Cheltenham by Royal Wessex Bitter (for Devenish/Greenalls), Bentley's and Trophy (following the closure of Exchange Brewery). One-off brews feature regularly.

The tankard symbol indicates the *Good Beer Guide Beers of the Year*, finalists in the *Champion Beer of Britain* contest held at the *Great British Beer Festival* at Olympia in August 1995.

The Nationals

West Country Pale Ale (WCPA)	(OG 1030.5, ABV 3%) Hoppy in aroma, but not as distinctive as it used to be. Light, refreshing and hoppy, with a clean, dry finish.
Fremlins Bitter*	(OG 1035.5, ABV 3.5%)
Bentley's Yorkshire Bitter*	(OG 1036, ABV 3.6%)
Flowers IPA	(OG 1036, ABV 3.6%) Pale brown, with little aroma, perhaps a faint maltiness. Moderately dry taste and finish, but no discernible hoppiness. Thin and uninspiring.
Trophy Bitter*	(OG 1036, ABV 3.6%)
Whitbread Best Bitter*	(OG 1036, ABV 3.6%) Also available in keg form.
Flowers Original	(OG 1045, ABV 4.5%) Hoppy aroma and hops in the taste, with some malt and a hint of fruit. A notably bitter finish.
	For Greenalls:
Royal Wessex Bitter*	(OG 1040.5, ABV 4%)

Whitbread Brew Pubs:

ALFORD ARMS

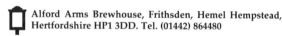 Alford Arms Brewhouse, Frithsden, Hemel Hempstead, Hertfordshire HP1 3DD. Tel. (01442) 864480

Brew pub opened in 1981, but only brewing again since 1993, after a long break. It is now working at full capacity, supplying malt extract beers to 20 other outlets. Tours by arrangement. Beers: Dark Mild (OG 1031 ABV 2.8%), New Cherry Pickers (OG 1040, ABV 3.9%), Olde Frithsden (OG 1042, ABV 4.2%), Pickled Squirrel (OG 1045, ABV 4.5%), Rub of the Brush (OG 1049, ABV 5%), Rudolf's Revenge (OG 1055, ABV 5.8%, winter), 500 Special Ale (OG 1057, ABV 6%, winter).

FOX & NEWT

 Fox & Newt, 9 Burley Street, Leeds, W. Yorkshire LS9 1LD. Tel. (0113) 2432612

Malt extract brew pub which also sells to other outlets. Tours by arrangement. Beers: Diesel (ABV 4.1%, a stout), Cushtie (ABV 4.2%), Black and Amber (ABV 4.5%), Ghostbuster (ABV 5.1%), The Bitch (ABV 6.5%).

FROG & PARROT

 Frog & Parrot, 64 Division Street, Sheffield, S. Yorkshire S1 4SG. Tel. (0114) 2721280

Malt extract brew pub. Beers are kept under a nitrogen blanket in casks and are sometimes available in a handful of other pubs. Beers: Old Croak (OG 1036, ABV 3.5%), Reckless (OG 1045, ABV 4.5%), Conqueror (OG 1066, ABV 6.9%), Roger & Out (OG 1125, ABV 12.5%).

LASS O'GOWRIE

 Lass O'Gowrie Brewhouse Ltd., 36 Charles Street, Manchester M1 7DB. Tel. (0161) 273 6932

Victorian pub, revamped and re-opened as a malt extract brew pub in 1983. The brewery in the cellar is visible from the bar. The beer is stored in tanks without a blanket of gas. No other outlets are supplied at present. Tours by arrangement. Beers: LOG 35 (OG 1035, ABV 3.8%), LOG 42 (OG 1042, ABV 4.5%).

OG stands for Original Gravity, the reading taken before fermentation of the amount of fermentable material in the brew. It is a rough indicator of strength. More reliable is the ABV (Alcohol by Volume) rating, which gives the percentage of alcohol in the finished beer.

Pub Groups

ASCOT ESTATES LTD
Bury House, 31 Bury Street, London EC3A 5AR.
Tel. (0171) 815 0805 Fax. (0171) 815 0808

Pub-owning company established as Belhaven Inns (a division of Control Securities) in 1987 with 68 pubs. The number rose to over 600 but has now been reduced to 497, spread across most of the country. Of these, 235 are tenanted, with the remaining 262 being leased out on 20-year contracts. Beers are supplied by Courage and Carlsberg-Tetley. No guest beers.

BEARDS OF SUSSEX LTD
West End, Herstmonceux, E. Sussex BN27 4NN.
Tel. (01323) 832777 Fax. (01323) 832833

Former brewing company (founded in 1797) which opted out of production in 1959. After contracting out its beers to Harveys from 1960 to 1986, Beards then abandoned brewing altogether and became a cask ale wholesaler as well as a pub company. The wholesaling division was sold off in 1994 and Beards currently runs 33 traditional pubs in Sussex (11 managed, 22 tenanted), which can sell any beers from the wide list offered by The Beer Seller wholesaler.

BODDINGTON PUB COMPANY
West Point, 501 Chester Road, Manchester M16 9HX.
Tel. (0161) 876 4292 Fax. (0161) 876 4260

Famous Manchester brewing name which sold its Strangeways and Higsons breweries to Whitbread in 1989. It now runs 475 pubs in the North-West, 275 managed and the rest tenanted, including 24 Henry's Tables pub restaurants. The pubs sell Whitbread Cask Collection beers, as well as Tetley, John Smith's and Theakston brews, plus Cains beers in the Liverpool area. There is also a selection from the group's Guest Ale Club and some pubs have been designated 'Boddingtons Ale Houses'.

CAFE INNS PLC
3 St Thomas's Road, Chorley, Lancashire PR7 1HP.
Tel. (01257) 262424 Fax. (01257) 260497

Company established in 1987 and now running 129, mostly tenanted pubs in the North-West. Fifty-one of the pubs are leased from Burtonwood and are operated under the Vantage Inns banner, a company jointly owned by Café Inns and Burtonwood. These pubs stock Burtonwood beers. The other pubs sell beers from Bass and S&N (Matthew Brown).

CENTURY INNS PLC
Belasis Business Centre, Coxwold Way, Billingham, Cleveland TS23 4EA.
Tel. (01642) 343426 Fax. (01642) 345603

Company formed in 1991 by Camerons employees with the purchase of 185 pubs from Bass. The intention was to establish a pub estate for a buy-out of the Camerons brewery, but this was scuppered by Brent Walker. The number of pubs now stands at 315, four managed and the rest traditionally tenanted (three-year agreements), with pubs located down the north-eastern side of the country, from Tyneside to Lincolnshire. Beer sales are still mostly confined to Bass products, with some Courage, Carlsberg-Tetley and S&N beers.

CM GROUP LTD
Magnet House, Station Road, Tadcaster, N. Yorkshire LS24 9JF.
Tel. (01937) 833311 Fax. (01937) 834236

Eighty-strong pub chain in North-East England, expanded from ten in 1992. Most of the pubs have been leased from Whitbread, with half tenanted, half managed. No guest beers are available to managers or tenants, with supplies coming from Whitbread, Courage, S&N and Carlsberg-Tetley.

CONQUEST INNS LTD
The Old Vicarage, 10 Church Street, Rickmansworth, Hertfordshire WD3 1BS.
Tel. (01923) 711118 Fax. (01923) 711128

Company set up to obtain 59 pubs from Bass in May 1994, backed by Jersey's Ann Street brewery. About half the pubs (now only 57 in total, nearly all three-year tenanted) are in London, with small pockets of houses in Sussex, the Midlands and East Anglia. Beers come solely from Bass and Courage, and tenants have no guest beer rights.

JT DAVIES
7 Aberdeen Road, Croydon, London CR0 1EQ.
Tel. (0181) 681 3222 Fax. (0181) 760 0390

Wine merchants now controlling around 30 tenancies and six managed houses in the South-East. Its main suppliers are Bass, Courage, Fuller's and Harveys.

DAVY'S OF LONDON LTD
59–63 Bermondsey Street, London SE1 3XF.
Tel. (0171) 407 9670 Fax. (0171) 407 5844

Long established (1870) wine merchants which has been opening wine bars and ale and port houses in the City since 1965, taking previously unlicensed property (largely basements) and creating a Dickensian, sawdust, nooks and crannies type of establishment. Two beers are sold: Davy's Ordinary Bitter (ABV 4%) and Davy's Old Wallop (ABV 4.8%), both re-badged brews of undeclared origin (though Courage Best and Directors fit the bill). The company currently runs 55 outlets.

DEAN ENTERTAINMENTS LTD
Dean House, Victoria Road, Kirkcaldy, Fife KY1 2SA.
Tel. (01592) 200417 Fax. (01592) 269501

Scottish-based company owning 44 pubs (nine managed, the rest tenanted), two hotels

Pub Groups

and three discos in the Fife and Tayside area. Many of the pubs came from Tennent Caledonian, whose beers are the only ones on sale. No guest beers are allowed. The tenanted side of the company has been earmarked for expansion.

DISCOVERY INNS
Unit 502, Discovery House, Worle Parkway, Worle, Weston-super-Mare, Avon BS22 0WA.
Tel. (01934) 520400 Fax. (01934) 520401

Company founded in 1992 and now running 280 pubs most of which it picked up from Whitbread on a freehold basis. The pubs are offered out on three-year tenancies but all guest beer rights have been taken away and only a limited choice from Whitbread's portfolio, with some Bass, Courage and regional brewers' beers, is offered to tenants. Many of the pubs are in the West Country and South Wales, with others in the North and London.

ENTERPRISE INNS LTD
Friars Gate, Stratford Road, Solihull, W. Midlands B90 4BN.
Tel. (0121) 733 7700 Fax. (0121) 733 6447

Midlands-based company founded in 1991 with the purchase of 372 pubs from Bass. The total now stands at around 500, over half run on a 21-year lease basis and the remainder tenanted, with beers provided by Bass, Whitbread, Carlsberg-Tetley, Courage and Wolverhampton & Dudley. Licensees are not allowed to buy beers outside the company, but the company is developing its own list of cask brands to increase the choice. The pubs are situated in the Midlands and the North.

SIR JOHN FITZGERALD LTD
Café Royal Buildings, 8 Nelson Street, Newcastle upon Tyne, Tyne & Wear NE1 5AW.
Tel. (0191) 232 0664 Fax. (0191) 222 1764

Long-established, family-owned, property and pubs company, dating from the end of the last century. Its pubs convey a 'free house' image, most offering a decent choice of cask beers. All 31 pubs (29 managed, two tenanted) are located in the North-East.

GRAY & SONS (CHELMSFORD) LTD
Rignals Lane, Galley Wood, Chelmsford, Essex CM2 8RE.
Tel. (01245) 475181 Fax. (01245) 475182

A brewery which ceased production at its Chelmsford brewery in 1974 and which now supplies its 49 Essex pubs with beers from Greene King (XX Mild, IPA, Rayments Special and Abbot Ale) and Ridleys (Mild, plus one other) instead.

GREENALLS GROUP PLC
Wilderspool House, Greenalls Avenue, Warrington, Cheshire WA4 6RH.
Tel. (01925) 651234 Fax. (01925) 444734

Former brewing giant which destroyed many fine independent breweries before turning its back on brewing in 1991. On a 1980s rampage, Greenalls stormed the Midlands, taking over and closing the Wem, Davenports, Simpkiss and Shipstone's breweries. Since the closure of its own Warrington brewery, Greenalls brands have been brewed by Carlsberg-Tetley. The company further demonstrated its contempt for brewing and pub traditions by bulldozing the famous Tommy Ducks pub in Manchester under the cover of night in 1993, ignoring local planning legislation. Following its acquisition of Devenish in the same year, the company now operates 1,068 tenancies and 870 managed houses. Another 112 pubs are leased out on seven-year contracts. The former Devenish beer, Royal Wessex Bitter (brewed by Whitbread), can be found in the former Devenish estate, alongside other Whitbread beers. Guest beers across the country include Tetley Bitter, Stones Best Bitter and, in a few outlets, ales from Cains, Adnams, Greene King, Young's and Coach House.

GROSVENOR INNS PLC
The Old Schoolhouse, London Road, Shenley, Hertfordshire WD7 9DX.
Tel. (01923) 855837 Fax. (01923) 857992

Group running around 40 pubs in the South-East, over half of which are leased from Inntrepreneur or other companies and are tied to Courage beers. The other pubs take beers from Whitbread, Fuller's and Wadworth, as well as Courage. Once known as Cromwell Taverns, it is now a publicly-quoted company and plans to develop its estate, establishing more of its Slug & Lettuces (currently 12 pubs). David 'Firkin' Bruce has joined the board to develop a subsidiary company of free house catering outlets, Belcher's Pubs Ltd. (currently seven pubs). The Hedgehog & Hogshead brew pubs are also part of the Grosvenor estate.

HEAVITREE BREWERY PLC
Trood Lane, Matford, Exeter, Devon EX2 8YP.
Tel. (01392) 58406 Fax. (01392) 411697

West Country brewery (established 1790) which gave up production in 1970 to concen-

trate on running pubs. The current estate (largely in Devon) stands at 110: 12 managed, and the rest tenanted or leased out (mostly on 21-year contracts). The pubs are tied to taking beers from The Whitbread Cask Collection, Bass and Eldridge Pope.

INN BUSINESS LTD
Tingewick Road, Buckingham MK18 1AN.
Tel. (01280) 822663 Fax. (01280) 823728

Inn Business Ltd. is now a subsidiary company of United Breweries PLC (the company which took over the former Premier Ales and Wiltshire Brewery operations). The original 74 Inn Business pubs, located in the northern Home Counties and on the South Coast (most on a six-year lease from Whitbread), have now been joined by the United Brewery pubs in the West Country and the Midlands, taking the estate total up to 140 houses. Pubs are tied to Whitbread, Bass, S&N and Courage products. United Breweries has no plans to resume brewing.

INNTREPRENEUR ESTATES LTD
Mill House, Aylesbury Road, Thame, Oxfordshire OX9 3AT.
Tel. (01844) 262000 Fax. (01844) 261332

The pub-owning company formed by Courage (Foster's) and Grand Metropolitan as part of the pubs-for-breweries swap in 1991. In the deal, Courage bought up all Grand Met.'s (Watney's) breweries, with most of Courage's pubs taken over by Inntrepreneur (330 went directly to Grand Met., which has since sold them to Scottish & Newcastle). Inntrepreneur has led the way with the long lease (20 years) as a replacement for the traditional tenancy, a move which has seen many valuable former Courage tenants leave the trade. The company currently operates 4,330 pubs, some of which are free houses though most are tied to Courage until 1998. In 1994 it was clarified that these pubs have the right to stock a guest beer of their own choosing, in addition to any guests supplied by Inntrepreneur/Courage. However, this is likely to change now that the S&N take-over of Courage has been allowed to go through. Inntrepreneur does not form part of the Courage package agreed for purchase by S&N from Foster's and therefore will no longer be considered to be owned or part-owned by a British brewer. Guest beer rights will be forfeited as a result. In addition, S&N has agreed to release 1,000 Inntrepreneur pubs from the Courage tie, but is not barred from renegotiating a supply deal with these pubs.

JOHN LABATT RETAIL LTD
Upper Ground, National Westminster House, Templar's Way, Chandler's Ford, Hampshire SD53 3RY.
Tel. (01703) 258200 Fax. (01703) 258222

John Labatt Retail controls some 530 (mostly tenanted) pubs across southern Britain, including 150 which were previously held by subsidiary company Maritime Taverns, and

168 purchased from S&N (former Chef & Brewer pubs). The head office-controlled beer list features mainly Whitbread and Bass products and guests.

MAGIC PUB COMPANY LTD
Corrie House, 48–54 London Road, Staines, Surrey TW18 4HQ.
Tel. (01784) 461460 Fax. (01784) 460909

Pub group established in June 1994 with the purchase of 260 pubs from S&N (former Chef & Brewer pubs). The pubs are nearly all managed and are mostly within the M25 ring, with others along the M4 corridor and some near Manchester. The head office beer list features ales from national and regional brewers.

MARR TAVERNS LTD
156 Tooley Street, London SE1 2NR.
Tel. (0171) 403 1140 Fax. (0171) 403 2891

Group owning around 150 pubs and aiming for over 700 by the end of the decade. Nearly all (most in South-East England) are tenanted on traditional three-year contracts, but there are no guest beer rights at present. Beers are supplied by Courage and Bass, plus some local suppliers. Fifty-one pubs in South Wales were sold to Ushers in 1995.

MERCURY TAVERNS PLC
Mercury House, Amber Business Village, Amington, Tamworth, Staffordshire B77 4RP.
Tel. (01827) 310000 Fax. (01827) 310530

Company running 111 pubs (97 tenanted, most others managed and one leased out on a ten-year contract). The pubs are scattered around from Cumbria to South Wales. Most have come from Bass, which, together with Carlsberg-Tetley and Banks's in some places, supplies the beer.

PARAMOUNT PLC
St Werburghs Chambers, Godstall Lane, Chester, Cheshire CH1 2EP.
Tel. (01244) 321171 Fax. (01244) 317665

Ambitious company founded in 1987 as Silver Bear, a games manufacturing company, becoming Paramount in 1988 when it began acquiring pubs. The company is now part-owned by Greenalls (25%), Burtonwood (20%) and Bass (10%), and most of its outlets were purchased from these three operators and S&N. Paramount has acquired 31 pubs from The Boddington Pub Company in the last year and now runs 273 pubs (85 as a partner in Real Inns with Labatts) and also manages 50 pubs for Whitbread under the Wirral Taverns name. The pubs are centred within 80 miles of Chester and nearly all are leased out on long contracts. Licensees are encouraged to sell cask ale, but are generally restricted to the Burtonwood, Bass and Whitbread lists. Two pubs acquired from The Boddington Pub Company continue as 'ale houses', with a greater choice, and there are plans for more such establishments.

Pub Groups

PUB MANAGEMENT CO. LTD
First Floor, North Barn, Tempest Court,
Broughton Hall Business Park, Skipton,
N. Yorkshire BD23 3AE.
Tel. (01756) 792717 Fax. (01756) 798613

Company running 68 pubs in Yorkshire, on a
mixture of short leases and tenancies, with
two managed houses. Formed in 1992, with
the purchase of 32 Bass pubs and 38 Allied
pubs, the company is still aiming for 100 pubs
in the next two years. Nearly all beers sold
come from the Carlsberg-Tetley list.

PUBMASTER LTD
26–27 Bedford Square, London WC1B 3HH.
Tel. (0171) 580 9966 Fax. (0171) 580 4900

Company formed in 1991 to take over the pub
estate of Brent Walker (ex-Camerons and
Tolly Cobbold pubs). In 1992, 734 houses
were leased from Allied, and 174 from Whitbread, and other acquisitions have been
made from Bass. Pubmaster currently runs
1,750 pubs across the country, 1,650 of which
are tenanted. Its most famous trading name is
Tap & Spile, a growing chain of traditional
alehouses (75 aimed for by the end of 1996)
offering an excellent choice of beers, including two house brews, Tap & Spile Bitter (ABV
3.8%, produced by Hadrian) and Tap & Spile
Premium (ABV 4.3%, from Ushers). The
small, new BieRRex chain of European-style
bars specialises in continental beers. The
other Pubmaster pubs stock beers from Bass,
Carlsberg-Tetley, Whitbread and some
regional independents. Pubmaster shares
control of 170 Maple Leaf Inns with Labatts.

RANDALLS VAUTIER LTD
PO Box 43, Clare Street, St Helier, Jersey JE4
8NZ.
Tel. (01534) 887788 Fax. (01534) 888350

Brewery which had produced no real ale for
some time but which stopped brewing
altogether in September 1992. It now runs 29
pubs on Jersey which sell beers from Bass,
Whitbread and Marston's. Not to be confused
with Randalls of Guernsey.

REGENT INNS PLC
Northway House, 1379 High Road,
Whetstone, London N20 9LP.
Tel. (0181) 445 5016 Fax. (0181) 446 0886

Company founded in 1980 and now owning
49 managed pubs in London and the Home
Counties. In 1994, rationalisation took place,
with ten pubs sold off and 17 acquired. Further acquisitions have since been sought. The
pubs are allowed to preserve their individual
identities and a wide range of beers are sold.

RYAN ELIZABETH HOLDINGS PLC
Ryan Precinct, 33 Fore Street, Ipswich,
Suffolk IP4 1JL.
Tel. (01473) 217458 Fax. (01473) 258237

This company's 54 pubs in East Anglia
(bought from national brewers) are leased to
individual operators on 35-year contracts.

Most are free, but around 40% have a tie to
Bass. A subsidiary company, Elizabeth
Hotels, runs six hotels.

SCORPIO INNS LTD
Zealley House, Greenhill Way, Newton
Abbot, Devon TQ12 3TB.
Tel. (01626) 334888 Fax. (01626) 332081

Pub group formed in 1991. After initially
managing pubs in Plymouth for Grand Met.,
it obtained over 100 houses from Whitbread
on short leases, bringing the number of pubs
controlled to 122, all now tenanted out. Despite being 'free of tie', these pubs stock Whitbread lagers and keg beers, plus a Whitbread
cask ale. A guest beer from a short list of
well-known brands is also available to tenants. Pubs are located in South Wales, the
Bristol and Hereford areas and along the M4
corridor to Swindon.

SMITHINNS PLC
Bridge House, Station Road, Scunthorpe,
Humberside DN15 6PY.
Tel. (01724) 861703 Fax. (01724) 861708

Seven-year-old company operating 28
managed pubs in Yorkshire, Humberside
and northern Lincolnshire. Eleven pubs are
leased from big brewers and tied to their
products, with the others selling beers from
national and certain regional brewers. There
are plans to develop the Honest Lawyer mini-
chain of pubs (three outlets) which offer at
least seven ales.

STAND INN SERVICES
21 Queen Anne's Place, Bush Hill Park,
Enfield, London EN1 2QB.
Tel. (0181) 360 5377 Fax. (0181) 360 6563

Chain of more than 50 pubs in the Home
Counties, over half on six-year leases from
Whitbread. Supply arrangements are in place
with Whitbread and Bass, and the company
has two ale house-style pubs, known as Beef
& Barrels, in the northern Home Counties.

SYCAMORE TAVERNS LTD
1 Guildford Street, Chertsey, Surrey KT16
9BG.
Tel. (01932) 571545 Fax. (01932) 571562

Company formed in 1992 and operating 235
traditionally-tenanted pubs across most
areas of England. The stock originally came
from Allied (308 pubs), but the estate has now
been rationalised. Tenants are allowed a
guest beer from the Bass and Courage lists,
though the main supplier is still Carlsberg-
Tetley.

TOM COBLEIGH PLC
Phoenix House, Oak Tree Lane, Mansfield,
Nottinghamshire NG18 4LF.
Tel. (01623) 21414 Fax. (01623) 28255

Company established in 1992 with two pubs.
Since then the estate has grown to 85, 48
tenanted, the remainder managed. The pubs,
which aim to conform to the company's

Pub Groups

slogan of 'unspoilt pubs for nice people', are located in Yorkshire, Humberside and the north-eastern Midlands. The tenanted pubs were acquired from Whitbread in 1994, though these are signed as belonging to The Nice Pub Company. Licensees choose beers from a head office range of national and regional ales, with Marston's, Whitbread, Bass and Courage the main suppliers.

TRENT TAVERNS LTD
PO Box 1061, Gringley on the Hill, Doncaster, S. Yorkshire DN10 4ED.
Tel. (01777) 817408 Fax. (01777) 816487

Company set up by a former S&N employee. Its 88 pubs in the Midlands (mainly in Warwickshire and Hereford & Worcester, but some on the south coast) are leased from Whitbread and sell only beers from the Whitbread and S&N lists.

JD WETHERSPOON ORGANISATION PLC
Wetherspoon House, Central Park, Reeds Crescent, Watford, Hertfordshire WD1 1QH.
Tel. (01923) 477777 Fax. (01923) 219810

Ambitious group, founded by Tim Martin, which opened its first pub in 1979 and went public in 1992. It currently owns 115 pubs in and around the capital, plus some in the Midlands, Bristol, Bournemouth and the North, all managed. The company continues to add about 25 pubs a year to its stock, many of which are conversions from shops, featuring standard wood and granite decor and common names like JJ Moon's and other 'Moon' titles. No music is played in any of the pubs, all offer no-smoking areas and food is served all day. There are six standard beers available to licensees: S&N Theakston Best, XB and Younger Scotch, Courage Directors, Wadworth 6X and Greene King Abbot Ale. Additional guest beers are chosen by managers from the head office list.

WHARFEDALE TAVERNS LTD
Croft House, Audby Lane, Wetherby, W. Yorkshire LS22 4DN.
Tel. (01937) 580805 Fax. (01937) 580806

Company set up in 1993 by former Tetley employees to lease 90 pubs from that company. The estate total currently stands at 75 pubs, nearly all traditionally tenanted (three-year agreements), and the main beer range still comes from Carlsberg-Tetley (Tetley Mild and Bitter), with guest beers supplied by S&N (Theakston). The pubs are situated mostly in West and South Yorkshire, and on the east coast.

WHITE ROSE INNS PLC
Chantrell House, 1 Chantrell Court, The Calls, Leeds, W. Yorkshire LS2 7HA.
Tel. (0113) 2461332

Group with 35 tenancies and two managed houses in Yorkshire. The main supplier is Carlsberg-Tetley.

JAMES WILLIAMS (NARBERTH)
7 Spring Gardens, Narberth, Dyfed SA67 7BP.
Tel. (01834) 860318 Fax. (01834) 860358

Privately-owned concern, founded in 1830 and operating 51 pubs in Dyfed (all tenanted). Tenants can choose selected beers from Brains, Crown Buckley and Felinfoel, as well as from the Bass, Carlsberg-Tetley, Courage and Whitbread lists.

YATES WINE LODGES LTD
Peter Yates House, Manchester Road, Bolton, Gtr. Manchester BL3 2PY.
Tel. (01204) 373737 Fax. (01204) 388383

Company founded in Oldham in 1884 and now expanded to run 53 pubs from Scotland to London. Beers are mainly from Courage and Bass, with some Cains ales in Liverpool.

Other notable chains (operated by, or divisions of, brewing companies or pub groups):
Artist's Fare (Morland)
Beefeater (Whitbread)
Bert's Bars (Alloa)
Big Steak (Allied)
Bill Bentley's Wine Bars (Young's)
Brewer's Fayre (Whitbread)
Calendars (Allied)
Exchanges (Taylor Walker)
Firkin (Carlsberg-Tetley)
Fork & Pitcher (Bass)
Harvester (Forte)
Hedgehog & Hogshead (Grosvenor Inns)
Henry's Café Bars (Greenalls)
Henry's Tables (Boddingtons Pub Group)
High Street Taverns (Grosvenor Inns)
Hogshead Ale Houses (Whitbread)
Honest Lawyer (Smithinns)
Hudsons (Greenalls)
JJ Moon's (Wetherspoon)
King's Fayre (Greene King)
Lacon Inns (Adnams)
Landlord's Table (Mansfield)
Maple Leaf Inns (Pubmaster/Labatts)
Maxwells (Taylor Walker)
Milestone Restaurants and Taverns
    (Wolverhampton & Dudley)
Millers Kitchen (Greenalls)
Mr Q's (Allied)
Nice Pub Company (Tom Cobleigh)
Pizza Hut (Whitbread)
Quincey's (Greenalls)
Real Inns (Labatts/Paramount)
Roast Inns (Greenalls)
Scruffy Murphy's (Allied)
Shakespeare Ale Houses (Forte)
Slug & Lettuce (Grosvenor Inns)
Southern Inns (S&N)
T&J Bernard's (S&N)
Tap & Spile (Pubmaster)
TGI Friday (Whitbread)
Toby Restaurants (Bass)
Tut 'n' Shive (Whitbread)
Vantage Inns (Burtonwood/Café Inns)
Wirral Taverns (Paramount)

The Beers Index

The Beers Index is your quick guide to Britain's most popular ales. Well over 1000 brews are highlighted in the following pages, together with page references to the breweries section, where you can find out more about each beer. Beers with only very limited availability have not been included.

534

The Beers Index

535

The Beers Index

536

The Beers Index

The Beers Index

538

The Beers Index

The Beers Index

The Beers Index

The Beers Index

MRA – JOIN FREE!

-obligation opportunity to sample the benefits of CAMRA membership.

MRA membership **now** stands at around 50,000, and thou-
ds of members **have** been part of the Campaign for many
rs, even decades. **This** is your chance to discover why they
so keen to be part **of** one of the world's great consumer
it needn't cost you **a** penny to do so.

nths', no strings, **trial** membership, just fill in the direct
eaf, sign the application form below and pop them in the
copies will do). If, **after** the three months are up, you do
in a CAMRA member, simply write to us returning your
d and you will owe **nothing**.

member (even for **these** three months), you will be able
s discounts on all CAMRA products (including the *Good*
you will receive the highly-rated monthly newspaper,
keep you up to date with events in the pub and brew-
ill also obtain the CAMRA members' handbook, packed
and figures about real ale, and can take advantage of
ice admission at many beer festivals.

member you can help to save pubs and breweries, enjoy
and brewery trips, and assist with surveying for the
d other CAMRA activities

to take up this offer, but wish to join anyway, just fill
orm below and return it to us with a cheque for your
tion. Do not fill in the direct debit form. To pay by
the Membership Secretary on (01727) 867201.

in CAMRA and protect your pleasure.

£12 ■ Joint membership £14
£120/£140

riate:

e advantage of the trial membership,
ed the instructions overleaf.

ome members of CAMRA.

de by the memorandum and articles of
company.

que/p.o. for £   (payable to CAMRA)

Road, St Albans, Herts. AL1 4LW

READERS' RECOMMENDATIONS
Suggestions for pubs to be included or excluded

All pubs are surveyed by the local branches of CAMRA. If you
would like to comment on a pub already featured, or any you
think should be featured, please fill in the form below (or a copy of
it) and send it to the address indicated. Your views will be passed
on to the branches concerned.

Pub Name:

Address:

Reason for recommendation/criticism:

Pub Name:

Address:

Reason for recommendation/criticism:

Your name and address:

lease send to: GBG, CAMRA, 230 Hatfield Road, St Albans, Herts. AL1 4LW

CAMRA BOOKS AND GIFTS

CAMRA produces a wide range of books and other items to complement the *Good Beer Guide*. The major titles are listed below, but a full catalogue of CAMRA products (including local guides) is available on request. Tear out or copy this form for ease of ordering. All prices include UK postage and packing.

	Quantity	Price each	Amount
GUIDES			
CAMRA Guide to Good Pub Food (4th edition)		£9.99	
Good Beer Guide to Belgium & Holland (2nd edition)		£9.99	
Good Beer Guide to Munich & Bavaria		£8.99	
OTHER TITLES			
CAMRA Guide to Home Brewing		£6.99	
Brew Your Own Real Ale at Home		£6.99	
Cellarmanship		£2.95	
Called to the Bar (CAMRA: the first 21 years)		£6.99	
OTHER PRODUCTS			
CAMRA Tie		£7.50	
CAMRA Lapel Badge		£2.50	
CAMRA T-shirt (white: M, L, XL, XXL – state size)		£7.50	
'Real Ale Masterclass' 30-minute video with Roger Protz		£12.95	
		Total	£

Please send to CAMRA, 230 Hatfield Road, St Albans, Herts. AL1 4LW (cheques made payable to CAMRA must accompany all orders). Allow 28 days for delivery. To place a credit card order, phone (01727) 867201 and ask for the Products Secretary.

Name

Address

Post Code

INSTRUCTIONS TO
TO PAY DIRECT

Please complete parts 1 to 4 to instruct your b
from your account.

Return the form to Campaign for Real Ale L
Albans, Herts. AL1 4LW

To the Manager

1 Please write the full postal address of

2 Name(s) of account holders(s)

Address

3 Account number

Banks may refuse to accept instructions
account.

Direct debit instructions should only b

CAMRA Computer Membership N

Originator's Identification No.

9	2	6	1	2	9

4 Your instructions to the bank
- I instruct you to pay direct debits
  Real Ale Limited.
- The amounts are variable and ar
- I understand that Campaign for
  giving me prior notice.
- PLEASE CANCEL ALL PREVIO
  FAVOUR OF CAMPAIGN FOR
- I will inform the bank in writin
- I understand that if any direct
  instruction, the bank will mak

Signature(s)

Date

CA
An

C   A
sa
ye
ar
movements, an

- For three-n
  debit form ove
  post to us (ph
  not wish to ren
  membership ca

- As a CAMR
  to enjoy genero
  Beer Guide) and
  What's Brewing,
  ing world. You
  with useful fact
  free or reduced-

- As a CAMRA
  local social even
  Good Beer Guide a

If you do not wan
in the application
first year's subscri
credit card, contac

- Full membershi
- Life membershi

Please delete as appr
- I/We wish to ta
  and have comple
- I/We wish to be
- I/We agree to ab
  association of the
- I/We enclose a c

Name(s)

Address

Signature(s)

CAMRA, 230 Hatfield